CCNP Self-Study

CCNP Practical Studies: Switching

Justin Menga, CCIE No. 6640

Cisco Press

800 East 96th Street
Indianapolis, IN 46240 USA

CCNP Practical Studies: Switching

Justin Menga

Copyright© 2004 Cisco Systems, Inc.

Published by:
Cisco Press
800 East 96th Street
Indianapolis, IN 46240 USA

Printed in the United States of America 2 3 4 5 6 7 8 9 0

Second Printing January 2004

Library of Congress Cataloging-in-Publication Number: 2001099911

ISBN: 1-58720-060-0

Warning and Disclaimer

This book is designed to provide information about switching. Every effort has been made to make this book as complete and as accurate as possible, but no warranty or fitness is implied.

The information is provided on an "as is" basis. The authors, Cisco Press, and Cisco Systems, Inc., shall have neither liability nor responsibility to any person or entity with respect to any loss or damages arising from the information contained in this book or from the use of the discs or programs that may accompany it.

The opinions expressed in this book belong to the author and are not necessarily those of Cisco Systems, Inc.

Feedback Information

At Cisco Press, our goal is to create in-depth technical books of the highest quality and value. Each book is crafted with care and precision, undergoing rigorous development that involves the unique expertise of members from the professional technical community.

Readers' feedback is a natural continuation of this process. If you have any comments regarding how we could improve the quality of this book, or otherwise alter it to better suit your needs, you can contact us through e-mail at feedback@ciscopress.com. Please make sure to include the book title and ISBN in your message.

We greatly appreciate your assistance.

Trademark Acknowledgments

All terms mentioned in this book that are known to be trademarks or service marks have been appropriately capitalized. Cisco Press or Cisco Systems, Inc., cannot attest to the accuracy of this information. Use of a term in this book should not be regarded as affecting the validity of any trademark or service mark.

Publisher	John Wait
Editor-in-Chief	John Kane
Executive Editor	Brett Bartow
Cisco Representative	Anthony Wolfenden
Cisco Press Program Manager	Sonia Torres Chavez
Manager, Marketing Communications, Cisco Systems	Scott Miller
Cisco Marketing Program Manager	Edie Quiroz
Production Manager	Patrick Kanouse
Acquisitions Editor	Michelle Grandin
Development Editor	Andrew Cupp
Project Editor	Marc Fowler
Copy Editor	Kevin Kent
Technical Editors	Andy Barkl
	Henry Benjamin
	Steve Daleo
	Drew Rosen
	Jeff Saxe
	Peter Welcher
Team Coordinator	Tammi Barnett
Book Designer	Gina Rexrode
Cover Designer	Louisa Adair
Compositor	Mark Shirar
Indexer	Larry Sweazy

CISCO SYSTEMS

Corporate Headquarters
Cisco Systems, Inc.
170 West Tasman Drive
San Jose, CA 95134-1706
USA
www.cisco.com
Tel: 408 526-4000
  800 553-NETS (6387)
Fax: 408 526-4100

European Headquarters
Cisco Systems International BV
Haarlerbergpark
Haarlerbergweg 13-19
1101 CH Amsterdam
The Netherlands
www-europe.cisco.com
Tel: 31 0 20 357 1000
Fax: 31 0 20 357 1100

Americas Headquarters
Cisco Systems, Inc.
170 West Tasman Drive
San Jose, CA 95134-1706
USA
www.cisco.com
Tel: 408 526-7660
Fax: 408 527-0883

Asia Pacific Headquarters
Cisco Systems, Inc.
Capital Tower
168 Robinson Road
#22-01 to #29-01
Singapore 068912
www.cisco.com
Tel: +65 6317 7777
Fax: +65 6317 7799

Cisco Systems has more than 200 offices in the following countries and regions. Addresses, phone numbers, and fax numbers are listed on the
Cisco.com Web site at www.cisco.com/go/offices.

Argentina • Australia • Austria • Belgium • Brazil • Bulgaria • Canada • Chile • China PRC • Colombia • Costa Rica • Croatia • Czech Republic
Denmark • Dubai, UAE • Finland • France • Germany • Greece • Hong Kong SAR • Hungary • India • Indonesia • Ireland • Israel • Italy
Japan • Korea • Luxembourg • Malaysia • Mexico • The Netherlands • New Zealand • Norway • Peru • Philippines • Poland • Portugal
Puerto Rico • Romania • Russia • Saudi Arabia • Scotland • Singapore • Slovakia • Slovenia • South Africa • Spain • Sweden
Switzerland • Taiwan • Thailand • Turkey • Ukraine • United Kingdom • United States • Venezuela • Vietnam • Zimbabwe

About the Author

Justin Menga is a dual-certified Cisco Certified Internetwork Expert (CCIE No. 6640) in the Routing and Switching and Security tracks. He has eight years of networking experience, working with many products from major vendors. Justin holds the premier qualifications for Cisco, Microsoft, and Check Point, demonstrating his understanding of both networks and applications and the underlying security required for both.

He is employed as a network design consultant for Logical CSI in New Zealand, a global network integration company with offices in more than 40 countries worldwide. Previously, he was employed by Compaq Global Services in a similar role. He is responsible for the pre-sales support, design, and proof-of-concept testing for complex networks that require a broad mix of technologies. These technologies include routing, switching, network, and wireless security and Voice over IP. Recently, Justin became CCIE certified in the Security track, demonstrating his diverse range of skills.

Justin has previously authored the book, *CCSA NG: Check Point Certified Security Administrator Study Guide.*

About the Technical Reviewers

Andy Barkl, CCNP, CCDP, has over 19 years of experience in the IT field. He's the owner of MCT & Associates LLC, a technical training and consulting firm in Phoenix, Arizona.

Henry Benjamin, CCIE No. 4695, is triple-CCIE-certified, having attained Routing and Switching in May 1999, ISP Dial in June 2001, and Communications and Services in May 2002. He has more than 10 years experience with Cisco networks including planning, designing, and implementing large IP networks running IGRP, EIGRP, BGP, and OSPF. Recently, Henry previously worked for a large IT organization based in Sydney, Australia, as a key Network Designer, designing and implementing networks all over Australia and Asia.

In the past two years, Henry has been a key member of the CCIE global team based in Sydney, Australia. As a senior and core member of the team, his tasks include writing new laboratory examinations and questions for the coveted CCIE R/S, CCIE Security, and CCIE C/S tracks, as well as the CCIE-written Recertification Examinations. Henry has authored three other titles—*CCIE Security Exam Certification Guide* and *CCNP Practical Studies: Routing* from Cisco Press and *CCIE Routing and Switching Exam Cram*. Henry holds a Bachelor of Aeronautical Engineering degree from Sydney University (1991).

Stephen A. Daleo, president of Golden Networking Consultants, Inc., is a network consultant whose clients include the University of South Florida—St. Petersburg and North Broward Hospital District (Fort Lauderdale, Florida). Steve was one of the course developers for Cisco Internet Learning Solutions Group—BCMSN 2.0 class. Steve is a frequent contributor to the technical content of Cisco Press books and an active Cisco Certified Systems Instructor (97025) teaching the BCMSN, BCRAN, CIPT, CIT, BSCI, and ICND Cisco courses.

Drew Rosen, CCIE No. 4365, is a Product Marketing Manager in Cisco's Internet Learning Solutions Group. In his present role, Drew manages a team of technical consultants focusing on educational products for enterprise and service provider markets. Previously, Drew spent 4 years as a systems engineer for Cisco, working on large named accounts in the enterprise space. He has been involved in the production and launch of numerous ILSG products including Building Scalable Cisco Internetworks (BSCI), Configuring BGP on Cisco Routers (CBCR), Configuring Cisco Routers for IS-IS (CCRI), Advanced MPLS VPN Solutions (AMVS), Building Metro Optical Networks (BCMON), and Implementing Quality of Service (QoS). Drew lives in Florida with his wife, Meredith, and daughter, Chelsea.

Jeff Saxe, CCIE No. 9376, is Network Engineer and a proud member of the IT Systems Group at Crutchfield Corporation, a mail-order/Web retailer of car stereo and home theater equipment founded in 1974. He has managed the company's LAN and WAN for a few years, including both Voice over Frame Relay and Voice over IP equipment for a remote call center. Jeff previously worked in computer support for the newspaper publishing and educational software industries. He graduated from the University of Virginia with a distinguished major in mathematics and a minor in chemistry. Jeff lives in Charlottesville, Virginia, with his wife, Laura, and their son, Nathan.

Dr. Peter J. Welcher, CCIE No. 1773, CCIP, has authored several advanced courses. He has written over 90 articles for *CiscoWorld Magazine* (now *Enterprise Networking Magazine*). Pete has reviewed many book proposals and books for Cisco Press, covering a wide variety of subjects. Pete currently is a partner in Chesapeake Netcraftsmen. For more information or the articles, see www.netcraftsmen.net/welcher.

Dedication

This book is dedicated to my beautiful wife Tania, who endured many late nights while I was busy tearing my hair out writing this book.

Contents at a Glance

Contents

Introduction

There are two fundamental components of modern networks today—routing and switching. The Cisco Certified Network Professional (CCNP) certification is a popular networking certification that is the next step in career certification following the Cisco Certified Network Associate (CCNA) certification. Cisco represents qualified individuals at three tiers, CCNP-qualified people represent the middle tier, while CCNA represents the lower tier, and CCIE the highest tier. Demand for CCNPs is high, especially for organizations that need people to implement and support Cisco-based networks. One of the requirements of obtaining CCNP is to pass the CCNP Switching exam, which tests your knowledge of switching concepts, protocols, and the configuration of Cisco Catalyst switches. This book is designed to provide you with a greater understanding of how to configure (and support) Cisco Catalyst switches.

Goals of this Book

The primary goal of this book is to provide a practical understanding of how to configure and support Cisco Catalyst switches. The CCNP certification provides you with the theoretical knowledge required to implement local-area networks (LAN) networks; however, it is important that when it comes to the crunch and you need to configure or troubleshoot a real-life network, you have the practical experience, knowledge, and confidence to respond quickly and effectively. The more ways you can learn about a subject, the better. This book is designed to provide a practical approach to not just CCNP switching objectives, but also LAN switching in general.

Audience

This book is targeted at networking professionals who possess a theoretical understanding of the concepts and principles of LAN switching but want to apply this knowledge to real-world scenarios. You need to possess at least CCNA-level knowledge of routing and switching if you want to use this book to its full extent. The value of practical experience in any type of work cannot be overstated, and this book gives you the practical experience and confidence to implement real-life switched networks. After reading this book, you should also possess a much deeper understanding of LAN switching theory and operation. It is amazing how a theoretical concept that might confuse you in reading becomes clearer after actually putting the concept into practice.

If you are purchasing this book for certification reasons, the primary certification audience of this book is obviously the prospective CCNP candidate. This book covers the material included in the new CCNP Switching 3.0 exam. This book is also an excellent book for any potential CCIE Routing + Switching candidates because the focus of the book is mainly around the Catalyst 3550 switch, which is the switch now used in the CCIE Routing + Switching lab. If you are not pursuing a certification and are considering buying this book because you need to implement and support Cisco Catalyst switches, this book is also perfect for you. The content covered is designed to take a real-world perspective on LAN switching, focusing on features that are common and important to real-life networks, rather than just focusing on the CCNP Switching exam objectives.

Chapter Organization

This book consists of 11 chapters and two appendixes. The first ten chapters focus on specific LAN switching technologies, with the final chapter providing a comprehensive switching self-study lab that incorporates content from all of the preceding chapters. The three appendixes provide solutions to this final lab chapter.

Each chapter begins with a brief introductory section, which backgrounds the key concepts and principles associated with the content covered in each chapter. Next, a number of scenarios are presented, each with a network topology and a set of requirements. Each scenario is designed to demonstrate how to implement and configure specific technologies and features related to the chapter content in a manner that allows you to relate to real-world networks. The scenarios are designed so that readers can build the topologies described in each scenario in their own labs at home or at work. If you have access to the equipment discussed in the scenarios of this book, you are encouraged to attempt as many scenarios as you can in your own lab.

After completing the configuration of each scenario, you are shown how to verify, monitor, and troubleshoot your configurations. The scenarios do not just contain purely practical information—detailed background and explanations of technologies are provided where deemed necessary, ensuring you gain a strong understanding of exactly what you are configuring and why you are configuring it in a certain way.

The following describes the content of each chapter and appendix.

- **Chapter 1, "Switching Connectivity"**—The first chapter introduces you to the basic Catalyst switch platforms and then shows you how to prepare both a CatOS-based and Cisco IOS-based Catalyst switch for placement on the network and to provide basic LAN connectivity for devices that allow basic communications between each device.

- **Chapter 2, "Virtual Operations"**—This chapter covers virtual LANs or VLANs. You are first introduced to the concept of VLANs and why they are such an integral component of modern LAN networks. You learn how to create and configure VLANs, placing switch ports into various VLANs, creating Layer 2 separations between devices.

- **Chapter 3, "Trunking and Bandwidth Aggregation"**—This chapter introduces both EtherChannel and Trunking, which are technologies used to link Cisco Catalyst switches together. You learn how to configure multiple physical interfaces as a single EtherChannel bundle, which allows you to increase the performance and resiliency of connections. Next, you learn about VLAN trunking protocol and how you must configure it. Trunking is then examined and you learn how to multiplex the traffic from multiple VLANs down a single physical trunk interface.

- **Chapter 4, "Spanning Tree"**—This chapter covers spanning tree, which is fundamental and very important protocol used in switched environments. The chapter introduces you to basic spanning-tree configuration and then moves into advanced spanning-tree features, such as how to implement load sharing and configuring spanning-tree enhancements.

- **Chapter 5, "Inter-VLAN Routing"**—This chapter covers inter-VLAN routing and how it is required for devices to communicate between VLANs. The basic inter-VLAN routing architectures are discussed; the chapter also delves into basic Layer 3 switching configuration, along with configuring Hot Standby Router Protocol (HSRP).

- **Chapter 6, "Layer 3 Switching"**—This chapter covers Layer 3 switching in depth and discusses the need for Layer 3 switches in modern LAN networks. This chapter focuses primarily on the Cisco Catalyst 6000/6500 series switch family and the components that make up the product, such as Supervisor engines, Policy Feature Cards (PFCs), and multilayer switching feature cards (MSFCs). You learn about Multilayer switching (MLS) and Cisco Express Forwarding (CEF) and how these provide the foundation for L3 switching on Catalyst switches.

- **Chapter 7, "Multicast Routing and Switching"**—This chapter covers multicast routing and how you can control multicast traffic on the LAN. You learn about multicast routing and how Cisco Layer 3 switches support this feature. You also learn how multicast routers can interoperate with switches, allowing switches to constrain multicast traffic to only those ports that wish to receive multicast traffic, using features such as Internet Group Management Protocol (IGMP) snooping and Cisco Group Management Protocol (CGMP).

- **Chapter 8, "Traffic Filtering and Security"**—This chapter shows you how you to secure your switching infrastructure by securing management access, securing device access to the switch, and implementing traffic filtering to ensure network security policy is conformed to. You learn how to secure the management interface for a Catalyst switch, enhance security by using AAA, provide user-based authentication and authorization to the LAN using 802.1x, and implement filtering of traffic received on ports and VLANs.

- **Chapter 9, "Quality of Service"**—This chapter shows you how to configure end-to-end quality of service (QoS) in a LAN switched network, as well as how to provide QoS classification and marking when looking at the entire network. You learn how to configure basic concepts of QoS—classification, marking, policing, and scheduling. The Cisco Catalyst switch platforms and how they implement QoS are discussed, which is important when selecting which switch platform you should implement. Voice over IP and how Cisco Catalyst switches can interact with Cisco IP phones is also covered.

- **Chapter 10, "Maintenance, Monitoring, and Troubleshooting"**—This chapter shows you how to monitor, maintain, and troubleshoot Cisco Catalyst switch networks. You learn about common issues in switched networks and how you can identify and resolve these issues. You also learn how to upgrade your switch and how you can recover from lost passwords or missing operating system files. Finally, you learn how to capture traffic from the switching backplane using SPAN, RSPAN, and VLAN access control lists (ACLs).

- **Chapter 11, "Comprehensive Switching Self-Study Lab"**—The final chapter provides a self-study lab scenario, which tests how well you understand the content provided in this book. The scenario consists of initially configuring a flat, Layer 2 topology and then converting it into a multilayer topology. Appendixes A and B provide full solutions to each part of the scenario.

- **Appendix A, "Comprehensive Switching Self-Study Lab Part I Solution"**—Provides complete solutions for the first section of the self-study lab in Chapter 11.

- **Appendix B, "Comprehensive Switching Self-Study Lab Part II Solution"**—Provides complete solutions for the second section of the self-study lab in Chapter 11.

How Best to Use This Book

While working through this book, you ideally want to have access to the equipment upon which the various scenarios are configured. By working through the scenarios on the actual equipment, you gain confidence in your ability to actually make features work in the real world. Of course, some of the equipment discussed in this book is very expensive, and you might not have access to some or all of the equipment. Because you might not, each configuration step is discussed in full where required, and full working configurations are provided, which ensures that you can follow each scenario. This means that you gain the same value out of this book, whether you have access to physical equipment or not.

Note that most scenarios in this book assume a basic configuration is already in place, which includes parameters such as device name and any other parameters indicated during the scenario.

Equipment Required for Practical Experience

NOTE   This section covers what equipment you need if you want to gain practical experience from the exercises in this book by actually following along with real equipment. Though this is the ideal way to benefit from this book, such equipment is not necessary due to the detailed explanations. If you do not have access to equipment, see the section, "How To Use This Book if You Do Not Have Access to This Equipment," later in this Introduction.

The features of Cisco Catalyst switches are much more based upon hardware than they are on software, unlike Cisco routers, where the software component (Cisco IOS) is common across all routers. This means that you find significant differences in the functionality provided by each Catalyst switch family. To learn how to configure all of the features provided by the Catalyst product family as a whole, it is often necessary for you to have access to a wide variety of Catalyst hardware platforms, some of them very expensive.

In this book, you work with three main Catalyst switch platforms:

- **Catalyst 3550**—Next-generation Cisco IOS-based switch with Layer 3/4 intelligence and Layer 3 switching capabilities. You can also use the Catalyst 2950 or Catalyst 2900/3500XL switches instead; however, some features supported on the Catalyst 3550 are not supported on these switches.

- **Catalyst 4000/4500**—Most Catalyst operating system (CatOS) configuration is based upon the Catalyst 4000/4500 switch. A cheap alternative to the Catalyst 4000/4500 is the Catalyst 2900 series switches, which are based upon the Catalyst 4000 switch (they run the same operating system image) but run on a fixed platform with a small form-factor.

- **Catalyst 6000/6500**—More advanced CatOS and Cisco IOS features are configured on the Catalyst 6000/6500 switch.

NOTE   Nearly all of the scenarios in this book require interconnection of Catalyst switches, which requires the use of crossover cables. If you are configuring your own lab equipment, always ensure you use crossover cables to connect each switch.

In addition to working with Catalyst switches, you also work with other types of devices as listed below:

- **Cisco routers**—Some scenarios include Cisco IOS routers to provide traditional routing functions. When selecting a router platform for use in each of the scenarios, the minimum recommended platform is the Cisco 2621 router, which includes 2 x 10/100BaseT network ports, although some scenarios may permit the use of lower end routers.

- **Hosts**—To test end-to-end connectivity, you must prove connectivity between different hosts on the network. Ideally, you should have a least two hosts on your network, each running Windows 2000/XP or the operating system of your choice.

- **Servers**—Some scenarios rely on external servers that provide supporting services. In Chapter 8, a Windows 2000 server with CiscoSecure ACS installed is required.

For all CatOS switches, all configuration examples are performed using CatOS version 7.6. For all Cisco IOS switches, the IOS version used varies depending on the switch platform used:

- **Catalyst 2950/3550**—Cisco IOS 12.1(13)EA1
- **Catalyst 4000/4500 with Supervisor 3/4**—12.1(12c)EW
- **Catalyst 4000 Layer 3 Router Module**—Cisco IOS 12.0(10)W5
- **Catalyst 6000/6500 with Native IOS**—Cisco IOS 12.1(13)E

NOTE   To conserve space, complete configurations for devices used in each scenario are not included in the text. Complete configurations are available at www.ciscopress.com/1587200600.

Obtaining Equipment

If you work for a company that has a lab or holds spares for the equipment used in this book, then you are in luck, and this will most likely become your source of equipment. If you do not have this luxury, you can always contact your local Cisco representatives and see if you can obtain loan equipment or gain access to customer lab facilities. Provided the aforementioned methods fail, you need to purchase the equipment. There are numerous sites on the Internet that sell cheap, used Cisco equipment; an example of this includes the eBay auction site at www.ebay.com. Another option is to use product simulators. For example, Cisco offers a product called the Cisco Interactive Mentor (CIM), which enables users to simulate the configuration of real-world networks.

It is important to note that Cisco switching equipment can be extremely expensive compared to more common devices such as routers; it is unlikely you will be able to afford the purchase of a Catalyst 6000 switch, even if it is second hand. Many of the configurations in this book can be completed on lower end Catalyst switches, such as the 2900 series switches (CatOS-based) or the Catalyst 2950 series switches (Cisco IOS-based). Realize that some features might not be supported on these platforms.

How To Use This Book if You Do Not Have Access to This Equipment

If you exhaust all possible avenues and find that you cannot get equipment, do not despair. Each scenario in this book takes you through configuration, verification, and troubleshooting processes step-by-step, providing you with all the necessary information, configurations, and figures to simulate the scenario in real life. Ensure that you pay closer attention to the examples included in each chapter, spending time to thoroughly analyze how features are configured and the outputs generated when verifying configuration.

Cisco Systems Networking Icon Legend

Cisco Systems, Inc., uses a standardized set of icons to represent devices in network topology illustrations. The icon legend that follows shows the most commonly used icons that you might encounter throughout this book.

Throughout this book, you will see the following icons used for networking devices:

Router

Bridge

Hub

DSU/CSU

Catalyst
Switch

Multilayer
Switch

ATM
Switch

ISDN/Frame Relay
Switch

Communication
Server

Gateway

Access
Server

The following icons are used for peripherals and other devices:

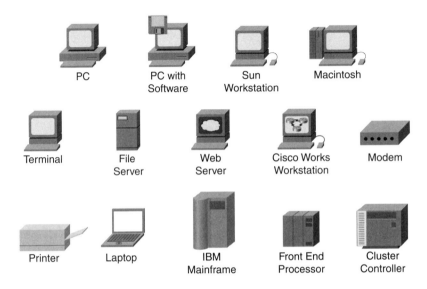

The following icons are used for networks and network connections:

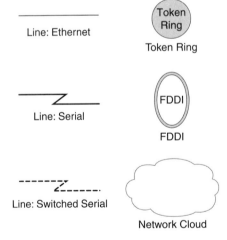

Command Syntax Conventions

The conventions used to present command syntax in this book are the same conventions used in the Cisco IOS Software Command Reference. The Command Reference describes these conventions as follows:

- Vertical bars (|) separate alternative, mutually exclusive elements.

- Square brackets ([ ]) indicate optional elements.

- Braces ({ }) indicate a required choice.

- Braces within brackets ([{ }]) indicate a required choice within an optional element.

- **Boldface** indicates commands and keywords that are entered exactly as shown.

- *Italics* indicates arguments for which you supply values.

## CHAPTER 1

Switching Connectivity

This book is all about switches, which are network devices that provide local-area network (LAN) connectivity for end devices such as servers, PCs, and printers. This book focuses almost entirely on Ethernet switches, which have become the most popular Layer 2 devices in modern networks. Cisco has traditionally been famous for their router, which is a Layer 3 device. In the past decade or so, Cisco has heavily invested in producing market-leading LAN switches, and consequently now holds the number one position worldwide in terms of LAN switch sales. In the past few years, switches have also evolved from being just Layer 2 devices that understand only Layer 2 operations to intelligent devices that possess an understanding of the Layer 3/4 parameters that define different types of traffic possess the ability to act as a high-performance Layer 3 router on the LAN in some platforms (referred to as *Layer 3 switching*). Cisco's switch portfolio is comprised of the Cisco Catalyst product family, which provides traditional Layer 2 switches, Layer 2 switches that possess Layer 3/4 intelligence, and Layer 3 switches that combine switching and routing features.

In this chapter, you learn the basics of configuring a Cisco Catalyst switch. You learn how to identify the switch and prepare it for placement on the network so that it can be remotely managed via IP and provide LAN connectivity for devices. It is important that you have a firm grasp of the concepts presented in this chapter, because they provide the underlying foundation for the enabling of other switching features that are presented in subsequent chapters. The chapter begins by giving a brief product view of the various Cisco Catalyst switches and then delves straight into some practical scenarios, where you learn how to configure Cisco Catalyst switches and provide connectivity for end devices attached to the LAN. The following scenarios are presented in this chapter:

- Scenario 1-1: Installing a Cisco Catalyst Switch onto the Network
- Scenario 1-2: Configuring Network Management Access to the Switch
- Scenario 1-3: Configuring Ethernet Device Connectivity
- Scenario 1-4: Configuring System Time
- Scenario 1-5: Monitoring and Troubleshooting Device Connectivity

Introduction to Cisco Catalyst Switches

The Cisco Catalyst switch family represents one of the most popular LAN switches on the market today. The Catalyst range is designed to meet the needs of a wide range of customers—from small to medium businesses, right up to large enterprise networks and service providers. Cisco Catalyst switches provide high performance, scalability, manageability, and many other intelligent features that ensure their success to date.

I find that Cisco Catalyst switches present one of more difficult product sets to work with, simply because of the large range of switch families available, the vast differences in features between low-end and high-end platforms, and the different operating systems used. When you select a switch platform and model to use to build a LAN network, you must bear in mind that these differences exist; otherwise, you might purchase one or more switches that don't quite do the job you expected.

Cisco Catalyst switches can physically described by one of two device types:

- Fixed-configuration switch
- Chassis-based switch

The *fixed-configuration switch* consists of a fixed number or ports contained within a fixed chassis that includes an internal switch processor. Some of these devices provide a limited degree of modularity in that they include modular slots that can be populated by variety of different modules. The major advantages of fixed-configuration switches are low cost and ease of deployment. The major disadvantages of a fixed-configuration switch are a lack of flexibility and the introduction of a multiple management points in the network when installing more than one switch. Scaling the network by introducing multiple fixed-configuration switches can also introduce bottlenecks between each switch.

NOTE	Some Catalyst switches support stacking, where a group of Catalyst switches can be managed as a single entity. Traditionally, the Catalyst 29xx and 35xx switches have supported stacking; however, inter-switch performance is limited for larger stacks and the ability to manage the stack as a single entity has had some restrictions. The recent Catalyst 3750 series of switches now include stacking technology that includes a high-speed 32 Gbps backplane and also allows the stack to be completely managed as a single switch.

The *chassis-based switch* provides a chassis as a starting point, after which you can add the various components of the switch as you require. You can determine a particular type of switch processor and switching module, and then install these options. Chassis-based switches provide slots, which support various types of modules. The major advantages of chassis-based switches include high performance, flexibility, simplified management, and extended product lifetime. Chassis-based switches also commonly offer redundancy features to ensure the failure of a module, power supply, or other component does not cause a network outage. The major disadvantage of chassis-based switches is the high cost involved.

Table 1-1 indicates the various models that comprise the Cisco Catalyst switch family.

Table 1-1   *Cisco Catalyst Switches*

Model	Format	Status
Catalyst 1900/2800	Fixed Configuration 10BASE-T + 100BASE-T Uplinks	End of Sale Recommended replacement = Catalyst 2950
Catalyst 2900XL/3500XL	Fixed Configuration 10/100BASE-T + 1000BASE-X Uplinks	End of Sale Recommended replacement = Catalyst 2950/3550
Catalyst 2900G	Fixed Configuration 10/100BASE-T + 1000BASE-X Uplinks	Legacy Recommended replacement = Catalyst 2950/3550
Catalyst 2950	**Fixed Configuration 10/100BASE-T + 1000BASE-X Uplinks**	**Current**
Catalyst 3550	**Fixed Configuration** **10/100BASE-T + 1000BASE-X Uplinks**	**Current**
Catalyst 3750	**Fixed Configuration** **10/100/1000BASE-T + 1000BASE-X Uplinks**	**Current**
Catalyst 4000/4500	**Chassis**	**Current**
Catalyst 4900	Fixed Configuration (*n* x 1000BASE-X)	Legacy Recommended replacement = Catalyst 3550/3750
Catalyst 5000/5500	Chassis	Legacy Recommended replacement = Catalyst 6000/6500
Catalyst 6000/6500	**Chassis**	**Current**
Catalyst 8000/8500	**Chassis**	**Current**

In Table 1-1, each of the Catalyst product families are listed, with the form factor and current status of each switch indicated. Each of the product families in **bold** are considered current products and are recommended for deployment for new networks or for network upgrades. All other product families are either end of sale or considered legacy products that should be purchased only for existing networks where a common platform needs to be maintained.

Each of the switches in Table 1-1 is targeted at a particular switching environment, based upon size, network traffic, and features required. One way of classifying the general role of a switch is to identify the hierarchical layer in which the switch is operating. Well-designed LAN networks can be divided into three key layers:

- **Access**—Provides access to the network for end devices, such as user PCs, servers, and printers.

- **Distribution**—Provides an aggregation point for access-layer devices and then connects directly to the core. Layer 3 switching can be applied at this point, which improves convergence and scalability and allows for the introduction of network policies.

- **Core**—Central portion of the network that interconnects all distribution layer devices. The core is normally redundant and high-speed. The main job of the core is to switch traffic as fast as possible, due to the high volumes of traffic within the core. The core layer can either be a Layer 2 only core or a Layer 3 core that relies on routing for redundancy and convergence.

For many networks, a network switch can provide the functions of two layers or even the entire three. Only the very large networks typically have distinct core, distribution, and access layers; smaller networks typically have a combined core/distribution layer and an access layer. Following the core/distribution/access layer design provides a hierarchical network that can easily scale as the network grows. Figure 1-1 illustrates the various layers of a LAN network and which platforms fit into each of the layers.

Figure 1-1 *Core/Distribution/Access Layers*

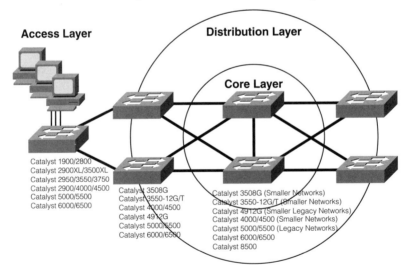

In Figure 1-1, notice that *all* of the Catalyst switches (bar the Catalyst 8500) can be used as an access layer switch. Most commonly, the access layer function is left to the switches up to the Catalyst 4000/4500 series; however, many larger networks use the Catalyst 5000/5500 and Catalyst 6000/6500 switch as a wiring closet switches, because they can provide very high port densities. When this happens, the high-end switch is normally providing distribution layer functionality as well.

Cisco Catalyst Switch Platforms

As described in Table 1-1, a number of Cisco Catalyst switch platforms are available, each of which are suitable for different switching environments depending on the size, complexity, features required and of course cost. In this section, each of the Cisco Catalyst switch platforms that are available for purchase and not considered legacy switches are described (i.e., the platforms highlighted bold in Table 1-1). This includes the following switch platforms:

- Catalyst 2950/3550 family
- Catalyst 3550/3750
- Catalyst 4000/4500
- Catalyst 6000/6500

NOTE	The Catalyst 8500 switch is not discussed in this section because the Catalyst 6000/6500 switches now outperform this switch

---

Catalyst 2950 Family

The Catalyst 2950 switches represent Cisco's entry-level switch product offering and are a fixed-configuration platform designed for access-layer/workgroup connectivity. Table 1-2 lists each of the Catalyst 2950 models and describes their hardware and software configurations. Each switch contains 8MB flash and 16MB memory.

Table 1-2   *Cisco Catalyst 2950 Family*

Model	Hardware Specifications	Performance		Software Image
		Forwarding Bandwidth	Forwarding Rate[1]	
2950-12	12 x 10/100BASE-T	2.4 Gbps	1.8 Mpps	Standard image (SI)
2950-24	24 x 10/100BASE-T	4.8 Gbps	3.5 Mpps	Standard image (SI)
2950C-24	24 x 10/100BASE-T 2 x fixed 1000BASE-SX	5.2 Gbps	3.9 Mpps	Standard image (SI)

continues

Table 1-2   *Cisco Catalyst 2950 Family (Continued)*

Model	Hardware Specifications	Performance		Software Image
		Forwarding Bandwidth	Forwarding Rate[1]	
2950SX-24	24 x 10/100BASE-T 2 x fixed 1000BASE-SX	8.8 Gbps	6.6 Mpps	Standard image (SI)
2950T-24	24 x 10/100BASE-T 2 x fixed 1000BASE-T	8.8 Gbps	6.6 Mpps	Enhanced image (EI)
2950G-12	12 x 10/100BASE-T 2 x fixed 1000BASE-X[2]	6.4 Gbps	4.8 Mpps	Enhanced image (EI)
2950G-24[3]	24 x 10/100BASE-T 2 x fixed 1000BASE-X[2]	8.8 Gbps	6.6 Mpps	Enhanced image (EI)
2950G-48	48 x 10/100BASE-T 2 x fixed 1000BASE-X[2]	13.6 Gbps	10.1 Mpps	Enhanced Image (EI)

[1]Mpps = million packets per second, based upon a packet size of 64 bytes

[2]1000BASE-X ports require a separate Gigabit Interface Converter (GBIC) of the appropriate Gigabit Ethernet technology (GigaStack, 1000BASE-T, 1000BASE-SX, 1000BASE-LX/LH or 1000BASE-ZX) to connect to the network.

[3]A model is available with DC power supply

As you can see from Table 1-2, many different models exist, each with different hardware and software specifications. In terms of software image, it is important to understand the difference between the standard image and enhanced image:

- **Standard image**—The standard image is a Layer 2 only image and provides traditional switching features. Standard image switches have no understanding of Layer 3/4 packets, meaning they look only at Ethernet headers and switch packets based upon those headers.

- **Enhanced image**—This image provides Layer 3/4 intelligence, allowing the switch to look deeper into frames to identify traffic generated by particular hosts and networks, as well as the applications that have generated a frame. These capabilities provide advanced security and quality of service (QoS) features for devices and applications in the network, all at wire speed without affecting switching performance. The enhanced image is essential for any network that runs converged voice, video, and data networks, because the switch can identify critical voice and video traffic, classify it as high priority, and then prioritize it when transmitting.

NOTE   It is important to understand that the Catalyst 2950 enhanced image does *not* provide Layer 3 routing capabilities, but rather the ability to understand the Layer 3 and Layer 4 properties of network traffic and apply security and/or QoS based upon those properties.

Figure 1-2 shows an example of the Catalyst 2950 switch (a Catalyst 2950G-48).

Figure 1-2   *The Catalyst 2950G-48 Switch*

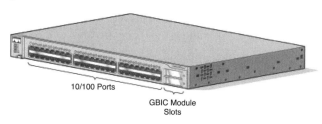

In Figure 1-2, notice the two GBIC slots, which provide connectivity for any combination of the following GBICs:

- **GigaStack (WS-X3500-XL)**—Provides a proprietary half-duplex or full-duplex gigabit Ethernet connectivity. These GBICs are used to stack up to 8 Catalyst switches in a cascaded or star configuration (star configuration requires an aggregation switch such as the 3550-12G) within close physical proximity.

- **1000BASE-T (WS-G5483)**—Provides copper-based gigabit Ethernet connectivity over UTP cable up to 100 m.

- **1000BASE-SX (WS-G5484)**—Provides short range fiber-based gigabit Ethernet connectivity over multimode fiber cable up to 550 m.

- **1000BASE-LX/LH (WS-G5486)**—Provides long range fiber-based gigabit Ethernet connectivity over single-mode fiber cable up to 10 km.

- **1000BASE-ZX (WS-G5487)**—Provides extended long range fiber-based gigabit Ethernet connectivity over single-mode fiber cable up to 100 km.

NOTE   All of the GBICs just described are supported on all gigabit-capable Cisco Catalyst switch platforms, with the exception of the GigaStack GBIC, which is only supported on Cisco Catalyst 29xx/35xx platforms. Support for the 1000BASE-T module on CatOS-based switches requires CatOS 7.2, and on the Catalyst 4000/4500 Supervisor 3/4 requires Cisco IOS 12.1(13)EW.

NOTE   Cisco also produces the Catalyst 2955 series of switches, which are 12-port switches with a variety of gigabit uplink options designed for industrial environments. The Catalyst 2955 ships with an industrial strength case, includes no moving parts, and ships with the enhanced software image.

Catalyst 3550 Family

The Catalyst 3550 switches represent the entry-level platform from Cisco that provides the ability to perform Layer 3 switching. Layer 3 switching is a feature that allows a switch to route traffic between different LAN segments (VLANs), without impacting performance. This allows organizations to gain the benefits of implementing a hierarchical Layer 3 routing topology in the LAN without sacrificing performance.

Cisco Catalyst 3550 switches still support traditional Layer 2 switching; in fact by default, a Catalyst 3550 operates as a Layer 2 switch. Layer 3 switching must be explicitly configured, and the features that you can configure for Layer 3 switching depend on the software image you have installed. Two software images are available when you purchase a Catalyst 3550 switch:

- **Standard Multilayer Image (SMI)**—The SMI image provides Layer 2 switching with Layer 3/4 intelligence to provide advanced security and quality of service features, as well as basic Layer 3 switching functionality. The SMI image supports only static routing and RIP and does not support other dynamic routing protocols such as Enhanced Interior Gateway Routing Protocol (EIGRP), Open Shortest Path First (OSPF), and Border Gateway Protocol (BGP). The EMI image is required for these protocols.

NOTE   Prior to Cisco IOS 12.1(13)a, the SMI image did not provide any Layer 3 switching features (i.e., static routing and RIP were not supported). With IOS 12.1(13)a and higher, Layer 3 switching using static routes and RIP is supported.

- **Enhanced Multilayer Image (EMI)**—The EMI image provides full Layer 2 switching and Layer 3 switching, with complete support for all popular IP routing protocols, including Routing Information Protocol (RIP), EIGRP, OSPF and BGP.

Table 1-3 provides a list of advanced features and describes there availability on the Catalyst 2950 SI and EI images, as well as the Catalyst 3550 SMI and EMI images.

Table 1-3   *Cisco Catalyst 2950/3550 Advanced Feature Comparison*

Category	Feature	Catalyst 2950		Catalyst 3550	
		SI	EI	SMI	EMI
Routing	IP routing (Static/RIP)	No	No	Yes	Yes
	IP routing (IGRP/EIGRP/OSPF/BGP)	No	No	No	Yes
	Multicast routing (PIM)	No	No	No	Yes
	Hot Standby Router Protocol (HSRP)	No	No	No	Yes
	Policy-based routing	No	No	No	Yes
	Multi-VRF CE	No	No	No	Yes
	WCCP	No	No	No	Yes

Table 1-3   *Cisco Catalyst 2950/3550 Advanced Feature Comparison (Continued)*

Category	Feature	Catalyst 2950		Catalyst 3550	
Switching	Maximum MAC addresses	8000	8000	8000	12000
	Maximum active VLANs	64	250	1000	1000
	Maximum STP instances	64	64	128	128
	ISL Trunking	No	No	Yes	Yes
	IGMP Snooping	Yes	Yes	Yes	Yes
	802.1s Multiple STP	No	Yes	Yes	Yes
	802.1w Rapid STP	No	Yes	Yes	Yes
	CrossStack UplinkFast	No	Yes	Yes	Yes
	Gigabit EtherChannel	No	Yes	Yes	Yes
Security	Port-based ACLs	No	Yes	Yes	Yes
	VLAN ACLs	No	No	Yes	Yes
	Router ACLs	No	No	Yes	Yes
	Secure Shell	No	Yes	Yes	Yes
	SNMPv3	No	Yes	Yes	Yes
	802.1x and per user ACLs	No	No	Yes	Yes
	802.1x and VLAN assignment	No	Yes	Yes	Yes
QoS	Class of Service (802.1p)	Yes	Yes	Yes	Yes
	DSCP support	No	Yes[1]	Yes[2]	Yes[2]
	IP Precedence support	No	No	Yes	Yes
	Ingress policing	No	Yes	Yes	Yes
	Egress policing	No	No	Yes	Yes
	WRED (gigabit ports)	No	No	Yes	Yes
	Auto QoS	No	Yes	Yes	Yes

[1]Only 13 DSCP values are support

[2]All DSCP values (64 values in total) are supported

As you can see from Table 1-3, the SI for the Catalyst 2950 provides hardly any advanced switching features at all. The Catalyst 3550 SMI possesses more features than the Catalyst 2950 EI, and the Catalyst 3550 EMI provides all features listed in Table 1-3.

Table 1-4 lists each of the Catalyst 3550 models and describes there hardware and software configuration. Each switch contains 16 MB flash and 64 MB memory.

Table 1-4   *Cisco Catalyst 3550 Models*

Model	Hardware Specifications	Performance		Software Image
		Forwarding Bandwidth	Forwarding Rate[1]	
3550-24FX	24 x 100BASE-FX 2 x 1000BASE-X	8.8 Gbps	6.6 Mpps	SMI or EMI
3550-24[2]	24 x 10/100BASE-T 2 x 1000BASE-X	8.8 Gbps	6.6 Mpps	SMI or EMI
3550-24PWR	24 x inline powered 10/100BASE-T 2 x 1000BASE-X	8.8 Gbps	6.6 Mpps	SMI or EMI
3550-48	48 x 10/100BASE-T 2 x 1000BASE-X	13.6 Gbps	10.1 Mpps	SMI or EMI
3550-12T	10 x 10/100/1000BASE-T 2 x 1000BASE-X	24 Gbps	17.0 Mpps	EMI only
3550-12G	10 x 1000BASE-X 2 x 10/100/1000BASE-T	24 Gbps	17.0 Mpps	EMI only

[1]Mpps = million packets per second, based upon a packet size of 64 bytes

[2]A model is available with DC power supply

In Table 1-4, notice the Catalyst 3500-12T and Catalyst 3550-12G, which provide 12 gigabit Ethernet ports and only ship with an EMI. These switches have a different physical layout to the other Catalyst 3550 models. Figure 1-3 and Figure 1-4 show examples of the Catalyst 3550 switches (the Catalyst 3550-48 and Catalyst 3550-12T).

Figure 1-3   *The Catalyst 3550-48 Switch*

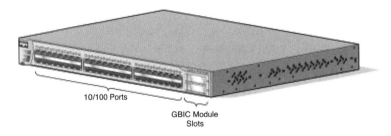

Figure 1-4   *The Catalyst 3550-12T Switch*

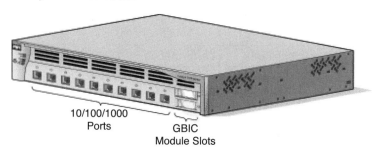

10/100/1000
Ports

GBIC
Module Slots

The GBIC options for 1000BASE-X ports on the Catalyst 3550 switches are the same as for the Catalyst 2950.

Catalyst 3750 Family

In April 2003, Cisco announced the Catalyst 3750 as a new product family. The Catalyst 3750 provides Cisco's first high density gigabit Ethernet over copper switch in a fixed chassis, providing up to 24 x 10/100/1000BASE-T ports + 4 x 1000BASE-X ports in a single 1.5RU chassis. The Catalyst 3750 is similar in many respects to the Catalyst 3550, with the same concept of SMI and EMI and full Layer 3 switching capabilities. It also provides several enhancements over the Catalyst 3550, which include the following:

- **Memory**—The Catalyst 3750 includes 128 MB memory (compared with 64 MB in Catalyst 3550), which allows for more unicast and multicast routes to be stored in the routing table.

- **Gigabit Ethernet over copper**—High-density 10/100/1000 gigabit Ethernet copper ports.

- **IP version 6 (IPv6)**—Support for hardware-based Layer 3 switching for IPv6 in future software releases.

- **Stackwise technology**—Enhances performance, scalability, and management by allowing up to 9 switches to be stacked using a 32-Gbps interconnect. All switches are managed as a single entity, with all ports from all switches appearing as part of a single virtual switch.

- **Jumbo frames**—Allows the 3750 to support oversized Ethernet frames on Gigabit Ethernet ports, which are important for high data transfer applications such as storage and video.

- **Support for SFP**—Provides 1000BASE-X connectivity with new small form-factor pluggable module technology, which replace the previous Gigabit Interface Converter (GBIC) technology. SFPs are much smaller than GBICs, allowing for up to 4 x 1000BASE-X connections on the Catalyst 3750 switch.

Table 1-5 lists each of the Catalyst 3750 switches. Each switch contains 16 MB flash and 128 MB memory.

Table 1-5   *Cisco Catalyst 3750 Models*

Model	Hardware Specifications	Performance		Software Image
		Forwarding Bandwidth	Forwarding Rate[1]	
3750-24TS	24 x 10/100BASE-T 4 x 1000BASE-X (SFP)	32 Gbps	6.5 Mpps	SMI or EMI
3750-48TS	48 x 10/100BASE-T 4 x 1000BASE-X (SFP)	32 Gbps	13.1 Mpps	SMI or EMI
3750-24T	24 x 10/100/1000BASE-T	32 Gbps	35.7 Mpps	SMI or EMI
3750-24TS	24 x 10/100/1000BASE-T 4 x 1000BASE-X (SFP)	32 Gbps	38.7 Mpps	SMI or EMI

[1]Mpps = million packets per second, based upon a packet size of 64 bytes

Catalyst 4000/4500 Family

The Catalyst 4000/4500 switch family represents the entry-level chassis-based switch offering from Cisco. The Catalyst 4000/4500 switches are made up of three basic components:

- **Chassis**—This includes the switch chassis, power supplies, and fans.
- **Supervisor engine**—This includes the switch processor and switching engine and is required to operate the switch.
- **Switching modules**—These provide ports for connecting various types of devices to the switch.

Each of these components are now discussed.

Catalyst 4000/4500 Chassis

The chassis provided by the Catalyst 4000/4500 series switches vary across the Catalyst 4000 and Catalyst 4500 family. The major difference between the Catalyst 4000 series chassis and Catalyst 4500 series chassis is power; the Catalyst 4500 has an improved power distribution system that is capable of supporting inline power (i.e., the ability to power phones and wireless access points over Ethernet cabling) without requiring an external power shelf (as is required with the Catalyst 4000). The Catalyst 4500 series also provides a chassis that allows for redundant supervisor engines, whereas the Catalyst 4000 series chassis do not provide this.

Within the Catalyst 4000 series, two chassis are provided:

- **Catalyst 4003**—3-slot chassis that provides one supervisor slot and two data slots.
- **Catalyst 4006**—6-slot chassis that provides one supervisor slot and five data slots.

Within the Catalyst 4500 series, three chassis are provided:

- **Catalyst 4503**—3-slot chassis that provides one supervisor slot and two data slots.
- **Catalyst 4506**—6-slot chassis that provides one supervisor slot and five data slots.
- **Catalyst 4507R**—7-slot chassis that provides two supervisor slots (one for redundancy) and five data slots.

Figure 1-5 and Figure 1-6 shows examples of the Catalyst 4000 and 4500 chassis (the Catalyst 4006 and 4507R).

Figure 1-5   *The Catalyst 4006 Chassis*

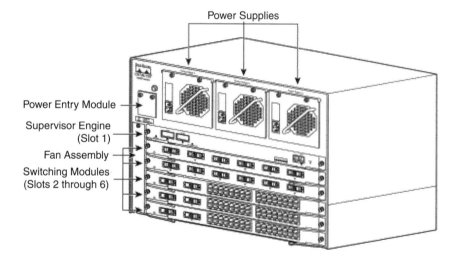

It is important to note that the Catalyst 2948G and Catalyst 2980G switches are essentially fixed configuration Catalyst 4000 switches with a Supervisor engine, power supply and a fixed configuration of 48 * 10/100BASE-T + 2 * 1000BASE-X ports (2948G) or 80 * 10/100BASE-T + 2 * 1000BASE-X ports (2980G). Figure 1-7 shows the Catalyst 2980G switch.

Figure 1-6 *The Catalyst 4507R Chassis*

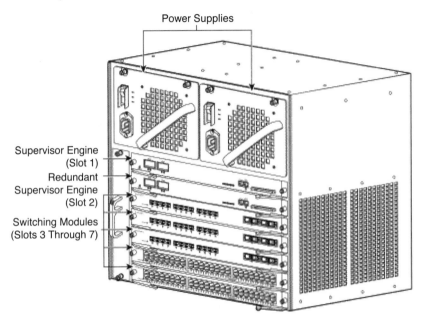

Figure 1-7 *The Catalyst 2980G Switch*

Supervisor Engines

The Catalyst 4000/4500 switch family consists of four Supervisor engines, which each vary in internal architecture, functionality, and operating system used for switch management. Table 1-6 describes each of the Catalyst 4000/4500 supervisors

Table 1-6   *Cisco Catalyst 4000/4500 Supervisor Engines*

Supervisor	Supported Chassis	Performance		Operating System
		Forwarding Bandwidth	Forwarding Rate[1]	
Supervisor 1	4003	24 Gbps	18 Mpps	CatOS
Supervisor 2	4006 4503 4506	64 Gbps[2]	18 Mpps	CatOS
Supervisor 3	4006 4503 4506	64 Gbps[2]	48 Mpps[3]	Cisco IOS
Supervisor 4	4006 4503 4506 4507R	64 Gbps[2]	48 Mpps[3]	Cisco IOS

[1]Mpps = million packets per second, based upon a packet size of 64 bytes

[2]Forwarding bandwidth is 28 Gbps in Catalyst 4503

[3]The same forwarding rate applies for Layer 2 and Layer 3 switched traffic

The Supervisor 1 and Supervisor 2 engines are Layer 2 switching only supervisors and are managed using the CatOS operating system. It is important to note that the Supervisor 2 contains a blocking architecture internally, meaning congestion is possible in certain configurations internally on the Supervisor. Figure 1-8 shows the internal blocking architecture of the Supervisor 2 switch.

Figure 1-8 *Internal Architecture of Supervisor 2 Switch*

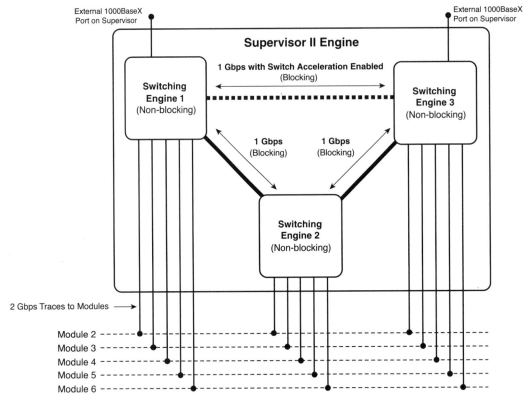

In Figure 1-8, notice that three separate switching engines (SEs) exist (each provide 24-Gbps internal non-blocking forwarding bandwidth), with each providing a 2-Gbps full-duplex trace to each module in the chassis (providing a total of 3 * 2-Gbps or 6-Gbps full-duplex bandwidth to each module).

Be careful of the "marketing terms" using by Cisco and other switch vendors to provide forwarding bandwidth performance figures. The quoted performance figures always refer to the total system bandwidth and not to the full-duplex bandwidth provided. For example, a 1-Gbps full-duplex connection is considered to provide a total of 2-Gbps bandwidth (1 Gbps in one direction, 1 Gbps in the other direction). In the case of SE1 and SE3 on a Catalyst 4000 Supervisor 2, each SE has 5 * 2-Gbps full-duplex connections to each line card, a single external 1-Gbps full-duplex 1000BASE-X connection on the supervisor and a 1-Gbps full-duplex connection to SE2. This provides a total of 12 Gbps full-duplex bandwidth (5 * 2 + 1 + 1), or a total forwarding bandwidth of 24 Gbps.

Although each SE is non-blocking internally, a single 1-Gbps full-duplex connection inter-connects the switching engines, which potentially causes blocking (congestion) on the interconnections between each SE if devices attached to one switching engine are commu-nicating with devices attached to another switching engine.

NOTE   If you are not using the two external 1000BASE-X ports on the Supervisor 2 module, you can disable them by configuring switch acceleration and introduce a third 1-Gbps interconnection between SE1 and SE3, reducing the amount of potential blocking (see dashed connection between SE1 and SE3 in Figure 1-8). You can also purchase a backplane channel module for the Supervisor 2, which doubles the bandwidth between each switching engine from 1 Gbps to 2 Gbps.

The Supervisor 3 and Supervisor 4 engines are Layer 2 and Layer 3 switching capable and are managed using the Cisco IOS operating system. These supervisors are completely non-blocking internally, unlike the Supervisor 1 and Supervisor 2, consisting essentially of one large non-blocking switching engine to which each module trace connects to. Just as for the Catalyst 3550/3750 switches, a basic image provides Layer 3 switching using static and RIP routing, whilst a separate enhanced image provides full Layer 3 switching using static, RIP, IGRP, EIGRP, OSPF, and BGP routing.

NOTE   The differences between the Supervisor 3 and Supervisor 4 include memory (128 MB in Supervisor 3, 256 MB in Supervisor 4); support for redundant supervisors (Supervisor 4); and the ability to add a NetFlow feature daughter card (Supervisor 4).

Switching Modules

The Catalyst 4000/4500 switch family provides for a wide variety of switching modules, allowing for high-density 10/100BASE-T, 10/100/1000BASE-T, and 1000BASE-X deployments. Other modules supported include a Layer 3 routing module (for Supervisor 1/2 deployment, not supported in Supervisor 3/4) and an access gateway module (provides voice gateway functionality). Table 1-7 lists some of the switching modules available for the Catalyst 4000/4500.

Table 1-7   *Cisco Catalyst 4000/4500 Switching Modules*

Module Part Number	Description
WS-X4148-RJ	48 x 10/100BASE-T RJ-45 ports
WS-X4148-RJ45V	48 x inline powered 10/100BASE-T RJ-45 ports
WS-X4148-RJ21	48 x 10/100BASE-T ports with RJ-21 Telco connectors
WS-X4232-GB-RJ	32 x 10/100BASE-T + 2 x 1000BASE-X
WS-X4232-L3	Layer 3 Router module 32 x 10/100BASE-T and 2 x 1000BASE-X ports
WS-X4424-GB-RJ45	24 x 10/100/1000BASE-T
WS-X4448-GB-RJ45	48 x 10/100/1000BASE-T
WS-X4448-GB-LX	48 x 1000BASE-LX
WS-X4306-GB	6 x 1000BASE-X
WS-X4418-GB	18 x 1000BASE-X

Catalyst 6000/6500 Family

The Catalyst 6000/6500 family represents the flagship of the Cisco Catalyst switching product range. The switch is aimed at the enterprise network and also at service provider networks. The Catalyst 6000/6500 is chassis-based, which means that it consists of the same fundamental components as a Catalyst 4000/4500 switch (i.e., chassis, supervisor engine, and switching modules), which are now discussed in more detail.

Catalyst 6000/6500 Chassis

The chassis provided by the Catalyst 6000/6500 series switches vary across the Catalyst 6000 and Catalyst 6500 family. The differences between the Catalyst 6000 series chassis and Catalyst 6500 series are listed below:

- **Backplane**—Both the Catalyst 6000 and Catalyst 6500 contain a shared 32-Gbps backplane; however, the Catalyst 6500 also supports an upgrade to a 256-Gbps crossbar switching matrix by adding an optional switch fabric module.

- **Scalability**—The Catalyst 6000 is provided only in a 6-slot chassis (6006) and 9-slot (6009) chassis, while the 6500 provides 3-slot (6503), 6-slot (6506), 9-slot (6509), and 13-slot (6513) chassis options.

Figure 1-9 and Figure 1-10 shows examples of the Catalyst 6000 and 6500 chassis (the Catalyst 6006 and 6509).

Figure 1-9   *The Catalyst 6006 Chassis*

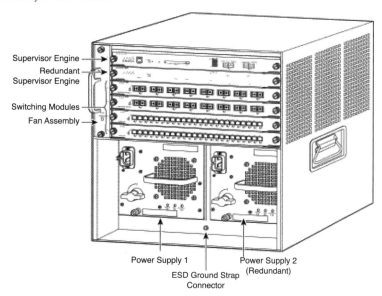

Supervisor Engine
Redundant Supervisor Engine
Switching Modules
Fan Assembly

Power Supply 1
ESD Ground Strap Connector
Power Supply 2 (Redundant)

Figure 1-10   *The Catalyst 6509 Chassis*

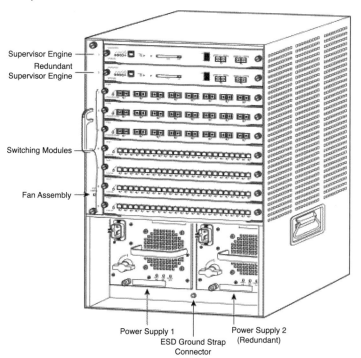

Supervisor Engine
Redundant Supervisor Engine
Switching Modules
Fan Assembly

Power Supply 1
ESD Ground Strap Connector
Power Supply 2 (Redundant)

Supervisor Engines

The Catalyst 6000/6500 switch family consists of three Supervisor engines, which each vary in terms of functionality and performance:

- **Supervisor 1A**—Provides support for advanced security and QoS features, as well as MLS-based (Multilayer switching) Layer 3 switching. The Supervisor 1A supports a backplane capacity of 32 Gbps and a Layer 2/Layer 3 forwarding rate of up to 15 Mpps.

- **Supervisor 2**—Provides support for advanced security and QoS features, as well as CEF-based (Cisco Express Forwarding) Layer 3 switching. The Supervisor 2 also supports the switch fabric module (SFM), which increases backplane capacity from 32 Gbps to 256 Gbps and supports a Layer 2/Layer 3 forwarding rate of up to 210 Mpps.

- **Supervisor 720**—Provides support for advanced security and QoS features, as well as advanced CEF-based Layer 3 switching. The Layer 3 switching engine supports IPv6 routing, network address translation, GRE tunneling, and MPLS all in hardware. The Supervisor 720 includes a crossbar switching matrix (formerly provided via the separate SFM in conjunction with the Supervisor 2), which provides a backplane capacity of 720 Gbps and a Layer 2/Layer 3 forwarding rate of up to 200 Mpps (IPv6) and 400 Mpps (IPv4). The Supervisor 720 also includes PFC3 and MSFC3 daughter cards (discussed later), which provide the Layer 3 switching capabilities of the Supervisor.

All supervisors can be installed in redundant pairs, ensuring maximum availability in the event of an active supervisor failure. Any additional add-on modules that extend system performance or functionality (e.g., SFM, PFC daughter card, and MSFC daughter card) can also be installed in a redundant configuration, ensuring the highest levels of availability

You have learned that the Supervisor 2 engine supports the SFM; each Supervisor also supports two types of add-on modules onboard the Supervisor itself (i.e., daughter cards), which extend the functionality and performance of the supervisor engine to provide the features and performance described above. These daughter cards are described as follows:

- **Policy feature card (PFC)**—The PFC provides Layer 3/4 intelligence, allowing for advanced security and QoS features to be applied based upon the Layer 3 and Layer 4 parameters of traffic. The PFC also provides the hardware forwarding engine when Layer 3 switching is enabled with the addition of an MSFC. The PFC can be installed just by itself, without the MSFC (discussed next).

- **Multilayer switching feature card (MSFC)**—The MSFC is essentially a router on a daughter card, providing full Layer 3 routing functionality and enabling the Catalyst 6000/6500 to perform Layer 3 switching. In a Layer 3 switching configuration, the MSFC provides the control plane component of L3 switching (i.e., populating and maintaining the routing table), while the PFC provides the data plane component of L3 switching (i.e., rewriting frame and packet headers and switching routed packets to the appropriate egress port), which means you must have a PFC installed before installing an MSFC. The MSFC also allows the switch to operate in *native IOS*, where the Supervisor and MSFC are managed via a single Cisco IOS-based management interface, integrating Layer 2 and Layer 3 switching management (similar to the Catalyst 3550 EMI and Catalyst 4000/4500 Supervisor 3/4).

NOTE   Without a MSFC, the Catalyst 6000/6500 Supervisor engines operate the CatOS operating system. When you add a MSFC, by default, the Supervisor still runs CatOS and the MSFC runs Cisco IOS (this configuration is known as referred to as *hybrid IOS*). You can then configure the switch to operate in native IOS mode, where the Supervisor and MSFC are managed by the same Cisco IOS management interface, as long as the switch has an MSFC installed.

There are three generations of PFC and MSFC modules, with various combinations of Supervisor engines and different versions of PFC and MSFC modules making it a reasonably complex task to understand which features are supported in each configuration. Chapter 6, "Layer 3 Switching," discusses the features of the various Supervisor, PFC, and MSFC configurations in more detail.

Switching Modules

On the Catalyst 6000/6500, you can purchase three types of line cards:

- **Classic**—A classic module connects to the 32-Gbps shared backplane only.

- **Fabric-enabled**—A fabric-enabled module connects to both the 32-Gbps backplane and also has an 8-Gbps full-duplex connection to the 256-Gbps crossbar switch matrix (requires Supervisor 720 or switch fabric module installed).

- **Fabric-only**—Connects only to the 256-Gbps crossbar switch matrix via dual 8-Gbps full-duplex connections (requires Supervisor 720 or switch fabric module installed).

Even though there are three types of modules, all modules can communicate with each other, even if they are attached to different switching backplanes (e.g., classic and fabric-only cards are not connected to the same bus). In this situation, an interconnection between the crossbar switching matrix is interconnected with the shared bus backplane allows classic cards and fabric-only cards to communicate. Table 1-8 lists some of the LAN switching modules available for the Catalyst 6000/6500.

Table 1-8   *Cisco Catalyst 6000/6500 Switching Modules*

Module Part Number	Description
WS-X6148-RJ-45	48 x 10/100BASE-T RJ-45 ports
WS-X6148-RJ-45V	48 x inline powered 10/100BASE-T RJ-45 ports
WS-X6148-RJ-21	48 x 10/100BASE-T with RJ-21 Telco connectors
WS-X6348-RJ-45	48 x 10/100BASE-T RJ-45 ports (Enhanced QoS)
WS-X6348-RJ-45V	48 x inline powered 10/100BASE-T RJ-45 ports (Enhanced QoS)
WS-X6348-RJ-21	48 x 10/100BASE-T with RJ-21 Telco connectors (Enhanced QoS)
WS-X6548-RJ-45	48 x 10/100BASE-T RJ-45 ports (Fabric enabled)
WS-X6548-RJ-45V	48 x inline powered 10/100BASE-T RJ-45 ports (Fabric enabled)
WS-X6548-RJ-21	48 x 10/100BASE-T with RJ-21 Telco connectors (Fabric enabled)
WS-X6408A-GBIC	8 x 1000BASE-X
WS-X6416-GBIC	16 x 1000BASE-X
WS-X6316-GE-TX	16 x 1000BASE-T
WS-X6516-GE-TX	16 x 1000BASE-T (Fabric enabled)

Perhaps one of the best features of the Catalyst 6000/6500 switch is the capability to extend switch functionality well outside the bounds of pure LAN switching and Layer 3 switching. The Catalyst 6000/6500 not only provides LAN switching modules, which allow for high-density 10/100BASE-T, 10/100/1000BASE-T, and 1000BASE-X deployments, but also provides a wide range of other modules called *services modules* that extend and enhance the functionality of the Catalyst 6000/6500. The following lists some examples of the services modules available for the Catalyst 6000/6500 switch:

- **Firewall services module (WS-SVC-FWM-1-K9)**—Essentially a PIX firewall on steroids, this module provides up to 5 Gbps firewall throughput, ensuring advanced security features can be implemented in the network without compromising performance.

- **IPSec virtual private network (VPN) services module (WS-SVC-IPSEC-1)**—Provides up to 1.9 Gbps of triple DES VPN performance, ensuring private data can be protected without comprising performance.

- **Intrusion detection system module (WS-SVC-IDS2BUNK9), also known as IDSM)**—Analyzes traffic from multiple VLANs for intrusive activity that might indicate an attack against the network, generating alarms and configuring security devices to block attacks. The latest IDSM can analyze up to 600 Mbps of traffic.

- **Content switching module (WS-SVC-CSG-1)**—Provides intelligent application-layer load balancing for web server farms and other application server farms, providing enhanced performance, availability, and scalability.

- **Network analysis module (WS-SVC-NAM-x)**—Provides intelligent network monitoring using Remote Monitoring (RMON) and network statistics using NetFlow capture.

As you can see from the preceding, the Catalyst 6000/6500 is not just a LAN switch; it is a platform that can integrate LAN switching features with advanced security, application, and network management features.

Catalyst Operating Systems

Today there are two main operating systems that are used on Cisco Catalyst switches:

- Catalyst Operating System (CatOS)
- Cisco Internetwork Operating System (Cisco IOS)

You are most likely familiar with Cisco IOS; Cisco IOS is the popular operating system installed on nearly all Cisco routers and is a very mature, feature-rich, and extensible operating system that offers Cisco customers significant value-add and return on investment. Historically, Cisco acquired a few major switch vendors in the early- to mid-1990s, which resulted in the introduction of what is now known as CatOS. CatOS is used to operate the following platforms:

- Catalyst 2900/4000/4500 with Supervisor 1/2
- Catalyst 5000/5500
- Catalyst 6000/6500

CatOS has a very easy to use command-line interface and has traditionally supported bulk administration tasks much more effectively than Cisco IOS. These are important features when configuring a device that potentially has more than 500 ports.

NOTE   The ability to perform bulk administration tasks has been addressed in later releases of Cisco IOS.

Unlike Cisco IOS, which has many configuration modes and different commands, CatOS provides three basic types of commands:

- **set**—These commands apply some configuration to the switch. For example, the **set system name** command is used to configure the switch name.
- **clear**—These commands remove some configuration from the switch.
- **show**—These commands display configuration status information, which allows you to verify the operational configuration.

Other commands are used for system management, such as **copy** and **write;** however, for configuration tasks, you will only ever use the **set** and **clear** commands and then use **show** commands to verify your configuration.

NOTE   Many chassis-based CatOS switches support optional Layer 3 routing modules (e.g., Catalyst 5000/5500 RSM, Catalyst 6000/6500 MSFC), which include their own Cisco IOS. This means that the module essentially just uses the switch chassis for power and network connectivity, with management of the module performed separately from the Supervisor that runs the switch. When CatOS is used to manage the Layer 2 switching component, and Cisco IOS is used to manage the Layer 3 routing component, the switch is said to be managed using hybrid IOS, because two different operating systems (CatOS and Cisco IOS) are used to manage the switch.

Cisco plans to eventually phase out CatOS, moving all switching platforms to Cisco IOS, which will allow for a uniform management interface across all Cisco switches and routers, as well as better integration of Cisco switching and routing features. Today, the following platforms are based upon Cisco IOS:

- Catalyst 2900XL/3500XL
- Catalyst 2950/3550/3750
- Catalyst 4000/4500 Supervisor 3/4
- Catalyst 6000/6500 with MSFC running native IOS

As you can see from the preceding list, the Catalyst 4000/4500 and Catalyst 6000/6500 switches can either run CatOS or Cisco IOS, which leads to the question: Which operating system should I run? On the Catalyst 4000/4500, the operating system is tied to the type of Supervisor engine, and normally the much higher performance capabilities and integrated Layer 3 switching capabilities of the Cisco IOS-based Supervisor 3/4 engines make them the obvious choice. It should be noted, however, that many features are still present in CatOS that are not present in Cisco IOS and that many new features are first released into CatOS code before Cisco IOS. This applies also to the Catalyst 6000/6500, where you can use either CatOS or Cisco IOS regardless of the Supervisor engine installed.

NOTE   Although CatOS still leads the development efforts in terms of new features over comparative Cisco IOS features, Cisco has indicated that this is short lived, with a goal of introducing feature parity and then focusing on the development of new features on Cisco IOS.

Although Cisco IOS might be the way of the future, for now and many years to come, there still exists a large deployment of CatOS-based switches. This means you must ideally be proficient in both Cisco IOS and CatOS if you want to design, implement, and support Cisco switched networks.

Scenario 1-1: Installing a Cisco Catalyst Switch onto the Network

The first step in successfully integrating Cisco Catalyst switches into the network is to install the switch and configure the switch so that it can operate correctly on the network. In this scenario you learn how to prepare Cisco Catalyst switches for operation on the network. It is important to implement a well-planned switch installation so that you can then attach devices and configure more advanced features with the knowledge that you have a stable platform to build upon. This scenario introduces fundamental configuration tasks of Cisco Catalyst switches that you should know and understand intimately.

Figure 1-11 illustrates the topology used for this scenario.

Figure 1-11   *Scenario 1-1 Topology*

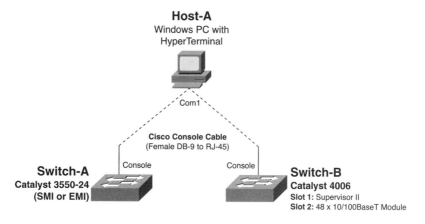

In Figure 1-11, Switch-A is a Catalyst 3550 switch, which enables you to learn how to prepare and install Cisco IOS-based switches. Switch-B is a Catalyst 4006 switch, which enables you to how to prepare and install CatOS-based switches. Notice that no devices are actually connected to either switch. In subsequent scenarios, you learn how to configure connectivity for end devices.

Configuration Tasks

In this scenario, you learn how to perform the following configuration tasks:

- Installing the switch
- Gaining initial management access
- Configuring system identity
- Configure management access

Installing the Switch

Before installing Cisco Catalyst switches onto the network, you must ensure that you have the appropriate hardware required for the switch to operate, as well as other physical requirements such as power, rack space, and the appropriate environmental conditions. On fixed configuration switches, such as the Catalyst 3550, the only hardware you might need to ensure you have are optional gigabit Ethernet GBICs. All other hardware is included with the switch. On chassis-based switches, however, you must ensure you have all the appropriate hardware to run your switch modules correctly. Obviously, at least one Supervisor is required, and you probably need a line card to connect devices to. However, of particular importance on chassis-based switches is power; you must have the appropriate power supplies installed to meet the power requirements of each of the modules installed, and you must understand the requirements for redundant power if this is desired.

Table 1-9 lists the AC power requirements for the Catalyst 4000/4500 switches. For the Catalyst 6000/6500 switches, see www.cisco.com/univercd/cc/td/doc/product/lan/cat6000/sw_6_2/confg_gd/admin.htm#46335.

Table 1-9 *Minimum Power Requirements for Cisco Catalyst Chassis-based Switches*

Platform	Configuration		Minimum Power Supply Requirements
	RPS (n+1)	**Inline Power[1]**	
Catalyst 4000	No	No	2 x 400W (WS-X4008)
	Yes	No	3 x 400W (WS-X4008)
	No	Yes	Provides up to 240 inline ports 2 x 400W (WS-X4008) 1 x 2100W DC External Power Shelf (WS-P4603-2PSU) 1 x DC Power Entry Module (WS-X4095-PEM)
	Yes	Yes	Provides up to 240 inline ports 3 x 400W (WS-X4008) 1 x 2100W DC External Power Shelf (WS-P4603-2PSU) 1 x 1050W Auxiliary PSU for External Power Shelf (WS-X4608) 1 x DC Power Entry Module (WS-X4095-PEM)

Table 1-9   *Minimum Power Requirements for Cisco Catalyst Chassis-based Switches (Continued)*

Platform	Configuration		Minimum Power Supply Requirements
	RPS (n+1)	**Inline Power[1]**	
Catalyst 4500[2]	No	No	1 x 1000W (PWR-C45-1000AC)
	Yes	No	2 x 1000W (PWR-C45-1000AC)
	No	Yes	Up to 126[3] inline ports: 1 x 1300W Up to 211 inline ports: 2 x 1300W in combined mode Up to 222 inline ports: 1 x 2800W Up to 240 inline ports: 2 x 2800W in combined mode
	Yes	Yes	Up to 126 inline ports: 2 x 1300W in redundant mode Up to 222 inline ports: 2 x 2800W in redundant mode

[1]Assumes each inline device requires 6.3W of power

[2]The Catalyst 4503 supports a maximum of 96 inline powered ports only, as only two slots are available for inline-powered Ethernet modules

[3]The Catalyst 4507R with dual Supervisor 4 engines only supports up to 111 inline devices with a single 1300W power supply

As you can see in Table 1-9, the power requirements for chassis-based switches vary, depending on if you require a redundant power supply and/or if you require inline-powered ports.

NOTE

For more information on inline power requirements for the Catalyst 4000, see www.cisco.com/warp/public/cc/pd/si/casi/ca4000/prodlit/c4k2_ds.htm. For more information on inline power requirements for the Catalyst 4500, see www.cisco.com/warp/public/cc/pd/si/casi/ps4324/prodlit/inpow_an.htm.

Assuming power, rack space, and environmental requirements have been met, in terms of hardware components, if you have a fixed configuration switch (e.g., Switch-A, which is a Catalyst 3550 switch), then the switch will work out of the box without requiring any other components. If you have a chassis-based switch, the following components are required to install the switch and begin configuration:

- **Switch chassis**—Provides slots for installing power supplies, supervisor engines, and line cards.
- **Power supplies**—All chassis-based switches require at least one power supply. Some switches (e.g., the Catalyst 4000 series) required at least two power supplies to properly power all line cards in the switch.
- **Supervisor engine**—Provides the switch processor and switching engine, which allows you to configure the switch and enable LAN switching between devices attached to line cards.
- **One or more line cards**—Provide LAN connectivity for end devices.

In this scenario, Switch-B is a chassis-based Catalyst 4006 switch, and it is assumed the following components are used:

- 1 x Catalyst 4006 chassis (WS-C4006)
- 1 x Supervisor 2 Engine (WS-X4013)
- 2 x AC power supplies (WS-X4008)
- 1 x 48-port 10/100 line card (WS-X4148-RJ)

Gaining Initial Management Access

After ensuring all of the physical components that make up the switch are installed and then physically installing the switch into the rack, the next task is to power on the switch, gain initial management access, and verify that the system has come up correctly and that the system software and hardware configuration is correct. This consists of the following tasks:

- Establishing a console connection
- Verifying system bootup
- Gaining privileged mode access
- Verifying system configuration

Establishing a Console Connection

On all Cisco Catalyst switches, a console port is provided, which allows serial access to a command-line interface (CLI) shell that allows you to manage the switch. To gain management access via the console port, the following components are required:

- A PC with a male DB-9 or DB-25 serial port
- A console cable with appropriate adapters that enables interconnection of the PC serial port and console port
- Terminal emulation software such as HyperTerminal

All Cisco Catalyst switches ship with the appropriate cables and adapters that allow you to connect the console port to a male DB-9 serial port on a PC or laptop. Newer Cisco Catalyst switches provide an RJ-45 physical interface for console access. However, older switches might provide a DB-9 or DB-25 interface. In this scenario, both the Catalyst 3550 and Supervisor 2 engine on the Catalyst 4006 provide an RJ-45 console port.

After physically connecting your PC or laptop to the console port of the switch, you must next start your terminal emulation application and establish a connection to the console port. All Cisco Catalyst switches provide console port access using the following connection parameters:

- Connection speed = 9600 bps
- Data bits = 8
- Parity = None
- Stop bits = 1
- Flow control = None

Figure 1-12 demonstrates configuring HyperTerminal with the appropriate serial port settings to gain management access via the console port.

Figure 1-12   *HyperTerminal Serial Connection Settings*

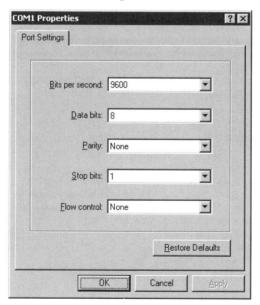

On HyperTerminal, the default speed setting is 2400 bps, with hardware-based flow control enabled, which must be modified to ensure a console connection can be established.

Verifying System Bootup

After establishing a console connection, your terminal emulation window just looks blank, because at this stage you have not powered on the switch. After powering on the switch, you should see the switch begin its boot sequence, which is important to monitor to ensure the switch boots correctly. Example 1-1 demonstrates the switch bootup sequence on Switch-A, which is a Cisco IOS-based Catalyst 3550 switch.

Example 1-1   *System Bootup on the Catalyst 3550 Switch*

```
Base ethernet MAC Address: 00:09:b7:bb:8d:08
Xmodem file system is available.
The password-recovery mechanism is enabled.
Initializing Flash...
flashfs[0]: 20 files, 3 directories
flashfs[0]: 0 orphaned files, 0 orphaned directories
flashfs[0]: Total bytes: 15998976
flashfs[0]: Bytes used: 6593024
flashfs[0]: Bytes available: 9405952
flashfs[0]: flashfs fsck took 15 seconds.
...done Initializing Flash.
Boot Sector Filesystem (bs:) installed, fsid: 3
Loading "flash:c3550-i5k2l2q3-mz.121-13.EA1a/c3550-i5k2l2q3-mz.121-13.EA1a.bin"
...############################################################################
##############################################################################
##############################################################################
##############################################################################
##############################################################################
##############################################################################
##########################################################

File "flash:c3550-i5k2l2q3-mz.121-13.EA1a/c3550-i5k2l2q3-mz.121-13.EA1a.bin"
uncompressed and installed, entry point: 0x3000
executing...

                  Restricted Rights Legend

Use, duplication, or disclosure by the Government is
subject to restrictions as set forth in subparagraph
 of the Commercial Computer Software - Restricted
Rights clause at FAR sec. 52.227-19 and subparagraph
 (1) (ii) of the Rights in Technical Data and Computer
Software clause at DFARS sec. 252.227-7013.

          cisco Systems, Inc.
          170 West Tasman Drive
          San Jose, California 95134-1706



Cisco Internetwork Operating System Software
IOS (tm) C3550 Software (C3550-I5K2L2Q3-M), Version 12.1(13)EA1a,
    RELEASE SOFTWARE (fc1)
Copyright  1986-2003 by cisco Systems, Inc.
```

Example 1-1   *System Bootup on the Catalyst 3550 Switch (Continued)*

```
Compiled Tue 25-Mar-03 23:56 by yenanh
Image text-base: 0x00003000, data-base: 0x008BA914


Initializing flashfs...
flashfs[1]: 20 files, 3 directories
flashfs[1]: 0 orphaned files, 0 orphaned directories
flashfs[1]: Total bytes: 15998976
flashfs[1]: Bytes used: 6593024
flashfs[1]: Bytes available: 9405952
flashfs[1]: flashfs fsck took 8 seconds.
flashfs[1]: Initialization complete.
...done Initializing flashfs.
POST: CPU Buffer Tests : Begin
POST: CPU Buffer Tests : End, Status Passed
POST: CPU Interface Tests : Begin
POST: CPU Interface Tests : End, Status Passed
POST: Switch Core Tests : Begin
POST: Switch Core Tests : End, Status Passed
POST: CPU Interface 2nd Stage Tests : Begin
POST: CPU Interface 2nd Stage Tests : End, Status Passed
POST: CAM Subsystem Tests : Begin
POST: CAM Subsystem Tests : End, Status Passed
POST: Ethernet Controller Tests : Begin
POST: Ethernet Controller Tests : End, Status Passed
POST: Loopback Tests : Begin
POST: Loopback Tests : End, Status Passed


This product contains cryptographic features and is subject to United
States and local country laws governing import, export, transfer and
use. Delivery of Cisco cryptographic products does not imply
third-party authority to import, export, distribute or use encryption.
Importers, exporters, distributors and users are responsible for
compliance with U.S. and local country laws. By using this product you
agree to comply with applicable laws and regulations. If you are unable
to comply with U.S. and local laws, return this product immediately.

A summary of U.S. laws governing Cisco cryptographic products may be found at:
http://www.cisco.com/wwl/export/crypto/tool/stqrg.html

If you require further assistance please contact us by sending email to
export@cisco.com.

cisco WS-C3550-24 (PowerPC) processor (revision C0) with 65526K/8192K
    bytes of memory.
Processor board ID CAT0620X0HV
Last reset from warm-reset
Bridging software.
Running Layer2/3 Switching Image

Ethernet-controller 1 has 12 Fast Ethernet/IEEE 802.3 interfaces
```

continues

Example 1-1 *System Bootup on the Catalyst 3550 Switch (Continued)*

```
Ethernet-controller 2 has 12 Fast Ethernet/IEEE 802.3 interfaces

Ethernet-controller 3 has 1 Gigabit Ethernet/IEEE 802.3 interface

Ethernet-controller 4 has 1 Gigabit Ethernet/IEEE 802.3 interface

24 FastEthernet/IEEE 802.3 interface(s)
2 Gigabit Ethernet/IEEE 802.3 interface(s)

The password-recovery mechanism is enabled.
384K bytes of flash-simulated non-volatile configuration memory.
Base ethernet MAC Address: 00:09:B7:BB:8D:08
Motherboard assembly number: 73-5700-99
Power supply part number: 34-0966-02
Motherboard serial number: CAT062843JA
Power supply serial number: LIT0636005A
Model revision number: C0
Motherboard revision number: B0
Model number: WS-C3550-24-EMI
System serial number: CAT0620Y1JJ


Press RETURN to get started!


00:00:34: %SPANTREE-5-EXTENDED_SYSID: Extended SysId enabled for type vlan
00:00:36: %SYS-5-CONFIG_I: Configured from memory by console
00:00:36: %SYS-5-RESTART: System restarted --
Cisco Internetwork Operating System Software
IOS (tm) C3550 Software (C3550-I5K2L2Q3-M), Version 12.1(13)EA1a,
    RELEASE SOFTWARE (fc1)
Copyright  1986-2003 by cisco Systems, Inc.
Compiled Tue 25-Mar-03 23:56 by yenanh

Switch>
```

In Example 1-1, the following processes occur during the boot process:

- Flash file system is initialized; an operating system image is found and is loaded.

- The operating system performs a series of Power-On Self-Test (POST) tests, ensuring system hardware is functioning correctly. In Example 1-1, notice that all POST tests pass, which indicates all hardware is functional.

- The operating system provides an indication as to the current interfaces installed on the system. This should match the physical interface configuration of the switch.

- After successful bootup, the Switch> prompt is provided, indicating management access via the CLI is available.

Example 1-2 demonstrates the switch bootup sequence on Switch-B, which is a CatOS-based Catalyst 4006 switch.

Example 1-2   *System Bootup on the Catalyst 4006 Switch*

```
0:00.574327: Please set IPAddr variable
0:00.574909: Please set Netmask variable
0:00.575267: Please set Broadcast variable
0:00.575633: No gateway has been specified
0:00.576177: Network is not configured
WS-X4013 bootrom version 6.1(4), built on 2001.07.30 14:43:26
H/W Revisions: Meteor: 4 Comet: 8 Board: 2
Supervisor MAC addresses: 00:10:7b:f7:2f:00 through 00:10:7b:f7:32:ff
    (1024 addresses)
Installed memory: 64 MB
Testing LEDs.... done!
The system will autoboot in 5 seconds.
Type control-C to prevent autobooting.
rommon 1 >
The system will now begin autobooting.
Autobooting image: "bootflash:cat4000-k8.7-6-1.bin"
...............................................................................
.............................................................
################################
Starting Off-line Diagnostics
Mapping in TempFs
Board type is WS-X4013
DiagBootMode value is "post"
Loading diagnostics...

Power-on-self-test for Module 1: WS-X4013
Status: (. = Pass, F = Fail)
processor: . cpu sdram: . temperature sensor: .
enet console port: . nvram: . switch sram: .
switch registers: . switch port 0: . switch port 1: .
switch port 2: . switch port 3: .       switch port 4: .
switch port 5: . switch port 6: . switch port 7: .
switch port 8: . switch port 9: . switch port 10: .
switch port 11: . switch bandwidth: .
Module 1 Passed
Power-on-self-test for Module 2: WS-X4148
Port status: (. = Pass, F = Fail)
1: . 2: . 3: . 4: . 5: . 6: . 7: . 8: .
9: . 10: . 11: . 12: . 13: . 14: . 15: . 16: .
17: . 18: . 19: . 20: . 21: . 22: . 23: . 24: .
25: . 26: . 27: . 28: . 29: . 30: . 31: . 32: .
33: . 34: . 35: . 36: . 37: . 38: . 39: . 40: .
41: . 42: . 43: . 44: . 45: . 46: . 47: . 48: .
Module 2 Passed

Exiting Off-line Diagnostics
IP address for Catalyst not configured
BOOTP/DHCP will commence after the ports are online
Ports are coming online ...
```

continues

Example 1-2   *System Bootup on the Catalyst 4006 Switch (Continued)*

```
Cisco Systems, Inc. Console

Enter password:
```

In Example 1-2, a similar sequence of events as Example 1-1 occurs, with the switch first loading and operating system from Flash, performing a series of successful POST tests on each module in the switch, and then providing an Enter password: prompt, which indicates the switch has successfully booted and initial management access is available.

Gaining Privileged Mode Access

After system bootup is complete, you should gain initial management access, which allows you to configure, manage, and monitor the switch.

NOTE   Cisco refers to the management access provided via CLI as *EXEC access*.

On Cisco IOS and CatOS, management access (EXEC access) is provided at two levels by default:

- **User mode**—Provides limited access to monitoring commands (**show** commands) and does not allow any configuration commands to be executed.

- **Privilege mode** (also known as *enable mode*)—Provides full access to all configuration, management and monitoring commands available.

The default levels of EXEC access provided vary, depending on whether or not you are configuring a Cisco IOS-based switch or a CatOS-based switch. On Cisco IOS, any access via the console is granted user mode access by default, which is indicated by the Switch> prompt (see Example 1-1). On CatOS, you must provide a password to gain user mode access via the console, which is indicated by the Enter password: prompt (see Example 1-2).

After gaining user mode access, you can then gain privileged mode access by executing the **enable** command. Each level of EXEC access requires a separate password to gain access; however, by default blank passwords are used to gain access.

Example 1-3 demonstrates gaining privileged level access to Switch-A.

Example 1-3   *Gaining Privileged Level Access on Cisco IOS*

```
Switch> enable
Switch#
```

In Example 1-3, user mode access is already granted by default via the console; hence, the **enable** command needs to be executed only to gain privilege mode access. Notice that privileged mode access is granted immediately, without any prompt for password, as by default no password is required for privileged mode access. The # portion of the Switch# prompt indicates that the current EXEC session has privileged mode access, whereas the > portion of the Switch> prompt indicates the current EXEC session has user mode access.

Example 1-4 demonstrates gaining privileged EXEC access to Switch-B.

Example 1-4   *Gaining Privileged Level Access on CatOS*

```
Cisco Systems, Inc. Console

Enter password: ↵
Console> enable

Enter password: ↵
Console> (enable)
```

In Example 1-4, a blank password is required to gain user mode access, after which the **enable** command is executed to gain privileged mode access. Notice that unlike Cisco IOS, CatOS prompts you for a password to gain privileged mode access, even though the default password is blank. The (enable) portion of the Console> (enable) prompt indicates that the current EXEC session has privileged mode access—if only the Console> prompt is displayed, the current EXEC session only has user mode access.

Verifying System Configuration

After gaining privileged mode access, you should next verify the system hardware and software configuration is correct. Although system hardware is tested during system bootup, you should also verify the operating system can see all switch hardware after system bootup. As with any operating system, various versions of operating systems exist on Cisco Catalyst switches, which contain various levels of features depending on the version of operating system software installed. Ensuring the appropriate version of operating system software is installed is important, so that you can maintain the same versions of operating system software throughout the network, as well as configure the features required for your network.

To verify system hardware and software on Cisco IOS, you can use the **show version** command, which displays hardware and software versions and other information, as demonstrated in Example 1-5.

Example 1-5   *Using the* **show version** *Command on Cisco IOS*

```
Switch# show version
Cisco Internetwork Operating System Software
IOS (tm) C3550 Software (C3550-I5K2L2Q3-M), Version 12.1(13)EA1a,
    RELEASE SOFTWARE (fc1)
```

Example 1-5 *Using the* **show version** *Command on Cisco IOS (Continued)*

```
Copyright  1986-2003 by cisco Systems, Inc.
Compiled Tue 25-Mar-03 23:56 by yenanh
Image text-base: 0x00003000, data-base: 0x008BA914

ROM: Bootstrap program is C3550 boot loader

Switch uptime is 51 minutes
System returned to ROM by power-on
System image file is "flash:c3550-i5k2l2q3-mz.121-13.EA1a/c3550-i5k2l2q3-mz.121-
  13.EA1a.bin"


This product contains cryptographic features and is subject to United
States and local country laws governing import, export, transfer and
use. Delivery of Cisco cryptographic products does not imply
third-party authority to import, export, distribute or use encryption.
Importers, exporters, distributors and users are responsible for
compliance with U.S. and local country laws. By using this product you
agree to comply with applicable laws and regulations. If you are unable
to comply with U.S. and local laws, return this product immediately.

A summary of U.S. laws governing Cisco cryptographic products may be found at:
http://www.cisco.com/wwl/export/crypto/tool/stqrg.html

If you require further assistance please contact us by sending email to
export@cisco.com.

cisco WS-C3550-24 (PowerPC) processor (revision C0) with 65526K/8192K
   bytes of memory.
Processor board ID CAT0620X0HV
Last reset from warm-reset
Bridging software.
Running Layer2/3 Switching Image

Ethernet-controller 1 has 12 Fast Ethernet/IEEE 802.3 interfaces

Ethernet-controller 2 has 12 Fast Ethernet/IEEE 802.3 interfaces

Ethernet-controller 3 has 1 Gigabit Ethernet/IEEE 802.3 interface

Ethernet-controller 4 has 1 Gigabit Ethernet/IEEE 802.3 interface

24 FastEthernet/IEEE 802.3 interface(s)
2 Gigabit Ethernet/IEEE 802.3 interface(s)

The password-recovery mechanism is enabled.
384K bytes of flash-simulated non-volatile configuration memory.
Base ethernet MAC Address: 00:09:B7:BB:8D:08
Motherboard assembly number: 73-5700-99
Power supply part number: 34-0966-02
Motherboard serial number: CAT062843JA
Power supply serial number: LIT0636005A
```

Example 1-5 *Using the* **show version** *Command on Cisco IOS (Continued)*

```
Model revision number: C0
Motherboard revision number: B0
Model number: WS-C3550-24-EMI
System serial number: CAT0620Y1JJ
```

In Example 1-5, the shaded lines indicate operating system software version, hardware interfaces recognized by the system, serial number information, and a lot of other information about the system.

To verify system hardware on CatOS, you can use the **show module** command, which lists the various hardware modules installed in chassis-based CatOS switches. You can also use **show version** command to display hardware and software versions and other information, as demonstrated in Example 1-6.

Example 1-6 *Verifying Hardware and Software on CatOS*

```
Console> (enable) show module
Mod Slot Ports Module-Type           Model              Sub Status
--- ---- ----- -------------------- ------------------- --- --------
1   1    2     Supervisor 2         WS-X4013            no  ok
2   1    48    10/100 Ethernet      WS-X4148            no  ok

Mod Module-Name         Serial-Num
--- ------------------- -------------------
1                       JAB05310GME
2                       JAB030200QX

Mod MAC-Address(es)                         Hw     Fw          Sw
--- --------------------------------------- ------ ---------- ----------------
1   00-30-24-48-d4-00 to 00-30-24-48-d7-ff 2.0    6.1(4)      7.6(1)
2   00-30-24-48-d7-9e to 00-30-24-48-d7-fd 2.0    .

Console> (enable) show version
WS-C4006 Software, Version NmpSW: 7.6(1)
Copyright  1995-2003 by Cisco Systems, Inc.
NMP S/W compiled on Apr 16 2003, 18:56:05
GSP S/W compiled on Apr 16 2003, 16:56:33

System Bootstrap Version: 6.1(4)

Hardware Version: 3.2  Model: WS-C4006  Serial #: FOX052202RB

Mod Port Model               Serial #              Versions
--- ---- ------------------- --------------------- -------------------------------
1   2    WS-X4013            JAB05310GME           Hw : 3.2
                                                   Gsp: 7.6(1.0)
                                                   Nmp: 7.6(1)
2   48   WS-X4148 JAB030200QX            Hw : 1.0

        DRAM                    FLASH              NVRAM
Module Total   Used    Free    Total   Used   Free   Total Used  Free
```

continues

Example 1-6 *Verifying Hardware and Software on CatOS (Continued)*

```
------ ------- ------- ------- ------- ------- ------- ----- ----- -----
1       65536K  36714K  28822K  16384K 4458K   11926K  480K  245K  235K

Uptime is 0 day, 3 hours, 0 minute
```

In Example 1-6, the **show module** command provides information specific to each module installed in the switch. You can see that the switch currently recognizes a Supervisor 2 module installed in module 1, and a 48-port module installed in module 2. The Status column indicates that each module is currently operational, as indicated by the value ok. The **show version** command also provides hardware and software information. The first line of the shaded output indicates the operating system version, while the second line indicates the read-only memory (ROM) software version used to boot the switch. The last shaded line indicates total system memory (64 MB) and Flash (16 MB) and also indicates current memory/Flash usage.

Configuring System Identity

After installing a Cisco Catalyst switch, gaining initial management access, and verifying the system configuration, you are ready to begin configuring the switch. Configuring a switch for operation on the network might comprise many different configuration tasks specific to your environment; however, several base configuration tasks most administrators will perform, which include the following:

- Configuring host name
- Saving and verifying your configuration

Configuring a Host Name

Configuring a host name for a switch is perhaps the most fundamental configuration task, because it enables you to uniquely identify a switch in the network.

Before configuring host name information, it is important to understand how you actually perform configuration on Cisco Catalyst switches. On Cisco IOS, configuration is provided via *configuration modes*, which are modes that are accessible via privileged mode access. A base configuration mode called *global configuration mode* provides the ability to configure settings that are applied globally to the switch. Other configuration modes exist for configuring specific components and features of the switch. To access any configuration mode on Cisco IOS, you must first access global configuration mode, which is performed using the **configure terminal** command via privileged mode access. Example 1-7 demonstrates accessing global configuration mode on a Cisco IOS switch.

Example 1-7   *Accessing Global Configuration Mode*

```
Switch# configure ?
  memory               Configure from NV memory
  network              Configure from a TFTP network host
  overwrite-network    Overwrite NV memory from TFTP network host
  terminal             Configure from the terminal
Switch# configure terminal
Enter configuration commands, one per line.  End with CNTL/Z.
Switch(config)#
```

In Example 1-7, the **configure ?** command is first executed, which provides online help for the various parameters that you can configure with the **configure** command. Cisco IOS includes online help as indicated in Example 1-7 for all commands, which can simply be accessed by using the **?** character. Notice that you can configure the switch using four different commands:

- **configure memory**—Loads the startup configuration saved in nonvolatile random-access memory (NVRAM) to the current configuration.

- **configure network**—Allows the current configuration to be modified by loading configuration commands via the network from a file located on a remote Trivial File Transfer Protocol (TFTP) server.

- **configure overwrite-network**—Allows the startup configuration in NVRAM to be overwritten by loading a configuration file via a remote Trivial File Transfer Protocol (TFTP) server.

- **configure terminal**—Allows an administrator to configure the switch using terminal (CLI) based access to the switch via an interface such as the console port or via Telnet access.

In Example 1-7, the **configure terminal** command is executed to allow configuration via the console port. Notice that the switch prompt changes to Switch(config)#, which indicates the switch is currently operating in global configuration mode and accepts global configuration commands. Once in global configuration mode, you can begin configuring the switch. To configure a host name on a Cisco IOS switch, you use the **hostname** global configuration command, as demonstrated in Example 1-8.

Example 1-8   *Configuring a Host Name on Cisco IOS*

```
Switch(config)# hostname ?
WORD   This system's network name
Switch(config)# hostname Switch-A ?
<cr>
Switch(config)# hostname Switch-A ⏎
Switch-A(config)# exit
Switch-A#
```

In Example 1-8, the **hostname ?** command is executed to determine the parameters that the command requires. Notice that Cisco IOS indicates a WORD is required that defines the host name. A *WORD* is essentially a free-text string that is used to describe some parameter on the switch, such as the switch host name. Next, the host name is configured as **Switch-A,** with another **?** character being used to see if any other parameters must be configured. Cisco IOS indicates that a carriage return is required (**<cr>**), which means the configuration of the command is complete. This means the full command to configure the host name is **hostname Switch-A**. After this command is executed, notice that the switch name in the command prompt is modified appropriately. Finally, notice that the **exit** command is used to exit global configuration mode and return to privileged mode access. The **exit** command can be used within any configuration mode on Cisco IOS to return to the previous mode.

On CatOS, all configuration is performed from privileged mode access, with no concept of configuration modes. All configuration commands begin predominantly with the **set** keyword, and the **clear** keyword is also used to reset some configuration parameters. To configure the host name of a CatOS-based switch, the **set system name** command is used, as demonstrated in Example 1-9.

Example 1-9 *Configuring the Host Name on CatOS*

```
Console> (enable) set system ?
Set system commands:
-------------------------------------------------------------------
set system baud            Set system console port baud rate
set system contact         Set system contact
set system help            Show this message
set system location        Set system location
set system modem           Set system modem control (enable/disable)
set system name            Set system name
Console> (enable) set system name ?
  <name_string>            Name for the system
  <cr>
Console> (enable) set system name Switch-B
System name set.
Switch-B> (enable)
```

In Example 1-9, notice that you can use the **?** character to provide a similar online help mechanism as provided on Cisco IOS. After executing the **set system name Switch-B** command, notice that the prompt is changed to include the system name.

Saving and Verifying Your Configuration

On Cisco IOS, any configuration changes made are made to a running configuration file, which is stored in memory and erased if the switch is rebooted or shut down. To ensure any configuration changes you have made are saved permanently, you must explicitly save the running configuration file to the startup configuration file, which is a file stored in nonvolatile RAM (NVRAM) that is read by the switch upon switch bootup. To save the current running configuration to the startup configuration file, you use the **copy running-config startup-config** command, as demonstrated in Example 1-10.

Example 1-10 *Configuring a Host Name on Cisco IOS*

```
Switch-A# copy running-config starup-config
Destination filename [startup-config]? ↵
Building configuration...
[OK]
Switch-A# show running-config
Building configuration...

Current configuration : 1475 bytes
!
version 12.1
no service pad
service timestamps debug uptime
service timestamps log uptime
no service password-encryption
!
hostname Switch-A
!
ip subnet-zero
!
spanning-tree mode pvst
spanning-tree extend system-id
!
interface FastEthernet0/1
 no ip address
!
interface FastEthernet0/2
 no ip address
!
interface FastEthernet0/3
 no ip address
!
interface FastEthernet0/4
 no ip address
!
interface FastEthernet0/5
 no ip address
!
interface FastEthernet0/6
 no ip address
!
interface FastEthernet0/7
 no ip address
!
interface FastEthernet0/8
 no ip address
!
interface FastEthernet0/9
 no ip address
!
```

continues

Example 1-10 *Configuring a Host Name on Cisco IOS (Continued)*

```
interface FastEthernet0/10
 no ip address
!
interface FastEthernet0/11
 no ip address
!
interface FastEthernet0/12
 no ip address
!
interface FastEthernet0/13
 no ip address
!
interface FastEthernet0/14
 no ip address
!
interface FastEthernet0/15
 no ip address
!
interface FastEthernet0/16
 no ip address
!
interface FastEthernet0/17
 no ip address
!
interface FastEthernet0/18
 no ip address
!
interface FastEthernet0/19
 no ip address
!
interface FastEthernet0/20
 no ip address
!
interface FastEthernet0/21
 no ip address
!
interface FastEthernet0/22
 no ip address
!
interface FastEthernet0/23
 no ip address
!
interface FastEthernet0/24
 no ip address
!
interface GigabitEthernet0/1
 no ip address
!
interface GigabitEthernet0/2
 no ip address
!
interface Vlan1
```

Example 1-10 *Configuring a Host Name on Cisco IOS (Continued)*

```
 no ip address
 shutdown
!
ip classless
ip http server
!
line con 0
line vty 5 15
!
end
```

In Example 1-10, after the running configuration file is saved to the startup configuration file, the **show running-config** command is executed, which displays the current configuration stored in memory. Notice the highlighted command **hostname Switch-A**, which you configured in Example 1-8. All other commands are default settings. You can also use the **show startup-config** command to view the startup configuration file.

NOTE   You can use the **copy startup-config running-config** command to copy the startup configuration to the current running configuration; however, be aware that this command is additive, in that any settings currently present in the running configuration file that are not present in the startup configuration file are still maintained. This is unlike the **copy running-config startup-config** command, where the existing startup configuration file is first erased and then replaced with the running configuration file.

On CatOS, all configuration changes are automatically saved, meaning you don't have to explicitly save your configurations. To verify your configuration, you can use the **show config** command, as demonstrated in Example 1-11.

Example 1-11 *Verifying Configuration on CatOS*

```
Switch-B> (enable) show config
This command shows non-default configurations only.
Use 'show config all' to show both default and non-default configurations.
...............
..

begin
!
# ***** NON-DEFAULT CONFIGURATION *****
!
#time: Wed Mar 3 1993, 02:34:54
!
#version 7.6(1)
!
#system web interface version(s)
```

continues

Example 1-11 *Verifying Configuration on CatOS (Continued)*

```
!
#system
set system name  Switch-B
!
#frame distribution method
set port channel all distribution mac both
!
#ip
set interface sl0 down
set interface me1 down
set ip alias default         0.0.0.0
!
#set boot command
set boot config-register 0x10f
set boot system flash bootflash:cat4000-k8.7-6-1.bin
!
#multicast filter
set igmp filter disable
!
#module 1 : 2-port Switching Supervisor
!
#module 2 : 48-port 10/100 Ethernet
end
```

In Example 1-11, the **show config** command is used to display all non-default configuration settings. You can use the **show config all** command to view all configuration settings; however, the output of this command is very long, limiting the usefulness of this command if you are trying to extract specific configuration information. You can see highlighted command **set system name Switch-B**, which you configured in Example 1-9. All other commands are default settings.

Scenario 1-2: Configuring Network Management Access to the Switch

In the previous scenario, you learned how to install a Cisco Catalyst switch on the network, verify system operation, and also configure switch identity information. The next configuration task is to configure management access so that the switch can be managed via the network. This scenario continues on from the previous scenario and shows you how to configure the various types of network management access available for Cisco Catalyst switches. For this scenario, a new connection is added to the network as shown in Figure 1-13.

Figure 1-13 *Scenario 1-2 Topology*

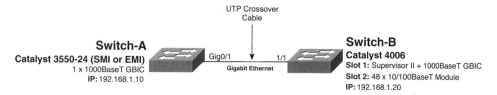

In Figure 1-13, notice that a gigabit Ethernet connection has been added between Switch-A and Switch-B, which enables IP connectivity and network management access to be tested between Switch-A and Switch-B. To enable gigabit Ethernet connectivity between the two switches, a copper gigabit Ethernet (1000BASE-T) GBIC (Cisco PN# WS-G5483) must be installed into the appropriate GBIC slots on each switch, with a gigabit Ethernet certified unshielded twisted-pair (UTP) crossover cable used to attach each GBIC.

NOTE   Although gigabit Ethernet is not required between the two switches for the purposes of verifying IP connectivity (you could just use a crossover cable between two Fast Ethernet ports), it is required for Scenario 1-3, where you learn how to configure gigabit Ethernet parameters.

By default, Cisco Catalyst switches can be managed only via the console port and require explicit configuration to enable management access using the network. Cisco Catalyst switches can be managed over the network via a variety of mechanisms, which include the following:

- **Remote EXEC access**—This provides EXEC access (i.e., access to the switch CLI) via network protocols such as Telnet and secure shell (SSH). To gain remote EXEC access to a switch, passwords and IP addressing must be configured.

- **Simple Network Management Protocol (SNMP)**—Cisco Catalyst switches allow SNMP management servers to monitor and manage the switch using SNMP. Cisco Catalyst switches support the generation of SNMP traps in response to system events and also support polling and configuration requests (GET and SET requests) from SNMP management servers. To allow a switch to be managed using SNMP, IP addressing and the appropriate SNMP parameters must be configured.

- **System logging (SYSLOG)**—Cisco Catalyst switches support the generation of SYSLOG messages in response to system events, which can be forwarded across the network to SYSLOG servers. To allow a switch to forward SYSLOG events to a SYSLOG server, IP addressing and the appropriate SYSLOG parameters must be configured.

Configuration Tasks

The following describes the configuration tasks required to enable network management access to Cisco Catalyst switches:

- Configuring passwords
- Configuring IP addressing and DNS
- Configuring SNMP support
- Configuring SYSLOG support

Configuring Passwords

Before you enable remote EXEC access (via Telnet or SSH) to a Cisco Catalyst switch, you should configure passwords to ensure only authorized administrators can gain EXEC access to the switch over the network. As you have already learned, the default passwords for access to Cisco Catalyst switches via the console are blank (null), and if you configure IP addressing, the same blank passwords are used for controlling Telnet/SSH access. This means your switch is extremely vulnerable if placed on an IP network with IP configured and with no password changes made.

Configuring Passwords on Cisco IOS

On Cisco IOS, any password that is used to gain initial user mode access is called a *line password*, while the password used to gain privileged mode access is called the *enable password*. On Cisco IOS, remote EXEC access is not granted until at least the line password used for Telnet/SSH access has been explicitly configured.

NOTE   Cisco IOS uses the concepts of *lines* to represent the various management interfaces for EXEC access to the switch. Console access is provided by a console line called **con 0**, while Telnet/SSH access is provided by virtual terminal lines called **vty**. A number of **vty** lines exist, which allow for multiple EXEC sessions using Telnet/SSH.

Assuming the line password has been configured and administrators can gain user mode access using Telnet/SSH, an enable password must also be explicitly configured if privileged mode access is required via Telnet/SSH.

To configure line passwords, you must first access line configuration mode, which is accessed using the **line con 0** command to configure the console line or the **line vty** command to access one or more of the virtual terminal lines. Once line configuration mode is obtained, you can then use the **password** command to configure a line password. To configure the switch to authenticate users using the line password (known as *line authentication*), you must also configure the **login** line configuration command. Example 1-12 demonstrates configuring a line password and enabling line authentication for console access and virtual terminal (telnet/SSH) access on Cisco IOS.

Example 1-12 *Configuring Line Passwords on Cisco IOS*

```
Switch-A# configure terminal
Switch-A(config)# line con 0
Switch-A(config-line)# password cisco
Switch-A(config-line)# login
Switch-A(config-line)# exit
Switch-A(config)# line vty 0 15
Switch-A(config-line)# password cisco
Switch-A(config-line)# login
Switch-A(config-line)# end
Switch-A#
```

In Example 1-12, notice the **line con 0** command is configured to gain access to line config- uration mode for the console line, as indicated by (config-line) in the prompt. A password of *cisco* is configured, and line authentication is enabled using the **login** command. The **exit** command is then used to return to the parent configuration mode of line configuration mode, which is global configuration mode. Next the **line vty 0 15** command is configured to gain access to line configuration mode for all of the virtual terminal lines on the switch (line vty 0 to line vty 15). After the line password is configured and line authentication enabled, notice that the **end** command is used to return immediately to privileged mode. The **end** command can be used to immediately exit any configuration mode and return to privileged mode.

TIP   You can also use the Ctrl--Z key sequence to immediately return from any configuration mode to privileged mode.

Now that you understand how to configure line passwords on Cisco IOS, if you want to authenticate privileged mode access after a user gains user mode access via console or virtual terminal access, you must configure an enable password. An enable password is used to prompt for authentication after the **enable** command is entered from user mode and provides a separate authentication mechanism for providing privileged mode access to the switch. To configure the enable password, you have two options:

- Use the **enable password** global configuration command
- Use the **enable secret** global configuration command. If configured, this takes precedence over the **enable password** command.

You should always use the **enable secret** command to configure the enable password, because it stores the password in a more secure fashion than the **enable password** command within the switch configuration file (see Chapter 8, "Traffic Filtering and Security," for more details). Example 1-13 demonstrates configuring an enable password using the **enable secret** command.

Example 1-13 *Configuring the Enable Password on Cisco IOS*

```
Switch-A# configure terminal
Switch-A(config)# enable secret cisco
```

In Example 1-13, an enable password of **cisco** is configured. This password is now required when attempting to gain privileged mode access from user mode access.

<table><tr><td>**NOTE**</td><td>Always avoid using a simple password like *cisco* for network devices, especially Cisco devices. This password is most likely the first password an attacker will use to attempt to gain unauthorized access. I only ever use this password in a lab environment, where the device is isolated from any external network. Using this password makes it easy for other co-workers to access the device if they need to perform their own lab testing. Try using passwords that contain a mixture of alphanumeric characters and do not resemble words. If you must use passwords that resemble a word to aid memorizing the password, try to configure the password as an alphanumeric password, replacing characters such as o with 0 and a with 4. It is also important to note that passwords are case sensitive.</td></tr></table>

Configuring Passwords on CatOS

On CatOS, the concept of a line does not exist, with a global user mode password used to authenticate user mode access no matter what management interface is used. Similarly, a global enable password is used to authenticate enable mode access. Unlike Cisco IOS, which does not permit Telnet/SSH access unless a line password has been explicitly configured or privileged mode access via Telnet/SSH unless an enable password has been explicitly configured, CatOS permits Telnet access using blank passwords. This means it is very important that you configure passwords on CatOS before connecting the switch to the network. To configure the password used for user mode access, the **set password** command is used. To configure the password used for privileged mode access, the **set enablepass** command is used. Example 1-14 demonstrates configuring passwords for user mode access and enable mode access.

Example 1-14 *Configuring Passwords on CatOS*

```
Switch-B> (enable) set password
Enter old password: ↵
Enter new password: *****
Retype new password: *****
Password changed.
Switch-B> (enable) set enablepass
Enter old password: ↵
Enter new password: *****
Retype new password: *****
Password changed.
```

In Example 1-14, notice that the **set password** and **set enablepass** commands are interactive, in that the switch prompts you for the old password (blank in Example 1-14) and then prompts you to enter and re-enter the new password (**cisco** in Example 1-14).

At this stage, if you logout from the current console EXEC sessions and attempt to access Switch-A or Switch-B via the console port, you should find that you are now prompted for authentication on Switch-A (Cisco IOS) and that blank passwords no longer work on Switch-B. Example 1-15 and Example 1-16 demonstrate logging out of Switch-A and Switch-B respectively and then reconnecting.

Example 1-15 *Testing Login Authentication on Cisco IOS*

```
Switch-A# logout

Switch-A con0 is now available

Press RETURN to get started.

User Access Verification

Password: ↵
Password: *****
Switch-A> enable
Password: ↵
Password: *****
Switch-A#
```

Example 1-16 *Testing Login Authentication on CatOS*

```
Switch-B> (enable) logout
Session Disconnected...


Cisco Systems, Inc. Console          Sun May 4 2003, 20:07:59


Enter password: ↵

Enter password: *****
Switch-B> enable

Enter password: ↵

Enter password: *****
Switch-B> (enable)
```

In Example 1-15 and Example 1-16, the **logout** keyword is used to disconnect the current console session, after which console access is reattempted. Notice in Example 1-15 that Switch-A now prompts the user for a password, because a line password has been configured for the console. In Example 1-15 and Example 1-16, a blank password is first attempted; however, notice that this fails. A password of "cisco" is then attempted (as indicated by the ***** input), which successfully authenticates providing user mode access. The **enable** command is then used to attempt access to privileged mode access, and again a password prompt is presented to the user. After an initial unsuccessful authentication attempt using a blank password, the user is successfully authenticating using the *cisco* enable password, providing privileged mode access to each switch.

Configuring IP Addressing and DNS

Once you have configured passwords to secure EXEC access to a Cisco Catalyst switch, you can safely attach the switch to the network and configure an IP address that the switch uses to enable network management. Before configuring IP addressing information, it is important to have a clear understanding of your current network topology and identify exactly where the switch attaches to the network. This enables you to determine the appropriate IP addressing and DNS parameters that are used to configure your switch. The parameters that you need to determine include the following:

- IP address of the switch
- Subnet mask
- Default gateway for communications to remote IP subnets
- Virtual LAN (VLAN) in which the switch management interface is placed

NOTE   In this scenario, the default VLAN, VLAN 1, is assumed; however, in Chapter 2, "VLAN Operations," you learn how to configure the management interface to reside in a different VLAN.

- Domain name to be used by the switch
- Domain Name System (DNS) servers to be used by the switch for resolving host names to IP addresses and vice versa.

Often you might configure only IP addressing and a default gateway, as configuring DNS provides only the ability to resolve host names to IP addresses, which is useful for utilities such as ping and traceroute but not essential to the ongoing management or operation of the switch.

Configuring IP Addressing and DNS on Cisco IOS

On Cisco IOS, you configure management interfaces based upon the VLAN that the switch should be managed from. Such an interface is called a switch virtual interface (SVI), which is an internal interface that attaches to the VLAN the SVI belongs to. By default, all Cisco

Catalyst switches ship with VLAN 1 as the default VLAN, and by default, the management interface on Cisco IOS is in VLAN 1 as well. To create or configure a management interface on Cisco IOS, you use the **interface vlan** global configuration command:

```
Switch(config)# interface vlan vlan-id
```

The *vlan-id* parameter defines the VLAN in which the interface belongs. If the management interface does not already exist (e.g., you are creating a management interface in another VLAN), then a new management interface is automatically created. By default, the VLAN 1 interface exists; however, the interface is placed in a shutdown state. To configure IP addressing on the VLAN 1 interface, you must not only configure an IP address for the interface, but also ensure the interface is enabled using the **no shutdown** interface configuration command. After enabling the interface, you can configure IP addressing using the **ip address** interface configuration command as follows:

```
Switch(config-if)# ip address address netmask
```

The *address* parameter defines the IP address, while the *netmask* parameter defines the subnet mask in dotted decimal format (e.g., 255.255.255.0). After configuring the IP address of the switch, if the switch is located on a routed network where multiple IP subnets exist, you normally need to configure a default gateway, so that the switch can route packets to destinations not attached to the local subnet. This is achieved using the **ip default-gateway** global configuration command:

```
Switch(config)# ip default-gateway next-hop-address
```

The *next-hop-address* defines the IP address of the router through which all non-local IP traffic should be sent.

Example 1-17 demonstrates configuring an IP address on Cisco IOS for the VLAN 1 management interface and also configuring a default gateway of 192.168.1.1, assuming a router with this IP address is connected to the network in later scenarios.

Example 1-17 *Configuring IP Addressing and Configuring a Default Gateway*

```
Switch-A# configure terminal
Switch-A(config)# interface vlan 1
Switch-A(config-if)# no shutdown
Switch-A(config-if)# ip address 192.168.1.10 255.255.255.0
Switch-A(config-if)# exit
Switch-A(config)# ip default-gateway 192.168.1.1
Switch-A(config)# exit
Switch-A# show interfaces vlan 1
Vlan1 is up, line protocol is down
  Hardware is EtherSVI, address is 0009.b7aa.9c80 (bia 0009.b7aa.9c80)
  Internet address is 192.168.1.10/24
  MTU 1500 bytes, BW 1000000 Kbit, DLY 10 usec,
     reliability 255/255, txload 1/255, rxload 1/255
  Encapsulation ARPA, loopback not set
  ARP type: ARPA, ARP Timeout 04:00:00
  Last input never, output never, output hang never
  Last clearing of "show interface" counters never
  Input queue: 0/75/0/0 (size/max/drops/flushes); Total output drops: 0
```

continues

Example 1-17 *Configuring IP Addressing and Configuring a Default Gateway (Continued)*

```
   Queueing strategy: fifo
   Output queue :0/40 (size/max)
   5 minute input rate 0 bits/sec, 0 packets/sec
   5 minute ouxtput rate 0 bits/sec, 0 packets/sec
      0 packets input, 0 bytes, 0 no buffer
      Received 0 broadcasts, 0 runts, 0 giants, 0 throttles
      0 input errors, 0 CRC, 0 frame, 0 overrun, 0 ignored
      0 packets output, 0 bytes, 0 underruns
      0 output errors, 0 interface resets
      0 output buffer failures, 0 output buffers swapped out
Switch-A# show ip route
Default gateway is 192.168.1.1

Host              Gateway          Last Use    Total Uses   Interface
ICMP redirect cache is empty
```

In Example 1-17, notice that after the **interface vlan 1** command is executed, interface configuration mode is entered, as indicated by the (config-if) prompt. After the **no shutdown** command is executed, the **ip address** command is used to configure an IP address of 192.168.1.10/24.

NOTE   Throughout this book, */nn* notation will be commonly used to indicate subnet mask configuration, where *nn* defines the number of 1s in the subnet mask. For example, a /24 mask represents 11111111 11111111 11111111 00000000, given a subnet mask of 255.255.255.0 in dotted decimal format.

After completing the IP addressing configuration, a default gateway of 192.168.1.10 is configured, after which the **show interfaces vlan 1** command is used to verify the current status of the VLAN 1 interface. Notice in the first shaded line that the interface is enabled (as indicated by the text "Vlan1 is up"); however, the line protocol (Layer 2 protocol) the interface is down. This is because currently no devices are connected to the switch, meaning there are no active ports in the default VLAN 1; hence, the VLAN 1 SVI stays down. If an active device is connected to the switch, the VLAN 1 SVI comes up, as an active port then exists in VLAN 1. The second shaded line in Example 1-17 indicates the IP address of the interface is now 192.168.1.10 with a subnet mask of 255.255.255.0. Finally, the **show ip route** command is used to verify the default gateway configuration, as indicated by the last shaded line in Example 1-17.

NOTE   In Scenario 1-3, where you connect devices to each switch, IP connectivity to Switch-A is
        verified.

To configure DNS on Cisco IOS, you normally configure a domain name to which the
switch belongs (used to append domain name information to any name resolution requests
for a host name only) and then configure one or more DNS servers that will be used for
name resolution. To configure the domain name to which the switch belongs, you use the
ip domain-name global configuration command:

```
Switch(config)# ip domain-name domain-name
```

NOTE   Configuring a domain name is required for enabling secure shell (SSH) server functionality,
        which allows for secure network-based EXEC access (instead of using Telnet). Configuring
        SSH is covered in Chapter 8.

To configure DNS servers for name resolution, you must first ensure that DNS lookup is
enabled using the **ip domain-lookup** command (enabled by default) and then configure the
ip name-server command:

```
Switch(config)# ip name-server dns-server-1 [dns-server-2] ... [dns-server-6]
```

You can configure up to six name servers, which are tried in the order specified in the **ip
name-server** command. Example 1-18 demonstrates configuring a domain name on Cisco
IOS and configuring DNS name resolution.

Example 1-18 *Configuring DNS on Cisco IOS*

```
Switch-A# configure terminal
Switch-A(config)# ip domain-name lanps.com
Switch-A(config)# ip domain-lookup
Switch-A(config)# ip name-server 192.168.1.100 192.168.1.200
Switch-A(config)# exit
Switch-A# ping host-x
Translating "host-x"...domain server (192.168.1.100) (192.168.1.200)
% Unrecognized host or address, or protocol not running.
```

In Example 1-18, a domain name of lanps.com is configured, which means that the fully
qualified domain name (FQDN) of Switch-A is Switch-A.lanps.com. Two DNS servers
(192.168.1.100 and 192.168.1.200) are configured, at which time an attempt is made to
ping a host by name. Notice the shaded line in Example 1-18, which shows the switch
trying to resolve the name "host-x". Because Switch-A is not connected to any devices, the
DNS name resolution process fails after waiting 10 seconds for a response from each
configured name server respectively.

NOTE   It is common practice to disable DNS name resolution using the **no ip domain-lookup** global configuration command on Cisco IOS. If DNS name resolution is enabled, Cisco IOS tries to resolve any mistyped commands that you configure, which takes up to 10 seconds to timeout if no DNS servers are configured (the switch attempts to broadcast DNS queries if no DNS servers are configured). During the name resolution process you cannot type in any other commands, making this occurrence extremely annoying and counter productive.

Configuring IP Addressing and DNS on CatOS

On CatOS, several different management interfaces are provided for the purposes of providing management access via an IP network:

- **sc0**—An in-band management interface that allows remote management from devices that are connected to the switch. The sc0 interface is connected to the switching back plane and can be configured to belong to any VLAN configured on the switch, which allows other devices connected to switch ports (that connect to the backplane) to communicate with the sc0 interface. This is the most common management interface used as it connects directly to the rest of your network.

- **sl0**—An out-of-band management interface that allows access via a Serial Line Internet Protocol (SLIP) connection. Access to sl0 is available only via the console port. The sl0 interface is most commonly used when a modem is attached to the console port, allowing remote CLI access by dialing the number associated with the modem.

- **me1**—An out-of-band physical management interface located on the front side of the Supervisor module of Catalyst 2900/4000/4500 switches. This Ethernet interface has no connection to the switch backplane, and hence can be used only for out-of-band management purposes. The me1 management interface is commonly used in secure networks (e.g., telco networks) that require out-of-band management and no in-band management.

By default, the sc0 interface is enabled and is assigned an IP address of 0.0.0.0. All other interfaces are disabled and must be manually enabled. The IP address 0.0.0.0 means that the switch attempts to automatically obtain its IP address via Dynamic Host Configuration Protocol (DHCP) or Reverse Address Resolution Protocol (RARP). If your switch is connected to an existing LAN network and a DHCP or RARP server exists, the switch is automatically assigned an IP address.

WARNING Because the sc0 interface attempts to automatically obtain an IP address, you should ensure you have configured a static IP address on the switch before connecting it to the network (unless, of course, you do want to use DHCP or RARP). Connecting the switch to the network before configuring an IP address could allow unauthorized Telnet access if you haven't configured new passwords.

To configure the sc0 interface, which allows for in-band management access, you use the **set interface sc0** configuration command:

```
Console> (enable) set interface sc0 [vlan-id] ip-address [netmask] [broadcast-
  address]
Console> (enable) set interface sc0 dhcp {renew | release}
Console> (enable) set interface sc0 {up | down}
```

Notice that the **set interface sc0** command has several different command syntaxes. The first command syntax is the most common syntax used, which defines a static IP address. The optional *vlan-id* parameter is used to define the VLAN the sc0 interface should attach to (default if omitted is VLAN 1). The required *ip-address* parameter defines the IP address of the switch, and the optional *netmask* parameter allows you to define the subnet mask. If the *netmask* parameter is omitted, a subnet mask based upon the class of the IP address configured (i.e., Class A, B, or C) is assumed. The second command syntax allows you to configure the sc0 for DHCP, while the third command syntax allows you to enable/disable the sc0 interface (default status for the sc0 interface is enabled).

After configuring the IP address of the sc0 interface, if the switch is located on a routed network where multiple IP subnets exist, you normally need to configure a default gateway, so that the switch can route packets to destinations not attached to the local subnet. This is achieved using the **set ip route default** configuration command:

```
Console> (enable) set ip route default gateway-addr [primary]
```

The *gateway-addr* parameter defines the IP address of the route to which all non-local traffic should be routed, while the optional **primary** keyword is used to define a primary default gateway if multiple default gateways are configured for redundancy purposes.

Example 1-19 demonstrates configuring IP addressing and a default gateway on CatOS.

Example 1-19 *Configuring IP Addressing on CatOS*

```
Switch-B> (enable) set interface sc0 192.168.1.20 255.255.255.0
Interface sc0 IP address and netmask set.
Switch-B> (enable) set ip route default 192.168.1.1
Route added.
Switch-B> (enable) show interface
sl0: flags=50<DOWN,POINTOPOINT,RUNNING>
        slip 0.0.0.0 dest 0.0.0.0
sc0: flags=63<UP,BROADCAST,RUNNING>
        vlan 1 inet 192.168.1.20 netmask 255.255.255.0 broadcast 192.168.1.255
me1: flags=62<DOWN,BROADCAST,RUNNING>
```

continues

Example 1-19 *Configuring IP Addressing on CatOS (Continued)*

```
           inet 0.0.0.0 netmask 0.0.0.0 broadcast 0.0.0.0
Switch-B> (enable) show ip route
Fragmentation   Redirect   Unreachable
-------------   --------   -----------
enabled         enabled    enabled


The primary gateway: 192.168.1.1
Destination     Gateway          RouteMask     Flags   Use      Interface
-------------   ---------------  ----------    -----   -------- ---------
default         192.168.1.1      0x0           UG      0        sc0
192.168.1.0     192.168.1.20     0xffffff00    U       0        sc0
```

In Example 1-19, the **set interface sc0** command is first used to configure a static IP address
of 192.168.1.20/24, with the sc0 interface placed into VLAN 1 by default as the optional
vlan-id parameter is omitted. Next the **set ip route default** command is used to configure
a default gateway of 192.168.1.1. The **show interface** command indicates that the sc0
interface is up, has an IP address of 192.168.1.20/24, and is in VLAN 1, while the **show ip
route** command verifies that 192.168.1.1 is configured as the default gateway.

To configure DNS on CatOS, you must configure a domain name to which the switch
belongs using the **set ip dns domain** command, enable DNS name resolution (disabled by
default) using the **set ip dns enable** command, and then define one or more DNS servers to
use for name resolution using the **set ip dns server** command. Example 1-20 demonstrates
configuring DNS on CatOS.

Example 1-20 *Configuring DNS on CatOS*

```
Switch-B> (enable) set ip dns domain lanps.com
Default DNS domain name set to lanps.com
Switch-B> (enable) set ip dns enable
DNS is enabled
Switch-B> (enable) set ip dns server 192.168.1.100 primary
192.168.1.100 added to DNS server table as primary server.
Switch-B> (enable) set ip dns server 192.168.1.200
192.168.1.200 added to DNS server table as backup server.
Switch-B> (enable) show ip dns
DNS is currently enabled.
The default DNS domain name is: lanps.com


DNS name server                              status
-------------------------------------------  -------
192.168.1.100                                primary
192.168.1.200                                backup
```

In Example 1-20, notice that the **primary** keyword is used with the **set ip dns server**
command to specify the primary DNS server. All other DNS servers configured without the
primary keyword are added as backup DNS servers. Finally, the **show ip dns** command is
used to verify DNS is enabled and to also view the name server configuration.

Verifying IP Connectivity

At this stage, both Switch-A and Switch-B have been configured with an IP address and the appropriate passwords have been configured to enable remote EXEC access using Telnet. Because a network connection (gigabit Ethernet connection—see Figure 1-13) is now in place between Switch-A and Switch-B, you can verify IP connectivity and also test remote EXEC access using Telnet, as both Cisco IOS and CatOS include Telnet client utilities.

NOTE   The default configuration on the gigabit Ethernet ports on Switch-A and Switch-B means that the connection come up as a trunk (discussed in Chapter 3, "Trunking and Bandwidth Aggregation"), enabling traffic from multiple virtual LANs (VLANs) to be transported across the link. This includes VLAN 1 traffic, which by default both management interfaces on Switch-A and Switch-B belong to, enabling IP communications between the two switches.

Both Cisco IOS and CatOS include the ping utility, which can be used to provide a basis test of IP connectivity. Example 1-21 demonstrates the use of the ping utility on Cisco IOS.

Example 1-21   *Verifying IP Connectivity on Cisco IOS*

```
Switch-A# ping 192.168.1.20

Type escape sequence to abort.
Sending 5, 100-byte ICMP Echos to 192.168.1.20, timeout is 2 seconds:
!!!!!
Success rate is 100 percent (5/5), round-trip min/avg/max = 8/10/20 ms
```

In Example 1-21, connectivity to the IP address of Switch-B (192.168.1.20) is tested. The ping utility generates five ICMP echo request messages, which are sent to the specified IP address. If these messages reach their intended destination, the destination generates an ICMP echo reply message in response to each echo request and then sent the echo reply to the source of the echo request. Notice the shaded output in Example 1-21, which shows five explanation marks—the ! character indicates the switch received an echo reply, indicating a successful response.

NOTE   Other possible characters that can be displayed include the following:

- .—Request timed out

- U—Destination unreachable

- ?—Unknown packet type

- &—Packet lifetime exceeded

- C—Congestion experience packet was received

- I—User interrupted test

Example 1-22 demonstrates the use of the ping utility on CatOS.

Example 1-22 *Verifying IP Connectivity on CatOS*

```
Switch-B> (enable) ping 192.168.1.10
!!!!!

----192.168.1.10 PING Statistics----
5 packets transmitted, 5 packets received, 0% packet loss
round-trip (ms)  min/avg/max = 5/7/10
```

To verify remove EXEC access on each switch, you can use the **telnet** command on both Cisco IOS and CatOS to establish a Telnet connection to the remote switch. Example 1-23 demonstrates establishing a Telnet connection from Switch-A to Switch-B.

Example 1-23 *Establishing a Telnet Connection from Cisco IOS*

```
Switch-A# telnet 192.168.1.20
Trying 192.168.1.20 ... Open

Cisco Systems, Inc. Console

Enter password: *****
Switch-B> enable

Enter password: *****
Switch-B> (enable) exit

[Connection to 192.168.1.20 closed by foreign host]
Switch-A#
```

Example 1-23 verifies that Telnet connectivity to Switch-B is working. Notice that the same interface provided via console access is provided using Telnet (indicated by the shaded output). The password configured for user mode access must be specified to gain initial user mode access, after which the enable password must be specified after the **enable** command is executed to gain privilege mode access.

Example 1-24 demonstrates establishing a Telnet connection from Switch-B to Switch-A.

Example 1-24 *Establishing a Telnet Connection from CatOS*

```
Switch-B> (enable) telnet 192.168.1.10
Trying 192.168.1.10...
Connected to 192.168.1.10.
Escape character is '^]'.

User Access Verification

Password: *****
Switch-A> enable
Password: *****
Switch-A# exit
Switch-B> (enable)
```

Example 1-24 verifies that Telnet connectivity to Switch-A is working. Notice that the same method of access to gain privileged mode access using a console connection is required when using a Telnet connection.

Configuring SNMP Support

Network management refers to the processes of configuring, monitoring, and trouble-shooting a network device. You've already seen the most direct form of network management for Cisco Catalyst switches—EXEC access through console or Telnet access. When your network starts to grow to hundreds of devices, to provide ongoing management you need to have a central management point that can query and configure each network device from a user-friendly interface. That said, even being able to manage a single switch from a common network management platform is useful as well. The following network management protocols are supported by Cisco Catalyst switches:

- **Simple Network Management Protocol (SNMP)**—Used to configure, monitor, and troubleshoot network devices.
- **SYSLOG**—Used for receiving system events from network devices.
- **RMON**—Used for monitoring network devices.

Simple Network Management Protocol (SNMP) is the *de facto* protocol used for monitoring IP-based networks. SNMP provides three key components that make up the management framework:

- SNMP manager
- SNMP agent
- SNMP protocol

Figure 1-14 shows the components of SNMP.

Figure 1-14 *SNMP Components*

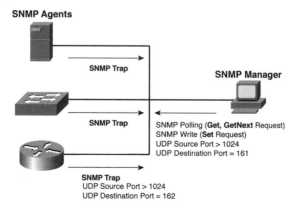

The SNMP manager is a network management station (NMS) that provides centralized management of a number of devices that can be geographically isolated from each other. The SNMP manager is the server portion of the SNMP client/server paradigm, while the SNMP agent is the client port and resides on the managed device. The manager and agent communicate using the SNMP protocol, which is UDP-based using a destination port 161 for messages originated by the SNMP manager and a destination port 162 for SNMP traps originated by SNMP agents (in other words, SNMP agents listen on UDP port 161 for SNMP Get, Set. or GetNext messages, while SNMP managers listen on UDP port 162 for SNMP traps). A manager can poll and configure a device by sending any one of three messages (Get, Set, or GetNext) to an SNMP agent. For example, an NMS might poll a device for its current CPU load by sending a Get request to the agent for the current CPU load. An SNMP agent generates a GetResponse message in response to any of these three messages. An agent can also initiate communications with an NMS by sending a trap or notification to the SNMP manager. This trap is normally sent based upon some event occurring or a specific threshold being exceeded. For example, an SNMP agent might send an SNMP trap to the SNMP manager if the number of errors on a port becomes excessive. Notice in Figure 1-14 that SNMP agents can include servers, routers, switches, and many other devices.

In Cisco product terms, Catalyst switches feature SNMP agent support since they are the devices being managed. Cisco has three main network management solutions that provide the SNMP manager component:

- **CiscoWorks for Windows**—Inexpensive network management platform that features a third-party SNMP manager called WhatsUp Gold.

- **CiscoWorks Small Network Management Solution**—Includes all components of CiscoWorks for Windows, as well as restricted version Resource Manager Essentials for managing up to 20 devices, which is a component of CiscoWorks 2000 that provides advanced network administration, inventory, and auditing capabilities.

- **CiscoWorks 2000**—Feature-packed network management platform that requires a third-party SNMP manager (e.g., HP OpenView) for SNMP monitoring.

The SNMP communications protocol features three access levels that define the type of access the NMS has on the SNMP agent:

- **Read-only**—This level allows an NMS to read/view configuration and performance information on an agent.

- **Read-write**—This level allows an NMS to both read and write configuration, but does not allow the NMS to read or configure the agent community strings.

- **Read-write-all**—This level allows an NMS to both read and write configuration and also allows the NMS to read and configure the agent community strings.

| NOTE | The read-write-all level of access is proprietary to Cisco switches and is not part of the SNMP specification. read-write-all is supported only on CatOS switches (not Cisco IOS-based switches). |

Each access level is authenticated by using an SNMP community string, which is essentially a password that enables the appropriate access. For the NMS to communicate with an agent at the required access level the NMS and SNMP agent must be configured with the same community string for each access level; otherwise, communications fail.

Configuring SNMP Support on Cisco IOS

Configuring SNMP support on Cisco IOS requires the following configuration tasks:

- **Configuring SNMP community strings**—Allows SNMP managers to obtain read-only and/or read-write access to the switch.

- **Configuring SNMP traps**—Configures the switch to generate and forward SNMP traps to an SNMP manager in response to system events.

To configure SNMP community strings, you use the **snmp-server community** global configuration command:

```
Switch(config)# snmp-server community string {ro | rw} [std-access-list]
```

The **ro** and **rw** keywords specify the read-only and read-write levels of access, respectively, with the optional *std-access-list* parameter used to restrict access to only SNMP managers defined in a standard access control list (in Chapter 8 you learn more about restricting SNMP access). Example 1-25 demonstrates enabling SNMP read-only and read-write access on Cisco IOS.

Example 1-25 *Enabling SNMP Access from SNMP Managers on Cisco IOS*

```
Switch-A# configure terminal
Switch-A(config)# snmp-server community readme ro
Switch-A(config)# snmp-server community writeme rw
Switch-A(config)# snmp-server contact Bob Jones (508)1112222
Switch-A(config)# snmp-server location 999 1st Street, Boston, MA
```

In Example 1-25, a community string of **readme** is configured for read-only access, and a community string of **writeme** is configured for read-write access. With this configuration in place, any SNMP manager that attempts to gain access to the switch via SNMP must use a matching community string for the required level of access. Notice the **snmp-server contact** and **snmp-server location** commands, which are used to define system information (i.e., contact and location information) about the switch.

WARNING	Many SNMP manager applications ship with a default read-only community string of public and a default read-write community string of private. Avoid using these community strings in your network, because they are well known and use of these strings can allow unauthorized access to devices on your network. It is also important to note that there are a number of SNMP vulnerabilities detailed on the Cisco Connection Online (CCO) website at www.cisco.com/warp/public/707/cisco-malformed-snmp-msgs-pub.shtml. It is advisable to read this document before configuring SNMP in your network, so that you understand the vulnerabilities that exist and how to mitigate them.

To configure SNMP traps, you must first enable traps to be generated using the **snmp-server enable** global configuration command:

```
Switch(config)# snmp-server enable {traps | informs} [trap-facility1]
    [trap-facility2...]
```

Notice that you can enable either traps or informs. The only difference between a trap and inform is that a trap is unacknowledged by the receiving SNMP manager, whereas an inform must be acknowledged by the receiving SNMP manager. Therefore, informs are more reliable, because they allow Cisco Catalyst switches to retransmit unacknowledged informs. The optional *trap-facility* parameters allow you to define the types of events for which traps will be generated. If you do not specify any of these parameters, all events generate traps.

After enabling SNMP traps/informs to be generated, you must next configure destination SNMP managers to which traps/informs should be sent using the **snmp-server host** global configuration command:

```
Switch(config)# snmp-server host manager-ip {traps | informs}
    [version {1 | 2c | 3}] community-string [trap-facility1]
    [trap-facility2...]
```

Notice the optional **version** command, which enables you to configure the version of the SNMP manager as SNMPv1, SNMPv2c, or SNMPv3. SNMPv1 and SNMPv2c rely on community-based authentication, with SNMPv2c supporting additional minor features such as bulk retrieval capabilities and enhanced error reporting. SNMPv3 includes a totally new security model for authenticating and protecting the privacy and integrity of SNMP communications; however, the use of SNMPv3 is not commonplace yet. If you specify a version of 1 or 2c, you must next configure a community string that is used for authenticating with the remote SNMP manager.

Example 1-26 demonstrates enabling SNMP traps and configuring a destination to which the traps should be sent.

Example 1-26 *Configuring SNMP Traps on Cisco IOS*

```
Switch-A# configure terminal
Switch-A(config)# snmp-server host 192.168.1.100 readme
Switch-A(config)# snmp-server enable traps ?
  bgp               Allow BGP state change traps
  bridge            Allow SNMP STP Bridge MIB traps
  cluster           Allow Cluster Member Status traps
  config            Allow SNMP config traps
  entity            Allow SNMP entity traps
  envmon            Allow environmental monitor traps
  flash             Allow SNMP FLASH traps
  hsrp              Allow SNMP HSRP traps
  mac-notification  Allow SNMP MAC Notification Traps
  port-security     Allow SNMP port-security traps
  rtr               Allow SNMP Response Time Reporter traps
  snmp              Allow SNMP-type notifications
  syslog            Allow SNMP syslog traps
  tty               Allow TCP connection traps
  udp-port          The notification host's UDP port number
  vlan-membership   Allow SNMP VLAN membership traps
  vlancreate        Allow SNMP VLAN created traps
  vlandelete        Allow SNMP VLAN deleted traps
  vtp               Allow SNMP VTP traps
Switch-A(config)# snmp-server enable traps
Switch-A(config)# exit
Switch-A# show snmp
Chassis: CAT0620X0HV
Contact: Bob Jones (508)1112222
Location: 999 1st Street, Boston, MA
0 SNMP packets input
    0 Bad SNMP version errors
    0 Unknown community name
    0 Illegal operation for community name supplied
    0 Encoding errors
    0 Number of requested variables
    0 Number of altered variables
    0 Get-request PDUs
    0 Get-next PDUs
    0 Set-request PDUs
1 SNMP packets output
    0 Too big errors (Maximum packet size 1500)
    0 No such name errors
    0 Bad values errors
    0 General errors
    0 Response PDUs
    1 Trap PDUs
SNMP global trap: enabled

SNMP logging: enabled
    Logging to 192.168.1.100.162, 0/10, 1 sent, 0 dropped.
SNMP agent enabled
```

In Example 1-26, an SNMP manager at 192.168.1.100 is configured as a trap destination, with a community string of readme configured for authentication. The **snmp-server enable traps ?** command is then executed, which provides an indication as to the various types of system events for which you can individually enable/disable SNMP traps for. Notice that the **snmp-server enable traps** command is then executed, which means all types of system events generate SNMP traps where supported. Finally, the **show snmp** command is used to verify the SNMP trap configuration. The shaded lines at the bottom of the output indicate that SNMP traps are enabled and are being sent to 192.168.1.100.

Configuring SNMP Support on CatOS

Configuring SNMP support on CatOS requires the same configuration tasks as on Cisco IOS, with the configuration of community strings enabling SNMP access to the switch, and the configuration of SNMP traps to allow traps to be forwarded to an external SNMP manager.

To configure SNMP community strings, the **set snmp community** command is used:

```
Console> (enable) set snmp community {read-only | read-write |
  read-write-all} community-string
```

Notice on CatOS the additional **read-write-all** access level, which is proprietary and not supported on Cisco IOS. Once the appropriate community strings have been configured, you can configure SNMP traps using the **set snmp trap** command:

```
Console> (enable) set snmp trap enable [trap-facility1] [trap-facility2...]
```

Example 1-27 demonstrates configuring SNMP management support on CatOS.

Example 1-27 *Configuring SNMP Community Strings*

```
Switch-B> (enable) set snmp community read-only readme
SNMP read-only community string set to 'readme'.
Switch-B> (enable) set snmp community read-write writeme
SNMP read-write community string set to 'writeme'.
Switch-B> (enable) set snmp community read-write-all
SNMP read-write-all community string cleared.
Switch-B> (enable) set snmp trap 192.168.1.100 readme
SNMP trap receiver added.
Switch-B> (enable) set snmp trap enable
All SNMP traps enabled.
Switch-B> (enable) show snmp
SNMP:                   Enabled
RMON:                   Disabled
Extended RMON Netflow:  Disabled
Memory usage limit for new RMON entries: 85 percent
EngineId: 00:00:00:09:00:30:24:48:d4:00:00:00
Chassis Alias:
Traps Enabled: auth,bridge,chassis,config,entity,entityfru,envfan,envpower,
envstate,ippermit,macnotification,module,port,stpx,syslog,system,vlancreate,
vlandelete,vmps,vtp
Port Traps Enabled: 1/1-2, 2/1-48
```

Example 1-27 *Configuring SNMP Community Strings (Continued)*

```
Community-Access    Community-String
----------------    --------------------
read-only           readme
read-write          writeme
read-write-all

Additional-                             Access-
Community-String    Access-Type     Number  View
------------------  --------------  ------- --------------------------------

Trap-Rec-Address Trap-Rec-Community Trap-Rec-Port Trap-Rec-Owner Trap-Rec-Index
---------------- ------------------ ------------- -------------- --------------
192.168.1.100    readme                    162       CLI                    1
```

In Example 1-27, SNMP community strings are configured for read-only and read-write access. Notice that the string for read-write-all access is cleared in Example 1-27 by specifying a null or blank community string, which means no access will be able to gain read-write-all access to the switch via SNMP, because this functionality has been explicitly disabled.

WARNING   By default on CatOS, all community strings are configured with default values of public, private, and secret for read-only, read-write, and read-write-all access, respectively. This means your switch is vulnerable to unauthorized parties that know the default community strings that are configured on the switch, with the potential for an unauthorized user to configure a switch using read-write access. As a best practice when installing a new CatOS-based switch, you should explicitly clear all SNMP community strings by specifying a null string for each access level and then configure SNMP community stings as required.

After SNMP community strings are configured, SNMP traps are then configured to be sent to the host 192.168.1.100, using a community string of readme. The **set snmp trap enable** command configures all traps to be generated based upon system events. Finally, the **show snmp** command is used to verify the current SNMP configuration. You can see that SNMP is enabled, and you can see the configured community strings for each level of access (notice the read-write-all string is empty) and information about trap destinations.

Configuring SYSLOG Support

SYSLOG is a protocol that is primarily used in UNIX systems and allows for system events to be sent to a central SYSLOG server in a standard message format that indicates the type (or facility) of the message, severity, and details of the message. Figure 1-15 shows how SYSLOG works:

Figure 1-15 *SYSLOG*

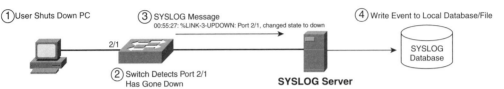

In Figure 1-15, the following events take place:

Step 1   The user shuts down his/her PC.

Step 2   The switch detects a link failure on port 2/1 due to the user shutting down the PC. An internal event is generated indicating the link failure.

Step 3   The switch determines that the event is severe enough to warrant notification to the SYSLOG server, and generates a message that details the event. A SYSLOG message is generated and sent to the SYSLOG server. The message includes a timestamp (00:55:27); a facility (LINK) which indicates the category the event relates to; a severity (3); the message type (UPDOWN); and a description (Port 2/1, changed state to down).

Step 4   The SYSLOG server receives the event, writes the event to a local database or file, and reacts in some way depending on how the server is configured.

TIP   You don't have a SYSLOG server to view SYSLOG messages; you can also configure Cisco Catalyst switches to output SYSLOG messages locally to your console and/or Telnet session, as well as store them in a logging buffer, which is a portion of memory of the switch. In fact by default, Cisco Catalyst switches display SYSLOG messages on the switch console.

Obviously, the event depicted in Figure 1-15 is a common occurrence, and as a network administrator, you probably wouldn't want to be flooded with lots of the events at 5 p.m. when users are shutting down to go home. Cisco Catalyst switches enable you to control the type of events and the severity of events for which SYSLOG messages are generated. The *facility* of a message relates to the category of the event. For example, on Cisco Catalyst switches a facility for system events exists (called *sys*) and a facility for link events (events related to link states and errors) exists. Within each facility, various messages exist that define events that relate to the facility.

NOTE   The facilities available vary, depending on the switch model. For an example, see
www.cisco.com/univercd/cc/td/doc/product/lan/c3550/12112cea/3550smg/
overview.htm#22819 for an example of the complete list of facilities support on a Catalyst
3550 switch.

Each message also has a severity that indicates how critical the event is. Table 1-10 shows
the severity levels that are used.

Table 1-10   *SYSLOG Severity Levels*

Severity Level	Keyword	Description
0	Emergencies	System unusable
1	Alerts	Immediate action required
2	Critical	Critical condition
3	Errors	Error conditions
4	Warnings	Warning conditions
5	notifications	Normal but significant conditions
6	informational	Information messages
7	Debugging	Debugging messages

As you can see from Table 1-10, severity level 0 is the highest and severity level 7 is the
lowest.

Each SYSLOG message has a common format that is displayed in Figure 1-16.

Figure 1-16   *SYSLOG Message Format*

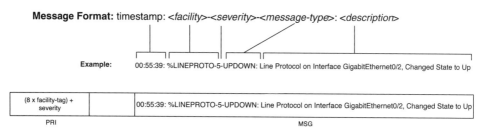

As you can see from Figure 1-16, SYSLOG messages are reasonably simple to read and
understand once you know their format.

It is important to understand that when SYSLOG messages are sent to a SYSLOG server, a facility tag is attached to each SYSLOG message, which allows the SYSLOG server to identify the application that has generated a SYSLOG message. The facility tag is separate from the actual SYSLOG message that is sent by an application and is always the same value regardless of the SYSLOG message that is attached. Table 1-11 lists the various facility tags that can be configured.

Table 1-11 *SYSLOG Facility Tags*

Facility Tag	Description
Auth	Authorization system
Cron	Cron/at facility
Daemon	System daemons
Kern	Kernel
Lpr	Line printer system
Mail	Mail system
News	USENET news
sys9	System use
sys10	System use
sys11	System use
sys12	System use
sys13	System use
sys14	System use
Syslog	Syslog itself
User	User process
Uucp	Unix-to-Unix copy system
local0	Local (custom) use
local1	Local (custom) use
local2	Local (custom) use
local3	Local (custom) use
local4	Local (custom) use
local5	Local (custom) use
local6	Local (custom) use
local7	Local (custom) use

On Cisco Catalyst switches, only a single facility tag can be configured, which is subsequently attached to all messages. Rather than relying on facility tags to identity the application or subsystem internally that generated a message, Cisco uses the facility field in the actual SYSLOG message (see Figure 1-16) to identify the subsystem that generated an event. This means that facility tags are useful only for identifying a particular Cisco device or type of device and are most commonly used to group different types of Cisco devices together. For example, a facility tag of local0 might be configured on all switches in the network, while a facility tag of local1 is configured for all routers in the network.

NOTE   It is very easy to get confused about the differences between facilities and facility tags. This is because Cisco refers to facility tags using the **facility** keyword in configuration commands.

Configuring SYSLOG Support on Cisco IOS

Configuration of SYSLOG on Cisco IOS is controlled via the **logging** global configuration command, which has many different parameters that control SYSLOG configuration. To configure support for an external SYSLOG server, you must perform the following configuration tasks:

- Ensure that SYSLOG logging is enabled using the **logging on** command (enabled by default)

- Define a SYSLOG server using the **logging** *server-ip-addr* command

- Enable SYSLOG event notification using the **logging trap** *severity-level* command (optional). The *severity-level* specifies the minimum severity alarms that should be generated using values or keywords from Table 1-10. By default, if you do not configure this command, a severity level of informational is assumed.

- Configure a SYSLOG facility tag (optional) using the **logging facility** *facility-tag* command.

- Configure the format of timestamps attached to each messages using the **service timestamps** global configuration command (optional).

If you also want to configure other destinations for SYSLOG messages (e.g., console, Telnet sessions), you can use the **logging** command as follows:

```
Switch(config)# [no] logging {console | monitor | buffered buffer-size}
  severity-level
```

By default, logging to the console is configured; however, in a production environment it is recommended that you disable console logging to avoid excessive CPU usage (every time an event is logged, an interrupt is sent to the CPU so that the message can be displayed on the console). Notice the **buffered** keyword, which allows you to allocate a portion of memory (specified in bytes using the *buffer-size* parameter) that can be used to store SYSLOG events.

As indicated in Figure 1-16, every SYSLOG message has a timestamp. On Cisco Catalyst switches, you can configure this timestamp to represent the system uptime or to represent the current date and time. By default on Cisco IOS, no timestamp information is included; however, you can enable timestamps and also modify the format of the timestamp attached to each SYSLOG message by using the **service timestamps log** global configuration command as follows:

```
Switch(config)# [no] service timestamps log {uptime | datetime [msec |
  localtime | show-timezone]}
```

The **uptime** keyword is used to specify that timestamps should be attached that include the system uptime, whereas the **datetime** keyword is used to specify that timestamps should be attached that include the current date and time. The optional **msec** keyword specifies the date/time format should include milliseconds, while the **localtime** specifies the local time should be used in the timestamp (by default UTC time is used) and the **show-timezone** keyword specifies time zone information should be included in the timestamp. You can use the **no service timestamps log** command to disable timestamps being used.

NOTE   The **service timestamps debug** global configuration command controls the timestamp added to any debugging messages that are displayed as a result of enabling debugging on Cisco IOS. This command has the same options as the **service timestamps log** command discussed previously.

Example 1-28 demonstrates configuring Cisco IOS to perform the following logging-related tasks:

- Sending SYSLOG messages with a severity of notifications (level 5) or higher to a SYSLOG server with an IP address of 192.168.1.100 with a facility of local0.
- Disabling logging to the console
- Enabling logging to Telnet sessions for critical events
- Enabling logging to a buffer of 256 KB for all events
- Configuring timestamps that show current date, local time, and time zone information to be appended to each message.

NOTE   To view SYSLOG messages from a Telnet session, you must execute the **terminal monitor** privileged mode command from within the Telnet session.

Example 1-28 *Configuring SYSLOG Server Support on Cisco IOS*

```
Switch-A# configure terminal
Enter configuration commands, one per line.  End with CNTL/Z.
Switch-A(config)# logging on
Switch-A(config)# logging 192.168.1.100
Switch-A(config)# logging trap notifications
Switch-A(config)# logging facility local0
Switch-A(config)# no logging console
Switch-A(config)# logging monitor critical
Switch-A(config)# logging buffered 256000 7
Switch-A(config)# service timestamps log datetime localtime show-timezone
Switch-A(config)# exit
Switch-A# show logging
Syslog logging: enabled (0 messages dropped, 0 messages rate-limited,
    0 flushes, 0 overruns)
    Console logging: disabled
    Monitor logging: level critical, 0 messages logged
    Buffer logging: level debugging, 1 messages logged
    Exception Logging: size (4096 bytes)
    File logging: disabled
    Trap logging: level notifications, 1 message lines logged
        Logging to 192.168.1.100, 1 message lines logged

Log Buffer (256000 bytes):

*Mar  1 01:07:53 UTC: %SYS-5-CONFIG_I: Configured from console by con0
```

In Example 1-28, the **logging on** command ensures that SYSLOG logging is enabled. The **logging 192.168.1.100** command defines a SYSLOG server with an IP address of 192.168.1.100 and the **logging trap notifications** command controls the severity of messages (Level 5 notifications) that are sent to the SYSLOG server. The **logging facility local0** command configures the local0 tag to be attached to all SYSLOG messages sent to the server (the default facility tag is local7). Logging to the console is next disabled, with logging to Telnet sessions for critical events enabled and logging to a 256 Kb buffer for all events (level 7 debugging) enabled. All messages are configured to include timestamp information, with the current local date, time, and time zone information included.

Finally, the **show logging** command is used to verify the logging configuration. The output of this command verifies the logging configuration of Example 1-28 and also displays the current log buffer. Notice that a single event exists in the buffer. This event represents exiting from global configuration mode in Example 1-28, which generates a %SYS-5-CONFIG event whenever this happens. You can see that the local date, time and time zone information is included. Because the date and time have not been configured on the switch, an asterisk is present at the beginning of the timestamp.

Configuring SYSLOG Support on CatOS

To configure SYSLOG support on CatOS, similar configuration tasks as described for Cisco IOS in the previous section are required, with the **set logging** command controlling SYSLOG configuration:

```
Console> (enable) set logging {server I console I telnet I session} {enable I
  disable}
Console> (enable) set logging server facility facility-tag
Console> (enable) set logging server severity severity-level
Console> (enable) set logging buffer message-size
Console> (enable) set logging history {message-size I severity severity-level}
Console> (enable) set logging level {all I facility} severity [default]
Console> (enable) set logging timestamp {enable I disable}
```

As you can see from the first command above, you can selectively enable or disable logging to a SYSLOG server (using the **server** keyword), to the console (using the **console** keyword), to all future Telnet sessions (using the **telnet** keyword), or to the current Telnet session (using the **session** keyword). The **set logging buffer** command allows you to define a local buffer in memory for SYSLOG messages, storing up to a maximum configurable number of messages defined by the *message-size* parameter. The **set logging history** command allows you to configure SYSLOG messages to be sent in batches to a SYSLOG server, rather than one by one (the default). The *message-size* parameter for the **set logging history** command specifies the number of messages that must be generated before sending all of the messages in a single batch to a locally configured SYSLOG server, while the **severity** *severity-level* option defines the minimum severity of messages that are stored in the history table. The **set logging level** command allows you to control the minimum severity of messages to log for each facility on the switch, and the **set logging timestamp** command allows you to add a timestamp (current system date and time) to each message that is generated (enabled by default).

Example 1-29 demonstrates configuring CatOS to perform the following logging-related tasks:

- Generating SYSLOG messages for all system logging facilities with a severity of notifications (level 5) or higher
- Sending SYSLOG messages with a severity of warnings (level 4) or higher to a SYSLOG server with an IP address of 192.168.1.100 with a facility of local0
- Configuring SYSLOG events of any severity to be sent to the SYSLOG server in batches of 10 messages
- Disabling logging to the console
- Enabling logging to Telnet sessions for critical events
- Enabling logging to a buffer of 100 messages for all events

Example 1-29 *Configuring SYSLOG Server Support on CatOS*

```
Switch-B> (enable) set logging level all 5 default
All system logging facilities set to severity 5(notifications)
Switch-B> (enable) set logging server 192.168.1.100
```

Example 1-29 *Configuring SYSLOG Server Support on CatOS (Continued)*

```
192.168.1.100 added to System logging server table.
Switch-B> (enable) set logging server severity 5
System logging server severity set to <5>
Switch-B> (enable) set logging server facility local0
System logging server facility set to <local0>
Switch-B> (enable) set logging history 10
System logging history table size set to <10>
Switch-B> (enable) set logging history severity 7
System logging history set to severity <7>
Switch-B> (enable) set logging server enable
System logging messages will be sent to the configured syslog servers.
Switch-B> (enable) set logging console disable
System logging messages will not be sent to the console.
Switch-B> (enable) set logging buffer 100
System logging buffer size set to <100>
Switch-B> (enable) show logging

Logging buffer size:        100
       timestamp option:    enabled
Logging history:
       size:                10
       severity:            debugging(7)
Logging console:            disabled
Logging telnet:             enabled
Logging server:             enabled
{192.168.1.100}
       server facility:     LOCAL0
       server severity:     warnings(4)

Facility            Default Severity        Current Session Severity
------------        ---------------------   ---------------------
cdp                 5                       5
dtp                 5                       5
dvlan               5                       5
earl                5                       5
ethc                5                       5
filesys             5                       5
gvrp                5                       5
ip                  5                       5
kernel              5                       5
mcast               5                       5
mgmt                5                       5
mls                 5                       5
protfilt            5                       5
pruning             5                       5
qos                 5                       5
radius              5                       5
security            5                       5
snmp                5                       5
spantree            5                       5
sys                 5                       5
tac                 5                       5
```

continues

Example 1-29 *Configuring SYSLOG Server Support on CatOS (Continued)*

```
tcp                  5                      5
telnet               5                      5
tftp                 5                      5
udld                 5                      5
vmps                 5                      5
vtp                  5                      5

0(emergencies)       1(alerts)          2(critical)
3(errors)            4(warnings)        5(notifications)
6(information)       7(debugging)
Switch-B> (enable) show logging buffer
Uptime at Mon May 5 2003, 14:24:33 is 0 day, 3 hours, 11 minutes.
2003 May 05 14:24:25 %SNMP-5-LINKTRAP:Link  Down Trap -- ifName=2/1
2003 May 05 14:24:25 %ETHC-5-PORTFROMSTP:Port 2/1 left bridge port 2/1
2003 May 05 14:24:25 %DTP-5-NONTRUNKPORTON:Port 2/1 has become non-trunk
2003 May 05 14:24:31 %SNMP-5-LINKTRAP:Link Up Trap -- ifName=2/1
2003 May 05 14:24:31 %SECURITY-5-DOT1X_PORT_AUTHORIZED:DOT1X: port 2/1
   authorized
```

In Example 1-29, the various configuration tasks described preceding the example are implemented. The **show logging** command is then executed, which displays the current logging configuration allowing you to verify your configuration. Notice the facility table, which lists all of the configurable facilities on the switch and the minimum severity level used to generate events by default and also for the current session. The minimum severity level for all events is 5, due to the **set logging level all 5** command executed in Example 1-29. Finally, the **show logging buffer** command is used to display the logging buffer. In Example 1-29, the events relating to a device being attached to port 2/1 are shown. You can use the **clear logging buffer** to remove events from the logging buffer.

NOTE   As a rule of thumb, you should not modify the default severity levels for each facility, because this might result in excessive messages (or a lack of messages) being logged. If you need to modify severity levels to aid in troubleshooting a specific problem, it is best to modify only the security level for the current session by omitting the **default** keyword in the **set logging level** command. To restore default security levels for each facility, use the **clear logging level** command.

Scenario 1-3: Configuring Ethernet Device Connectivity

The scenarios in this chapter have so far focused on preparing a switch for operation on the network. Of course the primary role of a switch is to provide LAN connectivity for end devices. In this scenario you learn how to configure Ethernet device connectivity on Cisco

Catalyst switches. Cisco Catalyst switches provide 10 Mbps, 100 Mbps, and 1000 Mbps connectivity for Ethernet-compliant devices. This scenario continues on from the previous scenarios; however, the scenario topology has changed somewhat with a few new devices and connections added as shown in Figure 1-17.

Figure 1-17 *Scenario 1-3 Topology*

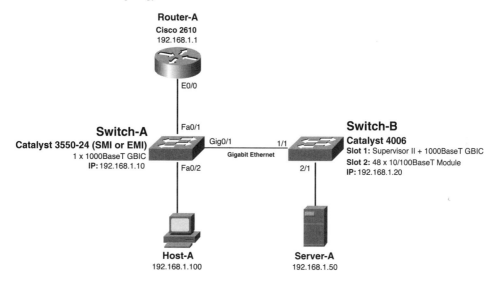

In Figure 1-17, notice that a Cisco router called Router-A has been added to the network, which has an Ethernet interface that supports only 10 Mbps Ethernet operation. Two hosts called Host-A and Server-A have also been attached to Switch-A and Switch-B, respectively, which support 10/100 Mbps Ethernet operation. You also learn how to configure parameters relating to the operation of the gigabit Ethernet connection between Switch-A and Switch-B, which although present in the previous scenario, was not configured whatsoever.

Scenario Prerequisites

Before beginning the configuration tasks specific to the requirements of this scenario, it is important to ensure that any prerequisite hardware and software configurations are in place. In this scenario, Router-A is added to the network and must be configured with a hostname, appropriate passwords and an IP address of 192.168.1.1. Example 1-30 shows the configuration required on Router-A before beginning this scenario.

Example 1-30 *Router-A Configuration for Scenario 1-3*

```
Router# configure terminal
Router(config)# hostname Router-A
Router-A(config)# enable secret cisco
Router-A(config)# line vty 0 4
Router-A(config-line)# password cisco
Router-A(config-line)# exit
Router-A(config)# interface Ethernet0/0
Router-A(config-if)# no shutdown
Router-A(config-if)# ip address 192.168.1.1 255.255.255.0
```

Table 1-12 describes the configuration that is assumed to be in place on all other devices in the scenario topology, such as servers and hosts, prior to beginning the configuration tasks. All other configuration parameters are assumed to have default values.

Table 1-12 *Scenario 1-3 Host Configuration Prerequisites*

Configuration Parameter	Host-A	Server-A
Operating System	Any[1]	Any[1]
IP Address/Mask	192.168.1.100/24	192.168.1.50/24
Ethernet NIC	10/100BASE-T	10/100BASE-T
Ethernet Speed/Duplex	Auto-negotiate	100 Mbps full-duplex (must be hardcoded)

[1] Any operating system is supported, as long as each can generate network traffic and supports other parameters defined in this chapter.

Configuration Tasks

To configure Ethernet device connectivity for this scenario, the following configuration tasks are required:

- Configuring Fast Ethernet ports
- Configuring gigabit Ethernet ports

Configuring Fast Ethernet Ports

To control the operation of Fast Ethernet ports on Cisco Catalyst switches, the following information must be determined prior to configuration:

- **Speed and duplex**—Cisco Catalyst switches can be configured to autosense speed and duplex settings (default) or can be configured for specific speed and duplex settings.

- **Flow control**—Some Fast Ethernet devices support flow control, where devices can send pause frames, which instruct the remote end to stop sending data for a specific period of time.

In this section, you only learn how to configure access port speed and duplex settings. Although flow control is supported on Fast Ethernet switches, the performance of modern switches means that it is never invoked on interfaces operating at 100 Mbps. Flow control is, however, a useful feature for gigabit Ethernet interfaces, and you learn how to configure flow control later in this scenario.

Configuring Speed and Duplex Settings

A fundamental requirement for successful and reliable Ethernet performance is to ensure that both ends of an Ethernet connection are operating using the same speed and duplex settings. Fast Ethernet ports on Cisco Catalyst switches support operating in one of the following modes of operation:

- 10 Mbps Half Duplex
- 10 Mbps Full Duplex
- 100 Mbps Half Duplex
- 100 Mbps Full Duplex

It is likely that the most common issues in any LAN environment are performance and connectivity issues related to speed and duplex misconfiguration, leading to situations where each end of an Ethernet connection is using a different mode of operation. Such a situation leads to two possible outcomes:

- **No connectivity whatsoever**—This happens when one side of the connection is configured for 10 Mbps operation, while the other side is configured for 100 Mbps operation. When the two devices connect, the clocking rates on the circuit do not match, and both devices cannot establish physical layer connectivity. In other words, a speed mismatch means connectivity is not possible between two Fast Ethernet devices.

- **Connectivity with impaired performance**—This happens when a duplex mismatch occurs, where both devices are configured for the same speed; however, one device is configured for half-duplex operation, and the other is configured for full-duplex operation. In this situation, connectivity is established between the devices. However, the performance of the connection is severely impaired, as one side (full-duplex side) of the connection does not exercise the CSMA/CD algorithm, causing excessive collisions, partial fragments (which cause CRC errors), and excessive retransmissions.

As you can see from the preceding information, ensuring the correct speed and duplex settings are configured on both sides of an Ethernet connection is important.

When configuring speed and duplex settings, you have two options available:

- **Auto-negotiation**—A Fast Ethernet interface attempts to auto-negotiate speed and duplex settings upon link initialization. Successful auto-negotiation relies on both devices that form the connection to be configured for auto-negotiation. Auto-negotiation is typically used for user devices, such as PCs and laptops, because these devices might move around and attach to different ports in your LAN infrastructure, making the task of attempting to maintain specific speed and duplex settings for each user device in the network very difficult and time consuming.

- **Manual configuration**—A Fast Ethernet interface is manually configured with specific speed and duplex settings. Manual configuration is typically used for servers, routers, firewalls, and other fixed devices, because these types of devices typically are fixed in the same location and are attached to the same Ethernet port. Hence, the administration associated with manually configuring speed and duplex settings is typically a one-time only effort, outweighing the potential performance issues that might result from auto-negotiation compatibility issues).

Fast Ethernet auto-negotiation is defined in the IEEE 802.3u specification, and uses Fast Link Pulse (FLP) to negotiate speed and duplex settings between two Ethernet devices when they are first attached. With FLP, each device sends a series of pulses that announces its capabilities to the remote device—capabilities include speed, duplex and the type of Ethernet operation supported (e.g., 100BASE-TX, 100BASE-T2, 100BASE-T4).

NOTE   Today the *de facto* Fast Ethernet standard is 100BASE-TX, which specifies Fast Ethernet operation using two pairs of Category 5 UTP and STP cabling. 100BASE-T2 and 100BASE-T4 are standards that allow Fast Ethernet operation over Category 3 cabling, using either two pairs or four pairs of wire respectively. It is very rare to find instances of 100BASE-T2 and 100BASE-T4 today.

On Cisco Catalyst switches, assuming a connecting device supports 10/100 Mbps and half-duplex modes of operation, both devices should auto-negotiate the most optimal mode of operation, which is 100 Mbps full duplex.

NOTE   Although the auto-negotiation feature is standards-based, it is common to find auto-negotiation compatibility issues between different Ethernet interface manufacturers. Auto-negotiation compatibility issues almost always result in duplex mismatches, which are hard to detect as connectivity is present. However, Ethernet performance is impaired due to the duplex mismatch. It is good practice to monitor port errors on Cisco Catalyst switches, so that you can detect possible duplex mismatches on ports where you believe devices should be communicating using full-duplex operation.

Myths of Auto-Negotiation

A common issue in many LAN environments is when one side of an Ethernet connection (typically the switch) has hardcoded speed and duplex settings, while the other side (normally a connecting device, such as a PC, laptop, or server) is configured to auto-negotiate speed and duplex settings. This is often due to the false belief that some administrators have that it is good practice to hardcode all of your switch ports to the most optimal speed and duplex settings (100 Mbps full duplex) with the mistaken impression that this will cause auto-negotiating devices that connect to the switch ports to negotiate to the most optimal mode of 100 Mbps full-duplex operation as well. In fact, this causes the opposite—when a Fast Ethernet interface is configured with hardcoded speed and duplex settings, it will not send any FLP messages upon link initialization, meaning the remote device (which is configured for auto-negotiation) does not receive any messages informing it of the capabilities of the local device. The auto-negotiating device can detect the correct speed, due to the clock rate that the hardcoded device applies to the connection; however, it cannot detect the appropriate duplex setting because it receives no FLP messages. When this happens, the auto-negotiating device assumes a mode of half-duplex operation, which, of course, causes a duplex mismatch, because the manually configured device is configured for full-duplex operation and the auto-negotiating device has assumed half-duplex operation, causing severe performance degradation on the Ethernet connection.

In conclusion, when configuring Fast Ethernet ports on Cisco Catalyst switches, if you manually hardcode settings on a switch port, always ensure that the connecting device also has hardcoded settings. When configuring auto-negotiation, always ensure the connecting device also is configured for auto-negotiation.

To configure speed and duplex settings for interfaces on Cisco IOS, you must first enter interface configuration mode, which is performed using the **interface** global configuration mode command:

```
Switch(config)# interface interface-type module/number
Switch(config-if)#
```

The *interface-type* parameter defines the type of interface you are configuring, while the *module/number* parameters identify the particular interface you are configuring. On Cisco IOS-based Catalyst switches, interfaces types include the following:

- **Fast Ethernet**—Specified using the **fastEthernet** keyword.
- **Gigabit Ethernet**—Specified using the **gigabitEthernet** keyword.
- **SVI**—Specified using the **VLAN** keyword, this configures a switch virtual interface (SVI) that is connected to the VLAN number specified by the *interface-id* parameter.

For identifying interfaces using the *module/number* parameter on fixed configuration switches that don't have modules (such as the Catalyst 2950/3550 switches), a module number of 0 is always used. Putting this all together, the first Fast Ethernet interface on a Catalyst 3550 is configured using the command **interface fastEthernet 0/1**. After you configure the **interface** command, you are placed into interface configuration mode, which is indicated by the **config-if** portion of the prompt.

You can also configure a range of interfaces at the same time, using the **interface range** command:

```
Switch(config)# interface range interface-type module/number
  [- number | , interface-type module/number] […]
Switch(config-if-range)#
```

You can specify a contiguous range of interfaces (e.g., fastEthernet 0/1 to fastEthernet 0/4), as well as specify a list of non-contiguous interfaces (e.g., fastEthernet0/1, fastEthernet 0/3, and fastEthernet0/7 to fastEthernet 0/9). It is very important that you follow the syntax of the **interface range** command carefully; otherwise, Cisco IOS interprets your command as invalid. If you are specifying a range of interfaces, you need only to specify an interface number for the upper bound of the range, ensuring a space is included between the lower *module/number* parameter of the range, the dash character that defines a range of interfaces is being configured, and the upper *number* parameter of the range. If you are specifying a list of interfaces, you must specify the full *module/number* designation for each interface in the list, separating each interface by a comma character, and must also ensure a space is in between any *module/number* designation and comma. For example, the following interface range command is valid:

```
Switch(config)# interface range fastEthernet 0/1 - 3 , fastEthernet0/6 ,
  fastEthernet0/8
```

However, the following interface range command is invalid because no space exists between the dash character and the full *interface-type module/number* designation is not used for specifying interface fastEthernet0/8:

```
Switch(config)# interface range fastEthernet 0/1-3 , fastEthernet0/6 , 0/8
                                              ^
% Invalid input detected at '^' marker.
```

TIP   If you work with a particular group of interfaces on a frequent basis, instead of explicitly specifying the group of interfaces using the **interface range** command each time you need to work with them, you can create an interface range macro using the **define interface-range** global configuration command, which allows you to define a group of interfaces and assign a group identifier to them. You can then easily configure the group of interfaces using the **interface range macro** *group-identifier*.

Now that you understand how to begin configuring an interface or range of interfaces, to configure speed and duplex settings for an interface you use the **speed** and **duplex** interface configuration commands, respectively:

```
Switch(config-if)# speed {10 | 100 | auto}
Switch(config-if)# duplex {half | full | auto}
```

By default, all ports on Cisco IOS switches are configured to auto-negotiate. If you need to hardcode speed and duplex settings, you must first hardcode the speed setting and then the hardcode duplex setting.

In this scenario (see Figure 1-17), Router-A is a network device connected to Switch-A, for which you would normally hardcode speed and duplex settings. Router-A is a Cisco 2610 router, which includes only 10 Mbps Ethernet ports and by default operates at 10 Mbps half-duplex operation. Host-A is a user device connected to Switch-A, for which you would normally configure auto-negotiation of speed and duplex settings. Example 1-31 demonstrates configuring speed and duplex settings on Switch-A.

Example 1-31 *Configuring Speed and Duplex Settings on Cisco IOS*

```
Switch-A# configure terminal
Switch-A(config)# interface fastEthernet0/1
Switch-A(config-if)# description ROUTER-A
Switch-A(config-if)# duplex half
Duplex can not be set until speed is set to non-auto value
Switch-A(config-if)# speed 10
Switch-A(config-if)# duplex half
Switch-A(config-if)# exit
Switch-A(config)# interface range fastEthernet0/2 - 23 , fastEthernet 0/24
Switch-A(config-if-range)# speed auto
Switch-A(config-if-range)# duplex auto
Switch-A(config-if-range)# exit
Switch-A(config)# define interface-range WORKSTATION-PORTS fastEthernet0/2 - 24
Switch-A(config)# interface range macro WORKSTATION-PORTS
Switch-A(config-if-range)# description WORKSTATION PORT
Switch-A(config-if-range)# end
Switch-A# show interface status
Port      Name            Status        Vlan    Duplex  Speed Type
Fa0/1                     connected     1         half     10 10/100BaseTX
Fa0/2                     connected     1       a-full  a-100 10/100BaseTX
Fa0/3                     notconnect    1         auto   auto 10/100BaseTX
Fa0/4                     notconnect    1         auto   auto 10/100BaseTX
… (Output truncated)
…
Switch-A# ping 192.168.1.1

Type escape sequence to abort.
Sending 5, 100-byte ICMP Echos to 192.168.1.1, timeout is 2 seconds:
!!!!!
Success rate is 100 percent (5/5), round-trip min/avg/max = 1/1/4 ms
Switch-A# ping 192.168.1.100

Type escape sequence to abort.
Sending 5, 100-byte ICMP Echos to 192.168.1.100, timeout is 2 seconds:
!!!!!
Success rate is 100 percent (5/5), round-trip min/avg/max = 8/8/12 ms
```

In Example 1-31, notice that the **description** interface configuration command can be used to assign some descriptive name to an interface. The first shaded line indicates that interface fastEthernet0/1 has a description of ROUTER-A, which is representative of the device (Router-A) attached to that interface. Next, an attempt is made to configure the duplex setting of the interface. Notice that when you attempt to hardcode duplex settings before speed settings, an error message is presented, indicating speed settings must be configured first.

After interface fastEthernet0/1 has been configured, notice that the **interface range** command is used to configure interfaces fastEthernet0/2 to fastEthernet0/23 and fastEthernet0/24, with a speed/duplex setting of auto configured (the command in Example 1-31 is used to demonstrate configuring a range and list in the same command and can be shortened to just **interface range fastEthernet0/2 – 24**). Using the **interface range** command reduces the number of configuration commands required to configure speed and duplex settings from 46 commands configuring each interface separately to just 2 commands.

NOTE | The speed/duplex configuration on the workstation interfaces is not actually required, because by default, all Fast Ethernet interfaces on Cisco Catalyst switches are configured for auto-negotiation.

Notice that an interface range macro is then defined, which defines interfaces fastEthernet0/2 to fastEthernet0/24 as belonging to the macro called **WORKSTATION-PORTS**. This macro is then referenced using the **interface range macro** command, which demonstrates how you can group interfaces and reference them using a descriptive name.

After each interface is configured, the **show interface status** command is executed, which provides a brief summary as to the current status and speed/duplex settings on each interface. The shaded output indicates that interface fastEthernet0/1 is operating 10 Mbps half duplex and that interface fastEthernet0/2 is operating at 100 Mbps full duplex, which has been auto-negotiated as indicate by the **a-** appended to the speed and duplex values. Finally, the **ping** command is used on Switch-A to successfully verify IP connectivity between the VLAN 1 management interface on Switch-A (configured in Scenario 1-2) to Router-A and Host-A.

NOTE | In Example 1-31, you need to wait for at least 30 seconds after connecting each device to allow the port to be placed into a forwarding state by spanning tree. Spanning tree is discussed in Chapter 4, "Spanning Tree."

To configure speed and duplex settings on CatOS, you use the **set port speed** and **set port duplex** commands, respectively:

```
Switch> (enable) set port speed mod/port(s) {10 | 100 | auto}
Switch> (enable) set port duplex mod/port(s) {half | full}
```

Notice that the **set port duplex** command does not have an **auto** option. If the **set port speed** command is configured with a setting of **auto**, then the duplex setting is automatically set to auto-negotiate. You can specify a single port, or a range and/or list of ports, in a similar fashion to the **interface range** command on Cisco IOS. Just as for Cisco IOS, if you need to hardcode speed and duplex settings, you must first hardcode the speed setting and then the hardcode duplex setting (by default, all ports on CatOS switches are configured to auto-negotiate). In this scenario, Server-A is a server device connected to Switch-B, for which you would normally hardcode speed and duplex settings. Assuming Server-A is hardcoded to operate at 100 Mbps full duplex, Example 1-32 demonstrates configuring a matching speed and duplex configuration on Switch-B and then configuring all remaining ports on module 2 to operate in auto-sensing mode.

Example 1-32 *Configuring Speed and Duplex Settings on CatOS*

```
Switch-B> (enable) set port name 2/1 SERVER-A
Port 2/1 name set.
Switch-B> (enable) set port duplex 2/1 full
Port 2/1 is in auto-sensing mode.
Switch-B> (enable) set port speed 2/1 100
Port(s)  2/1 speed set to 100Mbps.
Switch-B> (enable) set port duplex 2/1 full
Port(s)  2/1 set to full-duplex.
Switch-B> (enable) set port speed 2/2-24,2/25,2/26-48 auto
Ports 2/2-48 transmission speed set to auto detect.
Switch-B> (enable) show port status
Port  Name                Status       Vlan        Level  Duplex Speed Type
----- ------------------- ----------   ----------  ------ ------ ----- ------------
 2/1  SERVER-A            connected  1             normal full    100 10/100BaseTX
 2/2                      notconnect 1             normal auto   auto 10/100BaseTX
 2/3                      notconnect 1             normal auto   auto 10/100BaseTX
 2/4                      notconnect 1             normal auto   auto 10/100BaseTX
… (Output truncated)
…
Switch-B> (enable) ping 192.168.1.50
!!!!!

----192.168.1.50 PING Statistics----
5 packets transmitted, 5 packets received, 0% packet loss
round-trip (ms)  min/avg/max = 6/7/9
```

In Example 1-32, the **set port name** command is used to give a description of SERVER-A to port 2/1 on Switch-B. Notice that when you attempt to hardcode duplex settings before speed settings, an error message is presented, indicating the port is in auto-sensing mode (i.e., speed settings must be configured first). After configuring port 2/1, notice that the **set**

port speed command is used with a range and list of ports to configure a speed of auto for all remaining ports on module 2. When specifying a range or list of ports, similar rules apply as for Cisco IOS, except you don't need to ensure spaces are present between the - and , characters.

After 100 Mbps full-duplex operation is configured, the **show port status** command is used to display current status and speed/duplex settings on each port. The shaded output indicates that port 2/1 is connected and operating at 100 Mbps full duplex. Finally, the **ping** command is used on Switch-B to successfully verify IP connectivity between the sc0 interface on Switch-B (configured in Scenario 1-2) and Server-A (you need to wait for at least 30 seconds after connecting Server-A to allow the port to placed into a forwarding state by spanning tree).

Configuring Gigabit Ethernet Ports

To configure the physical characteristics of gigabit Ethernet port operation on Cisco Catalyst switches, the following information must be determined prior to configuration:

- **Port negotiation**—Gigabit Ethernet interfaces use port negotiation to negotiate some of the physical characteristics that determine how the interface operates. Port negotiation extends the concept of auto-negotiation on 10/100 Ethernet interfaces past just speed and duplex settings and enables other settings such as flow control and remote fault information.

- **Flow control**—Flow control is important for gigabit Ethernet connections, where it is reasonable for the receive buffers on a gigabit interface to become full due to the high speeds of data transfer, causing congestion on the interface.

- **Jumbo frames**—Many high data-transfer applications, such as network attached storage (NAS—not to be confused with network access server) support jumbo frames, which extend the maximum transmission unit (MTU) for Ethernet frames from 1518 bytes up to 9216 bytes. Using jumbo frames improves data throughput for data-intensive applications such as network attached storage.

Configuring Port Negotiation

Gigabit Ethernet interfaces use port negotiation to negotiate various parameters that relate to the physical operation of the interface. Port negotiation is used to exchange the following information:

- **Duplex settings**—All Cisco gigabit interfaces operate only in full-duplex mode.

- **Flow control capabilities**—Allows an interface to advertised whether or not it can support flow control features.

- Remote fault information

Notice in the preceding list that speed is not included in the list of auto-negotiated features, because gigabit Ethernet interfaces operate only at gigabit speeds. There is no requirement to negotiate speed.

NOTE
Cisco Catalyst switches also support 10/100/1000BASE-T auto-sensing interface, which obviously can operate at different speeds. On these ports, the switch first detects the clock rate on the interface. If a speed of 10/100 Mbps is detected, the auto-negotiation procedures for Fast Ethernet are invoked. If a speed of 1000 Mbps is detected, the port negotiation procedures for gigabit Ethernet are invoked.

On Cisco Catalyst switches, when configuring gigabit Ethernet interfaces, the following rules apply:

- You cannot modify speed or duplex settings on GBIC-based interfaces.
- You can modify speed and duplex settings for 10/100/1000BASE-T interfaces.
- You can disable port negotiation for 1000BASE-SX, 1000BASE-LX and 1000BASE-ZX GBIC-based interfaces.
- You cannot disable port negotiation for 1000BASE-T GBIC-based interfaces.
- If you enable port negotiation on a gigabit Ethernet interface, you must ensure port negotiation is configured on the other side of the connection. If port negotiation is enabled on one side but disabled on the other side, the interface configured for port negotiation does not come up.
- If port negotiation is disabled on both sides of a gigabit Ethernet connection, the link comes up; however, some features such as flow control might not be supported depending on your configuration.

By default, gigabit Ethernet interfaces have port negotiation enabled, and for most situations, this configuration should not require modification. The only time you need to disable port negotiation is if you are connecting to a device that does not support port negotiation.

To configure port negotiation on Cisco IOS, the **speed** interface configuration command is used, even though port negotiation on gigabit Ethernet has nothing to do with speed. On GBIC-based interfaces, the **speed** command has the following syntax:

```
Switch(config-if)# [no] speed nonegotiate
```

Example 1-33 demonstrates ensuring port negotiation is enabled on Switch-A.

Example 1-33 *Configuring Gigabit Ethernet Port Negotiation on Cisco IOS*

```
Switch-A# configure terminal
Switch-A(config)# interface gigabitEthernet0/1
Switch-A(config-if)# no speed nonegotiate
```

To configure port negotiation on CatOS, the more intuitive **set port negotiation** configuration command is used:

```
Console> (enable) set port negotiation mod/port(s) {enable | disable}
```

Example 1-34 demonstrates ensuring port negotiation is enabled on Switch-B.

Example 1-34 *Configuring Gigabit Ethernet Port Negotiation on Cisco IOS*

```
Switch-B> (enable) set port negotiation 1/1 enable
Port 1/1 negotiation enabled
Switch-B> (enable) show port negotiation 1/1
Port Link Negotiation
----- ----------------
1/1 enabled
```

In Example 1-34, the **show port negotiation** command is executed after enabling port negotiation, which verifies port negotiation is indeed enabled.

Configuring Flow Control

Flow control is a feature defined in the IEEE 802.3x specification, enabling a receiving device to signal congestion to a sending device, which allows for the sending device to temporarily halt transmission, alleviating congestion at the receiving device. Figure 1-18 demonstrates how flow control works.

Figure 1-18 *802.3x Flow Control*

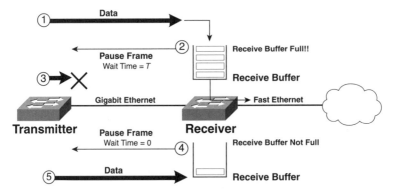

In Figure 1-18, the following events occur:

1 The transmitter is sending data (frames) to the receiver. Note that Figure 1-18 represents only one direction of the connection. The roles (transmitter and receiver) are swapped for frames sent in the reverse direction.

2 On the receiver, the receive buffers on the interface connected to the transmitter interface become full, causing a congestion condition. This is common when traffic is sent to a switch on a high-speed interface (e.g., gigabit Ethernet) and is then forwarded to a lower speed interface (e.g., Fast Ethernet). If the receiver now receives any more frames from the transmitter, they are discarded until the congestion is alleviated and the receive buffers emptied. To avoid this situation, the receiver sends a pause frame to the transmitter, which includes a wait time value. This instructs the transmitter to stop sending frames for the indicated wait time.

3 Assuming the transmitter supports 802.3x flow control, it now stops sending frames for the wait time period. After the wait time period is over, the transmitter starts transmitting frames again.

4 If the receiver clears the congestion before the wait period is over, it sends a pause frame with a wait time value of 0, which indicates to the transmitter it is okay to start transmitting again. This ensures that the connection is not idle if congestion is cleared before the transmitter is due to restart transmission.

5 The transmitter restarts transmission, either due to the wait time expiring or due to a pause frame being received with a wait time of 0.

If congestion occurs at the receiver interface once again, the process just described starts again, with the receiver generated a pause frame.

All Cisco Catalyst switches that include gigabit Ethernet capabilities include support for flow control; however, depending on the type of gigabit Ethernet port you are using, support for flow control might be limited. On all Cisco Catalyst switches, all gigabit Ethernet interfaces support the ability to *receive* and respond to pause frames (i.e., act like the transmitter in Figure 1-18). However, some gigabit Ethernet ports do not support the ability to send pause frames (i.e., act like the receiver in Figure 1-18). The ability to receive and respond to pause frames is referred to as *input flow control*, and the ability to send pause frames is referred to as *output flow control*. Table 1-13 describes the capabilities of the various gigabit Ethernet ports on each Cisco Catalyst switch and also describes the flow control capabilities.

Table 1-13   *Ethernet Flow Control Capabilities*

Model	Port Type	Receive	Send
Catalyst 2900 (CatOS)	All Fast Ethernet	No	No
	All gigabit Ethernet	Yes	No
Catalyst 2900XL/3500XL	All Fast Ethernet	No	No
	All gigabit Ethernet	Yes	Yes
Catalyst 2950	All Fast Ethernet	No	No
	All gigabit Ethernet	Yes	Yes

continues

Table 1-13   *Ethernet Flow Control Capabilities (Continued)*

Model	Port Type	Receive	Send
Catalyst 3550/3750	All Fast Ethernet	Yes	No
	All gigabit Ethernet	Yes	Yes
Catalyst 4000/4500	All Fast Ethernet	No	No
	Uplink gigabit Ethernet	Yes	No
	Oversubscribed gigabit Ethernet	Yes	Yes
Catalyst 5000/5500	Fast Ethernet	Varies[1]	Varies[1]
	All gigabit Ethernet except WS-X5410	Yes	Yes
	WS-X5410 Uplink gigabit Ethernet	Yes	No
	WS-X5410 Oversubscribed gigabit Ethernet	Yes	Yes
Catalyst 6000/6500	All Fast Ethernet	Yes	No
	All gigabit Ethernet	Yes	Yes
	All Ten gigabit Ethernet	Yes	Yes

[1]Check hardware module documentation or use **show port capabilities** command.

In Table 1-13, the Receive column indicates the ability to receive pause frames and pause transmission (input flow control), while the Send column indicates the ability to send pause frames in response to congestion on the receive buffers of a port (output flow control). Notice that the Catalyst 4000/4500 and Catalyst 5000/5500 include oversubscribed ports, which refers to oversubscription to the switch backplane, as well as uplink ports, which are non-oversubscribed ports (i.e., they have at least a 1 Gbps full-duplex connection to the switch backplane).

TIP

You can use the **show interface** *interface-type interface-id* **capabilities** command on Cisco IOS and the **show port capabilities** *mod/port* command on CatOS to determine whether or not a port supports send and/or receive flow control features.

To demonstrate the concept of oversubscribed and uplink ports, an example is now provided based upon the Catalyst 4000/4500 switch. On the Catalyst 4000/4500 switch, each module is provided with 3 * 2 Gbps full-duplex connections to the switching fabric. An example of a module for the Catalyst 4000/4500 that includes oversubscribed ports is the 18-port 1000BASE-X module (WS-X4418-GB) for the Catalyst 4000/4500 switch, which includes 2 * Uplink 1000BASE-X ports and 16 * oversubscribed 1000BASE-X ports. Figure 1-19 shows how bandwidth is allocated internally to the 18-port 1000BASE-X module on the Catalyst 4000/4500.

Figure 1-19   *Internal Bandwidth Allocation for the 18-port 1000BASE-X Module on the Catalyst 4000/4500 Switch*

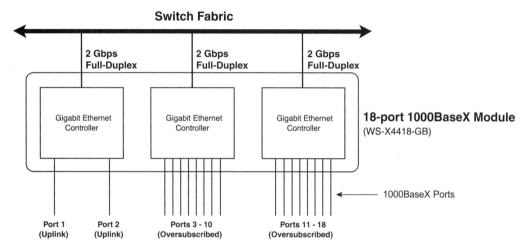

In Figure 1-19, Port 1 and Port 2 are uplink ports, which means they are each allocated 1 Gbps full-duplex bandwidth (i.e., non-blocking) to the switch backplane. This means that the receive buffers on these ports never experience congestion, because the ingress bandwidth is the same as the egress bandwidth. Even if frames received on an uplink port are eventually switched out a lower speed Fast Ethernet port, congestion occurs at the egress port, because the frames received have been emptied from the receive buffers of the uplink port and switched to the transmit buffers of the egress port. Hence, uplink ports have no requirement for the ability to send flow control pause frames. Looking back at Figure 1-19, ports 3–10 and ports 11–18 are oversubscribed ports, in that the total bandwidth of each group of ports (8 Gbps) is shared between a 2 Gbps connection to the backplane (i.e., possible blocking). This means an oversubscription of 4:1 exists, where if all ports in a group are connected and receiving traffic at the maximum possible rate of 1 Gbps, the bandwidth allocate to each port is only 250 Mbps, causing congestion on the receive buffers of each port. For this reason, the oversubscribed ports need to be able to signal congestion to transmitting devices, hence the ability to send flow control pause frames.

Now that you understand how flow control works, it is time to learn how to configure flow control on Cisco Catalyst switches. Before configuring flow control on the Catalyst 2950/3550 switches, it is important to understand that you should not configure flow control in conjunction with QoS features. This means you must disable all QoS features globally before configuring flow control. This restriction does not apply to Catalyst 4000/4500 switches or Catalyst 6000/6500 switches.

NOTE   QoS refers to the ability of a switch to classify certain types of traffic (e.g., voice, video, data), mark traffic, and then service each type of traffic appropriately. In other words, the ability to prioritize the forwarding of different types of traffic over other types of traffic. QoS is discussed in Chapter 9, "Quality of Service."

By default, QoS features are disabled globally on Cisco Catalyst 2950/3550 switches. However, it is good practice to verify that QoS is disabled and then disable QoS globally if required. To disable QoS globally on Cisco IOS, the **no mls qos** global configuration command is used. Example 1-35 demonstrates disabling QoS on Cisco IOS and then verifying that QoS is indeed disabled.

Example 1-35   *Disabling QoS Globally on Cisco IOS*

```
Switch-A# configure terminal
Switch-A(config)# no mls qos
Switch-A(config)# exit
Switch-A# show mls qos
QoS is disabled
```

In Example 1-35, after QoS is disabled, the **show mls qos** command is used to verify QoS is indeed disabled.

Getting back to configuring flow control, on Cisco Catalyst switches you have the ability to control whether or not a port responds to pause frames received and generate pause frames when congestion occurs (if supported). As indicated in the previous section on port negotiation, flow control capabilities are exchanged during the port negotiation process, and you can configure Cisco Catalyst switches to process pause frames received and/or send pause frames based on the flow control capabilities indicated by the remote device connected to a port.

To configure flow control on Cisco IOS switches, the **flowcontrol** interface configuration command is used to enable/disable flow control:

```
Switch(config-if)# flowcontrol {receive | send} {on | off | desired}
```

The **receive** keyword is used to enable/disable a port responding to pause frames, while the **send** keyword is used to enable/disable the sending of pause frames due to congestion. The **on** and **off** keywords enable or disable, respectively, the **send** or **receive** feature, while the **desired** keyword configures the interface to enable the **send** or **receive** feature only if the remote device indicates that capability to support flow control during port negotiation.

NOTE   By default on the Catalyst 2950/3550, the **receive** feature is set to **off** and the **send** feature is set to **desired** for gigabit Ethernet ports. The **receive** feature is set to off as the Catalyst 3550 is a non-blocking switch. Hence, if congestion does occur it normally happens at the transmit queue of a lower-speed port, not at the receive queue (buffer) of a Gigabit Ethernet port. For Fast Ethernet ports, the **receive** and **send** feature is set to **off** by default.

Example 1-36 demonstrates configuring interface gigabitEthernet 0/1 on Switch-A to enable the **send** and **receive** features only if the remote switch indicates the ability to support flow control during port negotiation.

Example 1-36 *Configuring Flow Control on Cisco IOS*

```
Switch-A# configure terminal
Switch-A(config)# interface gigabitEthernet0/1
Switch-A(config-if)# flowcontrol send desired
Switch-A(config-if)# flowcontrol receive desired
Switch-A(config-if)# end
Switch-A# show interfaces gigabitEthernet0/1
GigabitEthernet0/1 is up, line protocol is up (connected)
  Hardware is Gigabit Ethernet, address is 0009.b7aa.9c99 (bia 0009.b7aa.9c99)
  MTU 1500 bytes, BW 10000 Kbit, DLY 1000 usec,
     reliability 255/255, txload 1/255, rxload 1/255
  Encapsulation ARPA, loopback not set
  Keepalive set (10 sec)
  Auto-duplex, Auto-speed
  input flow-control is off, output flow-control is on
  ARP type: ARPA, ARP Timeout 04:00:00
... (Output Truncated)
...
```

In Example 1-36, after flow control is configured, the **show interfaces** command is used to verify the current flow control configuration of the interface. The shaded line indicates that input (receive) flow control is off, which is due to the fact that Switch-B has indicated it does not support output (send) flow control on its port (as port 1/1 on Switch-B is an uplink port, which does not support the **send** feature as indicated in Table 1-13). However, output (send) flow control is enabled, which is due to the fact that Switch-B has indicated the ability to support input flow control on its port during port negotiation.

To configure flow control on CatOS switches, the **set port flowcontrol** command is used to enable/disable flow control:

```
Console> (enable) set port flowcontrol mod/port(s) {receive | send}
   {on | off | desired}
```

Each of the **receive, send, on, off,** and **desired** keywords has the same meaning as it does for Cisco IOS.

NOTE   By default on CatOS, for uplink (non-oversubscribed) gigabit Ethernet ports, the **receive** feature is set to **off** and the **send** feature is set to **desired** (if **send** is supported). For oversubscribed gigabit Ethernet ports, the **receive** feature is set to **desired,** and the **send** feature is set to **on**. For CatOS platforms that support flow control for Fast Ethernet ports, the **receive** feature is set to **off** by default (the **send** feature is not supported on Fast Ethernet ports).

Example 1-37 demonstrates configuring port 1/1 on Switch-B to enable the **receive** feature only if the remote switch indicates the ability to support flow control during port negotiation.

Example 1-37 *Configuring Flow Control on CatOS*

```
Switch-B> (enable) set port flowcontrol send 1/1 desired
Port 1/1 flow control send administration status set to desired
(port will send flowcontrol to far end if far end supports it)
Switch-B> (enable) set port flowcontrol receive 1/1 desired
Port 1/1 flow control receive administration status set to desired
(port will allow far end to send flowcontrol if far end supports it)
Switch-B> (enable) show port flowcontrol 1/1
Port   Send-Flowcontrol   Receive-Flowcntl   RxPause   TxPause
       Admin   Oper       Admin   Oper
-----  ----------------   ----------------   -------   ------
 1/1   off     off        desired on         0         0
```

In Example 1-37, after flow control is configured, the **show port flowcontrol** command is used to verify the current flow control configuration of the port. The shaded line for receive (input) flow control indicates an administrative (configured) status of desired and an operational status of on, which is due to the fact that Switch-A has indicated the ability to support output flow control during port negotiation.

Configuring Jumbo Frames

In recent years, storage technologies such as storage area networking (SAN) and network attached storage (NAS) have become popular, because they allow organizations to consolidate storage, providing greater scalability and performance for data center environments.

NAS is a technology that allows storage devices, such as disk farms and tape libraries, to be accessible via the data network, reducing the costs associated with implementing other storage technologies such as SANs that implement out-of-band networks dedicated to storage. Protocols such as iSCSI (SCSI over IP) and Fiberchannel over IP have been developed, which enable servers to mount volumes located on a NAS as virtual file systems, transparent of the data network that separates the server and NAS. The amount of traffic generated by a NAS is significant, because file operations are typically data intensive, reading and/or writing sometimes gigabytes of information in a single file request. The relatively small default MTU of Ethernet frames (i.e., a maximum payload of 1500 bytes) means that six frames are required to execute even the most basic of I/O operations (i.e., read or write an 8 KB sector from disk).

For a NAS to effectively provide disk access for other network devices, it must be able to burst large amounts of data with very low latencies; having to generate large amounts of 1500-byte Ethernet frames increases system load and also increases latency. Jumbo frames extend the default MTU from 1500 bytes up to 9216 bytes (the actual value might vary depending on the Cisco Catalyst switch platform), which allows for greater data throughput for applications such as NAS.

Two types of oversized Ethernet frames exist, with jumbo frames being one of them. The other oversized frame is referred to as a *baby giant*. Each of these oversized frames is described as follows:

- **Baby giants**—These frames are up to 1600 bytes in size (MTU of 1548 or 1552 bytes) and accommodate applications such as MPLS, where one or more MPLS labels are attached to between the Ethernet header and IP header.

- **Jumbo frames**—These frames are up to 9216 bytes in size and are designed for applications such as storage that require a large MTU to burst larges amounts of information efficiently and with low latency.

Table 1-14 lists support for oversized frames on Cisco Catalyst switches, with the default MTU and largest MTU listed.

Table 1-14   *Oversized Frame Support on Cisco Catalyst Switches*

Platform	Minimum Software Version	Default MTU (Bytes)	Largest MTU (Bytes)
Catalyst 2900XL/3500XL	12.0(5.2)XU	1500	2018
Catalyst 2950 (SI)	Oversized frames not supported	1500	1500
Catalyst 2950 (EI)	12.1(6)EA2	1500	1530
Catalyst 3550 (Fast Ethernet switches)	12.1(6)EA1	1500	1546
Catalyst 3550-12G Catalyst 3550-12T	12.1(6)EA1	1500	2000[1]
Catalyst 3750	Supported in all versions	1500	1546 (10/100 ports) 900 (Gigabit ports)
Catalyst 4000/4500 Supervisor 1/2	Oversized frames not supported	1500	1500
Catalyst 4000/4500 Supervisor 3/IV	Cisco IOS 12.1(12c)EW	1500	1552
	Cisco IOS 12.1(13)EW	1500	9198
Catalyst 5000/5500 (CatOS)	CatOS 6.1(1)	1548	9000[2] 24000[2]
Catalyst 6000/6500 (CatOS)	CatOS 6.2(1)	1548	9216[3]

continues

Table 1-14 *Oversized Frame Support on Cisco Catalyst Switches (Continued)*

Platform	Minimum Software Version	Default MTU (Bytes)	Largest MTU (Bytes)
Catalyst 6000/6500 (Native IOS)	Cisco IOS 12.1(1)E	1500	9216

[1]Prior to 12.1(9)EA1, a MTU of 2025 is configurable. The time of writing, the Catalyst 3750 was not shipping, and no system documentation is available.

[2]The WS-X5213, WS-X5224, WS-X5225R, WS-X5234, and WS-X5410 modules support jumbo frames up to 9000 bytes. All other Ethernet ports support jumbo frames up to 24000 bytes.

[3]The WS-X6148-XX, WS-X6248-XX, and WS-X6348-XX modules support a maximum ingress MTU of only 8092 bytes. This also applies for the WS-6516-GE-TX module ports when operating at 100 Mbps.

As you can see from the preceding table, support for oversized frames varies, with some switches supporting baby giants and few supporting jumbo frames. If you are looking at implementing switches in a data center environment where you might run high data transfer applications (e.g., NAS) that will benefit from jumbo frames, then you must be careful about the switch models that you deploy.

NOTE   In this scenario, neither Switch-A (Catalyst 3550) nor Switch-B (Catalyst 4000 Supervisor 2) support jumbo frames; hence, you can't actually configure jumbo frames on the switches for this scenario. However, on Switch-A you can support baby giants, which is demonstrated in this chapter. The configuration of jumbo frames is also demonstrated, with examples provided from a Catalyst 4000 with Supervisor 4 (Cisco IOS) and a Catalyst 6500 (CatOS).

The way in which you configure oversized frames on Cisco Catalyst switches depends on the switch platform and operating system.

On the Catalyst 2950/3550 (Cisco IOS), the default MTU for all ports is 1500 bytes; however, you can modify this on a system-wide basis by configuring the **system mtu** global configuration command. Example 1-38 demonstrates configuring the maximum possible MTU on Switch-A to support baby giants.

Example 1-38 *Configuring Support for Baby Giants on the Catalyst 3550*

```
Switch-A# configure terminal
Switch-A(config)# system mtu 1546
Changes to the System MTU will not take effect until the next reload is done.
```

Example 1-38 *Configuring Support for Baby Giants on the Catalyst 3550 (Continued)*

```
Switch-A(config)# exit
Switch-A# show system mtu
System MTU size is 1500 bytes
On next reload, system MTU will be 1546 bytes
```

In Example 1-38, notice that after configuring the largest possible MTU on Switch-A (1546 bytes, which is the largest for Fast Ethernet–based Catalyst 3550 switches), Cisco IOS notifies you that the changes to the MTU are not applied until after the switch is rebooted. The **show system mtu** command is then used to view the current MTU, which indicates the MTU is currently 1500 bytes but will be 1546 bytes after the next reload.

On the Catalyst 4000/4500 Supervisor 3/IV with Cisco IOS, the default MTU for all ports is 1500 bytes; however, you can modify this by configuring the following:

- Enable baby giants (up to 1552 bytes) for all ports on a system-wide basis using the **system mtu** global configuration command.

- Enable jumbo frames (up to 9198 bytes) on a per-interface basis for gigabit Ethernet, switch virtual interfaces (SVI), and port channel interfaces (virtual interfaces that represent EtherChannel bundles), using the **mtu** interface configuration command.

Example 1-39 demonstrates configuring baby giants and configuring jumbo frames for a gigabit Ethernet interface on a Catalyst 4000 switch with Supervisor 4 engine.

Example 1-39 *Configuring Baby Giants and Jumbo Frames on a Catalyst 4000 with Supervisor 4*

```
cat4000-s4# configure terminal
cat4000-s4(config)# system mtu 1552
cat4000-s4(config)# interface gigabitEthernet 1/1
cat4000-s4(config-if)# mtu 9198
```

In Example 1-39, the MTU for all ports is configured to support baby giants up to 1552 bytes in size. The gigabitEthernet 1/1 interface is then configured to support jumbo frames up to 9198 bytes in size.

On the native IOS Catalyst 6000/6500 (Cisco IOS-based), the default MTU is 1500 bytes; however, you can increase the MTU by configuring the following:

- Enable jumbo frames (up to 9216 bytes) for all ports on a system-wide basis using the **system jumbomtu** global configuration command.

- Enable jumbo frames (up to 9216 bytes) on a per-interface basis for gigabit Ethernet, switch virtual interfaces (SVI), and port channel interfaces (virtual interfaces that represent EtherChannel bundles), using the **mtu** interface configuration command.

Example 1-40 demonstrates configuring a global system MTU of 9000 bytes and configuring jumbo frames with the largest MTU possible for a gigabit Ethernet interface on a native IOS Catalyst 6000 switch.

Example 1-40 *Configuring Jumbo Frames on a Native IOS Catalyst 6000 Switch*

```
Cat6000# configure terminal
Cat6000(config)# system jumbomtu 9000
Cat6000(config)# interface gigabitEthernet 1/1
Cat6000(config-if)# mtu 9216
```

On Catalyst 6000/6500 switches running CatOS, the default MTU is 1548 bytes; however, you can increase the MTU to 9216 bytes on a per-port basis by using the **set port jumbo** configuration command. Example 1-41 demonstrates configuring jumbo frames for a gigabit Ethernet interface on a Catalyst 6000 switch running CatOS.

Example 1-41 *Configuring Jumbo Frames on Catalyst 6000 Switch Running CatOS*

```
Cat6000> (enable) set port jumbo 1/1 enable
Jumbo frames enabled on port 2/1
Cat6000> (enable) show port jumbo
Jumbo frames MTU size is 9216 bytes
Jumbo frames enabled on port(s) 1/1
```

In Example 1-41, notice that you cannot specify the MTU on a Catalyst 6000/6500 switch running CatOS. If you enable jumbo frames, the MTU is automatically set to 9216 bytes, as confirmed by the **show port jumbo** command.

Scenario 1-4: Configuring System Time

In the previous scenarios you have learned how to install Cisco Catalyst switches, configure them for network management, and connect devices. The final base configuration task required is to configure system time, which is very important for ensuring logging information generated by Cisco Catalyst switches includes accurate timestamp information. Often when you are troubleshooting events in the network, you need to correlate external events with specific events that have occurred on your Cisco Catalyst switches. To enable accurate correlation of events, the system date and time must be accurate and ideally synchronized to a central time source used for all devices in the network.

This scenario continues on from the previous scenario and shows you how to configure the system clock on Cisco Catalyst switches, as well as configure Network Time Protocol (NTP), which enables Cisco Catalyst switches to obtain time from a trusted time source using IP. Cisco Catalyst switches support NTP client operation, while Cisco routers support both NTP client and NTP server operation. In this scenario, Router-A (see Figure 1-17) is configured as an NTP server, with Switch-A and Switch-B configured as NTP clients that obtains time from Router-A.

Scenario Prerequisites

This scenario requires NTP client support to be configured on Switch-A and Switch-B. Before configuring NTP client support, an appropriate NTP server configuration must be in place on Router-A. Example 1-42 demonstrates the configuration required on Router-A to enable NTP server functionality.

Example 1-42 *Configuring Router-A as an NTP Server*

```
Router-A# configure terminal
Router-A(config)# clock timezone NZST 12
Router-A(config)# ntp master
Router-A(config)# exit
Router-A# clock set 17:00:00 7 May 2003
Router-A# show clock
17:00:02.319 NZST Wed May 7 2003
```

In Example 1-42, the appropriate time zone (New Zealand Standard Time with a +12 UTC offset) is set using the **clock timezone** command. The **ntp master** command is then used, which configures Router-A as an NTP server in stratum 7 (default). The **clock set** command is then used to configure the current date and time.

Configuration Tasks

Configuring system time on Catalyst switches requires the following configuration tasks:

- Configuring the correct date and time
- Configuring NTP (optional)

As you can see from the preceding bullet, configuring network time protocol is optional. However, it is recommended that you use NTP for not just your Cisco Catalyst switches, but all devices in your network, including switches, routers, servers, PCs, and so on. Using the same time source for all your devices ensures that all devices are operating with the same perception of time as all other devices, which enables the job of correlating events collected from different devices much easier when troubleshooting or analyzing trends in the network.

Configuring the Correct Date and Time

All Cisco Catalyst switches possess a clock of some form, whether it is implemented in software, hardware, or both. Some Cisco Catalyst switches operate only a software clock, which is maintained by an operating system process while the switch operating system is loaded. Using just a software clock has the disadvantage that the date and time is reset to some value in the past every time the switch is reset. Some Cisco Catalyst switches operate a software clock and a hardware clock, which allows date and time to be maintained by the hardware clock (typically battery powered) while a switch is reset or if the switch is powered down.

Configuring the correct date and time consists of the following tasks:

- Configuring time zone information
- Configuring daylight saving information
- Configuring the current date and time

On Cisco IOS, the **clock timezone** global configuration command is used to configure time zone information, while the **clock summer-time** global configuration mode is used to configure daylight saving. The **clock set** privileged mode command is then used to configure the current date and time. Example 1-43 demonstrates configuring date and time on Switch-A.

Example 1-43 *Configuring the Correct Date and Time on Cisco IOS*

```
Switch-A# configure terminal
Switch-A(config)# clock timezone NZST 12
Router-A(config)# clock summer-time NZDT recurring first Sunday October 02:00
    3 Sunday March 02:00 60
Switch-A(config)# exit
Switch-A# clock set 17:15:00 7 May 2003
Switch-A# show clock
.17:15:03.947 NZST Wed May 7 2003
```

In Example 1-43, a time zone called NZST is created (the name could be anything; however, it might be appended to timestamps in some configurations), which indicates that the local time is 12 hours ahead of UTC time. Daylight saving is then configured, with the daylight saving time zone called NZDT. In Example 1-43, recurring daylight saving is configured that starts on the first Sunday in October at 2:00 a.m. and finishes in the third Sunday in March at 2:00 a.m., with clocks advanced by 60 minutes (1 hour) during the daylight saving period (these settings are the actual correct settings for New Zealand, otherwise known as Middle Earth to fans of "Lord of the Rings").

NOTE   If you just configure the **recurring** keyword for the **clock summer-time** command without any other parameters (e.g., **clock summer-time NZDT recurring**), U.S. daylight saving is assumed. The standard U.S. daylight saving configuration is to advance the clock one hour ahead at 2:00 a.m. on the first Sunday in April and then to move the clock back one hour at 2:00 a.m. on the last Sunday in October.

Finally, the software clock is set; it is important to set the clock after you configure time zone information, as the Cisco IOS advances or turn back the current system time when time zone information is configured.

TIP   Notice in the output of the **show clock** command that the time has a period in front of it (e.g., .17:15:03.947). This means the time is not yet synchronized with its master source. In Example 1-43 the router is synchronizing time using its local clock as the master, and it takes approximately 30 seconds for synchronization. Once the clock is synchronized (either locally as in Example 1-37 or via NTP if an NTP server is configured), the period disappears from the output of the **show clock** command.

On CatOS, the **set timezone** command is used to configure time zone information, the **set summertime** command is used to configure daylight saving, and the **set time** command is used to configure the current date and time. Example 1-44 demonstrates configuring date and time on Switch-B.

Example 1-44 *Configuring the Correct Date and Time on CatOS*

```
Switch-B> (enable) set timezone NZST 12
Timezone set to 'NZST', offset from UTC is 12 hours
Switch-B> (enable) set summertime recurring first Sunday October 02:00 third
    Sunday March 02:00 60
Summertime is disabled and set to ''
  Start : Sun Oct 5 2003, 02:00:00
  End   : Sun Mar 21 2004, 02:00:00
  Offset: 60 minutes
  Recurring: yes, starting at 02:00am of first Sunday of October and ending
    on 02:00am of third Sunday of March.
Switch-B> (enable) set summertime enable NZDT
Summertime is enabled and set to 'NZDT'
  Start : Sun Oct 5 2003, 02:00:00
  End   : Sun Mar 21 2004, 02:00:00
  Offset: 60 minutes
  Recurring: yes, starting at 02:00am of first Sunday of October and
    ending on 02:00am of third Sunday of March.
Switch-B> (enable) set time 05/07/2003 21:00:00
Wed May 7 2003, 21:00:00 NZST
```

In Example 1-44, notice the same time zone and daylight saving information configured on Switch-A in Example 1-43 is configured on Switch-B. Notice that to enable daylight saving, two commands are required. The first **set summertime** defines the period over which daylight savings is in effect, while the **set summertime enable** command is used to enable daylight savings and define a name for the daylight savings time zone.

Configuring Network Time Protocol

Network Time Protocol (NTP) is a client/server protocol specified for obtaining the correct time from time servers located on IP networks such as the Internet. Any network should have all network device clocks synchronized to aid management. A logging file generated by a network device that does not have the correct time configured is almost useless, because you have no idea as to when events actually occurred.

Cisco Catalyst switches can be configured as NTP clients, which obtain time from NTP servers. NTP defines a hierarchy of NTP servers, with the top-level hierarchy or stratum being the most authoritative time source. Lower level NTP servers synchronize time with upper-level NTP servers, which provide a scalable, hierarchical method of distributing accurate time from a root time source. Cisco routers can be configured as NTP servers, and they are commonly configured as the NTP server for other NTP clients, such as servers, other routers, switches, and other devices. The Cisco routers configured as NTP servers typically then obtain time themselves from another NTP server, such as an Internet time server, a server with a GPS device attached that synchronizes time via satellite, or perhaps even a server with an actual timekeeping device attached. Figure 1-20 demonstrates an NTP hierarchy.

Figure 1-20 *NTP Hierarchy*

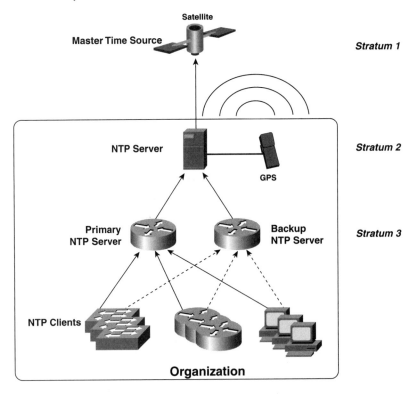

In Figure 1-20, notice that a pair of routers acting as NTP servers provide time for a large number of NTP clients, such as switches, other routers, servers, and PCs. One router acts as the primary NTP server, and the other router acts as a backup NTP server. Both NTP servers then obtain their time from a higher stratum NTP server, which has a GPS device used to obtain time from a master time source (satellite). The structure of how time is distributed to various devices in Figure 1-20 is very hierarchical.

In this scenario, Router-A is an NTP server that provides time for Switch-A and Switch-B. In the configuration prerequisites, the clock on Router-A was configured with the current date and time. Hence, Switch-A and Switch-B can be configured as NTP clients and obtain the correct date and time from Router-A.

NOTE	Router-A is a Cisco 2610 router that does not have a hardware clock, instead using a software clock that is reset every the switch is reloaded. In real-world scenarios, an accurate time source should be used to provide accurate time.

Configuring NTP on Cisco Catalyst switches requires the following configuration tasks:

- Configuring the correct time zone and enable daylight saving
- Defining an NTP server
- Configuring NTP authentication (optional)

In the previous section you learned how to configure time zone and daylight savings settings; therefore, only the configuration required to define an NTP server and configure NTP authentication is now discussed.

Defining an NTP Server

To configure the NTP client on Cisco IOS, you must define an NTP server using the **ntp server** global configuration command. Example 1-45 demonstrates configuring an incorrect date and time on Switch-A (assume the current date and time is May 8, 2003, at 2 p.m.), configuring Switch-A to use Router-A as an NTP server and then checking the date and time again after approximately 60 seconds.

Example 1-45 *Configuring the NTP Client on Cisco IOS*

```
Switch-A# clock set 23:59:59 31 December 1999
Switch-A# show clock
.00:00:00.207 NZDT Sat Jan 1 2000
Switch-A# configure terminal
Switch-A(config)# ntp server 192.168.1.1
Switch-A(config)# end
Switch-A# show clock
14:00:36.865 NZST Thu May 8 2003
Switch-A# show ntp associations

      address          ref clock       st  when  poll reach  delay  offset    disp
*~192.168.1.1         127.127.7.1       8    34    64  377     2.1    0.32      0.3
 * master (synced), # master (unsynced), + selected, - candidate, ~ configured
```

In Example 1-45, the date and time is first set in the past to 23:59:59 31 December 1999. Router-A is then configured as an NTP server for Switch-B, after which the **show clock** command is used to check the date and time (you might need to wait up to 60 seconds for the clock to synchronize with the NTP server). Notice that the date, time, and even time zone has been updated to the present. The **show ntp associations** command is then used to view information about the current status of the NTP server. Notice that *~ precedes the IP address of Router-A, which indicates that the local switch is configured with Router-A as an NTP server and local time is synchronized with Router-A.

To define the NTP client on CatOS, the **set ntp client** command is first used to enable the NTP client, after which an NTP server needs to be defined using the **set ntp server** command. Example 1-46 demonstrates configuring an incorrect date and time on Switch-B (again, assume the current date and time is approximately May 8, 2003, at 2 p.m.), configuring Switch-B to use Router-A as an NTP server and then checking the date and time again after approximately 60 seconds.

Example 1-46 *Configuring the NTP Client on CatOS*

```
Switch-B> (enable) set time 12/31/1999 23:59:59
Fri Dec 31 1999, 23:59:59 NZDT
Switch-B> (enable) show time
Sat Jan 1 2000, 00:00:00 NZDT
Switch-B> (enable) set ntp client enable
NTP Client mode enabled
Switch-B> (enable) set ntp server 192.168.1.1
NTP server 192.168.1.1 added.
Switch-B> (enable) show time
Thu May 8 2003, 14:04:40 NZST
Switch-B> (enable) show ntp
Current time: Thu May 8 2003, 14:04:55 NZST
Timezone: 'NZST', offset from UTC is 12 hours
Summertime: 'NZDT', enabled
  Start : Sun Oct 5 2003, 02:00:00
  End   : Sun Mar 21 2004, 02:00:00
  Offset: 60 minutes
Last NTP update: Thu May 8 2003, 14:34:33
Broadcast client mode: disabled
Broadcast delay: 3000 microseconds
Client mode: enabled
Authentication: disabled

NTP-Server                                 Server Key
---------------------------------------    ----------
192.168.1.1                                    -

Key Number    Mode
----------    --------
```

As you can see in Example 1-46, a similar result occurs on Switch-B after configuring NTP. The **show ntp** command is then used to verify the NTP configuration.

Configuring NTP Authentication

You can enhance the security of NTP by using NTP Authentication to enable your NTP client to accept time only from trusted NTP sources. NTP Authentication protects against spoofed NTP packets, where an unauthorized party attempts to change the time on your NTP client by masquerading as the NTP server. This is easily performed by modifying the source IP address of a forged NTP packet to the address of the NTP server.

NTP authentication works on the basis of a shared key, which must be configured identically on both the NTP server and client and must be known only to the NTP server and client. Figure 1-21 demonstrates how NTP authentication works.

Figure 1-21   *NTP Authentication*

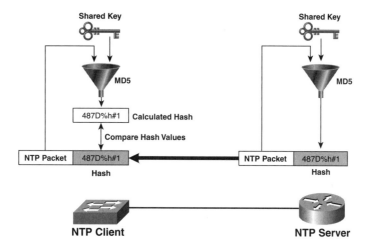

In Figure 1-21, the contents of each NTP packet sent from the NTP server are hashed together with the shared key using the message digest 5 (MD5) hashing algorithm to produce a hash value (digest) unique to the data input (i.e., it is very unlikely that the same hash value would be derived from different input data). The hash value also cannot be used to derive the original packet contents and key information that was input into the hash algorithm. The hash is then attached to each NTP packet by the NTP server and then sent to the NTP client; the NTP client performs the same hashing algorithm using the NTP packet contents and the locally configured secret key. If the hash value calculated by the client matches the hash value attached to the NTP packet, the client knows that the packet is from the NTP server (because only the NTP server knows the key) and that the integrity of the packet has been maintained in transit (if the packet contents were modified in transit, a different hash value would be calculated).

To configure NTP authentication, you must configure it on both the NTP server and NTP client. In this scenario, Router-A is the NTP server; hence, NTP authentication must be configured on Router-A. NTP configuration on Cisco routers and Cisco IOS-based Catalyst switches is the same. To configure NTP authentication on Cisco IOS you must perform the following tasks:

- Configuring authentication keys
- Configuring trusted authentication keys
- Enabling NTP authentication

To configure NTP authentication keys, you use the **ntp authentication-key** global configuration command:

```
Switch(config)# ntp authentication-key key-number md5 key
```

The *key-number* parameter is a non-zero integer and must match the key number defined on the remote NTP client/server. The **md5** keyword specifies MD5 hashing is to be used (at this time, no other hashing algorithms are supported) and the *key* parameter defines an ASCII secret key value.

Once you have defined one or more keys, you then must configure which of those keys are trusted, using the **ntp trusted-key** global configuration command:

```
Switch(config)# ntp trusted-key key-number
```

The *key-number* parameter is used to define the authentication key(s) that you want to trust.

NOTE   It is important that you configure a trusted key using the **ntp trusted-key** command, because if you do not, Cisco IOS assumes all keys (even those not configured locally) are trusted, which effectively bypasses NTP authentication.

Finally, after configuring one or more trusted keys, you must explicitly enable NTP authentication using the **ntp authenticate** global configuration command. Example 1-47 demonstrates configuring NTP authentication on Switch-A. For NTP authentication to work, an identical configuration is required on Router-A (the NTP server).

Example 1-47   *Configuring NTP Authentication on Cisco IOS*

```
Switch-A# configure terminal
Switch-A(config)# ntp authentication-key 1 md5 cisco123
Switch-A(config)# ntp trusted-key 1
Switch-A(config)# ntp authenticate
```

In Example 1-47, key #1 is configured with a value of **cisco123**. Assuming the configuration shown in Example 1-47 is configured on Router-A, Switch-A should be able to authenticate Router-A successfully as a trusted time source. This can be tested by changing the current date and time on Switch-A and then waiting for approximately 60 seconds to see if the date and time is re-synchronized with Router-A. Example 1-48 demonstrates testing NTP after authentication has been configured on Switch-A and Router-A.

Example 1-48 *Testing NTP Operation after NTP Authentication Is Configured*

```
Switch-A# clock set 23:59:59 31 December 1999
Switch-A# show clock
.00:00:00.207 NZDT Sat Jan 1 2000
Switch-A#
… (Wait for 60 seconds)
…
Switch-A# show clock
14:09:51.123 NZST Thu May 8 2003
```

In Example 1-48, notice that the clock on Switch-A resynchronizes with Router-A, which indicates NTP authentication is configured appropriately.

Now that NTP between Router-A and Switch-A is working with NTP authentication configured, it is now time to move on to Switch-B. To configure NTP authentication on CatOS, you perform the same configuration tasks as for Cisco IOS, configuring a trusted authentication key and enabling NTP authentication. However, you must also associate the appropriate authentication key with the appropriate NTP server.

To configure NTP authentication keys, you use the **set ntp key** configuration command:

```
Console> (enable) set ntp key key-number [trusted | untrusted] md5 key
```

Notice that you can define a key and also configure whether or not the key is trusted in a single command, unlike Cisco IOS which requires two commands. After configuring a trusted key for authentication, you must next associate the key with an NTP server, using the **set ntp server** command:

```
Console> (enable) set ntp server ntp-server-address key key-number
```

NOTE   You can also associate a trusted key with a particular NTP server on Cisco IOS, although this configuration is not required on Cisco IOS.

After associating a trusted key with an NTP server, all that remains is to enable NTP authentication, which is achieved using the **set ntp authentication** {**enable** | **disable**} command. Example 1-49 demonstrates configuring NTP authentication on Switch-B, modifying the date and time, and then waiting for approximately 60 seconds to see if NTP is still working.

Example 1-49 *Configuring and Testing NTP Authentication on CatOS*

```
Switch-B> (enable) set ntp key 1 trusted md5 cisco123
NTP key 1 added.
Switch-B> (enable) set ntp server 192.168.1.1 key 1
Key 1 set for NTP server 192.168.1.1
```

Example 1-49 *Configuring and Testing NTP Authentication on CatOS (Continued)*

```
Switch-B> (enable) set ntp authentication enable
NTP authentication feature enabled
WARNING: NTP client may not communicate with any server if none of
    the servers has a key configured and set to be trusted
Switch-B> (enable) set time 12/31/1999 23:59:59
Fri Dec 31 1999, 23:59:59 NZDT
Warning: NTP will override locally set time.
Switch-B> (enable)
… (Wait for approximately 60 seconds)
…
Switch-B> (enable) show time
Thu May 8 2003, 14:15:31 NZST
Switch-B> (enable) show ntp
Current time: Thu May 8 2003, 14:19:31 NZST
Timezone: 'NZST', offset from UTC is 12 hours
Summertime: 'NZDT', enabled
  Start : Sun Oct 5 2003, 02:00:00
  End   : Sun Mar 21 2004, 02:00:00
  Offset: 60 minutes
Last NTP update: Thu May 8 2003, 23:18:56
Broadcast client mode: disabled
Broadcast delay: 3000 microseconds
Client mode: enabled
Authentication: enabled

NTP-Server                                  Server Key
------------------------------------------- ----------
192.168.1.1                                      1

Key Number    Mode
----------    --------
1             trusted
```

In Example 1-49, notice that time is resynchronized successfully via NTP, indicated NTP authentication is working. The output of the **show ntp** command indicates that that NTP authentication is enabled and also lists the server key associated with the NTP server.

Scenario 1-5: Monitoring and Troubleshooting Device Connectivity

One of the most common issues on Cisco Catalyst switches is device connectivity. Device connectivity issues can be easy to discover (e.g., My PC can't connect to the network!); however, more commonly connectivity issues are less obvious, where connectivity is established between devices and switches with performance being impaired. These issues can be difficult to discover as they often rely on user perception. A power user might notice performance problems, while a normal user might not even notice performance problems because they rarely attempt to take advantage of the full speed of their LAN connection. Some users notice problems but just don't complain. Relying solely on user perception is simply not enough information to understand any device connectivity issues that might be present.

NOTE   A good tactic to discover issues relating to performance problems is to go to the lunch room and pretend you are reading a magazine. Listen out for comments like "Gee, the network is slow today" or "I really need a new PC." Seriously, implementing some form of monitoring procedure (could be implementing a network management system or could just be the regular execution of a few **show** commands) for your LAN switches help you to discover issues proactively, reducing the impact to users of any issues you discover. In this scenario you learn how to look for errors on switch ports that indicate possible performance problems.

This scenario is designed to give you tips on how to monitor and troubleshoot basic device connectivity. This scenario is based on the topology of the previous scenario (Scenario 1-4) and assumes the configuration at the end of Scenario 1-4 is in place on each switch.

Configuration Tasks

Successfully resolving device connectivity issues involves identifying a connectivity issue, troubleshooting the issue, and then resolving the issue. Identifying a device connectivity issue exists can happen in a number of ways. It might be that you've placed your switch on the network and configured an IP address, but you can't seem to get access to the rest of the network. It could be that you've connected a new server to your switch; however, your switch can't access rest of the network. Or it could be that a network management system has identified excessive errors on a particular port and generated an alarm.

Once you have identified a potential issue, the troubleshooting process begins. Whenever you are troubleshooting device connectivity issues, it is important to take a step-by-step layered approach, verifying connectivity exists at each layer of the network. Taking such an approach ensures you do not waste time troubleshooting an issue at a higher layer when there is a fundamental underlying issue at lower layers.

This section now shows you how to troubleshoot device connectivity issues by performing the following layered approach:

- Verifying layer 1 connectivity
- Verifying layer 2 connectivity
- Verifying layer 3 connectivity

Verifying Layer 1 Connectivity

Any form of network connectivity relies on a physical (Layer 1) connection being established. A working physical connection relies on an electrical or optical circuit being established between two devices, with some form of clocking established (assuming the connection is synchronous). Once a physical connection is established, devices can then establish Layer 2 connectivity.

On Cisco Catalyst switches, a working Layer 1 connection is verified as follows:

- Checking network cabling
- Checking port LEDs

Checking Network Cabling

Many physical layer connectivity problems are caused by faulty network cabling. All cabling between your switch and the rest of the network should be thoroughly tested prior to implementation using a professional cable tester. Ensure that you always use compatible cables for the protocol you are using.

A common source of cabling issue is the incorrect use of straight-thru and crossover RJ-45 cables. Any device-to-switch connection should use a straight-thru RJ-45 cable, while any device-to-device or switch-to-switch connection requires the use of a crossover RJ-45 cable. Figure 1-22 shows the cabling pinouts for a device-to-switch and switch-to-switch connection.

Figure 1-22 *RJ-45 Cabling Pinouts*

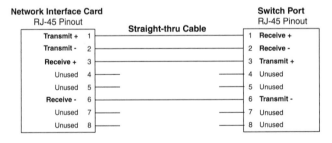

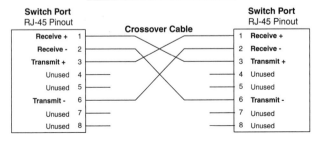

In Figure 1-22, for any Ethernet connection to work, the following wiring scheme must be used:

- Transmit + $\longleftrightarrow$ Receive +
- Transmit - $\longleftrightarrow$ Receive –
- Receive + $\longleftrightarrow$ Transmit +
- Receive - $\longleftrightarrow$ Transmit -

As you can see in Figure 1-22, for a device-to-switch connection, the switch port pinout is such that using a straight-thru cable ensures the wiring scheme above. For a switch-to-switch connection, however, if a straight-thru cable is used, Transmit + is incorrectly wired to Transmit + and so on, causing the connection to fail. A crossover cable ensures that when connecting like ports (i.e., switch port to switch port) the preceding wiring scheme is maintained. Of course, if a crossover cable is used for a device-to-switch connection, then Transmit + is incorrectly wired to Transmit + and so on, causing the connection to fail.

TIP	You can quickly distinguish a straight-thru cable from a crossover cable by lining up both ends of the cable and comparing the colors of the wires attached to the pin outs. If the wire positions are identical, then the cable is straight-thru; otherwise, the cable is a crossover cable.

All cabling should be well clear of possible sources of interference, such as power cords and air conditioning units. Always check that your cabling is properly connected. RJ-45 has a snap-in lever that ensures a proper physical, and you should avoid using RJ-45 connector where the snap-in lever has broken off.

Many cabling issues also arise when fiber cabling is being used. Make sure you understand the distance limitations of your fiber, and ensure that you are using the correct type of fiber cabling. Table 1-15 lists the distance limitations associated with the various fiber Gigabit Ethernet Interface Converters (GBICs) available for Cisco Catalyst switches.

Table 1-15   *GBIC Fiber Cabling Requirements and Distance Limitations*

GBIC (Wavelength)	Fiber Type	Core Size/ MFD (Micron)	Modal Bandwidth (MHz/km)	Maximum Distance (meters)
1000BASE-SX WS-G5484 (850 nm)	Multimode	62.5	160	220 meters
		62.5	200	275 meters
		50	400	500 meters
		50	500	550 meters

continues

Table 1-15 *GBIC Fiber Cabling Requirements and Distance Limitations (Continued)*

GBIC (Wavelength)	Fiber Type	Core Size/ MFD (Micron)	Modal Bandwidth (MHz/km)	Maximum Distance (meters)
1000BASE-LX/LH WS-G5486 (1310 nm)	Multimode[1]	62.5	500	550 meters
		50	400	550 meters
		50	500	550 meters
	Single-mode	8.3/9/10	-	10 km
1000BASE-ZX WS-G5487 (1550 nm)	Single-mode	8.3/9/10	-	70 km
		8	-	100 km[2]

[1]When using multimode fiber with the 1000BASE-LX/LH GBIC, you must install a mode-conditioning patch cord between the GBIC and multimode fiber at the both the transmit and receive ends if the distance is less than 100 m (to prevent overdrive) or greater than 300 m (reduce differential mode delay)

[2]Requires dispersion-shifted single-mode fiber

NOTE   An optical time domain reflector (OTDR) is a tool used by many cabling professionals to measure fiber distance and attenuation, locate fiber breaks, and measure any losses associated with splices or connectors. A good practice is to take a baseline measurement of attenuation and splice losses when fiber cabling is installed, which allows for future comparisons should a potential issue with the fiber cabling occur.

A common error with fiber cabling is to connect the transmit fiber on one end to the transmit fiber connector on the other end.

If you are certain that your cabling is installed and attached correctly, the next step is to move onto your devices and check physical layer status. With Ethernet, the physical layer status and Layer 2 status are tied together, because Ethernet is a connectionless protocol. For this reason, you'll examine the process of verifying both Layer 1 and 2 connectivity in the next section.

Checking Port LEDs

A simple way to check the current status of an Ethernet port is to physically look at the switch and check port LED state. Table 1-16 describes the various LED states for ports on Cisco Catalyst switches.

Table 1-16   *Port LED States for Cisco Catalyst Switches*

Platform	LED State		
	Off	Amber	Green
Catalyst 29xx/35xx[1]	No link	Software disabled (solid) Link fault (flashing green-amber)	Port is operational (solid) Network activity (flashing)
Catalyst 4000/4500 Catalyst 5000/5500 Catalyst 6000/6500	No link	Software disabled (solid) Hardware fault (flashing)	Port is operational (solid)

[1]The Catalyst 29xx/35xx switches support different LED display modes, which include STATUS, UTIL, DUPLX, and SPEED. The LED state for the port has different meaning depending on the LED display mode. By default, the STATUS display mode is selected.

As you can see in Table 1-16, the LED state provides a quick indication as to the nature of a fault. If the LED is off, either the port is disabled (e.g., **shutdown** interface configuration command on Cisco IOS or **set port disable** command on CatOS), or if the port is enabled, no electrical/optical connectivity is present, meaning a physical cabling issue exists.

If the port is a solid amber, this means the switch operating system has disabled the port for some reason. Typical reasons include:

- **Spanning tree** — By default, spanning tree stops the forwarding of data for 30 seconds during the listening and learning states (more on this in Chapter 4). This is a normal occurrence and should not cause any concerns, as long as the port transitions to an operational state (solid green).

- **Security violations** — Cisco Catalyst switches include a port security feature that enables you to shut down a port should an unauthorized device connect to a port.

- **Port misconfiguration** — There are many different types of misconfigurations, where protocol negotiation via mechanisms such as Dynamic Trunking Protocol (DTP) and Port Aggregation Protocol (PAgP) has determined an Ethernet connection between two switches is misconfigured, resulting in the port being disabled.

If the port is a flashing amber, this means the switch operating system has detected a hardware fault on the port (i.e., the port failed a hardware test during POST after bootup), or on the Catalyst 29xx/35xx, a flashing amber green LED indicates a link fault. A link fault refers to excessive errors on a port (e.g., excessive collisions, CRC errors, alignment errors, and jabbers).

Verifying Layer 2 Connectivity

Verifying Layer 2 connectivity involves checking switch ports and each connected device at an Ethernet level, ensuring Layer 2 connectivity has been established and also checking errors for a connection. Although all indications might be that a Layer 2 connection is operational, it is also good to actually confirm that Layer 2 traffic is being sent and received between two devices. Cisco Discovery Protocol (CDP) provides such functionality, verifying connectivity to locally connected Cisco devices. The following tasks related to verifying Layer 2 connectivity are now discussed:

- Verifying a Layer 2 connection is established
- Checking a Layer 2 connection for errors
- Using Cisco Discovery Protocol

Verifying a Layer 2 Connection is Established

On Cisco Catalyst switches, you can use the following commands to verify Layer 2 connectivity has been established:

- The **show interface** command (Cisco IOS)
- The **show port** command (CatOS)

Example 1-50 shows the output of the **show interface** command on Cisco IOS.

Example 1-50 *The **show interface** command on Cisco IOS*

```
Switch-A# show interface fastEthernet0/1
FastEthernet0/1 is up, line protocol is up (connected)
Hardware is Fast Ethernet, address is 0009.b7aa.9c86 (bia 0009.b7aa.9c86)
  MTU 1546 bytes, BW 10000 Kbit, DLY 1000 usec,
     reliability 246/255, txload 4/255, rxload 4/255
  Encapsulation ARPA, loopback not set
  Keepalive set (10 sec)
  Half-duplex, 10Mb/s
  input flow-control is off, output flow-control is off
  ARP type: ARPA, ARP Timeout 04:00:00
  Last input 00:00:46, output 00:00:00, output hang never
  Last clearing of "show interface" counters never
  Input queue: 0/75/0/0 (size/max/drops/flushes); Total output drops: 0
  Queueing strategy: fifo
  Output queue :0/40 (size/max)
  5 minute input rate 160000 bits/sec, 1 packets/sec
  5 minute output rate 160000 bits/sec, 1 packets/sec
     5990 packets input, 8324144 bytes, 0 no buffer
     Received 10 broadcasts, 859 runts, 0 giants, 0 throttles
     859 input errors, 0 CRC, 0 frame, 0 overrun, 0 ignored
     0 watchdog, 7 multicast, 0 pause input
     0 input packets with dribble condition detected
     6866 packets output, 8461183 bytes, 0 underruns
     0 output errors, 479 collisions, 1 interface resets
     0 babbles, 0 late collision, 70 deferred
     0 lost carrier, 0 no carrier, 0 PAUSE output
     0 output buffer failures, 0 output buffers swapped out…
```

In Example 1-50, the first shaded line provides an indication as to whether or not a Layer 2 connection is present. Notice that both the interface and line protocol are up, indicating Layer 1 and Layer 2 Ethernet is up. The next shaded line indicates the current speed and duplex settings. This is because Router-A has a 10BASE-T interface and is connected to interface fastEthernet0/1 on Switch-A (see Figure 1-11). Further down, you can see shaded portions of the output that indicate some errors on the port. Notice that there are 859 input errors, which have been exclusively caused by runts; a runt is frame received that is lower than the minimum 64 byte size permitted by Ethernet. Runts are normally caused by excessive collisions. Notice further that 479 collisions have been experienced. If you divide this figure by the highlighted total number of output frames (6866), this indicates a collision rate of approximately 7 percent, which is considered high.

NOTE   Collisions are a normal occurrence on a half-duplex connection, but should never be experienced on a full-duplex connection. Collisions on a full-duplex port indicate a duplex mismatch, where one side of the connection is operating in half-duplex mode and the other in full-duplex mode. A high collision rate on half-duplex connections can indicate the link is overloaded or can be an indication of a faulty network card if the link is not loaded.

Example 1-51 shows the output of the **show port** command on CatOS.

Example 1-51 *The **show port** command*

```
Switch-B> (enable) show port 2/3
* = Configured MAC Address

Port  Name              Status      Vlan       Level  Duplex Speed Type
----- ----------------- ----------- ---------- ------ ------ ----- -----------
 2/3                    connected   1          normal a-half a-10 10/100BaseTX

Port  AuxiliaryVlan AuxVlan-Status    InlinePowered      PowerAllocated
                                      Admin Oper   Detected mWatt mA @51V
----- ------------- --------------    ----- ------ -------- ----- --------
 2/3  none          none              -     -      -        -     -

Port  Security Violation Shutdown-Time Age-Time Max-Addr Trap     IfIndex
----- -------- --------- ------------- -------- -------- -------- -------
 2/3  disabled shutdown             0        0        1 enabled        10

Port  Num-Addr Secure-Src-Addr    Age-Left Last-Src-Addr     Shutdown/Time-Left
----- -------- ----------------   -------- ----------------- ------------------
 2/3         0                -          -                 -          -       -

Port  Flooding on Address Limit
----- -------------------------
 2/3                   Enabled
```

continues

Example 1-51 *The* **show port** *command (Continued)*

```
Port  Status     Channel              Admin Ch
                 Mode                 Group Id
-----  ---------- -------------------- ----- -----
 2/3  connected  auto silent           118   0

Port  Status     ErrDisable Reason    Port ErrDisableTimeout  Action on Timeout
----  ---------- ------------------- ----------------------- -----------------
 2/3  connected                   -   Enable                  No Change

Port  Align-Err  FCS-Err    Xmit-Err   Rcv-Err    UnderSize
-----  ---------- ---------- ---------- ---------- ---------
 2/3         -            1          2       1570       1403

Port  Single-Col Multi-Coll Late-Coll  Excess-Col Carri-Sen Runts      Giants
-----  ---------- ---------- ---------- ---------- --------- --------- ---------
 2/3         309        355          1          1         0       164          1

Last-Time-Cleared
------------------------
Fri May 9 2003, 07:57:54
```

In Example 1-51, the Status column at the top indicates the port is currently in a connected
state, indicating a Layer 2 Ethernet connection is up. Notice that the speed and duplex
settings are also displayed. At the bottom of the output, you can see port error information.

Checking Connections for Layer 2 Errors

In the previous section you saw how the **show interfaces** and **show port** command can be
used to view errors. On Cisco IOS, the **show controllers ethernet-controller** command
provides more detailed information about port errors. Example 1-52 demonstrates the use
of this command on Switch-A.

Example 1-52 *The* **show controllers ethernet-controller** *command on Cisco IOS*

```
Switch-A# show controllers ethernet-controller fastEthernet0/1
Transmit FastEthernet0/1            Receive
  15648658 Bytes                  15573710 Bytes
     12148 Unicast frames            11102 Unicast frames
        39 Multicast frames              1 Multicast frames
         8 Broadcast frames              0 Broadcast frames
         5 Discarded frames              7 No dest, unicast
         0 Too old frames                0 No dest, multicast
        18 Deferred frames               0 No dest, broadcast
      1212 1 collision frames
       151 2 collision frames
        41 3 collision frames            0 FCS errors
        15 4 collision frames            0 Oversize frames
         4 5 collision frames         1951 Undersize frames
         4 6 collision frames            0 Collision fragments
```

Example 1-52 *The* **show controllers ethernet-controller** *command on Cisco IOS (Continued)*

```
  20  7 collision frames          8 Minimum size frames
   5  8 collision frames          2 65 to 127 byte frames
   1  9 collision frames       1009 128 to 255 byte frames
   1 10 collision frames          1 256 to 511 byte frames
   1 11 collision frames          0 512 to 1023 byte frames
   0 12 collision frames      10090 1024 to 1518 byte frames
   0 13 collision frames
   0 14 collision frames          0 Flooded frames
   0 15 collision frames          0 Overrun frames
   0 Excessive collisions         0 VLAN filtered frames
   0 Late collisions              0 Source routed frames
1212 Good (1 coll) frames         0 Valid oversize frames
 243 Good(>1 coll) frames         0 Pause frames
   0 Pause frames                 0 Symbol error frames
   0 VLAN discard frames          0 Invalid frames, too large
   0 Excess defer frames          0 Valid frames, too large
   0 Too large frames             0 Invalid frames, too small
  50 64 byte frames            1951 Valid frames, too small
   2 127 byte frames
   0 255 byte frames
   4 511 byte frames
1010 1023 byte frames
11129 1518 byte frames
```

In Example 1-52, notice that a lot of information is provided in relation to interface statistics when using the **show controllers ethernet-controller** command. Of particular interest in Example 1-52 is the collision statistics, which provide an indication as to not only the number of collisions, but also the number of retries required before a frame could be sent. For example, there are 20 * *7 collision frames*, which means the switch attempted 7 retransmissions before the frame could be sent (i.e. 7 collisions occurred for the same frame). Notice that you can also view information as to the size distribution of frames—in Example 1-52, you can see a high proportion of 1518 byte frames transmitted (11129 out of 12148), indicating a large data transfer has taken place or is in progress.

Using Cisco Discovery Protocol

An extremely useful feature of Cisco network devices to test point-to-point Layer 2 connectivity is called Cisco Discovery Protocol (CDP). CDP is used by many Cisco devices to verify Layer 2 connectivity over a variety of LAN and WAN media. On Ethernet networks, Cisco devices multicast CDP Hello packets periodically, which includes information about the device, including name, capabilities, software version, and Layer 3 parameters such as IP addressing. CDP messages are only propagated to locally connected Cisco devices— each Cisco device that receives a CDP message reads the information in the message and then discards it, ensuring CDP messages to do not propagate further outwards.

NOTE	CDP is discussed in more detail in Chapter 10, "Maintenance, Monitoring, and Troubleshooting."

CDP is enabled by default on Cisco network devices, and both CatOS and Cisco IOS enable you to view CDP neighbor information, which makes it an invaluable tool for troubleshooting. Both operating systems use the **show cdp neighbors** command to display a summary of the CDP neighbor table, as shown in Example 1-53.

Example 1-53 *Viewing CDP Neighbors on Cisco IOS*

```
Switch-A# show cdp neighbors
Capability Codes: R - Router, T - Trans Bridge, B - Source Route Bridge
                  S - Switch, H - Host, I - IGMP, r - Repeater, P - Phone

Device ID         Local Intrfce     Holdtme    Capability  Platform  Port ID
Router-A          Fas 0/1           169          R         2610      Eth 0/0
JAB03375EKK(SwitcGig 0/1           162          T S       WS-C4006  1/1
```

In Example 1-53, you can see that Switch-A has two directly connected neighbors indicated in the Device ID column—Router-A and Switch-B (the serial number of Switch-B is displayed). The Local Intrfce column indicates with interface on the local switch each device is attached to, while the Capability column shows that Router-A is a router (R) and Switch-B is a switch (S) and transparent bridge (T). The Platform column indicates that Router-A is a 2610 router and that Switch-B is a Catalyst 4006, while the Port ID column indicates the port that the local switch is connected to on the remote device.

NOTE	You can view more information about a CDP neighbor using the **show cdp neighbors detail** command. See Chapter 10 for more details.

Example 1-54 demonstrates the **show cdp neighbors** command on Switch-B.

Example 1-54 *Viewing CDP Neighbors on CatOS*

```
Switch-B> (enable) show cdp neighbors
* - indicates vlan mismatch.
# - indicates duplex mismatch.
Port    Device-ID                            Port-ID                    Platform
------- ------------------------------------ -------------------------- ------------
 1/1      Switch-A                             GigabitEthernet0/1         cisco WS-C3550-24
```

In Example 1-54, notice that only a single neighbor (Switch-A) is shown, which is due to the fact that only Switch-A is directly connected to Switch-B (Server-A is as well; however, it is a non-Cisco device). You might expect Router-A to also be displayed as a neighbor, because Router-A is on the same VLAN as Switch-B; however, remember that CDP messages are propagated only to locally connected Cisco devices (whether they be switches, routers, or IP phones), at which point they are read and then discarded.

In Example 1-54, the output is abbreviated because the important line is the shaded line shown. The status field shows a value of connected, which indicates Layer 1 and Layer 2 connectivity to the switch. If Layer 1 and 2 are down, the status would show a value of not connected.

Verifying Layer 3 Connectivity

After verifying Layer 2 connectivity, you can next proceed to verify Layer 3 IP connectivity by using tools such as ping and traceroute. Refer to Chapter 10 for a discussion on Layer 3 connectivity tools.

Summary

Cisco Catalyst switches represent the best selling LAN switching product in the world today. A wide range of switching platforms are offered, which offer switches for all types of networks and customers. Cisco switches are offered either in a fixed-configuration form factor or in a chassis-based form factor. The major operating systems used to manage Cisco switches include Cisco IOS and Catalyst OS (CatOS). Cisco IOS is the future operating system for all Catalyst switches; however, CatOS is still the prevalent Cisco Catalyst operating system today.

Placing a Cisco Catalyst switch onto a network consists of physically installing the switch and any associated hardware, powering on the switch and verifying all software and hardware is functioning as expected, and then configuring basic parameters such as switch identification, network management support, and date/time. Once your base configuration is in place, you can enable connectivity for Ethernet devices, allowing these devices to communicate via the switch.

Although the tasks described in this chapter are simple and might seem straightforward, problems do still occur with these configurations. One of the most common troubleshooting issues in LAN networks is the mismatch of speed/duplex settings, caused by either misconfiguration or auto-negotiation problems. These issues are typically hard to detect. Often connectivity is achieved; however, performance is poor, and errors are detected on the Ethernet interface. By understanding how auto-negotiation can cause mismatches and disabling auto-negotiation where possible, you should be able to eliminate these issues. When interconnecting Cisco devices, you can use Cisco Discovery Protocol (CDP) to find any devices that are locally connected. CDP is enabled by default and is independent of any Layer 3 protocol. By viewing CDP information, you can detect IP addressing misconfiguration and speed/duplex mismatches.

## CHAPTER 2

VLAN Operations

This chapter explores probably the most fundamental concept of modern LAN switching: virtual LANs (VLANs). In legacy Ethernet networks of the 1980s and early 1990s, the concept of virtual LANs did not exist; instead, only the concept of physical LANs existed. Layer 1 and Layer 2 Ethernet devices such as hubs and bridges were dedicated to a single, physical LAN, and implementing another LAN required more hubs and bridges. Today, *LAN switches* have the capability to provide connectivity for multiple physical LANs by implementing the concept of virtual LANs. In this chapter you learn about transparent bridging, which is the function provided by a bridge on a single physical LAN. This concept is then extended to VLANs, and you learn how they work and how to configure them.

After some initial introductory material, this chapter presents the following configuration scenarios, which provide you with the practical knowledge required to implement spanning tree, which provide you with the practical knowledge required to implement VLANs:

- Scenario 2-1: Understanding Transparent Bridging
- Scenario 2-2: Configuring VLAN Trunking Protocol (VTP)
- Scenario 2-3: Configuring VLANs
- Scenario 2-4: Configuring the Management VLAN
- Scenario 2-5: Configuring Extended-Range VLANs

Introduction

In recent years, Ethernet has all but replaced Token Ring and FDDI technology on LANs. Many consider Ethernet to be a technology that is inferior in some ways to Token Ring and FDDI. These technologies provide more robust error-checking capabilities and more predictable access to media than Ethernet; however, the simplicity and low cost of Ethernet has seen it win over the other technologies.

With gigabit Ethernet well established and affordable, Ethernet is now also replacing aging, expensive, and very complex ATM equipment, which was popular in the mid-1990s for providing high-speed switch interconnectivity (also known as *trunking*).

Ethernet LANs use a concept called transparent bridging to enable the transmission of frames over multiple LAN devices called bridges. A *bridge* is a Layer 2 device that is used to segment collision domains and increase LAN performance. In this section, you learn about transparent bridging and the concepts of broadcast domains and collision domains which are important in understanding the benefits that switches and VLANs provide. You then learn about VLANs and how they are implemented on Cisco Catalyst switches. The following topics are discussed:

- Bridging overview
- VLAN concepts

Bridging Overview

To understand the primary operation of a switch, you must understand how transparent bridging works. All Ethernet LAN switches implement transparent bridging, so it is crucial that you be familiar with this process. Both bridges and switches offer performance benefits over using Layer 1 devices by providing *LAN segmentation*, which is the process of reducing large collision domains into smaller, more manageable collision domains. *Collision domains* are defined as an area of the LAN where only a single device can access the Ethernet network at any one time (i.e., multiple devices must contend for access to the network). The following are covered in this bridging overview:

- Transparent bridging
- LAN segmentation

Transparent Bridging

An *Ethernet switch* is a Layer 2 device that essentially operates as a transparent bridge. A *transparent bridge* is a device that understands Layer 2 addressing and can make intelligent Layer 2 forwarding decisions. The bridge operates by maintaining a table of MAC addresses and associated egress ports. The table tells the bridge where stations are located within the LAN, which enables the bridge to determine how to forward Layer 2 frames by reading the destination MAC address of each frame and looking up the corresponding egress port on the bridge. Table 2-1 shows a simple bridging table.

Table 2-1   *Bridging Table*

MAC Address	Egress Port	Age (Minutes)
0000.01a0.64b1	FastEthernet0/1	1
00a0.d1d0.20b9	FastEthernet0/2	0
0030.2448.d79e	FastEthernet0/3	4

In Table 2-1, each MAC address entry represents a destination host—for example if a frame is received with a destination MAC address of 0000.01a0.64b1, the frame will be sent out the FastEthernet0/1 interface.

The MAC address entries in the bridge table shown in Table 2-1 must somehow be populated, and this information must be accurate to ensure frames are delivered correctly. Transparent bridging allows a bridge or switch to learn the location of devices in the LAN based upon frames received on a particular port.

Figure 2-1 illustrates the algorithm that occurs when a frame is received on an interface.

Figure 2-1   *Transparent Bridging*

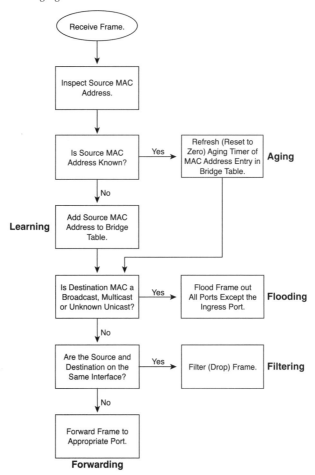

Figure 2-2 explains the processes shown in Figure 2-1 in terms of a sample network topology.

Figure 2-2 *Transparent Bridging Example*

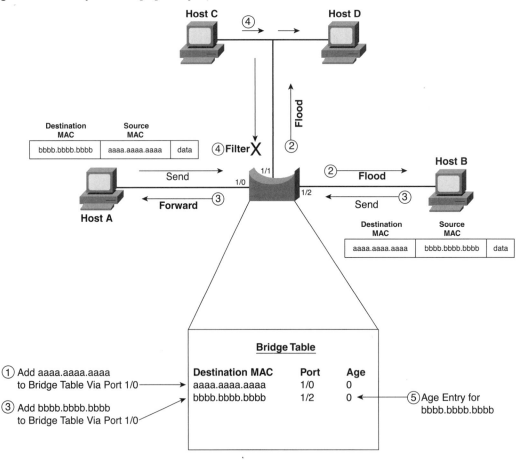

In Figure 2-2, assume that Host A (aaaa.aaaa.aaaa) is communicating with Host B (bbbb.bbbb.bbbb). The following processes occur:

1 **Learning**—Host A sends a frame to Host B. The bridge examines the source address (aaaa.aaaa.aaaa) of received frames and associates the ingress port (1/0) of the received frame with the source address of the frame by adding an entry to the bridging table.

2 **Flooding**—The bridge examines the destination address (bbbb.bbbb.bbbb), looks in the local bridging table, and finds no entry for the destination address. Because the received frame is sent to an unknown destination, the bridge floods the frame out all ports (except for the ingress port 1/0) to ensure the frame reaches the destination.

NOTE	Broadcast frames are always flooded by virtue of the fact that they are intended to be transmitted to all hosts within the LAN. Depending on the bridging device, multicast frames may also be flooded or may be forwarded out multiple egress ports if the bridging device supports multicast traffic control.

3 **Forwarding**—Host B receives the frame due to the flooding process. Host B replies to the frame. The bridge receives the frame, examines the source address (bbbb.bbbb.bbbb), and writes an entry to the bridge table, associating Host B with the port upon which the reply has been received (port 1/2). The bridge then examines the destination address (aaaa.aaaa.aaaa), looks in the bridging table, and finds the entry for Host A generated by step 1. Thus, the bridge only forwards the frame out the specified egress port (port 1/0) towards Host A.

4 **Filtering**—Assume that Host C and Host D are communicating and the bridge knows that these hosts exist and has respective entries for each in the local bridging table. When Host C sends a frame to Host D, the frame will be propagated to the bridge. The bridge follows the procedure of Figure 2-1 and finds that the source and destination address are associated with the same port (1/1). Thus, the bridge filters (drops) the frame, because the frame has already reached its destination.

5 **Aging**—When the entry for Host B is created in the bridging table, an idle timer is started for that entry. Every time a new frame is received from Host B, this idle timer is reset to zero. Assume Host B is shut down. No more traffic is generated from Host B; thus, the idle timer keeps on incrementing. Once the timer reaches the aging timeout value (e.g., 5 minutes), the entry for Host B is removed from the table, which saves precious memory resources and also ensures any location changes for Host B are reflected in the bridge table. If Host B comes back online, the bridging table is repopulated as soon as Host B sends a frame towards the bridge.

LAN Segmentation

One of the key requirements of a LAN protocol is performance; users expect to be able to transfer information between locally connected systems quickly and are not very forgiving when the LAN is running slow. LAN performance can be affected by many factors—one very important factor is the concept of LAN segmentation or rather the lack of. Ethernet is a shared media technology, and the performance of Ethernet diminishes as more and more devices contend for the shared bandwidth. LAN segmentation breaks up the LAN into smaller pieces, both at a physical level (Layer 1) and at a Layer 2 level. This segmentation ensures the performance and scalability of the LAN. LAN segmentation involves two key design parameters:

- Collision domains
- Broadcast domains

Collision Domains

A *collision domain* is an area of a single LAN where end stations contend for access to the network because all end stations are connected to a shared physical medium. If two connected devices transmit onto the media at the same time, a *collision* occurs. When a collision occurs, a JAM signal is sent on the network, indicating that a collision has occurred and that devices should ignore any fragmented data associated with the collision. Both sending devices back off sending their data for a random amount and then try again if the medium is free for transmission. Therefore, collisions effectively delay transmission of data, lowering the effective throughput available to a device. The more devices that are attached to a collision domain, the greater the chances of collisions; this results in lower bandwidth and performance for each device attached to the collision domain. Bridges and switches terminate the physical signal path of a collision domain, allowing you to segment separate collision domains, breaking them up into multiple smaller pieces to provide more bandwidth per user within the new collision domains formed.

Broadcast Domains

A *broadcast domain* is the area over which LAN broadcast frames are propagated, or the area over which LAN devices can communicate directly with each other using Ethernet. Unlike collision domains, which are bounded by a shared physical media, broadcast domains are not so restricted. The devices that terminate a broadcast domain are Layer 3 devices, such as routers, which will not normally forward LAN (Layer 2) broadcasts. A broadcast domain typically maps to a Layer 3 subnetwork, such as an IP subnet, and is also commonly referred to as a *LAN*. If a broadcast domain becomes too large, due to the sheer number of devices attached to the LAN, it is likely that the LAN will suffer from performance problems due to the high proportion of broadcast traffic. This varies depending on the operating system of your LAN devices, because some operating systems make use of broadcast traffic more than others. You can increase the performance of a broadcast domain by splitting it into two or more pieces, which in turn creates several smaller broadcast domains. You segment broadcast domains using a Layer 3 device, such as a router.

NOTE   It is important to understand that a broadcast domain can consist of multiple collision domains; however, a collision domain only ever belongs to a single broadcast domain. Routers, which separate broadcast domains, automatically terminate collision domains, preventing a collision domain from crossing a router.

Increasing Performance Using LAN Segmentation

In a worst-case scenario, a LAN consists of a single broadcast domain with one large collision domain. This arrangement means that all devices attached to the LAN are contending for access to the same physical shared media and that a broadcast sent by any device is propagated throughout the LAN.

LAN segmentation allows you to split a large collision domain into smaller collision domains, which increases the available bandwidth to devices because fewer devices are contending for shared bandwidth within the smaller collision domains. To segment large collision domains into smaller collision domains, you need bridges and switches.

LAN segmentation also allows you to split a large broadcast domain into several smaller broadcast domains, which reduces the proportion of broadcast traffic in each broadcast domain, increasing network efficiency and performance. You need Layer 3 switches or routers to segment broadcast domains into smaller broadcast domains.

Figure 2-3 shows a simple LAN, which has two broadcast domains, each with one or more collision domains.

Figure 2-3   *Two-LAN Internetwork*

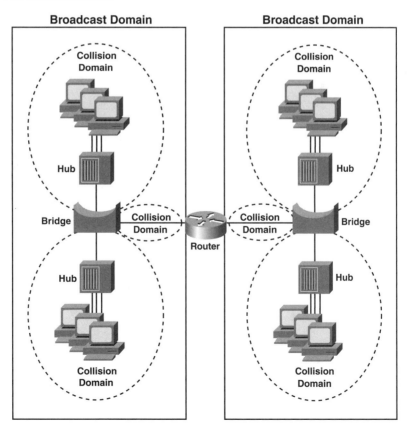

In Figure 2-3 notice that all hubs and connected devices comprise a collision domain, while each bridge terminates collision domains. This termination occurs because a bridge (or switch) terminates the electrical signal path, inspects frames received, and forwards the frames appropriately. A hub merely propagates signals (frames) out all other ports, effectively extending the electrical signal path.

Both bridges and switches allow you to reduce the size of collision domains in a LAN. A major and important difference between bridges and switches is that bridges typically connect only to other networking devices (such as hubs or bridges), while switches connect to both end devices and other networking devices. This difference is not a technical limitation, but rather one driven by cost. Bridges historically were expensive, with low port density, meaning it didn't make sense to connect users to bridges. Switches, however, are relatively cheap and have high port densities, so the benefits of a bridge/switch can be extended to user devices.

In a fully switched network, each switch port represents a separate collision domain, if half-duplex operation is used. You can totally eliminate all collision domains by configuring full duplex, provided of course that each device supports full-duplex 10-Mbps or 100-Mbps operation. Thus in Figure 2-3, if the router ports are working at full-duplex operation, no collision domain exists between the router and bridges, assuming of course that the connected bridge ports are also operating in full-duplex mode. Eliminating collision domains altogether means devices can use 80-90 percent of the available bandwidth (e.g., 80-90 Mbps on a Fast Ethernet port) because devices do not need to execute the carrier sense multiple access collision detect (CSMA/CD) algorithm. This available bandwidth is compared with a maximum of 40-50 percent on two or more devices sharing Ethernet media (i.e., when a collision domain exists).

Ethernet devices can operate at half duplex or full duplex when connected to LAN switches. In half-duplex operation, the transmit and receive wires on the network interface card (NIC) are connected to the same transmission circuit, so a collision can occur if the local device and remote switch port transmit at the same time. In full-duplex operation, the transmit circuit is wired directly to the remote receive circuit and vice versa, which eliminates the possibility of a collision at all. Figure 2-4 compares a 4-port switch containing 2 half-duplex ports and 2 full-duplex ports with a 4-port hub.

Figure 2-4   *Switch Versus Hub Comparison*

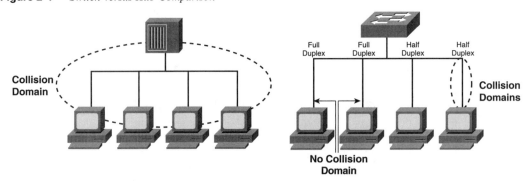

In Figure 2-4, notice that even if a device connected to a switch operates at half duplex, the collision domain is limited to just the device and the switch port it is connected to. If the device is connected using full-duplex operation, no collisions will ever occur, because the signal pathways are physically separate for transmit and receive on a full-duplex port. The switched environment experiences significantly fewer collisions than the hub environment, increasing network performance and efficiency.

NOTE   A common issue in switched LANs is duplex mismatches. For example, if a switch port is configured to operate at half duplex and a connected device is configured to operate at full duplex, the connected device disables the CSMA/CD algorithm because it should never experience collisions. However, this disabling seriously degrades performance and causes excessive errors because one party of the Ethernet connection is not using the CSMA/CD algorithm. This topic is covered in more detail in Chapter 10, " Maintenance, Monitoring, and Troubleshooting."

VLAN Concepts

VLANs provide a mechanism that enables you to split LAN infrastructure into multiple broadcast domains, in effect creating virtual LANs (hence, the name). Each VLAN places a group of physical ports into a logical broadcast domain, which allows devices within the VLAN to communicate at Layer 2. Multiple VLANs can be supported on a switch, meaning that although devices may be connected to the same physical switch, these devices can communicate at Layer 2 only with devices that belong to the same VLAN. VLANs can also be extended over multiple switches, which means that a user that belongs to a particular VLAN can move to another floor or building, connect to a physical port on a separate switch, and still belong to the same broadcast domain (VLAN). Cisco Catalyst switches all support VLANs because VLANs are an essential component of modern LANs. In this section the following topics are discussed:

- Introduction to VLANs
- Cisco Catalyst VLAN implementation

Introduction to VLANs

So far you have seen basically how LANs functioned up until the early to mid-1990s. Around this time, a new device known as the switch emerged. Essentially, a *switch* is a bridge and performs all the functions of a bridge; however, it does have some differences:

- A bridge is normally limited to a few ports and, hence, connects only to other networking equipment and not to end devices. A switch typically has high port densities that allow end devices to connect to it.
- A bridge normally operates in a single LAN; a switch can operate in multiple LANs, appearing as a virtual bridge for each LAN.

NOTE   This second statement is not strictly true; some bridges do support multiple LANs. For example, Cisco IOS routers can act as a bridge and do support multiple LANs. However, the major point here is that, from a purist point of view, a simple bridge operates only in a single LAN.

A bridge operates in software, while a switch typically operates in hardware, which means that a switch has much higher performance.

Today, the bridge has all but disappeared, supplanted by switches, which have much lower costs per port and much higher performance. The cost per port today for switches is low enough that many LANs are completely switched, which means all devices are connected to switches on the network. The most important technical feature of a switch is its ability to service multiple logical LANs or broadcast domains at once. Refer back to Figure 2-3; separate bridges and hubs service each LAN, which is the legacy method of LAN networking. Figure 2-5 shows the network of Figure 2-3, this time with a switch included.

Figure 2-5   *Two-LAN Internetwork with a Switch*

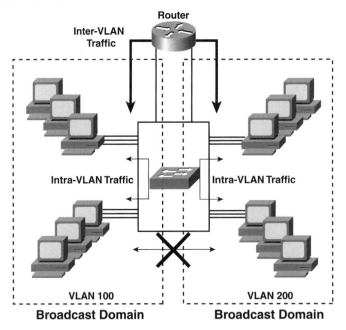

Notice in Figure 2-5 that a single physical switch is capable of servicing each broadcast domain. Within each broadcast domain, or VLAN, devices can communicate at a Layer 2 level (intra-VLAN communications). The switch maintains complete separation between each broadcast domain, which means that devices in separate VLANs cannot communicate directly with each other at a Layer 2 level. To enable inter-VLAN communications, a Layer 3 protocol, such as IP, is required; this means that any traffic between devices in separate VLANs must traverse the router.

NOTE   It is very important to understand that you require some form of Layer 3 router to allow devices from different VLANs to communicate. A switch with multiple VLANs configured with no router connected cannot enable communication between VLANs because this sort of communication is a routing function that the switch cannot understand. Layer 3 switches add Layer 3 routing functionality to a switch, which then removes the need for separate external routers.

Each LAN in Figure 2-5 is referred to as a virtual LAN (VLAN). The switch emulates a single LAN for each device connected to it (hence, the term *virtual*), yet supports devices from multiple LANs.

Cisco Catalyst VLAN Implementation

Cisco Catalyst switches support VLANs. Some newer Cisco Catalyst switches support up to 4096 VLANs, but traditionally, Cisco Catalyst switches support only up to 1024 VLANs. For most networks, 1024 VLANs are more than enough because implementing even 50 VLANs for a single LAN infrastructure can become impractical.

NOTE   Service providers are an exception because they are increasingly providing Ethernet services to customers and need to provide logical separation from other customers. The simplest method of creating this separation is to create a VLAN for each customer. However, this method must be able to scale; hence, the difference between 1024 and 4096 VLANs can be significant for a service provider.

Cisco Catalyst switches historically have supported only up to 1024 VLANs due to the use of 10-bit VLAN ID tag used in the Cisco proprietary Inter-Switch Link (ISL) trunking protocol. Trunking provides the ability for a single Layer 2 port to transport the traffic from multiple VLANs, rather than from just a single VLAN. To support this functionality, a tag is required that identifies the VLAN ID the frame is associated with. You learn more about trunking in Chapter 3, "Trunking and Bandwidth Aggregation." Later versions of ISL use a 15-bit VLAN ID tag and the standards-based IEEE 802.1Q trunking protocol uses a 12-bit VLAN ID tag, which provides for up to 4096 VLANs. ISL was used before 802.1Q protocol support was present; hence, a large number of Catalyst switches support only 1024 VLANs.

A Catalyst switch maintains a VLAN database, which is a listing of all VLANs, associated parameters such as VLAN ID and name, and a list of each port associated with each VLAN. Table 2-2 shows a sample VLAN database.

Table 2-2   *Sample VLAN Database*

VLAN ID	VLAN Parameter	Value
1	Name	VLAN0001
	Type	Ethernet
	MTU	1500
	Ports	2/1-10, 2/12, 2/15-24
2	Name	Marketing
	Type	Ethernet
	MTU	1500
	Ports	2/11, 2/13-14

Table 2-2 shows some of the basic parameters for each VLAN; many others are not shown. As you can see, each VLAN is associated with a set of ports. Only ports within the same VLAN can communicate with each other at a Layer 2 level (e.g., Ethernet). In Table 2-2, port 2/11 can communicate directly only with ports 2/13 and 2/14. If a device connected to port 2/11 wanted to communicate with a device on port 2/1, the frame has to be sent to a Layer 3 router with connectivity to both VLANs.

The VLAN database implementation varies based upon the Catalyst switch operating system. The next sections examine the VLAN database implementation for each of the following operating systems:

- Catalyst OS
- Cisco IOS

Catalyst OS

The Catalyst OS (CatOS) VLAN database implementation is simple to understand. It is stored in the switch configuration file that is loaded during bootup. This configuration file contains all of the configuration settings for the switch, so this makes it a single, central configuration storage point.

Cisco IOS

Cisco IOS-based switches differ from CatOS-based switches in that they store the VLAN database separately from the main configuration file. By default, the VLAN database is saved in a file called VLAN.DAT, which is located in the root file system on the local Flash storage device. That the VLAN database is stored separately is an important point to remember; even if you clear the main configuration of a Cisco IOS-based switch, the VLAN database is still maintained. The VLAN.DAT file is a binary file that you should not manually delete or edit. Make any configuration changes to the VLAN database through the Cisco IOS interface; the binary file is updated appropriately by Cisco IOS after changes have been made.

NOTE   In later versions of Cisco IOS, you can store VLAN configuration information in the main switch configuration file; however, the switch must be operating in VTP transparent mode (VTP is discussed in more detail in Chapter 3).

Scenario 2-1: Understanding Transparent Bridging

Before you learn how to configure VLANs, it is important that you have a firm under-standing of transparent bridging, because it is the underlying fundamental of Ethernet switching. Figure 2-1 described the transparent bridging algorithm that is used by switches, and Figure 2-2 demonstrated how frames are transparently bridged. In this scenario, you learn how to verify transparent bridging operation.

Figure 2-6 shows the topology used for this scenario.

Figure 2-6   *Scenario 2-1 Topology*

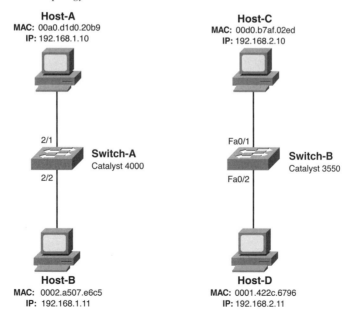

Host-A
MAC: 00a0.d1d0.20b9
IP: 192.168.1.10

Host-C
MAC: 00d0.b7af.02ed
IP: 192.168.2.10

2/1   Switch-A
Catalyst 4000
2/2

Fa0/1   Switch-B
Catalyst 3550
Fa0/2

Host-B
MAC: 0002.a507.e6c5
IP: 192.168.1.11

Host-D
MAC: 0001.422c.6796
IP: 192.168.2.11

In Figure 2-6, two separate LANs are used to demonstrate transparent bridging on a CatOS switch (Switch-A) and on a Cisco IOS switch (Switch-B). Each switch has hosts connected, with MAC addresses and IP addresses indicated. IP is required only to provide a protocol that requires transport via the LAN; the MAC addresses are required to verify transparent bridging operation.

Configuration Tasks

Cisco Catalyst switches inherently support transparent bridging, as this is how they forward frames between Layer 2 devices. As such, no explicit configuration is required to enable transparent bridging on Cisco Catalyst switches, which means you can conceivably power on a new switch, connect devices to it, and the devices will be able to communicate at a Layer 2 level without any configuration of the switch.

NOTE   The exceptions to needing no explicit configuration are the Catalyst 6000/6500 switches operating in native IOS mode (Cisco IOS-based). These switches are Layer 3 switches, which means they possess Layer 2 switching and Layer 3 routing capabilities. By default, all interfaces on these switches are routed interfaces (i.e., identical to Ethernet interfaces on a traditional router) and are in a shutdown state, meaning you must explicitly enable each interface and configure each as a Layer 2 interface to enable Layer 2 switching. The native IOS Catalyst 6000/6500 is discussed in detail in Chapter 6, " Layer 3 Switching."

In this scenario, you see how an unconfigured Cisco Catalyst switch performs transparent bridging by looking at the bridge table on each switch. The bridge table contains forwarding information that includes destination MAC addresses, the egress ports that frames with a particular destination MAC address should be sent out, and the age of each entry. The ability to view the bridge table on a switch is a fundamental skill that any LAN administrator or engineer should possess and provides you with the information you need to ensure transparent bridging is operating correctly.

Verifying Transparent Bridging on CatOS

To view the bridge table on a CatOS switch, use the **show cam dynamic** command. This command displays all entries within the bridge table that have been dynamically learned by the inspection of the source MAC address of frames received (i.e., the learning process of transparent bridging).

Example 2-1 demonstrates the use of this command on Switch-A, before any hosts have been connected to the switch.

Example 2-55 *Displaying the Bridge Table on Switch-A with No Hosts Connected*

```
Console> (enable) show cam dynamic
* = Static Entry. + = Permanent Entry. # = System Entry. R = Router Entry.
X = Port Security Entry $ = Dot1x Security Entry


VLAN  Dest MAC/Route Des     [CoS]  Destination Ports or VCs / [Protocol Type]
----  ----------------       -----  -------------------------------------------
Total Matching CAM Entries Displayed  =0
```

In Example 2-1, you can see that there are no dynamic entries in the bridge table, as no hosts are connected to the switch. The shaded line indicates the fields that make up the bridge table. The following describes each field:

- **VLAN**—Describes the VLAN for which the entry is valid. When a frame is received on a port, the VLAN of the port is noted, and the destination MAC address is matched only against entries in the bridge table that have the same VLAN as the port.

- **Dest MAC/Route Des**—Describes the destination MAC address.

- **CoS**—Describes the Class of Service (CoS) that should be attached to the frame when it is forwarded out the egress port. CoS is a quality of service (QoS) marking that indicates to other switches in the network the level of service the frame should receive (QoS is discussed in Chapter 9, "Quality of Service").

- **Destination Ports or VCs/[Protocol Type]**—Describes the destination port or egress port out which frames with the destination MAC address for the entry are to be forwarded. The [Protocol Type] parameter defines which Layer 3 protocols the entry is valid for (e.g., IP, IPX).

Now, assume that Host-A is attached to the switch and attempts to send data to Host-B. Because these hosts are using IP to communicate, Host-A sends an Address Resolution Protocol (ARP) request frame, which is sent to the ffff.ffff.ffff broadcast address, and asks for the MAC address of the host associated with the IP address of Host-B (192.168.1.11). The ARP request also includes a source MAC address of 00a0.d1d0.20b9, which is learned by the switch upon reception and placed into the bridge table. Because the ARP request is received on port 2/1, the destination port for the entry will be port 2/1. Host-B is not connected to the switch so the ARP request will never be answered; however, even though no communications have actually successfully taken place between devices connected to the switch, a bridge table entry has been generated. Example 2-2 demonstrates the use of the **show cam dynamic** command after Host-A has been attached to port 2/1 and has attempted to communicate with Host-B.

Example 2-56 *Displaying the Bridge Table after Host-A Transmits to Host-B*

```
Console> (enable) show cam dynamic
* = Static Entry. + = Permanent Entry. # = System Entry. R = Router Entry.
X = Port Security Entry $ = Dot1x Security Entry

VLAN  Dest MAC/Route Des    [CoS]  Destination Ports or VCs / [Protocol Type]
----  ------------------    -----  ------------------------------------------
1     00-a0-d1-d0-20-b9            2/1 [ALL]
Total Matching CAM Entries Displayed  =1
```

Notice in Example 2-2 that a single entry is now displayed. The VLAN indicated is VLAN 1 (which is the default VLAN that all ports are placed into), the destination MAC address is the MAC address of Host-A, and the destination port is port 2/1, which is indeed the port that Host-A is attached to. If frames are received in VLAN 1 by Switch-A that have a destination MAC address of 00-a0-d1-d0-20-b9, Switch-A now possesses the necessary information to forward the frame out port 2/1 to Host-A, instead of having to flood the frame out all ports (except the port the frame was received on).

Now, assume that Host-B is attached to Switch-A and that Host-A once again attempts to communicate with Host-B. The ARP request is a broadcast frame, so Switch-A forwards the frame out all ports, except for port 2/1. Host-B receives the broadcast and responds to the ARP request with an ARP reply, which indicates it is the host that possesses the IP address 192.168.1.11. The ARP reply is sent as a unicast frame back to Host-A, which means the source MAC address of the frame will be 00-02-a5-07-e6-c5 (Host-B) and the destination MAC address will be 00-a0-d1-d0-20-b9. When Switch-A receives this frame, it learns that Host-B is reachable via port 2/2, and it also forwards the frame out port 2/1 to Host-A, because of the entry in the bridge table for the MAC address of Host-A. Example 2-3 demonstrates the bridge table on Switch-A after the ARP reply is sent from Host-B to Host-A.

Example 2-57 *Displaying the Bridge Table on Switch-A After Host-B Replies to Host-A*

```
Console> (enable) show cam dynamic
* = Static Entry. + = Permanent Entry. # = System Entry. R = Router Entry.
X = Port Security Entry $ = Dot1x Security Entry

VLAN  Dest MAC/Route Des    [CoS]  Destination Ports or VCs / [Protocol Type]
----  ------------------    -----  ------------------------------------------
1     00-a0-d1-d0-20-b9            2/1 [ALL]
1     00-02-a5-07-e6-c5            2/2 [ALL]
Total Matching CAM Entries Displayed  =2
```

Notice in Example 2-3 that a new entry has been added for Host-B. Example 2-2 and Example 2-3 demonstrate how the bridge table can be populated very quickly, minimizing the flooding of traffic sent to an unknown destination MAC address.

It is important to note that you can also manually add static entries to the bridge table, with the option of making those entries permanent so that they remain in the bridge table even after a shutdown or reboot. To configure static bridge table entries on CatOS, use the following command:

```
set cam {static | permanent} mac_address mod/port vlan
```

If you specify the **static** keyword, the bridge table entry remains in the bridge table until the bridge table is cleared (using **clear cam** command) or until the switch is shutdown/ rebooted. If you specify the **permanent** keyword, the entry remains in the bridge table permanently, even after a switch reboot. Example 2-4 demonstrates configuring a static entry for Host-B.

Example 2-58 *Configuring a Static Bridge Table Entry on Switch-A*

```
Console> (enable) set cam static 00-02-a5-07-e6-c5 2/2 1
Static unicast entry added to CAM table.
```

It is important that you specify the MAC address as indicated in Example 2-4. The command configures a destination port of 2/2 and a VLAN of 1. To view static or permanent entries, you must use the **show cam static** or **show cam permanent** commands.

NOTE   You typically never need to configure static CAM entries on a switch, except possibly for multicast traffic, if you are not using multicast traffic control features on your switch. By configuring static CAM entries for a destination multicast address, you can constrain multicast traffic to a specific set of destination ports, instead of having the switch flooding the multicast out all ports.

Verifying Transparent Bridging on Cisco IOS

To view the bridge table on a Cisco IOS switch, use the **show mac-address-table dynamic** command. This command displays all entries within the bridge table that have been dynamically learned by the inspection of the source MAC address of frames received (i.e., the learning process of transparent bridging).

Example 2-5 demonstrates the use of this command on Switch-B, before any hosts have been connected to the switch.

Example 2-59 *Displaying the Bridge Table on Switch-B*

```
Switch# show mac-address-table dynamic
          Mac Address Table
-----------------------------------------

Vlan    Mac Address      Type       Ports
----    -----------      ----       -----
```

In Example 2-5, you can see that the bridge table is fairly similar in structure to the bridge table output on CatOS. The Type field indicates whether the entry is dynamic, static, permanent, and so on.

Now, assume that Host-C is attached to the switch and attempts to send data to Host-D. Following the same process as described in the previous section, Switch-B adds an entry to the bridge table for the MAC address of Host-C. Example 2-6 demonstrates the bridge table on Switch-B after Host-C has been attached to interface Fa0/1 and has attempted to communicate with Host-D.

Example 2-60 *Displaying the Bridge Table on Switch-B*

```
Switch# show mac-address-table dynamic
          Mac Address Table
-------------------------------------------

Vlan    Mac Address        Type       Ports
----    -----------        ----       -----
   1    00d0.b7af.02ed     DYNAMIC    Fa0/1
Total Mac Addresses for this criterion: 1
```

In Example 2-6, a new entry has been added to the bridge table that associates Host-C with the egress interface Fa0/1.

NOTE

Notice that on Cisco IOS the nomenclature for representing MAC addresses uses a *xxxx.xxxx.xxxx* format, as opposed to *xx-xx-xx-xx-xx-xx* on CatOS. There is absolutely no difference between MAC addresses represented in either format.

Now assume that Host-D is attached to Switch-B and that Host-C once again attempts to communicate with Host-D. Again following the same process as discussed in the previous section, an entry is added to the bridge table for the MAC address of Host-D. Example 2-7 demonstrates the bridge table on Switch-A after Host-D communicates with Host-C.

Example 2-61 *Displaying the Bridge Table on Switch-B*

```
Switch# show mac-address-table dynamic
          Mac Address Table
-------------------------------------------

Vlan    Mac Address        Type       Ports
----    -----------        ----       -----
   1    00d0.b7af.02ed     DYNAMIC    Fa0/1
   1    0001.422c.6796     DYNAMIC    Fa0/2
Total Mac Addresses for this criterion: 1
```

You can manually add static entries to the bridge table on Cisco IOS, which are placed permanently in the bridge table. To configure static bridge table entries on Cisco IOS, use the following global configuration mode command:

```
Switch(config)# mac-address-table static mac-address vlan vlan-id interface
   interface-id
```

The *mac-address* parameter must be specified in *xxxx.xxxx.xxxx* format. Unlike static entries on CatOS that are only placed into the bridge table until the switch is shutdown/rebooted, static entries on Cisco IOS are the equivalent of permanent entries on CatOS in that they remain in the bridge table even after a switch shutdown/reboot. Example 2-8 demonstrates configuring a static entry for Host-C on Switch-B:

Example 2-62 *Configuring a Static Bridge Table Entry on Switch-B*

```
Switch# configure terminal
Switch(config)# mac-address-table static 00d0.b7af.02ed vlan 1 interface fa0/1
```

To view static entries, use the **show mac-address-table static** command.

Scenario 2-2: Configuring VLAN Trunking Protocol (VTP)

The next three scenarios of this chapter (Scenarios 2-2 through 2-4) demonstrate how to configure VLANs for a simple network topology. You learn how to configure VLANs on both Cisco CatOS-based and IOS-based Catalyst switches. VLANs are an effective tool for modern networks, allowing you to restrict Layer 2 communications between devices by placing them into separate VLANs, yet to physically connect the devices to the same switching infrastructure. These VLANs have the effect of increasing security, as access between VLANs must pass through a Layer 3 router that can have access control lists configured. They also can break up large broadcast domains into smaller pieces, reducing the amount of broadcast traffic per LAN, increasing bandwidth and reducing host-processing overheads. Using VLANs also reduces costs, as your switch can service many VLANs simultaneously, meaning you don't have to buy dedicated switching equipment for each LAN.

Figure 2-7 demonstrates a legacy LAN topology for an organization that is to be replaced with Cisco Catalyst switches. In the legacy topology, hubs and bridges are used for three separate LANs.

Figure 2-7 *Legacy LAN Topology for Scenarios 2-2, 2-3, and 2-4*

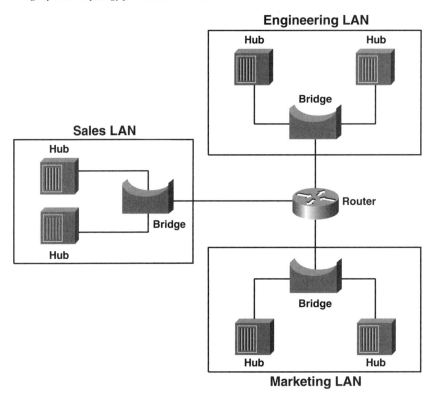

As you can see in Figure 2-7, dedicated hubs and bridges are used for each LAN, which increases ongoing management and maintenance costs because there are nine network devices in total for the entire network. To reduce ongoing management costs and to increase the performance of the network, new Cisco Catalyst switches are to be installed.

Figure 2-8 illustrates the new topology that is to replace the legacy LAN topology of Figure 2-7.

Figure 2-8   *New LAN Topology for Scenarios 2-2, 2-3, and 2-4*

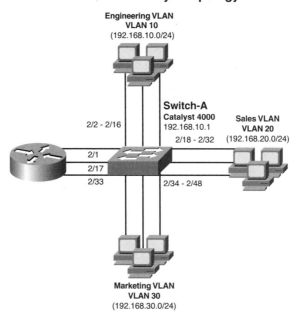

CatOS-based Catalyst Topology

Engineering VLAN
VLAN 10
(192.168.10.0/24)

Switch-A
Catalyst 4000
192.168.10.1

Sales VLAN
VLAN 20
(192.168.20.0/24)

2/2 - 2/16

2/18 - 2/32

2/1

2/17

2/33

2/34 - 2/48

Marketing VLAN
VLAN 30
(192.168.30.0/24)

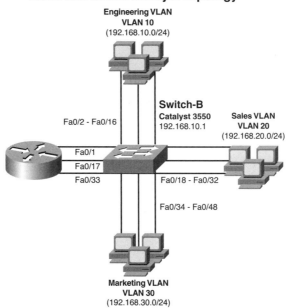

Cisco IOS-based Catalyst Topology

Engineering VLAN
VLAN 10
(192.168.10.0/24)

Switch-B
Catalyst 3550
192.168.10.1

Sales VLAN
VLAN 20
(192.168.20.0/24)

Fa0/2 - Fa0/16

Fa0/1

Fa0/17

Fa0/33

Fa0/18 - Fa0/32

Fa0/34 - Fa0/48

Marketing VLAN
VLAN 30
(192.168.30.0/24)

As you can see in Figure 2-8, two topologies are shown—one based upon a CatOS switch (Catalyst 4000) and the other based upon a Cisco IOS switch (Catalyst 3550). Both topologies provide the same functionality; the only difference is the hardware platform and administrative interface that provides that functionality. In each topology of Figure 2-8, a single Cisco Catalyst switch is used to replace the existing LAN topology (the router shown is for descriptive purposes only and is not configured in this scenario). Reducing the number of LAN devices from nine to one has clear benefits in terms of cost, simplicity, ongoing management, and ongoing maintenance.

VLAN Trunking Protocol

Before you can configure VLANs on a switch, you must configure a Cisco proprietary protocol called VLAN Trunking Protocol (VTP). VTP is designed for use in multi-switch, multi-VLAN networks, where administrators wish to configure VLANs centrally, as opposed to on each switch individually. VTP is covered in more depth in Chapter 3, but requires some coverage now because it must be configured before you can configure VLANs.

VTP defines administrative *domains*, which can be classed as a collection of switches under common administrative control. A switch can be a member of only a single VTP domain, and all switches within a VTP domain share the same VLAN database. All Cisco Catalyst switches use a VLAN database to store VLAN configuration information, such as VLAN ID, VLAN naming, and other related information. VTP allows that VLAN database information to be shared by all Cisco Catalyst switches that belong to the same VTP domain. For example, if you have a VTP domain called cisco.lab and 100 VLANs are configured in that VTP domain, all switches within the VTP domain have a VLAN database that includes all of the 100 VLANs.

The VLAN database can be configured centrally, which means that you can configure all of your VLANs centrally and VTP takes care of distributing the VLAN information to all other switches in the VTP domain. VTP propagates VLAN configuration information via multicast messages, which are sent out any trunks that are connected to the switch. A *trunk* is a Layer 2 connection to another switch (or other device) that transports data from multiple VLANs. When you connect switches together, you normally use trunks for the interconnections; hence, VTP needs to send VTP messages only out trunks as opposed to all ports on the switch.

Each switch that belongs to a VTP domain is configured with a *VTP mode*, which defines the role the switch plays in the VTP domain in terms of configuration and distribution of the VLAN database. The following lists the VTP modes that a switch can be configured in:

- **Server**—A switch that is configured as a VTP server can add, modify, and delete VLANs from the VLAN database shared in the VTP domain. A VTP server represents an administrative interface for VLAN configuration, allowing administrators to manage the VLAN configuration of the VTP domain.

- **Client**—A VTP client can read the VLAN database, but cannot modify or delete VLANs. VTP clients receive VTP messages that contain VLAN database information and ensure this information is updated in the local VLAN database.

- **Transparent**—In transparent mode, a switch does not actually participate in VTP but forwards VTP messages received out to other switches, ensuring that other VTP servers and clients connected to the switch receive these messages. The switch does not synchronize its VLAN configuration based upon VTP messages received or advertise its VLAN configuration in VTP messages.

- **Off**—The switch does not participate in VTP whatsoever. The switch operates in a similar fashion to transparent mode, but does not forward any VTP messages whatsoever.

Figure 2-9 illustrates the concept of VTP domains and how switches participate in VTP.

Figure 2-9   *VTP Domains*

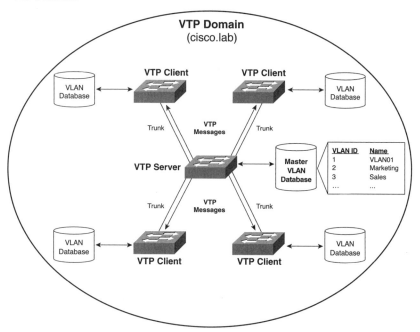

In Figure 2-9, a single switch acts as a VTP server, which means that administrators can use that switch to create, modify, and delete VLANs within the VLAN database. All other switches are VTP clients, which means that they cannot modify the VLAN database directly, and only update the VLAN database based upon VTP messages received from the VTP server. This restriction ensures that a single VLAN database is maintained throughout the VTP domain, with any modifications applied to the VTP server, after which VTP messages are sent to ensure all VLAN databases are synchronized.

Scenario Prerequisites

To successfully commence the configuration tasks required to complete this scenario, Table 2-3 describes the prerequisite configurations required on each device in the scenario topology. Any configurations not listed can be assumed as being the default configuration.

Table 2-3   *Scenario 2-2 Requirements*

Device	Required Configuration	
	Parameter	**Value**
Switch-A	Hostname	Switch-A
	Enable/Telnet Password	cisco
Switch-B	Hostname	Switch-B
	Enable/Telnet Password	cisco

Configuration Tasks

VTP is covered in depth in Chapter 3, so in this scenario you learn how to configure VTP in a single-switch environment. When you have only one switch in your LAN, you have only one VLAN database, and you don't need VTP to synchronize the VLAN database over multiple switches. This means that you can disable VTP by configuring a switch to operate either in transparent mode or in off mode.

NOTE   Off mode is supported on CatOS only at the time of writing.

You use transparent mode where a switch needs the ability to maintain its own VLAN database, but is connected to other switches that participate in a VTP domain and share a common VLAN database. By configuring transparent mode, the switch passes VTP messages through to other switches, but ignores them locally, keeping a separate VLAN database from the VTP domain. You use the off mode when a switch needs the ability to maintain its own VLAN database, and you don't want any VTP messages received to be propagated to other switches. Figure 2-10 demonstrates the difference between VTP transparent mode and VTP off mode in a multi-switch topology.

Figure 2-10   *VTP Transparent Mode Versus Off Mode*

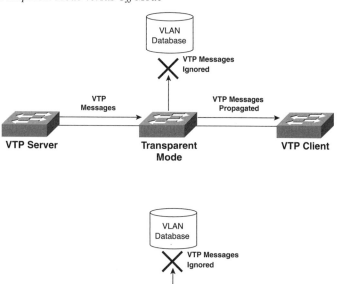

In transparent mode, you can see that the switch ignores the VTP messages received from the VTP server but does propagate the VTP messages to the VTP client, allowing the VTP server and VTP client to have synchronized VLAN database. In off mode, the switch ignores VTP messages received and also discards them, which cuts off the VTP client from the VTP server.

Disabling VLAN Trunk Protocol on CatOS

To configure the VTP mode on a CatOS switch you use the following command:

```
set vtp mode {server | client | transparent | off}
```

NOTE   If you choose to configure a mode of server or client, you must first configure a VTP domain using the **set vtp domain name** command (see Chapter 3 for more details).

In the topology for this scenario, Switch-A is the only switch on the network; hence, VTP should be configured in an off mode because there are no other switches connected that would benefit from configuring transparent mode. Example 2-9 shows an example of disabling VTP totally on Switch-A (i.e., configuring a VTP mode of off):

Example 2-63 *Disabling VTP on Switch-A*

```
Switch-A> (enable) set vtp mode off
VTP domain modified
```

Once you have completed your configuration of VTP, on CatOS you can use the **show vtp domain** command to verify your configuration. Example 2-10 demonstrates the use of this command after the configuration of Example 2-9 is applied to Switch-A.

Example 2-64 *Verifying VTP Configuration on Switch-A*

```
Switch-A> (enable) show vtp domain
Domain Name                     Domain Index VTP Version Local Mode  Password
------------------------------- ------------ ----------- ----------- ----------
                                1            2           off         -

Vlan-count Max-vlan-storage Config Revision Notifications
---------- ---------------- --------------- -------------
5          1023             0               disabled

Last Updater    V2 Mode   Pruning   PruneEligible on Vlans
--------------- --------- --------- -------------------------
0.0.0.0         disabled  disabled  2-1000
```

The local mode column in the output indicates that the current VTP mode is off. This mode enables administrators to configure and manage VLANs locally on the switch.

Disabling VLAN Trunk Protocol on Cisco IOS

It is important to understand on Cisco IOS that a VLAN database exists (separate from the switch configuration file) that holds all VTP and VLAN configuration information, unlike CatOS where all of this information is held within the switch configuration file.

Traditionally, to configure the VLAN database, you must enter *VLAN* configuration mode, which is accessed from privileged mode by using the **vlan database** command. Example 2-11 shows the use of the **vlan database** command to access VLAN configuration mode.

Example 2-65 *Accessing VLAN Configuration Mode*

```
Switch# vlan database
Switch(vlan)#
```

In Example 2-11, the (vlan) portion of the prompt indicates you have accessed VLAN configuration mode. From here you can configure VTP parameters and can add, modify, and delete VLANs. In VLAN configuration mode, all configuration commands entered are not applied to the VLAN database until you exit VLAN configuration mode, which you do by typing **exit**. Once you exit VLAN configuration mode, the switch modifies the binary VLAN database file appropriately, based upon the commands you entered.

TIP   You cannot add ports to a VLAN from VLAN configuration mode. You must add each of these via interface configuration mode for each interface or the range of interfaces that you wish to add to a VLAN.

In older releases of Cisco IOS, you must use VLAN configuration mode, which is a special configuration mode on Cisco IOS that directly modifies the VLAN database, to configure VTP parameters. To configure the VTP mode using VLAN configuration mode, use the following command:

```
Switch(vlan)# vtp {server | client | transparent}
```

Notice that on Cisco IOS, there is no option to configure a VTP mode of off because this mode is not supported in Cisco IOS. If you wish to disable the use of VTP, you must configure VTP transparent mode.

Once you have configured the VTP mode, you must exit VLAN configuration mode for the configuration to take effect. Example 2-12 demonstrates disabling VTP on Switch-B.

Example 2-66 *Disabling VTP on Switch-B*

```
Switch-B# vlan database
Switch-B(vlan)# vtp transparent
Setting device to VTP TRANSPARENT mode.
Switch-B(vlan)# exit
APPLY completed.
Exiting....
```

Newer versions of Cisco IOS allow you to alternatively use both EXEC mode and global configuration mode to configure VLANs and, in some instances, store this configuration in the main switch configuration file. The VLAN.DAT database file still exists; however, Cisco IOS simply applies configuration commands to the VLAN database from EXEC or global configuration mode as opposed to VLAN configuration mode.

NOTE   You might be wondering exactly what you can configure from EXEC mode, given that this mode is normally not used for configuration commands. You can configure VTP password, VTP pruning, and VTP version from EXEC mode, with all other VTP and VLAN parameters configured from global configuration mode.

You can configure the VTP mode from global configuration mode by using the following command:

```
Switch(config)# vtp mode {server | client | transparent}
```

Example 2-13 demonstrates using global configuration mode to disable VTP on Switch-B:

Example 2-67 *Disabling VTP on Switch-B*

```
Switch-B# configure terminal
Switch-B(config)# vtp mode transparent
Setting device to VTP TRANSPARENT mode.
```

NOTE   Using EXEC mode and global configuration mode for VTP and VLAN configuration is supported on the Catalyst 2950/3550 from IOS 12.1(9)EA, on the Catalyst 4000/4500 with Supervisor 3/4 from IOS 12.1(8a)EW, and on the native IOS Catalyst 6000/6500 from 12.1(8b)EX.

Once you have completed your configuration of VTP, you can use the **show vtp status** command on Cisco IOS to verify your configuration. Example 2-14 demonstrates the use of this command after the configuration of Example 2-4 is applied to Switch-B.

Example 2-68 *Verifying VTP Configuration on Switch-B*

```
Switch-B# show vtp status
VTP Version                     : 2
Configuration Revision          : 0
Maximum VLANs supported locally : 1005
Number of existing VLANs        : 5
VTP Operating Mode              : Transparent
VTP Domain Name                 :
VTP Pruning Mode                : Disabled
VTP V2 Mode                     : Disabled
VTP Traps Generation            : Disabled
MD5 digest                      : 0x9D 0x0E 0x94 0x5C 0xDE 0x33 0x4A 0x9C
Configuration last modified by 0.0.0.0 at 3-1-93 00:01:14
```

The shaded output indicates that Switch-B is operating in VTP transparent mode.

Scenario 2-3: Configuring VLANs

VLANs represent one of the most important and fundamental concepts of LAN switching, so it is important that you have a firm grasp of how to implement them. Before configuring VLANs, you need to plan exactly how many VLANs you are going to create, the parameters associated with each, and the switch ports that are going to be assigned to each VLAN. After the correct planning, you can then configure your VLAN requirements. The planning and configuration of VLANs can be split into the following tasks:

- Determine VLANs required
- Determine VLAN parameters
- Determine VLAN port assignments
- Configuring VLANs

Determine VLANs Required

Before you configure VLANs, you must determine how many VLANs you need for your network. The number of VLANs required is normally driven by high-level policy that requires VLANs to facilitate specific requirements of the policy. VLANs are the vessel for implementing high-level network policy—for example, a company may require separation of the sales, marketing, and engineering department information. Users from different departments may be co-located and connected to the same switching infrastructure, but their workstation should not be permitted to communicate directly across functional lines.

To extend this requirement to the LAN, VLANs can be created—one for each department. Users from the same department belong to the same VLAN, which allows Layer 2 communications within the same department. Users from different departments belong to different VLANs, which means inter-departmental communications must be sent via a Layer 3 router or firewall, which allows for policy to be applied at a single point in the network to control inter-departmental communications. Even if a user from sales is connected to port 1 on a switch (port 1 belongs to the sales VLAN) and a user from marketing is connected to port 2 on the same switch (port 2 belongs to the marketing VLAN), there is no way in which these two users can communicate unless the packets are sent to a router that connects to both VLANs. Figure 2-11 shows the concept of using VLANs to separate groups of users in a network.

Figure 2-11 *LAN Topology with Multiple VLANs*

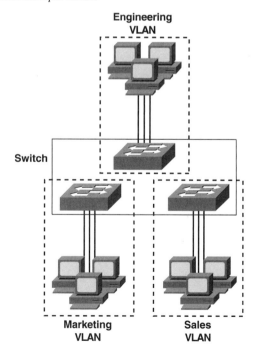

The requirement for VLANs can also be driven by other reasons, such as ensuring the network can perform appropriately by addressing existing network performance problems. A common issue with large VLANs is broadcasts; many network protocols use broadcasts periodically to maintain certain functions of the protocol. When a broadcast is sent, all hosts on the network must process the broadcast, even if the information contained within bears no importance to the host. An excessive number of broadcasts can degrade PC performance by expending CPU resources.

Certain guidelines exist as to the maximum number of devices per VLAN that should be used based upon the Layer 3 protocol used. Table 2-4 shows the recommended maximum devices per VLAN for Layer 3 protocols.

Table 2-4   *Maximum Devices per VLAN*

Layer 3 Protocol	Maximum Number of Devices
IP	500
IPX	300
AppleTalk	200
NetBIOS	200
Mixed	200

It is important to note that the numbers specified in Table 2-4 are guidelines only and were defined by Cisco several years ago. Today, CPUs are literally tens of times faster, and these limits may be extended. If you are looking to exceed the limits defined in Table 2-4, monitor the network regularly to ensure the network is performing appropriately. If you find that network performance is poor, consider splitting your network into more VLANs to reduce the number of broadcasts and increase network performance. As a rule of thumb, broadcast and multicast traffic should not account for more than 20 percent of the network utilization.

Once you have determined the list of VLANs required, you should also consider allocating a separate VLAN for device management purposes. This VLAN is commonly referred to as the *management VLAN* (as in network management, not workstations belonging to the corporate management of the company), and it is recommended that you keep all network management traffic separate from the data traffic by implementing this dedicated management VLAN. The most common VLAN used for management is VLAN 1. Separating management traffic from data traffic keeps network utilization to a minimum on the management VLAN, ensuring management communications are not affected by congestion or errors that may occur on the data VLAN.

Determine VLAN Parameters

Each VLAN has a list of parameters that you need to understand and configure to control the behavior of the VLAN. The following lists common Ethernet VLAN parameters supported on Cisco Catalyst switches:

- **ID**—Numeric ID that uniquely identifies the VLAN to the switch. By default a single Ethernet VLAN exists (VLAN 1), and all ports on the switch belong to this VLAN.

- **Name**—An alphanumeric string that describes the VLAN for human recognition purposes. For example, you might assign a name of *marketing* to a VLAN that connects marketing users.

- **Media Type**—Describes the media type of the VLAN. These media include Ethernet (the default), Token Ring, and Fiber Distributed Data Interface (FDDI).

- **MTU**—Describes the maximum transmission unit (MTU) in bytes that can be sent on the VLAN. The default MTU for Ethernet is 1500 bytes, meaning the largest frame sent on the VLAN contains 1500 bytes of data plus the Ethernet header.

- **State**—Defines the current operational state of the VLAN. When the VLAN is functioning and forwarding traffic, the state is said to be *active*. You can also *suspend* a VLAN, and the VLAN does not forward any traffic.

For Ethernet VLANs, you normally will only configure VLAN ID and name, as the defaults for the remaining parameters typically never require modification.

Referring back to the topology of Figure 2-8, you can see that for this scenario you need to create three new VLANs (VLAN 1 already exists by default and cannot be deleted). Table 2-5 describes each VLAN that will exist in the topology of Figure 2-8.

Table 2-5   *VLANs Used for Scenarios*

VLAN ID	Name	Description
1	VLAN0001	Default VLAN
10	Engineering	Engineering users
20	Sales	Sales users
30	Marketing	Marketing users

Determine VLAN Port Assignments

Now that have generated a list of VLANs, your final step is to determine which ports should be assigned each VLAN.

You can configure two basic roles for a port on a Catalyst switch:

- **Access port**—Belongs to a single VLAN and is designed to provide connectivity for an end device such as a server, PC, or printer.

- **Trunk port**—Transports traffic from multiple VLANs over a single connection. This port is normally used for interconnecting switches and sometimes routers. Trunks allow VLANs to be distributed over multiple switches. Chapter 3 discusses trunk ports in detail.

This chapter discusses only access ports, which are easy to understand because the port belongs only to a single VLAN. You place end devices in the correct VLAN by assigning each access port to the correct VLAN. Obviously, you need to know the port that each user connects to so that you can place the user (port) in the appropriate VLAN. Table 2-6 shows the port assignments required for the topology of Figure 2-8.

Table 2-6 *VLAN Port Assignments*

VLAN ID	VLAN Name	Port Assignment (Switch-A)	Interface Assignment (Switch-B)
1	—	—	—
10	Engineering	2/1–2/16	Fa0/1–Fa0/16
20	Sales	2/17–2/32	Fa0/17–Fa0/32
30	Marketing	2/33–2/48	Fa0/33–Fa0/48

Configuring VLANs

Once you have configured the appropriate VTP mode (server, transparent, or off), you can begin configuring VLANs. When you configure VLANs, you must first create a VLAN and then assign the applicable switch ports to the VLAN.

NOTE   You must create a VLAN first before assigning ports to the VLAN. You cannot create a VLAN and assign ports in the same configuration command.

Creating VLANs on CatOS

To create VLANs on CatOS, use the **set vlan** command as shown below:

```
set vlan vlan-id [name name] [type type] [state {active | suspend}]
```

When you create a VLAN, you must configure the *vlan-id* parameter, and you also normally configure a name that describes the VLAN. By default, the *type* parameter is set to **ethernet** (i.e., an Ethernet VLAN) and the **state** is set with **active**, meaning the VLAN is active (if this is set to **suspend**, the VLAN is not active but still exists).

Example 2-15 shows how to create each of the VLANs indicated in Figure 2-8 (see Table 2-5 also) on Switch-A.

Example 2-69 *Creating VLANs on Switch-A*

```
Switch-A> (enable) set vlan 10 name Engineering
Vlan 10 configuration successful
Switch-A> (enable) set vlan 20 name Sales
Vlan 20 configuration successful
Switch-A> (enable) set vlan 30 name Marketing
Vlan 30 configuration successful
```

After you have created your VLANs, you can then assign ports to the appropriate VLAN. Before you assign ports to a VLAN, you need to understand the default port mode on CatOS switches. By default, each port is configured in a *dynamic auto mode*, which means the port can negotiate to become a trunk port if the remote party connected to the port is configured appropriately (you learn about this in Chapter 3). If you wish to hard code a port to be only an access port (as is applicable for ports that are connected to end devices, such as workstations and printers), use the **set trunk** command to disable trunking all together:

set trunk *mod/port* **off**

NOTE   You should always hard code all access ports because it reduces the amount of delay introduced by *Dynamic Trunking Protocol (DTP)* negotiation when a port is first initialized. DTP is used to negotiate whether or not a trunk will form and adds a small amount of delay before a port moves into a forwarding state.

To assign ports to the appropriate VLAN on CatOS, you use the following variation of the **set vlan** command:

set vlan *vlan-id mod/ports*

Example 2-16 shows how to hard code each port as an access port and then assign each of the ports to the appropriate VLANs as indicated in Figure 2-8 (see Table 2-6 also) on Switch-B.

Example 2-70 *Configuring Access Ports and Assigning Ports to VLANs on Switch-A*

```
Switch-A> (enable) set trunk 2/1-48 off
Port(s) 2/1-48 trunk mode set to off.
Switch-A> (enable) set vlan 10 2/1-16
VLAN 10 modified.
VLAN 1 modified.
VLAN  Mod/Ports
----  ----------------------
10    2/1-16
Switch-A> (enable) set vlan 20 2/17-32
VLAN 20 modified.
```

continues

Example 2-70 *Configuring Access Ports and Assigning Ports to VLANs on Switch-A (Continued)*

```
VLAN 1 modified.
VLAN  Mod/Ports
----  ----------------------
20    2/17-32
Switch-A> (enable) set vlan 20 2/33-42,2/43-48
VLAN 30 modified.
VLAN 1 modified.
VLAN  Mod/Ports
----  ----------------------
30    2/33-48
```

The first command in Example 2-16 ensures that ports 2/1-48 are access ports, meaning that they can belong only to a single VLAN. Notice in Example 2-16 that CatOS permits you to specify ranges of ports, which means you can allocate multiple ports to a VLAN in a single command. You can also specify non-contiguous ports by using a comma to separate each port, and you can mix commas and hyphens as demonstrated in the shaded output of Example 2-16. Notice also that each command output shows that VLAN 1 has been modified, which indicates the ports configured were previously in VLAN 1.

Once you have completed your VLAN configuration, you can use the **show vlan** command to verify the VLAN configuration, as shown in Example 2-17.

Example 2-71 *Verifying VLAN Configuration on Switch-A*

```
Switch-A> (enable) show vlan
VLAN Name                             Status    IfIndex Mod/Ports, Vlans
---- -------------------------------- --------- ------- -----------------------
1    default                          active    4       1/1-2
10   Engineering                      active    59      2/1-16
20   Sales                            active    60      2/17-32
30   Marketing                        active    61      2/33-48
1002 fddi-default                     active    5
1003 token-ring-default               active    8
1004 fddinet-default                  active    6
1005 trnet-default                    active    7
... (Output abbreviated)
...
```

Notice that the output indicates that each of the ports on the switch is assigned to the correct VLAN.

Creating VLANs on Cisco IOS

To create VLANs on Cisco IOS, you can use either VLAN configuration mode or global configuration mode. In older versions of Cisco IOS, you must use the following VLAN configuration command to create a VLAN:

```
Switch(vlan)# vlan vlan-id [name name] [type type] [state {active | suspend}]
```

Example 2-18 shows how to create each of the VLANs indicated in Figure 2-8 on Switch-B using VLAN configuration mode.

Example 2-72 *Creating VLANs via VLAN Configuration Mode on Switch-B*

```
Switch-B# vlan database
Switch-B(vlan)# vlan 10 name Engineering
VLAN 10 added:
    Name: Engineering
Switch-B(vlan)# vlan 20 name Sales
VLAN 20 added:
    Name: Sales
Switch-B(vlan)# vlan 30 name Marketing
VLAN 30 added:
    Name: Marketing
Switch-B(vlan)# exit
APPLY completed.
Exiting....
```

You must exit VLAN configuration mode, as shown in Example 2-18, for the new VLAN configuration to take effect.

In newer versions of Cisco IOS, you can also use global configuration mode to configure VLANs. When you use this method, each VLAN that you create has its own config-vlan configuration mode, as demonstrated in Example 2-19.

Example 2-73 *Creating VLANs via Global Configuration Mode on Switch-B*

```
Switch-B# configure terminal
Enter configuration commands, one per line.  End with CNTL/Z.
Switch-B(config)# vlan 10
Switch-B(config-vlan)# name Engineering
Switch-B(config-vlan)# exit
Switch-B(config)# vlan 20
Switch-B(config-vlan)# name Sales
Switch-B(config-vlan)# exit
Switch-B(config)# vlan 30
Switch-B(config-vlan)# name Marketing
Switch-B(config-vlan)# exit
```

In Example 2-19, notice that you use the **vlan** *vlan-id* global configuration mode command to create/modify a VLAN, which then places you into config-vlan configuration mode for that VLAN. From here, you can configure the various VLAN parameters, and once you have completed this configuration, you must exit this mode for the changes to take effect. Once you exit, the configuration changes are written and applied to the VLAN database file.

You might be wondering whether or not the configuration of Example 2-19 is stored in the switch configuration file; the answer is yes, but only if the switch is configured in VTP transparent mode. When configured in transparent mode the switch saves global configuration mode VLAN configuration in the switch configuration file. When the switch boots, the VLAN database file is cleared; the VLAN configuration stored in the switch configuration file is read, which then populates the VLAN database. If you configure the VTP mode of the switch to server or client, the VLAN configuration is stored only in the VLAN database and is removed from the switch configuration file.

NOTE	If you configure a Cisco IOS switch using VLAN configuration mode (as shown in Example 2-18) or configure a Cisco IOS switch that is configured as a VTP server or VTP client in global configuration mode, ensure that you back up the VLAN.DAT file as well as the switch configuration file. If you don't back up the VLAN.DAT file, if you have to restore the switch, you need to recreate all VLANs, even if you have the original switch configuration file.

After you have created your VLANs, you can assign interfaces to the appropriate VLANs. Before you assign interfaces to a VLAN, you need to understand the default interface mode on Cisco IOS switches. By default, each interface is configured in a *dynamic desirable mode*, which is similar to CatOS in that an interface can negotiate to become a trunk port if the remote party connected to the interface is configured appropriately (you learn about this in Chapter 3). If you wish to hard code an interface to be only an access interface, use the **switchport mode access** command to disable trunking all together and configure the interface as an access interface.

```
Switch(config-if)# switchport mode access
```

NOTE	By default, on native IOS Catalyst 6000/6500 switches each interface is configured as a routed interface (identical to an interface on a router) as opposed to a switch (Layer 2) interface. You must use the **switchport** interface configuration command to configure an interface to become a switch interface.

To assign interfaces to the appropriate VLAN on Cisco IOS, you use the following interface configuration mode on a per-interface basis:

```
Switch(config-if)# switchport access vlan vlan-id
```

Example 2-20 demonstrates configuring a couple of interfaces as access interfaces and then assigning the interfaces to VLAN 10 on Switch-B.

Example 2-74 *Configuring Access Interfaces and Assigning Interfaces to VLANs on Switch-B*

```
Switch-B# configure terminal
Enter configuration commands, one per line.  End with CNTL/Z.
Switch-B(config)# interface fa0/1
Switch-B(config-if)# switchport mode access
Switch-B(config-if)# switchport access vlan 10
Switch-B(config-if)# exit
Switch-B(config)# interface fa0/2
```

Example 2-74 *Configuring Access Interfaces and Assigning Interfaces to VLANs on Switch-B (Continued)*

```
Switch-B(config-if)# switchport mode access
Switch-B(config-if)# switchport access vlan 10
Switch-B(config-if)# exit
```

If you use the method demonstrated in Example 2-20 to configure access interfaces and VLAN port assignments, you can see that you need to individually configure each interface, which clearly will take a lot longer than the performing the equivalent configuration on a CatOS switch (see Example 2-16). Cisco has recognized the administrative overhead of this common task on Cisco IOS-based switches and has introduced a new global configuration command **interface range** that allows you to apply commands to a range or list of interfaces at the same time. This command is actually a *macro*, which means that when used, the macro actually invokes a series of commands. This process is transparent to the administrator. The configuration file contains no reference to the interface range macro; instead it displays each of the configuration commands invoked by the macro.

NOTE   You can configure any interface configuration command when using the interface range macro, as long as the command is applicable to each interface in the range specified.

When you use the interface range macro, you must adhere to strict syntax rules. The following shows these rules applied for defining a contiguous range of interfaces (interface fa0/1 through fa0/16):

```
Switch(config)# interface range fa0/1 - 16
```

When specifying a range, you must ensure that a space is present between the lower bound (fa0/1), the hyphen, and the upper bound (16). The lower bound must be the full module/interface designation (e.g., fa0/1) while the upper bound can be only an interface number (e.g., 16) and cannot be a full module/interface designation. Example 2-21 demonstrates the incorrect use of the interface range macro, where the upper bound of the range is configured as a full module/interface designation.

Example 2-75 *Illegal Use of the Interface Range Macro*

```
Switch(config)# interface range fa0/1 - fa0/16
                                       ^
% Invalid input detected at '^' marker.
```

When you wish to specify a non-contiguous list of interfaces, you must use a comma to separate each interface, and you must use the full module/interface designation for each interface. The following shows an example of specifying interfaces fa0/1, fa0/3, fa0/7, and interfaces fa0/13 through fa0/20:

```
Switch(config)# interface range fa0/1 , fa0/3 , fa0/7 , fa0/13 - 20
```

Notice that a space is required between each interface and comma and that the full module/interface designation is required for each non-contiguous interface. If you include a range within the list, the upper bound of the range must specify the interface designation only (not the full module/interface designation).

Example 2-22 demonstrates the use of the interface range macro to assign each of the interfaces on Switch-B to the appropriate VLANs, as indicated in Table 2-6.

Example 2-76 *Using the Interface Range Macro*

```
Switch-B# configure terminal
Enter configuration commands, one per line.  End with CNTL/Z.
Switch-B(config)# interface range fa0/1 - 16
Switch-B(config-if-range)# switchport mode access
Switch-B(config-if-range)# switchport access vlan 10
Switch-B(config-if-range)# exit
Switch-B(config)# interface range fa0/17 - 32
Switch-B(config-if-range)# switchport mode access
Switch-B(config-if-range)# switchport access vlan 20
Switch-B(config-if-range)# exit
Switch-B(config)# interface range fa0/33 , fa0/34 - 48
Switch-B(config-if-range)# switchport mode access
Switch-B(config-if-range)# switchport access vlan 30
Switch-B(config-if-range)# exit
```

The shaded line in Example 2-22 demonstrates combining a list and range of interfaces.

Once you have completed your VLAN configuration, you can use the **show vlan** command to verify the VLAN configuration, as shown in Example 2-23.

Example 2-77 *Verifying VLAN Configuration on Switch-B*

```
Switch-B# show vlan
LAN Name                             Status    Ports
---- -------------------------------- --------- -------------------------------
1    default                          active    Gi0/1, Gi0/2
10   Engineering                      active    Fa0/1, Fa0/2, Fa0/3, Fa0/4
                                                Fa0/5, Fa0/6, Fa0/7, Fa0/8
                                                Fa0/9, Fa0/10, Fa0/11, Fa0/12
                                                Fa0/13, Fa0/14, Fa0/15, Fa0/16
20   Sales                            active    Fa0/17, Fa0/18, Fa0/19, Fa0/20
                                                Fa0/21, Fa0/22, Fa0/23, Fa0/24
                                                Fa0/25, Fa0/26, Fa0/27, Fa0/28
                                                Fa0/29, Fa0/30, Fa0/31, Fa0/32
30   Marketing                        active    Fa0/33, Fa0/34, Fa0/35, Fa0/36
                                                Fa0/37, Fa0/38, Fa0/39, Fa0/40
                                                Fa0/41, Fa0/42, Fa0/43, Fa0/44
                                                Fa0/45, Fa0/46, Fa0/47, Fa0/48
1002 fddi-default                     active
1003 token-ring-default               active
1004 fddinet-default                  active
1005 trnet-default                    active
... (Output abbreviated)
...
```

Removing VLANs

Sometimes you need to remove VLANs, and it is important that you understand how to do this and the implications of removing a VLAN.

When you remove a VLAN, you must understand that any ports assigned to that VLAN are placed into an inactive state because they still belong to the removed VLAN. Each port is effectively orphaned, and you need to reassign the ports to active VLANs to re-enable them. If you recreate the VLAN, any ports still configured to belong to the removed VLAN are automatically joined to the new VLAN once again.

To remove a VLAN completely on CatOS, use the **clear vlan** command, as demonstrated in Example 2-24.

Example 2-78 *Removing a VLAN on CatOS*

```
Switch-A> (enable) clear vlan 30
This command will deactivate all ports on vlan(s) 30
Do you want to continue(y/n) [n]?y
Vlan 30 deleted
```

Notice that you are warned that all ports on VLAN 30 will be deactivated by removing VLAN 30. If you issue a **show vlan** command, you will notice that all ports previously assigned to VLAN 30 have disappeared, as shown in Example 2-25.

Example 2-79 *Displaying VLAN Configuration after Removing a VLAN on CatOS*

```
Switch-A> (enable) show vlan
VLAN Name                             Status    IfIndex Mod/Ports, Vlans
---- -------------------------------- --------- ------- -----------------------
1    default                          active    4       1/1-2
10   Engineering                      active    59      2/1-16
20   Sales                            active    60      2/17-32
1002 fddi-default                     active    5
1003 token-ring-default               active    8
1004 fddinet-default                  active    6
1005 trnet-default                    active    7
... (Output abbreviated)
```

Notice that VLAN 30 has disappeared from the VLAN database and that the ports previously assigned to that VLAN (ports 2/33-48) no longer appear.

To remove a VLAN completely on Cisco IOS, use the **no vlan** *vlan-id* command in either VLAN configuration mode or global configuration mode, as demonstrated in Example 2-26.

Example 2-80 *Removing a VLAN on Cisco IOS*

```
Switch-B# vlan database
Switch-B(vlan)# no vlan 20
Deleting VLAN 20...
Switch-B(vlan)# exit
APPLY completed.
```

continues

Example 2-80 *Removing a VLAN on Cisco IOS (Continued)*

```
Exiting....
Switch-B# configure terminal
Enter configuration commands, one per line.  End with CNTL/Z.
Switch-B(config)# no vlan 30
Switch-B(config)# end
```

In Example 2-26, VLAN 20 is deleted using the older VLAN configuration method, while VLAN 30 is deleted using the global configuration method. Just as for CatOS switches, any ports assigned to removed VLANs are placed into an inactive state and must be assigned to a new VLAN if they are to be used.

Scenario 2-4: Configuring the Management VLAN

After you install switches into a network, it is important that you are able to manage them remotely using IP-based management protocols, such as Telnet and Simple Network Management Protocol (SNMP). Cisco Catalyst switches include a virtual management interface, which can be configured with an IP address and can provide a remote administration and management interface into the switch. These management interfaces are referred to as *in-band management interfaces* because they are attached to and can be accessed from the data network.

NOTE   Some Catalyst switches include an *out-of-band management interface*, which is simply a physical port allocated for management purposes only and is not connected to the switching backplane. This arrangement ensures that the data network is completely segregated from the management interface of each switch and the management network attached to the management interface, increasing the security of the network. For example, the Catalyst 4000 Supervisor 2 engine includes an Ethernet management interface called me0.

In a multi-VLAN environment, such as the topology shown in Figure 2-8, it is important to be able to place the management interface into the appropriate VLAN that uses the IP subnet addressing that your switch is configured to reside in. For example, in Figure 2-8, you can see that both Switch-A and Switch-B are configured with an IP address of 192.168.10.1.

NOTE   Switch-A and Switch-B reside in separate topologies, so the fact that they use the same IP addressing does not matter. If they resided in the same network, you would need to ensure the IP addresses of each were unique.

VLAN 10 (Engineering VLAN) is configured with the IP subnet 192.168.10.0/24, which means that the management interface of each switch needs to reside in VLAN 10 to ensure communications with other devices on the network.

On CatOS, the virtual management interface is called **sc0** and is configured via the **set interface sc0** command:

```
set interface sc0 [vlan] [ip-address] [mask]
```

If you don't specify a VLAN, the management interface is assigned to VLAN 1. If you specify an IP address but don't specify a subnet mask, the appropriate Class A, B, or C subnet mask is assumed for the mask. Example 2-27 demonstrates configuring the management interface on Switch-A.

Example 2-81   *Configuring the sc0 Management Interface on Switch-A*

```
Switch-A> (config) set interface sc0 10 192.168.10.1 255.255.255.0
Interface sc0 vlan set, IP address and netmask set.
```

On Cisco IOS, a virtual management interface is created, which can then be configured with an IP address to enable management access to the switch. Cisco IOS can attach to any VLAN by creating a *switched virtual interface* (*SVI*), which is essentially a virtual interface that can be configured with IP and is attached to a particular VLAN (you learn more about these in Chapters 5, "Inter-VLAN Routing" and 6, " Layer 3 Switching"). You can create multiple SVIs ; however, only a single SVI can be active at any one time for management purposes.

NOTE   The exception to this restriction is on Layer 3 switches, where any SVI or physical interface with an IP address can be used for management purposes.

It is important to note that by default an SVI for the default VLAN (VLAN 1) exists, which can be configured via the **interface vlan 1** global configuration command. This interface is shut down by default, so you must explicitly enable the interface by using the **no shutdown** interface configuration mode command. You can then configure an IP address for the VLAN 1 SVI. If you wish to use an SVI for another VLAN, you must create a new SVI. To create an SVI, you simply use the **interface** global configuration command as follows:

```
Switch(config)# interface vlan vlan-id
```

When you create an SVI, the default state of the interface is shutdown, which means you must explicitly enable the interface.

NOTEOn the Catalyst 2900XL/3500XL, if you use a management interface other than interface VLAN 1, you must designate the SVI as a management interface by using the **management** interface configuration command. Furthermore on IOS versions earlier than Release 12.0(5)XP, you cannot modify the management VLAN from VLAN 1.

After you have created the SVI, you need to configure an IP address on the interface, which then enables management access via the IP address configured. Example 2-28 demonstrates configuring a management interface on Switch-B and assigning the appropriate IP address.

Example 2-82 *Configuring a Management Interface on Switch-B*

```
Switch-B# configure terminal
Enter configuration commands, one per line.  End with CNTL/Z.
Switch-B(config)# interface VLAN 10
Switch-B(config-if)# no shutdown
Switch-B(config-if)# ip address 192.168.10.1 255.255.255.0
```

An SVI must have at least one device connected to a Layer 2 interface within the VLAN, otherwise the interface line protocol will be down.

Scenario 2-5: Configuring Extended-Range VLANs

Historically, Cisco Catalyst switches have supported only up to 1024 VLANs, with this number being derived from the 10-bit VLAN ID field included in Cisco's original trunking protocol, ISL. 802.1Q is the standards-based trunking protocol defined by the IEEE and is now the recommended trunking protocol for Cisco switched networks. 802.1Q includes a 12-bit VLAN ID field, which means that 802.1Q supports up to 4096 VLANs. Cisco refers to the VLANs between 1025 and 4096 as *extended-range VLANs*.

Cisco Catalyst switches support extended-range VLANs under the following restrictions:

* VTP cannot be used for VLAN management. In other words, VTP must be configured in transparent mode or off.

* Only Ethernet VLANs are supported.

* The spanning-tree extended system ID feature (also known as MAC address reduction) must be enabled, as the most MAC addresses that are allocated to Catalyst switches is 1024 (see Chapter 4, "Spanning Tree," for more details).

* When configuring extended-range VLANs, always use the highest numbers first because some Catalyst switch modules use VLANs from the lower portion of the extended VLAN range for internal use (e.g., the Catalyst 6000 FlexWAN module allocates VLANs for internal use starting from 1025 for ports on the FlexWAN module).

Configuration Tasks

To create extended-range VLANs, you must perform the following configuration tasks:

* Disable VTP
* Enable MAC address reduction
* Create extended-range VLANs

This scenario continues on from the previous scenarios. In Scenario 2-2, you disabled VTP by configuring a VTP mode of off for Switch-A and a VTP mode of transparent for Switch-B. Since you have already met that VTP requirement for configuring extended-range VLANs, the configuration task of disabling VTP is not presented again in the following sections.

Enabling MAC Address Reduction

On both switches, you must enable MAC address reduction before you can create extended VLANs. An explanation of MAC address reduction is outside the scope of this chapter and is discussed in Chapter 4. For now, understand that MAC address reduction removes the requirement for a switch to possess a unique MAC address per VLAN, meaning a switch does not require 4096 MAC addresses to be allocated to support 4096 VLANs.

On CatOS, MAC address reduction is disabled by default, so you must explicitly enable it to configure extended-range VLANs. To enable MAC address reduction, you use the **set spantree macreduction** command, as demonstrated in Example 2-29 on Switch-A.

Example 2-83 *Enabling MAC Address Reduction on Switch-A*

```
Switch-A> (enable) set spantree macreduction enable
MAC address reduction enabled
```

On Cisco IOS switches, MAC address reduction is enabled by default for switches with limited MAC addresses (e.g., the Catalyst 3550), but is disabled by default for switches with large numbers of MAC addresses (e.g., Catalyst 6000 running native IOS). To enable MAC address reduction (also referred to as *extended system ID* on Cisco IOS), use the **spanning-tree extend system-id** global configuration command, as demonstrated in Example 2-30 on Switch-A.

Example 2-84 *Enabling MAC Address Reduction on Switch-B*

```
Switch-B(config)# spanning-tree extend system-id
```

Creating Extended-Range VLANs

Once you have disabled VTP and enabled MAC address reduction, you can create extended-range VLANs. Creating these VLANs is no different than creating standard VLANs, you just simply specify a VLAN ID in the range of 1025 to 4095. Remember that you should avoid using the lower extended VLAN range; use higher VLAN IDs first.

NOTE   On Cisco Catalyst switches, VLANs 0, 1001-1025, and VLAN 4095 are reserved and cannot be configured.

Example 2-31 demonstrates creating VLAN 4000 on Switch-A and assigning port 2/3 to the new VLAN.

Example 2-85 *Creating an Extended-Range VLAN on Switch-A*

```
Switch-A> (enable) set vlan 4000 name EXTENDED
VTP advertisements transmitting temporarily stopped,
and will resume after the command finishes.
Not allowed to set name for extended range of vlans.
Switch-A> (enable) set vlan 4000 2/3
Vlan 4000 configuration successful
VLAN 4000 modified.
VLAN 10 modified.
VLAN  Mod/Ports
----  ----------------------
4000  2/3
```

Notice that you cannot configure a name for an extended-range VLAN, as indicated by the shaded line. Example 2-32 shows the output of the **show vlan** command after the new VLAN has been created.

Example 2-86 *Displaying Extended-Range VLANs*

```
Switch-A> (enable) show vlan
VLAN Name                             Status     IfIndex Mod/Ports, Vlans
---- -------------------------------- ---------  ------- ----------------------
1    default                          active     4       2/1-2,2/4-50
10   Engineering                      active     59      2/1-2,2/4-16
20   Sales                            active     60      2/17-32
30   Marketing                        active     61      2/33-48
1002 fddi-default                     active     5
1003 token-ring-default               active     8
1004 fddinet-default                  active     6
1005 trnet-default                    active     7
4000 VLAN4000                         active     62      2/3
... <output truncated>
```

To configure extended-range VLANs on Cisco IOS, you must use global configuration mode to create extended-range VLANs; you *cannot* use VLAN database configuration mode. Example 2-33 demonstrates creating VLAN 4000 on Switch-B and assigning interface fa0/3 to the new VLAN.

TIP   On Cisco IOS Switches, you can use the **show vlan internal usage** command to view VLANs currently used internally.

Example 2-87 *Creating an Extended-Range VLAN on Switch-B*

```
Switch-B# configure terminal
Switch-B(config)# vlan 4000
Switch-B(config-vlan)# name EXTENDED
Can't modify name for extended VLAN 4000.
Switch-B(config-vlan)# exit
Switch-B(config)# interface fastEthernet0/3
Switch-B(config-if)# switchport access vlan 400
```

Notice that you also cannot configure a name for an extended-range VLAN on Cisco IOS, as indicated by the shaded line.

Summary

Virtual LANs form the basis of modern local-area networks today. VLANs provide many benefits, including alleviating performance problems due to excessively large broadcast domains and securing devices by separating them into multiple VLANs, even though the devices may be connected to the same physical switch. Cisco Catalyst switches support up to 4096 VLANs (using 802.1Q trunking) or 1024 VLANs (using Cisco ISL trunking).

Each VLAN is totally separated from other VLANs on a switch. Devices within the same VLAN can communicate with each other directly at Layer 2 level. Devices that are in different VLANs can communicate only via a Layer 3 router that is attached to each VLAN. All VLANs are stored in a VLAN database. In its simplest form, a VLAN consists of an ID and a name. The VLAN ID uniquely identifies the VLAN, while the name gives the VLAN a descriptive meaning. Other parameters exist that define a VLAN, for example, the media type (e.g., Ethernet or Token Ring) and MTU (maximum transmission unit). Ethernet switches exclusively use transparent bridging to forward frames within a VLAN. Transparent bridging is aptly named because end devices are not aware that they connect to a bridging device such as a switch.

A fundamental requirement for any networking device is the ability to manage the device, both locally and remotely. Cisco Catalyst switches possess a virtual management interface that can be placed into any VLAN, ensuring the appropriate management devices can gain remote management access to the switch. The virtual management interface on a CatOS-based switch is called sc0, while on Cisco IOS-based switches, it is called a switched virtual interface (SVI).

## CHAPTER 3

Trunking and Bandwidth Aggregation

So far you have learned how to essentially configure a switch as a single independent device. However, such a configuration is not a very valid representation of the real world, because the size of many networks dictates that more than one switch is required to service the connectivity needs of the network. You've also learned about *virtual LANs (VLANs)* and how each switch can service multiple logical LANs simultaneously, maintaining separation between each VLAN.

Trunking refers to the interconnection of switches to allow devices attached to a particular switch to communicate with devices attached to another switch. Trunking allows switches to transmit traffic from multiple VLANs configured locally across the trunk, thus allowing a VLAN to be distributed over multiple switches. Cisco routers and other devices also support trunking, which ensures they can communicate over multiple VLANs without requiring a physical interface per VLAN. The configuration of the multiple VLANs transported by trunks requires *VLAN trunking protocol* (VTP), a protocol that propagates VLAN information across multiple switches, to be enabled. VTP also controls whether or not trunks form under certain conditions.

Bandwidth aggregation refers to the bundling of multiple physical interfaces to create a single virtual interface that supports the combined bandwidth of each physical interface. Not only does this offer a performance increase over using just a single physical interface to connect to a device, but it also offers redundancy because a physical interface failure does not take down the virtual interface (other physical interfaces are still operational). Cisco Catalyst switches and routers support *EtherChannel*, a well established proprietary protocol that enables the bundling of up to eight physical interfaces between Cisco Catalyst switches, routers and other devices.

In this chapter, you learn how to interconnect switches and routers using trunks and how to configure bandwidth aggregation between switches and routers.

After some initial introductory material, this chapter presents the following configuration scenarios, which enable you to learn how to implement the technologies and concepts discussed in this chapter:

- Scenario 3-1: Configuring VLAN Trunking Protocol
- Scenario 3-2: Configuring Trunking Between Switches
- Scenario 3-3: VTP Pruning
- Scenario 3-4: Configuring EtherChannel

Introduction

The following sections are presented as an introduction:

- Trunking
- VLAN Trunking Protocol
- Bandwidth aggregation

Trunking

Trunking allows switches to interconnect with each other and allows transport traffic from multiple VLANs over the same Layer 2 link. If you think about a normal access port on a switch, all traffic that enters or leaves the switch has no indication whatsoever as to the VLAN the traffic belongs to. When a frame is received on an access port, the switch internally assigns a VLAN tag to the frame based upon the VLAN configured for the access port. For example, if a frame is received on an access port that belongs to VLAN 100, internally the switch assigns a VLAN tag of 100 to the frame. This tag ensures that the switch knows which set of egress ports the frame can exit—only egress ports that belong to VLAN 100. Once the frame forwarding decision has been made by referencing the bridge table, the frame is forwarded to the appropriate egress port, at which point the internal VLAN tag is stripped, restoring the original frame, which is then transmitted out the egress port.

Trunking extends this VLAN tagging concept across multiple switches. Essentially, a VLAN tag is attached to all traffic over a trunk interface, allowing the receiving switch to identify the correct VLAN that traffic belongs to. Figure 3-1 illustrates the concept of trunking.

Figure 3-1   *Trunking*

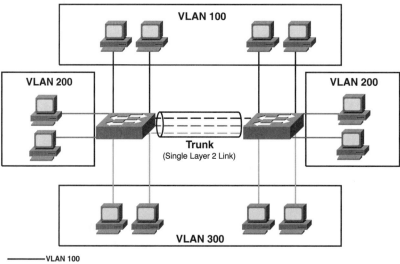

In Figure 3-1, three VLANs exist across two switches—VLANs 100, 200, and 300. The switches are interconnected by a *trunk* that transports (multiplexes) traffic from each VLAN. This arrangement means that the two PCs in VLAN 100 connected to the left-hand switch can communicate directly via Layer 2 with the two PCs in VLAN connected to the right-hand switch. To multiplex the traffic across a single physical link, each switch must *tag* each frame with the VLAN the frame belongs to. This tag allows the receiving switch to forward the frame out the correct ports.

Trunking Operation

Trunking operation defines the encapsulation a trunk uses for tagging VLANs and how trunks are negotiated. Three key considerations should be discussed with regards to trunking operation:

- Trunk encapsulations
- Trunk negotiation
- Controlling trunk traffic

Trunk Encapsulations

Trunk encapsulation refers to the protocol that is used to *tag* frames placed onto a trunk. On Ethernet networks, two trunking encapsulations are common within Cisco Catalyst switch networks:

- Cisco ISL
- IEEE 802.1Q

Historically, other trunking technologies, such as ATM LANE and 802.10, exist on such networks, but those technologies are outside the scope of this book.

Cisco *Inter-Switch Link (ISL)* is proprietary and was developed before the Institute of Electrical and Electronic Engineers (IEEE) 802.1Q standards-based approach was available. By default, two Cisco Catalyst switches will negotiate an ISL trunk on auto-negotiating trunk ports (as long as each side supports ISL). Many implementations still use ISL, so understanding ISL is important for your overall knowledge of trunking. Cisco ISL prepends a 26-byte ISL header and appends a 4-byte cyclic redundancy check (CRC) checksum to the original frame. The header contains various fields, including the all-important 10-bit VLAN ID, as shown in Figure 3-2.

Figure 3-2 *Inter-Switch Link Encapsulation*

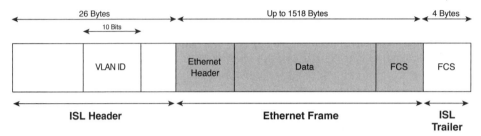

802.1Q was developed by the IEEE to allow multi-vendor support for VLANs. Another standard used within 802.1Q is *802.1p*, which allows for differentiation of the priority of different Layer 2 traffic. This standard is important for providing quality of service (QoS) at a Layer 2 level.

802.1Q is similar to ISL in that it tags frames; however, where it tags the frame is different. Figure 3-3 shows the structure of an 802.1Q-tagged Ethernet frame.

Figure 3-3 *802.1Q Ethernet Frame*

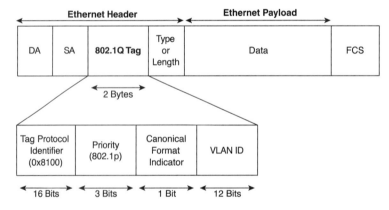

As you can see, the 802.1Q header is actually within the Ethernet frame. This arrangement is different from ISL, which encapsulates or wraps the Ethernet frame with an ISL header. Having the 802.1Q header within the frame introduces possible issues with the maximum transmission unit (MTU) for Ethernet. The IEEE *802.3ac* standard specifies an extension to the Ethernet MTU to allow for larger frames.

The priority field (802.1p) uses three bits to define the relative priority of the tagged traffic. This priority is designed to interoperate with the IP precedence field in IP packets (which surprisingly also uses 3 bits).

TIP	ISL has a *User* field that is used by Cisco Catalyst switches to carry priority information (identical to 802.1p) over ISL trunks. 802.1p is discussed in depth in Chapter 9, "Quality of Service."

Another notable difference between 802.1Q and ISL is that 802.1Q has the concept of a *native* VLAN, with all traffic belonging to the native VLAN being sent *without* an 802.1Q tag over the trunk. The purpose of the native VLAN is to allow interoperability with non-802.1Q ports (e.g., access ports). Because traffic is not tagged on the native VLAN, if a port configured as an 802.1Q trunk receives untagged traffic (for example, from a PC connected to the trunk), the switch assumes the traffic belongs to the native VLAN and is forwarded accordingly. Figure 3-4 demonstrates the concept of native VLANs.

Figure 3-4   *802.1Q Native VLAN*

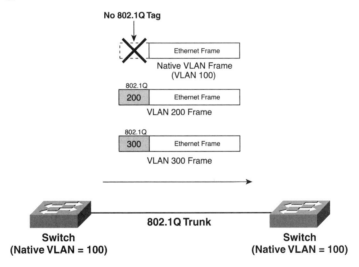

In Figure 3-4, the native VLAN is VLAN 100. Any VLAN 100 traffic transmitted across the trunk does *not* have an 802.1Q tag attached; however, all other VLAN traffic does have an 802.1Q tag attached. Because the native VLAN is not tagged, it is important that both sides of an 802.1Q trunk are configured correctly with the same native VLAN; otherwise, a switch may place native VLAN traffic into the wrong VLAN.

Trunking Negotiation

Trunking negotiation allows a port to auto-negotiate a trunk if the connected remote port supports trunking as well. This form of negotiation is similar in concept to EtherChannel negotiation. If both ends of a link support trunking, they can negotiate to form a trunk that transports traffic from multiple VLANs, rather than just a single VLAN.

Trunking uses a protocol called *Dynamic Trunking Protocol (DTP)* to facilitate the negotiation of trunks. Negotiation consists of sending DTP frames that specify various parameters to influence the negotiation process. DTP allows for the negotiation of the following:

- Whether or not the port becomes a trunk
- The trunk encapsulation used (i.e., ISL or 802.1Q)

By default, ISL encapsulation is preferred over 802.1Q, but encapsulation is dependent on the port capabilities of each end of the link, which are transmitted via DTP. You can hard code the encapsulation you wish to use and still allow DTP to negotiate whether a trunk comes up or not.

NOTE   DTP is derived from *Dynamic Inter-Switch Link* protocol, also known as *DISL*. DISL was developed by Cisco to specifically negotiate ISL-based trunks. DTP was then developed to include support for other trunk encapsulations, namely 802.1Q.

The *trunk mode* of a port determines whether or not it tries to negotiate a trunk using DTP. A port can be configured to five different modes:

- **On**—The port is hard coded to always be a trunk and sends DTP frames to indicate this.
- **Off**—The port is hard coded to *never* become a trunk (i.e., the port is an *access* port) and sends DTP frames that indicate the trunk mode is set to off.
- **Desirable**—The port tries to actively negotiate a trunk. This mode is the default mode of operation for Cisco IOS-based Catalyst switches.
- **Auto**—The port passively negotiates a trunk. The port does not actively send DTP frames, but responds to any received. This mode is the default mode for CatOS-based Catalyst switches.
- **Nonegotiate**—The port is hard coded to be a trunk and *never* sends DTP frames to try to negotiate a trunk.

As you can see from the preceding list, various modes exist that determine how a port negotiates (or doesn't negotiate) to become a trunk port (or non-trunk port). You learn about the compatible DTP modes in Scenario 3-2.

Allowed VLANs

By default, a trunk configured between two Cisco switches trunks traffic for *all* VLANs between the two switches. For example, if you have 100 active VLANs on each switch, when you set up a trunk, traffic from all 100 VLANs is trunked across the trunk. In some scenarios, this configuration may be undesirable because a switch might have devices connected to only a specific few VLANs. Cisco Catalyst switches allow you to configure a trunk to transport traffic from only a specific list of VLANs (called the *allowed VLAN list*).

VLAN Trunking Protocol

VLAN Trunking Protocol (*VTP*) is essentially a Cisco proprietary VLAN management tool that is designed to propagate VLAN information across a distributed switching environment that is interconnected via trunks. As you learned in Chapter 2, "VLAN Operations," VTP requires configuration before VLANs can be configured even on a single switch.

NOTE   A standards-based VLAN management protocol exists called Generic VLAN Registration Protocol (GVRP); it is an application of the Genetic Attribute Registration Protocol (GARP). GARP and GVRP are described in the IEEE 802.1p specification.

Figure 3-5 shows a scenario where four switches are interconnected via trunks in a distributed switching environment.

Figure 3-5   *Sample Distributed Switch Network*

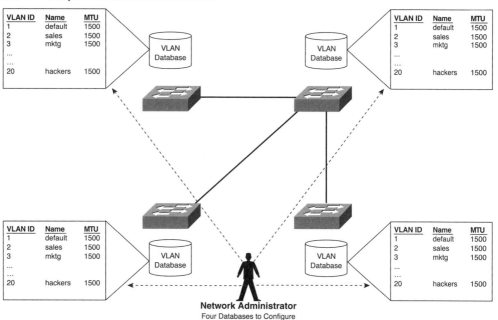

In Figure 3-5, 20 VLANs exist throughout the network, with devices existing in each VLAN located on any one of the four switches. You can see that 20 separate VLAN databases exist on each switch that define each VLAN, storing information such as VLAN ID, VLAN name, MTU, and more for each. If a network administrator had to manually define each database in this network and if a new VLAN were added or a change to an existing VLAN were made (e.g., changing a VLAN name), then the network administrator would need to configure the changes on each switch in the network (i.e., twenty times). Obviously, in large networks with many switches, this process becomes administratively prohibitive and prone to error.

VTP allows for the automatic propagation and distribution of VLAN database information throughout a Layer 2 network. VTP does not propagate port-based VLAN information (such as the ports belonging to each VLAN); it merely propagates information about each VLAN that exists in the network and the various administrative parameters (such as VLAN ID, name, MTU, and so on) associated with VLAN. Figure 3-6 shows the network of Figure 3-5 with a centralized VLAN database that is propagated to all other databases.

Figure 3-6   *Sample Distributed Switch Network with VTP*

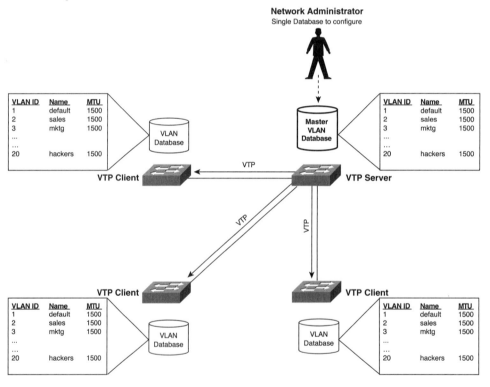

In Figure 3-6, a VTP *server* is defined that holds a master copy of the VLAN database. The VTP server has read-write access to the VLAN database, meaning administrators can configure the VLAN database only from the VTP server. The VTP server then distributes a copy of VLAN database to all the other switches, which are configured as VTP clients. A VTP client has only read access to the VLAN database, which ensures the VLAN database is kept in synchronization because only the VTP server can actually modify the VLAN database. As you can see in Figure 3-6, the VLAN database is configured centrally from a single point, and VTP distributes the VLAN information to the rest of the network.

VTP Operation

VTP is a client/server protocol that enables the propagation of VLAN information within an administrative collection of switches known as the *VTP domain*. Each switch can act as a VTP client or server, which determines if they have read-only or read-write access to the VLAN database. All VTP devices transmit *VTP advertisements*, which contain VLAN database information. The following components of VTP operation are now discussed:

- VTP domain
- VTP modes
- VTP advertisements

VTP Domain

A *VTP domain* defines a collection (or administrative boundary) of VTP devices that share the same VLAN database information. A VTP domain is a Layer 2 entity, meaning that a VTP domain can encompass only a Layer 2 network. Being a Layer 2 entity also means that Layer 3 devices, such as routers, terminate VTP domains.

The VTP domain is communicated in all VTP messages, which means that all devices within the same VTP domain must be configured with an identical VTP domain name. If a VTP message is received that includes a different VTP domain name from the local domain name, the VTP message is ignored. A Cisco Catalyst switch can belong only to a single VTP domain. Figure 3-7 demonstrates the concept of VTP domains.

In Figure 3-7, VTP advertisements sent between domain ABC and XYZ are rejected at the opposite domain because the VTP domain names are different and a switch can belong only to a single VTP domain. Notice also that the VTP domain ABC has been split into two due to the router that sits between each Layer 2 network. Although these VTP domains have the same name, they operate as separate entities because VTP messages cannot traverse the router.

VTP Modes

VTP is a client/server protocol that allows a VTP server read-write access to the VLAN database and allows a VTP client read-only access to the VLAN database. A Cisco Catalyst switch possesses the capability to act as a VTP server or client. The role that each switch plays in the VTP network is referred to as the *VTP mode*. The *server mode* is the default mode on Cisco Catalyst switches, ensuring that out of the box you can create VLANs (after setting a VTP domain name).

Figure 3-7 *VTP Domains*

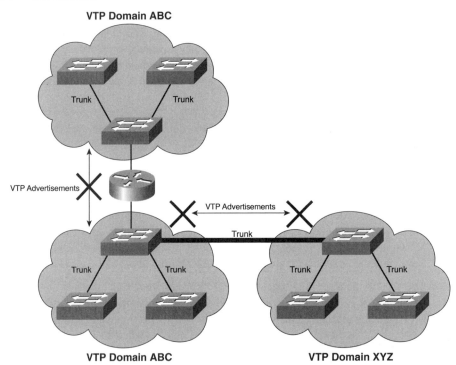

The VTP client/server architecture means you can configure a centralized VTP server switch from which you make any VLAN adds/moves or changes and all modifications to the VLAN database are propagated to each VTP client switch.

TIP   It is always good practice to enable at least two VTP servers in your network for redundancy purposes. A VTP server should be at or near the center of your LAN and should be the highest-performance switch available.

VTP also has another mode called *transparent*, in which the switch ignores any VTP messages but propagates the messages to ensure any VTP servers/clients connected to the switch receive VTP information.

TIP

A switch operating in VTP transparent mode and running VTP version 1 will not propagate any VTP messages that do not have the same VTP domain name as the locally configured VTP domain name. In VTP version 2, a VTP transparent switch propagates VTP messages, regardless of the VTP domain listed in each.

The final mode available is *off,* in which the VTP message is ignored and is not propagated to other switches. The VTP mode of off is available only on CatOS-based switches.

VTP Advertisements

VTP advertisements are the messages that are sent between VTP devices within a VTP domain. VTP advertisements are used to propagate VLAN database information. Each advertisement contains the following fields:

- **VTP Domain**—Defines the administrative scope of the advertisement. The advertisement is processed only by switches configured with the same VTP domain name.

- **VTP Version**—Defines the version of the VTP advertisement. VTP version 1 and version 2 currently exist today, with version 2 adding extra features.

TIP

All VTP devices throughout a VTP domain must operate the same VTP version. VTP clients learn the appropriate VTP version from VTP servers, so if you configure VTP version 2 on your VTP servers, all VTP clients automatically operate in version 2 mode providing they are version 2 compatible.

- **VTP Configuration Revision Number**—Indicates the revision of the configuration information version contained within the advertisement. This number is incremented each time a modification is made to the VLAN database and allows a switch to determine if the local VLAN database is up to date.

- **VLAN ID**—Indicates the ID of a VLAN that should be added, modified, or deleted from the VLAN database.

- **Other VLAN parameters relevant to the VLAN ID**—Includes parameters such as VLAN name.

VTP advertisements are sent periodically (every 30 seconds) or whenever a VLAN configuration change is made. VTP advertisements are multicast via Ethernet SNAP frames, using a multicast address of 01-00-0c-cc-cc-cc and a SNAP protocol type of 0x2003. Using multicast ensures that VTP advertisements are propagated across other network devices (such as hubs); they may be located between switches. VTP advertisements are only ever sent on trunk ports and are *always* sent on VLAN 1 (hence, one reason why VLAN 1 cannot be deleted).

Advanced VTP Features

VTP offers some advanced features, which includes the ability to authenticate VTP advertisements, allowing receiving switches to verify an advertisement is authentic. This verification is achieved via the use of a VTP password that is used to sign each VTP advertisement. VTP also allows for the *pruning* of trunks, which is the automatic clearing of unnecessary VLANs from trunks.

VTP Security

VTP provides a *VTP password* option that allows all messages to be signed with a message digest (MD5) *hash*. A hash is a one-way function that combines the contents of the message with the VTP password to create a unique hash value of fixed length, which is then appended to the VTP message. The VTP message cannot be derived from the hash because the hashing algorithm is one way. When a VTP device receives the message (with a hash attached), it runs the message through the same MD5 algorithm with the locally configured password. If the locally computed hash value matches the received hash value (this only happens if the passwords are identical on the sending device and receiving device), then the message is authentic.

VTP Pruning

VTP pruning is a feature that allows trunks to be pruned automatically of VLAN traffic. If you enable trunking and do not manually clear any VLANs from the trunk, traffic from all VLANs is propagated across the trunk. If a switch does not connect to any devices within a particular VLAN, the switch does not need to receive traffic for that VLAN.

VTP pruning enables each switch to dynamically signal (via VTP Join messages) to a remote switch if it needs to receive traffic for each VLAN in the database. This process allows trunks to dynamically prune unnecessary VLAN traffic.

Bandwidth Aggregation

Bandwidth aggregation is used to provide the aggregation of multiple physical links, creating a single virtual link that carries the bandwidth sum (or close to the sum) of each physical link. Bandwidth aggregation is used to provide both performance and redundancy. Figure 3-8 illustrates the basic concept of bandwidth aggregation, as it applies to LANs.

Figure 3-8   *Bandwidth Aggregation on a LAN*

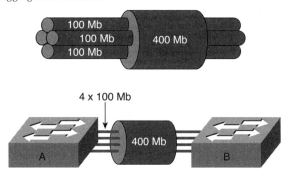

In Figure 3-8, four physical 100 Mbps full-duplex interfaces are aggregated to create a single virtual 400 Mbps full-duplex (800 Mbps bandwidth in total) interface, which boosts performance between the two switches. The aggregated interface is represented as a single Layer 2 link to each switch, which means spanning tree (discussed in Chapter 4, "Spanning Tree") sees only a single interface as opposed to four separate interfaces. If a physical interface fails, the virtual interface stays up (it just has one less physical interface, so obviously offers a lesser amount of performance), which means the spanning tree doesn't see the failure and does not react to the failure, preventing disruption to the Layer 2 network. In short, bandwidth aggregation provides physical layer redundancy that is transparent to higher layers, removing the requirement for protocols such as spanning tree to deal with redundant links.

Cisco was the first switch vendor to introduce a bandwidth aggregation protocol called *EtherChannel* for LAN switches, and EtherChannel is still popular today. Although Ether-Channel is proprietary, the demand for the feature is such that many third-party network card vendors offer support for the protocol.

NOTE   Recently, a standards-based bandwidth aggregation specification was released by the IEEE; it is known as the *IEEE 802.1ad* standard. Much of how this protocol works is derived from EtherChannel.

EtherChannel Operation

EtherChannel aggregates up to eight physical Ethernet links into a single virtual Layer 2 link (also known as an *EtherChannel bundle*), identical to the topology shown in Figure 3-1. The goals of EtherChannel are to provide the following:

- Performance
- Redundancy and high availability

EtherChannel enhances performance by transmitting frames over multiple physical links. EtherChannel provides redundancy in the event of a physical link failure, because other physical links are still up to transport frames. High availability is achieved by Ether-Channel's fast recovery times in the event of a failure, ensuring the impact to the network is zero or minimal at worst.

EtherChannel Performance

If you consider Figure 3-8, you can see that four physical links exist over which to transport a frame. By load sharing over each of these links, performance of up to the combined speed of the links is possible. To achieve the performance results possible by aggregating multiple physical links, EtherChannel supports the use of one or more of the following mechanisms to load share traffic over the bundle:

- Load sharing based upon Layer 2 (MAC) addressing
- Load sharing based upon Layer 3 (IP) addressing
- Load sharing based upon Layer 4 parameters (only supported on newer Cisco Catalyst switches)

The first and simplest implementation of EtherChannel loads shares based on the source or destination MAC address (Layer 2 address) of the frame being transmitted. Figure 3-9 illustrates this process.

Figure 3-9   *Load Sharing Using MAC Addresses*

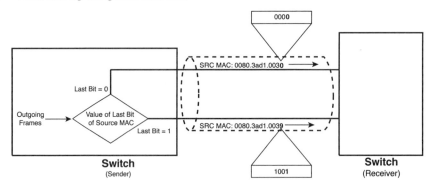

In Figure 3-9, load sharing based upon source MAC address is enabled. The source MAC address of each frame is examined, and the last bit of the MAC address is used to determine which physical link the frame should be transmitted over. If four links existed in the bundle, the last two bits of the MAC address are used, because this provides four possible values (one for each link). The scenario described in Figure 3-9 has a major issue. Because the load sharing is based upon the source MAC address, if a large number of frames originates from the same source MAC address, all of those frames are sent across the same link. Figure 3-10 illustrates this problem.

Figure 3-10   *Limitations of MAC-based Load Sharing*

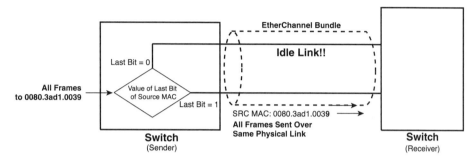

You could overcome the issue in Figure 3-10 by using destination MAC addresses to load share. However, this scenario also becomes a problem if the scenario in Figure 3-10 is reversed, where a large number of frames are sent to the same destination MAC address.

TIP   You don't have to configure the same method of load sharing at each end of an EtherChannel bundle. It is common to use source-based forwarding on a switch (connected to a router) and then use destination-based forwarding on the router. Because all communication to the router is performed using the same destination MAC address, source-based forwarding on the switch is configured to prevent frames from traversing only a single physical link in the bundle.

Some implementations also support load sharing based upon Layer 3 (IP addresses) and Layer 4 parameters (TCP/UDP ports), using similar principles to those shown in Figure 3-10 and just replacing Layer 2 addressing with Layer 3 addressing and/or Layer 4 parameters. Some Cisco Catalyst switches can combine source and destination addresses by performing an *Exclusive OR (XOR)* operation to both the source and destination addresses. At its simplest, this combining involves performing an XOR of the low-order bits of the source and destination addresses. In more recent Catalyst switches, the source and destination addresses are hashed to produce a much more random output than the low-order bits of a network address, with each hash then being XORed.

EtherChannel Redundancy and High Availability

If a link fails in an EtherChannel bundle, traffic that would normally be sent over the failed link is automatically redirected over the remaining active links. This failure is transparent to the network and is performed automatically by the switch. Obviously, the performance of the bundle is degraded while the failed link is down, and it is important to be able to detect and respond quickly to the failure. Cisco Catalyst switches can send a Simple Network Management Protocol (SNMP) trap or SYSLOG trap upon a link failure to notify network operations staff of the failure.

EtherChannel Negotiation (PAgP)

Port Aggregation Protocol (PAgP) enables EtherChannel bundles to be dynamically created between two devices, depending on the capabilities of each device's ports. When a port configured in an EtherChannel bundle comes up, the PAgP mode determines whether or not the port forms a bundle and whether or not it attempts to negotiate a bundle by sending PAgP frames. PAgP peers exchange information that identifies each other (which ensures that ports in a configured EtherChannel bundle that are connected to separate devices do not form a bundle) and information that indicates which ports specifically should bundle (which ensures that the correct ports form a bundle). PAgP peers also exchange information about features that cause known issues with EtherChannel, which then stops the bundle from forming.

NOTE PAgP frames are exchanged via SNAP Ethernet multicast frames with a destination address of 01-00-0c-cc-cc-cc and a SNAP protocol type of 0x0104. PAgP frames are always sent on VLAN 1 over trunk interfaces.

EtherChannel bundles can operate in one of the following PAgP modes:

- **On**—Forces the port to channel. The port does not use PAgP at all.
- **Off**—Disables the port from channeling. The port does not use PAgP at all.
- **Auto**—Enables the port to passively channel. The port does not actively send PAgP frames, but responds to any received.
- **Desirable**—Enables the port to actively channel. The port sends PAgP frames trying to negotiate a channel.

The sending of PAgP frames is disabled when you use the on or off modes, while PAgP frames are exchanged when you use the auto or desirable modes. Make sure you understand which PAgP modes are compatible with each other, so that an EtherChannel bundle will form. This topic is discussed in detail in Scenario 3-4.

NOTE The *IEEE 802.1ad* specification describes a bandwidth aggregation technique for LAN interfaces that is very similar to Cisco EtherChannel aggregation. Instead of using PAgP, link aggregation control protocol (LACP) is used to negotiate bundles. LACP defines four modes of operation, very similar to PAgP. At the time of this writing, support for LACP is offered only in the Catalyst 4000 and 6000 switches, beginning with the CatOS 7.1(1) release.

Scenario 3-1: Configuring VLAN Trunking Protocol

In Chapter 2, Scenario 2-2, you were introduced to VLAN Trunking Protocol (VTP), which was required in order to allow the configuration and creation of VLANs on a single Cisco Catalyst switch. You learned how to implement a basic VTP configuration so that you could create VLANs. In this scenario, you learn how to configure VTP in much more depth, because it is important when you start interconnecting switches via trunks and want to centralize your VLAN configuration.

Figure 3-11 shows the topology that is used for this scenario and the next two scenarios (Scenarios 3-1 to 3-3):

Figure 3-11 *Scenario 3-1, Scenario 3-2, and Scenario 3-3 Topology*

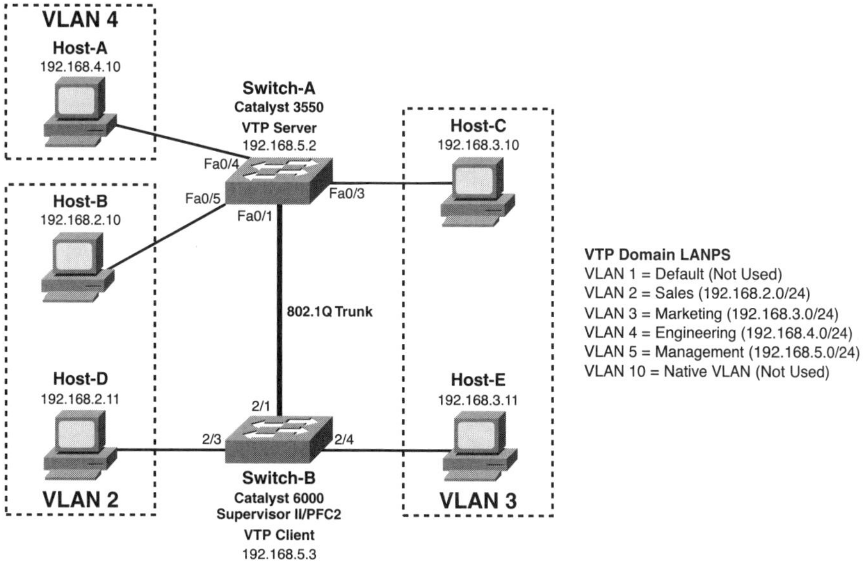

In Figure 3-11, six VLANs exist in the network—VLANs 1-5 and 10. The VLANs can be defined as follows:

- **VLAN 1**—The default VLAN on Cisco Catalyst switches that is used for a number of control communication protocols and cannot be disabled.

- **VLAN 2, 3, and 4**—User VLANs that host the actual data devices that make up the network. Data exchanged on these VLANs is referred to as user data.

- **VLAN 5**—Management VLAN used for managing network devices.

- **VLAN 10**—The native VLAN used on trunk between Switch-A and Switch-B. The native VLAN is used in 802.1Q trunks and defines the only VLAN over which traffic is sent untagged on the trunk.

NOTE	Many organizations commonly use VLAN 1 as the native VLAN and ensure user data is not present on this VLAN. This scenario uses VLAN 10 for the native VLAN to demonstrate how to change the native VLAN on trunks.

An 802.1Q trunk is to be configured between Switch-A and Switch-B for the purposes of extending each of these VLANs across both switches.

When configuring trunks, you normally configure VTP first, because that allows you to create all the appropriate VLANs required for the network. VTP also influences whether or not trunk interfaces operating in specific modes will form, so ensuring VTP configuration is in place first ensures trunks will form correctly.

Configuration Planning

With regards to VTP configuration, the following describes how the various VTP parameters need to be planned and how each parameter should be configured:

- **VTP domain name**—The VTP domain name determines the administrative boundary, and all switches within the domain must be configured with an identical domain name throughout. In this scenario, the VTP domain name is configured as LANPS on Switch-A and Switch-B.

- **VTP mode of operation**—VLAN configuration is performed on VTP servers, which then propagates the VLAN configurations to VTP clients. If you do not want to implement VTP on your network (more on this later), you can configure a VTP mode of transparent or off. If you are implementing VTP, you need to plan which switches are to be VTP servers. The ideal choices for VTP servers are core/distribution switches. You should always have at least one backup VTP server. In this scenario, Switch-A is configured as the VTP server, with Switch-B configured as a VTP client. This arrangement means that all VLAN configuration is implemented on Switch-A, with VTP updating the VLAN database on Switch-B.

- **VTP version**—All VTP switches must use the same version throughout (version 1 or 2). Version 2 adds some enhancements and is required for Token Ring VLAN support. For this scenario, VTP version 2 is used.

- **VTP password**—If you wish to secure the network against spoofed VTP advertisements, you can configure a password on each VTP switch. This password must be identical throughout the domain. In this scenario, a VTP password of *cisco* is configured.

- **VTP pruning**—You can control the VLAN traffic transported over trunks automatically by using VTP pruning. This pruning is recommended because it optimizes the network by eliminating unnecessary traffic propagation. In this scenario, VTP pruning is not configured; instead it is configured in Scenario 3-2.

Scenario Prerequisites

To successfully commence the configuration tasks required to complete this scenario, Table 3-1 describes the prerequisite configurations required on each device in the scenario topology. Any configurations not listed can be assumed as being the default configuration.

Table 3-1   *Scenario 3-1 Requirements*

Device	Required Configuration	
	Parameter	**Value**
Switch-A	Hostname	Switch-A
	Enable/Telnet Password	cisco
Switch-B	Hostname	Switch-B
	Enable/Telnet Password	cisco
Configuration Tasks		

When you first configure a switch that will be attaching to a VTP domain, do NOT connect the switch to the VTP domain until after the appropriate VTP configuration is in place. Waiting until after the configuration is in place ensures that the new switch does not accidentally overwrite the current VLAN database for the VTP domain with its own VLAN database.

Be aware that if a new switch is attached to an existing VTP domain and the new switch has the same VTP domain and has a VLAN database configuration revision that is higher than that which is currently present in the existing network, the existing VLAN database is overwritten with the VLAN database on the new switch, *regardless of whether the switch is a VTP server or client.* Yes, that's right; even if the switch is a VTP client, if it has the same VTP domain name and a higher VLAN database configuration revision number, the existing VLAN database is overwritten. If this happens, you will know about it quickly because the network usually comes to a grinding halt. This halt happens because any ports that belong to a VLAN that has been deleted by the new VLAN database introduced by the new switch are placed in an orphaned state, where they belong to no VLAN whatsoever and, thus, are not operational.

The safest method of configuring VTP for a new switch that is connecting to an existing VTP domain is to ensure it is disconnected from the network, configure the appropriate VTP domain name, ensure the VLAN database configuration revision number is lower than that of the current VTP domain, and then attach the switch to the network. Although this mechanism protects the VTP domain from accidental misconfiguration, it does not protect the VTP domain from intentional misconfiguration. Another mechanism that can be used to prevent against intentional misconfiguration is to implement VTP passwords on your domain to protect against rogue VTP servers intentionally erasing all or parts of your VLAN database.

NOTE	Out of the box, a new Cisco Catalyst switch has a VTP domain name set to NULL, but if you are redeploying old switches, the VTP domain might already be set. Be especially cautious with Cisco IOS switches because the VTP configuration is stored in the VLAN database file (VLAN.DAT), which is separate from the switch configuration file. When you erase the switch configuration file, the VTP and VLAN configuration, including VTP password configuration, is NOT erased, meaning just using VTP passwords to protect against the accidental deletion of VLANs might not be sufficient.

To configure VTP, you must perform the following tasks:

- Configure VTP servers
- Configure VTP clients
- Verify VTP operation

Configuring VTP Servers

VTP servers are the most important component of the VTP domain because they have full access to the VLAN database and are responsible for propagating VLAN database information to VTP clients. The following describes how you configure a VTP server:

- Configure a VTP domain
- Configure VTP server mode
- Configure VTP parameters such as VTP version, password, and pruning

In Figure 3-11, Switch-A is the VTP server and is Cisco IOS-based. You can configure VTP parameters on Cisco IOS switches from the following configuration modes:

- **VLAN configuration mode**—This is the original configuration mode for configuring the VLAN database and is supported on all Cisco IOS Catalyst switches.

- **Privileged EXEC mode**—On newer Cisco IOS Catalyst switches, you can configure the VTP password, VTP version, and VTP pruning from privileged EXEC mode. Using this mechanism is not recommended because it has been superseded by VTP configuration via global configuration mode.

- **Global configuration mode**—On newer Cisco IOS Catalyst switches, you can configure most or all VTP parameter names from global configuration mode, depending on the IOS version (the latest IOS supports the configuration of all VTP parameters). If supported, this mode is the recommended method of configuring VTP.

Configuring VTP via VLAN Configuration Mode

All Cisco IOS Catalyst switches support configuring VTP via VLAN configuration mode. To enter VLAN configuration mode, you must specify the **vlan database** privilege EXEC command, which places you into VLAN configuration mode, as demonstrated on Switch-A in Example 3-1.

Example 3-88 *Accessing VLAN Configuration Mode on Cisco IOS*

```
Switch-A# vlan database
Switch-A(vlan)#
```

The (vlan) portion of the prompt indicates that you are currently in VLAN configuration mode.

Once you are in VLAN configuration mode, the **vtp** command is used to configure each of the various VTP parameters.

```
Switch(vlan)# vtp {domain domain-name | password password | pruning | v2-mode |
  {server | client | transparent}}
```

Each of the keywords shown is self explanatory, except for **v2-mode**, which enables VTP version 2. The following bullet list describes the default VTP configuration on a Cisco IOS switch:

- **Domain name**—No domain name is defined
- **Mode**—Server mode
- **Password**—No password is defined
- **Pruning**—Disabled
- **Version**—Version 1 is enabled

When configuring a VTP server, you should configure all of the VTP parameters listed. When configuring a VTP client, you need to configure all the parameters listed except for the VTP version because it is propagated from the VTP server.

Example 3-2 demonstrates configuring VTP on Switch-A for this scenario.

Example 3-89 *Configuring VTP via VLAN Configuration Mode on Cisco IOS*

```
Switch-A# vlan database
Switch-A(vlan)# vtp domain LANPS
Changing VTP domain name from NULL to LANPS
Switch-A(vlan)# vtp server
Device mode already VTP SERVER.
Switch-A(vlan)# vtp password cisco
Setting device VLAN database password to cisco.
Switch-A(vlan)# vtp v2-mode
V2 mode enabled.
Switch-A(vlan)# exit
APPLY completed.
Exiting....
```

Notice that you must exit VLAN configuration mode by issuing the **exit** command, which ensures the configuration changes made in VLAN configuration mode are written to the VLAN.DAT database file.

Once you have configured VTP, you should verify your configuration using the **show vtp status** command, as demonstrated in Example 3-3.

Example 3-90 *Verifying VTP Configuration on Cisco IOS*

```
Switch-A# show vtp status
VTP Version                     : 2
Configuration Revision          : 1
Maximum VLANs supported locally : 1005
Number of existing VLANs        : 5
VTP Operating Mode              : Server
VTP Domain Name                 : LANPS
VTP Pruning Mode                : Disabled
VTP V2 Mode                     : Enabled
VTP Traps Generation            : Disabled
MD5 digest                      : 0xF8 0x79 0x2E 0x2D 0xF9 0xC1 0xCE 0x9E
Configuration last modified by 0.0.0.0 at 3-1-93 00:27:49
Local updater ID is 192.168.1.2 on interface Vl1
    (lowest numbered VLAN interface found)
```

In Example 3-3, you can see that the configuration of Example 3-2 has been implemented, as indicated by the shaded output. The MD5 digest line represents the current VTP configuration revision hashed with the configured password.

Configuring a VTP server that is connecting to an existing VTP domain should always be performed offline, with careful attention paid to the configuration revision numbers on the new VTP server and the existing VTP domain. Always ensure that the configuration revision number on the new VTP server is lower than the configuration revision number of the existing VTP domain so that when the new VTP server connects to the VTP domain, it accepts the VLAN database of the existing VTP domain instead of overwriting the existing VLAN database. You can use the **show vtp status** command on Cisco IOS (see Example 3-3) or the **show vtp domain** command on CatOS (see Example 3-6) to determine the current VLAN database revision number. If you find that the configuration revision number of the new VTP server is higher, you must reset the configuration revision number to zero. This reset is achieved by temporarily changing the VTP domain on the new VTP server to a temporary value and then changing the VTP domain name back to the appropriate value. Every time the VTP domain name is changed, the VLAN database configuration revision number is reset to zero.

Configuring VTP via Global Configuration Mode

NOTE   Although you can use privileged EXEC mode to configure some VTP parameters, using this mode is not recommended. Hence, no coverage is provided for using privileged EXEC mode configuration.

Newer Cisco IOS Catalyst switches support configuring VTP via global configuration mode. The **vtp** global configuration command is used to configure VTP, with most of the command syntax identical to the **vtp** VLAN configuration command. Example 3-4 demonstrates configuring VTP via global configuration mode on Switch-A.

Example 3-91   *Configuring VTP via Global Configuration Mode on Switch-A*

```
Switch-A# configure terminal
Switch-A(config)# vtp domain LANPS
Domain name already set to LANPS.
Switch-A(config)# vtp mode server
Device mode already VTP SERVER.
Switch-A(config)# vtp password cisco
Password already set to cisco.
Switch-A(config)# vtp version 2
VTP mode already in V2.
```

You can see that some of the VLAN configuration commands vary slightly from the global configuration commands shown in Example 3-4.

TIP   Although global configuration mode is used to configure VTP in Example 3-4, the configuration is stored only in the switch configuration file if the VTP mode is set to transparent. Regardless of how VTP is configured, all VTP parameters are stored in the VLAN database. In the case of VTP transparent operation, when a switch boots up, it reads the VTP configuration parameters from the switch configuration file and overwrites the VTP configuration in the VLAN database. If the VTP mode is server or client, the switch configuration file will not include the VTP commands. Instead, the VLAN database is used to read the VTP configuration.

Configuring VTP Clients

Once the VTP servers for the network are in place, you can configure VTP clients. In Figure 3-11, Switch-B is a VTP client and, hence, requires CatOS configuration of VTP. For this reason, this section demonstrates configuration of CatOS for VTP. However, be aware that on Cisco

IOS, configuring VTP clients follows the same concepts for configuring VTP servers on Cisco IOS.

To configure VTP parameters on a CatOS switch, use the **set vtp** command:

```
Console> (enable) set vtp [domain domain-name] [mode {client | server |
    transparent | off}] [passwd password] [pruning {enable | disable}]
    [v2 {enable | disable}]
```

Notice that CatOS supports the additional VTP mode of off, unlike Cisco IOS, which does not support this mode.

NOTE   The VTP off mode is supported from CatOS 7.*x*.

When configuring a VTP client, if the switch is to be connected to an existing VTP domain, ensure that VTP configuration is performed offline before the switch is connected to the network. This safeguard is to ensure that the VLAN database of the existing VTP domain is not overwritten accidentally by the VTP client (same concept as for VTP servers).

When configuring a VTP client, you must ensure that you configure VTP version and pruning parameters in VTP server or transparent mode, because CatOS (and Cisco IOS) does not allow you to modify these parameters in VTP client mode. Once these parameters have been defined, you can then enable VTP client mode. You can configure the VTP password and VTP domain name at any time, regardless of the VTP mode.

NOTE   VTP clients can automatically learn the appropriate VTP version and VTP pruning settings from VTP servers, meaning you don't necessarily need to explicitly configure these settings on VTP clients.

Example 3-5 demonstrates configuring Switch-B as a VTP client.

Example 3-92   *Configuring VTP Client Operation on Switch-B*

```
Switch-B> (enable) set vtp v2 enable
This command will enable the version 2 function in the entire management domain.
All devices in the management domain should be version2-capable before enabling.
Do you want to continue (y/n) [n]? y
VTP domain modified
Switch-B> (enable) set vtp mode client
VTP domain  modified
Switch-B> (enable) set vtp passwd cisco
Generating MD5 secret for the password ....
Switch-B> (enable) set vtp domain LANPS
VTP domain LANPS modified
```

To verify VTP configuration on CatOS, use the **show vtp domain** command, as demonstrated in Example 3-6 on Switch-B.

Example 3-93 *Verifying VTP Configuration on Switch-B*

```
Switch-B> (enable) show vtp domain
Domain Name                             Domain Index VTP Version Local Mode  Password
------------------------------- ------------ ----------- ----------- ----------
LANPS                                       1            2           server      configured

Vlan-count Max-vlan-storage Config Revision Notifications
---------- ---------------- ---------------- ------------
5          1023             1                disabled

Last Updater    V2 Mode  Pruning  PruneEligible on Vlans
--------------- -------- -------- -------------------------
0.0.0.0         enabled  disabled 2-1000
```

In Example 3-6, the shaded line verifies the various parameters configured in Example 3-5.

Verifying VTP Operation

Once you have implemented VTP on each switch in the network, assuming all switches are connected via trunks, you should be able to modify the VLAN database on your VTP server(s) and verify that the modifications are propagated to all VTP clients.

NOTE   VTP advertisements are sent only over trunk ports and are not sent over access ports (ports that belong only to a single VLAN).

In the topology of Figure 3-11, when you connect Switch-A and Switch-B, by default, the connections between each switch will actually form a trunk automatically, as the DTP mode of a Cisco IOS switch is desirable by default, and the DTP mode of a CatOS switch is *auto* by default. This means that without even configuring trunks on either Switch-A or Switch-B, both switches should be able to communicate via VTP.

NOTE   If you are connecting two CatOS switches, a trunk will not automatically form, because both sides are set to auto by default. If you are connecting two Cisco IOS switches, a trunk will automatically form, because both sides are set to dynamic by default.

Based upon this default behavior, you can now see how each of the VLANs in Figure 3-11 can be created on Switch-A (the VTP server), which is then propagated to Switch-B via VTP. Example 3-7 shows the creation of VLANs 2, 3, 4, and 10 on Switch-A:

Example 3-94 *Creating VLANs on Switch-A (VTP Server)*

```
Switch-A# configure terminal
Switch-A(config)# vlan 2
Switch-A(config-vlan)# name Sales
Switch-A(config-vlan)# exit
Switch-A(config)# vlan 3
Switch-A(config-vlan)# name Marketing
Switch-A(config-vlan)# exit
Switch-A(config)# vlan 4
Switch-A(config-vlan)# name Engineering
Switch-A(config-vlan)# exit
Switch-A(config)# vlan 5
Switch-A(config-vlan)# name Management
Switch-A(config-vlan)# exit
Switch-A(config)# vlan 10
Switch-A(config-vlan)# name Native
Switch-A(config-vlan)# exit
```

After the creation of the VLANs in Example 3-7, Switch-A should increment the VTP configuration revision number by 5 (one for each VLAN modification) and send VTP advertisements containing the VLAN modifications to Switch-B. Example 3-8 shows the output of the **show vlan** command on Switch-B after the configuration of Example 3-7 is implemented.

Example 3-95 *Verifying the VLAN Database is Synchronized with the VTP Server on Switch-B*

```
Switch-B> (enable) show vlan
VLAN Name                             Status    IfIndex Mod/Ports, Vlans
---- -------------------------------- --------- ------- -----------------------
1    default                          active    72      1/1-2,2/1-48
2    Sales                            active    77
3    Marketing                        active    78
4    Engineering                      active    79
5    Management                       active    80
10   Native                           active    81
1002 fddi-default                     active    73
1003 trcrf-default                    active    76
1004 fddinet-default                  active    74
1005 trbrf-default                    active    75      1003
...  <Output truncated>
...
```

Notice in Example 3-8 that VLAN 2 (Sales), VLAN 3 (Marketing), VLAN 4 (Engineering), VLAN 5 (Management), and VLAN 10 (Native) are present in the VLAN database.

Example 3-9 shows the output of the **show vtp domain** command on Switch-B after the configuration of Example 3-7 is implemented.

Example 3-96 *Viewing VTP Domain Information on Switch-B*

```
Switch-B> (enable) show vtp domain
Domain Name                          Domain Index VTP Version Local Mode  Password
------------------------------------ ------------ ----------- ----------- ----------
LANPS                                1            2           client      configured

Vlan-count Max-vlan-storage Config Revision Notifications
---------- ---------------- --------------- -------------
10         1023             6               disabled

Last Updater    V2 Mode  Pruning  PruneEligible on Vlans
--------------- -------- -------- ------------------------
192.168.1.2     enabled  disabled 2-1000
```

If you compare Example 3-6 (VTP domain information prior to configuration of VLANs) and Example 3-9 (VTP domain information after the configuration of VLANs), you might notice in Example 3-9 that the Config Revision field indicates that the revision number of the VLAN database is now 6, compared with 1 in Example 3-6. This change represents the five VLAN configuration changes that were made on Switch-A in Example 3-7. You can also see that the VLAN count has increased from 5 to 10, indicating new VLANs are present in the VLAN database.

VTP Recommendations

Although VTP has many positive benefits on the surface, many organizations do not implement VTP. As with making any decision about a feature, arguments exist both for and against implementing the feature. The following lists reasons why VTP should be implemented:

- VLAN administrative overhead is reduced because the VLAN database is configured and managed from a central location and distributed automatically to all switches in the VTP domain.

- VTP ensures VLAN databases on each switch are identical.

- VTP pruning enables the dynamic clearing of allowed VLANs on a trunk, increasing network efficiency.

The following lists reasons why many organizations do not implement VTP:

- The ability of VTP to distribute VLAN database information throughout the network means any configuration errors affect the entire network. For example, if a VLAN is accidentally deleted on a VTP server, the change is immediately propagated to all VTP clients, which causes loss of network connectivity for all devices attached to the deleted VLAN. Without VTP, the configuration error has local significance only.

- The risk of a VTP server or VTP client being added to the network with a higher revision number and overwriting the VLAN database is eliminated.

- If VTP passwords are not configured, the network is vulnerable to denial-of-service (DoS) attacks, where an attacker injects spoofed VTP messages that delete VLANs, causing network outages.

- Not having VTP requires the manual pruning of trunks, which has benefits over VTP pruning. With VTP pruning, even if trunks are cleared for VLANs, spanning tree still operates over the pruned VLANs. Spanning tree must operate throughout the entire network because pruned VLANs may need to be added back to trunks dynamically. With manual pruning, the spanning-tree topology for pruned VLANs stops where pruning is implemented, reducing spanning-tree diameter and eliminating the need for spanning-tree instances to be maintained on all switches for pruned VLANs.

As a general recommendation, it is best to not implement VTP in an ongoing fashion for the reasons just listed . If you are configuring a new network that has a large number of switches, you can use VTP for a temporary amount of time as a convenient method to distribute VLAN configuration to each switch. Once the VLAN configuration is in place, disable VTP by configuring VTP transparent mode on each switch. If you need to make VLAN configuration changes in the future and are worried about the administrative overhead of doing so without VTP, LAN management platforms such as CiscoWorks 2000 enable you to distribute VLAN configuration changes via alternative mechanisms (i.e., SNMP or Telnet) in an automated fashion. If you must implement VTP, *always* configure a VTP password and always preconfigure VTP before adding new switches to the network.

Scenario 3-2: Configuring Trunking Between Switches

Trunks are an essential part of any switched network and allow a set of distributed switches to appear as a single switching fabric. By implementing trunks, users within the same VLAN can be connected to different switches, with the trunks carrying intra-VLAN traffic across the distributed switch network. Trunks can also be used to connect to end devices such as routers or servers, providing connectivity to multiple VLANs without the need for multiple physical network interfaces. Trunks and distributed VLANs can be very flexible; devices are not constrained to physical switches to ensure that they are connected to the correct VLAN, which allows for devices to be easily moved between physical switches while still maintaining connectivity to the VLAN that the device is supposed to belong to. In a sense, trunks and distributed VLANs provide "virtual cabling." On the flip side, trunks and distributed VLANs also introduce extra complexity in the network and can be difficult to troubleshoot if planned poorly, so they should be used only with careful planning and only where required.

In this scenario, you will continue working on the topology from the last scenario, learning how to configure trunking between Switch-A and Switch-B.

Configuration Tasks

Before configuring a trunk, ensure that the appropriate VTP and VLAN configuration is in place. Trunks enable VTP communication—which are essentially control plane communications for VLANs—because VTP advertisements are forwarded only across trunks. Once VTP has distributed the appropriate VLAN configuration to each switch, ports can be placed into the appropriate VLANs and data forwarding can begin. If you are not using VTP, you need to ensure that each switch in the network is configured with the appropriate VLAN information, and you need to do this to manually define the list of VLANs that are transported across each trunk. You don't necessarily need to have VTP and VLAN configurations in place before creating trunks; for example, in Scenario 3-1, a trunk actually formed between Switch-A and Switch-B before any VTP and VLAN configurations were in place, because of the default DTP modes configured on each switch.

Assuming the appropriate VTP and VLAN configuration parameters are in place or are to be configured after configuring trunks, the following lists the configuration tasks required to configure a trunk:

- Configuring trunk encapsulation
- Configuring trunk mode
- Configuring the native VLAN (802.1Q)
- Configuring the allowed VLAN list
- Verifying trunk configuration

Configuring Trunk Encapsulation

On Ethernet networks, you have two options for trunk encapsulation:

- Cisco ISL
- 802.1Q

Your choice may be limited by the capabilities of the switch you are using. Table 3-2 describes trunking support on Cisco Catalyst switches.

Table 3-2 *Trunking Support on Cisco Catalyst Switches*

Platform	Encapsulations	Notes
1900/2800	ISL	Only DISL is supported DTP is not supported
2900XL/3500XL	ISL 802.1Q	DISL and DTP are not supported
2950	802.1Q	-
3550	ISL 802.1Q	-

continues

Table 3-2   *Trunking Support on Cisco Catalyst Switches (Continued)*

Platform	Encapsulations	Notes
2900/4000 (CatOS)	802.1Q	Use **show port capabilities** to determine if modules support trunking
4000 Supevisor 3/4 (Cisco IOS)	ISL 802.1Q	ISL is not supported on ports 3-18 of WS-X4418-GB ISL is not supported on WS-X4412-GB-T
5000/5500	ISL 802.1Q	Use **show port capabilities** to determine if modules support trunking
6000/6500 (CatOS and Cisco IOS)	ISL 802.1Q	ISL is not supported on 10 Gigabit Ethernet switching modules

For example, referring to Table 3-2 the Catalyst 2950 and 4000 series switches support only 802.1Q encapsulation, while the Catalyst 3550 series switches support both 802.1Q and ISL encapsulation. In this scenario, both Switch-A (Catalyst 3550) and Switch-B (Catalyst 6000) support both ISL and 802.1Q, so the encapsulation can be left as the default setting of negotiate. In this scenario, you configure the trunk to become an 802.1Q trunk.

On switches that support both ISL and 802.1Q trunking, DTP can be used to negotiate the appropriate trunking encapsulation. When negotiation is configured, ISL is always preferred, with 802.1Q being negotiated only if either side of the trunk does not support ISL.

If possible, try to use 802.1Q trunks. 802.1Q is standards-based and is now widely adopted by many vendors. Restrictions of the original 802.1Q standard (e.g., a single spanning-tree instance per Layer 2 network—see Chapter 4) have been overcome by Cisco .

Native VLAN Considerations

If you use 802.1Q trunks, you must ensure that you choose a common native VLAN for each port in the trunk. Failure to do this causes Cisco switches to partially shut down the trunk port because having mismatched native VLANs can result in spanning-tree loops. Native VLAN mismatches are detected via spanning tree and Cisco Discovery Protocol (CDP), not via DTP messages. If spanning tree detects a native VLAN mismatch, spanning tree blocks local native VLAN traffic and the remote switch native VLAN traffic on the trunk; however, the trunk still remains up for other VLANs.

Many people often ask, "What should I configure as the native VLAN?" The answer to this question is based upon two important considerations:

- Control Communications
- Security

The native VLAN has importance on Cisco Catalyst switches for control protocols, namely DTP and spanning tree. DTP messages are always sent on the native VLAN, and spanning-tree bridge protocol data units (BPDUs) are also sent untagged on the native VLAN, which ensures interoperability with other switch vendors. Because some interswitch control communications rely on the native VLAN, it is recommended that you forward no user data on the native VLAN (i.e., create VLANs separate from the native VLAN for user devices).

NOTE   The 802.1Q specification states that only one spanning-tree instance should exist for a Layer 2 network, regardless of the number of VLANs. This instance runs on the native VLAN and is referred to as the *Common Spanning Tree (CST)* instance. Cisco Catalyst switches operate a single spanning-tree instance per VLAN, which is important in redundant Layer 2 topologies. To ensure interoperability with other switches that only support a single spanning-tree instance on the native VLAN, Cisco switches operate the CST instance on the native VLAN.

If you are connecting 802.1Q trunks to switches from other vendors, it is recommended that you leave the native VLAN as VLAN 1 because many of these switches only support VLAN 1 as the native VLAN.

The second consideration in configuring your native VLAN is security. The SANS Institute, an independent security research organization that provides authoritative information on security vulnerabilities, has published a vulnerability at www.sans.org/newlook/resources/IDFAQ/vlan.htm that outlines how the native VLAN on 802.1Q trunks can be used to gain access to destination devices in a VLAN different from the VLAN that a source device is located in (referred to as *VLAN hopping*). Figure 3-12 demonstrates how VLAN hopping works.

Figure 3-12 *802.1Q VLAN Hopping*

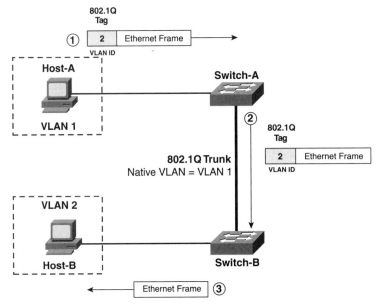

In Figure 3-12, the following events occur:

1 Host-A is attached to an access port on Switch-A that belongs to VLAN 1. Under normal operation, Host-A sends untagged Ethernet frames to Switch-A, which are interpreted by Switch-A as belonging to VLAN 1 and thus restricted to being forwarded only out ports that belong to VLAN 1 or trunks that include VLAN 1. In Figure 3-12, however, Host-A sends frames tagged with an 802.1Q tag, which specifies a VLAN ID of 2.

2 Switch-A receives the tagged frame from Host-A. Because 802.1Q headers are located within Ethernet frames (see Figure 3-6), Switch-A may not even be aware that an 802.1Q header exists because all Switch-A is interested in is reading the destination MAC address, which comes before the 802.1Q header, so that it can forward the frame. Assuming the destination MAC address of the frame is not in the bridge table on Switch-A, Switch-A regards the frame as an unknown unicast frame and floods the frame out all VLAN 1 ports and trunk ports that include VLAN 1. On the trunk to Switch-B, VLAN 1 is the native VLAN; thus, the frame is flooded towards Switch-B, with the 802.1Q header generated by Host-A intact.

3 Switch-B receives the tagged frame, and because the frame is received on an 802.1Q trunk port, looks for an 802.1Q header in the frame. Switch-B finds the 802.1Q header that was generated by Host-A in Step 1 and thinks the frame belongs to VLAN 2, as specified in the VLAN ID of the header. This mistake allows the frame to be forwarded to any device in VLAN 2, which includes Host-B. Assuming the

destination MAC address of the frame is Host-B's MAC address, the frame is forwarded to Host-B. At this point, Host-A has successfully been able to "hop" from VLAN 1 to VLAN 2 without the use of a router or firewall.

The vulnerability in the sequence of events described in Figure 3-12 is related to the fact that the sending device (Host-A) is located in the same VLAN as the native VLAN. If Host-A were in a different VLAN (e.g., VLAN 10), Switch-A would interpret the frame sent by Host-A as coming from VLAN 10, and when it came to forwarding the frame out the 802.1Q trunk, it would overwrite the 802.1Q header generated by Host-A with a new header indicating the frame belongs to VLAN 10. Because of this vulnerability, you need to ensure that the native VLAN used on 802.1Q trunks is not used by user devices (i.e., not assigned to any ports other than trunk ports). This arrangement ensures that user devices that attach to switches are never in the same VLAN as the native VLAN and cannot use the VLAN hopping vulnerability to breach the security of the network.

In summary, most organizations typically leave the default setting of VLAN 1 as the native VLAN and ensure that all user devices are placed on other VLANs. Taking this approach ensures interoperability with other switch vendors if required and also mitigates the VLAN hopping security vulnerability.

NOTE   In this scenario, VLAN 10 is configured as the native VLAN, with the management interfaces for Switch-A and Switch-B placed in this VLAN. As per the security recommendations above, this configuration is not recommended (the management interface of network devices should also be considered a user device). A better configuration would be to place the management interfaces of Switch-A and Switch-B in VLAN 1; however, for the purposes of demonstrating VLAN 1 trunk clearing (discussed later in this scenario), VLAN 10 is used instead.

Configuring Trunk Mode (DTP)

Trunk mode determines how a trunk port attempts to negotiate a trunk. You can configure a switch port to dynamically negotiate a trunk based upon the port capabilities of each end of the trunk, or you can configure a port to always form a trunk, regardless of the configuration of the remote switch. The recommended trunk mode to use for *interswitch links* (trunks that connect two switches together) is desirable mode, because this mode allows a trunk port to actively negotiate a trunk with both sides of the trunk supporting DTP. In desirable mode, the switch sends the locally configured VTP domain name, trunking mode, and supported encapsulations to the remote switch. This information ensures a trunk forms only if the VTP domain names match and the trunking capabilities are compatible. An exception to this restriction is if a remote switch has no VTP domain defined (i.e., the switch has a blank configuration) and the local switch has a VTP domain defined. In this situation, both switches form a trunk.

NOTE	A trunk operating in a DTP mode of auto also sends VTP domain name information.

If you configure the trunking mode to on, a switch can incorrectly force an interface to a trunking state while the remote switch has not formed a trunking state. By using a trunking mode of desirable, you can always be assured that a trunk has properly formed on both sides if one side reports that it has formed a trunk.

If you need to connect switches that belong to different VTP domains via a trunk, you cannot use desirable mode because each switch detects different VTP domains and stops the trunk from forming. In this situation, configure a DTP mode of on or nonegotiate because a trunk interface configured in on mode does not send the VTP domain during DTP negotiation. It sends only the configured DTP mode and supported trunk encapsulations (a trunk mode of nonegotiate disables the sending of any DTP frames whatsoever).

On trunks that connect to devices that don't use DTP (e.g., routers or servers), always configure a trunk to use the nonegotiate mode because this forces trunking without the use of any DTP whatsoever.

Figure 3-13 indicates the appropriate trunking modes that should be configured between various network devices.

Figure 3-13 *Recommended Trunking Modes*

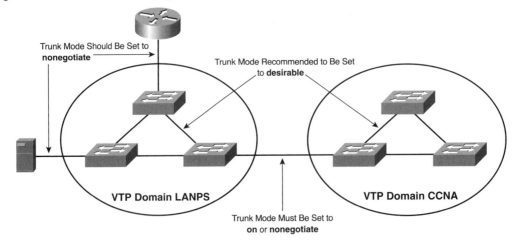

Table 3-3 shows a matrix of the various modes and how the combination of each mode at either end of the link determines whether or not a trunk is formed.

Table 3-3   *Trunk Mode Compatibility*

		Remote End				
		on	**off**	**desirable**	**auto**	**nonegotiate**
Local End	**on**	Local: Trunk Remote: Trunk	Local: Trunk Remote: Non-trunk	Local: Trunk Remote: Trunk	Local: Trunk Remote: Trunk	Local: Trunk Remote: Trunk
	off	Local: Non-Trunk Remote: Trunk	Local: Non-Trunk Remote: Non-Trunk	Local: Non-Trunk Remote: Non-Trunk	Local: Non-Trunk Remote: Non-Trunk	Local: Non-Trunk Remote: Trunk
	desirable	Local: Trunk Remote: Trunk	Local: Non-Trunk Remote: Non-Trunk	Local: Trunk Remote: Trunk	Local: Trunk Remote: Trunk	Local: Non-Trunk Remote: Trunk
	auto	Local: Trunk Remote: Trunk	Local: Non-Trunk Remote: Non-Trunk	Local: Trunk Remote: Trunk	Local: Non-Trunk Remote: Non-Trunk	Local: Non-Trunk Remote: Trunk
	nonegotiate	Local: Trunk Remote: Trunk	Local: Trunk Remote: Non-Trunk	Local: Trunk Remote: Non-Trunk	Local: Trunk Remote: Non-Trunk	Local: Trunk Remote: Trunk

Table 3-3 shows each the resulting trunk states that are reached based upon each combination of local and remote trunking mode. For example, if the local mode is set to auto and the remote mode is set to auto, both ends reach a non-trunk state because neither side actively attempts to negotiate.

Determining the VLANs Enabled on Each Trunk

By default, a trunk transports traffic from all active VLANs. This arrangement can waste precious bandwidth on links to switches that do not service any directly connected or downstream devices within specific VLANs. When you design your network, map out the VLANs that are to be serviced throughout the network. This mapping allows you to determine which VLANs require service over the various trunks in the network. A well-designed Layer 2 network limits large numbers of VLANs being serviced near the edge of the network as much as possible, reducing the amount of VLAN traffic on trunks at the edge of the network.

Once you have determined which VLANs you wish to transport over a trunk, you then have two options to actually implement the configuration:

- Manual configuration
- VTP pruning (automatic)

Manual configuration requires you to configure each trunk port with the appropriate list of VLANs to service, ensuring that each end point of a trunk has an identical VLAN list. In a network that contains hundreds of trunks, this manual configuration becomes tiresome and prone to error. The other option, VTP pruning, automates the process dynamically. If used, VTP pruning should be enabled on all switches within a VTP domain.

Notice in Figure 3-11 that no devices are connected to VLAN 4 on Switch-B. This configuration means that traffic for VLAN 4 does not need to be sent over the trunk between Switch-A and Switch-B Hence, VLAN 4 can be removed manually from the trunk, or VTP pruning can be enabled to dynamically remove the VLAN. In this scenario, you learn how to manually configure the allowed VLAN list on the trunk between Switch-A and Switch-B.

NOTE   Configuring VTP pruning and the rationale of manually configuring the allowed VLANs on a trunk versus using VTP pruning are explained further in Scenario 3-3.

VLAN 1 Considerations

VLAN 1 is the default VLAN configured on Cisco Catalyst switches (and switches from other vendors) and has special significance. On Cisco Catalyst switches, you cannot fully remove VLAN 1 from a trunk, even if you are not using it in your network. This characteristic exists because Cisco Catalyst switches always use VLAN 1 for control communications. VLAN 1 is used for the following control protocols on Cisco Catalyst switches:

- VLAN Trunking Protocol (VTP)
- Cisco Discovery Protocol (CDP)
- Port Aggregation Protocol (PAgP)
- Dynamic Trunking Protocol (DTP)

NOTE   DTP messages are always sent on VLAN 1 for ISL trunks. For 802.1Q trunks, DTP messages are always sent on the native VLAN.

It is important to understand that even if the native VLAN of an 802.1Q trunk is not VLAN 1, all of the above protocols (with the exception of DTP as indicated in the previous note) are still sent on VLAN 1, with a tag attached indicating VLAN 1 is not the native VLAN (if the native VLAN is VLAN 1, then messages are sent without a tag).

Because of the reliance of important Cisco Catalyst control protocols on VLAN 1, many low-end and older Cisco Catalyst switches do not allow you to clear VLAN 1 from a trunk. This restriction means that VLAN 1 traffic is propagated throughout the network, which is normally not a problem because Cisco recommends that VLAN 1 not be configured as a user VLAN. Hence, the volumes of traffic in VLAN 1 are very small. The problem with extending VLAN 1 throughout the network comes to play in larger switched networks where a spanning-tree instance for VLAN 1 must operate throughout the entire switched network. Finite limits exist for the network diameter of spanning-tree topologies (in Chapter 4, you learn that the maximum recommended network diameter of a spanning-tree topology is seven switches). Thus, extending VLAN 1 throughout a large switched network can lead to network instability.

NOTE   Cisco recommends you do not have VLANs that span the entire switched topology for large switched networks. Clearing VLANs from trunks is one approach to guard against such a span; however, Cisco recommends that you use a multilayer topology (discussed in Chapter 6, "Layer 3 Switching") to reduce the size of Layer 2 networks into smaller, more stable, and manageable chunks.

In newer Cisco Catalyst switches, you can clear VLAN 1 partially from a trunk. This feature is known as *VLAN 1 disable on trunk* and does not actually fully remove VLAN 1 traffic from the trunk.

NOTE   You can clear VLAN 1 from a trunk from CatOS 5.4 onwards on any CatOS-based switch. Prior to this release, you could not clear VLAN 1 from a trunk on a CatOS-based switch. The Cisco IOS-based Catalyst 2900XL/3500XL switches do not allow you to clear VLAN 1 from a trunk; however, the Catalyst 2950/3550, Cisco IOS 4000/4500, and native IOS 6000/6500 switches allow you to clear VLAN 1.

So what then is cleared from VLAN 1? Two important types of traffic are cleared from VLAN 1. The first is user data, meaning if, for example, you have users on Switch-A in VLAN 1 and users in Switch-B in VLAN 1, users cannot communicate if VLAN 1 is cleared from a trunk between Switch-A and Switch-B. The second type of traffic that is cleared is spanning-tree BDPU traffic, which is the important feature of VLAN 1 trunk clearing. Clearing VLAN 1 from a trunk reduces the size of the VLAN 1 spanning-tree domain, which allows network designers to control the extent of the VLAN 1 spanning-tree topology and ensures the stability of larger networks. Figure 3-14 demonstrates what happens when VLAN 1 is cleared from a trunk.

Figure 3-14 *Clearing VLAN 1 from a Trunk*

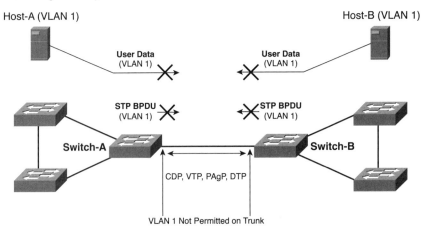

In Figure 3-14, VLAN 1 on the trunk between Switch-A and Switch-B has been cleared, which means that only VTP, CDP, PAgP, and VTP control communications are permitted across the trunk. All other communications, including spanning-tree BPDUs and user data, are blocked.

NOTE   The topology of Figure 3-14 is not recommended. You should never partition the same VLAN into two separate pieces because such a separation may cause problems with your Layer 3 protocols that operate on top of the VLAN. If you are clearing trunks from a VLAN, ensure that the VLAN is a single entity that is not partitioned within the network.

Configuration Tasks

This scenario is based upon the topology of Figure 3-11 and assumes the following configurations have already been implemented:

- All VLANs have been created, and VTP is configured (as per Scenario 3-1)

- All interfaces/ports have been placed in the appropriate VLANs as indicated, each interface/port is connected to the indicated devices, and each interface/port indicated is active.

- The appropriate VLAN and IP addressing configurations have been implemented on the appropriate management interfaces on Switch-A (VLAN 5 SVI) and Switch-B (sc0 interface).

Assuming the above configurations are in place, configuration of trunks for this scenario involves the following tasks:

- Configuring interswitch trunks
- Verifying trunks

Configuring Interswitch Trunks

In Figure 3-11, an interswitch trunk exists between Switch-A (Cisco IOS) and Switch-B (CatOS). The configuration on each of these switches is now examined in separate sections specific to the operating system on each.

Cisco IOS Configuration

On Cisco IOS, the **switchport mode**, **switchport nonegotiate**, and **switchport trunk** interface configuration commands are used to configure trunks.

The **switchport mode** command is used to configure the DTP mode that the trunk interface operates in and has the following syntax:

```
Switch(config-if)# switchport mode {access | dot1q-tunnel | dynamic
    {auto | desirable} | trunk}
```

If the **access** keyword is specified, then the interface is configured as an access port and trunking is disabled, which is equivalent to the DTP mode of off. If the **dynamic** keyword is specified, a DTP mode of auto or desirable can be selected by configuring the appropriate keyword. By default, all interfaces are configured to operate in a DTP mode of desirable, i.e., **switchport mode dynamic desirable**. Finally, if the **trunk** keyword is specified, this forces the interface to trunk unconditionally, which is equivalent to a DTP mode of on. If the **trunk** keyword is specified, you can also optionally use the **switchport nonegotiate** interface configuration command to force the DTP mode for the interface to nonegotiate.

```
Switch(config-if)# switchport nonegotiate
```

Table 3-4 describes each of the various options for configuring the **switchport mode** and **switchport nonegotiate** commands and how these affect the trunking mode of the interface on Cisco IOS Catalyst switches.

Table 3-4   *Trunk Modes on Cisco IOS Catalyst Switches*

Command	Resulting Trunking (DTP) Mode
switchport mode access	off
switchport mode dynamic auto	auto
switchport mode dynamic desirable	desirable (default)
switchport mode trunk	on[1]
switchport nonegotiate	nonegotiate[2]

[1]A resulting trunking mode of *nonegotiate* is configured if the **switchport nonegotiate** interface configuration command is also configured.

[2]Requires the **switchport mode trunk** interface configuration command to be configured.

NOTE   When configuring a trunk mode of on or nonegotiate, you must explicitly configure the trunk encapsulation as ISL or 802.1Q. By default, if a Cisco IOS Catalyst switch supports both 802.1Q and ISL, the trunk encapsulation is set to negotiate, which must be disabled if you wish to configure a trunk mode of on or nonegotiate.

The recommended trunking mode is desirable, because this mode ensures that the trunk forms only if both sides of the trunk are compatible.

Another recommendation is that you disable DTP on all switch ports that are to operate as access ports. This configuration removes DTP negotiation timeout delays of between 5-10 seconds that occur when a port first initializes. Configuring a DTP mode of off ensures access ports do not have to wait for this period, speeding up the time it takes for an access port to transition to a state where it is actively forwarding data.

Once the appropriate DTP mode has been configured, the **switchport trunk** interface configuration command is used to configure the various remaining trunking parameters. This command has the following syntax:

```
Switch(config-if)# switchport trunk {allowed vlan vlan-list} | {encapsulation
  {dot1q | isl | negotiate}} | {native vlan vlan-id} | {pruning vlan vlan-list}
```

- The following describes the trunking parameters configured by each of the keywords

- **Trunk encapsulation**—Defined by the **encapsulation** keyword. A specific encapsulation can be forced by specifying the desired encapsulation (e.g., **dot1q** or **isl**), or the encapsulation can be negotiated via DTP by specifying the **negotiate** keyword. On switches that support both ISL and 802.1Q encapsulations, negotiation via DTP is the default configuration. For switches that support only a single encapsulation type, only the supported encapsulation keyword is configurable.

- **Native VLAN**—Defined by the **native vlan** keywords, this parameter applies for 802.1Q trunks only and defines the native (untagged) VLAN that should be used for the trunk.

- **Allowed VLAN list**—The allowed VLAN list can be configured manually using the **allowed vlan** keywords followed by a listing of each VLAN permitted transport across the trunk.

- **Prune eligible VLANs**—If you are using VTP pruning to dynamically determine the allowed VLANs for a trunk, the **pruning vlan** keywords can be used to define which VLANs are eligible for VTP pruning.

In this scenario, an 802.1Q trunk is required between Switch-A and Switch-B, which at most needs to transport only VLANs 1, 2, 3, 4, and 10, because these are the only VLANs in the network. Using Cisco recommendations, a DTP mode of desirable should be configured on both Switch-A and Switch-B. An ISL trunk also needs to be configured between Switch-A and Router-A, and requires a DTP mode of nonegotiate on Switch-A because Cisco IOS routers do not support DTP. All access ports (non-trunk ports) also should have a DTP mode of off configured to reduce port initialization delays associated with DTP negotiation.

In terms of the VLANs that need to be transported across the trunk between Switch-A and Switch-B, only VLANs 2, 3, 5, and 10 are required, which means that VLAN 1 and VLAN 4 can be cleared from the trunk. In this scenario, you manually clear VLAN 1 from the trunk. In Scenario 2-3, you clear VLAN 4 from the trunk using VTP pruning.

NOTE   You cannot use VTP pruning to clear VLAN 1 from a trunk, which means you must manually remove VLAN 1 from the allowed VLAN list for a trunk.

The native VLAN should also be changed to a VLAN that is not used for user devices to bypass the VLAN hopping security vulnerability of 802.1Q trunking. In this scenario because VLAN 1 is not being used for user devices, it can be used as the native VLAN. However, to demonstrate how to configure a different native VLAN other than the default VLAN 1, VLAN 10 is to be configured as the native VLAN, which is also not used for user devices.

Example 3-10 demonstrates the trunking configuration required on Switch-A.

Example 3-97   *Configuring Trunking on Switch-A*

```
Switch-A# configure terminal
Switch-A(config)# interface fastEthernet0/1
Switch-A(config-if)# switchport trunk encapsulation dot1q
Switch-A(config-if)# switchport mode dynamic desirable
Switch-A(config-if)# switchport trunk native vlan 10
Switch-A(config-if)# switchport trunk allowed vlan 2-5,10,1002-1005
```

In Example 3-10, the trunk encapsulation is configured as 802.1Q (the default setting is to negotiate), and the trunk mode is set to desirable (this is the default setting, but is shown for demonstration purposes). Finally, the allowed VLAN list is set to VLANs 2-5, VLAN 10, and VLANs 1002 to 1005. This allowed VLAN list has cleared VLAN 1 from the trunk so that only control communications that require VLAN 1 (VTP, PAgP, and CDP) operate across the trunk.

NOTE   On the Catalyst 2900XL/3500XL and Catalyst 2950/3550 switches, VLANs 1002 to 1005 must always be transported across a trunk. For 802.1Q trunks, the native VLAN should also be enabled on the trunk. VLANs 1002 to 1005 are special VLANs used to represent Token Ring and Fiber Distributed Data Interface (FDDI) VLANs. On Cisco IOS-based Catalyst 4000/4500 and Catalyst 6000/6500 switches, you can remove all VLANs from a trunk.

During the configuration of Example 3-10, you may notice the following error messages are displayed on the console:

%SPANTREE-2-RECV_PVID_ERR: Received BPDU with inconsistent peer vlan id 1 on FastEthernet0/1 VLAN10.

00:10:56: %SPANTREE-2-BLOCK_PVID_PEER: Blocking FastEthernet0/1 on VLAN0001.

   Inconsistent peer vlan.

00:10:56: %SPANTREE-2-BLOCK_PVID_LOCAL: Blocking FastEthernet0/1 on VLAN0010.

   Inconsistent local vlan.

These errors are generated because the native VLAN is not matched on Switch-A and Switch-B (the native VLAN on Switch-B is currently the default setting, which is VLAN 1). The errors indicate that spanning tree has detected mismatched native VLANs and has shut down VLAN 1 and VLAN 10 on the trunk.

Once you have configured a trunk, you can use the **show interface switchport** command to verify your configuration, as demonstrated on Switch-A in Example 3-11.

Example 3-98   *Verifying Trunking on Switch-A*

```
Switch-A# show interface FastEthernet0/1 switchport
Name: Fa0/1
Switchport: Enabled
Administrative Mode: dynamic desirable
Operational Mode: trunk
Administrative Trunking Encapsulation: dot1q
Operational Trunking Encapsulation: dot1q
Negotiation of Trunking: On
Access Mode VLAN: 1 (default)
Trunking Native Mode VLAN: 10 (Native)
Administrative private-vlan host-association: none
Administrative private-vlan mapping: none
Operational private-vlan: none
Trunking VLANs Enabled: 2-5,10,1002-1005
Pruning VLANs Enabled: 2-1001

Protected: false
Unknown unicast blocked: disabled
Unknown multicast blocked: disabled

Voice VLAN: none (Inactive)
Appliance trust: none
```

In Example 3-11, notice that two types of state are described—administrative and operational. Administrative state refers to how the interface is configured, while operational state refers to how the interface is currently operating. For example, the administrative mode is dynamic desirable because this is how the interface was configured in Example 3-10. Notice that the operational mode is trunk, which indicates the interface is currently trunking. Although Switch-B has not yet been configured for trunking, because ports on CatOS-based Catalyst switches are configuring with a trunk mode or auto by default and the VTP domain names are matching (as previously configured in Scenario 3-1), a trunk has formed.

You can also use the **show interface trunk** command to verify the trunking configuration and status of each trunk interface, as demonstrated on Switch-A in Example 3-12.

Example 3-99 *Verifying Trunking on Switch-A*

```
Switch-A# show interface trunk
Port       Mode          Encapsulation  Status       Native vlan
Fa0/1      desirable     802.1q         trunking     10

Port       Vlans allowed on trunk
Fa0/1      2-5,10,1002-1005

Port       Vlans allowed and active in management domain
Fa0/1      2-5,10

Port       Vlans in spanning tree forwarding state and not pruned
Fa0/1      2-5
```

Notice on the last shaded line that only traffic for VLANs 2-5 is being forwarded on the trunk. Spanning tree has blocked VLAN 10 on the trunk due to the native VLAN mismatch currently present.

NOTE   Spanning tree also blocks the native VLAN configured on the remote switch on the trunk. In this scenario, this native VLAN is VLAN 1 because Switch-B has not yet been configured and the default native VLAN is VLAN 1. In Example 3-12, VLAN 1 is not included in any of the allowed VLAN lists because it has been manually cleared from the trunk (see Example 3-10). If VLAN 1 had not been cleared from the trunk, you would see VLAN 1 in the "Vlans allowed on trunk" column, but not in the "Vlans in spanning tree forwarding state…" column, due to spanning tree blocking VLAN 1 due to the native VLAN mismatch.

CatOS Configuration

On CatOS, the **set trunk** and **set vlan** commands are used to configure trunks.

The **set trunk** command is used to configure the following parameters of a trunk port:

- Trunk mode
- Trunk encapsulation
- Allowed VLAN list

The following shows the syntax for this command when configuring the trunk mode and encapsulation:

```
Console> (enable) set trunk module/port [on | off | auto | desirable |
  nonegotiate] [dot1q | isl | negotiate]
```

NOTE   The default trunking mode on CatOS is auto, and the default trunking encapsulation is to negotiate if multiple encapsulations are supported.

The following shows the syntax for this command when configuring the VLANs that are allowed to trunk:

```
Console> (enable) set trunk module/port vlan-list
```

When configuring the allowed VLAN list, the **set trunk** command is incremental, meaning it adds VLANs to the allowed VLAN list rather than overwriting the previous VLAN list. You must explicitly remove unwanted VLANs from the allowed VLAN list, using the **clear trunk** command:

```
Console> (enable) clear trunk module/port vlan-list
```

Because you normally want to specify a small number of VLANs in the allowed VLAN list, it is easiest to clear *all* VLANs from a trunk and then use the **set trunk** command to configure the specific VLANs allowed on the trunk.

Finally, the **set vlan** command is used to configure the native VLAN for 802.1Q trunks:

```
Console> (enable) set vlan vlan-id module/port
```

Unlike Cisco IOS, which has separate commands for assigning the VLAN for an access port and the native VLAN for a trunk port, CatOS uses the access port VLAN configuration to determine the native VLAN for 802.1Q trunks.

For this scenario, the trunk to Switch-A has already been configured on Switch-A as an 802.1Q trunk, with a trunking mode of desirable and an allowed VLAN list of 2-5, 10, and 1002-1005. The native VLAN must also be set to VLAN 10. Example 3-13 demonstrates configuring these parameters on Switch-B to ensure correct trunk operation with Switch-A.

Example 3-100 *Configuring Trunking on Switch-B*

```
Switch-B> (enable) set trunk 2/1 desirable dot1q
Port(s)  2/1 trunk mode set to desirable.
Port(s)  2/1 trunk type set to dot1q.
Switch-B> (enable) clear trunk 2/1 1-1005,1025-4094
Removing Vlan(s) 1-1005,1025-4094 from allowed list.
Port  2/1 allowed vlans modified to .
Switch-B> (enable) set trunk 2/1 2-5,10
Adding vlans 2-5,10 to allowed list.
Port(s)  2/1 allowed vlans modified to 2-5,10.
Switch-B> (enable) set vlan 10 2/1
VLAN 10 modified.
```

Example 3-100 *Configuring Trunking on Switch-B (Continued)*

```
VLAN 1 modified.
VLAN  Mod/Ports
----  ----------------------
10    2/1
```

Notice on Switch-B that VLAN 1 is manually cleared from the trunk. Also, notice that you don't need to include VLANs 1002-1005 in the allowed VLAN list, unlike Switch-A, which requires these VLANs.

NOTE   After the native VLAN is configured as VLAN 10 on Switch-B, spanning tree on both switches detects that the native VLANs are matched and unblocks any previously blocked VLANs on the trunk port.

Once you have configured a trunk, you should verify your configuration using the **show trunk** command. Example 3-14 demonstrates the use of the **show trunk** command on Switch-B.

Example 3-101 *Verifying Trunking on Switch-B*

```
Switch-B> (enable) show trunk
* - indicates vtp domain mismatch
Port      Mode         Encapsulation  Status        Native vlan
--------  -----------  -------------  ------------  -----------
2/1       desirable    dot1q          trunking      10

Port      Vlans allowed on trunk
--------  ----------------------------------------------------------------------
2/1       2-5,10

Port      Vlans allowed and active in management domain
--------  ----------------------------------------------------------------------
2/1       2-5,10

Port      Vlans in spanning tree forwarding state and not pruned
--------  ----------------------------------------------------------------------
2/1       2-5,10
```

Each of the shaded lines verifies the configuration of the trunk port in Example 3-13.

At this point, the real test is to ensure devices within each VLAN can communicate with each other. For example, Switch-A and Switch-B should be able to ping each other because VLAN 5 is forwarded across the trunk. Similarly, Host-B should be able to communicate with Host-D, and Host-C should be able to communicate with Host-E because VLAN 2 and VLAN 3 respectively are forwarded across the trunk.

Verifying Trunking

You can verify trunking operation using the various **show** commands described in the previous section. You can also verify trunking operation by monitoring trunking operation, which provides detailed low-level information that aids in troubleshooting problems.

On Cisco IOS, you can use the **debug dtp** command with various options to view DTP trunking events or errors as they occur. Example 3-15 shows a sample output of a trunk being established with the **debug dtp packets** command enabled.

Example 3-102 *Debugging DTP Packets on a Cisco IOS Switch*

```
Switch-A# debug dtp packets
DTP packet processing debugging is on
! The first DTP frame is sent by Switch-A. The TOS indicates the trunk
! operational status of the interface, which is currently an access interface
! as no trunk has formed
! The TAS indicates the trunk administrative status, which is DESIRABLE as this
! is the DTP mode configured for the port
! THE TOT/TAT similarly describe the operational and administrative trunk
! encapsulation, which is 802.1Q
03:27:02: DTP-pkt:Fa0/1:Sending packet ../dyntrk/dyntrk_process.c:1183
03:27:02: DTP-pkt:Fa0/1:  TOS/TAS = ACCESS/DESIRABLE
   ../dyntrk/dyntrk_process.c:1186
03:27:02: DTP-pkt:Fa0/1:  TOT/TAT = 802.1Q/802.1Q
   ../dyntrk/dyntrk_process.c:1189
03:27:02: DTP-pkt:Fa0/1:datagram_out ../dyntrk/dyntrk_process.c:1221
03:27:02: DTP-pkt:Fa0/1:datagram_out encap ../dyntrk/dyntrk_process.c:1233
03:27:02: DTP-pkt:Fa0/1:Invalid TLV (type 0, len 0) in received packet.
      ../dyntrk/dyntrk_core.c:1266

! An initial DTP frame is received from Switch-B, which includes the VTP domain,
! trunk mode and trunk encapsulation
03:27:02: DTP-pkt:Fa0/1:Good DTP packet received: ../dyntrk/dyntrk_core.c:1401
03:27:02: DTP-pkt:Fa0/1:  Domain: LANPS
   ../dyntrk/dyntrk_core.c:1404
03:27:02: DTP-pkt:Fa0/1:  Status: TOS/TAS = ACCESS/DESIRABLE
   ../dyntrk/dyntrk_core.c:1407
03:27:02: DTP-pkt:Fa0/1:  Type: TOT/TAT = 802.1Q/802.1Q
   ../dyntrk/dyntrk_core.c:1409
03:27:02: DTP-pkt:Fa0/1:  ID: 00507356C2F1 ../dyntrk/dyntrk_core.c:1412

! Because the VTP domain, mode, and encapsulation are compatible with Switch-A,
! a DTP frame is sent, this time to indicate that operation state (TOS) is TRUNK,
! indicating Switch-A is moving to a trunking status
03:27:03: DTP-pkt:Fa0/1:Sending packet ../dyntrk/dyntrk_process.c:1183
03:27:03: DTP-pkt:Fa0/1:  TOS/TAS = TRUNK/DESIRABLE
   ../dyntrk/dyntrk_process.c:1186
03:27:03: DTP-pkt:Fa0/1:  TOT/TAT = 802.1Q/802.1Q
   ../dyntrk/dyntrk_process.c:1189
03:27:03: DTP-pkt:Fa0/1:datagram_out ../dyntrk/dyntrk_process.c:1221
03:27:03: DTP-pkt:Fa0/1:datagram_out encap ../dyntrk/dyntrk_process.c:1233
03:27:04: DTP-pkt:Fa0/1:Invalid TLV (type 0, len 0) in received packet.
      ../dyntrk/dyntrk_core.c:1266
```

Example 3-102 *Debugging DTP Packets on a Cisco IOS Switch (Continued)*

```
! Switch-B sends responds with a DTP frame, which includes a TOS of TRUNK,
! indicating the port on Switch-B is also trunking
03:27:04: DTP-pkt:Fa0/1:Good DTP packet received: ../dyntrk/dyntrk_core.c:1401
03:27:04: DTP-pkt:Fa0/1:  Domain: LANPS ../dyntrk/dyntrk_core.c:1404
03:27:04: DTP-pkt:Fa0/1:  Status: TOS/TAS = TRUNK/DESIRABLE
    ../dyntrk/dyntrk_core.c:1407
03:27:04: DTP-pkt:Fa0/1:  Type: TOT/TAT = 802.1Q/802.1Q
    ../dyntrk/dyntrk_core.c:1409
03:27:04: DTP-pkt:Fa0/1:  ID: 00507356C2F1 ../dyntrk/dyntrk_core.c:1412

! Both switches have indicate a trunk operational status (TOS) of TRUNK,
! so the interface changes its Layer 2 status to UP
! DTP negotiation is complete
03:27:04: %LINK-3-UPDOWN: Interface FastEthernet0/1, changed state to up
...
...
```

In Example 3-15, you can see DTP packets being exchanged between the local and remote switch. Notice that DTP packets include the VTP domain (LANPS), which is why you must configure the same VTP domain name if you wish to negotiate a trunk. During trunk negotiation, DTP frames are sent every second; after successful negotiation, DTP frames are send every 30 seconds.

On CatOS switches, trunking can be monitored by setting a low SYSLOG severity level for the DTP facility and viewing SYSLOG messages as they are generated. Example 3-16 shows how to configure Switch-B to display all DTP SYSLOG events as they are generated.

Example 3-103 *Enabling All SYSLOG DTP Events for Switch-B*

```
Switch-B> (enable) set logging level dtp 7
System logging facility <dtp> for this session set to severity 7(debugging)
Switch-B> (enable) set logging console enable
System logging messages will be sent to the console.
%DTP-5-NONTRUNKPORTON:Port 2/1 has become non-trunk
%DTP-5-TRUNKPORTON:Port 2/1 has become dot1q trunk
```

In Example 3-16, you enable logging of all DTP events to the console, because the lowest severity level is configured. Port 2/1 is then disconnected and reconnected, and you can see the resulting SYSLOG event messages.

Scenario 3-3: VTP Pruning

In the previous scenario, the list of allowed VLANs is configured manually. This configuration is static, which means that if you need to enable a previously disallowed VLAN on a trunk, you must do so manually. In environments where users from different VLANs move around a lot, having to reconfigure the allowed VLAN list each time a user moves clearly starts to become tiresome and prone to error. VTP pruning offers a dynamic mechanism that automatically configures the allowed VLAN lists on trunks within a VTP domain. Based upon whether or not a switch has ports currently active within a VLAN, the switch dynamically indicates to the remote switch on the other side of a trunk that the traffic within the inactive VLAN not be forwarded across a trunk. The mechanism used by VTP to allow the communication of VTP pruning information is known as the *VTP Join message*. A VTP Join message includes a list of the VLANs that are currently active on the switch. Figure 3-15 demonstrates how VTP Join messages are used to prune trunks in the topology of Figure 3-11.

Figure 3-15 *VTP Join Messages and VTP Pruning*

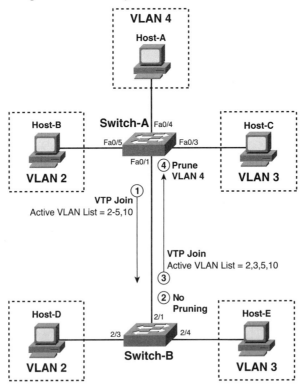

In Figure 3-15, the allowed VLAN list on both switches is VLANs 2-5 and VLAN 10, as configured in the previous scenario. Switch-A and Switch-B determine which VLANs are active within this the allowed VLAN list for the trunk and then send this list in VTP Joins to the remote switch.

The native VLAN of the trunk in Figure 3-15 is VLAN 10; hence, VLAN 10 must also be transported across the trunk. Both of the management interfaces for the switches are in VLAN 5; hence, VLAN 5 must also be transported across the trunk.

On Switch-A, notice that user VLANs 2-4 are active, which means that the active list of VLANs on Switch-A for the trunk is VLANs 2-5 and VLAN 10. The VTP Join message sent from Switch-A to Switch-B (Step 1) includes this list of active VLANs. When Switch-B receives the VTP Join (Step 2), it does not prune any VLANs from the trunk, because all VLANs allowed on the trunk are listed in the VTP Join message.

On Switch-B, notice that user VLANs 2 and 3 are active, while no users are attached to VLAN 4, which means that the active list of VLANs on Switch-B for the trunk is VLANs 2, 3, 5, and 10. The VTP Join message sent from Switch-B to Switch-A (Step 3), therefore, excludes VLAN 4 from the active list and Switch-A consequently prunes VLAN 4 from the trunk (Step 4).

To use VTP pruning, the feature must be enabled on all VTP servers and clients in the network (by default, VTP pruning is disabled). Fortunately, VTP pruning can be learned by VTP clients, meaning once you enable VTP pruning on VTP servers, each VTP client automatically enables VTP pruning. Of course, you might not want VTP pruning enabled on some VLANs. The classic example is VLAN 1, which Cisco Catalyst switches automatically ensure is not available for VTP pruning. If a VLAN is eligible for pruning, it is said to be *prune eligible*. By default, all VLANs on a Cisco Catalyst switches are prune eligible, except for VLAN 1. Cisco Catalyst switches can be configured with a custom prune eligible list, which ensures specific VLANs are never pruned from a trunk.

Configuration Tasks

To configure VTP pruning, the following configuration tasks are required:

- Enabling VTP pruning
- Configuring the prune eligible list
- Verifying VTP pruning

Enabling VTP Pruning

As previously indicated, VTP pruning needs to be enabled only on VTP servers, after which all VTP clients in the VTP domain automatically enable VTP pruning. VTP pruning can be enabled only on switches running in VTP server mode. If a switch is running in VTP client mode, an error is displayed. To enable VTP pruning on a Cisco IOS switch, you use the **vtp pruning** VLAN configuration or global configuration command. Example 3-17 demonstrates enabling VTP pruning on Switch-A.

Example 3-104 *Enabling VTP Pruning on Switch-A*

```
Switch-A# configure terminal
Switch-A(config)# vtp pruning
Pruning switched on
```

On CatOS, the **set vtp pruning** command is used to enable or disable VTP pruning.

```
Console> (enable) set vtp pruning {enable | disable}
```

Because Switch-B is a VTP client, you cannot enable VTP pruning explicitly on Switch-B without changing the VTP mode to server. However, you do not need to enable VTP pruning on Switch-B because it automatically inherits the VTP pruning configuration from Switch-A.

Configuring the Prune Eligible List

Once VTP pruning is enabled, you can optionally configure a prune eligible list if you wish to restrict the VLANs that can be pruned. On Cisco IOS, the prune eligible list can be configured on a per-trunk basis, allowing for flexible configuration options. On CatOS, the prune eligible list is configured globally for all trunks.

To configure the VTP prune list on Cisco IOS, you use the **switchport trunk pruning** interface configuration command on the trunk that you wish to configure.

```
Switch(config-if)# switchport trunk pruning vlan vlan-list
```

In Figure 3-11, VLAN 4 is only attached to Switch-A, and hence can be safely pruned from the trunk between Switch-A and Switch-B. In contrast, devices in VLANs 2 and 3 are attached to both switches, so these VLANs must be trunked in order for devices attached to different switches to communicate. VLAN 5 (used for management communications) and VLAN 10 (the native VLAN) are used for interswitch control communications, and thus, should never be pruned from the trunks. Example 3-18 demonstrates configuring a prune eligible list on Switch-A that permits only VLAN 4 to be pruned from the trunk to Switch-B.

Example 3-105 *Configuring a Prune Eligible List on Switch-A*

```
Switch-A# configure terminal
Switch-A(config)# interface fastEthernet0/1
Switch-A(config-if)# switchport trunk pruning vlan 4
```

To configure the VTP prune list on CatOS, you use the **set vtp pruneeligible** command.

```
Console> (enable) set vtp pruneeligible vlan-list
```

Just like the allowed VLAN list on CatOS, this command is additive in that it adds the VLANs configured in the *vlan-list* to the current prune eligible list instead of overriding the current list. By default, the prune eligible list includes VLANs 2–1000 on CatOS, which means that you must explicitly clear VLANs from the list using the **clear vtp pruneeligible** command if you do not want them to be on the prune eligible list.

```
Console> (enable) clear vtp pruneeligible vlan-list
```

Example 3-19 demonstrates configuring a prune eligible list on Switch-B that permits only VLAN 4 to be pruned from the trunk to Switch-A.

Example 3-106 *Configuring a Prune Eligible List on Switch-B*

```
Switch-B> (enable) clear vtp pruneeligible 2-1005
Vlans 1-4094 will not be pruned on this device.
VTP domain LANPS modified.
Switch-B> (enable) set vtp pruneeligible 4
Vlan 4 eligible for pruning on this device.
VTP domain LANPS modified.
```

Notice in Example 3-19 that the prune eligible list is first totally cleared and then VLAN 4 is added to the prune eligible list.

Verifying VTP Pruning

Once VTP pruning has been enabled and any VLANs have been added or removed from the prune eligible list, verify that the VTP pruning configuration is actually working. This scenario assumes that in Figure 3-11, Host-A has been connected to interface Fa0/4 on Switch-A and that interface Fa0/4 has been placed into VLAN 4. This configuration means that VLAN 4 is inactive on Switch-A. Each switch should detect this and will not send a VTP Join message for the inactive VLAN to the remote switch. For example, when Switch-B detects VLAN 4 is inactive on the switch, Switch-B does not include VLAN 4 in VTP Join messages sent to Switch-A, meaning Switch-A prunes VLAN 2 from the trunk, ensuring VLAN 2 traffic is not sent to Switch-B.

To verify VTP pruning on Cisco IOS, use the **show interface trunk** command, which includes the list of VLANs in a forwarding state on each trunk interface. Example 3-20 demonstrates this command on Switch-A:

Example 3-107 *Verifying VTP Pruning on Switch-A*

```
Switch-A# show interface trunk
Port      Mode        Encapsulation  Status       Native vlan
Fa0/1     desirable   802.1q         trunking     10

Port      Vlans allowed on trunk
Fa0/1     2-5,10,1002-1005

Port      Vlans allowed and active in management domain
Fa0/1     2-5,10

Port      Vlans in spanning tree forwarding state and not pruned
Fa0/1     2,3,5,10
```

In Example 3-20, notice that VLANs 2-5 and 10 are active and allowed on the Fa0/1 trunk interface, as indicated by the first shaded line. The second shaded line indicates that VLAN 4 is currently pruned from the trunk because Switch-B has not included this VLAN in the VTP Join messages sent to Switch-A.

TIP

Do not be confused by the fact that the output in Example 3-20 indicates VLANs 2, 3, 5, and 10 are in a "spanning tree forwarding state." This statement is misleading because it implies that spanning-tree BPDUs for VLAN 4 are not sent across the trunk. In fact, spanning-tree BPDUs for all VLANs in the manually-configured allowed VLAN list are sent across the trunk, regardless of whether they have been pruned or not pruned. This fact means that VTP pruning is useful only for reducing the unnecessary propagation of user data within pruned VLANs across trunks, but does not reduce the size of the spanning-tree topology for pruned VLANs.

To verify VTP pruning on CatOS, use the **show trunk** command, which includes the list of VLANS in a forwarding state on each trunk port. Example 3-21 demonstrates this command on Switch-B.

Example 3-108 *Verifying VTP Pruning on Switch-B*

```
Switch-B> (enable) show trunk
* - indicates vtp domain mismatch
Port      Mode         Encapsulation  Status        Native vlan
--------  -----------  -------------  -----------   -----------
 2/1      desirable    dot1q          trunking      10

Port      Vlans allowed on trunk
--------  -------------------------------------------------------------------
 2/1      2-5,10

Port      Vlans allowed and active in management domain
--------  -------------------------------------------------------------------
 2/1      2-5,10

Port      Vlans in spanning tree forwarding state and not pruned
--------  -------------------------------------------------------------------
 2/1      2-5,10
```

In Example 3-21, notice that the VLANs currently in a forwarding state are VLANs 2-5 and 10, which is identical to the manually configured allowed VLAN list. This is because all allowed VLANs are active on Switch-A, and hence are all included in VTP Join messages sent to Switch-B.

Scenario 3-4: Configuring EtherChannel

In this scenario you learn how to configure an EtherChannel bundle between two Cisco Catalyst switches. Figure 3-16 illustrates the topology used for this scenario, which extends the topology used for the previous scenarios.

Figure 3-16   *Scenario 3-4 Topology*

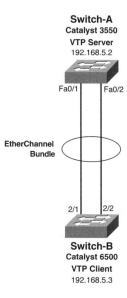

In Figure 3-16, the trunk between Switch-A and Switch-B is to operate over two physical interfaces configured as an EtherChannel bundle, rather than the single physical interface used in previous scenarios. This configuration increases the bandwidth of the connection between Switch-A and Switch-B and also protects against a single circuit or interface failure.

Understanding EtherChannel

Before configuring EtherChannel, you must understand how EtherChannel bundles negotiate and understand the load sharing mechanisms supported by your Cisco Catalyst switches. The following sections are now presented:

- PAgP negotiation
- Load sharing

PAgP Negotiation

Just as trunks use a negotiation protocol (DTP) between Cisco switches to determine whether or not a trunk should form, so to does EtherChannel, which uses PAgP as the protocol for negotiating an EtherChannel bundle.

It is important to understand which PAgP modes co-exist and form an EtherChannel. Table 3-5 describes all of the possible combinations of PAgP modes that can be configured between two directly connected PAgP peers, assuming the names of the peers are Switch-A and Switch-B.

Table 3-5   *PAgP Negotiation Matrix*

		Switch-B			
	PAgP Mode	**On**	**Off**	**Auto**	**Desirable**
Switch-A	On	Channel	Not Channel (ErrDisable)	Not Channel (ErrDisable)	Not Channel (ErrDisable)
	Off	Not Channel (ErrDisable)	Not Channel	Not Channel	Not Channel
	Auto	Not Channel (ErrDisable)	Not Channel	Not Channel	Channel
	Desirable	Not Channel (ErrDisable)	Not Channel	Channel	Channel

Notice that there are only three combinations of PAgP modes that will successfully channel (form a bundle):

- **Desirable and desirable**—Forms because both parties actively attempt to negotiate a channel. This combination is the recommended configuration.

- **Desirable and auto**—Forms because one side actively attempts to negotiate, while the other side responds only to PAgP negotiation.

- **On and on**—Always forms a channel because both parties are hard coded; no PAgP frames are sent.

It is very tempting to use a PAgP mode of on because normally a bundle is static and does not change. Therefore, why would you need to negotiate the bundle? However, if you decide to use a PAgP mode of on, notice in Table 3-5 that forcing a bundle to use a on mode results in the bundle not channeling if the PAgP mode of the other side is set to anything other than a mode of on as well. Notice also that an ErrDisable condition also occurs, which is caused by the on mode forcing an EtherChannel bundle to be always up while the other side of the connection is not configured as a bundle. This configuration can cause spanning-tree loops in the network. Cisco Catalyst switches detect and immediately shut down the looped ports, placing them into an ErrDisable state, which indicates a serious error caused the switch to shut down the ports. The following shows an example of the console message displayed on Switch-B when a spanning-tree loop is detected due to incorrect PAgP configuration:

2002 Oct 31 16:58:23 %SPANTREE-2-CHNMISCFG: STP loop

```
- channel 2/1-2 is disabled in vlan/instance 1
```

NOTE   Although the ErrDisable mechanism protects networks based upon Cisco Catalyst switch, occurrences of the ErrDisable are highly undesirable, indicating a serious problem with the network, and should be always avoided.

Even if both sides of a bundle are configured with a PAgP mode of on (which means a bundle forms), it is important to be aware that the redundancy of the link is compromised in the event of a failure on the link that is carrying spanning-tree traffic (see Chapter 4 for more detail on spanning tree). Basically, this means that spanning tree declares an entire bundle down if the link that carries spanning-tree traffic fails. Clearly, this result is undesirable and negates the redundancy benefits of EtherChannel. If, however, you configure a mode of desirable, each switch ensures that spanning-tree traffic is forwarded over the redundant link, ensuring the spanning-tree topology remains stable during a physical interface failure.

For all of the reasons described so far, it is recommended you use a mode of desirable on each end because configuring this mode ensures that an ErrDisable state is never generated (unless the remote side is configured with a PAgP mode of on) and also ensures the link failure scenario described does not affect the spanning-tree topology.

Of course if you are connecting a Cisco Catalyst switch to a device that does not support PAgP, such as a server or router, you need to configure a PAgP mode of on to ensure the bundle forms with the remote devices.

PAgP Negotiation Delays

If you configure a PAgP mode of auto or desirable, when a port first initializes due to a physical link being detected, the Layer 2 line protocol of the port does not come up until PAgP negotiates a bundle or until PAgP negotiation times out. If a bundle is successfully negotiated, this port coming up normally occurs within a matter of seconds, but if a PAgP negotiation timeout occurs, a port does not come up at Layer 2 for approximately 15-20 seconds. In other words, if a non-EtherChannel capable device connects to a switch port that has a PAgP mode of auto or desirable configured, it does get a Layer 2 connection for approximately 15-20 seconds. If workstations are connected, this situation can cause unacceptable delays when a workstation starts up, especially if the workstations are fast computers that boot up quickly. The workstation might not be able to obtain an IP address via Dynamic Host Configuration Protocol (DHCP), causing logon failures to the network among other problems.

TIP

On CatOS switches, a PAgP mode of auto is configured by default on EtherChannel capable ports, meaning by default all non-EtherChannel devices experience an unnecessary 18-19 second delay upon port initialization. This delay adds to other possible delays caused by DTP negotiation and spanning-tree initialization once the port is handed to spanning tree by PAgP, causing delays of up to a minute in extreme cases. To minimize port initialization delays, always configure a PAgP mode of off on ports that are connected to non-EtherChannel devices, such as workstations. On Cisco IOS switches, the default PAgP mode of ports is off, so the default configuration does not suffer this problem.

PAgP Silent and Non-Silent Operation

When a PAgP mode of auto or desirable is configured on a port, you also have the option of configuring either of the following operational parameters:

- **Non-Silent**—An EtherChannel bundle does not form, until bidirectional connectivity has been confirmed. This parameter means that ports in the EtherChannel bundle must receive data, as well as be able to transmit data, in order for the bundle to form. Non-silent is default on Catalyst 5000 fiber-based FastEthernet and fiber-based gigabit Ethernet ports. This mode protects against unidirectional failures, where one of the transmit or receive links may fail. These failures are common on fiber-based connections and can cause bridging loops.

- **Silent**—An EtherChannel bundle forms, even if data has not been received from the remote device. This mode is the default mode of operation on all Catalyst 4000, 6000, and Cisco IOS-based switch ports, as well as on Catalyst 5000 copper ports. For unidirectional failures on Cisco IOS-based Catalyst ports, Catalyst 4000 ports, and Catalyst 6000 ports, other protocols, such as *unidirectional link detection* (*UDLD*), which detect these failures much more quickly than non-silent PAgP operation, are used to protect against unidirectional failures.

Cisco recommends that you do not modify the default silent or non-silent mode of operation.

Load Sharing

If you are implementing EtherChannel for performance benefits, it is important that you understand that the load-sharing mechanism used by a bundle affects performance. Depending on the Cisco Catalyst switch platform, load sharing is supported based on Layer 2, Layer 3, and Layer 4 source and/or destination address/port values.

Table 3-6 shows the supported load sharing mechanisms based upon Catalyst platform.

Table 3-6   *Cisco Catalyst EtherChannel Load Sharing Capabilities*

Platform	Load Sharing Mechanisms
2900XL/3500XL 2950/3550 (Cisco IOS)	Source MAC Destination MAC
2900/4000/5000/5500 Early Catalyst 6000 Supervisor 1[1] (CatOS)	Source MAC XOR Destination MAC (Non-configurable)
Catalyst 6000/6500 Supervisor 1a with PFC/PFC2 (CatOS and Cisco IOS)	Source MAC Destination MAC Source MAC and Destination MAC Source IP Destination IP Source IP and Destination IP (default)
Catalyst 6000 Supervisor 2 with PFC2 (CatOS and Cisco IOS) and Catalyst 4000 Supervisor 3/4 (Cisco IOS)	Source MAC Destination MAC Source MAC and Destination MAC Source IP Destination IP Source IP and Destination IP (default) Source Port Destination Port Source Port and Destination Port

[1]Applies to early implementations of the Catalyst 6000 Supervisor 1. Issue the **show module** command, and if the sub-type is listed as "L2 Switching Engine I WS-F6020," then only a non-configurable distribution method based upon source and destination MAC addresses is supported.

The load sharing mechanism is particularly important when you provide connectivity to a small amount of devices via a bundle. In this situation, large amounts of traffic are being sent to and from a single or a few devices, which can overload a single link (refer Figure 3-10). Make sure you understand the major traffic flows between devices in your network to ensure your load sharing mechanism is adequate for your environment.

EtherChannel Support on Cisco Catalyst Switches

Most Cisco Catalyst switches support EtherChannel; however, it is important to understand that how EtherChannel is supported can vary from platform to platform. The following lists some important platform considerations you should well understand before implementing EtherChannel:

- What is the maximum number of EtherChannel bundles required?
- What is the maximum number of ports per bundle required?
- Are contiguous ports required?
- Are there specific restrictions on the collection of ports you can configure in a bundle?
- Do all ports need to be on the same switching module?
- Are there any load sharing considerations? (see Table 3-6)

The limitations of what you can or can't do are governed by the switch port hardware and software you are using. Table 3-7 shows the limitations of the various Catalyst platforms, assuming the hardware is EtherChannel capable.

Table 3-7   *EtherChannel Capabilities*

Platform	Maximum Number of Channels	Maximum Number of Ports per Channel	Contiguous Ports?	Specific collection of ports?	Same Module?
6000/6500 (Cisco IOS)	64 256[1]	8	No	No	No
6000/6500 (CatOS)	128	8	No	No	No
5000/5500[2] (CatOS)	-	4[3]	Yes[3] (2 or 4)	Yes[4]	Yes
4000 (Cisco IOS)	64	8	No	No	No
2900/4000 (CatOS)	126	8	No	No	No
3550	64	8	No	No	n/a
2950	6	8	No	No	n/a
2900XL/ 3500XL	12	8 (source-base) Unlimited (destination-based)	No	No	n/a

[1]Catalyst 6000/6500 Native IOS 12.1(2)E and earlier.

[2]Supported only on modules with an Ethernet Bundling Controller (EBC) onboard. These modules include the Supervisor 2/3 engines and some line cards.

[3]On the Catalyst 5000 family gigabit EtherChannel module (WS-X5010), an EtherChannel bundle can consist of any two to eight ports on the module. Ports in an EtherChannel do not have to be contiguous.

[4]For modules that support only a maximum of four ports, an EBC is allocated to each group of four ports. The ports that form a bundle must be managed by the same EBC, and bundles must use ports that start from the first port in the EBC group or ports. An exception to the latter is the WS-X5225R module, which allows you to configure bundles that do not start at the first port within a group (e.g., group = 2/1-4, bundle can be configured on 2/3-4).

As you can see from Table 3-7, each of the switch platforms has varying capabilities. The platform that has the most restrictions is the Catalyst 5000/5500 family, where most modules require EtherChannel to be configured on contiguous ports and only in certain configurations. An EtherChannel controller typically exists for every four ports on a module. For example, you might be able to configure a four-port bundle only on ports 2/1-4, 2/5-8, 2/9-12 and so on (you cannot configure a bundle from 2/3-2/6). If you want to configure a two-port bundle, you must start from the beginning of each range for a particular EtherChannel controller. For example, ports 2/1-2 are okay, but ports 2/3-4 are not OK because they do not start at the beginning of a range. Modern EtherChannel implementations do not have such strict limitations as the older Catalyst 5000/5500 family.

NOTE	You can use the **show port capabilities** command on CatOS to determine supported EtherChannel configurations. This command is demonstrated later in this scenario.

Configuration Tasks

Before you configure EtherChannel, you must ensure that you are aware of any restrictions that the hardware you are configuring might have. Refer to Table 3-7 for information on how EtherChannel might be configured on the various Cisco Catalyst platforms, and refer to Table 3-6 for information on the load sharing mechanisms that are supported.

Configuration of EtherChannel consists of the following tasks:

* Configuring physical port parameters
* Creating an EtherChannel bundle
* Configuring EtherChannel load distribution
* Verifying EtherChannel configuration

Configuring Physical Port Parameters

A very important prerequisite of configuring EtherChannel bundles is that each of the physical ports or interfaces that make up the EtherChannel bundle must be configured identically to ensure the bundle comes up and operates correctly. These physical port/interface parameters include the following:

* **Port speed/duplex settings**—Ensure all ports operate at the same speed and duplex setting.
* **VLAN configuration**—Ensure all ports belong to the same VLAN.

- **Trunking configuration**—Ensure trunking modes are identical and that the allowed VLANs for each trunk are the same. For 802.1Q trunks, ensure that the native VLAN for each trunk is identical (trunking is covered later in this chapter).

- **Spanning tree configuration**—Ensure path cost, port priority, and PortFast settings are identical (spanning tree is covered in Chapter 4).

- **SPAN destination ports**—You cannot configure an EtherChannel bundle that includes SPAN destination ports (SPAN is covered in Chapter 9).

- **Secure ports**—You cannot configure an EtherChannel bundle that includes secure ports (secure ports are covered in Chapter 7, "Multicast Routing and Switching").

- **Dynamic VLAN ports**—Do not configure EtherChannel ports as dynamic VLAN or 802.1x ports. Doing so can adversely affect switch performance (dynamic VLANs and 802.1x are covered in Chapter 7).

- **Protocol filtering**—EtherChannel bundles do not form if protocol filtering is configured differently on the ports (protocol filtering is covered in Chapter 7).

- **Quality of Service (QoS) configuration**—All ports must have identical QoS configurations; otherwise, an EtherChannel bundle does not form (QoS is covered in Chapter 8, " Traffic Filtering and Security").

- **Jumbo frames**—Ports with different jumbo frame configurations do not form a bundle.

As you can see, many configuration parameters must be set identically; otherwise, the switch operating system (CatOS or Cisco IOS) rejects the configuration.

Just as it is important to configure all ports on one side of an EtherChannel bundle identically, it is also very important that the ports on each switch that form each side of the bundle are also configured identically. In other words, you should ensure that the requirements just discussed are also applied to the remote switch ports that make up the other side of the EtherChannel bundle. Example 3-22 demonstrates configuring interfaces on Switch-A in Figure 3-16 to ensure that the interfaces form an EtherChannel bundle.

Example 3-109 *Configuring the Physical Interfaces of an EtherChannel Bundle on Cisco IOS*

```
Switch-A# configure terminal
Switch-A(config)# interface range FastEthernet0/1 - 2
Switch-A(config-if-range)# speed 100
Switch-A(config-if-range)# duplex full
Switch-A(config-if-range)# switchport trunk encapsulation dot1q
Switch-A(config-if-range)# switchport mode dynamic desirable
Switch-A(config-if-range)# switchport trunk native vlan 10
Switch-A(config-if-range)# switchport trunk allowed vlan 2-5,10,1002-1005
Switch-A(config-if-range)# switchport trunk pruning vlan 2-4
```

In Example 3-22, the configuration of both physical interfaces must be identical; hence, the trunk configurations applied in Scenarios 3-2 and 3-3 are applied to both interfaces to ensure the configurations on both are identical. The remote ports on Switch-B should also be configured with matching settings. Example 3-23 demonstrates configuring ports on Switch-B in Figure 3-16 to ensure that each port has the same configuration as other local ports and the remote interfaces on Switch-A.

Example 3-110 *Configuring the Physical Interfaces of an EtherChannel Bundle on CatOS*

```
Switch-B> (enable) set port speed 2/1-2 100
Ports 2/1-2 transmission speed set to 100Mbps.
Switch-B> (enable) set port duplex 2/1-2 full
Ports 2/1-2 set to full-duplex.
Switch-B> (enable) set trunk 2/1 desirable dot1q
Port(s)  2/1 trunk mode set to desirable.
Port(s)  2/1 trunk type set to dot1q.
Switch-B> (enable) set trunk 2/2 desirable dot1q
Port(s)  2/2 trunk mode set to desirable.
Port(s)  2/2 trunk type set to dot1q.
Switch-B> (enable) set vlan 10 2/1-2
VLAN 10 modified.
VLAN 1 modified.
VLAN  Mod/Ports
---- ----------------------
10    2/1-2
Switch-B> (enable) clear trunk 2/1 2-1005
Removing Vlan(s) 2-1005 from allowed list.
Port  2/1 allowed vlans modified to 1.
Switch-B> (enable) clear trunk 2/2 2-1005
Removing Vlan(s) 2-1005,1025-4094 from allowed list.
Port  2/2 allowed vlans modified to 1.
Switch-B> (enable) set trunk 2/1 2-5,10
Adding vlans 2-5,10 to allowed list.
Port(s)  2/1 allowed vlans modified to 2-5,10.
Switch-B> (enable) set trunk 2/2 2-5,10
Adding vlans 2-5,10 to allowed list.
Port(s)  2/2 allowed vlans modified to 2-5,10.
```

NOTE   If you are unsure of the current configuration of an interface or port, use the **show interface** command on Cisco IOS or the **show port** *mod/port* command on CatOS.

Configuring an EtherChannel Bundle

After ensuring that the settings for each of the physical interfaces/ports that make up an Ether-Channel bundle are compatible with EtherChannel and are configured identically across all local interfaces/ports and remote interfaces/ports, you can create EtherChannel bundles.

Cisco IOS Configuration

On Cisco IOS, an EtherChannel bundle is referred to as a *channel group* and is represented as a single logical interface known as a *port channel interface*. When configuring Layer 2 EtherChannel bundles (i.e., Layer 2 switch ports make up the bundle), you don't need to explicitly create the appropriate port channel interface for an EtherChannel bundle. Instead, the **channel-group** interface configuration mode command is used to assign the physical interface to an EtherChannel bundle, which automatically creates a new port channel interface if one does not already exist. The **channel-group** interface configuration mode has the following syntax:

```
Switch(config-if)# channel-group channel-group-number mode {auto | desirable
   [non-silent] | on}
```

The *channel-group-number* parameter defines the channel group number that is assigned to the bundle created. Valid values for this parameter range from 1 up to the maximum number of EtherChannel bundles supported on the switch (see Table 3-7). This number is also used to identify the logical port channel interface. The **mode** keyword allows you to specify the appropriate **auto**, **desirable**, or **on** keywords, which define the PAgP mode of operation. It is recommended that you always configure a mode of desirable because this mode ensures that interface failures do not cause issues with spanning tree. You also normally do not need to modify the silent or non-silent mode of operation (by default, the silent mode is configured on Cisco IOS switches). Example 3-24 demonstrates configuring an Ether-Channel bundle on Switch-A in Figure 3-16.

Example 3-111 *Creating an EtherChannel Bundle on Cisco IOS*

```
Switch-A# configure terminal
Switch-A(config)# interface range FastEthernet0/1 - 2
Switch-A(config-if-range)# channel-group 1 mode desirable
Switch-A(config-if-range)# end
```

The configuration of Example 3-24 automatically assigns interfaces FastEthernet0/1 and FastEthernet0/2 to channel group 1 and configures the interfaces to use the desirable mode for PAgP. If a new channel group has been created by the interface configuration (as is the case in Example 3-24), a new logical port channel interface is also created.

To verify that you have created an EtherChannel bundle, use the **show etherchannel summary** command, as demonstrated in Example 3-25.

Example 3-112 *Verifying EtherChannel Configuration*

```
Switch-A# show etherchannel summary
Flags:  D - down        P - in port-channel
        I - stand-alone s - suspended
        R - Layer3      S - Layer2
        u - unsuitable for bundling
        U - port-channel in use
        d - default port
Group Port-channel  Ports
-----+------------+-----------------------------------------------------------
 1     Po1(SU)      Fa0/1(P)   Fa0/2(P)
```

In Example 3-25, you can see the channel group #1, and that a port-channel interface has been created called Po1. The physical interfaces that comprise the group are listed in the Ports section. Notice the flags indicate that channel group #1 is a Layer 2 EtherChannel bundle (indicated by the S flag) and that each physical port is currently operating in the bundle (indicated by the P flag).

NOTE	Cisco Catalyst Layer 3 switches also support the configuration of Layer 3 EtherChannel bundles, which are equivalent to an EtherChannel bundle on a Cisco router. This feature is discussed in Chapter 5, "Inter-VLAN Routing."

Although Switch-B has not yet been configured for EtherChannel, notice that an Ether-Channel bundle has formed. By default CatOS switches operate in a PAgP mode of auto, which means that an EtherChannel bundle forms (see Table 3-5). Cisco IOS switches in contrast have a PAgP mode of off by default, requiring explicit configuration.

CatOS Configuration

On CatOS, an EtherChannel bundle is also referred to as a *channel group* and is formed based upon a logical entity known as an *administrative group*. A channel group represents an actual set of physical ports that currently form an active bundle. An administrative group on the other hand defines the list of available ports that a channel group may consist of. For example, an administrative group might specify a list of ports, say 2/1-2/4. Assume that a channel group is formed that initially includes each of these ports. Next consider what happens when a port (say port 2/3) fails. From a physical point of view, traffic must not be sent over the failed port; hence, the channel group needs to be updated to exclude the failed port (i.e., the channel group consists only of ports 2/1, 2/2, and 2/4). However, from a configuration point of view, the administrative group still needs to include ports 2/1-2/4 to ensure the channel group adds the failed port after that port has been restored.

Each channel group and administrative group is represented by a numeric identifier. With CatOS, you don't actually specify a channel group ID like you do with Cisco IOS. CatOS takes care of this automatically for you and then creates an administrative group. If you compare administrative groups with Cisco IOS, the equivalent Cisco IOS entity is a port channel interface. In Cisco IOS, the port channel interface ID is the same as the channel group ID; with CatOS, however, the administrative group ID is not the same as the channel group ID. However, at the end of the day, this numbering is essentially transparent to administrators, so if you find this scheme a little confusing, don't worry too much.

CatOS is also different to Cisco IOS in that any EtherChannel capable port is actually configured with a PAgP mode of *auto* by default. This default means that you don't actually necessarily need to configure anything for an EtherChannel bundle to form on a CatOS switch as long as the remote switch has ports configured with a PAgP mode of on or desirable. This characteristic explains why in Example 3-25 you saw that the EtherChannel bundle on Switch-A was up, without any configuration of Switch-B.

NOTE   Don't get lazy and forget to explicitly configure your EtherChannel bundles. Remember that the recommended EtherChannel PAgP mode to ensure physical interface failures do not affect spanning tree is desirable.

Before configuring EtherChannel on a CatOS switch, it is a good idea that you verify that the ports you wish to configure in an EtherChannel bundle do actually support Ether-Channel. You can use the **show port capabilities** command to verify whether or not a port supports EtherChannel. Example 3-26 demonstrates the use of this command on Switch-B in Figure 3-16.

Example 3-113 *Verifying a Port Supports EtherChannel on CatOS*

```
Switch-B> (enable) show port capabilities 2/1
Model                   WS-X6148-RJ45V
Port                    2/1
Type                    10/100BaseTX
Speed                   auto,10,100
Duplex                  half,full
Trunk encap type        ISL,802.1Q
Trunk mode              on,off,desirable,auto,nonegotiate
Channel                 2/1-48
Flow control            no
Security                yes
Dot1x                   yes
Membership              static,dynamic
... <output truncated>
...
```

In Example 3-26, the shaded line indicates that EtherChannel is supported on all ports of the module.

On CatOS by default, a set of administrative groups are already pre-configured, which can be displayed by using the **show channel group** command. Example 3-27 demonstrates the use of this command on Switch-B before any custom EtherChannel configuration has been applied.

Example 3-114 *Displaying Administrative Groups on CatOS*

```
Switch-B> (enable) show channel group
Admin Group  Ports
-----------  ----------------------------------------------
1            1/1-2
2            2/1-4
3            2/5-8
```

Example 3-114 *Displaying Administrative Groups on CatOS (Continued)*

```
4          2/9-12
5          2/13-16
6          2/17-20
7          2/21-24
8          2/25-28
9          2/29-32
10         2/33-36
11         2/37-40
12         2/41-44
13         2/45-48
```

In Example 3-27, you can see that on Switch-B each administrative group consists of four physical ports by default (except for the two gigabit Ethernet ports on the Supervisor). It is important that you understand the default grouping because it defines how the switch forms EtherChannel bundles by default. For example, in Example 3-25 you saw that Switch-B automatically formed an EtherChannel bundle on ports 2/1 and 2/2 with Switch-A. Referring to Example 3-27, ports 2/1 and 2/2 fall within an administrative group (#2); hence, a channel group can be formed as both ports are within the same administrative group. If, however, Switch-B were connected to Switch-A via ports 2/4 and 2/5, you can see that each port would be in separate administrative groups (port 2/4 is in group #2 and port 2/5 is in group #3). Because both ports would not be in the same administrative group, an EtherChannel bundle would not form. Understanding this point is why it is important you understand the default administrative groups.

NOTE   You are not locked into accepting the default port allocations used for the default administrative groups. For example, you can manually configure a new administrative group that includes ports 2/4 and 2/5, which would enable an EtherChannel bundle to form in the scenario just described .

The main point to take from the discussion about default administrative groups is that you are strongly recommended to configure your own administrative groups, which are specific to your requirements, encompassing the required amount of links and the desired ports that make up the bundle. Configuring your own administrative groups ensures your Ether-Channel bundles form as intended, without any nasty surprises.

To create a new EtherChannel bundle on CatOS, use the **set port channel** command.

```
Console> (enable) set port channel port-list {auto | desirable | on | off}
   [silent | non-silent]
```

The *port-list* parameter defines the list of ports that you wish to assign to the bundle. You must then specify the appropriate PAgP mode and optionally may specify silent or non-silent operation for desirable or auto modes (you can't configure silent or non-silent operation for a PAgP mode of on or off). After entering in the command, a new Ether-Channel bundle is created and automatically assigned an administrative group ID.

Example 3-28 demonstrates configuring an EtherChannel bundle that includes ports 2/1 and 2/2 on Switch-B in Figure 3-16.

Example 3-115 *Configuring an EtherChannel Bundle on CatOS*

```
Switch-B> (enable) set port channel 2/1-2 auto
Port(s) 2/1-2 are assigned to admin group 14.
Port(s) 2/1-2 channel mode set to auto.
```

In Example 3-28, notice that the new EtherChannel bundle is automatically assigned an administrative group ID of 14. This ID is one higher than the highest administrative group ID shown in Example 3-27 (CatOS automatically increments the administrative group ID created to ensure each administrative group ID is unique).

On CatOS, it is important that you do not confuse the following command with the command issued in Example 3-28:

```
Console> (enable) set port channel port-list mode {auto | desirable | on | off}
   [silent | non-silent]
```

Notice that this command includes the **mode** keyword. When the **mode** keyword is specified, no EtherChannel bundle is actually configured (i.e., no administrative group is created). Only the PAgP mode of the ports listed is modified according to the mode specified. In other words, using the **mode** keyword enables you to modify the PAgP mode of ports in existing administrative groups (the *port-list* specified can span multiple administrative groups) instead of creating a new administrative group. Example 3-29 demonstrates modifying the EtherChannel bundle created in Example 3-28 (administrative group 14) to use a PAgP mode of desirable.

Example 3-116 *Modifying PAgP Mode on CatOS*

```
Switch-B> (enable) set port channel 2/1-2 mode desirable
Port(s) 2/1-2 channel mode set to desirable.
```

If you compare Example 3-28 and Example 3-29, notice that in Example 3-29, a new administrative group is not created. Instead, only the PAgP mode of the ports has been modified.

Another variant of the **set port channel** command has the following syntax:

```
Console> (enable) set port channel port-list [admin-group]
```

This command allows you to create a new EtherChannel and manually specify the administrative group ID using the *admin-group* parameter. This command may be useful if you configure many EtherChannel bundles on your switch and wish to use a numbering scheme to ease management of administrative groups.

NOTE Valid values for the administrative group ID include 1 to 1024.

Example 3-30 demonstrates using this command on Switch-B in Figure 3-16 to create an EtherChannel bundle that has an administrative group ID of 100.

Example 3-117 *Manually Specifying Administrative Group ID on CatOS*

```
Switch-B> (enable) set port channel 2/1-2 100
```

Port(s) 2/1-2 are assigned to administrative group 100.

To verify that you have created an EtherChannel bundle, use the **show port channel** command, as demonstrated in Example 3-31 on Switch-B.

Example 3-118 *Verifying EtherChannel Configuration*

```
Switch-B> (console) show port channel
Port    Status      Channel                 Admin Ch
                    Mode                    Group Id
-----  ----------  -------------------     ----- -----
 2/1   connected   desirable silent         100   801
 2/2   connected   desirable silent         100   801


Port   Device-ID                           Port-ID                    Platform
-----  -------------------------------     -----------------------    ----------------
 2/1   Switch-A                            Fa0/1                      cisco WS-C3550-24
 2/2   Switch-A                            Fa0/2                      cisco WS-C3550-24
```

The first section of Example 3-31 indicates the current status of the EtherChannel bundle. You can see that both ports have a status of "connected," a channel mode of "desirable silent," and an administrative group ID of 100. The second section of Example 3-31 indicates port-specific information within the bundle. You can see that Switch-A (as indicated by the Device-ID column) is connected to both ports 2/1 and 2/2, that port 2/1 is connected to interface fa0/1, and that port 2/2 is connected to interface fa0/2 on Switch-A (as indicated by the Port-ID column). You can even see the Cisco Catalyst model of switch connected to Switch-B. Most of this information is exchanged via the PAgP negotiation process.

NOTE Platform information is derived from CDP information advertised via Cisco devices, not from PAgP.

Configuring EtherChannel Load Distribution

EtherChannel load distribution is an important consideration because it affects how Ether-Channel bundles perform in the network. How load distribution is configured is very much dependant on the network topology and the load distribution methods supported on the switches used in the network topology (see Table 3-6 for more information).

Cisco IOS Configuration

To configure the EtherChannel load sharing mechanism on Cisco IOS, use the **port-channel load-balance** global configuration mode command, as shown:

```
Switch(config)# port-channel load-balance {src-mac | dst-mac | src-dst-mac |
    src-ip | dst-ip | src-dst-ip | src-port | dst-port | src-dst-port}
```

Notice that a wide variety of load distribution mechanisms are indicated; however, depending on the switch platform you are using, the available load distribution methods vary as follows:

- Cisco Catalyst 2900XL/3500XL and Catalyst 2950/3550 switches support load distribution based only upon Layer 2 MAC addresses.

- Native IOS Catalyst 6000/6500 switches that include a PFC1 support load distribution based upon Layer 2 MAC addresses and Layer 3 IP addresses.

- Cisco Catalyst 4000 Supervisor 3/4 and native IOS Catalyst 6000/6500 switches that include a PFC2 support load distribution based upon Layer 2 MAC addresses, Layer 3 IP addresses, and Layer 4 TCP/UDP ports.

In this scenario, Switch-A is a Catalyst 3550 switch; hence, only load distribution based upon Layer 2 MAC addresses can be configured. This restriction means that on Switch-A the **port-channel load-balance** global configuration mode command has the following syntax:

```
Switch(config)# port-channel load-balance {src-mac | dst-mac}
```

The default is to load share based upon source MAC address. Example 3-32 shows how to configure load sharing on Switch-A based upon the destination MAC address of each frame sent across any EtherChannel bundle (this setting applies globally for all EtherChannel bundles).

Example 3-119 *Configuring EtherChannel Load Distribution on Cisco IOS*

```
Switch-A# configure terminal
Switch-A(config)# port-channel load-balance dst-mac
```

WARNING   There is one big caveat to configuring load sharing on the Cisco Catalyst series switches, whether they are CatOS-based or Cisco IOS-based—the load sharing method is implemented globally for all bundles. This restriction means you must choose the most optimal method for all scenarios.

CatOS Configuration

To configure the EtherChannel load sharing mechanism on CatOS, use the **set port channel all distribution** command as shown:

```
Console> (enable) set port channel all distribution {ip | mac | session}
    [source | destination | both]
```

The first set of configurable parameters specifies whether Layer 2 (indicated by the **mac** keyword), Layer 3 (indicated by the **ip** keyword), or Layer 4 (indicated by the **session** keyword) addressing should be used. The final set of configurable parameters indicates whether the source (indicated by the **source** keyword), destination (indicated by the **destination** keyword), or both source and destination (indicated by the **both** keyword) addressing should be used. Notice that a wide variety of load distribution mechanisms are indicated; however, depending on the switch platform you are using, the available load distribution methods vary as follows:

- Cisco Catalyst 2900/4000 and Catalyst 5000/5500 switches support only a single load distribution method based upon Layer 2 MAC addresses that cannot be modified.

- Catalyst 6000/6500 switches that include a PFC1 support load distribution based upon Layer 2 MAC addresses and Layer 3 IP addresses.

- Catalyst 6000/6500 switches that include a PFC2 support load distribution based upon Layer 2 MAC addresses, Layer 3 IP addresses, and Layer 4 TCP/UDP ports

In this scenario, Switch-A is a Catalyst 6500 switch with a Supervisor 2/PFC2; hence, all load distribution mechanisms are supported. The default load distribution mechanism on this switch is based upon both source IP address and destination IP address (i.e., **set port channel all distribution ip both**). Assume in Figure 3-16 that many client PCs are connected to Switch-B and that these PCs make client/server connections to servers attached to Switch-A. This situation means that most frames sent from Switch-B to Switch-A include a random Layer 4 source port (because client ports are normally chosen randomly) and a well-known Layer 4 destination port (because server ports normally listen on fixed, well-known ports). Configuring load sharing based upon Layer 4 source port should ensure an even load distribution because each source port value is essentially a random value. Example 3-33 shows how to configure load sharing on Switch-B based upon only the source Layer 4 ports of frames sent across any EtherChannel bundle (this setting applies globally for all EtherChannel bundles).

Example 3-120 *Configuring EtherChannel Load Distribution on Cisco IOS*

```
Switch-B> (config) set port channel all distribution session source
Channel distribution is set to mac both.
```

Verifying EtherChannel Configuration

Once you have completed your EtherChannel configuration, verify each configured bundle has come up and that the correct ports are included in each bundle. The first step in verifying EtherChannel configuration is to verify the bundle as a whole has been created and is up.

On Cisco IOS, you can use the **show etherchannel summary** command (see Example 3-25) to get a quick view of the status of each EtherChannel bundle, and on CatOS, you can use the **show port channel** command (see Example 3-31) to achieve a similar result.

Once you have checked the overall status of EtherChannel bundles, if you discover any problems, you can use the **show etherchannel port** command on Cisco IOS to view port-specific information about ports in an EtherChannel bundle, as demonstrated in Example 3-34.

Example 3-121 *Verifying a Port Within an EtherChannel Bundle on Switch-A*

```
Switch-A# show etherchannel port
                Channel-group listing:
                ----------------------

Group: 1
----------
                Ports in the group:
                -------------------
Port: Fa0/1
-----------

Port state      = Up Mstr In-Bndl
Channel group = 1          Mode = Desirable-Sl     Gcchange = 0
Port-channel  = Po1        GC   = 0x00010001     Pseudo port-channel = Po1
Port index    = 0          Load = 0x00

Flags:  S - Device is sending Slow hello.  C - Device is in Consistent state.
        A - Device is in Auto mode.         P - Device learns on physical port.
        d - PAgP is down.
Timers: H - Hello timer is running.        Q - Quit timer is running.
        S - Switching timer is running.    I - Interface timer is running.

Local information:
                              Hello    Partner  PAgP    Learning  Group
Port      Flags State   Timers Interval Count   Priority  Method  Ifindex
Fa0/1     SC    U6/S7   H      30s      1        128      Any      29

Partner's information:

          Partner              Partner          Partner          Partner Group
Port      Name                 Device ID        Port    Age Flags Cap.
Fa0/1     JAB03350EJR(Switch-B 0030.2448.d41b   2/1     23s SC    2

Age of the port in the current state: 00d:00h:27m:15s
... <Output Truncated>
...
```

In Example 3-34, you can see that a lot of information is provided. Each EtherChannel bundle is listed, followed by specific information for each port within the bundle. Within the information listed for each port, local information is provided, along with information about the remote device connected (see the "Partner's information" section).

At this point, you have verified that the EtherChannel bundle has formed, which means that the bundle should be up as a trunk. Example 3-35 demonstrates using the **show interface trunk** command to verify that the bundle has come up as an 802.1Q trunk between Switch-A and Switch-B.

Example 3-122 *Verifying the Trunk Between Switch-A and Switch-B Has Come Up on the EtherChannel Bundle*

```
Switch-A# show interface trunk
Port      Mode        Encapsulation  Status       Native vlan
Po1       desirable   802.1q         trunking     10


Port      Vlans allowed on trunk
Po1       2-5,10


Port      Vlans allowed and active in management domain
Po1       2-5,10


Port      Vlans in spanning tree forwarding state and not pruned
Po1       2,3,5,10
```

In Example 3-35, notice that the trunk port is now the port-channel 1 interface, indicating this interface is a logical Layer 2 interface.

As a final test, verify IP connectivity between the management interfaces on each switch and between devices within each VLAN.

Verifying Load Sharing and Redundancy

If you wish to verify that the load sharing and redundancy features are performing as you expect, you can use the **show interfaces counters** command on Cisco IOS to test load sharing and redundancy. Example 3-36 shows an example of the use of the **show interfaces counters** command.

Example 3-123 *Verifying Load Balancing and Redundancy on a Cisco IOS Switch*

```
Switch-A# show interfaces counters
Port          InOctets     InUcastPkts    InMcastPkts    InBcastPkts
Fa0/1           430066             443           5387              3
Fa0/2            85234             195            765              0
...<Output Truncated>
...
Port          OutOctets    OutUcastPkts   OutMcastPkts   OutBcastPkts
Fa0/1           181410             281           1189             10
Fa0/2           105111             502            440             69
...<Output Truncated>
...
```

Example 3-36 shows that you can determine load sharing based upon the unicast, multicast, and broadcast frame counts shown.

On CatOS you can use the **show channel traffic** command on CatOS to display traffic statistics for each physical interface within a bundle. This command displays both *received* and transmitted traffic, so you can verify how traffic is being load balanced locally over the channel (by viewing the transmitted statistics) and how it is being load balanced remotely over the channel (by viewing the received statistics). Example 3-37 shows a sample output of the **show channel traffic** command.

Example 3-124 *Verifying Load Balancing on a CatOS Switch*

```
Switch-B> (enable) show channel traffic
ChanId Port  Rx-Ucst Tx-Ucst Rx-Mcst Tx-Mcst Rx-Bcst Tx-Bcst
------ ----- ------- ------- ------- ------- ------- -------
   100  2/1   62.50%  44.50%  50.00%  75.75%  46.00%  42.50%
   100  2/2   37.50%  55.50%  50.00%  24.25%  54.00%  57.50%
...
...
```

In Example 3-37, you can easily verify traffic load distribution. For example, 44.50 percent of sent unicast traffic is being sent over port 2/1 and is then sent over the bundle.

Summary

In this chapter you have learned about one of the fundamentals of modern day switching — trunking. Trunks are high-speed highways of the LAN that aggregate VLAN traffic onto a single Layer 2 link. You have also learned about bandwidth aggregation of LAN interfaces and how this technique can improve the performance and redundancy of your network without costly upgrades to next generation switching speeds.

Cisco Catalyst switches support the proprietary Cisco Inter-Switch Link (ISL) trunking protocol, as well as the standards based 802.1Q protocol. Trunk ports can use Dynamic Trunking Protocol (DTP) frames to negotiate whether a trunk is formed and the encapsulation (ISL of 802.1Q) used. Trunk ports can exist in several modes that determine how they negotiate trunking. The on or off mode explicitly forces a trunk on or off, with the on mode supporting the use of DTP frames. The nonegotiate mode explicitly forces a trunk on and disables the use of DTP frames. The auto and desirable modes determine whether a port passively (auto) uses DTP or actively (desirable) uses DTP to negotiate a trunk.

VLAN Trunking Protocol (VTP) is used to propagate VLAN databases over trunk interfaces. This protocol allows the centralized configuration of VLANs, with the resulting configurations automatically propagated out to the remaining switches in the network. VTP messages are propagated within a VTP domain, which is a collection of switches under common administrative control. For VTP to work, various parameters such as the domain name, version, password, and pruning must be configured identically throughout a VTP domain. VTP pruning allows for the automatic pruning of VLAN traffic from trunks that don't service a particular VLAN and, therefore, don't need to receive the traffic for that

VLAN across a trunk. This pruning allows your network links to be optimized for the specific topology and distribution of users in your network.

EtherChannel is Cisco's proprietary bandwidth aggregation protocol, which all Cisco Catalyst switches support. EtherChannel forms bundles by using the Port Aggregation Protocol (PAgP), with each port operating in a specific PAgP mode. PAgP works by exchanging frames with remote ports to determine whether a bundle can be formed or not. The on or off mode explicitly forces an EtherChannel bundle on or off and disables the use of PAgP. The auto and desirable modes determine whether a port passively (auto) uses PAgP or actively (desirable) uses PAgP. The recommended PAgP mode for interswitch links between Cisco Switches is desirable because it handles link failures correctly.

CHAPTER 4

Spanning Tree

The *Spanning Tree Protocol (STP)* is a Layer 2 protocol that prevents loops in transparently bridged networks. Due to the nature of transparent bridging, when an active looped topology exists, a network meltdown generally occurs in a matter seconds. STP is a protocol that builds a logical loop-free topology, ensuring the network does not suffer from major problems such as a broadcast storm or bridge table corruption.

STP was originally developed by Digital Equipment Corporation in 1983 to address the issues of running transparent bridging in a looped Layer 2 topology. Today, STP exists in two flavors:

- **DEC**—The original Spanning Tree Protocol, created by Digital Equipment Corporation.
- **IEEE**—Standards-based Spanning Tree Protocol, specified in the 802.1d standard, initially developed by Radia Perlman. This protocol was developed from the DEC STP implementation; however, the versions are incompatible with each other. The IEEE 802.1d version is almost exclusively used in today's networks.

This chapter focuses exclusively on the IEEE 802.1d version of STP. After some initial introductory material, this chapter presents the following configuration scenarios, which provide you with the practical knowledge required to implement spanning tree:

- Scenario 4-1: Configuring the Root Bridge
- Scenario 4-2: Configuring STP Load Sharing
- Scenario 4-3: Configuring Root Guard
- Scenario 4-4: Configuring Spanning Tree PortFast
- Scenario 4-5: Configuring PortFast BPDU Guard
- Scenario 4-6: Configuring PortFast BPDU Filter
- Scenario 4-7: Configuring UplinkFast
- Scenario 4-8: Configuring BackboneFast
- Scenario 4-9: Improving Convergence and Load Sharing by Using a Multilayer Topology
- Scenario 4-10: Troubleshooting Spanning Tree

Introduction

Spanning tree is designed to ensure a loop-free forwarding topology is generated in a multi-switch LAN. Due to the nature of transparent bridging, if any loops are in the active Layer 2 topology, frames such as broadcast frames, multicast frames, and unknown unicast frames will continuously circle the looped network.

Transparent bridging defines no mechanism such as the TTL (time-to-live) field used in IP packets to prevent frames from continuously circling a looped network. This fact causes a snowball effect, with the number of broadcast, multicast, and unknown unicast frames looping the network increasing. Because broadcast frames must also be processed by the CPU of every device receiving the frame, CPU usage on every device increases as more and more frames loop the network. Eventually (normally within a matter of seconds), the entire network goes into a meltdown. CPU time and memory on each switch are consumed just processing each broadcast frame, and the available bandwidth on each link for valid traffic becomes less and less. As you can see, a looped Layer 2 topology is a catastrophe for any network, and you definitely need to prevent loops in the topology, while still providing redundant paths.

In this section, you are introduced to the concepts of spanning tree and how it can generate a loop-free topology that dynamically reconverges to a new loop-free topology in the event of failures.

Spanning Tree Operation

A looped Layer 2 topology causes serious issues. Simply blocking a port from sending and receiving data can prevent a looped topology. Spanning tree is the protocol responsible for determining a loop-free topology and blocking the appropriate ports as required. To create a loop-free topology, spanning tree forms a tree structure that is generated from a *root node* or *root bridge*.

NOTE   On Cisco Catalyst switches, by default, a separate, loop-free topology is created for each VLAN. A root bridge is selected for each VLAN, which means that while a physical port might be blocked for one VLAN, the same physical port might be forwarding for another VLAN. In spanning tree, each physical port contains a *logical port* per VLAN, which allows a logical port for one VLAN to be blocked while another logical port for another VLAN can be forwarding. Thus, spanning tree actually calculates a loop-tree *logical topology* for each VLAN.

The root bridge is the heart of the spanning-tree topology, and is used as a reference point to generate a loop-free topology. Once the root bridge is selected, each bridge determines the best path to reach the root bridge and blocks any other paths that introduce loops. In a converged spanning-tree topology, a port can be either in a *forwarding state* or in a *blocking state*. Only ports that are considered the best path to the root bridge are placed into a forwarding state; all other ports are placed into a blocking state.

When spanning tree first initializes, each switch generates a unique *bridge ID* per VLAN, which is used by spanning tree to uniquely identify the switch. The bridge ID consists of the bridge MAC address plus a 2-byte field called *bridge priority*, which can be altered to directly affect whether or not a bridge becomes the root bridge. The bridge priority can be configured as any value between 0 and 65535 and is 32768 on Cisco switches. Figure 4-1 shows the structure of the bridge ID.

NOTE   All Cisco Catalyst switches are assigned a set of MAC addresses that can be used for spanning tree and other purposes.

Figure 4-1   *Bridge ID*

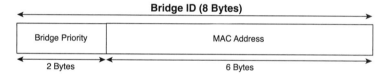

The bridge ID is used to select the root bridge; the bridge with the lowest bridge ID always becomes the root bridge. An example of a bridge ID is 32768.000d.7903.0c00. The first portion (32768) is the bridge priority, represented in decimal, while the remaining portion of the bridge ID (000d.7903.0c00) is the hexadecimal representation of the bridge MAC address. Once the bridge ID has been determined, each bridge starts out by assuming that it is the root bridge and begins to generate *configuration bridge protocol data units* (*BPDUs*). Configuration BPDUs are the main communication mechanism for spanning tree and are used to determine the root bridge as well as whether or not a port should be forwarding or blocking. A configuration BPDU has various fields that are used to indicate parameters that are important to the generation of the final spanning-tree topology. Table 4-1 describes the important fields that are present in each configuration BPDU.

Table 4-1   *Important Configuration BPDU Fields*

Field	Description
Type	Determines whether the BPDU is a configuration BPDU or a topology change BPDU.
Root bridge ID	Lists the bridge ID of what the sender of the BPDU considers is the root bridge. Once spanning tree has converged, the root bridge ID should be identical for all BPDUs in the network.
Root path cost	Lists the cost to the root bridge of the bridge sending the configuration BPDUs. This cost helps the receiving bridge to determine the shortest path to the root bridge when multiple configuration BPDUs are received from multiple bridges.
Sender bridge ID	Lists the bridge ID of the device that sent the configuration BPDU. This value is the same for all BPDUs by the same switch.
Port ID	A value that describes the port from which the BPDU was sent.
Max age (seconds)	Determines the maximum time a BPDU is considered valid. By default, this value is 20 seconds. If BPDUs stop being received, after 20 seconds the last BPDU received is considered invalid, which means the existing root bridge is considered down.
Hello time (seconds)	The interval at which configuration BPDUs are generated. By default this value is 2 seconds. It is important to note that the root bridge only ever generates configuration BPDUs. Each non-root bridge merely propagates the configuration BPDUs that are generated by the root bridge.
Forward delay	Indicates the time spent in the *listening* and *learning* phases. These phases are used to allow time for a root bridge to be elected and for a loop-free topology to be determined.

With regards to selecting the root bridge, the important field in Table 4-1 is the root bridge ID. If a bridge receives a configuration BPDU that lists a lower root bridge ID than what the bridge considers is the current root bridge ID, the bridge immediately considers the lower root bridge ID as the root bridge and begins propagating configuration BPDUs received from this root bridge. Eventually, in a Layer 2 network with multiple bridges, the bridge with the lowest bridge ID becomes known as the root bridge to all bridges. At this point, the root bridge has been selected, and each non-root bridge now begins the process of generating a loop-free topology. Figure 4-2 demonstrates the selection of a root bridge.

Figure 4-2   *Selecting the Root Bridge*

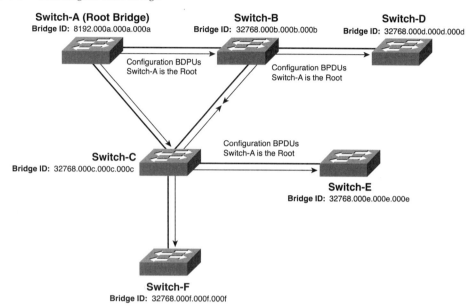

In Figure 4-2, Bridge A is selected as the root bridge, because it has the lowest bridge ID. Once the root bridge has been selected, all non-root bridges do not actually generate configuration BPDUs by themselves. Each non-root bridge generates configuration BPDUs only when a configuration BPDU originated by the root bridge is received. The non-root bridge updates certain fields in the configuration BPDU (such as root path cost and sender bridge ID) and then propagates the updated configuration BPDU out all ports, except the port upon which the BPDU was generated. This process ensures that configuration BPDUs are propagated throughout the entire network to all switches.

Once the root bridge has been selected, each non-root bridge attempts to build a topology that forms the lowest-cost path to the root bridge. To accommodate this requirement, spanning tree uses the concept of cost. The concept of *cost* in spanning tree is a measure of the how preferable a link or logical port is in comparison to other links. The lower the cost, the more preferable the link. For example, a 10-Mbps port is considered less preferable than a 100-Mbps port and, thus, has a higher cost to indicate this. Each logical port has a default cost associated with it, which is defined in the 802.1d standard and depends on the bandwidth of the link. The cost for a logical port can be modified to influence root port selection. Table 4-2 shows the 802.1d default costs for various bandwidths associated with a link.

Table 4-2   *IEEE 802.1d Default STP Costs*

Bandwidth (Mbps)	Cost
4	250
10	100
16	62
100	19
155	14
622	6
1000 (1 Gbps)	4
10000 (10 Gbps)	2

Generating a Loop-Free Topology

It is important to understand that every logical port within a spanning-tree instance transitions through several states upon port initialization. Table 4-3 summarizes each of the STP states a port can be in.

Table 4-3   *Spanning Tree Port States*

State	Description	User data being forwarded?
Disabled	The port is in a non-functional state, which might be due to a hardware failure or due to the port being administratively shut down.	No
Listening	The port is sending and receiving configuration BPDUs and is determining the root bridge and the role the port should take.	No
Learning	The switch is accepting user data on the port, but is not forwarding it, instead populating the bridge table with destination MAC address information. This ensures that the network is not suddenly flooded with unicast floods.	No
Forwarding	This state is transitioned to from the listening state. In this state, the port forwards all traffic. Only ports that represent the shortest path to the root bridge are placed into a forwarding state.	Yes
Blocking	The port is being blocked from sending or receiving any user data, but still sends and receives configuration BPDUs. A port is placed into the blocking state if it is determined to not represent the shortest path to the root bridge.	No

As you can see, user data is only forwarded when a port is in the forwarding state. Spanning tree takes this very cautious approach to prevent any loops from forming even for a short time, because a broadcast storm can bring down a network in seconds. Figure 4-3 illustrates how a port transitions through each of the various states to reach either a forwarding state or a blocking state.

Figure 4-3   *STP State Transition*

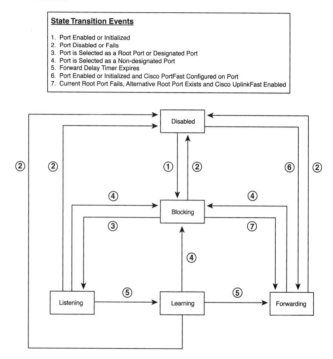

In Figure 4-3, you can see the various events that cause a transition in port state. Notice that a port in the Disabled state only ever transitions to a Blocking state (unless Cisco PortFast is configured), which ensures a loop cannot be created before the network topology is learned. Each of the phases listed in Table 4-3 and Figure 4-3 are now described.

Disabled

A port is disabled when the Layer 2 protocol is down on the port, whether it be because the port has been administratively shut down, because it is not connected, or because of some issue with processing BPDUs. A port transitions from the Disabled state to the Blocking state and then immediately to a Listening state after it is initialized at the Layer 2 level.

Listening

The Listening state is the phase where most of the important legwork of generating a loop-free topology is performed. To generate a loop-free topology, spanning tree goes through the following processes:

1 **Elect the root bridge**—You have already seen how a root bridge is elected. The bridge with the lowest bridge ID is selected as the root bridge.

2 **Select the root port**—Every non-root bridge selects a single *root port*, which is the port that provides the closest path to the root bridge. The concept of cost is used to determine which path is the most optimal—the port that provides a path with the lowest cost to the root bridge is selected as the root port.

3 **Select a designated bridge (port) for each segment**—Once the root bridge and root port have been determined, each switch determines whether or not it represents the shortest path to the root for each segment attached to the switch (excluding the segment attached to the root port). If the switch determines it represents the closest path to the root on a segment, it configures itself as the *designated bridge* for the segment and configures the port as a *designated port*. Each designated port is placed into a forwarding state, while all other non-designated ports are placed into a Blocking state. The exception to this configuration is if one of the non-designated ports represents the root port on another switch. In this case, the root port on the other switch remains in a Forwarding state, as well as remaining the designated port on the local switch.

When any of the decisions just listed for spanning-tree topology calculation are made, all those decisions are based upon the configuration BPDUs that are received by each bridge. No matter what the decision, whether it is selecting the root bridge or a root port, the same selection process is used for all decisions. This selection process is known as the *Spanning-Tree Algorithm (STA)* and is described in Table 4-4.

Table 4-4   *The Spanning-Tree Algorithm*

Priority	Criteria
1	Select the lowest root bridge ID
2	Select the lowest root path cost
3	Select the lowest sender bridge ID
4	Select the lowest port priority

Each of the criteria in Table 4-4 is processed one by one, by comparing the configuration BPDUs received on a port with the configuration BPDUs that are sent out a port, until a decision can be made. If parameters are equal, the next criterion is processed until a decision can be made. Referring back to Table 4-1, you can see that each of the selection criteria is a field in configuration BPDUs.

For example, consider the process of selecting the root bridge. If you take the STA and apply it to this process, you can see that the lowest root bridge ID becomes the root bridge. When it comes to selecting the root port, because a root bridge has been selected, the root bridge ID on all configuration BPDUs is the same, so this criteria cannot be used to make a selection. This fact means that the next criterion is evaluated (select the lowest root path cost). Again, if the criteria is the same on the configuration BPDUs being compared, the next criteria is evaluated, which is to select the lowest sender bridge ID.

Learning

During the Learning phase, the spanning-tree topology has normally been determined, and the switch is accepting user data. However, it is not forwarding it. The purpose of this phase is to populate the local bridging table on each switch, so that once traffic is actually forwarded, the switch does not need to flood a lot of traffic. Because the bridging table has been populated to a certain extent, the amount of unknown unicast destination MAC addresses is reduced, reducing the amount of flooding in the network.

Forwarding

After the Learning phase, if a port has been selected as either a root port or designated port, it is placed into the Forwarding state, which means that the port forwards user data. A port remains in the forwarding state until a topology change occurs where the path to the root bridge is affected or the root bridge itself fails. If this change occurs, the port transitions to the Listening phase and performs the appropriate selection processes.

NOTE   If a topology change occurs *downstream* from a switch (i.e., in an area of the network that is further away from the root bridge), no changes on the local switch should occur, unless superior configuration BPDUs are received from a downstream switch.

Spanning-Tree Timers

Spanning-tree timers are important because they determine how quickly or slowly a spanning-tree topology can react to a link or bridge failure and converge to a new topology. As indicated in Table 4-1, there are three spanning-tree timers:

- **Hello timer**—The interval at which each configuration BPDU is generated. The default is two seconds, meaning that a configuration BPDU is generated every two seconds.

- **Max age timer**—Controls how long a configuration BPDU is valid after being received. The default is 20 seconds, meaning that if a configuration BPDU is not received within 20 seconds of the previous, the previous configuration BPDU is no longer valid and a new root bridge must be selected.

- **Forward delay**—Controls the amount of time that a bridge port spends in each of the *Listening* and *Learning* phases before transitioning a blocking port to a Forwarding state.

NOTE   A failure in the spanning-tree topology can be detected either directly (if a physical interface goes down, the logical ports on that interface go down as well) or indirectly (a failure occurs that does not down a physical link, which can happen if an active device is in between two bridges). Detecting an indirect failure is simply a matter of not receiving configuration BPDUs for the Max Age timer interval.

It is important to ensure that the spanning-tree timers implemented are consistent throughout the spanning-tree topology. To ensure this, the root bridge configures the spanning-tree timers and attaches these to each configuration BPDU generated (see Table 4-1). Each non-root bridge inherits the spanning-tree timers in the configuration BPDUs, overriding any local configuration and ensuring the spanning-tree timers are consistent for the entire topology.

If a failure occurs in the spanning-tree topology, the various STP timers control how quickly the spanning-tree topology can converge. The following describes how to calculate the convergence time for different types of failures:

- **Direct failure**—A direct failure is detected immediately and enables a switch to immediately expire the Max Age timer, invalidating all current configuration BPDUs. At this point, the switch announces itself as the root bridge and must pass through the Listening and Learning phases before forwarding traffic. Because the forward delay timer determines how long the Listening and Learning phases are, the convergence time for a direct failure is defined as 2 × forward delay. For example, if the forward delay timer is the standard 15 seconds, the convergence time of a direct failure will be 2 × 15 seconds or 30 seconds.

- **Indirect failure**—An indirect failure is not detected immediately and relies upon configuration BPDUs not being received for the duration of the Max Age timer. Once the Max Age timer expires, the root bridge is considered down, and the switch will announce itself as the root bridge and must pass through the listening and learning phases before forwarding traffic. The convergence time for an indirect failure can be calculated as the Max age timer + 2 × forward delay. For example, if using the default STP timers, the convergence time of an indirect failure is 20 + (2 * 15) seconds or 50 seconds.

You can optimize spanning-tree timers to reduce the default convergence times, depending on your spanning-tree topology. Spanning-tree timers are dependant upon the *network diameter* of the Layer 2 network, which is defined as the maximum number of bridge hops between any two devices. The timers also depend on the value of the Hello timer, which can be reduced to ensure topology changes are learned of faster than when using the standard Hello timer value. Each timer is calculated so as to ensure that configuration BPDUs can be propagated throughout the network fully before decisions are made about forwarding or blocking ports. Clearly, if there are more bridge hops for a configuration BPDU to travel, the time required for propagation of BPDUs throughout the entire network is higher.

The default spanning-tree timers are designed to accommodate a spanning-tree topology that has a network diameter of seven. For some topologies, the network diameter might be lower than this; in these cases, the spanning-tree timers can safely be reduced. The 802.1d specification includes the correct formula for calculating spanning-tree timers based upon the Hello timer used and the network diameter. Cisco Catalyst switches provides tools that calculate the correct spanning-tree timers based upon network diameter and Hello timer interval.

NOTE   You can also use Cisco proprietary enhancements to STP to reduce convergence for common situations. These enhancements are discussed later in the chapter.

Recent Spanning Tree Developments

The IEEE has been busy at work recently and has released new specifications relating to spanning tree. Two important specifications are now supported by certain Cisco Catalyst switches:

- Rapid Spanning Tree Protocol (RSTP)
- Multiple Spanning Tree (MST)

Each of these new protocols is now discussed.

RSTP

The most significant development for spanning tree in recent times is the 802.1w specification, which is also known as *Rapid Spanning Tree Protocol (RSTP)*. RSTP is intended to replace the 802.1d standard and redefines the states that switch ports can be in, as well as how switches detect failure and the associated convergence time. With the advent of Layer 3 switching and the use of multilayer design to reduce the convergence times for modern switched networks, a primary goal of RSTP is to reduce convergence times to at least similar levels. RSTP achieves this and also includes standards-based implementations of PortFast, UplinkFast, and BackboneFast.

RSTP is supported from CatOS 7.1 and native IOS 12.1(11)EX on the Catalyst 6000/6500 platform. RSTP support is present from CatOS 7.2 on the Catalyst 4000, and at the time of this writing, it is not supported on the Cisco IOS-based Catalyst 4000 with Supervisor 3. It is supported from Cisco IOS 12.1(9)EA on the Cisco 2950 and 3550 platforms.

MST

The other important specification relating to spanning tree is the 802.1s specification, which is also known as *Multiple Spanning Tree* (*MST*). MST relates to how spanning tree interoperates with topologies that include multiple VLANs. On Cisco Catalyst switches, you can define the mode of spanning tree operation, which determines how the switch maintains STP for multiple VLANs. The following lists the common STP modes of operation:

- **CST (Common Spanning Tree)**—Prior to 802.1s, the only standards-based interpretation of STP and its relation to multiple VLANs was available in the 802.1q specification, which dictated that a *single* spanning-tree instance should be used for *all* VLANs. This feature is also known as CST. The reason for defining CST is to ensure interoperability with non-802.1q bridges, as all STP communication is sent untagged on the native VLAN. Having only a single spanning-tree instance means that each switch CPU needs to deal only with a single STP instance; however, you cannot implement load sharing (multiple STP instances are required for load sharing), which is a major drawback for many networks.

- **Cisco PVST+ (Per-VLAN spanning tree)**—Cisco developed the proprietary PVST+ mode of operation, which allows multiple STP instances to operate in a Layer 2 network, allowing for STP load sharing. PVST+ operates a unique STP instance per VLAN, which means that if you have 500 VLANs active in the Layer 2 network, 500 STP instances exist. Of course although 500 VLANs might exist in the network, only a handful of different paths through the network normally exist, meaning that you might require only several different STP topologies to implement load sharing. Thus, although PVST+ allows you to implement load sharing, the implementation is flawed in that a single STP instance is required for each VLAN, even if VLANs share the same STP topology. This flawed implementation can have a detrimental effect on CPUs in environments that support hundreds or thousands of VLANs.

NOTE   PVST+ is the default mode of spanning-tree operation on Cisco Catalyst switches.

- **Multiple Spanning Tree (MST)**—MST combines the best of both 802.1Q and PVST+. MST allows you to map a configurable number of VLANs to a single STP instance, which means that all VLANs that share the same STP topology can be supported by just one STP instance. Load sharing is achieved by having multiple STP instances, but the number of STP instances that must be maintained on each switch can be matched to the number of different logical topologies required for your network to implement load sharing.

NOTE   Cisco developed a proprietary version of MST before MST was released called multi-instance spanning tree protocol (MISTP), which has similar principles of MST.

Figure 4-4 demonstrates a simple STP topology that includes 1000 VLANs and shows how load sharing is achieved for each of the technologies just discussed.

Figure 4-4   *STP Load Sharing and 802.1Q, PVST+, and MST*

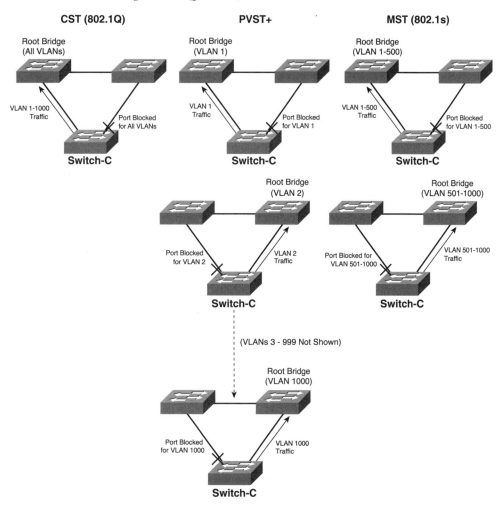

In Figure 4-4, the STP instances for each spanning tree mode are shown. In CST (802.1q) mode, a single STP instance exists for all VLANs, and only one active STP topology exists. This arrangement means that Switch-C can have only one active path uplink.

In PVST+ mode, a single STP instance exists for each VLAN, which means that 1000 STP instances exist in total. This arrangement allows for load sharing to be implemented by configuring 500 STP instances to use one uplink on Switch-C as the active forwarding path and the remaining 500 STP instances to use the other uplink on Switch-C. Although STP load sharing is now possible with PVST+, it comes at the expense of significant CPU load on every switch in the network because 1000 STP instances need to be maintained.

Finally, with MST (802.1s) mode, only two STP instances are required, because you need only two separate STP topologies to implement load sharing. The first STP instance is used for VLANs 1-500, and the second STP instance is used for VLANs 501-1000. MST achieves the same load sharing results as PVST+ (traffic for 500 VLANs are forwarded over each uplink on Switch-C), but does so only requiring two STP instances, which significantly reduces CPU load on all switches throughout the network.

MST is supported from CatOS 7.1 and native IOS 12.1(11)EX on the Catalyst 6000/6500 platform. MST support is present from CatOS 7.1 on the Catalyst 4000, and at the time of writing, it is not supported on the Cisco IOS-based Catalyst 4000 with Supervisor 3. MST is supported from Cisco IOS 12.1(9)EA on the Cisco 2950 and 3550 platforms.

NOTE   At present, configuring RSTP requires you to use the MST mode of operation; however, in future releases you will be able to use RSTP independently of MST (e.g., have a single RSTP instance per VLAN, similar to PVST+).

Scenario 4-1: Configuring the Root Bridge

Configuring spanning tree is relatively straightforward and consists of the following steps:

Step 1   Configure the root bridge (required)

Step 2   Configure STP load sharing (optional)

Step 3   Configure STP enhancements (optional)

The configuration scenarios show how to configure each of these steps, with a series of scenarios being presented for the many STP enhancements that are available and a final troubleshooting scenario.

In this scenario, you learn how to configure the root bridge. When you start configuring spanning tree, decide which switch will be the root bridge and then ensure that the desired root bridge becomes the root bridge. Figure 4-5 illustrates a network that consists of four switches connected in a looped topology.

Figure 4-5   *Scenario Network Topology*

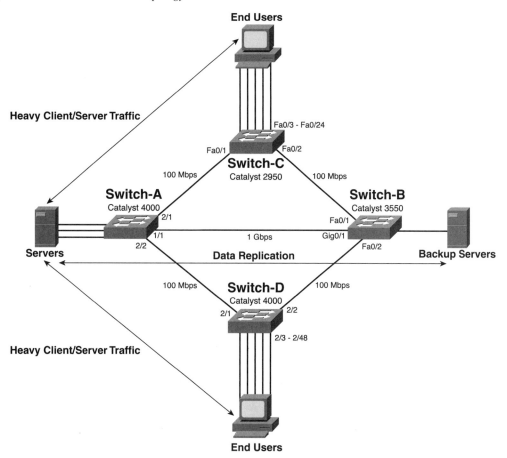

Switch-A is a Catalyst 4000 switch that connects servers and Switch-B is a Catalyst 3550 switch, also connecting servers. Switch-C (Catalyst 3550) and Switch-D (Catalyst 4000) are access layer switches that connect end user devices, such as PCs and printers.

The network in Figure 4-5 is using a single VLAN for all devices, and the heaviest client/ server traffic is between servers connected to Switch-A and clients on Switch-C and Switch-D. At all times, live data located on the servers attached to Switch-A is replicated to backup servers attached to Switch-B. The network must be configured so that the spanning-tree topology provides the most efficient route for the majority of traffic.

Root Bridge Placement

In this scenario and for any spanning-tree network, the most important component that needs to be decided is which switch becomes the root bridge. To demonstrate the design philosophy associated with spanning-tree root bridge selection, a few different choices for the root bridge are now considered, with the pros and cons of using each bridge as the root bridge described.

Figure 4-6 shows Switch-C as the root bridge and the spanning-tree topology calculated from this. The ports connected to Switch-C on Switch-A and Switch-B become root ports because they are closest ports to the root bridge. Next, consider the segment between Switch-A and Switch-B, where a designated port must be chosen for the segment. When a switch transitions from a shutdown state to the Listening state, each switch sends BPDUs listing Switch-C as the root, with a path cost of 19 (the cost of the link to Switch-C). Each switch receives the opposite switch configuration BPDUs and adds the cost of the gigabit link (4) to the advertised root path cost of 19, giving a root path cost of 23 on Switch-A via port 1/1 and on Switch-B via interface Gig0/1. Because the cost to the root is the same for both ports on the segment, the next selection criteria described in the STA (see Table 4-4) is the sender bridge ID. Assuming Switch-A has a lower bridge ID, Switch-A assumes the designated port on the segment (port 1/1) and Switch-B blocks interface Gig0/1.

Now, consider Switch-D. A similar process occurs, where Switch-D receives configuration BPDUs from both Switch-A and Switch-B, each with an equal path cost of 19. Switch-D adds the cost of each link (19) on which the configuration BPDUs were received to the root path cost and determines that the root bridge is reachable via both Switch-A and Switch-B with a total cost of 38. Switch-D chooses port 2/1 as its root port (because Switch-A has a lower bridge ID). On the segment attached to the non-root port 2/2, Switch-D next determines whether or not the port should be designated for the segment. Because Switch-B is advertising that it can reach the root bridge with a cost of 19, and the lowest cost to the root is 38 (via Switch-A), Switch-D chooses Switch-B as the designated bridge for the segment and places port 2/2 into a blocking state.

Switch-C has a direct connection to both Switch-A and Switch-B, which optimizes traffic for user PCs connected to Switch-C accessing servers on either Switch-A or Switch-B. However, it means that for servers on Switch-A to communicate with servers on Switch-B, the communications transit via Switch-C over 100-Mbps uplinks, as opposed to the gigabit link between Switch-A and Switch-B (Switch-B has blocked interface Gig0/1). This arrangement slows down the data replication process and introduces heavy congestion on the Switch-C switch and links during the day. Also, consider the effect on communications for Switch-D. With Switch-C as the root, the spanning tree is lopsided and long because Switch-C is at one edge of the network. This configuration causes inefficient and lengthy paths between devices, such as the four switch hops between end users on Switch-D and servers on Switch-B (the path will be Switch-D → Switch-A → Switch-C → Switch-B). If you choose Switch-D as the root bridge, the same spanning tree topology is created (a mirror image) with exactly the same problems just listed.

Figure 4-6 *Spanning Tree Topology with Switch-C as the Root Bridge*

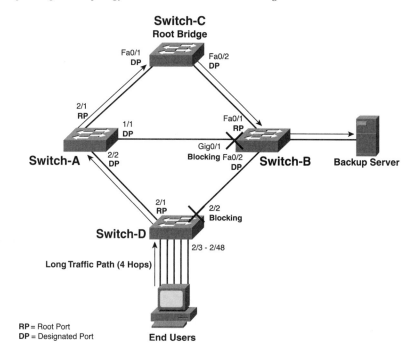

When you are selecting the root bridge, one of the most important objectives is to ensure the network diameter (the distance in switch hops between any two devices) is minimized. The simple rule of thumb to achieve this goal is to use a core switch at the center of the network; if you choose an edge switch, the maximum network diameter increases.

NOTE   You must also consider major traffic paths in the network when selecting the root bridge. The root bridge should be placed close to major servers and other sources of high network traffic to ensure the topology of the network is optimized to the traffic flows of the network.

In this scenario, either Switch-A or Switch-B should be configured as the root bridge because they are at the center of the network. So now that you have narrowed your selection to two choices, which bridge should be selected as the root bridge? Figure 4-7 shows the topology if Switch-B is chosen as the root bridge.

Figure 4-7 *Spanning Tree Topology with Switch-B as the Root Bridge*

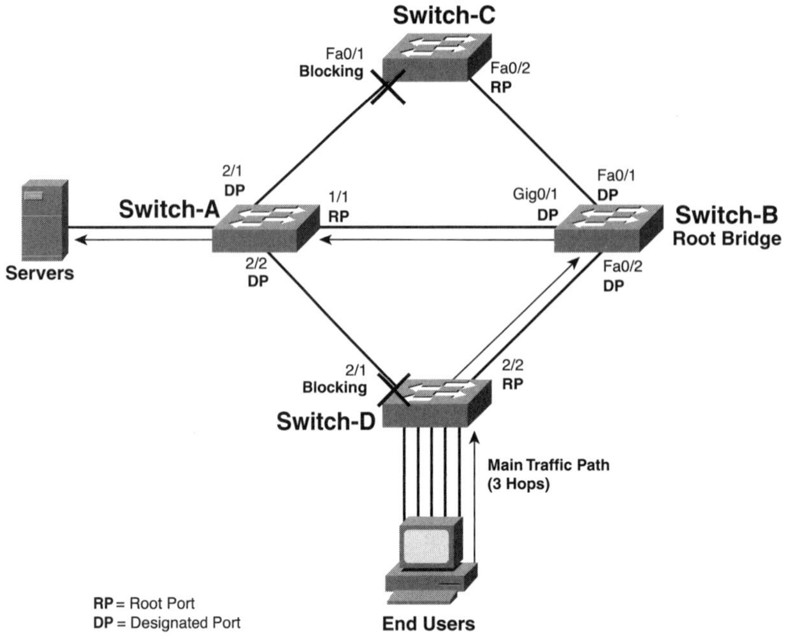

Clearly this is an improvement over the topology shown in Figure 4-6. The largest number of hops between any devices has been reduced from four to three (e.g., Switch-D → Switch-B → Switch-A). Now, consider the main traffic distribution path. Remember, this path is between clients on switches Switch-C or Switch-D and servers attached to Switch-A. With Switch-B as the root, all of this traffic must transit via the path Switch-C → Switch-B → Switch-A and vice versa. Ideally, you would like the connections between Switch-A and the client switches to be active because this configuration would reduce the path to Switch-C → Switch-A. How do you achieve this? By configuring Switch-A as the root bridge! Figure 4-8 shows the topology with Switch-A as the root bridge.

With Switch-A configured as the root bridge, the network topology is optimized for the traffic characteristics of the network. End user traffic needs to traverse only two switch hops, and data replication traffic is transported across the high-speed gigabit connection between Switch-A and Switch-B. It is important that you understand these characteristics to ensure that the network topology configured is performing correctly and adequately.

Figure 4-8   *Spanning Tree Topology with Switch-A as the Root Bridge*

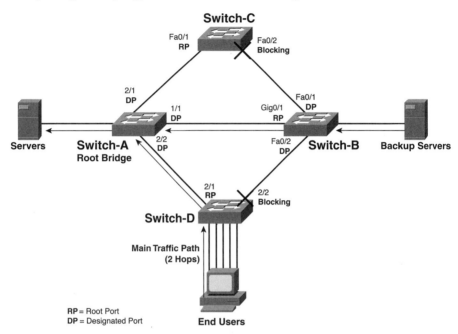

In summary, the main concepts to take into account when you are determining the root bridge are as follows:

- The root bridge needs to be placed so that the network diameter between any two devices is minimized. To achieve this goal, choose your root bridge to be a central, core switch. The key word here is *central*. In a well designed, symmetric network that has clearly defined core, distribution, and access layers, the choices for the root bridge should be fairly obvious.

- The root bridge should be chosen so that the major traffic distribution paths are given the most efficient routes. In our discussions, we initially proved that the center of the network should contain the root bridge. Then, we needed to decide which of the two central switches should become the root bridge. This choice became obvious based on the major traffic distribution path.

In this scenario, choosing Switch-A or Switch-B minimizes the network diameter. Because of the main servers being attached to Switch-A, choosing Switch-A as the root bridge is the correct choice because it optimizes the spanning-tree topology to the traffic paths between the end users and servers.

Secondary Root Bridge Placement

Now that you have chosen your root bridge, it's time to select a secondary or backup root bridge. The secondary root bridge becomes the root in the event of something going wrong with the root bridge, which includes root bridge failure, root bridge malfunction, or administrative error. Figure 4-9 shows the Layer 2 topology with Switch-A (the root bridge) having failed.

Figure 4-9   *Spanning Tree with Switch-A Having Failed*

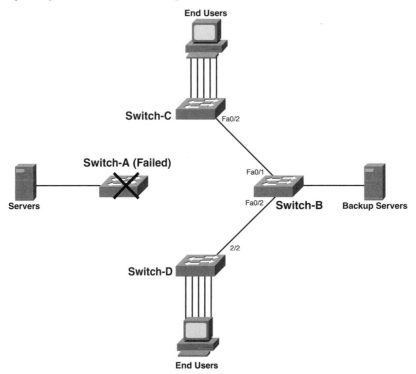

The new topology basically consists of three switches interconnected in a straight line. Because Switch-A has failed, all redundant paths have been removed from the network. You might now notice that with this particular topology, it really doesn't matter which bridge is the root bridge. The spanning tree topology is the same regardless of which bridge is the root bridge. You might now wonder why you should even bother thinking about a secondary root bridge. Well, assume that Switch-A is replaced, but the network administrator forgets to configure Switch-A with the appropriate bridge priority to force it to become the root bridge. Now a redundant topology exists, and you are working with the same issues shown in Figures 4-4 through 4-6. Clearly, in this scenario, you want Switch-B to become the root bridge because this configuration alleviates the issue of a long, inefficient spanning tree topology. So, you now have some motivation for choosing a secondary root bridge. In more complex LAN topologies, choosing a secondary root bridge is crucial because even with the root bridge having failed, redundant paths might still exist. Follow the same principles for choosing the root bridge when selecting the secondary root bridge; the resulting spanning tree topology should be balanced (a central root bridge means the maximum diameter of your network is minimized) and ensure that the major traffic distributions are given the fastest and most efficient path. In our lab topology, Switch-B should be chosen as the secondary root because it is in the center of the network, and has servers directly attached.

Scenario Prerequisites

To successfully commence the configuration tasks required to complete this scenario, Table 4-5 describes the prerequisite configurations required on each device in the scenario topology. Any configurations not listed can be assumed as being the default configuration.

Table 4-5   *Scenario 4-1 Requirements*

Device	Required Configuration	
	Parameter	**Value**
Switch-A	Hostname	Switch-A
	sc0 IP Address (VLAN)	192.168.1.1/24 (VLAN 1)
	Enable/Telnet Password	cisco
	VTP Mode	Transparent
	802.1q Trunks (DTP Mode)	2/1 (nonegotiate) 2/2 (nonegotiate) 2/3 (nonegotiate)
Switch-B	Hostname	Switch-B
	IP Address (VLAN)	192.168.1.2/24 (VLAN 1)
	Enable/Telnet Password	cisco
	802.1q Trunks (DTP Mode)	fa0/1 (nonegotiate) fa0/2 (nonegotiate) fa0/3 (nonegotiate)
Switch-C	Hostname	Switch-C
	IP Address (VLAN)	192.168.1.3/24 (VLAN 1)
	Enable/Telnet Password	cisco
	802.1q Trunks (DTP Mode)	fa0/1 (nonegotiate) fa0/2 (nonegotiate)
Switch-D	Hostname	Switch-B
	sc0 IP Address (VLAN)	192.168.1.4/24 (VLAN 1)
	Enable/Telnet Password	cisco
	802.1q Trunks (DTP Mode)	2/1 (nonegotiate) 2/2 (nonegotiate)

Example 4-1 through Example 4-4 shows the prerequisite configuration required on each switch.

Example 4-1   *Scenario 10-1 Prerequisite Configuration for Switch-A*

```
Console> (enable) set system name Switch-A
System name set.
Switch-A> (enable) set password
Enter old password: ø
Enter new password: *****
Retype new password: *****
Password changed.
Switch-A> (enable) set enablepass
Enter old password: ø
Enter new password: *****
Retype new password: *****
Password changed.
Switch-A> (enable) set interface sc0 192.168.1.1 255.255.255.0
Interface sc0 IP address and netmask set.
Switch-A> (enable) set vtp mode transparent
VTP domain  modified
Switch-A> (enable) set trunk 2/1 nonegotiate dot1q
Port(s)  2/1 trunk mode set to nonegotiate.
Port(s)  2/1 trunk type set to dot1q.
Switch-A> (enable) set trunk 2/2 nonegotiate dot1q
Port(s)  2/2 trunk mode set to nonegotiate.
Port(s)  2/2 trunk type set to dot1q.
Switch-A> (enable) set trunk 2/3 nonegotiate dot1q
Port(s)  2/3 trunk mode set to nonegotiate.
Port(s)  2/3 trunk type set to dot1q.
```

Example 4-2   *Scenario 10-1 Prerequisite Configuration for Switch-B*

```
Switch# configure terminal
Switch(config)# hostname Switch-B
Switch-B(config)# enable secret cisco
Switch-B(config)# line vty 0 15
Switch-B(config-line)# password cisco
Switch-B(config-line)# exit
Switch-B(config)# interface vlan 1
Switch-B(config-if)# no shutdown
Switch-B(config-if)# ip address 192.168.1.2 255.255.255.0
Switch-B(config-if)# exit
Switch-B(config)# vtp mode transparent
Setting device to VTP TRANSPARENT mode.
Switch-B(config)# interface range fastEthernet0/1 - 3
Switch-B(config-if)# switchport trunk encapsulation dot1q
Switch-B(config-if)# switchport mode trunk
Switch-B(config-if)# switchport nonegotiate
```

Example 4-3   *Scenario 4-1 Prerequisite Configuration for Switch-C*

```
Switch# configure terminal
Switch(config)# hostname Switch-C
Switch-C(config)# enable secret cisco
Switch-C(config)# line vty 0 15
Switch-C(config-line)# password cisco
Switch-C(config-line)# exit
Switch-C(config)# interface vlan 1
Switch-C(config-if)# no shutdown
Switch-C(config-if)# ip address 192.168.1.3 255.255.255.0
Switch-C(config-if)# exit
Switch-C(config)# vtp mode transparent
Setting device to VTP TRANSPARENT mode.
Switch-C(config)# interface range fastEthernet0/1 - 2
Switch-C(config-if)# switchport trunk encapsulation dot1q
Switch-C(config-if)# switchport mode trunk
Switch-C(config-if)# switchport nonegotiate
```

Example 4-4   *Scenario 4-1 Prerequisite Configuration for Switch-D*

```
Console> (enable) set system name Switch-D
System name set.
Switch-D> (enable) set password
Enter old password: ø
Enter new password: *****
Retype new password: *****
Password changed.
Switch-D> (enable) set enablepass
Enter old password: ø
Enter new password: *****
Retype new password: *****
Password changed.
Switch-D> (enable) set interface sc0 192.168.1.4 255.255.255.0
Interface sc0 IP address and netmask set.
Switch-D> (enable) set vtp mode transparent
VTP domain  modified
Switch-D> (enable) set trunk 2/1 nonegotiate dot1q
Port(s)  2/1 trunk mode set to nonegotiate.
Port(s)  2/1 trunk type set to dot1q.
Switch-D> (enable) set trunk 2/2 nonegotiate dot1q
Port(s)  2/2 trunk mode set to nonegotiate.
Port(s)  2/2 trunk type set to dot1q.
```

After the prerequisite configuration is implemented, you should verify PING connectivity
between each switch before proceeding.

Configuration Tasks

Now that you understand the design decisions for the network topology of Figure 4-5, you are ready to actually configure the network. For this scenario you need to perform the following tasks:

- Configure the root bridge (Switch-A)
- Configure the backup (secondary) root bridge (Switch-B)
- Verify the root bridge

Configuring the Root Bridge (Switch-A)

The simplest and quickest method to configure a root bridge is to use the spanning tree root macro commands. On Switch-A (CatOS), the syntax of the spanning tree root macro is as follows:

```
set spantree root [secondary] vlans [dia network-diameter] [hello seconds]
```

The *vlans* parameter allows you to define the VLANs for which the switch becomes the root bridge. It is important to remember that by default a Cisco Catalyst switch runs a separate spanning tree instance per VLAN, meaning it may be the root bridge for one VLAN, but not for another VLAN. When you execute the root macro command (and omit the **secondary** parameter), the switch looks at the priority of the root bridge and ensures that the priority of the local switch is set lower, forcing the local switch to become the root bridge. If the current root bridge has a priority higher than 8192, the local priority is set to 8192. If the current root bridge has a priority less than 8192, the local priority is set to one less than the current root bridge priority. For example, if a root bridge existed with a priority of 1000, the macro sets the priority of the local switch to 999.

The optional **secondary** parameter specifies that the root macro configures the bridge priority so that the bridge becomes a root bridge only in the event of a failure of the root bridge.

NOTE

The **secondary** keyword always sets the bridge priority to 16384. No mechanism in spanning tree allows a bridge to detect the second highest bridge priority. Even if the current priority of the root bridge is higher than 16384, the **set spantree root secondary** command does not take this priority into account, it merely sets the bridge priority to 16384. Always make sure your root bridge has a priority less than 16384 and that all other bridges have a priority greater than 16384. If you follow this rule, the command will always work as planned.

Example 4-5 demonstrates using the spanning tree root macro command for VLAN 1 on Switch-A.

Example 4-5   *Configuring Switch-A as a Root Bridge*

```
Switch-A> (enable) set spantree root 1
VLAN 1 bridge priority set to 8192.
VLAN 1 bridge max aging time set to 20.
VLAN 1 bridge hello time set to 2.
VLAN 1 bridge forward delay set to 15.
Switch is now the root switch for active VLAN 1.
```

As you can see, the bridge priority for VLAN 1 is set to 8192, which means that it becomes the root bridge (assuming there are no other switches that have a lower bridge priority, which by default is not the case). Notice that the STP timers can also be modified, although in Example 4-5 these are unchanged. Configuring the optional **dia** and **hello** parameters alters the timers, which are recalculated according to the 802.1d specification. Example 4-6 shows what happens when you configure a network diameter of 4, which is the maximum diameter of the topology shown in Figure 4-5 (e.g., Switch-D → Switch-A → Switch-B → Switch-C) and reduce the hello timer to one second (from the default of two seconds).

Example 4-6   *Modifying STP Timers using the Macro Command*

```
Switch-A> (enable) set spantree root 1 dia 4 hello 1
VLAN 1 bridge max aging time set to 8.
VLAN 1 bridge hello time set to 1.
VLAN 1 bridge forward delay set to 6.
Switch is now the root switch for active VLAN 1.
Switch is already the root switch for active VLAN 1.
```

Notice that the bridge priority for VLAN 1 is not modified because it has already been lowered in Example 4-1. The STP timers have now been modified from their defaults and are optimized for the topology of Figure 4-5 according to the 802.1d specification. Convergence of this network has been reduced from the default maximum of 50 seconds to a maximum of 20 seconds (max age + listening + learning).

If you look at the configuration on Switch-A, you find that there is no mention of the **set spantree root** command. It is a macro command, which actually configures other commands automatically. The commands that are configured automatically by the macro include the following:

```
set spantree priority priority [vlan-id]
set spantree hello hello-timer [vlan-id]
set spantree maxage maxage-timer [vlan-id]
set spantree fwddelay fwddelay-timer [vlan-id]
```

NOTE   You can reset all STP parameters modified by the root macro to their defaults by using the **clear spantree root** *vlan-id* command.

Example 4-7 demonstrates the process of configuring a root bridge and STP timers for
VLAN 1 on Switch-A without using the macro command.

Example 4-7   *Configuring Switch-A as the Root Bridge Manually*

```
Switch-A> (enable) set spantree priority 8192 1
VLAN 1 bridge priority set to 8192.
Switch-A> (enable) set spantree hello 1 1
VLAN 1 bridge hello time set to 1.
Switch-A> (enable) set spantree maxage 8 1
VLAN 1 bridge max aging time set to 8.
Switch-A> (enable) set spantree fwddelay 6 1
VLAN 1 bridge forward delay set to 6.
```

WARNING   When modifying spanning tree timers manually, ensure that you adhere to the
recommendations of 802.1d specification. 802.1d defines that STP timers are calculated on
network diameter and hello timer.

Configuring the Secondary Root Bridge (Switch-B)

On Switch-B (Cisco IOS), the syntax of the global configuration spanning tree root macro
is as follows:

```
spanning-tree vlan vlan-id root {primary | secondary} [diameter network-diameter]
   [hello-time seconds]
```

As you can see, the root macro command on Cisco IOS essentially has the same configuration parameters as the CatOS equivalent.

Example 4-8 demonstrates using the spanning tree root macro command to configure
Switch-A as the secondary root bridge for VLAN 1.

Example 4-8   *Configuring Switch-B as a Secondary Root Bridge*

```
Switch-B(config)# spanning-tree vlan 1 root secondary diameter 4 hello-time 1
   vlan 1 bridge priority set to 28672
   vlan 1 bridge max aging time set to 8
   vlan 1 bridge hello time set to 1
   vlan 1 bridge forward delay set to 6
```

The first thing that should stand out in Example 4-8 is that the priority is set to 28672,
instead of 16384, which is what the secondary root macro command sets the bridge priority
to on a CatOS switch.

If you configured Switch-B as the root bridge, the priority would be set to 24576, again
different from the 8192 set on a CatOS switch. Many Cisco IOS switches have a feature
called *extended system ID* enabled by default, which is a feature that extends the number of
spanning-tree instances that can be supported at any one time. The extended system ID is
defined in the IEEE 802.1t specification and is essentially just a subfield within the bridge

priority field of the bridge ID. Figure 4-10 shows the structure of a bridge ID that uses extended system ID.

Figure 4-10 *Bridge ID Structure with Extended System ID*

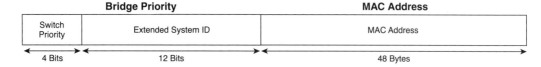

In Figure 4-10, the bottom of the figure shows that the last 12 bits of the bridge priority field are used for the extended system ID, while the 4 high-order bits are used for priority. The extended system ID feature allows a switch to support up to 4096 (2^{12}) VLANs (which equates to 4096 spanning-tree instances by default on a Cisco switch), as is required by the 802.1d and 802.1q standards, without requiring that 4096 unique MAC addresses be assigned to each switch. If you combine the values of the switch priority field and the extended system ID field, you get the traditional bridge priority value in bridge IDs that do not use extended system ID. For example, if the switch priority is configured as 32768 for VLAN 1 (therefore, the extended system ID is 1), the bridge priority field will be 32769. You can use the **show spanning-tree bridge** command to quickly view the bridge IDs associated with each VLAN on a switch, which is useful for illustrating the structure of a bridge ID that uses extended system ID. Example 4-9 demonstrates the use of this command on a switch with multiple VLANs.

Example 4-9 *Viewing the Bridge IDs for Multiple VLANs*

```
Switch-B# show spanning-tree bridge
Vlan                            Bridge ID              Time  Age  Dly  Protocol
---------------- ------------------------------------- ----- ---  ---  --------
VLAN0001            32769 (32768,1) 0009.b7aa.9c80     1     20   15   ieee
VLAN0002            32770 (32768,2) 0009.b7aa.9c80     2     20   15   ieee
```

When added, the switch priority and the extended system ID give the bridge ID. Notice that the same MAC address is used for each VLAN, with the extended system ID providing uniqueness for each bridge ID.

NOTE   Extended system ID is supported only in IOS version 12.1(8)EA or later on the Catalyst 2950 and Catalyst 3550 and is always enabled. The feature is supported on the native IOS Catalyst 6000 switch in IOS version 12.1(8)EX or later and can be enabled or disabled if the chassis supports up to 1024 MAC addresses (some chassis support only 64 MAC addresses, which means the feature cannot be disabled). At the time of this writing, the Catalyst 4000 Supervisor 3 does not support this feature because 1024 MAC addresses are allocated to each Supervisor 3.

On a switch such as the Catalyst 6000, up to 1024 MAC addresses have been traditionally assigned to the switch, which has in turn required up to 1024 unique STP instances using the traditional bridge ID shown in Figure 4-10. By using the extended system ID, a switch requires only a single MAC address to ensure the bridge ID is always unique, with the extended system ID being altered for each different spanning-tree instance (VLAN) on the switch. The extended system ID is automatically assigned as the VLAN ID per STP instance on the switch, which leaves only four configurable bits (2^4 or 16 configurable values) for switch priority. Because of the limitation on configurable options for switch priority, using higher switch priority values (24576 and 28672 as opposed to 8192 and 16384) in the root macro command allows for greater flexibility if you need to introduce new root bridges in the future.

TIP   Extended system ID is known as the STP MAC Address reduction feature on CatOS. This feature is disabled by default, but is automatically enabled (and cannot be disabled) if extended range VLANs (VLAN IDs above 1024) are enabled or a small number of MAC addresses have been allocated to the switch. If you are not using extended range VLANs and the switch has a large number of MAC addresses allocated, you can enable or disable the use of extended system ID on CatOS by using the **set spantree macreduction** command.

It is important to understand that just like CatOS, the root macro command on Cisco IOS is smart enough to detect if an existing root bridge has a priority that is lower than the normal values used by the root macro. Example 4-10 demonstrates configuring Switch-B as the root bridge for VLAN 1, with Switch-A already acting as the root bridge with a priority of 8192.

Example 4-10 *Configuring Switch-B as the Root Bridge with an Existing Root Bridge*

```
Switch-B(config)# spanning-tree vlan 1 root diameter 4 hello-time 1
 vlan 1 bridge priority set to 4096
 vlan 1 bridge max aging time unchanged at 8
 vlan 1 bridge hello time unchanged at 1
 vlan 1 bridge forward delay unchanged at 6
```

Notice that because Switch-A has a priority of 8192, Switch-B chooses the next lowest priority value. The next lowest value is 4096 (not 8191 as you might expect), because Switch-B is using the extended system ID feature, which means that switch priority can be modified only in increments of 4096.

After using the spanning tree macro command on Switch-B, if you look at the running configuration, you find that there is no mention of the **spanning-tree vlan 1 root** command. It is a macro command, which actually configures other commands automatically. The commands that are configured automatically by the macro include the following global configuration mode commands:

```
spanning-tree vlan vlan-id priority priority
```

```
spanning-tree vlan vlan-id hello-time hello-timer
spanning-tree vlan vlan-id max-age maxage-timer
spanning-tree vlan vlan-id forward-time fwddelay-timer
```

Example 4-11 demonstrates the process of configuring a secondary root bridge and STP timers for VLAN 1 on Switch-B without using the macro command.

Example 4-11 *Configuring Switch-B as the Secondary Root Bridge Manually*

```
Switch-B# configure terminal
Switch-B(config)# spanning-tree vlan 1 priority 28672
Switch-B(config)# spanning-tree vlan 1 hello-time 1
Switch-B(config)# spanning-tree vlan 1 max-age 8
Switch-B(config)# spanning-tree vlan 1 forward-time 6
```

Verifying the Root Bridge

On Switch-A, to verify that it is the root bridge for VLAN 1, you can use the **show spantree 1** command, as demonstrated in Example 4-12.

Example 4-12 *Verifying the Root Bridge on Switch-A*

```
Switch-A> (enable) show spantree 1
VLAN 1
Spanning tree mode          PVST+
Spanning tree type          ieee
Spanning tree enabled

Designated Root             00-01-96-a0-2c-00
Designated Root Priority    8192
Designated Root Cost        0
Designated Root Port        1/0
Root Max Age   8  sec    Hello Time 1   sec   Forward Delay 6   sec

Bridge ID MAC ADDR          00-01-96-a0-2c-00
Bridge ID Priority          8192
Bridge Max Age 8   sec   Hello Time 1   sec   Forward Delay 6   sec

Port                        Vlan Port-State    Cost      Prio Portfast Channel_id
----------------------      ---- ------------  --------- ---- -------- ----------
 1/1                        1    forwarding         4     32 disabled 0
 1/2                        1    not-connected      4     32 disabled 0
 2/1                        1    forwarding        19     32 disabled 0
 2/2                        1    forwarding        19     32 disabled 0
... (Output Abbreviated)
...
```

In Example 4-12, you can see that the designated root (root bridge) has a bridge ID 8192.0001.96a0.2c00, which matches the local bridge ID shown, as indicated by the Bridge ID MAC ADDR and Bridge ID Priority fields. This bridge ID means that Switch-A is the root bridge for VLAN 1. The root priority is configured as 8192, and the spanning-tree timers are optimized for the topology of Figure 4-5. Notice that Switch-A lists the designated root cost as 0 (which makes sense because Switch-A is the root bridge) and the root port as port 1/0 (which represents the internal CPU of Switch-A). You can also see that all connected ports on Switch-A are forwarding, as expected for the root bridge.

To verify who the root bridge is for VLAN 1 on Switch-B, use the **show spanning-tree vlan 1** command, as demonstrated in Example 4-13.

Example 4-13 *Verifying the Root Bridge on Switch-B*

```
Switch-B# show spanning-tree vlan 1

VLAN0001
  Spanning tree enabled protocol ieee
  Root ID    Priority    8192
             Address     0001.96a0.2c00
             Cost        4
             Port        25 (GigabitEthernet0/1)
             Hello Time  1 sec  Max Age  8 sec  Forward Delay  6 sec

  Bridge ID  Priority    28673  (priority 28672 sys-id-ext 1)
             Address     0009.b7aa.9c80
             Hello Time  1 sec  Max Age  8 sec  Forward Delay  6 sec
             Aging Time 300

Interface        Port ID                  Designated           Port ID
Name             Prio.Nbr    Cost Sts     Cost Bridge ID       Prio.Nbr
---------------- --------  --------- --- --------- ------------------- --------
Fa0/1            128.1          19 FWD       4 28673 0009.b7aa.9c80 128.1
Fa0/2            128.2          19 FWD       4 28673 0009.b7aa.9c80 128.2
... (Output Abbreviated)
Gig0/1           128.25          4 FWD       0  8192 0001.96a0.2c00  32.1
```

You can see that Switch-B thinks that Switch-A is the root bridge, as indicated by the Address field in the Root ID section. The root port is listed as GigabitEthernet0/1, and the cost to the root is listed as 4, which represents the default cost of the gigabit link to Switch-A. The bridge ID of Switch-B is listed as 28673.0009.b7aa.9c80. Notice that the local bridge priority is actually 28673 (not 28672 as configured in Example 4-8) because the extended system ID (indicated as sys-id-ext in Example 4-13) is 1, indicating this is the STP instance for VLAN 1. If you looked at the STP instance for VLAN 2, the priority would be 28674 (28672 + 2) because the extended system ID for VLAN 2 is 2. Because the priority of Switch-B is lower than the default switch priority of 32768, it becomes the root bridge if Switch-A fails. The final section of the output allows you to determine the state for each interface. You can see that interface Gig0/1 is in a forwarding state (as indicated by the text FWD), which is expected because Gig0/1 is the root port. Notice that the designated bridge for the Gig0/1 interface segment is the root bridge. Interfaces Fa0/1 and Fa0/2 are both forwarding, which means that they must be the designated ports on the segment attached to each. This information is confirmed as the bridge ID for Switch-B is listed in the Designated bridge section.

| NOTE | The **show spanning-tree interface** command can be used to list detailed information about each STP interface within a VLAN. The **show spanning-tree detail** command displays this detailed information for all STP interfaces in all VLANs. |

You can also use the **show spanning-tree root** command on Cisco IOS, which displays the root bridge for each VLAN, as well as STP timers, root cost, and the root port in a summarized format, as shown in Example 4-14.

Example 4-14 *Verifying the Root Bridge for Each VLAN on Switch-B*

```
Switch-B# show spanning-tree root
                                   Root   Hello Max Fwd
Vlan                   Root ID     Cost   Time  Age Dly  Root Port
---------------- -------------------- --------- ----- --- ---  ------------
VLAN0001          8192 0001.96a0.2c00      4    1    8   6  Gi0/1
```

It is also important to verify who is the root bridge on Switch-C and Switch-D. Example 4-15 demonstrates verifying the root bridge on Switch-C.

Example 4-15 *Verifying the Root Bridge on Switch-C*

```
Switch-C# show spanning-tree vlan 1

VLAN0001
  Spanning tree enabled protocol ieee
  Root ID    Priority    8192
             Address     0001.96a0.2c00
             Cost        19
             Port        1 (FastEthernet0/1)
             Hello Time  1 sec  Max Age  7 sec  Forward Delay  5 sec

  Bridge ID  Priority    32769  (priority 32768 sys-id-ext 1)
             Address     0009.b7ad.2700
             Hello Time  2 sec  Max Age 20 sec  Forward Delay 15 sec
             Aging Time 300

Interface        Port ID                   Designated            Port ID
Name             Prio.Nbr    Cost Sts    Cost Bridge ID          Prio.Nbr
---------------- -------- --------- --- --------- -------------------- --------
Fa0/1            128.1          19 FWD        0  8192 0001.96a0.2c00  32.65
Fa0/2            128.2          19 BLK       19 28673 0009.b7aa.9c80  128.2
```

Example 4-15 confirms that Switch-A is the root bridge. You can see that the bridge ID of Switch-C is 32769.0009.b7ad.2700 (the priority of Switch-C is 32769, again due to the extended system ID value of 1). The Root ID section indicates that interface FastEthernet0/1 is the root port and the cost to the root is 19 (the default cost for the 100-Mbps uplink to Switch-A). Notice that the STP timers configured on Switch-C are the default values (indicated in the Bridge ID section); however, the correct STP timers that are actually being used for VLAN 1 are being learned from the root bridge. The last lines of the output indicate the spanning-tree state of each interface in VLAN 1. Interface Fa0/1 is forwarding (as indicate by the text FWD), which is expected because interface Fa0/1 is the root port. Interface Fa0/2 (which is attached to Switch-B) is in a blocking state (as indicated by the text BLK), and you can see that Switch-B (as indicated by the bridge ID shown in the Designated section of the output) is the designated bridge for the segment attached to the interface. By blocking this port, the loop in the network is broken.

On Switch-D, you can use the **show spantree 1** command to verify spanning tree state for VLAN 1. You should be able to see that Switch-A is the root bridge, port 2/1 is forwarding (because it is the root port), and that port 2/2 is blocking.

Scenario 4-2: Configuring STP Load Sharing

An organization often implements redundancy in the network to ensure continued availability in the event of a device or link failure. Of course, redundancy means that two or more possible paths exist in the network, which may be via a different set of devices. If you have a redundant network that has high utilization, ideally you want to share traffic loads over the multiple paths and devices available in the network.

Spanning tree is a protocol that was designed to deal with the loops introduced as a result of implementing redundancy in the network; however, it was never designed with load sharing in mind. The only way you can load share with spanning tree is to use multiple spanning-tree topologies. By default, Cisco Catalyst switches use a separate spanning tree topology for each VLAN. This separate topology means that you can manipulate each spanning-tree topology to ensure that all redundant links in the network are utilized.

Figure 4-11 shows a similar topology to the previous scenario (see Figure 4-5), except with a few modifications that enable you to configure STP load sharing.

Figure 4-11   *Scenario 4-2 Network Topology*

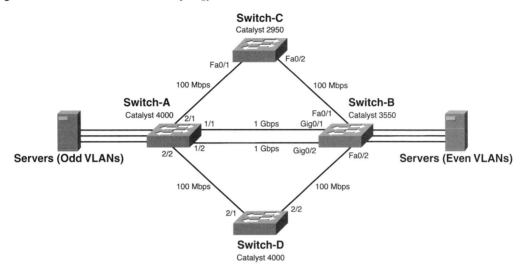

The following changes have been made to the topology:

* Four VLANs are now supported on the network (VLAN 1, 2, 3, and 4)

* The majority of servers on odd VLANs (VLAN 1 and VLAN 3) are attached to Switch-A

* The majority of servers on even VLANs (VLAN 2 and VLAN 4) are attached to Switch-B

* Switch-A and Switch-B are now connected by two separate gigabit trunks

Because now four different VLANs are in the network now, it is important that the network is configured to ensure it operates as efficiently as possible. To achieve the efficiency you need to load share VLAN traffic over different paths where multiple paths lead towards the traffic destination.

Several methods of implementing spanning-tree load sharing exist, each with advantages and disadvantages:

* Root bridge placement

* Port priority

* Port cost

Each of these methods is now discussed.

Scenario Prerequisites

Although this scenario continues on from the Scenario 4-1, to successfully commence the configuration tasks required to complete this scenario, you must first create each of the new VLANs that are needed to allow STP load sharing.

Example 4-16 through Example 4-19 show the VLAN configuration required on each switch.

Example 4-16 *Scenario 4-2 Prerequisite Configuration for Switch-A*

```
Switch-A> (enable) set vlan 2 name VLAN02
VTP advertisements transmitting temporarily stopped,
and will resume after the command finishes.
Vlan 2 configuration successful
Switch-A> (enable) set vlan 3 name VLAN03
VTP advertisements transmitting temporarily stopped,
and will resume after the command finishes.
Vlan 3 configuration successful
Switch-A> (enable) set vlan 4 name VLAN04
VTP advertisements transmitting temporarily stopped,
and will resume after the command finishes.
Vlan 4 configuration successful
```

Example 4-17 *Scenario 4-2 Prerequisite Configuration for Switch-B*

```
Switch-B# configure terminal
Switch-B(config)# vlan 2
Switch-B(config-vlan)# name VLAN02
Switch-B(config-vlan)# exit
Switch-B(config)# vlan 3
Switch-B(config-vlan)# name VLAN03
Switch-B(config-vlan)# exit
Switch-B(config)# vlan 4
Switch-B(config-vlan)# name VLAN04
Switch-B(config-vlan)# exit
```

Example 4-18 *Scenario 4-2 Prerequisite Configuration for Switch-C*

```
Switch-C# configure terminal
Switch-C(config)# vlan 2
Switch-C(config-vlan)# name VLAN02
Switch-C(config-vlan)# exit
Switch-C(config)# vlan 3
Switch-C(config-vlan)# name VLAN03
Switch-C(config-vlan)# exit
Switch-C(config)# vlan 4
Switch-C(config-vlan)# name VLAN04
Switch-C(config-vlan)# exit
```

Example 4-19 *Scenario 4-2 Prerequisite Configuration for Switch-D*

```
Switch-D> (enable) set vlan 2 name VLAN02
VTP advertisements transmitting temporarily stopped,
and will resume after the command finishes.
Vlan 2 configuration successful
Switch-D> (enable) set vlan 3 name VLAN03
VTP advertisements transmitting temporarily stopped,
and will resume after the command finishes.
Vlan 3 configuration successful
Switch-D> (enable) set vlan 4 name VLAN04
VTP advertisements transmitting temporarily stopped,
and will resume after the command finishes.
Vlan 4 configuration successful
```

Root Bridge Placement

An important concept to understand with regards to STP load sharing is that a unique spanning-tree instance (including root bridge, topology, timers, etc.) exists *per VLAN*, which means you can have different spanning-tree topologies per VLAN. In this scenario, four VLANs exist: VLANs 1 and 3 (with servers attached to Switch-A) and VLANs 2 and 4 (with servers attached to Switch-B). The major traffic distributions for each VLAN clearly take place via each respective switch. Figure 4-12 shows the network with Switch-A acting as the root bridge for all VLANs.

Figure 4-12 *Spanning Tree Topology with Switch-A as Root for All VLANs*

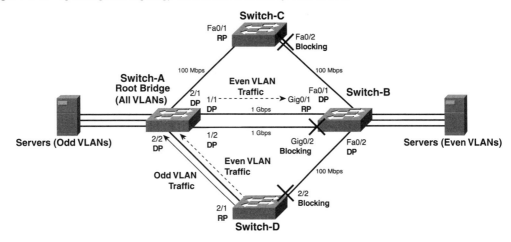

In this example, the root bridge is the same for all VLANs, and by default, the topology generated throughout the rest of the network is identical for each VLAN. Look at Switch-D (the same topology is used for all VLANs); only the uplink to Switch-A is active, with the uplink to Switch-B idle. This configuration means that the uplink to Switch-A is susceptible to oversubscription. The path for traffic in odd VLANs is also not ideal, because client/server traffic must traverse Switch-A to reach servers attached to Switch-B.

A simple technique to alter the spanning-tree topology for different VLANs is to change the root bridge for each VLAN. Figure 4-13 shows the network with Switch-A acting as the root bridge for odd VLANs (VLAN 1 and VLAN 3), and Switch-B acting as the root bridge for even VLANs (VLAN 2 and VLAN 4).

Figure 4-13   *Spanning Tree Topology with Switch-A as Root for Odd VLANs and Switch-B as Root for Even VLANs*

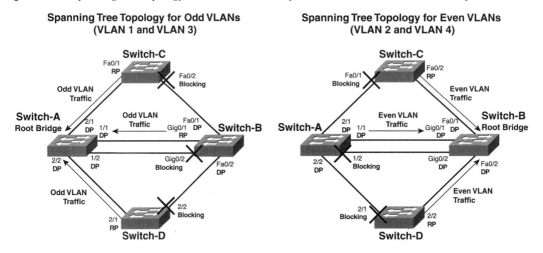

Switch-C and Switch-D now send odd VLAN traffic directly to Switch-A and even VLAN traffic directly to Switch-B. This topology is clearly more efficient than that shown in Figure 4-12, minimizing the number of switch hops and spreading the traffic load over the available uplinks. Notice, however, that the same link is used between Switch-A and Switch-B. This feature is the discussion of the next section.

Port Priority

Recall that spanning tree uses a simple algorithm (STA) to determine the spanning-tree topology, which involves the comparison of BPDUs as follows:

1   Choose the lowest root bridge ID.

2   Choose the lowest root path cost.

3   Choose the lowest sending bridge ID.

4   Choose the lowest port ID.

If you look at Figure 4-13, you may notice that for both VLAN topologies, the active link between Switch-A and Switch-B is the same link. A more efficient topology would be to have one link active for odd VLANs and the other active for even VLANs. Why does this not occur, even though the root bridges for each VLAN are different? To find the answer, you need to examine the spanning-tree topology calculation. First, consider VLAN 1 (an odd VLAN); because Switch-A is the root bridge, all ports on Switch-A are put into the forwarding state. Thus, the actual switch that determines which link is active is Switch-B. When the interfaces attached to Switch-A transition from a Shutdown state into a Listening state, Switch-B receives BPDUs from Switch-A on both links. Switch-B must choose a root port (the port on the switch that is closest to the root) and has received two candidate BPDUs. Figure 4-14 illustrates each of these BPDUs (assume the bridge ID of Switch-A is 8192.0001.96a0.2c00).

Figure 4-14 *BPDUs (VLAN 1) Received on Switch-B Interfaces Gig0/1 and Gig0/2*

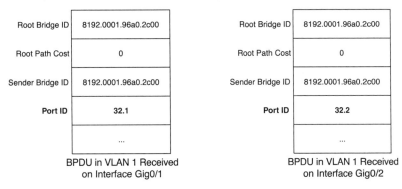

Because Switch-A is the root bridge it uses the following values for each field:

- Switch-A places its own bridge ID in the root bridge ID field because it is the root bridge.

- Switch-A specifies a root path cost of zero because it is the root bridge.

- Switch-A places its own bridge ID in the sending bridge ID field because it sent the BPDU.

- Switch-A places the port ID of the egress port the BPDU was sent from in the port ID field.

You can see that the BPDUs received are almost identical and that the only differentiator between the two is the *port ID*. The port ID is a 16-bit structure that includes a port priority value (default of 32 on CatOS, default of 128 on Cisco IOS) and a unique identifier that identifies the egress port that the BPDU was sent from. Figure 4-15 shows the port ID field structure.

Figure 4-15 *Port ID Structure*

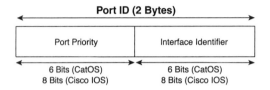

Notice that CatOS uses only 6 bits for the port priority value (allowing for a configurable range of $0 \rightarrow 63$), while Cisco IOS uses 8 bits (allowing for a configuration range of $0 \rightarrow 255$). The 802.1d standard specifies that 8 bits should be used for port priority; however, this causes problems on high-density switches, because only 8 bits are available for assigning interface IDs, allowing for only up to 256 ports. CatOS switches allocate 10 bits for the interface ID field, which allows up to 1024 ports, accommodating the high-density CatOS switches.

Referring back to Figure 4-14, you can see that the port ID received on interface Gig0/1 has a value of 32.1—the first portion (32) indicates a port priority of 32 and the second portion (1) indicates the egress port identifier on Switch-A. Because the BPDU received on interface Gig0/1 has the lower port ID (32.1) compared to that received on interface Gig0/2 (32.2), interface Gig0/1 is chosen as the root port and put into a Forwarding state. The next step for Switch-B in the Listening phase is to decide if interface Gig0/2 should be Forwarding or Blocking (choosing the designated port for the segment). Switch-B is receiving the BPDU shown in Figure 4-15 on interface Gig0/2 and compares this BPDU with the BPDU Switch-B sends out interface Gig0/2. Figure 4-16 compares the BPDU that Switch-B sends out interface Gig0/2, and the BPDU received from Switch-A on interface Gig0/2 of Switch-B (assume the bridge ID of Switch-B is 28673.0009.b7aa.9c80).

Figure 4-16 *BPDUs (VLAN 1) Sent and Received by Switch-B on Interface Gig0/2*

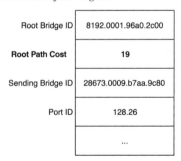

Switch-B decides if interface Gig0/2 is designated (Forwarding) for the segment attached by running the spanning-tree algorithm. Because the root bridge ID fields are the same, the next decision sequence is tested. This compares root path costs, with the lower root path cost winning. Switch-B sees that a switch (in this case the root bridge or Switch-A) has a lower cost (0 as compared to 19) to reach the root bridge, and hence, blocks interface Gig0/2, preventing a loop in the network.

Now, examine the same process for VLAN 2 (an even VLAN). In this case, Switch-B is the root bridge, and hence, all ports on Switch-B are put into the Forwarding state. Switch-A needs to choose a root port and performs the same procedures as discussed for Switch-B in VLAN 1. Figure 4-17 shows the BPDUs that are compared when deciding the root port on Switch-A (assume the bridge ID of Switch-B in VLAN 2 is 24578.0009.b7aa.9c80).

NOTE   The priority of Switch-B is 24578 because Switch-B has been configured using the root macro. This process assigns a switch priority of 24578, which is then added to the extended system ID for VLAN 2 (2), giving a bridge priority value of 24578.

Figure 4-17   *BPDUs (VLAN 2) Received on Switch-A Port 1/1 and Port 1/2*

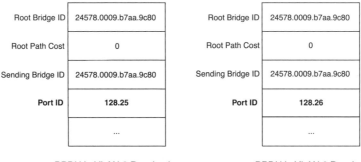

next decision sequence is tested. Notice that the port IDs received include a priority of 128, because Switch-B is a Cisco IOS-based switch. You should be able to quickly see that port 1/1 on Switch-A is chosen as the root port because the port ID of the configuration BPDU received on port 1/1 is lower than that the port ID of the configuration BPDU received on port1/2. Following the same logic for Switch-B in choosing the designated port on the segment attached to port 1/2, port 1/2 on Switch-A is placed into the Disabled state.

So far, the fact that the same link is used for traffic on both VLANs has been proved. The goal is to now change this behavior so that a different link is used per VLAN. The parameter that needs to vary is the selection of the root port on the non-root bridge. For example, if Switch-B chose port 1/1 as the root port for VLAN 1, and Switch-A chose port 1/2 as the root port for VLAN 2, the load sharing goal would be achieved. Now remember that the deciding factor in selecting the root port was the port ID, due to all of the other fields being identical. In each case, the port ID of configuration BPDUs received on port 1/1 on each switch was lower, hence, causing this port to be chosen as the root port for both VLANs. If you could alter the port ID for port 1/2 of the root bridge on one of the VLANs, then port 1/2 on the opposite switch would be chosen as the root port, and both links would be active for each different VLAN. The port ID field is a 16-bit field made up of a 6-bit priority subfield and a 10-bit port number subfield. The administratively configurable priority subfield is in the high-order bits of the port ID and, hence, directly controls the port ID value. The priority range is 0 to 255, and the lowest priority value is always considered the preferred value. By default, the port priority is 32 on CatOS-based switches and 128 on Cisco IOS-based switches. You can modify port priority for an entire physical port (all VLAN STP instances inherit the physical port priority), or you can modify the port priority on a per VLAN basis for each port. Figure 4-18 shows the BPDUs received by Switch-A if you lower the port ID for VLAN 2 on Switch-B to 127.

Figure 4-18 *BPDUs (VLAN 2) Received on Switch-A Port 1/1 and Port 1/2 after Port Priority Has Been Altered on Switch-B*

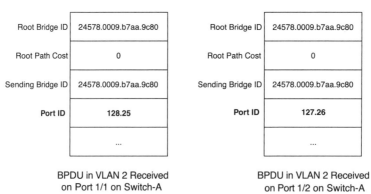

	BPDU in VLAN 2 Received on Port 1/1 on Switch-A		BPDU in VLAN 2 Received on Port 1/2 on Switch-A
Root Bridge ID	24578.0009.b7aa.9c80	Root Bridge ID	24578.0009.b7aa.9c80
Root Path Cost	0	Root Path Cost	0
Sending Bridge ID	24578.0009.b7aa.9c80	Sending Bridge ID	24578.0009.b7aa.9c80
Port ID	128.25	Port ID	127.26
	...		...

With the BPDUs received in Figure 4-18, when Switch-A is selecting its root port, it now selects port 1/2 as the root port because the port ID of the BPDU received on port 1/2 from Switch-B (127.26) is lower than the port ID received on port 1/1 (128.25). Notice how you needed to change the port ID on the opposing switch (Switch-B) and not the actual switch (Switch-A) that was making the decision. This concept of configuring the opposite switch from the switch that is actually making the decision is counterintuitive and can lead to some confusion.

Another limitation of altering port priority is where it has bearing on the selection of the spanning-tree topology. Because the port ID is used as the final selection criteria, it has effect only when you have multiple links to the same remote switch. The STA defines that the sender bridge ID is compared before port ID. If your switch has multiple links to different switches, then received sender bridge IDs are different and are used to select the active path before processing of the port ID is possible. If you have multiple links to the same switch, you receive the same sending bridge ID over each link, leaving the path selection to the port ID. The fact that the port ID is the last selection criteria used if all other criteria are equal is the biggest limiting factor for choosing to manipulate port ID to modify the spanning-tree topology.

Port Cost

Figure 4-13 showed a method of achieving load sharing by ensuring the root bridge for each VLAN was different. This method is actually a crude form of altering root path costs to ensure that a load sharing topology is chosen. Figure 4-19 shows Figure 4-13 with the root path costs for each link on every non-root switch. If you look at the costs on Switch-C and Switch-D for each STP topology, you can see that changing the root bridge for each VLAN has the effect of altering the root path cost so that a different uplink is used for each VLAN.

Figure 4-19   *Topology of Figure 4-13 with Root Path Costs*

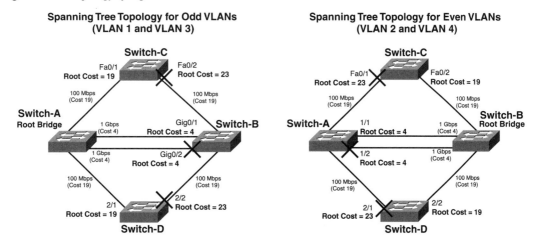

In more complex environments, changing the root bridge for a VLAN might not introduce the desired load sharing topology. Figure 4-20 shows a more complex LAN topology that supports multiple VLANs (VLAN 1 and VLAN 2), with a separate root bridge being configured for each VLAN:

Figure 4-20 *Complex LAN Topology with Different Root Bridge Configurations for VLAN 1 and 2*

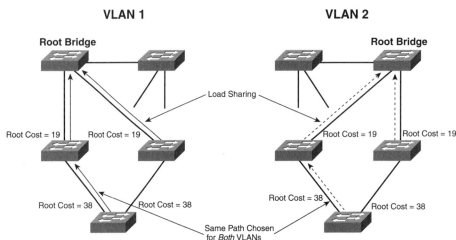

NOTE	The topology described in Figure 4-20 is for demonstration purposes and is not a recommended design. In modern networks, it is best to limit the reach of spanning tree, instead using a multilayer topology that benefits from the fast convergence and inherent load sharing capabilities of Layer 3 routing protocols.

In Figure 4-20, only the active paths in the STP topology for each VLAN are displayed. All switches are interconnected by 100-Mbps connections, which means each link has a default cost of 19. You can see that having the root bridge for each VLAN on a different core switch achieves a load sharing topology for the links that are directly attached to the root bridge (i.e., between the core and distribution switches). However, consider the links between the access switch and distribution switches. Because both distribution switches advertise the same root path cost (19) for *both* VLANs, the access switch bases its forwarding path decision on the lowest sending bridge ID because the root path cost (38) is the same via either switch (assume in this example that the left-hand distribution switch has the lower bridge ID). Thus, for both VLAN spanning-tree topologies, the access switch chooses the *same* forwarding path. For this topology, changing the root bridge for each VLAN does not have the desired load sharing effect throughout the entire network.

A much more effective method of configuring spanning tree load sharing is to use VLAN port cost to control selection of active links.

NOTE   You can modify port cost for an entire physical port (all VLAN STP instances that do no have an explicating configured VLAN port cost inherit the physical port cost), or you can modify the port cost on a per VLAN basis for each port (also known as the *VLAN port cost*).

For example, assume that for this scenario, you are restricted by the fact that Switch-A must be the root bridge for *all* VLANs. Without modifying VLAN port costs, the same spanning tree topology is now chosen for all VLANs. Figure 4-21 shows the topology for all VLANs using the default port costs.

Figure 4-21   *Scenario Topology with Default Port Costs*

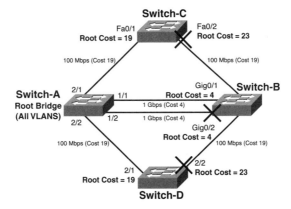

Switch-C forwards all traffic via port Fa0/1 because this port represents the lowest cost path (19) to the root bridge. Similarly Switch-D forwards all traffic via port 2/1. Figure 4-22 shows the topology in Figure 4-21 with manually configured port costs for the interface Fa0/1 on Switch-C and port 2/1 on Switch-D.

Figure 4-22 *Scenario Topology with Manually Configured Port Costs*

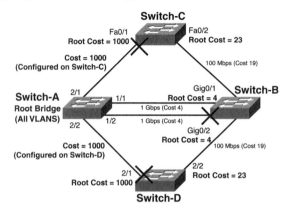

In Figure 4-22, the port cost of Switch-C interface Fa0/1 has been manually configured as 1000, giving a root path cost of 1000 via this interface. Because Switch-C can reach the root bridge via Switch-B with a cost of 23 (19 for the Switch-A ←→ Switch-B link + 4 for the Switch-B ←→ Switch-C link), Switch-C now forwards all traffic via interface Fa0/2. Similarly, Switch-D now forwards all traffic via port 2/2.

NOTE   It is important to understand that each switch receiving a configuration BPDU adds the root path cost advertised in the BPDU to the cost of the port that the BPDU was received upon. When a switch sends a configuration BPDU, it does *not* add the cost of the link of the port that the BPDU is being sent out; instead, this function is left to the receiving switch.

Cisco switches enable you to configure port cost on a per VLAN basis, so you can apply the configuration used in Figure 4-23 for a specific VLAN, controlling the traffic path for that particular VLAN. Figure 4-23 shows the scenario topology with manually configured port costs for each VLAN.

Figure 4-23 *Scenario Topology with Manually Configured VLAN Port Costs*

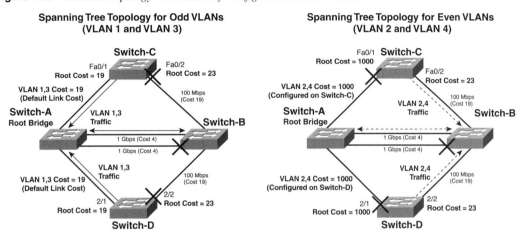

For Switch-C, the port cost on port Fa0/1 for VLAN 2 and VLAN 4 has been configured as 1000, forcing port Fa0/2 to be the active path toward the root bridge for these VLANs. On Switch-D, the port cost on port 2/1 for VLAN 2 and VLAN 4 has also been configured as 1000 to achieve the same result.

Configuring STP Load Sharing

To configure the requirements for the topology in Figure 4-11, you need to perform the following tasks:

- Configure STP load sharing on Switch-C
- Configure STP load sharing on Switch-D
- Configure STP load sharing between Switch-A and Switch-B
- Verify STP load sharing

NOTE   Before beginning configuration, if you are using the same topology used for Scenario 4-1, you should remove the custom spanning tree configuration of that scenario and then configure Switch-A as the root bridge for all VLANs.

Configuring STP Load Sharing on Switch-C

As discussed in this scenario, the recommended method of configuring STP load sharing is to modify the STP cost parameter for logical ports in each STP instance. Referring to Table 4-2, the default costs for the 100-Mbps links on Switch-C are 19, which means that for all

VLANs, Switch-C has a root path cost of 19 via Switch-A (the root bridge) and of 23 via Switch-B. So, by default, Switch-C forwards all traffic for all VLANS over the uplink to Switch-A, because Switch-A is the root bridge for both VLANs, leaving the uplink to Switch-B idle. To configure Switch-C so that traffic for even VLANs (VLAN 2 and VLAN 4) is forwarded out interface Fa0/2 to Switch-B instead of out interface Fa0/1, you must configure an STP cost greater than 23 (the cost via Switch-B to the root bridge) on the logical port associated with VLAN 1 on interface Fa0/1.

To modify STP costs on Cisco IOS for a logical port, you use the **spanning-tree vlan** interface configuration command, which has the following syntax:

```
spanning-tree vlan vlan-id cost cost
```

NOTE   You can configure the cost of a physical interface using the **spanning-tree cost** *cost* interface configuration command. Each logical port associated with the physical interface inherits this cost, unless the cost for the logical interface is explicitly configured.

Example 4-20 demonstrates the configuration required on Switch-C to force Switch-C to use the uplink to Switch-B as the forwarding path for VLAN 2 traffic.

Example 4-20   *Configuring STP Load Sharing*

```
Switch-C# configure terminal
Switch-C(config)# interface fa0/1
Switch-C(config-if)# spanning-tree vlan 2 cost 1000
Switch-C(config-if)# spanning-tree vlan 4 cost 1000
```

By configuring the logical ports in VLAN 2 and VLAN 4 with a cost of 1000, Switch-C calculates that for even VLANs, the cost to the root bridge is 1000 (1000 for fa0/1 on Switch-C + 0 for the root bridge Switch-A) via the uplink to Switch-A, and that the cost via the uplink to Switch-B is 23 (19 for Fa0/2 on Switch-C + 4 for Gig0/1 on Switch-B). Therefore, Switch-C always chooses interface Fa0/2 as its root port for even VLANs, and interface Fa0/1 becomes a blocked port as Switch-A becomes the designated bridge (because it is the root bridge) for the segment between Switch-A and Switch-C.

Although STP load sharing is now configured (VLAN 1 and VLAN 3 do not require config-uration because traffic for these VLANs is already being forwarded over the correct uplink), it is good practice to ensure that odd VLAN traffic is forwarded out the uplink to Switch-

A, by configuring a high cost for the logical port in the odd VLANs on the uplink to Switch-B (Fa0/2). Example 4-21 demonstrates this configuration.

Example 4-21 *Configuring STP Load Sharing*

```
Switch-C# configure terminal
Switch-C(config)# interface fa0/2
Switch-C(config-if)# spanning-tree vlan 1 cost 1000
Switch-C(config-if)# spanning-tree vlan 3 cost 1000
```

The root path cost for VLAN 1 and VLAN 3 via Switch-B has now increased to 1004, while the root path cost via Switch-A is 19. This configuration means it is very unlikely Switch-C will forward traffic for odd VLANs out interface Fa0/2, unless, of course, Switch-A fails.

Configuring STP Load Sharing on Switch-D

On Switch-D (CatOS), you need to perform the same tasks you performed on Switch-C. To configure the cost of an STP logical port within a VLAN on CatOS, you use the **set spantree portvlancost** command:

```
set spantree portvlancost mod/port cost cost [vlan_list]
```

The *vlan_list* parameter allows you to specify the VLANs (logical ports) that the cost will be applied to.

NOTE   You can configure the cost of a physical port using the **set spantree portcost** *mod/port* **cost** *cost* command. Each logical port associated with the physical port inherits this cost, unless the cost for the logical port is explicitly configured.

On CatOS, you can configure only a single **portvlancost** value per physical port. What this means is that if, for example, you configure a **portvlancost** of 1000 for VLAN 1 on port 2/1, you cannot also configure a separate **portvlancost** of 2000 for VLAN 2 on the same port. If you did this, the **portvlancost** for VLAN 1 would change to the second value you configured (2000). This limitation is implemented to reduce configuration file size, saving NVRAM usage.

NOTE   This limitation should not cause too many issues because you are merely using cost to influence whether or not a port forwards traffic. Because this decision has two possible outcomes for a logical port (forward or block), you need only two values to differentiate the two outcomes. For VLANs that you wish the port to forward traffic on, do not configure the **portvlancost** parameter; instead, allow the logical port to inherit a low (or the default) physical port (**portcost**) cost. For VLANs that you do not wish the port to forward traffic for, configure a high (**portvlancost**) cost and ensure each of the VLANs are assigned this cost.

Example 4-22 demonstrates the configuration required on Switch-D.

Example 4-22 *Configuring STP Load Sharing on Switch-D*

```
Switch-D> (enable) set spantree portvlancost 2/1 cost 1000 2,4
Port 2/1 VLANs 1,3,5-1005,1025-4094 have path cost 19.
Port 2/1 VLANs 2,4 have path cost 1000.
This parameter applies to trunking ports only.
Switch-D> (enable) set spantree portvlancost 2/2 cost 1000 1,3
Port 2/2 VLANs 2,4-1005,1025-4094 have path cost 19.
Port 2/2 VLANs 1,3 have path cost 1000.
This parameter applies to trunking ports only.
```

In Example 4-22 the first command ensures traffic for VLANs 2 and 4 is forwarded out port 2/2 over the uplink to Switch-C. The second command ensures traffic for VLANs 1 and 3 is forwarded out port 2/1 over the uplink to Switch-A, although this behavior is already implemented due to Switch-A being the root bridge.

Example 4-23 shows what happens when you configure the **portvlancost** for VLAN 6 as 2000 on port 2/1.

Example 4-23 *Modifying STP porvlancost on Switch-D*

```
Switch-D> (enable) set spantree portvlancost 2/1 cost 2000 6
Port 2/1 VLANs 1,3,5,7-1005,1025-4094 have path cost 19.
Port 2/1 VLANs 2,4,6 have path cost 2000.
This parameter applies to trunking ports only.
```

Notice that the **portvlancost** parameter for VLANs 2 and 4 is also modified when you configure the **portvlancost** parameter for VLAN 6. This change is due to the limitation of **portvlancost** on CatOS discussed earlier.

Configuring STP Load Sharing Between Switch-A and Switch-B

At this stage you have configured STP load sharing so that Switch-C and Switch-D load share odd and even VLAN traffic over separate links. With the configuration so far, all VLAN traffic is sent over the same link between Switch-A and Switch-B, which is not the most ideal use of the dual links configured between the two switches. As discussed earlier in this scenario, you can use port priority to implement load sharing across two links that are connected between the same switches.

On a CatOS switch, the default priority of every port is 32, with a configurable range of 0-63. You cannot modify the port index that uniquely represents each port, so you must lower the port priority to make the port ID more preferred. To modify the port priority for a particular VLAN, use the following command:

```
set spantree portvlanpri mod/port priority priority [vlan_list]
```

The *priority* configured must be a multiple of 16. If you specify a value that is not a multiple of 16, the port priority is converted to the nearest multiple. The *vlan_list* parameter allows you to specify the VLANs (logical ports) to which the port priority is applied.

NOTE	You can configure the priority of a physical port using the **set spantree portpri** *mod/port* **priority** *cost* command. Each logical port associated with the physical port inherits this cost, unless the cost for the logical port is explicitly configured.

Because Switch-B is the switch that decides which of the links to Switch-A should be forwarding based upon BPDUs received from Switch-A, you need to configure the VLAN port IDs on Switch-A to influence the active link selected for each VLAN. Example 4-24 demonstrates the configuration required on Switch-D.

Example 4-24 *Configuring STP Load Sharing on Switch-A*

```
Switch-A> (enable) set spantree portvlanpri 1/1 priority 16 1,3
Port 1/1 VLANs 2,4-1005,1025-4094 using portpri 32.
Port 1/1 VLANs 1,3 using portpri 16.
Switch-D> (enable) set spantree portvlanpri 1/2 priority 16 2,4
Port 1/2 VLANs 1,3,5-1005,1025-4094 using portpri 32.
Port 1/2 VLANs 2,4 using portpri 16.
```

In Example 4-24, the first command ensures that Switch-B places the port attached to port 1/1 on Switch-A into a Forwarding state for VLANs 1 and 3. The second command ensures that Switch-B places the port attached to port 1/2 on Switch-A into a Forwarding state for VLANs 2 and 4, allowing for load sharing of traffic.

Take note that the configuration of Example 4-24 is certainly not the recommended or best configuration for the topology between Switch-A and Switch-B. The best solution is to configure an EtherChannel bundle that is designed to automatically accommodate load sharing and redundancy at the physical layer, rather than at Layer 2, and that simplifies the spanning-tree topology. An EtherChannel bundle appears as a single Layer 2 connection to STP, and any link failure within the bundle is handled within seconds, in a fashion that is transparent to STP, improving stability (i.e., STP does not even know a failure has occurred because the Layer 2 protocol of the bundle remains up during the failure). The load sharing properties of EtherChannel are also much more granular than spanning tree, allowing traffic within a single VLAN to be load shared based upon parameters such as source/destination MAC address or IP address. STP does not provide load sharing to this detail; its load sharing can be implemented only on a per VLAN basis.

Example 4-25 demonstrates the configuration required on Switch-A to configure the links to Switch-B as an EtherChannel bundle.

Example 4-25 *Configuring an EtherChannel Bundle on Switch-A*

```
Switch-A> (enable) clear spantree portvlanpri 1/1 1,3
Port 1/1 vlans 1-1005, 1025-4094 using portpri 32
Switch-A> (enable) clear spantree portvlanpri 1/2 2,4
Port 1/2 vlans 1-1005, 1025-4094 using portpri 32
Switch-A> (enable) set port channel 1/1-2 mode desirable
Port(s) 1/1-2 are assigned to admin group 51.
Port(s) 1/1-2 channel mode set to desirable.
```

In Example 4-25, you first clear the spanning-tree configuration of Example 4-24 by resetting the port VLAN priority configuration of ports 1/1 and 1/2 to the default value of 32, because an EtherChannel bundle will not form if the spanning-tree parameters are not identical for all ports in the bundle.

TIP   Always set the PAgP mode to *desirable* for spanning-tree links. Using the *on* mode removes the monitoring capabilities of PAgP. On older Cisco IOS Catalyst switches, such as the 2900XL and 3500XL series, the switches do not support PAgP, so you must force ports on the remote switch connected to these older switches to form an EtherChannel bundle.

Example 4-26 demonstrates the configuration required on Switch-B to configure the links to Switch-A as an EtherChannel bundle.

Example 4-26 *Configuring an EtherChannel Bundle on Switch-B*

```
Switch-B# configure terminal
Switch-B(config)# interface range gig0/1 - 2
Switch-B(config-if-range)# channel-group 1 mode desirable
Creating a port-channel interface Port-channel1
```

At this stage, the EtherChannel bundle should form (assuming all ports and interfaces are configured identically). Example 4-27 verifies that the EtherChannel bundle has formed.

Example 4-27 *Verifying an EtherChannel Bundle on Switch-B*

```
Switch-B# show etherchannel summary
Flags:  D - down        P - in port-channel
        I - stand-alone s - suspended
        R - Layer3      S - Layer2
        u - unsuitable for bundling
        U - port-channel in use
Group Port-channel  Ports
--------------------------------------------------------------------------
1    Po1(SU)     Gig0/1(P)   Gig0/2(P)
```

In Example 4-27, you can see that a new logical interface Po1 (port-channel 1) has been created and that interfaces Gig0/1 and Gig0/2 are in port-channel. Spanning tree sees the logical interface as a single Layer 2 connection, which removes the loops between Switch-A and Switch-B. EtherChannel handles any physical failures transparently from spanning tree, increasing the stability of the network.

Verifying STP Load Sharing

In the topology of Figure 4-11, you can verify STP load sharing is occurring by determining which uplinks are forwarding or blocking for each VLAN on both Switch-C and Switch-D. On Switch-C, you can use the **show spanning-tree blockedports** command, which displays the blocked interfaces for each VLAN, as shown in Example 4-28.

Example 4-28 *Verifying STP Load Sharing on Switch-C*

```
Switch-C# show spanning-tree blockedports
Name                 Blocked Interfaces List
-------------------- -----------------------------------
VLAN0001             Fa0/2
VLAN0002             Fa0/1
VLAN0003             Fa0/2
VLAN0004             Fa0/1
```

You can quickly see that load sharing is configured properly because interface Fa0/2 is blocking for VLANs 1 and 3 (meaning traffic is forwarded over interface Fa0/2 for these VLANs) and interface Fa0/1 is blocking for VLANs 2 and 4 (meaning traffic is forwarded over interface Fa0/1 for these VLANs).

NOTE   You can also use the **show spanning-tree active** command to display ports that are only forwarding. This command also lists the costs configured for each port.

To verify STP load sharing on Switch-D (CatOS), use the **show spantree blockedports** command, as shown in Example 4-29.

Example 4-29 *Verifying STP Load Sharing on Switch-D*

```
Switch-D> (enable) show spantree blockedports
T = trunk
g = group
Ports       Vlans
-----       ----------
 2/1  (T)   2,4
 2/2  (T)   1,3
Number of blocked ports (segments) in the system : 4
```

The output in Example 4-29 shows that port 2/1 is blocking for VLANs 2 and 4, and port 2/2 is blocking for VLANs 1 and 3.

<table>
<tr><td>**NOTE**</td><td>You can use the **show spantree active** command to display ports that are only forwarding. This command also lists the costs configured for each port.</td></tr>
</table>

Finally, you should verify the configuration of the EtherChannel bundle between Switch-A and Switch-B. Example 4-30 shows the **show spantree 1** output of Switch-A, which specifies spanning-tree information for VLAN 1.

Example 4-30 *Verifying the STP Representation of the EtherChannel Bundle on Switch-A*

```
Switch-A> (enable) show spantree 1
VLAN 1
Spanning tree mode        PVST+
Spanning tree type        ieee
Spanning tree enabled

Designated Root           00-01-96-a0-2c-00
Designated Root Priority  8192
Designated Root Cost      0
Designated Root Port      1/0
Root Max Age  20  sec   Hello Time 2  sec   Forward Delay 15  sec

Bridge ID MAC ADDR        00-01-96-a0-2c-00
Bridge ID Priority        8192
Bridge Max Age  20  sec   Hello Time 2  sec   Forward Delay 15  sec

Port                     Vlan Port-State    Cost      Prio Portfast Channel_id
------------------------ ---- ------------- --------- ---- -------- ----------
 1/1-2                   1    forwarding           4  32 disabled 51
 2/1                     1    forwarding          19  32 disabled 0
 2/2                     1    forwarding          19  32 disabled 0
... (Output Abbreviated)
...
```

In Example 4-30, you can see that the EtherChannel bundle consisting of ports 1/1 and 1/2 is represented as a single port in spanning tree.

Example 4-31 shows the output of the **show spanning-tree vlan 1** command on Switch-B, which shows that the EtherChannel bundle is represented as a single STP port within VLAN 1.

Example 4-31 *Verifying the STP Representation of the EtherChannel Bundle on Switch-B*

```
Switch-B# show spanning-tree vlan 1

VLAN0001
  Spanning tree enabled protocol ieee
  Root ID     Priority    8192
              Address     0001.96a0.2c00
              Cost        4
              Port        65 (Port-channel1)
              Hello Time  2 sec  Max Age 20 sec  Forward Delay 15 sec

  Bridge ID   Priority    28673  (priority 28672 sys-id-ext 1)
              Address     0009.b7aa.9c80
              Hello Time  2 sec  Max Age 20 sec  Forward Delay 15 sec
              Aging Time 300

Interface       Port ID                    Designated              Port ID
Name            Prio.Nbr     Cost Sts     Cost Bridge ID           Prio.Nbr
--------------- -------- --------- ---     --------- -------------------- --------
Fa0/1           128.1          19 FWD        4 28673 0009.b7aa.9c80 128.1
Fa0/2           128.2          19 FWD        4 28673 0009.b7aa.9c80 128.2
Po1             128.65          4 FWD        0  8192 0001.96a0.2c00 32.65
```

In Example 4-31, notice that the root port is the Port-Channel1 interface, which is the Layer 2 interface representing the EtherChannel bundle. You can also see that interfaces Gig0/1 and Gig0/2 are not listed as spanning tree interfaces, instead Po1 (Port-Channel1) is listed.

Scenario 4-3: Configuring Root Guard

Root guard is a feature that can be used to influence which switches are eligible to become the root bridge. Although priorities are used to determine who becomes the root bridge, they provide no mechanism to determine who is eligible to become the root bridge. There is nothing to stop a new switch being introduced to the network with a lower bridge ID, which allows it to become the root bridge. The introduction of this new switch can affect the network, as new paths may be formed that are not ideal for the traffic flows of the network. Figure 4-24 demonstrates why you might need to configure root guard.

Figure 4-24 *Root Guard Topology*

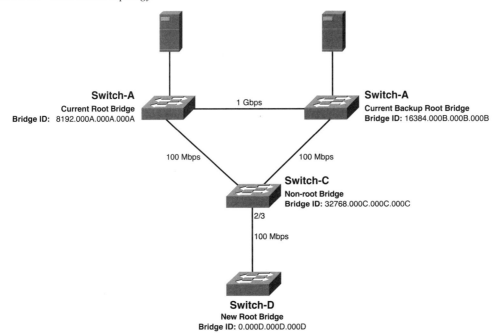

In Figure 4-24, a new switch (Switch-D) has been added to the network by connecting to Switch-C. Currently Switch-A is the root bridge and has a gigabit connection to Switch-B, which is the secondary root bridge. A lot of server-to-server traffic traverses the link between Switch-A and Switch-B. Switch-D has been configured with the lowest priority in the network (a priority of 0 as indicated by the bridge ID of Switch-D), and thus becomes the root bridge. This has the effect of blocking the gigabit port (port 2/1) on Switch-B, severely affecting the performance of the network, because server traffic must travel over 100-Mbps uplinks from Switch-A → Switch-C → Switch-B and vice versa.

To prevent the scenario in Figure 4-24 from occurring, you can configure the root guard feature to prevent unauthorized switches from becoming the root bridge. When you enable root guard on a port, if superior configuration BPDUs to the current configuration BPDUS generated by the root bridge are received, the switch blocks the port, discards the superior BPDUs and assigns a state of root inconsistent to the port.

NOTE   Once superior configuration BPDUs cease to be received, the blocked port once again resumes forwarding, meaning that the root guard feature is fully automated, requiring no human intervention.

In Figure 4-24, if you enable root guard on port 2/3 of Switch-C, when Switch-D starts sending superior configuration BPDUs, the port is immediately blocked, and the spanning-tree topology is not affected.

Configuration Tasks

To implement the root guart feature, you must complete the following configuration tasks:

- Enable root guard
- Test root guard

Enabling Root Guard

Figure 4-25 shows a simple spanning-tree network topology.

In Figure 4-25, Switch-A is the root bridge, and Switch-B is configured as the secondary root bridge. Switch-C and Switch-D are non-root bridges that connect end devices to the network.

Figure 4-25 *STP Topology*

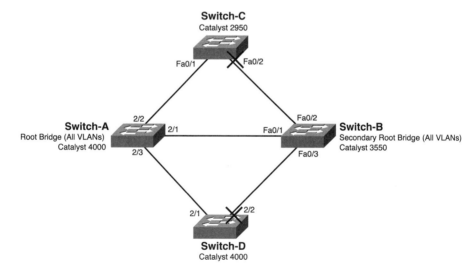

NOTE	This scenario assumes that a single VLAN (VLAN 1) is in use, and that Switch-A has been configured as the root bridge, with Switch-B configured as the secondary root bridge. All other spanning-tree parameters are configured as the default on all switches.

On CatOS switches, root guard is disabled by default, and you can either enable or disable the feature for physical interfaces. Root guard applies to the entire interface, meaning all STP instances have the configuration applied. To configure root guard on CatOS, you use the following command:

```
set spantree guard root mod/port
```

Root guard is disabled by default on Cisco IOS switch interfaces. Just as for CatOS, if you enable root guard on an interface, the feature applies to all STP instances. To configure root guard on Cisco IOS, you use the following interface configuration command:

```
spanning-tree rootguard
```

To configure root guard in the topology of Figure 4-25, you should configure the feature on all ports that are attached to switches that will *never* become root bridges. Switch-A and Switch-B are the only switches that should ever become root bridges, so you should enable root guard on the following ports:

- Switch-A: Ports 2/2 and 2/3
- Switch-B: Interfaces Fa0/2 and Fa0/3

Example 4-32 demonstrates configuring root guard on ports 2/2 and 2/3 on Switch-A.

Example 4-32 *Configuring Root Guard on Switch-A*

```
Switch-A> (enable) set spantree guard root 2/2-3
Enable rootguard will disable loopguard if it's currently enabled on the port(s).
Do you want to continue (y/n) [n]? y
Rootguard on ports 2/2-3 is enabled.
Warning!! Enabling rootguard may result in a topology change.
```

The configuration of Example 4-32 means that any switches connected to port 2/2 (i.e., Switch-C) and port 2/3 (i.e., Switch-D) cannot become the root bridge. If any superior configuration BPDUs are received on ports 2/2 or 2/3, Switch-A blocks the port, and the port has a state of *root inconsistent*. The following shows the SYSLOG message that is generated if a superior configuration BPDU is received on a port that has root guard enabled:

```
%SPANTREE-2-ROOTGUARDBLOCK: Port 2/2 tried to become non-designated in VLAN 2.
    Moved to root -inconsistent state
```

Once superior configuration BPDUs cease to be received on the blocked port, the switch restores the port as indicated by this message:

```
%SPANTREE-2-ROOTGUARDUNBLOCK: Port 2/2 restored in VLAN 2
```

Example 4-33 demonstrates configuring root guard on interfaces Fa0/2 and Fa0/3 on Switch-B.

Example 4-33 *Configuring Root Guard on Switch-B*

```
Switch-B# configure terminal
Switch-B(config)# interface range fa0/2 - 3
Switch-B(config-if)# spanning-tree rootguard
```

The configuration of Example 4-33 means that any switches connected to interface fa0/2 (i.e., Switch-C) and interface Fa0/3 (i.e., Switch-D) cannot become the root bridge. If any superior configuration BPDUs are received on either interface, Switch-B will block the port.

Testing Root Guard

To test Root Guard, configure root guard on Switch-B and then configure Switch-D so that it becomes the root bridge. You should be able to then see root guard in action.

Step 1   On Switch-B, ensure that root guard is enabled on interfaces Fa0/2 and Fa0/3, as shown in Example 4-34.

Example 4-34 *Configuring Root Guard on Switch-B*

```
Switch-B# configure terminal
Switch-B(config)# interface fa0/2 - 3
Switch-B(config-if)# spanning-tree guard root
14:46:27: %SPANTREE-2-ROOTGUARD_CONFIG_CHANGE: Root guard enabled on port
    FastEthernet0/2 on VLAN0001
14:46:27: %SPANTREE-2-ROOTGUARD_CONFIG_CHANGE: Root guard enabled on port
    FastEthernet0/3 on VLAN0001
```

Example 4-34 shows the console messages that appear when you enable root guard on a Cisco IOS switch.

Step 2   On Switch-D, configure a priority of 0 for VLAN 1, as shown in Example 4-35.

Example 4-35 Configuring IP on Switch-D

```
Switch-D> (enable) set spantree priority 0 1
Spantree 1 bridge priority set to 0.
```

At this stage, Switch-D has a lower bridge ID than the current root bridge (Switch-A). On Switch-B, you should see the following console message:

```
14:49:24: %SPANTREE-2-ROOTGUARD_BLOCK: Root guard blocking port
    FastEthernet0/3 on VLAN0001.
```

This message indicates that interface Fa0/3 connected to Switch-D has been blocked, because superior configuration BPDUs have been heard on the interface and root guard is enabled.

Step 3 On Switch-B, use the **show spanning-tree inconsistentports** command to display any interfaces that currently have an inconsistent STP state, as shown in Example 4-36.

Example 4-36 Viewing Inconsistent Ports on Switch-B

```
Switch-B# show spanning-tree inconsistentports

Name                  Interface               Inconsistency
------------------    --------------------    -----------------
VLAN0001              FastEthernet0/3         Root Inconsistent

Number of inconsistent ports (segments) in the system : 2
```

As you can see from Example 4-36, interface Fa0/3 in VLAN 1 is listed as *root inconsistent*.

Step 4 On Switch-D, reset the priority for VLAN 1 to 32768, as shown in Example 4-37.

Example 4-37 Configuring Priority on Switch-D

```
Switch-D> (enable) set spantree priority 32768 1
Spantree 1 bridge priority set to 32768.
```

At this stage, Switch-D has a higher bridge ID than the current root bridge (Switch-A). On Switch-B, you should see the following console message:

```
14:58:58: %SPANTREE-2-ROOTGUARD_UNBLOCK: Root guard unblocking port
FastEthernet0/3 on VLAN0001.
```

This message indicates that interface Fa0/3 connected to Switch-D is now forwarding once again, because inferior configuration BPDUs have been heard on the interface.

Scenario 4-4: Configuring Spanning Tree PortFast

Spanning tree PortFast is a Cisco enhancement to STP used to allow ports attached to end devices to transition from a Blocked or Disabled state to the Forwarding state, allowing devices to begin sending and receiving data immediately. PortFast is especially useful for ports that are connected to devices that shut down frequently. When you turn on such a device, the switch blocks the port for 30 seconds while the Listening and Learning phases occur. This blocking could cause problems if the device is quick to boot and tries to use the network (e.g., to get a DHCP address or to log on to the network). Enabling PortFast on a port eliminates this problem, because the port immediately begins forwarding traffic as soon as it is initialized.

NOTE	By default on Cisco Catalyst switches, both PAgP (used for EtherChannel negotiation) and DTP (used for trunk negotiation) are enabled, which increases the amount of time a port takes to initialize before forwarding data. You should also eliminate these sources of delay if you do not need EtherChannel bundles or trunks to form on your ports attached to workstations. See Chapter 10 "Maintenance, Monitoring, and Troubleshooting" for more details on this topic.

Before configuring PortFast, you must carefully consider which ports you are going to enable it for. It is recommended that you enable it only for ports that are connected to workstations, because it is very unlikely attaching these devices introduces loops in the network. Do not configure PortFast on ports that connect to other Layer 2 devices, such as a hub, bridge, or switch, and do not configure the feature on ports attached to servers and routers, because these devices are normally up at all times. If you do enable PortFast on a port that is attached to another switch and a loop is detected, the switch immediately blocks the port; however, there is a danger that it could be too late because the switch might already be overwhelmed by a broadcast storm. For this reason, PortFast should only ever be used on ports that are connected to a single host, because this ensures a loop could never be formed.

Diskless Workstations

A client once called me who was having issues imaging his new Windows 2000 Professional workstations. The client was using Microsoft RIS (Remote Installation Services), where the workstation boots from a PXE-compliant network card and downloads and installs the image. After various testing, he found that when he connected the workstations to a hub everything worked okay. However, when he connected them to a switch, nothing worked. The answer here was simple: The PXE-compliant NIC tries to get a DHCP lease to communicate with the RIS server and download the installation image. Because the switch was blocking the newly activated port for 30 seconds, this process failed. Of course, the solution was to enable PortFast.

Configuring PortFast

Figure 4-26 shows a topology where diskless workstations are connected to Switch-C and Switch-D, which boot from the network within a few seconds after powering up. A switch port takes 30 seconds (by default) to start forwarding traffic after initialization; this delay will cause problems for the diskless workstations, which must have network connectivity immediately. The solution to resolve this problem is to enable PortFast on the ports connected to the diskless workstations.

To configure PortFast on Switch-C (Cisco IOS), you use the following interface configuration command:

```
spanning-tree portfast
```

Example 4-38 demonstrates the configuration required on Switch-C to enable PortFast on interfaces Fa0/3 through Fa0/24.

Example 4-38 *Configuring PortFast on Switch-C*

```
Switch-C# configure terminal
Switch-C(config)# interface range fa0/3 - 24
Switch-C(config-if-range)# spanning-tree portfast
%Warning: portfast should only be enabled on ports connected to a single
 host. Connecting hubs, concentrators, switches, bridges, etc... to this
 interface  when portfast is enabled, can cause temporary bridging loops.
 Use with CAUTION

%Portfast has been configured on FastEthernet0/2 but will only
 have effect when the interface is in a non-trunking mode.
```

Figure 4-26   *PortFast Topology*

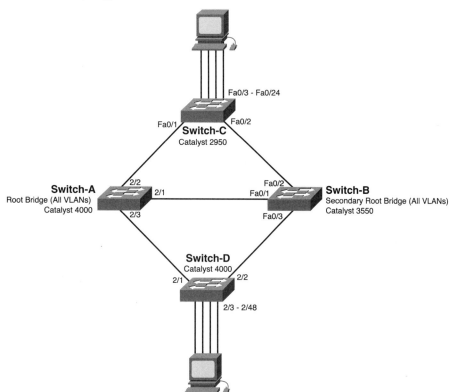

To verify your PortFast configuration on Cisco IOS, you can use the **show spanning-tree interface** *interface* **detail** command, as shown in Example 4-39.

Example 4-39   *Verifying PortFast on Switch-C*

```
Switch-C# show spanning-tree interface fa0/3 detail
Port 3 (FastEthernet0/3) of VLAN0001 is forwarding
    Port path cost 19, Port priority 128, Port Identifier 128.2.
    Designated root has priority 8192, address 0001.96a0.2c00
    Designated bridge has priority 28673, address 0009.b7aa.9c80
    Designated port id is 128.2, designated path cost 19
    Timers: message age 0, forward delay 0, hold 0
    Number of transitions to forwarding state: 1
    BPDU: sent 70, received 2
    The port is in the portfast mode
    Root guard is enabled
```

To configure PortFast on Switch-D (CatOS), you use the following command:

```
set spantree portfast mod/port {enable | disable}
```

Example 4-40 demonstrates the configuration required on Switch-D to enable PortFast on ports 2/3 through 2/48.

Example 4-40 *Configuring PortFast on Switch-D*

```
Switch-D> (enable) set spantree portfast 2/3-48 enable
Warning:Connecting Layer 2 devices to a fast start port can cause
temporary spanning tree loops. Use with caution.

Spantree ports 2/3-48 fast start enabled.
```

To verify your PortFast configuration, you can use the **show spantree** *module/port* command, which displays the PortFast state for the port, as shown in Example 4-41.

Example 4-41 *Verifying PortFast on Switch-D*

```
Switch-D> (enable) show spantree 2/3
Port                     Vlan Port-State   Cost      Prio Portfast Channel_id
---------------------    ---- ------------ --------- ---- -------- ----------
 2/3                       1    forwarding       100   32 enabled  0
```

In Example 4-41, you can see that PortFast (represented by the PortFast column) is enabled for port 2/3 on Switch-D.

Scenario 4-5: Configuring PortFast BPDU Guard

As previously discussed, it is important that you enable PortFast with caution, and only on ports that do not connect to multihomed devices such as hubs or switches. If you follow these rules, a PortFast port should *never* receive configuration BPDUs. If configuration BPDUs are received by a PortFast port, this reception indicates another bridge is somehow connected to the port, and it means that there is a possibility of a bridging loop forming during the Listening and Learning phases. In a valid PortFast configuration, configuration BPDUs should never be received, so Cisco switches support a feature called PortFast BPDU Guard, which is a feature that shuts down a PortFast-enabled port in the event a BPDU is received. This feature ensures that a bridging loop cannot form, because the switch's shutting down the port removes the possibility for a loop forming.

NOTE   A port that has been shutdown by the BPDU guard feature must be manually re-enabled by an administrator using the **no shutdown** interface configuration command on Cisco IOS or the **set port enable** command on CatOS.

If you do not have BPDU Guard configured on a PortFast-enabled port that is receiving configuration BPDUs, the configuration BPDUs are processed by the switch and eventually the port might be shut down to prevent a loop. However, because during this time the switch is forwarding traffic (because PortFast is enabled), a bridging loop might be formed that could bring down the network before the port is blocked.

Enabling PortFast BPDU Guard

On CatOS, the PortFast BPDU Guard feature is disabled by default. It can be enabled or disabled globally for all PortFast ports or explicitly enabled or disabled for each physical PortFast port. To enable or disable PortFast BPDU Guard globally on a CatOS switch, you use the following command:

```
set spantree global-default bpdu-guard {enable | disable}
```

To explicitly enable or disable PortFast BPDU Guard for a specific port on a CatOS switch, you use the following command:

```
set spantree portfast bpdu-guard mod/port {enable | disable | default}
```

Configuring the **default** option means that the port inherits the global configuration state of the BPDU Guard feature.

On Cisco IOS, you can configure BPDU Guard only globally, except for IOS 12.1(11b)E and later for native IOS Catalyst 6000/6500 switches, which allow you to configure BPDU guard explicitly on an interface. To enable PortFast BPDU Guard on a Cisco IOS-based switch, you use the following global configuration command:

```
spanning-tree portfast bpduguard
```

To disable PortFast BPDU Guard, simply use the no form of the command.

Referring back to Figure 4-26, assume that you need to enable BPDU Guard on Switch-C and Switch-D. Example 4-42 demonstrates enabling PortFast BPDU Guard on Switch-C.

Example 4-42 *Configuring PortFast BPDU Guard on Switch-C*

```
Switch-C# configure terminal
Switch-C(config)# spanning-tree portfast bpduguard
```

The configuration in Example 4-42 applies for all PortFast-enabled interfaces on Switch-C. Example 4-43 demonstrates enabling PortFast BPDU Guard both globally and for specific ports on Switch-D.

Example 4-43 *Configuring PortFast BPDU Guard on Switch-D*

```
Switch-D> (enable) set spantree global-default bpdu-guard enable
Spantree global-default bpdu-guard enabled on this switch.
Switch-D> (enable) set spantree portfast bpdu-guard 2/3-48 enable
Spantree ports 2/3-48 bpdu guard enabled.
```

In Example 4-43, if BPDU Guard were not enabled globally, only ports 2/3-48 would have BPDU Guard enabled.

Testing BPDU Guard

To test BPDU Guard, you first incorrectly configure PortFast and BPDU Guard on interface Fa0/3 (connected to Switch-D) of Switch-B in the topology of Figure 4-26. You then configure Switch-D with a priority of 0, which forces it to begin generating configuration BPDUs out the previously blocked port 2/2, because it assumes the root bridge role. Switch-B should hear these configuration BPDUs generated by Switch-D, which will invoke BPDU Guard and shut down interface Fa0/3.

Step 1 On Switch-B, ensure that PortFast and BPDU Guard are enabled on interface Fa0/3, as shown in Example 4-44.

Example 4-44 Configuring PortFast and BPDU Guard on Switch-B

```
Switch-B# configure terminal
Switch-B(config)# interface fa0/3
Switch-B(config-if)#spanning-tree portfast trunk
%Warning: portfast should only be enabled on ports connected to a single
 host. Connecting hubs, concentrators, switches, bridges, etc... to this
 interface  when portfast is enabled, can cause temporary bridging loops.
 Use with CAUTION
Switch-B(config-if)# spanning-tree bpduguard enable
```

In Example 4-44, the **trunk** keyword in the **spanning-tree portfast trunk** command forces PortFast to be enabled on the interface, even if it is a trunking interface.

Step 2 On Switch-D, set the priority for VLAN 1 as 0, as shown in Example 4-45.

Example 4-45 Configuring a Priority of 0 on Switch-D

```
Switch-D> (enable) set spanning-tree priority 0 1
Spantree 1 bridge priority set to 0.
```

Step 3 At this stage, Switch-D has a lower bridge ID than the current root bridge (Switch-A) and assumes that it is the root bridge. Switch-D starts sending configuration BPDUs out port 2/2 to Switch-B. On Switch-B, you should see the following console messages:

```
15:16:21: %SPANTREE-2-RX_PORTFAST: Received BPDU on PortFast enabled
port.
    Disabling FastEthernet0/3.
15:16:21: %PM-4-ERR_DISABLE: bpduguard error detected on Fa0/3,
    putting Fa0/3 in err-disable state
15:16:22: %LINEPROTO-5-UPDOWN: Line protocol on Interface
FastEthernet0/3,
    changed state to down
15:16:23: %LINK-3-UPDOWN: Interface FastEthernet0/3, changed state to
down
```

Notice that interface Fa0/3 is put into an *err-disable state*, which means that the interface has been administratively shut down.

Scenario 4-6: Configuring PortFast BPDU Filter

Even if you enable PortFast on a port, by default that port still generates configuration BPDUs. Any connected device receives and might process configuration BPDUs unnecessarily. You can configure a feature called *BPDU Filter*, which prevents a PortFast-enabled port from sending configuration BPDUs. If configuration BPDUs are received on the PortFast-enabled port, the port either loses its PortFast status (or is manually shut down if BPDU guard is configured), or it ignores the BPDUs, depending on how you configure BPDU Filter.

Configuring BPDU Filter so that all configuration BPDUs received on a port are dropped can be useful for service provider environments, where a service provider provides Layer 2 Ethernet access for customers. Figure 4-27 demonstrates such a scenario.

Figure 4-27   *Service Provider Scenario*

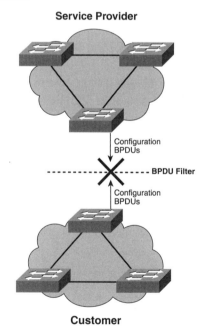

In Figure 4-27, the service provider has many customers attached via Layer 2 Ethernet connections. Ideally, the service provider does not want to share any spanning-tree information with customers, because such sharing might jeopardize the stability of the service provider's internal spanning-tree topology. By configuring PortFast and BPDU Filter on each customer access port, the service provider will not send any configuration BPDUs to customers and will ignore any configuration BPDUs sent from customers.

WARNING Configuring the BPDU Filter feature to ignore any configuration BPDUs received on a port can result in a loop forming that is never detected. Use this feature with care, ensuring there is no possibility for looping.

Enabling PortFast BPDU Filter

The PortFast BPDU Filter feature is currently supported only on CatOS and is not supported on any Cisco IOS-based switches, except for the native IOS Catalyst 6000/6500 from IOS release 12.1(11b)EX onwards. By default, the feature is disabled and can be enabled or disabled either globally or explicitly for each PortFast port. If you configure the feature globally, BPDU Filter applies to all PortFast-enabled ports, and if any configuration BPDUs are received on a PortFast-enabled port, the port immediately loses its PortFast status and returns to a normal STP port configuration. If you configure the feature explicitly on a PortFast-enabled port, any configuration BPDUs received are ignored and dropped.

To enable PortFast BPDU Filter globally on a CatOS switch, you use the following command:

```
set spantree global-default bpdu-filter [enable | disable]
```

To enable PortFast BPDU Filter for a specific port on a CatOS switch, you use the following command:

```
set spantree portfast bpdu-filter mod/port [enable | disable | default]
```

The **default** parameter configures the port to inherit the global BPDU Filter configuration.

Referring back to the topology of Figure 4-26, assume that you wish to enable the PortFast BPDU filter on each of the PortFast ports on Switch-D, and you want Switch-D to ignore any configuration BPDUs received on port 2/3. Example 4-46 demonstrates the configuration required on Switch-D.

Example 4-46 *Configuring PortFast BPDU Filter on Switch-D*

```
Switch-D> (enable) set spantree global-default bpdu-filter enable
Spantree global-default bpdu-filter enabled on this switch.
Switch-D> (enable) set spantree portfast bpdu-filter 2/3 enable
Warning:Ports enabled with bpdu filter will not send BPDUs and drop all
received BPDUs. You may cause loops in the bridged network if you misuse
this feature.

Spantree port  2/3 bpdu filter enabled.
```

In Example 4-46, because port 2/3 has BPDU Filter explicitly configured, it does not send any configuration BPDUs and ignores any configuration BPDUs received. All other PortFast-enabled ports inherit the global BPDU Filter configuration, which means they do not send any configuration BPDUs, but transition out of a PortFast state to a normal STP port if configuration BPDUs are received.

Scenario 4-7: Configuring UplinkFast

UplinkFast is a feature that greatly enhances the convergence time associated with a direct failure of an uplink attached to a leaf switch. You should only enable UplinkFast on leaf switches, and the feature works only with direct failures. Figure 4-28 shows the network topology used for this scenario.

Figure 4-28   *Converged STP Topology*

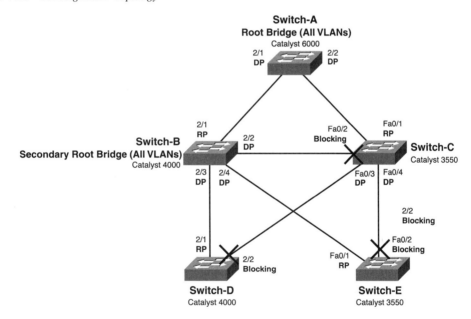

Switch-A is the root switch and connects two distribution-layer (intermediate) switches (Switch-B and Switch-C). Switch-B and Switch-C provide redundant uplinks to Switch-D and Switch-E, which are classified as leaf switches, because they are leaf nodes at the edge of the spanning tree and are not upstream from any other switches (a leaf switch is always downstream from all other switches in the network).

With regards to STP, *upstream* refers to the direction towards the root bridge, and *downstream* refers to the direction away from the root bridge. In Figure 4-28, Switch-D is downstream from Switch-B, because Switch-B is closer to the root bridge. In the reverse, Switch-B is upstream from Switch-D, because Switch-B is closer to the root bridge.

Assuming all costs are configured as defaults, Switch-D and Switch-E choose the uplink connected to Switch-B as the root port and, thus, place this port into a Forwarding state. The uplinks to Switch-C (port 2/2 on Switch-D and interface Fa0/2 on Switch-E) are placed into a Blocking state, because Switch-C always becomes the designated bridge for these segments as it is closer to the root bridge.

Now, assume that on Switch-D, the active uplink (port 2/1) fails or is shut down. Because the root port on Switch-D has failed, Switch-D has lost its path to the root, invalidating the last BPDU received on port 2/1. Switch-D is now in a situation similar to when it first initializes and must now determine who the new root bridge is, or determine the new path to the root bridge. Therefore, Port 2/2 transitions to a Listening state and discovers that the root bridge is reachable via Switch-C. Switch-D chooses port 2/2 as the new root port and transitions the port to a Learning state and then finally to a Forwarding state. Given the default STP timers, it takes 30 seconds after the failure for Switch-D to begin actually forwarding data again.

NOTE   The Max Age timer is not used with direct failures related to the root port because a direct failure is immediately detected, invalidating the root port and the configuration BPDUs received on that port.

If Switch-D were not a leaf switch, another uplink might be used to reach the root bridge. In this case, to prevent a loop from forming it is important that the Switch-D transitions through the Learning and Listening phases before forwarding any traffic. However, because Switch-D is a leaf switch with only two possible uplinks to the root bridge, if the primary uplink fails, the backup uplink will *always* be the uplink that begins forwarding. Therefore, no reason exists as to why Switch-D cannot just place the backup uplink into a Forwarding state immediately, as soon as the primary uplink goes down.

By enabling UplinkFast, a leaf switch notes a redundant uplink to the root and immediately allows the redundant uplink to forward user data if the primary uplink fails. This recognition reduces convergence from 30 seconds (using default STP timers) to almost nil.

NOTE   The Listening and Learning phases are still transitioned when the redundant uplink is activated. UplinkFast allows the port to send and receive user data during these phases.

Although the Forwarding state transition is immediate, you must also consider the bridging tables on each switch in the network. By default, the bridge table has an aging timer of 300 seconds, which means an idle entry remains in the bridge table for five minutes before disappearing. Figure 4-29 shows the topology of Figure 4-28 and what happens when UplinkFast is configured and invoked with relation to Switch-D (Switch-E is omitted to make the figure easier to read, but the same principles apply if UplinkFast is enabled on Switch-E).

Figure 4-29   *UplinkFast Operation*

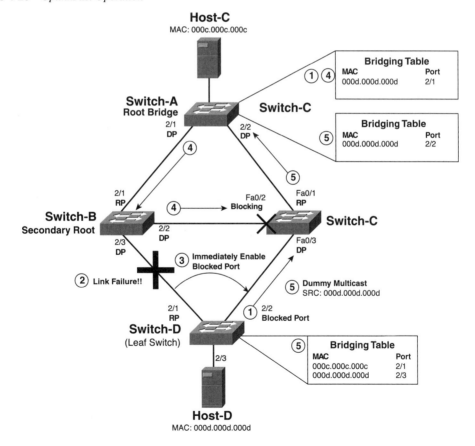

The following are the steps in Figure 4-29:

Step 1   The network is in its normal state, with port 2/1 on Switch-D running as the root port, and port 2/2 in a Blocking state. Notice the bridge table on Switch-A —because the active path to Host-D is via Switch-B, Host-D (000d.000d.000d) is listed as being reachable through interface port 2/1. Because UplinkFast is enabled on Switch-D, Switch-D notes that port 2/2 represents an alternative path to the root bridge.

Step 2   A link failure occurs between the Switch-D and Switch-B, bringing down the root port for Switch-D. Switch-D detects this failure immediately due to loss of physical link on the root port.

Step 3   Because UplinkFast is enabled on the Switch-D, it immediately designates the previously blocked port 2/2 (attached to Switch-C) as the new root port and allows the port to forward user data, while transitioning through the normal Listening and Learning phases. This operation is safe because Switch-D is a leaf switch and has no other paths to the root bridge that could cause loops.

Step 4   At this stage, although Switch-D is still connected to the rest of the network and can forward data out port 2/2, the bridge table on Switch-A is out of date, because it attempts to forward any data to Host-D out port 2/1, which arrives at Switch-B. Because the link to Switch-D on Switch-B is down, Switch-B has flushed its bridging table entry for Host-D and, therefore, floods the frame out all ports, except the port upon which the frame was received. The frame is flooded out port 2/2 towards Switch-C. Then, the flooded frame terminates at Switch-C, because Switch-C drops the frame because interface Fa0/2 is blocked. As you can see, the network cannot communicate with Host-D because the bridging table information cached on other switches is out of date.

Step 5   To ensure that the bridging tables of all other switches in the network are correct, Switch-D looks at its current bridge table and starts sending dummy multicasts out the new root port on behalf of every host that is directly attached to the switch (i.e., any MAC addresses in the bridge table that are associated with ports that are not attached to other switches). Each dummy multicast frame has an unused (dummy) destination multicast address, which ensures the frame is propagated throughout the entire Layer 2 topology. For example, in the bridge table of Switch-D, the 000d.000d.000d entry is considered directly attached because port 2/3 is not connected to any other switches. Switch-D, therefore, generates a dummy multicast with a source MAC address of 000d.000d.000d and sends it out port 2/2. Note that a multicast is *not* sent for the PC with MAC address 000c.000c.000c because the bridge table entry on Switch-D for this host has an egress port that is an uplink (port

2/1), indicating the host is not directly attached. When the multicast is received on interface Fa0/3, Switch-B updates the bridge table entry for 000d.000d.000d, listing a new egress port of Fa0/3. Switch-B then floods the multicast out all interfaces (except the interface the multicast was received on), allowing all other switches in the network to update their bridge tables correctly.

NOTE   Because the dummy multicasts have an unused destination multicast address, the multicasts are never actually received by any device and are only processed by switches for the purposes of updating bridge tables as part of normal transparent bridging operation.

At this stage, data is being forwarded by Switch-D, and the paths taken through network to reach devices attached to Switch-D are up-to-date and correct. In normal spanning-tree operation, the redundant uplink would have taken 30 seconds to transition through the Listening and Learning states before forwarding any data (the redundant uplink becomes the new root port). By enabling UplinkFast on the switch, the convergence time is reduced from 30 seconds to almost 0. The real key to the success of UplinkFast, however, is the clever way the switch generates dummy multicasts to update all bridge tables in the network appropriately.

NOTE   By default, Catalyst switches send dummy multicasts at a configurable rate of 15 frames per 100 milliseconds (150 frames per second). So if you had an edge switch with 450 directly connected hosts, it would take approximately 3 seconds for the network to converge fully after the upstream switch failure.

You should enable UplinkFast only on leaf switches because UplinkFast makes assumptions about your network topology based upon the fact that the switch is a leaf node. If you enable UplinkFast on a *transit switch* (a switch that is the root bridge or has downstream switches connected), unpredictable forwarding paths and loops can result. In Figure 4-29, Switch-B and Switch-C are transit switches because they connect downstream switches (e.g. Switch-D). Switch-D is a leaf switches because it connects only to upstream switches (Switch-B and Switch-C).

Enabling UplinkFast

Always remember that UplinkFast should only ever be configured on leaf switches. If you enable it on non-leaf switches, it is possible that loops could form in the network. To ensure that UplinkFast is enabled only on leaf switches, when you enable UplinkFast, the bridge priority and the cost of each port on the switch are increased.

NOTE This scenario assumes that a single VLAN (VLAN 1) is in use and that Switch-A has been configured as the root bridge, with Switch-B configured as the secondary root bridge. All other spanning tree parameters are configured as the default on all switches.

On CatOS, UplinkFast is disabled by default and can be globally enabled or disabled. To configure UplinkFast on a CatOS switch, you use the following command:

```
set spantree uplinkfast enable [rate station-update-rate]
```

The **rate** parameter allows you to specify the rate at which dummy multicast packets are generated every 100 milliseconds (the default is 15 packets per 100 milliseconds).

On Cisco IOS, UplinkFast is also disabled by default and can be globally enabled or disabled. To enable UplinkFast on a Cisco IOS switch, you use the following global configuration command:

```
spanning-tree uplinkfast [max-update-rate pkts-per-second]
```

The **max-update-rate** parameter allows you to specify the rate at which dummy multicast packets are generated every second (the default is 150 packets per second).

TIP You must explicitly configure the **spanning-tree uplinkfast** by itself to enable UplinkFast and then configure the **spanning-tree uplinkfast max-update-rate** command if you wish to modify the dummy multicast rate.

Referring back to Figure 4-28, to optimize the convergence time in the event of a direct uplink failure on any leaf switch (Switch-D and Switch-E), you can enable the UplinkFast feature.

Example 4-47 demonstrates how to enable UplinkFast on Switch-D (CatOS) and configure a custom dummy multicast rate of 250 packets per second.

Example 4-47 *Configuring UplinkFast on Switch-D*

```
Switch-D> (enable) set spantree uplinkfast enable rate 25
VLANs 1-4094 bridge priority set to 49152.
The port cost and portvlancost of all ports increased to above 3000.
Station update rate set to 25 packets/100ms.
uplinkfast all-protocols field set to off.
uplinkfast enabled for bridge.
```

You can see that by enabling UplinkFast, the bridge priority and cost of all ports are increased to ensure that the switch always becomes a leaf switch. Notice that the **rate** parameter is configured in packets per 100ms.

Verifying UplinkFast

Example 4-48 shows the output of the **show spantree** command after UplinkFast has been enabled.

Example 4-48 *Verifying Spanning-Tree Configuration on Switch-D after Enabling UplinkFast*

```
Switch-D> (enable) show spantree 1
VLAN 1
Spanning tree mode        PVST+
Spanning tree type        ieee
Spanning tree enabled

Designated Root           00-01-96-a0-2c-00
Designated Root Priority  8192
Designated Root Cost      38
Designated Root Port      2/1
Root Max Age  20  sec   Hello Time 2  sec   Forward Delay 15  sec

Bridge ID MAC ADDR        00-01-68-b1-1a-00
Bridge ID Priority        49152
Bridge Max Age 20  sec   Hello Time 2  sec   Forward Delay 15  sec

Port                    Vlan Port-State    Cost       Prio Portfast Channel_id
----------------------- ---- ------------- ---------- ---- -------- ----------
  2/1                   1    forwarding    3019       32 disabled 0
  2/2                   1    blocking      3019       32 disabled 0
... (Output Abbreviated)
...
```

Notice that the bridge priority of Switch-D is now 49152 and that the cost of ports 2/1 and 2/2 has been increased by 3000 from 19 (the default for 100-Mbps ports) to 3019.

To verify UplinkFast configuration, use the **show spantree uplinkfast** command after UplinkFast has been enabled, as shown in Example 4-49.

Example 4-49 *Verifying UplinkFast Configuration on Switch-D*

```
Switch-D> (enable) show spantree uplinkfast
Station update rate set to 25 packets/100ms.
uplinkfast all-protocols field set to off.

VLAN          port list
-----------------------------------------------
1             2/1(fwd), 2/2
```

You can see on Switch-D that port 2/1 is currently the active uplink (as indicate by the fwd text), and port 2/2 is a candidate port for fast failover should port 2/1 go down.

NOTE

If you want to disable UplinkFast, use the **set spantree uplinkfast disable** command. This command disables UplinkFast, but does not return the bridge priority and port cost values to their default values. To disable UplinkFast and configure the bridge priority and port cost values as their default values, use the **clear spantree uplinkfast** command instead.

Example 4-50 demonstrates how to enable UplinkFast on Switch-E (Cisco IOS) and configure a custom dummy multicast rate of 250 packets per second.

Example 4-50 *Configuring UplinkFast on Switch-E*

```
Switch-E# configure terminal
Switch-E(config)# spanning-tree uplinkfast
Switch-E(config)# spanning-tree uplinkfast max-update-rate 250
```

Notice in Example 4-50 that you must explicitly enable UplinkFast first and then configure the custom dummy multicast rate separately. Once you have enabled UplinkFast, the bridge priority is increased for 49152 for all VLANs, and the port cost of every physical port is increased by 3000, unless the port cost has been explicitly configured previously.

To verify UplinkFast on a Cisco IOS switch, use the **show spanning-tree uplinkfast** command, as demonstrated on Switch-E in Example 4-51.

Example 4-51 *Verifying Spanning-Tree Configuration on Switch-E After Enabling UplinkFast*

```
Switch-E# show spanning-tree uplinkfast
UplinkFast is enabled

Station update rate set to 250 packets/sec.

UplinkFast statistics
-----------------------
Number of transitions via uplinkFast (all VLANs)          : 1
Number of proxy multicast addresses transmitted (all VLANs) : 0

Name                    Interface List
------------------ ------------------------------------
VLAN0001                Fa0/1(fwd), Fa0/2
```

Notice that UplinkFast is enabled and the update rate is set to 250 packets per second. The rate is expressed in packets per second, unlike CatOS that specifies the rate in packets per 100 milliseconds. At the bottom of the table, you can see the interface list for each VLAN that UplinkFast uses for fast cutover. Interface Fa0/1 is listed as the uplink that is currently forwarding, with interface Fa0/2 listed as a candidate interface for fast failover. If Fa0/1 is detected as going down, Switch-D immediately places Fa0/2 into a forwarding state.

NOTE   To disable UplinkFast, use the **no spanning-tree uplinkfast** global configuration command. This command disables UplinkFast and return bridge priority and port cost values to their default values.

Testing UplinkFast

To test UplinkFast, configure IP addressing on Switch-B and Switch-D, which enables you to test ping connectivity between the switches. Then shut down the active root port on Switch-D and verify that you can still ping Switch-B immediately after the port is shut down.

Step 1   Create a virtual interface for VLAN 1 on Switch-B and configure an IP address of 192.168.1.2/24, as shown in Example 4-52.

Example 4-52 *Configuring IP on Switch-B*

```
Switch-B# configure terminal
Switch-B(config)# interface VLAN 1
Switch-B(config-if)# no shutdown
Switch-B(config-if)# ip address 192.168.1.2 255.255.255.0
```

Step 2   Configure the sc0 interface on Switch-D with an IP address of 192.168.1.4/24. Disable UplinkFast, as shown in Example 4-53. After you have completed your configuration, verify that you can ping Switch-B from Switch-D.

Example 4-53 *Configuring IP on Switch-D*

```
Switch-D> (enable) set interface sc0 192.168.1.4 255.255.255.0
Interface sc0 IP address and netmask set.
Switch-D> (enable) set spantree uplinkfast disable
uplinkfast disabled for bridge.
Use clear spantree uplinkfast to return stp parameters to default.
Switch-D> (enable) ping 192.168.1.2
!!!!!

-----192.168.1.2 PING Statistics------
5 packets transmitted, 5 packets received, 0% packet loss
round-trip (ms) min/avg/max = 1/1/1
```

In Example 4-53, you disable UplinkFast so that you can verify the normal convergence delays incurred when port 2/1 on Switch-D goes down.

Step 3   Disable the current root port on Switch-D (port 2/1) and then immediately try to ping Switch-B, as shown in Example 4-54. You should *not* be able to ping Switch-B, because port 2/2 is transitioning through the Listening and Learning phases and is now forwarding any user data. If you wait for approximately 30 seconds, you should then be able to ping Switch-B.

Example 4-54 *Testing Convergence Times on Switch-D*

```
Switch-D> (enable) set port disable 2/1
Port 2/1 disabled.
Switch-D> (enable) ping 192.168.1.2
.....

-----192.168.1.2 PING Statistics------
5 packets transmitted, 0 packets received, 100% packet loss
round-trip (ms) min/avg/max = -/-/-
```

Step 4   Re-enable the current root port on Switch-D (port 2/1) and allow 30 seconds for the port 2/1 to transition to a Forwarding state. Next, enable UplinkFast on Switch-D, verify the root port, and verify you can still ping Switch-D, as shown in Example 4-55.

Example 4-55 *Enabling UplinkFast on Switch-D*

```
Switch-D> (enable) set port enable 2/1
Port 2/1 enabled.
…
… (Wait for 30 seconds
Switch-D> (enable) set spantree uplinkfast enable
VLANs 1-1005 bridge priority set to 49152.
The port cost and portvlancost of all ports set to above 3000.
Station update rate set to 15 packets/100ms.
uplinkfast all-protocols field set to off.
uplinkfast enabled for bridge.
Switch-D> (enable) show spantree uplinkfast
Station update rate set to 15 packets/100ms.
uplinkfast all-protocols field set to off.

VLAN          port list
----------------------------------------------
1             2/1(fwd),2/2
Switch-D> (enable) ping 192.168.1.2
!!!!!

-----192.168.1.2 PING Statistics------
5 packets transmitted, 5 packets received, 0% packet loss
round-trip (ms) min/avg/max = 1/1/1
```

The **show spantree uplinkfast** command indicates that port 2/1 is forwarding and that port 2/2 is a candidate backup root port.

Step 5   Disable the current root port on Switch-D (port 2/1) and immediately try to ping Switch-B once again, as shown in Example 4-56. This time, you should be able to ping Switch-B immediately, because UplinkFast forwards traffic out port 2/2.

Example 4-56   *Testing UplinkFast on Switch-D*

```
Switch-D> (enable) set port disable 2/1
Port 2/1 disabled.
Switch-D> (enable) ping 192.168.1.2
!!!!!

-----192.168.1.2 PING Statistics------
5 packets transmitted, 5 packets received, 0% packet loss
round-trip (ms) min/avg/max = 1/1/1
```

Scenario 4-8: Configuring BackboneFast

BackboneFast is another Cisco enhancement designed to complement UplinkFast. UplinkFast is designed to detect *direct failures*, whereas BackboneFast is designed to detect *indirect failures*. An indirect failure is not immediately detected when it occurs, and under normal STP operation, the Max Age timer is used to detect an indirect failure by defining the maximum amount of time that must pass before the root bridge is considered down due to configuration BPDUs not being received from the root. By default, the Max Age timer is configured as 20 seconds, which means that it takes STP 20 seconds just to detect an indirect failure. After an indirect failure has been detected (i.e., the Max Age timer expires), the Listening and Learning phases (by default, a total of 30 seconds) are transitioned through until a Forwarding or Blocking state is reached for each port. This means that by default, an indirect failure requires 50 seconds to converge to a new topology that is actively forwarding user data.

BackboneFast effectively eliminates the Max Age timeout period associated with an indirect failure, lowering convergence from the default 50 seconds to 30 seconds. Note that it does *not* eliminate the Listening and Learning periods (30 seconds) like UplinkFast does.

BackboneFast should be enabled on *every* switch in your network (unlike UplinkFast). This recommendation comes because BackboneFast is a mechanism that detects a possible indirect failure and then queries the network to verify that an indirect failure has occurred. BackboneFast works on the assumption that if the designated bridge (and only the designated bridge) for a segment suddenly starts sending *inferior BPDUs* (i.e., root bridge ID is higher than current root bridge ID), then it is likely that an indirect failure has occurred. If the inferior BPDUs are being received from a non-designated bridge, then they are ignored because they indicate a failure further downstream in the topology and no action is required on any bridges upstream from the failure. If the inferior BPDUs are being received from the designated bridge, and no blocked ports exist on the switch (only one path to the root), then the switch immediately expires the Max Age timer because it knows it only has one path to the root bridge.

If the switch *does* have blocked ports, the process gets more complicated. The switch then sends *root link query* (*RLQ*) requests out all non-designated ports (except the port that received the inferior BPDU). An RLQ request is a Cisco-proprietary frame that is sent by a switch to query upstream switches if their (the upstream switch's) connection to the root bridge is stable. Each RLQ request is answered by an RLQ response that indicates that the path to the root is stable. Each switch that receives the RLQ request answers immediately if it is the root bridge or it knows that the root bridge connection has been lost. If neither of these conditions is the case, the switch propagates the RLQ request out the local root port, with this process continuing until the root bridge status is known. This method of propagating RLQ requests out the root ports of upstream switches ensures the RLQ request eventually reaches the root bridge or a switch that knows the root bridge is down.

NOTE   Because the RLQ mechanism is Cisco-proprietary, you must ensure that all switches in the network are Cisco switches and that BackboneFast is supported and enabled on each. If a Cisco switch does not have BackboneFast enabled, it ignores RLQ messages, which breaks the BackboneFast mechanism.

Once the RLQ request eventually reaches the root bridge (or a switch that knows the root bridge is down), because that switch is the root bridge, it generates an RLQ response, which is propagated in an identical manner to configuration BPDUs until the response reaches the requesting switch. If on the original switch that generated the RLQ request the RLQ response is *not* received on the root port, then the switch knows it has lost its connection to the root bridge and immediately expires its Max Age timer.

Figure 4-30 shows the topology used to demonstrate BackboneFast for this scenario.

Figure 4-30   *BackboneFast*

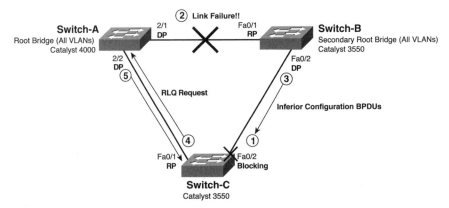

The following steps describe the events that occur in Figure 4-30:

Step 1   The network has converged to a stable STP topology, and interface Fa0/2 on Switch-C is in a blocking state, because Switch-B has a lower sender bridge ID than Switch-C. (Switch-B is the secondary root bridge.)

Step 2   A failure occurs on the link between Switch-A and Switch-B. Because the path to the root bridge (i.e., the root port) on Switch-B has gone down (interface Fa0/1), Switch-B immediately assumes that it is the new root bridge and starts sending configuration BPDUs out interface Fa0/2 listing Switch-B as the root.

Step 3   The new configuration BPDUs are received by Switch-C (remember BPDUs are sent and received on blocking ports), with Switch-B listed as the root bridge. Because Switch-C is still receiving BPDUs from Switch-A, the BPDUs received on interface Fa0/2 are considered inferior.

Step 4   Under normal STP operation, Switch-C ignores inferior BPDUs until the Max Age timer expires on the interface. At this point, assuming Switch-C is still receiving superior configuration BPDUs via its root port, Switch-C then starts sending the superior configuration BPDUs out interface Fa0/2, and the interface transitions through the Listening and Learning phases until a Forwarding state is reached. The total convergence of this process takes 50 seconds by default (Max Age of 20 seconds + 2 * Forward Delay of 15 seconds).

Step 5   Because BackboneFast is enabled on Switch-C, Switch-C reacts differently to the inferior configuration BPDU being received. The inferior configuration BPDU is received from the previously designated bridge for the segment (Switch-B), which indicates to Switch-C that Switch-B has lost its connection to the root bridge. The inferior configuration BPDUs could also indicate that Switch-C might have lost its connection to the root, so Switch-A generates an RLQ request frame that is sent out all non-designated (upstream) ports (i.e., blocked ports and root ports). The RLQ requests are not sent out designated ports, because these only lead to downstream switches and the root is always upstream. In Figure 4-30 then, a RLQ response is sent out interface Fa0/1 to Switch-A.

Step 6   Because Switch-A is the root bridge (and has BackboneFast enabled), it sends an RLQ response back to Switch-C. This response indicates to Switch-C that it still has a connection to the root bridge. Because Switch-C has a connection to the root bridge, it needs to expire only the Max Age timer on interface Fa0/2, not the Max Age timer on interface Fa0/1. If the RLQ response were received on another non-designated port, this would indicate that Switch-C had lost its connection to the root, and the Max Age timer would be immediately expired on the root port (Fa0/1).

Interface Fa0/2 still goes through the Listening and Learning phases because it may be found that Switch-B is still the designated bridge for the segment between Switch-B and Switch-C. Because the Max Age timer has been expired prematurely, convergence has been reduced from 50 seconds to 30 seconds, using the default STP timers. If the failure had also affected connectivity to the root bridge for Switch-C, the RLQ mechanism would have allowed Switch-C to also expire the Max Age timer prematurely for the root port.

NOTE   Remember, BackboneFast is designed to detect indirect failures only, and reduces only the Max Age timeout period. The Listening and Learning phases must still be transitioned through, as loops in the new topology must still be detected.

Enabling BackboneFast

Because of the proprietary RLQ Query/Response mechanism, BackboneFast needs to be enabled on *all* switches in the Layer 2 network, and all switches must be Cisco switches that support the feature.

NOTE   This scenario uses the topology of Figure 4-30, assumes that a single VLAN (VLAN 1) is in use and that Switch-A has been configured as the root bridge, with Switch-B configured as the secondary root bridge. All other spanning-tree parameters are configured as the default on all switches.

On CatOS, BackboneFast is disabled by default and can be enabled or disabled globally for the entire switch. To enable BackboneFast on a CatOS switch, use the following command:

```
set spantree backbonefast enable
```

You can verify BackboneFast is enabled by using the **show spantree backbonefast** command.

On Cisco IOS, BackboneFast is disabled by default and can be enabled or disabled globally for the entire switch. To enable BackboneFast on a Cisco IOS switch, use the following global configuration command:

```
spanning-tree backbonefast
```

In the topology of Figure 4-30, to reduce the convergence time associated with indirect failures in the network, you can enable BackboneFast, which eliminates the Max Age timer from the total convergence time required for an indirect failure. To enable BackboneFast, you must enable the feature on all switches. Example 4-57 through Example 4-59 demonstrates configuring BackboneFast on all switches in Figure 4-57.

Example 4-57 *Configuring BackboneFast on Switch-A*

```
Switch-A> (enable) set spantree backbonefast enable
Backbonefast enabled for all VLANs
```

Example 4-58 *Configuring BackboneFast on Switch-B*

```
Switch-B# configure terminal
Switch-B(config)# spanning-tree backbonefast
```

Example 4-59 *Configuring BackboneFast on Switch-C*

```
Switch-C# configure terminal
Switch-C(config)# spanning-tree backbonefast
```

Example 4-60 demonstrates verifying BackboneFast is configured on Switch-A (CatOS).

Example 4-60 *Verifying BackboneFast on Switch-A*

```
Switch-A> (enable) show spantree backbonefast
Backbonefast is enabled.
```

Example 4-61 demonstrates verifying BackboneFast is configured on Switch-B (Cisco IOS).

Example 4-61 *Verifying BackboneFast on Switch-B*

```
Switch-B# show spanning-tree summary
Root bridge for: none.
Extended system ID is enabled.
PortFast BPDU Guard is disabled
EtherChannel misconfiguration guard is enabled
UplinkFast is disabled
BackboneFast is enabled
Default pathcost method used is short

Name                     Blocking Listening Learning Forwarding STP Active
--------------------     -------- --------- -------- ---------- ----------
VLAN0001                     0        0        0         3          3
--------------------     -------- --------- -------- ---------- ----------
1 vlans                      0        0        0         3          3

BackboneFast statistics
-----------------------
Number of transition via backboneFast (all VLANs)      : 0
Number of inferior BPDUs received (all VLANs)          : 0
Number of RLQ request PDUs received (all VLANs)        : 0
Number of RLQ response PDUs received (all VLANs)       : 0
Number of RLQ request PDUs sent (all VLANs)            : 0
Number of RLQ response PDUs sent (all VLANs)           : 0
```

In Example 4-61, you can see that BackboneFast is enabled and can also see statistics for BackboneFast. Notice that the **show spanning-tree summary** command on Cisco IOS can also be used to determine if other spanning tree enhancements, such as UplinkFast and BPDU Guard, are enabled.

NOTE You can use **show spanning-tree backbonefast** command to just view the BackboneFast information shown in Example 4-61.

Testing BackboneFast

To test BackboneFast, you enable the debugging of spanning-tree Backbonefast events on Switch-C and simulate an indirect failure between Switch-A and Switch-B by shutting interface Fa0/1 on Switch-B. You should be able to see that the Max Age timer is expired prematurely and that interface Fa0/2 on Switch-C moves to a Forwarding state after 30 seconds, as opposed to the normal 50 seconds.

Step 1 On all switches in the network, ensure that BackboneFast is disabled. Examples 4-62 through 4-64 show the configuration required to disable BackboneFast on all switches.

Example 4-62 *Disabling BackboneFast on Switch-A*

```
Switch-A> (enable) set spantree backbonefast disable
Backbonefast disabled for all VLANs
```

Example 4-63 *Disabling BackboneFast on Switch-B*

```
Switch-B# configure terminal
Switch-B(config)# no spanning-tree backbonefast
```

Example 4-64 *Disabling BackboneFast on Switch-C*

```
Switch-C# configure terminal
Switch-C(config)# no spanning-tree backbonefast
```

Step 2 On Switch-C, ensure that logging of debug messages is enabled to the console and then enable the debugging of STP events, as shown in Example 4-65.

Example 4-65 *Debugging Spanning Tree BackboneFast Events on Switch-C*

```
Switch-C# configure terminal
Switch-C(config)# logging console debugging
Switch-C(config)# exit
Switch-C# debug spanning-tree events
Spanning Tree event debugging is on
```

Step 3   To simulate an indirect failure with regards to Switch-C, shut down the interface on Switch-B (interface Fa0/1) that is attached to Switch-A, as shown in Example 4-66.

Example 4-66   *Shutting Down an Interface on Switch-B*

```
Switch-B# configure terminal
Switch-B(config)# interface fa0/1
Switch-B(config-if)# shutdown
```

Step 4   On Switch-C, you see the following debugging output, as shown in Example 4-67.

Example 4-67   *Debug Output on Switch-C after an Indirect Failure*

```
Switch-C#
00:34:06: STP: VLAN0001 heard root 28673-0009.b7aa.9c80 on Fa0/1
00:34:07: STP: VLAN0001 heard root 28673-0009.b7aa.9c80 on Fa0/1
00:34:08: STP: VLAN0001 heard root 28673-0009.b7aa.9c80 on Fa0/2
00:34:09: STP: VLAN0001 heard root 28673-0009.b7aa.9c80 on Fa0/2
00:34:10: STP: VLAN0001 heard root 28673-0009.b7aa.9c80 on Fa0/2
00:34:11: STP: VLAN0001 heard root 28673-0009.b7aa.9c80 on Fa0/2
00:34:12: STP: VLAN0001 heard root 28673-0009.b7aa.9c80 on Fa0/2
00:34:13: STP: VLAN0001 heard root 28673-0009.b7aa.9c80 on Fa0/2
00:34:14: STP: VLAN0001 heard root 28673-0009.b7aa.9c80 on Fa0/2
00:34:15: STP: VLAN0001 heard root 28673-0009.b7aa.9c80 on Fa0/2
00:34:16: STP: VLAN0001 heard root 28673-0009.b7aa.9c80 on Fa0/2
00:34:17: STP: VLAN0001 heard root 28673-0009.b7aa.9c80 on Fa0/2
00:34:18: STP: VLAN0001 heard root 28673-0009.b7aa.9c80 on Fa0/2
00:34:19: STP: VLAN0001 heard root 28673-0009.b7aa.9c80 on Fa0/2
00:34:20: STP: VLAN0001 heard root 28673-0009.b7aa.9c80 on Fa0/2
00:34:21: STP: VLAN0001 heard root 28673-0009.b7aa.9c80 on Fa0/2
00:34:22: STP: VLAN0001 heard root 28673-0009.b7aa.9c80 on Fa0/2
00:34:23: STP: VLAN0001 heard root 28673-0009.b7aa.9c80 on Fa0/2
00:34:24: STP: VLAN0001 heard root 28673-0009.b7aa.9c80 on Fa0/2
00:34:24: STP: VLAN0001 Fa0/2 -> listening
00:34:25: STP: VLAN0001 Topology Change rcvd on Fa0/2
00:34:25: STP: VLAN0001 sent Topology Change Notice on Fa0/1
00:34:26: STP: VLAN0001 Topology Change rcvd on Fa0/2
00:34:26: STP: VLAN0001 sent Topology Change Notice on Fa0/1
00:34:39: STP: VLAN0001 Fa0/2 -> learning
00:34:54: STP: VLAN0001 sent Topology Change Notice on Fa0/1
00:34:54: STP: VLAN0001 Fa0/2 -> forwarding
```

In Example 4-67, notice that from 00:34:06 to 00:34:24 (approximate 20 seconds or the Max Age timer), Switch-C hears inferior configuration BPDUs on interface Fa0/2, due to the root port on Switch-B going down. Switch-C ignores these; however, after not hearing the correct configuration BPDUs on interface Fa0/2 for the Max Age time (20 seconds), interface Fa0/2 is placed into a Listening state (00:34:24). Interface fa0/2 then transitions to a Learning state and, finally, into a

Forwarding state, as it has become the designated port for the segment between Switch-C and Switch-B. Notice that the time between when the indirect failure actually occurred (approximately 00:34:06) and when interface Fa0/2 moved into a Forwarding state (at 00:34:54) is approximately 50 seconds, which is the expected convergence time for an indirect failure under normal STP operation.

Step 5 On all switches in the network, enable BackboneFast. Also re-enable interface Fa0/1 on Switch-B. Examples 4-68 through 4-70 show the configuration required to enable BackboneFast on all switches.

Example 4-68 *Enabling BackboneFast on Switch-A*

```
Switch-A> (enable) set spantree backbonefast enable
Backbonefast enabled for all VLANs
```

Example 4-69 *Enabling BackboneFast on Switch-B*

```
Switch-B# configure terminal
Switch-B(config)# spanning-tree backbonefast
Switch-B(config)# interface fa0/1
Switch-B(config-if)# no shutdown
```

Example 4-70 *Enabling BackboneFast on Switch-C*

```
Switch-C# configure terminal
Switch-C(config)# spanning-tree backbonefast
```

Step 6 On Switch-C, verify that interface Fa0/2 is now blocking again. Ensure that the debugging of spanning-tree events is enabled and also enable the debugging of BackboneFast events, as shown in Example 4-71.

Example 4-71 *Debugging Spanning Tree BackboneFast Events on Switch-C*

```
Switch-C# show spanning-tree blockedports
Name                    Blocked Interfaces List
------------------- -------------------------------------
VLAN0001                Fa0/2

Number of blocked ports (segments) in the system : 1
Switch-C# show debugging
Spanning Tree:
  Spanning Tree event debugging is on
Switch-C# debug spanning-tree backbonefast
Spanning Tree backbonefast general debugging is on
```

In Example 4-71, you can see that interface Fa0/2 is blocking once again because the link between Switch-A and Switch-B has been re-enabled. The **show debugging** output confirms that spanning-tree event debugging is already enabled.

Step 7 To simulate an indirect failure with regards to Switch-C, shut down the interface on Switch-B (interface Fa0/1) that is attached to Switch-A, as shown in Example 4-72.

Example 4-72 *Shutting Down an Interface on Switch-B*

```
Switch-B# configure terminal
Switch-B(config)# interface fa0/1
Switch-B(config-if)# shutdown
```

Step 8 On Switch-C, you should see the following debugging output, as shown in Example 4-73.

Example 4-73 *Debug Output on Switch-C after an Indirect Failure with BackboneFast Enabled*

```
Switch-C#
00:58:17: STP: VLAN0001 heard root 28673-0009.b7aa.9c80 on Fa0/2
00:58:17: STP FAST: received inferior BPDU on VLAN0001 FastEthernet0/2.
00:58:17: STP FAST: sending RLQ request PDU on VLAN0001 FastEthernet0/1
00:58:17: STP FAST: Received RLQ response PDU on VLAN0001 FastEthernet0/1.
00:58:17: STP: VLAN0001 Fa0/2 -> listening
00:58:18: STP: VLAN0001 Topology Change rcvd on Fa0/2
00:58:18: STP: VLAN0001 sent Topology Change Notice on Fa0/1
00:58:19: STP: VLAN0001 Topology Change rcvd on Fa0/2
00:58:19: STP: VLAN0001 sent Topology Change Notice on Fa0/1
00:58:32: STP: VLAN0001 Fa0/2 -> learning
00:58:47: STP: VLAN0001 sent Topology Change Notice on Fa0/1
00:58:47: STP: VLAN0001 Fa0/2 -> forwarding
```

In Example 4-73, at 00:58:17 an inferior configuration BPDU is received from Switch-B on Fa0/2. The next three events are STP FAST events, which relate to BackboneFast operation. Notice that BackboneFast detects an inferior BPDU has been received, sends a RLQ request out interface Fa0/1 towards the root bridge (Switch-A), and receives an RLQ response (from Switch-A). Because Switch-C knows that the connection to the root is stable, it then immediately expires the Max Age timer on interface Fa0/2 and places the interface into a Listening state (still at 00:58:17). The interface is then transitioned into the Learning state (at 00:58:32) and then finally into a Forwarding state (at 00:58:47). Notice that the time between when the indirect failure actually occurred (approximately 00:58:17) and when interface Fa0/2 moved into a Forwarding state (at 00:58:47) is approximately 30 seconds, which indicates that by enabling BackboneFast, the Max Age timer is expired almost immediately after an indirect failure.

Scenario 4-9: Improving Convergence and Load Sharing by Using a Multilayer Topology

Many of the convergence and load sharing limitations of spanning tree can be overcome by implementing a multilayer switch design, rather than a straight Layer 2 topology. Figure 4-31 shows a complex network topology, which is designed as a Layer 2 topology.

Figure 4-31 *Layer 2 Topology*

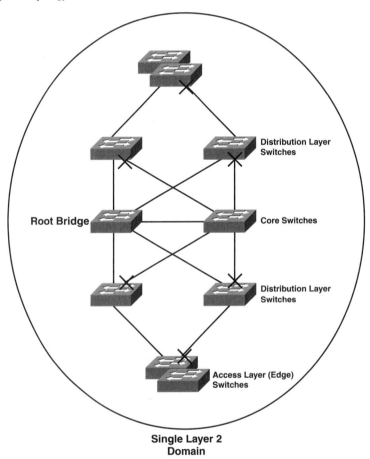

Distribution Layer
Switches

Root Bridge

Core Switches

Distribution Layer
Switches

Access Layer (Edge)
Switches

Single Layer 2
Domain

In Figure 4-31, the Layer 2 topology has been designed so that access layer switches can still connect to the rest of the network in the event of a single core or distribution switch failure. The STP topology for a single VLAN is shown, with blocked ports indicated. The topology has a network diameter of 5, which means that STP timers cannot be lowered significantly to reduce convergence. A different STP topology is required for other VLANs if load sharing is required. Although different STP topologies can be present in Figure 4-31, the network topology is a single Layer 2 domain. UplinkFast can be implemented at the edge of the network to reduce convergence for access layer switches in the event of a direct failure, and BackboneFast can be enabled to reduce the convergence for all switches if an indirect failure occurs. Even with these enhancements, the topology is complex and difficult to both configure and maintain.

Figure 4-32 demonstrates a multilayer equivalent topology for the Layer 2 topology shown in Figure 4-31.

Figure 4-32 *Multilayer Topology*

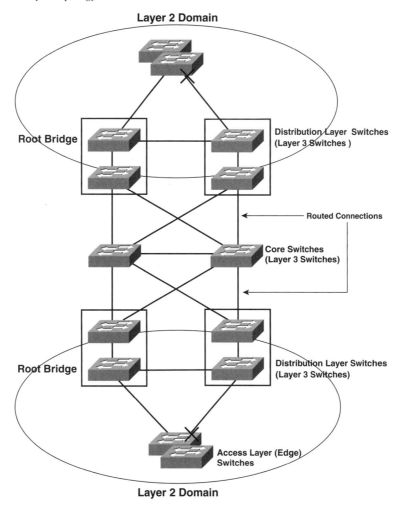

In Figure 4-32, all core and distribution switches are Layer 3 switches. Notice that each distribution switch is illustrated with the internal logical switch and router components that combine to make a Layer 3 switch. Each distribution layer switch has a routing component that terminates the Layer 2 domain that all of the access layer switches reside in, making the spanning-tree topology within the Layer 2 domain much simpler. All connections between the distribution layer switches and the core switches are routed connections, so no spanning-tree topology is present. There is essentially a single Layer 2 domain per redundant pair of distribution layer switches. The active spanning-tree topology within these Layer 2 domains is configured so that both uplinks from the access layer switches are active. UplinkFast is enabled on each access layer switch, which ensures the convergence related to a direct failure is limited to a few seconds. If a distribution layer switch fails, UplinkFast ensures convergence is in a matter of seconds. The STP topology for each Layer 2 domain is very simple, and spanning-tree timers can be significantly reduced within each Layer 2 domain, as the network diameter is significantly smaller.

From a Layer 3 perspective, at the edge of the network, the distribution layer switches are configured with Hot Standby Routing Protocol (HSRP), with one distribution layer switch acting as the active default gateway for a VLAN and the other acting as a backup default gateway. The active role is spread between the two switches for each VLAN. If a distribution layer switch is the root bridge for a VLAN, then it is also the primary default gateway for the VLAN, which ensures the IP traffic flow matches the active STP topology for each VLAN.

Within the core and distribution-to-core portions of the network, no spanning tree topology is in place, meaning all load sharing and redundancy is handled by Layer 3 routing protocols, which are much better at implementing these features than spanning tree.

NOTE	Don't worry if you don't fully understand the concepts discussed in Figure 4-32; they are discussed further in Chapter 5, "Inter-VLAN Routing" and Chapter 6, "Layer 3 Switching."

Scenario 4-10: Troubleshooting Spanning Tree

As with any protocol you configure, knowing how to verify, monitor and troubleshoot the ongoing operation of the protocol is crucial to effectively maintaining your network. In the previous scenarios, you have been shown how you can verify and monitor spanning-tree configuration and operation. This scenario is dedicated specifically to give you tips on how to troubleshoot spanning tree.

NOTE	No specific topology is provided for this scenario, because the content of this scenario has a very broad scope and no single topology can adequately cover the content.

Spanning-tree problems generally have a major impact on the network and can involve massive network meltdowns. Almost always, the problem is because of one simple issue — configuration BPDUs are not being propagated correctly on segments with blocking ports. This issue causes those blocking ports to forward traffic (even though a blocking port does not forward traffic, it is very important to understand that the port still receives BPDUs, which are processed by the switch). This forwarding has the effect of introducing loops, which quickly leads to total network chaos. Before troubleshooting, ensure you are familiar with the following:

- The full topology of the Layer 2 network
- The location of the root bridge
- Which ports should be blocked (i.e., the redundant links that loop the bridging topology)

Understanding all of the above ensures that you can easily identify what area of the network is malfunctioning and how the network topology should be configured. The following lists a guide for your troubleshooting process:

- Identify the loop
- Break the loop
- Check possible causes

Identifying the Loop

When you run into a spanning-tree problem, you will likely receive a sudden flood of calls saying the network is either down or running very slowly. The most definitive way to prove that a spanning-tree loop is the cause is to capture traffic on a link. However, you will normally be under pressure to provide a fix, and that is why the next sections discuss the quickest ways to identify a potential spanning-tree issue.

Catalyst OS

On CatOS, you can use the **show system** command to quickly identify the current load on the system backplane, as well as the time when peak load occurred. Example 4-74 demonstrates the use of this command:

Example 4-74 *Verifying Current and Historic System Load*

```
Switch-A (enable) show system
PS1-Status PS2-Status Fan-Status Temp-Alarm Sys-Status Uptime d,h:m:s Logout
---------- ---------- ---------- ---------- ---------- -------------- ---------
ok         none       ok         off        ok         0,12:16:25     20 min

PS1-Type   PS2-Type   Modem   Baud  Traffic Peak Peak-Time
---------- ---------- ------- ----- ------- ---- ------------------------
120w AC    none       disable 9600  5%      100% Thu Aug 15 2002, 16:01:20
```

continues

Example 4-74 *Verifying Current and Historic System Load (Continued)*

```
System Name              System Location         System Contact
----------------------   ----------------------  -----------------------
Switch-A
```

The Traffic column indicates the current traffic load, and the Peak and Peak-Time columns indicate the peak traffic load and when it occurred.

To drill down to the cause of the issue, you can check port utilization levels to see if anything appears out of the ordinary. Obviously, if you understand which ports should be blocking, you should check those ports first because the utilization should be very low. The **show mac** *mod/port* command displays sent/received frame statistics, as shown in Example 4-75.

Example 4-75 *Verifying Port Statistics*

```
Switch-C (enable) show mac 2/2
Port    Rcv-Unicast          Rcv-Multicast         Rcv-Broadcast
-------- -------------------- --------------------- --------------------
 2/2                   4467                   56170                 3059

Port    Xmit-Unicast         Xmit-Multicast        Xmit-Broadcast
-------- -------------------- --------------------- --------------------
 2/2                      0                     143                    0
... (Output truncated)
...
```

In Example 4-75, port 2/2 is a blocking port. You can see that very few multicast frames have been transmitted, which could represent configuration BPDUs sent during topology changes. You should see normal traffic statistics for received traffic, because another port of the segment is forwarding traffic to the segment.

Example 4-76 shows another useful command, the **show top** command, which displays the top traffic statistics for a variety of options on a per-port basis (the top 20 are shown by default). When checking for spanning tree loops, you will find the **show top bcst** command useful because it displays the top ports sorted by broadcast utilization.

Example 4-76 *Verifying Top Traffic Statistics*

```
Switch-D (enable) show top bcst 2/2
Start Time:      08/16/2002,04:42:42
End Time:        08/16/2002,04:43:13
PortType:        all
Metric:          bcst (Tx + Rx)
Port  Band- Uti Bytes              Pkts       Bcst       Mcst       Error Over
      width %   (Tx + Rx)          (Tx + Rx)  (Tx + Rx)  (Tx + Rx)  (Rx)  flow
----- ----- --- ------------------ ---------- ---------- ---------- ----- ----
 2/1   100   0              12726         174         60        114     0    0
 2/2   100   0               1237           8         43         65     0    0
... (Output truncated)
...
```

Cisco IOS

Cisco IOS provides the **show interface counters** command (see Example 4-77), which displays counters about frames sent and received on an interface. Again, you should check your blocked ports and verify that the transmit traffic utilization is very low.

Example 4-77 *Verifying Interface Traffic Statistics*

```
Switch-C# show interface fa0/2 counters
Port              InOctets   InUcastPkts   InMcastPkts   InBcastPkts
Fa0/2                64506          1023          1032           978

Port             OutOctets  OutUcastPkts  OutMcastPkts  OutBcastPkts
Fa0/2                  912             0            34             0
```

Breaking the Loop

In most organizations, the network has become a critical component of running an efficient and profitable business operation. Any downtime or poor performance can directly affect the bottom line of the organization, so chances are you need to restore the network as quickly as possible, before determining the cause of the problem. You should also be prepared for any reoccurrences to ensure that the problem does not reoccur again. The following strategies can be taken:

- Disabling ports
- Turning on event logging

Disabling Ports

An effective way to quickly eliminate loops is to manually disable ports that should be in a Blocking state. Performing this action should remove a loop if it has formed and will not affect the network because these ports are normally blocking. Use the **set port disable** command (CatOS) or the **shutdown** interface configuration command (Cisco IOS) to disable a port.

WARNING   Disable ports with caution, as you might accidentally disconnect your Telnet session if you are performing the configuration remotely or disrupt legitimate traffic by shutting down the wrong ports. If your network is in such a state that even your exec sessions (via Telnet or console) are not responding due to the high CPU utilization incurred by looping traffic causing 100 percent bandwidth utilization, you can resort to physically disconnecting the ports that you think are at fault.

Turning on Event Logging

After restoring the network, you should monitor the network closely for a few hours to ensure the problem does not resurface. An easy way to monitor the network is to turn on event logging/debug for spanning-tree events. Use the **set logging level spantree 7** command (CatOS) or the **debug spantree events** command (Cisco IOS).

Example 4-78 shows how to configure spanning-tree logging on CatOS.

Example 4-78 *Logging Spanning Tree Events*

```
Switch-A> (enable) set logging level spantree 7
Switch-A> (enable) set logging console
2002 Jan 16 03:13:52 %SPANTREE-6-PORTBLK: Port 2/1 state in VLAN 1
    changed to blocking
2002 Jan 16 03:13:52 %SPANTREE-5-PORTLISTEN: Port 2/1 state in VLAN 1
    changed to listening
2002 Jan 16 03:14:07 %SPANTREE-6-PORTLEARN: Port 2/1 state in VLAN 1
    changed to learning
2002 Jan 16 03:14:22 %SPANTREE-6-PORTFWD: Port 2/1 state in VLAN 1
    changed to forwarding
```

The first command in Example 4-78 enables logging of all spanning-tree events from level 7 (the lowest severity) up to the highest severity events. The second command enables the logging to be output to the console session—note that you can send the output to a SYSLOG server. The final lines show spanning-tree events as they occur; notice the timings between each state.

TIP   The **set logging level** command as used in the example sets the logging level only for the current session. To set the logging level permanently, add the **default** keyword to the end of the command (e.g., **set logging level spantree 7 default**). Be aware that setting a low severity level may generate a lot of useless information.

Cisco IOS offers real-time debugging tools that can provide in-depth, low-level monitoring and troubleshooting. Cisco IOS is a little light when it comes to debugging spanning tree, but does offer a couple of debugging options. It is important to note the distinction between logging and debugging. Logging is normally used on an ongoing basis, whereas debugging is used only for a session, indicating it is more a troubleshooting tool.

You can debug general spanning-tree events (**debug spanning-tree events**), or you can debug the actual BPDUs as they are received (**debug spanning-tree bpdu**). Example 4-79 demonstrates the use of the **debug spanning-tree events** command when an interface is initialized.

Example 4-79 *Debugging Spanning Tree Events*

```
Switch-C# debug spanning-tree events
12:58:06: set portid: VLAN0001 Fa0/1: new port id 8001
12:58:06: STP: VLAN0001 Fa0/1 -> listening
12:58:21: STP: VLAN0001 new root port Fa0/1, cost 19
12:58:21: STP: VLAN0001 sent Topology Change Notice on Fa0/1
12:58:21: STP: VLAN0001 Fa0/2 -> blocking
12:58:21: STP: VLAN0001 Fa0/1 -> learning
12:58:36: STP: VLAN0001 sent Topology Change Notice on Fa0/1
12:58:36: STP: VLAN0001 Fa0/1 -> forwarding
```

Checking Possible Causes

If a blocked port is not receiving configuration BPDUs, it eventually transitions to a Forwarding state to assume the designated bridge role. The following lists some possible reasons why a blocked port would not be receiving BPDUs:

- Duplex mismatch
- Unidirectional link
- Corrupted frames
- Lack of resources
- Incorrect timer configuration
- Incorrect use of PortFast

Duplex Mismatch

A duplex mismatch is a very common problem and is generally caused by one side being configured to full-duplex and the other side being configured to autosense. In this configuration, the autosensing side chooses half-duplex, which can cause collisions because the full-duplex side does not exercise the CSMA/CD algorithm. This will cause the half-duplex side to back off sending and can cause spanning-tree issues if the full-duplex port is a blocked port (the half-duplex side may back off sending configuration BPDUs, which could incorrectly transition the blocked port to a Forwarding state). Use the **show port** *mod/port* command (CatOS) or **show interface** command (Cisco IOS) to verify duplex settings.

Unidirectional Link

A unidirectional link occurs when traffic flows in one direction, but not the other. A unidirectional link is common on links that use fiber and/or transceivers, where a faulty fiber/transceiver may lead to a unidirectional link. If a link contains a blocking port, and BPDUs are not received due to a unidirectional link, then the port transitions to a Forwarding state, causing a loop. On high-end Catalyst switches, the unidirectional link detection (UDLD) protocol allows the switch to detect failures, so enabling this protocol is recommended if possible.

Corrupted Frames

Corrupted frames are, where configuration BPDUs are corrupted and ignored by the bridge with the blocked port, a less common problem. You can use the **show port** *mod/port* command (CatOS) or the **show interface** command (Cisco IOS) to check for corrupted frames.

Lack of Resources

Lack of resources refers to situations where the switch CPU is overloaded and cannot properly operate spanning tree, causing issues. The simple way to ensure that your switch has an acceptable CPU load is to use the **show inband** command (CatOS) or the **show processes cpu** command (Cisco IOS). The **show inband** command maintains a counter that is incremented every time the CPU has been too overloaded to perform a task.

Limitations exist as to how many STP instances a switch can run before CPU resource becomes an issue. The limitations are measured in a parameter called *logical ports*, with a logical port basically being a single spanning-tree port in a single VLAN (note that a trunk consists of multiple logical ports). The formula for calculating logical ports is as follows:

(number of non-ATM trunks * number of active VLANs on trunk) + 2 * (number of ATM trunks * number of active VLANs on trunk) + number of non-trunking ports

For example, if you have a switch that contains two trunks that actively trunk for ten VLANs and has 100 non-trunk ports, then the number of logical ports is (2 * 10) + (0) + 100, which is 120. Table 4-6 lists the logical port limitations on the Catalyst 4000/5000/6000 switches.

Table 4-6   *Logical Port Limits*

Platform	Supervisor Engine	Maximum Logical Ports
Catalyst 4000	Supervisor 1 and 2	1500
Catalyst 5000	Supervisor 1 (8 MB RAM)	200
	Supervisor 1 (20 MB RAM)	400
	Supervisor 2, 3F	1500
	Supervisor 2, 3G	1800
	Supervisor 3	4000
Catalyst 6000	All	4000

In the real world, if you are reaching the limits described in Table 4-5, your design has issues that will cause a lot of other problems as well. You should always limit the number of active VLANs in a Layer 2 network to no more than 50 or so. If you need to support more VLANs than this, you should look at implementing a Layer 3 topology that splits your Layer 2 network into smaller chunks that each have to support a smaller number of VLANs.

TIP   To reduce the number of logical ports, prune your trunks, enabling only the required VLANs on each trunk. This pruning eliminates logical ports for VLANs that are not used on the local switch. It is important to note that although VTP prunes unused VLANs from a trunk, STP ports still exist on the trunk. Therefore you must manually prune VLANs from a trunk by configuring the allowed list of VLANs for each trunk if you also wish to reduce the number of logical ports.

Summary

This chapter demonstrated both the basic and advanced spanning-tree configurations. The basic configuration process can be summarized as follows:

- Select and configure a root bridge
- Select and configure a secondary bridge

You should place your root bridge so that the calculated STP topology matches the major traffic paths of your network.

If you have multiple VLANs, a spanning-tree instance exists per VLAN, and you should adjust spanning-tree parameters to ensure any redundant links are load shared across. The following mechanisms exist for configuring spanning tree load sharing:

- Varying root bridge placement for each VLAN
- Modifying the per VLAN costs of links
- Modifying the per VLAN port priority of ports that send out configuration BPDUs

Modifying per VLAN costs is the recommended method of load sharing because root bridge placement affects load sharing only for switches connected directly to the root and port ID is seldom the deciding factor for path selection. Port ID is used only when two switches are connected by multiple connections. In this scenario you should consider combining the physical connections into an EtherChannel bundle, which is represented as a single logical Layer 2 connection to STP. EtherChannel handles failure and load sharing much more efficiently than STP.

Spanning tree does have considerable convergence delays, with the default convergence times ranging from 30 seconds (direct failure) to 50 seconds (indirect failure). Spanning-tree timers are calculated using a number of parameters, including the configurable Hello timer and network diameter parameters. Reducing your Hello timer speeds up how quickly the network learns about a failure; however, you must consider the effect on CPU load of the switch before reducing the Hello timer. By default, spanning-tree timers are configured to accommodate large Layer 2 networks with a network diameter of seven bridges or less. If your network diameter is smaller, you can reduce your spanning-tree timers to reflect this. Using the **set spantree root** command with the optional **dia** and **hello** parameters is the recommended method of adjusting spanning-tree timers because it uses the IEEE 802.1d calculations for each timer.

Cisco has developed a number of spanning-tree enhancements that are designed to reduce spanning-tree convergence in certain situations. These enhancements include the following:

- **PortFast**—Immediately puts a port into a Forwarding state from a Blocking state. This feature eliminates the normal 30-second interval required for the Listening and Learning states before the port can forward data. The most common use of this feature is to prevent issues with booting workstations not having network connectivity. PortFast should be enabled with caution, and Cisco provides the BDPU Guard feature that protects against PortFast misconfigurations. BPDU Filter is another feature that prevents PortFast-enabled ports from generating STP BPDUs.

- **UplinkFast**—Used on leaf nodes (edge switches) that have redundant uplinks towards the root bridge. If a direct failure occurs on a directly connected upstream switch, the edge switch immediately activates the redundant uplink, reducing spanning-tree convergence from 30 seconds to a few seconds.

- **BackboneFast**—This feature must be enabled on all switches throughout the network. BackboneFast reduces convergence by detecting indirect failures, which eliminates the Max Age timer period, reducing spanning-tree convergence by up to 20 seconds.

## CHAPTER 5

Inter-VLAN Routing

Networks are constantly evolving, and in the past few years a number of trends have become apparent. First of all, the Internet Protocol (IP) has become the Layer 3 protocol of choice for modern networks, with other Layer 3 protocols such as Internetwork Packet Exchange (IPX) and AppleTalk rapidly being phased out. IP interconnects the Internet. The increasing reliance of organizations on the Internet has promoted IP as the Layer 3 protocol of choice. Secondly, local-area networks (LANs) have seen tremendous advances in terms of performance, bandwidth, and lowering cost. The LAN provides the medium over which users and devices connect to the internal IP network and the Internet hence is an important component of networking. LAN topologies have evolved from traditionally being single, flat broadcast domains into multi-virtual LAN (VLAN) topologies, with inter-VLAN routing required to enable communications between each VLAN. Multiple VLANs increase network efficiency by reducing broadcast domain size, as well as providing a mechanism to allow network layer access control to be applied between VLANs. Using multiple VLANs also means that the resiliency of the network relies less on Layer 2 protocols such as Spanning Tree Protocol (STP), and more upon Layer 3 routing protocols. Modern Layer 3 routing protocols are much more intelligent than STP and as a result can converge much more quickly in the event of a network failure. Finally, segmenting a LAN network into VLANs allows for the isolation of problems to a smaller segment of network, allowed for reduced impact on the network and easier fault finding.

All of the above factors have caused the requirements for inter-VLAN routing within LAN networks to soar over the past few years. Even though this book is primarily about switches, which are traditionally Layer 2-only devices, it is important to understand the basics of inter-VLAN routing. Possessing this knowledge helps you to understand Layer 3 switches, which are becoming cost-effective, high performance alternatives to traditional routers for routing IP traffic between LAN segments. Possessing a fundamental understanding of inter-VLAN is important if you are to design multilayer topologies that are stable, available, and scaleable.

This chapter introduces you to the basic inter-VLAN routing architectures, using both traditional Cisco routers and basic Cisco Layer 3 switching. You also learn about multilayer LAN topologies and how a hierarchical design allows for scalability and a redundant topology that in the event of failure converges quickly and efficiently with minimal disruption to the network.

The following scenarios are presented in this chapter:

- Scenario 5-1: Configuring Basic IP Routing
- Scenario 5-2: Configuring Layer 3 Switching
- Scenario 5-3: Implementing a Redundant Multilayer Topology

Inter-VLAN Routing Architectures

Within a LAN topology, inter-VLAN routing is used to route packets between different VLANs. Three common inter-VLAN routing architectures are used in modern LAN networks today:

- Router-on-a-stick
- Router-on-a-stick using trunks
- Layer 3 switching

This section examines each of these in detail, outlining any restrictions or issues associated with each.

Router-on-a-Stick

The *router-on–a-stick* architecture is the most basic method of inter-VLAN routing. In this architecture, a router is simply connected to each VLAN and forwards inter-VLAN traffic between the appropriate VLANs. Figure 5-1 shows this architecture.

Figure 5-1   *Router-on–a-Stick*

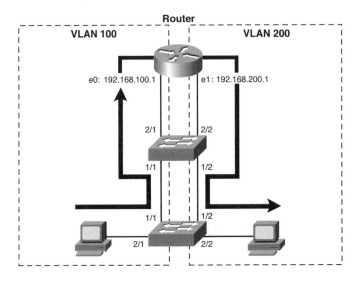

As you can see in Figure 5-1, the router has a physical Ethernet interface dedicated for each VLAN. If IP hosts on VLAN 100 need to communicate with hosts of VLAN 200, IP packets with the appropriate source and destination IP addresses are sent to the router, which looks up the destination IP address and forwards to the appropriate host on the destination VLAN. The router-on-a-stick architecture is simple to understand because the Layer 2 functions (provided by a switch) and Layer 3 functions (provided by a router) are physically separated.

The major issue with this architecture is performance. Because routers are software-based, they cannot route packets as fast as switches (hardware-based) can switch frames. Even if you are using high-performance routers, the physical interface connecting each VLAN to the router is a bottleneck because it can transmit packets only at 10 Mbps, 100 Mbps, or 1 Gbps depending on the interface type. This restriction means that the router becomes a performance bottleneck when routing between high-speed VLANs.

Another issue with this architecture is the number of routers and physical interfaces required to support multiple VLANs. A dedicated Ethernet interface is required per VLAN. Routers are low-density devices, meaning that there is a high cost per port and multiple routing devices might be required to support multiple VLANs, increasing the complexity of the network.

Finally, all inter-VLAN traffic must travel via the router. In Figure 5-1, even though the PCs in VLAN 100 and VLAN 200 are connected to the same switch, all inter-VLAN traffic between the PCs must be sent through the router, which is inefficient.

Router-on-a-Stick Using Trunks

As discussed in the last section, the router-on-a-stick architecture has physical limitations based upon a dedicated physical interface being required for each VLAN. This limitation can be removed by using trunk interfaces, where multiple VLANs are supported on a single physical interface by using tagging technologies such as 802.1Q or ISL. Rather than using physical interfaces to attach the router to each VLAN, virtual or logical interfaces are used to attach the router to each VLAN. Figure 5-2 shows this architecture.

In Figure 5-2, virtual interfaces (rather than physical interfaces) are used to connect the router to each VLAN. A single physical trunk interface transports tagged VLAN traffic to the router, with the tag determining to which virtual interface a frame should be forwarded for routing. Apart from the differences between using physical interfaces per VLAN as opposed to virtual interfaces per VLAN, this architecture is essentially identical to the traditional router-on-a-stick architecture and suffers the same performance limitations, because the routing engine is still software-based and the trunk interface is limited to 10 Mbps, 100 Mbps, or 1 Gbps.

Figure 5-2   *Router-on-a-Stick Using Trunks*

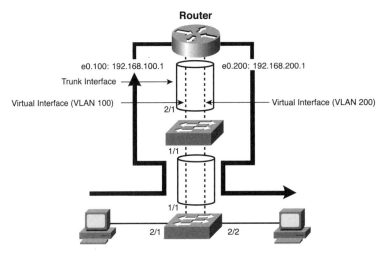

Routing Using Layer 3 Switches

The architectures discussed thus far represent the traditional inter-VLAN routing architectures. The major issue with these architectures is performance—if gigabit speed routing is required between VLANs, extremely high performance and costly routers are required. A new form of inter-VLAN routing on the LAN has emerged in recent years called *Layer 3 switching*. With a Layer 3 switch, the traditionally separated Layer 2 and Layer 3 functions are combined into a single device, eliminating the bottleneck associated with the cable between a router and switch by replacing the cable with a high-speed backplane connection. Layer 3 switches also typically perform routing in specially designed hardware circuitry rather than software, using specialized hardware that can perform routing functions at high speed. This means that the performance of Layer 3 switches is much higher than traditional router-on-a-stick architectures. For example, if you use a Cisco 3640 series router in the router-on-a-stick architecture, you can achieve routing speeds of up to 40,000 packets per second. If you compare this with a Cisco Catalyst 3550-24-EMI Layer 3 switch, which is actually cheaper than a Cisco 3640 router, you can route packets at up to 6.6 million packets per second. This is obviously quite a difference and highlights the limitations of using router-on-a-stick architectures for inter-VLAN routing on the LAN. Of course, the Cisco 3640 router still has a place in the network; it supports a wide variety of diverse media, including serial and ATM connections for WAN connectivity; also supports advanced features such as firewalling, encryption, and so on—all of which are not supported on Cisco Catalyst switches.

The Layer 3 switch uses application-specific integrated circuits (ASICs), which are hardware chips that can route traffic at very high speeds. These ASICs are installed on the switching engine of a Layer 3 switch, which traditionally switches frames at Layer 2. The ASICs allow the switching engine to also switch frames that contain packets sent between different VLANs. Each ASIC is programmed with the information required to route traffic from one VLAN to another, without having to pass the traffic through the CPU of the routing engine. This information includes the egress port, egress VLAN, and new destination MAC address that should be written for the frame that is sent. Some form of route cache is normally used to store such information, with the ASIC searching the cache for routing information for the destination IP address of packets as they are received. How this information is programmed into the route cache depends on the Layer 3 switch architecture used; however, the end result is essentially the same.

In addition to the high-speed routing feature, these ASICs also can apply security access control list (ACL) filtering and Layer 3 quality of service (QoS) classification, all at wire-speed, meaning these useful features can be turned on without affecting performance.

NOTE   The internal mechanics of Layer 3 switching are covered in more detail in Chapter 6, "Layer 3 Switching."

When examining the architecture of a Layer 3 switch, it is important to understand that several different approaches to Layer 3 switching implemented by Cisco exist:

- **Router-on-a-stick**—Some chassis-based Catalyst switches (e.g., the Catalyst 4000 and 5000) support routing modules, which are effectively routers on a blade. Apart from having a high-speed connection to the switch backplane, the routing module is essentially a router-on-a-stick, with all routed traffic requiring processing through the routing module. This architecture is not really Layer 3 switching at all because the switch hardware has no special ASICs for Layer 3 switching; instead, it is a high-speed, router-on-a-stick architecture.

- **Multilayer switching (MLS)**—In this architecture, hardware-based ASICs on the switching component of the Layer 3 switch refer to a cache that is populated with the required information to route a packet received on one VLAN to another VLAN, without having to pass the packet through the routing engine. With MLS, the Layer 3 switching cache is populated after the first packet of a particular flow (connection) is received and the route processor is queried for routing information.

- **Cisco Express Forwarding (CEF)**—This architecture is identical to MLS in terms of the hardware-based ASICs referring to a Layer 3 cache for information as to how to route packets between VLANs without involving the router processor. CEF differs from MLS in terms of the way the Layer 3 cache is populated. CEF pre-populates the caches with full routing information, which means the route processor never needs to be queried for the initial routing information that is required in a MLS architecture.

In this chapter, you learn how to configure the Catalyst 4000 using the Layer 3 routing module in a router-on-a-stick architecture. You also learn how to configure Layer 3 switching on the Catalyst 3550, which is based upon a CEF architecture. In Chapter 6, you learn about MLS and CEF on the Catalyst 6000/6500 family of switches.

Multilayer LAN Design

In the previous section, inter-VLAN routing architectures were discussed; however, the discussion was not based around how to split a LAN topology into VLANs and where you apply inter-VLAN routing. These issues delve into the topic of LAN design, where to are required to implement a LAN infrastructure that exhibits certain characteristics:

- **Performance**—Users expect the LAN to perform at high speeds. When implementing inter-VLAN routing, you must ensure the design does not affect such performance.

- **Availability**—The LAN is where all traffic generated by users, their PCs, and servers originates; hence, if the LAN is down, nobody can work and business comes to a grinding halt. A LAN failure is often more catastrophic than a wide-area network (WAN) failure; For example, if the WAN fails, at least users can still work locally on the LAN. Accordingly, the design of a LAN topology often needs to include high availability features, such as redundant paths and devices in the network. When designing such an infrastructure, you must ensure that the network fails over correctly and in a timeframe that causes minimal disruption to the network.

- **Manageability**—The LAN must be easy to support and troubleshoot. For example, if a workstation has a jabbering network interface card (NIC), the effect to the LAN should be minimized and ideally should not affect the entire LAN. Problems like this also should be easy to isolate.

- **Scalability**—As an organization grows, so to does the LAN, often at an equivalent rate. If a new employee is hired, that employee requires a new PC, which requires access to a switch port to gain access to the network. A LAN topology must be able to scale as users and other services are added to the network, without requiring a total redesign of the network. This requires not only capacity planning from a physical switch port perspective, but also consideration as to the bandwidth between switches and assurance that the number of devices within the same VLAN does not get too high.

- **Cost**—Cost is often one of the restricting factors as to how far you can go with "best practice" design. The key to successfully designing a LAN topology is to provide the requirements of the organization at the lowest cost to the organization.

Today, Two popular approaches exist when it comes to LAN design:

- Collapsed backbone design
- Multilayer design

When evaluating each design approach, you must consider each of the characteristics described previously and how the design meets the requirements of each of those characteristics. Each of the design approaches is now discussed, with reference to the previous characteristics to allow comparison of the two models.

Collapsed Backbone Design

The *collapsed backbone architecture* is the original LAN design methodology that includes inter-VLAN routing. In this design, the entire LAN infrastructure is configured as a Layer 2 domain with one or more VLANs. Because the Layer 2 domain spans the entire network, the collapsed backbone architecture is commonly referred to as being *flat*. To route between VLANs, a router installed in a router-on-a-stick configuration is attached at the edge of the network, allowing devices in different VLANs to communicate. Figure 5-3 demonstrates a collapsed backbone design.

Figure 5-3   *Collapsed Backbone*

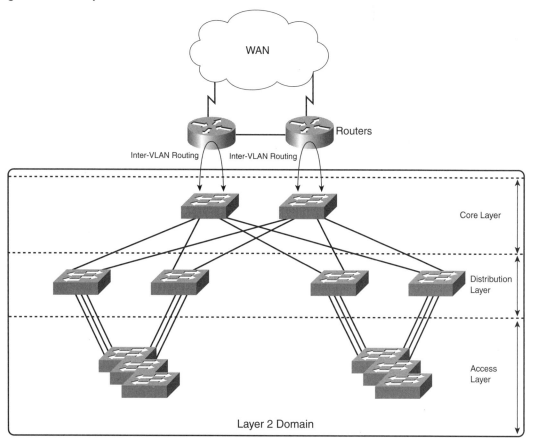

In Figure 5-3, the entire LAN topology is a single Layer 2 domain, with two routers attached to the LAN in a router-on-a-stick configuration. The network in Figure 5-3 is redundant—within the Layer 2 domain, spanning tree is used to build a loop-free topology, detect failures, and converge the network to a working topology should a failure occur. The routers are normally configured with a protocol such as Hot Standby Router Protocol (HSRP) to provide a single virtual router that can be serviced by either router (HSRP is discussed later in this chapter).

Multiple VLANs can be configured within the Layer 2 domain; however, to enable inter-VLAN communication, routing is required. The connection between the core switches and the routers are normally trunks, transporting traffic from VLANs within the Layer 2 domain for inter-VLAN routing. All traffic that requires inter-VLAN routing must be sent through the core of the network to the routers, and then back again. In a sense, each VLAN collapses onto one or more backbone routers, which provide inter-VLAN routing, as well as connectivity to the WAN.

Collapsed backbone architectures have some flaws, which are generally related to the scalability of the network. As a collapsed backbone architecture grows, the size of the Layer 2 domain grows. This has several consequences:

- **Availability**—A key fundamental of the collapsed backbone design is that the spanning-tree topology extends over the entire LAN, as a single Layer 2 domain encompasses the entire LAN. As the LAN grows, the spanning-tree topology built for each VLAN grows, which consequently affects the convergence of the network in the event of a failure. As per the IEEE 802.1d specification, spanning-tree timers must be calculated from a formula that relates to network diameter—the higher the network diameter, the higher the STP timers and the resulting convergence times. Some organizations might require the network to converge in no more than a few seconds; with spanning tree, this is not possible.

NOTE   The recent enhancements to spanning tree in the IEEE 802.1w specification (Rapid Spanning Tree Protocol or RSTP) allow for much faster convergence than traditional STP. However, this does not alleviate issues such as the size of each VLAN (broadcast domain) and the effect that excessive broadcast traffic has on the network.

- **Performance**—In a collapsed backbone architecture, each VLAN is a broadcast domain that spans the entire network. As the size of the network increases, so does the size of each broadcast domain, meaning more broadcasts are propagated further as devices are added. Excessive broadcast traffic decreases available bandwidth and network efficiency.
- **Manageability**—As the network grows, the size of each VLAN is such that it is difficult to monitor and support the network. For example, if a jabbering NIC is present on one VLAN, it can have an effect on all switches (and consequently all VLANs) in the network. Troubleshooting is also difficult, because the sheer size of each VLAN makes it hard to determine exactly where the cause of an issue is located.

  - **Scalability**—A collapsed backbone design lacks hierarchy from a Layer 3 perspective, and consequently, the network cannot be scaled in a modular and controlled fashion. Capacity to the network can be increased by adding more VLANs; however, at some point the physical port requirements of the network require the spanning-tree topology to be extended with new switches. Although hierarchy is in place within the Layer 2 domain (i.e., core, distribution, and access layers), the Layer 2 domain is limited in terms of scalability by spanning tree, which allows for a network diameter of only seven switches. Increasing the network diameter also has an effect on the convergence of the network, as STP timers must be increased to accommodate the larger network diameter.

As you can see in the next section, a multilayer design addresses many of the issues discussed above.

Multilayer Design

A multilayer design is hierarchical in nature, with the network separated into modular layers and with routing enabled for traffic sent between each layer. Instead of operating a single, large, flat Layer 2 domain, a multilayer design breaks up the network into smaller, more manageable Layer 2 domains at the edge of the network, and then relies on IP routing at the core of the network to route traffic between edge devices. Figure 5-4 demonstrates a multilayer design.

Figure 5-4   *Multilayer Design*

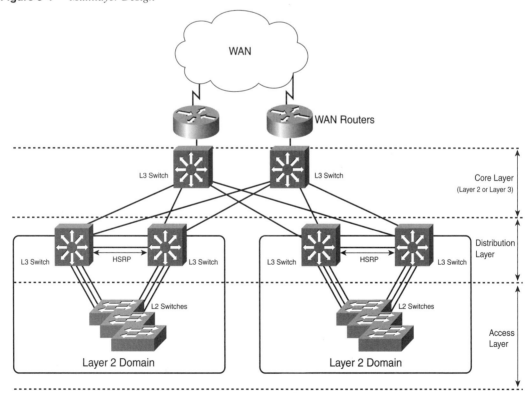

In Figure 5-4, the LAN topology is separated into multiple Layer 2 domains by introducing routing at the distribution and core layers. The core layer can be a Layer 2 or Layer 3 core. If a Layer 2 core is used, another Layer 2 domain is formed that encompasses the distribution layer switches and the core. Notice that the size of each Layer 2 domain is significantly reduced, which means the associated delays with spanning-tree convergence can be reduced because of the smaller network diameter. Even if you implement a Layer 2 core, you have still segmented the LAN into several smaller Layer 2 domains, allowing for scalability and reduced reliance on spanning tree for convergence.

NOTE   It is recommended to implement a Layer 3 core, especially for larger networks where you need maximum scalability and availability. However, many networks will implement a Layer 2 core because of the lower costs associated with such a design.

If you implement a Layer 3 core, only consider spanning-tree convergence issues at the access layer. Notice that the access layer, Layer 2 domains suit a spanning-tree UplinkFast configuration, where each access layer switch is configured with UplinkFast to enable fast convergence (in the order of a few seconds) in the event of a distribution layer switch failure. This means that the delays associated with spanning-tree convergence are minimal compared with the delays incurred on a collapsed backbone design. Load sharing can also be introduced at the access layer over each redundant uplink by altering spanning-tree costs associated with each uplink on a per-VLAN basis.

At the distribution layer, routing is provided that enables inter-VLAN routing between VLANs configured within the Layer 2 domain that comprises the access layer, as well as connectivity to the core of the network. Because the access layer contains end devices, such as PCs, servers, and printers, these devices will normally be configured with a default gateway pointing towards the distribution layer. To provide default gateway redundancy, HSRP (discussed in the next section) can be used to protect against the failure of a single distribution layer switch.

The core of the network can be either a Layer 2 core, based upon Ethernet or Asynchronous Transfer Mode (ATM), or a Layer 3 core. With a Layer 2 Ethernet core, the core is a Layer 2 domain and uses spanning tree as the protocol to provide redundancy and load sharing. The core of the network is typically limited to a few devices so the issues with spanning tree seen in a collapsed backbone architecture are not normally experienced with a Layer 2 core in a multilayer design. With a Layer 3 core, dynamic routing protocols are used to control traffic flows through the core and provide failure detection. Modern dynamic routing protocols, such as Open Shortest Path First (OSPF) and Enhanced IGRP (EIGRP) provide much more intelligent failure detection mechanisms than the spanning-tree mechanisms used in a collapsed backbone LAN, resulting in reduced convergence in the event of a network failure. Dynamic routing protocols also can load share traffic on a more granular basis than spanning tree, increasing the performance and efficiency of the network.

In summary, today for most modern networks, the collapsed backbone architecture is rapidly being replaced with a multilayer topology for the following reasons:

- **Availability**—Because the collapsed backbone architecture is essentially one large Layer 2 domain, spanning tree is used to provide redundancy in the network. Spanning tree can provide load sharing only on a per-VLAN basis and also can have rather long convergence delays after a switch failure.

- **Performance**—For larger networks, the size of the Layer 2 domain relates directly to the size of the broadcast domain. In such networks, the number of devices in each VLAN can grow to excessive amounts, reducing the overall performance within each VLAN because of excessive broadcasts.

- **Manageability**—The collapsed backbone architecture allows users and devices to be placed into any VLAN in the network, regardless of their location in the network. Although this is a useful feature, having VLANs that span the entire network means that a jabbering NIC can affect the entire network and issues in the network are harder to pinpoint. A multilayer design reduces the impact of any Layer 2 issues.

- **Scalability**—A multilayer LAN design is modular, allowing for much higher scalability than a collapsed backbone design. Because of the simplified Layer 2 topology at the access layer, the network can scale at the access layer by simply adding new access layer switches, without affecting the network diameter of the spanning-tree topology. If capacity runs out on distribution layer switches for additional access layer switches, additional distribution layer modules can be added, building a new access layer domain that is completely separate from other access layer domains in the network and does not impact the spanning tree topology in other access layer domains.

- **Cost**—Traditionally, the cost associated with a collapsed backbone architecture has been much lower in comparison to a multilayer architecture because of the high costs associated with Layer 3 switches that are typically used in a multilayer design. Today, the cost of Layer 3 switches is significantly lower than it was a few years ago, allowing for network designers to implement multilayer architectures without generating significant costs.

Hot Standby Router Protocol

Hot Standby Router Protocol (HSRP) is a protocol designed to provide redundancy for the routing services provided to the access layer or edge components of a multilayer LAN topology, where end devices, such as servers and workstations, connect to the network.

NOTE   HSRP is a topic that you must understand and be able to configure for the CCNP LAN Switching examination; hence, its coverage here and later on in Scenario 5-3.

HSRP is designed to provide Layer 3 redundancy where dynamic routing protocols, which support the ability to detect failures in the network and reroute traffic over a redundant path, cannot be used. End devices located at the edge of the network typically do not participate in dynamic routing protocols because they are designed for end-to-end communications rather than the delivery of those communications. This means that end devices typically are configured with a default gateway, which represents a routing device that handles all traffic destined for a system located remotely, offloading the task of routing traffic to a destination over the appropriate path in the network.

For example, a host might have an IP address of 192.168.10.100 with a subnet mask of 255.255.255.0 and a default gateway of 192.168.10.1. If the host needs to communicate with a host on the same subnet (for example, 192.168.10.200), the host communicates directly. If the host needs to communicate with a host on a different subnet (for example, 192.168.20.100), then packets are sent to the default gateway, and the default gateway is responsible for routing the packet to its correct destination. Figure 5-5 demonstrates this simple concept.

Figure 5-5   *Routing Using Default Gateways*

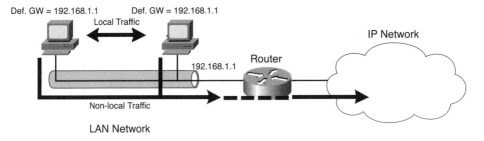

In Figure 5-5, the hosts on the LAN can reach the rest of the IP network via only one device—the locally attached router. If each host has the locally attached router (192.168.1.1) configured as the default gateway, all non-local traffic is sent to the router. Once the router receives the traffic, it and the other routers that lead to the final destination are responsible for ensuring that the packets sent reach their destination via the best path through the network.

Referring to Figure 5-5, if the default gateway fails for some reason, the hosts connected to the gateway are not able to communicate with the rest of the network. To implement redundancy, a second default gateway can be introduced. Figure 5-6 shows an example topology with two default gateways servicing a single VLAN.

Figure 5-6   *Using Two Default Gateways*

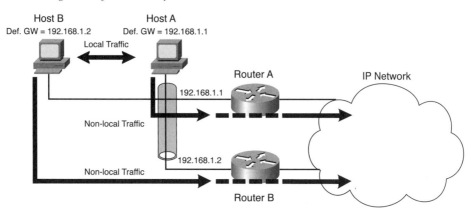

In Figure 5-6, a second router (Router B) has been introduced that connects to the rest of the IP network. Host A is configured with Router A as its default gateway and Host B is configured with Router B as its default gateway. Consider what happens when Router A fails. Because Host A is configured with Router A as its default gateway, Host A attempts to send any non-local traffic to Router A, which fails because Router A is down. To alleviate this, you can configure Host A with a new default gateway of Router B; this configuration solves the problem, but requires manual reconfiguration on each end device. You can also configure two default gateways (Router A and Router B) on each end device; however, most operating systems implement crude mechanisms for detecting a default gateway failure and switching to an alternate default gateway, making such mechanisms unreliable. For example, Microsoft operating systems require a reboot for an alternate default gateway to be used after the primary default gateway has gone down, which would cause disruption if the configuration of multiple default gateways were used to provide redundancy. Clearly, just simply installing a second gateway is not going to resolve the issue.

Another approach is to install two physical default gateway devices, but allow these devices to co-operatively interact so that they can appear as a single virtual default gateway for end devices connected to the LAN. This means that each end device is configured with a single virtual IP address for the default gateway. The routers are then configured as either active or standby for the virtual IP address. The active router services all communications to the virtual IP address from end devices. If the active router fails, then the standby router steps in and services all communications to the virtual default gateway. The active and standby routers know if the other is alive by communicating periodically between each other via the network. Figure 5-7 shows the concept of using redundant routers to implement a virtual router (default gateway).

Figure 5-7   *The Virtual Default Gateway*

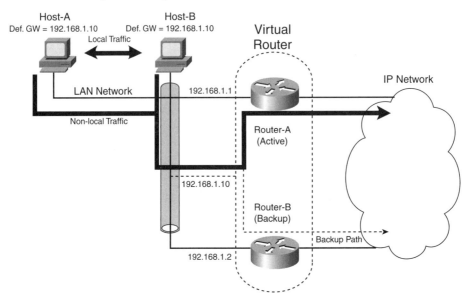

In Figure 5-7, Router-A and Router-B are configured to present a virtual router to the LAN network, which possesses a virtual IP address (192.168.1.10) that is configured as the default gateway on each host attached on the LAN. A virtual MAC address also exists for the virtual IP address, which is required to enable Layer 2 communications between end devices and the virtual router. In terms of physical operation, one of the physical routers (assume Router-A) is the active router, servicing the communications to the virtual IP address and MAC address from the hosts. Notice the path that packets take through the network while Router-A is operational (represented by the solid arrow). Each IP packet is encapsulated in Ethernet frames, which are addressed to the virtual MAC address. The active router listens for frames with the virtual MAC address, receipting these frames and then routing the packet contained within the frame towards the destination IP address of the packet. If the active router (Router-A) fails, then the backup router (Router-B) starts servicing the communications to the virtual IP address and MAC address, with the dashed arrow in Figure 5-7 showing the new path packets take in the network.

The hosts on the network believe they are always communicating through the virtual router (represented by the dashed line) and do not know that a physical router has failed because they are still talking to the same virtual IP address and another physical router services the virtual IP address in the event of a failure. Router-A and Router-B use a protocol to period-ically communicate with each other; this protocol serves as a mechanism to detect if a router fails, as communications will cease from the remote router.

Two common protocols are used to implement the concept of the virtual router, as shown in Figure 5-7:

- **Hot Standby Router Protocol (HSRP)**—This is a Cisco proprietary protocol that allows Cisco routers to service one or more virtual IP addresses in an active/standby configuration.

- **Virtual Router Redundancy Protocol (VRRP)**—This is a standards-based protocol derived from HSRP. VRRP lacks some features that HSRP provides.

The use of HSRP is very common in Cisco-only topologies, and to date only high-end Cisco routers support VRRP. Given that you normally implement two identical routing devices to implement HSRP or VRRP, if you are using Cisco routers, no benefits in using VRRP exist.

It is important to note that neither HSRP nor VRRP provides load sharing as a function. Both technologies are active/standby technologies, where a single active router always services the virtual IP address and a standby router services the virtual IP address only if the active router fails. For example, referring to Figure 5-7, Router-A is considered the active router and Router-B is considered the standby router. Under normal operation, all traffic flows through Router-A, leaving Router-B (and its link to the rest of the network) idle. You can implement load sharing by introducing multiple virtual IP addresses and alternating the active role between each physical router for each virtual IP address. Figure 5-8 demonstrates this concept.

In Figure 5-8, two virtual routers represented each by a virtual IP (VIP) address are configured. The top figure shows the first VIP (192.168.1.10), which is serviced by Router-A as the primary router, with Router-B acting as the standby router. The bottom figure shows the second VIP (192.168.1.20), which is serviced by Router-B as the primary router, with Router-A acting as the standby router. To enable the use of multiple VIPs to implement load sharing, half of the hosts on the network (i.e., Host-A) are configured with the first VIP (192.168.1.10) as their default gateway, and the other half of the hosts on the network (i.e., Host-B) are configured with the second VIP (192.168.1.20) as their default gateway. Although this form of load sharing might not provide equal distribution of traffic through each physical router, this ensures some form of load sharing, and both VIPs are protected against the failure of a single router. For example, if Router-A failed in Figure 5-8, Router-B would service both the 192.168.1.20 VIP, because it is configured as the active router for that VIP, and also the 192.168.1.10 VIP, because Router-A has failed and Router-B must assume the active router role for the VIP until Router-A is restored. This ensures all non-local communications continue to flow through the network.

Figure 5-8 *Using Multiple Virtual Routers for Load Sharing*

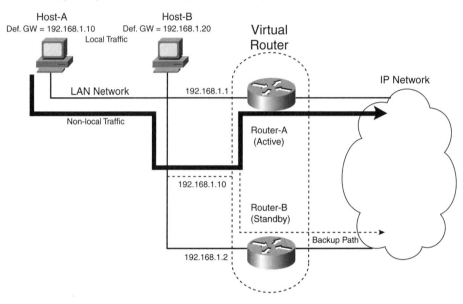

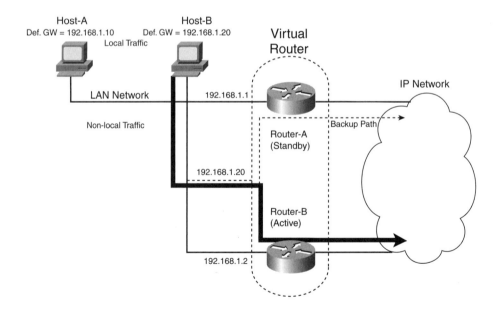

Scenario 5-1: Configuring Basic IP Routing

Before examining more advanced routing topics such as Layer 3 switching and multilayer switching, you must understand the fundamentals of basic IP routing. In today's networks, IP is the ubiquitous protocol that interconnects organizations and people globally. The principles of basic routing apply end-to-end over these networks; hence, ensuring you understand the basics is very important. In this scenario you essentially configure routers to route IP traffic This gives you a clear understanding of when a switch is just a switch and when a router is a router. After this you'll be ready to tackle switches that route and other blurred boundaries between routing and switch.

Figure 5-9 shows the topology used for this scenario. The topology is based on the traditional router-on-a-stick method of inter-VLAN routing, with separate physical devices providing routing and switching functions. From a switching point of view, the topology is very simple; only a single switch is required. The major focus of this lab is the two routers Router-A and Router-B. These routers are used to demonstrate inter-VLAN routing. VLANs are created on the switch and the routers are used to enable communications between the VLANs.

NOTE   The topology demonstrated in this scenario is somewhat outdated in terms of modern inter-VLAN routing design and should not be considered as a recommended architecture for implementing inter-VLAN routing. The scenario topology used is designed to introduce you to the basics of inter-VLAN routing by separating the switching and routing functions that can today be better implemented in an integrated fashion on a single physical platform.

Figure 5-9   *Scenario 5-1 Topology*

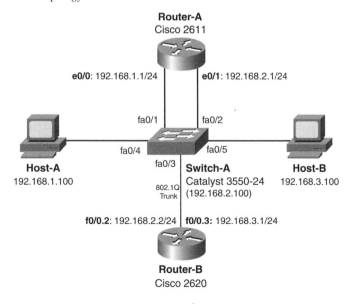

The following describes the function of each component of the scenario topology shown in Figure 5-9:

- Switch-A is a Catalyst 3550-24 switch that provides LAN connectivity for Router-A and Router-B, as well as Host-A and Host-B.

- Router-A is a Cisco 2611 router with two physical Ethernet interfaces that reside in different IP subnets (VLANs to the switch), demonstrating the earliest method of implementing a router-on-a-stick. Router-A must route traffic between VLAN 1 and VLAN 2 (and vice versa).

- Router-B is a Cisco 2620 router with a single FastEthernet interface that is configured as an 802.1Q trunk. The trunk interface allows Router-B to have two virtual interfaces that reside in different VLANs operate over the same physical interface, demonstrating a more scalable method of implementing a router-on-a-stick configuration than the physical interfaces used per VLAN on Router-A. Router-B must route traffic between VLAN 2 and VLAN 3 (and vice versa).

- Host-A and Host-B are workstations that are used to test inter-VLAN routing is configured to provide connectivity between each host.

Router-A demonstrates implementing a router-on-a-stick, using a physical interface on the router to attach to each VLAN (i.e., one physical interface per VLAN). Router-B demonstrates using a physical interface to attach to each VLAN.

Understanding the Inter-VLAN Routing Packet Flow

The goal of this scenario is to demonstrate basic inter-VLAN routing between different VLANs on a switch. A *switch* is a Layer 2 device that can enable intra-VLAN communications only between devices in the same VLAN; to enable communications between devices in different VLANs, a Layer 3 (IP) router is required.

When multiple routers are attached to the LAN infrastructure and multiple VLANs exist, it is important to understand how packets are routed throughout the switching and routing infrastructure. Understanding these packet flows helps determine the routes you must configure on each routing device and which switch ports should be assigned to each VLAN. It also aids in the troubleshooting of inter-VLAN routing issues that might arise. Figure 5-10 shows the topology of Figure 5-9 from an inter-VLAN routing and packet flow perspective.

Figure 5-10   *Scenario 5-1 Inter-VLAN Routing Topology*

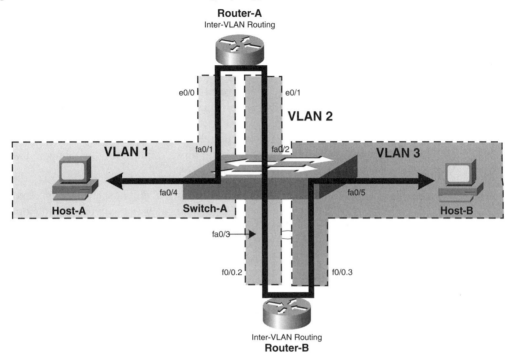

In Figure 5-10, you can see that three VLANs exist—VLAN 1, VLAN 2, and VLAN 3. To route traffic between VLAN 1 and VLAN 2, traffic from VLAN 1 must be sent to the interface of Router-A that is attached to VLAN 1 (e0/0). Because Router-A also has an interface attached to VLAN 2 (e0/1), traffic received from VLAN 1 can be routed to VLAN 2. To route traffic between VLAN 2 and VLAN 3, traffic must be sent from the VLAN 2 interface (e0/1) of Router-A to the interface of Router-B that is attached to VLAN 2 (f0/0.2). Notice in Figure 5-10 that each of the virtual interfaces configured on Router-B can be represented as logically separate interfaces. Because Router-B also has a virtual interface attached to VLAN 3 (f0/0.3), traffic received from the VLAN 2 interface can be routed to VLAN 3. It is important to note that the routers Router-A and Router-B are the devices that enable inter-VLAN routing. Switch-A can enable communications only between devices within the same VLAN. By ensuring that each router has a connection to at least two VLANs, the router can route traffic between each VLAN.

Planning Inter-VLAN Routing Configuration

The basic IP routing configuration required in this scenario is not difficult. The only real planning required is to ensure the appropriate routes are in place to reach remote networks from each router, each workstation has an appropriate default gateway configured, and the switch has the correct ports allocated to the correct VLANs.

In terms of routing, Router-A is directly connected to the 192.168.1.0/24 and 192.168.2.0/24 subnets and, therefore, automatically can route traffic to hosts within these subnets. To reach the 192.168.3.0/24 subnet, traffic must be routed via Router-B using the interface in VLAN 2 (192.168.2.2). In the reverse direction, Router-B requires a route to the 192.168.1.0/24 network, which should specify to forward traffic for this subnet to the VLAN 2 interface (192.168.2.1) address on Router-A.

To enable hosts connected to each subnet to communicate with hosts located on remote subnets, each host should have the appropriate default gateway configured on the local operating system TCP/IP stack. The default gateway defines the default route for all non-local traffic sent from the workstation. Host-A must send all non-local traffic to the VLAN 1 interface of Router-A (192.168.1.1) because this is the only router attached to the 192.168.1.0/24 subnet. Similarly, Host-B must send all non-local traffic to the VLAN 3 interface of Router-B (192.168.3.1). Router-A and Router-B then take care of the routing required to deliver packets between Host-A and Host-B (and vice versa).

Figure 5-11 illustrates the routing requirements of the scenario topology.

Figure 5-11 *Scenario 5-1 Inter-VLAN Routing Topology*

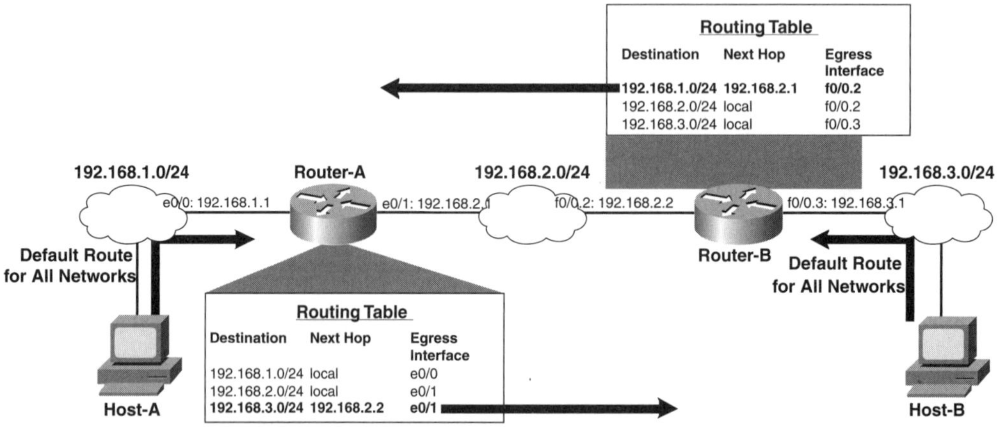

In Figure 5-11, you can see that each routing table entry has three parameters:

- **Destination network**—A range of destination addresses (normally a subnet, but can be a specific host address or a supernet)

- **Next hop**—The next closest routing device (hop) to the destination network

- **Egress interface**—The interface out which any packets addressed to an address within the destination network should be routed

For example on Router-A, a routing table entry exists for the destination network 192.168.3.0/24. The next hop is 192.168.2.2, which is required as 192.168.3.0/24 is reachable via Router-B. The egress interface is e0/1, as the next hop (Router-B) is reachable via the e0/1 interface. This route must be explicitly configured in the routing table, either manually configured using static routing or learned via a dynamic routing protocol.

In Figure 5-11, also notice that the routing table on each router has local routes (also known as *connected routes*), which can be identified as having a next hop of local. These connected routes are automatically generated for each subnet the router is directly attached to and enable the router to deliver packets to devices attached to these subnets. For example, on Router-A, connected routes are generated for 192.168.1.0/24 and 192.168.2.0/24, as Router-A has interfaces attached to each of these subnets. When a router discovers a destination is reachable via a connected route, assuming the egress interface is an Ethernet interface, the router generates an ARP request for the destination IP address to determine the MAC address of the host with the destination IP address. Once the MAC address of the destination host is known, the packet is delivered within an Ethernet frame addressed to the MAC address of the destination host.

Scenario Prerequisites

To successfully commence the configuration tasks required to complete this scenario, the following lists the prerequisite configuration tasks required on each device in the scenario topology:

- **Hostname**—each device should be configured with an appropriate hostname as per Figure 5-9.
- **Telnet/Enable password**—each device should be configured with an appropriate telnet and enable password.

This scenario assumes the configuration tasks listed above have already been implemented and hence does not include the configuration of these tasks.

Configuration Tasks

In this scenario you perform the following tasks:

- Configuring Layer 2 parameters
- Configuring inter-VLAN routing
- Verifying connectivity

Configuring Layer 2 Parameters

Before you can configure inter-VLAN routing, you must ensure that the appropriate Layer 2 configuration is in place. In this scenario, this requires the VLANs that packets are to be routed between actually exist and are configured. Each VLAN must be created and configured with the appropriate parameters, and then the appropriate switch ports must be placed into each VLAN. Any trunk connections must also be configured to ensure the trunk forms correctly and the appropriate VLANs are trunked across the physical trunk interface.

For this scenario, three VLANs must be configured on Switch-A, with the following port assignments (see Figure 5-10):

- **VLAN 1**—Interface fa0/1 and interface fa0/4
- **VLAN 2**—Interface fa0/2 and interface fa0/3 (trunk)
- **VLAN 3**—Interface fa0/3 (trunk) and interface fa0/5

All interfaces except for interface fa0/3 must be configured as access ports, meaning they belong only to a single VLAN. Interface fa0/3 must be configured as a trunk to Router-B and must transport traffic from VLAN 2 and VLAN 3. Example 5-1 shows the configuration required on Switch-A to create the required VLANs, assign the appropriate interfaces to each VLAN, and configure the trunk interface to Router-B.

Example 5-1   *Configuring VLANs on Switch-A*

```
Switch-A# configure terminal
Switch-A(config)# vtp mode transparent
Setting device to VTP TRANSPARENT mode.
Switch-A(config)# vlan 2
Switch-A(config-vlan)# name VLAN02
Switch-A(config-vlan)# exit
Switch-A(config)# vlan 3
Switch-A(config-vlan)# name VLAN03
Switch-A(config-vlan)# exit
Switch-A(config)# interface range FastEthernet 0/1 - 2 , FastEthernet 0/4 - 5
Switch-A(config-if-range)# switchport mode access
Switch-A(config-if-range)# exit
Switch-A(config)# interface FastEthernet 0/2
Switch-A(config-if)# switchport access vlan 2
Switch-A(config-if)# exit
Switch-A(config)# interface FastEthernet 0/5
Switch-A(config-if)# switchport access vlan 3
Switch-A(config-if)# exit
Switch-A(config)# interface FastEthernet 0/3
Switch-A(config-if)# switchport trunk encapsulation dot1q
Switch-A(config-if)# switchport mode trunk
Switch-A(config-if)# switchport nonegotiate
Switch-A(config-if)# switchport trunk allowed vlan 2,3,1002-1005
```

In Example 5-1, VLAN Trunking Protocol (VTP) is first configured to operate in transparent mode, which enables VLANs 2 and 3 to be created. Interfaces fa0/1, fa0/2, fa0/4, and fa0/5 are configured as access ports; then appropriate interfaces are then assigned to VLAN 2 and VLAN 3 (all other interfaces are assigned by default to VLAN 1). Interface fa0/3 is next configured as a trunk; then because Router-B is a router, the trunk is configured with a DTP mode of nonegotiate. Notice the allowed VLAN list on the trunk is restricted to VLAN 2 and VLAN 3, as only traffic from these VLANs needs to be forwarded over the trunk to Router-B.

NOTE   On the Catalyst 3550, you must always ensure VLAN 1002–1005 are in the allowed VLAN list, hence the inclusion of these VLANs in Example 5-1.

Configuring Inter-VLAN Routing

Once the required Layer 2 configuration is complete, the foundation is in place to begin configuring inter-VLAN routing. In this scenario, two types of key devices are involved in routing:

- **Hosts**—Hosts (end devices) are involved in the routing process because they must be configured with a default gateway so that packets sent to any unknown destination network are routed correctly.

- **Routers**—Routers require information about each subnet in the network to be configured in the local routing table with the correct next hop router to ensure correct routing through the network.

Configuration of each of these types of devices is now discussed.

Configuring Hosts

A fundamental concept of the IP routing paradigm is that routing is performed on a per-hop or per-device basis. This means that every device in the path between two communicating hosts (including the hosts themselves) must have the correct routing configuration in place; otherwise, end-to-end delivery might not be possible. When configuring inter-VLAN routing, this means that your inter-VLAN routing configuration must consider not only the normal devices associated with routing (i.e., routers), but also the routing configuration of the end devices (hosts) generate packets that require routing. As discussed previously, hosts generally are configured with a default gateway because hosts are not concerned with the intricacies of routing and require a simple routing configuration.

In this scenario, Host-A must be configured with a default gateway of 192.168.1.1, and Host-B must be configured with a default gateway of 192.168.3.1. Although there are two "hosts" (Host-A and Host-B), there is also a third "host" on the network. This third host is Switch-A, which can be considered a host because it includes a TCP/IP stack for network management purposes. Just as Host-A and Host-B require a default gateway to ensure the successful routing of packets generated by the hosts, so Switch-A requires a default gateway to ensure other devices in the network can communicate with it.

To configure the default gateway on a Cisco IOS-based Layer 2 switch, you use the **ip default-gateway** global configuration command as follows:

```
Switch(config)# ip default-gateway gateway-ip-address
```

It is important to note on Cisco IOS-based Layer 3 switches, such as the Catalyst 3550, that the **ip default-gateway** command can be used only if IP routing has been disabled on the switch. IP routing is disabled by default on all Cisco IOS-based Layer 3 switches (except for the Catalyst 6000/6500 operating in native IOS mode) and, if enabled, can be disabled by using the **no ip routing** global configuration command. If IP routing must be enabled, you can configure a default gateway of sorts by configuring a default route as demonstrated below:

```
Switch(config)# ip routing
Switch(config)# ip route 0.0.0.0 0.0.0.0 gateway-ip-address
```

Notice that the **ip routing** command must be configured to use the **ip route** command. If IP routing has been disabled, you must use the **ip default-gateway** command to configure a default gateway.

In this scenario, the management interface on Switch-A must be configured in VLAN 2 with an IP address of 192.168.2.100 (see Figure 5-9). Because Router-A and Router-B are both connected to VLAN 2, you can configure either router as the default gateway. For this scenario, it doesn't matter which router you choose as the default gateway because each router is configured with full routing information for all subnets in the network. Example 5-2 demonstrates the configuration required on Switch-A to create the management interface and configure Router-A as the default gateway.

Example 5-2   *Configuring a Default Gateway on Switch-A*

```
Switch-A# configure terminal
Switch-A(config)# interface vlan 2
Switch-A(config-if)# ip address 192.168.2.100 255.255.255.0
Switch-A(config-if)# exit
Switch-A(config)# ip default-gateway 192.168.2.1
```

Assuming Host-A has been configured with a default gateway of 192.168.1.1 and Host-B has been configured with a default gateway of 192.168.3.1, after the configuration of Example 5-2, all "hosts" in the network are configured correctly to communicate with remote destinations.

Configuring the Routers (Router-A and Router-B)

On Cisco IOS routers, although routing is enabled by default, no routes are explicitly configured; hence, a Cisco router configured with only the appropriate interface IP addressing and no routing configuration can route only between locally attached networks. In this section, the routing operation of a Cisco router before any routes have been configured is demonstrated, after which the required routing configuration for this scenario is implemented and the results are compared with the previous results.

The configuration required for Router-A to connect to the network and route between VLANs 1 and 2 is simple because multiple physical interfaces exist on Router-A for each VLAN. Example 5-3 shows the configuration required on Router-A to enable each interface to connect to the appropriate VLANs and also to enable Router-A to route between VLAN 1 and VLAN 2.

Example 5-3   *Configuring Router-A*

```
Router-A# configure terminal
Router-A(config)# interface ethernet 0/0
Router-A(config-if)# description CONNECTED TO VLAN 1
Router-A(config-if)# no shutdown
Router-A(config-if)# ip address 192.168.1.1 255.255.255.0
Router-A(config-if)# exit
Router-A(config)# interface ethernet 0/1
Router-A(config-if)# description CONNECTED TO VLAN 2
Router-A(config-if)# no shutdown
Router-A(config-if)# ip address 192.168.2.1 255.255.255.0
```

In Example 5-3, each Ethernet interface is configured with the appropriate IP addressing. By default, all interfaces on a router are in the shutdown state, with each interface requiring explicit enabling by using the **no shutdown** interface configuration mode command. Once each interface is enabled, Router-A accepts packets on each of these interfaces and is able to route packets between locally connected networks only (i.e., VLAN 1 and VLAN 2).

The configuration required for Router-B to connect to the network and route between VLANs 2 and 3 is a little more complex than the configuration required on Router-A because Router-B must be configured with a trunk interface. Example 5-4 shows the configuration required on Router-B to configure the trunk to Switch-A and to enable Router-B to route between VLAN 2 and VLAN 3.

Example 5-4   *Configuring Router-B*

```
Router-B# configure terminal
Router-B(config)# interface FastEthernet 0/0
Router-B(config-if)# no shutdown
Router-B(config-if)# exit
Router-B(config)# interface FastEthernet 0/0.2
Router-B(config-if)# description CONNECTED TO VLAN 2
Router-B(config-if)# encapsulation dot1q 2
Router-B(config-if)# ip address 192.168.2.2 255.255.255.0
Router-B(config-if)# exit
Router-B(config)# interface FastEthernet 0/0.3
Router-B(config-if)# description CONNECTED TO VLAN 3
Router-B(config-if)# encapsulation dot1q 3
Router-B(config-if)# ip address 192.168.3.1 255.255.255.0
```

In Example 5-4, notice you do not configure any IP addressing on the physical FastEthernet 0/0 interface. You create sub-interfaces (also known as *logical interfaces*) using the **interface FastEthernet 0/0.***x* command, where *x* is a unique sub-interface identifier. A sub-interface is created for each VLAN that you want to attach the router to, with the appropriate IP addressing configured on the sub-interface. The ID of the VLAN associated with each sub-interface is specified by the last parameter in the **encapsulation dot1q** *x* command.

After the configuration of Example 5-3 and Example 5-4, assuming all interfaces on Router-A and Router-B are connected to Switch-A, you should be able to successfully verify that each router can communicate with any device that is directly attached to the router. For example, Router-A should be able to ping both Host-A and Switch-A, while Router-B should be able to ping both Host-B and Switch-A. However, if at this stage either router attempts to ping any host on a subnet that is not locally connected (e.g., Router-A attempting to communicate with devices in VLAN 3), connectivity fails because routing has not been configured yet.

Example 5-5 demonstrates testing ping connectivity from Router-A to the interface attached to VLAN 3 on Router-B.

Example 5-5   *Testing* **ping** *Connectivity from Router-A to the VLAN 3 Interface on Router-B*

```
Router-A# ping 192.168.3.1
Type escape sequence to abort.
Sending 5, 100-byte ICMP Echos to 192.168.3.1, timeout is 2 seconds:
.....
Success rate is 0 percent (0/5)
```

Notice that you can't ping the VLAN 3 interface on Router-B. This is because the IP routing table on Router-A does not possess an entry for the 192.168.3.0/24 subnet, as is demonstrated by the **show ip route** command on Router-A in Example 5-6.

Example 5-6   *Viewing the Routing Table on Router-A*

```
Router-A# show ip route
Codes: C - connected, S - static, I - IGRP, R - RIP, M - mobile, B - BGP
       D - EIGRP, EX - EIGRP external, O - OSPF, IA - OSPF inter area
       N1 - OSPF NSSA external type 1, N2 - OSPF NSSA external type 2
       E1 - OSPF external type 1, E2 - OSPF external type 2, E - EGP
       i - IS-IS, L1 - IS-IS level-1, L2 - IS-IS level-2, ia - IS-IS inter area
       * - candidate default, U - per-user static route, o - ODR
       P - periodic downloaded static route

Gateway of last resort is not set

C    192.168.1.0/24 is directly connected, Ethernet0/0
C    192.168.2.0/24 is directly connected, Ethernet0/1
```

As you can see in Example 5-6, routes exist only for locally connected networks on Router-A, which means packets sent to any other destination are unroutable at this stage.

A useful command that can be used to verify routing operation is the **debug ip packet** command, which generates debugging output for any packet that is process-switched by the router. Example 5-7 demonstrates the use of this command on Router-A, after attempting to ping the VLAN 3 interface (192.168.3.1) on Router-B

WARNING   Avoid using the **debug ip packet** command in a live environment because excessive logging messages generated by packets to the console can freeze or crash the router.

Example 5-7   *Testing* **ping** *Connectivity from Router-A to the VLAN 3 Interface*

```
Router-A# debug ip packet
IP packet debugging is on
Router-A# ping 192.168.3.1

Type escape sequence to abort.
Sending 5, 100-byte ICMP Echos to 192.168.3.1, timeout is 2 seconds:

01:37:58: IP: s=192.168.1.1 (local), d=192.168.3.1, len 100, unroutable.
01:38:00: IP: s=192.168.1.1 (local), d=192.168.3.1, len 100, unroutable.
01:38:02: IP: s=192.168.1.1 (local), d=192.168.3.1, len 100, unroutable.
01:38:04: IP: s=192.168.1.1 (local), d=192.168.3.1, len 100, unroutable.
01:38:06: IP: s=192.168.1.1 (local), d=192.168.3.1, len 100, unroutable.
Success rate is 0 percent (0/5)
```

In Example 5-7, the shaded output shows the debugging messages generated for each ping packet that is sent. The important text within each message is the unroutable portion at the end, which has been shaded. This message means that the router does not possess a route to the destination network and, therefore, must discard the packet.

NOTE   By default a Cisco router sends ICMP unreachable messages to the source host of any unroutable traffic, which notifies the source host that the destination is unreachable. In this example no ICMP unreachable messages are sent because the traffic originates from the router itself.

To enable Router-A and Router-B to communicate with the VLANs that are not locally connected, static routes must be created on each router. Static routes are configured using the **ip route** global configuration command as follows:

```
Router(config)# ip route destination-network destination-mask
  next-hop-gateway [admin-distance]
```

Example 5-8 demonstrates configuring a static route for the 192.168.3.0/24 network on Router-A.

Example 5-8   *Configuring Static IP Routes on Router-A*

```
Router-A# configure terminal
Router-A(config)# ip route 192.168.3.0 255.255.255.0 192.168.2.2
```

In Example 5-8, the 192.168.3.0/24 subnet is defined as being reachable via Router-B (192.168.2.2). This means any packets received by Router-A with a destination IP address of 192.168.3.*x* are forwarded to Router-B. Example 5-9 shows the routing configuration required on Router-B.

Example 5-9   *Configuring Static IP Routing on Router-B*

```
Router-B# configure terminal
Router-B(config)# ip route 192.168.1.0 255.255.255.0 192.168.2.1
```

After configuring routing on Router-A and Router-B, the routing tables should now include the new static routes. Example 5-10 shows the output of the **show ip route** command on Router-A.

Example 5-10   *Verifying the IP Routing Table on Router-A*

```
Router-A# show ip route
Codes: C - connected, S - static, I - IGRP, R - RIP, M - mobile, B - BGP
       D - EIGRP, EX - EIGRP external, O - OSPF, IA - OSPF inter area
       N1 - OSPF NSSA external type 1, N2 - OSPF NSSA external type 2
       E1 - OSPF external type 1, E2 - OSPF external type 2, E - EGP
       i - IS-IS, L1 - IS-IS level-1, L2 - IS-IS level-2, ia - IS-IS inter area
       * - candidate default, U - per-user static route, o - ODR
       P - periodic downloaded static route

Gateway of last resort is not set

C    192.168.1.0/24 is directly connected, Ethernet0/0
C    192.168.2.0/24 is directly connected, Ethernet0/1
S    192.168.3.0/24 [1/0] via 192.168.2.2
```

In Example 5-10, the shaded output shows the static route configured in Example 5-9 loaded into the IP routing table.

NOTE   On Router-B, a single static route should also exist, except that it is for the 192.168.1.0/24 network and has a next hop of 192.168.2.1.

The S on the left-hand side indicates the route is a static route (see the codes section at the top of the **show ip route** command output), while the [1/0] indicates, firstly, the administrative distance of the route (1) and, secondly, the metric of the route (0). The administrative distance defines the preference of the route when multiple routing protocols offer up different routes to the same destination network. Different routing protocols possess different administrative distances—for example, OSPF possesses an administrative distance of 110 by default, while a static route possesses an administrative distance of 1 by default. The lower the administrative distance, the more preferable the route—administrative distance is always the primary entity used to select which routes should appear in the routing table.

The metric of the route defines how far away the route is and is used to differentiate between routes that possess the same administrative distance (this is normally routes from the same routing protocol). Routing protocols each possess different mechanisms for calculating metrics; in general, the lower the metric, the more preferred the route is. Importantly, administrative distance always takes precedence over the metric of a router. For example, a route with an administrative distance of 10 and a metric of 10,000 is preferred over a route with an administrative distance of 100 and a metric of 1, even though the second route has a lower metric because the administrative distance of the first route is lower and hence preferred.

NOTE   For static routing, the metric is not actually used; hence, all static routes have a metric of 0.

Verifying Connectivity

Now that the appropriate routing configuration is in place on Router-A and Router-B, hosts in VLAN 1 should be able to communicate with hosts in VLAN 3 (as well as VLAN 2).

Example 5-11 demonstrates using the **ping** command to verify connectivity to VLAN 3 from Router-A, with the **debug ip packet** command enabled.

Example 5-11 *Testing* **ping** *Connectivity from Router-A to the VLAN 3 Interface*

```
Router-A# debug ip packet
IP packet debugging is on
Router-A# ping 192.168.3.1

Type escape sequence to abort.
Sending 5, 100-byte ICMP Echos to 192.168.3.1, timeout is 2 seconds:
!!!!!
Success rate is 100 percent (5/5), round-trip min/avg/max = 1/3/4 ms
Router-A#
01:55:59: IP: s=192.168.2.1 (local), d=192.168.3.1 (Ethernet0/1), len 100, sending
01:55:59: IP: s=192.168.3.1 (Ethernet0/1), d=192.168.2.1 (Ethernet0/1), len 100,
  rcvd
01:55:59: IP: s=192.168.2.1 (local), d=192.168.3.1 (Ethernet0/1), len 100, sending
01:55:59: IP: s=192.168.3.1 (Ethernet0/1), d=192.168.2.1 (Ethernet0/1), len 100,
  rcvd
01:55:59: IP: s=192.168.2.1 (local), d=192.168.3.1 (Ethernet0/1), len 100, sending
```

continues

Example 5-11 *Testing* **ping** *Connectivity from Router-A to the VLAN 3 Interface (Continued)*

```
01:55:59: IP: s=192.168.3.1 (Ethernet0/1), d=192.168.2.1 (Ethernet0/1), len 100,
  rcvd
01:55:59: IP: s=192.168.2.1 (local), d=192.168.3.1 (Ethernet0/1), len 100, sending
01:55:59: IP: s=192.168.3.1 (Ethernet0/1), d=192.168.2.1 (Ethernet0/1), len 100,
  rcvd
01:55:59: IP: s=192.168.2.1 (local), d=192.168.3.1 (Ethernet0/1), len 100, sending
01:55:59: IP: s=192.168.3.1 (Ethernet0/1), d=192.168.2.1 (Ethernet0/1), len 100,
  rcvd
```

In Example 5-11, the VLAN 3 interface on Router-B (192.168.3.1) is successfully pinged, with the debug output providing details of the packets sent and received. If you compare the output of Example 5-11 with Example 5-7 (where routing was not configured), notice that the debug output is quite different. The first shaded line shows a ping packet (ICMP echo request) being sent by the router (as indicated by the text sending at the end of the line). Notice that the message indicates that the packet is being routed out the Ethernet0/1 interface, as indicated by the Ethernet0/1 text in the parentheses after the d=192.168.3.1 text. The second shaded line shows return ping replies (ICMP echo replies) received by the router, as indicated by the rcvd text at the end of the line.

If you take a closer look at the source and destination IP addresses of the ping packets generated in Example 5-11, you might notice that Example 5-11 is only verifying Router-A can route to VLAN 3 (192.168.3.0/24) and is not verifying that Router-B can route to VLAN 1 (192.168.1.0/24). This is because by default, the source IP address of each ping request generated by Router-A is the IP address of the egress interface out which the packet is sent. Because 192.168.3.0/24 is reachable via the egress interface Ethernet 0/0 on Router-A, the source IP address of each ping packet generated is 192.168.2.1. Router-B is directly attached to the 192.168.2.0/24 subnet, so even if Router-B does not have a route configured for VLAN 1, Router-B is able to successfully reply to the 192.168.2.1 source address of each ping request.

To verify that Router-B knows how to route to the 192.168.1.0/24 network, you can test connectivity between Host-A and Host-B, or you can ping the VLAN 1 interface on Router-A from Router-B. Another way to verify the routing configuration on Router-B is to issue an extended ping on Router-A, which allows you to modify the source IP address of the ping packets generated to be the VLAN 1 interface on Router-A. Example 5-12 demonstrates using the extended **ping** command on Router-A to verify both Router-A and Router-B have the appropriate routing configuration in place in a single step.

Example 5-12 *Testing Extended* **ping** *Connectivity from Router-A to Router-B*

```
Router-B# ping
Protocol [ip]: ip
Target IP address: 192.168.3.1
Repeat count [5]:
Datagram size [100]:
Timeout in seconds [2]:
Extended commands [n]: y
```

Example 5-12 *Testing Extended* **ping** *Connectivity from Router-A to Router-B (Continued)*

```
Source address or interface: 192.168.1.1
Type of service [0]:
Set DF bit in IP header? [no]:
Validate reply data? [no]:
Data pattern [0xABCD]:
Loose, Strict, Record, Timestamp, Verbose[none]:
Sweep range of sizes [n]:
Type escape sequence to abort.
Sending 5, 100-byte ICMP Echos to 192.168.3.1, timeout is 2 seconds:
!!!!!
Success rate is 100 percent (5/5), round-trip min/avg/max = 1/2/4 ms
```

In Example 5-12, you just specify the **ping** command to enter the interactive extended ping mode. In interactive mode, you are prompted for various parameters that are used to generate ping packets. The defaults are listed in square brackets for each prompt so if the default is sufficient you can just press the Enter key. In Example 5-12, the destination IP address is indicated with the use of extended commands enabled. Extended commands allow you to specify advanced parameters, such as the source address of the ping packet that is generated. In Example 5-12, notice that a source address of 192.168.3.1 is configured. After configuring the extended commands, the ping packets are generated, with successful replies received. This confirms two things:

- A valid route exists on Router-A for the destination network (192.168.3.0/24) of the ping traffic.

- A valid route exists on Router-B for the 192.168.1.0/24 network. This is true because the source IP address of the ping traffic (192.168.1.1) resides in the 192.168.1.0/24 network. For Router-B to successfully reply to the ping traffic from Router-A, it must have a route for the 192.168.1.0/24 network in its local route table.

At this point, the routing configuration on Router-A and Router-B has been successfully tested, and Host-A on VLAN 1 should be able to communicate with Host-B on VLAN 3. When verifying host connectivity to the network, it is good practice to first ensure that the host can ping its local default gateway and to then attempt to ping a remote network. Taking this approach ensures that you verify the path to remote networks in an incremental fashion, starting from the first hop in the path. Example 5-13 demonstrates verifying connectivity from Host-A to Host-B in such a fashion.

Example 5-13 *Testing ping Connectivity from Host-A*

```
C:\WINXP\SYSTEM32> ping 192.168.1.1
Pinging 192.168.1.1 with 32 bytes of data:

Reply from 192.168.1.1: bytes=32 time=1ms TTL=255
Reply from 192.168.1.1: bytes=32 time=1ms TTL=255
Reply from 192.168.1.1: bytes=32 time=1ms TTL=255
Reply from 192.168.1.1: bytes=32 time=1ms TTL=255

Ping statistics for 192.168.1.1:
   . Packets: Sent = 4, Received = 4, Lost = 0 (0% loss),
```

continues

Example 5-13 *Testing ping Connectivity from Host-A (Continued)*

```
Approximate round trip times in milli-seconds:
    Minimum = 1ms, Maximum = 1ms, Average = 1ms

C:\WINXP\SYSTEM32> ping 192.168.3.100
Pinging 192.168.3.100 with 32 bytes of data:

Reply from 192.168.3.100: bytes=32 time=1ms TTL=255
Reply from 192.168.3.100: bytes=32 time=1ms TTL=255
Reply from 192.168.3.100: bytes=32 time=1ms TTL=255
Reply from 192.168.3.100: bytes=32 time=1ms TTL=255

Ping statistics for 192.168.3.100:
    Packets: Sent = 4, Received = 4, Lost = 0 (0% loss),
Approximate round trip times in milli-seconds:
    Minimum = 1ms, Maximum = 1ms, Average = 1ms
```

In Example 5-13, connectivity to the local default gateway (Router-A) is first verified, after which connectivity to the desired remote network (VLAN 3) is verified.

Sometimes you might run into a situation where you want to verify the path traffic between two hosts takes through the network. The **tracert** (Windows) and **traceroute** (Cisco IOS and UNIX) utilities are useful tools that enable you to discover the path between two endpoints in the network. Example 5-14 demonstrates the use of the **tracert** utility on Host-A.

Example 5-14 *Verifying the Network Path from Host-A to Host-B*

```
C:\WINXP\SYSTEM32> tracert -d 192.168.3.100
Tracing route to 192.168.3.100 over a maximum of 30 hops

    1    1 ms     1 ms     1 ms   192.168.1.1
    2    2 ms     3 ms     1 ms   192.168.2.2
    3    3 ms     5 ms     5 ms   192.168.3.100

Trace Complete.
```

In Example 5-14, use the **–d** option to prevent the Windows operating system from performing a DNS query for the hostname associated with each IP address returned. Each routing device in the path to the destination is shown. You can see that Router-A (192.168.1.1) is the first router, Router-B (192.168.2.2) is the second router, with the third entry representing the traceroute packet reaching its final destination.

Scenario 5-2: Configuring Layer 3 Switching

Layer 3 (L3) switching is a technology that has become very popular in modern campus networks. L3 switching basically refers to a switch that can route. The main difference between a L3 switch and a traditional router is performance. L3 switches are used to route IP traffic at

LAN speeds (10/100/1000 Mbps) by utilizing hardware-based wire-speed routing, instead of software-based routing used on Cisco routers. L3 switches can route at speeds seen only in high-end Cisco routers, at a fraction of the cost, the trade-off being that L3 switches can route only between Ethernet media, whereas a Cisco router can route between a variety of LAN and WAN media. In this scenario you configure essentially the same IP topology of Scenario 5-1, but use L3 switches to implement routing instead of Cisco routers. It is very important to ensure you understand exactly how a L3 switch operates because these devices are becoming less expensive and are becoming more common in the marketplace.

Figure 5-12 shows the topology used for this scenario. The topology might not look like too much in terms of routing; however, each switch possesses both switched and routed interfaces that allow the switch to act as a L3 switch. In this lab, you enable connectivity between Host-A and Host-B, using the IP addressing and topology shown in Figure 5-12.

Figure 5-12 *Scenario 5-2 Topology*

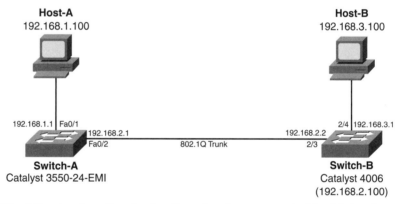

The following describes the function of each component of the lab topology shown in Figure 5-12:

- Switch-A is a Catalyst 3550-24-EMI L3 switch that provides LAN connectivity. This switch is loaded with an Enhanced Multilayer Image (EMI), which allows it to operate as a Layer 3 switch.

NOTE   The Catalyst 3550 can also operate with a Standard Multilayer Image (SMI), which does not support L3 switching and possesses only Layer 3/4 intelligence for security and quality of service features. The EMI software must be purchased as a separate cost.

- Switch-B is a Catalyst 4006 switch with a Supervisor 2 engine and a L3 switching module (WS-X4232-L3). The L3 switching module includes 32 x 10/100 ports as well as 2 gigabit Ethernet ports.

- Host-A and Host-B are workstations that are used to test that inter-VLAN routing is configured correctly to provide connectivity between each host.

Understanding the Catalyst 3550 Series Multilayer Switches

The Catalyst 3550 series is the next-generation switching family from Cisco for small to medium enterprises. The Catalyst 3550 switches are Layer 3/4 aware (can classify packets based upon Layer 3/4 information) and are also capable of performing Layer 3 routing. The Catalyst 3550 series switches consist of the following switches:

- Catalyst 3550-24 (24 * 10/100BaseT + 2 x 1000BaseX)
- Catalyst 3550-48 (48 * 10/100BaseT + 2 x 1000BaseX)
- Catalyst 3550-12T (10 * 10/100/1000BaseT + 2 x 1000BaseX)
- Catalyst 3550-12G (10 * 1000BaseX + 2 x 10/100/1000BaseT)

The Catalyst 3550-24 and 3550-48 switches are available with a Layer 2–only IOS image (known as SMI) or with a Layer 3–switching IOS image (known as EMI). The SMI version can be upgraded to the EMI version if required, which provides a low cost migration path for converting a Layer 2 switching architecture to a Layer 3 switching architecture. Both the Catalyst 3550-12T and 3500-12G are Layer 3 switches that run an EMI image and cannot be purchased as just a Layer 2 switch.

The new Cisco IOS-based L3 switches from Cisco are much more integrated than older L3 switch implementations because of the use of the same management interface (Cisco IOS only) for both Layer 2 and Layer 3 functionality, rather than the use of both CatOS (for Layer 2 functionality) and Cisco IOS (for Layer 3 functionality). To understand exactly how L3 switching works on the Catalyst 3550, it is often easier to draw out the L2 switch and L3 router components separately on a piece of paper. Figure 5-13 demonstrates separating out each of the L3 switch components used in Switch-A.

In Figure 5-13, you can see the concept of a L3 switch is essentially the same as a traditional separated L2 switch and L3 router topology. Within the L3 switch, a dedicated routing engine acts exactly like a normal router. The only real difference between a traditional L3 switch and router is that a L3 switch performs the L3 routing function in hardware, at much higher speeds than a software-based L3 router, and the internal connection between the routing engine and switching engine is not a bottleneck the way an external connection is.

Notice in Figure 5-13 the two types of routed interfaces on a L3 switch:

- Physical
- Switch virtual interface (SVI)

The physical interface is simply a port on the switch that acts exactly like an Ethernet port on a router. You can configure any port on the switch as a routed interface, making L3 switching much easier to understand and configure. The routed interface feature is available on all Catalyst 3550 L3 switches, as well as the Catalyst 4000/4500 with Supervisor 3/4 and the Cisco IOS-based Catalyst 6000/6500 with the Multilayer Switch Feature Card (MSFC) operating in native IOS mode.

Figure 5-13   *Layer 3 Switch (Switch-A) Logical Components*

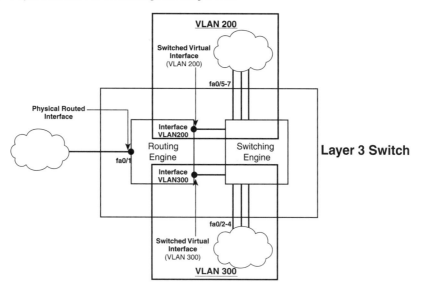

NOTE
On the switches listed above, a physical interface can be configured as a traditional switch (Layer 2) port or a routed interface. On older L3 switching modules, such as the Catalyst 4000 routing module, Catalyst 5000 RSM, and Catalyst 6000/6500 with MSFC running hybrid mode, you cannot configure a switched port on the switch as a routed interface — you can only use SVI routed interfaces, as the routing component has no control over any switched interfaces.

The SVI is an internal virtual interface that attaches to a particular VLAN on the switch. The SVI is essentially an internal routed interface attached to the L3 engine belonging to a particular VLAN. This allows other devices attached to switched physical ports within the VLAN to communicate at a Layer 3 level with the routing engine of the L3 switch. In Figure 5-13, two SVI interfaces are displayed — one for VLAN 200 and one for VLAN 300. Creating an SVI interface is simple; you simply create the SVI by using the IOS **interface VLAN** *x* global configuration mode command, where *x* is the VLAN ID to which you want to attach the SVI to. In Figure 5-13, the SVI for VLAN 200 is configured using the **interface VLAN 200** command, while the SVI for VLAN 300 is configured using the **interface VLAN 300** command. Once you have created the SVI, you configure it with normal L3 parameters (such as IP addressing) just as you would for a physical routed interface.

| NOTE | If you are familiar with configuring integrated routing and bridging (IRB) on Cisco routers, an SVI is similar in concept to a bridge virtual interface (BVI), and VLANs on Catalyst switches are similar to bridge groups on Cisco routers. |

Understanding the Catalyst 4000 Router Module (WS-X4232-L3)

This lab includes configuration of the Catalyst 4000 router module, which is the module used to turn the Catalyst 4000 with a Supervisor 1 or 2 module into a L3 switch.

| NOTE | The Catalyst 4000 has newer Supervisor 3 or Supervisor 4 modules available, which are Cisco IOS-based with integrated L3 switching functionality (similar to the Catalyst 3550). You cannot use the WS-X4232-L3 router module in Catalyst 4000 switches with the Supervisor 3/4 module installed. |

The router module is very popular with a large installation base worldwide and it is important that you understand the architecture of the router module before installing and configuring it.

The router module is essentially a standalone router that is powered by the Catalyst 4000 chassis and has gigabit interfaces that attach to the Catalyst 4000 backplane. The router module has its own processor, memory, flash, operating system (Cisco IOS), and management interface. All routing configuration is configured using the router module Cisco IOS interface. No routing configuration is provided by the CatOS management interface of the Catalyst 4000 switch. Figure 5-14 shows the internal architecture of the Catalyst 4000 router module.

In the Catalyst 4000 architecture, each module is provided with six internal gigabit links to the switch backplane. In Figure 5-14, you can see that two of these are attached to the Cisco IOS routing engine on the routing module, while the remaining internal gigabit links are attached to the 32-port 10/100 Ethernet card. The Catalyst 4000 Supervisor 1/2 sees the two gigabit links to the routing engine as ports $x/1$ and $x/2$, where x is the slot in which the routing module is installed (e.g., 2/1 and 2/2 if the routing module is installed in slot 2). The two external Gigabit Ethernet ports located on the routing module are directly attached routed interfaces on the routing engine and are not visible to the Supervisor engine. The 32-port 10/100 card is attached directly to the switching engine and has no relationship with the routing engine except that they both share the same physical chassis. The numbering of the ports starts from $x/3$ (port 1) and finishes at $x/34$ (port 32).

Figure 5-14 *Catalyst 4000 Router Module Architecture*

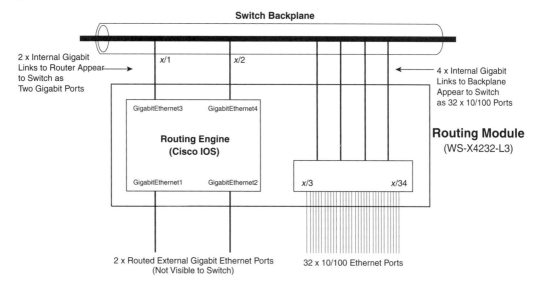

To allow Catalyst 4000 ports to communicate with the routing engine, the two internal gigabit links are normally configured as an EtherChannel bundle, which operates as an 802.1Q trunk. This means the throughput of the routing engine is limited to up to 2 Gbps full-duplex, and the routing engine can attach to any VLAN on the switch by use of the trunk. To attach the routing engine to a particular VLAN on the switch, an SVI must be created for the VLAN. This enables the routing engine to communicate on the VLAN at a Layer 3 level.

NOTE   The Catalyst 4000 L3 routing module can route IP packets at 6 million packets per second, although the actual performance achieved is limited to 2 Gbps based upon the backplane connection to the Catalyst 4000 switch engine.

Understanding the Inter-VLAN Routing Packet Flow

Now that you understand the architectures of both the Catalyst 3550 L3 switch and the Catalyst 4000 routing module, it is important that you understand how packets are routed between Host-A and Host-B in this scenario. Figure 5-15 shows the topology of Figure 5-12 from an inter-VLAN routing and packet flow perspective.

Figure 5-15 *Scenario 5-2 Inter-VLAN Routing Topology*

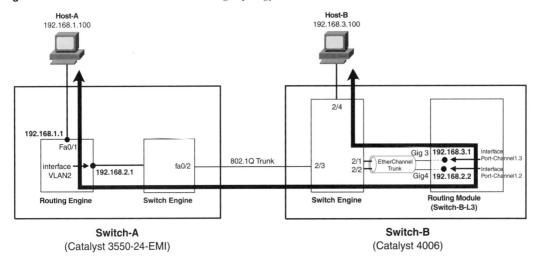

In Figure 5-15 notice the architectural differences between Switch-A and Switch-B. The Catalyst 4006 with router module is essentially a high-speed router-on-a-stick implementation, much like the relationship between Switch-A and Router-B in Scenario 5-1; however, the routing engine in the router module is much faster than a 2600 series router or similar (the router module is based upon the 7200 series platform). The fact that the Catalyst 4006 and router module are operating in a router-on-a-stick configuration is further indicated by the fact that each has a separate management interface. The Catalyst 3550 switch and other Cisco IOS L3 switches have an integrated management interface for both routing and switching.

Scenario Prerequisites

To successfully commence the configuration tasks required to complete this scenario, the following lists the prerequisite configuration tasks required on each device in the scenario topology:

- **Hostname**—each device should be configured with an appropriate hostname as per Figure 5-12.

- **Telnet/Enable password**—each device should be configured with an appropriate telnet and enable password.

This scenario assumes the configuration tasks listed above have already been implemented and hence does not include the configuration of these tasks.

Configuration Tasks

The configuration tasks for this scenario are essentially the same as for Scenario 5-1 because the basic goal of the scenario is the same (i.e., to enable routing for the network). The following lists the required configuration tasks:

- Configuring Layer 2 parameters
- Configuring inter-VLAN routing
- Verifying connectivity

Configuring Layer 2 Parameters

Just as configuring an inter-VLAN routing architecture that uses a router-on-a-stick, for an integrated Layer 3 switching inter-VLAN routing architecture, you must configure Layer 2 parameters first. The only difference with the router-on-a-stick architecture is that the Layer 2 configuration is on a separate Layer 2 switch With the integrated Layer 3 switching archi-tecture, you often find that you configure Layer 2 and Layer 3 attributes on the same switch device using the same management interface. The following lists the configuration tasks required to configure Layer 2 parameters for this scenario:

- Configuring Layer 2 parameters on Switch-A
- Configuring Layer 2 parameters on Switch-B

Configuring Layer 2 Parameters on Switch-A

When configuring VLANs on a L3 switch, you are controlling the way in which the switching engine of the L3 switch operates. When configuring VLANs on an integrated L3 switch such as the Catalyst 3550 (i.e., Switch-A in this scenario), you must create VLANs as you would on a Layer 2 switch. However, the way you configure VLAN port membership on the switch depends on whether or not the interface is configured as a Layer 3 (routed) interface or a Layer 2 interface. Understand that physical routed interfaces are not configured to belong to a specific VLAN because a routed interface connects directly to the routing engine (see Figure 5-15) and has no connection whatsoever to the switching engine, where VLANs are supported. The concept of a physical routed interface on an L3 switch is identical in concept to Ethernet interface on a normal Cisco router—Cisco routers do not support the concept of VLANs and do not require an interface to be configured to a specific VLAN.

NOTE   As you saw in Scenario 5-1, some Cisco routers do support the concept of VLANs in relation to an Ethernet port being configured as an ISL or 802.1Q trunk. On integrated Cisco IOS L3 switches, such as the Catalyst 3550, you cannot configure a routed interface as a routed trunk interface. To support routing sent via a trunk, you must configure a Layer 2 trunk and then create SVI interfaces for each VLAN on the trunk that requires routing.

With relation to Layer 2 ports on an L3 switch, VLAN membership is configured as per a normal Layer 2 switch. The routing engine of the L3 switch can process traffic sent and received on Layer 2 ports via an SVI interface created for the VLAN the Layer 2 ports are configured to belong to.

Now that you understand the VLAN configuration considerations for both Layer 2 and Layer 3 interfaces on Switch-A, it is time to implement the required VLAN configuration. On Switch-A, the following VLAN configuration is required:

- VTP must be configured so that VLANs can be created. In this scenario, both switches are configured to operate in VTP transparent mode, meaning VLANs must be manually created on each switch separately.

- VLAN 2 must be created. VLAN 3 does not need to be configured on Switch-A because no devices in VLAN 3 are attached to Switch-A.

- Interface fa0/2 must be configured as an 802.1Q trunk. To avoid VTP domain mismatches, the trunk should be configured with a DTP mode of on.

NOTE   For this scenario, interface fa0/2 doesn't actually need to be configured as a trunk because only traffic from VLAN 2 is being transported across it. In the real world, however, when connecting two switches, it is likely that the traffic from multiple VLANs will need to be transported across the interswitch link, requiring a trunk interface to be configured.

Example 5-15 shows the VLAN and trunking (i.e., Layer 2) configuration required on Switch-A.

Example 5-15   *Configuring VLANs and Trunking on Switch-A*

```
Switch-A# configure terminal
Switch-A(config)# vtp mode transparent
Setting device to VTP TRANSPARENT mode.
Switch-A(config)# vlan 2
Switch-A(config-vlan)# name VLAN02
Switch-A(config-vlan)# exit
```

Example 5-15 *Configuring VLANs and Trunking on Switch-A (Continued)*

```
Switch-A(config)# interface FastEthernet 0/2
Switch-A(config-if)# switchport trunk encapsulation dot1q
Switch-A(config-if)# switchport mode trunk
```

Notice in Example 5-15 that no configuration is performed on interface fa0/1. This is because interface fa0/1 is a routed interface and, therefore, does not require any Layer 2 configuration.

Configuring Layer 2 Parameters on Switch-B

Switch-B is a Catalyst 4006 switch with a L3 router module installed and is different from Switch-A in that the switching engine (Supervisor 2 engine) and the routing engine (L3 router module) have separate management interfaces. This means that the VLAN and other Layer 2 configuration required on Switch-B must be performed on the CatOS-based Supervisor engine. On Switch-B, the following VLAN and Layer 2 configuration is required:

* VTP transparent mode must be configured.

* VLAN 2 and VLAN 3 must be created. VLAN 2 is required for the trunk to Switch-A and for the connection to the L3 Router module, while VLAN 3 is required for the connection to Host-B and for the connection to the L3 Router module.

* Port 2/3 must be configured as an 802.1Q trunk, with VLANs. To avoid VTP domain mismatches, the trunk should be configured with a Dynamic Trunking Protocol (DTP) mode of on.

Example 5-16 shows the VLAN and Layer 2 configuration required on Switch-B.

Example 5-16 *Configuring VLANs on Switch-B*

```
Switch-B> (enable) set vtp mode transparent
VTP domain  modified
Switch-B> (enable) set vlan 2 name VLAN02
VTP advertisements transmitting temporarily stopped,
and will resume after the command finishes.
Vlan 2 configuration successful
Switch-B> (enable) set vlan 3 name VLAN03
VTP advertisements transmitting temporarily stopped,
and will resume after the command finishes.
Vlan 3 configuration successful
Switch-B> (enable) set vlan 3 name VLAN03
VTP advertisements transmitting temporarily stopped,
and will resume after the command finishes.
Vlan 3 configuration successful
Switch-B> (enable) set trunk 2/3 on dot1q
Port(s)  2/3 trunk mode set to on.
Port(s)  2/3 trunk type set to dot1q.
```

After the configuration of Example 5-16 is complete, assuming Switch-A and Switch-B are connected, a trunk should form between Switch-A and Switch-B. Example 5-17 demonstrates verifying a trunk has formed by using the **show trunk** command on Switch-B.

Example 5-17 *Verifying the Trunk Between Switch-A and Switch-B*

```
Switch-A> (enable) show trunk 2/3
Port      Mode         Encapsulation  Status        Native VLAN
--------  -----------  -------------  ------------  -----------
 2/3      on           dot1q          trunking      1
```

In Example 5-17, you can see by the shaded portion of the output that the trunk has successfully formed.

TIP   You can use the **show cdp neighbors** command on both switches to verify that each switch has Layer 2 connectivity with the other.

Configuring Inter-VLAN Routing

At this stage you have connected all devices as indicated in Figure 5-12 and enabled Layer 2 connectivity between Switch-A and Switch-B. In this section you enable the Layer 3 switching components of each switch, which ultimately allows Host-A to communicate with Host-B. On Switch-A, the inter-VLAN required routing configuration is performed using the same Cisco IOS management interface used to configure Layer 2 parameters earlier. On Switch-B, the inter-VLAN routing configuration required must be configured separately on the L3 router module, which has a separate Cisco IOS-based management interface from the CatOS management interface on Switch-B. The L3 router module on Switch-B is called *Switch-B-L3*, and in this section you learn how to configure the L3 router module.

The following lists the configuration tasks required to enable inter-VLAN routing for this scenario:

- Configuring Switch-A for inter-VLAN routing
- Configuring Switch-B for inter-VLAN routing

Configuring Switch-A for Inter-VLAN Routing

To enable L3 switching on Switch-A, you need to configure the interface connected to Host-A (fa0/1) as a routed interface and also need to create an SVI interface attached to VLAN 2 to enable inter-VLAN routing to the VLAN 2 interface on the L3 router module within Switch-B. You must also configure the appropriate routing for the remote 192.168.3.0/24 subnet attached to Switch-B to ensure Switch-A forwards packets to Host-B to the correct next hop. In this scenario, instead of configuring static routing, as was configured in Scenario 5-1, a dynamic routing protocol is configured.

To configure an interface as a routed interface, you must use the **no switchport** interface configuration command on the interface you want to convert. After you have completed this configuration, the interface becomes a Layer 3 interface and can be configured with Layer 3 parameters, such as IP addressing information. Example 5-18 shows the configuration required on Switch-A to configure interface fa0/1 as a routed interface.

Example 5-18   *Configuring a Routed Physical Interface on Switch-A*

```
Switch-A# configure terminal
Switch-A(config)# interface FastEthernet 0/1
Switch-A(config-if)# no switchport
Switch-A(config-if)# ip address 192.168.1.1 255.255.255.0
```

In Example 5-18, the **no switchport** command is used to configure the interface as a routed (Layer 3) interface rather than a switched (Layer 2) interface. Any routed interface on a Cisco IOS router or L3 switch is placed into a shutdown state by default, so you must explicitly enable the interface by using the **no shutdown** command.

NOTE   By default, all interfaces on the Catalyst 3550 and other Cisco IOS-based Layer 3 switches are Layer 2 interfaces and must be configured explicitly as routed interfaces. This does not apply to the Catalyst 6000/6500 operating in native IOS mode, where all interfaces are routed interfaces by default.

Finally, you assign an IP address to the interface, which you must do for any routed interface on a traditional Cisco IOS router.

NOTE   By default, any IP address associated with a routed interface on a L3 switch can be used for management access via Telnet. This means you do not have to create an SVI interface for switch management.

After configuring the routed interface on Switch-A, you next need to create SVI interfaces for each VLAN the L3 switch must route for. An SVI is created by using the **interface vlan** global configuration command:

```
Switch(config)# interface vlan vlan-id
```

In this scenario, Switch-A needs to route only for VLAN 2. Because interface fa0/2 is configured as a trunk, it cannot be configured as a routed interface (routed trunk interfaces are not supported) and instead must be configured as a Layer 2 trunk interface. To enable the routing engine of Switch-A to communicate with VLAN 2 on the switching engine, an SVI must be created for VLAN 2 as shown in Example 5-19.

Example 5-19 *Creating an SVI on Switch-A*

```
Switch-A# configure terminal
Switch-A(config)# interface vlan 2
Switch-A(config-if)# ip address 192.168.2.1 255.255.255.0
```

As you can see from Example 5-19, the procedure for creating an SVI on a L3 switch is identical to that for a traditional L2 switch. The only difference is that the SVI is used only for management connectivity on a L2 switch while the SVI is used for both routing and management connectivity on a L3 switch.

Now that the appropriate Layer 3 interfaces have been configured on Switch-A, you can configure IP routing. In this scenario, Switch-A is directly connected to the 192.168.1.0/24 and 192.168.2.0/24 subnets. However, it is not directly connected to the 192.168.3.0/24 subnet and, therefore, requires routing information for this subnet to be configured. Because EIGRP must be configured for this scenario, instead of configuring a static route on Switch-A, you must configure EIGRP so that Switch-A can learn about the 192.168.3.0/24 route dynamically and also advertise the 192.168.1.0/24 subnet. Example 5-20 shows the configuration required on Switch-A to perform these tasks.

Example 5-20 *Configuring IP Routing on Switch-A*

```
Switch-A# configure terminal
Switch-A(config)# ip routing
Switch-A(config)# router eigrp 1
Switch-A(config-router)# network 192.168.1.0
Switch-A(config-router)# network 192.168.2.0
```

In Example 5-20, notice that you must explicitly enable IP routing on Switch-A, because by default a Catalyst 3550 series L3 switch is configured as a Layer 2 switch and L3 switching is not enabled. EIGRP is then configured, placing interfaces in the 192.168.1.0/24 and 192.168.2.0/24 networks in the EIGRP routing domain.

Configuring Switch-B for Inter-VLAN Routing

To enable L3 switching on Switch-B, you must configure the router module installed in slot 2 of Switch-B. This router module is essentially a separate router that has its own Cisco IOS management interface and is configured independently of the main Switch-B chassis. To understand how to configure L3 switching using the Catalyst 4000 router module, you must view the router module as a separate router that is attached to the switch internally. This means that you need to provide an initial configuration (e.g., host name, passwords, and so on) for the router module before configuring inter-VLAN routing.

Before configuring inter-VLAN routing on Switch-B, it is a good idea to test connectivity over the trunk between Switch-A and Switch-B. This test can be achieved by configuring the sc0 management interface of Switch-B in VLAN 2 with an appropriate IP address and then attempting to ping the VLAN 2 SVI interface created in Example 5-21. Example 5-21 shows the configuration required on Switch-B.

Example 5-21 *Configuring the sc0 Management Interface on Switch-B*

```
Switch-B> (enable) set interface sc0 2 192.168.2.100 255.255.255.0
Interface sc0 vlan set, IP address and netmask set.
Switch-B> (enable) set ip route default 192.168.2.1
Route added.
Switch-B> (enable) ping 192.168.2.1
!!!!!

----192.168.2.1 PING Statistics----
5 packets transmitted, 5 packets received, 0% packet loss
round-trip (ms)  min/avg/max = 7/11/25
Switch-A> (enable) show arp
ARP Aging time = 1200 sec
+ - Permanent Arp Entries
* - Static Arp Entries
192.168.2.1                              at 00-09-b7-aa-9c-80 port  2/3 on VLAN 2
```

In Example 5-21, notice that the sc0 interface is configured, a default gateway is configured, connectivity to Switch-A is tested, and then the local ARP cache is viewed on Switch-B. When the **ping** command is executed, an ICMP echo request packet is generated from the sc0 interface (192.168.2.100) on Switch-B. The **show arp** command displays the local ARP cache, which contains IP address–to–MAC address mappings for devices on the VLAN the management interface is connected to. When the ICMP echo request packet is generated, assuming Switch-B does not know the MAC address of the SVI interface on Switch-A, Switch-B sends an ARP broadcast to determine the MAC address associated with the destination IP address (192.168.2.1). This broadcast is sent on VLAN 2 and is thus tagged and sent down the 802.1Q trunk to Switch-A. Because the broadcast is tagged with a VLAN ID of 2, the ARP broadcast is forwarded to the SVI interface in VLAN 2, which is configured with an IP address of 192.168.2.1. Switch-A sends an ARP reply back to Switch-B containing the virtual MAC address of the VLAN 2 SVI interface, enabling Switch-B to forward the ICMP echo packet to the VLAN 2 SVI interface on Switch-A. The ARP entry is indicated by the shaded output of the **show arp** command in Example 5-18.

So now that Layer 2 connectivity between Switch-A and Switch-B has been verified, it is time to begin configuring inter-VLAN routing. Before configuring inter-VLAN routing on the router module, you need to configure the gigabit connections to the router module on the backplane of Switch-B that the Supervisor engine manages. These connections are identified by the Supervisor engine as ports *x*/1 and *x*/2, where *x* is the slot in which the router module is installed, and must be configured in one of three ways:

- **Physical interfaces only**—Each gigabit connection to the L3 router module is configured as a separate access port. In this situation, you need only assign each gigabit port to the appropriate VLAN.

- **Physical trunks**—Each gigabit connection to the L3 router module is configured as a separate trunk port, allowing the L3 router module access to multiple VLANs. In this situation, you must configure trunking appropriately for each port and optionally define the allowed VLANs on each trunk.

- **EtherChannel bundle**—Both gigabit connections are configured as a single EtherChannel bundle, creating a single virtual Layer 2 connection between the Supervisor engine and the L3 router module. The physical ports bundle can be configured as access ports, meaning the EtherChannel bundle belongs only to a single VLAN, or as trunk ports, meaning the EtherChannel bundle is connected to multiple VLANs. In either case, each physical port must be configured identically to ensure the EtherChannel bundle forms.

In this scenario, you configure these connections as an EtherChannel 802.1Q trunk (see Figure 5-15). Example 5-22 demonstrates configuring the Supervisor engine on Switch-B to support the L3 router module.

Example 5-22 *Configuring Gigabit Ports on Switch-B to Router Module as an EtherChannel Trunk*

```
Switch-B> (enable) set trunk 2/1 nonegotiate dot1q
Port(s) 2/1 trunk mode set to nonegotiate.
Port(s) 2/1 trunk type set to dot1q.
Switch-B> (enable) set trunk 2/2 nonegotiate dot1q
Port(s) 2/2 trunk mode set to nonegotiate.
Port(s) 2/2 trunk type set to dot1q.
Switch-B> (enable) set port channel 2/1-2 on
Port(s) 2/1-2 are assigned to admin group 112.
Port(s) 2/1-2 channel mode set to on.
```

In Example 5-22, you must configure a trunking mode of nonegotiate because Cisco IOS routers (including the L3 router module) do not use or understand Dynamic Trunking Protocol (DTP). Similarly, you must also configure a PAgP mode of on for the Ether-Channel bundle, as Cisco IOS routers do not use or understand Port Aggregation Protocol (PAgP).

At this point, you are ready to begin configuring the Catalyst 4000 L3 router module. Because the L3 router module has its own management interface and cannot be configured from the CatOS interface of Switch-B, you must establish a new management connection to the router module. Catalyst 4000, 5000, and 6000 switches use the **session** command in conjunction with the slot number of the router module to access an internal console port attached to any module that has a separate management interface. Example 5-23 shows how to establish a connection to the router module.

NOTE   Most modules accessible via the **session** command also have a console port that allows
management access.

Example 5-23 *Establishing a Management Connection to the Router Module in Switch-B*

```
Switch-B> (enable) session 2
Trying IntlgLineCard-2...
Connected to IntlgLineCard-2.
Escape character is '^]'.
```

In Example 5-23, you use the **session 2** command, where the number 2 specifies the slot in
which the router module is installed. The switch then attempts to establish an internal
console connection to the management interface (CLI) of the module. Once established,
you are presented with a command-line interface within the router module operating
system (Cisco IOS), which is totally separate from the CatOS CLI of Switch-A. To return
back to the CatOS CLI of Switch-A, you simply use the **exit** command in the router module
IOS to logout of the session.

At this point, you have now successfully established a connection to the router module. The
router module is a totally separate device from the Catalyst 4000 switch, with its own
processor, memory, flash, and operating system. Use the **show version** command as shown
in Example 5-24 to get a feel for the hardware and software installed in the router module.

Example 5-24 *Checking the Router Module*

```
Router> show version
Cisco Internetwork Operating System Software
IOS (tm) L3 Switch/Router Software (CAT4232-IN-M), Version 12.0(10)W5(18f)
     RELEASE SOFTWARE
Copyright  1986-2000 by cisco Systems, Inc.
Compiled Mon 04-Dec-00 22:07 by integ
Image text-base: 0x60010928, data-base: 0x605F6000

ROM: System Bootstrap, Version 12.0(7)W5(15b) RELEASE SOFTWARE

Router uptime is 19 hours, 54 minutes
System restarted by power-on
Running default software

cisco Cat4232L3 (R5000) processor with 57344K/8192K bytes of memory.
R5000 processor, Implementation 35, Revision 2.1
Last reset from power-on
1 FastEthernet/IEEE 802.3 interface(s)
4 Gigabit Ethernet/IEEE 802.3z interface(s)
123K bytes of non-volatile configuration memory.

16384K bytes of Flash internal SIMM (Sector size 256K).
Configuration register is 0x2
```

Looking at the output of Example 5-24, you can pick out various pieces of information about the L3 router module, including the fact that the router module is Cisco IOS-based, includes a R5000 processor, 64 MB of memory, and 16 MB of flash memory.

The router module now needs to be configured as a new Cisco IOS router attached to Switch-B via the internal gigabit ports. This requires the router module to be configured with the following parameters:

- **Host identification information**—The router module routing engine is called Switch-B-L3.

- **Interface configuration**—The gigabit interfaces connected to the Supervisor engine must be configured as an EtherChannel bundle, with trunking configured over the bundle.

- **Routing configuration**—The router module must be configured to participate in the EIGRP routing domain so that Switch-B-L3 can exchange routes with the routing component of Switch-A.

Example 5-25 shows the configuration required to configure the host identification and interface configuration requirements just described.

Example 5-25 *Configuring the Router Module*

```
Router> enable
Router# configure terminal
Router(config)# hostname Switch-B-L3
Switch-B-L3(config)# interface GigabitEthernet 3
Switch-B-L3(config-if)# no shutdown
% Shutdown not allowed on this interface.
Switch-B-L3(config-if)# channel-group 1
Switch-B-L3(config-if)# exit
Creating a port-channel interface Port-channel1
Switch-B-L3(config)# interface GigabitEthernet 4
Switch-B-L3(config-if)# channel-group 1
Switch-B-L3(config-if)# end
Switch-B-L3# show interfaces port-channel 1
Port-channel1 is up, line protocol is up
  Hardware is GEChannel, address is 0004.4d19.e209 (bia 0000.0000.0000)
  MTU 1500 bytes, BW 2000000 Kbit, DLY 10 usec, rely 255/255, load 1/255
  Encapsulation ARPA, loopback not set, keepalive set (10 sec)
  Half-duplex, Unknown Speed, Media type unknown, Force link-up
  ARP type: ARPA, ARP Timeout 04:00:00
    No. of active members in this channel: 2
        Member 0 : GigabitEthernet3
        Member 1 : GigabitEthernet4
… (Output truncated)
…
```

In Example 5-25, interfaces GigabitEthernet 3 and GigabitEthernet 4 are added to a channel group, which creates a port-channel interface that represents the logical Layer 2 interface created by the EtherChannel bundle, as indicated by the shaded line directly below the first **channel-group** command that is executed. Notice the shaded lines in Example 5-25, which indicate that the internal gigabit interfaces connected to the switch backplane can never be shut down. In Example 5-25, also notice that no IP addressing is configured on the Ether-Channel (port-channel) interface because it is operating as an 802.1Q trunk and requires subinterfaces to be created for each VLAN that you want to attach to and route for. Finally, the **show interfaces port-channel 1** command is used to verify that the EtherChannel bundle has come up, which should happen immediately. As indicated by the shaded output, this interface is up at Layer 1 and Layer 2 and includes the GigabitEthernet 3 and GigabitEthernet 4 interfaces as active members.

TIP   It is important to note that when you configure the internal gigabit interfaces on the Layer 3 router module in an EtherChannel bundle, you cannot apply security access control lists (ACLs) to the port-channel interface that is used to represent the bundle. If you want to apply security ACLs for the purpose of filtering traffic sent or received by the Layer 3 router module on the internal gigabit interfaces, you must configure each port as a separate Layer 2 port.

All that now remains in terms of configuration on Switch-B-L3 is the creation of subinterfaces for each VLAN Switch-B-L3 must route for and the configuration of inter-VLAN routing. Example 5-26 shows the configuration required on Switch-B-L3 to create subinterfaces and verify connectivity from these subinterfaces to devices attached locally.

Example 5-26   *Configuring IP and Inter-VLAN Routing on Switch-B-L3*

```
Switch-B-L3# configure terminal
Switch-B-L3(config)# interface port-channel 1.2
Switch-B-L3(config-if)# encapsulation dot1q 2
Switch-B-L3(config-if)# ip address 192.168.2.2 255.255.255.0
Switch-B-L3(config-if)# exit
Switch-B-L3(config)# interface port-channel 1.3
Switch-B-L3(config-if)# encapsulation dot1q 3
Switch-B-L3(config-if)# ip address 192.168.3.1 255.255.255.0
Switch-B-L3(config-if)# end
Switch-B-L3# ping 192.168.2.100

Type escape sequence to abort.
Sending 5, 100-byte ICMP Echos to 192.168.2.100, timeout is 2 seconds:
!!!!!
Success rate is 100 percent (5/5), round-trip min/avg/max = 1/2/4 ms
Switch-B-L3# ping 192.168.2.1

Type escape sequence to abort.
Sending 5, 100-byte ICMP Echos to 192.168.2.1, timeout is 2 seconds:
!!!!!
Success rate is 100 percent (5/5), round-trip min/avg/max = 1/2/4 ms
```

continues

In Example 5-26, create a subinterface for each VLAN that you want the routing module to attach to. Referring to Figure 5-15, the routing module must route for VLAN 2 and VLAN 3; hence, two subinterfaces are created for each of these VLANs. The configuration here is identical to what was configured on the trunk from Router-B to Switch-A in Scenario 5-1 (see Example 5-4). The only difference here is that you are configuring an EtherChannel trunk rather than a physical trunk interface. After the configuration of each subinterface, connectivity to devices in VLAN 2 is tested. Notice that connectivity to the management interface (192.168.2.100) on the Supervisor engine of Switch-B is verified, as well as connectivity across the trunk to the VLAN 2 interface (192.168.2.1) on Switch-A.

Finally, inter-VLAN routing must be configured on Switch-B-L3, with the interfaces attached to VLAN 2 and VLAN 3 configured as part of the EIGRP routing domain. Example 5-27 shows the configuration required on Switch-B-L3.

Example 5-27 *Configuring Inter-VLAN Routing on Switch-B-L3*

```
Switch-B-L3# configure terminal
Switch-B-L3(config)# router eigrp 1
Switch-B-L3(config-router)# network 192.168.2.0
Switch-B-L3(config-router)# network 192.168.3.0
```

In Example 5-27, it is very important that you configure EIGRP for the same autonomous system number as configured on Switch-A, using the **router eigrp 1** command. This ensures that both routers are participating in the same routing domain and can exchange routes. Switch-B-L3 is then configured so that interfaces attached to the 192.168.2.0/24 and 192.168.3.0/24 networks belong to the routing domain.

After a few seconds, an EIGRP adjacency forms between Switch-A and Switch-B-L3 and routes exchange. On either device, you should be able to see any subnets not locally attached in the routing table, since they have been learned via EIGRP. Example 5-28 demonstrates the use of the **show ip route** command on Switch-B-L3.

Example 5-28 *Verifying IP Routing on Switch-B-L3*

```
Switch-B-L3# show ip route
Codes: C - connected, S - static, I - IGRP, R - RIP, M - mobile, B - BGP
       D - EIGRP, EX - EIGRP external, O - OSPF, IA - OSPF inter area
       N1 - OSPF NSSA external type 1, N2 - OSPF NSSA external type 2
       E1 - OSPF external type 1, E2 - OSPF external type 2, E - EGP
       i - IS-IS, L1 - IS-IS level-1, L2 - IS-IS level-2, * - candidate default
       U - per-user static route, o - ODR

Gateway of last resort is not set

D    192.168.1.0/24 [90/0] via 192.168.2.1
C    192.168.2.0/24 is directly connected, Port-channel1.2
C    192.168.3.0/24 is directly connected, Port-channel1.3
```

As you can see from the shaded output of Example 5-28, a route for the 192.168.1.0/24 network exists, which is reachable via 192.168.2.1. This route has been learned via EIGRP, as indicated by the code D to the left of the route entry.

Verifying Connectivity

You have now configured the scenario topology for full inter-VLAN routing between Host-A and Host-B. At this stage you should be able to ping any IP interface in the network from any location.

On Switch-A, you should be able to successfully ping the VLAN 3 interface on Switch-B-L3 (192.168.3.1), as shown in Example 5-29.

Example 5-29 *Testing* **ping** *Connectivity from Switch-A to Switch-B-L3*

```
Switch-A# ping 192.168.3.1
Type escape sequence to abort.
Sending 5, 100-byte ICMP Echos to 192.168.3.1, timeout is 2 seconds:
!!!!!
Success rate is 100 percent (5/5), round-trip min/avg/max = 0/1/4 ms
```

Example 5-29 confirms that Switch-A has the appropriate routing information for the 192.168.3.0/24 network.

On Switch-B, you should be able to successfully ping interface fa0/1 on Switch-B-L3 (192.168.1.1) as shown in Example 5-30.

Example 5-30 *Testing* **ping** *Connectivity from Switch-B-L3 to Switch-A*

```
Switch-B-L3# ping 192.168.1.1
Type escape sequence to abort.
Sending 5, 100-byte ICMP Echos to 192.168.1.1, timeout is 2 seconds:
!!!!!
Success rate is 100 percent (5/5), round-trip min/avg/max = 0/1/4 ms
```

Example 5-30 confirms that Switch-B-L3 has the appropriate routing information for the 192.168.1.0/24 network.

Finally, assuming Host-A and Host-B are connected to the network and configured appropriately, you should be able to successfully ping between these hosts. Example 5-31 shows an example of Host-A successfully pinging Host-B.

Example 5-31 *Testing* **ping** *Connectivity from Host-A to Host-B*

```
C:\WINXP\SYSTEM32> ping 192.168.3.100
Pinging 192.168.3.100 with 32 bytes of data:

Reply from 192.168.3.100: bytes=32 time=1ms TTL=255
Reply from 192.168.3.100: bytes=32 time=1ms TTL=255
Reply from 192.168.3.100: bytes=32 time=1ms TTL=255
Reply from 192.168.3.100: bytes=32 time=1ms TTL=255
```

continues

Example 5-31 *Testing* **ping** *Connectivity from Host-A to Host-B (Continued)*

```
Ping statistics for 192.168.3.100:
    Packets: Sent = 4, Received = 4, Lost = 0 (0% loss),
Approximate round trip times in milli-seconds:
    Minimum = 1ms, Maximum = 1ms, Average = 1ms
```

Scenario 5-3: Implementing a Redundant Multilayer Topology

In the previous two scenarios, you learned about inter-VLAN routing architectures, which
enable routing between VLANs in a LAN topology. In this scenario, it is time to demonstrate more of the big picture. Instead of focusing on a simple LAN topology, in this
scenario, you learn how to configure a reasonably complex network using a multilayer design.
Possessing a knowledge of inter-VLAN routing is a fundamental requirement for implementing a multilayer design. You learn how to apply the techniques learned in the first two
scenarios to enable a multilayer topology that is scalable, available, and performs well.

Figure 5-16 shows the topology used for this scenario.

Figure 5-16 *Scenario 5-3 Topology*

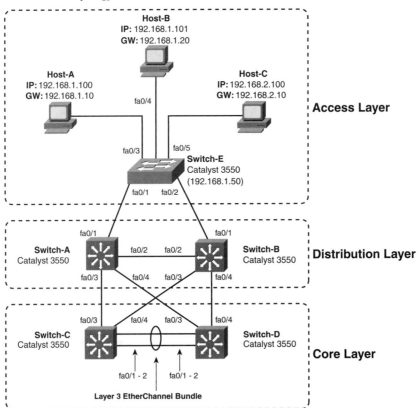

The following describes the function of each component of the scenario topology shown in Figure 5-16:

- Switch-E is a Catalyst 3550-24 switch that provides Layer 2 access for each of the hosts. Switch-E is considered an access layer switch, providing connectivity for hosts in two separate VLANs (VLAN 100 and VLAN 200).

- Switch-A and Switch-B are Catalyst 3550-24 Layer 3 switches that provide connectivity between VLAN 100 and VLAN 200, as well as the rest of the network. Switch-A and Switch-B are considered distribution layer switches.

- Switch-C and Switch-D are Catalyst 3550-24 L3 switches that represent the core of the network and are responsible for routing packets originated in VLAN 100 and VLAN 200 to other destinations in the network and vice versa.

- Host-A and Host-B are workstations attached to VLAN 100 and VLAN 200 respectively.

At the edge of the network, where Switch-A and Switch-B provide routing for the access layer, HSRP is configured to provide default gateway redundancy for all end devices in VLAN 100 and VLAN 200. Within the core and distribution layers, OSPF is configured as the dynamic routing protocol, which is the standards-based, link-state routing protocol of choice for many networks today.

Understanding the Scenario Layer 3 Topology

The physical topology shown in Figure 5-16 does not represent the logical topology of the lab well. Figure 5-17 illustrates the logical topology of the lab from an IP perspective.

In Figure 5-17, the network topology essentially consists of a single Layer 2 domain, which includes Switch-E and its connected hosts. Switch-A and Switch-B also connect to the Layer 2 domain but also include routing components that terminate the Layer 2 domain, routing traffic sent to and from the devices in the Layer 2 domain. The most important concept of Figure 5-17 is that the topology includes hierarchy. Hierarchy is achieved by splitting the network into layers as follows:

- **Access layer**—Provides LAN connectivity to the network for end devices. In a multilayer topology, access layer switches are typically Layer 2 switches. In Figure 5-17, Switch-E is an access layer switch.

- **Distribution layer**—In a multilayer LAN topology, the distribution layer forms the boundary between the Layer 2 domain that includes the access layer and the remaining Layer 2 or Layer 3 topology of the core. Layer 3 switches are implemented at this layer and are normally configured as the default gateway for devices in the access layer. In Figure 5-17, Switch-A and Switch-B are distribution layer devices.

- **Core layer**—The core layer can be based on either a high-speed Layer 2 backbone or a high-speed Layer 3 backbone. With modern core switches now supporting Layer 3 switching with no performance penalties, many organizations implement a Layer 3 backbone for the core, with all connections between core switches being routed connections rather than Layer 2 connections. In Figure 5-17, Switch-C and Switch-D are core devices.

Figure 5-17 *Scenario 5-3 IP Topology*

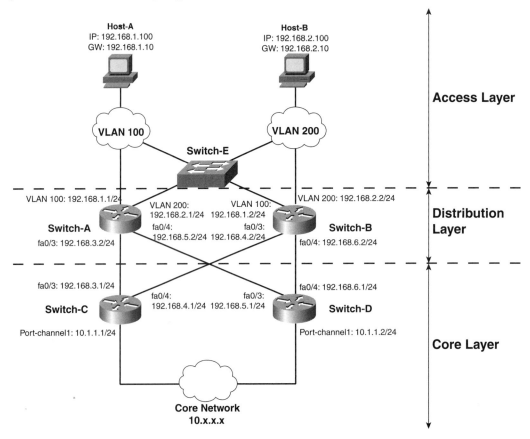

NOTE	The hierarchical nature of a multilayer design makes the network more scalable, available, and increases network performance.

Scenario Prerequisites

To successfully commence the configuration tasks required to complete this scenario, the following lists the prerequisite configuration tasks required on each switch in the scenario topology:

- **Hostname**—each switch should be configured with an appropriate hostname as per Figure 5-16.

- **Telnet/Enable password**—each switch should be configured with an appropriate telnet and enable password.

This scenario assumes the configuration tasks listed above have already been implemented and hence does not include the configuration of these tasks.

Table 5-1 describes the prerequisite configurations required on each host in the scenario topology. Any configurations not listed can be assumed as being the default configuration.

Table 5-1   *Scenario 5-3 Requirements*

Device	Required Configuration	
	Parameter	**Value**
Host-A	Operating System	Windows 2000 Professional or Windows XP
	IP Address	192.168.1.100/24
	Default Gateway	192.168.1.10
Host-B	Operating System	Windows 2000 Professional or Windows XP
	IP Address	192.168.2.100/24
	Default Gateway	192.168.2.10

Configuration Tasks

Configuring a multilayer LAN topology requires configuration of both Layer 2 and Layer 3 parameters on each of the various switching and routing devices in the network. To complete this scenario you need to perform the following tasks:

- Configuring Layer 2 parameters
- Configuring Layer 3 parameters
- Verifying connectivity

Configuring Layer 2 Parameters

In this scenario, the network can be viewed as two separate parts:

- **Layer 2 domain**—This encompasses Switch-E and the layer interfaces on Switch-A and Switch-B. Within this domain, all devices within the same VLAN can communicate directly at Layer 2.

- **Layer 3 domain**—This encompasses the entire network; however, it can be broken into separate IP subnets, which allows hierarchy to be introduced into the network. IP subnets exist for each VLAN in the Layer 2 domain, while IP subnets also exist for each routed link to the core of the network.

When working with Catalyst switches that integrate both Layer 2 and Layer 3 functionality, it is important to be able to recognize the separate Layer 2 and Layer 3 components of the network and then configure each component separately, starting with the Layer 2 component. Once the Layer 2 component is configured and verified, a stable foundation is in place to overlay the Layer 3 component of the network in a trouble-free manner. In this section, you configure the Layer 2 component of the scenario topology. The following lists the configuration tasks required to complete this configuration:

- Configuring the distribution layer switches
- Configuring the access layer switches

Configuring the Distribution Layer Switches

In this scenario, Switch-A and Switch-B are distribution layer switches (providing both Layer 2 and Layer 3 services) enabling communications between devices attached to the access layer and the rest of the network (reachable via the core). From a Layer 2 perspective, Switch-A and Switch-B form essentially the core of the Layer 2 domain that includes Switch-A, Switch-B, and Switch-E and, hence, must be configured appropriately for this role from a Layer 2 perspective. In a real-world network, there could be tens of access switches in the access layer, all connected to Switch-A and Switch-B. Switch-A and Switch-B are the center of the Layer 2 domain, qualifying their designation as the core of the Layer 2 domain.

Based upon the role of Switch-A and Switch-B in the Layer 2 domain, the following describes the various Layer 2 configuration parameters that must be implemented and how they should be configured on Switch-A and Switch-B:

- **VLAN Trunking Protocol**—VTP enables a central VLAN database to be configured that is shared between Switch-A, Switch-B, and all other access layer switches. In an environment where there are many access layer switches and VLANs, using VTP eases the administrative overhead of managing VLANs. Switch-A and Switch-B should be configured as VTP servers, providing VTP server redundancy, while any access layer switches should be configured as VTP clients.

- **VLANs**—After configuring VTP, you can then create VLANs that are distributed to other switches in the VTP domain. In this scenario, VLAN 100 and VLAN 200 must be created.

- **Trunks**—Trunk connections are required between the distribution layer switches and access layer switches to allow traffic from multiple VLANs to be transported over the same physical connection. A trunk is also required between Switch-A and Switch-B to enable redundancy in the network should any access layer switch uplink fail. In this scenario, the VLANs enabled on each trunk can be restricted to VLAN 1 (native VLAN), VLAN 100, and VLAN 200.

- **Spanning tree**—Spanning tree must be configured so that Switch-A is the root bridge and Switch-B is the secondary root bridge, or vice versa. This ensures that the Layer 2 topology formed between Switch-A, Switch-B, and access layer switches is optimal and loop free. In this scenario, to enable load sharing on the uplinks between the access layer and distribution layer, Switch-A should be configured as the root bridge for VLAN 100, while Switch-B should be configured as the root bridge for VLAN 200.

Example 5-32 shows the configuration required on Switch-A to configure VTP, VLANs, trunks, and spanning tree as just described.

Example 5-32 *Configuring Layer 2 Parameters on Switch-A*

```
Switch-A# configure terminal
Switch-A(config)# vtp mode server
Device mode already VTP SERVER.
Switch-A(config)# vtp domain lanps
Changing VTP domain name from NULL to lanps
Switch-A(config)# vlan 100
Switch-A(config-vlan)# name VLAN100
Switch-A(config-vlan)# exit
Switch-A(config)# vlan 200
Switch-A(config-vlan)# name VLAN200
Switch-A(config-vlan)# exit
Switch-A(config)# interface range FastEthernet 0/1 - 2
Switch-A(config-if-range)# switchport trunk allowed vlan 1,100,200,1002-1005
Switch-A(config-if-range)# exit
Switch-A(config)# spanning-tree vlan 1 root primary diameter 4
% This switch is already the root bridge of the VLAN0001 spanning tree
 vlan 1 bridge priority set to 24576
 vlan 1 bridge max aging time set to 14
 vlan 1 bridge hello time unchanged at 2
 vlan 1 bridge forward delay set to 10
Switch-A(config)# spanning-tree vlan 100 root primary diameter 4
% This switch is already the root bridge of the VLAN100 spanning tree
 vlan 100 bridge priority set to 24576
 vlan 100 bridge max aging time set to 14
 vlan 100 bridge hello time unchanged at 2
 vlan 100 bridge forward delay set to 10
Switch-A(config)# spanning-tree vlan 200 root secondary diameter 4
 vlan 200 bridge priority set to 28672
 vlan 200 bridge max aging time set to 14
 vlan 200 bridge hello time unchanged at 2
 vlan 200 bridge forward delay set to 10
```

In Example 5-32, VTP is first configured, with Switch-A being configured as a VTP server and a VTP domain defined; VLAN 100 and VLAN 200 are then created. Next, the trunk interfaces to Switch-E (fa0/1) and Switch-B (fa0/2) are configured, with the allowed VLAN list on the interfaces effectively restricted to VLAN 1, VLAN 100, and VLAN 200 (VLAN 1002–1005 are always required on trunk interfaces on the Catalyst 3550 and cannot be removed). Notice that you do not need to configure any other trunking parameters because by default Layer 2 interfaces on the Catalyst 3550 are configured with a DTP mode of desirable, meaning any interswitch connection between Catalyst 3550 switches forms a trunk by default (assuming the VTP domain name is identical on both switches). Finally, spanning tree is configured, with Switch-A configured as the root bridge for VLAN 1 and VLAN 100 and configured as the secondary root bridge for VLAN 200. Notice that the network diameter is configured as 4, while only three switches are present in the Layer 2 domain for this scenario. This is to reflect the network diameter when more than one access layer switch is present in the network.

Now that Switch-A is configured, Switch-B can be configured. When configuring Switch-B, because Switch-A is already present in the network as a VTP server, you should first configure VTP and then verify that VLAN 100 and VLAN 200 have been propagated to the VLAN database on Switch-B via VTP. Example 5-33 shows the process of configuring VTP and then verifying VLANs that have been propagated via VTP on Switch-B.

Example 5-33 *Configuring VTP and Verifying VLANs on Switch-B*

```
Switch-B# configure terminal
Switch-B(config)# vtp mode server
Device mode already VTP SERVER.
Switch-B(config)# vtp domain lanps
Changing VTP domain name from NULL to lanps
Switch-B(config)# exit
Switch-B# show vlan

VLAN Name                             Status    Ports
---- -------------------------------- --------- -------------------------------
1    default                          active    Fa0/1, Fa0/2, Fa0/3, Fa0/4, Fa0/6, Fa0/7,
                                                 Fa0/8, Fa0/9, Fa0/10, Fa0/11, Fa0/12,
                                                 Fa0/13, Fa0/14, Fa0/15, Fa0/16, Fa0/17,
                                                 Fa0/18, Fa0/19, Fa0/20, Fa0/21, Fa0/22,
                                                 Fa0/23, Fa0/24, Gi0/1, Gi0/2
100  VLAN0100                         active
200  VLAN0200                         active
1002 fddi-default                     active
1003 token-ring-default               active
1004 fddinet-default                  active
1005 trnet-default                    active

VLAN Type  SAID       MTU   Parent RingNo BridgeNo Stp  BrdgMode Trans1 Trans2
---- ----- ---------- ----- ------ ------ -------- ---- -------- ------ ------
1    enet  100001     1500  -      -      -        -    -        0      0
100  enet  100100     1500  -      -      -        -    -        0      0
200  enet  100200     1500  -      -      -        -    -        0      0
```

Example 5-33 *Configuring VTP and Verifying VLANs on Switch-B (Continued)*

```
1002 fddi   101002   1500 -     -     -       -   -   0   0
1003 tr     101003   1500 -     -     -       -   -   0   0
1004 fdnet  101004   1500 -     -     -     ieee  -   0   0
1005 trnet  101005   1500 -     -     -     ibm   -   0   0

Remote SPAN VLANs
------------------------------------------------------------------------


Primary Secondary Type             Ports
------- --------- ---------------- ---------------------------------------
```

As you can see in Example 5-33, VLAN 100 and VLAN 200 are present in the VLAN database of Switch-B. Now that the VLAN databases between Switch-A and Switch-B are synchronized, all remaining Layer 2 parameters can be configured on Switch-B. Example 5-34 shows the remaining Layer 2 configuration required on Switch-B.

Example 5-34 *Configuring Layer 2 Parameters on Switch-B*

```
Switch-B# configure terminal
Switch-B(config)# interface range FastEthernet 0/1 - 2
Switch-B(config-if-range)# switchport trunk allowed vlan 1,100,200,1002-1005
Switch-B(config-if-range)# exit
Switch-B(config)# spanning-tree vlan 1 root secondary diameter 4
 vlan 1 bridge priority set to 28672
 vlan 1 bridge max aging time set to 14
 vlan 1 bridge hello time unchanged at 2
 vlan 1 bridge forward delay set to 10
Switch-B(config)# spanning-tree vlan 100 root secondary diameter 4
 vlan 100 bridge priority set to 28672
 vlan 100 bridge max aging time set to 14
 vlan 100 bridge hello time unchanged at 2
 vlan 100 bridge forward delay set to 10
Switch-B(config)# spanning-tree vlan 200 root primary diameter 4
 vlan 200 bridge priority set to 24576
 vlan 200 bridge max aging time set to 14
 vlan 200 bridge hello time unchanged at 2
 vlan 200 bridge forward delay set to 10
```

In Example 5-34, the trunk interfaces to Switch-A and Switch-E are configured to effectively permit traffic only from VLAN 1, VLAN 100, and VLAN 200. Switch-B is then configured as the secondary root bridge for VLAN 1 and VLAN 100 and is configured as the primary root bridge for VLAN 200. It is a good idea to verify the spanning tree configuration, ensuring Switch-A is the root bridge for VLAN 1 and VLAN 100, while Switch-B is the root bridge for VLAN 200. Example 5-35 demonstrates the use of the **show spanning-tree summary** command on Switch-B.

Example 5-35 *Verifying Spanning Tree*

```
Switch-B# show spanning-tree summary
Root bridge for: VLAN0200.
Extended system ID is enabled.
PortFast BPDU Guard is disabled
EtherChannel misconfiguration guard is enabled
UplinkFast is disabled
BackboneFast is disabled
Default pathcost method used is short

Name                   Blocking Listening Learning Forwarding STP Active
---------------------- -------- --------- -------- ---------- ----------
VLAN0001                   0        0        0         2          2
VLAN0100                   0        0        0         2          2
VLAN0200                   0        0        0         2          2
---------------------- -------- --------- -------- ---------- ----------
3 vlans                    0        0        0         6          6
```

In Example 5-35, the shaded output indicates that Switch-B is the root bridge for VLAN 200. This implies that Switch-A is the root bridge for VLAN 1 and VLAN 100, although it is a good idea to check this explicitly on Switch-A.

Configuring the Access Layer Switches

Now that the distribution layer is in place from a Layer 2 perspective, the access layer can be configured. In this scenario, Switch-E is an access layer switch, as it provides Layer 2 connectivity for end devices, such as Host-A and Host-B. The following describes the Layer 2 parameters that must be configured on Switch-E:

- **VLAN Trunking Protocol**—Switch-E and any other access layer switch must be configured as a VTP client, which enables the VLANs configured on the VTP servers (Switch-A and Switch-B) to be learned automatically.

- **VLANs**—Interfaces fa0/3, fa0/4, and fa0/5 must be configured as access ports and placed into the appropriate VLANs. Interfaces fa0/3 and fa0/4 are to be placed into VLAN 100, and interface fa0/5 is to be placed into VLAN 200.

- **Trunks**—Interface fa0/1 and interface fa0/2 are trunk connections to each distribution layer switch and the configuration on these trunks should match the configuration on the distribution layer switches. This requires the allowed VLAN list to permit traffic only from VLAN 1, VLAN 100, and VLAN 200.

- **Spanning tree**—Spanning tree does not require modification in terms of bridge priority and spanning-tree timers because Switch-A or Switch-B is configured as the root bridge for each VLAN. To improve convergence in the event of an uplink failure, spanning tree UplinkFast should be enabled on Switch-E.

Example 5-36 shows the Layer 2 configuration required on Switch-E.

Example 5-36   *Configuring Layer 2 Parameters on Switch-E*

```
Switch-E# configure terminal
Switch-E(config)# vtp mode client
Setting device to VTP CLIENT mode.
Switch-E(config)# vtp domain lanps
Changing VTP domain name from NULL to lanps
Switch-E(config)# interface range FastEthernet 0/3 - 4
Switch-E(config-if-range)# switchport mode access
Switch-E(config-if-range)# switchport access vlan 100
Switch-E(config-if-range)# exit
Switch-E(config)# interface range FastEthernet 0/5
Switch-E(config-if-range)# switchport mode access
Switch-E(config-if-range)# switchport access vlan 200
Switch-E(config-if-range)# exit
Switch-E(config)# interface range FastEthernet 0/1 - 2
Switch-E(config-if-range)# switchport trunk allowed vlan 1,100,200,1002-1005
Switch-E(config-if-range)# exit
Switch-E(config)# spanning-tree uplinkfast
```

Configuring Layer 3 Parameters

Now that the appropriate Layer 2 configuration is in place, Layer 3 parameters such as inter-VLAN routing and HSRP can be configured. When configuring Layer 3 parameters in a topology similar to the one used for this scenario, where there are clear access, distribution, and core layers, configure each of these layers separately, starting from the core and finishing with the access layer. The following lists the configuration tasks required to configure inter-VLAN routing and HSRP for this scenario:

- Configuring the core
- Configuring the distribution layer
- Configuring the access layer

Configuring the Core

The core used for this scenario consists of Switch-C and Switch-D, with both switches providing connectivity to the "core" of the network (10.x.x.x) for the distribution layer switches (Switch-A and Switch-B). The configuration tasks for the core can be split into two:

- Configuring routed interfaces
- Configuring dynamic routing

Configuring Routed Interfaces   All connections on Switch-C and Switch-D are routed (Layer 3) connections, which means within the core the EtherChannel bundle between Switch-C and Switch-D must be configured as a Layer 3 interface, as opposed to a Layer 2 interface. So far in this book you have not learned how to configure Layer 3 EtherChannel bundles, so it is important to discuss the configuration required. Creating a Layer 3 Ether-

Channel bundle is almost identical to how you create a Layer 2 EtherChannel bundle. The only difference is that you assign Layer 3 (routed) interfaces to the bundle instead of Layer 2 (switched) interfaces.

NOTE   Note that on the Catalyst 3550, you cannot configure Layer 3 interfaces as trunks, unlike Cisco routers that support trunking. Layer 3 interfaces include SVI interfaces, routed physical interfaces, and Layer 3 EtherChannel bundles. If you need to support traffic from multiple VLANs over a routed connection, you must configure the connection as a Layer 2 trunk and then create an SVI for each VLAN on the trunk.

Example 5-37 and Example 5-38 shows the configuration required on Switch-C and Switch-D to configure the Layer 3 EtherChannel bundle between the switches.

Example 5-37   *Configuring a Layer 3 EtherChannel Bundle on Switch-C*

```
Switch-C# configure terminal
Switch-C(config)# interface range fastEthernet 0/1 - 2
Switch-C(config-if-range)# no switchport
Switch-C(config-if-range)# channel-group 1 mode desirable
Creating a port-channel interface Port-channel1
Switch-C(config-if-range)# exit
Switch-C(config)# interface Port-channel 1
Switch-C(config-if)# ip address 10.1.1.1 255.255.255.0
Switch-C(config-if)# exit
```

Example 5-38   *Configuring a Layer 3 EtherChannel Bundle on Switch-D*

```
Switch-D# configure terminal
Switch-D(config)# interface range fastEthernet 0/1 - 2
Switch-D(config-if-range)# no switchport
Switch-D(config-if-range)# channel-group 1 mode desirable
Creating a port-channel interface Port-channel1
Switch-D(config-if-range)# exit
Switch-D(config)# interface port-channel 1
Switch-D(config-if)# ip address 10.1.1.2 255.255.255.0
Switch-D(config-if)# exit
```

In Example 5-37 and Example 5-38, notice that the physical interfaces that comprise each bundle are first configured as routed interfaces using the **no switchport** command. The interfaces are then configured as an EtherChannel bundle using the **channel-group** interface configuration command, with a port-channel interface created that represents the bundle as a logical Layer 3 interface.

NOTE   Notice that you can configure PAgP on Layer 3 EtherChannel bundles on the Catalyst 3550. On traditional Cisco routers, PAgP is not supported, meaning you must configure a PAgP mode of on if you are connecting a Layer 3 EtherChannel bundle on the Catalyst 3550 to a Cisco router.

Once the physical interface configuration is complete, all subsequent Layer 3 configuration is performed on the port-channel interfaces created. After the configuration of Example 5-37 and Example 5-38, you should be able to verify IP connectivity between Switch-C and Switch-D, as demonstrated in Example 5-39.

Example 5-39 *Verifying IP Connectivity between Switch-C and Switch-D*

```
Switch-C# ping 10.1.1.2

Type escape sequence to abort.
Sending 5, 100-byte ICMP Echos to 10.1.1.2, timeout is 2 seconds:
.!!!!
Success rate is 80 percent (4/5), round-trip min/avg/max = 1/1/4 ms
```

In Example 5-39, the initial timeout is caused by the delays associated with the ARP process determining the MAC address associated with 10.1.1.2.

Now that the IP connectivity in the core has been established, it is time to configure IP connectivity to the distribution layer switches. Example 5-40 and Example 5-41 show the configuration required on Switch-C and Switch-D.

Example 5-40 *Configuring Routed Interfaces to Distribution Layer on Switch-C*

```
Switch-C# configure terminal
Switch-C(config)# interface fastEthernet 0/3
Switch-C(config-if)# description CONNECTED TO SWITCH-A
Switch-C(config-if)# no switchport
Switch-C(config-if)# ip address 192.168.3.1 255.255.255.0
Switch-C(config-if)# exit
Switch-C(config)# interface fastEthernet 0/4
Switch-C(config-if)# description CONNECTED TO SWITCH-B
Switch-C(config-if)# no switchport
Switch-C(config-if)# ip address 192.168.4.1 255.255.255.0
Switch-C(config-if)# exit
```

Example 5-41 *Configuring Routed Interfaces to Distribution Layer on Switch-D*

```
Switch-D# configure terminal
Switch-D(config)# interface fastEthernet 0/3
Switch-D(config-if)# description CONNECTED TO SWITCH-A
Switch-D(config-if)# no switchport
Switch-D(config-if)# ip address 192.168.5.1 255.255.255.0
Switch-D(config-if)# exit
```

continues

Example 5-41 *Configuring Routed Interfaces to Distribution Layer on Switch-D (Continued)*

```
Switch-D(config)# interface fastEthernet 0/4
Switch-D(config-if)# description CONNECTED TO SWITCH-B
Switch-D(config-if)# no switchport
Switch-D(config-if)# ip address 192.168.6.1 255.255.255.0
Switch-D(config-if)# exit
```

At this stage, you cannot verify connectivity to Switch-A and Switch-B because these switches have not yet been configured.

Configuring Dynamic Routing   The final configuration task for the core is to configure dynamic routing. For this scenario, OSPF is to be configured, with core network (10.1.1.0/24) configured in Area 0 and the networks connected to the distribution layer switches configured in Area 1. This requires both Switch-C and Switch-D to be configured as area border routers, meaning they are members of more than one area.

NOTE   An in-depth discussion as to OSPF theory and configuration is outside the scope of this book. The configuration of this scenario is included to give you exposure to the dynamic routing capabilities of the Catalyst 3550 switch. For more information on configuring OSPF in a practical lab environment, refer to *CCNP Practical Studies: Routing* by Henry Benjamin from Cisco Press.

Example 5-42 and Example 5-43 show the OSPF configuration required on Switch-C and Switch-D.

Example 5-42 *Configuring OSPF on Switch-C*

```
Switch-C# configure terminal
Switch-C(config)# ip routing
Switch-C(config)# router ospf 1
Switch-C(config-router)# network 10.1.1.0 0.0.0.255 area 0
Switch-C(config-router)# network 192.168.3.0 0.0.0.255 area 1
Switch-C(config-router)# network 192.168.4.0 0.0.0.255 area 1
Switch-C(config-router)# area 0 range 10.0.0.0 255.0.0.0
Switch-C(config-router)# area 1 range 192.168.0.0 255.255.248.0
```

Example 5-43 *Configuring OSPF on Switch-D*

```
Switch-D# configure terminal
Switch-D(config)# ip routing
Switch-D(config)# router ospf 1
Switch-D(config-router)# network 10.1.1.0 0.0.0.255 area 0
Switch-D(config-router)# network 192.168.5.0 0.0.0.255 area 1
Switch-D(config-router)# network 192.168.6.0 0.0.0.255 area 1
Switch-D(config-router)# area 0 range 10.0.0.0 255.0.0.0
Switch-D(config-router)# area 1 range 192.168.0.0 255.255.248.0
```

In Example 5-42 and Example 5-43, an OSPF routing process is first created using the **router ospf 1** command, with the number **1** indicating the process ID.

You can run multiple instances of OSPF on the same router, with a unique process ID required for each instance. The process ID has only local significance, meaning the router can participate in the same OSPF routing domains as other routers configured with a different process ID.

After the routing process is created, each interface is assigned to the appropriate OSPF area, using the **network** command. The **network** command specifies a range of IP addresses using a wildcard mask, which identifies the interfaces to be assigned to the specified area. For example, in Example 5-42, the **network 10.1.1.0 0.0.0.255 area 0** command configures any interfaces with an IP address in the address range 10.1.1.0 – 10.1.1.255 belong to 0. Finally, the **area range** command is used to generate summary routes for each area, reducing the number of inter-area routes in the OSPF routing domain. The **area 0 range 10.0.0.0 255.0.0.0** command configures a summary route of 10.0.0.0/8 that represents any networks in area 0 within the networks summarized by the summary route. The summary route suppresses all other inter-area routes encompassed by it, meaning Switch-C and Switch-D only advertise a route 10.0.0.0/8 from area 0 into area 1 (i.e., to Switch-A and Switch-B), with the 10.1.1.0/24 inter-area route not advertised because it is part of the 10.0.0.0/8 summary route. The **area 1 range 192.168.0.0 255.255.248.0** command ensures only a single route (192.168.0.0/21) from area 1 is advertised into area 0, which encompasses all of the /24 subnets within area 1 (192.168.1.0/24 – 192.168.6.0/24). Figure 5-18 illustrates how summarization of the inter-area routes works.

In Figure 5-18, you can see the inter-area routes advertised by the area border routers Switch-C and Switch-D. Notice that a single summary route is advertised into each area, as described earlier. Without the summary routes being configured, the number of routes advertised into area 0 would be six (192.168.1.0/24 to 192.168.6.0/24).

After completing the OSPF configuration, you should verify OSPF is configured and working correctly. At this stage, because Switch-A and Switch-B are not yet configured for OSPF, no OSPF routes are actually in the routing table of Switch-C or Switch-D. However, you can verify that OSPF neighbor adjacencies have formed correctly using the **show ip ospf neighbor** command, as demonstrated on Switch-C in Example 5-44.

Figure 5-18 *OSPF and Inter-Area Summarization*

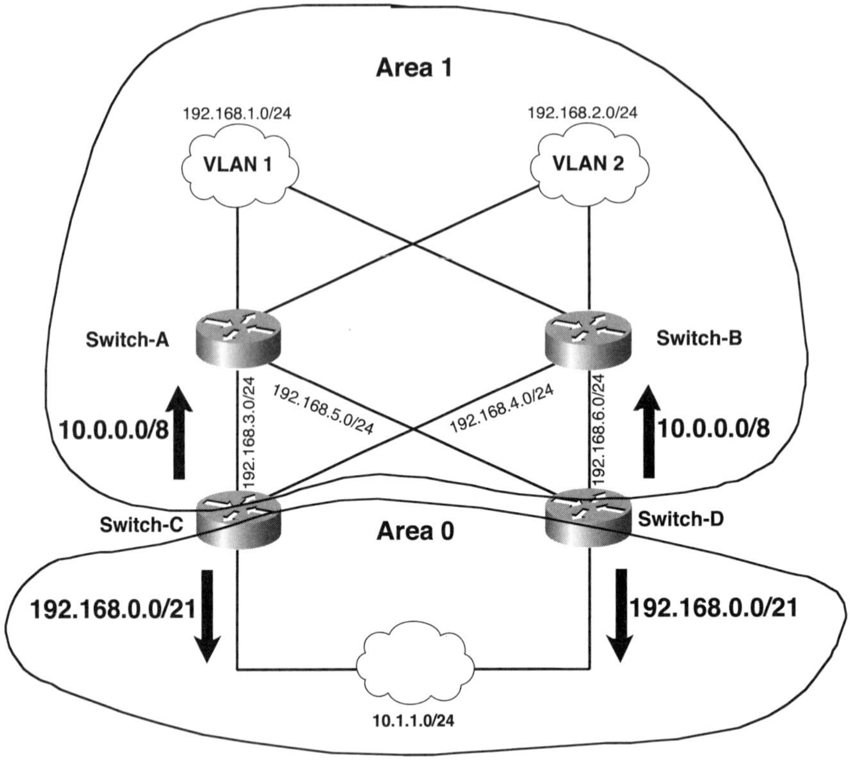

Example 5-44 *Verifying OSPF Neighbors on Switch-C*

```
Switch-C# show ip ospf neighbor

Neighbor ID     Pri   State       Dead Time   Address      Interface
192.168.6.1       1   FULL/DR     00:00:38    10.1.1.2     Port-channel1
```

In Example 5-44, notice that a single OSPF neighbor is known to Switch-C, via the Port-Channel1 interface (i.e., the 10.1.1.0/24 network). The key parameter to look for when verifying OSPF neighbors is the neighbor state, which is FULL/DR in Example 5-44. *FULL* means that a full adjacency has been formed with the neighbor, which means both OSPF routers recognize each other as valid neighbors and routes have been exchanged (this is a normal operational OSPF state). *DR* means that the neighbor is the designated router for the multi-access LAN segment. The DR is responsible for forming adjacencies with all OSPF routers on the same multi-access segment and distributing routes to each, eliminating the requirement for every OSPF router to form an adjacency with every other router.

OSPF also has the concept of a backup designated router (BDR), which in fact in this scenario is Switch-C. The BDR takes over the DR role if the DR fails. For every multi-access LAN segment, a DR and BDR are always elected, with the role chosen based upon the router with the highest router ID. On Switch-C you can see the router ID of Switch-D (the OSPF neighbor) is 192.168.6.1 The router ID is chosen as the highest loopback address on the router or, if no loopbacks are configured, the highest physical interface address. Because no loopbacks are configured on either Switch-C or Switch-D, Switch-C has a router ID of 192.168.4.1, and Switch-D has a router ID of 192.168.6.1. Hence, Switch-D is the DR and Switch-C is the BDR.

Configuring the Distribution Layer

The distribution layer consists of Switch-A and Switch-B, providing default gateway services for access layer devices and providing connectivity to the core. The configuration tasks required on the distribution layer switches are listed below:

- Configuring routed interfaces
- Configuring dynamic routing
- Configuring HSRP

Configuring Routed Interfaces   Switch-A and Switch-B require several routed interfaces to be configured as follows:

- **Interface fa0/3 and fa0/4**—These interfaces must be configured as physical routed interfaces, as they provide routed connections to the core of the network.

- **Interface VLAN 100 and VLAN 200**—These SVI interfaces must be created to allow routing for VLAN 100 and VLAN 200.

Example 5-45 and Example 5-46 show the configuration required on Switch-A and Switch-B to configure routed interfaces.

Example 5-45 *Configuring Routed Interfaces on Switch-A*

```
Switch-A# configure terminal
Switch-A(config)# interface FastEthernet 0/3
Switch-A(config-if)# no switchport
Switch-A(config-if)# ip address 192.168.3.2 255.255.255.0
Switch-A(config-if)# exit
Switch-A(config)# interface FastEthernet 0/4
Switch-A(config-if)# no switchport
Switch-A(config-if)# ip address 192.168.5.2 255.255.255.0
Switch-A(config-if)# exit
Switch-A(config)# interface vlan 100
Switch-A(config-if)# ip address 192.168.1.1 255.255.255.0
Switch-A(config-if)# exit
Switch-A(config)# interface vlan 200
Switch-A(config-if)# ip address 192.168.2.1 255.255.255.0
Switch-A(config-if)# exit
```

Example 5-46 *Configuring Routed Interfaces on Switch-B*

```
Switch-B# configure terminal
Switch-B(config)# interface FastEthernet 0/3
Switch-B(config-if)# no switchport
Switch-B(config-if)# ip address 192.168.4.2 255.255.255.0
Switch-B(config-if)# exit
Switch-B(config)# interface FastEthernet 0/4
Switch-B(config-if)# no switchport
Switch-B(config-if)# ip address 192.168.6.2 255.255.255.0
Switch-B(config-if)# exit
Switch-B(config)# interface vlan 100
Switch-B(config-if)# ip address 192.168.1.2 255.255.255.0
Switch-B(config-if)# exit
Switch-B(config)# interface vlan 200
Switch-B(config-if)# ip address 192.168.2.2 255.255.255.0
Switch-B(config-if)# exit
```

After implementing the configuration of Example 5-45 and Example 5-46, all connectivity between Switch-A, Switch-B, Switch-C, and Switch-D is in place, and you should be able to ping any of these devices from each other. Example 5-47 demonstrates verifying IP connectivity from Switch-A using the **ping** utility.

Example 5-47 *Verifying IP Connectivity from Switch-A*

```
Switch-A# ping 192.168.1.2

Type escape sequence to abort.
Sending 5, 100-byte ICMP Echos to 192.168.1.2, timeout is 2 seconds:
.!!!!
Success rate is 80 percent (4/5), round-trip min/avg/max = 1/1/4 ms
Switch-A# ping 192.168.3.1

Type escape sequence to abort.
Sending 5, 100-byte ICMP Echos to 192.168.3.1, timeout is 2 seconds:
.!!!!
Success rate is 80 percent (4/5), round-trip min/avg/max = 1/1/4 ms
Switch-A# ping 192.168.5.1

Type escape sequence to abort.
Sending 5, 100-byte ICMP Echos to 192.168.5.1, timeout is 2 seconds:
.!!!!
Success rate is 80 percent (4/5), round-trip min/avg/max = 1/1/4 ms
```

In Example 5-47, after an initial timeout due to delays associated with the ARP process, you can see that connectivity to interface VLAN 100 on Switch-B (192.168.1.2), interface fa0/3 on Switch-C (192.168.3.1), and interface fa0/3 on Switch-D (192.168.5.1) is confirmed. IP connectivity to Switch-B verifies the Layer 2 trunk between Switch-A and Switch-B (configured earlier in this scenario) is operational, while IP connectivity to

Configuring Dynamic Routing   As distribution layer switches, Switch-A and Switch-B are to be configured as OSPF routers, with both devices residing in OSPF area 1. OSPF must be configured so that routes for VLAN 100 and VLAN 200 are advertised to the core Layer 3 switches and also to allow Switch-A and Switch-B to learn the 10.0.0.0/8 route being advertised by the core.

Example 5-48 and Example 5-49 show the OSPF configuration required on Switch-A and Switch-B.

Example 5-48 *Configuring OSPF on Switch-A*

```
Switch-A# configure terminal
Switch-A(config)# ip routing
Switch-A(config)# router ospf 1
Switch-A(config-router)# network 192.168.0.0 0.0.255.255 area 1
```

Example 5-49 *Configuring OSPF on Switch-B*

```
Switch-B# configure terminal
Switch-B(config)# ip routing
Switch-B(config)# router ospf 1
Switch-B(config-router)# network 192.168.0.0 0.0.255.255 area 1
```

As you can in Example 5-48 and Example 5-49, the OSPF configuration required on Switch-A and Switch-B is identical and very simple. After IP routing is enabled using the **ip routing** command, an OSPF process is created; the **network** command is used to place all interfaces with an IP address in the address range 192.168.x.x into area 1. Refer back to the Layer 3 topology for this scenario (see Figure 5-17) and notice that all interfaces on Switch-A and Switch-B have IP addressing within the 192.168.x.x range. This means that the **network** command executed in Example 5-48 and Example 5-49 places all routed interfaces into the OSPF routing domain.

After completing the OSPF configuration of Switch-A and Switch-B, adjacencies should form across each of the routed connections, with link state information being exchanged that allows each OSPF router to install the appropriate routes into the local IP routing table. Example 5-50 shows the use of the **show ip ospf neighbor** command on Switch-A to initially verify that all expected adjacencies have formed correctly.

Example 5-50 *Verifying OSPF Neighbors on Switch-A*

```
Switch-A# show ip ospf neighbor

Neighbor ID     Pri   State      Dead Time   Address       Interface
192.168.4.1       1   FULL/BDR   00:00:36    192.168.3.1   FastEthernet0/3
192.168.6.1       1   FULL/DR    00:00:38    192.168.5.1   FastEthernet0/4
192.168.6.2       1   FULL/DR    00:00:32    192.168.1.2   Vlan100
192.168.6.2       1   FULL/DR    00:00:32    192.168.2.2   Vlan200
```

In Example 5-50, notice the four OSPF neighbors, when you might be expecting only three OSPF neighbors (Switch-B, Switch-C, and Switch-D). The reason for four neighbors is the fact that two directly connected paths exist between Switch-A and Switch-B, with an adjacency formed for each of these paths. This illustrates the fact that OSPF adjacencies are formed on a per-interface basis rather than a per-router basis. You can see that two adjacencies have been formed with the same router, as indicated by the two entries for the neighbor with a neighbor ID of 192.168.6.2 (the highest IP address on Switch-B). In Example 5-44, the Interface and Address columns allow you to determine over which interface an adjacency has formed and the IP address of the interface on the neighbor attached to the same Layer 2 segment as the local interface.

Referring again to Example 5-50, all of the adjacencies are operating in the FULL state, which means the adjacency is valid and link state information has been exchanged. This means that all the information required for the SPF calculations that generate OSPF routes has been obtained, and the IP routing table should contain OSPF routes. Example 5-51 demonstrates the use of the **show ip route** command on Switch-A to view the local IP routing table.

Example 5-51 *Viewing the IP Routing Table on Switch-A*

```
Switch-A# show ip route
Codes: C - connected, S - static, I - IGRP, R - RIP, M - mobile, B - BGP
       D - EIGRP, EX - EIGRP external, O - OSPF, IA - OSPF inter area
       N1 - OSPF NSSA external type 1, N2 - OSPF NSSA external type 2
       E1 - OSPF external type 1, E2 - OSPF external type 2, E - EGP
       i - IS-IS, L1 - IS-IS level-1, L2 - IS-IS level-2, ia - IS-IS inter area
       * - candidate default, U - per-user static route, o - ODR
       P - periodic downloaded static route

Gateway of last resort is not set

O IA 10.0.0.0/8 [110/2] via 192.168.3.1, 00:00:32, FastEthernet0/3
                        via 192.168.5.1, 00:00:34, FastEthernet0/4
C    192.168.1.0/24 is directly connected, Vlan100
C    192.168.2.0/24 is directly connected, Vlan200
C    192.168.3.0/24 is directly connected, FastEthernet0/3
O    192.168.4.0/24 [110/2] via 192.168.1.2, 00:00:40, Vlan100
                            via 192.168.2.2, 00:00:40, Vlan200
                            via 192.168.3.1, 00:00:32, FastEthernet0/3
C    192.168.5.0/24 is directly connected, FastEthernet0/4
O    192.168.6.0/24 [110/2] via 192.168.1.2, 00:00:40, Vlan100
                            via 192.168.2.2, 00:00:40, Vlan200
                            via 192.168.5.1, 00:00:34, FastEthernet0/4
```

In Example 5-51, each of the OSPF routes are shaded. The first route is an OSPF inter-area route, as indicated by the **O IA** designation at the beginning of the route entry. This route is the 10.0.0.0/8 summary route generated by Switch-C and Switch-D (see Figure 5-18). Notice that Switch-A has installed two next hop routers for this route—one via 192.168.3.1 (Switch-C) and the other via 192.168.5.1 (Switch-D). Because Switch-C and Switch-D advertise the 10.0.0.0/8 route with the same cost, the routes are considered equal-cost routes and, hence, are both installed into the routing table. The remaining OSPF routes are intra-area routes (i.e., routes within the OSPF area the router belongs to), as indicated by the **O** designation at the beginning of each route entry. These routes represent the subnets that are used to interconnect the distribution layer with the core and are unlikely to be used for normal traffic on the network.

NOTE	By default, Cisco routers and Layer 3 switches install up to four equal-cost routes into the local routing table. This number can be altered by using the **maximum-paths** command under the routing process that you want to modify.

Given that two next hop routers exist for the 10.0.0.0/8 route, you might wonder how traffic sent to a destination within the 10.0.0.0/8 network is actually routed. When equal-cost routes exist in the routing table, load sharing of traffic occurs on either a per-destination basis or per-packet basis.

When load sharing takes place on a per-destination basis, the next hop router chosen is alternated on a per-destination basis. This means that packets sent to the same destination always are sent over the same path; however, packets sent to multiple destinations are load balanced. For example, if a packet is received with a destination IP address of 10.1.1.1, the route via the next hop router 192.168.3.1 (Switch-C) is chosen. If another packet is received with a destination IP address of 10.1.1.1, that packet is always routed via the same next hop router originally chosen (i.e., Switch-C). If a packet is then received with a destination IP address of 10.1.1.2, assuming that for the last load-sharing decision Switch-C was selected as the next hop, Switch-D is selected as the next hop router. Any subsequent packets received with a destination IP address of 10.1.1.2 are always be routed via Switch-D.

When load sharing takes place on a per-packet basis, each packet is load shared, with the destination IP address of each packet having no bearing on the load-sharing decision. For example, if packets are received with the same destination IP address (e.g., 10.1.1.1), the next hop router chosen for delivery of each packet is alternated packet by packet. Load sharing on a per-packet basis is more accurate in terms of the amount of traffic that is actually sent over each path in the network. With per-destination load sharing, large amounts of traffic sent to the same destination can mean one path is used more than the other path.

Now that you understand about per-destination and per-packet load sharing, you might be wondering which load-sharing mechanism is selected. On the Catalyst 3550 switch, only per-destination load sharing is supported; per-packet load sharing is not supported. This means that you have no choice as to how traffic is load shared and must bear this in mind when considering the performance of redundant paths in the network.

Configuring HSRP   All that now remains in terms of Layer 3 configuration at the distribution layer is the configuration of HSRP. HSRP is required to enable redundancy for each default gateway address configured on hosts in the access layer.

HSRP is configured in terms of HSRP groups, where each HSRP group is configured with a number of parameters that define the behavior of the group. These parameters include the following:

- **Group ID**—The group ID identifies a specific HSRP group. HSRP groups are configured on a per-interface basis, and more than one HSRP group can exist on an interface, hence the requirement for a group ID. The group ID can be any value in the range of 0 to 255 (0 is the default group ID).

- **Virtual IP address (Group address)**—The virtual IP address is also known as the *group address* and is the IP address associated with an HSRP group. It is important to understand that routers participating in HSRP are configured with their own separate physical interface IP addresses and can communicate using these IP addresses. In fact, any router control communications, such as dynamic routing protocol packets, are sent using the physical IP address of an interface, rather than the virtual IP address. This extends to Layer 2 communications, where routers listen for frames addressed to both the burned-in address (BIA), as well as the virtual MAC address.

- **Virtual MAC address**—All Layer 3 communications over a LAN require Layer 2 communications to be operational. On Ethernet networks, devices must possess a MAC address to communicate. Hence, a virtual MAC address is required for the virtual IP address associated with an HSRP group. By default, the MAC address associated with a virtual IP address is assigned from a special MAC address pool designated by Cisco for HSRP groups. This MAC address pool is 0000.0c07.ac**, where ** represents the HSRP group number (0-255). For example, if the HSRP group number is 1, the virtual MAC address for the group is 0000.0c07.ac01. When a device on the LAN sends an ARP request for the virtual IP address, the virtual MAC address (e.g., 0000.0c07.ac01) is returned in the ARP reply by the active router. The active router then listens for any frames addressed to the virtual MAC address, ensuring it receives any communications associated with the virtual IP address.

NOTE   The virtual MAC address used can be manually configured, and you can also configure the burned-in address (BIA) to be used instead of the HSRP virtual MAC address (0000.0c07.ac**). The BIA is the hardware address that ships with the router. Some older Cisco routers that use Lance Ethernet controllers only support using a single MAC address at one time. These routers include the Cisco 1000, Cisco 2500, Cisco 3000, and Cisco 4500 series routers. When running HSRP, these routers use *only* the HSRP virtual MAC address if they are active and use the BIA when they are not. Because these routers support only a single MAC address, you cannot configure more than one HSRP group on any single interface.

- **Timers**—HSRP uses periodic Hello messages as a mechanism to detect the failure of other routers within an HSRP group. By default, the Hello timer is used to send Hello messages, and the value of this timer is 3 seconds by default. A remote router within an HSRP group is declared down if a Hello message is not received within the Hold down timer, which is 10 seconds by default. These timer values can be modified to reduce the convergence associated with a failure to milliseconds if required.

- **Priority**—Priority is used to determine which physical router is the active router for a specific HSRP group. Priority is transmitted in each Hello message sent by an HSRP router. The default priority value is 100, but this is configurable. The router with the highest priority in an HSRP group is selected as the active router, which services any communications associated with the virtual IP address and virtual MAC address of the HSRP group.

- **Operational state**—The operational state of a physical router within an HSRP group is non-configurable and is instead determined by the configured priority and current network conditions (e.g., if the active router is operational or if it has failed). An HSRP router can operate in one of four states—Active, Standby, Speaking + Listening, and Listening

- **Preempt**—Although the router with the highest priority is supposed to become the active router, whether this happens or not is often determined by the ability of physical routers to preempt the active router role. If a physical router is attached to the network and belongs to an HSRP group that already has an active router, by default, even if the new router has a higher priority, the existing active router actually remains as the active router. To override this behavior, you can configure physical routers to preempt the active role, which means they assume the active role if they detect they have the highest priority for the group, even if another router already exists as the active router.

- **Interface tracking**—Provides the ability for a physical router to decrement its priority for an HSRP group, based upon the failure of one or more interfaces. Other HSRP routers within the group detect a lower priority in the periodic Hello messages sent by the active router and can then assume the active role as long as their priority is higher than the decremented priority of the active router. The ability to preempt is important for interface tracking, because other standby routers must be able to assert themselves as the active router as soon as they have the highest priority for a group. Careful planning of group priorities is also required to ensure the decremented priority of the active router is lower than the priority of the appropriate standby router(s).

For this scenario, referring back to Figure 5-16, end devices are located within VLAN 100 and VLAN 200. Each host is to be configured with the virtual IP address of an HSRP group consisting of each physical distribution layer router (i.e., Switch-A and Switch-B). Separate HSRP groups are required for VLAN 100 and VLAN 200. To implement load sharing, the active routers for each HSRP group should be different. For VLAN 100, Switch-A is configured as the active router, while for VLAN 200, Switch-B is configured as the active router.

The first HSRP group that must be created is for the virtual IP address (VIP) 192.168.1.10 on VLAN 100. For this group, Switch-A is to be configured as the active router, with Switch-B operating as the standby router. Interface tracking should also be configured on Switch-A, so that if connectivity to the core is degraded (a single connection fails) or completely lost (both connections fail), Switch-A lowers its priority for the group so that Switch-B becomes the active router. To ensure that Switch-A and Switch-B assume the active role when appropriate, both devices must be configured to preempt the active role. Example 5-52 and Example 5-53 show the configuration required on Switch-A and Switch-B to configure HSRP for the 192.168.1.10 VIP.

Example 5-52 *Configuring HSRP for the 192.168.1.10 VIP on Switch-A*

```
Switch-A# configure terminal
Switch-A(config)# interface vlan 100
Switch-A(config-if)# standby 1 ip 192.168.1.10
Switch-A(config-if)# standby 1 priority 200 preempt
Switch-A(config-if)# standby 1 track FastEthernet0/3 50
Switch-A(config-if)# standby 1 track FastEthernet0/4 50
```

Example 5-53 *Configuring HSRP for the 192.168.1.10 VIP on Switch-A*

```
Switch-B# configure terminal
Switch-B(config)# interface vlan 100
Switch-B(config-if)# standby 1 ip 192.168.1.10
Switch-B(config-if)# standby 1 priority 150 preempt
```

The **standby 1 ip 192.168.1.10** command on Switch-A and Switch-B creates an HSRP group with an ID of 1 and a virtual IP address of 192.168.1.10. Switch-A is configured with a priority of 200 for the group, while Switch-B is configured with a priority of 150. This means that Switch-A assumes the active role for the group. Both Switch-A and Switch-B are also configured to preempt the active role.

Notice on Switch-A that the **standby track** command is configured, which enables interface tracking. Both interfaces that are connected to the core are tracked, and in the event that one of these interfaces fails, the priority of the group is configured to decrement by 50.

NOTE   If both interfaces fail on Switch-A in Example 5-48, the priority is decremented by the sum of the decrement values configured for each tracked interface (i.e., 100).

Because the priority of Switch-B is 175, a single interface failure causes the priority of Switch-A to fall to 150, with Switch-B assuming the active role. It is very important that Switch-B is configured to preempt the active role, which ensures it actively takes over active role as soon as the priority of Switch-A falls below 175.

The second HSRP group that must be created is for the virtual IP address (VIP) 192.168.2.10 on VLAN 200. For this group, Switch-B is to be configured as the active router, with Switch-A operating as the standby router. Interface tracking should be configured on the active router (Switch-B). Example 5-54 and Example 5-55 show the configuration required on Switch-A and Switch-B to configure HSRP for the 192.168.2.10 VIP.

Example 5-54 *Configuring HSRP for the 192.168.2.10 VIP on Switch-A*

```
Switch-A# configure terminal
Switch-A(config)# interface vlan 200
Switch-A(config-if)# standby ip 192.168.2.10
Switch-A(config-if)# standby priority 150 preempt
```

Example 5-55 *Configuring HSRP for the 192.168.2.10 VIP on Switch-B*

```
Switch-B# configure terminal
Switch-B(config)# interface vlan 200
Switch-B(config-if)# standby ip 192.168.2.10
Switch-B(config-if)# standby priority 200 preempt
Switch-B(config-if)# standby track FastEthernet0/3 50
Switch-B(config-if)# standby track FastEthernet0/4 50
```

In Example 5-54 and Example 5-55, notice that the group ID is not specified in the **standby** command, which means a group ID of 0 is assumed.

At this point, Switch-A is configured as the active router for the 192.168.1.10 VIP, while Switch-B is configured as the active router for the 192.168.1.20 VIP and 192.168.2.10 VIP. To verify that Switch-A and Switch-B have actually assumed these roles correctly, you can use the **show standby brief** command, as demonstrated in Example 5-56 on Switch-A.

Example 5-56 *Verifying HSRP*

```
Switch-A# show standby brief
                     P indicates configured to preempt.
                     |
                     |
Interface   Grp Prio P State    Active addr    Standby addr   Group addr
Vl100         1   200 P Active   local          192.168.1.2    192.168.1.10
Vl200         0   175 P Standby  192.168.2.2    local          192.168.2.10
```

In Example 5-56, notice that an entry exists for each group. The State column indicates the current status of the router; you can see that Switch-A is active for the group address 192.168.1.10, but is the standby router for the other group.

Configuring the Access Layer

At this stage, the Layer 3 configuration of the network is almost complete. All that remains is for devices in the access layer to be configured with the appropriate default gateway information to enable traffic generated by these devices to be routed correctly through the network. As indicated by Figure 5-16, the following default gateway addresses should be configured for each host:

- **Host-A** — 192.168.1.10

- **Host-B** — 192.168.2.10

Assuming the IP address on each host is configured correctly and the default gateway configuration listed previously is in place, you should be able to ping any interface on any device in the network from each host.

Each of the hosts listed previously are not the only access layer devices in this scenario; Switch-E is also an access layer device and should be configured with an IP address and default gateway to allow for remote network management. Example 5-57 shows the configuration required on Switch-E to configure an IP address and default gateway and then verify connectivity to the rest of the network.

Example 5-57 *Configuring IP on Switch-E*

```
Switch-E# configure terminal
Switch-E(config)# interface vlan 100
Switch-E(config-if)# ip address 192.168.1.50 255.255.255.0
Switch-E(config-if)# exit
Switch-E(config)# ip default-gateway 192.168.1.10
Switch-E(config)# exit
Switch-E# ping 192.168.1.10

Type escape sequence to abort.
Sending 5, 100-byte ICMP Echos to 192.168.1.10, timeout is 2 seconds:
.!!!!
Success rate is 80 percent (4/5), round-trip min/avg/max = 1/1/1 ms
Switch-E# ping 10.1.1.1

Type escape sequence to abort.
Sending 5, 100-byte ICMP Echos to 10.1.1.1, timeout is 2 seconds:
!!!!!
Success rate is 80 percent (5/5), round-trip min/avg/max = 4/4/6 ms
```

Example 5-58 demonstrates verifying connectivity to the second HSRP group on VLAN 100 (192.168.1.20) and each of the VLAN interface IP addresses on Switch-A and Switch-B and then using the **show arp** command to view the ARP cache on Switch-E, where the

MAC addresses associated with the HSRP group on VLAN 100, as well as the interfaces on Switch-A and Switch-B should be present.

Example 5-58 *Testing Connectivity and Viewing the ARP Cache on Switch-E*

```
Switch-E# ping 192.168.1.20

Type escape sequence to abort.
Sending 5, 100-byte ICMP Echos to 192.168.1.20, timeout is 2 seconds:
.!!!!
Success rate is 80 percent (4/5), round-trip min/avg/max = 1/1/1 ms
Switch-E# ping 192.168.1.1

Type escape sequence to abort.
Sending 5, 100-byte ICMP Echos to 192.168.1.1, timeout is 2 seconds:
.!!!!
Success rate is 80 percent (4/5), round-trip min/avg/max = 1/1/1 ms
Switch-E# ping 192.168.1.2

Type escape sequence to abort.
Sending 5, 100-byte ICMP Echos to 192.168.1.2, timeout is 2 seconds:
.!!!!
Success rate is 80 percent (4/5), round-trip min/avg/max = 1/1/1 ms
Switch-E# show arp
Protocol  Address        Age (min)  Hardware Addr   Type   Interface
Internet  192.168.1.1           0   0009.b7aa.9b40  ARPA   Vlan100
Internet  192.168.1.2           0   0009.b7aa.9c80  ARPA   Vlan100
Internet  192.168.1.10          0   0000.0c07.ac01  ARPA   Vlan100
```

In Example 5-58, the shaded lines indicate each of the entries in the ARP cache of Switch-E. Notice that the MAC addresses associated with the VLAN interface IP addresses of Switch-A and Switch-B (192.168.1.1 and 192.168.1.2, respectively) are physical MAC addresses (e.g., 0009.b7aa.9b40), while the MAC address associated with the HSRP group address is based upon the special MAC address family used for HSRP. You can see from the MAC address associated with the HSRP group address 192.168.1.10, that the HSRP group ID is 1, as indicated by the last two hex digits of the MAC address (01).

Verifying Connectivity

All of the required Layer 2 and Layer 3 configuration for the network is now in place. During the configuration tasks in this scenario, much of the network connectivity configured was verified immediately after configuration; hence, network connectivity under normal working operation has been verified. The only remaining verification required is to test how the network reacts during a network failure. In this section, the network path from the access layer to the core of the network is verified during normal operation, and then a network failure is simulated to ensure that the network converges to a working topology in a correct and timely manner.

To verify the path taken for packets sent while the network is in a fully operational state (i.e., all routing devices are operational), you can use the **tracert** utility on Windows (or **traceroute** on Cisco IOS). Example 5-59 demonstrates the use of this utility on Host-A in VLAN 100 for determining the path to the 10.1.1.0/24 network in the core.

Example 5-59 *Determining the Network Path from Host-A to the Core*

```
C:\WINXP\SYSTEM32> tracert -d 10.1.1.1
Tracing route to 10.1.1.1 over a maximum of 30 hops

  1     1 ms      1 ms      1 ms   192.168.1.1
  2    20 ms      8 ms      8 ms   10.1.1.1

Trace complete.
```

In Example 5-59, although the configured default gateway on Host-A is 192.168.1.10, the first response for both traceroutes is from 192.168.1.1 (physical interface on Switch-A), which confirms that Switch-A is indeed the active router for 192.168.1.10.

NOTE   The –d option used with the **tracert** command tells Windows not to attempt to resolve IP addresses to DNS names, which speeds up the traceroute process.

Example 5-60 demonstrates the use of the **tracert** utility on Host-B in VLAN 200 for determining the path to the 10.1.1.0/24 network in the core.

Example 5-60 *Verifying the Network Path from Host-B to the Core*

```
C:\WINXP\SYSTEM32> tracert -d 10.1.1.1
Tracing route to 10.1.1.1 over a maximum of 30 hops

  1     1 ms      1 ms      1 ms   192.168.1.2
  2    18 ms     12 ms      8 ms   10.1.1.1

Trace complete.
```

Notice in Example 5-60 that although the configured default gateway on Host-B is 192.168.1.20, the first response in the traceroute is from 192.168.1.2 (physical interface on Switch-B), which confirms that Switch-B is the active router for 192.168.1.20. This means that Switch-A and Switch-B are load sharing because each router is active for one of HSRP groups.

Now that the active routers have been verified on VLAN 100 and VLAN 200, it is time to test how the network responds to failure. When testing HSRP failover, it is useful to generate a constant stream of traffic between devices that are affected by the HSRP failover event, so you can monitor when connectivity is lost and how long it takes for connectivity to be restored. Example 5-61 shows how to generate a continuous ping on Host-A.

Example 5-61 *Establishing a Continuous **ping** Between Host-A and Host-B*

```
C:\WINXP\SYSTEM32> ping 192.168.2.100 -t
Pinging 192.168.2.100 with 32 bytes of data:

Reply from 192.168.2.100: bytes=32 time<1ms TTL=255
Reply from 192.168.2.100: bytes=32 time<1ms TTL=255
Reply from 192.168.2.100: bytes=32 time<1ms TTL=255
Reply from 192.168.2.100: bytes=32 time<1ms TTL=255
Reply from 192.168.2.100: bytes=32 time<1ms TTL=255
… (Output Repeated Continuously)
…
```

In Example 5-61, ping packets are generated continuously between VLAN 100 and VLAN 200, with replies received continuously while the network is up and running.

While you are keeping a close eye on the continuous ping established in Example 5-61, Example 5-62 shows what happens to the continuous ping after Switch-A is powered off.

Example 5-62 *Continuous **ping** Between Host-A and Host-B after Switch-A is Powered off*

```
Reply from 192.168.2.100: bytes=32 time=1ms TTL=255
Reply from 192.168.2.100: bytes=32 time=1ms TTL=255
Reply from 192.168.2.100: bytes=32 time=1ms TTL=255
Request timed out.
Request timed out.
Reply from 192.168.2.100: bytes=32 time=1ms TTL=255
Reply from 192.168.2.100: bytes=32 time=1ms TTL=255
```

In Example 5-62, the first shaded line shows what happens immediately after Switch-A is powered off. Because Switch-A is the active router for the default gateway (192.168.1.10) of Host-A, powering the switch off causes a disruption. However, the default HSRP timers are in place for the HSRP group, so Switch-B waits 10 seconds before declaring Switch-A to be down and assuming the active role for the 192.168.1.10 VIP. Because Host-A has a ping timeout of 5 seconds by default (the default on Windows XP), you see two Request timed out messages before connectivity is re-established, and the ping requests are responded to, as indicated by the second shaded line.

You should be able to verify that Switch-B is now the active router for the 192.168.1.10 group. Example 5-63 shows the output of the **show standby brief** command on Switch-B.

Example 5-63 *Verifying HSRP Status on Switch-B*

```
Switch-B# show standby brief
                     P indicates configured to preempt.
                     |
Interface   Grp Prio P State   Active addr   Standby addr   Group addr
Vl100        1   175 P Active   local         unknown        192.168.1.10
Vl200        0   175 P Active   local         unknown        192.168.2.10
```

Notice that Switch-B has become the active router for the 192.168.1.10 VIP. You can see that currently no HSRP communication with Switch-A exists, as indicated by the text "unknown" in the Standby addr column. This means that Switch-B cannot detect any other HSRP routers.

At this stage, if Switch-A is powered on, after bootup is complete, Switch-A should preempt the active router role for the 192.168.1.10 VIP. On Switch-B, you can monitor these events by using the **debug standby events** command. Example 5-64 demonstrates the use of this command while Switch-A boots up.

Example 5-64 *Monitoring HSRP Events*

```
Switch-B# debug standby events
HSRP Events debugging is on
01:07:39: SB1: V1100 Active: j/Coup rcvd from higher pri router (200/192.168.1.1)
01:07:39: SB1: V1100 Active router is 192.168.1.1, was local
01:07:39: SB1: V1100 Active -> Speak
01:07:39: %STANDBY-6-STATECHANGE: Vlan100 Group 1 state Active -> Speak
01:07:39: SB1: V1100 Redundancy "hsrp-V1100-1" state Active -> Speak
01:07:49: SB1: V1100 Speak: d/Standby timer expired (unknown)
01:07:49: SB1: V1100 Standby router is local
01:07:49: SB1: V1100 Speak -> Standby
01:07:49: SB1: V1100 Redundancy "hsrp-V1100-1" state Speak -> Standby
```

In Example 5-64, you can see that after Switch-A has been restored a Coup message is received from Switch-A indicating it has the highest priority for the HSRP group and is assuming the active role. Switch-B changes its state from Active to Speak, and then from Speak to Standby, because Switch-A has assumed the active role.

NOTE   When a router preempts to takeover the active role, you might notice a slight disruption to traffic using the VIP.

Now it is time to test the interface tracking feature. With interface tracking, an interface failure on the active router causes it to decrement its priority for a particular HSRP group, which might cause another router in the group to preempt the active role. Figure 5-19 demonstrates what happens during interface tracking.

Figure 5-19   *Interface Tracking*

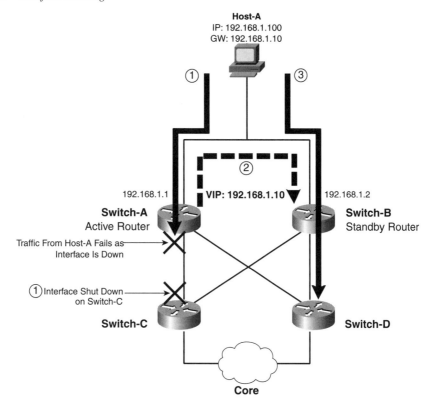

In Figure 5-19 the following events occur:

Step 1   Switch-A is the active router for the HSRP group. On Switch-C, the interface to Switch-A is shut down, causing the line protocol to go down on the interface. At this point, any traffic sent to Switch-A that is to be routed to Switch-C cannot be sent via Switch-C because the interface to Switch-C is down.

NOTE   In the topology of Figure 5-19, Switch-A actually reroutes traffic to Switch-B because of the dynamic routing protocols configured in the network.

Step 2   Switch-A decrements its group priority in response to a tracked interface going down. The decremented priority is immediately transmitted in a Hello message to all other HSRP routers.

Step 3   Switch-B receives the Hello message from Switch-A and detects that it now has a higher priority than Switch-A for the HSRP group. Assuming that Switch-B is configured to preempt, Switch-B assumes the active role. Traffic sent from Host-A is now routed by Switch-B.

Now that you understand how interface tracking works, it is time to see interface tracking in action. Assuming the continuous ping established in Example 5-61 is still running, Example 5-65 shows the process of shutting down interface fa0/3 on Switch-C. This causes the priority for the 192.168.1.10 VIP to be decremented to 150, meaning Switch-B preempts the active router role because it has a higher priority of 175. Example 5-66 shows the resulting effect on the continuous ping running on Host-A.

Example 5-65 *Shutting Down a Tracked Interface on Switch-C*

```
Switch-C# configure terminal
Switch-A(config)# interface FastEthernet 0/3
Switch-A(config-if)# shutdown
```

Example 5-66 *Continuous* **ping** *Between Host-A and Host-B after the FastEthernet0/3 Interface on Switch-C is Shut Down*

```
Reply from 192.168.2.100: bytes=32 time<1ms TTL=255
Reply from 192.168.2.100: bytes=32 time<1ms TTL=255
Reply from 192.168.2.100: bytes=32 time<1ms TTL=255
Reply from 192.168.2.100: bytes=32 time=2ms TTL=255
Reply from 192.168.2.100: bytes=32 time<1ms TTL=255
Reply from 192.168.2.100: bytes=32 time<1ms TTL=255
```

In Example 5-66, notice the response time for the shaded reply. The response time is 2 ms, as opposed to <1 ms response times for all other ping replies. This "glitch" represents the slight delay caused by the active router changing from Switch-A to Switch-B. Clearly, this slight delay has a negligible effect on end-to-end connectivity for the network. The "smooth" failover is due to the fact that Switch-A immediately transmits its decremented priority for the group to Switch-B when interface FastEthernet0/3 on Switch-A is shut down. Switch-B then immediately assumes the active role because it is configured to preempt.

To verify that Switch-A has indeed decremented its priority, Example 5-67 demonstrates the use of the **show standby** command on Switch-A.

Example 5-67 *Checking HSRP Status on Switch-A after Interface Failure*

```
Switch-A# show standby
Vlan100 - Group 1
  Local state is Standby, priority 150 (confg 200), may preempt
  Hellotime 3 sec, holdtime 10 sec
  Next hello sent in 2.343
  Virtual IP address is 192.168.1.10 configured
  Active router is 192.168.1.2 expires in 00:00:07
  Standby router is local
  Virtual mac address is 0000.0c07.ac01
Priority tracking 2 interfaces, 1 down:
    Interface            Decrement  State
    FastEthernet0/3         50      Down
    FastEthernet0/4         50      Up
... (Output Truncated)
...
```

In Example 5-67, notice in the first shaded line that the priority of the HSRP group for 192.168.1.10 is now 150 and that there is also an indication that the configured priority is 200. The current status for the group is also indicated as standby, which means Switch-B is the active router. The second to last shaded line of the output confirms that the current state of the FastEthernet0/3 is down.

Summary

Routing is a fundamental component of modern networking. A solid knowledge of routing is required no matter what area of network you specialize in.

In LAN networks, routing is used to allow VLANs to communicate with each other—such a process is referred to as inter-VLAN routing. Two main inter-VLAN routing architectures exist. The most simple is called the router-on-a-stick, where essentially all inter-VLAN packets in the source VLAN are sent to a router that routes the packet and forwards the packet back to the LAN network on another VLAN. The router-on-a-stick architecture requires that the router have an interface attached to each VLAN for which inter-VLAN routing is required. These interfaces can be multiple physical interfaces or can be multiple virtual interfaces operating over a single physical trunk interface (a trunk interface can also be operating over multiple physical links in an EtherChannel bundle). The second inter-VLAN routing architecture is called Layer 3 switching. L3 switching refers to what you might consider as a LAN switch being capable of routing packets. L3 switching increases the intelligence of the LAN network, allowing for high-performance inter-VLAN routing at wire speed and increasing the efficiency of traffic flows in the LAN network.

L3 switching has advanced as a technology to a point where it is cost effective to implement and provides the same level of performance as L2 switching. This is driving designers of LANs to design and recommend multilayer LAN topologies over traditional collapsed backbone architectures. A collapsed backbone architecture relies on a flat Layer 2 network consisting of Layer 2 switches, with a router-on-a-stick located at the edge of the network providing inter-VLAN routing. This architecture has issues in terms of availability because of the effect that spanning tree has on the convergence of large Layer 2 topologies. Performance is also affected for larger networks as the size of each broadcast domain (VLAN) increases. A multilayer design mitigates these issues by segmenting the LAN topology into smaller Layer 2 domains, with routing used to enable communications between each Layer 2 domain.

An important technology used with inter-VLAN routing architectures is Cisco's Hot Standby Router Protocol (HSRP). HSRP provides redundancy for inter-VLAN routing devices, where an active router services all inter-VLAN routing during normal operation, while a backup (standby) router provides inter-VLAN routing in the event the active router fails. HSRP is most commonly used at the edge of the IP network, where end devices are attached. End devices, such as servers and workstations, are not designed to be routers and thus are typically configured with a single next-hop IP address (default gateway) to which all inter-VLAN traffic is sent for routing. This provides a simple method of connecting to the rest of the network but does not offer any means of dynamically sending inter-VLAN traffic through another path should the configured path fail.

## CHAPTER 6

Layer 3 Switching

In the previous chapter, you were introduced to the concept of Layer 3 switching on the Catalyst 3550; however, the focus of the chapter was more on the fundamental concept of inter-VLAN routing and routing protocols rather than focusing specifically on Layer 3 switching. In this chapter, you learn about Layer 3 switching in detail and how to configure Layer 3 switching on the flagship of the Cisco Catalyst product family, the Catalyst 6000/6500.

NOTE   Although this chapter shows you how to configure Layer 3 switching on the Catalyst 6000/6500, the same concepts and configurations discussed in scenarios based around Layer 3 switching using Cisco Express Forwarding (CEF) can be applied to other CEF-based Cisco Catalyst Layer 3 switching platforms, such as the Catalyst 3550 and Catalyst 4000/4500 Supervisor 3/4 engines.

This chapter looks initially at software-only versus hardware-assisted Layer 3 (L3) switching (routing), examining the architectures used by each, which enables you to understand the limitations of software-based L3 switching and the advantages of hardware-based L3 switching. You learn about Multilayer switching (MLS), which represents an older Layer 3 switching technology used on older Catalyst switches and then learn about CEF-based Layer 3 switching, which is the current Layer 3 switching technology used on all next-generation Cisco Layer 3 switches (e.g., Catalyst 3550, Catalyst 4000/4500 Supervisor 3/4, and Catalyst 6000/6500 Supervisor 2 with PFC-2 + MSFC-2). You also learn about the architecture of the Catalyst 6000/6500, which represents the flagship of the Cisco Catalyst switching family.

Finally, the scenarios for this chapter are presented, which focus initially on MLS and then focus on the Catalyst 6000/6500 and how to configure CEF-based L3 switching on these switches. You also learn how to convert a Catalyst 6000/6500 from hybrid mode (CatOS) to native Cisco IOS, which is the future operating system for all Catalyst switches. After introductory material, the following scenarios are presented in this chapter:

- Scenario 6-1: Configuring MLS on the Catalyst 6000
- Scenario 6-2: Configuring CEF-based Layer 3 switching on the Catalyst 6000/6500 operating in hybrid mode

- Scenario 6-3: Upgrading from hybrid mode to native mode on the Catalyst 6000/6500
- Scenario 6-4: Configuring CEF-based Layer 3 switching on the Catalyst 6000/6500 operating in native mode

Introduction to Layer 3 Switching

In the previous chapter, you were introduced to the concept of inter-VLAN routing, which is required to enable hosts that belong to different VLANs on the same LAN network to communicate with each other. Implementing inter-VLAN routing introduces several benefits, which include the following:

- Reduces broadcast domains, increasing network performance and efficiency.
- Multilayer topologies based upon inter-VLAN routing are much more scalable and implement more efficient mechanisms for accommodating redundant paths in the network than equivalent flat Layer 2 topologies that rely on spanning tree alone.
- Allows for centralized security access control between each VLAN.
- Increases manageability by creating smaller "troubleshooting domains," where the effect of a faulty network interface card (NIC) is isolated to a specific VLAN rather than the entire network.

Of course, all of these features must be provided with a very important caveat—inter-VLAN routing should not affect performance, as users expect high performance from the LAN.

A popular approach to providing the benefits of inter-VLAN routing and also ensuring the performance of the LAN is not degraded has been to implement Layer 3 switches, which are essentially Layer 2 switches with a routing engine that is designed to specifically route traffic between VLANs in a LAN environment. Using Layer 3 switches for inter-VLAN routing as opposed to traditional routers is popular (and recommended) for the following reasons:

- **Performance versus Cost**—Layer 3 switches are much more cost effective than routers for delivering high-speed inter-VLAN routing. High performance routers are typically much more expensive than Layer 3 switches. For example, a Catalyst 3550-24 EMI switch sets you back $4,990 U.S. list, which provides a packet forwarding rate of 6.6 million packets per second with 24 * 10/100BASE-T ports and 2 * 1000BASE-X ports. A Cisco 7300 router with an NSE-100 engine provides a packet forwarding rate of 3.5 million packets per second, but sets you back $22,000 U.S. list and has only 2 * 1000BASE-T ports in its base configuration. Of course, the Cisco 7300 router has many more features and can support a wide variety of WAN media options; however, many of these extra features are not required for inter-VLAN routing.
- **Port density**—Layer 3 switches are enhanced Layer 2 switches and, hence, have the same high port densities that Layer 2 switches have. Routers on the other hand typically have a much lower port density.

- **Flexibility**—Layer 3 switches allow you to mix and match Layer 2 and Layer 3 switching, meaning you can configure a Layer 3 switch to operate as a normal Layer 2 switch, or enable Layer 3 switching as required.

Layer 3 switching is cheap because Layer 3 switches are targeted specifically for inter-VLAN routing, where only Ethernet access technologies are used in high densities. This makes it easy for Layer 3 switch vendors such as Cisco to develop high performance Layer 3 switches, as vendors can develop hardware chips (known as *application-specific integrated circuits* or *ASICs*) that specifically route traffic between Ethernet networks, without having to worry about the complexities of also supporting WAN technologies such as Frame Relay or ATM. Routing over WAN networks can still be supported, simply by plugging a traditional router that connects to the WAN networks into the LAN network. Figure 6-1 illustrates the concept of Layer 3 switching.

Figure 6-1   *Layer 3 Switching*

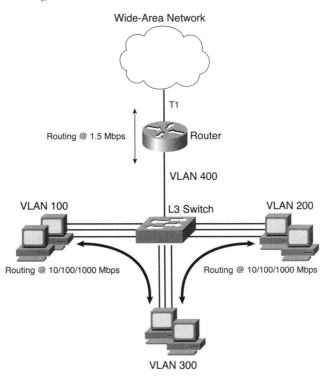

In Figure 6-1, a L3 switch provides switched LAN connections for each device in the network. Three user VLANs are present, and a routing engine on the L3 switch enables communications between each VLAN. The L3 switch possesses specialized hardware chips called application-specific integrated circuits (ASICs) that are preprogrammed and designed to route between Ethernet ports at high speed. A traditional router is connected to the L3 switch and handles the routing of any traffic that needs to be sent across the WAN. Because the L3 switch does not need the flexibility required of the router to support different WAN protocols, it can use ASICs to route traffic at the 100-Mbps speeds expected of the LAN network. The router in the network is designed to handle the requirements of routing at T1 (1.5 Mbps) speeds and would cause a bottleneck if it had to route between VLANs, as routing is performed in software, not hardware. Of course, you could purchase an expensive high-performance router with three Ethernet ports and a T1 interface; however, the cost associated with this approach is much higher. The cost associated with adding more routed Ethernet ports to the router (e.g., if a new VLAN was added to the network) is also high.

Layer 3 Routing Versus Layer 3 Switching

It is important to understand the difference between Layer 3 routing and Layer 3 switching. Both terms are open to some interpretation; however, the distinction between both can perhaps be best explained by examining how an IP packet is routed. The process of routing an IP packet can be divided into two distinct processes:

- **Control plane**—The control plane process is responsible for building and maintaining the IP routing table, which defines where an IP packet should be routed to based upon the destination address of the packet, which is defined in terms of a next hop IP address and the egress interface that the next hop is reachable from. Layer 3 routing generally refers to control plane operations.

- **Data plane**—The data plane process is responsible for actually routing an IP packet, based upon information learned by the control plane. Whereas the control plane defines where an IP packet should be routed to, the data plane defines exactly how an IP packet should be routed. This information includes the underlying Layer 2 addressing required for the IP packet so that it reaches the next hop destination, as well as other operations required on for IP routing, such as decrementing the time-to-live (TTL) field and recomputing the IP header checksum. Layer 3 switching generally refers to data plane operations.

Figure 6-2 illustrates the differences between control plane operation and data plane operation by providing an example of how an IP packet is routed.

NOTE   Some Cisco Catalyst Layer 3 switches support the Layer 3 switching of Internetwork Packet Exchange (IPX) packets as well. For this chapter, the discussion focuses purely on IP packets.

Figure 6-2   *Control Plane and Data Plane Operation*

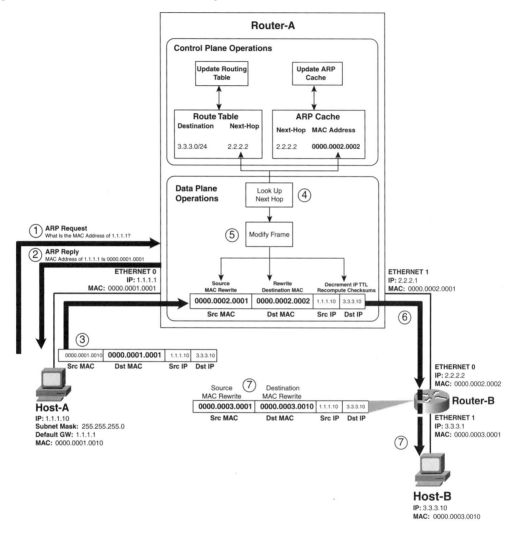

In Figure 6-2, Host-A is sending an IP packet to Host-B over a LAN network that includes a couple of routers. The following describes the events that occur in Figure 6-2.

Step 1   Host-A (1.1.1.10) needs to send an IP packet to Host B (3.3.3.10). Host-A determines (by considering its own IP address, its subnet mask, and the IP address of Host-B) that Host-B is a non-local host and, therefore, must send the IP packet to the configured default gateway of 1.1.1.1 (Router-A). Because Host-A is connected to the network via Ethernet, Host-A must deliver the original IP packet in an Ethernet frame to Router-A. To place the packet in an Ethernet frame that can be delivered to Router-A, Host-A must know the MAC address of Router-A's 1.1.1.1 interface. Host-A checks the local Address Resolution Protocol (ARP) cache to see whether or not it knows the MAC address of Router-A (1.1.1.1). Assuming Host-A does not know the MAC address, Host-A broadcasts an ARP request, which is sent to all devices on the local LAN and asks for the MAC address associated with the IP address 1.1.1.1.

Step 2   Because Router-A is configured with an IP address of 1.1.1.1 on the interface attached to Host-A, it responds to the ARP request by sending a unicast ARP reply, which provides its MAC address (0000.0001.0001).

Step 3   Host-A can now encapsulate the IP packet in an Ethernet frame and send it to Router-A. The destination MAC address of the frame is the MAC address of Router-A, which ensures that Router-A receives the IP packet contained within for routing. The destination IP address, however, is not that of Router-A; it's that of Host-B, the true eventual destination of the packet (in other words, the IP addresses in the packet are not modified).

Step 4   Router-A receives the Ethernet frame and the data plane operations begin. For Router-A to forward the packet on to the appropriate next hop, it must know who the next hop is and the MAC address of the next hop. To determine the next hop, the router inspects the destination IP address of the IP packet (IP routing is always based upon the destination IP address). Router-A references the local route table for an entry that matches the destination IP address (3.3.3.10) and finds that 3.3.3.0/24 is reachable via a next hop IP address of 2.2.2.2 (Router-B).

Step 5   Because Router-A is connected to Router-B via Ethernet, Router-A must send the IP packet inside an Ethernet frame addressed to Router-B. To determine the MAC address associated with the next hop router, the local ARP cache on the router is checked to see if an entry exists for the IP address of the next hop. If no entry exists, then the router must generate an ARP request, asking for the MAC address associated with the next hop IP address (this is a control plane operation). Once the correct destination MAC address is known, the routed frame destination MAC address can be rewritten. The source MAC address is also rewritten to the MAC address of the Ethernet 1 interface on Router-A so that Router-B knows it received the frame from Router-A. It is this process of rewriting the frame MAC addresses that represents the key concept of data plane operations—A router does not modify the source or destination IP addresses of IP packets that are being delivered, but rather it must *rewrite* the destination and source MAC address so that the IP packet can be delivered over the LAN to the next hop.

NOTE   Router-A actually does have to modify some information in the IP header. Router-A must decrement the IP time-to-live (TTL) field and also must recompute the IP header checksum, since the TTL field has been changed. IP addressing might also be modified if network address translation (NAT) is configured; however, this operation is performed by a separate process outside of the control plane and data plane operations of routing.

Step 6   The rewritten Ethernet frame containing the IP packet is sent to Router-B.

Step 7   Router-B receives the frame from Router-A and examines the destination IP address of the packet. Because the destination IP address is that of a host that is locally connected, Router-B can complete the delivery by sending the packet to Host-B. Because Host-B is connected via Ethernet to Router-B, Router-B must send the IP packet inside an Ethernet frame addressed to Host-B. The same rewrite of the destination (and source) MAC address that was described in Step 5 takes place, and the frame is delivered to its final destination, Host-B.

NOTE   It is important to understand that the MAC addresses are specific only to each local LAN. For example, Host-A does not know and does not need to know Host-B's MAC address or even Router-B's MAC address. Host-A needs to know only the MAC address of Router-A so that it can deliver IP packets in Ethernet frames locally to Router-A, with Router-A then forwarding the packet on appropriately and with this process occurring on a hop-by-hop basis until the final destination is reached.

Control Plane and Data Plane Implementation

Control plane operations require an understanding of routing protocols and hence require some intelligence that is capable of supporting the complex algorithms and data structures associated with protocols such as Open Shortest Path First (OSPF) and Border Gateway Protocol (BGP). Depending on the routing protocol(s) configured, the control plane operations required might vary dramatically between different routing devices. On the other hand, data plane operations are simple and fixed in their implementation because how a packet is routed is the same, regardless of the routing protocol that was used to learn where a packet should be routed. Although data plane operations are simple, they are also performed much more frequently than control plane operations because data plane operations must be performed for every packet that is routed, while control plane operations must be performed only for routing topology changes once the routing table is built. This means that the performance of the data plane implementation ultimately dictates how fast a routing device can route packets.

Because control plane operations are complex, most vendors use a general purpose CPU capable of supporting a high-level programming language so that vendors can easily develop and maintain the complex code associated with support the various routing protocols. In this respect, the control plane is implemented in *software,* which means that code (software) developed from a high-level programming language provides control plane operation. Both traditional routers and Layer 3 switches normally take the same approach to implementing the control plane operations associated with IP routing, using software that requires a general purpose CPU.

In contrast to control plane operations, data plane operations are very simple. In fact, the data plane operations required can be presented in a single table. Table 6-1 describes the data plane operations that must take place, assuming a packet is addressed from a host called Host-A to another host called Host-B and is sent via a router.

Table 6-1   *Data Plane Operations Required on Received Frames*

	Layer 2 Ethernet Header		Layer 3 IP Header				Data	FCS
	Destination MAC	Source MAC	Destination IP	Source IP	TTL	Checksum		
Received Frame	Router MAC Address	Host-A MAC Address	Host-B	Host-A	n	value1		
Rewritten Frame	Next Hop MAC Address	Router MAC Address	Host-B	Host-A	n-1	value2		

In Table 6-1, the details of the received frame are indicated and then the details required for the rewritten frame that is transmitted after routing are shown. Notice that the following fields must be modified for the rewritten frame that is forwarded to the next hop routing device:

- **Destination MAC address**—The MAC address of the next hop must be written to the rewritten frame.

- **Source MAC address**—The source MAC address must be written to the MAC address of the router.

- **IP TTL**—This must be decremented by one, as per the normal rules of IP routing.

- **IP Header Checksum**—This must be recalculated, as the TTL field changes.

The process of how the data plane operations shown in Table 6-1 are implemented is where the difference between a traditional router and Layer 3 switch lie. A traditional router uses the same general purpose CPU used to perform control plane operations to also implement data plane operations, meaning data plane operations are handled in software. A Layer 3 switch on the other hand uses an ASIC to perform data plane operations because it is very easy to program the very simple operations required for the data plane into an ASIC. In this respect, the data plane is implemented in hardware because a series of hardware operations are programmed into the ASIC that perform the data plane operations required for routing a packet.

NOTE   It should be noted that many high-end routers use ASICs for data plane operations in a similar fashion to Layer 3 switches. In fact, much of the ASIC technology used in Layer 3 switches is derived from the ASICs used in high-end routers.

So how does this affect performance? Well, a general purpose CPU is designed to support many different functions, where as an ASIC is designed to support a single function or a handful of specific functions such as performing the data plane operations required to route a packet. This means that an ASIC can operate much faster because the internal architecture of the ASIC can be optimized just to perform the operations required for data plane operations, whereas a general purpose CPU must be designed to support a series of generic functions that do not relate to data plane operations whatsoever (as the CPU must support other applications). A high-level language combines the generic functions of the general purpose CPU to provide the higher specific functions required to perform data plane operations. This approach allows flexibility but comes at the price of performance. Hence, a Layer 3 switch that performs data plane operations using ASICs route packets much faster than a traditional router that performs data plane operations using a general purpose CPU.

NOTE   The term *software* when applied to Layer 3 routing means that a general purpose CPU performs routing, along with other tasks such as system maintenance and providing command-line access. The term *hardware* when applied to Layer 3 switching means an ASIC dedicated to the process of Layer 3 switching, whose sole purpose in life is to route packets.

Hardware-Based Layer 3 Switching Architectures

Although the data plane operations required for routing IP packets can easily be accelerated by the use of ASICs, it is important to understand that a fundamental requirement for data plane operation is the process of determining the next hop IP address for the destination IP address of the packet and the MAC address associated with the next hop so that the correct destination MAC address can be written to the rewritten frame. The components that implement data plane operations must "look up" this information (see the lookup operation in Figure 6-2); this lookup operation in itself can become a bottleneck. To ensure the lookup process does not significantly delay the rewrite processes of data plane operation, Layer 3 switches use specialized data structures that allow for fast lookups. These data structures can be split into two categories:

- **Route cache**—A route cache is populated with information that defines how to Layer 3 switch frames associated with a particular *flow*. A flow uniquely identifies specific traffic conversations in the network (e.g., one flow might be Host-A communicating with Host-B, while another flow might be Host-A communicating with Host-C), and each flow entry contains the required information to Layer 3 switch packets received for that flow. The flow entries are built by routing the first packet in software, with the relevant values in the rewritten first frame used to fill out the required information for a flow entry. Subsequent packets associated with the flow are then Layer 3 switched in hardware based upon the information learned in the flow entry. Cisco's implementation of route caching on Cisco Catalyst switches is called *Multilayer switching* (*MLS*), and is discussed in more detail in Scenario 6-1.

- **Optimized route lookup table**—One approach to the lookup process could be to use the routing table; however, this contains information not relevant to data plane operations, such as the routing protocol that learned a route, metric associated with a route, and the administrative distance of a route. The routing table also does not contain MAC address information for the next hop. This must be determined either via a control plane operation (using ARP) or by reading the ARP cache. Next-generation Cisco Catalyst Layer 3 switches use an optimized route lookup table, which organizes only the required routing information for data plane operations (e.g., destination prefix, next hop, egress interface) and also includes a pointer to another optimized adjacency table, which describes the MAC address associated with the various next hop devices in the network. Cisco's implementation of using optimized route lookup tables on Cisco Catalyst switches is called *Cisco Express Forwarding* (*CEF*) and is discussed in more detail in Scenario 6-2 and Scenario 6-4.

It is important to note that in addition to possessing a high performance lookup mechanism, many Layer 3 switches also possess specialized hardware that can be used to provide QoS classification and security access control (using access control lists) for packets at the same time the next hop lookup is being implemented. This means that these features can be turned on with affecting performance.

Cisco Catalyst 6000/6500 Switch Architecture

The Catalyst 6000/6500 is the flagship of the Cisco Catalyst switching family and represents one of the most popular switches used for enterprise networks and service providers. If you are tasked with the procuring a Catalyst 6000/6500 switch, it is important to understand the various Supervisor modules available and the technologies that are used with each to perform both Layer 2 and Layer 3 switching.

The following topics are now discussed:

- Supervisor architectures
- Catalyst 6000/6500 operating systems

Supervisor Architectures

Several architectural options are available when designing a Catalyst 6000/6500 switch, each of which varies in terms of Layer 3 capabilities. Layer 3 capabilities are added to the Catalyst 6000/6500 switch by two key components:

- **Policy feature card (PFC)**—The PFC provides the necessary ASICs to perform hardware-based Layer 3 switching, quality of service (QoS) classification, and access control list (ACL) filtering. The PFC requires a *route processor* to populate the route cache or optimized route table structure used by the L3 switching ASIC. If no route processor is present, the PFC can perform only Layer 3/4 QoS classification and ACL filtering and cannot perform L3 switching.

- **Multilayer switching feature card (MSFC)**—The MSFC is essentially a Cisco IOS router based upon the high-performance 7200 series router. This provides the route processor functions required by the PFC to implement L3 switching. The MSFC provides the necessary routing information in the PFC route cache so that the PFC can L3 switch packets.

When you purchase the Catalyst 6000/6500, you have a choice as to the generation of Supervisor that you wish to purchase, as well as the L3 components (i.e., the PFC and/or MSFC) that you require depending on your Layer 3 requirements. These options include the following:

- Supervisor 1A
- Supervisor 2
- Supervisor 720—Next-generation Supervisor engine that includes an integrated PFC-3, MSFC-3, and 720-Gbps crossbar switching matrix.

Each of the various configuration options is now examined.

Supervisor 1A with no PFC

The simplest configuration option available for the Catalyst 6000 is just the Supervisor 1 module with no policy feature card (PFC) or MSFC. In this configuration, the switch is essentially a Layer 2 switch and possesses no Layer 3 switching or classification capabilities. A Supervisor 1A can provide a Layer 2 switch up to 15 million packets per second (Mpps).

Supervisor 1A with PFC-1

The next option available for the Catalyst 6000/6500 is the Supervisor 1 module with a policy feature card (PFC-1) installed. The PFC-1 enables Layer 3 and 4 classification for QoS classification and security ACL filtering; however, L3 switching is not supported unless an MSFC is added to provide route processor functions. The Supervisor 1A with PFC-1 is capable of processing frames through the QoS and ACL engines without degrading Layer 2 switching performance, at speeds of up to 15 Mpps. Figure 6-3 demonstrates the architecture of the Supervisor 1A with PFC-1.

Figure 6-3   *Supervisor 1A with PFC-1 Architecture*

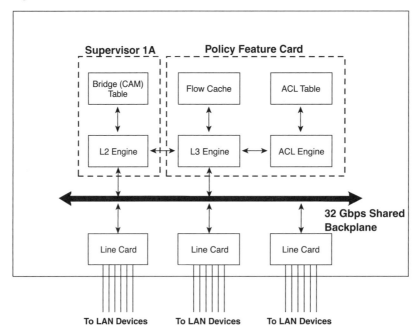

In Figure 6-3, the Supervisor 1A contains the basic Layer 2 engine that references the local bridge table for determining the egress port for switching decisions. The PFC contains a Layer 3 engine, flow cache, ACL engine, and ACL table. In this configuration, the PFC is not used for L3 switching, because no route processor (provided by an MSFC) is installed that provides the required next hop information. However, the PFC can be used for Layer 3/4 QoS classification and ACL filtering; the ACL engine is responsible for providing these functions. The ACL table is stored in *ternary content addressable memory (TCAM)*, which stores ACL information in a format that can be referenced very quickly by the ACL engine. When a packet arrives that requires ACL filtering, while the L2 engine determines the forwarding decision to be made based upon the information contained within the L2 bridge table, at the same time, the ACL engine determines whether or not the packet is permitted or denied. Because the L2 lookup and ACL lookup occur in parallel, applying ACLs or QoS classification to traffic does not affect the forwarding rate of the switch (15 Mpps).

Supervisor 1A with PFC-1 and MSFC-1/MSFC-2

The last Supervisor 1A option and only L3 switching option for the Catalyst 6000/6500 using the Supervisor 1A is the Supervisor 1A module with PFC-1 and MSFC-1 or MSFC-2 installed. The MSFC-1 is now end of sale, so you can only purchase the MSFC-2 if you want to add Layer 3 switching capabilities to existing Supervisor 1A configurations.

NOTE	The MSFC-1 and MSFC-2 differ only in performance. The MSFC-1 has an R5000 200-MHz processor, supports up to 128MB memory, and can route packets at up to 170 Kpps in software. The MSFC-2 has an R7000 300-MHz processor, supports up to 512 MB memory, and can route packets at up to 650 Kpps in software. The Layer 3 switching performance in hardware is still 15 Mpps, regardless of the MSFC used.

In this architecture, the L3 engine onboard the PFC-1 can perform L3 switching, because a route processor is now present in the form of the MSFC. Figure 6-4 shows the architecture of the Supervisor 1A with PFC-1 and MSFC.

Figure 6-4   *Supervisor 1A with PFC-1 and MSFC*

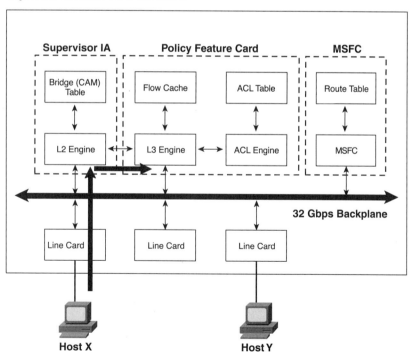

In Figure 6-4, the addition of the MSFC allows for the L3 engine to L3 switch inter-VLAN traffic. All other features of the PFC, such as QoS classification and ACL filtering are also supported. The PFC-1 and MSFC-1/MSFC-2 use *multilayer switching (MLS)* to perform L3 switching; this means that a flow cache exists on the PFC which is used to L3 switch packet flows through the switch. The first packet within a flow must always be routed by the MSFC, which references the routing table to determine the next hop information for a packet. Once the MSFC has made a routing decision and forwarded the frame back to the L3 engine, the L3 engine reads the routed frame information and writes this information into the flow cache. Subsequent packets received and that match flow cache entries can now be L3 switched by the L3 engine, rather than the MSFC. A limitation of the MLS L3 switching mechanism is the initial route lookup performed in software by the MSFC. The first packet in an IP flow must be passed to the MSFC route processor for routing. In an environment that has many connections being established at the same time, this can cause performance problems for the MSFC. This problem in particular applies to service provider environments, which typically must handle conditions where many short term connections (e.g., downloading a web page might open several HTTP connections that are terminated immediately once the page is downloaded) are being established at once. The Supervisor 1 with PFC-1 and MSFC can L3 switch packets at 15 Mpps.

Supervisor 2 with PFC-2

The first configuration available for the Catalyst 6000/6500 with a Supervisor 2 module is the Supervisor 2 with a policy feature card 2 (PFC-2) installed (the Supervisor 2 is integrated with PFC-2; you can't purchase either separately). The PFC-2 is similar in function to the PFC-1, enabling Layer 3 classification for QoS classification and security ACL filtering; however, it is twice as fast as the PFC-1 and supports more ACLs that can be stored in hardware for QoS and Security. The Supervisor 2 with PFC-2 is capable of switching packets and performing Layer 3/4 QoS classification and ACL filtering at up to 30 Mpps; however, this requires switch fabric enabled modules and a switch fabric module to be installed. Because no MSFC is present in this configuration, L3 switching is not possible. Figure 6-5 demonstrates the architecture of the Supervisor 2 with PFC-2.

Comparing the architecture of the Supervisor 1A with PFC-1, notice that the PFC-2 is actually an integrated part of the Supervisor 2 module. The most notable difference is that the Layer 2 and ACL engine are now combined into a single L2/L4 engine, which boosts the performance capabilities of L2 switching combined with Layer 3/4 QoS classification and ACL filtering up to 30 Mpps. The L3 engine is not used for L3 switching, because an MSFC-2 (route processor) is required to generate information contained in the CEF table.

Figure 6-5   *Supervisor 2 with PFC-2 Architecture*

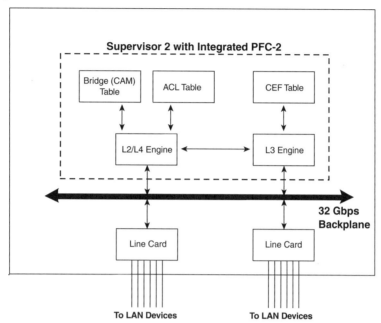

Supervisor 2 with PFC-2 and MSFC-2

To enable Layer 3 switching on a Supervisor 2 with PFC-2, the only option is to add an MSFC-2 (the MSFC-1 is not supported on the Supervisor 2). In this architecture, the L3 engine onboard the PFC-2 can perform L3 switching, because a route processor is now present in the form of the MSFC-2. Figure 6-6 shows the architecture of the Supervisor 2 with PFC-2 and MSFC-2.

In Figure 6-6, the addition of the MSFC allows for the L3 engine to L3 switch inter-VLAN traffic. All other features of the PFC, such as QoS classification and ACL filtering, are also supported. The PFC-2 and MSFC-2 use CEF to perform L3 switching; the MSFC-2 is responsible for generating the appropriate CEF tables (the FIB table and adjacency table, discussed in Scenario 6-2) upon PFC initialization. This means that as soon as packets need to be L3 switched, the L3 engine has the necessary information to L3 switch the packet, without having to send the first packet associated with a flow to the MSFC (as is the case with MLS). This architecture eliminates the issue that MLS has for supporting an environment that has thousands of connections being established every second. The Supervisor 2 with PFC-2 and MSFC-2 can L3 switch packets at 30 million packets per second.

Figure 6-6   *Supervisor 2 with PFC-2 and MSFC-2*

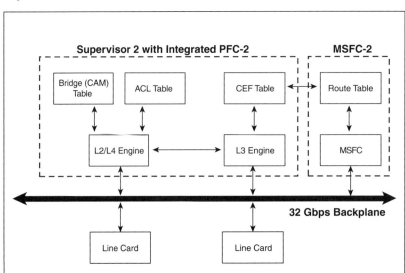

The Switch Fabric Module

The *switch fabric module (SFM)* is a module that includes a switching backplane that increases the forwarding rate of the Catalyst 6500 backplane from 32 Gbps to 256 Gbps.

NOTE   The SFM is available only for the Catalyst 6500 with Supervisor 2 and must be installed in Slot 5. A redundant SFM is available and must be installed in Slot 6 if used.

The SFM provides a crossbar switching matrix for the switching backplane, which allows multiple frames to be switched between different line cards at the same time. For example, a frame can be switched across the matrix from line card #2 to line card #4 at exactly the same time as another frame is being switched from line card #3 to line card #8. This is not possible on the traditional shared 32-Gbps backplane of the Catalyst 6000/6500; thus the crossbar matrix can support much higher packet forwarding rates. The SFM provides 16 * 8-Gbps full-duplex connections into the switching matrix. Figure 6-7 shows the SFM and how it provides connections to the other switch modules in the switch chassis.

Figure 6-7 *The Switch Fabric Module*

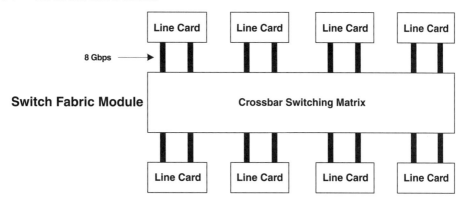

Each switch module has two available 8-Gbps connections to the SFM. Depending on the type of line cards installed, a line card might take advantage of zero, one, or both of the 8-Gbps connections. Three types of switch modules (line cards) relate to the SFM:

- **Non fabric-enabled card**—These cards are not compatible with the SFM and connect only to the 32-Gbps backplane.

- **Fabric-enabled card**—These cards are compatible with both the SFM and 32-Gbps backplane. A single 8-Gbps connection is provided to the SFM, as well as a single connection to the traditional 32-Gbps backplane.

- **Fabric-only card**—These cards connect solely to the SFM via dual 8-Gbps connections. These cards do not connect directly to the traditional 32-Gbps backplane.

It is important to understand that all of the cards listed above can communicate with each other. The fabric-only card can communicate with non fabric-enabled cards because the SFM has a connection to the traditional Catalyst 6000/6500 32-Gbps backplane.

The Distributed Feature Card (DFC)

The *Distributed Feature Card (DFC)* allows fabric-enabled line cards to make L3 forwarding decisions locally without requiring the L3 switching engine located on the Supervisor PFC. The DFC consists of the same components as the PFC located on the Supervisor module, however it does not contain the MSFC routing engine. Figure 6-8 shows the DFC architecture.

NOTE   Only fabric-enabled line cards support the DFC. If you are using the DFC, you must install a switch fabric module card.

Figure 6-8 *The Distributed Feature Card*

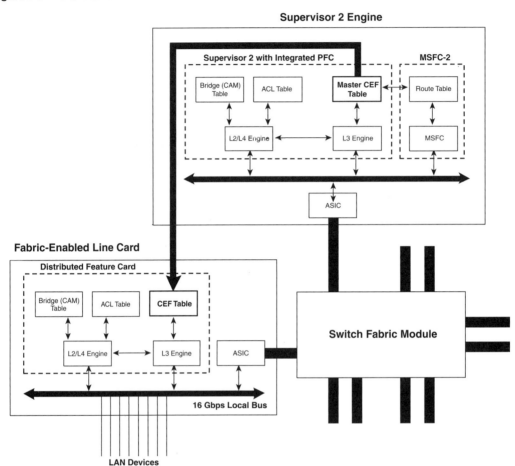

In Figure 6-8, you can see a fabric-enabled line card that has a DFC installed. The DFC looks exactly like a PFC and performs the same functions as the PFC, except for frames received on local ports. The key to the DFC is the use of distributed CEF (dCEF). A master CEF table resides on the Supervisor 2 PFC-2, which is generated by the MSFC routing table. The master CEF table is downloaded (mirrored) to each DFC, which enables the L3 engine on each DFC to make routing decisions locally. If a route table change occurs, the CEF tables on the PFC and each DFC are updated immediately. If frames are received on a DFC-enabled line card that require routing, the L3 engine on the DFC inspects the destination IP address of the IP packet contained within the frame and looks up the CEF table to determine the next-hop MAC address and egress port. If the egress port is local, the L3 engine rewrites the destination MAC address and forwards the frame out the appropriate local egress port. If the egress port is located on another module, the L3 engine rewrites the destination MAC address and forwards the frame onto the SFM matrix, prepending a tag that identifies the egress port the frame should be switched out of. The tagged frame is forwarded to the appropriate switch module, with the local switching engine forwarding the frame out the appropriate egress port. This forwarding of frames across the SFM matrix does not require any intervention by the main Supervisor 2 PFC L3 engine. Given that a DFC can L3 switch up to 30 Mpps, if a Catalyst 6509 has a single Supervisor 2 with PFC-2 and MSFC-2, a SFM, and seven fabric-enabled line cards each with a DFC installed, the total system capacity theoretically is 210 Mpps (7 * 30 Mpps).

Supervisor 720

A recent new addition to the Catalyst 6500 family is the Supervisor 720 engine, which is the third-generation supervisor engine that integrates the following components into a single module:

- PFC-3
- MSFC-3
- Crossbar Switching Fabric that provides 720 Gbps of backplane bandwidth

The Supervisor 720 significantly increases the number of slots available for data modules. For example, in a non-redundant Catalyst 6509 configuration, the Supervisor 720 takes up only a single slot, leaving eight slots for data modules. In comparison, a Supervisor 2 with SFM installed takes up two slots, leaving only seven slots for data modules. In a redundant configuration, the Supervisor 720 engines take up only two slots while the Supervisor 2 engines and redundant SFMs take up four slots.

NOTE   For the Catalyst 6506, 6509, and 6513, the primary Supervisor 720 must be installed in Slot 5, while the redundant Supervisor 720 must be installed in Slot 6. You must also install a minimum of 2500W power supplies to power the Supervisor 720 on all Catalyst 6500 switches.

The Supervisor 720 also provides a large number of feature enhancements, which include the following:

- Hardware-based MPLS forwarding
- Hardware-based IPv6 Layer 3 switching
- Support for hardware assisted NAT and generic routing encapsulation (GRE)
- Backplane bandwidth increases to 2 * 20 Gbps, up from 2 * 8 Gbps with the SFM
- Maximum throughput of 400 Mpps, almost twice that of the Supervisor 2 with SFM

Catalyst 6000/6500 Operating Systems

On the Catalyst 6000/6500, it is important to understand that the switch can operate in one of three different modes, depending on the hardware installed and operating systems used to manage the switch. These modes include the following:

- **CatOS**—In this mode, the switch only operates a single operating system: CatOS. No MSFC is installed, because this uses its own operating system.

- **Hybrid mode**—Hybrid mode refers to the configuration where an MSFC is installed that is running Cisco IOS, whilst the switch is running CatOS. This means two separate management interfaces are required—one for the switch and one for the MSFC.

- **Native mode**—In this configuration, a single Cisco IOS operating system is used to manage both the switch and the MSFC. This allows for a single management interface to manage both the switching and routing components of the switch (native mode requires an MSFC).

Scenario 6-1: Configuring MLS on the Catalyst 6000

In this scenario, you learn how to configure *Multilayer switching* (*MLS*), which represents the first Layer 3 switching technology used by Cisco Catalyst switches to provide wire-speed routing of inter-VLAN traffic. Although MLS is no longer considered the ideal L3 switching architecture, many installations still use MLS, and hence, you as a Cisco engineer must be able to configure and troubleshoot MLS.

Figure 6-9 illustrates the topology used for this scenario. In Figure 6-9, an MLS configuration is to be used to provide the high-speed Layer 3 switching of inter-VLAN traffic on Switch-A. Router-A is required to provide routing control plane operation, initially routing the first packet of each flow sent through the Switch-A, allowing Switch-A to learn the required MAC address rewrite operations for Layer 3 switching.

Figure 6-9   *Scenario 6-1 Topology*

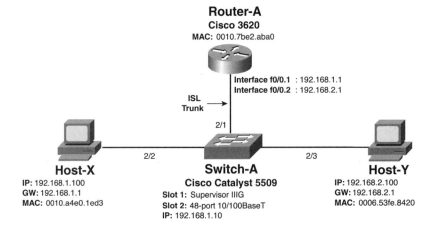

The following describes the function of each component of the lab topology shown in Figure 6-9:

- Switch-A is a Catalyst 5509 switch with a Supervisor 3G module installed. In this scenario, Switch-A acts as the *MLS Switching Engine (MLS-SE)*, which is responsible for the data plane operations required for Layer 3 switching.

- Router-A is a Cisco 3620 router with a physical FastEthernet interface that connects as an 802.1Q to Switch-A. Two virtual interfaces are required on the trunk to provide inter-VLAN routing between each VLAN. Router-A acts as an *MLS Route Processor (MLS-RP)*, which is responsible for making routing decisions for the first packet associated with an MLS flow.

- Host-X and Host-Y are workstations that are used to test that inter-VLAN routing works with MLS configured.

Understanding MLS

MLS represents the first hardware-based Layer 3 switching mechanism used by Cisco Catalyst switches, supported on switches such as the Catalyst 5000/5500 and Catalyst 6000/6500. This section explains the operation of MLS and how Layer 3 switches use MLS.

MLS Overview

MLS is designed to support a distributed L3 switching architecture, which means the various components of MLS do not need to be located on the same physical device. MLS consists of the following two main components:

- **MLS Route Processor (MLS-RP)**—This component represents the *control plane* of the routing process. The MLS-RP maintains the route table and is responsible for updating the route table as changes in the network topology occur.

- **MLS Switching Engine (MLS-SE)**—This component represents the *data plane* of the routing process. The MLS-SE is responsible for determining the next hop and egress interface information for each frame received that requires routing, and then rewriting the frame as required and forwarding the frame to the correct egress interface.

The route table is maintained on the MLS-RP, and this control plane information must somehow be communicated to the MLS-SE. The MLS-RP and MLS-SE communicate using the *MLS protocol (MLSP)*, which is a Cisco proprietary protocol that uses multicast Ethernet frames to communicate.

Flows are used to represent routing information in the route cache located on the MLS-SE. A flow can be defined based upon a unique destination IP address, a unique combination of source and destination IP address, or a unique combination of source and destination IP address, as well as source and destination Layer 4 (i.e., TCP or UDP) ports. For example, all packets that are sent from any source IP address to a destination IP address of 192.168.2.1 can be represented as a flow. All packets sent from a source IP address of 192.168.2.1 to a destination IP address of 192.168.2.2 can be represented by a flow, with the return packets represented as another flow.

For each flow, the MLS-SE builds the required frame rewrite information for Layer 3 switching (i.e., source and destination MAC address rewrite information) by allowing the MLS-RP to perform the normal routing process for the first frame of each new flow. This allows the MLS-SE to learn the required rewrites for the source and destination MAC address of a framed IP packet after it has been routed, with the appropriate information stored in an MLS cache. Figure 6-10 demonstrates the MLS architecture and how packets are routed using MLS using flows.

Figure 6-10 *MLS Architecture*

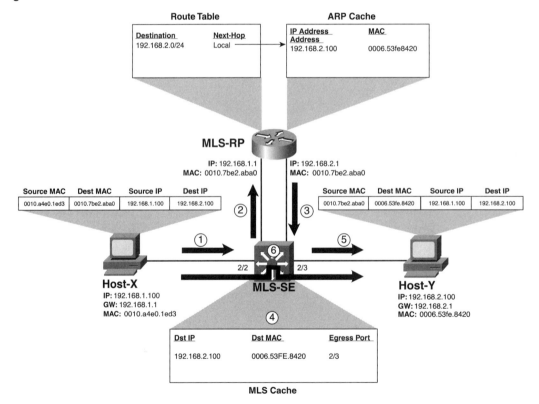

The following describes the events that occur in Figure 6-10:

Step 1   Host-X sends an IP packet to Host-Y (192.168.2.100). Because the packet is on a different IP subnet from Host-X, Host-X addresses the Ethernet frame containing the IP packet to the configured default gateway (MLS-RP) for routing, meaning the frame has a destination MAC address of 0010.7be2.aba0.

Step 2   The frame is received by the MLS-SE, which initially examines the destination MAC address of the frame. Because the destination MAC address is the MAC address of the MLS-RP (0010.7be2.aba0), the MLS-SE immediately marks the frame as a *candidate frame* for L3 switching (as any L3 switched frame always has a destination MAC address of a routing device). The MLS-SE inspects the destination IP address in the packet and checks the MLS cache for a flow. Because this is the first packet sent to Host-Y, no entry is present so the packet is sent to the MLS-RP for routing. An incomplete flow entry is written in the MLS cache, which includes only information that identifies the flow at this stage (e.g., destination IP address).

Step 3   The MLS-RP receives the frame and performs normal IP routing, inspecting the destination IP address and determining from the local route table that the destination is locally attached. The MLS-RP determines the MAC address of Host-Y by checking the ARP cache (and sending an ARP request if the ARP cache does not contain the entry) and generates a new Ethernet frame to transport the IP packet to its intended destination.

Step 4   The MLS-SE receives the routed frame and writes the destination MAC address of the routed frame into the incomplete flow entry that was initially created in Step 2. The switch also consults the local bridge table to determine the egress port associated with the destination MAC address and writes this information into the flow entry as well. The flow entry information is used for future rewriting and forwarding of packets sent to Host-Y without having to forward the packets to the MLS-RP.

Step 5   The frame is switched out the appropriate egress port (2/3) to Host-Y.

Step 6   Host-X sends another IP packet to Host-Y. The MLS-SE sees from the destination MAC address that the frame is destined to the MLS-RP and is therefore a candidate for L3 switching. The MLS-SE inspects the destination IP address (192.168.1.200) and matches it against the flow entry completed in Step 4. The MLS-SE rewrites the destination MAC address of the frame and performs other necessary L3 switching operations (such as decrementing the IP TTL and computing the IP and Ethernet checksums).

Step 7 The rewritten frame is switched out the correct egress port (2/3) to Host-Y. All subsequent IP packets from Host-X to Host-Y are L3 switched as described in Step 6 and Step 7 as long as the flow entry created in Step 4 is valid.

As you can see from Figure 6-10, MLS requires the first packet in a flow to be routed through the MLS-RP, which allows the MLS-SE to determine the appropriate information that must be rewritten by the MLS-SE for the subsequent L3 switching of packets to Host-Y.

The MLS-RP and MLS-SE also communicate regularly, so that if the MLS-SE can detect if an MLS-RP goes down, the MLS-SE can flush the appropriate flow entries in the MLS cache. This is important in a redundant topology where two or more MLS-RPs provide inter-VLAN routing, because it ensures the redundant MLS-RP can be used if the primary MLS-RP fails.

MLS Flows

Because the MLS architecture is based on flows, it is important to understand the different type of flows that exist. Each flow can be categorized as belonging to a particular flow mask. A flow in MLS terms represents one of the following (the name of the flow mask that categorizes the flow is indicated in parentheses):

- **Destination IP address (destination-only)**—A single destination IP address can represent a flow. All traffic sent to the destination IP address is part of a single flow. In Figure 6-10, flows were represented by destination IP address.

- **Source and Destination IP address (source-destination)**—All traffic sent between a specific source and destination IP address is part of a single flow. This means that several flows might exist for the same destination IP address; each flow is differentiated by the source IP address.

- **Full flow (full)**—A full flow represents all traffic associated with a specific source IP address, destination IP address, source TCP/UDP port, and destination TCP/UDP port. For example, a Telnet connection between 192.168.1.1 and 192.168.2.1 would be represented by a separate flow from an HTTP connection between the same two hosts.

Flows are important because the route cache used by MLS uses flows to store the information for the hardware-based rewrites required for Layer 3 switching process. The flow you use depends on the requirements of your network. For example, if you are using simple routing (where routing decisions only need to be made based solely upon the destination IP address of each packet), destination IP address flows are only required. However, if you are using access control lists (ACLs) on a routed interface through which a packet would normally travel, you need to use source and destination IP address or full flows depending on the granularity of the ACLs. For example, Figure 6-11 shows the topology of Figure 6-10 with an extended ACL configured on an interface on the MLS-RP.

Figure 6-11 *MLS Architecture and ACLs*

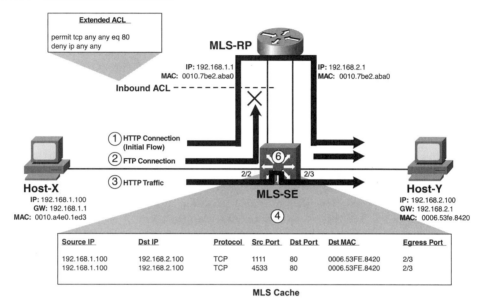

The following describes the events that occur in Figure 6-11:

Step 1   Host-X attempts to establish an HTTP connection to Host-Y, sending an
IP packet with a source IP address of 192.168.1.100, destination IP
address of 192.168.2.100, protocol number of 6 (TCP), destination TCP
port of 80, and a random source TCP port of 1111. The frame for the IP
packet is addressed to the MLS-RP, because Host-Y is not on the local
subnet. The MLS-SE receives the frame, marks it as a candidate frame,
and routes the frame to the MLS-RP, because no flow entry exists that
matches the packet. When the MLS-RP receives the packet, it is inspected
against the ACL and is permitted because the packet is a TCP packet with
a destination port of 80. The MLS-SE receives the routed packet,
allowing it to write a complete flow entry in the MLS cache.

Step 2   Host-X next attempts to establish an FTP connection to Host-Y. Because
the flow cache on the MLS-SE is now using a full flow mask, the FTP
packet sent does not match the flow entry created in Step 1 and hence is
forwarded to the MLS-RP. The MLS-RP inspects the packet against the
ACL and drops the packet because it is not an HTTP packet. This means
that the MLS-SE never sees the return routed frame come back from the
MLS-RP that includes the required information to complete the entry for
the flow, meaning the MLS-SE can never complete the incomplete flow
entry created when the packet was first received by the MLS-SE. Any

subsequent FTP connection requests (or any other non-HTTP traffic) is always forwarded to the MLS-RP (because no complete flow entries ever exist on the MLS-SE), at which point the traffic is dropped.

Step 3   All traffic associated with the HTTP connection established in Step 1 is Layer 3 switched by the MLS-SE. If a new HTTP connection is established between Host-X and Host-Y, a new flow entry must be built (as per Step 1), because the source TCP port is different for each connection. In Figure 6-11, you can see two flow entries, which each represent separate HTTP connections established from Host-X to Host-Y.

In Figure 6-11, a full flow *must* be used because the MLS-RP must be able to permit traffic based on specific combinations of source and destination IP address and source and destination TCP/UDP ports. If a destination or destination-source flow were used in Figure 6-11, the MLS-SE would not differentiate HTTP packets from FTP packets and FTP packets would be incorrectly L3 switched (permitted) to Host-Y.

NOTE   The MLS-RP can communicate the required flow mask to the MLS-SE, which ensures that if an ACL is applied in an existing MLS configuration, the appropriate flow mask is immediately used on the MLS-SE ensuring packets are not incorrectly permitted if they have been denied in the ACL.

MLS Communications

MLS requires some internal communications between the MLS-RP and MLS-SE to ensure L3 switching on the MLS-SE is performed accurately and correctly. Two major events that can cause the MLS cache to become invalid:

- Routing topology changes
- ACL configuration

If a routing topology change occurs, it is possible that flow information in the MLS cache needs to be updated. This is also the case if an ACL is applied to an interface (or modified) on the MLS-RP. The MLS-RP and MLS-SE use MLSP messages to communicate with each other. The MLS-RP sends MLSP messages to the MLS-SE if either of the above events occur, which indicate to the MLS-SE that it should flush the MLS cache and possibly modify the flow mask used. An example of when the flow mask would be changed is when an extended ACL is applied to a previously unfiltered interface. As you saw in Figure 6-11, a full flow mask is required when extended ACLs are used, so the MLS-RP sends an MLSP message to the MLS-SE to flush its MLS cache and update the flow mask.

NOTE	MLSP communications are also used to verify that MLS components are still alive via the exchange of hello packets. These messages are sent every 15 seconds by default.

In an environment where multiple MLS-RPs are present, the MLS-SE must be able to differentiate between each MLS-RP. This can be done based upon the MAC address of each MLS-RP; however, if there are thousands of flow entries in the MLS cache and if each of the entries associated with an MLS-RP that has just gone down need to be flushed, searching through the cache based upon a 48-bit MAC address value can take some time. To facilitate faster cache purges, an 8-bit XTAG value is assigned to MLS-RP, which acts like an index for each MLS-RP, allowing the MLS-SE to differentiate between the flow entries associated with each MLS-RP much more quickly.

Cisco Platform Support for MLS

It is important to understand that MLS is now considered a legacy technology and as such is not supported on many newer Cisco Catalyst switches. Table 6-2 lists the Cisco Catalyst switch platforms that the MLS-SE component is supported on.

Table 6-2   *MLS-SE Supported Platforms*

Platform	Hardware Requirements	Software Requirements
Catalyst 5000/5500	Supervisor 2G/3G/3/3F NetFlow Feature Card	CatOS 4.1(1)
Catalyst 6000/6500[1]	Policy Feature Card	5.1(1)

[1]The Catalyst 6000/6500 MLS-SE supports only operation with a locally installed MSFC as the MLS-RP. No support for an external MLS-RP is currently provided.

Table 6-3 lists the router platforms that the MLS-RP component is supported on.

Table 6-3   *MLS-RP Supported Platforms*

Platform	Software Requirements
3600	12.0(2)
4500/4700 7200/7500	11.3(2)WA4(4)
Catalyst 5000 RSM/RSFC	12.0(3c)W5(8a)
Catalyst 6000 MSFC	All software trains

NOTE	It is important to note that the Catalyst 6000/6500 Supervisor 1A with PFC can act only as an MLS-SE in conjunction with the Catalyst 6000/6500 MSFC; in this configuration, the MLS-SE (the PFC) and MLS-RP (the MSFC) do not communicate over IP, instead communicating via an internal bus. However, the MSFC can act as an MLS-RP with other MLS-SEs such as a Catalyst 5000 with NetFlow Feature Card (NFFC).

Scenario Prerequisites

To successfully commence the configuration tasks required to complete this scenario, Table 6-4 describes the prerequisite configurations required on each device in the scenario topology. Any configurations not listed can be assumed as being the default configuration.

Table 6-4   *Scenario 6-1 Requirements*

Device	Required Configuration	
	Parameter	**Value**
Switch-A	Hostname	Switch-A
	sc0 IP Address (VLAN)	192.168.1.10/24 (VLAN 1)
	Enable/Telnet Password	cisco
	VTP Mode	Transparent
	VTP Domain Name	lanps
	VLANs (Name)	VLAN 2 (VLAN02)
	VLAN Assignments	VLAN 2: port 2/3
	ISL Trunks (DTP Mode)	2/1 (nonegotiate)
Router-A	Hostname	Router-A
	Enable/Telnet Password	cisco
	ISL Trunks	FastEthernet0/0
	ISL Trunk Subinterfaces	FastEthernet0/0.1 (VLAN 1)
	IP Address	FastEthernet0/0.2 (VLAN 2)
	(Interface)	192.168.1.1/24 (fa0/0.1) 192.168.2.1/24 (fa0/0.2)
Host-X	Operating System	Windows 2000 Professional or Windows XP
	IP Address	192.168.1.100/24
	Default Gateway	192.168.1.1

Table 6-4   *Scenario 6-1 Requirements (Continued)*

Device	Required Configuration	
	Parameter	**Value**
Host-Y	Operating System	Windows 2000 Professional or Windows XP
	IP Address	192.168.2.100/24
	Default Gateway	192.168.2.1
	Applications	Telnet server (e.g. Microsoft Telnet Server)

Example 6-1 and Example 6-2 shows the configuration required on Switch-A and Router-A before you can begin this scenario.

Example 6-68 *Scenario 6-1 Prerequisite Configuration for Switch-A*

```
Console> (enable) set system name Switch-A
System name set.
Switch-A> (enable) set password
Enter old password: ⏎
Enter new password: *****
Reenter new password: *****
Switch-A> (enable) set enablepass
Enter old password: ⏎
Enter new password: *****
Retype new password: *****
Switch-A> (enable) set interface sc0 192.168.1.10 255.255.255.0
Interface sc0 IP address and netmask set.
Switch-A> (enable) set vtp mode transparent
VTP domain modified
Switch-A> (enable) set vtp domain lanps
VTP domain lanps modified
Switch-A> (enable) set vlan 2 name VLAN2
Vlan 2 configuration successful
Switch-A> (enable) set trunk 2/1 nonegotiate isl
Port(s)  2/1 trunk mode set to nonegotiate.
Port(s)  2/1 trunk type set to isl.
Switch-A> (enable) set vlan 2 2/3
VLAN 2 modified.
VLAN 1 modified.
VLAN  Mod/Ports
----  ---------------------
2     2/3
```

Example 6-69 *Scenario 6-1 Prerequisite Configuration for Router-A*

```
Router# configure terminal
Router(config)# hostname Router-A
Router-A(config)# enable secret cisco
Router-A(config)# line vty 0 4
```

continues

Example 6-69 *Scenario 6-1 Prerequisite Configuration for Router-A (Continued)*

```
Router-A(config-line)# password cisco
Router-A(config-line)# exit
Router-A(config)# interface FastEthernet0/0
Router-A(config-if)# no shutdown
Router-A(config-if)# exit
Router-A(config)# interface FastEthernet0/0.1
Router-A(config-if)# encapsulation isl 1
Router-A(config-if)# ip address 192.168.1.1 255.255.255.0
Router-A(config-if)# exit
Router-A(config)# interface FastEthernet0/0.2
Router-A(config-if)# encapsulation isl 2
Router-A(config-if)# ip address 192.168.2.1 255.255.255.0
```

After the prerequisite configuration is implemented, you should attach each device as indicated in Figure 6-9 and verify PING connectivity between devices in the network before proceeding.

Configuration Tasks

As you have learned, MLS consists of an MLS-SE and MLS-RP, which must each be configured separately. Configuring MLS requires the following configuration tasks:

- Configuring the MLS-RP
- Configuring the MLS-SE
- Verifying MLS operation

Configuring the MLS-RP

When configuring MLS on the MLS-RP, you must configure MLS globally on the router, which then enables you to configure global MLS parameters as well as specific interfaces for MLS. Before you can enable any MLS interface, you must configure the same VTP domain used by the MLS-SE on each MLS-enabled interface. This is because MLSP communications between MLS components cannot cross VTP domain boundaries. You must also configure an MLS management interface, which is the interface used to send and receive MLSP messages. Once you have completed all these tasks, you can then enable MLS on the required interfaces. In summary, this requires the following configuration tasks:

- Enabling MLS globally
- Configuring MLS on interfaces

Enabling MLS Globally

The first configuration task for configuring MLS on an MLS-RP is to enable MLS globally, which enables further configuration of specific MLS parameters. To enable MLS globally, the **mls rp ip** global configuration command is used, as demonstrated in Example 6-3 on Router-A.

Example 6-70   *Enabling IP MLS on Router-A*

```
Router-A# configure terminal
Router-A(config)# mls rp ip
```

Configuring MLS on Interfaces

After enabling MLS globally on the MLS-RP, you next configure MLS on each interface that needs to communicate with MLS-SEs. Each interface that needs to communicate with an MLS-SE requires the following configuration:

- The VTP domain of the MLS-SE switches that the MLS-RP communicates with via the interface must be configured.

- MLS must be explicitly enabled on the interface.

An MLS-RP also requires a single interface to be designated as a *management interface*, which defines the interface used for MLS-RP ←→ MLS-SE communications. Without a management interface, the MLS-RP does not function.

To configure MLS on an interface, the **mls** interface configuration command is used, which has the following syntaxes:

```
Switch(config-if)# mls rp vtp-domain vtp-domain-name
Switch(config-if)# mls management-interface
Switch(config-if)# mls rp ip
```

The following describes each of the command syntaxes listed above:

- **mls rp vtp-domain**—Defines the VTP domain of the MLS-SEs connected to the interface. The configured VTP domain must match the VTP domain configured on MLS-SEs; otherwise, MLS communications fail.

- **mls management-interface**—Defines the interface as the MLS management interface. Only one interface can be configured as a management interface.

- **mls rp ip**—Enables MLS operation on the interface.

WARNING   Always configure the VTP domain first, *before* configuring any other MLS commands on an interface. If you do not specify the VTP domain first, as soon as you configure another MLS command (e.g., enable MLS or configure a management interface), a null VTP domain will be assumed and configured. To change the VTP domain, all MLS interface configuration must be removed. Hence, to save time and frustration, always configure the appropriate VTP domain first.

In this scenario, Router-A has two subinterfaces configured (fastEthernet0/0.1 and fastEthernet0/0.2) over a physical trunk to Switch-A, which belong in VLAN 1 and VLAN 2 respectively. MLS must be enabled on both these interfaces, and a management interface must also be configured. Example 6-4 demonstrates enabling MLS on both interfaces and configuring fastEthernet0/0.1 as the management interface.

Example 6-71   *Enabling IP MLS on MLS-RP Interfaces*

```
Router-A# configure terminal
Enter configuration commands, one per line.  End with CNTL/Z.
Router-A(config)# interface fastEthernet0/0.1
Router-A(config-if)# mls rp vtp-domain lanps
Router-A(config-if)# mls management-interface
Router-A(config-if)# mls rp ip
Router-A(config-if)# exit
Router-A(config)# interface fastEthernet0/0.2
Router-A(config-if)# mls rp vtp-domain lanps
Router-A(config-if)# mls rp ip
```

In Example 6-4, notice that the VTP domain is configured first with a value of *lanps,* which matches the VTP domain configured on Switch-A in the "Configuration Prerequisites" section earlier in this chapter. The fastEthernet0/0.1 interface is specified as the management interface, meaning Router-A must be configured as an MLS-RP with an IP address of 192.168.1.1 on the MLS-SE.

Configuring the MLS-SE

After you have configured the MLS-RP, you can then configure the MLS-SE. Configuring the MLS-SE requires the following configuration tasks:

- Configuring VTP
- Enabling MLS
- Configuring optional MLS parameters

Configuring VTP

As indicated in the previous section on configuring the MLS-RP, the VTP domains configured on the MLS-RP and MLS-SE must match. In the configuration prerequisites section of this scenario, VTP was configured on Switch-A with a VTP domain name of *lanps*, which matches the VTP domain configured on the MLS-RP earlier, ensuring MLS communications succeed.

Enabling MLS

After ensuring VTP is configured correctly, you can begin to configure MLS. The first MLS configuration task is to enable MLS globally on the switch, which enables MLS-SE functionality. If the MLS-RP is integrated with the Catalyst switch (i.e., the RSM/RSFC on the Catalyst 5000/5500 or the MSFC on the Catalyst 6000/6500), MLS is already enabled automatically and you do not need to configure MLS, unless you wish to modify certain MLS parameters. If the MLS-RP is external (as is the case for this scenario), you must explicitly enable MLS and also define at least one MLS-RP.

To enable MLS, the **set mls enable** command is used without any other parameters. After enabling MLS, you can then define up to 16 external MLS-RPs using the **set mls include** command:

```
Console> (enable) set mls include mls-rp-address
```

The *mls-rp-address* parameter must be the IP address of the MLS management interface configured on the MLS-RP. Example 6-5 demonstrates enabling MLS on Switch-A and then defining Router-A as an MLS-RP.

Example 6-72 *Enabling IP MLS and Configuring an MLS-RP on CatOS*

```
Switch-A> (enable) set mls enable
IP Multilayer switching is enabled.
Switch-A> (enable) set mls include 192.168.1.1
Multilayer switching is enabled for router 192.168.1.1
```

In Example 6-5, notice that after MLS is enabled, the VLAN 1 interface IP address on Router-A is defined as an MLS-RP, which is the management interface on Router-A (see Example 6-4).

Configuring Optional MLS Parameters

At this stage, Switch-A has been configured as a fully functional MLS-SE and begins to use MLS as Router-A is operational as an MLS-RP. You can also configure other optional MLS parameters, which mainly affect the how the flow cache is operated and maintained. Some of these optional parameters include the following:

- Configuring the minimum flow mask
- Configuring MLS timers

Configuring the Minimum Flow Mask

The first optional parameter defines the *minimum* flow mask for the flow cache. By default, a flow mask of *destination* is used, which means flow entries are generated on a per-destination IP address basis. As you have already learned, three different flow masks exist— *destination*, *source-destination,* and *full flow.* You normally don't need to modify the default flow mask of *destination*, as the configuration of features that require a higher resolution masks, such as implementing ACLs on the MLS-RP, is performed automatically. If you do wish to configure the minimum flow mask to a higher resolution flow mask, you can use the **set mls flow** command:

```
Console> (enable) set mls flow {destination | destination-source | full]
```

Example 6-6 demonstrates configuring the minimum flow mask as source and destination IP address on Switch-B, which means a new flow entry is generated for each unique source and destination pair of IP addresses.

Example 6-73 *Configuring the Minimum Flow Mask on CatOS*

```
Switch-A> (enable) set mls flow destination-source
Configured flow mask is set to destination-source flow.
```

WARNING   The full flow mask generates a lot of entries in the MLS cache and should be used with caution. For example, in this scenario, an HTTP connection between Host-X and Host-Y is represented by a separate flow from an FTP connection between Host-X and Host-Y.

Configuring MLS Timers

The flow cache is a finite resource that only can maintain a certain amount of flow entries before the cache becomes full. If the cache becomes full, the MLS-SE can no longer write new entries for new flows, meaning any new flows that require routing cannot be Layer 3 switched. Instead they are routed normally via the router-on-stick topology of the MLS-RP. The MLS cache can accommodate 128 K (128 * 1024) entries; however, when the number of entries is above 32 K, there is a chance that the MLS-SE forwards some flows to the MLS-RP for forwarding. To avoid the flow cache from exceeding 32 K entries, the MLS-SE operates two timers, which are both used to age out idle flow entries after a configurable period of time:

- **MLS fast aging timer**—Used to age out flows that have not exceeded sending a configurable number of packets (the *packet threshold*) within the fast aging timer. By default, the fast aging timer is set to 0 (not used) and is normally configured only to reduce the size of the MLS cache when it is consistently exceeding 32K entries. You can configure the fast aging timer as 32, 64, 96, or 128 seconds; you can configure a packet threshold of 0, 1, 3, 7, 15, 31, or 63 packets. For example, if you configured a fast aging timer of 32 seconds and a packet threshold of 15, any flow that does not send more than 15 packets within 32 seconds is aged out. If the MLS cache exceeds 32 K, reduce the fast aging timer; if the MLS cache continues to exceed 32 K, you should decrease the MLS aging timer (described next).

- **MLS aging timer**—Used to age out idle flows that have not sent a single packet (if one or more packets is sent, the aging timer is reset) during the aging timer interval. The MLS aging timer is 256 seconds by default and the aging time can be configured in 8-second increments between 8 and 2032 seconds.

NOTE   You should only ever modify the MLS aging time after you have first tuned the IP MLS fast aging timer.

To configure the MLS fast aging timer and aging timer, the **set mls agingtime** command is used:

```
Console> (enable) set mls agingtime {aging-timer | fast
  fast-aging-timer packet-threshold}
```

You configure the MLS aging timer by just specifying an aging timer value, while you configure the MLS fast aging timer by specifying the **fast** keyword and then configuring the fast aging timer and packet threshold. Example 6-7 demonstrates configuring the MLS fast aging timer and aging timer on Switch-A.

Example 6-74 *Configuring the MLS Aging Timer and MLS Fast Aging Timer on CatOS*

```
Switch-A> (enable) set mls agingtime 480
Multilayer switching aging time set to 480
Switch-A> (enable) set mls agingtime fast 128 7
Multilayer switching fast aging time set to 128 seconds for entries
    with no more than 7
packets switched.
```

In Example 6-7, the MLS aging timer is set to 480 seconds, meaning any flow entry that is idle for 480 seconds is aged out. The MLS fast aging timer is also configured, aging out any flow entry that does not send more than 7 packets within a 128 second period.

Verifying MLS Operation

At this stage, you have configured an MLS-RP and MLS-SE, configured a minimum flow mask on the MLS-SE so that the MLS cache on the MLS-SE contains flows that represent unique source and destination IP address combinations and also configured MLS timers on the MLS-SE. To verify the MLS configuration on the MLS-RP and MLS-SE, Host-X and Host-Y need to communicate so that MLS operation can be observed and verified.

Before testing inter-VLAN communications, it is a good idea to verify the MLS configuration on the MLS-RP and MLS-SE. On the MLS-RP (Cisco IOS-based), the **show mls rp** command can be used to verify MLS configuration. Example 6-8 demonstrates using this command on Router-A after both the MLS-RP and MLS-SE have been configured.

Example 6-75 *Verifying MLS Configuration on the MLS-RP*

```
Router-A# show mls rp
ip multilayer switching is globally enabled
ipx multilayer switching is globally disabled
ipx mls inbound acl override is globally disabled
mls id is 0010.7be2.aba0
```

continues

Example 6-75 *Verifying MLS Configuration on the MLS-RP (Continued)*

```
mls ip address 192.168.1.1
mls ip flow mask is destination
mls ipx flow mask is unknown
number of domains configured for mls 1

vlan domain name: lanps
   current ip flow mask: destination-source
  ip current/next global purge: false/false
  ip current/next purge count: 0/0
  current ipx flow mask: destination
  ipx current/next global purge: false/false
  ipx current/next purge count: 0/0
  current sequence number: 4280145038
  current/maximum retry count: 0/10
  current domain state: no-change
  domain uptime: 00:14:43
  keepalive timer expires in 9 seconds
  retry timer not running
  change timer not running
  fcp subblock count = 2

  1 management interface(s) currently defined:
     vlan 1 on fastEthernet0/0.1

  2 mac-vlan(s) configured for multi-layer switching

  2 mac-vlan(s) enabled for ip multi-layer switching:

     mac 0010.7be2.aba0
        vlan id(s)
        1    2

0 mac-vlan(s) enabled for ipx multi-layer switching:

router currently aware of following 1 switch(es):
     switch id 0030.f2b8.3fff
```

Notice in Example 6-8 that IP MLS is enabled on Router-A, and that the IP address of the MLS-RP is 192.168.1.1. You can see that interface fastEthernet0/0.1 is the management interface and that two VLANs are enabled for MLS (VLAN 1 and VLAN 2, which are provided physically by fastEthernet0/0.1 and fastEthernet0/0.2, respectively). You can also see that a single VTP domain called *lanps* is configured and that Router-A is aware of Switch-A as an MLS-SE. Notice that the flow mask is indicated as being destination, as opposed to destination-source as has been configured on Switch-A. This is because Router-A has no knowledge of the flow mask on Switch-A and, therefore, has a flow mask that is independent of the switch.

You can also you the **show mls ip** command on the MLS-SE (CatOS). Example 6-9 demonstrates using this command on Switch-A after both the MLS-RP and MLS-SE have been configured.

Example 6-76 *Verifying MLS Configuration on the MLS-SE*

```
Switch-A> (console) show mls ip
IP Multilayer switching enabled
IP Multilayer switching aging time = 480 seconds
IP Multilayer switching fast aging time = 128 seconds, packet threshold = 7
IP Current flow mask is Destination-source flow
Configured flow mask is Destination-source flow
Active IP MLS entries = 1
Netflow Data Export disabled
Netflow Data Export port/host is not configured.
Total packets exported = 0

IP MLS-RP IP      MLS-RP ID     XTAG MLS-RP MAC-Vlans
---------------   -----------   ---- --------------------------------
192.168.1.1       00107be2aba0   2 00-10-7b-e2-ab-a0  1-2
```

In Example 6-9, you can see that MLS is enabled and can also see the aging timers configured for MLS. Notice that the flow mask on the MLS-SE is destination-source, because this has been configured as the minimum flow mask. The last line in the output of Example 6-9 shows the IP address, MAC address, XTAG, and VLANs for which each interface of the MLS-RP is configured.

Now that the MLS configuration on both the MLS-RP and MLS-SE has been verified, it is time to actually test that inter-VLAN is routing and that MLS is being performed as it should. Before testing inter-VLAN routing, it is a good idea to clear any current flow entries from the MLS cache using the **clear mls entry ip all** command so that you can easily see when entries are generated in response to various events. Example 6-10 demonstrates clearing all current entries from the MLS cache on the MLS-SE.

Example 6-77 *Clearing the MLS Cache on Switch-A*

```
Switch-A> (enable) clear mls entry ip all
Multilayer switching entries cleared.
Switch-A> (enable) show mls entry ip
                              Last     Used
Destination IP  Source IP     Prot DstPrt SrcPrt Destination Mac   Vlan Port
--------------- ------------- ---- ------ ------ ----------------- ---- -----
MLS-RP 192.168.1.1:
No entries
```

In Example 6-10, after all entries in the MLS cache are cleared, the **show mls entry ip** command is used to verify no entries exist in the cache.

After the MLS cache is emptied, the process of testing inter-VLAN routing can now begin. To simulate traffic that requires inter-VLAN routing, Host-X (in VLAN 1) can be used to ping Host-Y (in VLAN 2), which causes inter-VLAN routing between VLAN 1 and VLAN 2 to occur. Example 6-11 demonstrates pinging Host-Y from Host-X.

Example 6-78 *Generating Inter-VLAN on Host-X*

```
C:\> ping 192.168.2.100

Pinging 192.168.2.100 with 32 bytes of data:

Reply from 192.168.2.100: bytes=32 time=4ms TTL=128
Reply from 192.168.2.100: bytes=32 time<1ms TTL=128
Reply from 192.168.2.100: bytes=32 time<1ms TTL=128
Reply from 192.168.2.100: bytes=32 time<1ms TTL=128

Ping statistics for 192.168.2.100:
    Packets: Sent = 4, Received = 4, Lost = 0 (0% loss),
Approximate round trip times in milli-seconds:
    Minimum = 1ms, Maximum = 4ms, Average = 2ms
```

In Example 6-11, the first packet sent by Host-X is routed through the MLS-RP, with the MLS-SE learning the information required for Layer 3 switching based upon the routed Ethernet frame that is sent from the MLS-RP to Host-Y in VLAN 2. Each subsequent packet is then Layer 3 switched in hardware on the MLS-SE, ensuring high performance inter-VLAN routing. Example 6-12 demonstrates verifying that a flow entry has indeed been generated on the MLS-SE (Switch-A) using the **show mls entry ip** command, after traffic has been generated in Example 6-11 between Host-X and Host-Y.

Example 6-79 *Viewing the MLS Cache on Switch-A*

```
Switch-A> (enable) show mls entry ip
                                   Last    Used
Destination IP   Source IP         Prot DstPrt SrcPrt Destination Mac    Vlan Port
--------------- ---------------    ---- ------ ------ ----------------- ---- -----
MLS-RP 192.168.2.2:
 No entries
MLS-RP 192.168.1.1:
 192.168.1.100   192.168.2.100     -    -      -      00-10-a4-e0-1e-d3 1    2/2
 192.168.2.100   192.168.1.100     -    -      -      00-06-53-fe-84-20 2    2/3
```

Notice in Example 6-12 that two new entries are in the MLS cache for the MLS-RP at 192.168.1.1 (Router-A). The first entry indicates that any IP packet with a source IP address of 192.168.2.100 (Host-Y) and a destination IP address of 192.168.1.100 (Host-X) should be L3 switched by rewriting the destination MAC address of the frame to 00-10-a4-e0-1e-d3 (the MAC address of Host-X) and then switching the frame out port 2/2 (which is attached to Host-X). Similarly, the second entry describes the information required to L3 switch traffic from Host-X (192.168.1.100) to Host-Y (192.168.2.100). Example 6-12 demonstrates that a bidirectional communications session between two devices generates two flow entries—one for each direction packets are sent.

You can see that the flow entries generated on the MLS-SE in Example 6-12 have a flow mask of destination-source, which means only a single pair of flow entries are generated for any communications between Host-X and Host-Y. If on Host-X you attempt to establish another form of connectivity to Host-Y (e.g., access a file share or establish a Telnet connection), no new flow entries are generated.

Verifying MLSP Operation

MLSP is used to communicate information between the MLS-RP and MLS-SE. Events such as routing topology changes and access control list configuration changes are communicated to the MLS-SE by the MLS-RP via MLSP messages. In the event of a routing topology change, the MLS-SE flushes the MLS cache to ensure that packets are not L3 switched in error. In the event of an access control list (ACL) being applied to an interface on the MLS-RP, the MLS-SE adjusts the flow mask to that specified by the MLS-RP to ensure traffic cannot bypass the ACL.

Example 6-13 demonstrates configuring an extended ACL on Router-A and then applying it to interface fastEthernet0/0.1, which is attached to VLAN 1 on Switch-B. After this configuration is implemented, Router-A (as the MLS-RP) should immediately notify Switch-A (the MLS-SE) that the flow mask needs to be modified.

Example 6-80 *Configuring an Extended Access Control List on Switch-A*

```
Router-A# configure terminal
Router-A(config)# access-list 100 permit tcp any any eq telnet
Router-A(config)# access-list 100 deny ip any any log
Router-A(config)# interface fastEthernet0/0.1
Router-A(config-if)# ip access-group 100 in
```

In Example 6-13, the ACL configured permits only Telnet traffic, denying all other traffic. After applying the ACL to interface fastEthernet0/0.1, Router-A communicates via MLSP to the MLS-SE that the flow mask needs to be modified to a full flow mask to ensure the MLS-SE does not permit other types of traffic. Example 6-14 demonstrates checking the MLS configuration on Switch-A after the ACL is applied on Router-A in Example 6-13.

Example 6-81 *Checking the MLS Cache on Switch-A*

```
Switch-A> (console) show mls ip
Total packets switched = 1748724
Total Active MLS entries = 0
IP Multilayer switching enabled
IP Multilayer switching aging time = 480 seconds
IP Multilayer switching fast aging time = 128 seconds, packet threshold = 7
IP Current flow mask is Full flow
Configured flow mask is Destination-source flow
Active IP MLS entries = 0
```

In Example 6-14, notice that the configured flow mask is destination-source; however, the current flow mask is full, which is due to the ACL configuration on Router-A causing Router-A to indicate to Switch-A that the flow mask needs to be changed to a full flow mask.

At this point, Host-X is able to establish only Telnet connections to Host-Y based upon the ACL configured in Example 6-13 (ping requests should fail). Because a full flow mask is now configured on Switch-A, a new flow entry should be generated for each connection routed through the Layer 3 switching engine of Switch-A. Figure 6-12 demonstrates establishing two Telnet connections to Host-Y from Host-X, and then Example 6-15 demonstrates checking the MLS cache after the connections have been established.

Figure 6-12 *Establishing Two Telnet Connections From Host-X to Host-Y*

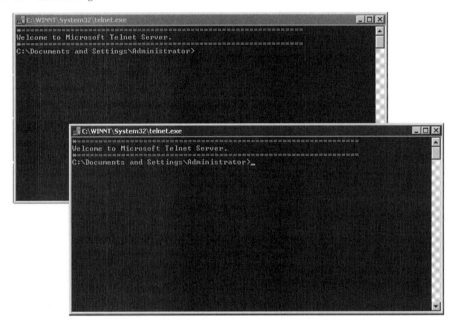

Example 6-82 *Viewing the MLS Cache on Switch-A*

```
Switch-A> (enable) show mls entry ip
Destination IP  Source IP       Prot DstPrt SrcPrt Destination Mac    Vlan Port
--------------- --------------- ---- ------ ------ ----------------- ---- -----
MLS-RP 192.168.2.2:
 No entries
MLS-RP 192.168.1.1:
 192.168.2.100   192.168.1.100   TCP  Telnet 3779   00-06-53-fe-84-20 2    2/3
 192.168.2.100   192.168.1.100   TCP  Telnet 3780   00-06-53-fe-84-20 2    2/3
 192.168.1.100   192.168.2.100   TCP  3780   Telnet 00-10-a4-e0-1e-d3 1    2/2
 192.168.1.100   192.168.2.100   TCP  3779   Telnet 00-10-a4-e0-1e-d3 1    2/2
```

Notice in Example 6-15 that four new flows are cached in the MLS cache, one for each direction of traffic for each connection. Because the source TCP port (on Host-X) of each connection is different, separate pairs of flow entries in the MLS cache are present due to the flow mask being now configured as full (see Example 6-14). With the ACL configured, you should never see any completed flow entries for traffic other than Telnet traffic. Because the access list on Router-A drops all non-Telnet traffic, Switch-A never sees any traffic associated with non-Telnet packets return from Router-A and thus never completes a flow entry for the non-Telnet traffic in the MLS cache.

Scenario 6-2: Configuring CEF-based Layer 3 Switching on the Catalyst 6000/6500 Operating in Hybrid Mode

The next-generation of Cisco Catalyst Layer 3 switches are all based upon Cisco Express Forwarding (CEF). CEF is also the next-generation route caching mechanism for interrupt context switching on Cisco routers so understanding how CEF works and how to configure it is important for network engineers. CEF offers significant improvements over MLS, the most notable being that the first packet in a flow does not need to process-switched by the control plane routing component, as is the case with MLS. With CEF, all packets (even the first) associated with a flow are Layer 3 switched in hardware. This is an important consideration in environments where many new flows are being established continuously (e.g., an Internet service provider environment), because large amounts of new flows in an MLS configuration reduces performance.

In this scenario you learn how to configure Layer 3 switching using CEF on a *hybrid mode* Catalyst 6000/6500 switch, which refers to a configuration where the Supervisor engine runs CatOS and the MSFC runs a separate Cisco IOS operating system. In later scenarios, you learn how to upgrade from a hybrid mode system to a native mode system and then configure Layer 3 switching using native mode.

Figure 6-13 shows topology used for this scenario.

In Figure 6-13, Switch-A is a Catalyst 6509 switch a Supervisor 2 engine installed, which includes a PFC-2 and MSFC-2. Switch-A is running hybrid mode, with CatOS running on the Supervisor 2 engine and Cisco IOS running on the MSFC-2. The goal of this scenario is simply to enable inter-VLAN routing between Host-X and Host-Y, using CEF-based Layer 3 switching.

Figure 6-13 *Topology for Scenario 6-2*

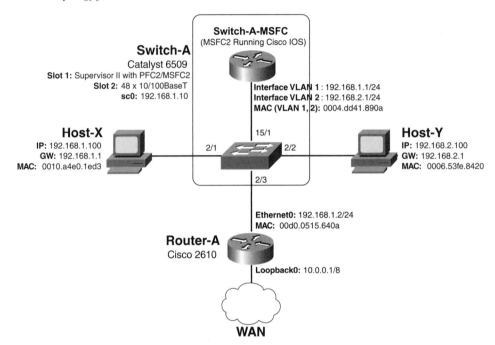

Introduction to Cisco Express Forwarding

Cisco Express Forwarding (CEF) allows the appropriate information required for the data plane operations of Layer 3 routing (e.g., MAC address rewrites on an Ethernet network and determining the egress port out which a routed frame should be sent) to be stored in a compact data structure optimized for fast lookup.

NOTE　　CEF is not only used by Cisco Catalyst Layer 3 switches; it is also used by Cisco routers (in fact, CEF was originally developed on high-end Cisco routers). CEF represents the recommended "route caching" mechanism that should be configured on all Cisco Layer 3 devices if possible.

You have learnt that MLS uses a *flow-based* caching mechanism, where packets must first be process-switched by the MLS-RP to generate flow entries in the cache. In environments where thousands of new flows are being created per second, this can cause the MLS-RP to become a bottleneck. CEF was developed to eliminate the performance penalty of the first-packet process-switched lookup, allowing the route cache used by the hardware-based L3 routing engine to contain all the necessary information to L3 switch in hardware before any packets associated with a flow are received. To achieve this, CEF creates two data structures in the route cache:

- **Forwarding Information Base (FIB)**—The FIB is generated directly from the route table and contains the next-hop IP address information for each destination (IP route) in the network.

- **Adjacency table**—The adjacency table defines each next-hop IP address in terms of MAC address and egress interface. MAC address information is collected via the ARP cache.

Figure 6-14 illustrates how the route table, FIB, adjacency table and ARP cache work together.

Figure 6-14 *CEF Components*

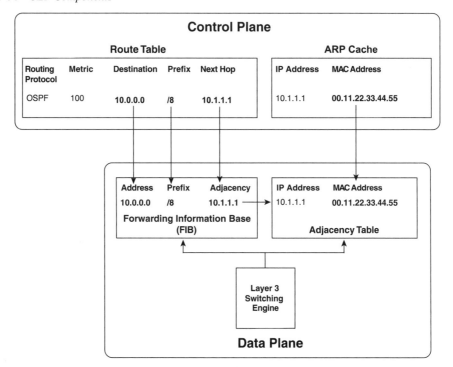

In Figure 6-14, the route table and ARP cache are both control plane entities, meaning that both are generated and maintained via the control plane processor. From these tables, the FIB and adjacency tables are built, which are data structures optimized for fast lookup by the data plane processor In Figure 6-14, the Layer 3 switching engine uses the FIB and adjacency table to determine the MAC address of the next hop device for a packet, providing the Layer 3 switching engine the required information for MAC address to rewritten in hardware rather than software. Notice how the FIB is built in the route table; the destination address, subnet mask (or prefix), and next hop gateway are extracted from the route table (the remaining information in the route table is not relevant to the Layer 3 switching process). The adjacency table then builds the MAC address details that are used to rewrite the destination MAC address of each Layer 3 switched frame, using the ARP cache (populated via the control plane using ARP requests).

NOTE   The MAC address of the router must also be known to the Layer 3 switching engine, which is used to rewrite the source MAC address of the Layer 3 switched frame. This MAC address is always the same value and hence does not need to be included in the FIB/adjacency tables.

You might notice that all of the information contained in the FIB and adjacency table is the same information contained within the route and ARP tables. The FIB and adjacency exist purely for organizing the specific information required for Layer 3 switching into a structure that is optimized for fast lookups by the data plane.

Distributed and Accelerated CEF

By default, all CEF-based Cisco Catalyst switches use a central Layer 3 switching engine to provide CEF-based Layer 3 switching, where a single processor makes all Layer 3 switching decisions for traffic received on all ports in the switch. Even though the Layer 3 switching engines used in Cisco Catalyst switches provide high performance, in some networks, having a single Layer 3 switching engine to all the Layer 3 switching does not provide sufficient performance. *Distributed CEF (dCEF)* and *Accelerated CEF (aCEF)* are technologies that implement multiple Layer 3 switching engines so that simultaneous Layer 3 switching operations can occur in parallel, boosting overall system performance.

dCEF can be used in Cisco Catalyst 6500 switches and refers to the use of multiple CEF tables distributed across multiple line cards installed in the chassis. Each line card that supports dCEF has its own dedicated hardware-based L3 routing engine and CEF route cache, allowing for multiple L3 data plane operations to be performed simultaneously within a single chassis-based system. The main route processor of the switch is responsible for generating a central master FIB and adjacency table and distributing these tables out to each dCEF line card. Figure 6-15 demonstrates the dCEF architecture.

Figure 6-15 *L3 Switching Using dCEF*

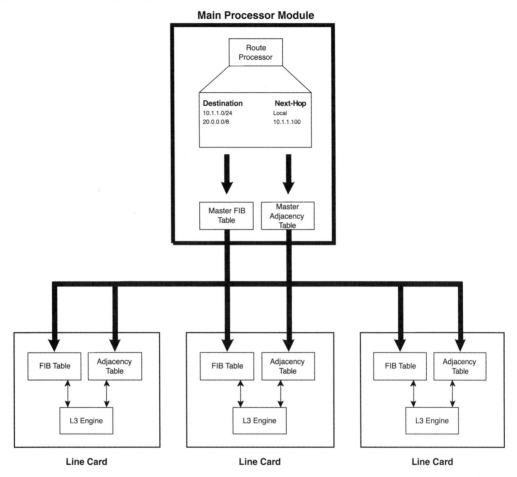

aCEF is a new feature supported in conjunction with the new Supervisor 720 engine which works in a similar fashion to MLS. In MLS, line cards send the initial packet of a flow to the Supervisor engine, where the packet is switched in hardware using the master CEF table. The forwarding decision made is then stored in a local scaled-down CEF table on the line card where the flow enters the switch, with the local line card making any subsequent forwarding decisions for packets associated with a flow in the local CEF table.

The Cisco CEF Implementation

The use of CEF-based L3 switching is supported on the following Cisco Catalyst switches:

- Catalyst 3550/3750 series with L3 enhanced image
- Catalyst 4000/4500 series with Supervisor 3/4
- Catalyst 6000/6500 series with Supervisor 2, PFC-2, and MSFC-2
- Catalyst 6000/6500 series with Supervisor 720 (includes PFC-3 and MSFC-3)

NOTE CEF is also supported on all Cisco routers from IOS 12.0 upwards. It is important to understand that the CEF implementation on low-end routers (i.e., Cisco 3700 series and lower) still uses the main processor for data plane operations, whereas L3 switches use a dedicated hardware chip (ASIC) for data plane operations (e.g., PFC-2) instead of the main processor. Using CEF still provides a performance advantage over older route caching technologies, such as fast switching. On higher end routers (e.g., 7500 series, 10000 series, and 12000 series), data plane operations are performed in specialized hardware-based ASICs.

Scenario Prerequisites

To successfully commence the configuration tasks required to complete this scenario, Table 6-5 describes the prerequisite configurations required on each device in the scenario topology. Any configurations not listed can be assumed as being the default configuration.

Table 6-5   *Scenario 6-2 Requirements*

Device	Required Configuration	
	Parameter	Value
Switch-A	Hostname	Switch-A
	sc0 IP Address (VLAN)	192.168.1.10/24 (VLAN 1)
	Enable/Telnet Password	cisco
	VTP Mode	Transparent
	VLANs (Name)	VLAN 2 (VLAN02)
	VLAN Assignments	VLAN 2: port 2/2
Router-A	Hostname	Router-A
	Enable/Telnet Password	cisco
	IP Address (Interface)	192.168.1.2/24 (Ethernet0/0)

Table 6-5   *Scenario 6-2 Requirements (Continued)*

Device	Required Configuration	
	Parameter	**Value**
Host-X	Operating System	Windows 2000 Professional or Windows XP
	IP Address	192.168.1.100/24
	Default Gateway	192.168.1.1
Host-Y	Operating System	Windows 2000 Professional or Windows XP
	IP Address	192.168.2.100/24
	Default Gateway	192.168.2.1

Example 6-16 and Example 6-17 shows the configuration required on Switch-A and Router-A before you can begin this scenario.

Example 6-83   *Scenario 6-2 Prerequisite Configuration for Switch-A*

```
Console> (enable) set system name Switch-A
System name set.
Switch-A> (enable) set password
Enter old password: ø
Enter new password: *****
Reenter new password: *****
Switch-A> (enable) set enablepass
Enter old password: ø
Enter new password: *****
Retype new password: *****
Switch-A> (enable) set interface sc0 192.168.1.10 255.255.255.0
Interface sc0 IP address and netmask set.
Switch-A> (enable) set vtp mode transparent
VTP domain modified
Switch-A> (enable) set vlan 2 name VLAN2
Vlan 2 configuration successful
Switch-A> (enable) set vlan 2 2/2
VLAN 2 modified.
VLAN 1 modified.
VLAN  Mod/Ports
----  ----------------------
2     2/2
```

Example 6-84   *Scenario 6-2 Prerequisite Configuration for Router-A*

```
Router# configure terminal
Router(config)# hostname Router-A
Router-A(config)# enable secret cisco
Router-A(config)# line vty 0 4
Router-A(config-line)# password cisco
```

continues

Example 6-84 *Scenario 6-2 Prerequisite Configuration for Router-A (Continued)*

```
Router-A(config-line)# exit
Router-A(config)# interface Ethernet0/0
Router-A(config-if)# no shutdown
Router-A(config-if)# ip address 192.168.1.2 255.255.255.0
```

After the prerequisite configuration is implemented, you should attach each device as indicated in Figure 6-13 and verify PING connectivity between devices in the network (where possible) before proceeding.

Configuration Tasks

Configuring CEF-based L3 switching on the Catalyst 6000/6500 operating in hybrid mode is very simple. On the Supervisor 2 engine (running CatOS), all that is required is for a PFC-2 and MSFC-2 daughtercard to be installed. No CatOS software configuration is required; however, you can tune and monitor the PFC-2 from CatOS. All configuration is controlled via the Cisco IOS running on the MSFC-2, where the IP route table is generated from the various routing protocols configured on the MSFC which then automatically populates the CEF table on the PFC-2. In summary, the following is required to configure CEF-based L3 switching:

- Configuring the MSFC
- Configuring the PFC (optional)
- Verifying CEF operation

Configuring the MSFC

To configure the MSFC on a hybrid mode Catalyst 6000/6500, the following tasks are required:

- Establishing management connectivity to the MSFC
- Configuring the MSFC-2

Establishing Management Connectivity to the MSFC-2

On a hybrid mode Catalyst 6000/6500 switch, configuration of the MSFC requires a management connection to be established to the MSFC operating system (Cisco IOS), which is separate from the CatOS running on the Supervisor engine. On the Catalyst 6000/6500, the MSFC is accessible via module 15, which is an internal designation for the internal interface between the MSFC daughtercard and Supervisor engine. You can access the MSFC management interface using the **session 15** command (where 15 represents the slot number of the MSFC), or alternatively, you can also use the **switch console** command. Example 6-18 demonstrates gaining access to the MSFC from CatOS.

Example 6-85 *Gaining Management Access to the MSFC*

```
Switch-A> (enable) switch console
Trying Router-15...
Connected to Router-15.
Type ^C^C^C to switch back...

Router>
```

TIP   The **session** command can be used only if the Supervisor detects the MSFC. If the MSFC has problems booting (for example, the IOS image is corrupted) and boots to ROMMON mode, the Supervisor does not detect the MSFC, and you cannot use the **session** command to connect to the MSFC console. In this situation, use the **switch console** command, because this accesses a console connection that is permanently wired to an internal console port on the MSFC.

Configuring the MSFC-2

After establishing initial management connectivity to the MSFC-2, you can next configure the MSFC-2 for routing. In Example 6-18, the MSFC should have a blank configuration because it has not yet been configured and, therefore, requires not only configuration relevant to Layer 3 switching but also any relevant base configuration. Example 6-19 shows the base configuration required on the MSFC-2.

Example 6-86 *Base Configuration for MSFC-2 on Switch-A*

```
Router> enable
Router# configure terminal
Router(config)# hostname Switch-A-MSFC
Switch-A-MSFC(config)# enable secret cisco
Switch-A-MSFC(config)# line vty 0 4
Switch-A-MSFC(config-line)# password cisco
```

In Example 6-19, the MSFC host name, Telnet password, and enable password is configured.

After the base configuration is complete, Layer 3 interfaces need to be created so that IP routing can take place. In this scenario, two Layer 3 switched virtual interfaces (SVIs) are required, which each attach to VLAN 1 and VLAN 2, respectively. Example 6-20 demonstrates configuring the required SVIs on the MSFC.

Example 6-87 *Configuring SVIs on the MSFC*

```
Switch-A-MSFC# configure terminal
Switch-A-MSFC(config)# interface VLAN 1
Switch-A-MSFC(config-if)# no shutdown
Switch-A-MSFC(config-if)# ip address 192.168.1.1 255.255.255.0
Switch-A-MSFC(config-if)# exit
Switch-A-MSFC(config)# interface VLAN 2
Switch-A-MSFC(config-if)# ip address 192.168.2.1 255.255.255.0
```

At this stage, you should be able to ping the sc0 interface (192.168.1.10) on the Supervisor engine of Switch-A because the VLAN 1 interface in Example 6-20 has been configured with an IP address. You should also be able to ping Router-A (192.168.2.2), Host-X, and Host-Y from Switch-A assuming these devices are connected and configured as per the earlier configuration prerequisites section.

Once IP connectivity has been verified, you can then configuring Layer 3 routing on the MSFC. In this scenario, the MSFC is part of an OSPF routing domain and must be configured to exchange routes with Router-A. Example 6-21 demonstrates configuring OSPF on the MSFC.

Example 6-88 *Configuring IP Routing on the MSFC*

```
Switch-A-MSFC# configure terminal
Switch-A-MSFC(config)# router ospf 1
Switch-A-MSFC(config-router)# network 192.168.1.0 0.0.0.255 area 0
Switch-A-MSFC(config-router)# network 192.168.2.0 0.0.0.255 area 0
Switch-A-MSFC(config-router)# end
Switch-A-MSFC# show ip ospf neighbors

Neighbor ID     Pri   State         Dead Time    Address        Interface
192.168.1.2      1    FULL/BDR      00:00:38     192.168.1.2    Vlan1
Switch-A-MSFC# show ip route
Codes: C - connected, S - static, I - IGRP, R - RIP, M - mobile, B - BGP
       D - EIGRP, EX - EIGRP external, O - OSPF, IA - OSPF inter area
       N1 - OSPF NSSA external type 1, N2 - OSPF NSSA external type 2
       E1 - OSPF external type 1, E2 - OSPF external type 2, E - EGP
       i - IS-IS, L1 - IS-IS level-1, L2 - IS-IS level-2, ia - IS-IS inter area
       * - candidate default, U - per-user static route, o - ODR
       P - periodic downloaded static route

Gateway of last resort is not set

O IA 10.0.0.0/8 [110/2] via 192.168.1.2, 00:00:32, Vlan1
C    192.168.1.0/24 is directly connected, Vlan1
C    192.168.2.0/24 is directly connected, Vlan2
```

In Example 6-21, both VLAN interfaces are configured as part of OSPF area 0. After the configuration, the **show ip ospf neighbors** command is executed, which verifies an OSPF adjacency has formed with Router-A. The **show ip route** command verifies that Switch-A-MSFC has learned the 10.0.0.0/8 network from Router-A.

Configuring the PFC (Optional)

No configuration is required of the PFC using the Supervisor engine to enabled CEF operation. CEF-based Layer 3 switching is solely enabled by configuring the MSFC.

One area where you can configure the Supervisor engine for CEF-based Layer 3 switching is in configuring *NetFlow statistics*. NetFlow is a protocol that is used in many service provider and enterprise networks which provides statistics to a NetFlow data collector about each flow or connection that passes through a routing device. This information is often for billing purposes in a service provider, making NetFlow a crucial feature of the network. NetFlow information can also be used for traffic analysis, which is common in enterprise networks. Traditionally, routers have been used for NetFlow; however, with the advent of Layer 3 switching, NetFlow has also moved to the switch. On a Layer 3 switch, the flow-based architecture of MLS (discussed in Scenario 6-1) fits well with NetFlow because the information about flow entries stored in cache can be directly exported to NetFlow. In a CEF-based Layer 3 switching architecture, however, the route caching mechanism is not flow-based, instead being based on routing topology and Layer 2 adjacency information rather than flows.

Cisco Catalyst 6000/6500 switches that perform CEF-based Layer 3 switching also collect flow information, purely for the purposes of supporting NetFlow statistics collection. On the Supervisor engine, you configure NetFlow statistics collection much like you configure MLS. The various commands that affect how information is stored in the MLS flow cache are the same commands used to determine how information is stored for NetFlow statistics on a CEF-based switch (all NetFlow information is stored in the *NetFlow table*). These commands include the following:

* **set mls agingtime**—Used to control how long an entry remains in the NetFlow table.
* **set mls flow**—Used to control the flow mask that defines the granularity of the NetFlow table.
* **set mls exclude protocol**—Used to exclude TCP and/or UDP flows from the NetFlow table.

NOTE   You can use the **show mls statistics** command to view information about the various flows stored in the Netflow table.

---

continues

Verifying CEF Operation

At this stage, the configuration of the network is complete. Host-X and Host-Y should be able to communicate with each other and also should be able to ping the loopback 0 interface on Router-A (10.0.0.1). This verifies that inter-VLAN routing is working; however, just because inter-VLAN routing is working doesn't necessarily mean that Layer 3 switching using CEF is working. Packets possibly could be routed in software via the MSFC, which of course in a production environment on a busy network degrades performance. If you are configuring CEF for Layer 3 switching, you must understand how to verify not only inter-VLAN routing, but also how to verify CEF operation.

To verify CEF operation on a hybrid mode Catalyst 6000/6500, you use various **show mls** commands, which display information relating to CEF operation. The **show mls cef mac** command can be used to view the MAC address that is used by the MSFC, which allows the PFC on the Supervisor engine to identify a candidate frame for Layer 3 switching. Example 6-22 demonstrates the use of this command.

Example 6-89 *Displaying the MSFC MAC Address on CatOS*

```
Switch-A> (enable) show mls cef mac
Module 15: Physical MAC-Address 00-04-dd-41-89-0a
Module 15 is the designated MSFC for installing CEF entries
```

In Example 6-22, you can see that Switch-A knows that the MAC address of the MSFC is 00-04-dd-41-89-0a, meaning any frames received with a destination MAC address of this address require Layer 3 switching.

As discussed in the introduction of this chapter, CEF uses two tables to represent control plane routing operation in a format that can be quickly looked up by the L3 engine on the PFC-2. The first table is the Forwarding Information Base (FIB). To view the FIB, you can use the **show mls entry cef ip** command, as demonstrated on Switch-A in Example 6-23.

Example 6-90 *Displaying the FIB on CatOS*

```
Switch-A> (enable) show mls entry cef ip
Mod FIB-Type Destination-IP  Destination-Mask NextHop-IP      Weight
--- -------- --------------- ---------------- --------------- ------
 15 receive  255.255.255.255 255.255.255.255
 15 receive  127.0.0.12      255.255.255.255
 15 receive  127.0.0.0       255.255.255.255
 15 receive  127.255.255.255 255.255.255.255
 15 resolved 127.0.0.11      255.255.255.255  127.0.0.11           1
 15 receive  192.168.2.1     255.255.255.255
 15 receive  192.168.2.0     255.255.255.255
 15 receive  192.168.2.255   255.255.255.255
 15 resolved 192.168.2.100   255.255.255.255  192.168.2.100        1
 15 receive  192.168.1.1     255.255.255.255
 15 receive  192.168.1.0     255.255.255.255
 15 receive  192.168.1.255   255.255.255.255
 15 resolved 192.168.1.100   255.255.255.255  192.168.1.100        1
 15 receive  224.0.0.0       255.255.255.0
```

Example 6-90 *Displaying the FIB on CatOS (Continued)*

```
15 connected 192.168.2.0      255.255.255.0
15 connected 192.168.1.0      255.255.255.0
15 resolved  10.0.0.0         255.0.0.0         192.168.1.2           1
15 connected 127.0.0.0        255.0.0.0
15 drop      224.0.0.0        240.0.0.0
15 wildcard  0.0.0.0          0.0.0.0
```

The FIB table is generated by the MSFC from the MSFC route table and written to the CEF FIB table in the route cache on the PFC-2. In Example 6-23, the *Mod* column indicates the module number of the MSFC (module 15) that generated each FIB entry. The *FIB-Type* column describes the type of FIB entry. The following describes each of the FIB types shown in Example 6-23:

- **resolved**—Indicates an entry that represents the route to a host on the local subnet or remote destination subnet derived from the routing table on the MSFC. Every resolved FIB entry includes a next hop IP address.

- **receive**—Indicates that any packet that matches the indicated destination IP address or IP subnet should be sent to the MSFC for processing. For example, these entries are used for any management traffic to a local IP address on the MSFC.

- **connected**—Indicates an entry that represents a locally connected IP subnet.

- **drop**—Indicates that any packet that matches the indicated destination IP address or IP subnet should be dropped. In Example 6-23, because multicast routing is not enabled on the MSFC, all multicast traffic (indicated by a destination IP address in the range of 224.0.0.0 → 239.255.255.255) is dropped.

- **wildcard**—Indicates the entry that matches any packets that do not match other FIB entries. The actions for this entry is to drop the traffic, as it is deemed unroutable.

The important entries in Example 6-23 are shaded. For example, the last shaded entry specifies a destination prefix of 10.0.0.0/8 and indicates that the next hop for this destination is 192.168.1.2 (Router-A).

The next table related to CEF is the adjacency table, which can be displayed by executing the **show mls entry adjacency** command, as shown in Example 6-24.

Example 6-91 *Displaying the CEF Adjacency Table on CatOS*

```
Switch-A> (enable) show mls entry cef adjacency
Mod:                15
Destination-IP:     192.168.2.100      Destination-Mask:    255.255.255.255
FIB-Type:           resolved

AdjType  NextHop-IP      NextHop-Mac       Vlan Encp Tx-Packets   Tx-Octets
-------  --------------- ----------------- ---- ---- ------------ -------------
connect  192.168.2.100   00-06-53-fe-84-20  2 ARPA           4           256
**************************************************************************
Mod:                15
```

continues

Example 6-91 *Displaying the CEF Adjacency Table on CatOS (Continued)*

```
Destination-IP:      127.0.0.11          Destination-Mask:   255.255.255.255
FIB-Type:            resolved

AdjType  NextHop-IP      NextHop-Mac       Vlan Encp Tx-Packets   Tx-Octets
-------- --------------- ----------------- ---- ---- ------------ -------------
connect  127.0.0.11      00-00-11-00-00-00    0 ARPA           0             0
*****************************************************************************
Mod:                 15
Destination-IP:      192.168.1.100       Destination-Mask:   255.255.255.255
FIB-Type:            resolved

AdjType  NextHop-IP      NextHop-Mac       Vlan Encp Tx-Packets   Tx-Octets
-------- --------------- ----------------- ---- ---- ------------ -------------
connect  192.168.1.100   00-10-a4-e0-1e-d3    1 ARPA           4           256
*****************************************************************************
Mod:                 15
Destination-IP:      10.0.0.0            Destination-Mask:   255.255.255.0
FIB-Type:            resolved

AdjType  NextHop-IP      NextHop-Mac       Vlan Encp Tx-Packets   Tx-Octets
-------- --------------- ----------------- ---- ---- ------------ -------------
connect  192.168.1.2     00-d0-05-15-64-0a    2 ARPA           5           420
```

In Example 6-24, notice that asterisked lines are included to show each of the separate adjacency entries. The output shows each of the next hop devices listed in the FIB table (see Example 6-23) and indicates the next hop interface and the number of IP packets and bytes transmitted. For example, the last entry in Example 6-24 is for the FIB prefix 10.0.0.0/8. In the adjacency information, you can see that the next hop address is 192.168.1.2 (Router-A). This information is generated from the routing table on the MSFC. The **NextHop-Mac** address column represents the destination MAC address of the next hop router, which is required as the address used to rewrite the destination MAC address for the relevant prefix. The MAC address information is built from the ARP cache. Finally, the **Tx-Packets** and **Tx-Octets** columns indicate how many packets and bytes have been L3 switched that match the adjacency entry.

TIP

A much tidier method of displaying the CEF adjacencies is to use the **show mls entry cef long** command. This command is not demonstrated here as the output is displayed in a table format that is very wide.

Scenario 6-3: Upgrading from Hybrid Mode to Native Mode on the Catalyst 6000/6500

At the beginning of this chapter, you learned that there are two different modes in which you can operate a Cisco Catalyst 6000/6500 Layer 3 switch. The first mode is hybrid mode, where a separate and different operating system (CatOS and Cisco IOS) runs on the Supervisor engine and MSFC respectively; in the previous scenario, you learned how to configure a Catalyst 6000/6500 switch running in hybrid mode. The second mode is native mode, where a single operating system (Cisco IOS) controls and configures both the Supervisor engine and MSFC and is considered the way of the future for the Cisco Catalyst 6000/6500 switch. By default, all Cisco Catalyst 6000/6500 switches that include an MSFC ship in hybrid mode, so if you wish to run native mode, you must upgrade your switch to native mode yourself.

In this scenario, you learn how to upgrade a hybrid mode Catalyst 6000/6500 switch to native mode and also learn about some of the restrictions of running native mode. This scenario follows on from the previous scenario with the goal of ensuring the same level of functionality as the previous scenario; the only difference being that Switch-A is to operate in native mode as opposed to hybrid mode.

Understanding Native Mode

Before examining native mode, it is important to understand that the Supervisor module has its own processor, which is referred to as the *switch processor*. The switch processor is responsible for managing the Layer 2 components of the switch, as well as the PFC card that provides Layer 3/4 data plane operations. The MSFC also has its own processor, which is referred to as the *route processor*; this is responsible for managing Layer 3 control plane operations.

When a Cisco Catalyst 6000/6500 is installed with a MSFC, the switch can be described as operating in two modes:

- **Hybrid mode**—In hybrid mode (or Hybrid mode), separate operating systems manage the Supervisor module and the MSFC. The Supervisor module operating system (CatOS) has control over the Layer 2 switching functions and hardware-based L3 switching (data plane) functions, while the MSFC operating system (Cisco IOS) has control over the Layer 3 routing control plane functions. Hybrid mode is the default mode of operation, and the Supervisor and MSFC require separate management.

- **Native mode**—In native mode (or Native mode), a single operating system is used to manage both the Supervisor module and the MSFC. The operating system, which is Cisco IOS, has control over all Layer 2 and Layer 3 functions of the switch. Native mode represents the future direction of the Cisco Catalyst 6000/6500; however, it is important to note that at this time, native mode requires an MSFC to be installed alongside the Supervisor, and some line cards and features are not currently supported in native mode.

Hybrid mode represents the majority of Catalyst 6000/6500 installations today; this will .remain so for the foreseeable future because there are some specific requirements and restrictions when using native mode.

Native Mode Requirements

To upgrade to native mode (if your Catalyst 6000/6500 switch has a Supervisor 1 module installed) it must meet the following prerequisites:

- Policy feature card (PFC-1) installed.
- Multilayer switching feature card (MSFC-1 or MSFC-2) installed.
- Supervisor 1 must have at least 16 MB Flash (default) and 64 MB DRAM (default) installed.
- MSFC-1 or MSFC-2 must have at least 16 MB Flash (default) and 128 MB DRAM (default for MSFC-2) installed. For larger and more complex networks, 256 MB or 512 MB of DRAM is recommended.
- A 32 MB PCMCIA flash card is recommended at least temporarily for rollback purposes, as you must format the internal flash file system to a Cisco IOS format.

If your Catalyst 6000/6500 switch has a Supervisor 2 module installed, it must meet the following prerequisites:

- Policy Feature Card (PFC-2) that is integrated into the Supervisor 2 module.
- Multilayer Switching Feature Card (MSFC-2) installed (the Supervisor 2 does not support the MSFC-1).
- Supervisor 2 must have at least 32 MB Flash and 128 MB DRAM (default) installed.
- MSFC-2 must have at least 16 MB Flash (default) and 256 MB DRAM (default) installed.
- A 32 MB PCMCIA Flash card is recommended at least temporarily for rollback purposes because you must format the internal Flash file system to a Cisco IOS format.

NOTE   If your Catalyst 6000/6500 switch has a Supervisor 720 engine installed, this engine in its default configuration meets the requirements for upgrading to native mode.

The main requirement for native mode (and also the main limiting factor for choosing to upgrade to native mode) is the MSFC. The MSFC certainly isn't cheap and is obviously not required for many LAN topologies where the switch is required to L2 switch packets and classify packets only at L3/L4 (the PFC is only required to classify packets at L3/L4).

Native Mode Limitations

It is important to understand that there are some restrictions on both the hardware and software features you can use with native mode. At the time of writing, hybrid mode supports more features than native mode, although at some stage in the not too distant future, Cisco has indicated native mode will become equal with hybrid mode in terms of features. From there native mode will be the primary development platform for the Catalyst 6000/6500.

In terms of hardware limitations, the following modules are not supported in the latest Cisco IOS release at the time of writing (12.1(14)E):

- Voice modules (WS-X6624-FXS, WS-X6608-T1, WS-X6608-E1)
- ATM LANE modules (WS-X6101-OC12-MMF, WS-X6101-OC12-SMF)
- Multilayer Switch Module (WS-X6302-MSM)
- 2-port OC-12/STM-4 ATM OSM, MM (WS-X6101-OC12-MMF)
- 2-port OC-12/STM-4 ATM OSM, SM-IR (WS-X6101-OC12-SMF)

If you have these modules installed in a native mode system, the modules remain powered down and do not interfere with the operation of the switch.

In terms of software limitations, quite a number of features are still not supported in native mode, although this list will grow smaller with each new release of Cisco IOS. Notable features that are not supported include:

- High availability
- Dynamic VLANs using VLAN Membership Policy Server (VMPS)
- Multi-Instance Spanning Tree Protocol (MISTP)
- MAC address filtering
- Layer 2 traceroute

Probably the most important feature not available is high availability. A feature called Route Processor Redundancy Plus (RPR+) is supported; however, the failover time is in the order of 30 to 60 seconds. For many Catalyst 6000/6500 installations with redundant Supervisor configurations, this failover time is unacceptable and is definitely a limiting factor in the migration to native mode. Hybrid mode supports the high availability feature, which synchronizes the various state tables between each Supervisor (e.g., spanning tree, bridge table) and allows failover within three seconds.

NOTE	Other ways of implementing faster convergence for high availability networks exist, such as using Hot Standby Routing Protocol (HSRP), which can provide sub-second failover when operating redundant Layer 3 chassis. If you want a redundancy in a single chassis, however, native mode does not support the fast failover high availability brings to hybrid mode installations.

The Hybrid Mode versus Native Mode Boot Process

It is important to understand the differences in the boot process of both hybrid mode and native mode so that you can understand the file system and image requirements of upgrading to native mode. This information also helps you to revert back to hybrid mode if required.

The Hybrid Mode Boot Process

With hybrid mode, the following describes the files that the Supervisor and MSFC modules boot from:

- **Supervisor Image**—The Supervisor CatOS image is normally installed in the *bootflash:* device (the onboard flash device) of the Supervisor and always begins with a prefix of cat6000-sup—e.g., cat6000-sup2k8.7-2-2.bin.

- **MSFC Boot Loader**—The MSFC uses two files. The first is the boot loader file, which is required to initially boot the MSFC. This file is normally stored in the *bootflash:* device of the MSFC (not the Supervisor), and begins with a prefix of c6msfc-boot (for MSFC-1) or c6MSFC-2-boot (for MSFC-2)—e.g., c6MSFC-2-boot-mz.121-8a.E4.

- **MSFC Image**—The MSFC Cisco IOS operating system image is normally stored in the *bootflash:* device of the MSFC and begins with a prefix of c6msfc (for MSFC-1) or c6MSFC-2 (for MSFC-2)—e.g., c6MSFC-2-jsv-mz.121-8a.E4.

When a hybrid mode switch first boots, the switch processor on the Supervisor module reads a boot environment variable, which specifies the full path to the operating system image that should be booted. This image is a CatOS-based image, which boots the Supervisor module. The Supervisor module initializes the various modules installed, runs systems diagnostics, and loads the CatOS operating system into Supervisor memory. If an MSFC is installed, once it has been initialized by the switch processor, the MSFC boot loader image is loaded, after which the main MSFC image is loaded by the route processor on the MSFC. This image is a Cisco IOS-based image which initializes the various hardware components on the MSFC, runs system diagnostics, and loads the Cisco IOS operating system into MSFC memory. Once the Supervisor and MSFC boot processes are complete, two separate operating systems exist, which each provide separate management interfaces to configure and manage each component.

The Native Mode Boot Process

With native mode, the following describes the files that each module boots from:

- **MSFC Boot Loader**—The MSFC-1 still requires the boot loader file in native mode (the MSFC-2 does not require this file). This file is identical to the boot loader file used in hybrid mode. If you have an MSFC-2, you don't need this file; however, it is recommended to keep this file so that you can revert back to hybrid mode.

- **Combined Supervisor and MSFC Image**—A single combined Supervisor and MSFC Cisco IOS operating system image is normally stored in the *bootflash:* device of the Supervisor and always begins with a prefix of c6sup, following by two digits that identify the Supervisor module and MSFC that the image is compatible for. For example, the file c6sup22-jsv-mz.121-11b.E4 is a native mode image for a Supervisor 2 module (indicated by the first number 2 digit) and MSFC-2 (indicated by the second number 2 digit).

When a native mode switch first boots, the switch processor on the Supervisor module reads a boot environment variable, which specifies the full path to the operating system image that should be booted. This image is a native mode (Cisco IOS) image, which boots the Supervisor module. The Supervisor module initializes the various modules installed, runs systems diagnostics, and loads the Cisco IOS operating system into Supervisor memory. Once complete, system control is then handed to the MSFC route processor, which boots from a portion of the native mode image. The MSFC hardware is initialized, system diagnostics are run and the Cisco IOS image is loaded into MSFC memory. At this point, both the switch processor and route processor have each loaded a separate Cisco IOS-based operating system that actually run independently of each other to some extent.

The MSFC Cisco IOS operating system has control over the console port on the Supervisor module and provides a single management interface that you as the administrator see from the switch console port, which allows you to perform all system configuration tasks. In the background the route processor handling the commands executed by administrators actually passes the tasks that require handling by the switch processor to the switch processor for execution. This serves to give the look and feel of a unified switch management interface that manages all components of the switch.

Configuration Prerequisites

Before beginning this scenario, it is important that you have an appropriate operating system file required for native mode operation and that this file is somehow distributed to a local file system on Switch-A. The easiest way of distributing the new native mode operating system image to Switch-A is used the network, which requires a TFTP server to be accessible from Switch-A. This scenario assumes that the appropriate native mode image has been obtained (if you are a registered cisco.com user and have sufficient rights to download software, you can obtain a native mode operating system image from www.cisco.com/cgi-bin/tablebuild.pl/cat6000-sup-ios) and that this image has been installed to a PCMCIA Flash card in Switch-A via TFTP.

Configuration Tasks

It is important to ensure you fully understand the native mode upgrade process and that you follow the process correctly to ensure a smooth upgrade to native mode. Upgrading from hybrid mode to native mode requires the following configuration tasks:

- Backing up existing configuration and operating system files
- Obtaining the appropriate native mode operating system files
- Upgrading to native mode operation

Backing up Existing Configuration and Operating System Files

The first thing that you must do before upgrading to native mode is to ensure that you have full backups of your current configuration and hybrid mode files. When upgrading to native mode a blank configuration is initially loaded, so you must manually reconfigure the switch to your previous configuration.

TIP   An automatic configuration converter is available on CCO at www.cisco.com/cgi-bin/ Support/CatCfgConversion/catcfg_xlat.pl, which allows you to paste an existing CatOS hybrid mode configuration and outputs an equivalent native mode Cisco IOS configuration. This converter is available only for registered CCO users.

It is a good idea to also keep a copy of your hybrid mode files, just in case you need to revert back to hybrid mode. The ideal situation is to have enough flash so that you can leave the old hybrid mode image intact alongside the new native mode image. This makes it very quick and easy to revert back to hybrid mode if required.

At this stage, it is a good idea to have an understanding of the files that the Supervisor 2 engine and MSFC-2 on Switch-A are using for hybrid mode operation, so that you are aware of the files required to run hybrid mode if a roll back should be required. Example 6-25 demonstrates viewing the files used by the Supervisor engine on Switch-A and then establishing a console connection to the MSFC-2 on Switch-A by using the **session** command and viewing the files present on the MSFC-2 internal Flash file system.

Example 6-92 *Viewing Hybrid Mode Files on an MSFC-2*

```
Switch-A> (enable) dir bootflash:
-#- -length- -----date/time------ name
  1  6199068 Apr 26 2002 13:18:19 cat6000-sup2k8.7-2-2.bin
```

Example 6-92 *Viewing Hybrid Mode Files on an MSFC-2 (Continued)*

```
25782500 bytes available (6199068 bytes used)
Switch-A> (enable) session 15
Trying Router-15...
Connected to Router-15.
Escape character is '^]'.

Switch-A-MSFC> enable
Password: *****
Switch-A-MSFC# dir bootflash:
Directory of bootflash:/

    1  -rw-      1686724   Jun 04 2002 13:32:23  c6MSFC-2-boot-mz.121-8a.E4
    2  -rw-     12263928   Jun 04 2002 13:37:19  c6MSFC-2-jsv-mz.121-8a.E4

15204352 bytes total (1253444 bytes free)
```

In Example 6-25, you initially can see the CatOS operating system file used for the Supervisor 2 engine (cat6000-sup2k8.7-2-2.bin) present in the bootflash: file system on Switch-A (the internal Supervisor engine Flash). On the MSFC-2, you can see two files present in the bootflash: file system (not to be confused with the bootflash: file system on the Supervisor), which represents the internal Flash on the MSFC-2. The first file is the boot image (c6MSFC-2-boot-mz.121-8a.E4), which is required to initially boot the MSFC-2 when operating in hybrid mode. The second file is the actual operating system file (c6MSFC-2-jsv-mz.121-8a.E4) for the MSFC-2, which is designed to operate in hybrid mode.

With Switch-A running in native mode, the CatOS operating system file on the Supervisor bootflash: device is replaced with a single native mode Cisco IOS operating system image, which manages both the Supervisor 2 engine and MSFC-2 without any additional files. This means you don't actually need the boot image and operating system image files located on the MSFC-2 bootflash: device. However, it is a good idea to maintain these files, at least during the upgrade process, just in case you need to revert to hybrid mode.

TIP   If you are upgrading a Supervisor 1 with MSFC-1 to native mode (instead of MSFC-2), you must keep the boot loader image in the MSFC flash file system, as it is used to boot the MSFC-1 in native mode.

Obtaining the Appropriate Native Mode Operating System Files

Before beginning the native mode upgrade process, you must ensure that you use the correct native mode image for your Catalyst 6000/6500 supervisor/MSFC configuration. A separate native mode image exists for the various combinations of Supervisor 1/2 modules and MSFC-1/MSFC-2 modules. For example, a different native mode image is required for a Supervisor 1 module with MSFC-2, compared with a Supervisor 2 module with MSFC-1. To determine which native mode image is suitable for your system, refer to the prefix of the native mode image filename. The first five characters of the filename should contain the text c6sup, which indicates the file is a native mode image. The next character (the sixth character of the filename) indicates the Supervisor engine that the native mode image is suitable for, while the following character (the seventh character of the filename) indicates the MSFC module that the native mode image is suitable for. For example, the prefix c6sup12 indicates the image is suitable for a Supervisor 1 with MSFC-2, while the prefix c6sup22 indicates the image is suitable for Supervisor 2 with MSFC-2.

If you have an MSFC-1 installed with the Supervisor 1, you must also ensure that the boot loader file used to initially boot the MSFC in hybrid mode is also present in native mode (i.e., the c6MSFC-2-boot-xxxx file). This file is already required for hybrid mode operation, so the correct boot loader file should already be in place.

After you have determined the appropriate files required for native mode, you must ensure the files are present on the Flash file system of the switch. Because the Supervisor module initially boots from the native mode image, the native mode image must be present on a file system that the Supervisor can initially read at system startup. This includes the following flash devices:

- **Supervisor internal Flash**—This is the internal Flash included with every Supervisor 2 module. This device is referred to by the Supervisor module as *bootflash:* and by the MSFC as *sup-bootflash:*.

- **PCMCIA Flash**—If your internal Flash does not have enough space to accommodate the native mode image, you must install PCMCIA-based Flash in the external PCMCIA slots on the Supervisor module. It is recommended that you have PCMCIA Flash available during the native mode upgrade, as you need to format all file systems after the upgrade to allow native mode to write to each file systems. PCMCIA Flash can be used as temporary storage whilst the internal Flash file system is being formatted.

In this scenario, assume that Switch-A has a PCMCIA flash card installed which allows for the native mode image to be stored here temporarily while the Supervisor Flash file system is formatted; this is required to ensure the file system is compatible with the native mode Cisco IOS operating system.

NOTE A switch running in native mode can read a hybrid mode file system, but cannot write to the hybrid mode file system due to differences in the file system format. This is the reason why all file systems used by native mode must be reformatted.

Assuming a native mode image has been downloaded to the PCMCIA Flash card via TFTP or some other means, Example 6-26 demonstrates verifying a native mode image is present on the PCMCIA card.

Example 6-93 *Verifying Native Mode Image is Available on File System*

```
Switch-A> (enable) dir slot0:
-#- -length- -----date/time------ name
  1 21611516 Jun 03 2002 09:12:08 c6sup22-jsv-mz.121-11b.E4

10370052 bytes available (21611516 bytes used)
```

In Example 6-26, **slot0:** represents the Flash file system on the PCMCIA Flash card. An image called c6sup22-jsv-mz.121-11b.E4 is present. This is the new native mode image that you configure the switch to boot from. You can tell that the image is a native mode image for the Supervisor 2 with MSFC-2 because the filename prefix is c6sup22.

Upgrading to Native Mode Operation

Once the appropriate native mode files are in place within Flash, you are ready to begin the process of upgrading the switch to operate in native mode. Configuring the switch to operate in native mode requires the following configuration tasks:

- Boot into ROMMON mode
- Boot into native mode for the first time
- Convert Flash file systems to native mode format
- Set boot parameters
- Reboot the switch

Booting into ROMMON Mode

When you upgrade to native mode, you must alter the BOOT environment variables that the switch processor reads (stored in the ROMMON configuration) so that the switch processor boots the native mode image, rather than a hybrid mode CatOS image. You need to specify the correct file system path, so it is important you understand the Flash device upon which the Native mode image is stored, and the full name of the image. The full path includes the Native mode image filename, preceded by the Flash device name (e.g., bootflash:c6sup22-jsv-mz.121-11b.E4 refers to a native mode image installed on the internal Flash of the Supervisor).

NOTE   It is important to understand that you cannot use any file system device that is attached to the MSFC to store the native mode image because the Supervisor module must have access to the image upon initialization (remember the MSFC is not initialized until after the Supervisor has initially booted from the native mode image).

continues

To reconfigure the boot environment variables, you need to initially boot the switch into ROMMON mode and then modify the boot environment variables. This can be achieved by modifying the boot variables of the configuration register on the Supervisor engine using the **set boot config-register** command, so that the switch always boots to ROMMON mode and then physically rebooting the switch. Example 6-27 demonstrates configuring Switch-A to always boot into ROMMON mode and then rebooting the switch into ROMMON mode.

Example 6-94 *Booting the Catalyst 6000/6500 into ROMMON Mode*

```
Switch-A> (enable) set boot config-register 0x0
Configuration register is 0x0
ignore-config: disabled
auto-config: non-recurring, overwrite, sync disabled
console baud: 9600
boot: the ROM monitor
Switch-A> (enable) reset
This command will reset the system.
Do you want to continue (y/n) [n]? y
2002 Jul 01 11:48:47 %SYS-5-SYS_RESET:System reset from Console
Powering OFF all existing linecards
System Bootstrap, Version 6.1(4)
Copyright  1994-2001 by cisco Systems, Inc.
c6k_sup2 processor with 131072 Kbytes of main memory

rommon 1 >
```

In Example 6-27, notice that the configuration register is set to **0x0** (short for 0x0000), which configures the switch to boot to ROMMON mode as indicated by the shaded output of the command. The switch is then rebooted using the **reset** command, with the switch booting into ROMMON mode due to the new value of the configuration register.

Booting into Native mode for the First Time

Before you can boot into native mode, you must clear a boot variable called CONFIG_FILE, which is used by hybrid mode to locate the configuration file that contains the configuration of the switch. The reason for this is that although native mode does not use this variable, there have been some issues with leaving this variable set a value other than null. Example 6-28 demonstrates clearing this variable in ROMMON mode on Switch-A.

Example 6-95 *Clearing the CONFIG_FILE Environment Variable*

```
rommon 1 > set
PS1=rommon ! >
BOOT=bootflash:cat6000-sup2k8.7-2-2.bin,1;
CONFIG_FILE=bootflash:switch.cfg
rommon 2 > CONFIG_FILE=
rommon 3 > sync
```

In Example 6-28, the **set** ROMMON command is used to display the various environment variables—notice the CONFIG_FILE variable is currently set to **bootflash:switch.cfg**, which represents a hidden CatOS binary configuration file stored in the internal flash file system (bootflash:) on Switch-A. This variable is then set to a null value using the command **CONFIG_FILE=**, after which the **sync** command must be used to write the environment variable changes permanently. At this point, for the environment variable change to take effect, the switch must once again be rebooted. The switch reboots back into ROMMON mode because the configuration register is still set to 0x0. Example 6-29 demonstrates rebooting Switch-A after clearing the CONFIG_FILE environment variable.

Example 6-96 *Rebooting Switch-A To Clear the CONFIG_FILE Environment Variable*

```
rommon 4 > reset

System Bootstrap, Version 6.1(4)
Copyright  1994-2001 by cisco Systems, Inc.
c6k_sup2 processor with 131072 Kbytes of main memory

rommon 1 > set
PS1=rommon ! >
BOOT=bootflash:cat6000-sup2k8.7-2-2.bin,1;
CONFIG_FILE=
```

In Example 6-29, notice that the CONFIG_FILE variable now has a null value, which ensures the switch doesn't boot with a value for this variable.

After clearing the CONFIG_FILE variable, the switch can now be booted from the native mode operating system image file. This can be achieved by using the **boot** ROMMON command, specifying the full path to the native mode image, which in this scenario is stored in PCMCIA Flash and can be referenced by the path **slot0:c6sup22-jsv-mz.121-11b.E4** (see Example 6-26). Example 6-30 demonstrates booting Switch-A in ROMMON mode from the native mode operating system image file.

Example 6-97 *Booting Native Mode Manually from ROMMON Mode*

```
rommon 2 > boot slot0:c6sup22-jsv-mz.121-11b.E4
Self decompressing the image : ########################################
########################################################################
########################################################################
########################################################################
########################################################################
[OK]
Restricted Rights Legend
Use, duplication, or disclosure by the Government is
subject to restrictions as set forth in subparagraph
 of the Commercial Computer Software - Restricted
Rights clause at FAR sec. 52.227-19 and subparagraph
 (1) (ii) of the Rights in Technical Data and Computer
Software clause at DFARS sec. 252.227-7013.
cisco Systems, Inc.
170 West Tasman Drive
San Jose, California 95134-1706
```

continues

Example 6-97 *Booting Native Mode Manually from ROMMON Mode (Continued)*

```
Cisco Internetwork Operating System Software
IOS (tm) c6sup2_sp Software (c6sup2_sp-SPV-M), Version 12.1(11b)E4,
    EARLY DEPLOYMENT RELEASE SOFTWARE (fc1)
Synced to mainline version: 12.1(11b)
TAC:Home:Software:Ios General:CiscoIOSRoadmap:12.1
Copyright  1986-2001 by cisco Systems, Inc.
Compiled Wed 28-Mar-01 18:36 by hqluong
Image text-base: 0x30020980, data-base: 0x306B8000
Start as Primary processor
00:00:05: %SYS-3-LOGGER_FLUSHING: System pausing to ensure console
    debugging output.
00:00:03: Currently running ROMMON from S (Gold) region
00:00:05: %OIR-6-CONSOLE: Changing console ownership to route processor
System Bootstrap, Version 12.1(3r)E2, RELEASE SOFTWARE (fc1)
Copyright  2000 by cisco Systems, Inc.
Cat6k-MSFC2 platform with 131072 Kbytes of main memory
rommon 1 > boot
Self decompressing the image : ###############################################
###############################################################################
## [OK]
Restricted Rights Legend
Use, duplication, or disclosure by the Government is
subject to restrictions as set forth in subparagraph
 of the Commercial Computer Software - Restricted
Rights clause at FAR sec. 52.227-19 and subparagraph
 (1) (ii) of the Rights in Technical Data and Computer
Software clause at DFARS sec. 252.227-7013.
cisco Systems, Inc.
170 West Tasman Drive
San Jose, California 95134-1706
Cisco Internetwork Operating System Software
IOS (tm) MSFC2 Software (C6MSFC2-BOOT-M), Version 12.1(8a)E4,
    EARLY DEPLOYMENT RELEASE SOFTWARE (fc1)
Copyright  1986-2000 by cisco Systems, Inc.
Compiled Sat 14-Oct-00 05:33 by eaarmas
Image text-base: 0x30008980, data-base: 0x303B6000
cisco Cat6k-MSFC2 (R7000) processor with 114688K/16384K bytes of memory.
Processor board ID SAD04430J9K
R7000 CPU at 300Mhz, Implementation 39, Rev 2.1, 256KB L2, 1024KB L3 Cache
Last reset from power-on
X.25 software, Version 3.0.0.
509K bytes of non-volatile configuration memory.
16384K bytes of Flash internal SIMM (Sector size 512K).
Press RETURN to get started!

--- System Configuration Dialog ---
Continue with configuration dialog? [yes/no]: n
Router> enable
```

In Example 6-30, you can see the native mode boot process. First of all, the Supervisor engine is booted, as indicated in the first shaded line by the text, c6sup2 sp Software (Catalyst 6000 Supervisor 2 switch processor software). After the supervisor engine boots, notice the next shaded line, which states that console ownership is being changed to the route processor (MSFC):

```
00:00:05: %OIR-6-CONSOLE: Changing console ownership to route processor
```

This message indicates that the switch processor (Supervisor) is handing management control of the system to the route processor (MSFC). When a Catalyst 6000/6500 switch running native mode boots, the Supervisor initially executes startup code and then hands off the boot process to the MSFC. The MSFC then boots. At this stage, the MSFC still boots from the hybrid mode files located on the MSFC internal Flash. Once boot up by the MSFC is complete, notice that the switch loads with a blank configuration, as indicated by the System Configuration Dialog prompt. After specifying **n** at the System Configuration Dialog prompt, notice that a normal Cisco IOS **Router>** prompt is presented, as per the default operation when booting up a Cisco IOS-based Catalyst switch with a blank configuration.

At this point, it is a good idea to issue a **show version** command so that you can verify the switch has booted from the image you think it has booted from and to also verify that native mode has recognized each of the physical interfaces installed in the switch. Example 6-31 demonstrates using **show version** to verify the hardware configuration and operating system version on Switch-A.

Example 6-98 *Verifying a Native Mode Catalyst 6000/6500 Switch*

```
Router# show version
Cisco Internetwork Operating System Software
IOS (tm) c6sup2_rp Software (c6sup2_rp-JSV-M), Version 12.1(11b)E4,
    EARLY DEPLOYMENT
Synced to mainline version: 12.1(11b)
TAC:Home:Software:Ios General:CiscoIOSRoadmap:12.1
Copyright  1986-2001 by cisco Systems, Inc.
Compiled Wed 28-Mar-01 17:52 by hqluong
Image text-base: 0x30008980, data-base: 0x315D0000
ROM: System Bootstrap, Version 12.1(3r)E2, RELEASE SOFTWARE (fc1)
BOOTFLASH: c6sup2_rp Software (c6sup2_rp-JSV-M), Version 12.1(8a)EX,
    EARLY DEPLOYMENT
Router uptime is 2 hours, 33 minutes
System returned to ROM by power-on (SP by power-on)
Running default software
cisco Catalyst 6000 (R7000) processor with 114688K/16384K bytes of memory.
Processor board ID SAD04430J9K
R7000 CPU at 300Mhz, Implementation 39, Rev 2.1, 256KB L2, 1024KB L3 Cache
Last reset from power-on
Bridging software.
X.25 software, Version 3.0.0.
SuperLAT software (copyright 1990 by Meridian Technology Corp).
TN3270 Emulation software.
1 Virtual Ethernet/IEEE 802.3 interface(s)
48 FastEthernet/IEEE 802.3 interface(s)
2 Gigabit Ethernet/IEEE 802.3 interface(s)
381K bytes of non-volatile configuration memory.
16384K bytes of Flash internal SIMM (Sector size 512K).
Configuration register is 0x0
```

In Example 6-31, notice that the switch is running Cisco IOS 12.1(11b)E4 and that the switch has recognized 1 virtual Ethernet interface (the VLAN 1 interface), 48 FastEthernet interfaces (located in slot 2 of Switch-A), and 2 gigabit Ethernet interfaces, which are onboard the Supervisor 2 engine.

Converting the Flash File Systems to Native mode Format

Assuming the switch has booted correctly as shown in Example 6-30 and verified in Example 6-31, the switch is now operating in native mode which confirms the switch is compatible with the native mode image. The next step is to convert the existing Flash file systems to native mode format, so that native mode can write to these file systems. This involves the following tasks:

- Formatting existing hybrid mode file systems
- Copying native mode image to new native mode file systems

To format the Flash file systems, you use the **format** command which takes a single parameter indicated the Flash device that you wish to format. At a minimum, you must format the Flash from which the switch normally boots. This is normally the internal Flash on the Supervisor engine; however, it could also be a PCMCIA Flash card. In this scenario, although Switch-A is currently booted from the slot0: Flash device (i.e., a PCMCIA Flash card), this is only temporary with the intention of Switch-A normally booting from the internal Flash on the Supervisor engine. It is important to understand that in native mode, the MSFC refers to the internal Flash device on the Supervisor engine as **sup-bootflash:** (as the MSFC already has its own bootflash: internal flash device).

NOTE   It is recommended that all Flash file systems on the switch be formatted so that the switch can both read and write to all file systems.

Example 6-32 demonstrates formatting the onboard Flash file system of the Supervisor module and then verifying that the file system has been formatted.

Example 6-99 *Formatting Supervisor Flash from Native Mode*

```
Router# format sup-bootflash:
Format operation may take a while. Continue? [confirm] y
Format operation will destroy all data in "sup-bootflash:".
    Continue? [confirm] y
Formatting sector 1
Format of sup-bootflash complete
Router# dir sup-bootflash:
Directory of sup-bootflash:/

No files in directory

31981568 bytes total (31981568 bytes free)
```

In Example 6-32, after the format of the Supervisor internal Flash is complete, the **dir** command is used to verify that the file system is accessible.

NOTE   If you have an MSFC-2 installed, the native mode image will be larger than 16 MB. This means that your Supervisor Flash must be 32 MB to store the native mode image for the MSFC-2. If the onboard Flash is only 16 MB, you must store the native mode image on a 32-MB PCMCIA card permanently installed into the Supervisor engine.

After formatting the appropriate Flash file system that is used for booting the switch, you must next copy the native mode image to the newly formatted file system so that the switch boots. In this scenario, the Supervisor Flash (sup-bootflash:) is to be used to boot the switch, and the native mode image is currently stored on PCMCIA flash (slot0:). Example 6-33 demonstrates copying the native mode image on slot0: of Switch-A to the sup-bootflash: Flash device.

Example 6-100 *Copying Native Mode Image to Onboard Flash*

```
Router# copy slot0:c6sup22-jsv-mz.121-11b.E4 sup-bootflash:
c6sup22-jsv-mz.121-11b.E4
CCCCCCCCCCCCCCCCCCCCCCCCCCCCCCCCCCCCCCCCCCCCCCCCCCCCCCCCCCCCCCCCCCCCCCCCCCCCCCCCCC
CCCCCCCCCCCCCCCCCCCCCCCCCCCCCCCCCCCCCCCCCCCCCCCCCCCCCCCCCCCCCCCCCCCCCCCCCCCCCCCCCC
CCCCCCCCCCCCCCCCCCCCCCCCCCCCCCCCCCCCCCCCCCCCCCCCCCCCCCCCCCCCCCCCCCCCCCCCCCCCCCCCCC
CCCCCCCCCCCCCCCCCCCCCCCCCCCCCCCCCCCCCCCCCCCCCCCCCCCCCCCCCCCCCCCCCCCCCCCCCCCCCCCCCC
CCCCCCCCCCCCCCCCCCCCCCCCCCCCCCCCCCCCCCC
21611516 bytes copied in 371.077 secs (58340 bytes/sec)
Router# dir sup-bootflash:
Directory of sup-bootflash:/

    1  -rw-     21611516   July 01 2001 16:15:11   c6sup22-jsv-mz.121-11b.E4
31981568 bytes total (10370052 bytes free)
```

In Example 6-33, after the **copy** command is used for copying the native mode image, the **dir** command is then used to verify the image has been successfully copied to Flash.

NOTE   You can also copy the native mode image via other means such as over the network using TFTP or FTP; however, this requires some configuration of the switch because the switch loads with a blank configuration the first time you boot native IOS. Using the network is required when you have only a single Flash file system to boot the switch from initially (i.e., sup-bootflash:) because you must erase the native mode image when formatting the sup-bootflash: device in this situation.

At this stage, the native mode image is located in the appropriate Flash device, with the switch able to read and write from the file system because it is now formatted for native mode. It is a good idea at this point to also format all other Flash file systems for native mode operation, although you might want to leave this until such time that you are confident that the switch is operating correctly in native mode. If you format all other Flash file systems immediately, you lose the ability to rollback quickly to hybrid mode (you can still rollback; it just takes longer to do).

Set Boot Parameters

Finally, you need to modify the boot parameters so that the switch automatically boots from Flash and boots from the native mode image. At present, the configuration register of the Supervisor engine is set to boot to ROMMON mode, and the boot environment variable is set to the previous CatOS image file.

When working with boot variables in native mode, it is important to understand that just as in hybrid mode, the supervisor engine and MSFC each possess their own bootstrap code and associated boot variables. Although the MSFC controls the switch during normal operation, the switch initially boots from the Supervisor engine first, and then control is handed over to the MSFC. This means that you must ensure you modify the boot variables of both the Supervisor engine and MSFC.

To view the current boot environments on the MSFC, you can use the **show bootvar** command, as shown in Example 6-34.

Example 6-101 *Verifying Boot Parameters on the MSFC in Native Mode*

```
Router# show bootvar
BOOT variable = bootflash:c6MSFC-2-jsv-mz.121-8a.E4,1;
CONFIG_FILE variable does not exist
BOOTLDR variable = bootflash:c6MSFC-2-mz.121-8a.E4
Configuration register is 0x2102
```

In Example 6-34, the boot variables of the MSFC are actually the old boot variables of the MSFC in hybrid mode. This is quite reasonable because no modification of the MSFC environment variables has so far taken place. Also notice that the configuration register is 0x2102. This is a normal configuration register value that indicates the MSFC should boot normally from flash. The point of Example 6-34 is to show that the MSFC has separate boot environment variables from the Supervisor engine. For example, the configuration register of the Supervisor engine is currently 0x0 (boot to ROMMON mode), which is different from the configuration register on the MSFC.

To ensure both the Supervisor engine and MSFC boot correctly, you can set the boot environment variable from native mode using the **boot system** global configuration command. When executed, this command not only modifies the boot environment variables on the MSFC, it also modifies the boot environment variables on the Supervisor, as a single file is now used to boot both the Supervisor and MSFC. You must also modify the configuration register on the Supervisor engine so that the switch boots from Flash. This can be achieved by executing the **config-register** global configuration command in native mode. Example 6-35 demonstrates configuring the switch to boot from the new native mode image.

Example 6-102 *Setting Native Mode Boot Parameters*

```
Router# configure terminal
Router(config)# boot system sup-bootflash:c6sup22-jsv-mz.121-11b.E4
Router(config)# end
Router# copy running-config startup-config
Building configuration...
[OK]
Router# show bootvar
BOOT variable = sup-bootflash:c6sup22-jsv-mz.121-11b.E4,1;
CONFIG_FILE variable does not exist
BOOTLDR variable = bootflash:c6MSFC-2-mz.121-8a.E4
Configuration register is 0x2102
```

In Example 6-35, the **boot system** global configuration command is used to modify the BOOT environment variable to the native mode image path. The configuration is then saved, which ensures the environment variables are saved permanently. If you are using the MSFC-2 with native mode, the BOOTLDR variable is ignored. This is required only on the MSFC-1.

The configuration of Example 6-35 sets the boot environment variable for both the MSFC and the supervisor engine. To prove this, you can actually access the Supervisor engine switch processor from native mode and then view the boot environment variables for the Supervisor. To access the switch processor and view environment variables, you use the **remote login switch** command to access the switch processor and then use the **show bootvar** command to view the current boot parameters for the Supervisor engine itself, as shown in Example 6-36.

Example 6-103 *Viewing the Supervisor Engine Boot Environment Variables*

```
Router# remote login switch
Trying Switch ...
Entering CONSOLE for Switch
Type "^C^C^C" to end this session

Switch-sp# show bootvar
BOOT variable = bootflash:c6sup22-jsv-mz.121-11b.E4,12
CONFIG_FILE variable =
BOOTLDR variable does not exist
Configuration register is 0x0 (will be 0x2102 at next reload)
Switch-sp# exit

[Connection to Switch closed by foreign host]
Router#
```

You can see from Example 6-36 that native mode allows you to run Cisco IOS commands (not CatOS commands) from the Supervisor processor (switch processor). You shouldn't need to do this often, as commands executed on the MSFC in native mode are automatically passed to the appropriate switch processor or MSFC processor for handling. In Example 6-34, you need to use the switch processor to read the boot environment variables for the Supervisor engine rather than the MSFC. Notice that the BOOT variable is correctly set. This is because when you modify boot parameters in native mode, both the MSFC and Supervisor boot parameters are updated. The last shaded line indicates that the configuration register value on the Supervisor is 0x0, which means the switch still boots into ROMMON mode. You need to change this to ensure that the switch boots from Flash and loads the native mode image.

NOTE   The **remote command switch** privileged command can be used to execute commands on the switch processor from native mode, without having to first log in to the switch processor (see Example 6-37 for a demonstration).

To configure the switch to ensure it boots from Flash rather than into ROMMON mode as is currently the case, you can use the **config-register** global configuration mode command to modify the configuration register on both the MSFC and supervisor engine. Example 6-37 demonstrates modifying the configuration register and then using the **remote command switch** command to verify the new configuration register value on the Supervisor engine.

Example 6-104 *Modifying the Supervisor Engine Configuration Register*

```
Router# configure terminal
Router(config)# config-register 0x2102
Router(config)# end
Router# copy running-config startup-config
Building configuration...
[OK]
Router# remote command switch show bootvar

Switch-sp#
BOOT variable = bootflash:c6sup22-jsv-mz.121-11b.E4,1;
CONFIG_FILE variable =
BOOTLDR variable does not exist
Configuration register is 0x0 (will be 0x2102 at next reload)

Router#
```

In Example 6-37, after the configuration register is modified, the **remote command switch** command is used to execute the **show bootvar** command on the switch processor. Notice that the configuration register has been modified so that the Supervisor boots from Flash at the next reload (i.e., 0x2102).

Rebooting the Switch

Congratulations, you have successfully completed upgrading a Catalyst 6000/6500 switch with MSFC to native mode. At this stage, it is a good idea to reboot the switch to verify that the switch does boot automatically into native mode with no problems. After rebooting the switch, you can then configure the switch for native mode operation, which is discussed in the next scenario.

Scenario 6-4: Configuring CEF-Based Layer 3 Switching on the Catalyst 6000/6500 Operating in Native Mode

In the previous scenario, you learned how to upgrade a Cisco Catalyst 6000/6500 switch from hybrid mode to native mode. When you upgrade to native mode, you lose both the Supervisor engine and MSFC configurations, meaning you must manually reconfigure the functionality previously in place when the switch was in hybrid mode. In Scenario 6-2, you learned how to configure the Catalyst 6000/6500 for CEF-based Layer 3 switching in hybrid mode. In this scenario, you configure the newly converted Switch-A for CEF-based Layer 3 switching in native mode, maintaining the same functionality as in Scenario 6-2. Figure 6-16 shows the new topology of Switch-A for this scenario.

Figure 6-16 *Topology for Scenario 6-4*

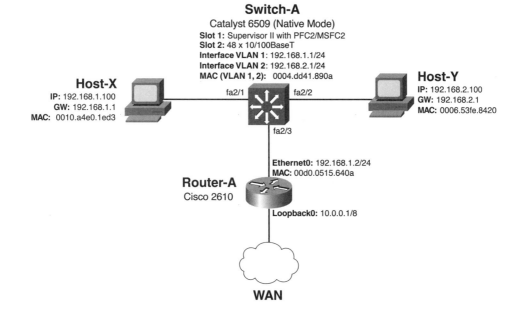

Configuration Tasks

The goal of this scenario is to implement the same functionality configured on Switch-A in Scenario 6-2. When upgraded to native mode, a Cisco Catalyst 6000/6500 switch loses its configuration, meaning you must reconfigure the switch from scratch. This requires the following configuration tasks:

- Configuring system settings
- Configuring Layer 2 interfaces
- Configuring Layer 3 interfaces
- Configuring Layer 3 routing
- Verifying connectivity

Configuring System Settings

In this book so far, you have learned how to configure Cisco IOS-based Catalyst switches using the Catalyst 3550 switch. Because the native mode Catalyst 6000/6500 switch runs the same base operating system as the Catalyst 3550 (Cisco IOS), the commands used on the Catalyst 6000/6500 are identical to those used on the Catalyst 3550.

NOTE   Some minor differences exist in the command set supported on each switch, due to differences in the features supported.

This means that the same commands used to create and configure VLANs on the Catalyst 3550 are also used on the Catalyst 6000/6500. The same applies for all features that both switches have in common.

Example 6-38 demonstrates configuring Switch-A with a host name and passwords and configuring VLANs as required.

Example 6-105 *Configuring System Settings on Switch-A in Native Mode*

```
Router# configure terminal
Router(config)# hostname Switch-A
Switch-A(config)# enable secret cisco
Switch-A(config)# line vty 0 15
Switch-A(config-line)# password cisco
Switch-A(config-line)# exit
Switch-A(config)# vtp mode transparent
Setting device to VTP TRANSPARENT mode.
Switch-A(config)# vlan 2
Switch-A(config-vlan)# name VLAN02
```

Configuring Layer 2 Interfaces

On the native mode Catalyst 6000/6500, it is important to understand that by default, all interfaces are configured as routed interfaces, as opposed to switched interfaces as is the default on other Cisco IOS-based Catalyst switches. This means that all interfaces are shut down by default (this is the default state for a routed interface on Cisco IOS) so if you wish to configure an interface for Layer 2 or Layer 3 operation, you must explicitly enable the interface. If you want to configure a Layer 2 interface (i.e. switched interface), you must also explicitly configure this, because all interfaces are Layer 3 interfaces by default.

You might also be wondering how interfaces are named in native mode. All interfaces are named using the *interface-type interface-id* convention used on other Cisco IOS-based Catalyst switches, with the *interface-id* defined in the format *module/port*. For example, port 2/4 on a 10/100BASE-T module is represented as **interface fastEthernet2/4** on native mode.

In this scenario, interface fastEthernet0/1 through interface fastEthernet0/3 are all Layer 2 interfaces, with interface FastEthernet0/2 belonging to VLAN 2. Example 6-37 demonstrates configuring each of the above interfaces as Layer 2 interfaces and assigning the appropriate interface to VLAN 2.

Example 6-106 *Configuring Layer 2 Parameters on Switch-A in Native Mode*

```
Switch-A# configure terminal
Switch-A(config)# interface range fastEthernet2/1 - 3
Switch-A(config-if-range)# no shutdown
Switch-A(config-if-range)# switchport
Switch-A(config-if-range)# exit
Switch-A(config)# interface fastEthernet2/2
Switch-A(config-if)# switchport access vlan 2
```

In Example 6-39, notice that the **interface range** command is support on the native mode Catalyst 6000/6500, just like the Catalyst 3550. The **no shutdown** command takes each interface out of its default shutdown state and then the **switchport** command configures each interface as a Layer 2 interface, as opposed to a Layer 3 router interface. Finally, interface fastEthernet2/2 is assigned to VLAN 2, as this interface is connected to Host-Y.

Configuring Layer 3 Interfaces

On the native mode Catalyst 6000/6500, the same types of Layer 3 interfaces supported on other Cisco IOS-based Layer 3 Catalyst switches are also supported:

- Physical interface
- Switch virtual interface (SVI)

In this scenario, an SVI must be created for VLAN 2 (an SVI for VLAN 1 exists by default, but is in a shutdown state) so that Switch-A can route between VLAN 1 and VLAN 2.

Example 6-40 demonstrates configuring SVIs for each VLAN and configuring the appropriate IP addressing for each SVI.

Example 6-107 *Configuring Layer 2 Parameters on Switch-A in Native Mode*

```
Switch-A# configure terminal
Switch-A(config)# interface vlan 1
Switch-A(config-if)# no shutdown
Switch-A(config-if)# ip address 192.168.1.1 255.255.255.0
Switch-A(config-if)# exit
Switch-A(config)# interface vlan 2
Switch-A(config-if)# ip address 192.168.2.1 255.255.255.0
```

As you can see in Example 6-40, the configuration required on Switch-A is identical to the configuration required on the MSFC when creating SVIs in hybrid mode (see Example 6-39).

Configuring Layer 3 Routing

Finally, Layer 3 routing needs to be configured. In this scenario, Switch-A needs to participate in OSPF area 0, with Router-A as an OSPF neighbor. Example 6-41 shows the configuration required on Switch-A.

Example 6-108 *Configuring Layer 2 Parameters on Switch-A in Native Mode*

```
Switch-A# configure terminal
Switch-A(config)# router ospf 1
Switch-A(config-router)# network 192.168.1.0 0.0.0.255 area 0
Switch-A(config-router)# network 192.168.2.0 0.0.0.255 area 0
Switch-A(config-router)# end
Switch-A# show ip ospf neighbors

Neighbor ID      Pri   State          Dead Time    Address        Interface
192.168.1.2        1   FULL/BDR       00:00:33     192.168.1.2    Vlan1
Switch-A# show ip route
Codes: C - connected, S - static, I - IGRP, R - RIP, M - mobile, B - BGP
       D - EIGRP, EX - EIGRP external, O - OSPF, IA - OSPF inter area
       N1 - OSPF NSSA external type 1, N2 - OSPF NSSA external type 2
       E1 - OSPF external type 1, E2 - OSPF external type 2, E - EGP
       i - IS-IS, L1 - IS-IS level-1, L2 - IS-IS level-2, ia - IS-IS inter area
       * - candidate default, U - per-user static route, o - ODR
       P - periodic downloaded static route

Gateway of last resort is not set

O IA 10.0.0.0/8 [110/2] via 192.168.1.2, 00:00:37, Vlan1
C    192.168.1.0/24 is directly connected, Vlan1
C    192.168.2.0/24 is directly connected, Vlan2
```

The configuration and subsequent Layer 3 routing configuration verification shown in Example 6-41 is identical to the hybrid mode configuration of an MSFC (see Example 6-40).

Verifying Connectivity

At this point, the native mode configuration of Switch-A is in place. Having a single operating system to manage all components of the Catalyst 6000/6500 simplifies management and ensures only a single configuration file and operating system image file needs to be maintained. To verify your configuration, Host-X should be able to ping Host-Y and vice versa, and both hosts should also be able to ping the loopback interface on Router-A.

To view the MAC address used by the MSFC for routing, you use the **show mls cef mac** command, which is demonstrated in Example 6-42 on Switch-A.

Example 6-109 *Displaying the MSFC MAC Address in Native Mode*

```
Switch-A# show mls cef mac

Switch-A-sp#
Router MAC address: 0004.dd41.890a
```

If you compare the output of Example 6-42 with the output of the **show mls cef mac** command on the Supervisor engine of Switch-A in Scenario 6-2 (see Example 6-41), notice that the same router MAC address (00d0.0515.640a) is displayed. Even though Switch-A is now operating in native mode, the fundamental components of Layer 3 switching are still present (PFC and MSFC), so it is important that the L2 engine passes any frames with a destination MAC address of the MSFC to the L3 engine for possible L3 switching. Notice in Example 6-42 that the **show mls cef mac** command is actually executed by the switch processor rather than the MSFC processor, as indicated by the **Switch-A-sp#** prompt at the beginning of the command output. This is because the L2 engine is a component of the switch processor (Supervisor engine).

To view the FIB table in native mode, you use the **show mls cef** command, as demonstrated in Example 6-43.

Example 6-110 *Displaying the FIB in Native Mode*

```
Switch-A# show mls cef

Switch-A-sp#
Index     Prefix           Mask             Adjacency
0         0.0.0.0          255.255.255.255  punt
1         255.255.255.255  255.255.255.255  punt
2         127.0.0.12       255.255.255.255  punt
3         127.0.0.0        255.255.255.255  punt
4         127.255.255.255  255.255.255.255  punt
5         192.168.1.1      255.255.255.255  0004.dd41.890a
6         192.168.1.2      255.255.255.255  00d0.0515.640a
7         192.168.1.100    255.255.255.255  0010.a4e0.1ed3
8         192.168.1.0      255.255.255.255  punt
9         192.168.1.255    255.255.255.255  punt
10        192.168.2.1      255.255.255.255  0004.dd41.890a
11        192.168.2.100    255.255.255.255  0006.53fe.8420
```

continues

Example 6-110 *Displaying the FIB in Native Mode (Continued)*

```
12        192.168.2.0      255.255.255.255   punt
13        192.168.2.255    255.255.255.255   punt
6400      224.0.0.0        255.255.255.0     punt
6401      192.168.1.0      255.255.255.0     punt
6402      192.168.2.0      255.255.255.0     punt
6403      10.0.0.0         255.0.0.0         00d0.0515.640a
115200    0.0.0.0          0.0.0.0           drop
```

In Example 6-43, notice that each destination prefix and associated mask are listed, along with adjacency information. The adjacency information does not specify next hop IP information as is the case in hybrid mode (see Example 6-42). Instead, the MAC address of the next hop device is listed. Notice that many prefixes have the punt adjacency associated with them. This means that any packets with a destination IP address that matches the prefix should be forwarded (punted) to the route processor (MSFC) for processing. For example, entry 5 shows that traffic destined to 192.168.1.1 should be sent to the route processor, which is the correct action because this is the IP address configured on the VLAN 1 interface. Notice that the last entry (numbered 115200) specifies a prefix of 0.0.0.0 and mask of 0.0.0.0, which matches any destination IP address not matched by the preceding FIB entries. The adjacency is a drop adjacency, which means any packets not matched by other FIB entries are dropped. This is the correct action to take because if no FIB entry for a destination exists, then no route for the destination exists and the destination is deemed unreachable.

Also in Example 6-43, the shaded entries indicate FIB entries that have a remote adjacency to which any packets that match the entry should be forwarded. The remote adjacency is indicated by a MAC address in the adjacency column. Referring to the MAC addresses for Host-X, Host-Y, and Router-A in Figure 6-16, you can see in Example 6-43 that the appropriate IP addresses are associated with the correct MAC addresses. For example, entry 6403 specifies a destination prefix of 10.0.0.0/8 (which is reachable via Router-A) and lists the adjacency as 00d0.0515.640a, which is the MAC address of Router-A.

Finally, to view the adjacency table in native mode, you use the **show mls cef adjacency** command, as demonstrated in Example 6-44.

Example 6-111 *Displaying the CEF Adjacency Table in Native Mode*

```
Switch-A# show mls cef adjacency

Switch-A-sp#
Index 17416 :  mac-sa: 0004.dd41.890a, mac-da: 0006.53fe.8420
               interface: Fa2/2, mtu: 1514
               packets: 0000000000000010, bytes: 0000000000000960

Index 17417 :  mac-sa: 0004.dd41.890a, mac-da: 00d0.0515.640a
               interface: Fa2/3, mtu: 1514
```

Example 6-111 *Displaying the CEF Adjacency Table in Native Mode (Continued)*

```
                  packets: 0000000000000010, bytes: 0000000000000960

Index 17418 :   mac-sa: 0004.dd41.890a, mac-da: 0010.a4e0.1ed3
                  interface: Fa2/1, mtu: 1514
                  packets: 0000000000000020, bytes: 0000000000001920

Index 262140:   mac-sa: 00d0.0515.640a, mac-da: 0000.0000.0202
                  interface: unknown, mtu: 1514
                  packets: 0000004294967295, bytes: 0002199023255551
```

Notice in Example 6-44 that an adjacency entry exists per destination MAC address. The output is rather different from the comparative command on a hybrid mode switch and is much easier to understand. Each adjacency entry contains the information required for the hardware-based L3 engine on the PFC-2 to perform Layer 3 switching. Remember that Layer 3 switching occurs at the data plane of IP routing; at this level, a rewrite of the destination and source MAC addresses is required, along with knowledge of the egress interface. You can see in Example 6-44 that each adjacency specifies the source MAC address to rewrite, destination MAC address to rewrite, and egress interface. You can also see the number of packets and associated bytes that have been matched to each adjacency. This is useful for verifying that CEF-based Layer 3 switching is actually taking place.

If you put together all of the information in Example 6-43 and Example 6-44, you begin to see exactly how L3 switching works using CEF. Suppose a packet from Host-X (192.168.1.100) is passed to the L3 engine on the PFC-2 that is addressed to Host-Y (192.168.2.100). The L3 engine inspects the destination IP address (192.168.2.100) and looks up the FIB table (see Example 6-44) for the most specific entry that matches the destination IP address. Entry #11 is matched, which specifies an adjacency of 0006.53fe.8420. The L3 engine then looks up the adjacency table (see Example 6-44) for an adjacency with a destination MAC address of 0006.53fe.8420. Entry #17416 is matched, which provides the L3 engine with the values for the rewriting of the source MAC address (0004.dd41.890a—i.e., the MSFC) and destination MAC address (0006.53fe.8420—i.e., Host-Y), as well as the interface (Fa2/2) out which the packet should be sent. The L3 engine rewrites the frame waiting to be routed, performs other required tasks (such as TTL decrement and checksum recomputation), and then forwards the packet to the egress interface for transmission. Figure 6-17 shows the process described above.

Figure 6-17 *CEF Operation on Switch-A*

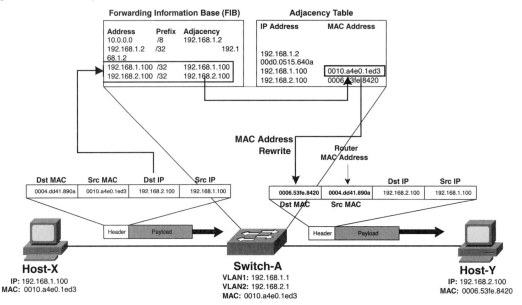

At this stage, you have successfully verified CEF-based Layer 3 switching operation. As a final verification task, you can use the **show mls cef statistics** command to view the NetFlow statistical information that is collected. Example 6-45 demonstrates executing the **show mls cef statistics** command, generating some traffic on the network (in this example, a continuous ping is generated between Host-X and Host-Y), and then executing the **show mls cef statistics** command again.

Example 6-112 *Displaying NetFlow Statistics*

```
Switch-A# show mls cef statistics

Switch-A-sp#
Total CEF switched packets:   0000000000021720
Total CEF switched bytes:     0000000032444268
... (Generate traffic between Host-X and Host-Y, wait a few minutes)
...
Switch-A# show mls cef statistics

Switch-A-sp#
Total CEF switched packets:   0000000000021926
Total CEF switched bytes:     0000000032753268
```

In Example 6-45, the second **show mls cef statistics** command is executed approximately 3 minutes after the first. Notice that the number of packets L3 switched by CEF has increased by 206 (from 21720 to 21926), and the total number of bytes has also increased due to the continuous ICMP traffic being sent from Host-X to Host-Y.

You can also use the **show interfaces** command on a native mode switch to view the number of packets that have been Layer 2 switched and Layer 3 switched on a particular interface. Example 6-46 shows the output of the **show interfaces** command on interface FastEthernet 2/2, which is connected to Host-Y.

Example 6-113 *Displaying Interface Statistics in Native Mode*

```
Switch-A# show interface FastEthernet2/2
FastEthernet2/2 is up, line protocol is up
  Hardware is C6k 10/100Mb 802.3, address is 0004.dd41.890a (bia 0004.dd41.890a)
… (Output truncated)
…
  L2 Switched: ucast: 3993 pkt, 354635 bytes - mcast: 569 pkt, 46508 bytes
  L3 in Switched: ucast: 75329 pkt, 112930074 bytes - mcast: 0 pkt, 0 bytes mcast
  L3 out Switched: ucast: 75337 pkt, 112929372 bytes
… (Output truncated)
…
```

In Example 6-46, the shaded output indicates how many packets have been L2 switched on the interface as well as how many packets have been L3 switched in and out of the interface. This command is useful for verifying L3 switching on a particular interface.

TIP   The L2 and L3 switching interface counters are updated approximately every 180 seconds.

Summary

The routing of IP traffic can be represented by two distinct planes of operation—the control plane and the data plane. The control plane deals with determining the information about where each destination IP address in the network is. Each destination IP address is associated with a next-hop IP address, which represents the next closest router to the destination. The data plane deals with the physical operations that are required to actually forward the packet to the next hop; this refers to the operation of storing the packet in memory while control plane information (such as the next hop address and egress interface) is determined, placing the appropriate Layer 2 addressing and encapsulation (depending on the egress interface Layer 2 protocol) on the frame, and then forwarding the packet out the appropriate egress interface to the next hop.

Layer 3 switching represents the data plane operations that are required to route IP traffic. Layer 3 switching can be performed in software, where an operating system application is responsible for the data plane operations, or in hardware, where a hardware chip (or ASIC) designed specifically for L3 switching is responsible for the data plane operations. Performing L3 switching in software allows for more flexibility because code can be written that uses as a common processor to perform the specific data plane operations required for each Layer 2 protocol. Performing L3 switching in hardware increases performance because all operations are performed by a function-specific chip, leaving the main processor free to perform other duties. Using hardware L3 switching is less flexible and more expensive because a hardware chip must be designed for each Layer 2 protocol (e.g., separate ASIC for Ethernet, separate ASIC for Token Ring).

Modern LAN design methodology recognizes the business requirements for the separation of functional groups within the LAN by using multiple VLANs. Separating functional groups increases network performance and efficiency and also allows for security access controls to be applied between each functional group (VLAN). From an IP perspective, each VLAN represents an IP subnet. For each IP subnet to communicate with remote IP subnets, IP routing or inter-VLAN routing is required. From a Layer 2 (Ethernet) perspective, IP routing is required between high-speed Ethernet networks which means that performance is a major consideration for inter-VLAN routing within the LAN. Hardware-based L3 switching within Ethernet LAN networks overcomes the performance limitations of software-based L3 switching and does not suffer the flexibility or cost disadvantages associated with hardware-based L3 switching, because only Ethernet-to-Ethernet L3 switching is required. This means only a single ASIC design is required.

Cisco Catalyst switches support two methods of hardware-based L3 switching. The methods differ in how the data plane components of L3 switching can get the necessary control plane information required to place in the Layer 2 framing. Multilayer switching (MLS) represents the first method of hardware-based L3 switching used by Cisco Catalyst switches and uses a flow-based model to populate a cache that includes the necessary control plane information for the data plane to L3 switch a packet. A flow simply represents a collection of IP packets that each shares a number of identical parameters, such as the same destination IP address or same destination TCP port. An MLS Route Processor (MLS-RP) provides control plane operations, while an MLS Switching Engine (MLS-SE) provides data plane operation. MLS requires that the first packet of a new flow (candidate packet) received by the MLS-SE be routed to the MLS-RP, which makes a control plane decision and routes the packet in software to its destination. The MLS-SE sees the control plane information in the return packet (enabler packet) that is sent to the destination and populates the MLS cache with the necessary control plane information required to L3 switch packets that belong to the flow. Subsequent packets received by the MLS-SE can be L3 switched in hardware without requiring the packet to be sent to the MLS-RP because the MLS cache includes the required control plane information.

The next-generation method of hardware-based L3 switching is based upon Cisco Express Forwarding (CEF). In the CEF architecture, the cache (that is used to store the necessary control plane information required for the data plane hardware ASICs to L3 switch each packet) is pre-populated with all the necessary control plane information (the CEF table). This means that the L3 switching ASIC can switch all IP packets in hardware, unlike MLS which requires the first packet of a flow to be switched in software (by the MLS-RP). This architecture is more efficient and scalable and resolves performance limitations of MLS in environments where thousands of new flows are established every second. The CEF architecture is also very easy to scale because CEF caching information can be distributed to multiple L3 switching ASICs. This means that a L3 switch can perform multiple L3 switching operations simultaneously—one per CEF cache and ASIC. The route processor (control plane) component of IP routing is responsible for generating the information in the CEF table and updating it as routing topology changes occur. The CEF table actually consists of two tables—the Forwarding Information Base (FIB) and the adjacency table.

## CHAPTER 7

Multicast Routing and Switching

The growing level of multimedia content available on corporate networks and the Internet has increased many organizations bandwidth requirements. Streaming video and audio applications are becoming more commonplace, with many of these audio/video streams originating from a single source and being sent to many receivers. For example, a video server may transmit a single video feed to thousands of receivers, which raises concerns about bandwidth usage and CPU overheads. The video server could send a video feed to each individual receiver, but doing so means the server has to generate thousands of video streams. So many streams would most likely saturate the link connected to the server and render the server useless due to the high CPU load incurred. Multicasting allows a one-to-many transmission that consists of a single data stream that is propagated to any host that wants to receive the data stream, without unnecessarily sending that data stream to hosts that do not want to receive the data stream. That means multicast traffic must be controlled in some fashion at both a Layer 2 level and Layer 3 level.

This chapter focuses on controlling multicast traffic in both Layer 2 and Layer 3 networks. After some initial introductory material, this chapter presents the following configuration scenarios, which provide you with the practical knowledge required to implement multicast traffic control on Layer 2 and Layer 3 networks:

- Scenario 7-1: Configuring PIM Dense Mode Multicast Routing
- Scenario 7-2: Configuring PIM Sparse Mode and PIM Sparse-Dense Mode Multicast Routing
- Scenario 7-3: Multicast Traffic Control on the LAN
- Scenario 7-4: Configuring IGMP Snooping
- Scenario 7-5: Configuring Cisco Group Management Protocol (CGMP)

Introduction

Most networking professionals are very familiar with the concept of unicast traffic and broadcast traffic. A *unicast packet* is sent from a single source to a single destination and is also known as one-to-one communications. A *broadcast* packet is sent from a single source to all hosts on a VLAN and is also known as one-to-all communication. *Multicast traffic* is designed to enable a host to send network data to a group of hosts (i.e., one-to-many communications) without requiring the data to be broadcast throughout the network or replicated as multiple unicast communications to each receiving host. This process ensures only a single copy of a one-to-many transmission is sent and that the transmission is forwarded only over the paths necessary to reach the group of hosts that need to receive it. This control allows for a reduction in bandwidth usage, increasing network efficiency and performance.

Multicast is important for any application that needs to send large amounts of the same information to multiple devices. Common uses for multicast traffic include:

- Multimedia applications that consume high bandwidth, such as streaming video and TV servers
- Voice-conferencing applications
- Software distribution applications
- Routing protocols such as Open Shortest Path First (OSPF), Enhanced Interior Gateway Routing Protocol (EIGRP), and Routing Information Protocol (RIP) version 2
- Any application that requires a central host to efficiently send the same message to multiple peers

The following topics are now introduced to ensure that you are familiar with fundamental multicast concepts:

- Multicast addressing
- Internet Group Management Protocol (IGMP)
- Multicast routing
- Multicast on the LAN
- Multicast performance considerations on Cisco Catalyst switches

Multicast Addressing

For both IP (Layer 3) and Ethernet (Layer 2) communications, special addressing is required to identify multicast packets and frames. A multicast address identifies a specific group of receivers that want to receive the information transmitted to the multicast address.

IP Multicast Addressing

For IP multicast addressing, the Class D address range is used (224.0.0.0-239.255.255.255) in the destination IP address field to identify a multicast packet. The source IP address of a multicast packet is always a unicast address (Class A, B, or C). Within the Class D address range, some smaller address ranges are reserved for special use. The first is the 224.0.0.x range, which is reserved for the use of various communications protocols. Table 7-1 describes some common reserved multicast addresses.

Table 7-1   *Reserved Multicast Addresses*

Address	Description
224.0.0.1	All multicast receivers on a subnet
224.0.0.2	All multicast routers on a subnet
224.0.0.5	All OSPF routers on a subnet
224.0.0.6	All OSPF designated routers on a subnet
224.0.0.9	All RIPv2 routers on a subnet
224.0.0.10	All EIGRP routers on a subnet
224.0.0.13	All Protocol Independent Multicast (PIM) routers on a subnet
224.0.0.18	All Virtual Redundancy Router Protocol (VRRP) routers on a subnet (VRRP is a standards-based implementation of HSRP)
224.0.0.102	All Hot Standby Router Protocol (HSRP) routers on a subnet

The 224.0.0.x multicast range has a local scope. The *scope* of a multicast packet is basically the number of router hops the multicast is allowed to travel and is implemented using the IP TTL (time-to-live) field. A *local scope* means that the multicast is never forwarded by routers and is isolated to a single VLAN. If you are familiar with routing protocols, this is the reason why OSPF and EIGRP multicast communications are never forwarded off the subnet they originated in.

The other important reserved address range is 239.0.0.0 through 239.255.255.255, which is reserved for private use. This reservation is a similar concept to the RFC 1918 private IP address ranges (10.x.x.x, 172.16.x.x-172.31.x.x, and 192.168.x.x) and is designed to be used for multicast traffic that is restricted to a closed area of a private network.

Ethernet Multicast Addressing

Ethernet multicast addresses are derived directly from IP multicast addresses, as shown in Figure 7-1.

Figure 7-1 *Layer 2 Multicast Addressing*

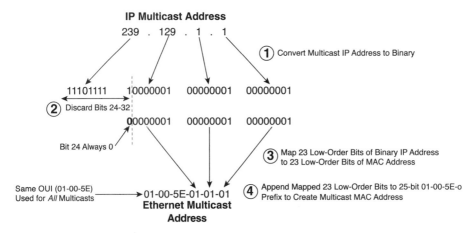

Figure 7-1 shows that an Organizational Unique Identifier (OUI) of 01-00-5E is always used to allow a receiving host to identify the frame as an IP multicast (other OUIs are used to identify multicasts for other Layer 2 protocols). The first bit in the second octet (bit 24) is *always* 0, and the remaining low-order 23 bits are mapped directly from the first 23 low-order bits of the matching IP multicast address. With Class D IP addressing, the first four bits are always 1110, with the remaining 28 bits identifying each IP multicast group. When the conversion to Ethernet multicast addressing is performed, 5 bits from the IP multicast address (bits 24-28) are lost, which means that there are 32 (2^5) IP multicast addresses that map to the same Ethernet multicast address.

Internet Group Management Protocol

Multicast packets are transmitted to a particular multicast address, which represents a group of receivers interested in the packets. Internet Group Management Protocol (IGMP) facilitates the concepts of joining a group, maintaining group membership and leaving a group. IGMP exists in three versions (version 1, 2, and 3), of which version 2 is the most common. In this chapter, assume version 2 unless otherwise stated. IGMP uses several different messages that provide the following various functions:

- **Allows a receiver to join a multicast group**—Facilitated by IGMP Membership Report messages

- **Allows a router to query a LAN segment for receivers that want to join a multicast group**—Facilitated by IGMP General Query messages

- **Allows a receiver to notify a router that it wants to leave a multicast group**—Facilitated by IGMP Leave Group messages and verified by IGMP Group-Specific Query messages.

IP Multicast Routing

IGMP deals with allowing receivers to register that they want to receive a particular multicast transmission, but does not deal with routing multicast traffic across the network from the source to each receiver. This task is left to a multicast routing protocol, several of which exist for IP networks:

- Distance Vector Multicast Routing Protocol (DVMRP)
- Protocol Independent Multicast (PIM)
- Multicast OSPF (MOSPF)
- Multicast BGP (MBGP)

Of the routing protocols listed above, PIM represents the most commonly used routing protocol used on Cisco routers.

The primary goal of IP multicast routing is to define exactly which IP subnets contain receiving hosts for a particular multicast transmission and to forward the multicast transmission only out interfaces connected to subnets that contain receivers, or out interfaces that lead to receivers connected to other multicast routers. Each multicast router determines via a multicast routing protocol which interfaces multicast traffic should be forwarded over, which builds a path or tree topology over which multicast traffic is forwarded. This tree is commonly referred to as a *multicast distribution tree.*

NOTE   Cisco routers and Cisco Catalyst Layer 3 switches both support multicast routing, and either type of device may be represented as a multicast router in this chapter.

Two basic types of multicast distribution trees are used with multicast routing:

- Source trees
- Shared trees

NOTE   Another less common type of multicast distribution tree used is called a *Core-Based Tree (CBT)*. Discussion of this distribution tree is outside the scope of this book.

Source Trees

A *source tree*, as the name implies, is rooted at the source of a multicast group, with a tree built from the source out to each receiver that belongs to the group. The paths that are used to deliver traffic to each receiver are the shortest possible paths between the source and receiver; hence, a source tree is also commonly known as a *shortest path tree* (*SPT*). With an SPT, the multicast tree is defined around two important parameters:

- The source of a multicast group (S)

- The multicast group (G)

An SPT can be identified using (S,G) nomenclature. For example, if a source with an IP address of 10.1.1.10 is sending multicast traffic to a group with an IP address of 239.1.1.1, then the SPT that is built to distribute this particular traffic can be defined as (10.1.1.10,239.1.1.1). For each unique (S,G) entity in the network, a separate SPT exists for each (S,G) entity. Understand that an STP only supports unidirectional traffic; it flows only from the source to receivers, and not vice versa. Figure 7-2 shows an SPT.

Figure 7-2   *Shortest Path Trees*

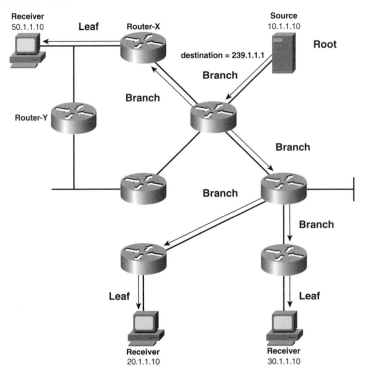

In Figure 7-2, the source is 10.1.1.10 and the multicast group is 239.1.1.1; hence, the SPT in Figure 7-2 can be represented as (10.1.1.10,239.1.1.1).

Shared Trees

A *shared tree* is a multicast distribution tree that can be shared by multiple sources for the same group. For example, if two separate sources are generating traffic for the same group, the traffic generated by each of these flows down the same shared tree. Because multiple sources share the same tree for a specific group, the (S,G) notation for a shared tree is (*,G), with the asterisk indicating any source. For example, if multiple sources are sending to a group address of 239.1.1.1, the shared tree is represented as (*,239.1.1.1).

Shared trees are not rooted at the source of a multicast group, because multiple sources can exist that use the shared tree. Instead, a shared tree is rooted at some common point in the network, which can be arbitrarily defined by an administrator. This common point is referred to as a *shared root*. The shared tree is built from the shared root to ensure that all receivers on the network can receive multicast traffic for the group. With a unidirectional shared tree, multicast traffic flows from the shared root across the shared tree to each receiver.

For multicast traffic to be placed upon the shared tree, each source that uses the shared tree for multicast delivery must somehow be able to deliver multicast traffic to the shared root. The multicast router locally attached to the source is responsible for ensuring that multicast traffic is forwarded to the shared root either by using a SPT, where the shared root joins an SPT rooted at the source, or by encapsulating the multicast traffic in a unicast packet and forwarding this directly to the shared root. Figure 7-3 demonstrates shared trees.

In Figure 7-3, Router-A is configured as the shared root for the network, and a shared tree is built for (*,239.1.1.1) that ensures each receiver receives transmissions from any source associated with the 239.1.1.1 group. Notice that an SPT (10.1.1.10,239.1.1.1) enables the source to deliver multicast traffic to the shared root, which then forwards the traffic down the shared tree. Instead of using an SPT to ensure traffic from the source is sent to the shared root, Router-B could be configured to forward all multicast traffic encapsulated in unicast packets to the shared root.

NOTE   One important advantage of a shared tree over an SPT is that a shared tree can be either unidirectional or bidirectional. A bidirectional tree enables traffic to be sent either up or down a shared tree. In Figure 7-3, a bidirectional tree means that multicast traffic generated from the source and received at Router-B can be immediately forwarded to Router-X as well as forwarded to Router-A, instead of having to forward the traffic only to Router-A, which then simply forwards the traffic down the shared tree to Router-B if the tree is unidirectional.

Figure 7-3   *Shared Trees*

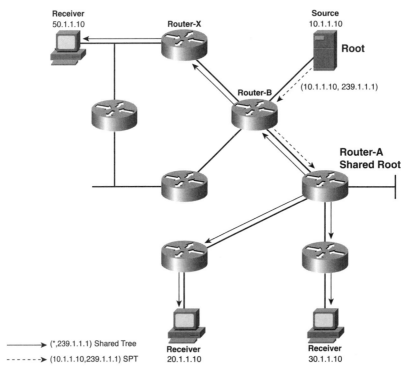

Multicast Forwarding

A *multicast distribution tree* is a logical entity that is defined by the collective forwarding states of each multicast router that makes up the multicast distribution tree. Multicast routers maintain this state information in a *multicast routing table*, which is similar in concept to a unicast routing table, but just engineered for multicast forwarding as opposed to unicast forwarding. Each SPT (S,G) and shared tree (*,G) is defined as an entry in the multicast routing table, and each of these entries contains a forwarding state.

To build forwarding state for a particular multicast route entry, each router defines the following:

- Incoming interface
- Outgoing interface

The incoming interface defines the closest interface on the router to the source (S), which represents the interface on which multicast traffic should (and must) be received from the source. Depending on the multicast routing protocol in use, a multicast router might use the multicast routing protocol's own mechanism to determine the closest interface to the source (e.g., DVMRP) or might rely on the unicast routing table (e.g., PIM).

The incoming interface is determined using what is known as a *reverse path forwarding* (*RPF*) check. For example, with the PIM multicast routing protocol, when a multicast packet arrives on an interface, the source IP address is examined against the unicast IP routing table. The outgoing interface associated with the source IP address is determined, and if this is the same interface that the multicast packet was received on, the multicast router knows that the packet has arrived via the shortest path to the source. At this point, the multicast packet is said to have passed the RPF check.

Any multicast packet that passes the RPF check is accepted for subsequent multicast routing; any multicast packet that does not pass the RPF check (i.e., is received on an interface that is not the closest interface to the source) is dropped. The RPF check is primarily designed to prevent multicast routing loops from forming in the network, as demonstrated in Figure 7-4.

NOTE	For SPT (S,G) entries, the incoming interface is defined as the closest interface to the source (S). For shared tree (*,G) entries, no incoming interface can be defined based upon a source (as a shared tree can be shared by multiple sources). Instead, the incoming interface is defined as the closest interface to the shared root.

Figure 7-4   *Preventing Multicast Routing Loops*

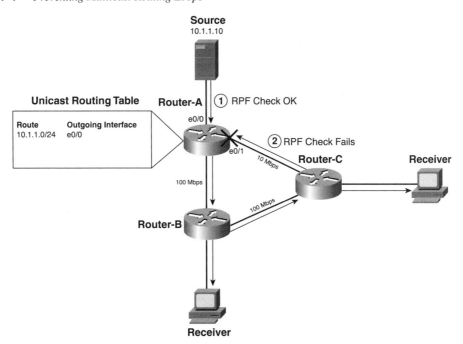

In Figure 7-4, multicast traffic is being sent from a source attached to Router-A. When a packet arrives from the source on Ethernet0/0, an RPF check takes place. The source IP address of the multicast packet (10.1.1.10) is examined against the unicast routing table, with the outgoing interface associated with the source IP address found to be the same interface (Ethernet0/0) that the packet arrived on. This means that the RPF check succeeds, and the multicast traffic is accepted and forwarded appropriately. Notice that the packet then is forwarded to Router-B and then to Router-C. Router-C then forwards the multicast packet back to Router-A. At this point, Router-A performs an RPF check on the same IP address of the original packet (10.1.1.10). This time, it is determined that the packet has arrived on a different interface than that listed in the unicast routing table; hence, the RPF check fails and the multicast packet is dropped. Note that if Router-A accepted this packet for forwarding, a multicast routing loop would form. The RPF check ensures multicast routing loops don't form.

Once a multicast packet passes an RPF check (i.e., it is received on the interface that is defined as the incoming interface for the (S,G) STP or (*,G) shared tree), it must be forwarded appropriately. The outgoing interface list defines which interfaces a multicast packet should be forwarded out to ensure that the network forwards multicast packets to all receivers. This list is built using both IGMP (which indicates any local receivers attached to local interfaces) and the multicast routing protocol configured for the network (which indicates any receivers attached to remote multicast routers). Once the list is built, any multicast packets received that match a specific (S,G) or (*,G) route entry and pass an RPF check are forwarded out the outgoing interface list.

Figure 7-5 demonstrates how a multicast router forwards multicast traffic. In Figure 7-5, take a close look at the multicast distribution tree and Router-B. You can see that multicast traffic generated by the source is received on interface Fa0/1 on Router-B. This interface is defined as the incoming interface because multicast packets are received on this interface. Notice that Router-B must forward multicast packets received out interface Fa0/2 and interface Fa0/3 to ensure that the two receivers located further downstream receive multicast traffic. Because there are no receivers or downstream multicast routers attached to interface Fa0/5, Router-B does not need to forward multicast traffic out this interface. The outgoing interface list, therefore, consists of interface Fa0/2 and interface Fa0/3.

Figure 7-5   *Multicast Forwarding*

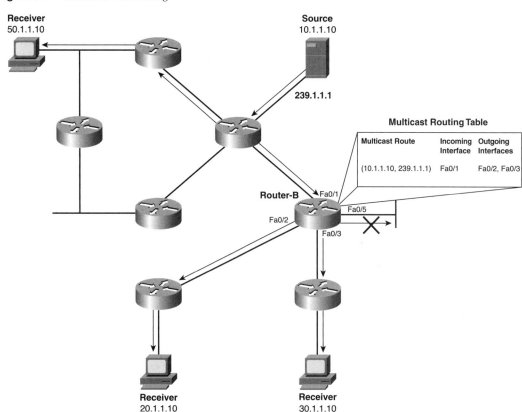

Multicast on the LAN

Multicast routing gets the traffic for a particular multicast group to only the Layer 2 segments that need to receive the group traffic. Once the multicast transmission is on the Layer 2 network, multicast routing has no control over which Layer 2 links or ports the transmission is sent to. This control is left to the Layer 2 device (such as a switch) that interconnects the segment.

Ideally, the Layer 2 device should forward the multicast transmission only out ports to which receivers are connected and also out any ports that are connected to downstream multicast routers. This configuration requires a Layer 2 device to be able to determine the ports on which multicast routers and receivers for each separate (S,G) or (*,G) multicast group are located. To facilitate intelligent forwarding of multicast traffic on the LAN, Cisco Catalyst switches support two mechanisms:

- **IGMP snooping**—The switch listens in or "snoops" IGMP communications between receivers and multicast routers. This snooping enables the switch to determine which ports are connected to receivers for each multicast group and which ports are connected to multicast routers.

- **Cisco Group Management Protocol (CGMP)**—The switch communicates with multicasts routers, with multicast routers relaying group membership information to switches.

Once a switch has learned the appropriate port information, the Layer 2 bridging table is updated for the each Ethernet multicast MAC address to include the ports associated with all multicast routers on the LAN and each receiver that belongs to each group represented by a specified multicast MAC address.

NOTE   To control multicast bandwidth usage, you can use a feature called *multicast/broadcast control*, where multicast and broadcast traffic on a port that exceeds a configurable threshold over a defined time interval is dropped. This feature is considered a legacy and can have serious side effects. For example, a large multicast stream may reach the allowable multicast/broadcast threshold on a port. After this point, all multicasts and broadcasts are dropped (including crucial spanning tree BPDUs), which can cause network instability. For this reason, it is recommended that you don't use multicast/broadcast control in an attempt to reduce the bandwidth usage of multicast traffic.

Multicast Routing Performance Considerations on Cisco Catalyst Layer 3 Switches

Cisco Catalyst Layer 3 switches are designed to route IP packets at high performances, so the mechanisms used by Cisco Catalyst Layer 3 switches to forward IP multicast traffic must be understood to determine how multicast routing impacts on Layer 3 switching. To ensure that multicast traffic does not have a negative effect on the network, Cisco Catalyst Layer 3 switches all perform hardware-based Layer 3 switching of multicast traffic, ensuring wire-speed performance for such traffic.

If you think about the differences between unicast traffic and multicast traffic, you should be able to quickly realize that it is much more difficult for a Layer 3 switch to route multicast traffic in hardware. For example, unicast routing requires only knowledge of the destination IP address of packets, whereas multicast routing requires knowledge of both the source and destination IP address (S,G). To further complicate things, Layer 3 switches that also provide Layer 2 functions for VLANs with receivers attached must also ensure that traffic is forwarded only out ports with receivers attached if IGMP snooping is enabled.

The various Cisco Catalyst Layer 3 switching platforms vary in their approach as to the specifics of how they implement Layer 3 switching of multicast traffic. The end result is that Cisco Catalyst Layer 3 switches not only forward unicast traffic in hardware, but also multicast traffic as well. This forwarding ensures that you can run multicast applications on top of Layer 3 switching infrastructure without any performance degradations.

Scenario 7-1: Configuring PIM Dense Mode Multicast Routing

Before you can configure multicast features on Cisco Catalyst switches, you must have a network that supports IP multicast routing. IP multicast routing is traditionally supported on most Cisco routers and is also supported on Cisco Catalyst Layer 3 switches, such as the Catalyst 3550 with EMI image, the Catalyst 4000 with Supervisor 3, and the native IOS Catalyst 6000/6500. In this scenario, you learn how to configure a routed IP multicast network based upon PIM, using both Cisco IOS routers and Cisco Layer 3 switches. Figure 7-6 shows the network topology that is used to demonstrate the configuration of IP multicast routing for all scenarios in this chapter.

Figure 7-6   *Chapter 7 Scenario Topology*

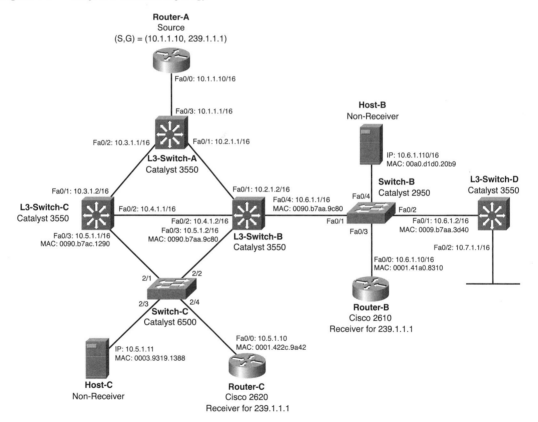

In Figure 7-6, four Cisco Catalyst 3550 switches with Enhanced Multilayer Image (EMI) software are used to provide Layer 3 switching functionality. These switches are named L3-Switch-A through L3-Switch-D. Switch-B and Switch-C provide Layer 2 LAN connectivity for various hosts attached to the network, which consist of a mixture of multicast receivers and non-multicast receivers.

PIM can be configured to operate in one of the following modes:

* Dense mode
* Sparse mode
* Sparse-dense Mode

In this scenario you will learn how to configure PIM dense mode (PIM-DM). Before configuring PIM, you need to understand a little bit about how PIM operates — how PIM routers discover and communicate with each other and how PIM routers operating in dense mode build multicast distribution trees. The following sections provide an introduction to PIM-DM operation:

* Unicast routing considerations
* Neighbor discovery
* Building multicast trees in PIM dense mode networks
* Configuration tasks

Unicast Routing Considerations

Before configuring PIM to operate in any mode, you must ensure that unicast routing protocol(s) are configured throughout the network to ensure that all devices can communicate with each other using unicast communications. PIM relies on unicast routing protocols for anything related to unicast IP addresses. For example, multicast traffic by definition has a unicast source IP address, and PIM relies on the unicast routing table to perform a RPF check, which determines the closest interface on a multicast router that leads to the source of a multicast transmission. The RPF check is crucial because it prevents multicast traffic from looping continuously in the network by ensuring that multicast traffic received is forwarded only if the traffic has been received on the closest interface (in terms of the unicast routing table) to the source.

A detailed discussion on how to implement unicast routing protocols is outside the scope of this book, so it is assumed for all scenarios that you understand that a unicast routing topology has been configured and is in place.

Neighbor Discovery

The first event that occurs in a multicast network configured for PIM is *neighbor discovery*. Each multicast router announces its presence to the network by multicasting PIM Hello messages every PIM-enabled interface every 30 seconds (by default). These messages are sent to the 224.0.0.13 group address, which is reserved for all PIM routers. All directly attached neighbors hear each other's Hello messages and form adjacencies with each other.

On a multi-access network (such as an Ethernet segment), if multiple PIM routers are attached to the network, a *designated router* (*DR*) is selected for the segment. If you are familiar with OSPF, the DR selection is similar in concept to the OSPF DR selection on multi-access networks. In PIM-DM networks, the DR is not actually used, except for the situation where a multi-access network has IGMPv1 receivers attached. IGMPv1 specifies that if more than one multicast router is attached to a multi-access segment, the multicast routing protocol is used to select the IGMP Querier role. With PIM, the DR is selected to perform the IGMPv1 Querier role, which is responsible for determining if receivers exist on the network for a specific group address.

NOTE   With IGMPv2 routers, the IGMP Querier is determined independently from the multicast routing protocol in use; it is determined by the IGMPv2 router with the highest IP address on the LAN.

Building Multicast Trees in PIM Dense Mode Networks

PIM-DM uses a source distribution tree or shortest path tree (SPT) for each group address present in the network. The goal of using multicast is to form a tree that includes only the necessary branches and leaves required to transport the multicast traffic to each receiver. Understanding how PIM-DM forms a source distribution tree is most easily explained by using an example. Assume that the topology of Figure 7-6 has been configured for PIM-DM operation, and that Host-A is multicast source. After neighbor discovery is complete, Figure 7-7 shows what happens when a PIM-DM network detects the new group address associated with Host-A (i.e., Host-A starts sending traffic to a new multicast address).

Figure 7-7 *Scenario 7-1 Topology Configured for PIM-DM*

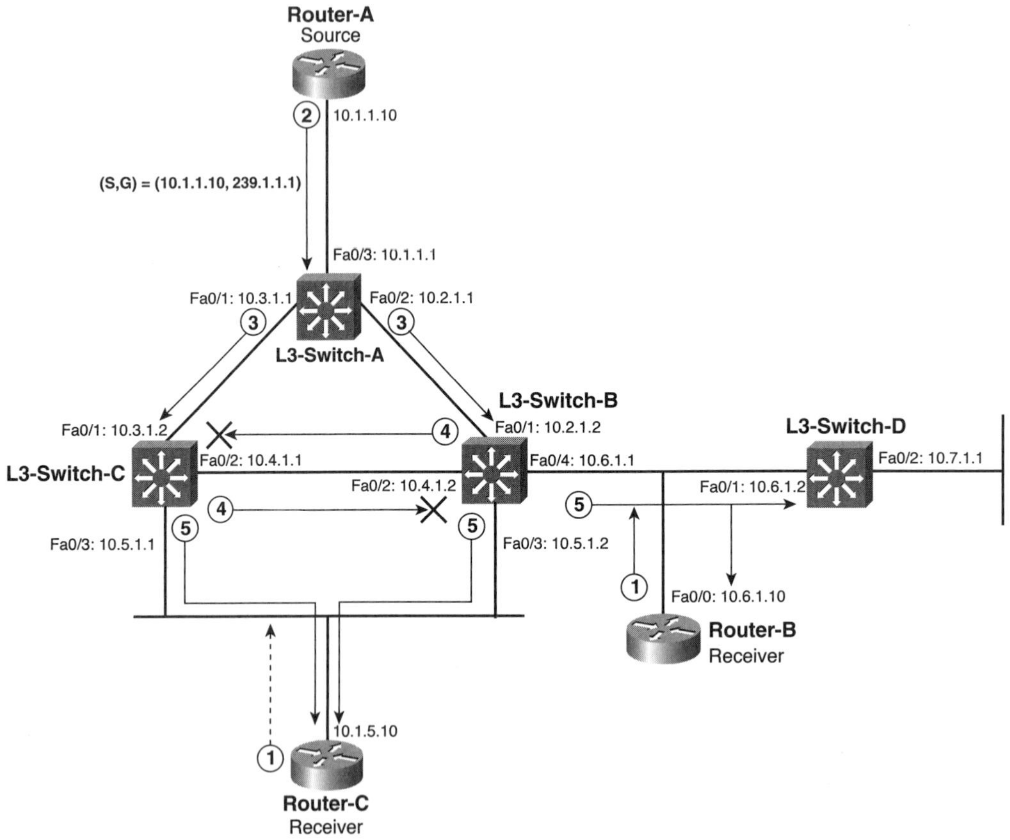

In Figure 7-7 the following events occur:

1. Router-B and Router-C, as receivers of the multicast group 239.1.1.1, send IGMP membership reports to all multicast routers attached to the local segments.

2. Router-A starts generating multicast traffic, sending the first multicast packet towards L3-Switch-A, which arrives at L3-Switch-A on the routed interface Fa0/3. L3-Switch-A performs an RPF check to ensure that the source IP address of the packet is reachable via the interface the packet was received on. L3-Switch-A then looks at its PIM neighbor list and forwards the multicast packet out any interfaces that have a PIM neighbor attached. If L3-Switch-A has any connected receivers for the multicast group address, it also forwards the multicast out the interfaces connected to these receivers.

3. L3-Switch-A has PIM neighbors (L3-Switch-B and L3-Switch-C) and, consequently, forwards the multicast out interfaces Fa0/1 and Fa0/2. L3-Switch-B and L3-Switch-C both receive the multicast packet and perform an RPF check to ensure that the source of the multicast packet is reachable via the interface the packet was received on.

4 L3-Switch-B and L3-Switch-C now forward the multicast packet out any interface that has a PIM neighbor attached (excluding L3-Switch-A, as this is where the multicast was forwarded from). Notice that L3-Switch-B and L3-Switch-C forward the multicast to each other. For example, L3-Switch-B forwards the multicast out interface Fa0/2 towards L3-Switch-C. When L3-Switch-C receives the multicast from L3-Switch-B, it immediately performs an RPF check. Because the source IP address of the multicast packet (Host-A or 192.168.1.10) is reachable via interface Fa0/1 (L3-Switch-A) rather than the interface the packet is received on (interface Fa0/2), L3-Switch-C discards the multicast from L3-Switch-B. The same happens on L3-Switch-B, where the multicast forwarded from L3-Switch-C and received on interface Fa0/2 is discarded due to the RPF check.

5 L3-Switch-B and L3-Switch-C also forwards the multicast packet out any interface that has receivers attached that you have registered as wanting to receive multicast traffic for the group address. This setting means that L3-Switch-C forwards the multicast out interface Fa0/3 towards Router-C (a receiver). L3-Switch-B forwards the multicast out interface Fa0/3 towards Router-C and also out interface Fa0/4. L3-Switch-D does not forward the packet out Fa0/2, because it is a leaf multicast router and has no receivers connected to the 10.7.0.0/16 subnet.

NOTE   Notice that a receiver may receive multiple copies of the same multicast packet at this stage. For example, Router-C receives two copies of the multicast traffic from L3-Switch-B and L3-Switch-C. Receivers must be able to deal with duplicate packet delivery.

Understand that the tree shown in Figure 7-7 is specific only to the source (S) and the multicast group the source is sending traffic to. In other words, Figure 7-7 represents the (10.1.1.10,239.1.1.1) tree. If other sources are present in the network for the same group or a different group, totally separate (S,G) trees exist for each unique (S,G) combination.

Notice in Figure 7-7 that although multicast traffic is being successfully forwarded to all receivers, the distribution of the multicast traffic is not ideal. For example, multicast traffic does not need to be sent on the link between L3-Switch-B and L3-Switch-C, and Router-C is receiving two copies of multicast traffic (one from Switch-B and one from Switch-C). With PIM-DM operation, multicast traffic is initially flooded throughout the multicast-enabled network, which is inefficient. Once initial multicast packets have been flooded throughout the multicast network down the initial broadcast tree, the tree is shaped to the optimal shape so that only the necessary branches and leaves of the tree are active. This process is referred to as pruning.

PIM-DM Pruning

Pruning is the process of removing unnecessary branches in the SPT that is generated for each group. PIM routers can generate a PIM prune message, which indicates to PIM neighbors that they should not forward multicast traffic towards the router. PIM prune messages are generated based upon the following conditions:

- Traffic arrives on a non-RPF point-to-point interface.

- The router is a leaf router (has no downstream PIM neighbors) and has no connected receivers.

- The router is a non-leaf router on a point-to-point link that has received a prune from its neighbor.

- The router is a non-leaf router on a multi-access segment with no receivers that has received a prune from a neighbor on the LAN segment, and no other neighbors on the segment have overridden the prune.

It is important to understand that pruning operates differently on point-to-point interfaces (e.g., serial interfaces) than it does on multi-access interfaces (e.g., Ethernet interfaces). In Figure 7-6, there are no point-to-point interfaces, even though multicast routers/L3 switches are directly connected to each other because Ethernet by definition is a multi-access network.

Figure 7-8 demonstrates how pruning works on the multi-access networks of the topology of Figure 7-6 and Figure 7-7.

In Figure 7-8, because L3-Switch-D is a leaf router and has no receivers attached to the 10.7.0.0/16 subnet, L3-Switch-D generates a prune message for the (S,G) entry (10.1.1.10, 239.1.1.1) and sends the prune (Step 1) to its upstream PIM neighbor (L3-Switch-B). L3-Switch-B ignores this prune message because Router-C is a receiver and is attached to the 10.6.0.0/16 subnet. L3-Switch-D continues to generate prune messages every three minutes. Also in Figure 7-8, both L3-Switch-B and L3-Switch-C prune the multi-access network connecting both switches (Step 2) without sending PIM prune messages to each other because no receivers are attached to this network and each multicast router can reach the source via L3-Switch-A.

PIM-DM Asserts

Asserts are a mechanism used on multi-access networks, such as Ethernet segments, to determine which multicast router forwards multicast traffic to the segment. In Figure 7-7, you can see that in Step 5 both L3-Switch-B and L3-Switch-C are forwarding multicast traffic onto the Ethernet segment that attaches to Router-C (a receiver). Having both switches forwarding the multicast traffic is both a waste of bandwidth and performance drain because the application running on receivers must constantly handle duplicate packets, which may affect the performance of the multicast application.

Figure 7-8   *PIM Dense Mode Pruning*

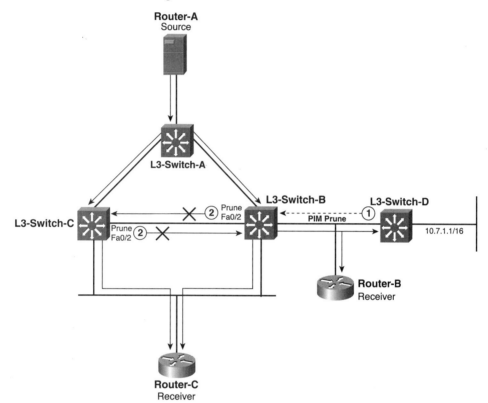

To ensure only a single multicast router forwards on a multi-access segment, PIM-DM uses asserts. An assert message is generated by a multicast router every time it receives traffic associated with a multicast group on a multi-access interface that is listed in the outgoing interface list for the multicast group. Figure 7-9 demonstrates how asserts are used in the topology described in Figure 7-7.

Figure 7-9 *PIM Dense Mode Asserts*

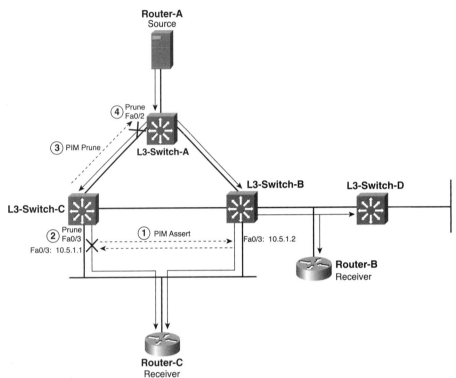

In Figure 7-9, both L3-Switch-B and L3-Switch-C receive multicast traffic from each other on interface Fa0/3, which is an outgoing interface for the multicast group. In response to this, each switch sends a PIM assert message (indicated by step 1), which includes the routing protocol administrative distance and the routing protocol metric that each router can reach the source by. The administrative distance parameter determines how believable the routing information is. For example, EIGRP has an administrative distance of 90 for an internal route, whilst OSPF has an administrative distance of 110. The lower the administrative distance, the more believable it is. The administrative distance value is considered first, with the router sending the assert with the lowest administrative distance asserting itself successfully as the forwarding multicast router for the segment. If the administrative distance values are equal, the routing metric to the source is compared with each, with the lowest routing metric determining which is the assertive router. In Figure 7-9, assume that EIGRP is in use throughout the network and that both L3-Switch-B and L3-Switch-C both have equal cost routes (metrics) to the source. In this tiebreaker situation, where the administrative distance and route metrics are identical, the router with the highest IP address on the multi-access network asserts itself as the forwarding router for the segment. This principle means that L3-Switch-B becomes the forwarding router for the segment, because L3-Switch-B has the highest IP address (10.5.1.2). Thus, L3-Switch-C prunes back interface F0/3 from the outgoing interface list (as indicated by Step 2).

At this point, L3-Switch-C has pruned back both interface Fa0/2 and interface Fa0/3 and, therefore, no longer needs to receive multicast traffic from L3-Switch-A. Thus, L3-Switch-C generates a prune message and sends the prune to L3-Switch-A. This causes both L3-Switch-A to prune the interface attached to L3-Switch-C (interface Fa0/2) from the outgoing interface list.

PIM-DM Grafting

The scenario topology is now fully pruned, meaning that the multicast group traffic is forwarded only down the paths necessary to reach each receiver in the network. You might be wondering what happens if a new receiver attaches onto the network in an area that has been pruned from the SPT. Because networks are dynamic, receivers may come and go, and a multicast routing protocol must be able to adapt to these changes. PIM-DM uses a mechanism known as *grafting*, which in essence grafts a previously pruned network path to the SPT. Figure 7-10 demonstrates the process of grafting, after a new multicast receiver enters the network.

Figure 7-10 *PIM Dense Mode Grafting*

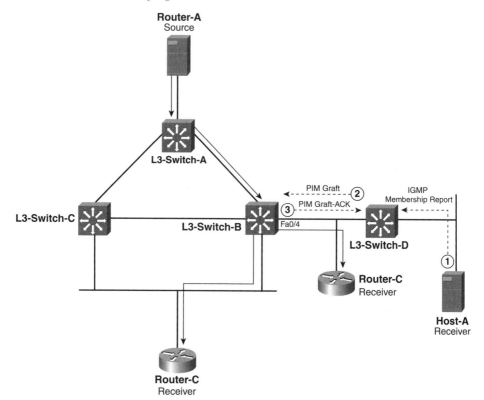

In Figure 7-10, the solid arrows indicate the SPT after the prune and assert mechanisms of Figure 7-9 are complete. The dashed lines indicate the following new events:

1 Host-A is a new receiver for the 239.1.1.1 multicast group and sends an IGMP membership report to L3-Switch-D, indicating that it wants to receive traffic for the multicast group.

2 Because L3-Switch-D has pruned all interfaces (see Figure 7-8), L3-Switch-D sends a PIM Graft message to the next upstream multicast router, which is L3-Switch-B. In Figure 7-10, L3-Switch-B is still forwarding multicast to the segment that L3-Switch-D is attached to, so you might wonder what the point is of sending a PIM graft message. If no receivers were attached to the segment between L3-Switch-B and L3-Switch-D, then L3-Switch-B would have pruned back its interface attached to the segment, so L3-Switch-D must notify L3-Switch-B that it needs to graft the interface back onto the outbound interface list.

3 Upon receiving the graft message, L3-Switch-B ensures that the interface that received the graft message (interface Fa0/4) is added to the outgoing interface list (in Figure 7-10, it already is because Router-C is a receiver attached to the same segment as the interface). L3-Switch-B also sends a Graft-Ack to L3-Switch-D to indicate it has grafted the interface that connects to L3-Switch-D back into the SPT.

At this point, the multicast forwarding tree has been extended to include L3-Switch-D and the segment that Host-A attaches to. Figure 7-10 demonstrates that PIM can dynamically adapt to changes that are required in the multicast forwarding tree to ensure all receivers can receive multicast traffic.

NOTE   PIM-DM networks age out pruning information after three minutes by default, at which time multicast routers once again flood the network, as described in Figure 7-8, with the appropriate pruning and assert mechanisms, described in Figure 7-9 and Figure 7-10, occurring all over again. To prevent this periodic flood and prune behavior, a recent enhancement to PIM-DM allows the multicast router(s) directly connected to the source of an (S,G) SPT to periodically send a PIM state refresh message to the multicast group G, which is flooded to all multicast routers and indicates that each router should keep any pruned interfaces for the (S,G) SPT in the pruned state, without using the clumsy flood and prune mechanism.

Scenario Prerequisites

To successfully commence the configuration tasks required to complete this scenario, Table 7-2 describes the prerequisite configurations required on each device in the scenario topology. Any configurations not listed can be assumed as being the default configuration.

Table 7-2   *Scenario 7-1 Requirements*

Device	Required Configuration	
	Parameter	**Value**
L3-Switch-A	Hostname	L3-Switch-A
	Enable/Telnet Password	cisco
	IP Routing	Enabled
	Routed Interfaces	FastEthernet0/1 FastEthernet0/2 FastEthernet0/3
	IP Addresses (interface)	10.2.1.1/16 (fa0/1) 10.3.1.1/16 (fa0/2) 10.1.1.1/16 (fa0/3)
L3-Switch-B	Hostname	L3-Switch-B
	Enable/Telnet Password	cisco
	IP Routing	Enabled
	Routed Interfaces	FastEthernet0/1 FastEthernet0/2 FastEthernet0/3 FastEthernet0/4
	IP Addresses (interface)	10.2.1.2/16 (fa0/1) 10.4.1.2/16 (fa0/2) 10.5.1.2/16 (fa0/3) 10.6.1.2/16 (fa0/4)
L3-Switch-C	Hostname	L3-Switch-C
	Enable/Telnet Password	cisco
	IP Routing	Enabled
	Routed Interfaces	FastEthernet0/1 FastEthernet0/2 FastEthernet0/3
	IP Addresses (interface)	10.3.1.2/16 (fa0/1) 10.4.1.1/16 (fa0/2) 10.5.1.1/16 (fa0/3)

continues

Table 7-2   *Scenario 7-1 Requirements (Continued)*

Device	Required Configuration	
	Parameter	**Value**
L3-Switch-D	Hostname	L3-Switch-D
	Enable/Telnet Password	cisco
	IP Routing	Enabled
	Routed Interfaces	FastEthernet0/1 FastEthernet0/2
	IP Addresses (interface)	10.6.1.2/16 (fa0/1) 10.7.1.1/16 (fa0/2)
Switch-C	Hostname	Switch-C
	Enable/Telnet Password	cisco
	sc0 IP Address (VLAN)	10.5.1.3/24
	Default Gateway	10.5.1.1
Switch-B	Hostname	Switch-B
	Enable/Telnet Password	cisco
	sc0 IP Address (VLAN)	10.6.1.3/24
	Default Gateway	10.6.1.1
Router-B	Hostname	Router-B
	Enable/Telnet Password	cisco
	IP Addresses	Fa0/0: 10.6.1.10/24
Router-C	Hostname	Router-C
	Enable/Telnet Password	cisco
	IP Addresses	Fa0/0: 10.5.1.10/24

Example 7-1 demonstrates the configuration required on a Layer 3 switch (L3-Switch-A) before you can begin this scenario. Example 7-2 demonstrates the configuration required for Router-A.

Example 7-1   *Scenario 7-1 Prerequisite Configuration for L3-Switch-A*

```
Switch# configure terminal
Switch(config)# hostname L3-Switch-A
L3-Switch-A(config)# enable secret cisco
L3-Switch-A(config)# line vty 0 15
L3-Switch-A(config-line)# password cisco
L3-Switch-A(config-line)# exit
L3-Switch-A(config)# ip routing
L3-Switch-A(config)# interface FastEthernet0/1
L3-Switch-A(config-if)# no switchport
L3-Switch-A(config-if)# ip address 10.2.1.1 255.255.0.0
```

Example 7-1 *Scenario 7-1 Prerequisite Configuration for L3-Switch-A (Continued)*

```
L3-Switch-A(config-if)# exit
L3-Switch-A(config)# interface FastEthernet0/2
L3-Switch-A(config-if)# no switchport
L3-Switch-A(config-if)# ip address 10.3.1.1 255.255.0.0
L3-Switch-A(config-if)# exit
L3-Switch-A(config)# interface FastEthernet0/3
L3-Switch-A(config-if)# no switchport
L3-Switch-A(config-if)# ip address 10.1.1.1 255.255.0.0
```

Example 7-2 *Scenario 7-1 Prerequisite Configuration for Router-A*

```
Router# configure terminal
Router(config)# hostname Router-A
Router-A(config)# enable secret cisco
Router-A(config)# line vty 0 4
Router-A(config-line)# password cisco
Router-A(config-line)# exit
Router-A(config)# interface FastEthernet0/0
Router-A(config-if)# no shutdown
Router-A(config-if)# exit
Router-A(config)# interface FastEthernet0/0.1
Router-A(config-if)# encapsulation isl 1
Router-A(config-if)# ip address 192.168.1.1 255.255.255.0
Router-A(config-if)# exit
Router-A(config)# interface FastEthernet0/0.2
Router-A(config-if)# encapsulation isl 2
Router-A(config-if)# ip address 192.168.2.1 255.255.255.0
```

After the prerequisite configuration is implemented, you should attach each device as indicated in Figure 7-6 and verify ping connectivity between devices in the network before proceeding.

Configuration Tasks

This scenario demonstrates the configuration of Catalyst 3550 Layer 3 switches for IP multicast routing using PIM dense mode operation. Configuration of multicast routing on the Catalyst 3550 switches is identical to the configuration required on Cisco routers because both devices use Cisco IOS. The tasks required to enable multicast routing using PIM dense mode are very simple and include the following:

- Configuring unicast routing
- Configuring PIM dense mode multicast routing
- Verifying PIM dense mode multicast routing
- Testing PIM dense mode multicast routing

NOTE   This scenario assumes that the IP configuration indicated in Figure 7-6 has been implemented on each routing device

Configuring Unicast Routing

As previously discussed, PIM relies on the unicast routing table to perform RPF checks, which protect against multicast traffic being looped continuously in the network. If you are implementing multicast routing in a network, unicast routing is likely already in place, because a network is not much use if devices cannot communicate with each other. Before implementing PIM, ensure that you have confirmed that complete and correct unicast routing protocols are in place and that all devices in the network can communicate with each other. Implementing PIM on a solid and reliable unicast routing topology ensures that PIM is much less likely to encounter issues.

For the scenario topology of Figure 7-6, EIGRP is assumed to be the unicast routing protocol implemented on all routers and Layer 3 switches in the network. Because all subnets in the network fall within the 10.x.x.x Class A network, the EIGRP configuration required on each router and Layer 3 switch is very simple, as demonstrated in Example 7-3.

Example 7-3   *Configuring EIGRP on Routers and Layer 3 Switches for Scenario 7-1*

```
L3-Switch-A# configure terminal
L3-Switch-A(config)# ip routing
L3-Switch-A(config)# router eigrp 10
L3-Switch-A(config-router)# network 10.0.0.0
```

NOTE   When configuring EIGRP, ensure that the autonomous system number matches on each router. In Example 7-3, the autonomous system is configured as 10.

Notice that the global configuration command **ip routing** is required because by default all Cisco Catalyst Layer 3 switches (except for native IOS Catalyst 6000/6500 switches) have IP unicast routing disabled by default.

After configuring IP unicast routing, verify that all routing devices have full knowledge of all subnets throughout the network. Example 7-4 demonstrates the unicast routing table on L3-Switch-A after all routing devices in Figure 7-6 have been configured for unicast routing.

Example 7-4   *Verifying IP Unicast Routing*

```
L3-Switch-A# show ip route
Codes: C - connected, S - static, I - IGRP, R - RIP, M - mobile, B - BGP
       D - EIGRP, EX - EIGRP external, O - OSPF, IA - OSPF inter area
       N1 - OSPF NSSA external type 1, N2 - OSPF NSSA external type 2
       E1 - OSPF external type 1, E2 - OSPF external type 2, E - EGP
       i - IS-IS, L1 - IS-IS level-1, L2 - IS-IS level-2, ia - IS-IS inter area
       * - candidate default, U - per-user static route, o - ODR
       P - periodic downloaded static route

Gateway of last resort is not set
```

Example 7-4   *Verifying IP Unicast Routing (Continued)*

```
     10.0.0.0/8 is variably subnetted, 7 subnets
C       10.1.0.0/16 is directly connected, FastEthernet0/3
C       10.2.0.0/16 is directly connected, FastEthernet0/1
C       10.3.0.0/16 is directly connected, FastEthernet0/2
D       10.4.0.0/16 [90/30720] via 10.3.1.2, 00:03:00, FastEthernet0/2
                    [90/30720] via 10.2.1.2, 00:03:20, FastEthernet0/1
D       10.5.0.0/16 [90/30720] via 10.3.1.2, 00:03:00, FastEthernet0/2
                    [90/30720] via 10.2.1.2, 00:03:20, FastEthernet0/1
D       10.6.0.0/16 [90/30720] via 10.2.1.2, 00:03:20, FastEthernet0/1
D       10.7.0.0/16 [90/33289] via 10.2.1.2, 00:03:20, FastEthernet0/1
```

Example 7-4 demonstrates the configuration required on a Layer 3 switch (L3-Switch-A) before you can begin this scenario. Example 7-3 demonstrates the configuration required for Router-A.

In Example 7-4, the important route from a multicast point of view for this scenario is the shaded connected route. This represents the route that indicates where the source of the multicast is located (Router-A—10.1.1.10). Whenever multicast traffic is received that is generated by Router-A (i.e., Router-A is the source), L3-Switch-A performs an RPF check to determine which is the next-hop interface for the source IP address (10.1.1.10). By referring to the route table in Example 7-4, you can see that the next-hop interface is FastEthernet0/3. If multicast packets from the source are received on this interface, then L3-Switch-A forwards the multicast packet out all interfaces in the outbound interface list, because L3-Switch-A knows that the multicast packet has arrived on the nearest interface that faces the source. If the multicast packets from the source are received on any other interface, the packet is dropped, because this situation indicates that the packet must somehow have looped back around to L3-Switch-A.

The same concepts relating to the unicast routing table and RPF checks apply to each of the multicast routers in Figure 7-6. The following lists each of the multicast routers and the RPF interfaces that should be determined via the unicast routing table on each.

- L3-Switch-A—interface Fa0/3
- L3-Switch-B—interface Fa0/1
- L3-Switch-C—interface Fa0/1
- L3-Switch-D—interface Fa0/1

If multicast packets are received with a source IP address of Router-A (10.1.1.10) on the interfaces listed, the multicast packets are forwarded. If multicast packets with a source IP address of 10.1.1.10 are received on any other interface, the packets are dropped.

Configuring PIM Dense Mode Multicast Routing

Refer back to Figure 7-6 and note that the only devices that require multicast routing to be configured are as follows:

- L3-Switch-A
- L3-Switch-B
- L3-Switch-C
- L3-Switch-D

Router-A, Router-B, and Router-C do not require multicast routing configuration, because Router-A is a multicast source and Router-B and Router-C are receivers. Even though each of these devices are routers fully capable of participating in a multicast routing topology, for the purposes of this chapter, each of these devices are used only to provide the source and receiver components of the overall multicast-enabled network.

Before you configure PIM dense mode, you must globally enable multicast routing, which is performed using the following global configuration mode command:

```
Router(config)# ip multicast-routing
```

Once multicast routing is enabled, you must then explicitly configure PIM on each routed interface on the Layer 3 switch (or router) that you want to participate in the multicast routing topology. When you are configuring Layer 3 switches, which often have a combination of routed and switched interfaces, understand that you can configure PIM only on *routed interfaces*. A routed interface on a Cisco Layer 3 switch can be either a physical interface or a switch virtual interface (SVI).

NOTE   For each scenario in this chapter, it is assumed that each interface on L3-Switch-A thru L3-Switch-D shown in Figure 7-6 has been confiugred as a routed interface using the **no switchport** interface configuration command and configured with an appropriate IP address.

To configure a routed interface for PIM operation, you must first enable PIM on the interface, specifying the appropriate PIM version (version 1 or version 2). The default and recommended PIM version is version 2, which is the default version of PIM used in Cisco IOS from Cisco IOS Release 11.3(2)T onwards. To enable PIM on a routed interface, use the **ip pim** interface configuration command:

```
Router(config-if)# ip pim [version {1 | 2}]
```

If you don't specify the **version** parameter, the interface operates in PIM version 2 mode.

After enabling PIM on the interface, you must next configure the appropriate PIM mode of operation. The following modes of operation are supported in Cisco IOS:

- Dense mode
- Sparse mode
- Sparse-dense mode

To configure the PIM mode of operation on a routed interface, you also use the **ip pim** interface configuration command as follows:

```
Router(config-if)# ip pim {dense-mode | sparse-mode | sparse-dense-mode}
```

TIP   If you don't need to explicitly configure the IP PIM version (i.e., you are using PIM version 2), you can use the **ip pim dense-mode** command to both enable PIM on the interface and configure dense mode operation, without specifying the **ip pim** command separately.

Example 7-5 shows the full configuration required on L3-Switch-A to enable multicast routing and PIM dense mode operation on all routed interfaces (see Figure 7-5 for these interfaces).

Example 7-5   *Configuring PIM Dense Mode Multicast Routing on Router-A*

```
L3-Switch-A# configure terminal
L3-Switch-A(config)# ip multicast-routing
L3-Switch-A(config)# interface range FastEthernet 0/1 - 3
L3-Switch-A(config-if-range)# ip pim dense-mode
```

Notice that only a single interface configuration command is required to enable PIM on each interface, because the PIM version being used is the default (version 2) and does not need to be explicitly configured.

Example 7-6 shows the full configuration required on L3-Switch-B to enable multicast routing and PIM dense mode operation on all routed interfaces (see Figure 7-6 for these interfaces).

Example 7-6   *Configuring PIM Dense Mode Multicast Routing on Router-B*

```
L3-Switch-B# configure terminal
L3-Switch-B(config)# ip multicast-routing
L3-Switch-B(config)# interface range FastEthernet 0/1 - 3
L3-Switch-B(config-if-range)# ip pim dense-mode
```

Example 7-7 shows the full configuration required on L3-Switch-C to enable multicast routing and PIM dense mode operation on all routed interfaces (see Figure 7-6 for these interfaces).

Example 7-7 *Configuring PIM Dense Mode Multicast Routing on Router-C*

```
L3-Switch-C# configure terminal
L3-Switch-C(config)# ip multicast-routing
L3-Switch-C(config)# interface range FastEthernet 0/1 - 4
L3-Switch-C(config-if-range)# ip pim dense-mode
```

Example 7-8 shows the full configuration required on L3-Switch-D to enable multicast routing and PIM dense mode operation on all routed interfaces (see Figure 7-6 for these interfaces).

Example 7-8 *Configuring PIM Dense Mode Multicast Routing on Router-D*

```
L3-Switch-D# configure terminal
L3-Switch-D(config)# ip multicast-routing
L3-Switch-D(config)# interface range FastEthernet 0/1 - 2
L3-Switch-D(config-if-range)# ip pim dense-mode
```

As you can see from the above examples, configuring PIM dense mode multicast routing is very simple. All of the internal mechanics of PIM, such as pruning, asserting and grafting, are automatically performed by Cisco IOS.

Verifying PIM Dense Mode Multicast Routing

Once you have configured PIM dense mode multicast routing on each multicast router, assuming that the unicast routing topology is in place correctly, you should first verify your interface configuration and then verify that all multicast routers can see each other as PIM neighbors. To list all of the PIM neighbors known to a particular multicast router, use the **show ip pim neighbor** command, as demonstrated on L3-Switch-B in Example 7-9.

Example 7-9 *Displaying PIM Neighbors*

```
L3-Switch-B# show ip pim neighbor
PIM Neighbor Table
Neighbor Address   Interface          Uptime     Expires    Ver   Mode
10.2.1.1           FastEthernet0/1    00:43:50   00:01:35   v2
10.4.1.1           FastEthernet0/2    00:41:33   00:01:19   v2
10.5.1.1           FastEthernet0/3    00:41:33   00:01:31   v2
10.6.1.2           FastEthernet0/4    00:39:07   00:01:29   v2    (DR)
```

Notice on L3-Switch-B that you can see the PIM neighbors for each subnet attached to L3-Switch-B. L3-Switch-B sees L3-Switch-C as a neighbor twice (via the 10.4.0.0/16 and 10.5.0.0/16) because both are connected to these subnets. The mode column indicates whether or not a neighbor is the PIM designated router (DR) for the subnet.

NOTE   The DR function is applicable only to multi-access networks such as Ethernet. The DR function for a specific multi-access network is performed by the router with the highest IP addressed interface on the network.

The DR function is not used by PIM dense mode and is only used in PIM dense mode operation if IGMP version 1 is in use by receivers on a subnet, because IGMPv1 relies on the multicast routing protocol (PIM dense mode) to provide the role of IGMP Query router for the subnet. You can also use the **show ip pim interface** command to display information about PIM interfaces, the version and mode configuration as well as the DR for multi-access segments. Example 7-10 demonstrates the use of this command on L3-Switch-A.

Example 7-10 *Displaying PIM Interface Information*

```
L3-Switch-A# show ip pim interface FastEthernet0/1
Address           Interface            Version/Mode      Nbr   Query    DR
                                                         Count Intvl
10.3.1.1          FastEthernet0/1      v2/Dense          1     30       10.3.1.2
```

Once you have verified that all multicast routers can see all neighbors, it is a good idea to verify that RPF checks are going to work correctly when your multicast sources start to transmit traffic. The **show ip rpf** command can be used to perform an RPF check manually for any source address, allowing you to verify that the correct unicast routing information is in place. Example 7-11 demonstrates the use of this command on L3-Switch-D for the multicast source used in this scenario (10.1.1.10).

Example 7-11 *Performing an RPF Check*

```
L3-Switch-D# show ip rpf 10.1.1.10
RPF information for ? (10.1.1.10)
  RPF interface: FastEthernet0/1
  RPF neighbor: ? (10.6.1.1)
  RPF route/mask: 10.1.0.0/16
  RPF type: unicast (eigrp 10)
  RPF recursion count: 0
  Doing distance-preferred lookups across tables
```

Notice in Example 7-11, you can see the RPF interface (FastEthernet0/1), the next-hop neighbor (RPF neighbor) to the source (10.6.1.1 or L3-Switch-C), the route used to determine the RPF information (10.1.0.0/16), and the type of routing information used (unicast routing using the EIGRP 10 process). If you refer to Figure 7-6, the RPF check indicates that the routing information on L3-Switch-D matches the actual network topology.

Finally, it is good to have a look at the multicast routing table, so that you know what the multicast routing table looks like before any multicast sources are active in the network. To display the multicast routing table, use the **show ip mroute** command, as shown in Example 7-12 on L3-Switch-A.

Example 7-12 *Displaying the Multicast Routing Table*

```
L3-Switch-A# show ip mroute
IP Multicast Routing Table
Flags: D - Dense, S - Sparse, s - SSM Group, C - Connected, L - Local,
       P - Pruned, R - RP-bit set, F - Register flag, T - SPT-bit set,
       J - Join SPT, M - MSDP created entry, X - Proxy Join Timer Running
       A - Advertised via MSDP, U - URD, I - Received Source Specific Host
           Report
Outgoing interface flags: H - Hardware switched
Timers: Uptime/Expires
Interface state: Interface, Next-Hop or VCD, State/Mode

(*, 224.0.1.40), 01:40:01/00:02:42, RP 0.0.0.0, flags: DJCL
  Incoming interface: Null, RPF nbr 0.0.0.0
  Outgoing interface list:
    FastEthernet0/2, Forward/Dense, 01:39:54/00:00:00
```

In Example 7-12, you can see a single multicast route entry, which is indicated by the shaded output. You might wonder why there is an entry in the multicast route table when no multicast sources are currently active in the network. The entry represents multicast packets generated by a feature known as Auto-RP, which is used to discover rendezvous points (RPs) in a PIM sparse mode network. The 224.0.1.40 address is used for RP discovery messages.

NOTE   Because this scenario focuses on PIM dense mode, you don't need to worry about the current multicast route entry, just understand why it is there.

Testing PIM Dense Mode Operation

Once the PIM configuration of the network has been verified, the network is ready to begin forwarding multicast traffic. As described previously in this scenario, a number of steps take place during the initial forwarding of multicast traffic for a particular (S,G). These steps are generally completed in a manner of seconds, so once you start generating multicast traffic, you can quickly determine that the appropriate links in the network are pruned to ensure an optimal multicast tree.

In this scenario, a single Cisco router (Router-A) with an IP address of 10.1.1.10 is used as the source of multicast traffic for the group address 239.1.1.1, and several Cisco routers (Router-B and Router-C) are configured as multicast receivers for the 239.1.1.1 group address. This configuration means that for Figure 7-6, the (S,G) notation for multicast traffic on the network is (10.1.1.10, 239.1.1.1).

To configure Router-A as the source of multicast traffic, you simply need to ensure the router is configured with an appropriate IP address (10.1.1.10) that represents the source of the multicast traffic you want to generate. Once Router-A is configured and attached to the network, you can issue pings (ICMP echo requests) to the multicast group address (e.g., 239.1.1.1), which generates multicast traffic with a source IP address of 10.1.1.10 and a destination IP address of 239.1.1.1.

To configure Router-B and Router-C as receivers, you need to ensure that both Router-B and Router-C are attached to the network and also have the necessary routing information to respond to the ICMP echo requests generated by Router-A. Once the base IP configuration is in place, you then use the **ip igmp join-group** interface configuration command, which configures an interface on the router to become a receiver for a specified multicast group address.

NOTE   Cisco routers acting as receivers by default use IGMP version 2.

Example 7-13 demonstrates configuring Router-B to become a receiver (i.e., join) for the multicast group address of 239.1.1.1.

Example 7-13 *Joining a Multicast Group*

```
Router-B# configure terminal
Router-B(config)# interface FastEthernet0/0
Router-B(config-if)# ip igmp join-group 239.1.1.1
```

Example 7-14 demonstrates configuring Router-C to become a receiver (i.e., join) for the multicast group address of 239.1.1.1.

Example 7-14 *Joining a Multicast Group*

```
Router-C# configure terminal
Router-C(config)# interface FastEthernet0/0
Router-C(config-if)# ip igmp join-group 239.1.1.1
```

The **ip igmp join-group** command is very useful because it enables you to use your network devices to test multicast operation without having to implement actual hosts. As soon as you configure this command, Router-B and Router-C immediately multicast an IGMP membership report on the LAN indicating that they are receivers for the 239.1.1.1 group. At this point, any attached multicast routers create a (*,G) entry in the multicast route table for the group address (*,239.1.1.1). The (*,239.1.1.1) entry is like a template route entry; it is created in preparation for actual (S,239.1.1.1) entries, with S being one or more sources. Example 7-15 shows the routing table on L3-Switch-B after Router-B and Router-C have sent IGMP membership reports.

Example 7-15 *Viewing the Multicast Route Table After Router-B and Router-C Send IGMP Membership Reports*

```
L3-Switch-B# show ip mroute
IP Multicast Routing Table
Flags: D - Dense, S - Sparse, s - SSM Group, C - Connected, L - Local,
       P - Pruned, R - RP-bit set, F - Register flag, T - SPT-bit set,
       J - Join SPT, M - MSDP created entry, X - Proxy Join Timer Running
       A - Advertised via MSDP, U - URD, I - Received Source Specific Host
          Report
Outgoing interface flags: H - Hardware switched
Timers: Uptime/Expires
Interface state: Interface, Next-Hop or VCD, State/Mode

(*, 239.1.1.1), 01:25:49/00:02:32, RP 0.0.0.0, flags: DJC
  Incoming interface: Null, RPF nbr 0.0.0.0
  Outgoing interface list:
    FastEthernet0/4, Forward/Dense, 01:09:34/00:00:00
    FastEthernet0/3, Forward/Dense, 01:25:49/00:00:00
    FastEthernet0/2, Forward/Dense, 01:16:04/00:00:00
    FastEthernet0/1, Forward/Dense, 01:25:49/00:00:00

(*, 224.0.1.40), 01:40:01/00:02:42, RP 0.0.0.0, flags: DJCL
  Incoming interface: Null, RPF nbr 0.0.0.0
  Outgoing interface list:
    FastEthernet0/2, Forward/Dense, 01:39:54/00:00:00
```

The concept of a (*,G) entry can be a little confusing at first, because you might think that it represents a shared tree in a PIM-DM network that doesn't use shared trees. The (*,G) entry simply allows Cisco IOS to build a list of interfaces to which receivers or PIM neighbors are attached, so that when a source does start sending to the group, Cisco IOS simply has to copy this interface list to the new (S,G) entry in the route table. In Example 7-15, because either receivers and/or PIM neighbors are attached to all interfaces on L3-Switch-B, all interfaces are listed in the outgoing interface list.

At this point, the network is ready to begin generating multicast traffic. Example 7-16 shows how to start a continuous ping using the extended **ping** command on Router-A.

Example 7-16 *Starting a Continuous ping on Router-A*

```
Router-A# ping ip
Target IP address: 239.1.1.1
Repeat count [5]: 100000000
Datagram size [100]: 1500
Timeout in seconds [2]: 0
Extended commands [n]:
Sweep range of sizes [n]:
Type escape sequence to abort.
Sending 100000000, 1500-byte ICMP Echos to 10.1.1.10, timeout is 2 seconds:
Reply to request 0 from 10.5.1.10, 96 ms
```

Example 7-16 *Starting a Continuous ping on Router-A (Continued)*

```
Reply to request 0 from 10.6.1.10, 104 ms
Reply to request 1 from 10.5.1.10, 88 ms
Reply to request 1 from 10.6.1.10, 96 ms
Reply to request 2 from 10.5.1.10, 88 ms
Reply to request 2 from 10.6.1.10, 96 ms
Reply to request 3 from 10.5.1.10, 88 ms
Reply to request 3 from 10.6.1.10, 100 ms
Reply to request 4 from 10.5.1.10, 88 ms
Reply to request 4 from 10.6.1.10, 96 ms
Reply to request 5 from 10.6.1.10, 92 ms
Reply to request 5 from 10.6.1.10, 100 ms
...
...
```

In Example 7-16, 100,000,000 ping packets are sent to the multicast group address of 239.1.1.1. Because Router-A and Router-B are receivers of this group, they generate replies to these packets, as indicated in Example 7-16.

Now that there is active multicast traffic in the network, you should be able to see new multicast routes generated in the multicast routing table on each multicast router. Example 7-17 shows the multicast routing table on L3-Switch-B.

Example 7-17 *The IP Multicast Route Table on L3-Switch-B After (10.1.1.10,239.1.1.1) Is Activated*

```
L3-Switch-B# show ip mroute
IP Multicast Routing Table
Flags: D - Dense, S - Sparse, B - Bidir Group, s - SSM Group, C - Connected,
       L - Local, P - Pruned, R - RP-bit set, F - Register flag,
       T - SPT-bit set, J - Join SPT, M - MSDP created entry,
       X - Proxy Join Timer Running, A - Candidate for MSDP Advertisement,
       U - URD, I - Received Source Specific Host Report
Outgoing interface flags: H - Hardware switched
Timers: Uptime/Expires
Interface state: Interface, Next-Hop or VCD, State/Mode

(*, 224.0.1.40), 03:21:51/00:00:00, RP 0.0.0.0, flags: DCL
  Incoming interface: Null, RPF nbr 0.0.0.0
  Outgoing interface list:
    FastEthernet0/1, Forward/Dense, 00:39:00/00:00:00
    FastEthernet0/2, Forward/Dense, 00:39:00/00:00:00
    FastEthernet0/3, Forward/Dense, 00:39:00/00:00:00
    FastEthernet0/4, Forward/Dense, 00:39:00/00:00:00

(*, 239.1.1.1), 00:23:05/00:02:59, RP 0.0.0.0, flags: DC
  Incoming interface: Null, RPF nbr 0.0.0.0
  Outgoing interface list:
    FastEthernet0/1, Forward/Dense, 00:23:05/00:00:00
    FastEthernet0/2, Forward/Dense, 00:23:05/00:00:00
    FastEthernet0/3, Forward/Dense, 00:23:05/00:00:00
    FastEthernet0/4, Forward/Dense, 00:23:05/00:00:00

(10.1.1.10, 239.1.1.1), 00:02:20/00:02:04, flags: CT
```

continues

Example 7-17 *The IP Multicast Route Table on L3-Switch-B After (10.1.1.10,239.1.1.1) Is Activated*

```
Incoming interface: FastEthernet0/1, RPF nbr 10.2.1.1
Outgoing interface list:
  FastEthernet0/2, Prune/Dense, 00:02:20/00:00:00
  FastEthernet0/3, Forward/Dense, 00:02:20/00:02:02
  FastEthernet0/4, Forward/Dense, 00:02:20/00:02:02
```

In Example 7-17, you can see a new entry represented as (10.1.1.10, 239.1.1.1). Look at this new multicast route entry while I dissect the various pieces of information that make up the entry.

The first piece of information is (10.1.1.10, 239.1.1.1), which represents the (S,G) SPT that has a source of 10.1.1.10 and a group address of 239.1.1.1. The next piece of information is 00:02:20/00:02:04, which represents how long the route has been installed in the route table (i.e., 2 minutes and 20 seconds) and the expiry time on the route, which is currently 2 minutes and 4 seconds in Example 7-17 (the expiry timer is reset to a default value of 3 minutes every time a multicast packet associated with the route is received and forwarded).

The next line lists the incoming interface information, which represents the RPF interface associated with the source. Notice that the FastEthernet0/1 interface on L3-Switch-B has been selected as the RPF interface because this represents the closest interface to the source of the multicast traffic. The next-hop address is listed as 10.2.1.1, which is L3-Switch-A, a switch connected directly to the source.

The next line lists the outgoing interface list, which describes how multicast traffic associated with the route is forwarded. A key concept demonstrated in Example 7-17 is that the incoming interface is *never* in the outgoing interface list, which ensures loops do not form in the network. Notice that interface FastEthernet0/2 indicates a state of Prune/Dense. Multicast traffic is not forwarded out this interface because FastEthernet0/2 has no receivers attached to it and L3-Switch-C, which is connected, has another shorter path to the source; hence, FastEthernet0/2 is not considered a downstream multicast router. Interfaces FastEthernet0/3 and FastEthernet0/4 have a state of Forward/Dense, which means that multicast packets arriving on the incoming interface are forwarded out these interfaces. If you refer to Figure 7-9, this output is correct, because interface FastEthernet0/3 on L3-Switch-B is asserted as the forwarding multicast router for the 10.5.0.0/16 subnet, interface FastEthernet0/4 has Router-B (a receiver) connected, and L3-Switch-B represents the closest (and only) multicast router that leads to the source.

To view multicast groups that are currently active and sending traffic in your network, you can use the **show ip mroute active** command, which displays all active multicast groups that are generating greater than 4 kbps of traffic on average. Example 7-18 demonstrates this command on L3-Switch-B.

Example 7-18   *Using the* **show ip mroute active** *Command*

```
L3-Switch-B# show ip mroute active
Active IP Multicast Sources - sending >= 4 kbps

Group: 239.1.1.1, (?)
   Source: 10.1.1.10 (?)
      Rate: 42 pps/323 kbps(1sec), 323 kbps(last 10 secs), 310 kbps(life avg)
```

You can see that the continuous ping is generating 42 packets per second and an average bandwidth consumption of 323 kbps. Because multicast traffic is commonly used for high-bandwidth multimedia applications, this command is useful for determining the effects of the multicast traffic on the network.

Debugging PIM Dense Mode Operation

Cisco IOS provides debugging of IP PIM operation using the **debug ip pim** command. Example 7-19 demonstrates the use of the **debug ip pim** command on L3-Switch-C immediately after multicast traffic is generated in Example 7-14. This debug is intended to demonstrate both PIM pruning and asserting.

Example 7-19   *Debugging PIM Dense Mode Operation*

```
L3-Switch-C# debug ip pim
PIM debugging is on
! Normal PIM Hellos (sent out every PIM enabled interface every 30 seconds)
03:44:01: PIM: Send v2 Hello on FastEthernet0/1
03:44:01: PIM: Send v2 Hello on FastEthernet0/2
03:44:01: PIM: Send v2 Hello on FastEthernet0/3

! Multicast Traffic is Received. L3-Switch-C detects
! duplicate multicast packets on
! FastEthernet0/3 and begins the ASSERT process.
03:44:04: PIM: Send v2 Assert on FastEthernet0/3 for 239.1.1.1, source 10.1.1.10,
   metric [90/30720]
03:44:04: PIM: Assert metric to source 10.1.1.10 is [90/30720]
03:44:04: PIM: We win, our metric [90/30720]
03:44:04: PIM: (10.1.1.10/32, 239.1.1.1) oif FastEthernet0/3 in Forward state

! An ASSERT is received from L3-Switch-B.
! The administrative distance and metrics to the
! source are equal for each router (90/30720), so L3-Switch-B
! wins as it has the highest
! IP address on the subnet.  L3-Switch-C then immediately prunes FastEthernet0/3.
03:44:04: PIM: Received v2 Assert on FastEthernet0 from 10.5.1.2
03:44:04: PIM: Assert metric to source 10.1.1.10 is [90/30720]
03:44:04: PIM: We lose, our metric [90/30720]
03:44:04: PIM: Prune FastEthernet0/3/239.1.1.1 from (10.1.1.10/32, 239.1.1.1)
```

continues

Example 7-19 *Debugging PIM Dense Mode Operation*

```
03:44:04: PIM: (10.1.1.10/32, 239.1.1.1) oif FastEthernet0/3 in Prune state

! L3-Switch-C also prunes FastEthernet0/2, as no receivers or
! downstream PIM neighbors
! are connected to this interface
03:44:38: PIM: Prune FastEthernet0/2/239.1.1.1 from (10.1.1.10/32, 239.1.1.1)
03:44:38: PIM: (10.1.1.10/32, 239.1.1.1) oif FastEthernet0/2 in Prune state
```

Example 7-20 demonstrates the use of the **debug ip pim** command on L3-Switch-D when Host-A attaches to the 10.7.0.0/16 subnet as described in Figure 7-10. This debug output is intended to demonstrate PIM Grafting operation.

Example 7-20 *Debugging PIM Dense Mode Operation*

```
L3-Switch-D# debug ip pim
PIM debugging is on
! Host-A attaches and issues an IGMP Membership Report.  Because L3-Switch-D has
! previously had all interfaces pruned for the 239.1.1.1 group.
! L3-Switch-D generates a
! PIM-DM Graft message, to indicate to the upstream PIM neighbor (L3-Switch-C)
! that it
! now needs to receive traffic for the group.
04:23:49: PIM: Building Graft message for 239.1.1.1, FastEthernet0/1: no entries
04:23:49: PIM: Building Graft message for 239.1.1.1, FastEthernet0/1:
     10.1.1.10/32
04:23:49: PIM: Send v2 Graft to 10.6.1.1 (FastEthernet0/1)

! L3-Switch-C sends a PIM Graft-Ack message,
! to indicate that its interface has been
! added back to the multicast tree.
04:23:49: PIM: Received v2 Graft-Ack on FastEthernet0/1 from 10.2.1.1
04:23:49:     Group 239.1.1.1:
     10.1.1.10/32
```

Scenario 7-2: Configuring PIM Sparse Mode and PIM Sparse-Dense Mode Multicast Routing

In the previous scenario, you learned how to configure PIM dense mode multicast routing. PIM dense mode is normally a good place to start learning about PIM because it certainly represents the simplest mode of operation. However, PIM dense mode is inefficient because it initially floods all multicast traffic throughout the network and then prunes back the multicast forwarding tree to only those links required to ensure all receivers for a particular group can receive the multicast traffic for the group. Taking this approach is similar to the concept of throwing a bucket of water over a cup of water in order to fill the cup of water—clearly an inefficient mechanism.

NOTE   Before bagging PIM dense mode to your fellow network engineers, there is absolutely no reason why you can't use PIM dense mode in a high-bandwidth network that has plenty of bandwidth to throw around. Unfortunately, this scenario is seldom the case and PIM dense mode often causes congestion in low-bandwidth networks when a new multicast source comes online.

In this scenario you learn how to configure PIM sparse mode multicast routing, as well as a special mode of PIM called sparse-dense mode routing.

NOTE   The same topology of Scenario 7-1 is used for this scenario (see Figure 7-6), however it is assumed that each device has the base configuration as described in the scenario prerequisites section of Scenario 7-1 (see Table 7-2), as well as a complete unicast routing topology as configured in Example 7-2.

The unicast routing considerations and neighbor discovery mechanisms in PIM sparse mode and sparse-dense mode are identical to PIM dense mode, but how multicast forwarding trees are built differs. The following sections provide an introduction to PIM sparse mode and sparse-dense operation and then show you how to configure PIM sparse and PIM sparse-dense mode:

- Building multicast trees in PIM sparse mode networks
- Configuration tasks
- Configuring PIM sparse-dense mode operation

Building Multicast Trees in PIM Sparse Mode Networks

PIM sparse mode (PIM-SM) is reasonably complex in how multicast distribution trees are formed because a variety of multicast distribution trees are used to forward traffic for a multicast group. PIM-SM initially uses a shared tree that flows from a shared root (multicast router) in the network known as a *rendezvous point* (*RP*) and also uses a shortest path tree (SPT) to allow each source to forward traffic to the rendezvous point. The rendezvous point then receives multicast traffic from the source via the SPT and then forwards the multicast traffic down the shared tree to the various receivers. The goal of these two initial multicast distribution trees is to allow new multicast sources to be added to the multicast routing topology, without flooding multicast traffic to all links in the network (as is the case with PIM-DM). Once a new source is known to the network, PIM-SM can then form a SPT rooted at the source of a group, which ensures the most optimal multicast distribution tree is formed, without requiring the inefficient flooding that occurs with PIM-DM.

The following describes the various stages that exist in PIM-SM operation:

- Building the shared tree
- Building a shortest path tree from the source to the rendezvous point
- Building a shortest path tree from the source to all receivers

Each of these stages of PIM-SM operation is now discussed in detail.

Building the Shared Tree

The first phase of PIM-SM operation is when receivers initially indicate their intention to join a group. At this point, assuming no sources are active for the group on the network, each multicast router that has receivers attached will join a shared tree that is rooted at a configured RP in the network. Figure 7-11 demonstrates this process.

In Figure 7-11, assume that the network has been configured for sparse mode operation. Router-C is a receiver that has just attached to the network and wants to join the 239.1.1.1 group.

1 When Router-C attaches to the LAN, it joins the 239.1.1.1 multicast group by sending an IGMP Membership Report.

2 L3-Switch-B receives the IGMP Membership Report, immediately creates a (*,239.1.1.1) entry in the multicast routing table, and sends a multicast PIM Join message towards the RP (L3-Switch-D). The purpose of the PIM Join message is to build a new shared tree (or attach to an existing shared tree) for the group (239.1.1.1) that is rooted at the RP. In Figure 7-11, the RP must somehow be known to L3-Switch-B (and any other PIM sparse mode router in the network), either via manual configuration or by using an RP discovery protocol such as Auto-RP (more on Auto-RP later in the chapter). For now, assume that the L3-Switch-B (and all other multicast routers) is manually configured with the IP address of the RP (10.6.1.2). The unicast routing table is used to determine which interface is the closest to the RP (Fa0/4 in Figure 7-11), and the PIM Join message is then multicast out this interface. Notice that the multicast routing table entry created on L3-Switch-B specifies an incoming interface of Fa0/4 (because this interface is closest to the RP) and an outgoing interface of Fa0/3 (because this interface is attached to the LAN that the receiver is on).

Figure 7-11   *Building the Shared Tree in PIM-SM Operation*

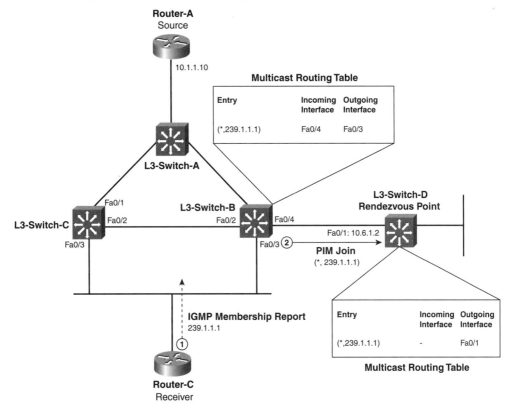

NOTE

On a multi-access network that has multiple multicast routers attached (such as the LAN that Router-C is connected to), only the PIM designated router (DR) sends PIM Join messages. The PIM DR is chosen as the multicast with the highest IP addressed interface on the LAN. For example, in Figure 7-11 on the 10.5.0.0/16 subnet, L3-Switch-B is the PIM DR because it has a higher IP address on the subnet than L3-Switch-C. Consequently, only L3-Switch-B generates PIM Joins for receivers attached to the 10.5.0.0/16 subnet because it is the PIM DR for this subnet.

If multiple hops exist between the initial multicast router that generates the (*,G) PIM Join and the RP, each upstream PIM router accepts PIM Joins from downstream routers, creates the appropriate (*,G) entry in the multicast routing table, and then sends a PIM Join to the next upstream router. This process is repeated until the PIM Join finally reaches the RP and creates a (*,G) shared tree that includes the shortest path in the network between the RP and the receiver that originally caused the PIM Join to be sent.

Once the RP (L3-Switch-D) receives the PIM Join, it also creates a (*,239.1.1.1) entry in the local multicast routing table, which specifies an outgoing interface of Fa0/1. This entry ensures that any traffic received from a source for the 239.1.1.1 group is forwarded down the shared tree generated in Figure 7-11.

NOTE   The concept of an incoming interface for the (*,239.1.1.1) entry on the RP does not apply, as the RP is the root of the shared tree.

Building a Shortest Path Tree from the Source to the Rendezvous Point

In Figure 7-11, a (*,239.1.1.1) shared tree has been generated that enables the RP to forward multicast traffic to receivers for the 239.1.1.1 group. At this point, however, no source is actually sending multicast traffic to the RP, and some mechanism must be available to ensure the RP receives traffic from a source if a source comes online. A source has no concept of PIM, let alone rendezvous points, and sends multicast traffic only out onto the LAN the source is connected to, relying on the network to forward the traffic to any receivers for the group. Therefore, the first multicast router that receives multicast traffic from the source must somehow ensure that the multicast traffic received is forwarded to the RP. Figure 7-12 demonstrates how this is achieved.

In Figure 7-12, the (*,239.1.1.1) shared tree built in Figure 7-11 is shown as the thick black arrows. Router-A (a source) is about to start sending multicast packets to the 239.1.1.1 group. The following describes the events that occur:

1   The source (Router-A) starts generating multicast traffic, sending the first multicast packet towards L3-Switch-A. The packet arrives at L3-Switch-A.

2   L3-Switch-A is configured for PIM-SM operation, which means that it must somehow get the multicast packet to the RP. L3-Switch-A could just flood the multicast packet out all interfaces (as in PIM dense mode operation); however, that strategy would defeat the goal of PIM sparse mode operation. Instead, L3-Switch-A creates a PIM Register message, which is a unicast packet that includes the multicast packet received from the source. The PIM Register message is addressed to the IP address of the RP (which means the RP for the network must be manually configured or dynamically learned) and is forwarded out the appropriate interface (Fa0/1), based upon the unicast routing table. In Figure 7-12, this means that the PIM Register message is forwarded towards L3-Switch-B, which then simply routes the unicast packet on towards the RP (L3-Switch-D).

Figure 7-12 *Building an SPT from the Source to the RP*

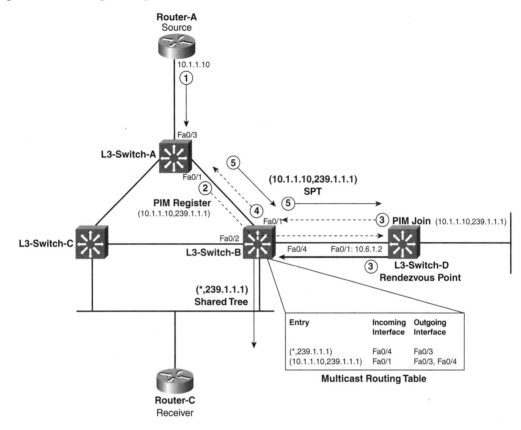

3 The RP (L3-Switch-D) receives the PIM Register message and extracts the original multicast packet sent. Because the multicast packet has been sent to an active group (239.1.1.1), the L3-Switch-D forwards the multicast packet down the (*,239.1.1.1) shared tree, which ensures that any receivers for the 239.1.1.1 group receive the packet. The RP also now attempts to build an SPT from the source to the RP so that the multicast packets sent by the source do not need to be always encapsulated in unicast PIM Register messages. To build the SPT, L3-Switch-D sends PIM Join messages for the (10.1.1.10,239.1.1.1) SPT out the closest interface to the source (Fa0/1), which indicates to any upstream routers to the source that L3-Switch-D wants to join the SPT.

4 L3-Switch-B receives the PIM Join from L3-Switch-D and creates an (S,G) entry in its multicast routing table. The incoming interface for this entry is determined by performing an RPF check on the IP address of the source (10.1.1.10), which determines that Fa0/1 (attached to L3-Switch-A) is the closest interface to the source.

The interface on which the PIM Join was received (Fa0/4) is added to the outgoing interface list for the entry, because L3-Switch-D has indicated via the Join that it wants to receive traffic from the SPT. It is important to also note the L3-Switch-B also adds interface Fa0/3 to the outgoing interface list, because this interface is specified as an outgoing interface for the (*,239.1.1.1) shared tree. Although this interface is not required to ensure receivers receive multicast traffic from the host, because the RP always forwards any multicast traffic for the group down the shared tree, it is more efficient if L3-Switch-B forwards group traffic down the shared tree because it is closer to the receiver (Router-C) than the RP. After creating the (S,G) entry, L3-Switch-B then sends a PIM Join for (10.1.1.10,239.1.1.1) towards the source to ensure any upstream routers add L3-Switch-B to the SPT.

5 L3-Switch-A receives the PIM Join from L3-Switch-B, which completes the construction of an SPT from the source (10.1.1.10) to the 239.1.1.1 group. L3-Switch-A updates the (10.1.1.10,239.1.1.1) entry in its multicast routing table to include Fa0/1 as an outgoing interface. At this point, any multicast packets received from the source for the 239.1.1.1 group are no longer unicast via PIM Register messages. Instead, they are forwarded down the (10.1.1.10,239.1.1.1) SPT that has been built in Steps 3 and 4. This configuration reduces the overhead on L3-Switch-A because it no longer has to encapsulate each multicast packet in a unicast packet.

When L3-Switch-B receives multicast traffic for the (10.1.1.1,239.1.1.1) SPT from L3-Switch-A, it forwards the multicast traffic out Fa0/4 (towards the RP) and also out Fa0/2. This configuration ensures that the RP receives multicast traffic via the shortest path possible from the source, which it can then forward down the shared tree to receivers. Because the RP is now receiving multicast traffic for the (S,G) SPT via native multicast packets, as opposed to unicast PIM Register messages, the RP sends a unicast PIM Register-Stop message to L3-Switch-A, which informs L3-Switch-A (the originator of PIM Register messages in Step 2) to stop sending PIM Register messages.

This completes the building of the SPT between the source and the RP, ensuring traffic flows down the SPT from the source to the RP and then down the shared tree from the RP to any receivers. Notice that because the SPT and shared trees intersect at L3-Switch-B, multicast traffic sent down the (10.1.1.10,239.1.1.1) SPT towards the RP are actually forwarded down the shared tree at L3-Switch-B bypassing the RP because this represents a more efficient path to reach receivers.

NOTE   L3-Switch-B ignores any (10.1.1.10,239.1.1.1) multicast packets received on the interface attached to the RP, because these packets fail an RPF check. Ignoring these packets ensures receivers do not receive duplicate multicast packets sent via L3-Switch-B and via the RP.

Building a Shortest Path Tree from the Source to All Receivers

If you look at the multicast distribution trees that have been generated so far, the combination of the SPT from the source to the RP and the shared tree from the RP to each receiver ensures multicast traffic can be forwarded to all receivers, but does not represent the most efficient multicast forwarding path through the network. For example, the most efficient path between Router-A (source) and Router-C (a receiver) is via L3-Switch-A ◊ L3-Switch-C or via L3-Switch-A ◊ L3-Switch-B. At the moment, multicast traffic between Router-A and Router-C is traveling via L3-Switch-A ◊ L3-Switch-B, but only because the topology is reasonably simple. Consider Figure 7-13, where a direct link between L3-Switch-A and L3-Switch-D has been added to the topology of Figure 7-12.

Figure 7-13   *Demonstrating the Inefficiencies of a Combined SPT and Shared Tree Multicast Distribution Tree*

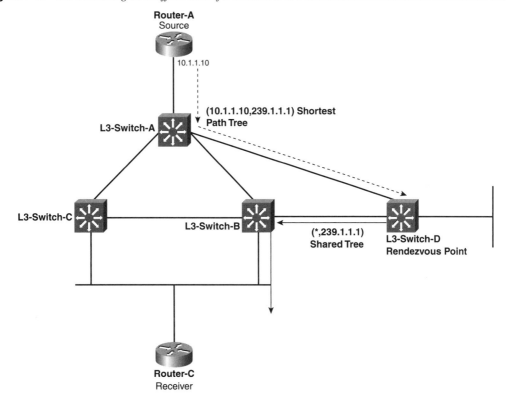

In Figure 7-13, because the SPT and shared tree intersect only at the RP, all traffic sent from the source must be sent across three hops (L3-Switch-A ◊ L3-Switch-D ◊ L3-Switch-B), while a more efficient path exists (via L3-Switch-A ◊ L3-Switch-B).

Once a receiver starts receiving multicast traffic from a source, both the receiver and the multicast routers attached to the receiver know the IP address of the source. This knowledge means that the locally connected multicast routers can join the (S,G) SPT, so that the most optimal multicast forwarding path is taken between the source and receivers. Figure 7-14 demonstrates this for the topology of Figure 7-13.

Figure 7-14   *Building the SPT from the Source to Receivers*

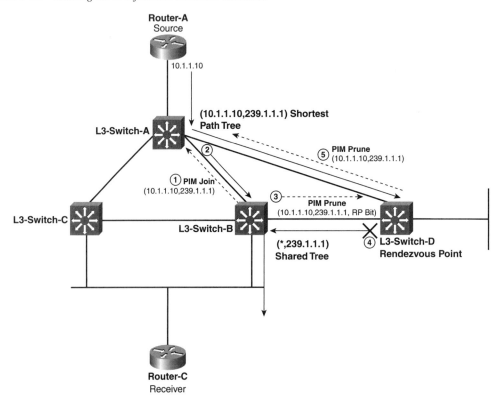

In Figure 7-14, the following events occur:

1 L3-Switch-B detects that it is actively forwarding traffic from a valid source to a multicast group over the shared tree for the group from the RP. As soon as the first packet for a valid source is detected on L3-Switch-B, it immediately attempts to join the (S,G) SPT, which means that L3-Switch-B sends a PIM Join for (10.1.1.10,239.1.1.1) out the interface that is closest to the source.

NOTE   You can configure the amount of traffic that must be seen from a valid source before a PIM sparse mode router attempts to join the (S,G) SPT. This parameter is known as the *SPT-Threshold* and is expressed as a bandwidth parameter in kbps. By default on Cisco IOS, the SPT-Threshold is 0 kbps, which means that a multicast router immediately attempts to join the (S,G) SPT.

2   L3-Switch-A receives the PIM Join, and adds the interface connected to L3-Switch-B to the outgoing interface list of the (S,G) entry. Any subsequent multicast traffic sent from the source (10.1.1.10) to the group (239.1.1.1) is forwarded directly to L3-Switch-B, in addition to the RP.

3   L3-Switch-B now has specific entry in the multicast routing table for (10.1.1.10,239.1.1.1) that is more preferred than the shared tree entry. L3-Switch-B no longer needs to receive (10.1.1.10,239.1.1.1) traffic sent via the RP and thus sends a special PIM prune message known as a Prune RP-Bit message. This message has a flag in the PIM prune message known as the RP-bit set, which indicates to any upstream routers on the shared tree that only the traffic sent from the source specified in the prune message should be pruned from the shared tree.

4   The RP prunes traffic for (10.1.1.10,239.1.1.1) from the interface attached to L3-Switch-B. This pruning stops multicast packets from the RP from being sent unnecessarily out the interface attached to L3-Switch-B. Note that the shared tree (*,G) still exists, which means receivers that may expect traffic from another source are forwarded this traffic initially across the shared tree.

5   Because the RP has no more active paths for the (10.1.1.10,239.1.1.1) shared tree, the RP sends a PIM prune message to L3-Switch-A, which indicates the RP no longer needs to receive traffic from L3-Switch-A.

At this point, an SPT has been formed between the source and receiver, ensuring only the most optimal path in the network is chosen to route multicast traffic to receivers.

NOTE   Multicast routers cannot initially form an (S,G) SPT to the source (S) when a receiver first announces its membership to the group , if no source currently exists for the group. Each PIM-SM multicast router that has receivers attached joins the (*,G) shared tree to the RP, which ensures that once a source does come online for the group, each multicast router receives the traffic. Once a PIM-SM multicast router receives actual multicast packets from a source, the multicast router now knows the IP address of the source and can form an SPT to the source. Essentially, the RP provides a mechanism for PIM-SM multicast routers to discover sources and then form an SPT to each source.

You might be wondering why you even use PIM sparse mode, if all it ultimately provides is an SPT between source and receiver. PIM dense mode also does this, so why go to the trouble of implementing PIM sparse mode, which is clearly much more complex for multicast routers to deal with? The answer is that PIM sparse mode removes the inefficient requirement of PIM dense mode to initially flood all multicast traffic throughout the network and then prune back the multicast distribution tree as required. Instead, PIM sparse mode requires only initial forwarding of traffic from the source to the RP (initially via unicast and then via multicast once an SPT is built from the source to the RP) and then from the RP down to each receiver via the shared tree. This forwarding is clearly more efficient than that offered by PIM dense mode because significantly less multicast traffic is initially flooded on the network. Once PIM sparse mode multicast routers know about a source that is sending multicast traffic, they can immediately create or join the (S,G) SPT by sending PIM Joins upstream toward the source.

Configuration Tasks

This scenario demonstrates the configuration of Catalyst 3550 Layer 3 switches for IP multicast routing using PIM sparse mode operation. Configuration of multicast routing on the Catalyst 3550 switches is identical to the configuration required on Cisco routers because both devices use Cisco IOS. The tasks required to enable multicast routing using PIM-SM include the following:

- Configuring unicast routing
- Configuring the rendezvous point
- Configuring PIM sparse mode multicast routing
- Verifying PIM sparse mode multicast routing

The unicast routing configuration required for PIM-SM is identical to that required for PIM-DM; hence, this configuration task is not covered in this scenario (refer to Scenario 7-1 for coverage of this task). All subsequent configuration tasks presented in this scenario assume a complete unicast routing topology is in place.

Configuring the Rendezvous Point

As indicated previously in this scenario, the RP provides a very important role in PIM sparse mode operation. Without an RP, there is no way for PIM-SM routers with receivers attached to join the appropriate (*,G) shared tree, and there is also no way for PIM-SM routers with sources attached to send PIM Register messages to the root of the shared tree.

It is important to understand that the RP is a multicast router and, therefore, requires multicast routing to be configured. On an RP, the following multicast routing configuration is required:

- Multicast routing is globally enabled.

- PIM sparse mode operation is configured on the interface whose IP address is configured as the RP IP address on other multicast routers (it is recommended that you configure PIM sparse mode on all interfaces).

- The RP IP address must be configured on the RP itself.

To globally enable multicast routing, use the **ip multicast-routing** global configuration command. To configure an interface to support PIM sparse mode, use the **ip pim** interface configuration mode command:

```
Router(config-if)# ip pim sparse-mode
```

Once you have configured the prerequisites for an RP, you can next configure the RP feature itself. The method by which you configure the RP depends on how you want the multicast network to discover the RP. If you manually configure the RP on each multicast router in the network, you simply need to configure the RP with an RP IP address that points to itself. This configuration is performed using the **ip pim rp-address** command:

```
Router(config)# ip pim rp-address ip-address [access-list-number] [override]
```

NOTE   If you configure RP discovery protocols for discovery of the RP, you do not need to configure the previous command on the RP.

The *access-list-number* parameter specifies the number of a standard access control list configured on the router that defines all groups for which the router is the RP. The **override** keyword indicates that if a different RP for a group is learned via a mechanism such as Auto-RP, the IP address configured for this command takes precedence.

TIP   If multiple paths to an RP exist in the network, you should create a loopback interface on the RP, assign an IP address to the loopback interface, and use the loopback IP address for the RP. If you use a physical interface for the RP and if that physical interface goes down, the RP stops working.

If you want for the network to use an automated discovery mechanism to locate the RP, you need to configure the RP to support the appropriate discovery mechanism. For this scenario, assume that the RP is configured manually on each multicast router. Example 7-21 demonstrates the configuration required on the RP (L3-Switch-D) if the RP is configured manually on all other multicast routers.

Example 7-21 *Configuring an RP*

```
L3-Switch-D# configure terminal
L3-Switch-D(config)# access-list 1 permit 239.1.1.0 0.0.0.255
L3-Switch-D(config)# ip pim rp-address 10.6.1.2 1
L3-Switch-D(config)# ip multicast-routing
L3-Switch-D(config)# interface range FastEthernet0/1 - 2
L3-Switch-D(config-if-range)# ip pim sparse-mode
```

In Example 7-21, an access control list (ACL) is created and defined as the list of groups that the RP represents. The ACL permits only multicast groups in the 239.1.1.x range (all ACLs have an implicit drop at the end of the ACL). Notice that the configured IP address of the RP is 10.6.1.2, which is the Fa0/1 interface on L3-Switch-D. All other multicast routers must be configured with this IP address for the RP to ensure correct PIM sparse mode operation.

Configuring PIM Sparse Mode Multicast Routing

After the RP is configured, you should then configure all other multicast routers in the network. Before you can configure PIM sparse mode, you must globally enable multicast routing, which is performed using the **ip multicast-routing** global configuration command. Once multicast routing is in place, if the network is using manual configuration to define the IP address of the RP, you must manually configure the IP address of the RP on each multicast router. This configuration ensures that each multicast router can join (*,G) shared trees rooted at the RP and send PIM Register messages to the RP. To configure the IP address of the RP, you use the same **ip pim rp-address** global configuration command that is also configured on the RP.

Example 7-22 demonstrates the configuration required on L3-Switch-A to enable multicast routing and configure PIM sparse mode.

Example 7-22 *Configuring a PIM Sparse Mode Router*

```
L3-Switch-A# configure terminal
L3-Switch-A(config)# access-list 1 permit 239.1.1.0 0.0.0.255
L3-Switch-A(config)# ip multicast-routing
L3-Switch-A(config)# ip pim rp-address 10.6.1.2 1
L3-Switch-A(config)# interface range FastEthernet0/1 - 3
L3-Switch-A(config-if-range)# ip pim sparse-mode
```

In Example 7-22, because the RP has been configured to act as the RP only for groups in the 239.1.1.x address range, you should also configure all other multicast routers with this information, using ACLs as indicated. Notice that you use the same command (**ip pim rp-address**) that was used on the RP itself to configure the RP on other routers. The configuration of Example 7-22 must be configured on all other multicast routers in the network to ensure each router knows where the RP is located in the network.

NOTE   Dynamic RP discovery mechanisms eliminate the requirement to manually configure the RP and the groups the RP represents. For this reason, use dynamic RP discovery mechanisms in larger networks to save administrative overheads.

Example 7-23 demonstrates the configuration required on L3-Switch-B to enable multicast routing and configure PIM sparse mode.

Example 7-23   *Configuring PIM Sparse Mode Operation on L3-Switch-B*

```
L3-Switch-B# configure terminal
L3-Switch-B(config)# access-list 1 permit 239.1.1.0 0.0.0.255
L3-Switch-B(config)# ip multicast-routing
L3-Switch-B(config)# ip pim rp-address 10.6.1.2 1
L3-Switch-B(config)# interface range FastEthernet0/1 - 4
L3-Switch-B(config-if-range)# ip pim sparse-mode
```

Example 7-24 demonstrates the configuration required on L3-Switch-C to enable multicast routing and configure PIM sparse mode.

Example 7-24   *Configuring PIM Sparse Mode Operation on L3-Switch-C*

```
L3-Switch-C# configure terminal
L3-Switch-C(config)# access-list 1 permit 239.1.1.0 0.0.0.255
L3-Switch-C(config)# ip multicast-routing
L3-Switch-C(config)# ip pim rp-address 10.6.1.2 1
L3-Switch-C(config)# interface range FastEthernet0/1 - 4
L3-Switch-C(config-if-range)# ip pim sparse-mode
```

Verifying PIM Sparse Mode Multicast Routing

Once you have configured PIM sparse mode multicast routing on each multicast router (assuming that the unicast routing topology is in place correctly), verify your interface configuration. Then verify that all multicast routers can see each other as PIM neighbors using the **show ip pim neighbor** command (see Example 7-9 in Scenario 7-1). This command is important for PIM sparse mode operation because it enables you to determine the PIM DR on each multi-access network. The PIM DR is the multicast router that sends PIM Joins for (*,G) shared trees to the RP.

Once you have verified that all multicast routers can see all neighbors, it is a good idea to verify that RPF checks are going to work correctly when your multicast sources start to transmit traffic. The **show ip rpf** command can be used to perform an RPF check manually for any source address, allowing you to verify that the correct unicast routing information is in place (see Example 7-11 in Scenario 7-1).

Testing PIM Sparse Mode Operation

Once the PIM sparse mode configuration of the network has been verified, the network is ready to begin forwarding multicast traffic. In this scenario, the topology of Figure 7-6 is used, where a single Cisco router (Router-A) with an IP address of 10.1.1.10 is used as the source of multicast traffic for the group address 239.1.1.1, and several Cisco routers (Router-B and Router-C) are configured as multicast receivers for the 239.1.1.1 group address. L3-Switch-D is configured as the RP for the network.

As described in this scenario, several multicast distribution trees are used to forward multicast traffic over a PIM sparse mode network. Initially, when receivers for groups are attached to the network but no sources are sending, a shared tree (*,G) exists for each group that is rooted at the RP and extends to the appropriate multicast routers with receivers attached. In this scenario, a (*,239.1.1.1) shared tree is initially formed from the RP to all receivers. Assume that Router-C has just come online and has sent an IGMP Membership Report for the 239.1.1.1 group. L3-Switch-B is the PIM DR for the 10.5.0.0/16 subnet because it has the highest IP addressed interface of any PIM router on the subnet, so L3-Switch-B sends PIM Joins for the (*,239.1.1.1) shared tree when Router-B (or any receiver on the 10.5.0.0/16 subnet) comes online. Example 7-25 shows the output of the **debug ip igmp** and **debug ip pim** commands on L3-Switch-B when Router-C comes online and sends an IGMP Membership Report.

Example 7-25 *Building the (*,G) Shared Tree to the RP*

```
L3-Switch-B# debug ip igmp
IGMP debugging is on
L3-Switch-B# debug ip pim
PIM debugging is on
! Router-C sends an IGMP Membership Report for the 239.1.1.1 Group
00:42:32: IGMP: Received v2 Report on FastEthernet0/3 from 10.5.1.10
     for 239.1.1.1
00:42:32: IGMP: Received Group record for group 239.1.1.1, mode 2 from
     10.5.1.10 for 0 sources
00:42:32: IGMP: WAVL Insert group: 239.1.1.1 interface: FastEthernet0/3Successful
00:42:32: IGMP: Switching to EXCLUDE mode for 239.1.1.1 on FastEthernet0/3
00:42:32: IGMP: Updating EXCLUDE group timer for 239.1.1.1

! Router-C creates (*,239.1.1.1) entry and sends PIM Join to the RP
00:42:32: PIM: Check RP 10.6.1.2 into the (*, 239.1.1.1) entry
00:42:32: PIM: Building triggered (*,G) Join / (S,G,RP-bit) Prune message
     for 239.1.1.1
00:42:32: PIM: v2, for RP, Join-list:10.6.1.2/32, RP-bit, WC-bit,S-bit
00:42:32: PIM: batch v2 Join on FastEthernet0/4 to 10.6.1.2 for
     (10.6.1.2/32, 239.1.1.1), WC-bit, RPT-bit, S-bit
00:42:32: PIM: Building batch join message for 239.1.1.1
00:42:32: PIM: Send v2 batch join to 10.6.1.2 (FastEthernet0/4)
```

The various events indicated by the output of Example 7-23 are illustrated in Figure 7-11. You can see that as soon as Router-C sends the IGMP Membership Report (Step 1 in Figure 7-11), L3-Switch-B generates a PIM Join for the (*,239.1.1.1) shared tree to the RP (Step 2 in Figure 7-11).

Example 7-26 shows the multicast routing table on L3-Switch-B after the events of Example 7-25, using the **show ip mroute** command.

Example 7-26   *The Multicast Routing Table on L3-Switch-B After Joining the (*,239.1.1.1) Shared Tree*

```
L3-Switch-B# show ip mroute
IP Multicast Routing Table
Flags: D - Dense, S - Sparse, s - SSM Group, C - Connected, L - Local,
       P - Pruned, R - RP-bit set, F - Register flag, T - SPT-bit set,
       J - Join SPT, M - MSDP created entry, X - Proxy Join Timer Running
       A - Advertised via MSDP, U - URD, I - Received Source Specific Host
          Report
Outgoing interface flags: H - Hardware switched
Timers: Uptime/Expires
Interface state: Interface, Next-Hop or VCD, State/Mode

(*, 239.1.1.1), 00:29:06/00:02:34, RP 10.6.1.2, flags: SJC
  Incoming interface: FastEthernet0/4, RPF nbr 10.6.1.2
  Outgoing interface list:
    FastEthernet0/3, Forward/Sparse, 00:29:06/00:00:00, H
... <output truncated>
...
```

The output shows that an entry for (*,239.1.1.1) has been created. You can see that the RP associated with the entry is 10.6.1.2 (L3-Switch-D), with the flags (SJC) indicating that the entry is a sparse mode entry (S) and that a receiver is directly connected to the router. The J flag (Join SPT) indicates that the SPT threshold is being exceeded (remember that by default, this threshold is 0 kbps), which means that the next (S,G) packet that is seen and has the same group address as the (*,G) entry (i.e., 239.1.1.1) triggers a PIM (S,G) Join to be sent towards the source, forming an SPT to the source. Notice that the incoming interface is listed as FastEthernet0/4, which is the closest interface to the RP. The outgoing interface list includes only FastEthernet0/3, because this is the interface to which the receiver (Router-C) is attached. The H flag indicates that any multicast packets received that for the 239.1.1.1 group are Layer 3 switched in hardware, as opposed to routed in software.

Example 7-27 shows the multicast routing table on L3-Switch-D after the events of Example 7-26, using the **show ip mroute** command.

Example 7-27   *The Multicast Routing Table on L3-Switch-D After Joining the (*,239.1.1.1) Shared Tree*

```
L3-Switch-D# show ip mroute
IP Multicast Routing Table
Flags: D - Dense, S - Sparse, B - Bidir Group, s - SSM Group, C - Connected,
       L - Local, P - Pruned, R - RP-bit set, F - Register flag,
       T - SPT-bit set, J - Join SPT, M - MSDP created entry,
       X - Proxy Join Timer Running, A - Candidate for MSDP Advertisement,
       U - URD, I - Received Source Specific Host Report
Outgoing interface flags: H - Hardware switched
Timers: Uptime/Expires
Interface state: Interface, Next-Hop or VCD, State/Mode
```

continues

Example 7-27 *The Multicast Routing Table on L3-Switch-D After Joining the (*,239.1.1.1) Shared Tree (Continued)*

```
(*, 239.1.1.1), 00:00:45/00:03:19, RP 10.6.1.2, flags: S
  Incoming interface: Null, RPF nbr 0.0.0.0
  Outgoing interface list:
    FastEthernet0/1, Forward/Sparse, 00:00:45/00:03:19
... <Output Truncated>
...
```

If you compare the (*,239.1.1.1) entries of Example 7-26 and Example 7-27, you can see that the entry for L3-Switch-D in Example 7-27 is a little different because it is the RP. The incoming interface is listed as Null because the RP is the root of (*,G) shared trees and, thus, has no concept of an incoming interface that leads to upstream routers. The outgoing interface is listed as FastEthernet0/1, which is attached to L3-Switch-B. This entry is present because L3-Switch-B sent the original PIM Join for (*,239.1.1.1). If the RP received any PIM joins for the shared tree on any other interfaces, these interfaces are also listed in the outgoing interface list.

Example 7-26 and Example 7-27 verify the PIM sparse mode operation is working properly when receivers join a multicast group, with a shared tree being formed that is rooted at the RP. At this point, no sources are actually sending traffic. Now assume that Router-A (source) comes online and begins forwarding traffic. You can simulate this by issuing an extended ping on Router-A to the multicast group address of 239.1.1.1 (see Example 7-16 in Scenario 7-1). Once multicast traffic is sent from a source in a PIM sparse mode network, the first multicast router that receives the traffic (L3-Switch-A in this scenario) sends a PIM Register message to the RP, as indicated in Figure 7-12. Example 7-28 shows the output of the **debug ip pim** command on L3-Switch-A, after Router-A sends traffic to the 239.1.1.1 group.

Example 7-28 *Demonstrating the PIM Register Process*

```
L3-Switch-A# debug ip pim
! Multicast packet is received from Router-A (source).
! L3-Switch-A sends a unicast PIM
! Register message to the RP for (10.1.1.10,239.1.1.1),
! which includes the multicast packet
03:19:28: PIM: Check RP 10.6.1.2 into the (*, 239.1.1.1) entry
03:19:28: PIM: Send v2 Register to 10.6.1.2 for 10.1.1.10, group 239.1.1.1

! A PIM Join for (10.1.1.10,239.1.1.1) is received from L3-Switch-B.
! This is the final
! Join used to build the SPT from the RP to the source
03:19:28: PIM: Received v2 Join/Prune on FastEthernet0/1 from 10.2.1.2, to us
03:19:28: PIM: Join-list: (10.1.1.10/32, 239.1.1.1), S-bit set
03:19:28: PIM: Add FastEthernet0/1/10.2.1.2 to (10.1.1.10/32, 239.1.1.1),
    Forward state

! Because the (10.1.1.10,239.1.1.1) SPT has been built,
! the RP receives multicast traffic
! down the SPT and sends a PIM Register-Stop message to L3-Switch-A
03:19:30: PIM: Received v2 Register-Stop on Ethernet1 from 10.6.1.2
03:19:30: PIM:    for source 10.1.1.10, group 239.1.1.1
03:19:30: PIM: Clear register flag to 10.6.1.2 for (10.1.1.10/32, 239.1.1.1)
```

In Example 7-28, you can see that all of the events described in Figure 7-12 take place extremely quickly. You can't see the final step of PIM sparse mode operation, where a multicast router joins the (S,G) SPT, because the (S,G) SPT generated from the RP to the source effectively builds the (S,G) SPT from L3-Switch-B to the source. Thus, the L3-Switch-B doesn't actually need to join the (S,G) SPT when it forwards the first multicast packet to receivers.

Example 7-29 demonstrates the events that occur on the RP after Router-A starts generating multicast traffic by using the **debug ip pim** command on L3-Switch-D.

Example 7-29 *Demonstrating the PIM Register Process on the RP*

```
L3-Switch-D# debug ip pim
! PIM Register is received from L3-Switch-A
! Multicast packet in PIM Register message is forwarded down the shared tree
04:25:05: PIM: Received v2 Register on FastEthernet0/1 from 10.2.1.1
04:25:05:       for 10.1.1.10, group 239.1.1.1
04:25:05: PIM: Forward decapsulated data packet for 239.1.1.1 on FastEthernet0/1

! RP is sending PIM Join for (10.1.1.10,239.1.1.1) towards source to build SPT
04:25:05: PIM: Send v2 Join on FastEthernet0/1 to 10.6.1.1 for
    (10.1.1.10/32, 239.1.1.1), S-bit

! PIM Register-Stop message is sent to L3-Switch-A (10.2.1.1),
! as multicast packets are
! now being received via SPT instead of via PIM Register messages
04:25:07: PIM: Send v2 Register-Stop to 10.2.1.1 for 10.1.1.10, group 239.1.1.1

! PIM Prune is sent for (10.1.1.10,239.1.1.1) from L3-Switch-B to the RP.
! The RP bit is set, to indicate that only (S,G) traffic should be pruned
! from the (*,239.1.1.1) tree
04:25:08: PIM: Received v2 Join/Prune on FastEthernet0/1 from 10.6.1.1, to us
04:25:08: PIM: Prune-list: (10.1.1.10/32, 239.1.1.1) RPT-bit set
```

Example 7-29 shows the PIM Register messages generated from L3-Switch-A when Router-A begins sending multicast packets. The PIM messages are followed by the RP joining the (10.1.1.10,239.1.1.1) SPT. Once the SPT is built, native multicast packets are received instead of unicast PIM Register messages, and a PIM Register-Stop is sent to L3-Switch-A. Figure 7-12 illustrates each of these events. The final event in Example 7-29 is the sending of a PIM prune message from L3-Switch-B to the RP, after L3-Switch-B forms an SPT to the source. If you refer back to Figure 7-14, Step 3 illustrates this event. In Example 7-29, the last line of the output indicates that the RPT-bit is set. The RPT portion of this output indicates flags with R representing the RP bit (i.e,. the RP bit is set), P indicating the message is a prune, and T (the SPT bit) indicating that packets have been received on the SPT, as opposed to the shared tree. The prune message ensures that L3-Switch-D doesn't unnecessarily forward multicast packets towards L3-Switch-B, because L3-Switch-B is already receiving the packets down the (10.1.1.10,239.1.1.1) SPT.

Configuring PIM Sparse-Dense Mode Operation

PIM sparse-dense mode represents a simple extension to PIM sparse mode operation that enables PIM routers to use PIM dense mode operation for any multicast groups that do not have an RP configured. If a multicast router has all interfaces configured for PIM sparse mode operation and a receiver joins a group that is not serviced by any known RP, a shared tree can never be joined for the group because there is no RP known to the multicast router for the group. Similarly, if a multicast router receives traffic from a source for a group that is not serviced by any known RP, the multicast router simply cannot forward the traffic because it has no RP to which it can send PIM Register messages.

Using the configuration presented so far in this book, the situations discussed in the previous paragraph are not really a problem because each multicast router is configured with an RP and, thus, knows where to forward multicast traffic. However, sparse mode operation does present a problem when you want to use RP discovery protocols instead of manually configuring the RP, because these protocols use multicast transmissions themselves to communicate information about RPs in the network. This situation presents an interesting problem—a router must know about at least one RP to forward multicast traffic, but the protocols used to advertise the location of RPs use multicast communications. The solution to this problem is to use PIM dense mode operation for the RP discovery protocols, which means that the RP discovery messages are flooded throughout the network without requiring knowledge of an RP. If you configure PIM dense mode, however, you lose the benefits of PIM sparse mode. What is needed is some mode of operation that uses PIM dense mode when an RP is not present for a group, but uses PIM sparse mode when an RP is present for a group.

PIM sparse-dense mode is a mode of operation that provides this exact functionality. For each group present on the network, multicast routers configured in PIM sparse-dense mode operate in PIM sparse mode if the RP is known for the group or, alternatively, operate in PIM dense mode if the RP is unknown. Configuring PIM sparse-dense mode has no effect on your existing sparse mode network, but ensures that messages sent to groups without an RP configured (e.g., RP discovery protocols) are flooded throughout the network using PIM dense mode operation.

NOTE   Cisco recommends that the PIM sparse-dense mode operation always be configured over other PIM modes where possible in the network.

To configure PIM sparse-dense mode operation, you simply change the PIM mode on each interface to sparse-dense mode, using the **ip pim** interface configuration command:

```
Router(config-if)# ip pim sparse-dense-mode
```

All other PIM sparse mode multicast routing configuration remains the same and is not affected by sparse-dense mode operation. The only difference in functionality is that multicast routers use PIM dense mode operation if an RP is not present for a particular multicast group. Example 7-30 demonstrates the configuration required on L3-Switch-A to enable IP PIM sparse-dense mode operation.

Example 7-30 *Configuring IP PIM Sparse-Dense Mode Operation*

```
L3-Switch-A# configure terminal
L3-Switch-A(config)# interface FastEthernet0/1 - 3
L3-Switch-A(config-if-range# ip pim sparse-dense-mode
```

Configuring Auto-RP

In the scenario so far, each multicast router has been manually configured with the RP. In a small network, this configuration is not too much of a problem, but in a large multicast network that has several RPs that each service separate multicast groups, manually configuring RP information on each and every multicast router in the network requires high administrative overhead and is prone to error. To avoid the issues of manually configuring RP information, several dynamic RP discovery mechanisms are available that automate the discovery of one or more RPs in the network and the groups that each RP services. With these mechanisms, you no longer have to manually configure every single multicast router in the network with RP information; instead, each multicast router can dynamically learn RP information.

Two RP discovery protocols are available and commonly used in PIM multicast networks:

* Auto-RP
* PIMv2 bootstrap router (BSR)

In general, Auto-RP is the recommended dynamic RP protocol because it uses multicast trees to distribute RP information. In contrast, PIMv2 BSR floods traffic throughout the network, which is less efficient than using multicast. Accordingly, this section provides information only on how to configure Auto-RP.

Auto-RP is a Cisco proprietary mechanism that was invented before the PIM version 2 specification, which includes the alternative BSR RP discovery protocol. Auto-RP introduces *mapping agents*, which are routers that listen to messages sent to a well-known group called *Cisco-RP-Announce*. The Cisco-RP-Announce group has an IP address of 224.0.1.39, and any Cisco RP that is configured to announce its presence as an RP sends RP-Announce messages to this group. An RP-Announce message contains the IP address of the RP and a list of the groups that the RP services, which can be defined as a *Group-to-RP mapping*. Each mapping agent that receives these messages writes the Group-to-RP mappings contained in each message to a Group-to-RP mapping cache, which is stored locally in memory. These mappings contain the IP address of each RP and the groups that each RP services. The mapping agent then transmits this information to the network in RP-Discovery multicast messages, which are sent to the well-known Cisco-RP-Discovery group (224.0.1.40). All Cisco multicast routers join this group and, hence, receive all RP-

Discovery messages sent by mapping agents, which enables all multicast routers to receive RP information dynamically, in a manner that is highly efficient and scalable.

Figure 7-15 demonstrates how the Auto-RP works on the topology used for this scenario.

Figure 7-15 *Auto-RP Operation*

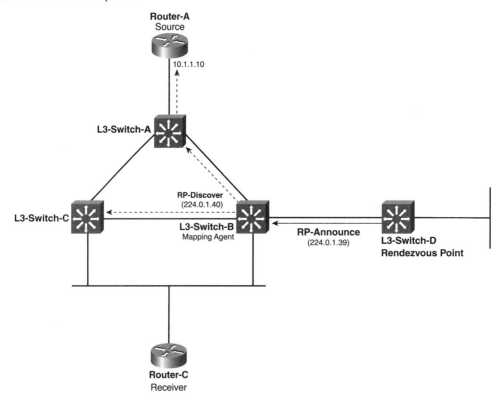

In Figure 7-15, L3-Switch-D is the RP and is configured to send RP-Announce messages to the Cisco-RP-Announce group. L3-Switch-B is configured as a mapping agent and, thus, listens to the RP-Announce messages sent from L3-Switch-D. L3-Switch-B then propagates this information to all other multicast routers in the network by sending RP-Discovery messages to the Cisco-RP-Discovery group. L3-Switch-B essentially becomes a source for the 224.0.1.40 group, with an SPT being built to the remaining multicast routers in the network because they are receivers of this group. PIM sparse-dense mode operation is required on all multicast routers because the RP-Announce and RP-Discovery groups require PIM dense mode to flood traffic to all mapping agents and multicast routers, ensuring all multicast routers in the network can discover all available RPs.

Once your network is configured for PIM sparse-dense mode operation, to configure auto-RP you must perform the following configuration tasks:

- Configuring candidate rendezvous points
- Configure mapping agents

NOTE The configurations presented in this section assume that you have removed all manual configuration of the RP on L3-Switch-A, L3-Switch-B, and L3-Switch-C to ensure this information is not used to find the RP.

Configuring Candidate Rendezvous Points

When Auto-RP is configured, all RPs in the network must be configured to belong to the Cisco-RP-Announce group, which means they periodically send RP-Announce messages indicating the IP address of the RP and the groups it services (Group-to-RP mapping). To configure an RP to do this, use the **ip pim send-rp-announce** global configuration command:

```
Router(config)# ip pim send-rp-announce interface-id scope ttl
   group-list access-list-number interval seconds
```

The **scope** keyword defines the IP TTL value that is set on the RP-Announce messages, which can be used to control how far RP-Announce messages propagate once sent. You must ensure that the TTL is large enough to reach all mapping agents in the network. The **group-list** keyword allows you to specify which groups the RP services by configuring an ACL that specifies each group. The **interval** keyword defines how often RP-Announce messages are sent; the default is every 60 seconds.

NOTE If multiple RPs advertise that they service the same groups, the RP with the highest IP address is chosen as RP. This mechanism enables you to implement RP redundancy, with the highest IP addressed RP normally performing the RP role and other lower IP addressed RPs providing backup in case the primary RP fails.

Example 7-31 demonstrates configuring L3-Switch-D to generate RP-Announce messages.

Example 7-31 *Configuring an RP for Auto-RP*

```
L3-Switch-D# configure terminal
L3-Switch-D(config)# interface loopback 0
L3-Switch-D(config-if)# ip address 10.10.10.4 255.255.255.255
L3-Switch-D(config-if)# ip pim sparse-dense-mode
L3-Switch-D(config-if)# exit
L3-Switch-D(config)# ip pim send-rp-announce loopback 0 scope 2 group-list 1
```

In Example 7-31, a loopback interface is created to ensure that a physical interface failure does not stop RP-Announce messages from being generated. So, RP-Announce messages are sent via the (10.10.10.4,224.0.1.39) SPT. The scope is set to 2, which means the RP-Announce messages are propagated only two hops to L3-Switch-B (the local router is considered a single hop), which is a mapping agent. The **group-list** keyword references ACL #1, which was created in Example 7-21 and means that L3-Switch-D only advertises that it is the RP for groups that are within the 239.1.1.x address range.

NOTE   In Example 7-31, notice that you don't need to configure the **ip pim rp-address** command on the RP, which you do need to configure if using manual RP configuration. The **ip pim send-rp-announce** command tells the RP which interface it should listen on.

Configuring Mapping Agents

Once all RPs are configured to send RP-Announce messages, you must configure mapping agents to generate RP-Discover messages in response to RP-Announce messages received. The mapping agent essentially acts as a *relay* agent—when RP-Announce messages are received by the mapping agent, the information contained in these messages is relayed to all multicast routers on the network using RP-Discover messages.

NOTE   You might wonder why all multicast routers don't just listen to RP-Announce messages to determine RP information. The answer is scalability. You may have many RPs in your network. Those RPs represent multiple sources of RP-Announce messages, each of which generates an SPT (because RP-Announce messages are sent to a multicast group). If all multicast routers listened to the RP-Announce messages, the SPTs for each source would span the entire network, which does not scale well in large networks. By using mapping agents, each RP-Announce SPT needs to span only all mapping agents, which then can aggregate all of the RP information onto a single SPT tree that is rooted at the mapping agent and distributed to all multicast routers. In short, mapping agents allow network designers to exercise tight control over the traffic flows associated with RP discovery protocols.

To configure a mapping agent, use the **ip pim send-rp-discovery** global configuration command:

```
Router(config)# ip pim send-rp-discovery [interface-id] [scope ttl]
```

When configuring mapping agents, create a loopback interface and configure this interface as the *interface-id* parameter. This configuration ensures only a single SPT is generated from the mapping agent to multicast routers. If you specify a physical interface and if that interface goes down, then the mapping agent feature stops working. If you omit the *interface-id* parameter, all interfaces are used to send RP-discovery messages, which means an SPT exists for each interface on the mapping agent, because each interface has a different IP address, which in turn means a separate SPT must be generated for each different IP address. However, using a loopback interface ensures only a single SPT is formed and also protects against interface failures. The **scope** keyword defines the IP TTL value that is set on the RP-Discovery messages, which can be used to control how far RP-Discovery messages propagate once sent. You must ensure that the TTL is large enough to reach all multicast routers in the network.

Example 7-32 demonstrates configuring L3-Switch-B as a mapping agent.

Example 7-32 *Configuring an Auto-RP Mapping Agent*

```
L3-Switch-B# configure terminal
L3-Switch-B(config)# interface loopback 0
L3-Switch-B(config-if)# ip address 10.10.10.2 255.255.255.255
L3-Switch-B(config-if)# ip pim sparse-dense-mode
L3-Switch-B(config-if)# exit
L3-Switch-B(config)# ip pim send-rp-discovery loopback 0 scope 16
```

In Example 7-32, a loopback interface is created to ensure that only a single SPT is created (10.10.10.2,224.0.1.40) for sending RP-Discovery messages to the other multicast routers. Notice that you must configure PIM sparse-dense-mode operation on the loopback interface if you want to use it as the source of the RP-Discovery SPT.

At this point, all multicast routers in the network should be learning RP information from the mapping agent, because all Cisco multicast routers join the 224.0.1.40 (RP-Discovery group). To verify multicast routers have indeed learned Group-to-RP mapping information, use the **show ip pim rp mapping** command, as demonstrated on L3-Switch-A in Example 7-33.

Example 7-33 *Verifying Auto-RP Operation*

```
L3-Switch-A# show ip pim rp mapping
PIM Group-to-RP Mappings

Group(s) 239.1.1.0/24
  RP 10.10.10.4 (?), v2v1
    Info source: 10.10.10.2 (?), via Auto-RP
        Uptime: 00:01:26, expires: 00:02:33
```

In Example 7-33, notice that L3-Switch-D (10.10.10.4) is listed as the RP for groups within the 239.1.1.0/24 address range, which is the address range that was specified with the **group-list** keyword in Example 7-31 on L3-Switch-D. The source of this Group-to-RP mapping is indicated as 10.10.10.2, which is the loopback 0 interface of L3-Switch-B. At this point, if Router-A (source) starts transmitting packets to the 239.1.1.1 group, PIM sparse mode operation should occur because the RP is known to each multicast router via the Auto-RP mechanism.

Scenario 7-3: Multicast Traffic Control on the LAN

The primary goal of multicast is to enable traffic to be sent from a single source to a specific group of devices, without requiring the traffic to be flooded throughout the network to meet the goal of ensuring all receivers interested in the traffic receive the traffic. Scenarios 7-1 and 7-2 showed you how to implement multicast routing, which is a Layer 3 function that is independent of Layer 2 (the only effect Layer 2 has on multicast routing is related to how PIM operates on point-to-point and multi-access Layer 2 networks). Multicast routing is concerned with providing multicast traffic control in Layer 3 topologies, where multicast traffic is sent across the minimum number of Layer 3 paths in the network to ensure all receivers can receive multicast traffic. Multicast routing gets the traffic for a particular multicast group to only the Layer 2 segments that need to receive the group traffic. Once the multicast transmission is on the Layer 2 network, multicast routing has no control over which Layer 2 links or ports the transmission is sent to. This control is left to the Layer 2 device (such as a switch) that interconnects the segment.

You can allow the Layer 2 device to forward the multicast out all ports, treating multicasts in an identical fashion to broadcasts. This strategy certainly makes multicasts much easier to deal with from the Layer 2 device point of view, but it defeats the whole concept of multicasting. The real problem with taking the broadcast approach to multicasting is performance. If you are multicasting a large video stream out all ports, the bandwidth available to all network devices decreases. To control the multicast bandwidth usage, you can use a technique known as *broadcast control*, where excessive multicast (and broadcast) traffic over a certain threshold is dropped. However, this technique can have serious side effects. For example, a large multicast stream might reach the allowable multicast/broadcast threshold on a port. After this point, all multicasts and broadcasts are dropped (including crucial spanning tree BPDUs), which can cause network instability.

Ideally, the Layer 2 device should forward the multicast transmission only out ports to which receivers are connected and also out any ports that are connected to downstream multicast routers. Figure 7-16 illustrates this concept.

Figure 7-16 shows that it is the responsibility of the switch (rather than the router) to control which ports the multicast is flooded to. The switch must forward the multicast out ports 2/2 and 2/3 to ensure that the locally attached receiver and the rest of the multicast network receive the multicast; however, the non-receiver attached to port 2/4 does not need to receive the multicast. Layer 2 devices, such as the switch in Figure 7-16, must possess some understanding of multicast in order to control the forwarding of multicast traffic out each Layer 2 link.

Cisco Catalyst switches can use the following methods of controlling multicast transmissions, which are discussed in this section:

- Static bridge table (CAM) entries
- IGMP snooping

- Cisco Group Management Protocol (CGMP)
- GARP Multicast Registration Protocol or GMRP (not discussed in this chapter)

This scenario continues on from the previous scenario and examines using static bridge table entries to constrain multicast traffic on the LAN to specific ports attached to multicast receivers.

Figure 7-16 *Multicast Forwarding on a Layer 2 Network*

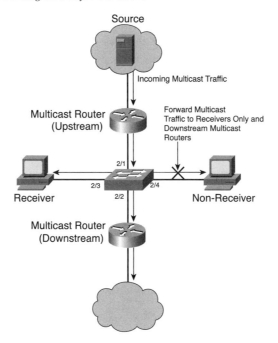

NOTE	*GMRP* is a standards-based protocol that provides constrained multicast flooding on Layer 2 networks, in a similar fashion to IGMP snooping (see Scenario 7-4) and CGMP (see Scenario 7-5). A major drawback to GMRP is that multicast receivers (hosts) must support GMRP and send GMRP joins in addition to IGMP joins. The GMRP joins are received by a GMRP-aware switch, which uses this information to associate the ports attached to receivers with a particular multicast group. IGMP snooping and CGMP achieve the same results, but do so transparently to multicast receivers (i.e., multicast receivers need to use IGMP only to register to a multicast group and do not need to understand another protocol).

Static Bridge Table Entries

The simplest and most easily understood method of controlling multicast traffic on Layer 2 networks is to manually associate the appropriate destination ports with each multicast address. Because a multicast address is always a destination address, an entry can be placed in the bridge table of a switch that lists the appropriate egress ports for the multicast transmission. Forwarding of the multicast frames operates in identical fashion to that of unicast frames—the multicast destination MAC address is located in the local bridge table, the egress ports are found, and then a copy of the multicast frame is forwarded out each egress port. If the multicast destination MAC address is not present in the bridge table, then the frame is flooded out all ports within the VLAN, in an identical fashion to how frames to unknown unicast destination MAC addresses are flooded. Referring back to Figure 7-6, notice that on the 10.6.0.0/16 subnet, Switch-B has four devices connected:

- **L3-Switch-B**—An upstream PIM multicast router with respect to the (10.1.1.10,239.1.1.1) multicast tree

- **L3-Switch-D**—A downstream PIM multicast router with respect to the (10.1.1.10,239.1.1.1) multicast tree

- **Router-B**—A receiver for the (10.1.1.10,239.1.1.1) group

- **Host-B**—A non-receiver

Because L3-Switch-B is the upstream multicast router for (10.1.1.10,239.1.1.1), multicast frames are received from L3-Switch-B inbound on interface Fa0/1 on Switch-B. Switch-B then needs to forward the multicast frame out interface Fa0/3 (connected to Router-B) and interface Fa0/2 (connected to L3-Switch-D), but does not need to forward the multicast frame out interface Fa0/4 (connected to the non-receiver Host-B). Figure 7-17 illustrates how you can use static bridge table entries to control multicast traffic on the 10.6.0.0/16 subnet in Figure 7-6.

Notice in Figure 7-17 that a static bridge table entry exists that indicates that frames with a destination MAC of address 0100.5e01.0101 (the Ethernet multicast address for the 239.1.1.1 IP multicast address) are forwarded out interface Fa0/2 (to L3-Switch-D) and interface Fa0/3 (to Router-B). If the frames are received on interface Fa0/1, they are not forwarded back out interface Fa0/1, even though interface Fa0/1 is in the egress interface list. Also, notice that the age of the entry in the bridging table is not specified because this entry is a static bridge table entry that always remains in the bridge table and, thus, never ages out.

NOTE   You might be wondering why interface Fa0/1 is included in the egress interface list when group traffic is normally received on this interface. Because receivers periodically send IGMP membership reports to the group address (in response to IGMP general queries), to ensure that these messages are sent to multicast routers all interfaces with multicast routers attached must be added to the egress interface list. When configuring static bridge table entries, ensure that all groups configured include all multicast router interfaces in the egress interface list.

A few issues with static bridge table entries make it difficult to use in anything but the simplest multicast networks:

- If a new host needs to receive a multicast transmission, an administrator must manually add the host's connected port or interface to the bridge table entry.

- If a host does not need to receive a multicast transmission any longer, an administrator must manually remove the host's connected port or interface from the bridge table entry.

- If a host is moved to another port or interface, an administrator must update the bridge table entry manually.

Figure 7-17   *Multicast Traffic Control Using Static Bridge Table Entries*

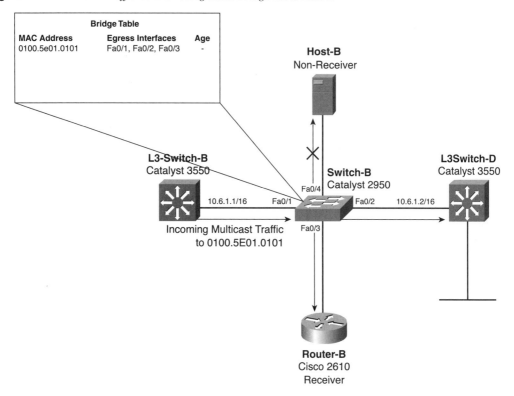

The underlying problem is the lack of ability to dynamically adapt to changes in the network. The switch cannot dynamically add or remove an egress port/interface from the bridge table entry; an administrator must manually configure it. In all but the very simplest networks, the administrative overhead of implementing static bridge table entries to constrain multicast traffic on the LAN is far too high.

Configuration Tasks

As already indicated, implementing static bridge table entries to constrain multicast flooding on the LAN is very simple. The configuration of static bridge table entries for multicast is identical to the configuration required for static bridge table entries that reference unicast addresses (see Chapter 2, "VLAN Operations"), except you may need to specify more than one egress port or interface for the entry, depending on the number of receivers and downstream multicast routers connected to the LAN.

In Figure 7-6, a single multicast source and group is present on the network. This source/group is represented in (S,G) notation as (10.1.1.10,239.1.1.1), where 10.1.1.10 (Router-A) is the source and 239.1.1.1 is the multicast group address. On the LAN segments in Figure 7-6, the Ethernet multicast address for the 239.1.1.1 IP multicast address is 0100.5e01.0101 (see Figure 7-1 if you are unsure how this is derived). Two LAN segments in the network contain receivers—the 10.5.0.0/16 subnet, which is provided LAN connectivity by Switch-C (CatOS Catalyst 6500), and the 10.6.0.0/16 subnet, which is provided LAN connectivity by Switch-B (Cisco IOS Catalyst 2950). Both segments have non-receivers and receivers that are connected locally; hence, both of these switches should ensure that multicast traffic is constrained to receivers only (and downstream multicast routers if applicable).

To configure static bridge table entries for multicast frames on CatOS (also referred to as *CAM entries on CatOS switches*), you should first disable IGMP snooping if applicable (IGMP snooping is supported and enabled by default on the Catalyst 5000/5500 and Catalyst 6000/6500 switches) by using the **set igmp** command:

```
Console> (enable) set igmp disable
```

Once IGMP snooping has been disabled, you can then configure static bridge table entries by using the **set cam** command:

```
Console> (enable) set cam {static | permanent} destination-mac mod/port [vlan-id]
```

If you use the **static** keyword, the entry remains in the bridge table only until the bridge table is cleared or the switch is rebooted. To ensure the entry is always present in the bridge table even after a switch reboot, use the **permanent** keyword. If you don't specify the optional *vlan-id* parameter, VLAN 1 is assumed as the VLAN for which the entry applies. Thus if you need to control multicast traffic in a VLAN other than VLAN 1, ensure that you specify the *vlan-id* to indicate to which VLAN an entry should apply.

In Figure 7-6 on the 10.5.0.0/16 subnet, Router-C is the only connected receiver for (10.1.1.10,239.1.1.1), with L3-Switch-B forwarding IP multicast frames onto the subnet (L3-Switch-B has asserted the role of the multicast router from L3-Switch-C for the LAN, as described in Figure 7-9). This means that on Switch-C, multicast frames need to be forwarded out port 2/1, 2/2, and 2/4. Example 7-34 demonstrates configuring a static bridge table entry on Switch-C.

Example 7-34 *Configuring Static Bridge Table Entries on Switch-C*

```
Switch-C> (enable) set igmp disable
IGMP Snooping is disabled.
CGMP is disabled.
Switch-C> (enable) set cam permanent 01-00-53-01-01-01 2/1-2,2/4 1
Permanent multicast entry added to CAM table.
Switch-C> (enable) show cam permanent
* = Static Entry. + = Permanent Entry. # = System Entry. R = Router Entry.
X = Port Security Entry $ = Dot1x Security Entry

VLAN   Dest MAC/Route Des     [CoS]   Destination Ports or VCs / [Protocol Type]
----   ------------------     -----   ------------------------------------------
1      01-00-5e-01-01-01  +           2/1-2,2/4 ! Permanent Bridge Table Entry
Total Matching CAM Entries Displayed  =1
```

The **show cam permanent** command verifies the configuration and indicates that any frame received with a destination MAC address of 0100.5e01.0101 is forwarded out port 2/4. The + symbol next to the entry indicates that this is a permanent entry.

To configure static bridge table entries for multicast frames on Cisco IOS, you must first ensure that IGMP snooping is disabled (IGMP snooping is enabled by default on Cisco IOS Catalyst switches). To disable IGMP snooping, use the **no ip igmp snooping** global configuration command:

```
Switch(config)# no ip igmp snooping
```

Once IGMP snooping is disabled, you can use the **mac-address-table static** global configuration command to add a new entry to the bridge table:

```
Switch(config)# mac-address-table static multicast-mac-address vlan
   vlan-id interface interface-id1 interface-id2 ...
```

In Cisco IOS, the **static** keyword means that the entry is always present in the bridge table even after a switch reboot, unlike the CatOS **set cam** command where the **static** keyword saves the entry only until the bridge table is cleared or the switch is rebooted (i.e., the **static** keyword in Cisco IOS is equivalent to the **permanent** keyword in CatOS). Notice that you must also specify the appropriate VLAN ID for which the entry applies.

In Figure 7-6, Router-B is the only connected receiver on the 10.6.0.0/16 subnet for (10.1.1.10,239.1.1.1), with L3-Switch-B forwarding frames onto the LAN and L3-Switch-D acting as a downstream multicast router. This configuration means that multicast frames need to be forwarded out interface Fa0/1, Fa0/2, and Fa0/3. Example 7-35 demonstrates configuring a static bridge table entry on Switch-B.

Example 7-35 *Configuring Static Bridge Table Entries on Switch-B*

```
Switch-B# configure terminal
Switch-B(config)# no ip igmp snooping
Switch-B(config)# multicast-address-table static 0100.5e01.0101 vlan 1
  interface FastEthernet0/1 FastEthernet0/2 FastEthernet0/3
Switch-B(config)# end
Switch-B# show mac-address-table multicast
Vlan   Mac Address      Type      Ports
----   -----------      ----      - - --
   1   0100.5e01.0101   USER      Fa0/1 Fa0/2 Fa0/3 ! Permanent Entry
```

Example 7-35 shows that you can use the **show mac-address-table** multicast command to view all bridge table entries that reference multicast destination MAC addresses. The Type field indicates a type of USER, which means that a user has manually configured the entry.

Scenario 7-4: Configuring IGMP Snooping

In the previous scenario, you learned how to constrain multicast flooding on the LAN by directly configuring the bridge table on your switches. As highlighted in the scenario, although this method is very simple and easy to understand, it is totally static in that any modifications required to the configuration are not performed dynamically and must be manually configured.

Cisco Catalyst switches can provide intelligent multicast forwarding on Layer 2 (Ethernet) networks, by using features such as IGMP snooping, CGMP, and GMRP. These features dynamically learn which ports are connected to receivers or downstream multicast routers and automatically constrain multicast flooding to just these ports. When a receiver attaches, moves, shuts down, or disconnects from the network, this event is learned by the switch and the bridge table entries are automatically modified as appropriate. This scenario discusses IGMP snooping and shows you how to configure it on Cisco Catalyst switches. The topology of Figure 7-6 is used to demonstrate IGMP snooping for this scenario, and it is assumed that the multicast routing configurations of the previous scenarios have been implemented.

IGMP Snooping Operation

IGMP snooping allows a switch to dynamically determine which hosts connected to a particular VLAN in the switch need to receive a particular multicast transmission. The switch basically listens (snoops) to the various IGMP messages (such as Join, Query, Response, Leave), as well as other multicast protocol transmissions, and dynamically determines which egress ports are associated with each multicast transmission. The switch still uses a bridge table entry to control multicast forwarding, except the entry is dynamic and not statically configured. Based upon IGMP messages snooped, a switch performs the following actions:

- Adding a receiver to a group
- Removing a receiver from a group
- Maintaining group membership

Adding a Receiver to a Group

Before receivers attach to the LAN, multicast routers that are also attached to the LAN are normally already operational and have sent IGMP General Query messages in an attempt to locate any receivers attached to the LAN. IGMP snooping switches can use these messages to determine where multicast routers are located, which is important because switches must forward all multicast traffic to every multicast router on the LAN to ensure that IGMP group maintenance messages are always passed to the multicast routers and also to ensure that any multicast traffic that requires forwarding off the LAN by multicast routers is forwarded.

When a receiver attaches to the LAN, it immediately indicates its desire to join multicast groups by sending an IGMP Membership Report to each group address the receiver wants to join.

Figure 7-18 illustrates IGMP snooping operation on the 10.6.0.0/16 subnet of Figure 7-6.

Figure 7-18   *IGMP Snooping*

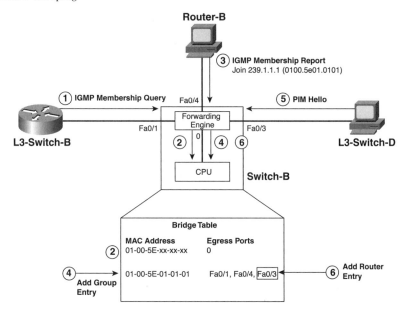

In Figure 7-18, assume that L3-Switch-B is the IGMP Querier for the LAN segment:

1 L3-Switch-B (a multicast router) sends an IGMP General Query (to the 224.0.0.1 all hosts address or 0100.5e00.0001) every 60 seconds as part of the normal IGMP maintenance process.

2 The switch receives the periodic IGMP General Query sent by L3-Switch-B. Notice that a permanent bridge table entry exists that forwards any IP multicast frames (0100.5eXX.XXXX) to port 0. Port 0 represents the switch CPU, which must receive all multicast frames to properly snoop IGMP Membership Reports and Leave Group messages. The General Query is forwarded to the CPU, and because multicast routers only ever send IGMP General Query messages, the switch knows that a multicast router is connected to interface Fa0/1, which is important because the interface attached to the multicast router should be included in all bridge table entries that reference a multicast address. This configuration ensures that the router receives any membership reports that are sent for multicast groups and also ensures that the switch can forward multicast frames generated by local sources only out interfaces attached to multicast routers. The IGMP General Query is then flooded out all interfaces on the switch to ensure it reaches all potential receivers on the LAN.

NOTE   In the real world on a live network, forwarding all multicast frames to the switch CPU can cause major performance issues. For example, if the switch CPU has to process every single frame sent of multiple video streams that each consume 1.5 Mbps and generate 20 frames per second, the CPU becomes quickly overwhelmed, causing the switch to crash or to not perform other more important functions, such as generating and processing spanning tree BPDUs. Cisco Catalyst switches do not forward all multicast frames to the switch CPU; only multicast frames that have an IP protocol type of 2 (IGMP) are forwarded to the switch CPU (after all, IGMP snooping requires only IGMP messages to be snooped).

---

3 Router-B attaches to the network and sends an IGMP Membership Report message, which is addressed to the group address (0100.5e01.0101) that Router-B wants to join.

4 The switch receives the IGMP Membership Report message from Router-B. Because the group address (0100.5e01.0101) is not currently in the bridge table, the multicast is flooded out all interfaces, except the interface the multicast was received upon. Switch-B also creates a new bridge table entry for the 0100.5e01.0101 address and adds the multicast router interface (Fa0/1) and the ingress interface of the frame (Fa0/4, attached to Router-B) to the egress port list. At this point, if multicast frames sent to 0100.5e01.0101 are received from the source (via L3-Switch-B), the bridge

table entry means that the multicast is forwarded only out interface Fa0/4 (the multicast is not forwarded out interface Fa0/1, because this is the ingress interface for frames generated by the source).

NOTE	Notice that the process of populating the bridge table with multicast MAC addresses is based upon inspection of the destination MAC address, unlike unicast MAC addresses where the source MAC address of unicast frames is examined to generate bridge table entries.

5 The discussion so far has disregarded L3-Switch-D, which is a downstream multicast router for the 239.1.1.1 group. Because L3-Switch-B is the IGMP Querier for the segment, L3-Switch-D does not send any IGMP messages to the segment, which means Switch-B can't detect L3-Switch-D via IGMP messages. If L3-Switch-D has receivers attached further downstream, it is important that multicast frames are also forwarded to L3-Switch-D. To detect other multicast routers on the LAN, Cisco Catalyst switches also listen for other messages that indicate the presence of another multicast router. In Figure 7-18, L3-Switch-D generates PIM hellos every 30 seconds by default, as part of normal PIM operation. The switch hears these PIM Hello message generated by L3-Switch-D on interface Fa0/3 and thus ensures that interface Fa0/3 is added to the egress port list for all multicast addresses in the bridge table.

Figure 7-18 describes what happens when a single receiver joins a multicast group. If another receiver joins the multicast group, Switch-B receives the IGMP Membership Report sent by the receiver and simply appends the interface attached to the new receiver to the bridge table entry for the multicast group address, ensuring the new receiver also receives multicast frames. Because the group already exists and has active receivers on the LAN, the switch does not actually need to forward the IGMP Membership Report to the multicast router (L3-Switch-B). The Cisco Catalyst implementation of IGMP snooping forwards no more than one IGMP Membership Report for an existing group within a 10 second period, which reduces load on the multicast router if a large number of receivers attach to an existing group within a small period of time. This feature is known as *proxy reporting* and is also used for maintaining group membership, which is discussed later in this scenario.

Removing a Receiver from a Group

Now that you understand how IGMP snooping works when receivers join a group, you need to understand that IGMP snooping must also detect when receivers leave a group, because multicast frames no longer need to be forwarded out the interface attached to the receiver that has just left the group. Figure 7-19 illustrates what happens when Router-B (the receiver) wants to leave the multicast group 239.1.1.1.

In Figure 7-19, the following events occur:

1 Router-B wants to leave the multicast group and sends an IGMP Leave Group message to the 224.0.0.2 (0100.5e00.0002) all multicast routers multicast address. This message includes the group that the receiver wants to leave.

2 Switch-B receives the IGMP Leave Group message and passes the message to the switch CPU, based upon the bridge table entry that forwards all IGMP multicast messages to the CPU. Switch-B then sends an IGMP Group-Specific Query message out the interface attached to the receiver (Fa0/4) that sent the Leave Group message to ensure that other receivers are not attached to the interface (this could happen if another switch or hub is connected to the interface, with receiver and other receivers connected to the remote switch or hub).

3 Because Router-B is directly attached to interface Fa0/4 and wants to leave the group, the Group-Specific Query sent by Switch-B is not answered. Switch-B can safely assume that no more receivers are attached to the interface and subsequently remove the interface from the egress port list for the multicast group.

4 At this point, Switch-B examines the egress port list for the multicast group to determine whether any non-router interfaces are still present. If there are still non-router interfaces in the egress port list, it means that receivers are connected to the LAN and the switch discards the original IGMP Leave Group message sent in Step 1. (The multicast router attached to the LAN does not need to receive this message because it still has receivers attached that it would unnecessarily try to determine whether or not to forward the Leave Group message to.) In Figure 7-19, because Router-B is the only receiver (and therefore, last receiver) on the LAN, only router interfaces remain in the egress port list for the group address, indicating to Switch-B that no more receivers are connected to the LAN. Because of this indication, Switch-B forwards the original Leave Group message sent in Step 1 to the multicast routers, which ensures that the multicast routers can prune the locally attached interface from the LAN off the multicast routing tree if applicable.

Notice that IGMP snooping is more intrusive (although still transparent to receivers) for the leave process. The IGMP snooping switch actually acts almost like a proxy, accepting Leave Group messages from receivers and then querying the receivers' interface. Consequently, the IGMP leave process is more efficient because the Leave Group messages are forwarded to multicast routers only if no more receivers are attached to the LAN.

NOTE   Some Cisco Catalyst switches support *IGMP fast-leave processing*, which means that the switch immediately removes the interface attached to a receiver upon reception of the Leave Group message (i.e., the Group-Specific Query sent in Step 2 of Figure 7-19 is not sent). This feature speeds up leave processing, but should only be used when receivers are directly attached to the switch.

Figure 7-19   *Removing Receivers Using IGMP Snooping*

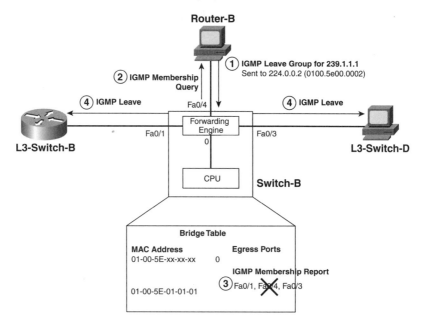

Maintaining Group Membership

Once a receiver has joined a multicast group, it must periodically indicate that it still wants to be a receiver for the group. The IGMP Querier (multicast router) for a LAN periodically sends IGMP General Query messages, every 60 seconds by default, and receivers attached to the LAN respond to the General Query with an IGMP Membership Report. If multiple receivers are attached to the LAN, once a Membership Report has been sent by one receiver for a multicast group, then all other receivers in the group suppress sending a Membership Report in response to the General Query, because one Membership Report message is sufficient to ensure the multicast router continues to forward multicast traffic onto the LAN.

The report suppression mechanism causes an issue for IGMP snooping switches because the switch needs to know which specific receivers are attached to the LAN, whereas a multicast router needs to know only that at least one receiver is attached to the LAN. The report suppression mechanism is designed for eliminating redundant membership report messages, but the result of the suppression is that IGMP snooping switches are not able to determine whether or not a receiver is still attached to a specific port, which in turn determines whether or not the port remains in the egress port list for a group address in the bridge table. You might argue that an IGMP snooping switch could simply maintain a receiver port in the egress port list for a group and remove the receiver port from the list when the receiver sends an IGMP Leave Group message. Although in theory this strategy might work, in reality, it is possible that a receiver might not get a chance to send a Leave Group message (due to the receiver being accidentally powered off or disconnected from the LAN). Also, only IGMPv2 receivers send Leave Group messages, so you still have a problem for IGMPv1 receivers.

To circumvent the issues just described that are introduced by the report suppression mechanism, Cisco Catalyst switches that implement IGMP snooping ensure that IGMP Membership Reports that are sent in response to IGMP General Queries are not heard by other receivers (i.e., each Membership Report is forwarded only to the switch CPU and not flooded to all ports that are specified in the egress port list for the group address). Consequently, every receiver on the LAN responds to the IGMP General Query because each receiver does not hear any other Membership Report messages. This process ensures the switch has an accurate picture of exactly which receivers are still attached to the LAN and can add, remove, or maintain the egress port list for group addresses in the bridge table appropriately.

Of course, the multicast router that sent the General Query message must receive at least one Membership Report response to ensure that the multicast router does not remove the interface attached to the LAN from outgoing interface list for the multicast group. Because a single response is sufficient to maintain the group state on multicast routers, Cisco Catalyst switches implement the proxy report feature, which ensures no more than one Membership Report is sent within a 10 second period in response to the General Query. This mechanism is the same one used when new receivers join an existing group.

IGMP Snooping Support on Cisco Catalyst Switches

Not all Cisco Catalyst switches support IGMP snooping. Table 7-3 lists the various Cisco Catalyst platforms and indicates whether or not IGMP snooping is supported and what minimum software is required.

Table 7-3 *IGMP Snooping Support on Cisco Catalyst Switches*

Platform	IGMP Snooping Supported	Minimum Software
Catalyst 1900/2820	No	—
Catalyst 2900XL/3500XL	No	—
Catalyst 2950/3550	Yes	All IOS Releases
Catalyst 4000 (Supervisor 1/2)	No	—
Catalyst 4000 (Supervisor 3/4)	Yes	All IOS Releases
Catalyst 5000/5500	Yes (Supervisor 2G/3G or Sup 3 with NFFC only)	CatOS 4.1
Catalyst 6000/6500	Yes	All CatOS Releases

Configuration Tasks

The configuration of IGMP snooping is very simple and consists of the following tasks:

- Enabling IGMP snooping
- Enabling IGMP fast-leave processing
- Enabling the IGMP Querier function

Enabling IGMP Snooping

By default, most recent CatOS and Cisco IOS software images that support IGMP snooping have the feature enabled by default. To enable IGMP snooping on CatOS, use the **set igmp enable** command:

```
Console> (enable) set igmp {enable | disable}
```

Example 7-36 demonstrates enabling IGMP snooping on Switch-C in Figure 7-6.

Example 7-36 *Enabling IGMP Snooping on Switch-C*

```
Switch-C> (enable) set igmp enable
IGMP Snooping is enabled.
```

Once you have enabled IGMP snooping, the switch starts listening to IGMP messages and updates its bridge table entries for multicast addresses dynamically. The switch also automatically learns about the multicast routers attached to each VLAN. On CatOS, you can use the **show multicast router** command to verify that the switch has automatically learned about all of the multicast routers attached to the switch, as demonstrated in Example 7-37 on Switch-C.

Example 7-37 *Verifying Multicast Router Information on Switch-C*

```
Switch-C> (enable) show multicast router
IGMP enabled

Port      Vlan
--------- ----------------
 2/1      1
 2/2      1

Total Number of Entries = 2
'*' - Configured
```

In Example 7-37, you can see that Switch-C has detected both L3-Switch-B and L3-Switch-C, which are connected to ports 2/2 and 2/1 respectively.

TIP   You can statically configure multicast router ports using the **set multicast router** command.

CatOS also provides the **show multicast group** command, which allows you to view information related to active multicast groups detected by the switch and has the following syntax:

```
Console> (enable) show multicast group [group-mac-address] [vlan-id]
```

Example 7-38 demonstrates the use of this command on Switch-C.

Example 7-38 *Verifying Multicast Group Information on Switch-C*

```
Switch-C> (enable) show multicast group
IGMP enabled

VLAN  Dest MAC/Route Des  Destination Ports or VCs / [Protocol Type]
----  ------------------  ------------------------------------------------------
1     01-00-5e-00-01-28   2/1-2
1     01-00-5E-01-01-01*  2/1-2,2/4

Total Number of Entries = 1
```

Notice in Example 7-38 that a single group address exists for the 239.1.1.1 group address (01-00-5E-01-01-01). The destination ports associated with this entry are indicated as ports 2/1, 2/2, and 2/4. Port 2/3 is correctly not included in the destination port list because no receivers are attached to this port.

TIP   The 01-00-5e-00-01-28 entry represents the 224.0.1.40 group, which is used for rendezvous point discovery and is automatically enabled on Catalyst 3550 Layer 3 switches.

To enable IGMP snooping on Cisco IOS, use the **ip igmp snooping** global configuration command:

```
Switch(config)# ip igmp snooping vlan vlan-id mrouter learn {cgmp | pim-dvmrp}
```

The **mrouter learn** keywords define how the switch learns about interfaces that are attached to multicast routers. If you choose the **cgmp** option, multicast router ports are determined by listening to CGMP packets sent from routers (CGMP is covered in the next section). If you choose the **pim-dvmrp** option, multicast router ports are determined by listening to IGMP, PIM, and DVMRP packets (this is the default learning method).

NOTE   Choosing the CGMP learning method just means that the switch determines where multicast routers are located on the LAN by listening to CGMP messages sent by multicast routers. It does not mean that the switch is configured to support full CGMP operation.

Example 7-39 demonstrates enabling IGMP snooping on Switch-B in Figure 7-6.

Example 7-39 *Enabling IGMP Snooping on Switch-B*

```
Switch-B# configure terminal
Switch-B(config)# ip igmp snooping vlan 1 mrouter learn pim-dvmrp
```

Notice that the multicast router learning mode is set to **pim-dvmrp**, which is required because L3-Switch-B and L3-Switch-D are PIM neighbors. Once you have enabled IGMP snooping, you should use the **show ip igmp snooping mrouter** command to verify that the switch has automatically learned about all of the multicast routers attached to the switch, as is demonstrated in Example 7-40 on Switch-C.

Example 7-40 *Verifying Multicast Router Information on Switch-B*

```
Switch-B# show ip igmp snooping mrouter
Vlan    ports

....    .....
   1    Fa0/1(dynamic)
   1    Fa0/2(dynamic)
```

In Example 7-40, you can see that Switch-B has detected both L3-Switch-C and L3-Switch-D, which are connected to interfaces Fa0/1 and Fa0/2 respectively. The "dynamic" text indicates that the switch has automatically learned the entries.

TIP   You can statically configure multicast router interfaces using the **ip igmp snooping vlan** *vlan-id* **mrouter interface** *interface-id* command.

Once you have verified the switch can see each multicast router, you can then verify that the appropriate interfaces are listed in the egress port list for the multicast group address in the bridge table. On Cisco IOS, this information can be verified by using the **show mac-address-table multicast** command, which allows you to view information related to active multicast groups detected by the switch. Example 7-41 demonstrates the use of this command on Switch-B.

Example 7-41 *Verifying Multicast Group Information on Switch-B*

```
Switch-B# show mac-address-table multicast
Vlan    Mac Address       Type       Ports
----    -----------       ----       -----
 1      0100.5e01.0101    IGMP       Fa0/1 Fa0/2 Fa0/3
```

Notice in Example 7-41 that a single group address exists for the 239.1.1.1 group address (01-00-5E-01-01-01). The destination ports associated with this entry are indicated as interfaces Fa0/1, Fa0/2, and Fa0/3. Interface Fa0/4 is correctly not included in the destination port list because no receivers are attached to this interface. The Type field indicates that the entry was learned dynamically via IGMP (compare with Example 7-35 which displayed a static entry).

TIP
You can use either the **mac-address-table static** *mac-address* **vlan** *vlan-id* **interface** *interface-id* global configuration command or the **ip igmp snooping vlan** *vlan-id* **static** *mac-address* **interface** *interface-id* command to statically associate a receiver with an interface.

Enabling IGMP Fast-Leave Processing

IGMP fast-leave processing modifies the default IGMP snooping process implemented on Cisco Catalyst switches when an IGMP Leave Group message is received from a receiver that wants to leave a multicast group. By default, Cisco Catalyst switches send an IGMP Group-Specific Query message out the interface upon which the Leave Group message was received to ensure that no other receivers are connected to the interface. If receivers are directly attached to the switch, there is no point in sending the membership query because the receiver wanting to leave is the only connected host.

NOTE
IGMP fast-Leave processing is also referred to as *immediate leave processing* on some Cisco Catalyst switches.

IGMP fast-leave processing caters to the situation where all receivers are directly attached to the switch and eliminates the IGMP Group-Specific Query message, allowing the switch to immediately remove an interface from the bridge table upon receiving the Leave Group message. This processing speeds up the overall leave process and also eliminates the CPU overhead of having to generate an IGMP Group-Specific Query message.

To enable fast-leave processing on CatOS, use the **set igmp fastleave enable** command, as shown in Example 7-42 on Switch-C.

Example 7-42 *Enabling IGMP Fast Leave on Switch-C*

```
Switch-C> (enable) set igmp fastleave enable
IGMP fastleave set to enable.
```

To enable fast-leave processing on Cisco IOS, use the **ip igmp snooping** global configuration command, as follows:

```
Switch(config)# ip igmp snooping vlan vlan-id immediate-leave
```

Notice that you must specify each VLAN that you want enable immediate leave processing for.

NOTE   Only use IGMP fast-leave processing if all receivers (ideally all hosts) are directly attached to the switch. IGMP fast-leave processing also works only with IGMPv2 receivers because IGMPv1 receivers don't sent Leave Group messages whatsoever.

Enabling the IGMP Querier Function

The IGMP implementation on Cisco Catalyst 6000/6500 switches also caters to a special situation where no multicast routers are present on the LAN, yet you have a source and receivers for multicast groups and want to constrain this traffic to just the ports attached to the receivers. Because no multicast routers are present on the LAN, no device is querying hosts via IGMP for the multicast groups that they want to receive (this is normally the function of a multicast router). In this scenario, a Cisco Catalyst 6000/6500 switch can be configured to act as an IGMP Querier for the LAN, ensuring that the switch can constrain multicast traffic correctly, based upon the information gathered via the IGMP query process.

NOTE   If multiple IGMP Querier-enabled Catalyst 6000/6500 switches reside on the LAN, the IGMP Querier for the LAN is chosen as the switch with the lowest IP address. If the switch becomes the active IGMP Querier for the LAN, it sends IGMP General Queries every 125 seconds.

The IGMP Querier feature is supported only on the Catalyst 6000/6500 switch, starting from CatOS 7.1. To enable the IGMP Querier, use the **set igmp querier** command, as follows:

```
Console> (enable) set igmp querier {enable | disable} vlan-id
```

Assume in Figure 7-6 that Switch-C (Catalyst 6500) has been disconnected from the rest of the network, but still has a source and receivers attached. Example 7-43 demonstrates how to enable the IGMP Querier function on VLAN 1 for Switch-B to ensure that multicast traffic within VLAN 1 can be constrained correctly.

Example 7-43 *Enabling the IGMP Querier Function on Switch-B*

```
Switch-B> (enable) set igmp querier enable 1
```

Scenario 7-5: Configuring Cisco Group Management Protocol (CGMP)

Cisco Group Management Protocol (*CGMP*), as the name suggests, is a proprietary protocol that is used to constrain multicast traffic on the LAN for networks that use Cisco routers and switches. In the previous scenario, you learned about IGMP snooping, where Cisco Catalyst switches monitor IGMP conversations between multicast routers and receivers, allowing a switch to dynamically determine the ports that frames with a specific multicast group address should be forwarded out. With IGMP snooping, multicast routers and receivers have no idea that a switch is monitoring IGMP traffic, so IGMP snooping is transparent to the multicast routers and receivers. Multicast routers see IGMP Membership Reports from receivers, and receivers see IGMP Queries generated by multicast routers—the fact that a switch might be monitoring the IGMP traffic between multicast routers and receivers is unbeknownst to either.

NOTE   IGMP snooping is not really transparent when it comes to the IGMP leave process. As indicated in Figure 7-19, if IGMP snooping is enabled on a Cisco Catalyst switch, a multicast router will not see IGMP Leave Group messages until the last receiver for a group leaves the LAN segment. This quality actually enhances the IGMP leave process, because multicast routers do not need to unnecessarily query the LAN for more receivers when a receiver leaves a group and there are still other receivers on the LAN for the group.

To implement IGMP snooping properly, switches must possess knowledge of the IGMP protocol and must be able to look at information located much deeper within IGMP frames than normal frames that the switch receives and forwards. Switches need to be able to forward frames at high speeds because the switches attach to high-speed LAN networks. Thus, switches that support IGMP snooping require more expensive hardware-based components such as IGMP-aware ASICs (as opposed to implementing IGMP snooping in software) to ensure that IGMP snooping does not have an effect on frame-forwarding performance.

CGMP provides an alternative approach to IGMP snooping and offloads much of the intelligence required to determine group membership at a Layer 2 level to the multicast routers attached to the LAN. For this reason, CGMP is supported on many earlier low-end Cisco switches, with IGMP snooping supported only on high-end or recent Cisco Catalyst switches that possess enhanced hardware that enables the intelligence required for IGMP snooping while maintaining the frame-forwarding performance of the switch.

NOTE   Although CGMP requires less switch intelligence and, therefore, offers a multicast traffic control solution for low-end switches, today's low-end switches possess enough intelligence to implement IGMP snooping at a low cost. Because IGMP snooping is essentially transparent to the rest of the network and works with any multicast routers that supports IGMP, it is considered superior in benefits over CGMP, and CGMP is considered a legacy protocol that should be implemented only where IGMP snooping is not supported. Proof of this concept is shown on the next-generation Catalyst 2950 and Catalyst 3550 switches, which support only IGMP snooping and do not support CGMP. That said, there are still major deployments of switches that support only CGMP (e.g., the Catalyst 4000 running CatOS), so it is important you understand CGMP.

CGMP Operation

CGMP takes quite a different approach to multicast traffic control from IGMP snooping. With CGMP, the intelligence required to determine the multicast groups present on a LAN segment and the receivers attached to the LAN is performed by CGMP-enabled multicast routers attached to the LAN (known as *CGMP servers*). Multicast routers already possess the required intelligence to a certain extent because they must be able to determine whether a Layer 3 subnet has receivers attached so that they can build the outgoing interface list for routes in the multicast route table. With CGMP enabled, multicast routers take this process one step further by transmitting host-specific group membership information to CGMP-enabled LAN switches (known as *CGMP clients*) using CGMP messages. Using this mechanism creates a communications channel between multicast routers and switches on the LAN, which is separate to normal IGMP communications. It also reduces the computational requirements for switches because they do not need to perform the logic required to determine multicast group membership. Instead this computation is performed by the multicast router and then transmitted to each switch, with switches simply updating bridge table information based upon the information received.

For example, when a receiver attaches to the LAN and sends an IGMP Membership Report message to a local multicast router, the multicast router performs normal IGMP operations, but also sends a CGMP message to the switch that indicates a new receiver exists for a group. Because the multicast router receives the IGMP Membership Report message as an IP packet within an Ethernet frame, the multicast router knows the MAC address of the receiver, which is the source MAC address of the Ethernet frame. The multicast router then sends a CGMP Join message to all switches on the LAN, which includes the multicast group address and the MAC address of the new receiver. The CGMP-enabled switches that receive the message then look up the egress port associated with the MAC address of the receiver and add that port to the egress port list for the group address.

CGMP communications are one-way in that CGMP servers (multicast routers) communicate information to CGMP clients (switches), but because CGMP operates separately to IGMP and is used purely to provide CGMP clients with receiver membership for each group, CGMP clients are not required to communicate with CGMP servers. CGMP servers communicate with CGMP clients using CGMP messages, which are sent to a special multicast Ethernet address of 01-00-0C-DD-DD-DD. CGMP messages are made up of the following fields:

- **Version**—1 or 2
- **Message Type**—Join or Leave
- **Count**—The number of multicast/unicast address pairs in the message
- **Group Destination Address (GDA)**—The MAC address of the multicast group address
- **Unicast Source Address (USA)**—The MAC address of the host that is joining or leaving the multicast group indicated by the GDA

Each CGMP message contains a pair of GDA and USA entries that define a specific host (USA) joining or leaving a specific multicast group (GDA). Table 7-4 shows the various combinations of GDA, USA, and Join/Leave fields and each combination's respective meaning.

Table 7-4 *CGMP Message Types*

GDA	USA	Message Type	Meaning
Group MAC	Host MAC	Join	Add receiver to group
Group MAC	Host MAC	Leave	Remove receiver from group
0000.0000.0000	Router MAC	Join	Assign router port
0000.0000.0000	Router MAC	Leave	Remove router port
Group MAC	0000.0000.0000	Leave	Delete Group
0000.0000.0000	0000.0000.0000	Leave	Delete all Groups

As you can see from Table 7-4, CGMP messages can be used to indicate several different events that are part of normal multicast operation. Important multicast events on the LAN include the following, which normally occur in the order specified:

- Assigning a router port
- Adding receivers to a group
- Removing receivers from a group
- Maintaining group membership

Each of these events and how CGMP communicates these events to CGMP-enabled switches is now examined in detail.

Assigning a Router Port

When a multicast router starts up that has CGMP enabled, the router generates a CGMP Join message with the GDA set to all zeroes and the USA set to the MAC address of the router. This message is multicast out all CGMP-enabled interfaces, ensuring all switches on the LANs the multicast router is attached to receive the message. Referring back to Figure 7-6, assume that L3-Switch-B and L3-Switch-C have just started up, with L3-Switch-B having CGMP configured on interfaces Fa0/3 and Fa0/4, and L3-Switch-C having CGMP configured on interface Fa0/3. This means that on the 10.5.0.0/16 subnet, two CGMP-enabled routers exist (L3-Switch-B and L3-Switch-C). On the 10.6.0.0/16 subnet, even though two multicast routers are attached (L3-Switch-B and L3-Switch-D), only L3-Switch-B is a CGMP-enabled router and, therefore, must communicate information on behalf of L3-Switch-D as well. Also, assume that Switch-B and Switch-C are both CGMP clients. Figure 7-20 demonstrates the process of L3-Switch-B and L3-Switch-C announcing their presence to Switch-C, and L3-Switch-B announcing its presence to Switch-B.

Figure 7-20   *Assigning a Router Port via CGMP*

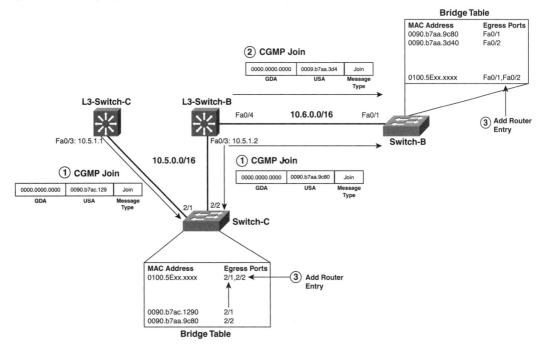

In Figure 7-20, the following events occur:

1 When L3-Switch-B and L3-Switch-C start up, they send a CGMP Join message out all interfaces that are enabled for CGMP. The CGMP Join message contains a GDA set to all zeroes and a USA of the router's own MAC address (e.g., 0090.b7aa.9c80 for L3-Switch-B). This message is intended to inform any connected switches of the multicast router's existence.

2 On the 10.6.0.0/16 subnet, L3-Switch-B is the only CGMP-enabled router and, for proper IGMP operation, needs to ensure that Switch-B knows about L3-Switch-D, which is another multicast router attached to Switch-B. Therefore, L3-Switch-B is configured as a *CGMP proxy*, which means that it will also send CGMP Joins on behalf of other multicast routers on the LAN that do not have CGMP enabled. In Figure 7-20, L3-Switch-B also sends a CGMP Router Join for L3-Switch-D, which informs Switch-B of the presence of L3-Switch-D.

NOTE   To perform the CGMP proxy function, a multicast router must be the IGMP Querier (DR) for the LAN. In IGMPv1, the IGMP Querier is elected via the multicast routing protocol (e.g., PIM), while in IGMPv2, the IGMP Querier is elected based upon the lowest IP addressed router on the LAN. Because all multicast routers in Figure 7-6 are configured for IGMPv2, L3-Switch-B is the IGMP Querier for the 10.6.0.0/16 subnet (because it has the lowest IP address on the subnet of 10.6.1.1) and, therefore, can act as a CGMP proxy.

---

3 Switch-B and Switch-C receive the CGMP Join messages on the 10.6.0.0/16 and 10.5.0.0/16 subnets, respectively. Each switch examines the GDA and USA, determines that the message indicates a CGMP router announcing itself, and ensures that the egress port associated with the router MAC address specified in the USA field (the egress port is determined by looking up the unicast entry for the router MAC address in the bridge table) is added to all future bridge table entries for multicast group addresses. For example, on Switch-C, the bridge table indicates that the MAC address of L3-Switch-B is reachable via port 2/2 and that L3-Switch-C is reachable via port 2/1. This means that any future multicast group entries in the bridge table include port 2/1 and port 2/2 in the egress port list.

The CGMP Router Join mechanism ensures that any new multicast group entries added to the bridge table (because receivers send Membership Reports to the new group addresses) contain the port or interface that attaches to each CGMP-enabled multicast router on the LAN. This process ensures that multicast routers always receive IGMP Membership Reports from receivers for groups in response to IGMP General Queries that are sent periodically as part of normal IGMP maintenance.

Adding Receivers to a Group

When receivers attach to the LAN and want to join a multicast group, they issue IGMP Membership Report messages, indicating the multicast group that they want to join. Once the multicast routers attached to the LAN receives these messages, they ensure the router interface that the Membership Report was received on is added to the multicast routing topology. If CGMP is enabled on the interface, the multicast router also sends a CGMP Join message out the interface to communicate the fact that a new receiver has joined a multicast group to all CGMP-enabled switches.

Figure 7-21 demonstrates this process on the 10.6.0.0/16 subnet of Figure 7-6, assuming Router-B (a receiver) has just attached to the network.

Figure 7-21 *Adding Receivers to a Group via CGMP*

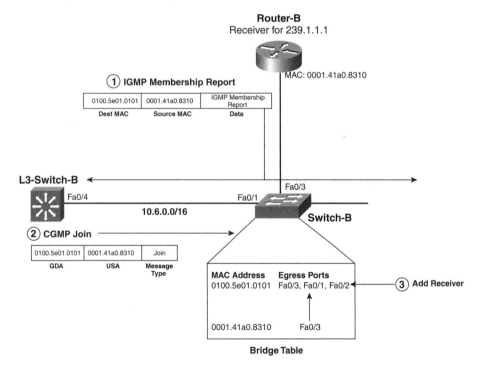

In Figure 7-21 the following events occur:

1 Router-B (a receiver for the 239.1.1.1 group) starts up and generates an IGMP Membership Report message to indicate that it wants to join the 239.1.1.1 group. This message is sent to the group multicast address at both the IP and Ethernet layers. The destination MAC address of the Membership Report is 0100.5e01.0101, which is the Ethernet group address for the 239.1.1.1 IP group address. Assuming that Router-B is

the first receiver on the LAN for the group, Switch-B does not have any bridge table entries for the group address and thus floods the Membership Report out all interfaces except the ingress interface.

2 L3-Switch-B receives the flooded Membership Report and ensures that interface Fa0/ 4 (attached to the LAN that Router-B is attached to) is in the outgoing interface for the (*,239.1.1.1) entry in the multicast routing table, as well as any (S,G) entries that include a group address of 239.1.1.1. Assuming CGMP is enabled on the interface, L3-Switch-B generates a CGMP Join message and sends this message out the interface the Membership Report was received on. The GDA of the CGMP Join message is copied from the destination MAC address of the IGMP Membership Report frame (0100.5e01.0101), and the USA is copied from the source MAC address of the IGMP Membership Report frame (0001.41a0.8310). The multicast router sends an IGMP Group-Specific Query to check if any hosts on the segment belong to multicast groups. This query indicates to all CGMP-enabled switches on the LAN that a new receiver with a MAC address of 0001.41a0.8310 has joined the multicast group with a MAC address of 0100.5e01.0101.

3 Switch-B receives the CGMP Join message and, assuming that this is the first receiver on the LAN for the group, creates a new entry in the bridge table for the group address indicated by the GDA of the message. All CGMP router interfaces (which are known to Switch-B based upon the process described in Figure 7-6) are added to the egress port list for the new bridge table entry. Switch-B also reads the USA of the message and searches the bridge table for the bridge table entry that matches the MAC address specified by the USA. Once this entry has been found, the egress port associated with the entry (i.e., the interface attached to Router-B) is added to the egress port list of the bridge table entry for the multicast group.

If subsequent receivers attach to the LAN for the multicast group, the same events as described in Figure 7-20 occur, except that Switch-B updates an existing bridge table entry for the multicast group, rather than creating a new bridge table entry.

NOTE   It is important to understand that when multiple CGMP-enabled routers are attached to a LAN segment, only the IGMP Querier (DR) sends CGMP Join messages for receivers that have joined a group. Consequently, on the 10.5.0.0/16 subnet of Figure 7-6, L3-Switch-C sends CGMP Join messages for attached receivers because L3-Switch-C is the IGMP Querier for this subnet (because IGMPv2 is being used and L3-Switch-C has the lowest IP address on this subnet). The same rule applies to CGMP Leave messages (discussed in the next section).

Removing Receivers from a Group

When receivers want to leave a group, they generate IGMP Leave Group messages. When a CGMP-enabled router receives these messages, it generates a CGMP Leave message and sends this to the LAN to which the receiver is attached to ensure that any CGMP-enabled switches can remove the appropriate port from the egress port list. This process is identical to the events illustrated in Figure 7-21. However, the IGMP Membership Report message is replaced with an IGMP Leave Group message that is addressed to the all multicast routers address (224.0.0.2), and the CGMP Join message is replaced with a CGMP Leave message. If the receiver that is leaving is not the last receiver on the LAN (i.e., other receivers are still attached), the CGMP Leave message specifies the following GDA and USA values:

- **GDA**—Multicast group address (e.g., 0100.5e01.0101 for the topology used in Figure 7-21)
- **USA**—MAC address of the leaving receiver (e.g., 0001.41a0.8310 for the topology used in Figure 7-21)

Each CGMP-enabled switch that receives the CGMP Leave message reads the GDA and USA and removes the interface associated with the USA from the egress port list for the GDA.

If the receiver that is leaving is the last receiver on the LAN, the CGMP Leave message includes the multicast group address in the GDA, but includes a USA value of all zeroes (0000.0000.0000), which indicates to all CGMP-enabled switches that there are no more receivers on the LAN and that the bridge table entry for the group address should be deleted from the bridge table.

CGMP Local Leave Processing

Later versions of CGMP on Cisco Catalyst switches include a feature known as *local leave processing*. This feature is similar to how leave processing is handled with IGMP snooping. When CGMP local leave is enabled, the switch intercepts any IGMP Leave Group messages that are received and then sends an IGMP General Query message out the port that the Leave Group message was received on. If no receivers for the group respond to the General Query, the switch knows that no more receivers for the group are attached to the port, and the port is removed from the egress port list of the bridge table entry for the group address. At this point, if other receivers are still attached to other ports on the switch for the group, the original IGMP Leave Group message is discarded and not forwarded to any multicast routers. However, if there are no more receivers for the group, the switch forwards the IGMP Leave Group message to all multicast routers to ensure that they can prune the LAN interface from the outgoing interface list in the multicast route table entry for the group.

NOTE   Just as with IGMP snooping, the benefits of local leave processing are realized only for IGMPv2 receivers, because IGMPv2 requires a receiver that wants to leave a group to send a Leave Group message to the 224.0.0.2 (0100.5e00.0002) all multicast routers address, which provides a distinct indication to the switch that a Leave Group message has been generated and the switch CPU should inspect the message. IGMPv1 receivers do not generate a message that indicates they want to leave a group. Rather, they just ignore IGMP General Queries sent by routers to ensure receivers are still active on a segment.

In more recent Cisco Catalyst switches, the CGMP local leave feature has been extended to include a fast leave feature, which is identical in function to the IGMP snooping fast leave feature. When fast leave is enabled, Cisco Catalyst switches do not send an IGMP General Query message out the port the Leave Group message was received on, instead assuming that the receiver wanting to leave a group is the only device attached to the switch port. Only enable CGMP fast leave processing if all receivers are directly attached to the switch.

Maintaining Group Membership

As discussed in the IGMP snooping scenario (Scenario 7-4), maintaining group membership is an important consideration for constraining multicast traffic on the LAN. The multicast router that performs the IGMP Querier role for the LAN sends General Query messages periodically to ensure that at least one receiver for every group previously active on the LAN is still active. Receivers use the report suppression mechanism if they hear other IGMP Membership Reports sent by other receivers in response to the General Query messages, which causes an issue for switches that need to know about all receivers attached to the switch.

With IGMP snooping, switches ensure that IGMP Membership Reports sent from receivers are not heard by any other receivers on the LAN, which solicits a response from all receivers, ensuring that the switch knows exactly which receivers are still active on the LAN. With CGMP, because this feature lacks a detailed understanding of IGMP, each CGMP-enabled switch simply relies on the multicast routers attached to the LAN to indicate when receivers have left a group. Unfortunately, using this mechanism to maintain group membership on a CGMP-enabled switch is not ideal in the following situations:

- When an IGMPv1 receiver leaves a group
- When an IGMPv2 receiver leaves a group without sending a Leave Group message

NOTE	The IGMPv2 specification, unfortunately, does not mandate that receivers must send an IGMP Leave Group message when a receiver wants to leave a group, instead recommending that an IGMP Leave Group should be sent. Consequently, some TCP/IP stacks might implement of IGMPv2 and not generate a Leave Group message when the receiver wants to leave a group.

In both of these situations, there is no way for the multicast router attached to a LAN to verify that the receiver has left a group. Hence, no CGMP Leave messages can be generated to indicate to a CGMP-enabled switch that an attached receiver has left a group. The switch continues to forward multicast traffic to receivers who have left the group in the situations just described. These ports cannot be cleared from the egress port list until the group as a whole is removed from the bridge table (i.e., no more receivers are on the LAN for a group).

CGMP and IGMP Snooping Interoperability

In some networks, due to hardware limitations, you might not be able to run IGMP snooping on all switches, which might create a special scenario where you might need to run CGMP on some switches and also run IGMP snooping in the same LAN.

Because CGMP operation relies on multicast routers generating CGMP Joins in response to IGMP Membership Reports sent from receivers, all IGMP Membership Reports must be seen by multicast routers to ensure the appropriate CGMP Joins are generated. IGMP snooping uses a proxy reporting mechanism, which means that not all IGMP Membership Report messages are sent to the multicast router if a group already exists. If CGMP-enabled switches exist in the network, proxy reporting must be disabled on the switches running IGMP snooping, which then ensures all Membership Reports are sent to the multicast router. Cisco Catalyst switches that are running IGMP snooping can detect CGMP messages and can detect that some switches in the network are running CGMP, because they see CGMP multicast messages sent by CGMP-enabled multicast routers. Each switch moves to a special IGMP-CGMP mode that automatically disables the proxy reporting, which ensures CGMP works correctly on the LAN.

CGMP Support on Cisco Catalyst Switches

It is important to understand that not all Cisco Catalyst switches support CGMP. Table 7-5 lists the various Cisco Catalyst platforms and indicates whether or not CGMP is supported and what minimum software is required. As you can see, CGMP is supported only on the older Cisco Catalyst switches, indicating that CGMP is considered a legacy protocol.

Table 7-5   *CGMP Support on Cisco Catalyst Switches*

Platform	CGMP Support	Minimum Software
Catalyst 1900/2820	No	—
Catalyst 2900XL/3500XL	Yes	All IOS Releases
Catalyst 2950/3550	No	—
Catalyst 4000 (Supervisor 1/2)	Yes	All CatOS Releases
Catalyst 4000 (Supervisor 3/4)	No	—
Catalyst 5000/5500	Yes	All CatOS Releases
Catalyst 6000/6500	No	—

Configuration Tasks

The configuration of CGMP consists of the following tasks, which are both required to ensure CGMP operation works correctly:

- Configuring CGMP on a Cisco multicast router
- Configuring CGMP on a Cisco switch

This scenario uses the topology of Figure 7-6, and referring to Table 7-5, you can see that none of the switches in Figure 7-6 actually support CGMP. For this scenario, assume that Switch-C is a Catalyst 4000 switch running CatOS and that Switch-B is a Catalyst 3500XL switch running Cisco IOS (both of these switches support CGMP). The configuration of CGMP on the 10.5.0.0/16 and 10.6.0.0/16 subnets are demonstrated.

Configuring CGMP on a Cisco Multicast Router

CGMP operation on a multicast router (referred to as a *CGMP Server*) is supported from Cisco IOS version 11.1(2) onwards in all IOS features sets and is supported on all current Cisco router platforms. CGMP Server operation is also supported on Cisco Catalyst Layer 3 Switches, such as the Catalyst 3550, Catalyst 4000/4500 with Supervisor 3/4, and native IOS Catalyst 6000/6500.

To enable CGMP on a multicast router, you simply need to enable it on each routed LAN interface that has CGMP-enabled switches attached, which on Cisco Catalyst Layer 3 switches means any physical routed interface or SVI that connects to a VLAN that has CGMP-enabled switches attached.

NOTE   Each interface that you want to enable CGMP on must have PIM enabled.

To enable CGMP on a routed LAN interface that has PIM enabled, use the **ip cgmp** interface configuration command:

```
Router(config-if)# ip cgmp [proxy | router-only]
```

The optional **proxy** keyword indicates that the multicast router should generate CGMP Join messages not only for all receivers attached to the LAN and itself, but also for any other non-CGMP multicast routers on the LAN. This feature is known as CGMP proxy and can be configured only on the IGMP Querier (DR) for the LAN.

The **router-only** keyword indicates that the multicast router should generate CGMP Join messages only for itself and other non-CGMP multicast routers on the LAN, *without* generating CGMP Join messages for receivers on the LAN. This mode of operation is required if you want to use CGMP as the router learning mechanism for IGMP snooping, because the multicast router generates a CGMP Join messages only for itself.

Example 7-44 demonstrates configuring CGMP on L3-Switch-C in Figure 7-6 for the interface attached to the 10.5.0.0/16 subnet.

Example 7-44 *Enabling CGMP on L3-Switch-C*

```
L3-Switch-C# configure terminal
L3-Switch-C(config)# interface range FastEthernet0/3
L3-Switch-C(config-if-range)# ip cgmp proxy
```

Example 7-45 demonstrates configuring CGMP on L3-Switch-B in Figure 7-6 for the interfaces attached to the 10.5.0.0/16 and 10.6.0.0/16 subnets, assuming that on the 10.6.0.0/16 subnet L3-Switch-D is not configured to support CGMP.

Example 7-45 *Enabling CGMP on L3-Switch-B*

```
L3-Switch-B# configure terminal
L3-Switch-B(config)# interface FastEthernet0/3
L3-Switch-B(config-if)# ip cgmp
L3-Switch-B(config-if)# exit
L3-Switch-B(config)# interface FastEthernet0/4
L3-Switch-B(config-if)# ip cgmp proxy
```

Notice in Example 7-44 that the CGMP proxy feature has been enabled only on interface FastEthernet0/4 and not interface FastEthernet0/3. The CGMP proxy feature is not required on the 10.5.0.0/16 subnet (attached to interface FastEthernet0/3 on L3-Switch-B), because L3-Switch-C is also configured for CGMP on this subnet.

On the 10.6.0.0/16 subnet, however, L3-Switch-D is not configured for CGMP; hence, L3-Switch-B must be configured as a CGMP proxy. Because L3-Switch-B has the lowest IP address (10.6.1.1) on the 10.6.0.0/16 subnet, it becomes the IGMP Querier and the CGMP proxy feature works.

Configuring CGMP on a Cisco Switch

Once you have enabled CGMP on all multicast routers on a LAN, or enabled CGMP on at least one multicast router with the CGMP proxy feature configured, you must next enable CGMP on all switches in the LAN. Cisco Catalyst switches operate as CGMP clients, meaning that they are the Layer 2 devices that receive receiver information from multicast routers (CGMP servers).

To enable or disable CGMP on a CatOS switch, use the **set cgmp** command as follows:

```
Console> (enable) set cgmp {enable | disable}
```

By default, CGMP support is disabled. You can also configure CGMP leave and fast leave processing as follows:

```
Console> (enable) set cgmp {leave [enable | disable]} |
  {fastleave [enable | disable]}
```

The **leave** keyword enables the CGMP leave processing feature, while the **fastleave** keyword enables the CGMP fast leave feature. Example 7-46 demonstrates enabling CGMP on Switch-C (a Catalyst 4000 switch for this scenario) in Figure 7-6 and also enabling the CGMP fast leave feature.

Example 7-46 *Enabling CGMP on a CatOS Switch*

```
Switch-C > (enable) set cgmp enable
CGMP support for IP multicast enabled.
Switch-C > (enable) set cgmp fastleave enable
CGMP fastleave processing enabled.
```

Once you have enabled CGMP, you should verify that the switch can see the multicast routers attached to the LAN. Example 7-47 demonstrates the **show multicast router cgmp** command, which is used to display all multicast routers that have been learned via CGMP router joins.

Example 7-47 *Displaying Multicast Routers Learned via CGMP on CatOS*

```
Switch-C> (enable) show multicast router cgmp
Port      Vlan
--------- ----------------
 2/1       1
 2/2       1

Total Number of Entries = 2
'*' - Configured
'+' - RGMP-capable
```

Notice that both L3-Switch-B (connected to port 2/2) and L3-Switch-C (connected to port 2/1) have been learned, because CGMP is configured on both switches.

After verifying that the switch can see all multicast routers on the LAN, you should next verify that the correct receiver information is being reported for each group. Example 7-48 demonstrates using the **show multicast group** command on Switch-C.

Example 7-48 *Verifying Multicast Group Information Learned via CGMP on CatOS*

```
Switch-C> (enable) show multicast group
VLAN  Dest MAC/Route Des     [CoS]  Destination Ports or VCs / [Protocol Type]
----  ------------------     -----  ------------------------------------------
1     01-00-5e-00-01-28             2/1-2
1     01-00-5e-01-01-01             2/1-2,2/4

Total Number of Entries = 1
```

In Example 7-48, you can see that the switch has a multicast group entry for 01-00-5e-01-01-01, which is the Ethernet multicast address for the 239.1.1.1 group. Notice that port 2/3 is not included in the destination port list because no receivers are attached to that port.

NOTE   The 01-00-5e-00-01-28 entry represents the 224.0.1.40 group, which is used for RP discovery and is automatically enabled on Catalyst 3550 Layer 3 switches.

On Cisco IOS-based Catalyst switches that support CGMP, such as the Catalyst 2900XL/3500XL, CGMP support is enabled by default, with the CGMP fast leave feature disabled by default. If you want to enable CGMP fast leave, use the **cgmp leave-processing** global configuration command.

```
Switch(config)# cgmp leave-processing
```

Cisco IOS also allows you to tune a parameter called the *CGMP router hold-time*, which is the number of seconds the switch waits before removing a router entry after a CGMP Router Leave message has been received. Once a router entry is aged out, all groups associated with that router are also removed. By default this parameter is configured as 400 seconds; however, you can tune this parameter if you want to accelerate the removal of expired group information by using the **cgmp holdtime** global configuration command:

```
Switch(config)# cgmp holdtime seconds
```

Example 7-49 demonstrates configuring CGMP fast leave and modifying the CGMP router hold-time on Switch-B (a Catalyst 3500XL switch for this scenario).

Example 7-49 *Enabling CGMP Fast Leave and Modifying CGMP Router Hold-Time on Cisco IOS*

```
Switch-B# configure terminal
Switch-B(config)# cgmp leave-processing
Switch-B(config)# cgmp holdtime 60
```

In Example 7-49, remember that CGMP is enabled by default on Cisco IOS switches, so you don't need to explicitly enable CGMP. The CGMP router hold-time has been altered to 60 seconds to allow faster aging out of group information associated with CGMP routers that have send CGMP router leave messages.

Once you have configured CGMP on Cisco IOS switches, you should verify that CGMP is working correctly. On Cisco IOS, you can use the **show cgmp** command to view all CGMP router and group information, as demonstrated on Switch-B in Example 7-50.

Example 7-50 *Verifying CGMP on Cisco IOS*

```
Switch-B# show cgmp

CGMP is running.
CGMP Fast Leave is running.
CGMP Allow reserved address to join GDA.
Default router timeout is 60 sec.

vLAN    IGMP MAC Address    Interfaces
------  ----------------    -----------
     1  0100.5e01.0028      Fa0/1, Fa0/2
     1  0100.5e01.0101      Fa0/1, Fa0/2, Fa0/3


vLAN    IGMP Router         Expire    Interface
------  ----------------    --------  -----------
     1  0090.b7aa.9c80      191 sec   Fa0/1
     1  0009.b7aa.3d40      191 sec   Fa0/2
```

In Example 7-49, you can see that Switch-C knows about both L3-Switch-C and L3-Switch-D, as indicated by the last two shaded lines of the output. The CGMP proxy configuration on L3-Switch-B has ensured that L3-Switch-D is also advertised as a multicast router via CGMP. You can also see that a multicast group entry exists for 0100.5e01.0101, with the appropriate interfaces listed (Fa0/1, Fa0/2, Fa0/3) for multicast forwarding.

Summary

Due to the growing requirement for networks to support multimedia applications that must transmit the same video and voice information to many people, the need for multicast traffic has arisen. Multicast traffic provides one-to-many delivery, unlike one-to-one (unicast) and one-to-all (broadcast) traffic types. Multicast traffic control allows you to control where a multicast transmission is flooded. Ideally you want this transmission flooded only to receivers that have subscribed to the multicast.

To enable multicast on your network, you must support multicast at both the Layer 2 and Layer 3 level. From a Layer 3 perspective, a multicast network determines which router interfaces (segments) a multicast should be forwarded to. Multicast routing topologies are used to build the Layer 3 paths over which multicast traffic flows. PIM is an example of a common multicast routing protocol used today. It operates in three modes:

- PIM dense mode
- PIM sparse mode
- PIM sparse-dense mode

PIM dense mode uses a flood and prune mechanism to build SPTs between a source and receivers. PIM sparse mode uses a combination of shared trees and SPTs to eventually build an SPT between a source and receivers, without requiring the flooding mechanism used by PIM dense mode operation. A key component of PIM sparse mode is the RP, which is where all shared trees are rooted. PIM sparse-dense mode allows PIM routers to use PIM sparse mode when an RP is known for a group or PIM dense mode when no RP is known for a group. PIM sparse-dense mode enables RP discovery protocols, such as Auto-RP, by using PIM dense mode for Auto-RP messages, ensuring all multicast routers receive RP information.

Once a multicast leaves routers to transit a LAN segment, the multicast router has no control over the multicast. Instead of flooding the multicast out all ports on a switch, you can limit the multicast transmission to only hosts that are receivers of a particular group. The following dynamic mechanisms exist for controlling multicast traffic on the LAN:

- IGMP snooping
- CGMP

IGMP snooping works by having the switch inspect IGMP traffic sent between a multicast router and receiving hosts. IGMP is the protocol used to maintain multicast group membership. By understanding which hosts belong to a particular group, the switch can flood the multicast group traffic only to those hosts.

CGMP (proprietary) works by having a multicast router relay IGMP messages to a LAN switch in a CGMP message. The multicast router provides notification of router and host joins and leaves.

## CHAPTER 8

Traffic Filtering and Security

Network security is a topic that grows in importance every day. With an increased reliance on business-to-business and business-to-consumer communication, secure Internet connectivity has become mission critical for many organizations. For these companies, an Internet security breach can cause embarrassment, loss of consumer confidence, and ultimately fiscal loss.

When it comes to network security, one of the most neglected network devices is the switch. Organizations often enforce strict security policies on routers and firewalls, yet fail to recognize the dangers of leaving a switch unsecured. The switch is the most accessible device in your network, and often, it unwittingly provides unauthorized access to your network.

NOTE   It is a common misconception that most network security breaches occur from an external party (e.g., a hacker on the Internet). In fact, most breaches occur from an internal party (e.g., a disgruntled employee).

Review of the following topics can help you secure your switched network infrastructure.

- Securing management access
- Securing network access
- Traffic filtering

Securing Management Access

Cisco networking devices provide rich management access capabilities that give the network administrator powerful configuration and diagnostics tools.

The most common form of management access to a Cisco networking device is via an *EXEC session*. An EXEC session is similar to a UNIX shell and is accessible via Telnet, secure shell, or the console port. Cisco devices also support management via Simple

Network Management Protocol (SNMP) and Hypertext Transfer Protocol (HTTP). Figure 8-1 illustrates the various management interfaces and how they interact with a Cisco switch.

Figure 8-1   *Cisco Management Interfaces*

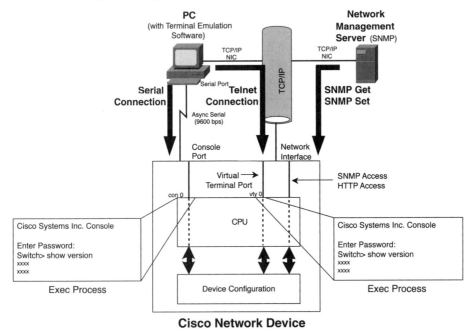

The first step to securing your switching infrastructure is to secure the switch's management interfaces. Next, you should implement techniques that improve the overall security of the switch.

The following switch security techniques are available:

*   Configuring authentication, authorization, and accounting (AAA)
*   Restricting management access
*   Using secure management protocols
*   Reducing other vulnerabilities

Configuring Authentication, Authorization, and Accounting (AAA)

The default authentication policy on a Cisco CatOS switch is extremely lax. Cisco IOS-based switches are slightly more secure by default, but the security of both platforms can be significantly improved. Table 8-1 shows the default authentication methods for accessing a CatOS and IOS switch.

Table 8-1   *Default Authentication Procedures*

Platform	Access Type	User EXEC Mode	Privileged EXEC Mode
CatOS	Console	None	Blank Password
	Telnet	Blank Password	Blank Password
IOS	Console	None	None
	Telnet	Password Required	Password Required

Table 8-1 represents the *access policy* for obtaining management access to the switch. Since default passwords should never be used in a production environment, the first thing you should do is configure passwords for all access methods (e.g., console, Telnet) and then configure an enable secret to protect privileged access.

You can further secure switch management access through the implementation of the techniques detailed in Table 8-2.

Table 8-2   *Techniques To Secure Switch Management Access*

Technique	Description
Local user authentication	Provides a per-user username and password, which can eliminate the need to share the enable secret, and adds username information to relevant log entries (e.g., configuration changes). The primary disadvantage of this technique is a lack of centralized account management. On CatOS, local user authentication is in CatOS 7.5.
Lockout parameters (CatOS only)	This feature disables access to a switch when a number of failed login attempts have occurred. This is meant to thwart brute force login attacks.
Privilege levels (IOS only)	Ranging from 0 to 15, 16 privilege levels exist. By default 1 is the user EXEC mode, and 15 is privileged EXEC mode. Commands can be assigned to each privilege level, which are then secured with a level specific enable secret.
Login banners (CatOS and IOS)	Login banners provide a means to communicate with anyone attempting to access a device. Typically these are used to inform visitors of their unwelcome status.
Session timeouts (CatOS and IOS)	Simply used to disconnect idle EXEC sessions.
Centralized AAA (CatOS and IOS)	Provides centralized user account management and accounting. Requires a TACACS+ or RADIUS server.

Restricting Management Access

In most networks, only a select handful of people need management access to switches. CatOS and Cisco IOS allow you to restrict which hosts can establish management sessions based on the source IP address.

Figure 8-2 illustrates restricting management access.

Figure 8-2 *Restricting Management Access*

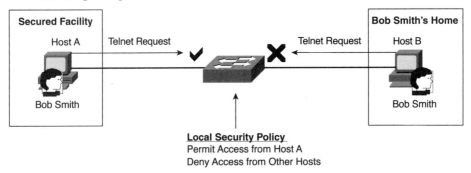

Through the use of permit lists on CatOS and access classes on IOS, management sessions can be controlled on a source IP address basis for the following protocols:

- Telnet
- Secure shell
- SNMP
- HTTP

Using Secure Management Protocols

In previous sections, we discussed secure access control mechanisms. Most of the time, management access is remote, which means that management communications are passed through the network. These communications could contain sensitive information, such as username/password combinations or device configuration information. If your management communications are transmitted in clear text, it is possible for other parties on the network to eavesdrop on your management session, gleaning sensitive information such as a username/password pair. To circumvent this issue, you need to employ secure management protocols that protect the confidentiality of your management session.

Table 8-3 details the secure management protocols available on CatOS and IOS devices.

Table 8-3 *The Secure Management Protocols Available on CatOS and IOS Devices*

Protocol	Description
Secure shell	Provides encrypted Telnet-like terminal emulation to remote network devices. Secure shell client software and an SSH-enabled IOS or CatOS image is required.
SNMPv3	SNMPv3 greatly improves on the security of SNMP versions 1 and 2c by providing message confidentiality, authentication, and integrity. SNMPv3 is not in widespread use and device support is very limited.

Reducing Other Vulnerabilities

So far we have discussed switch access methods and protocols; now you can leverage a few other configuration tips to protect against some of the less common security vulnerabilities.

- **Password encryption**—Cisco IOS enables you to encrypt all passwords in the configuration file. This type of encryption is not secure and is meant only to prevent casual onlookers from learning passwords.

TIP   Don't rely on password encryption used in conjunction with the standard enable password, because many tools available can decrypt the encrypted password.

- **Enable secret**—Cisco IOS can use two types of enable passwords, known as the enable password and enable secret. The enable password uses a weak algorithm that can easily be decrypted. The enable secret, however, uses MD5, a one-way encryption algorithm that greatly increases password security.
- **Disabling unnecessary services**—Various services are enabled by default that might not be required on your network. An example of this is the *Cisco Discovery Protocol (CDP)*, which multicasts information about Cisco devices. Since CDP is a very valuable troubleshooting tool, it is common practice to disable CDP only on interfaces connecting to untrusted or insecure networks.

Securing Network Access

Once you have secured your switch, you are now ready to configure it to enforce your organization's security policy. Cisco Catalyst switches provide the security features aimed at securing network access found in Table 8-4.

Table 8-4   *Cisco Catalyst Switch Security Features Aimed at Securing Network Access*

Feature	Description
Port security	Binds a specific MAC address or group of addresses to a particular switch port. Configured on a per-port basis and disables the port if an unauthorized MAC address is seen.
VLAN membership policy server	Uses a central database to bind a MAC address to a specific VLAN. This awkward technology has many restrictions and does not enjoy widespread success.
802.1x	Based on the Extensible Authentication Protocol (EAP), 802.1x provides user-level authentication of devices wanting to connect to the network. RADIUS is used to authenticate users against a centrally managed user database.

Traffic Filtering

Traffic filtering has traditionally been used on routers and firewalls to enforce access control policies. Most traffic filtering is performed at Layer 3 and Layer 4; hence, traffic filtering on switches (traditionally being Layer 2 devices) is a relatively new practice. With the importance of security and quality of service, switches need extra intelligence to provide the features that enable end-to-end security and quality of service.

NOTE   Support for these features varies by platform. For up to date feature support information, use the Feature Navigator at www.cisco.com/go/fn (CCO registration required).

Table 8-5 details the available traffic filtering features.

Table 8-5   *Available Traffic Filtering Features*

Feature	Description
Protocol filtering (CatOS only)	Filters Layer 2 frames based on Layer 3 protocol. Can explicitly permit or deny IP, IPX, and Group (includes AppleTalk and DECnet). Can automatically filter the protocols not in use on each switch port.

Table 8-5   *Available Traffic Filtering Features (Continued)*

Feature	Description
VLAN access control lists (Catalyst 6500 with CatOS only)	Applies IP- or MAC-based access control lists to a VLAN. The applied VLAN access control list (VACL) is used to filter traffic bridged within the VLAN, as well as traffic routed into the VLAN.
VLAN maps (Catalyst 3550 and 6500 with IOS)	Provides identical functionality to VACLs but with a different name.
Port-based access control lists (Catalyst 2950, 3550 and Cat6K with Supervisor 720)	On a Layer 2 port, Ccan filter inbound Layer 2 frames using MAC addresses as well as IP packets based on Layer 3 and Layer 4 information.
Routed access control lists	Identical to access control lists implemented on Cisco routers, these can be used on SVI and physical routed interfaces on Cisco Catalyst Layer 3 switches.
Private VLANs	Creates the idea of hierarchical VLANs with restricted Layer 2 connectivity. Promiscuous ports can communicate with any port in the VLAN, community ports can talk with any port in the same community and any promiscuous ports, and isolated ports can talk only with promiscuous ports.

Scenario 8-1: Securing the Management Interface

In this scenario, you secure both a CatOS-based switch and an IOS-based switch. By securing each switch, you are not only reducing their vulnerabilities, but also increasing the security of the entire network.

Scenario Exercise

Figure 8-3 illustrates the scenario topology used for Scenarios 8-1, 8-2, and 8-3. Corporation XYZ requires their existing switches to be secured using best practices. They are also about to acquire a larger corporation and need to add new switches to the network. The Corporation XYZ CIO has specified that the current network must be secured, to ensure the new network maintains a tight security policy.

Figure 8-3   *Scenarios 8-1, 8-2, and 8-3 Topology*

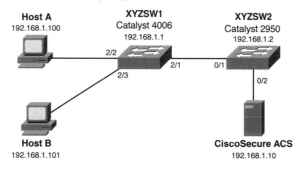

A Catalyst 4006 (XYZSW1) provides access for Hosts A and B. Host A is a dedicated network administration workstation that is used to manage the network. Host B is a user's PC, and should not be allowed management access to any network devices. A Catalyst 2950 (XYZSW2) provides connectivity to the company servers, including a recently installed CiscoSecure asynchronous communications server (ACS). Both switches are interconnected by a single Fast Ethernet trunk.

Scenario Objectives

The scenario objectives are as follows:

- Configure local user-level authentication (Cisco IOS only)
- Configure a lockout policy (CatOS only)
- Configure a login banner
- Configure session timeouts
- Configure local authorization (Cisco IOS only)
- Restrict management access
- Enable SSH support (CatOS only)

Equipment Needed

The equipment needed is as follows:

- The workstations and servers in the diagram recommended set up and installed as per the scenario diagram
- One CatOS and one IOS switch

Command Syntax

This covers the following:

- Securing a CatOS Switch
- Securing a Cisco IOS Switch
- The following sections describe the commands used for each part of the scenario

CatOS Command Syntax

The following new CatOS commands are introduced in this scenario:

- **set authentication**
- **set banner motd**
- **set logout**

- **set ip permit**
- **set crypto key rsa**

The **set authentication** Command Syntax

Login authentication is configured using the **set authentication login** command. You can also control access to privileged configuration mode (enable mode) separately by using the **set authentication enable** command.

You can individually specify the maximum number of unsuccessful login or enable attempts using the following syntax:

```
set authentication {login | enable} attempt maximum_attempts [console | telnet]
```

Once the maximum number of attempts is reached, you can define a lockout policy by using the following syntax:

```
set authentication {login | enable} lockout time [console | telnet]
```

The time parameter is configurable between 30 and 600 seconds, with a value of 0 disabling any lockout; 0 is the default configuration.

NOTE   Unlike a console lockout, which completely blocks console access, a Telnet lockout blocks only the IP address from which the login attempts failed.

The **set banner motd** Command Syntax

You configure a login banner on CatOS using the **set banner motd** command, as shown in Example 8-1.

Example 8-1   *Configuring a Banner on CatOS*

```
Switch (enable) set banner motd #
*********************************
* Unauthorized access prohibited *
*********************************
#
MOTD banner set
```

Notice the use of the # character as a delimiter, which allows you to enter a banner as free text until you terminate the input with the same delimiter. The delimiter can be any character, as long as it does not appear in the desired banner.

The **set logout** Command Syntax

The **set logout** command controls how long a session (e.g., a console or Telnet session) can remain idle before being disconnected by the system:

```
set logout timeout
```

The *timeout* parameter is specified in minutes and is configurable from 0 (no timeout) to 10000 minutes. The default setting is 20 minutes.

The **set ip permit** Command Syntax

The **set ip permit** command restricts management access for Telnet, SSH, and SNMP on CatOS. All restrictions are controlled by the **set ip permit** command. You must initially specify which hosts are to be permitted management access:

```
set ip permit ip-address [mask] [telnet | ssh | snmp | all]
```

You can specify network address ranges by configuring the optional *mask* parameter and you can specify different access policies based upon each management access protocol (e.g., Telnet or SNMP).

Once you have defined your permitted hosts, you then need to enable the permit list:

```
set ip permit enable [telnet | ssh | snmp | all]
```

You can selectively enable the permit list based upon management protocol, or you can enable all permit lists.

The **set crypto key rsa** Command Syntax

To enable SSH support, you must create a public/private key pair on the switch using the following syntax:

```
set crypto key rsa nbits
```

The argument *nbits* is used to specify the length of the key in bits; valid values are from 512 to 2048. Once this key pair has been created, you are able to connect to the switch using a SSH client.

Cisco IOS Command Syntax

The following new Cisco IOS commands are introduced in this scenario:

- The **username** command
- The **login local** command
- The **banner** command
- The **exec-timeout** command
- The **privilege** command
- The **access-class** command

The **username** Command and **login local** Command Syntax

When enabling user-level authentication, the first step is to create user accounts for each user that requires access to the switch. This is achieved by executing the **username** global configuration command:

username *name* **password** *secret*

Next you need to configure each management interface to use local authentication. This is achieved by executing the **login local** line configuration command, as shown in Example 8-2.

Example 8-2 *Enabling Local User-Level Authentication*

```
Switch(config)# line con 0
Switch(config-line)# login local
Switch(config-line)# line vty 0 4
Switch(config-line)# login local
```

In Example 8-2, both the console and vty ports are configured to use the local user account database to authenticate users.

The **banner** Command Syntax

You configure a login banner on Cisco IOS using the **banner motd** global configuration command, as shown in Example 8-3.

Example 8-3 *Configuring a Banner on Cisco IOS*

```
Switch(config)# banner motd #
**********************************
* Unauthorized access prohibited *
**********************************
#
```

Notice the use of the # character as a delimiter, which allows you to enter a banner as free text until you terminate the input with the same delimiter.

It is also possible to display other banners by using one of the arguments to the **banner** global configuration command listed in Table 8-6.

Table 8-6 *Arguments to the **banner** Global Configuration Command*

Argument	Description
exec	Displayed when an exec session is created
incoming	Displayed when a reverse Telnet session is established through a router
login	Displayed after the message of the day (MOTD) but before the username and password prompt

The **exec-timeout** Command Syntax

The **exec-timeout** command is used to control how long a session (e.g., a console or telnet session) can remain idle before being disconnected by the switch. The command is applied in line configuration mode as shown in Example 8-4.

Example 8-4   *Configuring Session Timeouts on Cisco IOS*

```
Switch(config)# line con 0
Switch(config-line)# exec-timeout 20 30
```

The first numeric parameter of the **exec-timeout** command specifies the number of minutes, while the second numeric parameter specifies the number of seconds. In Example 8-4, the console idle session timeout is set to 20 minutes and 30 seconds.

The **privilege** Command Syntax

The **privilege** global configuration mode command is used to define custom, local authorization levels for Cisco IOS commands. You can assign a particular command (or set of commands) to a particular privilege level using the following syntax:

```
privilege {configure | exec | interface} level privilege-level command
```

You must specify which configuration mode the command exists in (e.g., configure, exec, interface); indicate the desired privilege level; and then specify the command you want to assign. You can replace the **level** *privilege-level* portion with the **reset** keyword to reset the command to its default privilege level.

Once you have assigned the appropriate commands to the privilege level, you must now create an enable password for the new privilege level. This is configured by using the **enable password** or **enable secret** (recommended) command:

```
enable secret level privilege-level secret
```

To access the new privilege level, a user simply appends the desired privilege level when executing the **enable** command in user mode as shown in Example 8-5.

Example 8-5   *Accessing a Custom Privilege Level*

```
Switch> enable 10
Password: ********
Switch#
```

By adding the level to the **enable** command (e.g., **enable 10**), the desired level is accessed rather than the default enable mode (level 15).

TIP   If you access a higher privilege level, you can use any commands specified in lower privilege levels. When creating privilege levels, it is a good idea to simulate all the commands a user would execute and then add them to the privilege level. Don't forget commands such as **configure terminal** and **exit**.

The **access-class** Command Syntax

The **access-class** line configuration command is used to apply access lists to management interfaces such as vty ports. To restrict Telnet and SSH access, you first create a simple access list that defines the source addresses of authorized hosts and then apply that access list to the management interface (e.g., line vty 0 4), as shown in Example 8-6. SSH connections are treated as coming in via the virtual terminal (vty) ports and, hence, are configured identically.

Example 8-6 *Restricting Telnet and SSH Access on Cisco IOS*

```
Switch(config)# access-list 1 permit 192.168.1.0 0.0.0.255
Switch(config)# line vty 0 4
Switch(config-line)# access-class 1 in
```

In Example 8-6, only hosts on the 192.168.1.0/24 subnet are able to access the switch via Telnet or SSH. You must bind the access list that defines the source hosts to the vty ports using the **access-class** command.

Configuration Tasks

In this scenario, you perform the following tasks:

- Step 1—Preparing the switches
- Step 2—Securing the Catalyst OS switch (XYZSW1)
- Step 3—Securing the Cisco IOS switch (XYZSW2)

Step 1—Preparing the Switches

In this step you:

- Configure the system name and management IP address
- Interconnect each switch and ensure ping connectivity
- Provide connectivity for Hosts A, B, and the AAA server

Configuring the System name and Management IP Address

On each switch, ensure you can access the switch via the console port.

Step 1   On XYZSW1, configure system name, Telnet/enable password of "cisco" and an IP address of 192.168.1.1/24, as shown in Example 8-7.

Example 8-7   *Configuring Basic Parameters on XYZSW1*

```
Console enable
Enter password:
Console (enable) set system name XYZSW1
System name set.
XYZSW1 (enable) set password
Enter old password: *****
Enter new password: *****
Retype new password: *****
Password changed.
XYZSW1 (enable) set enablepass
Enter old password: *****
Enter new password: *****
Retype new password: *****
Password changed.
XYZSW1 (enable) set interface sc0 192.168.1.1 255.255.255.0
```

Step 2   On XYZSW2 configure system name, Telnet/enable password of *cisco* and an IP address of 192.168.1.2/24, as shown in Example 8-8.

Example 8-8   *Configuring Basic Parameters on XYZSW2*

```
Switch> enable
Password:
Switch# configure terminal
Switch(config)# hostname XYZSW2
XYZSW2(config)# enable secret cisco
XYZSW2(config)# line vty 0 4
XYZSW2(config-line)# password cisco
XYZSW2(config-line)# login
XYZSW2(config-line)# interface VLAN1
XYZSW2(config-if)# ip address 192.168.1.2 255.255.255.0
XYZSW2(config-if)# end
XYZSW2# copy running-config startup-config
Building configuration...
[OK]
```

Interconnecting the switches

For this scenario you interconnect the switches using crossover unshielded twisted-pair (UTP) cables between Fast Ethernet 802.1Q trunk ports (you can use gigabit Ethernet trunks if you have these). Refer to Figure 8-1 for port assignments.

Step 1   On XYZSW1, configure 100 Mbps speed and full duplex on port 2/1 and enable trunking using 802.1Q, as shown in Example 8-9.

Example 8-9   *Configuring Trunks on XYZSW1*

```
XYZSW1> (enable) set port speed 2/1 100
Port 2/1 transmission speed set to 100Mbps.
XYZSW1> (enable) set port duplex 2/1 full
Port 2/1 to full-duplex.
XYZSW1> (enable) set trunk 2/1 on dot1q
Port(s)  2/1 trunk mode set to on.
Port(s)  2/1 trunk type set to dot1q.
```

Step 2   On XYZSW2, configure 100 Mbps speed and full duplex on port 0/1 and enable trunking using 802.1Q, as show in Example 8-10.

Example 8-10   *Configuring Trunks on XYZSW2*

```
XYZSW2# configure terminal
XYZSW2(config)# interface fastEthernet0/1
XYZSW2(config-if)# no shutdown
XYZSW2(config-if)# speed 100
XYZSW2(config-if)# duplex full
XYZSW2(config-if)# switchport mode trunk
XYZSW2(config-if)# switchport trunk encapsulation dot1q
XYZSW2(config-if)# end
XYZSW2# copy running-config startup-config
Building configuration...
[OK]
```

Once these configurations are complete, wait for at least 50 seconds to allow the spanning-tree state of the trunk ports to transition to forwarding.

Step 3   Verify you are able to ping XYZSW1 from XYZSW2 as shown in Example 8-11.

Example 8-11   *Verifying ping Connectivity Between XYZSW1 and XYZSW2*

```
XYZSW1> (enable) ping 192.168.1.2
!!!!!
```

Connecting the Hosts and AAA Server

Ensure all hosts are configured with an IP address, as shown in Figure 8-3. Then, connect each host as shown in Figure 8-3 to the appropriate switch and port.

Step 1   On XYZSW1, configure 100 Mbps speed, full duplex, and spanning-tree PortFast for ports 2/2 and 2/3 as shown in Example 8-12.

Example 8-12   *Configuring Access Ports on XYZSW1*

```
XYZSW1> (enable) set port speed 2/2-3 100
Ports 2/2-3 transmission speed set to 100Mbps.
XYZSW1> (enable) set port duplex 2/2-3 full
Port(s)  2/2-3 to full-duplex.
XYZSW1> (enable) set spantree portfast 2/2-3 enable
Warning: Spantree port fast start should only be enabled on ports connected
to a single host.  Connecting hubs, concentrators, switches, bridges, etc. to
a fast start port can cause temporary spanning tree loops.  Use with caution.
Spantree ports 2/2-3 fast start enabled.
```

Step 2   On XYZSW2, configure 100 Mbps speed and full duplex for port 0/2, as shown in Example 8-13.

Example 8-13   *Configuring Access Ports on XYZSW2*

```
XYZSW2# configure terminal
XYZSW2(config)# interface fastEthernet0/2
XYZSW2(config-if)# no shutdown
XYZSW2(config-if)# speed 100
XYZSW2(config-if)# duplex full
XYZSW2(config-if)# switchport mode access
XYZSW2# copy running-config startup-config
Building configuration...
[OK]
```

Step 3   Ensure that all devices in the network (switches, hosts, servers) can ping each other, as shown in Example 8-14.

Example 8-14   *Verifying ping Connectivity Between XYZSW1 and Hosts A, B, and the AAA Server*

```
XYZSW1> (enable) ping 192.168.1.10
!!!!!
XYZSW1> (enable) ping 192.168.1.100
!!!!!
XYZSW1> (enable) ping 192.168.1.101
!!!!!
```

Step 2—Securing the Catalyst OS Switch (XYZSW1)

On XYZSW1, you now perform minor security configurations to enhance the security of Telnet and console access to XYZSW1. In this step you:

- Set banner, lockout, and session Timeout Parameters
- Restrict Telnet and SNMP access
- Enable SSH support

Setting Banner, Lockout, and Session Timeout Parameters

Step 1   On XYZSW1, configure a banner that is displayed at each login prompt, as shown in Example 8-15.

Example 8-15   *Configuring a Banner on XYZSW1*

```
XYZSW1> (enable) set banner motd #
************************************
*              WARNING             *
* Unauthorized access prohibited   *
************************************
#
```

Step 2   On XYZSW1, configure a maximum of three unsuccessful login attempts for Telnet access and five for console access, and set a lockout of 180 seconds for Telnet access and 300 seconds for console access. Also configure a maximum of three unsuccessful enable mode login attempts for all modes of access, with a lockout of 300 seconds, as shown in Example 8-16. You also need to set the idle session timeout to be 5 minutes.

Example 8-16   *Configuring Lockout Policy on XYZSW1*

```
XYZSW1> (enable) set authentication login attempt 3 telnet
Login authentication attempts for telnet set to 3.
XYZSW1> (enable) set authentication login attempt 5 console
Login authentication attempts for console set to 5.
XYZSW1> (enable) set authentication login lockout 180 telnet
Login lockout time for telnet set to 180.
XYZSW1> (enable) set authentication login lockout 300 console
Login lockout time for console set to 300.
XYZSW1> (enable) set authentication enable attempt 3
Enable mode authentication attempts for console and telnet logins set to 3.
XYZSW1> (enable) set authentication enable lockout 300
Enable mode lockout time for console and telnet logins set to 300.
XYZSW1> (enable) set logout 5
Sessions will be automatically logged out after 5 minutes of idle time.
```

Restricting Telnet Access on XYZSW1

For this scenario, you permit Telnet access only from Host A (192.168.1.100), SNMP access from an SNMP management system at 192.168.1.20, and block Telnet access from all other hosts for both switches.

Step 1   On XYZSW1, add Host A (192.168.1.100) to the Telnet permit list and add 192.168.1.20 to the SNMP permit list, as shown in Example 8-17.

Example 8-17   *Creating Telnet and SNMP Permit Lists on XYZSW1*

```
XYZSW1> (enable) set ip permit 192.168.1.100 telnet
192.168.1.100 added to Telnet permit list.
XYZSW1> (enable) set ip permit 192.168.1.20 snmp
192.168.1.20 added to Snmp permit list.
```

Step 2   On XYZSW1, enable the Telnet and SNMP permit lists, as shown in Example 8-18.

Example 8-18   *Enabling Telnet and SNMP Permit Lists on XYZSW1*

```
XYZSW1 (enable) set ip permit enable telnet
Telnet permit list enabled.
XYZSW1 (enable) set ip permit enable snmp
SNMP permit list enabled.
```

Step 3   Verify that you now cannot Telnet to XYZSW1 from Host B. Next verify the permit lists on XYZSW1, as shown in Example 8-19.

Example 8-19   *Verifying Telnet and SNMP Permit Lists on XYZSW1*

```
XYZSW1> (enable) show ip permit
  Telnet permit list enabled.
  Ssh permit list disabled.
  Snmp permit list enabled.
Permit List        Mask                 Access-Type
---------------    ----------------     -------------
192.168.1.20                            snmp
192.168.1.100                           telnet
Denied IP Address Last Accessed Time Type
192.168.1.101     01/30/02,03:13:44  Telnet
```

As you can see, the Telnet and SNMP permit lists are enabled, and the switch has logged the unauthorized Telnet connection attempt from Host B. Example 8-20 shows what a denied host receives when trying to Telnet to XYZSW1.

Example 8-20   *Denied Telnet Connection*

```
C:\>telnet 192.168.1.100
Connecting To 192.168.1.100...
Access not permitted.  Closing connection...
Connection to host lost.
C:\>
```

Enabling SSH Support

For this section, you enable SSH support and then disable Telnet access to XYZSW1.

Step 1   On XYZSW1, generate a 1024-bit RSA public/private key pair as shown in Example 8-21.

Example 8-21   *Generating an RSA Key Pair on XYZSW1*

```
XYZSW1> (enable) set crypto key rsa 1024
Generating RSA keys.... [OK]
```

Step 2   On XYZSW1, configure an IP permit list for SSH access, allowing only Host A (192.168.1.100) to connect via SSH. Then enable the IP permit list (for SSH) as shown in Example 8-22.

Example 8-22   *Configure an IP Permit List for SSH on XYZSW1*

```
XYZSW1> (enable) set ip permit 192.168.1.100 ssh
192.168.1.100 added to Ssh permit list.
XYZSW1> (enable) set ip permit enable ssh
SSH permit list enabled.
```

Step 3   On XYZSW1, verify the creation of the RSA keys, shown below as Example 8-23.

Example 8-23   *show crypto key on XYZSW1*

```
XYZSW1> (enable) show crypto key
```

Step 3—Securing the Cisco IOS Switch (XYZSW2)

On XYZSW2, you now perform minor security configurations to enhance the security of Telnet and console access to XYZSW2. In this step you:

- Set banner, lockout, and session timeout parameters
- Restrict Telnet and SNMP access
- Configure privilege levels to provide command authorization

Setting Banner, Lockout, and Session Timeout Parameters

Step 1   On XYZSW2, configure a banner that is displayed at each login prompt, as shown in Example 8-24.

Example 8-24   *Configuring a Banner on XYZSW2*

```
XYZSW2(config)# banner motd #
Enter TEXT message.  End with the character '#'.
***********************************
```

continues

Example 8-24   *Configuring a Banner on XYZSW2 (Continued)*

```
*              WARNING              *
* Unauthorized access prohibited  *
***********************************
#
```

Step 2   On XYZSW2, configure the idle session timeout to be 5 minutes for all management ports, as shown in Example 8-25.

Example 8-25   *Configuring Idle Session Timeouts on XYZSW2*

```
XYZSW2(config)# line vty 0 4
XYZSW2(config-line)# exec-timeout 5 0
XYZSW2(config-line)# line con 0
XYZSW2(config-line)# exec-timeout 5 0
XYZSW2(config-line)# end
```

Restricting Telnet Access on XYZSW2

In this section, you permit Telnet access only from Host A (192.168.1.100), SNMP access from an SNMP management system at 192.168.1.20, and block Telnet access from all other hosts.

Step 1   On XYZSW2, create two simple access lists to allow only the source IP address of Host A and the SNMP manager, as shown in Example 8-26.

Example 8-26   *Creating Access Lists on XYZSW2*

```
XYZSW2(config)# access-list 1 permit host 192.168.1.100
XYZSW2(config)# access-list 2 permit host 192.168.1.20
```

Step 2   On XYZSW2, configure the vty lines (Telnet management interfaces) to restrict management access based on the first access list you created in Step 1, as shown in Example 8-27.

Example 8-27   *Restricting Telnet Access on XYZSW2*

```
XYZSW2(config)# line vty 0 4
XYZSW2(config-line)# access-class 1 in
```

Step 3   On XYZSW2, configure the SNMP read-only and read-write community strings to be accepted only from the hosts specified in the second access list you created in Step 1, as shown in Example 8-28.

Example 8-28   *Restricting SNMP Access on XYZSW2*

```
XYZSW2(config)# snmp-server community cisco123 ro 2
XYZSW2(config)# snmp-server community cisco321 rw 2
```

Step 4   Verify that you can connect to XYZSW2 only via Telnet from Host A and cannot connect from Host B (see Example 8-29).

Example 8-29   *Failed Telnet to XYWSW2 from Host B*

```
C:\>telnet 192.168.1.2
Connecting To 192.168.1.2...Could not open a connection to host: Connect failed
C:\>
```

Configuring Privilege Levels to Provide Command Authorization

For this section, you configure privilege levels that allow network operators to view the system configuration and allow the operator to add a description to an interface.

The following commands are added to a custom privilege level; then a password is assigned to allow operators to gain access to the command set:

- **show running-config** (exec mode)
- **configure terminal** (exec mode)
- **interface** (global configuration mode)
- **description** (interface configuration mode)

Step 1   On XYZSW2, add the appropriate commands to a custom privilege level of 5, as shown in Example 8-30.

Example 8-30   *Assigning Commands to a Custom Privilege Leve*

```
XYZSW2(config)# privilege exec level 5 configure terminal
XYZSW2(config)# privilege exec level 5 show running-config
XYZSW2(config)# privilege configure level 5 interface
XYZSW2(config)# privilege interface level 5 description
```

Be sure that you understand the configuration mode (e.g., global configuration or exec) of the commands that you want to add.

Step 2   On XYZSW2, configure an enable secret password for the custom privilege level, as shown in Example 8-31.

Example 8-31   *Configuring an Enable Secret for a Custom Privilege Level*

```
XYZSW2(config)# enable secret level 5 cisco123
```

In Example 8-31, a password of "cisco123" is assigned to privilege level 5.

Step 3   Test your new privilege level by connecting to the switch via Telnet and
logging into the new privilege level. Try all the permitted commands, as
well as non-permitted commands (e.g., **erase**), as shown in Example 8-32.

Example 8-32 *Testing Custom Privilege Levels*

```
User Access Verification

Password: ******
XYZSW2> enable 5
Password:
XYZSW2# show running-config
Building configuration...

Current configuration:
interface FastEthernet0/1
...
...
XYZSW2# configure terminal
XYZSW2(config)# interface fastEthernet0/1
XYZSW2(config-if)# description TESTING
XYZSW2(config-if)# end
XYZSW2# erase flash
              ^
% Invalid input detected at '^' marker.
```

In Example 8-32, you access the custom privilege level by using the **enable 5** command.
Notice that you can execute all the required commands, but when you try to execute an
unauthorized command (e.g., **erase**), IOS notifies you that the command is invalid.

Scenario 8-2: Enhancing Security by Using AAA

In this scenario, you secure both a Catalyst CatOS-based switch and an IOS-based switch.
In doing so, you increase the security of each device and consequently the network. This
exercise builds on the previous scenarios by including the configuration of AAA.

Scenario Exercise

Figure 8-3 illustrates the topology used for this scenario. Corporation XYZ requires their
existing switches to be secured using best practices. Corporation XYZ is about to acquire
a larger corporation and needs to add new switches to the network. A new CiscoSecure ACS
3.2 server has been installed to allow Corporation XYZ to evaluate the use of both
TACACS+ and RADIUS to provide a suitable access control model. It is through the
configuration of AAA that the ACS server can be used.

Scenario Objectives

The scenario objectives are as follows:

- Configure security server support
- Configure AAA authentication
- Configure AAA authorization
- Configure AAA accounting

Additional Equipment Needed

Building on the previous scenario, only the following additional equipment is required to complete the following steps:

- A server with CiscoSecure ACS v3.2 software installed. CiscoSecure ACS software requires Windows 2000 Server with Service Pack 3 installed and Internet Explorer 6.0 SP1.

Scenario Planning

Planning AAA can seem reasonably complex at first, with many options available for authentication, authorization, and accounting. Many AAA configuration options are designed towards Point-to-Point Protocol (PPP) access (such as dial-up access to an Internet service provider, ISP), so the number of options that you actually need to secure network devices is reduced.

The first step in configuring any AAA services is to establish a relationship with a security server on the network. The TACACS+ and RADIUS security server protocols require the IP address of the security server and a shared secret key (password) be defined on the switch. The security server must also be configured with the IP address of the switch and must share the same shared secret key to successfully communicate. Once you have configured security server support, you are ready to complete the implementation of AAA.

Planning Authentication

The following services can be authenticated on both CatOS and IOS:

- **Login**—This refers to a user attempting to initially login to the switch via Telnet or the console.
- **Enable**—This refers to a user attempting to login to enable mode on the switch via Telnet or the console.

For example, login access is required to establish a user mode connection to a switch, while enable access is required to establish privileged access to the switch.

Planning Authorization

The following services can be authorized on both CatOS and Cisco IOS:

- **Exec**—This refers to a user attempting to start an *exec* process. An exec process is basically the shell (or command-line interface (CLI)) you use to input commands from a console or Telnet connection.

- **Enable (CatOS only)**—This refers to a user attempting to access privileged mode (enable mode). This occurs when a user executes the **enable** command in user mode.

- **Commands**—All commands that are executed can be authorized by the security server. This allows restricted use of dangerous commands such as **erase** or **copy**.

Authorization requires that a user be authenticated so that the switch can query the security server with a username and type of service required.

Planning Accounting

The following events can be accounted for on both CatOS and Cisco IOS:

- **Exec**—Records are generated for each exec process (e.g., console or telnet session) and include the user who invoked the process and the duration of the session.

- **System**—Records are generated every time a non-user system event occurs (such as a system reset).

- **Command**—Records are generated every time a command is issued. This enables you to see exactly what a user did during their exec session

- **Connect**—Records are generated every time a user running an exec session attempts a connection (such as Telnet or rlogin) to a remote device.

When you configure accounting, you also specify when to create accounting records. The following options are available:

- **Start-Stop**—Records are generated at both the start and completion of each event.

- **Stop-Only**—Records are generated at the completion of each event.

- **Wait-Start (Cisco IOS only)**—Records are generated at both the start and completion of each event. However, the switch does not allow the service to commence until an accounting acknowledgement is received from the security server.

NOTE   Wait-Start should be used with great caution. For example, if Wait-Start is configured for EXEC sessions, you will not be able to log on to the network device if the AAA server is unavailable for any reason.

Command Syntax

The following sections describe the commands used for CatOS and Cisco IOS in this scenario.

CatOS Command Syntax

The following new CatOS commands are introduced in this scenario:

- The **set radius** command
- The **set tacacs** command
- The **set authentication** command
- The **set authorization** command
- The **set accounting** command

The set radius Command Syntax

The **set radius server** command is used to define the IP address of a RADIUS server:

```
set radius server ip-address [auth-port port] [acct-port port] [primary]
```

The **auth-port** and **acct-port** keywords specify the server User Datagram Protocol (UDP) ports that should be used for authentication and accounting communications (the various RADIUS products available differ; by default, ports 1812 and 1813 are used). If you specify the **primary** keyword and have multiple RADIUS servers defined, then this RADIUS server is contacted first. You can have up to three RADIUS servers defined. You must also specify a RADIUS secret key by using the **set radius key** command:

```
set radius key secret
```

This command sets the RADIUS key for *all* configured RADIUS servers.

The **set tacacs** Command Syntax

The **set tacacs server** command is used to define the IP address of a TACACS+ server:

```
set tacacs server ip-address [primary]
```

The **primary** keyword specifies that this TACACS+ server should always contacted first if multiple TACACS+ servers are defined. You can have up to three TACACS+ servers configured. You must also specify a TACACS+ secret key by using the **set tacacs key** command:

```
set tacacs key secret
```

This command sets the TACACS+ key for all configured TACACS+ servers.

The **set authentication** Command Syntax

To configure authentication, you use the **set authentication** command:

```
set authentication {login | enable} {radius | tacacs | kerberos}
   enable [all | console | telnet | http] [primary]
```

You can specify the authentication method for either login authentication (access to exec mode) or enable authentication (access to privileged configuration mode). You then specify the use of RADIUS or TACACS+ and can apply the configuration to whichever management interfaces you require. The **primary** keyword is used when you have multiple authentication methods (e.g., using TACACS+ and RADIUS simultaneously), and you want to specify which authentication method is attempted first. You can also disable local authentication by using the following command:

```
set authentication {login | enable} local disable
   [console | telnet | http | all]
```

WARNING Be careful when disabling local authentication. If you disable local authentication for every management interface, if your security server is down you will be unable to access the switch. A common practice is to disable local authentication for Telnet access, but leave it enabled for console access.

The set authorization Command Syntax

To configure authorization, you use the **set authorization** command. To configure authorization for exec mode and/or enable mode access use the following syntax:

```
set authorization {enable | exec} enable option fallback
   [both | console | telnet]
```

The *option* parameter specifies which security server protocol to use. Because RADIUS authorization is integrated with the authentication process, only tacacs is a valid option here. The fallback parameter specifies what action you should take if communication with the TACACS+ server fails (for example, you can specify **none**, meaning the service requested is granted if the TACACS+ server is down). Valid fallback options are **tacacs+**, **deny**, **if-authenticated**, and **none**.

To configure authorization for commands that can be executed use the following syntax:

```
set authorization commands enable {config | enable | all}
   option fallback [both | console | telnet]
```

Using the **config** parameter limits command authorization to configuration commands only (i.e., **show** commands do not need to be authorized).

The **set accounting** Command Syntax

To configure accounting, you use the **set accounting** command. To configure accounting for connect, exec, and system events, use the following syntax:

```
set accounting {connect | exec | system} enable
   {start-stop | stop-only} {tacacs+ | radius}
```

To configure accounting for *command* events, use the following syntax:

```
set accounting commands {config | enable | all} [stop-only] tacacs+
```

Notice that your only security server protocol option is **tacacs+**, because RADIUS does not support command authorization and accounting.

Cisco IOS Command Syntax

The following new Cisco commands are introduced in this scenario:

- The **radius-server** command
- The **tacacs-server** command
- The **aaa authentication** command
- The **aaa authorization** command
- The **aaa accounting** command

The **radius-server** Command Syntax

Before configuring RADIUS support, you must enable AAA by using the **aaa new-model** global configuration mode command:

```
aaa new-model
```

The **radius-server** global configuration command can then be used to configure the IP address of the RADIUS server:

```
radius-server host ip-address [auth-port port] [acct-port port] [key secret]
```

If you do not specify a key using the optional **key** keyword, you must specify a RADIUS secret key by using the **radius-server key** global configuration command, as shown here:

```
radius-server key secret
```

This command sets the RADIUS key for all RADIUS servers defined (unless a host has a specific key configured via the **radius-server host** command).

The **tacacs-server** Command Syntax

The **tacacs-server** global configuration command is used to define the IP address of a TACACS+ server:

```
tacacs-server host ip-address
```

You must also specify a TACACS+ secret key by using the **tacacs-server key** global configuration command:

```
tacacs-server key secret
```

This command sets the TACACS+ key for all configured TACACS+ servers. The key can optionally be configured on a per-server basis using the **key** parameter to the **tacacs-server host** global configuration command.

The **aaa authentication** Command Syntax

Before configuring AAA on Cisco IOS, you must enable AAA support explicitly using the **aaa new-model** command:

```
aaa new-model
```

To configure authentication for login (exec) access, you use the **aaa authentication login** global configuration command:

```
aaa authentication login {default | list} method1 [method2..]
```

The preceding command creates a profile that can be applied to different interfaces (e.g., a console port), allowing you to create different policies for different access methods. The **default** keyword specifies the default login authentication profile that is used for all management interfaces. You can specify multiple methods of authentication (e.g., RADIUS, TACACS+, line, none). To use a custom profile that you have created, you must bind the profile to the management interface that you want to control. The **login authentication** line configuration mode command is used to bind a profile to a management interface, as shown in Example 8-33.

Example 8-33   *Creating and Applying an AAA Authentication Profile*

```
Switch(config)# aaa authentication login PROFILE-A radius line
Switch(config)# line con 0
Switch(config-line)# login authentication PROFILE-A
```

In Example 8-33, an AAA authentication profile is created called PROFILE-A that uses RADIUS authentication as its primary method, and line authentication (i.e., the password assigned to the line to which access is being attempted) is used if the configured RADIUS server is down. The profile is then bound to the console port, meaning this profile is applied when access is attempted from the console port.

WARNING   When you enable AAA by using the **aaa new-model** command, the default method of login authentication for Telnet access is to use the local method. The local method requires users to be defined locally using the **username** command. If no users are defined when you turn on AAA, you will be unable to gain Telnet access to the switch. A good rule of thumb is to set the default authentication method as the line method, which uses the line password (e.g., the vty password) as the default mechanism.

To configure authentication for enable mode access, you use the **aaa authentication enable** global configuration command:

```
aaa authentication enable default method1 [method2..]
```

You can create only a single (the default) enable authentication profile, and you do not need to bind this to any management interface because enable mode access is independent from a management interface.

The **aaa authorization** Command Syntax

To configure authorization, you use the **aaa authorization** global configuration command:

```
aaa authorization {network | exec | commands level} {default | list}
    method1 [method2..]
```

Similar to authentication, the preceding command creates a profile that can be applied to different interfaces. You can control authorization for either exec access (i.e., starting a command session on the switch), or you can control authorization for commands entered at a specific privilege level. Example 8-34 shows a sample AAA authorization configuration:

Example 8-34   *Creating and Applying an AAA Authorization Profile*

```
Switch(config)# aaa authorization exec PROFILE-EXEC radius none
Switch(config)# line vty 0 4
Switch(config-line)# authorization exec PROFILE-EXEC
```

In Example 8-34, an AAA authorization profile called PROFILE-EXEC is created that authorizes exec access using RADIUS. If the RADIUS server is down, the switch permits the access as indicated by the use of the **none** keyword.

TIP

When configuring both AAA authentication and authorization, it is good practice to configure backup methods, as shown in Example 8-34. It is important to understand that these methods are invoked only if the primary security server is down. If the primary security server rejects a request, the switch rejects the requested access (and does not try the second method).

The **aaa accounting** Command Syntax

To configure *accounting*, you use the **aaa accounting** global configuration command:

```
aaa accounting {network | exec | connection | system | commands level}
    {default | list} {start-stop | stop-only | wait-start}
    method1 [method2..]
```

Similar to both authentication and authorization, the preceding command creates a profile that can be applied to different interfaces. You can specify accounting for exec, connection, system, or command events. You can also control when the accounting events are created.

Configuration Tasks

In this scenario, you perform the following tasks:

- Step 1—Configuring the CiscoSecure server for AAA support
- Step 2—Configuring each switch for AAA support
- Step 3—Confirming your AAA configuration

Step 1—Configuring the CiscoSecure Server for AAA Support

This scenario assumes that you have installed CiscoSecure ACS and performed preliminary switch configurations from Scenario 8-1. CiscoSecure ACS 3.2 must be installed on a Windows 2000 Server.

Once you have installed CiscoSecure ACS, you need to create an AAA client definition for each switch and then create user accounts for network administrators.

Step 1   Start the web-based CiscoSecure administration application by opening the URL *http://127.0.0.1:2002* from the ACS server.

Step 2   Click on the *Network Configuration* button and click on the *Add Entry* button, as shown in Figure 8-4.

Figure 8-4   *Creating an AAA Client*

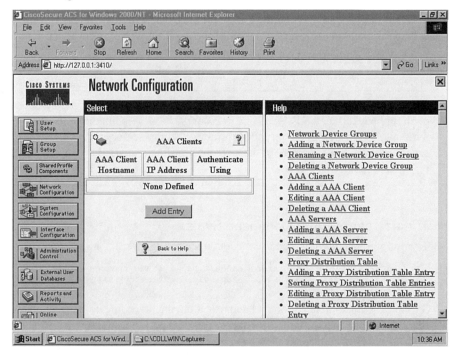

Step 3   Enter the appropriate parameters for XYZSW1, using a secret key of *cisco123* and ensuring *RADIUS (Cisco IOS/PIX)* is selected as the authentication protocol. Once complete, click the Submit + Restart button, as shown in Figure 8-5.

Figure 8-5   *Creating an AAA Client*

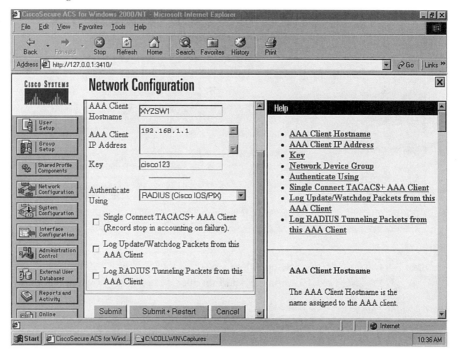

Step 4   Repeat Steps 2 and 3 for XYZSW2, except ensure that TACACS+ is selected as the authentication protocol. The AAA Client list should now contain entries for both XYZSW1 and XYZSW2, as shown in Figure 8-6.

Figure 8-6 *Verifying AAA Clients*

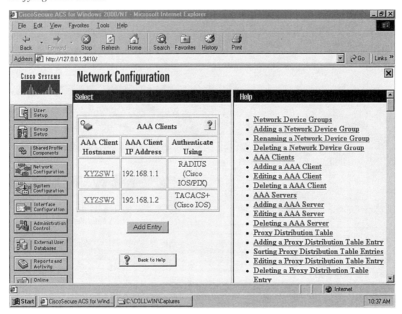

Step 5 Click on the User Setup button, and enter the username "administrator" in the User field. Click on the Add/Edit once complete as shown in Figure 8-7.

Figure 8-7 *Creating a User*

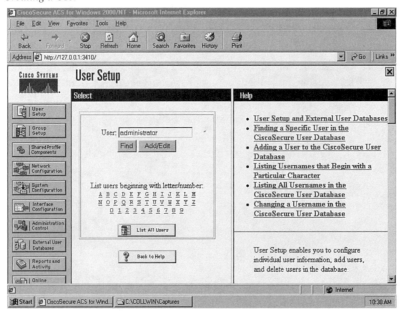

Step 6   In the User Setup page, scroll down to the Password Authentication section, configure a password of "password," and then click the *Submit* button as shown in Figure 8-8.

Figure 8-8   *Configuring a User Password*

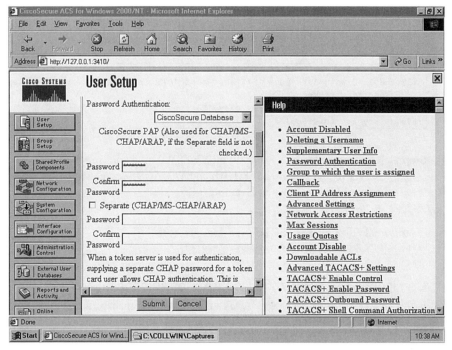

Step 2—Configuring Each Switch for AAA Support

In this section, you configure each switch to use AAA. The following actions are required:

- Configuring the appropriate security server protocol support
- Configuring each switch to use AAA for authentication
- Configuring each switch to use AAA for management access authorization
- Configuring each switch to use AAA for management access accounting

Configuring the Appropriate Security Server Protocol Support

In this section, you configure both RADIUS (on XYZSW1) and TACACS+ (on XYZSW2) support.

Step 1 Configure RADIUS support on XYZSW1 by specifying the RADIUS server IP address (192.168.1.10) and RADIUS server secret key (cisco123), as shown in Example 8-35.

Example 8-35 *Configuring RADIUS Support on XYZSW1*

```
XYZSW1> (enable) set radius server 192.168.1.10
192.168.1.10 with auth-port 1812 acct-port 1813 added to radius server table
   as primary server.
XYZSW1> (enable) set radius key cisco123
Radius key set to cisco123
```

Step 2 Configure TACACS+ support on XYZSW2 by specifying the TACACS+ server IP address (192.168.1.10) and TACACS+ server secret key (cisco123), as shown in Example 8-36.

Example 8-36 *Configuring TACACS+ Support on XYZSW2*

```
XYZSW2(config)# tacacs-server host 192.168.1.10
XYZSW2(config)# tacacs-server key cisco123
```

Configuring Each Switch to Use AAA for Authentication

In this section, you learn how to use AAA authentication for management access on each switch.

Step 1 Configure XYZSW1 to use RADIUS authentication and authorization for Telnet logins only, as shown in Example 8-37.

Example 8-37 *Configuring RADIUS Authentication for Telnet Login on XYZSW1*

```
XYZSW1> (enable) set authentication login radius enable telnet
radius login authentication set to enable for telnet session.
```

In Example 8-37, the use of the **telnet** keyword enables RADIUS authentication for Telnet access only.

Step 2 Configure XYZSW2 to use TACACS+ authentication for Telnet logins only, as shown in Example 8-38.

Example 8-38 *Configuring TACACS+ Authentication for Telnet Login on XYZSW2*

```
XYZSW2(config)# aaa new-model
XYZSW2(config)# aaa authentication login default line
XYZSW2(config)# aaa authentication login TELNET group tacacs+ line
XYZSW2(config)# line vty 0 4
XYZSW2(config-line)# login authentication TELNET
XYZSW2(config)# line con 0
XYZSW2(config-line)# password cisco
XYZSW2(config-line)# end
```

In Example 8-38, notice that you have to globally enable AAA by using the **aaa new-model** command. The next command tells the switch to use the locally configured **line** password as the default login authentication mechanism. Next, you create a login authentication profile called **TELNET**, which uses TACACS+ as the authentication method, and uses the **line** authentication method as a backup in case the TACACS+ server is down. The last step is to apply the profile (TELNET) to the vty lines, which then enables TACACS+ authentication for Telnet access.

WARNING   Be careful when setting the default authentication mechanism as the line password. If your console port does not have a line password configured, access is denied to the console port. Ensure that you set a line password for the console port if you are using line password as the default authentication mechanism.

Configuring Each Switch to Use AAA for Management Access Authorization

In this section, you learn how to use AAA authorization to allow enable mode management access on each switch and to deny the use of the **erase** command on XYZSW2 using TACACS+.

NOTE   You can enable mode authorization with two approaches. The first is to apply enable mode authentication when an authenticated user types in the **enable** command. The second is to authorize enable mode access when a user first attempts management access (e.g., authenticates at a Telnet prompt), which takes the user straight to enable mode if authenticated and authorized. TACACS+ supports both of these methods, while RADIUS supports only the second method (RADIUS does support the first, but not very well). For this reason, we look exclusively at the second method of enable mode authorization.

Step 1   On the CiscoSecure ACS server, click on the *Group Setup* button, ensure the *Default Group* is selected (which contains the user *administrator*), and click on the *Edit Settings* button, as shown in Figure 8-9.

Figure 8-9 *Configuring Group Settings*

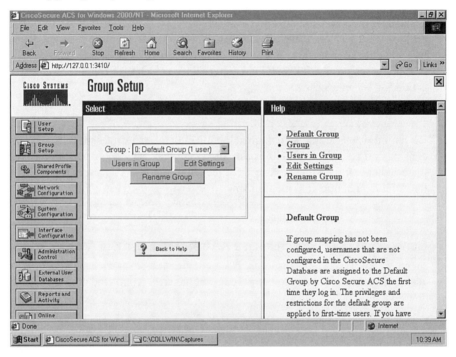

Step 2 On the Group Setup page, scroll down to the *TACACS+ Settings* section and enable the Shell (exec) setting and configure Privilege level to be 15 (enable mode), as shown in Figure 8-10. This authorizes the user for enable mode (privilege level 15) access via TACACS+.

Figure 8-10   *Enabling TACACS+ Enable Mode Authorization*

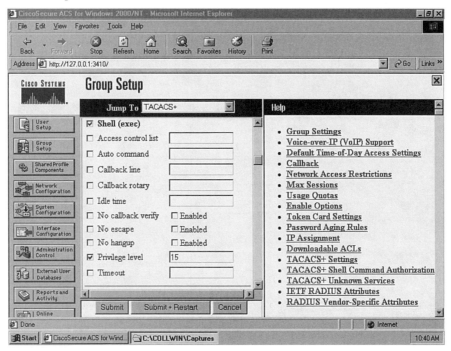

Step 3   On the Group Setup page, scroll down to the *IETF RADIUS Attributes* section and enable the *[006] Service-Type* attribute, changing the attribute value to *Administrative*. This *authorizes* the user for enable mode access via RADIUS. Once complete, click on the *Submit + Restart* button to apply the configuration, as shown in Figure 8-11.

Figure 8-11 *Enabling RADIUS Enable Mode Authorization*

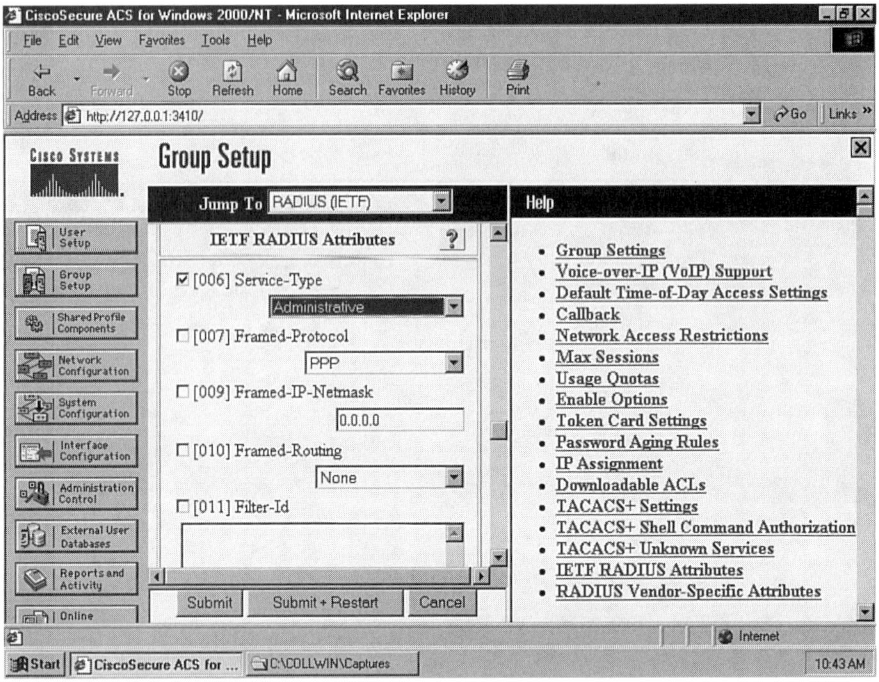

Step 4 Remaining on the Group Setup page, scroll down to the *Shell Command Authorization Set* section and enable the *Per Group Command Authorization* setting. Configure the *Unmatched Cisco IOS commands* setting to *Permit*, and then disable the **erase** command, as shown in Figure 8-12. This prevents the user from using the **erase** command.

Step 5 Configure XYZSW2 to use TACACS+ authorization for enable mode access, as shown in Example 8-39.

Example 8-39 *Configuring TACACS+ Authorization for Enable Mode Access on XYZSW2*

```
XYZSW2(config)# aaa authorization exec TELNET group tacacs+ none
XYZSW2(config)# line vty 0 4
XYZSW2(config-line)# authorization exec TELNET
XYZSW2(config-line)# end
```

Figure 8-12   *Enabling TACACS+ Command Authorization*

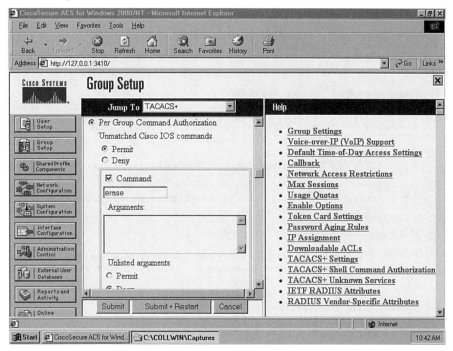

In Example 8-39, you use the **exec** keyword to tell the switch to contact the TACACS+ server for authorization when a user starts an exec process. Notice the use of the **none** keyword to ensure the user can at least get user mode access if the TACACS+ server is down (if you omitted this and the TACACS+ server is down, you would not be able to access the switch via Telnet).

Step 6   Configure XYZSW2 to use TACACS+ authorization for commands, as shown in Example 8-40.

Example 8-40   *Configuring TACACS+ Authorization for Commands on XYZSW2*

```
XYZSW2(config)# aaa authorization commands 15 TELNET group tacacs+ none
XYZSW2(config)# line vty 0 4
XYZSW2(config-line)# authorization commands TELNET
XYZSW2(config-line)# end
```

In Example 8-40, you use the **commands** keyword to tell the switch to contact the TACACS+ server for authorization of commands when in enable mode (privilege level 15). Notice that this authorization is used only for Telnet access because we have created a specific AAA profile (TELNET) and applied it only to the vty lines.

Configuring Each Switch to Use AAA for Management Access Accounting

In this section, you learn how to use AAA accounting to audit exec events (e.g., starting a Telnet session) and command events (invoked each time a command is issued).

Step 1   On XYZSW1, configure AAA accounting for exec events (audit both the start and stop of each event), as shown in Example 8-41.

Example 8-41   *Configuring AAA Accounting on XYZSW1*

```
XYZSW1> (enable) set accounting exec enable start-stop radius
Accounting set to enable for exec events in start-stop mode.
```

Step 2   On XYZSW2, configure AAA accounting for exec events (audit both the start and stop of each event) and enable mode command events (ensure you can contact the TACACS+ server before allowing commands to proceed) for Telnet sessions, as shown in Example 8-42.

Example 8-42   *Configuring AAA Accounting on XYZSW2*

```
XYZSW2(config)# aaa accounting exec TELNET start-stop group tacacs+
XYZSW2(config)# aaa accounting commands 15 TELNET-CMD wait-start group tacacs+
XYZSW2(config)# line vty 0 4
XYZSW2(config-line)# accounting exec TELNET
XYZSW2(config-line)# accounting commands 15 TELNET-CMD
XYZSW2(config)# end
```

You create two separate profiles for each event category you are accounting and then apply the profiles to the vty lines. Notice the use of the **wait-start** keyword to ensure enable mode command events are always audited.

Step 3   Now you are ready to test your accounting configuration. From Host A, make a Telnet connection to XYZSW1 logging in as the administrator user you created earlier, leaving the session open for 30 seconds or so, and then disconnect. On the CiscoSecure ACS server, click on the *Reports and Activity* button, then click the *RADIUS Accounting* hyperlink, and then click the *RADIUS Accounting active.csv* hyperlink. Figure 8-13 shows the accounting information that you should see.

Figure 8-13 shows a start and stop record around 09:09 a.m. The *Service Type* column indicates this is a *NAS Prompt* (exec) event, and the *Acct-Session-Time* column for the *stop* record indicates the session lasted for 35 seconds. The *User-Name* column indicates that the user administrator established the exec connection.

Step 4   From Host A, make a Telnet connection to XYZSW2, perform some minor configuration changes (e.g., change an interface description), and then disconnect. On the CiscoSecure ACS server, click on the *Reports and Activity* button, then click the *TACACS+ Accounting* hyperlink, and then click the *TACACS+ Accounting active.csv* hyperlink. Figure 8-14 shows the accounting information that you should see.

Figure 8-13 *Viewing RADIUS Accounting Information*

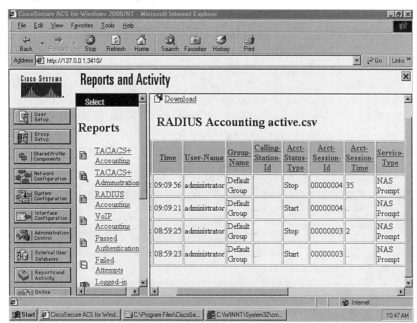

Figure 8-14 *Viewing TACACS+ Accounting Information*

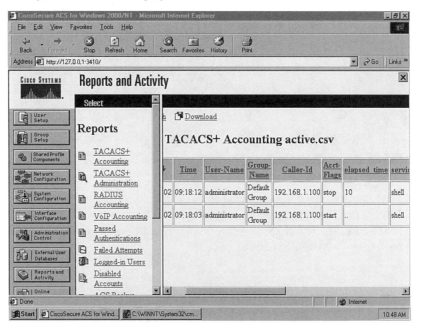

Figure 8-14 shows a start and stop record around 09:18 a.m. The *Service* column indicates this is a *shell* (exec) event, and the *elapsed time* column for the *stop* record indicates the session lasted for 10 seconds. The *User-Name* column indicates that the user *administrator* established the exec connection, and the *Caller-Id* column indicates that the exec session was initiated from 192.168.1.100 (Host A).

Notice that no events are related to commands in Figure 8-14. This is because command accounting records are stored in the TACACS+ Administration database on CiscoSecure ACS. On the CiscoSecure ACS server, click on the *Reports and Activity* button, then click the TACACS+ Administration hyperlink, and then click the TACACS+ Administration active.csv hyperlink. Figure 8-15 shows the accounting information that you should see.

Figure 8-15 *Viewing TACACS+ Administration Information*

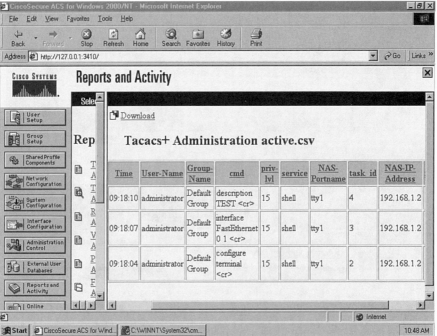

Figure 8-15 shows three command events that occurred around 09:18 a.m. The events indicate that the user administrator configured a description of TEST for interface fastEthernet0/1. The NAS-IP-Address column indicates the configuration was performed on 192.168.1.2 (XYZSW2).

Step 3—Confirming Your AAA Configuration

Now it is time to test your configuration by attempting Telnet access to both switches and requesting various services.

Step 1   From Host A, attempt a Telnet connection to XYZSW1. Enter in the administrator credentials (password = *password*), as shown in Example 8-43.

Example 8-43   *Testing Telnet Access to XYZSW1*

```
C:\> telnet 192.168.1.1
Cisco Systems, Inc. Console
Username: administrator
Password: ********
XYZSW1> (enable)
```

Notice that once you have successfully authenticated, you are taken directly to enable mode on the switch. This is because the RADIUS server returned the *006 Service-Type* attribute with a value of *Administrative*, which tells the switch to grant the user enable mode access.

Step 2   From Host A, attempt a Telnet connection to XYZSW2. Enter in the administrator credentials (password = *password*), as shown in Example 8-44.

Example 8-44   *Testing Telnet Access to XYZSW2*

```
C:\> telnet 192.168.1.2
Username: administrator
Password: ********
XYZSW2#
```

Again, you have been granted enable mode access directly. This is because you configure the switch to authorize exec access, and the TACACS+ server authorized the user with a privilege level of 15 (enable mode).

Step 3   In the Telnet session established in Step 2, try entering configuration mode, execute a few commands, and then exit back to enable mode. Then attempt to erase the startup configuration of the switch, as shown in Example 8-45.

Example 8-45   *Testing Command Authorization on XYZSW2*

```
XYZSW2# configure terminal
XYZSW2(config)# interface fastEthernet0/10
XYZSW2(config-if)# description Just Mucking around here…
XYZSW2(config-if)# end
XYZSW2# erase startup-config
Command authorization failed.
```

In Example 8-45, notice how you can execute normal configuration commands, but once you attempt to execute the **erase** command, you cannot. This is because every time the user executes a command, the switch contacts the TACACS+ server to authorize the command and we had previously denied it.

Step 4   (Optional) Access each switch via the console port. Notice that you do not need to enter user credentials (only a line password or local username authentication), and you can perform all commands. This is because you have applied the AAA configurations only for Telnet access.

Scenario 8-3: Securing Device Access

In this scenario, you secure Catalyst switch ports using the various techniques available. Although in the real world you would generally not configure all of these techniques on a single network, the scenario shows you how to configure each technology.

Scenario Exercise

Figure 8-16 illustrates the scenario topology used for this scenario.

Figure 8-16   *Scenario 8-3 Topology*

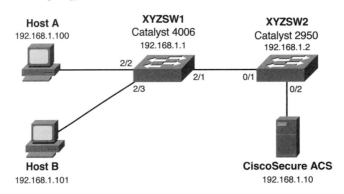

Corporation XYZ wants to try the various port security techniques available to determine which technique works best for the network. You learn how to configure the following port security techniques:

- Simple port security
- 802.1x authentication

Scenario Objectives

The scenario objectives are as follows:

- Configure basic port security
- Configure 802.1x authentication

Additional Equipment Needed

The additional equipment Needed is as follows:

- Hosts B must be Windows XP or Windows 2000 SP4 hosts

Scenario Planning

Securing device access is a process that must be well-planned before implementation. Implementing port security techniques without careful planning can cause administrative headaches, with users being unable to connect to certain ports or users being granted access to the network when they shouldn't be. In this scenario, you configure the following methods of securing device access:

- Basic port security
- 802.1x authentication

Planning Basic Port Security

Basic port security is easily configured and allows you to secure access to a port based upon a MAC address basis. It does not allow you to dynamically determine the VLAN a port should be placed into, so make sure you understand this. Basic port security is also configured locally and has no mechanism for controlling port security in a centralized fashion for distributed switches. Basic port security is normally configured on ports that connect servers or fixed devices, because the likelihood of the MAC address changing on that port is low. A common example of using basic port security is applying it to a port that is in an area of the physical premises that is publicly accessible. This could include a meeting room or reception area that might have an IP telephone available. By restricting the port to accept only the MAC address of the IP telephone, you prevent unauthorized access if somebody plugged another device into the port.

When configuring port security, you should be aware of the default configurations:

- **The maximum number of secure MAC addresses permitted**—Depending on the platform, both CatOS and Cisco IOS switches can permit multiple hosts on a port when port security is configured. If you don't manually specify these addresses, they are auto-learned in the order MAC addresses are heard on the port. If your goal is to allow only a single MAC address on the port, you might be required to manually configure the maximum MAC addresses on each port as one.

- **The security violation action**—The default security violation action on both CatOS and Cisco IOS switches is to shut down the port, requiring manual re-enabling of the port by an administrator. This action could be used as a denial of service attack, so consider this action very carefully.

Planning 802.1x Authentication

The IEEE 802.1x standard provides a framework that allows users (rather than MAC addresses) to be authenticated for switch access to a port. 802.1x can use a centralized security database to provide authentication information, which allows for scalability and ease of management. On Cisco platforms, 802.1x support requires a RADIUS server, so you must configure this server and enable RADIUS support on the switch before proceeding. In recent versions of Cisco IOS and CatOS, RADIUS authorization attributes can also be associated with a user, which define the VLAN a user belongs to as well a port-based access control list that should be applied to traffic received from the user.

A restriction of 802.1x is the requirement for the host connecting to the switch port to be 802.1x aware. This means the operating system must have 802.1x client support. Microsoft Windows XP and Windows 2000 are the only operating systems that currently support 802.1x natively, although third-party clients do exist for other operating systems.

NOTE   802.1x client support is available for Windows 2000 starting in Service Pack 4.

Command Syntax

The following sections describe the commands used for configuring standard port security and 802.1x security in this scenario.

Standard Port Security Command Syntax

The following commands, which are used to configure port security, are introduced in this scenario:

- The **set port security** command (CatOS)
- The **switchport security** command (Cisco IOS)

The set port security Command Syntax

To enable port security on CatOS, you use the **set port security** command. The first step you must take is to enable port security on a particular port. You then can allow one or more MAC addresses to use a secured port. You can manually specify these addresses, allow the switch to auto-learn the addresses, or use a mixture of both. Finally, you can specify a *violation* action (either shut down the entire port or block unauthorized traffic), which occurs when an unauthorized MAC address is detected on the port. The **set port security** command has the following syntax:

```
set port security mod/port [enable | disable] [mac_addr] [age age_time]
    [maximum limit] [shutdown shutdown-time] [violation {shutdown | restrict}]
```

Example 8-46 illustrates configuring port security.

Example 8-46   *Configuring Port Security*

```
Switch> (enable) set port security 2/1 enable
Port 2/1 port security enabled with the learned mac address.
Trunking disabled for Port 2/1 due to Security Mode
Switch> (enable) set port security 2/1 maximum 10
Maximum number of secure addresses set to 10 for port 2/1.
Switch> (enable) set port security 2/1 00-d0-b5-11-22-33
Mac address 00-d0-b5-11-22-33 set for port 2/1.
Switch> (enable) set port security 2/1 violation restrict
Port security violation on port 2/1 will cause insecure packets to be dropped.
```

NOTE   When following this scenario, do not use the MAC addresses shown in the text; use the correct MAC address of your Host A instead.

Example 8-46 sets port 2/1 to allow a maximum of ten hosts. A single static host is permitted, with the remaining nine MAC addresses added dynamically as new hosts send traffic through the port. If an insecure packet is received, the port drops the packets (as opposed to the default configuration of shutting down the entire port).

The **switchport security** Command Syntax

To enable port security on Cisco IOS, you use the **switchport security** interface configuration command syntax:

```
switchport port-security [maximum number] [mac-address mac-address]
```

If you omit the optional parameters, port security is enabled and allows for up to 132 secure MAC addresses. The optional **maximum** keyword allows you to specify the maximum number of MAC addresses allowed on the interface. The optional **mac-address** keyword allows you to add specific MAC addresses to the secure MAC address list (if you do not do this, then the switch auto-learns the secure MAC addresses).

By default, if an unauthorized MAC address is detected on a secure port, the port is shut down and must be administrative enabled. To configure what happens when an unauthorized MAC address is detected on the interface, you use the **switchport security violation** command:

```
switchport port-security violation {protect | restrict | shutdown}
```

The **protect** keyword drops any frames from unauthorized hosts, but still forwards traffic for authorized hosts. The **restrict** keyword generates a trap violation (SNMP and SYSLOG), which is sent to the network management station.

Example 8-47 shows a sample configuration that allows only a single host (MAC address of 00-01-02-00-D8-1D) on the switch port. If another host connects to the port, the port is shut down and must be re-enabled by an administrator.

Example 8-47 *Configuring Port Security on Cisco IOS*

```
Switch(config)# interface fastEthernet0/1
Switch(config-if)# switchport port-security
Switch(config-if)# switchport port-security maximum 1
Switch(config-if)# switchport port-security mac-address 00-01-02-00-D8-1D
Switch(config-if)# switchport port-security violation shutdown
```

802.1x Security Command Syntax

The following commands, which are used to configure 802.1x security, are introduced in this scenario:

- The **set dot1x** and **set port dot1x** command (CatOS)
- The **aaa authentication dot1x** command (Cisco IOS)
- The **dot1x port-control** command (Cisco IOS)

The **set dot1x** and **set port dot1x** Command Syntax (CatOS)

When configuring 802.1x, you must have a RADIUS server configured before enabling 802.1x support. Once you have configured RADIUS support, you must globally enable 802.1x support using the **set dot1x system-auth-control** command:

```
set dot1x system-auth-control {enable | disable}
```

Once 802.1x is enabled globally for the switch, you can then configure individual ports to use 802.1x security by using the **set port dot1x** command. By default, each port has a specific 802.1x port state of *force-authorized*, which means that each port is automatically authorized to forward traffic (in effect, 802.1x is turned off). You must set the port state to *auto* to enable 802.1x on the port, using the **set port dot1x port-control** command:

```
set port dot1x mod/port port-control {auto | force-authorized | force-unauthorized}
```

Once you have set the 802.1x port state, you must initialize the port using the set **port dot1x initialize** command:

```
set port dot1x mod/port initialize
```

TIP   802.1x supports the use of multiple hosts attached to a single port. This can occur when a hub is connected to the switch. To enable support for multiple hosts, you must configure the **set port dot1x** *mod/port* **multiple-host enable** command on the appropriate port.

The **aaa authentication dot1x** Command Syntax (Cisco IOS)

To configure 802.1x support on Cisco IOS Catalyst switches, the following prerequisites must be configured:

- AAA enabled (using the **aaa new-model** command)
- RADIUS support configured (using the **radius-server** command)

Once these prerequisites have been configured, you must configure the 802.1x authentication profile to use RADIUS, using the **aaa authentication dot1x** global configuration command:

```
aaa authentication dot1x default method1 [method2...]
```

Example 8-48 shows how to configure 802.1x using RADIUS authentication.

Example 8-48   *Enabling 802.1x Authentication*

```
Switch(config)# aaa authentication dot1x default group radius
```

NOTE   You can configure 802.1x authentication to use the local switch user database by specifying the **local** keyword. This method is recommended only for testing purposes.

The **dot1x port-control** Command Syntax (Cisco IOS)

Once 802.1x authentication has been enabled on a Cisco IOS switch, you must then configure 802.1x on each port that you want to use it. As for CatOS, all ports by default are in the force-authorized state and must be set to the auto state to enable 802.1x support. The **dot1x port-control** interface configuration command is used to enable 802.1x on a port:

```
dot1x port-control {auto | force-authorized | force-unauthorized}
```

TIP   To enable support for multiple hosts on Cisco IOS, you must configure the **dot1x multiple-hosts** interface configuration command on the appropriate port.

Configuration Tasks

In this scenario, you perform the following tasks:

- Step 1—Configure basic port security
- Step 2—Configure 802.1x authentication

Step 1   Configuring Basic Port Security

Basic port security is supported on both Cisco IOS and CatOS switches. In this scenario, you configure basic port security for the ports connected to Host A and the CiscoSecure ACS server. In this step:

- Configure XYZSW1 for basic port security
- Configure XYZSW2 for basic port security
- Verify that port security is functioning

Configuring XYZSW1 for Basic Port Security

On XYZSW1 you permit only Host A's MAC address on port 2/2, and block access from any other source MAC addresses detected on the port.

On XYZSW1, configure port security for port 2/2, allowing only Host A (MAC address = 00-40-96-39-FA-0A) access to the switch port (see Example 8-49).

Example 8-49   *Configure Port Security on XYZSW1*

```
XYZSW1 (enable) set port security 2/2 enable 00-40-96-39-FA-0A violation restrict
Port 2/2 security enabled, violation mode restrict.
Mac address 00-40-96-39-fa-0a set for port 2/2.
```

The **restrict** keyword configures the port to reject frames from unauthorized MAC addresses (also known as the *violation action*). The default violation action is to shut down the port if an unauthorized MAC address is detected.

Configuring XYZSW2 for Basic Port Security

On XYZSW2 you permit only the CiscoSecure ACS server MAC address on port 0/2 and shut down the port if any other source MAC addresses are detected on the port.

On XYZSW2, configure port security for port 0/2 allowing only one MAC address on the port, as shown in Example 8-50.

Example 8-50   *Configure Port Security on XYZSW2*

```
XYZSW2(config)# interface fastEthernet0/2
XYZSW2(config-if)# switchport port-security
XYZSW2(config-if)# switchport port-security maximum 1
XYZSW2(config-if)# switchport port-security mac-address 00-01-02-00-D8-1D
XYZSW2(config-if)# switchport port-security violation shutdown
```

The maximum 1 configuration means that only a single MAC address is allowed on the switch port (the default is 132). The **violation shutdown** configuration means that any frames received from unauthorized MAC addresses causes a shut down of the port.

NOTE   The **switchport port-security** command replaces the **port security** interface configuration command used in older IOS versions on the Catalyst 2900XL/3500XL switches.

Verifying That Port Security Is Functioning

The following outlines how to verify that port security is functioning:

Step 1   On XYZSW1, disconnect Host A from port 2/2 and plug in Host B to port 2/2. Try and ping any other hosts in the network as shown in Example 8-51.

Example 8-51   *Testing Connectivity from an Unauthorized Host*

```
C:\WINNT\System32> ping 192.168.1.100
Pinging 192.168.1.101 with 32 bytes of data:
Request timed out.
Request timed out.
Request timed out.
Request timed out.
```

You should not be able to ping anywhere in the network from Host B, because a security violation has occurred and the port blocks frames from unauthorized hosts.

Step 2 On XYZSW2, disconnect the CiscoSecure ACS server from port 0/2 and plug in Host B to port 0/2. Verify the port security status, as shown in Example 8-52.

Example 8-52 *Verifying Port Security Status on XYZSW2*

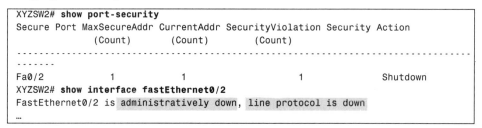

```
XYZSW2# show port-security
Secure Port MaxSecureAddr CurrentAddr SecurityViolation Security Action
            (Count)       (Count)     (Count)
------------------------------------------------------------------------------
--------
Fa0/2          1             1                 1             Shutdown
XYZSW2# show interface fastEthernet0/2
FastEthernet0/2 is administratively down, line protocol is down
...
```

The **show port-security** output in Example 8-52 shows the switch has registered a security violation. The **show interface** command indicates the port has been shut down and must manually be re-enabled by issuing the **no shutdown** interface configuration command.

Step 2 Configuring 802.1x Authentication

You now configure 802.1x authentication, which authenticates switch port access based on user credentials rather than MAC address. Cisco's current 802.1x implementation requires the use of a RADIUS server, although the standard allows for any authentication mechanism to be used. In this step:

- Configure XYZSW2 for RADIUS support
- Configure 802.1x support
- Configure the host operating system 802.1x support

Configuring XYZSW2 for RADIUS Support

In Scenario 8-1, you configured RADIUS support on XYZSW1. You now need to configure RADIUS support on XYZSW2 to enable 802.1x authentication.

Step 1 On the CiscoSecure ACS server, add a new NAS definition for XYZSW2 (call it XYZSW2_RADIUS) to use RADIUS, as shown in Figure 8-17. Click on the *Network Configuration* button, then the *XYZSW2 AAA Client*, and modify the *Authenticate Using* field to *RADIUS (Cisco IOS/ PIX)*. Then click the *Submit + Restart* button to apply your changes.

Example 8-54 shows that enabling 802.1x support disables trunking and turns on the spanning-tree PortFast feature on that port.

Step 2 On XYZSW2, configure RADIUS support as shown in Example 8-53.

Example 8-53 *Configuring RADIUS support on XYZSW2*

```
XYZSW2(config)# radius-server host 192.168.1.10 key cisco123
```

Figure 8-17 *Configuring RADIUS Support for XYZSW2*

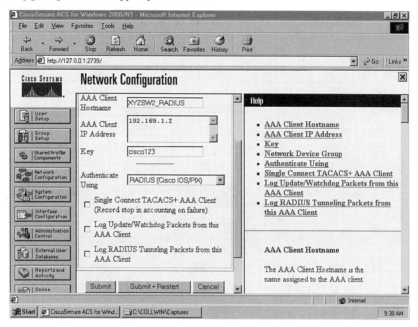

TIP   You can dynamically determine VLAN membership for a user using 802.1x. This is
             achieved by configuring the following RADIUS attributes on a per-user or per-group basis:

- **[64] Tunnel-Type** indicates the tunnel attributes returned relates to VLANs. For
  802.1x, this value must always be VLAN.
- **[65] Tunnel-Medium-Type** indicates the tunnel attributes returned relate to LAN
  access. For 802.1x, this value must always be 802.
- **[81] Tunnel-Private-Group-ID** indicates the VLAN name (not VLAN ID) the user
  should be assigned to.

You can also apply per-user ACLs to restrict traffic for a user using either the [11] Filter-ID
attribute or the [026/009/001] cisco-av-pair attribute.

Configuring 802.1x Support

Do the following to configure 802.1x support:

Step 1   On XYZSW1, enable 802.1x support globally for the switch, and
              configure port 2/3 for 802.1x, as shown in Example 8-54.

Example 8-54 *Configuring 802.1x Support on XYZSW1*

```
XYZSW1 (enable) set dot1x system-auth-control enable
dot1x system-auth-control enabled.
XYZSW1 (enable) set port dot1x 2/3 port-control auto
Port 2/3 dot1x port-control is set to auto.
```

continues

Example 8-54 *Configuring 802.1x Support on XYZSW1 (Continued)*

```
Trunking disabled for port 2/3 due to Dot1x feature.
Spantree port fast start option enabled for port 2/3.
XYZSW1 (enable) set port dot1x 2/3 initialize
Port 2/3 initializing...
Port 2/3 dot1x initialization complete.
```

Step 2 On XYZSW1, verify your 802.1x configuration, as shown in Example 8-55.

Example 8-55 *Verifying 802.1x Configuration on XYZSW1*

```
XYZSW1 (enable) show port dot1x 2/3
Port  Auth-State           BEnd-State Port-Control        Port-Status
----- -------------------- ---------- ------------------- -------------
 2/3  connecting           finished   auto                unauthorized
Port  Multiple Host Re-authentication
----- ------------- ----------------
 2/3  disabled      enabled
```

Example 8-55 shows that the port status of the port is unauthorized, indicating the 802.1x client on the port is not present or is providing invalid credentials.

Step 3 On XYZSW2, enable 802.1x support globally for the switch and configure port 0/3 for 802.1x, as shown in Example 8-56.

Example 8-56 *Configuring 802.1x Support on XYZSW2*

```
XYZSW2(config)# aaa authentication dot1x default group radius
XYZSW2(config)# interface fastEthernet0/3
XYZSW2(config-if)# dot1x port-control auto
XYZSW2(config-if)# end
```

Configuring Host Operating System Support for 802.1x

Configuring host operating system support for 802.1x is done as follows:

Step 1 On Host A, try pinging any other network device (e.g. 192.168.1.1). You should not be able to ping because you have not yet authenticated on the switch port.

Step 2 On Host A, click on Start → All Programs → Accessories → Communications → Network Connections. Right-click on the icon that represents the local LAN interface and select Properties. Next, select the Authentication tab and select the *Enable network access control using IEEE 802.1X* check box, choosing the EAP type as *MD5-Challenge,* as shown in Figure 8-18. Click on the OK button to complete the configuration:

Figure 8-18 *Configuring 802.1x Support on Windows XP*

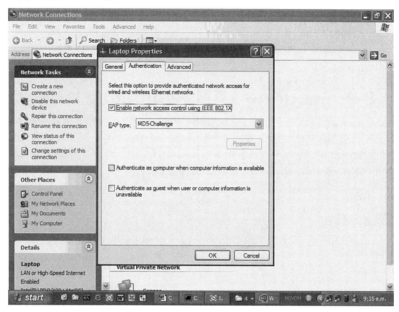

Step 3 Connect the LAN interface to XYZSW1 port 2/3. You should receive a notification, asking you to authenticate LAN access, as shown in Figure 8-19. Enter *administrator* as the username and *password* as the password, leaving the domain field blank.

Figure 8-19 *Authenticating LAN Access Using 802.1x*

Step 4   Now try pinging another device on the network. If you entered the correct credentials, you should be able to ping okay.

Step 5   Repeat Steps 1 to 4 for Host B. This demonstrates the 802.1x functionality via a Cisco IOS-based switch.

Scenario 8-4: Securing LAN Segments

In this scenario, you enhance the security of a DMZ segment that is used to provide public access from the Internet for web content and Internet e-mail. The DMZ architecture used in this scenario is a very common architecture in use today, so learning how to secure the segment gives you valuable real world experience.

Scenario Exercise

Figure 8-20 illustrates the scenario topology used for this scenario.

Figure 8-20   *Topology*

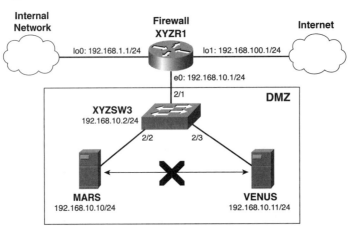

Corporation XYZ is providing public Internet access for the two external web sites on a DMZ segment, as shown in Figure 8-20. Hosts MARS and VENUS are Windows 2000 web servers. Corporation XYZ wants to provide as much security as possible for this segment and also wants to restrict communications between hosts on the DMZ segment.

The following access control policy must be implemented:

- The DMZ hosts must reside in the same IP subnet, but cannot directly communicate with each other.
- The DMZ hosts must accept inbound HTTP connections.

- The DMZ hosts must be able to issue echo requests and DNS queries to any external network.

- All other access to/from the DMZ hosts must be blocked.

Scenario Objectives

The scenario objectives are as follows:

- Configure private VLANs to prevent communications between hosts on the same IP subnet

- Configure VLAN access control lists (ACLs) to provide access control of traffic flowing between hosts in the same VLAN

Equipment Needed

The equipment needed is as follows:

- One CatOS Catalyst 6000/6500 switch

- One Cisco IOS router with at least one Ethernet interface

- The two hosts in this example are not required, but to verify the objectives you need these two hosts present.

Scenario Planning

Private VLANs are an excellent security feature that allows you to reduce the number of VLANs required to implement access control in the network. By restricting access between devices on the same VLAN (IP subnet), you reduce the need for firewalls with multiple interfaces and the complexity of your firewall security policy. Because the switch provides isolation between devices rather than the firewall, this leaves the firewall free to perform other security functions.

When planning a private VLAN architecture you need to consider the following:

- Which devices require isolation?

- Which devices are to be connected to promiscuous ports?

- Do you have a group of devices that require connectivity within the group, but isolation from the remaining hosts on a segment?

In this scenario, you have two hosts that require isolation from each other. Rather than placing these hosts in separate VLANs and using multiple physical or virtual interfaces on a firewall device to restrict access between the two hosts, you attach each host to an isolated port that can communicate only with the a promiscuous port which connects the firewall. Straight away, you have isolated each host, and even though they are on the same logical IP subnet, they cannot communicate.

One way to bypass the security of private VLANs is to add static host routes on each host, directing frames for another isolated host to the promiscuous port router/firewall, rather than trying to send the frame directly. You can circumvent this issue by using traffic filtering on either the router/firewall or the switch. In this scenario, you use VLAN access control lists on the switch to prevent this.

Command Syntax

This section describes the commands used for configuring private VLANs and VLAN access control lists on the Catalyst 6000/6500 series switches. The following commands are introduced in this scenario:

- The **set vlan** *vlan-id* **pvlan-type** command
- The **set pvlan** command
- The **set security acl** command

The **set vlan** *vlan-id* **pvlan-type** Command

When creating private VLANs, you create the following types of VLANs to implement your required security configuration:

- Primary VLAN
- Isolated VLAN
- Community VLAN

You use the **set vlan** *vlan-id* **pvlan-type** command to create a new VLAN and assign it the appropriate private VLAN role:

```
set vlan vlan-id pvlan-type {primary | isolated | community | twoway-community}
```

The **set pvlan** Command

Once you have created your private VLANs, you must now perform the following tasks:

- Assign ports to isolated and community VLANs.
- Map the isolated and community (secondary) VLANs to the primary VLAN and promiscuous port.

To assign ports to isolated/community VLANs, you use the **set pvlan** command:

```
set pvlan primary-vlan-id secondary-vlan-id {mod/port | sc0}
```

The *mod/port* parameter represents the isolated or community port, and you must repeat the command for each secondary VLAN.

Once primary and secondary VLANs have been created, you use the **set pvlan mapping** command to associate secondary VLANs with a primary VLAN and promiscuous port:

```
set pvlan mapping primary-vlan-id {isolated-vlan | community-vlan} mod/port
```

The *mod/port* parameter represents the promiscuous port, and you must repeat the command for each secondary VLAN.

The **set security acl** Command

The **set security acl** command is used to create VLAN access control lists (VACLs). VACLs allow you to filter upon Layer 3 and Layer 4 parameters and are applied for all inbound access on the entire VLAN. Although very similar to router ACLs, VACLs can be applied only in the inbound direction and can also filter traffic switched within a VLAN. The following tasks are required to configure VACLs:

- Create the VACL
- Commit the VACL to hardware
- Apply the VACL to a VLAN

To create a VACL for IP traffic, you use the **set security acl ip** command:

```
set security acl ip acl-name {permit | deny} {ip | tcp | udp} source destination
```

Example 8-57 shows a VACL called EXAMPLE that filters on IP UDP and TCP traffic.

Example 8-57 *VACL Example*

```
Switch> (enable) set security acl ip EXAMPLE permit ip host 10.1.1.1 any
Switch> (enable) set security acl ip EXAMPLE permit tcp 10.1.1.0 0.0.0.255 any eq 80
Switch> (enable) set security acl ip EXAMPLE permit udp 10.1.1.0 0.0.0.255 any eq 53
Switch> (enable) set security acl ip EXAMPLE deny ip any any
```

Once you have created your VACL, you need to commit the VACL to the Policy Feature Card (PFC), PFC2 or PFC3 on the Catalyst 6000/6500 Supervisor using the **commit security acl** command:

```
commit security acl {vacl-name | all}
```

Finally, you apply the VACL to a particular VLAN using the **set security acl map** command:

```
set security acl map vacl-name vlan
```

Configuration Tasks

The following steps are required to successfully perform the scenario configuration:

- Step 1—Prepare the switch and router
- Step 2—Configure private VLANs and VLAN ACLs
- Step 3—Confirm the desired access control has been achieved

Step 1 Preparing the Switch and Router

In this step, you:

- Configure the system name and IP parameters of the switch
- Configure the router (IP addressing only required)
- Provide connectivity for the router and hosts

Configuring the System Name and IP Parameters of the Switch

Configuring the system name and IP parameters of the switch is done as follows:

Step 1 On the switch, configure the system name, prompt, an IP address of 192.168.10.2/24, and the appropriate default route, as shown in Example 8-58.

Example 8-58 *Configuring Basic Parameters on XYZSW1*

```
Console enable
Enter password: *****
Console (enable) set system name XYZSW3
System name set.
XYZSW3 (enable) set interface sc0 192.168.10.2 255.255.255.0
XYZSW3 (enable) set ip route default 192.168.10.1
Route added.
```

Configuring the Router

Do the following to configuring the router:

Step 1 On the router, configure the system name (XYZR1), Ethernet interfaces, loopback interfaces, and the appropriate IP addressing, as shown in Example 8-59. Refer to Figure 8-20 for the correct IP addressing.

Example 8-59 *Configuring the router*

```
Router(config)# hostname XYZR1
XYZR1(config)# interface ethernet0
XYZR1(config-if)# no shutdown
XYZR1(config-if)# ip address 192.168.10.1 255.255.255.0
XYZR1(config-if)# interface loopback0
XYZR1(config-if)# ip address 192.168.1.1 255.255.255.0
XYZR1(config-if)# interface loopback1
XYZR1(config-if)# ip address 192.168.100.1 255.255.255.0
```

Providing Connectivity for the Router

Step 1 On XYZSW3, configure port 2/1 as 10 Mbps half-duplex and ports 2/2-3 as 100Mbps full-duplex, also naming each port appropriately.

Step 2   Connect the router and hosts with the appropriate cabling to the switch. After at least 30 seconds, ensure that you can ping all hosts and all interfaces on the router as demonstrated in Example 8-60.

Example 8-60   *Confirming Connectivity*

```
XYZSW3> (enable) ping 192.168.10.1
!!!!!
XYZSW3> (enable) ping 192.168.10.10
!!!!!
XYZSW3> (enable) ping 192.168.10.11
!!!!!
XYZSW3> (enable) ping 192.168.1.1
!!!!!
XYZSW3> (enable) ping 192.168.100.1
!!!!!
```

NOTE   Try pinging MARS from VENUS or vice versa. Notice that you are able to ping each other because this is normal behavior when both hosts are in the same VLAN, on the same IP subnet with a switch interconnecting the devices. The goal of this scenario is to prevent this intra-VLAN communication using the switch.

Step 2   Configuring Private VLANs and VLAN ACLs

In this step you:

- Configure the required VLANs to implement private VLANs
- Configure the appropriate VLAN ACLs to enforce the required access control

Configuring the Required VLANs to Implement Private VLANs

Figure 8-21 illustrates the VLANs that you use to implement private VLANs.

Figure 8-21   *Private VLANs Used for Scenario 8-4*

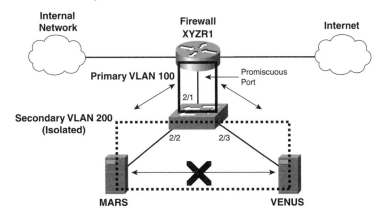

VLAN 100 is designated as the primary VLAN, to which any promiscuous ports are assigned. VLAN 200 is designated as a secondary VLAN, to which any isolated ports are assigned. You assign the server ports *and* the management interface port sc0 to the isolated VLAN. This ensures the hosts cannot communicate with each other and also cannot communicate with the switch IP address (if you assigned the sc0 interface to the primary VLAN, it is designated as a promiscuous port and, hence, would be open to communications from the isolated ports).

NOTE   In production environments, the switch management interface should not be placed on the same VLAN as users or servers, especially where security is critical.

Step 1   The switch must operate in VTP transparent mode to support private VLANs, so configure this first. Next, create the primary VLAN (100) on XYZSW3, assigning it a private VLAN type of primary, as shown in Example 8-61.

Example 8-61   *Creating the Primary VLAN on XYZSW3*

```
XYZSW3> (enable) set vtp mode transparent
VTP domain  modified
XYZSW3> (enable) set vlan 100 pvlan-type primary
Vlan 100 configuration successful
```

Step 2   Create the secondary VLAN (200) on XYZSW3 assigning it a private VLAN type of *isolated* and assign ports 2/2 and 2/3 to the isolated VLAN. Also assign the management interface sc0 to the isolated VLAN, as shown in Example 8-62.

Example 8-62   *Creating the Secondary (Isolated) VLAN on XYZSW3*

```
XYZSW3> (enable) set vlan 200 pvlan-type isolated
Vlan 200 configuration successful
XYZSW3> (enable) set pvlan 100 200 2/2-3
Successfully set the following ports to Private Vlan 100,200: 2/2-3
XYZSW3> (enable) set pvlan 100 200 sc0
Successfully set the following ports to Private Vlan 100,200: sc0
```

Step 3   Map the secondary (isolated) VLAN to the primary VLAN on the promiscuous port, as shown in Example 8-63.

Example 8-63   *Mapping the Secondary (Isolated) VLAN to the Primary VLAN Promiscuous Port 2/1*

```
XYZSW3> (enable) set pvlan mapping 100 200 2/1
Successfully set mapping between 100 and 200 on 2/1
```

Step 4   Verify your private VLAN configuration by using the **show pvlan** command, as shown in Example 8-64.

Example 8-64   *Verifying the Private VLAN Configuration*

```
XYZSW3> (enable) show pvlan
Primary Secondary Secondary-Type Ports
------- --------- -------------- -----------
100    200        isolated       2/2-3, sc0
XYZSW3> (enable) show pvlan mapping
Port  Primary  Secondary
----- -------- ----------
2/1   100      200
```

The first **show pvlan** command verifies which ports are isolated, while the second **show pvlan mapping** command shows the promiscuous ports.

Step 5   Verify that the private VLANs are working as desired by performing the same ping tests described in Example 8-60.

Configuring the Appropriate VLAN ACLs to Enforce the Required Access Control

You now configure VACLs to provide the required access control on the switch, enhancing the overall security of the architecture. You configure a VACL on the primary VLAN and a VACL on the secondary VACL.

The VACL on the primary VLAN is used to prevent the hosts on the DMZ from routing local traffic (e.g., traffic from MARS to VENUS) to the router to bypass the private VLAN security.

The VACL on the secondary VLAN is used to restrict the services that are allowed for each host. In this scenario, you allow only HTTP and Domain Name System (DNS) traffic.

Step 1   Configure a VACL for the primary VLAN called PROTECT-DMZ on XYZSW3, as shown in Example 8-65.

Example 8-65   *Creating the VACL for the Primary VLAN*

```
XYZSW3> (enable) set security acl ip PROTECT-DMZ permit ip host
   192.168.10.1 192.168.10.0 0.0.0.255
XYZSW3> (enable) set security acl ip PROTECT-DMZ deny ip
   192.168.10.0 0.0.0.255 192.168.10.0 0.0.0.255
XYZSW3> (enable) set security acl ip PROTECT-DMZ permit ip any
   192.168.10.0 0.0.0.255
```

This VACL allows the router to communicate with the DMZ segment, then prevents any hosts on the DMZ from routing local traffic via the router, and then allows the DMZ hosts to communicate with remote networks. Note the importance of the ordering of the VACL.

TIP This VACL is applied to traffic coming from the router only. Traffic from the hosts is not filtered as you might expect (VACLs normally filter inbound traffic to the VLAN), because the VACL is not applied when the secondary to primary VLAN mapping is performed. The reverse applies for the secondary VACL (i.e., only traffic from the hosts is filtered).

Step 2 Configure a secondary VACL called *DMZ-OUT* on XYZSW3, as shown in Example 8-66.

Example 8-66 *Creating the Secondary VACL*

```
XYZSW3> (enable) set security acl ip DMZ-OUT deny icmp any any fragment
XYZSW3> (enable) set security acl ip DMZ-OUT permit tcp host 192.168.10.10
  eq 80 any established
XYZSW3> (enable) set security acl ip DMZ-OUT permit tcp host 192.168.10.11
  eq 80 any established
XYZSW3> (enable) set security acl ip DMZ-OUT permit udp host 192.168.10.10
  any eq 53
XYZSW3> (enable) set security acl ip DMZ-OUT permit udp host 192.168.10.11
  any eq 53
XYZSW3> (enable) set security acl ip DMZ-OUT permit icmp host 192.168.10.10
  any echo
XYZSW3> (enable) set security acl ip DMZ-OUT permit icmp host 192.168.10.11
  any echo
```

This VACL enforces the access control policy for the DMZ. This configuration can be much more effective than filtering on a firewall or router because VACL filtering is performed at wire speed and any dropped packets have no effect on performance (which means denial-of-service attacks can't bring down the switch).

Step 3 Commit the VACLs to hardware and bind them to the appropriate VLANs, as shown in Example 8-67.

Example 8-67 *Committing and Binding the VACLs*

```
XYZSW3> (enable) commit security acl all
ACL commit in progress.
ACL PROTECT-DMZ is committed to hardware.
ACL DMZ-OUT is committed to hardware.
XYZSW3> (enable) set security acl map PROTECT-DMZ 100
ACL PROTECT-DMZ mapped to vlan 100
XYZSW3> (enable) set security acl map DMZ-OUT 200
ACL DMZ-OUT mapped to vlan 200
```

Step 3   Confirm the Desired Access Control Has Been Achieved

The final task is to confirm that you have implemented the correct access control policy. Perform the following traffic tests to verify your configuration:

Step 1   Verify that you can ping all router interfaces from both MARS and VENUS, as shown in Example 8-68 (this verifies that your secondary VACL is allowing outbound ICMP echo requests).

Example 8-68   *Pinging XYZR1 Interfaces from MARS*

```
M:\>ping 192.168.10.1
Pinging 192.168.10.1 with 32 bytes of data:
Reply from 192.168.10.1: bytes=32 time<1ms TTL=255
...
M:\>ping 192.168.1.1
Pinging 192.168.1.1 with 32 bytes of data:
Reply from 192.168.1.1: bytes=32 time<1ms TTL=255
...
M:\>ping 192.168.100.1
Pinging 192.168.100.1 with 32 bytes of data:
Reply from 192.168.100.1: bytes=32 time<1ms TTL=255
...
```

Step 2   Verify that you cannot ping MARS from VENUS and vice versa, as shown in Example 8-69 (this indicates that your private VLAN configuration is working).

Example 8-69   *Pinging VENUS from MARS*

```
M:\>ping 192.168.10.11
Pinging 192.168.10.11 with 32 bytes of data:
Request timed out.
Request timed out.
Request timed out.
```

Step 3   Add a static route on both MARS and VENUS, which routes traffic for the other DMZ host to the router IP address on the DMZ segment (192.168.10.1). For example, on MARS you would add a route defining VENUS (192.168.10.11) as being reachable via XYZR1 (192.168.10.1). Now verify that you still *cannot* ping MARS from VENUS and vice versa, as shown in Example 8-70 (this indicates that your primary VACL is working).

Example 8-70   *Adding a Static Route on MARS and Pinging VENUS from MARS*

```
M:\>route add 192.168.10.11 mask 255.255.255.0 192.168.10.1

M:\>ping 192.168.10.11
Pinging 192.168.10.11 with 32 bytes of data:
Request timed out.
Request timed out.
Request timed out.
```

Step 4   Verify that you can Telnet to MARS and VENUS on port 80 from the
router XYZR1, using a source interface address of loopback 1, as shown
in Example 8-71 (this verifies that your secondary VACL is allowing the
appropriate access). Press Enter a few times once you have connected to
get the HTTP Bad Request output shown.

Example 8-71   *Verifying HTTP Connectivity to MARS from XYZR1*

```
XYZR1# telnet 192.168.10.10 80 /source-interface loopback 1
HTTP/1.1 400 Bad Request
Server: Microsoft-IIS/5.1
Date: Sun, 03 Feb 2002 12:03:10 GMT
Content-Type: text/html
Content-Length: 87
<html><head><title>Error</title></head><body>The parameter is incorrect. </body>
</html>
```

Step 5   Verify that you *cannot* perform an extended ping to MARS and VENUS
from the router XYZR1 using a source interface address of loopback 1,
as shown in Example 8-72 (this verifies that your secondary VACL is
blocking any unauthorized services).

Example 8-72   *Verifying ICMP Traffic Is Dropped to MARS from XYZR1*

```
XYZR1# ping ip
Target IP Address: 192.168.10.10
Repeat Count [5]:
Datagram size [100]:
Timeout in seconds [2]:
Extended commands [n]: y
Source address or interface: 192.168.100.1
…
Sending 5, 100-byte ICMP Echos to 192.168.10.10, timeout is 2 seconds:
.....
Success rate is 0 percent (0/5), round-trip min/avg/max = 0/0/0 ms
```

Summary

In this chapter, you have learned how to secure your switch infrastructure. Securing your
switch infrastructure comprises the following key components:

- Securing management access to the switch

- Securing network access

- Implementing traffic filtering

The first step you should take is to secure management access to the switch. Because the switch has substantial control over the network and how traffic is directed, you must ensure it is secure, as secure as possible. Securing management access consists of the following:

- Configuring banners, lockout parameters, and session timeouts
- Configuring user-level authentication and privilege levels
- Using secure protocols such as SSH and SNMPv3 to protect against eavesdropping

Once you have secured your switch, you can place it on your network and implement security features for connecting devices. Port security and 802.1x allow the switch to control access to ports for hosts based upon parameters such as MAC address or a login name and password. The following methods are available for implementing port security:

- **Standard port security**—All port security is configured locally on the switch and is based upon a list of secure MAC addresses for the interface.
- **802.1x security**—Port access is controlled via the use of the IEEE 802.1x standard. The 802.1x standard allows for switch access to be controlled independently of hardware (MAC address) on a per-user basis. 802.1x uses RADIUS to provide centralized authentication and authorization.

Finally, Cisco Catalyst switches include traffic filtering features that allow you to filter traffic based upon Layer 2, 3, and 4 criteria. From a protocol perspective, you can specify that a port forwards only IP, IPX, or AppleTalk/DEC traffic, allowing you to eliminate unnecessary protocols where they are not required. For a more finely grained approach, Catalyst 6000/6500 switches have a VLAN access control list (VACL) feature that filters IP, IPX, or Ethernet traffic at wire speed (requires PFC, PFC2, or PFC3) for an entire VLAN.

## CHAPTER 9

Quality of Service

To increase communications efficiency, both businesses and service providers are looking to IP-based networks to transport voice, video, and data services. Voice and video have special networking requirements, which IP networks must be able to provide. This means IP networking devices, such as local-area network (LAN) switches and routers require enhanced intelligence, with the ability to differentiate between various traffic types, identify applications such as voice or video, and provide the appropriate network resources as required.

A common question that is asked about quality of service (QoS) on the LAN is a simple one—why? It is a simple yet valid question. Modern switched networks are high-speed networks that are more than capable of handling many organization's bandwidth requirements. With the recent push to converge voice and video onto the data network, QoS has moved from being a wide-area network (WAN)–only feature (where the links are relatively slow) to a feature that is required throughout the WAN and LAN. Voice traffic is not bandwidth-hungry; it is delay and jitter-sensitive. A LAN must be able to provide minimal delay and jitter; it is these requirements that make QoS on the LAN a real requirement.

This chapter discusses quality of service (QoS), which in the context of network devices refers to the identification of a particular type of network traffic (that relates to a application or service) and the allocation of network resources to ensure the traffic gets the appropriate level of service from the network. The exciting topic of Cisco's IP Telephony offering is also introduced, with a discussion of how Cisco switches complement and enhance a Cisco IP Telephony network. The following topics are discussed:

- Introducing to quality of service
- Implementing quality of service

Introducing to QoS

QoS is a generic term that defines the level or measure of service that is provided for a particular application or network service. For example, consider the various passenger classes on an international air flight. Typically, first class, business class, and economy class exist. The first-class passengers get the highest degree of service (e.g., better food, bigger seats, personalized service) because these passengers pay extra for that service. Similarly, business-class passengers get a higher degree of service than economy-class passengers, but do not enjoy some of the service that first-class passengers enjoy. The business-class passenger pays more than an economy class passenger, but less than a first-class passenger. Taking this example a step further, those passengers on standby might be equated to a best-effort service.

The same concepts apply to data networks. Specific applications and services might be more important for an organization than others. These applications require a higher quality of service (QoS). Referring back to the airline example, certain characteristics of the whole flying experience define the level of service you receive. For example, these characteristics could include quality of food, leg room, in-flight entertainment, and baggage clearance priority. Each passenger class receives a varying level of service for each characteristic, with the overall quality of service being defined by the sum of these service levels.

On data networks, the characteristics of the network that define quality of service are described in Table 9-1.

Table 9-1 *Characteristics of the Network that Define Quality of Service*

Characteristic	Description
Bandwidth	The amount of data transferred over a certain time frame defines the bandwidth used by the application.
Latency	The amount of time required for a piece of information to travel from source to destination.
Jitter	This term applies to the variation in latency. Certain applications can compensate for latency, but require that the latency be consistent.
Packet loss	Packet loss can occur when congestion occurs in the network. It is possible to assign a preference to certain applications, reducing the likelihood that they can experience packet loss.

Now that you understand a little about QoS, it is time to examine how network devices actually implement and apply QoS. The following topics are now discussed:

- QoS models
- DiffServ model
- QoS functions

QoS Models

Three models define how quality of service can be implemented in modern networks today:

- **Best effort**—This model provides no quality of service. All traffic received is sent on a best-effort basis (normally first come, first served).

- **Integrated Services (IntServ)**—In this model, applications need to signal their QoS requirements to the network before sending data. Network devices receive signaling messages from the application and allocate the requested network resources.

- **Differentiated Services (DiffServ)**—In this model, each packet in the network contains a marking that indicates the required QoS. Each network device applies QoS based upon this marking.

Cisco LAN switches implement the DiffServ model, where they inspect or mark QoS information contained within each frame or packet and apply QoS based upon these values.

DiffServ Model

The DiffServ model requires applications to indicate QoS requirements in every data packet that is sent. This means that applications do not need to explicitly signal QoS requirements to the network before sending data (which is required in the IntServ model). Figure 9-1 demonstrates the DiffServ approach.

Figure 9-1   *The DiffServ Model*

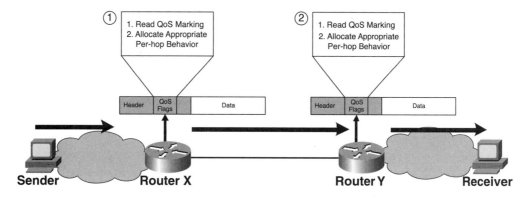

In Figure 9-1, the following steps occur:

Step 1   The sender immediately sends session data, with each packet of the session being marked with QoS information in the header of each packet. Router X receives this packet, reads the QoS marking in the header, and applies the appropriate behavior based upon the QoS marking.

Step 2   Router Y receives the packet from Router X, reads the QoS marking in the header, and behaves according to the QoS marking. Router Y then forwards the packet to its final destination.

The DiffServ model signals QoS requirements by using the following markers in each packet or frame transmitted:

- Type of service (applies to IP traffic)
- Class of service (applies to Layer 2 traffic)
- Differentiated Services Code Point (DSCP)—Applies to IP traffic

Type of Service (ToS)

The most common form of QoS marking present in IP networks today is the use of the type of service (ToS) field. Interpreted by routers, the ToS field is a part of the IP header and allows for a QoS marking to be applied on a per-packet basis. Figure 9-2 illustrates the ToS field.

Figure 9-2   *The Type of Service Field*

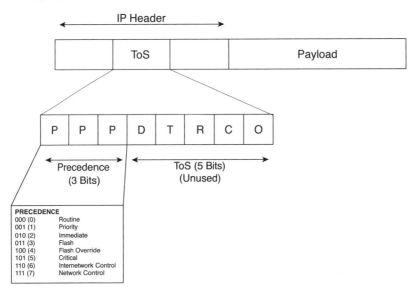

Figure 9-2 shows two subfields that exist within the ToS field. The ToS subfield is not used, with the Precedence subfield being the only portion of the ToS field actually used today. The IP Precedence value is simply a 3-bit binary value, which in decimal terms represents a value of 0 through 7. The value indicates the relative priority of the packet, with 0 representing the lowest priority and 7 representing the highest priority. Each priority level is also assigned a name; for example, an IP Precedence value of 6 represents Internetwork Control traffic.

Class of Service (CoS)

Class of service (*CoS*) refers to the marking of Layer 2 frames to indicate the quality of service requirements of the frame. CoS is required for Layer 2 devices to apply QoS within a Layer 2 network. If we consider Ethernet as the Layer 2 technology, none of the various Ethernet frame types include a CoS field. A CoS field is created on tagged traffic, where the tag is primarily used to identify the VLAN that the tagged frame belongs to. Two major tagging techniques (trunking protocols) are supported by Cisco switches today—IEEE 802.1Q and ISL.

Figure 9-3 illustrates the tag format used for 802.1Q tags.

Figure 9-3   *802.1Q Tag Format*

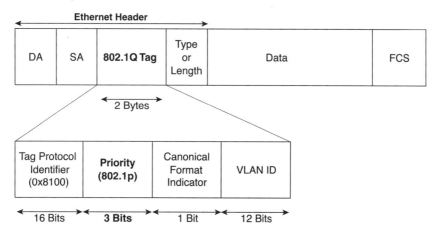

Notice that the tag is contained within the actual Ethernet frame and that a 3-bit 802.1p priority field exists that provides up to 8 CoS values.

Differentiated Services Code Point (DSCP)

The IP Precedence marking mechanism provides up to eight different indications of QofS. Eight levels of QoS is not sufficient for many large networks, causing scalability issues. Recently, the IETF has developed a new standard (see RFC 2474) that defines a *Differentiated Services Field* (*DS Field*) that obsoletes the old ToS and Precedence fields, and uses the first six high-order bits (up to 64 levels of QoS) for QoS marking. The value defined in the DS Field is known as the *Differentiated Services Code Point* (*DSCP*), and is designed to be backward compatible with older routers that only understand IP precedence. Figure 9-4 illustrates the DiffServ field.

Figure 9-4   *The DiffServ Field*

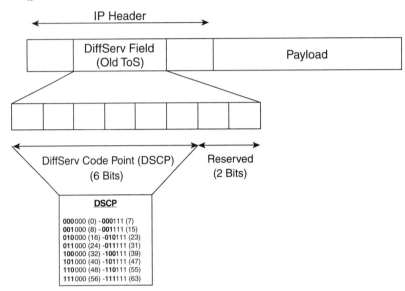

In the Diffserv model, each device that can provide QoS is able to provide a per-hop behavior (PHB) for different classes of traffic. The PHB is simply the way in which the queueing and scheduling mechanisms on a forwarding device are implemented for a particular class of traffic. Diffserv-compliant networks support the following PHBs:

- **Default PHB**—Defined in RFC 2474, this defines that traditional best-effort service (first-in, first-out) should be applied. RFC 2474 states that a DSCP value of 0 should be used to indicate that the default PHB be applied to a packet.

- **Class-Selector PHB**—Defined in RFC 2474, this is used to preserve backward compatibility with IP precedence, by setting the three low-order bits to 000 (DSCP values are in the format *xxx*000, where *xxx* is equivalent to IP precedence). With this PHB, forwarding devices must apply queueing and scheduling in same fashion as IP precedence is applied. For example, a packet with a DSCP value of 111000 (equivalent IP precedence of 7), is provided preferential treatment over a packet with a DSCP value of 101000 (equivalent IP precedence of 5).

- **Assured Forwarding PHB**—Defined in RFC 2597, this defines four classes of traffic called AF1, AF2, AF3 and AF4, each of which can be assigned a different level of QoS. For example, a forwarding device might allocate 10%, 20%, 30% and 40% of a links bandwidth to the AF1, AF2, AF3 and AF4 classes respectively. Within each class, three sub-classes exist (AFx1, AFx2 and AFx3), with each sub-class defining a relative *drop precedence*, which is used to determine which packets should be dropped first if a queue is full. For example, in the AF3 class, traffic assigned to the AF33 sub-class will be discarded before traffic in the AF32 sub-class, which in turn will be discarded before traffic in the AF31 sub-class. Table 9-2 describes each of the AF classes and subclasses and also indicates the DSCP value used to identify each subclass.

Table 9-2   *IP Precedence and DSCP Backward Compatibility*

Drop Precedence	Class 1 (AF1)	Class 2 (AF2)	Class 3 (AF3)	Class 4 (AF4)
Low Drop Precedence	AF11 DSCP = 10	AF21 DSCP = 18	AF31 DSCP = 26	AF41 DSCP = 34
Medium Drop Precedence	AF12 DSCP = 12	AF22 DSCP = 20	AF32 DSCP = 28	AF42 DSCP = 36
High Drop Precedence	AF13 DSCP = 14	AF23 DSCP = 22	AF33 DSCP = 30	AF43 DSCP = 38

In Table 9-2, each class of traffic is allocated a specific amount of bandwidth; for example, class 1 might be allocated 10% of the available bandwidth, whilst class 4 might be allocated 50% of the available bandwidth. Within each class, if the queue that services the class becomes full, packets are discarded according to their drop precedence. For example, packets with a DSCP value of 10, 12 or 14 are assigned to class 1. If the queue that these packets are placed into is full, packets in the class with a high drop precedence (for example, AF13 or DSCP 14) are discarded first, before packets with a medium and low drop precedence.

- **Expedited Forwarding PHB**—This PHB is designed for applications that required guaranteed bandwidth, low latency, and low jitter, such as voice and video. To provide this service, a forwarding device will typically place packets into a priority queue that is serviced before any other queues. RFC 2598 defines a DSCP value of 46 to indicate the expedited forwarding PHB is required.

QoS Functions

In previous sections, you have learned about the various QoS models. In the next few sections, you learn how each network device (in this case a LAN switch) implements QoS using the DiffServ model. Figure 9-5 summarizes the steps that occur when data is received by a LAN switch and how the appropriate QoS policy is determined and applied for that data.

Figure 9-5   *QoS Process in a Catalyst Switch*

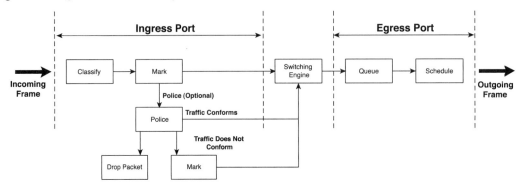

As Figure 9-5 shows, certain functions are performed on the ingress port (the port that receives the packet), while other functions are performed at the egress port (the port the sends the packet towards its destination). These functions are discussed in Table 9-3.

Table 9-3   *Ingress and Egress Port Functions*

Function	Description
Classification and marking	*Classification* allows the switch to determine the QoS that should be assigned to a received frame, while marking sets the CoS, ToS, or DiffServ bits in the frame or packet.
Policing	*Policing* on a LAN switch refers to the switch monitoring the bandwidth used by traffic and ensuring a specific bandwidth threshold is not exceeded. If the threshold is exceeded, the switch *polices* the traffic in excess, either dropping it or marking it with a lower QoS marking (e.g., DSCP) value.
Queuing	*Queuing* is applied to traffic at the egress switch port. Queuing allows for the preferential treatment (in terms of transmission priority or loss characteristics) of certain traffic classes.
Scheduling	The process of *scheduling* determines how each queue is serviced. The scheduling process takes a frame from a queue and transmits the frame onto the wire.

Implementing Quality of Service on Cisco Switches

It is important to understand the features and limitations of the various Catalyst platforms to ensure your network can deliver the QoS your applications require. The following platforms are considered the most common Cisco switches available today; the scenario for this chapter includes each of the following:

- Catalyst 2900XL/3500XL
- Catalyst 2950/3550
- Catalyst 4000 Supervisor 1/2
- Catalyst 4000 Supervisor 3
- Catalyst 6000/6500

Each platform is now discussed, with the discussion focusing on the classification, marking, policing, queuing, and scheduling features available. You also learn how to configure QoS on each platform to aid your understanding of this complex subject.

Catalyst 2900XL/3500XL

The Catalyst 2900XL/3500XL family consists of workgroup switches designed as an access layer switch for small to medium businesses. Their QoS features are very basic when compared to the newer Catalyst switches. However, a large installed base of these switches exists, and due to the inline power capabilities of the Catalyst 3524PWR-XL, this family of switches is common in Cisco IP Telephony deployments.

Classification and marking is supported only at a Layer 2 level by using 802.1p CoS values. The default classification process of the Catalyst 2900XL/3500XL is to *trust* the CoS of tagged frames received on a port and is described below:

- If untagged traffic is received on a port, assign the default 802.1p priority of the port to the frame tag.
- If tagged traffic is received on a port, trust the 802.1p priority value in the tag.

The default priority (CoS) of a port is zero, so by default any traffic received on access ports (non-trunk ports) are assigned a CoS of zero. The default priority can be changed per-port and is applied to all untagged traffic received on the port. You can also optionally override the CoS assigned to all ingress tagged traffic on a particular port.

TIP The Catalyst 2900XL/3500XL switches do not support policing of any kind.

The queuing mechanism used on the Catalyst 2900XL/3500XL switches consists of a single ingress queue and two egress queues per port. A high-priority queue and normal-priority queue make up the egress queues, with the high-priority queue being a strict priority queue, where it is always serviced ahead of the normal-priority queue. Traffic in the normal-priority queue is serviced only if the high-priority queue is empty. The traffic that is placed into each queue is determined by the CoS priority value in the 802.1Q or Inter-Switch Link (ISL) tag:

- **Priority 0 to 3**—This traffic is placed into the normal-priority queue.
- **Priority 4 to 7**—This traffic is placed into the high-priority queue.

NOTE   The queuing placement configuration just listed is fixed and is non-configurable.

Catalyst 2950/3550

The Catalyst 2950/3550 switches are the successors to the current 2900XL/3500XL switches and include more advanced quality of service features.

NOTE   The first release of Catalyst 2950 switches, running on the IOS 12.0(5.2)WC(1) Release software image support only the QoS features described for the 2900XL/3500XL switches. The next software release (IOS 12.1(6)EA2) Release introduced the advanced QoS features discussed in this section.

Before you can use QoS features, you must ensure QoS is globally enabled by issuing the **mls qos** privileged configuration mode command:

```
[no] mls qos
```

The switches use the DiffServ model in order to support end-to-end QoS, where all IP traffic is classified using a DSCP value. Switches also maintain class of service information for any tagged traffic, with mapping options available to generate the CoS from the DSCP value and vice versa. In terms of classification, the Catalyst 2950/3550 offers the following options:

- Classification based upon Layer 2, 3 or 4 access lists
- Classification based upon the trust state of the port
- Classification based upon the default priority (CoS) of the port

Classification based upon access lists is relatively straightforward to understand. Incoming traffic is compared to an access list; if traffic matches the access list, a QoS action (such as marking the packet with a particular DSCP value) is taken. This form of classification is normally performed on access layer switches, at the edge of the network.

Classification based upon the trust state of the port is a little more complicated to understand, but much simpler for switches to implement. Remember that a switch marks two places within each frame that contains an IP packet—the CoS value in the Layer 2 trunk header and the DSCP value in the IP packet. The switch can be configured to trust either the received CoS value or the received DSCP value. If the switch trusts the CoS value, the CoS value is maintained, and a DSCP value is written to the IP header based upon a map table called the *CoS-to-DSCP map*. Similarly, if the switch trusts the DSCP value, the DSCP value is maintained; however, the CoS value can be modified based upon another map table called the *DSCP-to-CoS map*.

NOTE   The Catalyst 3550 switches support a few more marking and trust features compared to the Catalyst 2950. The Catalyst 3550 can also trust IP Precedence and has an IP-Precedence-to-DSCP map to generate the appropriate DSCP value for each packet. Also, if an interface trusts DSCP state, you can modify the DSCP value using a DSCP-to-DSCP-mutation map, which translates a particular DSCP value to a new value.

If you do not explicitly configure classification based upon trust or access lists, the switch automatically overrides received QoS markings with the default priority of the port. This is limited to modification of the CoS value only (DSCP is not considered). You can modify the CoS assigned to any untagged traffic that is received or optionally overwrite the CoS values of any received tagged traffic.

Once an incoming frame has been classified appropriately, the switch can police traffic on a per-class basis only. Traffic that does not conform to the configured rate can be dropped or marked with a different DSCP value.

The last step in the QoS process is queuing and scheduling. The available options differ between the Catalyst 2950 and the 3550. On the Catalyst 2950, each port has four egress queues, which can be configured using one of the following scheduling options:

- **Strict priority**—Each queue is assigned a priority between 0 and 7. All traffic in higher priority queues is always serviced before traffic in lower priority queues. This mechanism is identical to the priority queuing implementation used on Cisco IOS routers. As such, care must be taken to ensure that all queues are serviced appropriately.

- **Weighted round robin (WRR)**—Each queue is assigned a weight, with each queue guaranteed service. The amount of traffic sent from each queue as it is serviced depends on the weight of the queue, with higher-weighted queues sending more traffic per scheduling cycle than lower-weighted queues.

Traffic is placed into each queue based upon a configurable CoS-to-Queue mapping table. Table 9-4 shows the default CoS-to-Queue mappings.

Table 9-4 *Default CoS-to-Queue Map on Catalyst 2950*

Priority (CoS)	Queue
0,1	1
2,3	2
4,5	3
6,7	4

Notice in Table 9-4 that the CoS value (rather than the DSCP value) determines which queue (and ultimately the actual QoS) a frame is placed into. This means it is very important that your DSCP-to-CoS map is accurate and consistent throughout the network.

WARNING On the Catalyst 2950, all queueing and scheduling configuration can only be applied on a global basis, meaning only a single policy can be used. On the Catalyst 3550, a unique queueing and scheduling policy can be configured per-port, allowing for much more flexibility.

- **Tail drop**—All traffic exceeding a queue threshold is dropped. If a tail drop condition occurs, all traffic can suddenly be dropped, which can cause phenomenon such as TCP slow start, where all TCP applications suddenly slow their data transmission rates in response to lost (dropped) TCP packets. In slow start, bandwidth efficiency is low because the network is sending at full bandwidth and then suddenly at half bandwidth due to TCP slow start. This bandwidth usage slowly increases until another tail drop occurs.

- **Weighted Random Early Detection (WRED)**—Traffic exceeding a queue threshold is randomly discarded, with frames coming from heavier data sources more likely to be dropped. WRED prevents a combined TCP slow start by dropping only a few select packets, causing TCP slow start for those sessions only. This increases the efficiency of the network.

Catalyst 4000

The Catalyst 4000 series of switches (including the 2948G and 2980G but excluding the Catalyst 4000 with Supervisor 3/4 module) offer very limited QoS functionality. In terms of classification, the Catalyst 4000 switches can only provide the following functions:

- Any untagged traffic can be assigned a default CoS value. This CoS value can be configured only on a per-switch basis.
- Any tagged traffic CoS values are maintained and cannot be overridden.

As you can see, you can configure the CoS value for untagged traffic only on a per-switch basis. This does not provide much flexibility, and you must bear this limitation in mind when designing your QoS architecture.

In terms of policing, the Catalyst 4000 switches do not provide any policing capabilities. In terms of queuing and scheduling, each port features two egress queues with a single drop threshold (of 100 percent), at which point tail drop occurs. A configurable CoS-to-Transmit Queue mapping exists, which defines the queue each frame is placed into based upon the CoS value of the frame. For example, you could place frames with a CoS value of 0–3 into one queue, and frames with a CoS value of 4–7 into the other queue.

Catalyst 4000 with Supervisor 3/4

The Supervisor 3/4 module for the Catalyst 4000 is a Cisco IOS-based module that includes many new features, including many new QoS features. The QoS features available on the Supervisor 3/4 are similar to those offered on the Catalyst 2950/3550 series switches, except a few interesting extras are included on the Supervisor 3/4.

Classification on the Catalyst 4000 is identical to the classification options available for the Catalyst 2950/3550, which in summary are as follows:

* Classification based upon Layer 2, 3, or 4 access lists
* Classification based upon the trust state of the port
* Classification based upon the default priority (CoS) of the port

If using CoS for classification, a CoS-to-DSCP map exists that generates the appropriate DSCP value for each IP packet. When using DSCP classification, if a CoS value needs to be generated for a frame, a DSCP-to-CoS map is referenced.

Policing is available on the Supervisor 3/4, with policing options on an individual basis, where each matched traffic class in a policy is policed separately, or on an aggregate basis, where all traffic classes within a policy are policed all together. Traffic that does not conform to a configured rate can either be dropped or marked with a new DSCP value.

Once classification and policing are complete, each frame needs to be queued and scheduled for transmission. Each egress port features four queues, and the placement of traffic into each queue is determined by the DSCP value of each packet by using a DSCP-to-queue map. For scheduling, the egress queues can be serviced using one of the following options:

* **Round robin**—Traffic is serviced on a round-robin basis, queue by queue. In essence this provides best-effort QoS and is the default scheduling mode.
* **Weighted round robin**—Each queue is assigned a portion of the available bandwidth of the egress port. Traffic in each queue is serviced according to this bandwidth value. By default, the user configurable weights are tied to IP Precedence.
* **Strict priority**—One of the queues is designated a priority queue, which is always serviced ahead of other queues.

A useful QoS feature also available on the Supervisor 3/4 is traffic shaping on each egress queue. This feature allows you to shape traffic to a maximum rate on each queue. Unlike a policer that typically drops traffic that exceeds the configured rate, the traffic shaper uses the egress queue to buffer traffic that exceeds the rate. The shaper can queue excess traffic only for a small time, and if traffic continuously exceeds the configured rate, the shaper discards traffic. Traffic shaping is useful for bursty applications, where the shaper allows short bursts of data, whereas a policer drops traffic bursting above the configured rate.

Catalyst 6000/6500

The Catalyst 6000/6500 switch is the flagship of the Cisco switch product line and as such includes the most advanced quality of service features available. The QoS features available are quite complex and are dependent on the type of switching engines installed in the Catalyst 6000/6500 switch. Two major switching engines exist on the Catalyst 6000/6500 switch:

- **Layer 2 switching engine**—This includes the Supervisor 1 or Supervisor 1a without the policy feature card (PFC) installed.

- **Layer 3 switching engine**—Includes the Supervisor 1/1a with PFC or the Supervisor 2 (which includes an integrated PFC2).

TIP	The policy feature card (PFC) is a Layer 3 switching engine that allows the Catalyst 6000/6500 to perform Layer 3 switching at wire speed. To perform true routing, the PFC requires a multiLayer switch feature card (MSFC), which is basically a Cisco IOS router. The MSFC operates in the control plane for Layer 3 routing, generating a route table, and then downloading this information to the PFC that operates in the data plane for Layer 3 routing. The PFC also provides hardware-based Layer 3 classification for QoS and security purposes, allowing these features to be applied at wire speed. The PFC does not require the MSFC for Layer 3 classification, only for performing Layer 3 routing.

It is important to note that the QoS model used by the Catalyst 6000/6500 features both egress and ingress classification, policing, and queuing mechanisms. The Catalyst 6000/6500 allows you to perform all QoS actions on the ingress port and egress port, not just some actions on the ingress and some actions on the egress.

For classification, the L2 switching engine can classify based upon Layer 2 access lists and VLANs and mark using CoS values. The Layer 3 engine can classify based upon Layer 3/4 access lists and mark using CoS, IP Precedence, or DSCP. If you classify traffic using the CoS trust option, you can queue received traffic in ingress queues. If you classify traffic using any other option (such as via access control lists (ACLs), non-trusted ports, trust DSCP, or trust IP Precedence), the traffic is passed directly to the switching engine.

The ingress queuing mechanism depends on the capability of the switch port. You can issue a **show port capabilities** command to view the ingress port queues and thresholds available. For example, a port might support a single queue with four thresholds, while another might support a priority queue and a standard queue with no thresholds. The thresholds are used to implement congestion avoidance mechanisms, such as tail drop or WRED. For example, if a queue reaches a threshold of 75 percent full, the switch might start dropping frames (tail drop) or randomly dropping frames (WRED). With multiple thresholds, traffic with a lower CoS can be assigned to a lower threshold (e.g., 50 percent), while higher CoS traffic can be assigned to a higher threshold (e.g., 100 percent). This ensures that lower priority traffic is dropped before higher priority traffic.

NOTE   The **show port capabilities** command shows queuing capabilities using a special naming convention. For example, an ingress (receive) queue that features a single queue with four thresholds is represented as rx-(1q4t). The *rx* identifies this applies to the ingress, the *1q* specifies a single queue, and the *4t* specifies four configurable thresholds on the queue. The rx-(1p1q8t) representation specifies on ingress the port supports a single priority queue (*1p*) and a single queue with eight configurable drop thresholds.

For policing functionality, only the Layer 3 switching engine supports policing. Policing can be applied on a *microflow basis*, where a single *flow* that matches an access list entry is policed at the configured rate. Policing can also be applied on an *aggregate basis*, where all flows that match an access control entry are policed at the configured rate. Any traffic that does not conform to the configured rate can be dropped or marked down.

NOTE   Do not confuse the microflow and aggregate policing features with the individual and aggregate policing functions on the Catalyst 4000 with Supervisor 3. On the Catalyst 4000, individual policers apply to a single traffic class (i.e., all traffic matched by a single ACL), and the aggregate policer applies to an entire policy (collection of ACLs).

So far, you have learned about the ingress classification, queuing and policing functions of the Catalyst 6000/6500 switch. Once the egress port for the received frame has been determined, the frame is placed into an egress queue for transmission. Similar to the ingress port, each egress port has particular queuing characteristics, which can be determined by using the **show port capabilities** command. For example, the port might indicate a capability of tx-1p3q1t, where the *tx* indicates this is for the egress side of the port, the *1p* indicates a single priority queue, and the *3q1t* indicates three standard queues, each with a single drop threshold. The CoS value of each frame dictates which queue traffic is placed into; the CoS value is also used within each queue to determine which drop threshold applies to traffic. The drop threshold relates to how full each queue is (e.g., 75 percent full) and determines the point at which traffic is subject to congestion avoidance. As for the ingress queues, the congestion avoidance mechanisms include tail drop and WRED.

TIP   The Catalyst 6000/6500 switch with a Layer 3 switching engine also supports the IntServ QoS model by supporting both the Resource Reservation Protocol (RSVP) and the Common Open Policy Service. The configuration of this is outside the scope of this book.

Scenario 9-1: Configuring QoS Features

In this scenario, you configure QoS on both Catalyst CatOS-based switches and Cisco IOS-based switches. Rather than present a series of scenarios that configure specific QoS features, this chapter presents a single, longer scenario that shows you how to configure QoS throughout the LAN environment.

Scenario Exercise

Figure 9-6 illustrates the topology used for this scenario. Corporation XYZ has recently implemented a pilot Cisco Architecture for Voice, Video, and Integrated Data (AVVID) IP Telephony network to replace the legacy PBX system. Initially, Corporation XYZ pilots the Cisco IOS IP Telephony Service software, before introducing a Cisco CallManager platform. To ensure that voice functionality operates with the same quality and reliability in both solutions, you must configure quality of service. The configuration of QoS ensures voice traffic receives the appropriate bandwidth and latency characteristics. The Corporation XYZ network includes an intranet web server that at certain times has caused LAN congestion. Corporation XYZ would like the capability to rate limit web traffic to a maximum rate if required. You must ensure all of the quality of service requirements mentioned are met by the LAN switches.

Figure 9-6   *Scenario 9-1 Topology*

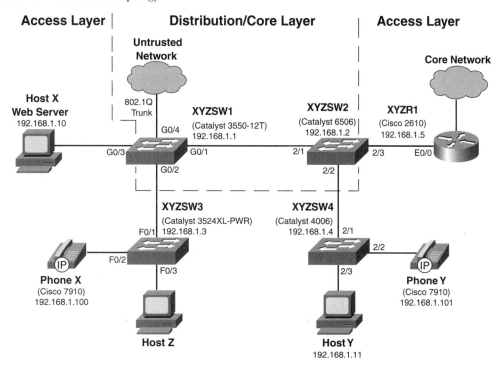

The LAN consists of an access layer that is used to provide network access for devices such as IP telephones. A combined distribution/core layer provides connectivity for the access switches to core network services and applications. The following describes the function of each component of the scenario topology shown in Figure 9-6:

- XYZSW1 is a Catalyst 3550-12T access/distribution switch that provides connectivity for the XYZSW3 switch. XYZSW1 interconnects with XYZSW2, the other distribution switch, via an 802.1Q trunk. XYZSW1 also provides access layer functions by connecting directly to Host X.

- XYZSW2 is a Catalyst 6506 access/distribution switch that provides access for the XYZSW4 switch. XYZSW2 interconnects with XYZSW1, the other distribution switch, via an 802.1Q trunk. XYZSW2 also provides access layer functions by connecting directly to XYZR1.

- XYZSW3 is a Catalyst 3524XL-PWR switch that provides access for Cisco IP telephones. This is a common access switch used in IP Telephony deployments, because it provides inline power for Cisco IP telephones.

NOTE   The Catalyst 3550 switch family now includes a 24-port switch that provides inline power. In the future, a Catalyst 3750 switch will be produced that offers inline power based upon the IEEE 802.3af standard.

- The Catalyst 3550 switch family now includes a 24-port switch that provides inline power. In the future, a Catalyst 3750 switch will be produced that offers inline power based upon the IEEE 802.3af standard.

- XYZSW4 is a Catalyst 4006 switch that also provides network access for Cisco IP telephones. This is also a common workgroup/departmental access switch used in IP Telephony deployments, because an inline power module is available for the Catalyst 4000 series switches.

- XYZR1 is a Cisco 2610 router that runs the Cisco IOS IP Telephony service.

- Phone X and Phone Y are Cisco 7910 IP Telephones.

- Host X is an intranet server that uses Microsoft NetMeeting to stream audio to web clients.

- Host Y is a web client that connects to Host X for Intranet web access.

Scenario Objectives

The scenario objectives are as follows:

- Configure Catalyst 2900XL/3500XL QoS features
- Configure Catalyst 2950/3550 QoS features
- Configure Catalyst 2980/4000 QoS features
- Configure Catalyst 6000/6500 QoS features
- Configure the Cisco IOS IP Telephony Service to support Cisco IP Phones
- Establish a phone call over an IP network

Equipment Needed

The equipment needed is a follows:

- One CatOS Catalyst 6000/6500 Switch with Supervisor 2 installed *or* Supervisor 1/1a with policy feature card installed.
- One Cisco IOS Catalyst 3550-12T or 3550-12G switch.
- One Cisco IOS Catalyst 4003 or 4006 switch.
- One Cisco IOS Catalyst 3524PWR-XL inline power switch.
- One Cisco 2610 Router running a 12.2(2)XB image (or higher) with an IP Plus feature set.
- Two Cisco 7910, 7940, or 7960 IP Phones.
- Two PCs running a Windows operating system with network card installed and configured to use TCP/IP. To verify some QoS configurations, Host X requires a web server and File Transfer Protocol (FTP) server running.

Scenario Planning

The first goal of this scenario is to show you how to configure QoS on Cisco Catalyst switches. The second, and more important, goal is to make you aware of the need for end-to-end QOS. This scenario shows you how to implement end-to-end QoS on a LAN, but you should understand that in the real world a QoS implementation must include the devices of the wide-area network as well. In fact, it is in the wide-area network that QoS is the most critical.

When you are planning for end-to-end QoS, you should create a table that lists each of the various QoS markings and the level of QoS they represent on the network. Table 9-5 shows the QoS markings used in this scenario.

Table 9-5 *QoS Markings Used in Scenario 9-1*

Type	Marking	Description
CoS	0	Low priority traffic
	1	Internal company traffic
	3	Business critical traffic
	5	VoIP control traffic
DSCP	0	Low priority traffic
	8	Internal company traffic
	24	Business critical traffic
	41	VoIP traffic
	46	VoIP traffic (EF)

As you can see in Table 9-5, traffic is represented in both CoS and DSCP markings. CoS is required for non-DSCP aware switches, which include XYZSW3 (Catalyst 3500XL) and XYZSW4 (Catalyst 4000). It is also a good idea to define key traffic flows on your network, so that you can determine where QoS needs to be applied. Figure 9-7 shows the Scenario 9-1 network with each of the traffic types shown in Table 9-5.

In Figure 9-7, you can see that business critical traffic is transmitted only between devices connected to XYZSW1 and XYZSW2, and not to devices connected to XYZSW3 or XYZSW4. Therefore, no business critical traffic tagged with a CoS of 3 is being sent or received from these switches. This is important to understand, as you can then assign a DSCP value of 46 (voice traffic) to all traffic with a CoS of 5 from XYZSW3 and XYZSW4. In this scenario, you configure XYZSW3 and XYZSW4 to tag only voice with a CoS of 5, so no other traffic should be tagged with this CoS.

Figure 9-7 *Scenario 9-1 Traffic Types*

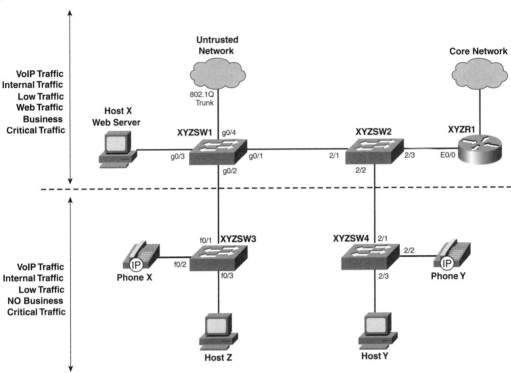

Command Syntax

The requirements for configuring QoS vary immensely for each platform, and providing command syntax for all of these commands would require a significant section, which would only serve to bore you. If you need command syntax help for any of the commands, visit the Cisco documentation web site at www.cisco.com/univercd/home/home.htm.

Configuration Tasks

In this scenario, you perform the following tasks:

- Step 1—Prepare the network
- Step 2—Configure the IOS IP Telephony service
- Step 3—Configure QoS at the access layer
- Step 4—Configure QoS at the distribution layer

Step 1—Preparing the Network

In this step, you perform the following to prepare the network:

- Configure basic parameters on each switch
- Interconnect each switch
- Connect the router, host, and IP Phones
- Configure basic parameters on XYZR1

Configuring Basic Parameters on Each Switch

Before beginning, ensure you have a working console connection on a PC running terminal emulation software and then confirm you can access each switch via the console port.

Step 1 On XYZSW1, configure system name, disable Domain Name System (DNS) name resolution, add a Telnet/enable password of *cisco*, an IP address of 192.168.1.1/24, and a default gateway of 192.168.1.5 (XYZR1), as shown in Example 9-1.

Example 9-1 *Configuring Basic Parameters on XYZSW1*

```
Switch> enable
Password:
Switch# configure terminal
Switch(config)# hostname XYZSW1
XYZSW1(config)# no ip domain-lookup
XYZSW1(config)# enable secret cisco
XYZSW1(config)# line vty 0 4
XYZSW1(config-line)# password cisco
XYZSW1(config-line)# interface VLAN1
XYZSW1(config-if)# no shutdown
XYZSW1(config-if)# ip address 192.168.1.1 255.255.255.0
XYZSW1(config-if)# exit
XYZSW1(config)# ip default-gateway 192.168.1.5
XYZSW1(config)# end
```

Step 2 On XYZSW2, configure the system name, a Telnet/enable password of *cisco*, an IP address of 192.168.1.2/24, and a default gateway of 192.168.1.5 (XYZR1), as shown in Example 9-2.

Example 9-2 *Configuring Basic Parameters on XYZSW2*

```
Console enable
Enter password:
Console (enable) set system name XYZSW2
System name set.
XYZSW2> (enable) set password
Enter old password:
Enter new password: *****
Retype new password: *****
Password changed.
XYZSW2> (enable) set enablepass
```

continues

Example 9-2 *Configuring Basic Parameters on XYZSW2 (Continued)*

```
Enter old password:
Enter new password: *****
Retype new password: *****
Password changed.
XYZSW2> (enable) set interface sc0 192.168.1.2 255.255.255.0
XYZSW2> (enable) set ip route default 192.168.1.5
Route added.
```

Step 3 On XYZSW3, configure the system name, add a Telnet/enable password of "cisco," disable DNS name resolution, an IP address of 192.168.1.3/24, and a default gateway of 192.168.1.5 (XYZR1), as shown in Example 9-3.

Example 9-3 *Configuring Basic Parameters on XYZSW3*

```
Switch> enable
Password:
Switch# configure terminal
Switch(config)# hostname XYZSW3
XYZSW3(config)# no ip domain-lookup
XYZSW3(config)# enable secret cisco
XYZSW3(config)# line vty 0 4
XYZSW3(config-line)# password cisco
XYZSW3(config-line)# interface VLAN1
XYZSW3(config-if)# no shutdown
XYZSW3(config-if)# ip address 192.168.1.3 255.255.255.0
XYZSW3(config-if)# exit
XYZSW3(config)# ip default-gateway 192.168.1.5
XYZSW3(config)# end
```

Step 4 On XYZSW4, configure the system name, add a Telnet/enable password of "cisco," an IP address of 192.168.1.4/24, and a default gateway of 192.168.1.5 (XYZR1), as shown in Example 9-4.

Example 9-4 *Configuring Basic Parameters on XYZSW4*

```
Console enable
Enter password:
Console (enable) set system name XYZSW4
System name set.
XYZSW4> (enable) set password
Enter old password:
Enter new password: *****
Retype new password: *****
Password changed.
XYZSW4> (enable) set enablepass
Enter old password:
Enter new password: *****
Retype new password: *****
Password changed.
XYZSW4> (enable) set interface sc0 192.168.1.4 255.255.255.0
XYZSW4> (enable) set ip route default 192.168.1.5
Route added.
```

Interconnecting the Switches

For this scenario, you interconnect all switches using crossover UTP cables between Fast Ethernet 802.1Q trunk ports (you can use gigabit Ethernet trunks if you have these).

Step 1   On XYZSW1, configure 100 Mbps speed and full duplex on ports GigabitEthernet0/1–3 and enable trunking using 802.1Q, as shown in Example 9-5.

Example 9-5   *Configuring Trunks on XYZSW1*

```
XYZSW1# configure terminal
XYZSW1(config)# interface GigabitEthernet0/1
XYZSW1(config-if)# description TRUNK TO XYZSW2
XYZSW1(config-if)# no shutdown
XYZSW1(config-if)# speed 100
XYZSW1(config-if)# duplex full
XYZSW1(config-if)# switchport trunk encapsulation dot1q
XYZSW1(config-if)# switchport mode trunk
XYZSW1(config-if)# interface GigabitEthernet0/2
XYZSW1(config-if)# description TRUNK TO XYZSW3
XYZSW1(config-if)# no shutdown
XYZSW1(config-if)# speed 100
XYZSW1(config-if)# duplex full
XYZSW1(config-if)# switchport trunk encapsulation dot1q
XYZSW1(config-if)# switchport mode trunk
XYZSW1(config-if)# exit
XYZSW1(config)# interface GigabitEthernet0/3
XYZSW1(config-if)# description TRUNK TO UNTRUSTED NETWORK
XYZSW1(config-if)# no shutdown
XYZSW1(config-if)# speed 100
XYZSW1(config-if)# duplex full
XYZSW1(config-if)# switchport trunk encapsulation dot1q
XYZSW1(config-if)# switchport mode trunk
XYZSW1(config-if)# end
```

NOTE   In this scenario, GigabitEthernet0/4 is not connected to anything, but for the purposes of the scenario, assume some network is connected for GigabitEthernet0/4.

Step 2   On XYZSW2, configure 100 Mbps speed and full duplex on port 2/1 and port 2/2 and enable trunking using 802.1Q, as show in Example 9-6.

Example 9-6   *Configuring Trunks on XYZSW2*

```
XYZSW2> (enable) set port speed 2/1-2 100
Port(s)  2/1-2 transmission speed set to 100Mbps.
XYZSW2> (enable) set port duplex 2/1-2 full
Port(s)  2/1-2 to full-duplex.
```

continues

Example 9-6 *Configuring Trunks on XYZSW2 (Continued)*

```
XYZSW2> (enable) set trunk 2/1 on dot1q
Port(s)  2/1 trunk mode set to on.
Port(s)  2/1 trunk type set to dot1q.
XYZSW2> (enable) set trunk 2/2 on dot1q
Port(s)  2/2 trunk mode set to on.
Port(s)  2/2 trunk type set to dot1q.
```

Step 3 On XYZSW3, configure 100 Mbps speed and full duplex on port fastEthernet0/1 and enable trunking using 802.1Q, as shown in Example 9-7.

Example 9-7 *Configuring Trunks on XYZSW3*

```
XYZSW3# configure terminal
XYZSW3(config)# interface fastEthernet0/1
XYZSW3(config-if)# description TRUNK TO XYZSW1
XYZSW3(config-if)# no shutdown
XYZSW3(config-if)# speed 100
XYZSW3(config-if)# duplex full
XYZSW3(config-if)# switchport trunk encapsulation dot1q
XYZSW3(config-if)# switchport mode trunk
XYZSW3(config-if)# end
```

Step 4 On XYZSW4, configure 100 Mbps speed and full duplex on port 2/1 and enable trunking using 802.1Q, as shown in Example 9-8.

Example 9-8 *Configuring Trunks on XYZSW4*

```
XYZSW4> (enable) set port speed 2/1 100
Port 2/1 transmission speed set to 100Mbps.
XYZSW4> (enable) set port duplex 2/1 full
Port 2/1 to full-duplex.
XYZSW4> (enable) set trunk 2/1 on dot1q
Port(s)  2/1 trunk mode set to on.
Port(s)  2/1 trunk type set to dot1q.
```

Once these configurations are complete, wait for at least 30 seconds to allow the spanning-tree state of the trunk ports to progress from the learning → listening → forwarding state.

Step 5 Verify that you are able to ping all other switches from any switch in the network, as shown in Example 9-9.

Example 9-9 *Verifying Ping connectivity*

```
XYZSW2> (enable) ping 192.168.1.1
!!!!!
XYZSW2> (enable) ping 192.168.1.3
!!!!!
```

Connecting the Router, Host, and IP Phones

Connect each end device to the appropriate switch and port and prepare each port for the devices.

Step 1   On XYZSW1, configure 100 Mbps speed, full duplex for port GigabitEthernet0/3 and configure the port as an *access* port, as shown in Example 9-10.

Example 9-10   *Configuring Ports on XYZSW1*

```
XYZSW1# configure terminal
XYZSW1(config)# interface GigabitEthernet0/3
XYZSW1(config-if)# no shutdown
XYZSW1(config-if)# speed 100
XYZSW1(config-if)# duplex full
XYZSW1(config-if)# switchport mode access
XYZSW1(config-if)# end
```

Step 2   On XYZSW2, configure 10 Mbps speed, half duplex for port 2/3 (connected to XYZR1) and configure the port as an access port, as shown in Example 9-11.

Example 9-11   *Configuring Ports on XYZSW2*

```
XYZSW2> (enable) set port speed 2/3 10
Port 2/3 transmission speed set to 10Mbps.
XYZSW2> (enable) set port duplex 2/3 half
Port 2/3 to half-duplex.
```

Step 3   On XYZSW3, configure port fa0/2 to *autosense,* configure the port as an *access* port, and ensure inline power is enabled (if you want to use this feature). Also, configure port fastEthernet0/3 as an 802.1Q trunk, as shown in Example 9-12.

Example 9-12   *Configuring Ports on XYZSW3*

```
XYZSW3# configure terminal
XYZSW3(config)# interface fastEthernet0/2
XYZSW3(config-if)# description PHONE X
XYZSW3(config-if)# no shutdown
XYZSW3(config-if)# speed auto
XYZSW3(config-if)# duplex auto
XYZSW3(config-if)# switchport mode access
XYZSW3(config-if)# power inline auto
XYZSW3(config-if)# exit
XYZSW3(config)# interface fastEthernet0/3
XYZSW3(config-if)# description TRUNK TO HOST Z
XYZSW3(config-if)# no shutdown
XYZSW3(config-if)# speed 100
XYZSW3(config-if)# duplex full
XYZSW3(config-if)# switchport trunk encapsulation dot1q
XYZSW3(config-if)# switchport mode trunk
XYZSW3(config-if)# end
```

TIP   When connecting Cisco IP Phones, configure the switch port as autosensing. Do not hard code the port speed and duplex settings, because the phone must negotiate these settings.

Step 4   On XYZSW4, configure port 2/2 to autosense and hard code port 2/3 to 100 Mbps, full duplex, as shown in Example 9-13.

Example 9-13 *Configuring Ports on XYZSW4*

```
XYZSW4> (enable) set port speed 2/2 auto
Port 2/2 transmission speed set to auto.
XYZSW2> (enable) set port duplex 2/2 auto
Port 2/2 to auto.
XYZSW2> (enable) set port speed 2/3 100
Port 2/3 transmission speed set to 100Mbps.
XYZSW2> (enable) set port duplex 2/3 full
Port 2/3 to full-duplex.
```

Step 5   Verify that you can ping from Host X to Host Y, as shown in Example 9-14.

Example 9-14 *Verifying End-to-End Connectivity*

```
C:\WINXP\system32>ping 192.168.1.11
Pinging 192.168.1.11 with 32 bytes of data:
Reply from 192.168.1.11: bytes=32 time=1ms TTL=255
Reply from 192.168.1.11: bytes=32 time=1ms TTL=255
Reply from 192.168.1.11: bytes=32 time=1ms TTL=255
Reply from 192.168.1.11: bytes=32 time=1ms TTL=255
Ping statistics for 192.168.1.11:
    Packets: Sent = 4, Received = 4, Lost = 0 (0% loss),
Approximate round trip times in milli-seconds:
    Minimum = 1ms, Maximum = 1ms, Average = 1ms
```

Configuring Basic Parameters on XYZR1

Do the following to configuring basic parameters on XYZR1:

Step 1   On XYZR1, configure host name, Telnet/enable passwords of "cisco," IP addressing, and the correct date and time, as shown in Example 9-15.

Example 9-15 *Configuring XYZR1*

```
Router> enable
Router# configure terminal
Router(config)# hostname XYZR1
XYZR1(config)# enable secret cisco
XYZR1(config)# clock timezone NZT 12
XYZR1(config)# line vty 0 4
XYZR1(config-line)# password cisco
XYZR1(config-line)# interface ethernet0/0
```

Example 9-15 *Configuring XYZR1 (Continued)*

```
XYZR1(config-if)# no shutdown
XYZR1(config-if)# ip address 192.168.1.5 255.255.255.0
XYZR1(config)# exit
XYZR1# clock set 12:00:00 23 March 2002
```

Step 2   On XYZR1, verify you can ping all switches in the network, as shown in Example 9-16.

Example 9-16 *Verifying XYZR1 Connectivity*

```
XYZR1#ping 192.168.1.1
Type escape sequence to abort.
Sending 5, 100-byte ICMP Echos to 192.168.1.1, timeout is 2 seconds:
!!!!!
Success rate is 100 percent (5/5), round-trip min/avg/max = 4/8/12 ms
XYZR1#ping 192.168.1.2
Type escape sequence to abort.
Sending 5, 100-byte ICMP Echos to 192.168.1.1, timeout is 2 seconds:
!!!!!
Success rate is 100 percent (5/5), round-trip min/avg/max = 4/8/12 ms
...
```

Step 2—Configuring the IOS IP Telephony Service

In this step, you perform the following on XYZR1:

- Configure DHCP server support
- Configure the IOS IP Telephony service
- Configure IP Phone support

WARNING   The IP Plus feature set on the Cisco 2600 series router supports the IP Telephony service features detailed in this section out of the box. However, you must license the use of this feature by purchasing a separate license from Cisco. You also require a Cisco login to download IP Phone images from Cisco.

Configuring DHCP Server Support

Configuring DHCP server support is done as follows:

Step 1   Configure a DHCP exclusion range that prevents XYZR1 from providing DHCP addresses within the reserved range of 192.l68.1.1-192.168.1.99, as shown in Example 9-17.

Example 9-17 *Creating a DHCP Exclusion Range on XYZR1*

```
XYZR1# configure terminal
XYZR1(config)# ip dhcp excluded-address 192.168.1.1 192.168.1.99
```

Step 2   Configure the DHCP server on XYZR1, creating a DHCP address pool
for the 192.168.1.0/24 subnet, ensuring the TFTP Server option (option
150) is set to the IP address of XYZR1, as shown in Example 9-18.

Example 9-18   *Creating a DHCP Pool on XYZR1*

```
XYZR1(config)# ip dhcp pool QOSLAB
XYZR1(dhcp-config)# network 192.168.1.0 255.255.255.0
XYZR1(dhcp-config)# option 150 ip 192.168.1.5
XYZR1(dhcp-config)# default-router 192.168.1.5
XYZR1(dhcp-config)# end
```

In Example 9-18, you first configure the DHCP server to exclude the address range
192.168.1.1 through 192.168.1.99 from the DHCP scope. Then, in Example 9-18, you
create a DHCP scope called QOSLAB, which provides DHCP address leases for the
192.168.1.0/24 subnet. You configure the TFTP Server option (option 150) with the IP
address of XYZR1, because this is required for the phones to download their firmware
image from XYZR1 when they boot up. The address leases provided start from
192.168.1.100 (not 192.168.1.1) because of the exclusion range configured in Example 9-17.

Configuring the IP Telephony Service

Do the following to configure the IP telephony service:

Step 1   Configure basic IP Telephony service parameters, as shown in Example 9-19.

Example 9-19   *Configuring the XYZR1 Keyswitch*

```
XYZR1# configure terminal
XYZR1(config)# telephony-service
XYZR1(config-telephony)# ip source-address 192.168.1.5
XYZR1(config-telephony)# load 7910 P004G302
XYZR1(config-telephony)# max-ephones 24
XYZR1(config-telephony)# max-dn 48
XYZR1(config-telephony)# dialplan-pattern 1 508339.... extension-length 4
XYZR1(config-telephony)# end
```

In Example 9-19, you enter telephony configuration mode and then first configure the IP
address that the telephony service binds to. You must also configure the phone load that
each phone model (e.g., 7910, 7940) should use by configuring the **load** command. Next,
you specify the maximum number of phones allowed (**max-ephones 24**), the maximum
number of directory numbers/extensions allowed (**max-dn 48**), and also an expansion dial
pattern that is appended to all outgoing calls in calling ID information (**dial-plan pattern**).

Step 2   Using the **show flash** command, verify that your Flash file system contains the appropriate phone load files (.bin files) and that the initial keyswitch configuration has created a SEPDEFAULT.cnf file, as shown in Example 9-20.

Example 9-20   *Verifying the Appropriate Files Are Present on XYZR1*

```
XYZR1# show flash
System flash directory:
File   Length     Name/status
   1   12273948   c2600-is-mz.122-2.XB.bin
   2   14         SEPDEFAULT.cnf
   3   258360     P004G302.bin
[12535980 bytes used, 4241236 available, 16777216 total]
16384K bytes of processor board System flash (Read/Write)
```

In Example 9-20, the P004G302.bin file represents a phone load file, while the SEPDE-FAULT.cnf file contains global configuration information for each phone.

Step 3   Configure XYZR1 as a TFTP server, enabling phones to download the appropriate phone files (SEPDEFAULT.cnf and any phone load files) stored in Flash, as shown in Example 9-21.

Example 9-21   *Configuring TFTP Server Support on XYZR1*

```
XYZR1# configure terminal
Enter configuration commands, one per line.  End with CNTL/Z.
XYZR1(config)# tftp-server flash:SEPDEFAULT.cnf
XYZR1(config)# tftp-server flash:P004G302.bin
XYZR1(config)# end
```

Configuring the IP Phones

Do the following to configure the IP phones:

TIP   A directory number tag is not the directory (extension) number itself, just an identifier for the directory number. You configure the directory extension number in the next step.

Step 1   Configure the extension numbers and a display name for each of the directory number (DN) tags, as shown in Example 9-22.

Example 9-22   *Configuring Directory Numbers*

```
XYZR1# configure terminal
Enter configuration commands, one per line.  End with CNTL/Z.
XYZR1(config)#ephone-dn 1
XYZR1(config-ephone-dn)#number 4001
```

continues

Example 9-22   *Configuring Directory Numbers (Continued)*

```
XYZR1(config-ephone-dn)#name PHONE X
XYZR1(config-ephone-dn)#exit
XYZR1(config)#ephone-dn 2
XYZR1(config-ephone-dn)#number 4002
XYZR1(config-ephone-dn)#name PHONE Y
XYZR1(config-ephone-dn)#end
```

In Example 9-22, you assign the extension number 4001 and the display name of PHONE X to the DN tag of 1 and the extension number 4002 with a display name of PHONE Y to the DN tag 2.

Step 2   Configure phone support by creating a definition for each IP Phone that defines the MAC address of the phone and the directory number tag assigned to each button on the phone, as shown in Example 9-23 (every Cisco IP Phone is labeled with its MAC address).

Example 9-23   *Configuring IP Phones*

```
XYZR1# configure terminal
Enter configuration commands, one per line.  End with CNTL/Z.
XYZR1(config)#ephone 1
XYZR1(config-ephone)#mac-address 0007.0ea6.398d
XYZR1(config-ephone)#button 1:1
XYZR1(config-ephone)#exit
XYZR1(config)#ephone 2
XYZR1(config-ephone)#mac-address 0007.0ea6.33da
XYZR1(config-ephone)#button 1:2
XYZR1(config-ephone)#end
```

In Example 9-23, you create a definition for each phone (for example, **ephone 1**) that includes the MAC address of each phone (**mac-address** *xxxx.xxxx.xxxx*) and the directory number (DN) tag associated with each button on the phone (**button** *x:x*). For example, the command **button 1:2** assigns the DN tag 2 to button 1 on the phone.

Step 3   Ensure your IP Phones are connected to the correct ports on each switch. The phones should eventually receive an IP address via DHCP and register with XYZR1. Phone X should receive an extension number of 4001, while Phone Y should receive an extension number of 4002. You should be able to make calls between Phone X and Phone Y.

Step 3—Configuring QoS at the Access Layer

In this step, you configure QoS functions at the edge of the network, the access layer switches. XYZSW3 and XYZSW4 are dedicated access layer switches, so you configure these switches in this section. XYZSW1 and XYZSW2 provide both access layer and distribution layer connectivity; you configure the access layer features on XYZSW1 and XYZSW2. You now perform the following:

- Configure access layer QoS on XYZSW3 and XYZSW4
- Configure access layer QoS on XYZSW1
- Configure access layer QoS on XYZSW2

Configuring Access Layer QoS on XYZSW3 and XYZSW4

XYZSW3 and XYZSW4 offer the most limited QoS features of the switches in the scenario and are the simplest to configure. In this section, you configure the following:

- Configure XYZSW3 to tag all voice frames from Phone X with a CoS of 5. You configure Phone X to tag any frames received from a PC connected to the phone with a CoS of 1. You then configure XYZSW3 to override the CoS on all frames received from Host Z, tagging each frame with a CoS of 0.

- Configure XYZSW4 to tag all frames from Phone Y with a CoS of 5. You configure the default CoS for frames from Host Y to be set to 1, which is applied to all frames because Host Y sends untagged frames. You then assign traffic with a CoS value of 5 to the strict priority queue on XYZSW4.

On the queuing and scheduling side, both XYZSW3 and XYZSW4 offer only a single priority queue and a normal queue on an egress port. The placement of frames into each queue is determined by the CoS of the frame; hence, it is important to classify frames correctly to ensure the correct placement of high priority traffic into the priority queue.

Step 1   Configure XYZSW3 to identify voice traffic on port fastEthernet0/2 and instruct Phone X to tag voice traffic with an 802.1p priority of 5 using the native VLAN. Also configure Phone X so that it sets the CoS to 1 for all untagged frames received from the PC by the phone. This means any data frames from a PC connected to Phone X (the 7940/7960 phones support connecting your PC directly to the phone, saving switch port capacity) are tagged with an 802.1p value of 1. Example 9-24 demonstrates the configuration required.

Example 9-24   *Enabling Voice Prioritization over Data on the Same VLAN*

```
XYZSW3# configure terminal
XYZSW3(config)# interface fastEthernet0/2
XYZSW3(config-if)# switchport voice vlan dot1p
XYZSW3(config-if)# switchport priority extend cos 1
XYZSW3(config-if)#end
```

Step 2 Verify the voice VLAN configuration, as shown in Example 9-25.

Example 9-25 *Verifying Voice VLAN Configuration*

```
XYZSW3#show interface fastEthernet0/2 switchport
Name: Fa0/2
Switchport: Enabled
Administrative mode: trunk
Operational Mode: trunk
Administrative Trunking Encapsulation: dot1q
Operational Trunking Encapsulation: dot1q
Negotiation of Trunking: Disabled
Access Mode VLAN: 0 ((Inactive))
Trunking Native Mode VLAN: 1 (default)
Trunking VLANs Enabled: ALL
Trunking VLANs Active: 1
Pruning VLANs Enabled: 2-1001
Priority for untagged frames: 0
Override vlan tag priority: FALSE
Voice VLAN: dot1p
Appliance trust: extend cos 1
```

As you can see from Example 9-25, the voice VLAN configuration is dot1p (i.e., use a single VLAN for voice and data and tag the voice traffic with a CoS of 5) and the appliance trust is set to override the 802.1p value of all PC data frames to 1.

Step 3 You also want to ensure traffic from Host Z has a CoS set to 0, because this host supports 802.1p tagging, and you do not want traffic from Host Z to affect the quality of service provided to voice within your network. Configure XYZSW3 to override the 802.1p priority of any tagged frames arriving on port fastEthernet0/3 to a value of 0, as shown in Example 9-26.

Example 9-26 *Enabling 802.1p Priority Override on Port fa0/3 of XYZSW3*

```
XYZSW3# configure terminal
XYZSW3(config)# interface fastEthernet0/3
XYZSW3(config-if)# switchport priority default 0
XYZSW3(config-if)# switchport priority override
XYZSW3(config-if)#end
```

Step 4 Verify the 802.1p priority configuration on fastEthernet0/3, as shown in Example 9-27.

Example 9-27 *Verifying Voice VLAN Configuration*

```
XYZSW3# show interface fastEthernet0/3 switchport
Name: Fa0/3
Switchport: Enabled
Administrative mode: trunk
Operational Mode: trunk
Administrative Trunking Encapsulation: dot1q
Operational Trunking Encapsulation: dot1q
Negotiation of Trunking: Disabled
```

Example 9-27 *Verifying Voice VLAN Configuration (Continued)*

```
Access Mode VLAN: 0 ((Inactive))
Trunking Native Mode VLAN: 1 (default)
Trunking VLANs Enabled: ALL
Trunking VLANs Active: 1
Pruning VLANs Enabled: 2-1001
Priority for untagged frames: 0
Override vlan tag priority: TRUE
Voice VLAN: none
Appliance trust: none
```

Example 9-27 shows that the switch is set to override the VLAN tag priority with the default priority of untagged frames, which is 0.

Step 5   Enable qualify of service features on XYZSW4, as shown in Example 9-28.

Example 9-28 *Enabling QoS on XYZSW4*

```
XYZSW4> (enable) set qos enable
QoS is enabled.
```

Step 6   On XYZSW4, configure the default CoS value for any untagged frames received by the switch to 1, as shown in Example 9-29.

Example 9-29 *Setting the Default CoS on XYZSW4*

```
XYZSW4> (enable) set qos defaultcos 1
qos defaultcos set to 1
```

Step 7   On XYZSW4, determine the number of egress queues and thresholds available on port 2/1 (the uplink to XYZSW2) by using the **show port capabilities** command, as shown in Example 9-30.

Example 9-30 *Determining QoS Port Capabilities on XYZSW4*

```
XYZSW4> (enable) show port capabilities 2/1
Model                 WS-X4148
Port                  2/1
Type                  10/100BaseTX
Speed                 auto,10,100
Duplex                half,full
Trunk encap type      802.1Q
Trunk mode            on,off,desirable,auto,nonegotiate
Channel               2/1-48
Flow control          no
Security              yes
Dot1x                 yes
Membership            static,dynamic
Fast start            yes
QOS scheduling        rx-(none),tx-(2q1t)
CoS rewrite           no
ToS rewrite           no
Rewrite               no
...
```

Example 9-30 shows that the port has no QoS scheduling capabilities on the ingress (rx) side, but has two queues, each with a single drop threshold on the egress side.

Step 8 On XYZSW4, configure only traffic with a CoS of 5 (voice traffic) to be placed in queue 2 as shown in Example 9-31.

Example 9-31 *Configuring Queuing on XYZSW4*

```
XYZSW4> (enable) set qos map 2q1t 2 1 cos 5
Qos tx priority queue and threshold mapped to cos successfully.
```

The configuration in Example 9-31 places any traffic with a CoS of 5 into queue 2. Queue 2 is the strict priority queue that is always serviced over queue 1.

Step 9 Verify the queuing configuration on XYZSW4 by using the **show qos info** command, as shown in Example 9-32.

Example 9-32 *Verifying Queuing on XYZSW4*

```
XYZSW4> (enable) show qos info config
QoS is enabled
All ports have 2 transmit queues with 1 drop thresholds (2q1t).
Default CoS = 1
Queue and Threshold Mapping:
Queue Threshold CoS
----- --------- ---------------
1     1         0 1 2 3 4 6 7
2     1         5
```

Example 9-32 shows that the default CoS has been set to 1, and only traffic with a CoS of 5 is transmitted out the priority queue (queue 2).

Configuring Access Layer QoS on XYZSW1

XYZSW1 is a combined access/distribution layer that provides access layer connectivity for Host X, as well as a trunk connection to an untrusted network. In this section, you configure the QoS for the access layer port connected to Host X, classifying traffic (based upon access control lists) and rate limiting particular types of traffic received from Host X. You also configure QoS for the trunk port (port GigabitEthernet0/4), classifying and marking voice traffic received on the trunk, and applying an aggregate rate limit of 1 Mbps for all incoming traffic on the trunk.

Step 1 Globally enable the qualify of service features on XYZSW1, as shown in Example 9-33.

Example 9-33 *Enabling QoS on XYZSW1*

```
XYZSW1(config)# mls qos
```

Step 2   Configure XYZSW1 to classify audio traffic by using an access control list that defines H.323 and skinny call control protocol (SCCP) control traffic and another ACL that defines the RTP audio stream used for transporting actual voice packets. Create an access list that defines HTTP traffic and then create another access list that defines mission-critical traffic for Corporation XYZ (a custom application that runs on a TCP server port of 10000), as shown in Example 9-34.

Example 9-34   *Configuring ACLs on XYZSW1*

```
XYZSW1# configure terminal
XYZSW1(config)# ip access-list extended VOIP
XYZSW1(config-ext-nacl)# remark THIS ACL DEFINES VOIP TRAFFIC
XYZSW1(config-ext-nacl)# permit udp any range 16384 32767 any range 16384 32767
XYZSW1(config-ext-nacl)# exit
XYZSW1(config)# ip access-list extended VOIP-CONTROl
XYZSW1(config-ext-nacl)# remark THIS ACL DEFINES VOIP CONTROL TRAFFIC
XYZSW1(config-ext-nacl)# permit tcp any any eq 1720
XYZSW1(config-ext-nacl)# permit tcp any any range 11000 11999
XYZSW1(config-ext-nacl)# permit tcp any any eq 2000
XYZSW1(config-ext-nacl)# exit
XYZSW1(config)# ip access-list extended WEB
XYZSW1(config-ext-nacl)# remark THIS ACL DEFINES DOWNLOADED HTTP CONTENT FROM HOSTX
XYZSW1(config-ext-nacl)# permit tcp any eq www any
XYZSW1(config-ext-nacl)# exit
XYZSW1(config)# ip access-list extended BUSINESS
XYZSW1(config-ext-nacl)# remark THIS ACL DEFINES BUSINESS TRAFFIC SENT FROM HOSTX
XYZSW1(config-ext-nacl)# permit tcp any any eq 10000
XYZSW1(config-ext-nacl)# end
```

In Example 9-34, each access control entry (ACE) defines the criteria that each packet examined must meet in order to provide a match.

Step 3   Create a policy map called HOSTX that includes separate class maps for each of the QoS ACLs you defined in Step 2. Configure the VoIP traffic class to set the DSCP value of voice traffic to 46 and the VoIP control traffic class to set the DSCP value to 26. Configure the business-critical traffic class to set the DSCP to 28. Configure the web traffic class to set the DSCP value to 8 and to police the bandwidth rate to 128 Kbps with a burst size of 8000 bytes, with any web traffic that exceeds this rate being dropped. Example 9-35 shows the configuration required.

Example 9-35   *Creating a Class Map on XYZSW1*

```
XYZSW1# configure terminal
XYZSW1(config)# policy-map HOSTX
XYZSW1(config-pmap)# class-map VOIP access-group name VOIP
XYZSW1(config-pmap-c)# set ip dscp 46
XYZSW1(config-pmap-c)# exit
XYZSW1(config-pmap)# class-map VOIP-CONTROL access-group name VOIP-CONTROL
XYZSW1(config-pmap-c)# set ip dscp 26
XYZSW1(config-pmap-c)# exit
XYZSW1(config-pmap)# class-map BUSINESS access-group name BUSINESS
```

continues

Example 9-35 *Creating a Class Map on XYZSW1 (Continued)*

```
XYZSW1(config-pmap-c)# set ip dscp 28
XYZSW1(config-pmap-c)# exit
XYZSW1(config-pmap)# class-map WEB access-group name WEB
XYZSW1(config-pmap-c)# set ip dscp 8
XYZSW1(config-pmap-c)# police 128000 8000 exceed-action drop
XYZSW1(config-pmap-c)# end
```

Step 4 Verify the policy you just created by checking the access lists you created, as well as the policy map you created, as shown in Example 9-36.

Example 9-36 *Verifying QoS Policy Configuration on XYZSW1*

```
XYZSW1# show access-list
Extended IP access list VOIP
    permit udp any range 16384 32767 any range 16384 32767
Extended IP access list VOIP-CONTROL
    permit tcp any any eq 1720
    permit tcp any any range 11000 11999
    permit tcp any any eq 2000
Extended IP access list BUSINESS
    permit tcp any any eq 10000
Extended IP access list WEB
    permit tcp any eq www any
XYZSW1# show policy-map
 Policy Map HOSTX
  class  BUSINESS
   set ip dscp 28
  class  VOIP
   set ip dscp 46
  class VOIP-CONTROL
   set ip dscp 26
  class  WEB
   set ip dscp 8
   police 128000 8000 exceed-action drop
```

Step 5 Bind the policy you created to the interface attached to Host X (GigabitEthernet0/3) in the ingress direction, as shown in Example 9-37.

Example 9-37 *Binding QoS Policy on the Ingress to Interface gig0/3*

```
XYZSW1# configure terminal
XYZSW1(config)# interface GigabitEthernet0/3
XYZSW1(config-if)# service-policy input HOSTX
XYZSW1(config-if)# end
```

Step 6 Verify the policy is bound on ingress to the interface by using the **show mls qos interface** command, as shown in Example 9-38.

Example 9-38 *Verifying QoS policy Is Bound to an Interface*

```
XYZSW1# show mls qos interface GigabitEthernet0/3
GigabitEthernet0/3
Attached policy-map for Ingress: HOSTX
```

Example 9-38   *Verifying QoS policy Is Bound to an Interface (Continued)*

```
trust state: not trusted
COS override: dis
default COS: 0
DSCP Mutation Map: Default DSCP Mutation Map
```

> **Step 7**   On Host Y, attempt to download a file via HTTP from Host X, as shown
> in Figure 9-8. In Figure 9-8, even though the switched network provides
> up to 100 Mbps bandwidth between Host X and Y, the download speed is
> limited to approximately 13 kBps (104 kbps), which is consistent with
> the 128 kbps limit configured in the policing configuration.

Figure 9-8   *Verifying an HTTP Download Is Being Policed*

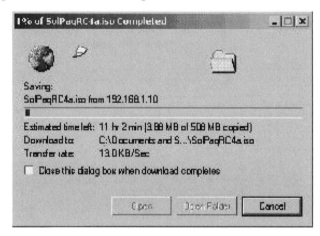

Steps 1 to 7 demonstrated how to apply QoS configuration to the access port connected to
Host X. You now configure QoS on the trunk port (GigabitEthernet0/4) to the untrusted
network.

> **Step 8**   Create an aggregate policer called UNTRUSTED, that defines a traffic
> rate of 1 Mbps and a burst size of 64000 bytes. Any traffic that does not
> conform to the rate should be dropped. Example 9-39 shows the
> configuration required.

Example 9-39   *Creating an Aggregate Policer*

```
XYZSW1# configure terminal
XYZSW1(config)# mls qos aggregate-police UNTRUSTED 1000000 64000 exceed-action drop
```

Step 9 Create a policy map called UNTRUSTED, and configure a voice traffic class to set the DSCP value of voice traffic to 46. Apply the aggregate policer you created in Step 7 to each class map to rate limit all traffic processed by the entire policy map. Example 9-40 shows the configuration required.

Example 9-40 *Creating a Class Map on XYZSW1*

```
XYZSW1# configure terminal
XYZSW1(config)# policy-map UNTRUSTED
XYZSW1(config-pmap)# class-map VOICE access-group 100
XYZSW1(config-pmap-c)# set ip dscp 46
XYZSW1(config-pmap-c)# police aggregate UNTRUSTED
XYZSW1(config-pmap-c)# exit
XYZSW1(config-pmap)# end
```

Step 10 Bind the policy you created to the interface attached to the untrusted network (GigabitEthernet0/4) in the ingress direction, as shown in Example 9-41.

Example 9-41 *Binding QoS Policy on the Ingress to Interface gig0/3*

```
XYZSW1# configure terminal
XYZSW1(config)# interface GigabitEthernet0/4
XYZSW1(config-if)# service-policy input UNTRUSTED
XYZSW1(config-if)# end
```

Step 11 Repeat Step 6 to verify the UNTRUSTED policy map configuration and ensure it is bound to the correct interface.

Configuring Access Layer QoS on XYZSW2

XYZSW2 is a combined access/distribution layer Catalyst 6000/6500 switch that provides access layer connectivity for XYZR1. In this section, you configure the QoS for the access layer port connected to XYZR1 to classify traffic based upon access control lists.

Step 1 Enable quality of service features on XYZSW2, as shown in Example 9-42.

Example 9-42 *Enabling QoS on XYZSW2*

```
XYZSW2> (enable) set qos enable
QoS is enabled.
```

Step 2 Configure the trust state of port 2/3 (connected to XYZR1) as untrusted, as shown in Example 9-43.

Example 9-43 *Configuring Port Trust State on XYZSW2*

```
XYZSW2> (enable) set port qos 2/3 trust untrusted
Port 2/3 qos set to untrusted
```

NOTE   The default port trust configuration is untrusted, so the configuration shown in Example 9-43 is not necessary but is for demonstration purposes only.

Step 3   Configure a QoS ACL on XYZSW2 to identify voice traffic between XYZR1 and the rest of the network. Configure the ACL to mark VoIP traffic with a DSCP value of 46, mark VoIP control traffic with a DSCP value of 26, mark business critical traffic with a DSCP value of 28 and to mark all other traffic with a DSCP value of 8, as shown in Example 9-44.

Example 9-44   *Configuring a QoS ACL on XYZSW2*

```
XYZSW2> (enable) set qos acl ip XYZR1 dscp 46 udp any range 16384 32767
  any range 16384 32767
XYZR1 editbuffer modified. Use 'commit' command to apply changes.
XYZSW2> (enable) set qos acl ip XYZR1 dscp 26 tcp any any eq 1720
XYZR1 editbuffer modified. Use 'commit' command to apply changes.
XYZSW2> (enable) set qos acl ip XYZR1 dscp 26 tcp any any range 11000 11999
XYZR1 editbuffer modified. Use 'commit' command to apply changes.
XYZSW2> (enable) set qos acl ip XYZR1 dscp 26 tcp any any eq 2000
XYZR1 editbuffer modified. Use 'commit' command to apply changes.
XYZSW2> (enable) set qos acl ip XYZR1 dscp 28 tcp any any eq 10000
XYZR1 editbuffer modified. Use 'commit' command to apply changes.
XYZSW2> (enable) set qos acl ip XYZR1 dscp 8 any
XYZR1 editbuffer modified. Use 'commit' command to apply changes.
```

Step 4   Commit the QoS ACL to hardware and attach the ACL to port 2/3, as shown in Example 9-45.

Example 9-45   *Committing a QoS ACL and Binding a QoS ACL to an Interface*

```
XYZSW2> (enable) commit qos acl XYZR1
Hardware programming in progress...
ACL XYZR1 is committed to hardware.
XYZSW2> (enable) set qos acl map XYZR1 2/3
Hardware programming in progress...
ACL XYZR1 is attached to port 2/3.
```

Step 5   Verify the QoS ACL you just created by using the **show qos acl** command, as shown in Example 9-46.

Example 9-46   *Verifying QoS ACL Configuration on XYZSW2*

```
XYZSW2> (enable) show qos acl info XYZR1
set qos acl ip XYZR1
--------------------------------------------------
1. dscp 46 udp any range 16384 32767 any range 16384 32767
2. dscp 26 tcp any any eq 1720
3. dscp 26 tcp any any range 11000 11999
```

continues

Example 9-46 *Verifying QoS ACL Configuration on XYZSW2 (Continued)*

```
4. dscp 26 tcp any any eq 2000
5. dscp 28 tcp any any 10000
2. dscp 8 any
XYZSW2> (enable) show qos acl map XYZR1
ACL name    Vlan #           Ports
---------   ---------------  ---------------
XYZR1       1                2/3
```

Step 4—Configuring QoS at the Distribution Layer

In this step, you configure QoS functions at the distribution layer of the switched network, which includes the switches XYZSW1 and XYZSW2. You now perform the following:

- Configure distribution layer QoS on XYZSW1
- Configure distribution layer QoS on XYZSW2

Configuring Distribution Layer QoS on XYZSW1

In this section, you configure distribution layer QoS features on XYZSW1. This includes configuration of each of the inter-switch trunks to XYZSW2 and XYZSW3. The goal of a well-designed end-to-end QoS network is to move as much classification policy to the edge (access layer) of the network, which simplifies the distribution and core layers QoS configuration. In this section, you also configure egress queuing and scheduling.

Step 1   Configure XYZSW1 to trust the DSCP on IP packets received from XYZSW2 (port GigabitEthernet0/1) and then verify your configuration, as shown in Example 9-47.

Example 9-47 *Configuring XYZSW1 Port Trust*

```
XYZSW1# configure terminal
XYZSW1(config)# interface GigabitEthernet0/1
XYZSW1(config-if)# mls qos trust dscp
XYZSW1(config-if)# end
XYZSW1#show mls qos interface GigabitEthernet0/1
GigabitEthernet0/2
trust state: trust dscp
COS override: dis
default COS: 0
DSCP Mutation Map: Default DSCP Mutation Map
```

Step 2   Configure XYZSW1 to trust the CoS on tagged frames received from
XYZSW3 (port GigabitEthernet0/2) and then verify your configuration
as shown in Example 9-48.

Example 9-48   *Configuring XYZSW1 Port Trust*

```
XYZSW1# configure terminal
XYZSW1(config)# interface GigabitEthernet0/2
XYZSW1(config-if)# mls qos trust cos
XYZSW1(config-if)# end
XYZSW1#show mls qos interface GigabitEthernet0/2
GigabitEthernet0/2
trust state: trust cos
COS override: dis
default COS: 0
DSCP Mutation Map: Default DSCP Mutation Map
```

In Steps 1 and 2, you have configured the ingress on each inter-switch trunk to trust QoS
information received in each frame. Because you have performed the required classification
and marking at the edge of the network, XYZSW1 can simply trust the QoS marking on
each frame, simplifying the QoS processing at the distribution layer.

Step 3   Configure the CoS-to-DSCP map on XYZSW1 to assign a DSCP value
of 46 to any frames that possess a CoS of 5 as shown in Example 9-49.

NOTE   When you modify the CoS-to-DSCP map you must configure all the DSCP values that
correspond to each CoS, modifying only the DSCP values you want. Table 9-6 shows the
default CoS-to-DSCP map.

Table 9-6   *The Default CoS-to-DSCP map*

Class of Service	0	1	2	3	4	5	6	7
DSCP	0	8	16	24	32	40	48	56

Example 9-49   *Configuring the CoS-to-DSCP Map on XYZSW1*

```
XYZSW1# configure terminal
XYZSW1(config)# mls qos map cos-dscp 0 8 16 24 32 46 48 56
XYZSW1(config-if)# end
XYZSW1# show mls qos maps cos-dscp
   Cos-dscp map:
        cos:   0  1  2  3  4  5  6  7
   --------------------------------
       dscp:   0  8 16 24 32 46 48 56
```

In Example 9-49, you configure the Cos-to-DSCP map so that any frames received with a CoS of 5 are marked with a DSCP value of 46 (instead of the default 40). This is required because XYZSW3 is capable of marking only CoS values. When XYZSW3 sends voice traffic to XYZSW1 for transport, it contains a CoS of 5 in the 802.1p field of the 802.1Q tag. If you use the default CoS-to-DSCP map, XYZSW1 generates a DSCP of 40. By modifying the map, you now effectively classify voice traffic from XYZSW3 with a DSCP of 46, which is consistent with the QoS policy you have configured on XYZSW1 so far.

NOTE   The CoS-to-DSCP map applies globally to the switch and is used for any ports that are configured to trust CoS.

You have now configured the classification and marking functions on XYZSW1. Next, you configure queuing and scheduling on XYZSW1.

Step 4   Configure the CoS-to-Queue map on the GigabitEthernet0/1, GigabitEthernet0/2, and GigabitEthernet0/4 trunks of XYZSW1 to assign the CoS values of 0–2 to queue 1, CoS values of 3–4 to queue 2, CoS values of 6–7 to queue 3, and the CoS value of 5 to queue 4. Assign a weight of 10 to queue 1, a weight of 40 to queue 2, a weight of 50 to queue 3, and a weight of 0 to queue 4. Configure queue 4 to be a priority queue, ensuring service before any other queue. Example 9-50 shows how to perform this configuration.

Example 9-50   *Configuring the CoS-to-Queue Interface gig0/1 Map on XYZSW1*

```
XYZSW1# configure terminal
XYZSW1(config)# interface GigabitEthernet0/1
XYZSW1(config-if)# wrr-queue cos-map 1 0 1 2
XYZSW1(config-if)# wrr-queue cos-map 2 3 4
XYZSW1(config-if)# wrr-queue cos-map 3 6 7
XYZSW1(config-if)# wrr-queue cos-map 4 5
XYZSW1(config-if)# wrr-queue bandwidth 10 40 50 0
XYZSW1(config-if)# priority-queue out
XYZSW1(config-if)# exit
XYZSW1(config)# interface GigabitEthernet0/2
XYZSW1(config-if)# wrr-queue cos-map 1 0 1 2
XYZSW1(config-if)# wrr-queue cos-map 2 3 4
XYZSW1(config-if)# wrr-queue cos-map 3 6 7
XYZSW1(config-if)# wrr-queue cos-map 4 5
XYZSW1(config-if)# wrr-queue bandwidth 10 40 50 0
XYZSW1(config-if)# priority-queue out
XYZSW1(config-if)# exit
XYZSW1(config)# interface GigabitEthernet0/4
XYZSW1(config-if)# wrr-queue cos-map 1 0 1 2
XYZSW1(config-if)# wrr-queue cos-map 2 3 4
XYZSW1(config-if)# wrr-queue cos-map 3 6 7
XYZSW1(config-if)# wrr-queue cos-map 4 5
XYZSW1(config-if)# priority-queue out
XYZSW1(config-if)# wrr-queue bandwidth 10 40 50 0
XYZSW1(config-if)# end
```

In Example 9-50, the default queuing configuration is modified using the **wrr-queue cos-map** command so that all voice traffic (CoS of 5) is placed into queue 4. Queue 4 is then enabled as the strict priority queue by the use of the **priority-queue out** command, meaning all voice traffic (any traffic with a CoS of 5) is given priority service on the interface. The weighting of each of the remaining queues (queue 1–3) is configured using the **wrr-queue bandwidth** command such that low-priority traffic (CoS 0–2) is apportioned 10 percent (10/100), medium-priority traffic (CoS 3–4) is apportioned 40 percent (40/100), and high-priority traffic (CoS 6-7) is apportioned 50 percent (50/100) of the bandwidth. The bandwidth weighting for queue 4 is ignored because queue 4 has been enabled as the priority queue and is always serviced before any other queues.

Step 5   Configure WRED on egress queue 2 for interfaces GigabitEthernet0/1, GigabitEthernet0/2, and GigabitEthernet0/4 of XYZSW1. Configure the first drop threshold of queue 2 at 60 percent and the second drop threshold of queue 2 at 80 percent. Then configure the DSCP-to-threshold map to apply any traffic with a DSCP of 28 (business critical traffic) to the first drop threshold and any traffic with a DSCP of 26 (VoIP control traffic) to the second drop threshold. Example 9-51 shows the required configuration.

Example 9-51   *Configuring WRED on XYZSW1*

```
XYZSW1# configure terminal
XYZSW1(config)# interface GigabitEthernet0/1
XYZSW1(config-if)# wrr-queue random-detect max-threshold 2 60 80
XYZSW1(config-if)# wrr-queue dscp-map 1 28
XYZSW1(config-if)# wrr-queue dscp-map 2 26
XYZSW1(config-if)# exit
XYZSW1(config)# interface GigabitEthernet0/2
XYZSW1(config-if)# wrr-queue random-detect max-threshold 2 60 80
XYZSW1(config-if)# wrr-queue dscp-map 1 28
XYZSW1(config-if)# wrr-queue dscp-map 2 26
XYZSW1(config-if)# exit
XYZSW1(config)# interface GigabitEthernet0/4
XYZSW1(config-if)# wrr-queue random-detect max-threshold 2 60 80
XYZSW1(config-if)# wrr-queue dscp-map 1 28
XYZSW1(config-if)# wrr-queue dscp-map 2 26
XYZSW1(config-if)# end
```

In Example 9-51, you have set the drop thresholds for queue 2 on each egress interface at 60 percent and 100 percent. This means that when the queue buffer fills to 60 percent capacity, business critical packets will begin to be randomly discarded with heavier flows more likely to experience drops. When the queue buffer fills to 80 percent capacity, VoIP control traffic will also start to be randomly discarded. Having this configuration makes it less likely for voice control traffic to be dropped, and also avoids a tail drop condition for all traffic when the queue reaches 100 percent capacity.

NOTE	WRED is only supported on weighted round robin queues. If strict priority scheduling is configured for a queue, any WRED configuration for the queue is ignored.

Step 6   Verify your queuing and scheduling configuration by using the **show mls qos interface** command, as shown in Example 9-52.

Example 9-52   *Verifying Egress Queuing and Scheduling Configuration on XYZSW1*

```
XYZSW1# show mls qos interface GigabitEthernet0/1 queuing
GigabitEthernet0/1
Ingress expedite queue: dis
Egress  expedite queue: ena
wrr bandwidth weights:
qid-weights
 1 - 10
 2 - 40
 3 - 50
 4 - 0    when expedite queue is disabled
Dscp-threshold map:
     d1 :  d2 0  1  2  3  4  5  6  7  8  9
     ---------------------------------------
      0 :    01 01 01 01 01 01 01 01 01 01
      1 :    01 01 01 01 01 01 01 01 01 01
      2 :    01 01 01 01 01 01 02 01 01 01
      3 :    01 01 01 01 01 01 01 01 01 01
      4 :    01 01 01 01 01 01 01 01 01 01
      5 :    01 01 01 01 01 01 01 01 01 01
      6 :    01 01 01 01
Cos-queue map:
cos-qid
 0 - 1
 1 - 1
 2 - 1
 3 - 2
 4 - 2
 5 - 4
 6 - 3
 7 - 3
XYZSW1# show mls qos interface GigabitEthernet0/1 buffers
GigabitEthernet0/1
Notify Q depth:
qid-size
 1 - 25
 2 - 25
 3 - 25
 4 - 25
qid WRED thresh1 thresh2
1    dis  100     100
2    ena  60      80
3    dis  100     100
4    dis  100     100
```

In Example 9-52, the **show mls qos interface GigabitEthernet0/1 queuing** command verifies the following information:

- Priority queuing is enabled, indicated by the Egress expedite queue status.

- The DSCP-threshold map shows that the DSCP value of 24 is mapped to the second discard threshold.

- The CoS-queue map shows the CoS values that are mapped to each queue. For example, the CoS value of 5 is mapped to queue 4.

- The **show mls qos interface GigabitEthernet0/1 buffers** command shows that WRED is enabled for queue 2 only, with the first threshold (thresh1) set to 60 percent and the second threshold (thresh2) set to 80 percent.

Configuring Distribution Layer QoS on XYZSW2

In this section, you configure distribution layer QoS features on XYZSW2. This includes configuration of classification and queuing/scheduling on each of the inter-switch trunks to XYZSW1 and XYZSW4.

Step 1   Configure XYZSW2 to trust the DSCP on IP packets received from XYZSW1 (port 2/1) and then verify your configuration, as shown in Example 9-53.

Example 9-53   *Configuring XYZSW2 Port Trust*

```
XYZSW2> (enable) set port qos 2/1 trust trust-dscp
Port 1/1 qos set to trust-dscp
XYZSW2> (enable) show port qos 2/1
QoS is enabled for the switch.
QoS policy source for the switch set to local.

Port  Interface Type Interface Type Policy Source Policy Source
      config         runtime        config        runtime
----- -------------- -------------- ------------- -------------
 2/1               -              -         local         local

Port  TxPort Type  RxPort Type  Trust Type   Trust Type    Def CoS Def CoS
                                config       runtime       config  runtime
----- ------------ ------------ ------------ ------------- ------- -------
 2/1         2q2t         1q4t   trust-dscp   trust-dscp         0       0
...
```

Step 2   Configure XYZSW2 to trust the CoS on tagged frames received from
XYZSW4 (port gig2/2), as shown in Example 9-54.

Example 9-54 *Configuring XYZSW2 Port Trust*

```
XYZSW2> (enable) set port qos 2/2 trust trust-cos
Port 1/1 qos set to trust-cos
```

In Steps 1 and 2, you have configured the ingress on each inter-switch trunk to trust the QoS
information received in each frame, because each trunk is connected to a switch that has
correctly configured QoS policy.

Step 3   Configure and verify the CoS-to-DSCP map on XYZSW2 to assign a
DSCP value of 46 to any frames that possess a CoS of 5, as shown in
Example 9-55.

Example 9-55 *Configuring the CoS-to-DSCP map on XYZSW1*

```
XYZSW2> (enable) set qos cos-dscp-map 0 8 16 24 32 46 48 56
QoS cos-dscp-map set successfully.
XYZSW2> (enable) show qos maps cos-dscp-map
CoS - DSCP map:
CoS   DSCP
---   --------------
 0     0
 1     8
 2    16
 3    24
 4    32
 5    46
 6    48
 7    56
```

You have now configured the classification and marking functions on XYZSW2. Next, you
configure queuing and scheduling on XYZSW2.

Step 4   Verify the port capabilities of the trunk ports on XYZSW2 by using the
show port capabilities command, as shown in Example 9-56.

Example 9-56 *Verifying Port Capabilities on XYZSW2*

```
XYZSW2> (enable) show port capabilities 2/1
Model                 WS-X6348
Port                  2/1
Type                  10/100BaseTX
Speed                 auto,10,100
Duplex                half,full
Trunk encap type      802.1Q
Trunk mode            on,off,desirable,auto,nonegotiate
Channel               2/1-48
Flow control          no
Security              yes
```

Example 9-56   *Verifying Port Capabilities on XYZSW2 (Continued)*

```
Dot1x                   yes
Membership              static,dynamic
Fast start              yes
QOS scheduling          rx-(1q4t),tx-(2q2t)
...
```

Example 9-56 shows that a single queue with four drop thresholds (1q4t) exists on the receive (rx) or ingress side, while two queues, each with two drop thresholds (2q2t), exist on the transmit (tx) or egress side.

Step 5   Configure the CoS values that are associated with each queue and drop threshold, as shown in Example 9-57. Table 9-7 shows the required configuration.

Table 9-7   *CoS to Queue/Threshold Mappings for XYZSW2*

CoS	Queue Number	Threshold Number
0	1	1
1	1	1
2	1	1
3	1	2
4	1	2
5	2	2
6	2	1
7	2	1

Example 9-57   *Configuring CoS to Queue/Threshold Mappings on XYZSW2*

```
XYZSW2> (enable) set qos map 2q2t tx 1 1 0,1,2
Qos tx priority queue and threshold mapped to cos successfully.
XYZSW2> (enable) set qos map 2q2t tx 1 2 3,4
Qos tx priority queue and threshold mapped to cos successfully.
XYZSW2> (enable) set qos map 2q2t tx 2 1 6,7
Qos tx priority queue and threshold mapped to cos successfully.
XYZSW2> (enable) set qos map 2q2t tx 2 2 5
Qos tx priority queue and threshold mapped to cos successfully.
```

As you can see from Example 9-57, the Catalyst 6000/6500 queues traffic based upon CoS and also uses CoS to determine the drop threshold the traffic is subject to within the queue. This differs from the Catalyst 3550 implementation, where traffic is placed into queues based upon CoS, while traffic is assigned to a drop threshold based upon DSCP rather than CoS. Also notice that the queuing configuration on the Catalyst 6000/6500 is applied globally (i.e., to all ports that are 2q2t), whereas the Catalyst 3550 allows you to specify a custom queuing configuration per-interface.

Step 6 Configure the weightings for each queue, so that queue 1 is allocated 20 percent of bandwidth and queue 2 is allocated 80 percent of the bandwidth, as shown in Example 9-58.

Example 9-58 *Configuring the Queue Weightings on XYZSW2*

```
XYZSW2> (enable) set qos wrr 2q2t 12 48
QoS wrr ratio is set successfully.
```

In Example 9-58, the weighting ratio is set to 12:48, which works out to 20 percent:80 percent. You could have set the weighting to 2:8 or 1:4; however, this will not achieve the same results. Each unit of weight is equivalent to 256 bytes and is the actual amount of traffic that the scheduler services before moving to the next queue. For example, if you configure a weight of 20, then the scheduler services 5120 bytes before moving to the next queue. If you use a weighting of 2:8, in byte terms, this works out to 512 bytes:2048 bytes. Now, consider if queue 1 contains a frame that is 1500 bytes in size (this is feasible, since the Ethernet MTU is 1500 bytes). The scheduler cannot chop up the frame into 512 byte pieces; it must send the full frame, even though it exceeds the 512 byte queue servicing limit. You should always set a weighting that services at least the MTU of the interface. On Ethernet networks (MTU = 1500 bytes), therefore, the minimum weighting you should use is 6 (6 * 256 bytes = 1536 bytes).

TIP

As a rule of thumb on Ethernet interfaces, when configuring queue weights on the Catalyst 6000/6500, I recommend working with multiples of six.

Step 7 Configure the drop thresholds for the second queue (queue 2) on 2q2t ports, configuring 60 percent as the first drop threshold and 80 percent as the second drop threshold. Example 9-59 shows the required configuration.

Example 9-59 *Configuring the 2q2t Drop Thresholds on XYZSW2*

```
XYZSW2> (enable) set qos drop-threshold 2q2t tx queue 2 60 80
Transmit drop thresholds for queue 2 set at 60% and 80%
```

The 2q2t ports support only tail drop as the congestion mechanism and do not support WRED. Because you did not configure the first queue (queue 1), the default configuration of 80 percent for the first threshold and 100 percent for the second threshold applies for queue 1.

Step 8   Verify your configuration of steps 5 through 7 by using the **show qos info** command, as shown in Example 9-60.

Example 9-60   *Verifying QoS Configuration on XYZSW2*

```
XYZSW2> (enable) show qos info config 2q2t tx
QoS setting in NVRAM for 2q2t transmit:
QoS is enabled
 CoS = 0
Queue and Threshold Mapping:
Queue Threshold CoS
----- --------- ---------------
 1       1        0 1 2
 1       2        3 4
 2       1        6 7
 2       2        5
Tx drop thresholds:
Queue #  Thresholds - percentage (abs values )
-------  -------------------------------------
 1         80% 100%
 2         60% 80%
Queue Sizes:
Queue #  Sizes - percentage (abs values )
-------  -------------------------------------
 1         80%
 2         20%
WRR Configuration:
Ports have transmit ratios between queue 1 and 2 of
12:48
```

The **config** keyword used with the **show qos info** command displays the QoS configuration as configured in NVRAM. Example 9-60 verifies the following:

- The correct CoS values are mapped to the appropriate queue and drop threshold within the queue as configured in Step 5. This is shown in the Queue and Threshold Mapping section of the output.

- The drop thresholds for queue 2 are 50 percent and 100 percent as configured in Step 7. This is shown in the Tx drop thresholds section of the output.

- The transmit ratio between queue 1 and queue 2 is 12:48. This is shown in the *WRR* Configuration section of the output.

Step 9   Use the **show qos info runtime** command to display the actual byte values used on port 2/1 for the weighted round robin servicing of each queue, as shown Example 9-61.

Example 9-61   *Verifying QoS Configuration on XYZSW2*

```
XYZSW2> (enable) show qos info runtime 2/1
Run time setting of QoS:
QoS is enabled on 2/1
Port 2/1 has 2 transmit queue with 2 drop thresholds (2q2t).
```

continues

Example 9-61   *Verifying QoS Configuration on XYZSW2 (Continued)*

```
Port 2/1 has 1 receive queue with 4 drop thresholds (1q4t).
The qos trust type is set to trust-dscp.
 CoS = 0
Queue and Threshold Mapping:
Queue Threshold CoS
..... ......... ...............
1     1          0 1 2
1     2          3 4
2     1          6 7
2     2          5
Rx drop thresholds:
Queue #  Thresholds - percentage (abs values )
.......  ------------------------------------
1        50% (38912 bytes) 60% (46688 bytes) 80% (62240 bytes) 100% (73696 bytes)
Tx drop thresholds:
Queue #  Thresholds - percentage (abs values )
.......  ------------------------------------
1        80% (288332 bytes) 100% (360416 bytes)
2        60% (38896 bytes) 80% (77792 bytes)
Queue Sizes:
Queue #  Sizes - percentage (abs values)
.......  ------------------------------------
1        80% (360416 bytes)
2        20% (81888 bytes)
WRR Configuration:
Ports with speed 100Mbps have ratio of 12:48 between transmit queue 1
and 2 (3072:12288 bytes)
```

Example 9-61 shows you all the byte values used for each QoS parameter. This gives you a perspective on how the switch hardware is actually implementing QoS.

Summary

In this chapter you learned about quality of service and why it is becoming more important for many. With the advent of voice and video convergence, QoS is now required end-to-end on all network devices between application end points. This includes not only Layer 3 routers, but also LAN switches. The LAN switch is a key component of an end-to-end QoS design; the LAN switch is the first device that receives traffic that requires a particular QoS level. In a DiffServ QoS implementation, where QoS for traffic is indicated within each frame or packet, marking is required at the network entry point to ensure end-to-end QoS. Cisco Catalyst switches allow seamless integration of QoS between Layer 2 and Layer 3 networks, reducing the cost and complexity of providing end-to-end QoS.

QoS is provided on Cisco Catalyst switches through the implementation of key QoS functions, such as classification and marking at the ingress, policing at the ingress or egress, and queuing and scheduling at the egress. Cisco Catalyst switches support the use of 802.1p class of service, IP Precedence, and DiffServ Code Point (DSCP) markings, with the ability to trust or override existing QoS markings. Cisco has recently invested much research and development into providing advanced QoS features, the benefits of which are now available on the next generation of Cisco Catalyst switches. Even switches at the workgroup level can classify traffic based upon Layer 3 or 4 parameters and support next-generation QoS features such as DSCP. You need to be aware of the differences in QoS support between each Catalyst platform and understand that the configuration syntax for QoS also varies.

## CHAPTER 10

Maintenance, Monitoring, and Troubleshooting

The ability to maintain, monitor, and troubleshoot networks is important. You might design a switched LAN network that meets the requirements of the organization using the network today, but over time these requirements might exceed the current capabilities of your design. It is very important that you understand how to monitor and troubleshoot your network, ensuring that you can identify key issues in your network and resolve them quickly and efficiently.

To ensure the continuing operation and stability of your LAN switches, you must put in place mechanisms that allow for the fast restoration of configuration files and other files in the event of a switch failure or file corruption. Understanding how you can work with key files on your LAN switches in terms of transferring these files to and from other locations for both backup and restoration purposes is paramount in ensuring your ability to maintain the availability of the LAN network.

It is always important to put the LAN network in perspective; it exists to allow organizations to run network applications and permit the exchange of information vital to the ongoing operation of the organization. The ability to troubleshoot these network applications is vital; you might often need to view the traffic that is being transmitted between the end points of a network application to aid in troubleshooting a specific problem. Cisco Catalyst switches enable you to capture network traffic, even though traffic capture has been traditionally impossible to perform on a switch. In a switched environment, capturing traffic is difficult because the fabric that forms each broadcast domain is not shared and the traffic destined for a specific host on a specific switch port is not normally sent to any other ports. Traffic capture also enables you to monitor the performance of your network, looking for possible issues such as excessive broadcast and multicast traffic or an excess of corrupted frames.

In this chapter, you first learn about basic troubleshooting tools on Cisco IOS and then learn how to troubleshoot common issues on Cisco Catalyst switches. Next you learn how to maintain Cisco Catalyst switches, how to back up, recover, and upgrade configuration files and operating system files. Finally, you learn how to configure the various packet capture features provided on Cisco Catalyst switches. The following scenarios are presented in this chapter:

- Scenario 10-1: Using IP and LAN connectivity tools
- Scenario 10-2: Troubleshooting workstation startup problems

- Scenario 10-3: Troubleshooting the errDisable status
- Scenario 10-4: Password recovery
- Scenario 10-5: File management on Cisco Catalyst switches
- Scenario 10-6: Capturing traffic using SPAN, RSPAN, and VACLs

Scenario 10-1: Using IP and LAN Connectivity Tools

An important feature of Cisco Catalyst switches is the troubleshooting tools that are provided as part of the operating system, which enable you to quickly diagnose problems that might arise in your switched environment. Cisco Catalyst switches provide the following troubleshooting tools:

- IP connectivity tools, such as **ping** and **traceroute**
- LAN connectivity tools, such as Cisco Discovery Protocol (CDP) and Layer 2 traceroute
- Debugging tools
- Monitoring tools, such as switch port analyzer (SPAN)

In this scenario, you learn about the IP and LAN connectivity tools. The use of debugging has been demonstrated throughout this book; monitoring tools are covered later in Scenario 10-6.

Understanding IP and LAN Connectivity Tools

The tools provided for verifying connectivity to the network are important features of any networking device. As a network engineer, when you install networking equipment and attach it to the network, you want confirmation that the equipment is configured correctly and is communicating with the network. Cisco Catalyst switches provide traditional IP connectivity tools, such as ping and traceroute, which are used for verifying management communications on Layer 2 switches and are useful for verifying Layer 3 routing on Layer 3 switches. Cisco Catalyst switches also provide LAN (Layer 2) connectivity tools, such as the Cisco Discovery Protocol (CDP) and Layer 2 traceroute (**l2trace**), which are useful for verifying interswitch communications and the Layer 2 transmission paths within a Layer 2 domain. In summary, the following tools are provided on Cisco Catalyst switches for verifying Layer 2 and Layer 3 (IP) connectivity:

- The ping utility
- The traceroute utility
- Cisco Discovery Protocol (CDP)
- Layer 2 traceroute (**l2trace**)

Each of these tools is now discussed and demonstrated.

IP Connectivity Tools—the ping Utility

The ping utility represents the most fundamental tool used for verifying Layer 3 connectivity. ping can quickly provide you with information indicating whether or not a remote device is alive, as well as the end-to-end delay of the network path to the remote device. In this book, you have used the ping utility numerous times to verify basic IP connectivity between systems; as a network engineer you will probably use ping on a daily basis to ensure networks that you are configuring are working as expected or to aid in the diagnosis of faults that are affecting connectivity.

On Cisco IOS-based Catalyst switches, you can use either the *basic ping* or *extended ping* utilities for testing connectivity. The basic ping sends just five ICMP echo requests to a remote destination and indicates whether or not an ICMP echo reply was received and how long it took for each reply to be received. The extended ping allows you much more flexibility, by allowing you to send a configurable number of ICMP echo requests, with the packet size of your choice along with many other parameters. Example 10-1 demonstrates the use of the extended ping utility on Cisco IOS:

Example 10-1   *Using the extended ping Utility*

```
Switch# ping
Protocol [ip]: ip
Target IP address: 192.168.1.1
Repeat count [5]: 10
Datagram size [100]: 1500
Timeout in seconds [2]:
Extended commands [n]: y
Source address or interface: VLAN 1
Type of service [0]: 7
Set DF bit in IP header? [no]:
Validate reply data? [no]:
Data pattern [0xABCD]:
Loose, Strict, Record, Timestamp, Verbose[none]:
Sweep range of sizes [n]: n
Type escape sequence to abort.
Sending 10, 1500-byte ICMP Echos to 192.168.1.1, timeout is 2 seconds:
!!!!!!!!!!
Success rate is 100 percent (10/10), round-trip min/avg/max = 1/2/4 ms
```

In Example 10-1, you just initially specify the command **ping** to invoke the interactive extended ping utility. If you are using extended ping for testing IP connectivity, you can also use the **ping ip** command to invoke an extended IP ping. Notice the round-trip time statistics, which provide an indication of the current end-to-end latency in the network.

NOTE   If you specify an IP address after the **ping** command, a basic ping is assumed, and five 100-byte ICMP echo request packets are sent.

By using the extended ping utility, you can modify the parameters of the ping test such as increasing the number of packets sent and the size of each packet sent. You can also specify the source IP address used in each packet, which is useful if you want to ensure that the return path from the destination being tested has the necessary routing information to reach the source IP address specified.

NOTE   The source IP address specified must be a valid IP address on the local switch itself; you can't use extended ping to spoof (masquerade) a source IP address of another device.

You can configure other advanced features such as setting the type of service (useful for testing quality of service), setting the don't fragment (DF) bit (useful for determining the lowest maximum transmission unit [MTU] of a transmission path by testing whether or not IP packets of a particular length can reach a destination), and more.

On CatOS, the ping utility is much simpler than the extended ping available on Cisco IOS because Cisco IOS was originally designed for Layer 3 routers rather than Layer 2 switches that essentially act only like an end device in terms of IP. You can use the –s switch with the **ping** command to send a continuous stream of Internet Control Message Protocol (ICMP) traffic until you interrupt the utility. Example 10-2 shows the syntax of the ping utility on CatOS.

Example 10-2   *Using the ping utility on CatOS*

```
Console> (enable) ping <host>
Console> (enable) ping -s <host> [packet_size] [packet_count]
```

In Example 10-2, if you use the **ping** command with no options, a basic ping is assumed and five 56-byte ICMP echo requests are sent to the host specified. If you use the –s option, you can optionally specify a custom packet size and packet count. If you do not specify a custom packet size and packet count with the –s option, an almost infinite amount (2,147,483,647) of 56-byte ICMP echo requests are sent to the host specified.

NOTE   To interrupt the **ping –s** command, use the Ctrl-C key sequence.

Example 10-3 shows an example of using the different methods available to the ping utility on a CatOS-based Catalyst switch.

Example 10-3   *Using the ping utility on CatOS*

```
Console> (enable) ping 192.168.1.1
!!!!!

-----192.168.1.1 PING Statistics------
5 packets transmitted, 5 packets received, 0% packet loss
round-trip (ms) min/avg/max = 1/1/1

Console> (enable) ping -s 192.168.1.1 1400 2
PING 192.168.1.1: 1400 data bytes
1408 bytes from 192.168.1.1: icmp_seq=0. time=18 ms
1408 bytes from 192.168.1.1: icmp_seq=1. time=10 ms

----192.168.1.1 PING Statistics----
2 packets transmitted, 2 packets received, 0% packet loss
round-trip (ms)  min/avg/max = 10/14/18

Console> (enable) ping -s 192.168.1.1
PING 192.168.1.1: 56 data bytes
64 bytes from 192.168.1.1: icmp_seq=0. time=7 ms
64 bytes from 192.168.1.1: icmp_seq=1. time=11 ms
64 bytes from 192.168.1.1: icmp_seq=2. time=10 ms
64 bytes from 192.168.1.1: icmp_seq=3. time=6 ms
64 bytes from 192.168.1.1: icmp_seq=4. time=10 ms
64 bytes from 192.168.1.1: icmp_seq=5. time=9 ms
64 bytes from 192.168.1.1: icmp_seq=6. time=8 ms
64 bytes from 192.168.1.1: icmp_seq=7. time=7 ms
64 bytes from 192.168.1.1: icmp_seq=8. time=9 ms
^C

----192.168.1.1 PING Statistics----
9 packets transmitted, 9 packets received, 0% packet loss
round-trip (ms)  min/avg/max = 6/8/11
```

In Example 10-3, the base **ping** utility with no options is first demonstrated. Next, the **ping –s 192.168.1.1 1400 2** command is executed, which generates two 1400-byte ICMP echo requests (1400 bytes represents the data payload of the ICMP. Notice that the ICMP header adds an additional 8 bytes to the packet). Finally, the **ping –s 192.168.1.1** command is executed, which generates continuous ICMP echo requests every second, until the Ctrl-C break sequence (**^C**) is executed.

The traceroute Utility

The traceroute utility is a useful tool that is used to determine the Layer 3 path taken to reach a destination host from a source host. Figure 10-1 illustrates what is meant by the path between a source and destination host.

Figure 10-1   *Network Path to a Destination Host*

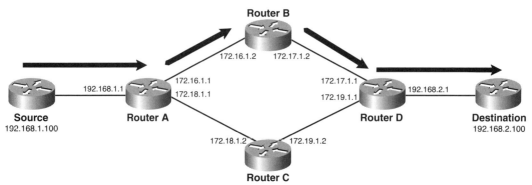

In Figure 10-1, the source and destination "hosts" are routers. The arrows indicate the path that traffic takes from the source host to the destination host. In Figure 10-1, you might think that it does not matter which path is taken. However, the links between Switch-A and Switch-B might be faster and more reliable; hence, the path via Switch-B should be preferred. On the other hand, the dual paths via Switch-B and Switch-C might be equal-cost paths, designed for redundancy and load sharing; hence, traffic should alternate over each path. The traceroute utility allows you to verify that IP traffic is flowing over the correct and desired path(s) in your network.

NOTE   The traceroute utility verifies the network path only from the source to destination (as indicated by the arrows in Figure 10-1), but does not verify return traffic from the destination to source. When the return path is different from the forward path, this is described as *asymmetric routing* (as opposed to *symmetric routing*). Asymmetric routing can be undesirable because although traffic might take the most optimum path to a destination, return traffic takes a less optimum path back. Asymmetric routing also causes issues for firewalls, as most firewalls classify traffic in terms of connections and must see both the forward and return traffic on a connection (for example, if a firewall receives a return packet associated with a connection, but has not seen the connection setup packets sent in the forward direction, the firewall rejects the packet as part of an invalid connection).

Traditionally, because the traceroute utility is useful only for routed IP networks, it has not been used too often on Layer 2 devices such as switches. However, with the growing number of Layer 3 switched networks, the traceroute utility has become a useful trouble-shooting utility for L3 switched LAN networks. The traceroute utility works by using the time-to-live (TTL) field inside an IP packet header. Every IP packet header has a TTL field, which specifies how long the packet should "live," and this field is used to prevent IP packets from continuously circulating around *routing loops*. A routing loop exists when a packet bounces back and forth between two or more routers and can be present due to the convergence behavior of older distance-vector routing protocols after a network failure. Each router that routes an IP packet decrements the TTL field; if a routing loop exists in the network, the TTL field is eventually decremented to 0 and the IP packet is dropped. When an IP packet is dropped due to the TTL field reaching zero (or expiring), the router that drops the packet sends an ICMP TTL expired in transit message back to the source of the IP packet, to inform the source that the packet never reached its destination. The source IP address of the ICMP message is the router that dropped the packet, which therefore indicates to the sender that the router is part of the network path to the destination

The goal of traceroute is to determine the network path taken, hop-by-hop to reach a destination IP address. traceroute works by generating ICMP echo request packets addressed to the desired destination, initially starting with a TTL of 1 and then generating subsequent ICMP echo request packets with an incrementing TTL (i.e., 1,2,3,4 and so on). This has the effect of causing each router in turn along the transmission path to the destination to receive an ICMP echo request packet with a TTL of 1, which each switch discards and then generates an ICMP TTL Expired in Transit message that is sent back to the source. Figure 10-2 demonstrates how traceroute works in the network of Figure 10-1.

Figure 10-2   *How the traceroute Utility Works*

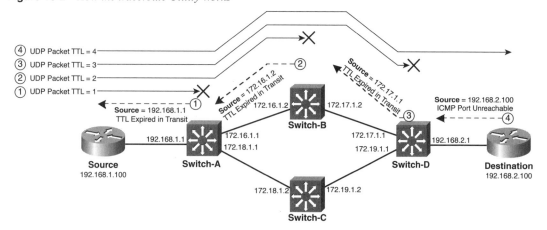

In Figure 10-2, the following events occur:

 1   The source (192.168.1.100) generates a UDP packet (also known as a *probe*) with a destination IP address of 192.168.2.100 and a destination UDP port of an unused port on the destination. The TTL on this packet is set to 1 and is then routed to Switch-A. Switch-A receives the packet, discards the packet (as the TTL is set to 1), and generates an ICMP TTL Expired in Transit message that is sent to the source. This

message includes the source IP address of the interface on Switch-A that originally received the packet, which indicates to the source the IP address of the first hop to the destination.

NOTE   On UNIX systems, Cisco IOS, and CatOS, the probes used are UDP-based and sent to a starting destination port of 33434, with each probe sent incrementing the destination port by 1. On Windows systems, the probes used are ICMP echo requests.

2   After receiving the TTL Expired in Transit message from Switch-A, the source next generates a new UDP probe to 192.168.2.100 and increments the TTL on the packet to 2. The packet is then routed to Switch-A. Switch-A receives the packet and routes the packet towards Switch-B, as the TTL is set to 2, and, therefore, the packet is still valid. Switch-A also decrements the TTL by one (as per the rules of IP routing), meaning the packet received by Switch-B has a TTL of 1. When Switch-B receives the packet, it discards the packet (because the TTL is 1) and generates an ICMP TTL Expired in Transit message that is sent to the source with a source IP address of the interface on Switch-B that originally received the packet. This indicates to the source the IP address of the second hop to the destination.

3   After receiving the TTL Expired in Transit message from Switch-B, the source next generates a new UDP probe to 192.168.2.100 and increments the TTL on the packet to 3. The packet is then routed through Switch-A and Switch-B, who each decrement the TTL by 1, with the packet sent from Switch-B to Switch-D having a resulting TTL of 1. When Switch-D receives the packet, it discards the packet (because the TTL is 1) and generates an ICMP TTL Expired in Transit message that is sent to the source with a source IP address of the interface on Switch-D that originally received the packet. This indicates to the source the IP address of the third hop to the destination.

4   After receiving the TTL Expired in Transit message from Switch-D, the source next generates a new UDP probe to 192.168.2.100 and increments the TTL on the packet to 4. This time the packet is routed through Switch-A, Switch-B, and Switch-D, who each decrement the TTL by 1, with the packet sent from Switch-D to the destination having a resulting TTL of 1. Because the packet has arrived at its destination, the destination host processes the packet (it does not discard the packet as the packet does not require further routing) and generates an ICMP Port Unreachable message to the source (because no UDP service on the destination host is listening on the destination UDP port of the probe). Because the source receives an ICMP Port Unreachable message, it knows it has finally made contact with the destination and the traceroute is complete.

NOTE   In the case of using traceroute on Windows-based hosts, where ICMP echo replies are used for probes, an ICMP Echo Reply message is sent back from the destination host.

Example 10-4 demonstrates the use of the traceroute utility on the source in Figure 10-2, assuming the source is a CatOS-based Catalyst switch.

Example 10-4   *Using the traceroute Utility*

```
Console> (enable) traceroute 192.168.2.100
traceroute to 192.168.2.100 (192.168.2.100), 30 hops max, 40 byte packets
1 192.168.1.1 (192.168.1.1) 12 ms 8 ms 12 ms
2 172.16.1.2 (172.16.1.2) 24 ms 20 ms 23 ms
3 172.17.1.1 (172.17.1.1) 28 ms 23 ms 28 ms
4 192.168.2.100 (192.168.2.100) 32 ms 30 ms 31 ms
```

In Example 10-4, you can see that each hop to the destination is indicated, as described in Figure 10-2. Notice that three response times are listed for each hop; this is because the traceroute utility actually generates three probes for determining each hop.

Example 10-5 demonstrates the use of the traceroute utility on the source in Figure 10-2, assuming the source is a Cisco IOS-based Catalyst switch.

Example 10-5   *Using the traceroute Utility*

```
Switch# traceroute 192.168.2.100

Type escape sequence to abort.
Tracing the route to 192.168.2.100

1 192.168.1.1 12 msec 8 msec 12 msec
2 172.16.1.2 24 msec 20 msec 23 msec
3 172.17.1.1 28 msec 23 msec 28 msec
4 192.168.2.100 32 msec 30 msec 31 msec
```

NOTE   Remember that the traceroute utility verifies only the Layer 3 path throughout the network and has no visibility of the Layer 2 switches a packet might traverse. In other words, only Layer 3 routers decrement the TTL of traceroute probes and only Layer 3 routers generate TTL Expired in Transit messages, which allow a source to collect transmission path information. The Layer 2 traceroute utility (**l2trace**) enables you to determine the Layer 2 hops a frame takes to reach a particular destination within a Layer 2 domain.

Using Cisco Discovery Protocol (CDP)

Cisco Discovery Protocol (CDP) is a proprietary protocol that is useful for troubleshooting networks that use Cisco devices. All Cisco routers and switches support CDP, which is used to discover other directly connected Cisco devices. CDP runs on top of the Layer 2 protocol for a connection, relying on the underlying Layer 2 protocol for transport of CDP messages. Within a LAN environment, CDP messages are sent in Ethernet frames, with a multicast destination address of 01-00-0C-CC-CC-CC. A Cisco device receiving CDP messages processes each CDP message but does not propagate the message, instead discarding it after the appropriate information has been retrieved from the message. In this way, CDP is a protocol that can be used to verify connectivity to other directly connected devices only— it cannot provide information about remotely connected devices. Figure 10-3 demonstrates the generation of CDP messages.

Figure 10-3   *CDP Message Propagation*

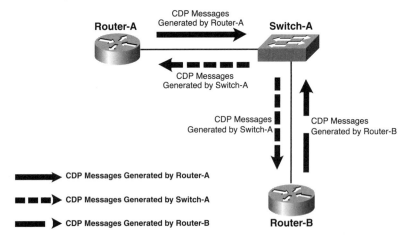

In Figure 10-3, each Cisco device generates CDP messages that are periodically sent out each interface over the appropriate Layer 2 encapsulation. Any receiving Cisco device passes the CDP message to the main CPU, where the contents are read and the CDP packet discarded (i.e., CDP packets received by Cisco devices are never propagated). This means that even though Router-A and Router-B are on the same VLAN, they never see CDP messages from each other because Switch-A is a Cisco device and hence absorbs the CDP messages generated by each router. If Switch-A were a non-Cisco device, because CDP is a proprietary protocol and uses multicast addressing, any CDP messages received would be flooded based upon the destination multicast MAC address, meaning Router-A and Router-B would see CDP messages advertised by each other.

Of course, you might be wondering exactly what these periodic CDP messages contain and what they are used for. CDP is used primarily for two main functions:

- For a Cisco device to indicate its presence to other locally attached Cisco devices. This allows administrators to verify Layer 2 connectivity between directly attached Cisco devices (e.g., an interswitch trunk) is operational.

- For a Cisco device to communicate certain configuration parameters and/or capabilities about itself to locally attached Cisco devices.

CDP is essential for some inter-device communications. For example, in the case of Cisco IP phones that are attached to Catalyst switches the IP phone can learn the virtual LAN (VLAN) ID that should be used to tag voice traffic via CDP messages sent by the switch; this means that you have to program only your switch, and all Cisco IP phones auto-learn the correct voice VLAN ID. Again on IP phones, some Catalyst switches support inline power, which allows an IP phone to be powered over the RJ-45 Ethernet cables. CDP messages are used by the IP phones to indicate to the switch the power requirements of the phone.

CDP also provides an effective troubleshooting tool, especially in pure Cisco environments. If you need to troubleshoot problems with connectivity to locally connected Cisco devices, CDP can be used to confirm that devices can actually see each other. CDP can also be used to find out more details about locally connected devices such as Layer 3 protocol (e.g., IP or IPX) addressing, host name, Cisco device type and model and serial number. In LAN environments, CDP messages also pass information about the speed, duplex, and VLAN configuration of the interface over which the CDP message is sent, which allows remotely connected devices to detect if a duplex or native VLAN mismatch is present; this is particularly useful in switched LAN network. The following shows an example of a SYSLOG message that is generated when a duplex mismatch is detected on a Cisco Catalyst switch:

```
2002 Jul 09 01:10:43 %CDP-4-DUPLEXMISMATCH:Full/half duplex mismatch
    detected on port 2/1
```

The preceding message is useful for detecting duplex mismatches, which do not affect LAN connectivity but do affect the performance of the connection significantly. Notice that the message even indicates the port that you should be investigating.

CDP is also useful for detecting native VLAN mismatches. As you learned in Chapter 3, "Trunking and Bandwidth Aggregation," the 802.1Q trunking protocol supports the concept of a native VLAN. Frames belonging to the native VLAN do not have an 802.1Q tag attached, meaning it is very important that both ends of a trunk are configured with the same native VLAN. If a native VLAN mismatch occurs, one side of the trunk believes untagged frames belong to a different VLAN than the other side. This situation causes spanning tree to shut down both of the conflicting native VLANs on both sides of the trunk to avoid possible bridging loops. The following shows an example of a SYSLOG message that is generated when a native VLAN mismatch is detected on a Cisco Catalyst switch:

```
2003 Apr 26 01:01:39 %CDP-4-NVLANMISMATCH:Native vlan mismatch
    detected on port 2/1
```

CDP is enabled by default and periodically sends messages every 60 seconds by default. A CDP neighbor represents a remote device from which CDP messages have been received; if a CDP message is not heard from a neighbor for more than 180 seconds, the device is considered down and removed from the list of neighbors. On both CatOS and Cisco IOS, the **show cdp neighbors** command provides a summary of each CDP neighbor. The **show cdp neighbors detail** command allows you to view detailed information about each neighbor. Example 10-6 demonstrates the **show cdp neighbors** command on a Catalyst 4000 switch.

Example 10-6 *Using the* **show cdp neighbors** *Command*

```
Console> (enable) show cdp neighbors
* - indicates vlan mismatch.
# - indicates duplex mismatch.
Port    Device-ID               Port-ID                  Platform
-----   ----------------------  -----------------------  -----------
 2/1    Switch-A                FastEthernet0/1*         cisco WS-C3550-24
```

In Example 10-6, notice that the shaded entry indicates a Cisco Catalyst 3550-24 switch (WS-C3550-24) is attached to port 2/1 on the local switch. The interface on the remote switch that attaches to the local switch is FastEthernet0/1, and the * character after this interface indicates a native VLAN mismatch.

Example 10-7 demonstrates the **show cdp neighbors detail** command on the same Catalyst 4000 switch in Example 10-6.

Example 10-7 *Using the* **show cdp neighbors detail** *Command*

```
Console> (enable) show cdp neighbors detail
Port (Our Port): 2/1
Device-ID: Switch-A
Device Addresses:
  IP Address: 192.168.1.1
Holdtime: 173 sec
Capabilities: ROUTER SWITCH IGMP
Version:
  Cisco Internetwork Operating System Software
  IOS (tm) C3550 Software (C3550-I5K2L2Q3-M), Version 12.1(13)EA1a, RELEASE SOFTWARE
  (fc1)
  Copyright  1986-2003 by cisco Systems, Inc.
  Compiled Tue 25-Mar-03 23:56 by yenanh
Platform: cisco WS-C3550-24
Port-ID (Port on Neighbors's Device): FastEthernet0/1
VTP Management Domain: LANPS
Native VLAN: 10 (Mismatch)
Duplex: full
System Name: unknown
System Object ID: unknown
Management Addresses: unknown
Physical Location: unknown
```

In Example 10-7, you can see several useful pieces of information transmitted in CDP messages from the remote device. Notice that you can see the IP address of the remote switch (192.168.1.1); you also can see that the switch is running Cisco IOS 12.1(13)EA1a software. The command output also displays the VTP domain configured on a neighbor, as well as native VLAN and duplex information.

WARNING   CDP messages are unencrypted and as such pose a security risk by potentially transmitting device configuration parameters to unauthorized parties attached to the LAN. CDP should be disabled in any secure LAN environment. See Chapter 8, "Traffic Filtering and Security," for more details.

Layer 2 Traceroute

The Layer 2 traceroute utility (**l2trace**) is an extremely useful utility that is supported on the following Cisco Catalyst switch platforms:

- Catalyst 2950/3550 switches running Cisco IOS 12.1(12c)EA1 or higher
- Catalyst 4000/4500 switches running CatOS 6.2 or higher
- Catalyst 5000/5500 switches running CatOS 6.1 or higher
- Catalyst 6000/6500 switches running CatOS 6.1 or higher

The **l2trace** utility is similar in functionality to the IP traceroute utility; instead of indicating the router hops in the path to a destination IP address, the **l2trace** utility indicates the switch hops in the path to a destination MAC address within a Layer 2 network. This is very useful if you want to verify that traffic is flowing over the correct paths in a complex switched network and is most commonly used to verify spanning-tree topologies are being generated as planned. The only limitations of the **l2trace** utility are that all switches in the **l2trace** path must support the utility, CDP must be enabled on all switches, and it is supported only between devices in the same VLAN.

To demonstrate the use of Layer 2 traceroute, consider the following redundant LAN topology illustrated in Figure 10-4.

In Figure 10-4, a redundant LAN topology includes three Catalyst switches that are connected in a looped Layer 2 topology. The Catalyst 4000 switch (Switch-A) is configured as the root bridge for spanning tree and Figure 10-4 shows each of the spanning tree port roles (RP = root port, DP = designated port, and BP = blocked port). Interface FastEthernet0/2 on Switch-C is placed in a blocking state to remove the loop from the Layer 2 topology. The expected Layer 2 transmission path between Host-A and Host-B is indicated in Figure 10-4. To verify this is indeed the path taken through the network, the Layer 2 traceroute utility can be used.

Figure 10-4 *Redundant LAN Topology*

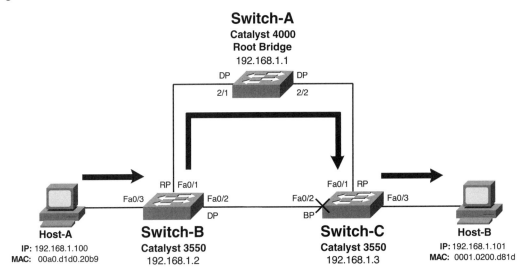

Before the use of the Layer 2 traceroute utility is demonstrated in Figure 10-4, you need to understand the configuration prerequisites that must be implemented before the Layer 2 traceroute works:

- CDP must be enabled on all switches through which the Layer 2 traceroute is performed.

- All switches must support the Layer 2 traceroute feature.

- All switches must be reachable from all other switches via IP.

- The Layer 2 traceroute feature traces the path between a source MAC address and destination MAC address; hence it requires both MAC addresses to be present in the CAM tables of the switches the source and destination hosts are connected to. This means the source and destination hosts must be active on the network or static CAM entries must be configured.

- The maximum number of switch hops supported is 10.

- Only unicast destinations are supported.

In Figure 10-4, assume that CDP is running on all switches. You can use the **show cdp neighbors** command on each switch to verify this. Each switch in Figure 10-4 supports the Layer 2 traceroute, and assuming the indicated IP addressing for each switch is in place, all switches should be reachable from each other via IP (this should be tested using **ping**). Host-A and Host-B are active hosts on the network; therefore, their MAC addresses can be populated in the CAM tables of the appropriate switches by simply generating traffic between the two hosts.

On Cisco IOS, the same **traceroute** command used to perform Layer 3 traceroutes is also used to perform Layer 2 traceroutes when configured with the following syntax:

```
Switch# traceroute mac [interface interface-type interface-id]
   source-mac [interface interface-type interface-id]
   destination-mac [vlan vlan-id] [detail]

Switch# traceroute mac ip source-ip destination-ip [detail]
```

Notice that the **mac** or **mac ip** keywords are used to indicate a Layer 2 traceroute as opposed to a Layer 3 traceroute. If you use the **traceroute mac** command, you must specify the source MAC address and destination MAC address for the traffic flow between the hosts that you want to trace. The optional **interface** parameters are used to define the interfaces on the source and destination switches, the optional **vlan** keyword allows to specify the VLAN through which the Layer 2 traceroute should be performed, and the optional **detail** keyword enables more detail trace information.

NOTE A useful feature of the Layer 2 traceroute is that you don't have to execute the command from the switch that is connected to the source specified in the trace. For example in Figure 10-4, you can execute a Layer 2 traceroute between Host-A and Host-B from any switch in the network, not just Switch-B.

If you use the **traceroute mac ip** command, you need to specify only the source IP address and destination IP address for the traffic flow between the hosts that you want to trace. Because a Layer 2 traceroute works only for paths within a Layer 2 network (i.e., VLAN), you must ensure the source and destination IP address represent hosts within the same IP subnet/VLAN. The switch executing the trace consults its local ARP cache to determine the MAC addresses of the source and destination. If no Address Resolution Protocol (ARP) entries are cached, then the switch issues ARP requests for each IP address and begins the trace once the required source and destination MAC address information is known.

It is very important that you understand that the bridge tables on each switch contain entries for at least the destination MAC address specified in the Layer 2 traceroute. If this is not the case, the Layer 2 traceroute fails with a message indicating the MAC address could not be found on one of the switches in the transmission path. To ensure the appropriate bridge table entries are populated on all switches, generate traffic between the source and destination hosts (preferably a continuous stream of traffic). Example 10-8 demonstrates generating a continuous ping between Host-A and Host-B, which ensures all switches in the network contain bridge table entries for both hosts.

Example 10-8 *Generating Traffic Between Host-A and Host-B*

```
c:\> ping -t 192.168.1.101
Pinging 192.168.1.101 with 32 bytes of data:

Reply from 192.168.1.101: bytes=32 time=2ms TTL=255
```

continues

Example 10-8   *Generating Traffic Between Host-A and Host-B (Continued)*

```
Reply from 192.168.1.101: bytes=32 time=1ms TTL=255
Reply from 192.168.1.101: bytes=32 time=1ms TTL=255
etc... (Output truncated)
etc...
```

Now that the appropriate bridge table entries are populated on each switch, Example 10-9 demonstrates using the **traceroute mac** command on Switch-B to trace the path used for traffic sent between Host-A (00a0.d1d0.20b9) and Host-B (0001.0200.d81d).

Example 10-9   *Using the* **traceroute mac** *Command on Cisco IOS*

```
Switch-B# traceroute mac 00a0.d1d0.20b9 0001.0200.d81d detail
Source 00a0.d1d0.20b9 found on Switch-B[WS-C3550-24] (192.168.1.2)
Switch-B / WS-C3550-24 / 192.168.1.2 :
                Fa0/3 [auto, auto] => Fa0/1 [full, 100M]
Switch-A / WS-C4006 / 192.168.1.1 :
                 2/1 [full, 100M] =>  2/2 [full, 100M]
Switch-C / WS-C3550-24 / 192.168.1.3 :
                Fa0/1 [full, 100M] => Fa0/3 [auto, auto]
Destination 0001.0200.d81d found on Switch-C[WS-C3550-24] (192.168.1.3)
Layer 2 trace completed.
```

In Example 10-9, notice that each switch in the transmission path between the specified source and destination MAC address is specified, with ingress and egress port information included. The first entry reads as follows:

```
Switch-B / WS-C3550-24 / 192.168.1.2 :
                Fa0/3 [auto, auto] => Fa0/1 [full, 100M]
```

This entry means that Switch-B is the first hop in the Layer 2 path between Host-A and Host-B and that the ingress port is Fa0/3 (attached to Host-A) and the egress port is Fa0/1 (attached to the next hop switch, Switch-A) In other words, traffic from Host-A enters interface Fa0/3 and exits interface Fa0/1. Notice also that speed and duplex settings are indicated for each ingress/egress port in the format [*duplex, speed*]. From the first entry in the preceding entry, you can see that Host-A is connected to an auto-sensing port (as indicated by the output **[auto, auto]**), while each of the interswitch trunks are configured as 100 Mbps full-duplex (as indicated by the output **[full, 100M]**). Example 10-9 verifies that the spanning-tree topology of Figure 10-4 is working correctly. The transmission path between Host-A and Host-B is Switch-B → Switch-A → Switch-C.

Example 10-10 demonstrates using the **traceroute mac ip** command on Switch-B to trace the path used for return traffic sent between Host-B and Host-A.

Example 10-10   *Using the* **traceroute mac ip** *Command on Cisco IOS*

```
Switch-B# traceroute mac ip 192.168.1.101 192.168.1.100 detail

Translating IP to mac .....
192.168.1.101 => 0001.0200.d81d
```

Example 10-10 *Using the* **traceroute mac ip** *Command on Cisco IOS (Continued)*

```
192.168.1.100 => 00a0.d1d0.20b9

Source not directly connected, tracing source .....
Source 0001.0200.d81d found on Switch-C[WS-C3550-24] (192.168.1.3)
Switch-C / WS-C3550-24 / 192.168.1.3 :
                Fa0/3 [auto, auto] => Fa0/1 [full, 100M]
Switch-A / WS-C4006 / 192.168.1.1 :
                2/2 [full, 100M] =>  2/1 [full, 100M]
Switch-B / WS-C3550-24 / 192.168.1.2 :
                Fa0/1 [full, 100M] => Fa0/3 [auto, auto]
Destination 00a0.d1d0.20b9 found on Switch-B[WS-C3550-24] (192.168.1.2)
Layer 2 trace completed.
```

In Example 10-10, notice that because the **traceroute mac ip** command is used, the switch first determines the MAC addresses associated with the specified IP addresses. Once these MAC addresses are known, notice that because the specified source (192.168.1.101 or Host-B) is not directly connected to Switch-B, Switch-B traces the switch to which Host-B is connected. This is found to be Switch-C, and the Layer 2 traceroute begins. As you can see from Example 10-9 and Example 10-10, traffic between Host-A and Host-B is taking the same forward and return path through the network (as it should, since spanning tree always provides symmetrical forwarding paths in the network).

On CatOS, the **l2trace** command is used to perform Layer 2 traceroutes, which has the following syntax options:

```
Console> (enable) l2trace source-mac-address destination-mac-address
  [vlan] [detail]
Console> (enable) l2trace source-ip-address destination-ip-address [detail]
```

If you use the **l2trace** command where you specify source and destination IP addresses, the switch checks its local ARP cache to allow the IP addresses to be mapped to MAC addresses or issues ARP requests if no mappings are present in the ARP cache.

Example 10-11 demonstrates using the **l2trace** command with MAC addresses on Switch-A to trace the path used for traffic sent between Host-A (00a0.d1d0.20b9) and Host-B (0001.0200.d81d), while Example 10-12 demonstrates using the **l2trace** command to trace the return path for traffic sent from Host-B to Host-A, specifying IP addresses instead of MAC addresses.

Example 10-11 *Using the* **l2trace** *command with MAC Addresses on CatOS*

```
Switch-B> (enable) l2trace 00-a0-d1-d0-20-b9 00-01-02-00-d8-1d detail
Starting L2 Trace

l2trace vlan number is 1.

Attention: Source 00-a0-d1-d0-20-b9 is not directly attached to this system.
Tracing the Source...
Completed Source Tracing.
Source 00-a0-d1-d0-20-b9 found in WS-C3550-24 : 192.168.1.2
```

continues

Example 10-11   *Using the* **l2trace** *command with MAC Addresses on CatOS (Continued)*

```
WS-C3550-24 : Switch-B : 192.168.1.2: Fa0/3  -> Fa0/1 100MB full duplex
WS-C4006 : Switch-A : 192.168.1.1:  2/1 100MB full duplex ->  2/2 100MB full duplex
WS-C3550-24 : Switch-C : 192.168.1.3: Fa0/1 100BM full duplex  -> Fa0/3

Destination 00-01-02-00-d8-1d found in WS-C3550-24 named Switch-C on port Fa0/3
```

Example 10-12   *Using the* **l2trace** *Command with IP Addresses on CatOS*

```
Switch-B> (enable) l2trace 192.168.1.101 192.168.1.100 detail
Mapping IP address to MAC address
192.168.1.101  ->  00-01-02-00-d8-1d
192.168.1.100  ->  00-a0-d1-d0-20-b9
Starting L2 Trace

l2trace vlan number is 1.

Attention: Source 00-01-02-00-d8-1d is not directly attached to this system.
Tracing the Source...
Completed Source Tracing.
Source 00-01-02-00-d8-1d found in WS-C3550-24 : 192.168.1.3
WS-C3550-24 : Switch-C : 192.168.1.3: Fa0/3  -> Fa0/1 100MB full duplex
WS-C4006 : Switch-A : 192.168.1.1:  2/2 100MB full duplex ->  2/1 100MB full duplex
WS-C3550-24 : Switch-B : 192.168.1.2: Fa0/1 full duplex -> Fa0/3

Destination 00-01-02-00-d8-1d found in WS-C3550-24 named Switch-B on port  fa0/3
```

As you can see from Example 10-11 and Example 10-12, the same functionality and similar output is provided by the **l2trace** utility on CatOS. Example 10-11 and Example 10-12 verify the spanning-tree topology of Figure 10-4, as traffic between Host-A and Host-B travels from Switch-B → Switch-A → Switch-C and vice versa.

Scenario 10-2: Troubleshooting Workstation Startup Problems

A very common issue with switched networks is a lack of initial LAN connectivity when workstations are powered on or rebooted. Core network devices such as routers, switches, and servers are rarely powered off or rebooted. Workstations are often powered down or rebooted at least once a day, which means that the problem is much more apparent to workstation users. Workstations also typically boot much faster than servers, to the extent that you might have a user expecting access to the network in a matter of seconds. If you have read through the previous chapters of this book, you probably have a good idea as to why LAN connectivity is not immediately granted. The issue stems from the fact that physical connectivity is lost on the switch port when a workstation is powered off, and even sometimes when a workstation is rebooted (depending on the network interface card). Once the workstation powers up (or starts the boot process) and physical connectivity is restored, the default operation of Cisco switches is to not forward traffic on the port until various protocol negotiations have occurred and checks have been made (via spanning tree) to ensure that forwarding traffic in and out of the switch port does not introduce Layer 2 loops into the LAN. You can break down the delay factors for placing a switch port into a forwarding state as follows:

- Protocol negotiation
- Spanning-tree listening and learning

In this scenario, you learn how to reduce port startup delays for switch ports. Figure 10-5 shows the topology used for this scenario.

Figure 10-5   *Scenario 10-2 Topology*

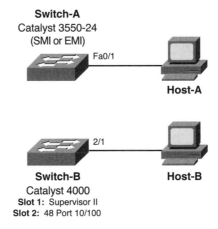

In Figure 10-5, two standalone switches each attach a single host. Each host is assumed to contain a standard 10/100BaseT network interface card (NIC) and requires only an access port connection with no requirements for trunking or EtherChannel. Therefore, the startup delay for the ports attached to each workstation can (and should be) significantly reduced. In this scenario, the default startup delay of each port is measured, with the startup delay then measured after the various techniques available to reduce port delay are implemented.

Understanding the Causes of Port Startup Delays

Before implementing and testing techniques to reduce port startup delay, you need to understand exactly what causes startup delays. The causes of port startup delay can be broadly categorized into two categories:

- **Protocol negotiation delays**—Speed/duplex auto-negotiation (802.1u), Dynamic Trunking Protocol (DTP), and Port Aggregation Protocol (PAgP)
- **Spanning-tree delays**—Spanning-tree listening and learning states

Each of the listed delays occurs in sequential order. In other words, protocol negotiation delays occur first, which determine how a port is going to operate at both the physical layer and at Layer 2. Once these attributes are known, the port comes up at Layer 2 (i.e., spanning tree sees the port as just having come up), and the delays associated with the spanning-tree listening and learning phases take place. Figure 10-6 illustrates the causes of port startup delays.

Figure 10-6   *Port Startup Delays*

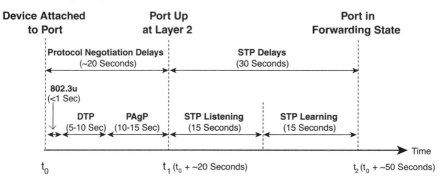

In Figure 10-6, you can see the sequence in which each contributing factor to port startup delay occurs. Protocol negotiation delays, related to 802.1u speed/duplex auto-negotiation, DTP negotiation, and PAgP negotiation, take approximately 20 seconds. Next, the spanning-tree listening and learning phases take 30 seconds, for a total of approximately 50 seconds before a port can start forwarding data. During the initial startup delay period, any traffic sent from an attached device is discarded.

Each of the causes of startup delay is now discussed in more detail.

Protocol Negotiation Delays

On Cisco Catalyst switches, a number of default settings enabled on each port introduce protocol negotiations, each of which introduces some factor of delay. The following lists the various protocol negotiations that take place by default when a port is initialized:

- **Speed/duplex auto-negotiation**—The default speed and duplex settings for 10/100BaseT and 10/100/1000BaseT Ethernet ports on Catalyst switches is to auto-negotiate. The auto-negotiation process takes a few seconds.

- **Dynamic Trunking Protocol (DTP)**—DTP is used to negotiate whether a switch port becomes a trunk port that transports traffic from multiple VLANs. The default DTP setting on CatOS-based Catalyst switches is "auto," while the default DTP setting on Cisco IOS-based Catalyst switches is "desirable." For both DTP modes of operation, this means the port listens for DTP messages from the remote device. The switch normally listens for 5 to 10 seconds before assuming the port will not trunk.

- **Port Aggregation Protocol (PAgP)**—PAgP is similar in nature to DTP, except it is used to negotiate EtherChannel bundles. The default PAgP setting on most Catalyst switches is "auto," which means the port listens for PAgP messages from the remote device. The switch normally listens for approximately 10 to 15 seconds before assuming the port will not form a bundle.

If you add the times listed in the preceding list, you come out with a figure of somewhere between 15 and 25 seconds. During this time, the port is not even up at a Layer 2 level, as attributes specific to how the interface operates at both a physical level (i.e., EtherChannel) and Layer 2 level (i.e., trunking) are attempting to be determined. In other words, once DTP and PAgP negotiations are complete, a port comes up at Layer 2. At this point, the port becomes available for spanning tree, which then applies spanning-tree delays

Reducing Ethernet Auto-Negotiation Delays

To eliminate delays associated with speed and duplex auto-negotiation, you must hard code speed and duplex settings. On Cisco IOS, you can achieve this by using the **speed** and **duplex** interface configuration commands, as demonstrated in Example 10-13.

Example 10-13 *Hard Coding Speed and Duplex Settings on Cisco IOS*

```
Switch# configure terminal
Switch(config)# interface fastEthernet 0/1
Switch(config-if)# speed 100
Switch(config-if)# duplex full
```

On CatOS, you use the **set port speed** and **set port duplex** configuration commands to hard code speed and duplex settings, as demonstrated in Example 10-14.

Example 10-14 *Hard Coding Speed and Duplex Settings on CatOS*

```
Console> (enable) set port speed 2/1 100
Port(s)  2/1 speed set to 100Mbps.
Console> (enable) set port duplex 2/1 full
Port(s)  2/1 set to full-duplex.
```

NOTE   On Cisco IOS and CatOS, you must hard code interface speed before you can hard code the duplex setting.

It is important to note that it is *not* recommended to hard code speed and duplex settings unless each device that attaches to a hard coded port has hard coded speed and duplex settings as well. Most organizations leave user workstation NIC settings in an auto-sensing configuration to reduce administrative overheads and to accommodate the capabilities of the various user workstation NICs that might be present within the organization. For this reason, it is recommended you leave auto-negotiation on for ports connected to user workstations (turning it off only saves a couple of seconds). For ports connected to servers and other network devices (e.g., routers and firewalls), it is also recommended to hard code speed and duplex where possible, although primarily to reduce the chance of negotiation mismatches, rather than for reducing port startup delay (as most servers and network devices are rarely rebooted or cycled).

Reducing DTP and PAgP Negotiation Delays

To eliminate delays associated with DTP and PAgP negotiation, you must configure each protocol to operate in an off mode, meaning the protocol is essentially disabled. By default on Cisco IOS, all interfaces are configured with a DTP mode of desirable; however, PAgP is disabled by default. You can configure a DTP mode of off by using the **switchport mode access** interface configuration command, and if you do need to disable PAgP for some reason (for example, because an interface has previously been part of an EtherChannel bundle), then you can use the **no channel-group** interface configuration command. Example 10-15 demonstrates disabling DTP and ensuring PAgP is disabled.

Example 10-15 *Disabling DTP and PAgP on Cisco IOS*

```
Switch# configure terminal
Switch(config)# interface fastEthernet 0/1
Switch(config-if)# switchport mode access
Switch(config-if)# no channel-group
```

On CatOS, the default DTP mode and PAgP mode is auto, which means you must explicitly disable both DTP and PAgP (unlike Cisco IOS, where PAgP is already disabled by default). To disable DTP, you use the **set trunk** command, and to disable PAgP, you use the **set port channel** command, as demonstrated in Example 10-16.

Example 10-16 *Disabling DTP and PAgP on CatOS*

```
Console> (enable) set trunk 2/1 off
Port(s)  2/1 trunk mode set to off.
Console > (enable) set port channel 2/1 mode off
Port(s) 2/1 channel mode set to off.
```

Spanning-Tree Listening and Learning

Once the protocol negotiation phases are complete, the port is placed into an up state at Layer 2, at which point in time spanning tree sees the port. Spanning-tree delays are now incurred before traffic is actually forwarded on the port. Spanning tree listens for 15 seconds by default, determining whether or not a loop would be formed by placing the port into a forwarding state. Next, spanning tree learns the MAC addresses of devices transmitting into the port and place entries into the bridge table. This continues for a period of 15 seconds and prevents the large-scale flooding of frames (due to the bridge table being empty) when the port starts forwarding frames. So by default, a delay of 30 seconds is incurred by the spanning-tree behavior of the switch. If you add the protocol negotiation and spanning-tree delays, you are looking at a total delay of 45 to 55 seconds before a port starts forwarding data after it has detected physical connectivity.

Reducing Spanning-Tree Timers

The first option to reduce spanning-tree delays is to reduce the *forward delay timer*, which defines the length of the Spanning Tree Protocol (STP) listening and learning periods. The default spanning-tree timers are designed for a Layer 2 network that has a network diameter (maximum number of hops between any device) of 7. By using a hierarchical, star topology, you can significantly reduce the network diameter to 2 or 3 hops. This means that if your network is smaller than 7 hops, you can use shorter spanning-tree timers because the amount of time taken for spanning-tree messages to reach the entire Layer 2 network is shorter. For example, assuming a network diameter of 3, you can reduce the spanning-tree delay for a new port from 30 seconds to 18 seconds. You can also reduce timers further by lowering the Hello timer from the default value of 2 seconds to 1 second (the Hello timer affects the calculation of other STP timers). For example, assuming a network diameter of 3 and a Hello timer of 1 second, you can reduce the spanning-tree delay for a new port from 30 seconds to 10 seconds (compared with 18 seconds if the hello timer is 2 seconds).

When modifying spanning-tree timers, you must use the formulas specified in the IEEE 802.1d specification. Both Cisco IOS and CatOS include spanning-tree macros, which automatically calculate and configure the appropriate spanning-tree timers according to the 802.1d specification based upon the network diameter input to the macro. Example 10-17 and Example 10-18 demonstrate the use of the spanning-tree macros on Cisco IOS and CatOS, respectively, to reduce the spanning tree timers for a switched network with a network diameter of three switches.

Example 10-17 *Reducing Spanning-Tree Delays on Cisco IOS*

```
Switch# configure terminal
Switch(config)# spanning-tree vlan 1 root primary diameter 3 hello-time 1
Switch(config)# exit
Switch# show spanning-tree vlan 1

VLAN0001
  Spanning tree enabled protocol ieee
  Root ID    Priority    24577
             Address     0009.b7aa.9c80
             This bridge is the root
             Hello Time   1 sec  Max Age  7 sec  Forward Delay  5 sec

  Bridge ID  Priority    24577  (priority 24576 sys-id-ext 1)
             Address     0009.b7aa.9c80
             Hello Time   1 sec  Max Age  7 sec  Forward Delay  5 sec
             Aging Time 15

Interface        Role Sts Cost      Prio.Nbr Type
---------------- ---- --- --------- -------- --------------------------------
Fa0/1            Desg FWD 19        128.1    P2p
```

Example 10-18 *Reducing Spanning-Tree Delays on CatOS*

```
Console> (enable) set spantree root 1 dia 3 hello 2
VLAN 1 bridge priority set to 8192.
VLAN 1 bridge max aging time set to 7.
VLAN 1 bridge hello time set to 1.
VLAN 1 bridge forward delay set to 9.
Switch is now the root switch for active VLAN 1.
```

In Example 10-17 and Example 10-18, the shaded lines indicate the *forward delay timer*, which is the timer that determines the length of the listening and learning STP states. In both examples, the network diameter is configured as 3; however, notice that the forward delay for each example is different. This is because in Example 10-17, the Hello timer is reduced to one second (resulting in a forward delay of 5 seconds, or a combined listening and learning delay of 10 seconds), while in Example 10-18, the Hello timer is configured as the default setting of one second (resulting in a forward delay of 9 seconds, or a combined listening and learning delay of 18 seconds).

Enabling Spanning Tree PortFast

The other option to reduce spanning-tree delays is to eliminate them completely by enabling the PortFast feature, which is a proprietary Cisco enhancement that places a switch port immediately into a forwarding state while the listening and learning phases take place. This reduces the normal STP delay of 30 seconds to 0—clearly quite an improvement. The restriction with PortFast is that you should only ever use it on ports that have single-homed (single network card) connections. You should never use PortFast on a port that connects to another Layer 2 network device, such as a switch or hub. You can enable PortFast for multi-homed routing devices (e.g., routers, firewalls, and multi-homed workstations); however, you must ensure that the multi-homed device is in no way bridging traffic between local interfaces. PortFast is the most common method used to reduce spanning-tree delays, as it totally eliminates any delay. In fact, it can be used in conjunction with reduced spanning-tree timers, where reducing the spanning-tree timers reduces the convergence time of other parts of the Layer 2 network.

To enable PortFast on Cisco IOS, you use the **spanning-tree portfast** interface configuration command, and on CatOS, you use the **set spantree portfast** configuration command. Example 10-19 and Example 10-20 demonstrate enabling spanning-tree PortFast on Cisco IOS and CatOS, respectively, to eliminate spanning-tree delays completely.

Example 10-19 *Enabling Spanning-Tree PortFast on Cisco IOS*

```
Switch# configure terminal
Switch(config)# interface fastEthernet0/1
Switch(config-if)# spanning-tree portfast
%Warning: portfast should only be enabled on ports connected to a single
  host. Connecting hubs, concentrators, switches, bridges, etc... to this
  interface  when portfast is enabled, can cause temporary bridging loops.
  Use with CAUTION
```

Example 10-20 *Enabling Spanning-Tree PortFast on CatOS*

```
Console> (enable) set spantree portfast 2/1 enable

Warning: Connecting Layer 2 devices to a fast start port can cause
temporary spanning tree loops. Use with caution.

Spantree port  2/1 fast start enabled.
```

The switchport host and set port host Macros

At this point, it is appropriate to discuss the **switchport host** interface configuration macro (Cisco IOS) and the **set port host** macro (CatOS), which are macros that automatically configure all the various commands used implement the following configuration tasks:

- Disabling DTP
- Disabling PAgP
- Enabling spanning-tree PortFast

The **switchport host** and **set port host** macros reduce the administrative overhead and errors associated with having to manually perform each of the configuration tasks mentioned in the preceding list. Example 10-21 and Example 10-22 demonstrate the use of these macros on Cisco IOS and CatOS.

Example 10-21 *Using the* **switchport host** *Macro on Cisco IOS*

```
Switch# configure terminal
Switch(config)# interface range fastEthernet0/1 - 24
Switch(config-if)# switchport host
! switchport mode will be set to access
! spanning-tree portfast will be enabled
channel group will be disabled
```

Example 10-22 *Using the* **set port host** *Macro on CatOS*

```
Console> (enable) set port host 2/1-48
Port(s) 2/1-48 channel mode set to off.

Warning: Connecting Layer 2 devices to a fast start port can cause
temporary spanning tree loops. Use with caution.

Spantree port  2/1-48 fast start enabled.
Port(s)  2/1-48 trunk mode set to off.
```

As you can see in Example 10-21 and Example 10-22, DTP is disabled, PAgP is disabled, and spanning-tree PortFast is enabled after executing the macro.

Configuration Tasks

In this scenario, reducing the port startup delay on a CatOS-based switch is demonstrated, with each contributing delay factor incrementally eliminated and tested to determine the effect it has on reducing the total port startup delay. This requires the following configuration tasks:

- Measuring the default port startup delay
- Measuring the delay associated with spanning-tree timers and protocol negotiation

Measuring the Default Port Startup Delay

Before commencing configuration and testing, enable spanning tree informational event logging (level 6) so that a switch generates SYSLOG events when spanning tree events occur to detect when spanning tree sees a port first come up (i.e., after protocol negotiations occur) and to detect when a port is placed into a forwarding state (i.e., after the STP listening and learning phases). By default, the logging level is critical (level 2), which does not generate the required SYSLOG messages upon normal spanning tree events. Example 10-23 demonstrates configuring the spanning tree logging level as informational on Switch-A.

Example 10-23 *Configuring Spanning-Tree Logging Level*

```
Switch-A> (enable) set logging level spantree 6
System logging facility <spantree> for this session set to severity 6(information)
```

Now that the appropriate events are displayed as they occur, testing can begin. To emulate when a port is physically not connected and when a port transitions to a physically connected state, you can use the **set port disable** command to physically disable a port and then use the **set port enable** command to bring the port up (effectively emulating the port being physically connected). In this scenario, Host-A is always connected to Switch-A physically; the **set port disable** command is used to emulate Host-A being physically disconnected from the switch.

To begin the first port delay test, port 2/1 on Switch-A is disabled, to emulate Host-A being disconnected from the switch. The **show time** command is then used to display the current time in hh:mm:ss format. Immediately after this command is entered, the **set port enable 2/1** command is executed. Doing this emulates bringing up the port from a physical point of view; the faster you enter the **set port enable 2/1** command after entering the **show time** command, the more accurate timing is. After port startup delays are completed and the port goes up from a Layer 2 perspective, a "%PAGP-5-PORTTOSTP" message is displayed, which includes a timestamp that can be used to determine how long protocol negotiation took to bring up the port. Once spanning tree places the port into a forwarding state, a "%SPANTREE-6-PORTFWD" message is displayed, which also includes a timestamp. This enables measurement of exactly how long spanning tree takes to place the port into a forwarding state, as well as the total delay from when the port goes up physically to when the port actually starts forwarding data. Example 10-24 demonstrates the entire process just described.

Example 10-24 *Timing the Default Startup Delay of a Port*

```
Switch-A> (enable) set port disable 2/1
Port 2/1 disabled.
2002 Jul 08 19:28:30 %ETHC-5-PORTFROMSTP:Port 2/1 left bridge port 2/1
Switch-A> (enable) show time
Mon Jul 8 2002, 19:28:16
Switch-A> (enable) set port enable 2/1
Port 2/1 enabled.
2002 Jul 08 19:28:36 %PAGP-5-PORTTOSTP:Port 2/1 joined bridge port 2/1
2002 Jul 08 19:28:36 %SPANTREE-6-PORTBLK: Port 2/1 state in VLAN 1 changed to
  blocking
2002 Jul 08 19:28:36 %SPANTREE-5-PORTLISTEN: Port 2/1 state in VLAN 1 changed to
  listening
2002 Jul 08 19:28:50 %SPANTREE-6-PORTLEARN: Port 2/1 state in VLAN 1 changed to
  learning
2002 Jul 08 19:29:06 %SPANTREE-6-PORTFWD: Port 2/1 state in VLAN 1 changed to
  forwarding
```

In Example 10-24, the **show time** command is issued to determine the current time, and then the **set port enable 2/1** command is entered immediately. It is paramount that this command is entered as quickly as possible after the **show time** command to ensure timing is accurate.

TIP To obtain the most accurate timing, in your favorite text editor type the **show time** command, press Enter, type the **set port enable 2/1** command, and then press Enter again. Select all of the text including the last blank line (you need this to apply a carriage return after **set port enable 2/1**) and copy this to the clipboard. Pasting this into your terminal emulation package automatically implements the commands shown in Example 10-24 in the quickest fashion possible.

After the port is enabled physically (at 19:28:16), 20 seconds later (at 19:28:36) the port is placed into an up state at the Layer 2 level. This is determined by subtracting the first two shaded timestamps in Example 10-24. After another 30 seconds, the port is placed into a forwarding state as indicated by the "%SPANTREE-6-PORTFWD" event. Thus in total, it takes 50 seconds for the port to actually be in a state that forwards data from the time it first comes up physically.

Measuring the Delay Associated with Spanning-Tree Timers and Protocol Negotiation

At this point, a baseline default time delay of 50 seconds has been measured, during which time a switch port is physically up but not actually forwarding data. To reduce this delay, spanning-tree PortFast can be enabled, which should reduce the startup delay by 30 seconds. Example 10-25 shows the process of enabling PortFast on Switch-A.

Example 10-25 *Enabling PortFast on Switch-A*

```
Switch-A> (enable) set spantree portfast 2/1 enable

Warning: Spantree port fast start should only be enabled on ports connected
to a single host.  Connecting hubs, concentrators, switches, bridges, etc. to
a fast start port can cause temporary spanning tree loops.  Use with caution.

Spantree port 2/1 fast start enabled.
```

Now that PortFast is enabled, the same testing procedure used in Example 10-24 must be repeated to measure the effect that PortFast has on reducing startup delay. Example 10-26 demonstrates measuring startup delay with PortFast enabled.

Example 10-26 *Timing the Startup Delay of a Port with PortFast Enabled*

```
Switch-A> (enable) set port disable 2/1
Port 2/1 disabled.
2002 Jul 08 19:34:35 %PAGP-5-PORTFROMSTP:Port 2/1 left bridge port 2/1

Switch-A> (enable) show time
Mon Jul 8 2002, 19:35:08
Switch-A> (enable) set port enable 2/1
Port 2/1 enabled.
2002 Jul 08 19:35:28 %PAGP-5-PORTTOSTP:Port 2/1 joined bridge port 2/1
2002 Jul 08 19:35:28 %SPANTREE-6-PORTFWD: Port 2/1 state in VLAN 1 changed to
  forwarding
```

Notice in Example 10-26 that the time between when the port comes up at a Layer 2 level (20 seconds after the port is physically enabled) and when the port starts forwarding data is instantaneous. This means the port startup delay has been reduced from 50 seconds (see Example 10-24) to just 20 seconds by enabling spanning-tree PortFast.

To further reduce startup delays, PAgP can be disabled by configuring a PAgP mode of off. Example 10-27 demonstrates viewing the default PAgP configuration on Switch-A for port 2/1 and then disabling PAgP on port 2/1.

Example 10-27 *Disabling PAgP for Port 2/1 on Switch-A*

```
Switch-A> (enable) show port channel 2/1
Port   Status      Channel              Admin Ch
                   Mode                 Group Id
-----  ----------  -------------------- ----- -----
 2/1   connected   auto silent             27     0
```

Example 10-27 *Disabling PAgP for Port 2/1 on Switch-A (Continued)*

```
Port  Device-ID                         Port-ID                  Platform
----- ------------------------------- ------------------------- ----------------
 2/1
Switch-A> (enable) set port channel 2/1 mode off
Port(s) 2/1 channel mode set to off.
```

As you can see in Example 10-27, the default PAgP mode is auto, which means PAgP negotiations and the associated delay take place when port 2/1 comes up. By disabling PAgP in Example 10-27, the delays associated with PAgP negotiations are eliminated.

Now that PortFast is enabled and PAgP is disabled, the same testing procedure used in Example 10-24 and Example 10-26 must be repeated to measure the effect that PortFast and disabling PAgP has on reducing startup delay. Example 10-28 demonstrates measuring startup delay with PortFast enabled and PAgP disabled.

Example 10-28 *Timing the Startup Delay of a Port with PortFast Enabled and PAgP Disabled*

```
Switch-A> (enable) set port disable 2/1
Port 2/1 disabled.
2002 Jul 08 19:39:57 %PAGP-5-PORTFROMSTP:Port 2/1 left bridge port 2/1

Switch-A> (enable) show time
Mon Jul 8 2002, 19:40:13
Switch-A> (enable) set port enable 2/1
Port 2/1 enabled.
2002 Jul 08 19:40:24 %PAGP-5-PORTTOSTP:Port 2/1 joined bridge port 2/1
2002 Jul 08 19:40:24 %SPANTREE-6-PORTFWD: Port 2/1 state in VLAN 1 changed to
  forwarding
```

Notice in Example 10-28 that the time between when the port is physically enabled (19:40:13) and when the port comes up at a Layer 2 level (19:40:24) is now reduced to just 11 seconds from 20 seconds in Example 10-26. This means that the reduction in delay due to the disabling of PAgP is 9 seconds.

To further reduce startup delays, DTP can be disabled by configuring a DTP mode of off. Example 10-29 demonstrates viewing the default DTP configuration on Switch-A for port 2/1 and then disabling DTP for port 2/1.

Example 10-29 *Disabling DTP for Port 2/1 on Switch-A*

```
Switch-A> (enable) show trunk 2/1
* - indicates vtp domain mismatch
Port      Mode          Encapsulation  Status        Native vlan
--------  ------------  -------------  ------------  -----------
 2/2      auto          dot1q          not-trunking  1

Port      Vlans allowed on trunk
--------  ------------------------------------------------------------------------
 2/2      1-1005,1025-4094
```

continues

Example 10-29 *Disabling DTP for Port 2/1 on Switch-A (Continued)*

```
Port      Vlans allowed and active in management domain
--------  ------------------------------------------------------------------
 2/2      1

Port      Vlans in spanning tree forwarding state and not pruned
--------  ------------------------------------------------------------------
 2/2
Switch-A> (enable) set trunk 2/1 off
Port(s)  2/1 trunk mode set to off.
```

Notice that the default (DTP) mode in the **show trunk** output is set to auto, which means the port listens for DTP messages until a timeout period expires. By disabling DTP in Example 10-29, the delays associated with DTP negotiations are eliminated.

Now that PortFast is enabled, PAgP is disabled, and DTP is disabled, the same testing procedure used in Example 10-24, Example 10-26 and Example 10-28 must be repeated to measure the effect that enabling PortFast, disabling PAgP, and disabling DTP has on reducing startup delay. Example 10-30 demonstrates measuring startup delay with PortFast enabled, PAgP disabled, and DTP disabled.

Example 10-30 *Timing the Startup Delay of a Port with PortFast Enabled and PAgP and DTP Disabled*

```
Switch-A> (enable) set port disable 2/1
Port 2/1 disabled.
2002 Jul 08 19:44:06 %PAGP-5-PORTFROMSTP:Port 2/1 left bridge port 2/1

Switch-A> (enable) show time
Mon Jul 8 2002, 19:44:18
Switch-A> (enable) set port enable 2/1
Port 2/1 enabled.
2002 Jul 08 19:44:22 %PAGP-5-PORTTOSTP:Port 2/1 joined bridge port 2/1
2002 Jul 08 19:44:22 %SPANTREE-6-PORTFWD: Port 2/1 state in VLAN 1 changed to
  forwarding
```

Notice in Example 10-30 that the time between when the port is physically enabled and when the port is placed up at Layer 2 is now reduced to just 4 seconds in total, compared with 11 seconds in Example 10-28. This means that the reduction in delay due to disabling DTP is 7 seconds.

Finally, to reduce startup delays as much as possible, speed and duplex settings can be configured on port 2/1, eliminating the delays associated with Ethernet auto-negotiation on port 2/1. To ensure optimal performance on the port, the speed and duplex settings on Host-A must also be hard coded with a matching speed and duplex configuration. Assuming the speed and duplex settings on Host-A are configured as 100 Mbps full-duplex, Example 10-31 demonstrates hard coding the speed and duplex settings for port 2/1 on Switch-A.

Example 10-31 *Disabling Auto-Negotiation for Port 2/1 on Switch-A*

```
Switch-A> (enable) set port speed 2/1 100
Port(s)  2/1 speed set to 100Mbps.
Switch-A> (enable) set port duplex 2/2 full
Port(s)  2/1 set to full-duplex.
```

Now that all startup delay factors have been eliminated (i.e., PortFast, DTP, PAgP, and Ethernet auto-negotiation), a final test of startup delay is required. Example 10-32 demonstrates measuring startup delay with PortFast enabled, PAgP disabled, DTP disabled, and Ethernet speed/duplex auto-negotiation disabled.

Example 10-32 *Timing the Startup Delay of a Port with PortFast Enabled, PAgP + DTP Disabled and Ethernet Auto-negotiation Disabled*

```
Switch-A> (enable) set port disable 2/1
Port 2/1 disabled.
2002 Jul 08 19:52:07 %PAGP-5-PORTFROMSTP:Port 2/1 left bridge port 2/1

Switch-A> (enable) show time
Mon Jul 8 2002, 19:52:10
Switch-A> (enable) set port enable 2/1
Port 2/1 enabled.
2002 Jul 08 19:44:12 %PAGP-5-PORTTOSTP:Port 2/1 joined bridge port 2/1
2002 Jul 08 19:44:12 %SPANTREE-6-PORTFWD: Port 2/1 state in VLAN 1 changed to
  forwarding
```

Notice in Example 10-32 that the time between when the port is physically enabled and when the port is placed up at Layer 2 is now reduced to just 2 seconds in total, compared with 4 seconds in Example 10-30. This means that the reduction in delay due to disabling auto-negotiation is 2 seconds. You would normally not disable auto-negotiation on a workstation port, because this would require the disabling of auto-negotiation on the workstation NIC as well to ensure proper duplex matching.

NOTE   The 2-second delay that still remains can be attributed to processing and port initialization delays that cannot be eliminated.

Scenario 10-3: Troubleshooting the errDisable Status

The *errDisable status* is a feature utilized by Cisco Catalyst switches that is designed to protect the network from issues resulting from switch misconfiguration and other errors in the network. The errDisable status describes a port that has been shut down by the switch operating system due to an error being detected on the port. Once a port is placed into the errDisable state, an administrator must manually re-enable the port. This feature is reserved for errors that might seriously jeopardize the stability of the switch or the entire LAN network.

NOTE   You can also configure Cisco Catalyst switches to automatically enable errDisabled ports after a configurable timer expires.

The following lists common reasons why a port might be placed into an errDisable state:

- **Spanning-tree BPDU Guard**—This feature is used on ports that have the spanning-tree PortFast feature enabled. Because PortFast places a port into a forwarding state immediately upon activation, it should be used only for ports that are connected to a single-homed device, and not any bridging device, such as another LAN switch. If another LAN switch is connected to the port, the port receives spanning-tree bridge protocol data units (BPDUs). This indicates to the receiving switch that a multi-homed device is connected to the PortFast-enabled port (in error). If BPDU Guard is enabled, the switch shuts down the port and places the port into an errDisable state.

- **EtherChannel misconfiguration**—A common cause of the ports being placed into an errDisable is EtherChannel misconfiguration. When configuring EtherChannel, you must ensure that various parameters are identical for all ports on both sides of the bundle. For example, all ports must belong to the same VLAN or if using trunks, all ports must be configured as trunks with the same native VLAN (when using 802.1Q trunking). A common misconfiguration problem is when incompatible PAgP modes are used on the endpoints of the bundle or when speed and duplex settings are not matched.

- **Unidirectional Link Detection (UDLD)**—This features is used to detect unidirectional failures. Unidirectional failures are common with fiber-based connections where a pair of physically separated fiber strands represents the transmit and receive for the connection. If one of these fibers is damaged or broken, while the other fiber still operates okay, traffic can flow only in one direction. This introduces an unforeseen situation that was probably not anticipated by the designers of spanning tree. STP assumes that all links can send traffic in both directions, which is a reasonable assumption for any network connection that is useful. Having traffic being sent only in one direction can cause loops to form in a spanning-tree topology when a blocked spanning-tree port fails to received BDPUs from the designated bridge for the link, due to the failure of the receive fiber on the blocked port. After spanning-tree timers expire, the blocked port is placed into a forwarding state, generating a loop in the network. UDLD is designed to ensure a Layer 2 connection is bidirectional at all times by detecting unidirectional failures. If a unidirectional failure is detected, the switch places the port into an errDisable state to prevent spanning-tree loops from forming.

- **Port security**—Port security enables administrators to define a list of source MAC addresses permitted on a port and by default shuts down a port if a security violation, where a frame is received that contains an unauthorized MAC address, occurs. The fact that ports are disabled due to port security violations is often by design; the security policy of an organization might dictate that such an action is appropriate for a port security violation.

- **Other issues**—Other issues can cause a port to be placed into the errDisable state, including invalid GBICs (i.e., GBICs inserted manufactured by a non-Cisco approved manufacturer), excessive late collisions, duplex mismatches, link flapping, PAgP flapping, and Dynamic Host Configuration Protocol (DHCP) snooping rate-limiting.

Troubleshooting Steps

As with any problem that you might try to solve, you should take clear troubleshooting steps, depending on the issue you are trying to tackle. The following describes each of the troubleshooting steps you should take when trying to determine the cause of the errDisable state of a port:

Step 1   Determine an issue exists

Step 2   Determine why the port(s) were disabled

Step 3   Resolve the issue(s)

Step 4   Re-enable the port(s)

Each of these troubleshooting steps is now examined in detail.

Step 1—Determining an Issue Exists

When a port is placed into an errDisable state, the visibility of such an event to network operations personnel responsible for maintaining the network is important, so that the issue can be resolved and so that the port can be restored to an operational state. An errDisable event can be detected in several ways:

- Port LED changes color from green to orange
- Loss of functionality in the network
- Notification via network management systems (e.g., SYSLOG messages or SNMP traps)

The first indication of a port being placed in the errDisable state is the physical status of the port as displayed on the switch itself. Cisco Catalyst switches include LEDs for each switch port, with a color of green indicating a port is connected and operating normally and a color of orange indicating the port has been placed into an errDisable state.

The next and most apparent indication of a port being in the errDisable state is that traffic ceases to be forwarded in and out of the port. If the disabled port is a workstation port, it might take a while for the problem to be detected by the end user whose workstation is connected to the port. However, if the port is connected to an important server or is an inter-switch link, you generally know about the problem fairly quickly, as it has a major impact on the network.

Aside from the functional visibility and impact on the network of a port being placed into an errDisable state, operationally on the switch, as soon as a port is placed into an errDisable state, a SYSLOG message can be generated that is displayed on the console and forwarded to a SYSLOG server.

NOTE   A Simple Network Management Protocol (SNMP) trap can also be generated and forwarded to an SNMP management server if SNMP is configured appropriately on the switch.

Depending on the error event that causes a port to be placed in the errDisable state, SYSLOG messages are generated that give you clues to the reason for disabling the port. For example, Example 10-33 and Example 10-34 show what happens on a Cisco IOS switch and CatOS switch respectively when a BPDU is detected on a port that has spanning-tree PortFast enabled and BPDU guard is also enabled.

Example 10-33 *SYSLOG Messages Indicating BDPU Guard Has Been Invoked on Cisco IOS*

```
00:54:17: %SPANTREE-2-BLOCK_BPDUGUARD: Received BPDU on port FastEthernet0/1
    with BPDU Guard enabled. Disabling port.
00:54:17: %PM-4-ERR_DISABLE: bpduguard error detected on Fa0/1, putting
    Fa0/1 in err-disable state
00:54:18: %LINEPROTO-5-UPDOWN: Line protocol on Interface FastEthernet0/1,
    changed state to down
```

Example 10-34 *SYSLOG Message Indicating BDPU Guard Has Been Invoked on CatOS*

```
21:00:09 %SPANTREE-2-RX_PORTFAST:Received BPDU on PortFast enable port.
    Disabling 2/1
21:00:09 %PAGP-5-PORTFROMSTP:Port 2/1 left bridge port 2/1
```

In Example 10-33, the first message indicates a critical spanning tree event (as indicated by the "%SPANTREE-2" portion of the message). The message description indicates that a BPDU has been received on a port configured with PortFast (FastEthernet0/1) and that the port is being disabled as a result. The second message ("%PM-4-ERR DISABLE") indicates that an errDisable event has occurred, with interface FastEthernet0/1 placed into an errDisable state. In Example 10-34, a similar message sequence also occurs.

Example 10-35 and Example 10-36 demonstrate the messages generated when Ether-Channel misconfiguration causes a ports to be disabled.

Example 10-35 *SYSLOG Message Indicating EtherChannel Misconfiguration on Cisco IOS*

```
01:06:56: %PM-4-ERR_DISABLE: channel-misconfig error detected on Po1,
    putting Fa0/1 in err-disable state
01:06:56: %PM-4-ERR_DISABLE: channel-misconfig error detected on Po1,
    putting Fa0/2 in err-disable state
```

Example 10-36 *SYSLOG Message Indicating EtherChannel Misconfiguration on CatOS*

```
21:00:09 %PAGP-5-PORTTOSTP:Port 1/1 joined bridge port 1/1-2
21:00:09 %PAGP-5-PORTTOSTP:Port 1/2 joined bridge port 1/1-2
21:00:09 %SPANTREE-2-CHNMISCFG: STP loop - channel 1/1-2 is disabled in vlan 1
21:00:09 %PAGP-5-PORTFROMSTP:Port 1/1 left bridge port 1/1-2
21:00:09 %PAGP-5-PORTFROMSTP:Port 1/2 left bridge port 1/1-2
```

In Example 10-35 and Example 10-36, the local ports are configured with a PAgP mode of on, which means they always form a bundle and don't send PAgP negotiation packets. The remote switch to which the ports are connected has PAgP disabled for the connected ports. This means that an EtherChannel bundle is formed on one side, but not formed on the other side. When an EtherChannel bundle is formed, spanning-tree BPDUs are sent down only one physical link. In Example 10-35 and Example 10-36, the remote switch sends BPDUs out both ports and the local switch receives these BPDUs on both ports of the EtherChannel bundle.

Once you have detected something is wrong in your network, and suspect that it is related to a port being disabled by the switch, you can use the **show interfaces** (Cisco IOS) and **show port** (CatOS) command to check the status of a port. Example 10-37 and Example 10-38 demonstrate checking the status of an interface on a Cisco IOS-based switch and a CatOS-based switch.

Example 10-37 *Checking Interface Status on Cisco IOS*

```
Switch# show interfaces fastEthernet0/1
FastEthernet0/1 is down, line protocol is down (err-disabled)
  Hardware is Fast Ethernet, address is 0009.b7aa.9c81 (bia 0009.b7aa.9c81)
… (Output truncated)
```

Example 10-38 *Checking Port Status on CatOS*

```
Console> (enable) show port 2/1
Port  Name               Status     Vlan       Level  Duplex Speed Type
----- ------------------ ---------- ---------- ------ ------ ----- ------------
2/1                      errDisable 1                 normal   auto  auto 10/100BaseTX
… (Output truncated)
```

In Example 10-37 and Example 10-38, the shaded output indicates the port in each example is in an errDisable state.

Step 2—Determining Why a Port is Disabled

Once you have confirmed that a port has been disabled, the next step is to determine why the port was disabled. You could re-enable the port at this point; however, it is more than likely that the problem will manifest itself again. Re-enabling the port might give users a few minutes of access and then another outage, but this can actually portray an image that the network is unstable because it is flapping up and down. A much better approach is to determine the cause of the issue and resolve it before re-enabling the port.

As discussed in Step 1, depending on the event that caused a port to be disabled, messages that indicate the cause of the port being disabled can be displayed by the switch operating system. For example, Example 10-33 and Example 10-34 show the messages that are generated when a port is disabled due to BPDU guard being invoked, while Example 10-35 and Example 10-36 show the messages that are generated when an EtherChannel misconfiguration causes a spanning-tree loop.

Cisco Catalyst switches possess an errDisable recovery mechanism, where a timer can be invoked that automatically re-enables a port that has been shut down due to an errDisable condition. Although this feature is primarily used for recovery purposes, it also allows administrators to determine the exact reason why a port has been disabled. When errDisable recovery is enabled, the switch keeps track of the interfaces currently in an errDisable state and the conditions that caused the errDisable state to be invoked. Administrators can then view this information, allowing them to determine what caused the errDisable status.

To enable the errDisable recovery mechanism on Cisco IOS, the **errdisable recovery cause** global configuration command is used, which can enable the feature for some or all conditions that can cause an errDisable state. Example 10-39 demonstrates enabling the errDisable recovery mechanism on Cisco IOS.

Example 10-39 *Enabling errDisable Recovery on Cisco IOS*

```
Switch# configure terminal
Switch(config)# errdisable recovery cause ?
  all                 Enable timer to recover from all causes
  bpduguard           Enable timer to recover from BPDU Guard error disable state
  channel-misconfig   Enable timer to recover from channel misconfig disable state
  dtp-flap            Enable timer to recover from dtp-flap error disable state
  gbic-invalid        Enable timer to recover from invalid GBIC error disable state
  l2ptguard           Enable timer to recover from l2protocol-tunnel error disable
    state
  link-flap           Enable timer to recover from link-flap error disable state
  loopback            Enable timer to recover from loopback detected disable state
  pagp-flap           Enable timer to recover from pagp-flap error disable state
  psecure-violation   Enable timer to recover from psecure violation disable state
  security-violation  Enable timer to recover from 802.1x violation disable state
  udld                Enable timer to recover from udld error disable state
  vmps                Enable timer to recover from vmps shutdown error disable state
Switch(config)# errdisable recovery cause all
```

In Example 10-39, the **errdisable recovery cause ?** command is executed, which displays all of the individual causes of the errDisable status. The **errdisable recovery cause all** command is then executed to enable errDisable recovery for any event that causes an errDisable state on a port.

To enable the errDisable recovery mechanism on CatOS, the **errdisable-timeout enable** configuration command is used, which can enable the feature for some or all conditions that can cause an errDisable state. Example 10-40 demonstrates enabling the errDisable recovery mechanism on CatOS.

Example 10-40 *Enabling errDisable Recovery on CatOS*

```
Console> (enable) set errdisable-timeout enable ?
  bpdu-guard             BPDU Port-guard
  channel-misconfig      Channel misconfiguration
  udld                   UDLD
  other                  Reasons other than the above
  all                    Apply errDisable timeout to all reasons
Console> (enable) set errdisable-timeout enable all
Successfully enabled errdisable-timeout for all.
```

After enabling errDisable recovery, if an errDisable event occurs, you can use the **show errdisable recovery** (Cisco IOS) and **show errdisable-timeout** (CatOS) commands to determine exactly what caused an errDisable event. Example 10-41 and Example 10-42 demonstrate the output of these commands on a Cisco IOS switch and CatOS switch respectively.

Example 10-41 *Determining the Reason for errDisable Events on Cisco IOS*

```
Switch# show errdisable recovery
ErrDisable Reason    Timer Status
-----------------    -------------
udld                 Enabled
bpduguard            Enabled
security-violatio    Enabled
channel-misconfig    Enabled
vmps                 Enabled
pagp-flap            Enabled
dtp-flap             Enabled
link-flap            Enabled
gbic-invalid         Enabled
l2ptguard            Enabled
psecure-violation    Enabled
loopback             Enabled

Timer interval: 300 seconds

Interfaces that will be enabled at the next timeout:

Interface    Errdisable reason    Time left(sec)
---------    -----------------    --------------
Fa0/1             bpduguard             281
```

Example 10-42 *Determining the Reason for errDisable Events on Cisco IOS*

```
Console> (enable) show errdisable-timeout
ErrDisable Reason       Timeout Status
--------------------    --------------
bpdu-guard              enable
channel-misconfig       enable
udld                    enable
other                   enable

Interval: 300 seconds

Port  ErrDisable Reason    Port ErrDisableTimeout  Action on Timeout
----  ------------------   ----------------------  -----------------
 2/1  bpdu-guard           Enable                  Enabled
```

In Example 10-41 and Example 10-42, the bottom line of each output indicates the current ports that are in the errDisable state and the reason why the port is in such a state. As you can see from both examples, a port on each switch has been disabled due to the BPDU guard feature being invoked.

Step 3—Resolving the Issue

Once you know the issues that are responsible for ports being disabled, you should take the necessary steps to resolve the issue(s). Obviously, the course of action taken depends on the issue. The following lists how you should approach common issues that disable ports:

- **BPDU Guard**—Check your spanning-tree PortFast configurations and either connect devices that are generating BPDUs to ports that do not have PortFast enabled or disable PortFast on ports that have PortFast incorrectly enabled.

- **EtherChannel misconfiguration**—Ensure that the various parameters configured for each port of a bundle on both sides of the bundle are identical. This includes speed/duplex settings, port VLAN membership, if the ports are trunks, and compatible PAgP modes.

- **UDLD**—This normally indicates a cable fault or possibly a faulty transceiver on one side of the link. Verify the physical cabling, and if this is okay, try replacing any fiber-based transceivers or active equipment in between the switch ports.

Step 4—Re-enabling Disabled Ports

Once you are confident that you have resolved the issue that has caused ports to be disabled by the switch, you can re-enable the disabled port(s) using the **shutdown** and **no shutdown** interface configuration commands on Cisco IOS and **set port enable** command on CatOS.

Example 10-43 and Example 10-44 demonstrate manually re-enabling a port that has been placed into an errDisable state on Cisco IOS and CatOS respectively.

Example 10-43 *Manually Re-enabling errDisabled Ports on Cisco IOS*

```
Switch# configuration terminal
Switch(config)# interface fastEthernet0/1
Switch(config-if)# shutdown
Switch(config-if)# no shutdown
01:22:06: %LINK-3-UPDOWN: Interface FastEthernet0/1, changed state to up
01:22:07: %LINEPROTO-5-UPDOWN: Line protocol on Interface FastEthernet0/1,
    changed state to up
```

Example 10-44 *Manually Re-enabling errDisabled Ports on CatOS*

```
Console> (enable) set port enable 2/1
Port 2/1 enabled.
21:24:17 %ETHC-5-PORTTOSTP:Port 2/1 joined bridge port 2/1
```

In Example 10-43, notice that to re-enable an errDisabled port, you must first execute the **shutdown** command and then execute the **no shutdown** command to bring the interface up. This is somewhat different to the normal process of enabling an interface on Cisco IOS, where you need to issue only the **no shutdown** command.

The process demonstrated in both examples above is totally manual and obviously incurs some administrative overhead. As discussed earlier, Cisco IOS and CatOS include an automated errDisable recovery feature, which enables the switch operating system to re-enable errDisabled ports after a configurable timeout value. You learned how to configure errDisable recovery on Cisco IOS in Example 10-39; however, you did not learn how to configure the errDisable timer, which is a global timer that determines how long the switch should wait before re-enabling a port. On Cisco IOS, this timer is configured using the **errdisable recovery interval** global configuration command and has a value of 300 seconds by default. On Cisco IOS, you can also enable/disable errDisable detection, which means if Cisco IOS is incorrectly detecting a condition that causes a port to be placed in an errDisable status, you can disable errDisable detection for the feature that is at fault. Example 10-45 demonstrates configuring errDisable detection, enabling errDisable recovery, and configuring an interval of 30 seconds on Cisco IOS.

Example 10-45 *Configuring errDisable Detection, Recovery, and Timeouts on Cisco IOS*

```
Switch# configuration terminal
Switch(config)# errdisable detect cause ?
  all          Enable error detection on all cases
  dtp-flap     Enable error detection on dtp-flapping
  gbic-invalid Enable error detection on gbic-invalid
  l2ptguard    Enable error detection on l2protocol-tunnel
  link-flap    Enable error detection on linkstate-flapping
  loopback     Enable error detection on loopback
  pagp-flap    Enable error detection on pagp-flapping
  vmps         Enable error detection on vmps
```

continues

Example 10-45 *Configuring errDisable Detection, Recovery, and Timeouts on Cisco IOS (Continued)*

```
Switch(config)# no errdisable detect cause gbic-invalid
Switch(config)# errdisable recovery cause all
Switch(config)# errdisable recovery interval 30
Switch(config)# exit
Switch# show errdisable detect
ErrDisable Reason    Detection status
----------------     ----------------
pagp-flap            Enabled
dtp-flap             Enabled
link-flap            Enabled
l2ptguard            Enabled
gbic-invalid         Disabled
loopback             Enabled
Switch# show errdisable recovery
ErrDisable Reason    Timer Status
----------------     -------------
udld                 Enabled
bpduguard            Enabled
security-violatio    Enabled
channel-misconfig    Enabled
vmps                 Enabled
pagp-flap            Enabled
dtp-flap             Enabled
link-flap            Enabled
gbic-invalid         Enabled
l2ptguard            Enabled
psecure-violation    Enabled
loopback             Enabled

Timer interval: 30 seconds

Interfaces that will be enabled at the next timeout:
```

In Example 10-45, the switch is configured to not place a port into an errDisable state due to an invalid GBIC being inserted. Next, the errDisable recovery timer is configured as 30 seconds. The **show errdisable detect** command is used to verify the errDisable detection configuration, which verifies that invalid GBIC detection is disabled. The **show errdisable recovery** command is then used to verify the new recovery timer, which is 30 seconds as indicated by the shaded output.

On CatOS, a similar recovery timer exists which determines the amount of time the switch should wait before re-enabling an errDisabled port. Unlike Cisco IOS, you cannot enable/disable detection of specific events that can cause an errDisable event—all events supported are always enabled. You learned how to enable errDisable recovery on CatOS in Example 10-40 using the **set errdisable-timeout enable** command; however, to modify the recovery timer from the default setting of 300 seconds, you use the **set errdisable-timeout interval** command as demonstrated in Example 10-46.

Example 10-46 *Configuring errDisable Recovery and Timeouts on CatOS*

```
Console> (enable) set errdisable-timeout enable all
Successfully enabled errdisable-timeout for all.
Console> (enable) set errdisable-timeout interval 30
Successfully set errdisable timeout to 30 seconds.
Console> (enable) show errdisable-timeout
ErrDisable Reason      Timeout Status
--------------------   -------------
bpdu-guard             enable
channel-misconfig      enable
udld                   enable
other                  enable

Interval: 30 seconds

Port  ErrDisable Reason    Port ErrDisableTimeout  Action on Timeout
----  ------------------   --------------------- ----------------
```

In Example 10-46, the errDisable recovery feature is first enablcd for all events, and then the errDisable recovery timer is configured to automatically re-enable ports after 30 seconds. The **show errdisable-timeout** command is then used to verify that the timer has been configured correctly.

Scenario 10-4: Password Recovery

A common problem with any type of device that has some form of access control to the management interface is the loss of administrative passwords. If you haven't come across a situation where you need to recover a forgotten or lost password, it is just a matter of time before you will be faced with the situation. The password recovery mechanisms for Cisco Catalyst switches vary depending on the specific switch platform. In this scenario, examples of password recovery on CatOS-based switches and the Cisco IOS-based Catalyst 3550 switch are provided. For password recovery details for other switch platforms, see www.cisco.com/warp/public/474.

Password Recovery on CatOS-based Switches

The techniques described in this section apply to all CatOS-based switches including the Catalyst 2900, 4000, 5000/5500, and 6000/6500 series switches. Password recovery on CatOS-based switches is relatively simple, where CatOS allows you to gain management access to the switch with a blank password and reconfigure passwords for a 30-second period just after switch bootup.

Password recovery on CatOS-based switches requires access to the console port of the switch and also the ability to be able to cycle (power off and then power on again) the switch. The cycle is required, because password recovery on CatOS requires the switch to be rebooted so that the initial blank password period is made available.

NOTE   The requirement to cycle the switch normally means you require physical access to the switch. Although you can use the **reset system** command to reboot the switch, this is a privileged mode command that requires enable mode access. If you are attempting to recover a password and have enable mode access, all you need to do is simply reconfigure the password, as you have the right to do so under privileged configuration mode. If you can't gain access to privileged mode because of a lost password, then the only way to cycle the switch is to manually pull the power plug.

Assuming console access has been established to the switch and the switch has been cycled, after the switch boots up, the "Enter password:" prompt is presented. As soon as the prompt is presented, the switch allows access to the switch using a blank password. During this 30-second period, the switch also allows you to modify switch passwords using the **set password** and **set enablepass** privileged configuration commands. After the "Enter password:" prompt has been displayed for 30 seconds or more, you can only gain user mode access and enable mode access using the appropriate passwords configured on the switch. It is also important to understand that even though you might have privileged mode access to the switch during the initial 30-second blank password period, you are not able to configure new passwords unless you know the existing passwords once the 30-second period has expired. This is because CatOS prompts you for existing passwords when you configure the **set password** and **set enablepass** commands.

Example 10-47 shows an example of the boot up process, accessing enable mode and then reconfiguring the existing passwords on the switch.

Example 10-47 *Password Recovery on CatOS-based Switch*

```
WS-X2948G bootrom version 6.1(4), built on 2001.07.30 14:43:26
H/W Revisions:    Fin: 2    Head: 11    Board: 1
Supervisor MAC addresses: 00:30:24:48:d4:00 through 00:30:24:48:d7:ff (1024
  addresses)
Installed memory: 64 MB
Testing LEDs.... done!
The system will autoboot in 5 seconds.
Type control-C to prevent autobooting.
rommon 1 >
The system will now begin autobooting.
Autobooting image: "bootflash:cat4000-k8.7-4-2.bin"
CCCCCCCCCCCCCCCCCCCCCCCCCCCCCCCCCCCCCCCCCCCCCCCCCCCCCCCCCCCCCCCCCCCCCCCCCCCCCCCC
CCCCCCCCCCCCCCCCCCCCCCCCCCCCCCCCCCCCCCCCCCCCCCCCCCCCCCC#######################
########
```

Example 10-47 *Password Recovery on CatOS-based Switch (Continued)*

```
Starting Off-line Diagnostics
Mapping in TempFs
Board type is WS-X2948
DiagBootMode value is "post"
Loading diagnostics...

Power-on-self-test for Module 1:  WS-X2948
Status: (. = Pass, F = Fail)
processor: .          cpu sdram: .          eprom: .
nvram: .              flash: .              enet console port: .
switch registers: .   switch sram: .
Module 1 Passed

Exiting Off-line Diagnostics

Cisco Systems, Inc. Console

Enter password: ↵
! (blank password)
Switch-A> enable
Enter password: ↵
! (blank password)
Switch-A> (enable) set password
Enter old password: ↵
! (blank password)
Enter new password: *****
Retype new password: *****
Switch-A> (enable) set enablepass
Enter old password: ↵
! (blank password)
Enter new password: *****
Retype new password: *****
```

In Example 10-47, notice that blank passwords are accepted to gain access to user mode
and enable mode, and then blank passwords are also accepted for the old password prompts
when resetting passwords using the **set password** and **set enablepass** commands. It is very
important that you understand blank passwords for user mode access, enable mode access,
the **set password** command, and the **set enablepass** command are accepted for only 30
seconds after the initial "Enter password:" prompt is displayed. Example 10-48 demonstrates what happens after 30 seconds have expired when you try to modify the enable
password using the **set enablepass** command using a blank password for the old password.

Example 10-48 *Attempting to Reset a Password after 30-second Initial Blank Password Period Expires*

```
Switch-A> (enable) set enablepass
Enter old password: ↵
! (blank password entered)
Sorry password incorrect.
```

As you can see in Example 10-48, CatOS rejects the blank password because the 30-second blank password period has expired. At this stage, the only way to reconfigure the password is to enter the correct old password or to cycle the switch and reattempt password recovery.

Password Recovery on Cisco IOS-based Switches

As you saw in the last section, password recovery on CatOS is reasonably simple. Password recovery on Cisco IOS is a little bit more complex because Cisco IOS does not support an initial 30-second blank password period. In this section, you learn how to recover a password on the Catalyst 3550 switch, with the same recovery procedure also applying to the Catalyst 2900XL/3500XL and Catalyst 2950 switch families.

To recover lost passwords, the following configuration tasks are required:

- Configuring the switch to bypass the startup configuration
- Gaining privileged mode access and restore the original configuration
- Resetting passwords and save the new configuration

Configuring the Switch to Bypass the Startup File

The first configuration task in password recovery is to configure the switch to bypass the startup configuration file, forcing the switch to load with a default configuration, allowing privileged mode access to be accessed using blank passwords. Because you normally don't have privileged mode access to the switch when you have lost a password, you must configure to bypass the startup configuration by interrupting the boot process, which can be performed only if you have physical access to the switch and have a console connection to the switch.

To interrupt the boot process, you must first power down the switch (by disconnecting the power cord) and then hold down the MODE button on the front of the switch, which is on the left hand side of the switch directly below the Cisco Systems emblem and just to the left of the main switch LEDs. Keeping the MODE button held down, you must then power on the switch by reconnecting the power cord. When the switch initializes, all port LEDs are lit green; the MODE button must continue to be held down until the port LED above interface fastEthernet 0/1 turns off. Once this LED turns off, you can let go of the MODE button and on the console connection to the switch, you should notice that the boot process has been interrupted. Example 10-49 demonstrates how the boot process is interrupted.

Example 10-49 *Interrupting the Boot Process on the Catalyst 3550*

```
The system has been interrupted prior to initializing the flash file system.
The following commands will initialize the flash file system, and finish loading
the operating system software:

    flash_init
    boot

switch:
```

In Example 10-49, the shaded output is a prompt, which provides recovery access to the Flash file system of the switch.

On the Catalyst 3550 switch, the startup configuration file is actually stored in the Flash file system in a file called config.text. This is unlike other Cisco IOS devices, which store the startup configuration file in nonvolatile random-access memory (NVRAM). The Catalyst 3550 represents the config.text file as virtual NVRAM, allowing Cisco IOS to think it stores its startup configuration in NVRAM. To bypass the startup configuration file, you must rename the file from config.text to something else; if no config.text file exists on bootup, Cisco IOS creates a config.text file that contains a default startup configuration (i.e., blank passwords). To rename the config.text file in Flash, you must first mount the Flash file system by using the **flash_init** command, followed by the **load_helper** commands. Once mounted, you should be able to use the **dir** command to view the contents of the Flash file system. Example 10-50 demonstrates mounting the Flash file system.

Example 10-50 *Mounting the Flash File System*

```
switch: flash_init
switch: load_helper
switch: dir flash:
Directory of flash:
    2  -rwx        0    Jan 01 1970 00:01:18  env_vars
    3  -rwx      342    Jan 01 1970 00:01:18  system_env_vars
    4  -rwx      676    Jul 01 2002 12:47:23  vlan.dat
    5  -rwx     1460    Mar 01 1993 06:45:10  config.text
    9  drwx      192    Mar 01 1993 00:03:18  c3550-i5q3l2-mz.121-8.EA1c66 -rwx

15998976 bytes total (10891264 bytes free)
```

In Example 10-50, the **dir flash:** command, where **flash:** represents the Flash file system (the colon is important and must be specified) displays the contents of Flash. Notice that the config.text file is present on the Flash file system. To rename this file, you must use the **rename** command. Once the config.text file has been renamed, the switch can be booted normally using the **boot** command. Example 10-51 demonstrates renaming the config.text file and then booting the switch.

Example 10-51 *Renaming the Startup Configuration File*

```
switch: rename flash:config.text flash:config.old
switch: boot
Loading "flash:c3550-i5k2l2q3-mz.121-13.EA1a/c3550-i5k2l2q3-mz.121-
  13.EA1a.bin"...############################################################
  ############################################################################
  ##################
… (Output Truncated)
  …
```

Notice the syntax for renaming the config.text file. The full path to the original file must be specified first (i.e., flash:config.text), after which the new filename, which can be anything other than config.text, must be specified (i.e., config.old). After renaming the file, the switch is booted using the **boot** command.

Gaining Privileged Mode Access and Restoring the Original Configuration

After issuing the **boot** command in Example 10-51, the switch boots as normal. Once the boot process is complete, because the startup configuration file (config.text) is not present, the switch generates a new blank configuration file and starts the configuration setup wizard. At this point, you should exit the configuration setup wizard, after which you are provided user mode access via the console. You can now access privileged mode without any password, because only a blank configuration currently exists on the switch. Example 10-52 demonstrates exiting the configuration wizard and then gaining privileged mode access.

Example 10-52 *Gaining Privileged Mode access*

```
Continue with the configuration dialog? [yes/no]: no
Switch> enable
Switch#
```

In Example 10-52, notice that the enable password is not prompted for because the enable password is blank.

Resetting Passwords and Saving the New Configuration

At this stage, you have gained privileged mode access to the switch. The old switch configuration file now needs to be applied to the current configuration to ensure that the switch is still configured as previously. Of course restoring the old configuration also means restoring the old passwords; however, because you now have privileged mode access to the switch (which is not lost when you restore the configuration), you can reset the passwords after the configuration is restored. Example 10-53 demonstrates restoring the old switch configuration file.

Example 10-53 *Restoring the Old Switch Configuration File and Resetting Passwords*

```
Switch# copy flash:config.old system:running-config
Source filename [config.text]? ↵
Destination filename [running-config]? ↵
Switch-A#
```

In Example 10-53, the **copy flash:config.old system:running-config** command ensures the renamed configuration file (renamed in Example 10-51) is restored to the current running configuration of the switch. Notice that the switch name changes from Switch to

Switch-A in Example 10-53, giving an indication that the previous switch configuration has been restored.

The switch is now configured identically to how it was before you began the password recovery procedure, with the only difference being that you now have privileged mode access to the switch. This allows the **enable secret** global configuration command to be executed, resetting the enable secret password to "cisco123." After passwords have been reset, the new configuration must be saved to the startup configuration file, to ensure the switch boots with the new passwords next time.

TIP   After resetting passwords, if the VLAN 1 interface is enabled in the normal switch configuration, you must ensure you issue the **no shutdown** interface configuration command because the default Catalyst configuration is to place the VLAN 1 interface in a shutdown state using the **shutdown** command. Because configuration files do not store the command **no shutdown**, when you overwrite the default configuration with the startup configuration (Step 2), the default **shutdown** command is not overwritten, leaving VLAN 1 down.

Example 10-54 demonstrates configuring a new enable password, ensuring interface VLAN 1 is enabled and then saving the configuration.

Example 10-54   *Configuring a New Password*

```
Switch-A# configure terminal
Switch-A(config)# enable secret abc123
Switch-A(config)# interface vlan 1
Switch-A(config-if)# no shutdown
00:19:06: %LINK-3-UPDOWN: Interface Vlan1, changed state to up
00:19:07: %LINEPROTO-5-UPDOWN: Line protocol on Interface Vlan1, changed state to up
Switch-A(config)# end
Switch-A# copy running-config startup-config
Building configuration...
[OK]
```

At this stage, if you exit the management interface of the switch and attempt to reconnect or reboot the switch, the new enable secret configured in Example 10-54 should be in use.

Scenario 10-5: File Management on Cisco Catalyst Switches

Every Catalyst switch requires an operating system to ensure the ongoing operation of the switch, as well as ensure the configuration applied to the switch is implemented by the various hardware components. Cisco Catalyst switches include a main operating system that is loaded into memory on switch boot. On most Catalyst switches, an operating system image file comprises the code that is loaded to form the operating system, and a configuration file also exists that contains the various configuration parameters that are applied to the switch. Obviously, without these files, a switch cannot operate properly if at all so it is important that you understand how to work with these files should you need to back up, recover, or upgrade them. Other files might also exist that might or might not be crucial to the operation of the switch.

In this scenario you learn how to work with the various files that are essential for Cisco Catalyst switch operation, learning how to back up files to remote network locations, upgrade operating system files, and recover from a lost or corrupted operating system image file. Figure 10-7 shows the topology used for this scenario.

Figure 10-7 *Scenario 10-5 Topology*

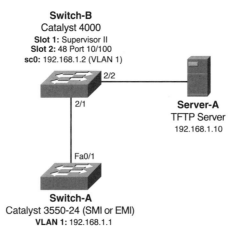

In Figure 10-7, Server-A is a Windows 2000 host that has a TFTP Server application installed, which allows Switch-A and Switch-B to send and receive files across the network using Trivial File Transfer Protocol (TFTP).

Understanding File Management on Cisco Catalyst Switches

Before delving into the specifics of managing files, you must understand the different types of files that exist and the management requirements for each file type on each different Catalyst switch platform. This section describes file management on Cisco IOS-based switches and CatOS-based switches.

File Management on Cisco IOS-based Switches

On Cisco IOS-based switches several files on Cisco IOS enable the switch to operate:

- **Operating system image**—This file includes the code that enables the switch to perform all operations required to implement the various features of the switch.

- **Configuration file**—This file includes custom configuration attributes that control how the switch behaves. When you configure a switch, you are working with the commands that are placed into the configuration file.

- **VLAN Database file**—This file includes all VLANs and associated parameters known to the switch. The VLAN Trunking Protocol (VTP) configuration is also stored in this file.

- **HTML files**—These files are used to provide HTTP management of the switch via cluster management software (CMS). Currently, only the Cisco Catalyst 2900XL, 3500XL, 2950, 3550, and 3750 series switches support CMS.

The operating system image is normally stored on a local Flash file system, with the image being copied and loaded into dynamic memory when the switch boots. The configuration file is saved as a text file called config.text located on the Flash file system; however, this file is emulated as virtual nonvolatile RAM (NVRAM) to Cisco IOS, which is a special file system used purely for the storage of the configuration file on Cisco IOS devices. The switch reads the configuration file on boot up and loads the configuration into memory. The configuration file stored in virtual NVRAM is known as the *startup configuration file*, while the configuration loaded into memory is known as the *running configuration file*. When you make configuration changes to a Cisco IOS-based switch, you are actually modifying the running configuration file loaded into memory. If you want to save the configuration changes permanently, you must explicitly overwrite the startup configuration file (in NVRAM) with the running configuration file (in memory). The VLAN database is a binary file that is used to store information about each configured VLAN on the switch. You cannot work with this file directly; you must use the operating system (Cisco IOS) to modify the file. The VLAN database file is called VLAN.DAT.

TIP

In newer releases of IOS (12.1(8a)EW and higher), VLAN configuration can now be stored within the startup configuration file if VTP transparent mode is configured. A VLAN database file still exists; however, each time the switch boots, the VLAN configuration in the startup configuration file is loaded and stored in the VLAN database file.

File Management on CatOS-based Switches

On CatOS-based switches, two main files enable the switch to operate:

- **Operating system image**—This file includes the code that enables the switch to perform all operations required to implement the various features of the switch.

- **Configuration file**—This file includes custom configuration attributes that control how the switch behaves. When you configure a switch, you are working with the commands that are placed into the configuration file.

The operating system image is normally stored on a local Flash file system, with the image being copied and loaded into dynamic memory when the switch boots. By default, the configuration file on a CatOS-based file is saved as a binary file in non-volatile RAM (NVRAM), which is a special file system used purely for the storage of the configuration file. The switch reads the configuration file on boot up and loads the configuration into memory. The switch operating system converts the binary information stored in the configuration file into the text-based configuration commands that you as the administrator work with. Similarly, when you enter commands, the switch operating system applies the configuration parameters and also converts these parameters appropriately into the binary format of the saved configuration file. When using the binary storage mechanism, you don't need to explicitly save your configuration on a CatOS-based switch; any changes you make are immediately saved as the new, permanent configuration.

TIP

You can configure CatOS-based switches to save the configuration file as a text-based file in either NVRAM or Flash using the **set config mode** command. Using this method reduces the size of the configuration file because only the commands that specify a non-default configuration must be stored. When using text-based storage, you must explicitly save any configuration changes you have made (just as you must for Cisco IOS-based switches) by using the **write memory** command (the **copy running-config startup-config** command is not supported on CatOS).

Configuration Tasks

This scenario demonstrates file management on Cisco Catalyst switches. In this section you learn how to perform the following configuration tasks:

- Transferring Files using TFTP
- Upgrading/Rolling Back the Operating System Image
- Copying and Deleting Operating System Files
- Modifying the Boot Environment Variable
- Recovering from a Corrupt Operating System Image

Transferring Files using TFTP

A key requirement for managing operating system files is to possess the capability to back up, recover, and upgrade these files. All of these operations normally require that the operating system files are either read from or written to a remote location other than the local switch itself. For example, you would hardly back up an important configuration file to another file located locally on the same switch; for the best result you would back this file up to a remote location, where you could then implement a more robust backup solution such as using a tape backup mechanism.

Cisco Catalyst switches allow you to transfer files remotely across an IP-based network using a protocol known as Trivial File Transfer Protocol or TFTP. TFTP is a very simple client/server protocol. Cisco Catalyst switches normally act as the TFTP client, while a remote TFTP server (which can be running on a Windows or UNIX-based host) provides both read and write access to files stored on the remote server. Some Cisco Catalyst switches also support File Transfer Protocol (FTP), which provides slightly more security than TFTP (both are considered insecure protocols). When a Cisco Catalyst switch uses TFTP to read or write files, it does so using its management interface IP address. For example, on a CatOS-based switch, this is normally via the sc0 interface, while on a Cisco IOS-based switch this is normally via the vlan 1 interface. This means that you must configure IP correctly on each switch, ensuring that the correct routes are also configured if the TFTP server does not reside on the same subnet as the switch.

Historically, Cisco has provided a free TFTP server application called Cisco TFTP Server that runs on any Windows-based platform. As of February 2003, however, this software is no longer available, with Cisco recommending the use of freeware or shareware TFTP servers instead. This is perhaps due to a serious security vulnerability found in the software where attackers can gain access to any file on the Cisco TFTP server system (see www.securityfocus.com/bid/2886/discussion for more details). A good TFTP server product that is free and supports multiple simultaneous TFTP send and receive operations is SolarWinds TFTP Server product, downloadable from www2.solarwinds.net/downloads/SolarWinds-TFTP-Server.exe.

NOTE   UNIX-based systems typically include TFTP server functionality as part of the operating system.

Upgrading/Rolling Back the Operating System Image

The most common reason for transferring operating system images across the network is to upgrade (or rollback) the switch operating system. Upgrading a Cisco Catalyst switch is relatively easy and requires three tasks:

- Verifying current operating system boot settings (optional)
- Copying and deleting operating system files
- Modifying the boot environment variable

Verifying Current Operating System Boot Settings

Before upgrading your Cisco Catalyst switch, it is a good idea to have a firm understanding of the current boot environment so that you can easily rollback after an upgrade if problems surface that are associated with the new operating system upgrade. This requires the collection of the following information:

- The current file(s) stored in Flash
- The value of the switch boot environment variable used to boot the switch

To view the current files stored in Flash, you must have an understanding of the current file storage devices installed on your Catalyst switch. By default, Catalyst switches include internal Flash devices, which are referred to as follows:

- **CatOS**—The internal Flash device is referred to as bootflash:.
- **Cisco IOS**—The internal Flash device is referred to as flash: on Cisco Catalyst 29xx, 35xx, and 3750 switches. On Cisco IOS-based Catalyst 4000/4500 and Catalyst 6000/6500 native IOS switches, the Supervisor internal Flash device is referred to as bootflash:.

Some Catalyst switches with Supervisor modules include PCMCIA slots that enable you to install additional Flash memory. Each PCMCIA Flash card is normally referred to as slot0: or slot1: depending on the number of PCMCIA cards installed. In this scenario, Switch-A is a Cisco Catalyst 3550 switch, which supports only a single internal Flash device, while Switch-B is a Cisco Catalyst 4006 switch with only a single internal Flash device (PCMCIA Flash is supported on the Supervisor 2; however, is not present for this scenario).

On Cisco IOS and CatOS, to view the files contained within a Flash device, you use the **dir** command:

```
dir [device-name]
```

The optional *device-name* parameter allows you to view the contents of a specific file system. Example 10-55 and Example 10-56 demonstrate the use of the **dir** command on Switch-A and Switch-B respectively.

Example 10-55 *Viewing the Contents of the Default Flash Device on Cisco IOS*

```
Switch-A# dir flash:
Directory of flash:/

    3  drwx        192   Mar 01 1993 04:12:16  c3550-i5k2l2q3-mz.121-13.EA1a
   22  -rwx          0   Mar 01 1993 04:12:16  env_vars
   23  -rwx        348   Mar 01 1993 04:12:17  system_env_vars
   20  -rwx       4277   Mar 01 1993 01:08:02  config.text
   21  -rwx        796   Mar 01 1993 00:00:36  vlan.dat
   25  -rwx         24   Mar 01 1993 01:08:02  private-config.text

15998976 bytes total (9402368 bytes free)
Switch-A# cd c3550-i5k2l2q3-mz.121-13.EA1a
Switch-A# dir
```

Example 10-55 *Viewing the Contents of the Default Flash Device on Cisco IOS (Continued)*

```
Directory of flash:/c3550-i5k2l2q3-mz.121-13.EA1a/

    4  drwx         832    Mar 01 1993 04:10:43  html
   18  -rwx     4578754    Mar 01 1993 04:12:16  c3550-i5k2l2q3-mz.121-13.EA1a.bin
   19  -rwx         261    Mar 01 1993 04:12:16  info

15998976 bytes total (9404928 bytes free)
```

Example 10-56 *Viewing the Contents of the Default Flash Device on CatOS*

```
Switch-B> (enable) dir bootflash:

-#- -length- -----date/time------ name
  1  4309944 Feb 22 2002 14:00:00 cat4000-k8.7-4-2.bin
  2  4111884 Feb 22 2002 14:00:00 cat4000.6-3-2a.bin


8355388 bytes available (8421828 bytes used)
```

In Example 10-55, you can see the various files and directories that comprise the Catalyst 3550 Flash file system. Notice that c3550-i5k2l2q3-mz.121-13.EA1a is a directory, not a file, as indicated by the d in the field drwx near the beginning of the first shaded line in Example 10-55. The **cd** command is used to change the present working directory to the c3550-i5k2l2q3-mz.121-13.EA1a, and then the **dir** command is used to list the contents of this directory. Within this directory, the operating system file (c3550-i5k2l2q3-mz.121-13.EA1a.bin) and cluster management software (html directory) are installed.

In Example 10-56, you can see that currently two files are located in bootflash on Switch-B. Each is an operating system file, as indicated by the .bin extension, with the appropriate version number included in the file name.

Now that you know exactly what files are present on both switch's file systems, it is time to determine exactly which file is booted from by each switch. This information can be found by inspecting the boot environment variable on a Cisco Catalyst switch. On Cisco IOS, the command used for viewing the boot environment variable differs, depending on the switch platform. On the Catalyst 3550, the **show boot** command is used to display current boot settings, as shown in Example 10-57.

Example 10-57 *Viewing Boot Environment Variables*

```
Switch-A# show boot
BOOT path-list:          flash:c3550-i5k2l2q3-mz.121-13.EA1a/c3550-i5k2l2q3-mz.
   121-13.EA1a.bin
Config file:             flash:/config.text
Private Config file:     flash:/private-config.text
Enable Break:            no
Manual Boot:             no
HELPER path-list:
NVRAM/Config file
     buffer size:        393216
```

In Example 10-57, you can see that Switch-A is booting from the file flash:/c3550-i5k2l2q3-mz.121-13.EA1a/c3550-i5k2l2q3-mz.121-13.EA1a.bin and the configuration file used is the file /config.text.

NOTE   On the Cisco IOS-based Catalyst 4000/4500 and Catalyst 6000/6500 native IOS switches, the **show boot var** command is used to display boot environment variables.

On CatOS, the **show boot** command is used for viewing the boot environment variables, as shown in Example 10-58.

Example 10-58 *Viewing Boot Environment Variables on CatOS*

```
Switch-B> (enable) show boot
BOOT variable = bootflash:cat4000-k8.7-4-2.bin,1;
CONFIG_FILE variable = bootflash:switch.cfg

Configuration register is 0x1
ignore-config: disabled
auto-config: recurring
console baud: 9600
boot: image specified by the boot system commands
```

The BOOT variable determines which file the switch should boot off. Notice that the current file the switch boots from is the file cat4000-k8.7-1-1a.bin.

Copying and Deleting Operating System Files

At this stage, you are ready to begin the process of transferring the new operating system image to the Flash file system over the network from a remote TFTP server. Before doing so, however, it is a good idea to back up your current operating system file and configuration file first and then proceed with the upgrade.

Backing up Files

All file transfer operations on Cisco IOS and CatOS use the **copy** command, which copies files within the same file system or from one file system to another file system (which could be another file system on the local switch or a remote file system accessed using TFTP). Example 10-59 demonstrates copying both the operating system and configuration files on Cisco IOS.

NOTE   Example 10-59 and Example 10-60 assume a working IP address has been configured on each switch as per Figure 10-7 and that the TFTP server (Server-A) has been set up and configured to allow read and write access from network devices.

Example 10-59 *Backing Up Files on Cisco IOS*

```
Switch-A# copy startup-config tftp
Address or name of remote host []? 192.168.1.10
Destination filename [switch-a-confg]? Switch-A.cfg
!!
4277 bytes copied in 0.052 secs (82250 bytes/sec)
Switch-A# copy flash tftp
Source filename []? flash:c3550-i5k2l2q3-mz.121-13.EA1a/c3550-i5k2l2q3-mz.121-13
    .EA1a.bin
Address or name of remote host []? 192.168.1.10
Destination filename []? c3550-i5k2l2q3-mz.121-13.EA1a.bin
!!!!!!!!!!!!!!!!!!!!!!!!!!!!!!!!!!!!!!!!!!!!!!!!!!!!!!!!!!!!!!!!!!!!!!!!!!!!!!!!!!!!
!!!!!!!!!!!!!!!!!!!!!!!!!!!!!!!!!!!!!!!!!!!!!!!!!!!!!!!!!!!!!!!!!!!!!!!!!!!!!!!!!!!!
!!!!!!!!!!!!!!!!!!!!!!!!!!!!!!!!!!!!!!!!!!!!!!!!!!!!!!!!!!!!!!!!!!!!!!!!!!!!!!!!!!!!
!!!!!!!!!!!!!!!!!!!!!!!!!!!!!!!!!!!!!!!!!!!!!!!!!!!!!!!!!!!!!!!!!!!!!!!!!!!!!!!!!!!!
!!!!!!!!!!!!!!!!!!!!!!!!!!!!!!!!!!!!!!!!!!!!!!!!!!!!!!!!!!!!!!!!!!!!!!!!!!!!!!!!!!!!
!!!!!!!!!!!!!!!!!!!!!!!!!!!!!!!!!!!!!!!!!!!!!!!!!!!!!!!!!!!!!!!!!!!!!!!!!!!!!!!!!!!!
!!!!!!!!!!!!!!!!!!!!!!!!!!!!!!!!!!!!!!!!!!!!!!!!!!!!!!!!!!!!!!!!!!!!!!!!!!!!!!!!!!!!
!!!!!!!!!!!!!!!!!!!!!!!!!!!!!!!!!!!!!!!!!!!!!!!!!!!!!!!!!!!!!!!!!!!!!!!!!!!!!!!!!!!!
!!!!!!!!!!!!!!!!!!!!!!!!!!!!!!!!!!!!!!!!!!!!!!!!!!!!!!!!!!!!!!!!!!!!!!!!!!!!!!!!!!!!
!!!!!!!!!!!!!!!!!!!!!!!!!!!!!!!!!!!!!!!!!!!!!!!!!!!!!!!!!!!!!!!!!!!!!!!!!!!!!!!!!!!!
!!!!!!!!!!!!!!!!!!!!
4578754 bytes copied in 18.876 secs (242570 bytes/sec)
```

In Example 10-59, the **copy startup-config tftp** command is used to copy the startup configuration file to a TFTP server. Notice that this command interactively prompts for TFTP server address and what the name of the file should be on the destination TFTP server. Next, the **copy flash tftp** command is used to copy the operating system file to a TFTP server.

NOTE   You can specify the full path to the file that you want to copy, as well as the full path to the file on the destination TFTP server, instead of specifying just the **flash** and **tftp** parameters. For example, the **copy flash:config.text tftp://192.168.1.10/config.text** command copies the config.text file in Flash to a TFTP server of 192.168.1.10 and saves the copied file as config.text on the destination server.

On the Catalyst 2950/3550 switches, the Flash file system not only contains an operating system image file, but also contains many other files used for the *cluster management software (CMS)*. CMS is a Web-based management application that enables the configuration of multiple Cisco Catalyst 29xx/35xx switches in a single physical location, removing the requirement to use command-line interface (CLI) for configuration by allowing all configuration to be performed via CMS. It is important to understand that the CMS files are matched to a specific version of operating system image file (as CMS must support new features as they are released in new versions); hence, you should always back up and restore the operating system image together with the matching CMS files. This can be achieved by using the **archive** command, as demonstrated in Example 10-60 on Switch-A.

Example 10-60 *Backing Up Files on CatOS*

```
Switch-A#archive upload-sw tftp://192.168.1.10/c3550-i5k2l2q3-mz.121-13.EA1a.tar
Image info:
     Version Suffix: i5k2l2q3-121-13.EA1a
     Image Name: c3550-i5k2l2q3-mz.121-13.EA1a.bin
     Version Directory: c3550-i5k2l2q3-mz.121-13.EA1a
     Ios Image Size: 4580864
     Total Image Size: 6596096
     Image Feature: LAYER_3¦MIN_DRAM_MEG=64
     Image Family: C3550
archiving info (261 bytes)
archiving c3550-i5k2l2q3-mz.121-13.EA1a (directory)
archiving c3550-i5k2l2q3-mz.121-13.EA1a/html (directory)
archiving c3550-i5k2l2q3-mz.121-13.EA1a/html/homepage.htm (3992 bytes)!
archiving c3550-i5k2l2q3-mz.121-13.EA1a/html/not_supported.html (1392 bytes)
archiving c3550-i5k2l2q3-mz.121-13.EA1a/html/common.js (9529 bytes)!!
archiving c3550-i5k2l2q3-mz.121-13.EA1a/html/cms_splash.gif (22152 bytes)!!!!!
archiving c3550-i5k2l2q3-mz.121-13.EA1a/html/cms_13.html (1211 bytes)
archiving c3550-i5k2l2q3-mz.121-13.EA1a/html/cluster.html (2823 bytes)!
archiving c3550-i5k2l2q3-mz.121-13.EA1a/html/Redirect.jar (4195 bytes)!
archiving c3550-i5k2l2q3-mz.121-13.EA1a/html/mono_disc.sgz (16232 bytes)!!!
archiving c3550-i5k2l2q3-mz.121-13.EA1a/html/CMS.sgz (1343769
  bytes)!!!!!!!!!!!!!!!!!!!!!!!!!!!!!!!!!!!!!!!!!!!!!!!!!!!!!!!!!!!!!!!!!!!!!!!!!!!!
  !!!!!!!!!!!!!!!!!!!!!!!!!!!!!!!!!!!!!!!!!!!!!!!!!!!!!!!!!!!!!!!!!!!!!!!!!!!!!!!!!!
  !!!!!!!!!!!!!!!!!!!!!!!!!!!!!!!!!!!!!!!!!!!!!!!!!!!!!!!!!!!!!!!!!!!!!!!!!!!!!!!!!!
  !!!!!!!!!!!!!!!!!!!!!!!!!!!!!!!!!
archiving c3550-i5k2l2q3-mz.121-13.EA1a/html/images.sgz (86920 bytes)!!!!!!!!!!!!
  !!!!!!
archiving c3550-i5k2l2q3-mz.121-13.EA1a/html/help.sgz (316438 bytes)
  !!!!!!!!!!!!!!!!!!!!!!!!!!!!!!!!!!!!!!!!!!!!!!!!!!!!!!!!
archiving c3550-i5k2l2q3-mz.121-13.EA1a/html/CiscoChartPanel.sgz (135599 bytes)
  !!!!!!!!!!!!!!!!!!!!!!!!!!!
archiving c3550-i5k2l2q3-mz.121-13.EA1a/html/cms_boot.jar (58861 bytes)!!!!!!!!!!
  !!!
archiving c3550-i5k2l2q3-mz.121-13.EA1a/c3550-i5k2l2q3-mz.121-13.EA1a.bin
  (4578754 bytes)!!!!!!!!!!!!!!!!!!!!!!!!!!!!!!!!!!!!!!!!!!!!!!!!!!!!!!!!
  !!!!!!!!!!!!!!!!!!!!!!!!!!!!!!!!!!!!!!!!!!!!!!!!!!!!!!!!!!!!!!!!!!!!!!!!!!!!!!!!!!
  !!!!!!!!!!!!!!!!!!!!!!!!!!!!!!!!!!!!!!!!!!!!!!!!!!!!!!!!!!!!!!!!!!!!!!!!!!!!!!!!!!
  !!!!!!!!!!!!!!!!!!!!!!!!!!!!!!!!!!!!!!!!!!!!!!!!!!!!!!!!!!!!!!!!!!!!!!!!!!!!!!!!!!
  !!!!!!!!!!!!!!!!!!!!!!!!!!!!!!!!!!!!!!!!!!!!!!!!!!!!!!!!!!!!!!!!!!!!!!!!!!!!!!!!!!
  !!!!!!!!!!!!!!!!!!!!!!!!!!!!!!!!!!!!!!!!!!!!!!!!!!!!!!!!!!!!!!!!!!!!!!!!!!!!!!!!!!
```

Example 10-60 *Backing Up Files on CatOS (Continued)*

```
!!!!!!!!!!!!!!!!!!!!!!!!!!!!!!!!!!!!!!!!!!!!!!!!!!!!!!!!!!!!!!!!!!!!!!!!!!!!!!!!!!!!!!!
!!!!!!!!!!!!!!!!!!!!!!!!!!!!!!!!!!!!!!!!!!!!!!!!!!!!!!!!!!!!!!!!!!!!!!!!!!!!!!!!!!!!!!!
!!!!!!!!!!!!!!!!!!!!!!!!!!!!!!!!!!!!!!!!!!!!!!!!!!!!!!!!!!!!!!!!!!!!!!!!!!!!!!!!!!!!!!!
!!!!!!!!!!!!!!!!!!!!!!!!!!!!!!!!!!!!!!!!!!!!!!!!!!!!!!!!!!!!!!!!!!!!!!!!!!!!!!!!!!!!!!!
!!!!!!!!!!!!!!!!!!!!!!!!!!!!!!!!!!!!!!!!!!!!!!!!!!!!!!!!!!!!!!!!!!!!!!!!!!!!!!!!!!!!!!!
!!!!!!!!!!!!!!!!!!!!!!!!!!!!!!!!!!!!!!!!!
archiving c3550-i5k2l2q3-mz.121-13.EA1a/info (261 bytes)!
archiving info.ver (261 bytes)
```

In Example 10-60, the **archive upload-sw** command is used to archive all current operating system files (including operating system image and CMS files) into a single file, which is specified as c3550-i5k2l2q3-mz.121-13.EA1a.tar, and then "upload" the archive file to the TFTP server 192.168.1.10. The **archive upload-sw** command works by checking the current boot environment variable (flash:c3550-i5k2l2q3-mz.121-13.EA1a/c3550-i5k2l2q3-mz.121-13.EA1a.bin—see Example 10-57) and then checking the directory the operating system image is located in for a file called info. This file contains the information indicated in the shaded output of Example 10-60 and allows the switch to determine the current Cisco IOS version and the directory in which all files related to the current IOS version are stored. The switch then archives all files within the directory and copies the archive to the configured destination in the **archive** command.

NOTE   The **archive** command is used to create tape archive (TAR) files, which are common in UNIX environments for backing up a collection of files into a single file, allowing for easy restoration. The **archive** command is supported only on the Catalyst 2950/3550 switches and is not supported on the Catalyst 2900XL/3500XL, 4000/4500, or 6000/6500 Cisco IOS-based platforms.

Example 10-61 demonstrates copying both the operating system and configuration files on CatOS.

Example 10-61 *Backing Up Files on CatOS*

```
Switch-B> (enable) copy config tftp
This command uploads non-default configurations only.
Use 'copy config tftp all' to upload both default and non-default
    configurations.
IP address or name of remote host []? 192.168.1.10
Name of file to copy to [Switch-B.cfg]? ↵

Upload configuration to tftp:Switch-B.cfg, (y/n) [n]? y
..............
.......................
..
/
```

Example 10-61   *Backing Up Files on CatOS (Continued)*

```
Configuration has been copied successfully.
Switch-B> (enable) copy flash tftp
Flash device [bootflash]? ↵
Name of file to copy from []? cat4000-k8.7-4-2.bin
IP address or name of remote host []? 192.168.1.10
Name of file to copy to []? cat4000-k8.7-4-2.bin
CCCCCCCCCCCCCCCCCCCCCCCCCCCCCCCCCCCCCCCCCCCCCCCCCCCCCCCCCCCCCCCCCCCCCCCCCCCCCCCCCC
CCCCCCCCCCCCCCCCCCCCCCCCCCCCCCCCCCCCCCCCCCCCCCCCCCCCCCCC¦
File has been copied successfully.
Switch-B> (enable) copy bootflash:cat4000-k8.7-4-2.bin tftp
IP address or name of remote host [192.168.1.10]? ↵
Name of file to copy to [cat4000-k8.7-2-2.bin]? ↵
CCCCCCCCCCCCCCCCCCCCCCCCCCCCCCCCCCCCCCCCCCCCCCCCCCCCCCCCCCCCCCCCCCCCCCCCCCCCCCCCCC
CCCCCCCCCCCCCCCCCCCCCCCCCCCCCCCCCCCCCCCCCCCCCCCCCCCCC/
File has been copied successfully.
```

In Example 10-61, the **copy config tftp** command is used to copy the current non-default configuration to a TFTP server. Just like Cisco IOS, a series of interactive prompts are presented to collect information, such as the TFTP server and filename on the destination server. The **copy flash tftp** command is then used to copy the operating system file. Notice that you can specify the full path to the file that you are copying, as demonstrated by the **copy bootflash:cat4000-k8.7-4-2.bin tftp** command.

Deleting Files

After backing up the current operating system files and configuration files, you are almost ready to upgrade/restore the operating system. When copying files from the network to Flash, it is important that enough Flash is available for the new file. If there is not enough Flash, you need to delete files to make space. This is achieved by using the **delete** command and, depending on the switch model, might also require the use of the **squeeze** command. If you attempt to copy a file to Flash and there is not enough space, the copy is interrupted as soon as the file system is filled.

TIP   To determine the amount of free space, you can use the **dir** command (see Example 10-55 and Example 10-56).

Example 10-62 demonstrates deleting files on Cisco IOS to free up Flash space.

Example 10-62 *Deleting Files on Cisco IOS*

```
Switch-A# cd flash:c3550-i5k2l2q3-mz.121-13.EA1a
Switch-A# delete c3550-i5k2l2q3-mz.121-13.EA1a.bin
Delete filename [c3550-i5k2l2q3-mz.121-13.EA1a.bin]? ↵
Delete flash:c3550-i5k2l2q3-mz.121-13.EA1a/c3550-i5k2l2q3-mz.121-13.EA1a.bin?
 [confirm] y
```

In Example 10-62, notice the use of the **cd** (change directory) command, which is used to change the current working directory. Because the current operating system file is located in the c3550-i5k2l2q3-mz.121-13.EA1a directory (see Example 10-55), your working directory must be changed to this directory for the delete c3550-i5k2l2q3-mz.121-13.EA1a.bin command to work (alternatively you could specify the full path to the file in the delete command). Notice after executing the **delete** command, you are prompted with the **Delete filename [...]** prompt; at this prompt, always just press Enter, which confirms that you want to delete the filename you specified in the **delete** command. Many administrators not familiar with using file management commands often mistake this as a prompt for confirmation of file deletion (which is in fact performed during the next prompt), and enter in **y** or **yes.** The switch interprets this as meaning "delete the file called y" (or yes), which of course causes the delete process to fail as it is unlikely such a file exists.

WARNING   On the Catalyst 29xx/35xx switches, it is not recommended to delete operating system files because a large number of files comprise the operating system (i.e., image file and CMS files) that are all related to each other and deleting specific files might break interdependencies.

Example 10-63 demonstrates deleting files on Cisco IOS to free up Flash space.

Example 10-63 *Deleting Files on CatOS*

```
Switch-B> (enable) dir bootflash:
-#- -length- -----date/time------ name
  1  4309944 Feb 22 2002 14:00:00 cat4000-k8.7-4-2.bin
  2  4111884 Feb 22 2002 14:00:00 cat4000.6-3-2a.bin

8355388 bytes available (8421828 bytes used)
Switch-B> (enable) delete cat4000.6-3-2a.bin
Switch-B> (enable) dir bootflash:
-#- -length- -----date/time------ name
  1  4309944 Feb 22 2002 14:00:00 cat4000-k8.7-4-2.bin

8355388 bytes available (8421828 bytes used)
Switch-B> (enable) undelete
Usage: undelete <index> [[m/]device:]
```

continues

Example 10-63 *Deleting Files on CatOS (Continued)*

```
Switch-B> (enable) undelete 2
Switch-B> (enable) dir
-#- -length- -----date/time------ name
  1  4309944 Feb 22 2002 14:00:00 cat4000-k8.7-4-2.bin
  2  4111884 Feb 22 2002 14:00:00 cat4000.6-3-2a.bin

8355388 bytes available (8421828 bytes used)
Switch-B> (enable) delete cat4000.6-3-2a.bin
Switch-B> (enable) squeeze bootflash:

All deleted files will be removed, proceed (y/n) [n]? y

Squeeze operation may take a while, proceed (y/n) [n]? y
Erasing squeeze log
Switch-B> (enable) dir
-#- -length- -----date/time------ name
  1  4309944 Feb 22 2002 14:00:00 cat4000-k8.7-4-2.bin

12467272 bytes available (4309944 bytes used)
```

In Example 10-63, the **dir** command is first used to view files currently in Flash. Next the **delete** command is used to remove the file cat4000.6-3-2a.bin, with the **dir** command being used immediately afterwards to verify the file has been deleted. Notice that although the file is no longer listed, the bytes available and used in Flash are the same as when the file was present before the deletion. This is because CatOS does not delete files completely when you use the **delete** command, instead just removing the file system pointer to the file. This allows the **undelete** command to be used, which can be used to restored deleted files. In Example 10-63, you can see that the **undelete** command is used to restore the deleted file, by specifying the index of the file. The index is the first number on the left for each file listed using the **dir** command. If you look at the first **dir** command executed in Example 10-63, you can see that the index of the cat4000.6-3-2a.bin file is **2**; consequently, the **undelete 2** command restores this file. After the undelete process is demonstrated, the file is once again deleted, and this time, the **squeeze** command is used to permanently erase any deleted files on the bootflash: device.

NOTE   If you want to permanently erase a deleted file on CatOS, you must always delete the file using the **delete** command and then perform the **squeeze** operation. The same applies on some Cisco IOS-based switches such as the Catalyst 4000/4500 Supervisor 3/4 and Catalyst 6000/6500 running native IOS.

Upgrading/Restoring Operating System Files

After verifying the current file system contents, backing up important files and ensuring enough space is available on Flash, you can copy new operating system files to perform an upgrade. As you might expect, copying files from a TFTP server to Flash is performed using the **copy** command. You can use this command to upgrade the operating system, as well as restore or apply a new configuration.

Example 10-64 demonstrates copying the configuration file and operating system file backed up in Example 10-59 from the TFTP server to Switch-A.

Example 10-64 *Copying Files from TFTP on Cisco IOS*

```
Switch-A# copy tftp startup-config
Address or name of remote host []? 192.168.1.10
Source filename []? Switch-A.cfg
Destination filename [startup-config]? ↵
Accessing tftp://192.168.1.10/Switch-A.cfg...
Loading Switch-A.cfg from 192.168.1.10 (via Vlan1): !
[OK - 4277 bytes]

4277 bytes copied in 0.088 secs (48602 bytes/sec)
01:40:22: %SYS-5-CONFIG_NV_I: Nonvolatile storage configured from
    tftp://192.168.1.10/Switch-A.cfg by console
Switch-A# cd flash:/
Switch-A# mkdir temp
Create directory filename [temp]? ↵
Created dir flash:/temp
Switch-A# copy tftp flash
Address or name of remote host []? 192.168.1.10
Source filename []? c3550-i5k2l2q3-mz.121-13.EA1a.bin
Destination filename [c3550-i5k2l2q3-mz.121-13.EA1a.bin]? flash:/temp/c3550-
  i5k2l2q3-mz.121-13.EA1a.bin
Accessing tftp://192.168.1.10/c3550-i5k2l2q3-mz.121-13.EA1a.bin...
Loading c3550-i5k2l2q3-mz.121-13.EA1a.bin from 192.168.1.10 (via Vlan1):
!!!!!!!!!!!!!!!!!!!!!!!!!!!!!!!!!!!!!!!!!!!!!!!!!!!!!!!!!!!!!!!!!!!!!!!!!!!!!!!!
!!!!!!!!!!!!!!!!!!!!!!!!!!!!!!!!!!!!!!!!!!!!!!!!!!!!!!!!!!!!!!!!!!!!!!!!!!!!!!!!
!!!!!!!!!!!!!!!!!!!!!!!!!!!!!!!!!!!!!!!!!!!!!!!!!!!!!!!!!!!!!!!!!!!!!!!!!!!!!!!!
!!!!!!!!!!!!!!!!!!!!!!!!!!!!!!!!!!!!!!!!!!!!!!!!!!!!!!!!!!!!!!!!!!!!!!!!!!!!!!!!
!!!!!!!!!!!!!!!!!!!!!!!!!!!!!!!!!!!!!!!!!!!!!!!!!!!!!!!!!!!!!!!!!!!!!!!!!!!!!!!!
!!!!!!!!!!!!!!!!!!!!!!!!!!!!!!!!!!!!!!!!!!!!!!!!!!!!!!!!!!!!!!!!!!!!!!!!!!!!!!!!
!!!!!!!!!!!!!!!!!!!!!!!!!!!!!!!!!!!!!!!!!!!!!!!!!!!!!!!!!!!!!!!!!!!!!!!!!!!!!!!!
!!!!!!!!!!!!!!!!!!!!!!!!!!!!!!!!!!!!!!!!!!!!!!!!!!!!!!!!!!!!!!!!!!!!!!!!!!!!!!!!
!!!!!!!!!!!!!!!!!!!!!!!!!!!!!!!!!!!!!!!!!!!!!!!!!!!!!!!!!!!!!!!!!!!!!!!!!!!!!!!!
!!!!!!!!!!!!!!!!!!!!!!!!!!!!!!!!!!!!!!!!!!!!!!!!!!!!!!!!!!!!!!!!!!!!!!!!!!!!!!!!
!!!!!!!!!!!!!!!!!!!!
[OK - 4578754 bytes]

4578754 bytes copied in 70.248 secs (65180 bytes/sec)
Switch-A# verify flash:/temp/c3550-i5k2l2q3-mz.121-13.EA1a.bin
Verified flash:/temp/c3550-i5k2l2q3-mz.121-13.EA1a.bin
```

In Example 10-64, the **copy tftp startup-config** command is used to copy the file Switch-A.cfg on the TFTP server to startup configuration (NVRAM). Next, the **cd flash:/** command is used to ensure the present working directory on Switch-A is the root directory. The **mkdir** command is then used to create a directory called temp, after which the **copy tftp flash** command is used to copy the operating system image file to Flash. Notice that the destination path of /temp/ c3550-i5k2l2q3-mz.121-13.EA1a.bin is specified, meaning the file is to be copied to the new temp folder. Finally, the **verify** command is used to ensure the copied file is not corrupt; Cisco IOS operating system files include a checksum, which allows for any changes to the content of a filc to bc detected. If a file is corrupted, you should immediately delete the file and copy the file from the TFTP server once again.

On Cisco Catalyst 2950/3550 switches, rather than using **copy tftp flash** to upgrade operating system software, it is recommended to use the **archive** command (previously demonstrated in Example 10-60 for backup purposes) because this can upgrade not just the operating system image file but also the related CMS files, ensuring CMS is compatible with the upgraded operating system. Example 10-65 demonstrates using the **archive** command on Switch-A to restore the operating system archive created in Example 10-60.

Example 10-65   *Upgrading the Operating System Using* **archive** *on Cisco IOS*

```
Switch-A# archive download-sw ?
  /force-reload    Unconditionally reload system after successful sw upgrade
  /imageonly       Load only the IOS image
  /leave-old-sw    Leave old sw installed after successful sw upgrade
  /no-set-boot     Don't set BOOT -- leave existing boot config alone
  /overwrite       OK to overwrite an existing image
  /reload          Reload system (if no unsaved config changes) after successful
                   sw upgrade
  /safe            Always load before deleting old version
  flash:           Image file
  ftp:             Image file
  rcp:             Image file
  tftp:            Image file
Switch-A# archive download-sw /overwrite tftp://192.168.1.10/c3550-i5k2l2q3-mz
.121-13.EA1a.tar
examining image...
Loading c3550-i5k2l2q3-mz.121-13.EA1a.tar from 192.168.1.10 (via Vlan1): !
extracting info (261 bytes)
!!!!!!!!!!!!!!!!!!!!!!!!!!!!!!!!!!!!!!!!!!!!!!!!!!!!!!!!!!!!!!!!!!!!!!!!!!!!!!!!!
!!!!!!!!!!!!!!!!!!!!!!!!!!!!!!!!!!!!!!!!!!!!!!!!!!!!!!!!!!!!!!!!!!!!!!!!!!!!!!!!!
!!!!!!!!!!!!!!!!!!!!!!!!!!!!!!!!!!!!!!!!!!!!!!!!!!!!!!!!!!!!!!!!!!!!!!!!!!!!!!!!!
!!!!!!!!!!!!!!!!!!!!!!!!!!!!!!!!!!!!!!!!!!!!!!!!!!!!!!!!!!!!!!!!!!!!!!!!!!!!!!!!!
!!!!!!!!!!!!!!!!!!!!!!!!!!!!!!!!!!!!!!!!!!!!!!!!!!!!!!!!!!!!!!!!!!!!!!!!!!!!!!!!!
[OK - 6596096 bytes]
Image info:
    Version Suffix: i5k2l2q3-121-13.EA1a
    Image Name: c3550-i5k2l2q3-mz.121-13.EA1a.bin
    Version Directory: c3550-i5k2l2q3-mz.121-13.EA1a
    Ios Image Size: 4580864
    Total Image Size: 6596096
    Image Feature: LAYER_3¦MIN_DRAM_MEG=64
```

Example 10-65 *Upgrading the Operating System Using* **archive** *on Cisco IOS (Continued)*

```
        Image Family: C3550
Extracting files...
Loading c3550-i5k2l2q3-mz.121-13.EA1a.tar from 192.168.1.10 (via Vlan1): !
extracting info (261 bytes)
c3550-i5k2l2q3-mz.121-13.EA1a (directory)
c3550-i5k2l2q3-mz.121-13.EA1a/html (directory)
extracting c3550-i5k2l2q3-mz.121-13.EA1a/html/homepage.htm (3992 bytes)!
extracting c3550-i5k2l2q3-mz.121-13.EA1a/html/not_supported.html (1392 bytes)
extracting c3550-i5k2l2q3-mz.121-13.EA1a/html/common.js (9529 bytes)!!
extracting c3550-i5k2l2q3-mz.121-13.EA1a/html/cms_splash.gif (22152 bytes)!!!!!
extracting c3550-i5k2l2q3-mz.121-13.EA1a/html/cms_13.html (1211 bytes)
extracting c3550-i5k2l2q3-mz.121-13.EA1a/html/cluster.html (2823 bytes)!
extracting c3550-i5k2l2q3-mz.121-13.EA1a/html/Redirect.jar (4195 bytes)!
extracting c3550-i5k2l2q3-mz.121-13.EA1a/html/mono_disc.sgz (16232 bytes)!!!
extracting c3550-i5k2l2q3-mz.121-13.EA1a/html/CMS.sgz (1343769
  bytes)!!!!!!!!!!!!!!!!!!!!!!!!!!!!!!!!!!!!!!!!!!!!!!!!!!!!!!!!!!!!!!!!!!!!!!!!!!!
  !!!!!!!!!!!!!!!!!!!!!!!!!!!!!!!!!!!!!!!!!!!!!!!!!!!!!!!!!!!!!!!!!!!!!!!!!!!!!!!!!
  !!!!!!!!!!!!!!!!!!!!!!!!!!!!!!!!!!!!!!!!!!!!!!!!!!!!!!!!!!!!!!!!!!!!!!!!!!!!!!!!!
  !!!!!!!!!!!!!!!!!!!!!!!!!!!!!!!!!
extracting c3550-i5k2l2q3-mz.121-13.EA1a/html/images.sgz (86920 bytes)!!!!!!!!!!
  !!!!!!!
extracting c3550-i5k2l2q3-mz.121-13.EA1a/html/help.sgz (316438
  bytes)!!!!!!!!!!!!!!!!!!!!!!!!!!!!!!!!!!!!!!!!!!!!!!!!!!!!!!!!!!!
extracting c3550-i5k2l2q3-mz.121-13.EA1a/html/CiscoChartPanel.sgz (135599
  bytes)!!!!!!!!!!!!!!!!!!!!!!!!!!!!!
extracting c3550-i5k2l2q3-mz.121-13.EA1a/html/cms_boot.jar (58861 bytes)!!!!!!!!!
  !!!!
extracting c3550-i5k2l2q3-mz.121-13.EA1a/c3550-i5k2l2q3-mz.121-13.EA1a.bin
    (4578754 bytes)!!!!!!!!!!!!!!!!!!!!!!!!!!!!!!!!!!!!!!!!!!!!!!!!!!!!!!!!!!!!!!!!!
  !!!!!!!!!!!!!!!!!!!!!!!!!!!!!!!!!!!!!!!!!!!!!!!!!!!!!!!!!!!!!!!!!!!!!!!!!!!!!!!!!
  !!!!!!!!!!!!!!!!!!!!!!!!!!!!!!!!!!!!!!!!!!!!!!!!!!!!!!!!!!!!!!!!!!!!!!!!!!!!!!!!!
  !!!!!!!!!!!!!!!!!!!!!!!!!!!!!!!!!!!!!!!!!!!!!!!!!!!!!!!!!!!!!!!!!!!!!!!!!!!!!!!!!
  !!!!!!!!!!!!!!!!!!!!!!!!!!!!!!!!!!!!!!!!!!!!!!!!!!!!!!!!!!!!!!!!!!!!!!!!!!!!!!!!!
  !!!!!!!!!!!!!!!!!!!!!!!!!!!!!!!!!!!!!!!!!!!!!!!!!!!!!!!!!!!!!!!!!!!!!!!!!!!!!!!!!
  !!!!!!!!!!!!!!!!!!!!!!!!!!!!!!!!!!!!!!!!!!!!!!!!!!!!!!!!!!!!!!!!!!!!!!!!!!!!!!!!!
  !!!!!!!!!!!!!!!!!!!!!!!!!!!!!!!!!!!!!!!!!!!!!!!!!!!!!!!!!!!!!!!!!!!!!!!!!!!!!!!!!
  !!!!!!!!!!!!!!!!!!!!!!!!!!!!!!!!!!!!!!!!!!!!!!!!!!!!!!!!!!!!!!!!!!!!!!!!!!!!!!!!!
  !!!!!!!!!!!!!!!!!!!!!!!!!!!!!!!!!!!!!!!!!!!!!!!!!!!!!!!!!!!!!!!!!!!!!!!!!!!!!!!!!
  !!!!!!!!!!!!!!!!!!!!!!!!!!!!!!!!!!!!!!!!!!!!!!!!!!!!!!!!!!!!!!!!!!!!!!!!!!!!!!!!!
  !!!!!!!!!!!!!!!!!!!!!!!!!!!!!!!!!!!!!!!!
extracting c3550-i5k2l2q3-mz.121-13.EA1a/info (261 bytes)!
extracting info.ver (261 bytes)
[OK - 6596096 bytes]

New software image installed in flash:c3550-i5k2l2q3-mz.121-13.EA1a
Configuring system to use new image...done.
```

In Example 10-65, the **archive download-sw** command is used to download a TAR archive and extract the archive. Notice the options that you can specify with the command. In Example 10-63, the **archive download-sw** command is used with the **/overwrite** switch to overwrite any existing files if required, and the archive is obtained via TFTP. After the archive is obtained, it is then extracted and the entire directory structure and associated files restored to a root directory specific to the version of software (e.g., the c3550-i5k2l2q3-mz.121-13.EA1a directory in Example 10-65). Once the archive extraction process is complete, notice that the **archive** command even configures the system to use the new image, meaning the boot environment variables are automatically modified.

Example 10-66 demonstrates copying the configuration file and operating system file backed up in Example 10-61 from the TFTP server to Switch-B.

Example 10-66 *Copying Files from TFTP on CatOS*

```
Switch-B> (enable) copy tftp config
IP address or name of remote host []? 192.168.1.10
Name of file to copy from []? Switch-B.cfg

Configure using tftp:Switch-B.cfg (y/n) [n]? y

Finished network download.  (8602 bytes)
>> set password $2$p8hX$98Gs/eXM2L/jjCTGhLPec.
Password changed.
>> set enablepass $2$NMK/$VnHGG4PHSDFPFG28d7IpP0
Password changed.
>> set system name  Switch-B
System name set.
… (Output Truncated)
…
Switch-B> (enable) copy tftp flash
IP address or name of remote host []? 192.168.1.10
Name of file to copy from []? cat4000-k8.7-4-2.bin
Flash device [bootflash]? ⏎
Name of file to copy to [cat4000-k8.7-4-2.bin]? ⏎

Overwrite image file (y/n) [n]? y

12467272 bytes available on device bootflash, proceed (y/n) [n]? y
CCCCCCCCCCCCCCCCCCCCCCCCCCCCCCCCCCCCCCCCCCCCCCCCCCCCCCCCCCCCCCCCCCCCCCCCCCCCCCCC
CCCCCCCCCCCCCCCCCCCCCCCCCCCCCCCCCCCCCCCCCCCCCCCCCCCCCCC

File has been copied successfully.
Switch-B> (enable) verify bootflash:cat4000-k8.7-4-2.bin
CCCCCCCCCCCCCCCCCCCCCCCCCCCCCCCCCCCCCCCCCCCCCCCCCCCCCCCCCCCCCCCCCCCCCCCCCCCCCCCC
CCCCCCCCCCCCCCCCCCCCCCCCCCCCCCCCCCCCCCCCCCCCCCCCCCCCCCC
Starting verification on file bootflash:cat4000-k8.7-2-2.bin.
...............................................................................
...............................................................................
...............................................................................
...............................................................................
...............................................................................
..............................
File bootflash:cat4000-k8.7-2-2.bin verified and is Ok.
```

In Example 10-66, the **copy tftp config** command is used to copy a configuration file from TFTP to the current configuration on CatOS. Notice that after the configuration file has been copied via TFTP, it is immediately applied to the current configuration. Next, the **copy tftp flash** command is used to copy a new operating system file via TFTP. If you are attempting to overwrite the current operating system file, notice that you are prompted if you want to do so. After the file is copied, the **verify** command is used to verify the new file.

Modifying the Boot Environment Variable

If you are upgrading or rolling back the switch operating system file, after the appropriate operating system files are copied to Flash, you must modify the boot environment variable so that the switch boots from the new operating system image file. After this has been performed, the next time the switch is rebooted, the switch should boot from the new operating system image.

On Cisco IOS, the **boot system** global configuration command is used to set the boot environment variable, as demonstrated in Example 10-67.

NOTE   If you use the **archive download-sw** command to upgrade Catalyst 29xx/35xx switches, you do not need to modify the boot environment variable as this is performed automatically during the upgrade process (see Example 10-63).

Example 10-67 *Modifying the BOOT Environment Variable on Cisco IOS*

```
Switch-A# configure terminal
Switch-A(config)# boot system flash:temp/c3550-i5k2l2q3-mz.121-13.EA1a.bin
Switch-A(config)# exit
Switch-A# show boot
BOOT path-list:          flash:temp/c3550-i5k2l2q3-mz.121-13.EA1a.bin
Config file:             flash:/config.text
Private Config file:     flash:/private-config.text
Enable Break:            no
Manual Boot:             no
HELPER path-list:
NVRAM/Config file
      buffer size:       393216
```

In Example 10-67, notice that after modifying the boot environment variable, the **show boot** command confirms the switch is now configured to boot from the new operating system file located in the temp directory (see Example 10-59).

On CatOS, the **clear boot** command is first used to clear the boot environment variable, and then the **set boot** configuration command is used to set the boot environment variable, as demonstrated in Example 10-68.

Example 10-68 *Modifying the BOOT Environment Variable on CatOS*

```
Switch-B> (enable) clear boot system all
BOOT variable =
Switch-B> (enable) set boot system flash bootflash:cat4000-k8.7-4-2.bin
BOOT variable = bootflash: cat4000-k8.7-4-2.bin,1;
```

In Example 10-68, the BOOT variable is first cleared, as the **set boot** command does not overwrite the BOOT variable (just appends or prepends to the variable). After clearing the BOOT variable, the switch is then configured to boot from the new image file. You can add further files to boot from (only booted if primary files are not present) by using the **set boot** command again.

At this point, an upgraded switch should be rebooted to ensure that the new operating system file is loaded. After reboot, the switch should boot from the new image file, which you can verify using the **show version** command after the switch has rebooted.

Recovering from a Corrupt Operating System Image

In the previous section you learned how you can copy new image files to Flash and modify the switch to boot from these new files. Sometimes, the CatOS image file might get corrupted or (more likely) you accidentally copy in the wrong version of software or maybe even install an image that requires more RAM than your switch contains. In these circumstances, the switch fails to boot, instead booting to ROM Monitor (ROMMON) mode. Depending on the hardware platform, the ROM monitor provides one or more basic mechanisms that allow you to restore or boot from a new operating system image file. These mechanisms might include one or more of the following:

- Transferring the file via the console port using a serial file transfer protocol such as XMODEM or KERMIT.
- Transferring the file from another PCMCIA Flash device installed locally.
- Transferring the file from an IP network using TFTP.

The mechanisms available vary based upon the hardware platform. Table 10-1 describes the mechanisms available for the various CatOS-based platforms from ROM Monitor mode.

Table 10-1   *Operating System Recovery Options from ROM Monitor for Cisco Catalyst Switches*

Platform	Recovery Mechanism
Catalyst 2900XL/3500XL Catalyst 2950/3550/3750 (Cisco IOS)	XMODEM (via console)
Catalyst 2900 Catalyst 4000 (Sup 1/2) (CatOS)	TFTP (via management port)
Catalyst 4000/4500 (Supervisor 3/4) (Cisco IOS)	Local Flash TFTP (via management port)
*Catalyst 5000/5500 (Sup. 1/2/2G/3G) (CatOS)	KERMIT (via console) TFTP (via linecard)
Catalyst 5000/5500 (Supervisor 3) Catalyst 6000/6500 (CatOS)	PCMCIA Flash XMODEM (via console)
Catalyst 6000/6500 (Native IOS)	Local Flash XMODEM (via console)

*To access ROM Monitor mode, you must enable jumpers on the Supervisor module. See www.cisco.com/warp/public/473/26.html#recovery2 for more details.

Operating system recovery is now demonstrated on Switch-A (Catalyst 3550) and on Switch-B (CatOS).

Operating System Recovery on a Catalyst 29xx/35xx Switch (Cisco IOS)

Operating system recovery on the Catalyst 29xx/35xx switches can be performed only via a console connection using XMODEM. Most terminal emulation programs (e.g., Hyper-Terminal on Windows) support the transfer of files via XMODEM and in this scenario, you learn how to transfer files via XMODEM using HyperTerminal.

If the operating system image becomes corrupted or is deleted, when a switch starts up you will find that the switch cannot boot because it no longer has an operating system image to boot from. This causes the switch to be placed into ROM Monitor mode, as demonstrated in Example 10-69.

Example 10-69 *Boot Failure on the Catalyst 3550*

```
Base ethernet MAC Address: 00:09:b7:aa:9c:80
Xmodem file system is available.
The password-recovery mechanism is enabled.
Initializing Flash...
flashfs[0]: 0 files, 1 directories
flashfs[0]: 0 orphaned files, 0 orphaned directories
flashfs[0]: Total bytes: 15998976
flashfs[0]: Bytes used: 1024
flashfs[0]: Bytes available: 15997952
flashfs[0]: flashfs fsck took 12 seconds.
...done Initializing Flash.
Boot Sector Filesystem (bs:) installed, fsid: 3
Loading ""...: permission denied

Error loading ""

Interrupt within 5 seconds to abort boot process.
Boot process failed...

The system is unable to boot automatically.  The BOOT
environment variable needs to be set to a bootable
image.

switch:
```

Example 10-69 shows the boot process when no files are present in Flash. Notice that a message is displayed, indicating the boot process failed, with the switch being placed into ROM monitor mode as indicated by the switch: prompt.

At this point, the Flash file system has been mounted during the boot process in an attempt to boot the switch; hence, you do not need to explicitly mount the Flash file system using the **flash_init** and **load_helper** commands.

NOTE   If you enter ROM monitor mode by holding down the MODE button while powering on the switch, you must use the **flash_init** and **load_helper** commands to mount the Flash file system.

Assuming the Flash file system is mounted, to ensure the XMODEM file transfer is as fast as possible, you should change the baud rate used for the console connection from 9600 bps to 57600 bps, using the **set BAUD** command (case sensitive) as demonstrated in Example 10-70.

NOTE   Although a speed of 115200 bps is supported on the Catalyst 3550, setting such a speed results in numerous CRC errors, with the copy process failing.

Example 10-70 *Configuring a High-Speed Baud Rate*

```
switch: set BAUD 57600
                    ÿÍ¿∆
```

In Example 10-70, notice after the baud rate is configured as 57600 bps that some garbled text appears (shaded), due to the console operating at a 9600 bps baud rate. At this stage, you must reconnect to the switch using a new console connection operating at 57600 bps.

After connecting at 57600 bps to the console port, you should be able to once again see the switch: prompt. At this stage, the appropriate operating system file can now be transferred via XMODEM using the **copy xmodem: flash:**<*file-name*> command, as demonstrated in Example 10-71.

Example 10-71 *Starting File Download via XMODEM*

```
switch: copy xmodem: flash:c3550-i5k2l2q3-mz.121-13.EA1a.bin
Begin the Xmodem or Xmodem-1K transfer now...
CC
```

After the **copy xmodem:** command is executed, the switch begins waiting for the XMODEM transfer to begin as indicated by the shaded output in Example 10-71. At this point the file transfer must be initiated from the terminal emulation being used for console access. Assuming HyperTerminal is being used, you can select **Transfer** → **Send File** from the main menu, which displays the Send File dialog box and allows you to transmit a file via the console connection. Figure 10-8 demonstrates specifying the appropriate path to the image file and ensuring the file transfer protocol is set to XMODEM.

Figure 10-8 *Preparing HyperTerminal to Send a File via XMODEM*

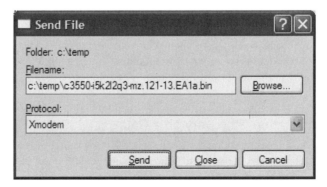

NOTE   There is no **archive** command in ROM Monitor mode, so you must ensure you copy an operating system image file if recovering from ROM Monitor mode. After the switch has booted from the recovered operating system image, you can then use the **archive** command to completely restore the entire operating system and CMS files.

Once the Send button is clicked, the file transfer begins. Figure 10-9 shows the HyperTerminal XModem file send screen.

Figure 10-9   *Using HyperTerminal to Send a File via XMODEM*

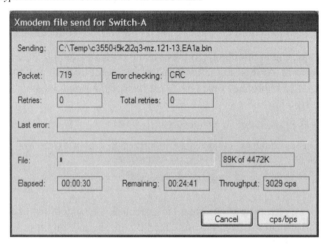

Depending on the size of the image and the baud rate configured, the XMODEM file copy could take hours to complete. Notice in Figure 10-9 that at 57600 bps, the file transfer takes approximate 25 minutes.

Once the XMODEM file copy is complete, you should set the console speed to 9600 bps using the **set BAUD 9600** command, re-establish a console connection at 9600 bps, and then use the **boot** command to boot the switch from the new image (e.g., boot flash:c3550-i5k2l2q3-mz.121-13.EA1a.bin). Once the switch has booted, you should restore the complete operating system using the **archive** command, or at least ensure the boot environment variable is set to boot from the new image using the **boot system** global configuration command.

Operating System Recovery on a Catalyst 2900/4000 Switch (CatOS)

Operating system recovery on the Catalyst 2900/4000 switches is a lot quicker than on the Catalyst 3550 because the onboard Ethernet management interface can be accessed from

ROM Monitor mode, allowing for an operating system image file to be recovered using TFTP rather than a slow serial file transfer protocol such as XMODEM.

If the operating system image on a CatOS switch becomes corrupted or is deleted, when the switch starts up, you will find that the switch cannot boot because it no longer has an operating system image to boot from. This causes the switch to be placed into ROM Monitor mode, as demonstrated in Example 10-72.

Example 10-72 *Boot Failure on the Cisco Catalyst 2900/4000*

```
0:00.575648: Please set IPAddr variable
0:00.576244: Please set Netmask variable
0:00.576605: Please set Broadcast variable
0:00.577211: Please set TftpServer variable to do tftp downloads
0:00.577757: Network is not configuredWS-X2948G bootrom version 6.1(4), built on
  2001.07.30 14:43:26
H/W Revisions:    Fin: 2     Head: 11     Board: 1
Supervisor MAC addresses: 00:30:24:48:d4:00 through 00:30:24:48:d7:ff (1024
  addresses)
Installed memory: 64 MB
Testing LEDs.... done!
The system will autoboot in 5 seconds.
Type control-C to prevent autobooting.
rommon 1 >
The system will now begin autobooting.
Autobooting image: "bootflash:cat4000-k8.7-4-2.bin"
loadprog: error - on file open
Booting "bootflash:cat4000-k8.7-4-2.bin" failed. (loadprog() returned -1.)
Resetting system...

WS-X2948G bootrom version 6.1(4), built on 2001.07.30 14:43:26
H/W Revisions:    Fin: 2     Head: 11     Board: 1
Supervisor MAC addresses: 00:30:24:48:d4:00 through 00:30:24:48:d7:ff (1024
  addresses)
Installed memory: 64 MB
Testing LEDs.... done!
rommon 1> dir bootflash:
        File size          Checksum    File name
```

In Example 10-72, the switch cannot find an operating system file to boot from, and eventually the switch is placed into ROM monitor mode. Notice that the **dir bootflash:** command is used to check the Flash file system. No files are present on Flash; hence, the reason why the switch cannot boot.

The Catalyst 2900 series and Catalyst 4000 Supervisor 1/2 series include an external Ethernet management interface, which can be used to recover an operating system image from an IP network using TFTP. Assuming that the management interface is either directly attached to a TFTP server using a crossover cable or attached to LAN infrastructure that provides connectivity to the TFTP server, you can configure an IP address for the management interface that allows TFTP communications. This is achieved using the **set interface me1** ROMMON command, where **me1** refers to the Ethernet management interface. You must also configure a route using the **set ip route default** ROMMON command if your TFTP server is not attached to the same IP subnet. Example 10-73 demonstrates the configuration of an IP address on the management interface (**me1**) and a default gateway.

Example 10-73 *Configuring the Management Interface in ROMMON Mode*

```
rommon 2> set interface me1 192.168.1.2 255.255.255.0
15:46.811393: Please set TftpServer variable to do tftp downloads
15:46.813026: ig0: 00:30:24:48:d7:fe is 192.168.1.2
15:46.813619: netmask: 255.255.255.0
15:46.813973: broadcast: 192.168.1.255
15:46.814336: gateway: 0.0.0.0
rommon 3> set ip route default 192.168.1.1
```

NOTE   Other CatOS Catalyst switches might not include a dedicated Ethernet management interface and require the new operating system image to be downloaded via the console connection (using a protocol such as XMODEM). For example, the Catalyst 6000/6500 Supervisor 1 and 2 require you to download a new image via the console port that runs at 9600 bps by default, which can be changed to operate at speeds of up 115200 bps by modifying configuration registers on the switch.

Notice in Example 10-73 that you must set an environment variable called TftpServer if you want to download a file via TFTP. Example 10-74 demonstrates setting this variable with the IP address of the TFTP server and then verifying the configuration.

Example 10-74 *Configuring the TFTP Server Environment Variable*

```
rommon 4> TftpServer=192.168.1.10
rommon 5> set
PS1=rommon ! >
DiagBootMode=post
MemorySize=64
ResetCause=198
TmpfsAddr=2197815296
TmpfsSize=12582912
TmpfsDirectorySize=10240
DiagFreePageLimit=12288
AutobootStatus=fail
TftpServer=192.168.1.10
?=0
BOOT=bootflash:,1;
CONFIG_FILE=bootflash:switch.cfg
WHICHBOOT=bootflash:cat4000.7-4-2.bin
ROMVERSION=5.4(1)
```

In Example 10-74, the **set** command is used to display all environment variables. Notice that the **TftpServer** variable is now set to 192.168.1.10.

After setting the TFTP server IP address, you can next begin the process of operating system recovery. The Catalyst 2900/4000 ROM Monitor program allows you to boot from an image operating system file located on the network (via TFTP), rather than allowing you to download the file from a TFTP server to Flash and then booting from Flash. The **TftpServer** environment variable is used by the **boot** command to locate the TFTP server on which an image is located. Example 10-75 demonstrates configuring the switch to boot from an operating system image file located on the TFTP server.

Example 10-75 *Booting the Switch via TFTP*

```
rommon 6> boot cat4000-k8.7-4-2.bin
2:52.639673: Loading file 192.168.1.10:cat4000-k8.7-4-2.bin
3:42.148276: 4458444 bytes received (checksum 0x9dbb)
###############################
Starting Off-line Diagnostics
Mapping in TempFs
Board type is WS-X2948
DiagBootMode value is "post"
Loading diagnostics...

Power-on-self-test for Module 1:  WS-X2948
Status: (. = Pass, F = Fail)
processor: .          cpu sdram: .          eprom: .
nvram: .              flash: .              enet console port: .
switch registers: .   switch sram: .
Module 1 Passed

Exiting Off-line Diagnostics

Cisco Systems, Inc. Console
Enter password: *****
Switch-B> enable
Enter password: *****
Switch-B> (enable)
```

Notice that you don't need to specify any indication in the **boot** command that you are using TFTP; the switch first looks in the local Flash file system for the file and, if it is not present, assumes that the file is reachable via the TFTP server configured using the **TftpServer** variable. The shaded line indicates that the switch is using 192.168.1.10 to load the image via TFTP. After the file is downloaded via TFTP, it is used to boot the switch. Notice that the switch configuration is maintained, even though the Flash file system is empty. This is because the switch configuration is stored in separate NVRAM.

Now that the full CatOS image is loaded, the appropriate image can be restored to a Flash device on the switch. If you suspect that the file system on the device is corrupted, you must first format the file system, as demonstrated in Example 10-76.

WARNING   All files on the formatted Flash device are erased during the format process. If you don't need to format the file system, ignore this step and proceed to the next step.

Example 10-76 *Formatting the Flash File System on CatOS*

```
Switch-B> (enable) format bootflash:
All sectors will be erased, proceed (y/n) [n]? y

Enter volume id (up to 31 characters): ↵

Formatting sector 1
Format device bootflash completed
```

After optionally formatting the file system, you can obtain the operating system image file using TFTP, either using the sc0 interface or the me1 (external management) interface.

NOTE   The me1 interface has no connection to the switch backplane whatsoever, meaning you must connect this interface directly to the appropriate network you are trying to access.

Example 10-77 shows the process of downloading a new image to Flash and the subsequent verification of the image.

Example 10-77 *Downloading a New Operating System Image*

```
Switch-A> (enable) copy tftp flash
IP address or name of remote host []? 192.168.1.10
Name of file to copy from []? cat4000-k8.7-4-2.bin
Flash device [bootflash]? ↵
Name of file to copy to [cat4000-k8.7-4-2.bin]? cat4000-k8.7-4-2.bin
15599146 bytes available on device bootflash, proceed (y/n) [n]? y
/
CCCCCCCCCCCCCCCCCCCCCCCCCCCCCCCCCCCCCCCCCCCCCCCCCCCCCCCCCCCCCCCCCCCCCCCCCCCC
CCCCCCCCCCCCCCCCCCCCCCCCCCCCCCCCCCCCCCCCCCCCCCCCCCCCCCCCCCCCCCCCCCCCCCCCCCCC
CCCCCCCCCCCCCCCCCC

...

...
File has been copied successfully.
Switch-A> (enable) verify cat4000-k8.7-4-2.bin

CCCCCCCCCCCCCCCCCCCCCCCCCCCCCCCCCCCCCCCCCCCCCCCCCCCCCCCCCCCCCCCCCCCCCCCCCCCC
CCCCCCCCCCCCCCCC
File bootflash:cat4000-k8.7-4-2.bin verified OK
```

Finally, the BOOT environment variable must be configured correctly to ensure that the switch boots from the new image, as demonstrated in Example 10-78.

Example 10-78 *Configuring the BOOT Environment Variable on CatOS*

```
Switch-B> (enable) clear boot system all

BOOT variable =
XYZSW1> (enable) set boot system flash bootflash:cat4000-k8.7-4-2.bin

BOOT variable = bootflash:cat4000-k8.7-4-2.bin,1;
```

At this point, the operating system image is restored to Flash and the switch is configured to boot from the restored image file. If the switch is rebooted, the switch should boot normally with no problems.

Scenario 10-6: Capturing Traffic Using SPAN, RSPAN, and VACLs

The ability to capture traffic on the network is a fundamental requirement for any network engineer that requires low-level protocol monitoring and troubleshooting capabilities. Traditionally, in hub-based LAN environments, traffic capture has been an easy process; by simply attaching to the shared LAN segment, all traffic is seen by a monitoring device. In the modern era of the LAN switch however, Ethernet segments are no longer shared. Instead, Layer 2 unicast traffic between devices is isolated to the ports to which each device is connected, meaning a monitoring device connected to another port has no visibility of traffic. To enable the ability to capture traffic sent and received on other switch ports, Cisco Catalyst switches include a feature called the switch port analyzer feature (SPAN), as well as remote SPAN (RSPAN) and VLAN access control lists (VACLs).

In this scenario you learn how to capture traffic using the SPAN, RSPAN, and VACLs. SPAN, RSPAN, and VACLs are all techniques that have been developed that enable administrators to troubleshoot and monitor LAN communications in a switched environment. This capability is a very important troubleshooting and monitoring tool when verifying the data communications between devices in your LAN network. Figure 10-10 illustrates the topology used for this scenario.

Figure 10-10 *Scenario 10-6 Topology*

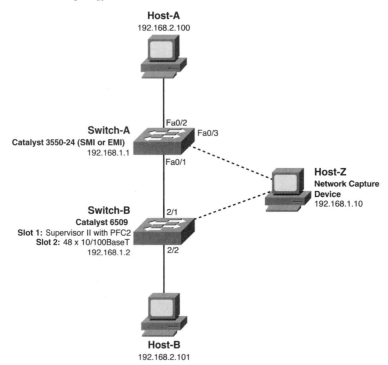

In this scenario you learn how to use SPAN and VLAN access control lists to monitor traffic on a single switch and learn how to use RSPAN to monitor traffic across multiple switches. To generate traffic and to verify that the traffic capturing features are working correctly, you need two hosts that simulate LAN communications, as well as another host that has some form of network capture software.

Understanding Traffic Capture

The ability to capture traffic on any network is important for both troubleshooting and monitoring purposes. In traditional shared hub environments, capturing traffic from the local LAN is not a problem because all traffic is seen by all devices attached to the shared media. In switched networks, however, this does not happen because a switch only forwards unicast traffic out the port attached to the destination and not to any other ports. To monitor traffic in a switched network, Cisco Catalyst switches provide three features:

- SPAN
- RSPAN
- VACLs

SPAN

SPAN is the traditional method of monitoring LAN traffic on Cisco switches. SPAN uses the concept of mirroring traffic from a set of source ports to a single destination port, which has a network capture tool connected to it. Figure 10-11 demonstrates SPAN operation.

Figure 10-11 *SPAN Operation*

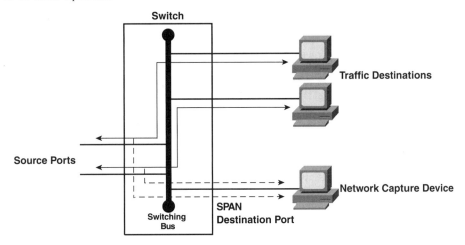

In Figure 10-11, the traffic received on a group of source ports is mirrored out a single destination port to some form of network capture device. Figure 10-11 represents a SPAN session, which is essentially a relationship between a set of source ports and a single, unique destination port.

With SPAN, only a single destination port can be configured, while multiple source ports can be configured per session. Looking at source ports, you can configure a SPAN session to mirror traffic either received, transmitted, or both transmitted and received on the source ports. You can also specify a VLAN as a source, which means that the Catalyst switch automatically mirrors the traffic from all ports in the VLAN to the destination port. This feature is sometimes referred to as *VLAN SPAN* or *VSPAN*.

Depending on the direction of traffic that is mirrored, a SPAN session can be defined as one of the following session types:

- **Ingress SPAN session**—Refers to a SPAN session where at least one source interface is configured to mirror traffic received (rx) or configured to mirror traffic sent and received on an interface (both).

- **Egress SPAN session**—Refers to a SPAN session where all source interfaces are configured to mirror traffic transmitted (tx) only.

Differentiating between ingress and egress SPAN sessions is important because some Catalyst switches have different limitations as to the maximum number of ingress and egress SPAN sessions that you can run.

While SPAN meets the requirements of many traffic capture environments, it does have a few limitations of which you need to be aware:

- **Session limitations**—Catalyst switches have limitations on how many simultaneous SPAN sessions you can run. These limitations are based upon the direction of traffic that you capture. For example, the Catalyst 6000/6500 allows only up to two ingress SPAN sessions (traffic received or received and transmitted on source ports) and up to four egress SPAN sessions (only traffic transmitted on source ports).

- **Lack of granularity**—SPAN can be controlled only to a per-port or per-VLAN level. You cannot selectively capture specific types of traffic sent or received on a source port. All traffic is mirrored to the destination port. This means you must filter traffic at your network capture device, which is inefficient if you want to capture only a specific type of traffic and want to avoid oversubscribing the destination port.

- **Destination port oversubscription**—The traffic mirrored to the destination port is the bandwidth sum of all source ports in the SPAN session. If you have multiple source ports, your destination port can easily become oversubscribed, meaning some mirrored traffic might be dropped. For example, if you had a single 100 Mbps destination port and two 100 Mbps source ports, you already run the risk of oversubscription. The main issue with oversubscription and SPAN is that you cannot filter specific traffic sent or received on a source port.

RSPAN

One useful feature of SPAN is an extension of SPAN called *remote SPAN* or *RSPAN*. RSPAN allows you to monitor traffic from source ports distributed over multiple switches, which means that you can centralize your network capture devices. RSPAN works by mirroring the traffic from the source ports of an RSPAN session onto a VLAN that is dedicated for the RSPAN session. This VLAN is then trunked to other switches, allowing the RSPAN session traffic to be transported across multiple switches. On the switch that contains the destination port for the session, traffic from the RSPAN session VLAN is simply mirrored out the destination port. Figure 10-12 demonstrates RSPAN operation.

In Figure 10-12, Switch-A hosts the source ports of an RSPAN session and is configured to mirror all traffic received on these ports to VLAN 300, which is a special VLAN created for the RSPAN session. The mirrored traffic is tagged with a VLAN ID of 300 and then forwarded across the trunk to Switch-B, which simply forwards the tagged traffic across the trunk to Switch-C. Switch-C is configured to mirror all traffic received on the RSPAN VLAN (VLAN 300) to the destination port, enabling the network capture device to monitor ports on a remote switch.

Figure 10-12 *RSPAN Operation*

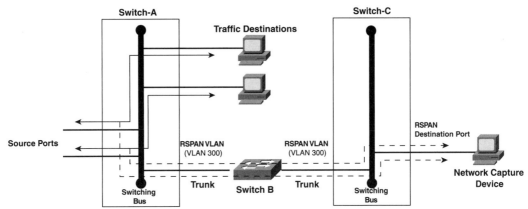

Because an RSPAN session spans many switches, various types of RSPAN components comprise an overall RSPAN session. An RSPAN session actually consists of three different components:

- **RSPAN source session**—This refers to an RSPAN session configured on the switch that has source interfaces from which traffic is captured and then mirrored to an RSPAN VLAN. In Figure 10-12, Switch-A must have an RSPAN source session configured.

- **RSPAN destination session**—This refers to an RSPAN session configured on the switch where traffic received on an RSPAN VLAN is mirrored to a local destination port. In Figure 10-12, Switch-C must have an RSPAN destination session configured.

- **Transit switches**—This refers to any switch in the LAN that only transports RSPAN VLAN traffic, but does not contain any source or destination ports for an RSPAN session. In Figure 10-12, Switch-C is a transit switch.

A major requirement for RSPAN to work is that all switches with RSPAN source and RSPAN destination sessions, as well as any transit switch that transports RSPAN traffic, must support RSPAN. Understanding the different types of RSPAN components is important, because there are limitations as to the number of RSPAN source and destination sessions you can configure on a switch.

Table 10-2 describes the platforms that currently support RSPAN.

Table 10-2 *Cisco Catalyst Support for RSPAN*

Platform	Minimum Software Version
Catalyst 2950/3550 (Cisco IOS)	IOS 12.1(11)EA1 or higher
Catalyst 4000/4500 Supervisor 1/2 (CatOS)	CatOS 7.5 or higher
Catalyst 6000/6500 (CatOS)	CatOS 5.3 or higher Requires PFC
Catalyst 6000/6500 (Native IOS)	IOS 12.2SX or higher Requires PFC

VACLs

VACLs are a feature supported on the Catalyst 6000/6500 that was discussed in Chapter 8 in the context of network security. Although VACLs are primarily used for providing network access control at Layer 3/4 between devices attached to the same VLAN, they can also be used to capture traffic that is subsequently mirrored to a list of capture ports. Figure 10-13 demonstrates VACL operation.

Figure 10-13 *VACL Operation*

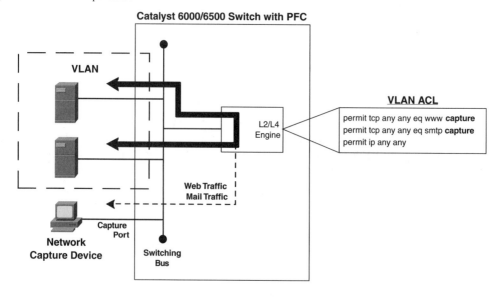

In Figure 10-13, a VACL is applied to the VLAN shown. This means that all traffic within the VLAN is passed through the VACL by the L2/L4 engine (on the Supervisor 2 with PFC-2) or on the ACL engine (with the Supervisor 1 with PFC-2). Notice that the VACL specifies the **capture** keyword at the end of the access control entries (ACEs) that match web and mail traffic. Any traffic that matches an ACE that specifies the **capture** keyword is mirrored to a list of capture ports. In Figure 10-13, the bottom port is a member of the capture port list and thus receives World Wide Web and SMTP traffic on the VLAN shown.

The following describes the advantages of using VACLs to capture traffic:

- **No session limitations**—There is no limitation as to how many ACEs you can configure that specify the **capture** keyword.

- **Layer 3/4 traffic flow granularity**—Traffic can be captured based upon layer 3/4 parameters, which allows you to filter what is captured at the switch, rather than at the network capture device.

- **Support for gigabit interfaces**—A major benefit of VACLs is that you can specify a gigabit Ethernet interface as a capture port, which ensures that you can avoid oversubscription on the capture device.

- **No performance overheads**—VACLs are processed in hardware during the L2 switching lookup and hence incur no penalty in terms of switching throughput. Because of the way in which data is forwarded over the backplane on the Catalyst 6000/6500, there is also no performance penalty for mirroring the captured traffic to the capture port list.

The only real restriction of using VACLs to capture traffic is that it is supported only on the Catalyst 6000/6500 with a policy feature card (PFC) installed. If you are using another platform, or do not have a PFC installed, you must use SPAN to capture traffic.

TIP You can use VACLs (without the **capture** keyword) to filter traffic on an RSPAN session VLAN, allowing you to effectively control the traffic at a Layer 3/4 level that is mirrored out the destination port in the RSPAN session. You simply would create a VACL that explicitly permits the traffic that you want mirrored and drops all other traffic. Such a technique is most effective when applied on the switch that contains the source ports of the RSPAN session.

SPAN and RSPAN Session Limitations

Before learning how to configure SPAN and RSPAN, it is important to understand that Cisco Catalyst switches have limitations as to the number of SPAN and RSPAN sessions that are supported running at the same time. Table 10-3 lists the SPAN and RSPAN session limitations of the various Cisco Catalyst switch platforms.

Table 10-3   *Maximum SPAN Sessions on Cisco IOS-based Catalyst Switches*

Platform	SPAN/RSPAN Session Limitations
Catalyst 2950	Maximum of 1 SPAN/RSPAN source session in total 1 ingress/egress SPAN session (**tx**, **rx**, or **both**) 1 RSPAN source session 1 RSPAN destination session (if 1 x SPAN/RSPAN source session configured) 2 RSPAN destination sessions (if no SPAN/RSPAN source session configured)
Catalyst 3550	Maximum of 2 SPAN/RSPAN sessions in total 2 ingress/egress SPAN sessions (**tx**, **rx**, or **both**) 2 RSPAN source/destination sessions
Catalyst 2900/4000/4500 Supervisor1/2	Maximum of 5 SPAN/RSPAN sessions in total 5 ingress/egress SPAN sessions (**tx**, **rx**, or **both**) 5 RSPAN source/destination sessions
Catalyst 4000/4500 Supervisor 3/4	2 ingress SPAN sessions (**rx** or **both**) 4 egress SPAN sessions (**tx**) No RSPAN support
Catalyst 5000/5500	1 ingress SPAN session (**rx** or **both**) 4 egress SPAN session (**tx**) No RSPAN support
Catalyst 6000/6500 (CatOS)	Maximum of 2 ingress SPAN/RSPAN source sessions in total 2 ingress SPAN sessions(**rx** or **both**) 4 egress SPAN sessions(**tx**) 1 RSPAN source session 24 RSPAN destination sessions
Catalyst 6000/6500 (Native IOS)	Maximum of 2 SPAN/RSPAN source sessions in total 2 ingress/egress SPAN sessions (**tx**, **rx**, or **both**) 1 RSPAN source session 64 RSPAN destination sessions

NOTE   Transit switches for an RSPAN session (e.g., Switch-B in Figure 10-12), where traffic for the session is transported via an RSPAN VLAN but no source or destination ports for the RSPAN session are configured on the transit switch, do not have a limitation as to the number of RSPAN sessions that can transit the switch. Transit switches must support RSPAN, however, because RSPAN VLANs have special properties not understood by switches that do no support RSPAN.

Scenario Prerequisites

To successfully commence the configuration tasks required to complete this scenario, Table 10-4 describes the prerequisite configurations required on each device in the scenario topology. Any configurations not listed can be assumed as being the default configuration.

Table 10-4 *Scenario 10-6 Requirements*

Device	Required Configuration	
	Parameter	**Value**
Switch-A	Hostname	Switch-A
	IP Address (VLAN)	192.168.1.1/24 (VLAN 1)
	Enable/Telnet Password	cisco
	VTP Mode	Transparent
	VLANs (Name)	VLAN 2 (VLAN02)
	VLAN Assignments	VLAN 2: interface fa0/2
	802.1q Trunks (DTP Mode)	fa0/1 (nonegotiate)
Switch-B	Hostname	Switch-B
	IP Address (VLAN)	192.168.1.2/24 (VLAN 1)
	Enable/Telnet Password	cisco
	VTP Mode	Transparent
	VLANs (Name)	VLAN 2 (VLAN02)
	VLAN Assignments	VLAN 2: port 2/2
	802.1q Trunks (DTP Mode)	2/2 (nonegotiate)
Host-A	Operating System	Windows 2000 Professional or Windows XP
	IP Address	192.168.2.100/24
Host-B	Operating System	Windows 2000 Professional or Windows XP
	IP Address	192.168.2.101/24
Host-Z	Operating System	Windows 2000 Professional or Windows XP
	IP Address	192.168.1.10/24
	Applications	Traffic Capture Software (e.g. Microsoft Network Monitor)

Example 10-79 and Example 10-80 shows the prerequisite configuration required on Switch-A and Switch-B respectively.

Example 10-79 *Scenario 10-6 Prerequisite Configuration for Switch-A*

```
Switch# configure terminal
Switch(config)# hostname Switch-A
Switch-A(config)# enable secret cisco
Switch-A(config)# line vty 0 15
Switch-A(config-line)# password cisco
Switch-A(config-line)# exit
Switch-A(config)# interface vlan 1
Switch-A(config-if)# no shutdown
Switch-A(config-if)# ip address 192.168.1.1 255.255.255.0
Switch-A(config-if)# exit
Switch-A(config)# vtp mode transparent
Setting device to VTP TRANSPARENT mode.
Switch-A(config)# vlan 2
Switch-A(config-vlan)# name VLAN02
Switch-A(config-vlan)# exit
Switch-A(config)# interface fastEthernet0/1
Switch-A(config-if)# switchport trunk encapsulation dot1q
Switch-A(config-if)# switchport mode trunk
Switch-A(config-if)# switchport nonegotiate
Switch-A(config)# interface fastEthernet0/2
Switch-A(config-if)# switchport access vlan 2
```

Example 10-80 *Scenario 10-6 Prerequisite Configuration for Switch-B*

```
Console> (enable) set system name Switch-B
System name set.
Switch-B> (enable) set password
Enter old password: ø
Enter new password: *****
Retype new password: *****
Password changed.
Switch-B> (enable) set enablepass
Enter old password: ø
Enter new password: *****
Retype new password: *****
Password changed.
Switch-B> (enable) set interface sc0 192.168.1.2 255.255.255.0
Interface sc0 IP address and netmask set.
Switch-B> (enable) set vtp mode transparent
VTP domain  modified
Switch-B> (enable) set vlan 2 name VLAN02
VTP advertisements transmitting temporarily stopped,
and will resume after the command finishes.
```

Example 10-80 *Scenario 10-6 Prerequisite Configuration for Switch-B (Continued)*

```
Vlan 2 configuration successful
Switch-B> (enable) set vlan 2 2/2
VLAN 2 modified.
VLAN 1 modified.
VLAN  Mod/Ports
----  ---------------------
2     2/1,2/2
Switch-B> (enable) set trunk 2/1 nonegotiate dot1q
Port(s)  2/1 trunk mode set to nonegotiate.
Port(s)  2/1 trunk type set to dot1q.
```

After the prerequisite configuration is implemented, you should attach each host as indicated in Figure 10-10 and verify PING connectivity between devices where possible in before proceeding. Host-A and Host-B should be able to ping each other, whilst Host-Z should also be able to ping both Switch-A and Switch-B.

Configuration Tasks

This scenario demonstrates the use of SPAN, RSPAN, and VACLs to provide the capturing of traffic sent and/or received by one or more interfaces or VLANs on a Cisco Catalyst switch. This requires the following configuration tasks:

- Configuring SPAN
- Configuring RSPAN
- Configuring VACLs

Configuring SPAN

In this scenario, SPAN is configured on both Switch-A and Switch-B, to demonstrate the configuration of SPAN on Cisco IOS and CatOS. This requires the following configuration tasks:

- Configuring SPAN on Cisco IOS
- Configuring SPAN on CatOS

Configuring SPAN on Cisco IOS

In this section, a continuous traffic stream in VLAN 2 between Host-A and Host-B is generated, as well as a continuous traffic stream in VLAN 1 between Switch-B and Switch-A. Switch-A is configured to mirror this traffic to Host-Z (which must be connected to interface Fa0/3 on Switch-A) using SPAN. This requires the following configuration tasks to be implemented:

- Generating network traffic
- Configuring Switch-A for SPAN
- Performing a packet capture of network traffic on Host-Z

To generate traffic between Host-A and Host-B in VLAN 2, the **ping** utility can be used with the –**t** option on Windows, which generates a continuous stream of ping packets. Example 10-81 demonstrates generating a continuous ping on Host-B between Host-B and Host-A.

Example 10-81 *Generating a Continuous Traffic Stream on VLAN 2 Between Host-B and Host-A from Host-B*

```
C:\> ping -t 192.168.2.100

Pinging 192.168.2.100 with 32 bytes of data:

Reply from 192.168.2.100: bytes=32 time=1ms TTL=255
Reply from 192.168.2.100: bytes=32 time=1ms TTL=255
Reply from 192.168.2.100: bytes=32 time=1ms TTL=255
Reply from 192.168.2.100: bytes=32 time=1ms TTL=255
Reply from 192.168.2.100: bytes=32 time=1ms TTL=255
...
...
```

In Example 10-81, the –**t** switch is used with the Windows **ping** utility to continuously generate ping traffic. ICMP Echo Requests are sent from 192.168.2.101 (Host-B) to 192.168.2.100 (Host-A), with ICMP Echo Replies sent from 192.168.2.100 (Host-A) to 192.168.2.101 (Host-B).

NOTE   At this point, if you start capturing network traffic on Host-Z, you should notice that the traffic generated in Example 10-79 is not being captured because SPAN is not configured at present. The only traffic that should be captured is flooded unicast traffic, multicast and broadcast traffic, or unicast traffic generated locally by Host-Z.

Now that a particular type of traffic is being generated in the network, SPAN can be configured to mirror that traffic to Host-Z. On Cisco IOS, the **monitor session** global configuration command is used to create SPAN sessions.

When configuring SPAN, you must configure the source interfaces/VLANs and the destination interface separately. The following shows the syntax for configuring source interfaces and/or VLANs:

```
Switch(config)# monitor session session-id source interface interface-type
    interface-id [tx | rx | both]
Switch(config)# monitor session session-id source vlan vlan-id [rx]
```

Notice that if you specify a source interface, you can capture traffic sent, received, or sent and received using the **tx**, **rx**, or **both** keywords respectively. If you specify a source VLAN, you can capture only traffic received by interfaces belonging to the VLAN.

NOTE   You can configure source interfaces and source VLANs for the same SPAN session.

After configuring the source interfaces/VLANs, you must next configure the destination port. Only a single destination port can be configured, which is created using the **monitor session** command as follows:

```
Switch(config)# monitor session session-id destination interface
    interface-type interface-id [encapsulation]
    {dot1q | isl | replicate}] [ingress vlan vlan-id]
```

Notice the two optional parameters you can define along with the destination interface. The optional **encapsulation** command allows you to tag frames mirrored to the monitoring device with their VLAN ID, using either 802.1q (**dot1q**), ISL (**isl**), or the tagging of the original packet (**replicate**). The optional **ingress vlan** *vlan-id* configuration ensures that frames input on the destination SPAN port (i.e., received from the packet capture device) will be accepted and placed into the VLAN specified.

In this scenario, Host-B is currently generating continuous ICMP echo requests to Host-A, with ICMP echo replies sent back from Host-A to Host-B. To capture this traffic on Switch-A, you can create a SPAN session that specifies interface fastEthernet 0/2 (attached to Host-A) as the source interface and interface fastEthernet 0/3 (attached to Host-Z) as the destination interface. Alternatively, you could configure VLAN 2 as the source VLAN, which would automatically add interface fastEthernet 0/3 as a source port given that it belongs to VLAN 2. Example 10-82 demonstrates configuring a SPAN session on Switch-A to capture traffic transmitted and received on the interface attached to Host-A.

Example 10-82 *Configuring a SPAN Session on Cisco IOS*

```
Switch-A# configure terminal
Switch-A(config)# monitor session 1 source interface fastEthernet0/2 both
Switch-A(config)# monitor session 1 destination interface fastEthernet0/3
Switch-A(config)# exit
Switch-A# show monitor
Session 1
---------
Type              : Local Session
Source Ports      :
    Both          : Fa0/2
Destination Ports : Fa0/3
    Encapsulation: Native
        Ingress: Disabled
```

In Example 10-82, the first command creates a new SPAN session with an ID of 1 and defines a source interface for the SPAN session (interface Fa0/2). The second command specifies that traffic both sent and received (indicated by the **both** keyword) on the source interfaces should be mirrored to the destination interface. After the SPAN session is created, the **show monitor** command is executed to verify the SPAN configuration.

At this stage, if the network capture software on Host-Z is started, Host-Z should be able to see the traffic sent between Host-A and Host-B, even though the interface attached to Host-Z is not even on the same VLAN as Host-A and Host-B. Figure 10-14 demonstrates a network capture performed on Host-Z (using Microsoft Network Monitor, which ships as a free, optional component with Windows 2000 server) after the configuration of Example 10-79 is implemented.

Figure 10-14 *Network Capture Output on Host-Z*

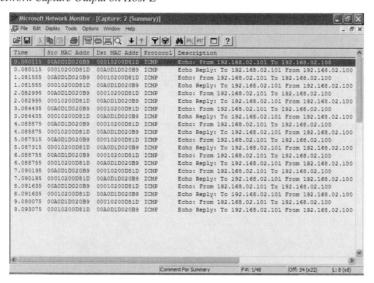

In Figure 10-14, the output has actually been filtered to display only ICMP packets because any traffic between Host-A and Host-B is captured. Notice in the Description column (other columns are hidden from view), you can see each ICMP Echo packet sent from 192.168.2.101 (Host—B) to 192.168.2.100 (Host-A) and the corresponding ICMP Echo Reply packet sent from Host-A to Host-B. This verifies that SPAN is working and that the SPAN session is mirroring traffic sent and received on the interface attached to Host-A.

If you now try and attempt to communicate from Host-Z within VLAN 1, you should find that Host-Z is unable to communicate at all. This is easily verified by attempting to ping either Switch-A or Switch-B from Host-Z, which should fail, as demonstrated in Example 10-83.

Example 10-83 *Attempting Communications from Host-Z*

```
C:\> ping 192.168.1.1
Pinging 192.168.1.1 with 32 bytes of data:

Request timed out.
Request timed out.
Request timed out.
Request timed out.

Ping statistics for 192.168.1.1:
    Packets: Sent = 4, Received = 0, Lost = 4 (100% loss),
```

The reason why Host-Z cannot communicate is because the destination interface for the SPAN session has not been configured to enable incoming packets on the destination port (using the optional **ingress** keyword).

Now that configuring a SPAN session with source interfaces has been demonstrated, it is time to demonstrate configuring a VSPAN session, where one or more VLANs can be configured as the source for the SPAN session. To demonstrate configuring multiple VLANs as the source, traffic needs to be generated in VLAN 1. Example 10-84 demonstrates configuring a continuous ping from Switch-B to Switch-A, which generates continuous traffic in VLAN 1.

Example 10-84 *Configuring a Continuous ping on Switch-B*

```
Switch-B> (enable) ping -s 192.168.1.2
PING 192.168.1.2: 56 data bytes
64 bytes from 192.168.1.2: icmp_seq=0. time=5 ms
64 bytes from 192.168.1.2: icmp_seq=1. time=1 ms
64 bytes from 192.168.1.2: icmp_seq=2. time=1 ms
64 bytes from 192.168.1.2: icmp_seq=3. time=1 ms
64 bytes from 192.168.1.2: icmp_seq=4. time=1 ms
64 bytes from 192.168.1.2: icmp_seq=5. time=1 ms
64 bytes from 192.168.1.2: icmp_seq=6. time=1 ms
...
...
```

Example 10-85 demonstrates removing the SPAN session configured in Example 10-82 on Switch-A, creating a new SPAN session that specifies both VLAN 1 and VLAN 2 as source VLANs, and this time configuring the destination interface to Host-Z to accept incoming packets.

Example 10-85 *Configuring a VSPAN Session on Cisco IOS with Incoming Packets Enabled*

```
Switch-A# configure terminal
Switch-A(config)# no monitor 1
Switch-A(config)# monitor session 1 source vlan fastEthernet0/2 rx
Switch-A(config)# monitor session 1 destination interface fastEthernet0/3 ingress
  vlan 1
Switch-A(config)# exit
Switch-A# show monitor
Session 1
----------
Type            : Local Session
Source VLANs    :
    RX Only     : 1-2
Destination Ports : Fa0/3
    Encapsulation: Native
            Ingress: Enabled, default VLAN = 1
```

After removing the previous SPAN session, notice that next only traffic received on the source VLANs is mirrored to the destination port because this is the only direction supported for source VLANs on the Catalyst 3550. The destination interface configured for the SPAN session is configured to accept incoming packets and place them in VLAN 1, as indicated by the **ingress vlan 1** keywords.

At this stage on Host-Z, if you perform another packet capture, this time you should see ICMP traffic being generated in VLAN 1 (between Switch-A and Switch-B), as well as in VLAN 2 (between Host-A and Host-B). Figure 10-15 demonstrates a network capture performed on Host-Z after the configuration of Example 10-85 is implemented.

In Figure 10-15, again the output has actually been filtered to display only ICMP packets. Notice that ICMP echo traffic between Host-A and Host-B is still being captured, with packets captured sent in both directions. Although only traffic received on VLAN 2 is captured, this captures the ICMP echo requests from Host-B to Host-A received on interface fastEthernet0/1 (the trunk between Switch-A and Switch-B) and also captures the ICMP echo replies from Host-A to Host-B received on interface fastEthernet0/2. If you compare Figure 10-14 and Figure 10-15, you can notice that ICMP echo traffic sent from Switch-B (192.168.1.2) to Switch-A (192.168.1.1) is being captured, in addition to the Host-A ←→ Host-B traffic. However, the return ICMP echo reply from Switch-A to Switch-B is not being captured. This is because traffic generated by the switch CPU on the Catalyst 3550 is not mirrored to a SPAN session. The CPU on Switch-A must generate ICMP echo replies to the echo requests sent from Switch-B; hence, these replies are not mirrored to the destination SPAN interface. The ICMP echo request traffic from Switch-B to Switch-A is being captured, as this traffic is received on interface fastEthernet0/1 within VLAN 1.

Figure 10-15 *Network Capture Output on Host-Z*

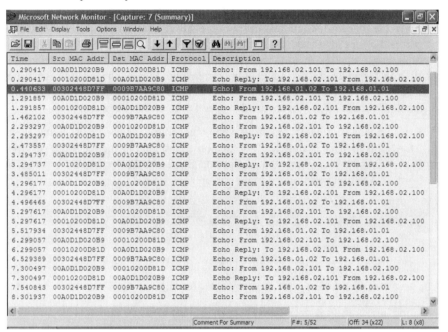

Time	Src MAC Addr	Dst MAC Addr	Protocol	Description
0.290417	00A0D1D020B9	00010200D81D	ICMP	Echo: From 192.168.02.101 To 192.168.02.100
0.290417	00010200D81D	00A0D1D020B9	ICMP	Echo Reply: To 192.168.02.101 From 192.168.02.100
0.440633	00302448D7FF	0009B7AA9C80	ICMP	Echo: From 192.168.01.02 To 192.168.01.01
1.291857	00A0D1D020B9	00010200D81D	ICMP	Echo: From 192.168.02.101 To 192.168.02.100
1.291857	00010200D81D	00A0D1D020B9	ICMP	Echo Reply: To 192.168.02.101 From 192.168.02.100
1.462102	00302448D7FF	0009B7AA9C80	ICMP	Echo: From 192.168.01.02 To 192.168.01.01
2.293297	00A0D1D020B9	00010200D81D	ICMP	Echo: From 192.168.02.101 To 192.168.02.100
2.293297	00010200D81D	00A0D1D020B9	ICMP	Echo Reply: To 192.168.02.101 From 192.168.02.100
2.473557	00302448D7FF	0009B7AA9C80	ICMP	Echo: From 192.168.01.02 To 192.168.01.01
3.294737	00A0D1D020B9	00010200D81D	ICMP	Echo: From 192.168.02.101 To 192.168.02.100
3.294737	00010200D81D	00A0D1D020B9	ICMP	Echo Reply: To 192.168.02.101 From 192.168.02.100
3.485011	00302448D7FF	0009B7AA9C80	ICMP	Echo: From 192.168.01.02 To 192.168.01.01
4.296177	00A0D1D020B9	00010200D81D	ICMP	Echo: From 192.168.02.101 To 192.168.02.100
4.296177	00010200D81D	00A0D1D020B9	ICMP	Echo Reply: To 192.168.02.101 From 192.168.02.100
4.496465	00302448D7FF	0009B7AA9C80	ICMP	Echo: From 192.168.01.02 To 192.168.01.01
5.297617	00A0D1D020B9	00010200D81D	ICMP	Echo: From 192.168.02.101 To 192.168.02.100
5.297617	00010200D81D	00A0D1D020B9	ICMP	Echo Reply: To 192.168.02.101 From 192.168.02.100
5.517934	00302448D7FF	0009B7AA9C80	ICMP	Echo: From 192.168.01.02 To 192.168.01.01
6.299057	00A0D1D020B9	00010200D81D	ICMP	Echo: From 192.168.02.101 To 192.168.02.100
6.299057	00010200D81D	00A0D1D020B9	ICMP	Echo Reply: To 192.168.02.101 From 192.168.02.100
6.529389	00302448D7FF	0009B7AA9C80	ICMP	Echo: From 192.168.01.02 To 192.168.01.01
7.300497	00A0D1D020B9	00010200D81D	ICMP	Echo: From 192.168.02.101 To 192.168.02.100
7.300497	00010200D81D	00A0D1D020B9	ICMP	Echo Reply: To 192.168.02.101 From 192.168.02.100
7.540843	00302448D7FF	0009B7AA9C80	ICMP	Echo: From 192.168.01.02 To 192.168.01.01
8.301937	00A0D1D020B9	00010200D81D	ICMP	Echo: From 192.168.02.101 To 192.168.02.100

NOTE   Because ingress packets have been enabled on the destination SPAN interface, Host-Z should now be able to ping Switch-A and Switch-B in Example 10-81, even with the SPAN session configured.

Configuring SPAN on CatOS

In this section, the configuration of SPAN on CatOS (Switch-B) is demonstrated. Before configuring and testing SPAN on Switch-B, Host-Z must be disconnected from Switch-A and attached to port 2/3 on Switch-B.

To configure a SPAN session on CatOS, the **set span** command is used to create SPAN sessions. The following describes the syntax to create SPAN sessions that include source ports and SPAN sessions that include source VLANs.

```
Console> (enable) set span {source-vlans | source-mod/port}
   destination-mod/port [both | rx | tx] [filter vlan-list]
   [inpkts {enable | disable}] [learning {enable | disable}] [create]
```

Notice that you can specify either VLANs or ports as the source for the SPAN session. The **both, rx,** and **tx** keywords define the direction(s) of traffic to be monitored. If you specify one or more VLANs as the source, then only the **both** option is applicable. The **inpkts** keyword enables input packets on the destination SPAN port, while the **learning** keyword is relevant only when the **inpkts** setting is configured and controls whether or not the switch learns the source MAC address of frames received from devices attached to the destination port and places MAC addresses into the bridge table. The **filter** keyword is used where a trunk port is configured as the source port, with the *vlan-list* parameter defining specific VLANs for which traffic should only be mirrored. Finally, the **create** keyword must be specified when you first create a SPAN session. If you subsequently modify parameters of the SPAN session, you do not need to specify the **create** keyword.

Assuming the continuous ping traffic being generated between Host-B and Host-A in VLAN 2 is in place, Example 10-86 demonstrates configuring the trunk port (port 2/1) on Switch-B as the source port and configuring port 2/3 as the destination port with only traffic from VLAN 2 received on the trunk mirrored.

Example 10-86 *Configuring a SPAN session on CatOS with VLAN Filtering*

```
Switch-B> (enable) set span 2/1 2/3 both filter 2 inpkts enable create
2003 May 01 04:08:19 %SYS-5-SPAN_CFGSTATECHG:local span session inactive for
  destination port 2/3
Overwrote Port 2/3 to monitor transmit/receive traffic of Port 2/1
Incoming Packets enabled. Learning enabled.
2003 May 01 04:08:19 %SYS-5-SPAN_CFGSTATECHG:local span session active for
  destination port 2/3
Switch-B> (enable) show span

Destination       : Port 2/3
Admin Source      : Port 2/1
Oper Source       : Port 2/1
Direction         : transmit/receive
Incoming Packets: enabled
Learning          : enabled
Filter            : 2
Status            : active

-------------------------------------------------------------------
Total local span sessions:  1
```

In Example 10-86, notice that the **filter** keyword is configured, with a VLAN-ID of 2 defined as the permitted VLAN from the source interface configured. Inbound packets on the destination port are also permitted, as the **inpkts enable** option has been configured. After configuration SPAN, the **show span** command is used to verify the configuration.

After the configuration of Example 10-86 is in place, Host-Z should be able to capture ICMP traffic sent between Host-B and Host-A with a similar capture of Figure 10-14. Because the VLAN filter configured for the span session permits only traffic to/from VLAN 2 sent/received on the trunk to be mirrored, Host-Z is not able to capture any of the continuous ICMP traffic being generated between Switch-A and Switch-B. Because incoming packets are enabled for the SPAN session, Host-Z should be able to communicate with Switch-A and Switch-B.

Configuring RSPAN

In this scenario, RSPAN is configured on both Switch-A and Switch-B to demonstrate how you can mirror traffic using RSPAN to any device connected in the LAN. The configuration of RSPAN on Cisco IOS and CatOS requires the following configuration tasks:

- Creating VLANs for RSPAN
- Configuring RSPAN on Cisco IOS
- Configuring RSPAN on CatOS
- Verifying RSPAN operation

NOTE   This section assumes that any SPAN sessions configured earlier in the scenario have been removed, using the **no monitor session** global configuration command on Cisco IOS and the **set span disable all** command on CatOS.

Creating VLANs for RSPAN

To enable the transportation of mirrored traffic over multiple switches, RSPAN requires dedicated VLANs that are used to carry RSPAN traffic. When an RSPAN session is created on the source switch, the traffic sent and/or received on the source interfaces/VLANs must be mirrored to an RSPAN VLAN, which can then be transported across one or more switches to a destination switch where the destination port for the RSPAN session is located.

To create a VLAN for RSPAN on Cisco IOS, you must create the VLAN via the config-vlan configuration mode, as opposed to using the older VLAN database configuration mode. During the process of defining VLAN parameters, you must specify that the new VLAN is an RSPAN VLAN by configuring the **remote-span** VLAN configuration command. Example 10-87 demonstrates creating an RSPAN VLAN with a VLAN ID of 100 on Switch-A.

Example 10-87 *Creating an RSPAN VLAN on Cisco IOS*

```
Switch-A# configure terminal
Switch-A(config)# vlan 100
Switch-A(config-vlan)# remote-span
Switch-A(config-vlan)# end
Switch-A# show vlan remote-span
Remote SPAN VLANs
------------------------------------------------------------------------------
100
```

In Example 10-87, the **remote-span** command is used to specify that the newly created VLAN 100 is an RSPAN VLAN, via the config-vlan configuration mode. If you attempted to create VLAN 100 using the older VLAN database method, you would not be able to configure the VLAN as an RSPAN VLAN. The configuration is verified by displaying the current RSPAN VLANs using the **show vlan remote-span** command.

On CatOS, the process used to create RSPAN VLANs is very similar to creating normal VLANs, except you must explicitly configure the new VLAN as an RSPAN VLAN. Example 10-88 demonstrates creating a VLAN on Switch-B, which will be used as an RSPAN VLAN.

Example 10-88 *Creating RSPAN VLANs on CatOS*

```
Switch-B> (enable) set vlan 100 name VLAN100 rspan
vlan 100 configuration successful
Switch-B> (enable) show vlan 100
VLAN Name                             Status    IfIndex Mod/Ports, Vlans
---- -------------------------------- --------- ------- -----------------------
100  VLAN0100                         active    61      2/1


VLAN Type  SAID       MTU   Parent RingNo BrdgNo Stp  BrdgMode Trans1 Trans2
---- ----- ---------- ----- ------ ------ ------ ---- -------- ------ ------
100  enet  100100     1500  -      -      -      -    -        0      0


VLAN MISTP-Inst DynCreated RSPAN
---- ---------- ---------- --------
100  -          static     enabled
```

In Example 10-88, the **rspan** keyword is used within the **set vlan** command to specify that the VLAN should be used to transport RSPAN traffic. The **show vlan 100** command verifies that the new VLAN 100 is configured as an RSPAN VLAN, as indicated in the RSPAN column of the shaded output.

Configuring RSPAN on Cisco IOS

Before learning how to configure RSPAN on Cisco IOS, it is important to understand exactly how Cisco IOS implements RSPAN. An RSPAN session is very similar to a SPAN session, where multiple source VLANs or interfaces can be mirrored to a destination port. The difference with RSPAN sessions is that you don't also require a destination port on the same switch.

In Figure 10-12, a simple explanation of RSPAN was provided, which indicated that on the switch configured with an RSPAN source session, traffic mirrored from the source ports or VLANs for the session is mirrored directly to an RSPAN VLAN. Although this description explains the concept of RSPAN reasonably well, it is not entirely accurate. On the Catalyst 2950/3550 switches, it is important to understand the concept of a *reflector port*, which is used literally to "reflect" traffic captured from source ports or source VLANs to an RSPAN VLAN.

Figure 10-16 demonstrates the concept of a reflector port.

Figure 10-16 *Reflector Ports for RSPAN Source Sessions*

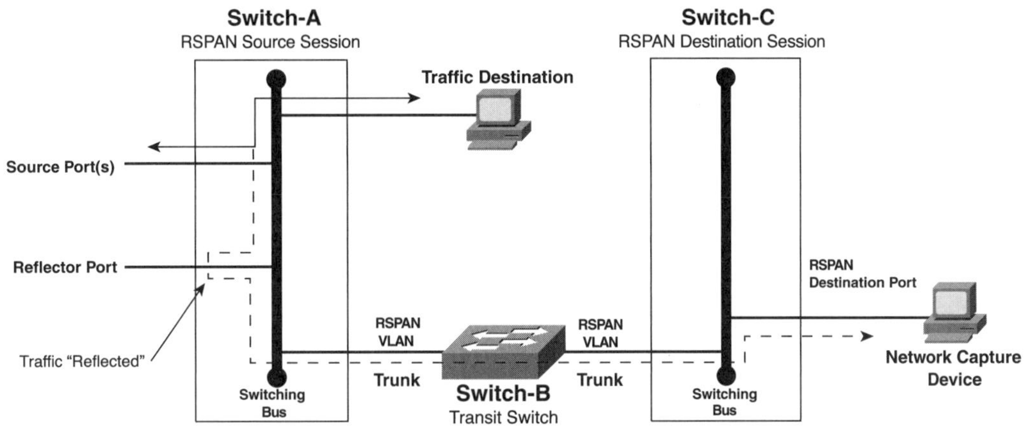

In Figure 10-16, the diagram of Figure 10-12 has been updated. On Switch-A, where the RSPAN source session is configured, only a single source port is shown, although this can be multiple source ports/VLANs. Notice that traffic captured from the source port is mirrored to a reflector port, which simply acts like a loopback interface in that it reflects the captured traffic to the RSPAN VLAN. No traffic is actually sent out the reflector port; it merely provides an internal loopback mechanism for RSPAN source sessions. Notice that a reflector port exists only for an RSPAN source session. On Switch-C, where the RSPAN destination session is configured, no reflector port is required. It is important to understand that on the Catalyst 2950/3550, when you configure an RSPAN source session, you must allocate a physical interface as a reflector port, which cannot be used for any other purposes other than reflecting RSPAN traffic. This means you must have a spare physical interface when you want to configure an RSPAN source session. If you remove an RSPAN source session, you can resume using the reflector port as a normal interface.

NOTE   Each RSPAN source session requires a separate reflector port. Traffic reflected by a reflector port also is placed on the RSPAN VLAN with any VLAN tagging information from the original frames removed, to ensure the traffic is not sent over the wrong VLAN.

Now that you understand RSPAN session limitations on Cisco IOS-based switches and how RSPAN works on the Catalyst 2950/3550 switches, it is time to learn how to configure RSPAN sessions on Cisco IOS.

NOTE   The only other Cisco IOS platform that supports RSPAN is the native IOS Catalyst 6000/
6500 running IOS 12.2SX. On this switch, you do not need to configure a reflector port
because the switch handles the process of mirroring traffic from source ports to the RSPAN
VLAN internally.

Unlike SPAN, where the source and destination ports exist on the same switch, the source and
destination ports for an RSPAN session reside on different switches. This requires a separate
RSPAN source session to be configured, as well as a separate RSPAN destination session to be
configured. The following shows the syntax used to configure an RSPAN source session:

```
Switch(config)# monitor session session-id source {interface interface-type
   interface-id | vlan vlan-id] {both | rx | tx}

Switch(config)# monitor session session-id destination remote vlan rspan-vlan
   reflector-port interface-type interface-id
```

Notice that when configuring an RSPAN source session, you must first define the source
ports for the session and then use a separate command to define the reflector port. Within
the reflector port configuration, you also specify the RSPAN VLAN to which captured
traffic should be placed. The following shows the syntax used to configure an RSPAN destination session:

```
Switch(config)# monitor session session-id source remote vlan rspan-vlan

Switch(config)# monitor session session-id destination interface interface-type
   interface-id [encapsulation {dot1q | isl}]
```

In this scenario, Host-Z is currently connected to port 2/3 on Switch-B; hence, Switch-A is
initially configured with an RSPAN source session, with Switch-B configured with an
RSPAN destination session. Later on when RSPAN operation is verified, the RSPAN roles
of Switch-A and Switch-B are swapped, with Switch-A configured with an RSPAN destination session. Example 10-89 demonstrates configuring an RSPAN source session on
Switch-A that captures traffic received from Host-A. This requires configuring interface
fastEthernet0/2 attached as the source port, VLAN 100 created in Example 10-87 as the
RSPAN VLAN, and an unused interface on the switch as a reflector port.

Example 10-89 *Configuring an RSPAN Source Session on Cisco IOS*

```
Switch-A# configure terminal
Switch-A(config)# monitor session 1 source interface fastEthernet0/2 rx
Switch-A(config)# monitor session 1 destination remote vlan 100
   reflector-port fastEthernet0/24
Switch-A(config)# exit
Switch-A# show monitor
Session 1
----------
Type              : Remote Source Session
Source Ports      :
    Rx            : Fa0/2
Reflector Port    : Fa0/24
Dest RSPAN VLAN   : 100
```

In Example 10-89, an RSPAN source session is created with a session ID of 1, which specifies traffic received on fastEthernet 0/2 should be captured and should subsequently be mirrored to the RSPAN VLAN 100 using a reflector port of interface fastEthernet0/24. The **show monitor** command is used to verify the configuration. Notice that the session type indicates the SPAN session is an RSPAN source session and also indicates the reflector port and destination RSPAN VLAN.

Configuring RSPAN on CatOS

In this section, the configuration of RSPAN on CatOS (Switch-B) is demonstrated. Before learning how to configure RSPAN on CatOS, it is important to understand how RSPAN is implemented on CatOS. On CatOS, the implementation of RSPAN varies depending on the switch platform used. On the Catalyst 2900/4000 switches, the same concept of a reflector port used on Cisco IOS is used, where you must explicitly configure an unused port as a reflector port. On the Catalyst 6000/6500 switch, you do not need to configure reflector ports; the switch automatically provides the reflector port functionality internally without using up a physical port.

To configure an RSPAN source session on a Catalyst 2900/4000 switch, the **set rspan source** command is used:

```
Console> (enable) set rspan source {mod/port(s) | vlan-id(s)}_rspan-vlan
   reflector mod/port [rx | tx | both] [filter vlan-id(s)] [create]
```

The **rspan-vlan** parameter allows you to configure the RSPAN VLAN, while the **reflector** keyword allows you to configure the reflector port. All other configuration parameters have the same meaning as when configuring a SPAN session.

To configure an RSPAN source session on a Catalyst 6000/6500 switch, the same **set rspan source** command is used; however, you do not configure a reflector port:

```
Console> (enable) set rspan source {mod/port(s) | vlan-id(s)}
   [rx | tx | both] [filter vlan-id(s)] [create]
```

To configure an RSPAN destination session on all CatOS platforms, the **set rspan destination** command is used:

```
Console> (enable) set rspan destination mod/port rspan-vlan
   [inpkts {enable | disable}] [learning {enable | disable}] [create]
```

The **rspan-vlan** parameter specifies the RSPAN VLAN from which traffic should be mirrored to the specified destination port. All other configuration parameters have the same meaning as when configuring a SPAN session.

In this scenario, Switch-B is a Catalyst 6000/6500 with Host-Z (the network capture device) attached. In the previous section, Switch-A was configured with an RSPAN source session; hence, Switch-B requires an RSPAN destination session to be configured. Example 10-90 demonstrates creating an RSPAN destination session on Switch-B, which mirrors traffic received on the RSPAN VLAN 100 to the port attached to Host-Z and also enables Host-Z to still communicate with the network.

Example 10-90 *Creating an RSPAN Destination Session on CatOS*

```
Switch-B> (enable) set rspan destination 2/3 100 inpkts enable create
Rspan Type        : Destination
Destination       : Port 2/3
Rspan Vlan        : 100
Admin Source      : -
Oper Source       : -
Direction         : -
Incoming Packets: enabled
Learning          : enabled
Filter            : -
Status            : active
```

In Example 10-90, the output displayed after executing the **set rspan destination** command indicates that the RSPAN session is a destination session, the destination port is port 2/3 and the RSPAN VLAN from which traffic is mirrored is VLAN 100.

NOTE   You can use the **show rspan** command to display the same output as Example 10-90 for all RSPAN sessions currently configured.

Verifying RSPAN Operation

At this stage, Switch-A has been configured with an RSPAN source session, mirroring only traffic received by Host-A to the RSPAN VLAN 100, which is then sent across the trunk to Switch-B. On Switch-B, an RSPAN destination has been configured, which mirrors traffic received via the RSPAN VLAN 100 to port 2/3, which is attached to Host-Z. Assuming the continuous ping between Host-B and Host-A established in Example 10-81 is still operating, the network capture software on Host-Z should capture all traffic received by Host-A, as shown in Figure 10-17.

In Figure 10-17, the display has been configured to display only ICMP traffic. Comparing Figure 10-17 with Figure 10-14, notice that only ICMP echo replies sent from Host-A to Host-B have been captured, which is due to the fact that the RSPAN source session configured on Switch-A mirrors only traffic received on interface fastEthernet0/2 from Host-A, or in other words, traffic sent by Host-A.

After verifying RSPAN operation with Switch-A configured as the RSPAN source and Switch-B configured as the RSPAN destination, it is a good idea to configure RSPAN in the reverse direction, where Switch-B is configured as the RSPAN source and Switch-A is configured as the RSPAN destination. This requires Host-Z to be attached on interface fastEthernet0/3 on Switch-A, which enables Host-Z to capture traffic mirrored from Host-B attached to Switch-B.

Figure 10-17 *Traffic Received by Host-A Captured on Host-Z Using RSPAN*

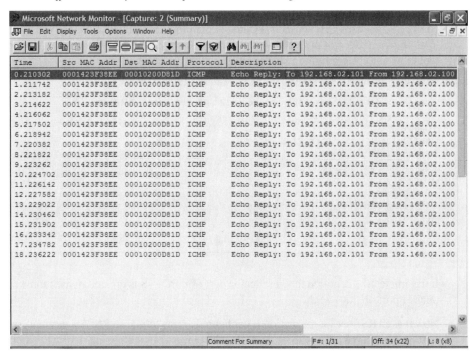

Example 10-91 demonstrates clearing current RSPAN sessions on Switch-B and creating
an RSPAN source session that mirrors only traffic received on port 2/2 from Host-B.

Example 10-91 *Creating an RSPAN Source Session on CatOS*

```
Switch-B> (enable) set rspan disable destination all
This command will disable all remote span destination session(s).
Do you want to continue (y/n) [n]? y
Disabled monitoring of remote span traffic for all rspan destination ports.
Switch-B> (enable) set rspan source 2/2 100 rx
Rspan Type       : Source
Destination      : -
Rspan Vlan       : 100
Admin Source     : Port 2/2
Oper Source      : Port 2/2
Direction        : receive
Incoming Packets: -
Learning         : -
Filter           : -
Status           : active
```

In Example 10-91, the RSPAN destination session previously configured is removed, using the **set rspan disable destination all** command. Next, an RSPAN source session is configured. Because Switch-B is a Catalyst 6000/6500 switch, notice that you don't have to configure a reflector port. If Switch-B were a Catalyst 2900/4000 switch, a reflector port would need to be configured, as demonstrated in Example 10-92.

Example 10-92 *Creating an RSPAN Source Session on the Catalyst 2900/4000*

```
cat4000> (enable) set rspan source 2/2 100 reflector 2/48 rx
Rspan Type       : Source
Destination      : -
Reflector        : Port 2/48
Rspan Vlan       : 100
Admin Source     : Port 2/2
Oper Source      : Port 2/2
Direction        : receive
Incoming Packets: -
Learning         : -
Filter           : -
Status           : active
```

In Example 10-92, notice that a reflector port of port 2/48 is created, which must be an unused port on the switch.

Now that an RSPAN source session is configured on Switch-B, an RSPAN destination session is required on Switch-A. Example 10-93 demonstrates clearing all RSPAN source sessions on Switch-A and then creating an RSPAN destination session.

Example 10-93 *Configuring an RSPAN Destination Session on Cisco IOS*

```
Switch-A# configure terminal
Switch-A(config)# no monitor session remote
Switch-A(config)# monitor session 1 source remote vlan 100
Switch-A(config)# monitor session 1 destination interface fastEthernet0/3 ingress
  vlan 1
Switch-A(config)# exit
Switch-A# show monitor
Session 1
---------
Type              : Remote Destination Session
Source RSPAN VLAN : 100
Destination Ports : Fa0/3
    Encapsulation: Native
          Ingress: Enabled, default VLAN = 1
```

In Example 10-93, the **no monitor session remote** command is used to remove any current RSPAN sessions (the **no monitor session all** command can also be used to remove all SPAN and RSPAN sessions). Next, VLAN 100 is configured as the source RSPAN VLAN and interface fastEthernet0/3 is then configured as the destination interface to which traffic received from the source RSPAN VLAN should be mirrored. The **ingress vlan 1** configuration allows Host-Z to still communicate with the rest of the network on VLAN 1.

At this point, assuming the continuous ping between Host-B and Host-A established in Example 10-81 is still operating, the network capture software on Host-Z should capture all traffic received by Host-B, as shown in Figure 10-18.

Figure 10-18 *Traffic Received by Host-B Captured on Host-Z Using RSPAN*

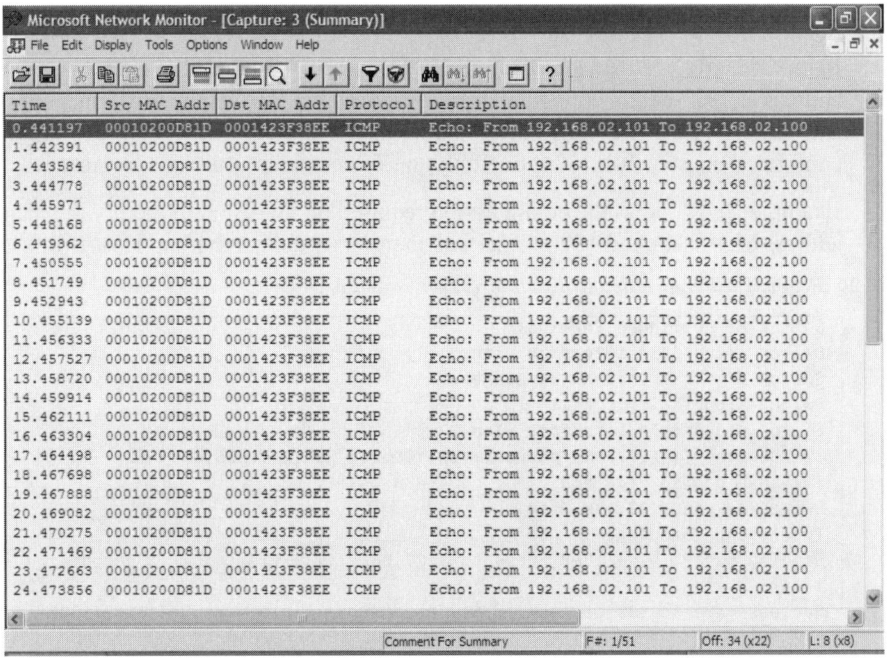

In Figure 10-18, the display has been configured to display only ICMP traffic. Comparing Figure 10-18 with Figure 10-14, notice that only ICMP echo requests sent from Host-B to Host-A have been captured, which is due to the fact that the RSPAN source session configured on Switch-B in Example 10-91 only mirrors traffic received on port 2/3 from Host-B, or in other words, traffic sent by Host-B.

Configuring VACLs

As a final configuration task, you now learn how to configure the capture feature of VLAN access control lists to capture traffic. Using VACLs to capture traffic is a feature supported only on the Catalyst 6000/6500 switch and requires a policy feature card (PFC) installed. Using VACLs to capture traffic provides some benefits over the use of SPAN, in that you can specify what types of traffic you want to capture based upon Layer 3 (IP) and Layer 4 (e.g., TCP, UDP, and ICMP) parameters. There are also no SPAN or RSPAN session limitations to worry about. The only limitation when using VACLs to capture traffic is TCAM usage, which is unlikely to be exhausted in most environments.

Configuring VACLs to capture traffic requires the following configuration tasks:

- Defining VACL(s) that specify which type of traffic should be captured
- Defining one or more capture ports to which traffic should be mirrored
- Applying VACL(s) to the appropriate VLANs that you want to capture traffic from

In this scenario, the management address of Switch-A is placed into VLAN 2, with an IP address of 192.168.2.1 configured. This enables Host-B to establish a Telnet connection to Switch-A, while at the same time generate ICMP traffic to Host-A. VACLs are then configured on Switch-B to capture only the Telnet traffic generated by Host-B.

Example 10-94 shows the configuration required on Switch-A to modify the management address of Switch-A to 192.168.2.1 and then verify connectivity to Host-B in VLAN 2.

Example 10-94 *Reconfiguring the Management Address on Switch-A*

```
Switch-A# configure terminal
Switch-A(config)# interface vlan 1
Switch-A(config-if)# no ip address
Switch-A(config-if)# exit
Switch-A(config)# interface vlan 2
Switch-A(config-if)# ip address 192.168.2.1 255.255.255.0
Switch-A(config-if)# end
Switch-A# ping 192.168.2.101
Type escape sequence to abort.
Sending 5, 100-byte ICMP Echos to 192.168.2.101, timeout is 2 seconds:
!!!!!
Success rate is 100 percent (5/5), round-trip min/avg/max = 1/200/1000 ms
```

Now that the management address of Switch-A has been modified, configuration of VACLs on Switch-B can begin.

NOTE   The configuration syntax for VACLs was discussed in Chapter 8, so if you are unsure of the syntax required, please refer back to Chapter 8.

When configuring VACLs to capture traffic, you can selectively specify that traffic classified by each access control entry (ACE) in the VACL should be captured by simply specifying the **capture** keyword at the end of the ACE. Example 10-95 demonstrates creating a VACL on Switch-B that captures Telnet traffic.

Example 10-95 *Creating a VLAN ACL*

```
Switch-B> (enable) set security acl ip TELNET permit tcp any any eq telnet
  capture
TELNET editbuffer modified. Use 'commit' command to apply changes.
Switch-B> (enable) set security acl ip TELNET permit any
TELNET editbuffer modified. Use 'commit' command to apply changes.
Switch-B> (enable) commit security acl all
ACL commit in progress.
ACL TELNET is committed to hardware.
```

In Example 10-95, the first ACE is used to specify that any Telnet traffic should be permitted and should also be captured as indicated the **capture** keyword. The second ACE specifies that any other IP traffic should be permitted but not captured. If you don't configure the second ACE in Example 10-91, all other IP traffic is dropped by the VACL because there is an implicit deny all at the end of a VLAN ACL. After the VACL is configured, it is programmed to the PFC using the **commit security acl all** command.

Now that a VACL has been configured that specifies the traffic you want to capture, the next configuration task is to define the list of capture ports to which the captured traffic will be mirrored. On the Catalyst 6000/6500, only a single list of capture ports exists, which is configured using the **set security acl capture-ports** command as demonstrated in Example 10-96.

Example 10-96 *Configuring the VLAN ACL Capture Port List*

```
Switch-B> (enable) set security acl capture-ports 2/3
Successfully set the following ports to capture ACL traffic:
2/3
```

In Example 10-96, port 2/3 (connected to Host-Z) is configured as a capture port.

It is important to understand that capture ports receive traffic from all VACLs. The **set security acl capture-ports** command defines a global capture port list for the entire switch. If multiple VACLs are configured that capture traffic from multiple VLANs, and you want to capture traffic only from a specific VLAN, you can control exactly what traffic is mirrored out a capture port by configuring the port as an access port in the VLAN that you want.

Now that the VACL has been configured and capture ports have been defined, the final configuration task is to map the VACL to the VLAN(s) for which you want to capture traffic. Example 10-97 demonstrates mapping the Telnet VACL created in Example 10-95 to VLAN 2, where Host-A, Host-B, and Switch-A are connected.

Example 10-97 *Mapping a VLAN ACL to a VLAN*

```
Switch-A> (enable) set security acl map TELNET 2
Mapping in progress.
VLAN 2 successfully mapped to ACL TELNET.
```

After you have mapped the VLAN ACL to VLAN 2, all traffic within VLAN 2 is inspected against the VLAN ACL.

At this stage, the VACL configuration is complete on Switch-B and it is time to verify the VACL capture configuration. On Host-B, the continuous ping to Host-A should still be operational. However, some Telnet traffic now needs to be generated to test the VACL on Switch-B. Before this happens, Host-Z must be connected to port 2/3 and must be configured to start capturing traffic.

Assuming the continuous ping to Host-A is still running (established in Example 10-81) and that Host-Z has been connected to port 2/3 on Switch-A and is capturing traffic, Example 10-98 demonstrates establishing a Telnet connection to the new management IP address of Switch-A.

Example 10-98 *Generating Telnet Traffic in VLAN 2*

```
C:\> telnet 192.168.2.1
Connecting To 192.168.2.1...
User Access Verification

Password: *****
Switch-A>
```

On Host-Z, the traffic capture software should capture only the Telnet traffic generated in Example 10-98. The ICMP traffic generated between Host-B and Host-A should not be captured due to the VACL configuration, as demonstrated in Figure 10-19.

Figure 10-19 *Traffic Captured on Host-Z Using VACL Capture*

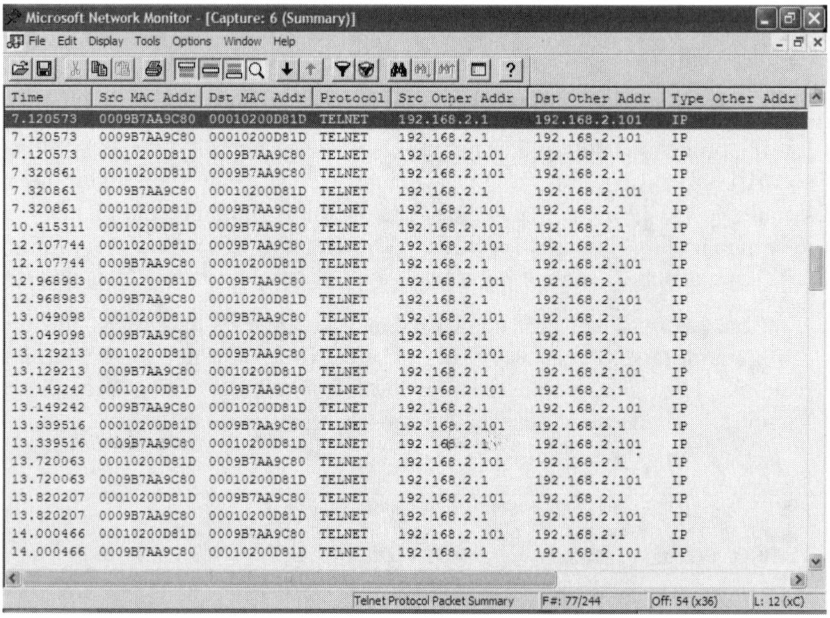

In Figure 10-19, you can see that only Telnet traffic has been captured between Host-B and Switch-A. No ICMP packets or any other type of packets have been captured, indicating the VACL capture configuration is working.

Summary

Cisco Catalyst LAN switches possess many features that make them much more than just a "dumb" Layer 2 switch. All Catalyst switches offer a rich operating system interface that enables you to perform advanced maintenance, monitoring, and troubleshooting tasks. In terms of maintenance, Catalyst switches are easy to upgrade, allowing you to protect your investment by adding new features to your existing switches as they become available. Flexible backup mechanisms allow you to store configuration files and image files at a remote network location using TFTP; you can also use TFTP to restore files as you want. All backup, restore, and upgrade operations can be performed across the network, reducing the administrative overhead of these tasks and allowing switches to be maintained remotely. You learned about common troubleshooting issues within LAN networks and how you can identify and resolve these issues. Common issues include port startup delays, which can cause a workstation to not have network connectivity when it first boots. Another common issue on CatOS-based switches is the errDisable port state, which means that the switch has shut down the port in response to some error condition. A variety of reasons why the errDisable state is invoked exist, and you learned how to identify and resolve them.

The ability to capture traffic within a switched network is also important. Traditionally, in hub-based networks, traffic capture has simply been a process of attaching to a hub port and because of the shared nature of hubs, all traffic can be captured. Switches are designed for efficiency and send only unicast traffic out the ports upon which destination systems are located. This makes it much more difficult to capture traffic in a switched environment. Cisco provides SPAN, RSPAN, and VLAN ACLs as mechanisms by which you can capture traffic on a switch.

## CHAPTER 11

Comprehensive Switching Self-Study Lab

This chapter presents a complex LAN topology and requires you to configure it to certain specifications. The content of this lab draws upon the content covered in the previous chapters and is designed to allow you to apply the content you have learned throughout the book to a real-world network. This lab is particularly useful if you are a CCIE lab candidate and want to gain experience configuring features on the Catalyst 3550 series switch.

NOTE	You can find detailed solutions to these labs in Appendixes A, "Comprehensive Switching Self-Study Lab Part I Solution" and B, "Comprehensive Switching Self-Study Lab Part II Solution".

The lab consists of two portions. In Part I, the entire LAN topology is Layer 2 based, relying on spanning tree to ensure convergence in the event of a switch or link failure. Part I uses a router-on-a-stick architecture to provide inter-VLAN routing. Figure 11-1 shows the network topology for Part I.

Figure 11-1 *Part I Lab Topology*

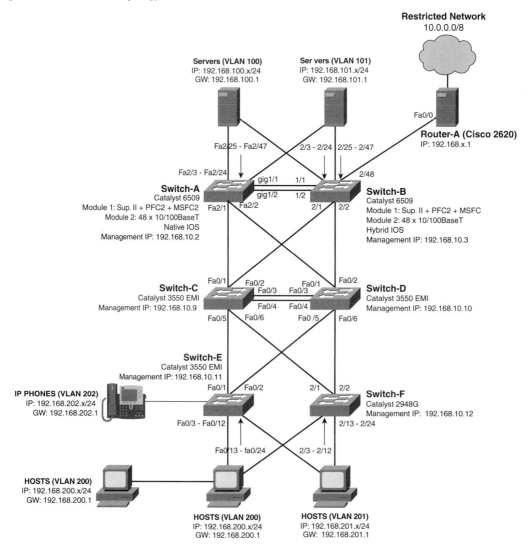

In Part II, you migrate the flat Layer 2 topology of Part I to a multilayer topology, which relies more on IP routing protocols (rather than spanning tree) for convergence. Figure 11-2 shows the network topology for Part II.

Figure 11-2   *Part II Lab Topology*

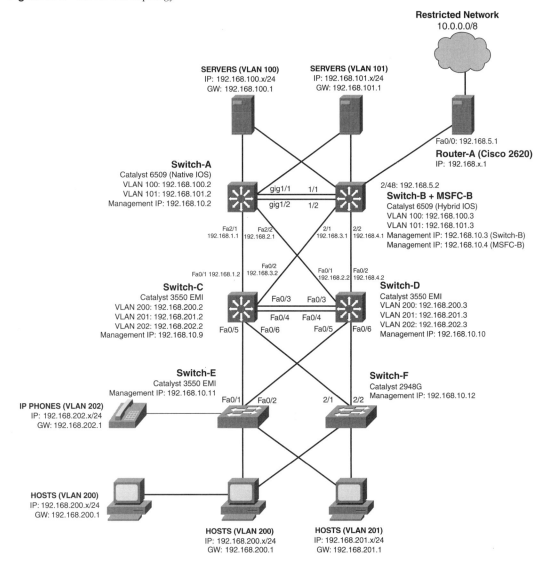

Lab Hardware Requirements

If you wish to attempt to complete this lab on your own hardware, Table 11-1 lists the hardware platforms and software versions that were used when creating this lab. Don't worry if you don't have any hardware with which to complete this lab, the solutions provided in the appendices are explained in a manner that is very helpful without the actual hardware.

Table 11-1   *Lab Hardware Requirements*

Device	Modules (per device)	Software Version
3 × Catalyst 3550-24 EMI	—	Cisco IOS Release 12.1(12)EA
1 × Catalyst 2948G	—	CatOS 7.4
2 × Catalyst 6509	Supervisor 2 MSFC-2 48-port 10/100BASE-T 4 × 1000BASE-SX GBIC	CatOS 7.4 Cisco IOS Release 12.1(8a)E4[1] Cisco IOS Release 12.1(11b)E4[2]
1 × Cisco 2620 Router	1 × 10/100BASE-T	Cisco IOS Release 12.1(5)T

[1]This image is required on MSFC-A.

[2]This image is required for Switch-B in native IOS mode.

Part I: Configuring a Layer 2 Switching Infrastructure

The following are the tasks you are required to complete in this part of the Self-Study Lab:

- Connecting the network
- Port, EtherChannel, and Trunking configuration
- VLAN configuration
- Spanning-tree configuration
- Inter-VLAN routing configuration
- Management and security configuration
- Quality of Service configuration

NOTE   A detailed solution to this part of the Self-Study Lab is in Appendix A.

Connecting the Network

Step 1   Connect the network as show in Figure 11-1. All Fast Ethernet connections between switches require crossover UTP cables. For the two gigabit Ethernet connections between Switch-A and Switch-B, multi-mode fiber is required with SC connectors.

Step 2   Configure each switch with the appropriate host name and configure a Telnet/enable password of "cisco."

Port, EtherChannel, and Trunking Configuration

Step 1   On all switches, configure all Fast Ethernet ports that connect to other switches for 100-Mbps full-duplex operation. On gigabit Ethernet ports, configure speed and duplex according to Cisco's recommendations.

Step 2   Configure the two physical links that attach Switch-A and Switch-B so that they appear as a single Layer 2 connection. Ensure the configuration meets the following requirements:

- A single physical link failure must not affect the spanning-tree topology.

- Traffic should be distributed across the links based upon IP source and destination addressing.

- Configure the links so that they are optimized for frames exchanged between two network attached storage (NAS) devices.

- If receive buffers on either switch become full, configure both switches to send 802.3Z pause frames to temporarily stop the sending of frames.

Step 3   Configure the two physical links that attach Switch-C and Switch-D so that they appear as a single Layer 2 connection. Ensure the configuration meets the following requirement:

- Switch-C should always try to actively negotiate the use of both links, while Switch-D should respond only to negotiations from Switch-C.

Step 4   Configure trunks for all Inter-Switch Links (ISLs) in the network as follows:

- Trunks between the core switches (Switch-A and Switch-B) must tag all frames with an appropriate VLAN ID. Configure Dynamic Trunking Protocol (DTP) so that the trunk always comes up.

- All other trunks should be configured with a standards-based trunking protocol and should always try to actively negotiate trunking where possible.

VLAN Configuration

Step 1   Configure VLAN Trunking Protocol (VTP) parameters as follows:

- Switch-A, Switch-B, and Switch-F should belong to a VTP domain called "ciscolab."

- All other switches must be configured to belong to a VTP domain called "ccnp."

- Switch-D should ignore VTP messages, but must propagate them to other switches.

- All VTP communications must be secured.

- Broadcast and multicast traffic within each VLAN should be propagated only to switches that connect active hosts on the VLAN.

- Switch-A and Switch-C can write only to the VLAN database. All other switches must be able to read only the VLAN database.

Step 2 Create the following VLANs, each with a name as indicated in the parenthesis:

- VLAN 10 (management)

- VLAN 100 (servers100)

- VLAN 101 (servers101)

- VLAN 200 (users200)

- VLAN 201 (users201)

- VLAN 202 (phones)

Step 3 On Switch-A and Switch-B, configure the following VLAN memberships for each interface:

- **VLAN 100**—Ports 2/3 to 2/24

- **VLAN 101**—Ports 2/25 to 2/47

Step 4 On Switch-E, configure the following VLAN memberships for each interface:

- **VLAN 200**—Fa0/3 to Fa0/12

- **VLAN 201**—Fa0/13 to Fa0/24

Step 5 On Switch-F, configure the following VLAN memberships for each interface:

- **VLAN 200**—2/3 to 2/12

- **VLAN 201**—2/13 to 2/24

- Disable ports 2/25 to 2/48

Step 6 On all switches, configure all 802.1Q trunks so that any traffic sent on VLAN 10 is not tagged.

Spanning-Tree Configuration

Step 1   Configure spanning tree so that Switch-A is the root bridge for all even VLANs and Switch-B is the root bridge for all odd VLANs. Switch-A should be configured as the secondary bridge for all odd VLANs, and Switch-B should be configured as the secondary root bridge for all even VLANs. Configuring spanning-tree timers to ensure that the convergence time of the topology is the most optimal configuration, without placing any additional CPU load on each switch.

Step 2   Configure the network so that all traffic within even VLANs follows the most optimal path towards the root bridge for even VLANs (Switch-A). Ensure that all traffic within odd VLANs follows the most optimal path towards the root bridge for odd VLANs (Switch-B).

Step 3   Ensure that all workstation ports attached to VLAN 201 on Switch-E and Switch-F provide network connectivity within a few seconds after being activated. Configure Switch-E and Switch-F so that BPDUs are not sent out these ports by default.

Step 4   Configure the network so that Switch-E and Switch-F can recover from direct link failures to Switch-C or Switch-D within 3 seconds. Assume that the MAC address tables of Switch-E and Switch-F hold 600 local MAC addresses.

Step 5   Devices in VLAN 100 and VLAN 101 are attached only to the core switches (Switch-A and Switch-B). Ensure that no spanning-tree instance runs for these VLANs on Switch-C, Switch-D, Switch-E ,and Switch-F. You cannot explicitly disable spanning tree on any VLAN for this task.

Inter-VLAN Routing Configuration

Step 1   Configure the connection to Router-A as an 802.1Q trunk, ensuring that Switch-A is configured with the appropriate DTP mode of operation that is compatible with Router-A.

Step 2   Configure Router-A for inter-VLAN routing. Router-A should use an IP address of 192.168.x.1 on each VLAN, where x represents the VLAN ID. For example, on VLAN 10, Router-A should be configured with an IP address of 192.168.10.1. Also, configure an interface that represents a restricted network attached to Router-A (see Figure 11-1).

Step 3   Configure all switches in the network with the management IP addressing as indicated in Figure 11-1. Ensure that all switches can ping any device in the network.

Management and Security Configuration

Step 1   Configure Simple Network Management Protocol (SNMP) on all switches. Configure a read-only string of "cisco" and enable traps for all events to be sent to an SNMP host at 192.168.100.50.

Step 2   Restrict Telnet access on all switches to only hosts that reside in VLAN 100. Also, restrict SNMP access to the SNMP host at 192.168.100.50.

Step 3   An Network Time Protocol (NTP) server is available on the network. Configure all switches so that each has similar clock settings as follows:

- NTP server has an IP address of 192.168.100.50.

- Clock zone is Eastern Standard Time (GMT -5 hours).

Step 4   To ensure the security of the IP phones in VLAN 202, configure the network so that only the communications required to support the IP phones are permitted. All other traffic must be discarded and you must ensure that unauthorized traffic is discarded as soon as possible. The following lists the protocols that must be permitted from the perspective of communications originating from the IP phones:

- **Skinny Call Control Protocol (SCCP)**—TCP traffic sent to a destination port of 2000 on Cisco CallManager

- **Voice traffic**—User Datagram Protocol (UDP) traffic with source and destination ports in the range of 16384–32767

- **HTTP traffic**—TCP traffic sent to a destination port 80

- **Trivial File Transfer Protocol (TFTP) traffic**—UDP traffic sent to a destination port of 69

- **Dynamic Host Configuration Protocol (DHCP) traffic**—UDP traffic using a source port of 67 and destination port of 68

- **Internet Control Message Protocol (ICMP) traffic (for diagnostic purposes)**—ICMP echo and echo replies

Step 5   Configure Switch-E to permit access only to a PC with a MAC address of 0010.0010.0010 on interface Fa0/24. No other devices should be permitted access to the interface. If another device attempts to use the interface, the interface should be shut down immediately.

Step 6   Configure the core of the network (Switch-A and Switch-B) to permit communications only between VLANs within the local switching infrastructure, ensuring local devices cannot communicate with the protected network (10.0.0.0/8). Configure these requirements using the least amount of configuration possible.

Quality of Service Configuration

Step 1 Ensure that all traffic generated by all end devices attached to Switch-E is classified as follows upon entry to the network:

- All voice traffic should be marked with a Differentiated Services Code Point (DSCP) of 46. Voice control traffic (SCCP) should be marked with a DSCP value of 26.

- All SQL server traffic (TCP traffic sent to a destination port of 1433) should be marked with a DSCP of 24.

- All other traffic is marked with a DSCP of 8.

Step 2 Configure Switch-E so that IP phones connected to interfaces Fa0/3–Fa0/12 transmit voice in VLAN 202 and data from any attached PCs in VLAN 200. Also ensure that any data received from PCs connected to an IP phone has a class of service (CoS) of three.

Step 3 Web servers are attached to Switch-A and Switch-B. On the client side of HTTP connections, limit HTTP traffic to 1 Mbps per device (devices connected to Switch-E are considered client side). On the server side, limit HTTP traffic to 1 Mbps per connection (devices connected to Switch-A and Switch-B are considered server side).

Step 4 Configure the network so that the quality of service (QoS) policy configured at the edge is honored throughout the network. Ensure that all voice packets marked with a DSCP of 46 are placed into a priority queue for transmission where possible (assume that the Ethernet modules on Switch-A are WS-X6148-RJ45 with a transmit port type of 2q2t). Trust the IP precedence of traffic received from Router-A.

Part II: Multilayer Configuration

The following are the tasks you are required to complete in this part of the Self-Study Lab:

- Core layer configuration
- Distribution and access layer configuration
- Routing and multicast routing configuration

NOTE A detailed solution to this part of the Self-Study Lab is in Appendix B.

Core Layer Configuration

Step 1   To avoid any IP addressing conflicts with Router-A while you convert the network, disconnect Router-A from Switch-B.

Step 2   The new multilayer topology has split the Layer 2 domain into smaller pieces. Ensure that Switch-A and Switch-B are configured appropriately to ensure the VTP, VLAN, and spanning-tree parameters configured in the first lab are maintained in the new core Layer 2 topology that connects servers.

Step 3   Configure Switch-A and Switch-B as Layer 3 switches using the IP addressing indicated in Figure 11-2. Assume a 24-bit subnet mask for all subnets. Switch-B has an Multilayer Switch Feature Card (MSFC) installed that provides Layer 3 switching and is to be named "MSFC-B." Ensure that physical interfaces are configured as routed interfaces wherever possible, instead of using switch virtual interfaces (SVIs). If required, you are permitted to create new VLANs.

Step 4   Ensure that devices connected to VLANs 100 and 101 can still connect to the rest of the network without reconfiguration of the IP addressing parameters on any edge device in these VLANs. Traffic for VLAN 100 should be routed through Switch-A and traffic for VLAN 101 should be routed through MSFC-B. However, should either of the routing engines on either core switch fail, the remaining working routing engine should take over.

Distribution and Access Layer Configuration

Step 1   The new multilayer topology has split the Layer 2 domain into smaller pieces. Ensure that Switch-C, Switch-D, Switch-E, and Switch-F are configured appropriately to ensure the VTP, VLAN, and spanning-tree parameters configured in the first lab are maintained in the new Layer 2 topology. You should configure all switches to belong to the same VTP domain.

Step 2   Configure Switch-C and Switch-D as Layer 3 switches using the IP addressing shown in Figure 11-2. Ensure that physical interfaces are configured as routed interfaces wherever possible, instead of using SVIs. If required, you are permitted to create new VLANs.

Step 3   Configure the network so that devices connected to VLANs 200, 201, and 202 can still connect to the rest of the network without reconfiguration of the IP addressing parameters on any edge device in these VLANs. You must ensure that edge devices can still connect to the rest of the network within 5 seconds after the failure of either Switch-C or Switch-D. The routed traffic load should be shared for even and odd VLANs by Switch-C and Switch-D, respectively.

Routing and Multicast Routing Configuration

Step 1 Configure Router-A as indicated in Figure 11-2. The FastEthernet0/0 interface should now be configured as a non-trunk port with a single IP address configured, as shown in Figure 11-2. Once complete, reconnect Router-A to Switch-B.

Step 2 Ensure that all switches can be managed using the 192.168.10.x addressing used in Part I. The management IP addresses configured on each device cannot be altered, although you may alter the subnet mask and default gateway configuration.

Step 3 Configure Enhanced Interior Gateway Routing Protocol (EIGRP) on all routing devices so that any device in the network can communicate with any other device, regardless of the location in the network.

Step 4 Configure multicast routing on all routing devices, which includes all switches except for Switch-E and Switch-F. Configure a shared tree that is rooted at Router-A, which should be used for initial forwarding of multicast traffic. You are not permitted to manually configure Router-A as the root of the shared tree on any other multicast router. Ensure all interfaces enabled for multicast routing are operating in the appropriate mode as recommended by Cisco.

Step 5 Configure Switch-E to join the multicast group 239.1.1.1 on VLAN 10. Ensure that any edge device can ping the 239.1.1.1 address with a response from Switch-E.

Step 6 Ensure that all switches constrain multicast traffic to multicast routers and receivers within each Layer 2 network.

Step 7 Ensure that any access control configurations on the core switches are still compatible with the new topology.

APPENDIX **A**

Comprehensive Switching Self-Study Lab Part I Solution

Configuring a Layer 2 Switching Infrastructure Solution

This appendix provides step-by-step solutions for each configuration task required for Part I of the Chapter 11, "Comprehensive Switching Self-Study Study Lab." Each configuration task is listed, followed by the solution for each task. At the end of this appendix, the complete configurations for each network device relevant to Part I of the lab are provided.

Connect the Network Solution

Step 1   Connect the network as show in Figure 11-1. All Fast Ethernet connections between switches require crossover UTP cables. For the two gigabit Ethernet connections between Switch-A and Switch-B, multi-mode fiber is required with SC connectors.

Step 2   Configure each switch with the appropriate host name and configure a Telnet/enable password of "cisco."

Example A-1 and Example A-2 demonstrate the required configurations on Switch-A (Cisco IOS) and Switch-B (CatOS). Refer to the complete configuration examples at the end of this appendix if you want to view the relevant configuration for this task on any other switches.

Example A-1   *Configuring Switch-A*

```
Switch> enable
Switch# configure terminal
Enter configuration commands, one per line.  End with CNTL/Z.
Switch(config)# hostname Switch-A
Switch-A(config)# enable secret cisco
Switch-A(config)# line vty 0 15
Switch-A(config-line)# password cisco
Switch-A(config-line)# end
```

In Example A-1, using the **enable secret** command instead of the **enable password** command ensures the secret password is stored in a secure, encrypted fashion on the switch.

Example A-2   *Configuring Switch-B*

```
Console> enable
Enter password:
Console> (enable) set system name Switch-B
```

continues

Example A-2 *Configuring Switch-B (Continued)*

```
System name set.
Switch-B> (enable) set password
Enter old password:
Enter new password: *****
Retype new password: *****
Password changed.
Switch-B> (enable) set enablepass
Enter old password:
Enter new password: *****
Retype new password: *****
Password changed.
```

On Switch-A, you must explicitly enable and configure each switch interface because Switch-A is running native IOS and, by default, all interfaces are Layer 3 interfaces in a shutdown state. On all other switches, all interfaces are enabled and configured as Layer 2 interfaces by default. Example A-3 shows the configuration required on Switch-A.

Example A-3 *Enabling and Configuring Layer 2 Interfaces on Switch-A*

```
Switch-A# configure terminal
Enter configuration commands, one per line.  End with CNTL/Z.
Switch-A(config)# interface range GigabitEthernet1/1 - 2
Switch-A(config-if-range)# no shutdown
Switch-A(config-if-range)# switchport
Switch-A(config-if-range)# exit
Switch-A(config)# interface range FastEthernet2/1 - 48
Switch-A(config-if-range)# no shutdown
Switch-A(config-if-range)# switchport
```

In Example A-3, all interfaces indicated on Figure 11-1 are enabled and configured as Layer 2 interfaces using the **switchport** interface configuration command.

Once you have connected the switches together, use the **show cdp neighbors** command to verify that each switch can see the correct locally connected neighbors. Example A-4 shows an example of using this command on Switch-A.

Example A-4 *Verifying Connectivity to Local Neighbors on Switch-A*

```
Switch-A# show cdp neighbors
Capability Codes: R - Router, T - Trans Bridge, B - Source Route Bridge
                  S - Switch, H - Host, I - IGMP, r - Repeater

Device ID       Local Intrfce    Holdtme    Capability  Platform  Port ID
Switch-B        Gig 1/1          173        T S I       WS-C6509  1/1
Switch-C        Fas 2/1          168        T S I       WS-C3550  0/1
Switch-D        Fas 2/2          157        T S I       WS-C3550  0/1
```

Example A-4 shows that Switch-A is connected to Switch-B, Switch-C, and Switch-D and that Layer 2 connectivity is present to each switch.

Port, EtherChannel, and Trunking Configuration Solution

Step 1   On all switches, configure all Fast Ethernet ports that connect to other switches for 100-Mbps full-duplex operation. On gigabit Ethernet ports, configure speed and duplex according to Cisco's recommendations.

Cisco recommends that all gigabit Ethernet ports be configured as autosensing, which is the default setting and thus requires no extra configuration. Autosensing on gigabit Ethernet passes a lot more information (such as flow control parameters) than is passed in the Fast Ethernet/ Ethernet auto-negotiation process.

Example A-5 and Example A-6 demonstrate configuring 100-Mbps full-duplex operation on Switch-A (Cisco IOS) and Switch-B (CatOS).

Example A-5   *Configuring Interface Speed and Duplex Settings on Switch-A*

```
Switch-A# configure terminal
Enter configuration commands, one per line.  End with CNTL/Z.
Switch-A(config)# interface range FastEthernet 2/1 - 2
Switch-A(config-if-range)# speed 100
Switch-A(config-if-range)# duplex full
Switch-A(config-if-range)# exit
```

Example A-6   *Configuring Interface Speed and Duplex Settings on Switch-B*

```
Switch-B> (enable) set port speed 2/1-2 100
Ports 2/1-2 transmission speed set to 100Mbps.
Switch-B> (enable) set port duplex 2/1-2 full
Ports 2/1-2 set to full-duplex.
```

Step 2   Configure the two physical links that attach Switch-A and Switch-B so that they appear as a single Layer 2 connection. Ensure the configuration meets the following requirements:

- A single physical link failure must not affect the spanning-tree topology.

- Traffic should be distributed across the links based upon IP source and destination addressing.

- Configure the links so that they are optimized for frames exchanged between two network attached storage (NAS) devices.

- If receive buffers on either switch become full, configure both switches to send 802.3Z pause frames.

The feature required for this configuration task is EtherChannel, which allows you to configure multiple physical interfaces as a single, virtual Layer 2 interface. The requirements dictate how you must configure Port Aggregation Protocol (PAgP) and how you need to configure load distribution. For spanning tree to work correctly with EtherChannel bundles, you configure an EtherChannel mode of desirable on both sides. This PAgP mode ensures that spanning tree does not detect a physical link failure. The second requirement is straightforward and simply requires configuration of load sharing based upon source and destination IP address. The third and fourth requirements are physical interface parameters that should be configured on each interface within the EtherChannel bundle. To optimize the links for NAS operation, enable jumbo frames, which permit an MTU of 9216 bytes for higher data throughput. You must also configure flow control on each link so that 802.3z flow control frames are exchanged if queue congestion is experienced on either switch.

Example A-7 and Example A-8 show the configuration required on Switch-A and Switch-B.

Example A-7 *Configuring EtherChannel, Jumbo Frames, and 802.3z Flow Control on Switch-A*

```
Switch-A# configure terminal
Enter configuration commands, one per line.  End with CNTL/Z.
Switch-A(config)# interface range GigabitEthernet 1/1 - 2
Switch-A(config-if-range)# mtu 9216
Switch-A(config-if-range)# flowcontrol receive on
Switch-A(config-if-range)# flowcontrol send on
Switch-A(config-if-range)# channel-group 1 mode desirable
Switch-A(config-if-range)# exit
Switch-A(config)# port-channel load-balance src-dst-ip
```

Jumbo frames are enabled on Cisco IOS software by simply modifying the maximum transmission unit (MTU) of the appropriate interface(s), as shown in Example A-7 on the Gig0/1 and Gig0/2 interfaces. Notice that you must configure each switch to both send and receive (i.e., respond to) flow control frames for flow control to correctly work.

Example A-8 *Configuring EtherChannel, Jumbo Frames, and 802.3z Flow Control on Switch-B*

```
Switch-B> (enable) set port jumbo 1/1-2 enable
Jumbo frames enabled on ports 1/1-2
Switch-B> (enable) set port flowcontrol 1/1-2 receive on
Ports 1/1-2 flow control receive administration status set to on
(ports will require far end to send flowcontrol)
Switch-B> (enable) set port flowcontrol 1/1-2 send on
Ports 1/1-2 flow control send administration status set to on
(ports will send flowcontrol to far end)
Switch-B> (enable) set port channel 1/1-2 mode desirable
Port(s) 1/1-2 channel mode set to desirable.
Switch-B> (enable) set port channel all distribution ip both
Channel distribution is set to ip both.
```

Example A-9 shows how you can verify an EtherChannel bundle has formed on Switch-B.

Example A-9 *Verifying EtherChannel Configuration*

```
Switch-B> (enable) show port channel
Port  Status    Channel            Admin Ch
```

Example A-9   *Verifying EtherChannel Configuration (Continued)*

```
                  Mode                   Group Id
-----  ----------  --------------------  -----  -----
 1/1   connected   desirable silent        40    801
 1/2   connected   desirable silent        40    801


Port   Device-ID                          Port-ID                   Platform
-----  ---------------------------------  ------------------------  ----------------
 1/1   Switch-A                           Gig1/1                    WS-C6509
 1/2   Switch-A                           Gig1/2                    WS-C6509
```

Step 3   Configure the two physical links that attach Switch-C and Switch-D so that they appear as a single Layer 2 connection. Ensure the configuration meets the following requirement:

- Switch-C should always try to actively negotiate the use of both links, while Switch-D should respond only to negotiations from Switch-C.

This task requires an EtherChannel bundle configured between Switch-C and Switch-D. You must configure Switch-C with a PAgP mode of desirable to allow it to actively negotiate and Switch-D with a PAgP mode of auto so that it responds only to PAgP negotiations. Example A-10 and Example A-11 show the configurations required on Switch-C and Switch-D.

Example A-10   *Configuring EtherChannel on Switch-C*

```
Switch-C# configure terminal
Enter configuration commands, one per line.  End with CNTL/Z.
Switch-C(config)# interface range FastEthernet 0/3 - 4
Switch-C(config-if-range)# channel-group 1 mode desirable
```

Example A-11   *Configuring EtherChannel on Switch-D*

```
Switch-D# configure terminal
Enter configuration commands, one per line.  End with CNTL/Z.
Switch-D(config)# interface range FastEthernet 0/3 - 4
Switch-D(config-if-range)# channel-group 1 mode auto
```

Step 4   Configure trunks for all Inter-Switch Links (ISLs) in the network as follows:

- Trunks between the core switches (Switch-A and Switch-B) must tag *all* frames with an appropriate VLAN ID. Configure Dynamic Trunking Protocol (DTP) so that the trunk always comes up.

- All other trunks should be configured with a standards-based trunking protocol and should always try to actively negotiate trunking where possible.

For the trunk between Switch-A and Switch-B, all frames must be tagged, which requires the use of ISL for trunking because 802.1Q trunks do not tag traffic sent on the native VLAN. A DTP mode of on must also be configured on both switches so that the trunk always comes up.

All other switches must be configured with 802.1Q trunks, because 802.1Q is a standards-based protocol, and must all be configured to operate in a DTP mode of desirable to ensure trunks are always actively negotiated.

Example A-12 and Example A-13 show the configuration required on Switch-A and Switch-B for the ISL trunk that must be configured between them, as well as the 802.1Q trunks that must be configured to Switch-C and Switch-D. Refer to the examples at the end of this appendix for the trunk configurations of the other switches.

Example A-12 *Configuring Trunking on Switch-A*

```
Switch-A# configure terminal
Enter configuration commands, one per line.  End with CNTL/Z.
Switch-A(config)# interface range GigabitEthernet 1/1 - 2
Switch-A(config-if-range)# switchport trunk encapsulation isl
Switch-A(config-if-range)# switchport mode trunk
Switch-A(config-if-range)# exit
Switch-A(config)# interface range FastEthernet 2/1 - 2
Switch-A(config-if-range)# switchport trunk encapsulation dot1q
Switch-A(config-if-range)# switchport mode dynamic desirable
```

Example A-13 *Configuring Trunking on Switch-B*

```
Switch-B> (enable) set trunk 1/1 on isl
Port(s)  1/1 trunk mode set to on.
Port(s)  1/1 trunk type set to isl.
Switch-B> (enable) set trunk 1/2 on isl
Port(s)  1/2 trunk mode set to on.
Port(s)  1/2 trunk type set to isl.
Switch-B> (enable) set trunk 2/1 desirable dot1q
Port(s)  2/1 trunk mode set to desirable.
Port(s)  2/1 trunk type set to dot1q.
Switch-B> (enable) set trunk 2/2 desirable dot1q
Port(s)  2/2 trunk mode set to desirable.
Port(s)  2/2 trunk type set to dot1q.
```

When configuring trunks on CatOS, you must configure each trunk port separately, as shown in Example A-13. You can configure a range of trunk ports only when you disable trunking (i.e., configure a mode of off).

Once configuration is complete, verify each trunk. Example A-14 and Example A-15 demonstrate verifying that each trunk is functioning on a Cisco IOS-based switch (Switch-A) and a CatOS-based switch (Switch-B).

Example A-14 *Verifying Trunking on Switch-A*

```
Switch-A# show interface trunk

Port       Mode        Encapsulation  Status      Native vlan
Gi1/1      on          isl            trunking    1
Gi1/2      on          isl            trunking    1
Fa2/1      desirable   802.1q         trunking    1
Fa2/2      desirable   802.1q         trunking    1
... <output truncated>
...
```

Example A-15 *Verifying Trunking on Switch-B*

```
Switch-B> (enable) show trunk
* - indicates vtp domain mismatch
Port       Mode         Encapsulation  Status       Native vlan
--------   -----------  -------------  -----------  -----------
1/1        on           isl            trunking     1
1/2        on           isl            trunking     1
2/1        desirable    dot1q          trunking     1
2/2        desirable    dot1q          trunking     1
15/1       nonegotiate  isl            trunking     1
...<output truncated>
...
```

Notice in Example A-15 that port 15/1 is currently trunking. This port represents the internal port to the MSFC-2 that is installed on the Supervisor 2 of Switch-B.

VLAN Configuration Solution

Step 1 Configure VLAN Trunking Protocol (VTP) parameters as follows:

- Switch-A, Switch-B, and Switch-F should belong to a VTP domain called "ciscolab."

- All VTP communications must be secured.

- All other switches must be configured to belong to a VTP domain called "ccnp."

- Switch-D should ignore VTP messages, but must propagate them to other switches.

- All VTP communications must be secured.

- Broadcast and multicast traffic within each VLAN should be propagated only to switches that connect active hosts on the VLAN.

- Switch-A and Switch-C can write only to the VLAN database. All other switches must be able to read only the VLAN database.

In the description in the previous bullet list, two VTP domains must be configured. Such a configuration is not normally the case in a LAN infrastructure under common administrative control; however, this lab is designed to thoroughly test your knowledge and understanding of LAN switching, hence the unorthodox configuration requirements described here. When switches reside in separate VTP domains, be aware of several key considerations:

- VLAN database information cannot be shared between different VTP domains. You must configure any VLAN requirements for this lab separately for each VTP domain.

- Under certain conditions, trunks will not form between switches in different VTP domains. This situation occurs when a trunk is configured with a DTP mode of desirable or auto, because these modes include VTP domain information. Therefore, for any trunks configured between switches in different VTP domains, you must configure a DTP mode of on to ensure trunks are maintained.

- When a switch is operating in VTP transparent mode, VTP version 2 must be configured to allow the transparent switch to propagate VTP messages from a different VTP domain to the VTP domain configured locally.

Because Switch-A is permitted read and write access to the VLAN database for the ciscolab VTP domain, it must be configured as a VTP server. Similarly, Switch-C must be configured as a VTP server in the ccnp VTP domain. All other switches (excluding Switch-D) are configured as VTP clients in their respective VTP domains, because VTP clients are permitted only read access to the VLAN database.

Switch-D must be configured with a VTP mode of transparent because it must ignore all VTP messages but still propagate them to other switches. Switch-D is to be configured with a VTP domain of ccnp; however, it is located between Switch-B and Switch-F, which are both in the ciscolab VTP domain. To ensure VTP messages from the ciscolab domain are propagated between Switch-B and Switch-F, VTP version 2 must be configured on Switch-D.

The other requirements are for VTP communications to be secured and for broadcast and multicast traffic in a VLAN to be propagated only to switches with active hosts within the VLAN. This configuration requires configuring VTP passwords and VTP pruning on all switches (except Switch-D).

Example A-16 shows the VTP configuration required on Switch-A, along with the reconfiguration of trunks to Switch-C and Switch-D (both of which are configured with a different VTP domain name).

Example A-16   *Configuring VTP on Switch-A*

```
Switch-A# configure terminal
Enter configuration commands, one per line.  End with CNTL/Z.
Switch-A(config)# vtp domain ciscolab
Changing VTP domain name from null to ciscolab
```

Example A-16 *Configuring VTP on Switch-A (Continued)*

```
Switch-A(config)# vtp mode server
Setting device to VTP SERVER mode
Switch-A(config)# vtp password cisco
Setting device VLAN database password to cisco.
Switch-A(config)# vtp pruning
Pruning switched on
Switch-A(config)# interface range FastEthernet 2/1 - 2
Switch-A(config-if-range)# switchport mode trunk
```

In Example A-16, the last shaded line of the output configures a DTP mode of on, which ensures the trunks to Switch-C and Switch-D form.

Example A-17 shows the VTP and trunk configuration required on Switch-B, which is identical to the configuration required on Switch-F because both switches are CatOS switches in the ciscolab domain and both are VTP clients.

Example A-17 *Configuring VTP on Switch-B*

```
Switch-B> (enable) set vtp domain ciscolab
VTP domain ciscolab modified
Switch-B> (enable) set vtp pruning enable
This command will enable the pruning function in the entire management domain.
All devices in the management domain should be pruning-capable before enabling.
Do you want to continue (y/n) [n]? y
VTP domain ciscolab modified
Switch-B > (enable) set vtp passwd cisco
Generating MD5 secret for the password ....
VTP domain ciscolab modified
Switch-B> (enable) set vtp mode client
VTP domain ciscolab modified
Switch-B> (enable) set trunk 2/1 on dot1q
Port(s)  2/1 trunk mode set to on.
Port(s)  2/1 trunk type set to dot1q.
Switch-B> (enable) set trunk 2/2 on dot1q
Port(s)  2/2 trunk mode set to on.
Port(s)  2/2 trunk type set to dot1q.
```

In Example A-17, you don't actually need to enable VTP pruning, because this feature is automatically learned from Switch-A (a VTP server).

On Switch-C, you need to apply the same configuration applied to Switch-A (see Example A-16); however, you must configure a VTP domain name of ccnp. You must also configure the trunks to Switch-A, Switch-B, and Switch-F with a DTP mode of on to ensure the trunks form. The configuration on Switch-E is the same as that configured on Switch-C, except you must configure a VTP mode of client instead of server and you do not need to modify the configuration of any trunks because each trunk connects to a switch in the ccnp VTP domain.

Finally, Example A-18 shows the VTP and trunk configuration required on Switch-D.

Example A-18 *Configuring VTP on Switch-D*

```
Switch-D# configure terminal
Enter configuration commands, one per line.  End with CNTL/Z.
Switch-D(config)# vtp domain ccnp
Changing VTP domain name from null to ccnp
Switch-D(config)# vtp version 2
Switch-D(config)# vtp mode transparent
Setting device to VTP TRANSPARENT mode
Switch-D(config)# interface range FastEthernet 0/1 - 2 , FastEthernet0/6
Switch-D(config-if-range)# switchport mode trunk
```

In Example A-18, notice that VTP version 2 is configured to ensure that Switch-D propagates VTP messages for the ciscolab domain sent from Switch-B to Switch-F. The last configuration of Example A-18 configures each trunk connected to a switch in the ciscolab domain with a DTP mode of on to ensure the trunks form.

Once your VTP configurations are in place, verify that all trunks are still functioning using the **show trunk** command (CatOS) and **show interface trunk** command (Cisco IOS).

Step 2   Create the following VLANs, each with a name as indicated in the parenthesis:

- VLAN 10 (management)
- VLAN 100 (servers100)
- VLAN 101 (servers101)
- VLAN 200 (users200)
- VLAN 201 (users201)
- VLAN 202 (phones)

For this task, create the VLANs on the VTP servers in each VTP domain (remember, you can't create VLANs on VTP clients). You also need to create the VLANs on Switch-D because Switch-D is operating in VTP transparent mode and, therefore, uses only a locally configured VLAN database. Example A-19 demonstrates the configuration required on Switch-A, which is a VTP server for the ciscolab domain. The exact same configuration is also required on Switch-C (VTP server for ccnp domain) and on Switch-D.

TIP   VTP communications are passed only over trunk interfaces, so you must verify in advance that all trunks are working to ensure that the VLAN information is propagated to all switches.

Example A-19 *Configuring VLANs on Switch-A*

```
Switch-A# configure terminal
Enter configuration commands, one per line.  End with CNTL/Z.
Switch-A(config)# vlan 10
Switch-A(config-vlan)# name management
Switch-A(config-vlan)# exit
Switch-A(config)# vlan 100
Switch-A(config-vlan)# name servers100
Switch-A(config-vlan)# exit
Switch-A(config)# vlan 101
Switch-A(config-vlan)# name servers101
Switch-A(config-vlan)# exit
Switch-A(config)# vlan 200
Switch-A(config-vlan)# name users200
Switch-A(config-vlan)# exit
Switch-A(config)# vlan 201
Switch-A(config-vlan)# name users201
Switch-A(config-vlan)# exit
Switch-A(config)# vlan 202
Switch-A(config-vlan)# name phones
Switch-A(config-vlan)# exit
```

Once complete, verify your configuration is correct on each VTP server and on all other VTP client switches to ensure VTP is working correctly. Also verify the VLAN configuration is correct on Switch-D. The real test that everything is configured correctly is to verify that all VLANs are present in the VLAN database of Switch-F, because VTP messages must be propagated through Switch-D to Switch-F. Example A-20 demonstrates verifying VLAN configuration on Switch-F.

Example A-20 *Verifying VLAN Configuration on Switch-F*

```
Switch-F> (enable) show vlan
VLAN Name                             Status    IfIndex Mod/Ports, Vlans
---- -------------------------------- --------- ------- ----------------------
1    default                          active    4       2/1-50
10   management                       active    62
100  servers100                       active    63
101  servers101                       active    64
200  users200                         active    65
201  users201                         active    66
202  phones                           active    67
1002 fddi-default                     active    5
1003 trcrf-default                    active    6
1004 fddinet-default                  active    7       2003
1005 trbrf-default                    active
… <Output truncated>
…
```

As you can see, each VLAN is present in the VLAN database on Switch-F. This output confirms that Switch-D is propagating VTP messages from Switch-B to Switch-F.

Step 3   On Switch-A and Switch-B, configure the following VLAN memberships for
each interface:

- VLAN 100—Ports 2/3 to 2/24

- VLAN 101—Ports 2/25 to 2/47

Once the VLAN database has been populated via VTP, you can assign ports to VLANs.
Example A-21 and Example A-22 show the configuration required on Switch-A and Switch-B.

Example A-21   *Configuring VLAN Port Membership on Switch-A*

```
Switch-A# configure terminal
Enter configuration commands, one per line.  End with CNTL/Z.
Switch-A(config)# interface range FastEthernet 2/3 - 24
Switch-A(config-if-range)# switchport access vlan 100
Switch-A(config-if-range)# exit
Switch-A(config)# interface range FastEthernet 2/25 - 47
Switch-A(config-if-range)# switchport access vlan 101
```

Example A-22   *Configuring VLAN Port Membership on Switch-B*

```
Switch-B> (enable) set vlan 100 2/3-24
VLAN 100 modified.
VLAN 1 modified.
VLAN  Mod/Ports
----  ----------------------
100   2/3-24
Switch-B> (enable) set vlan 101 2/25-47
VLAN 101 modified.
VLAN 1 modified.
VLAN  Mod/Ports
----  ----------------------
101   2/25-47
```

Once you have completed your configuration, verify the new VLAN port membership settings.
Example A-23 demonstrates verifying VLAN port membership on Switch-B.

Example A-23   *Verifying VLAN Port Membership on Switch-B*

```
Switch-B> (enable) show vlan
VLAN Name                             Status    IfIndex Mod/Ports, Vlans
---- -------------------------------- --------- ------- -----------------------
1    default                          active    5       1/1-2
                                                        2/1-2,2/48
10   management                       active    37
100  servers100                       active    38      2/3-24
101  servers101                       active    39      2/25-47
... <output truncated>
...
```

Step 4   On Switch-E, configure the following VLAN memberships for each
interface:

- VLAN 200—Fa0/3 to Fa0/12

- VLAN 201—Fa0/13 to Fa0/24

Once the VLAN database has been populated via VTP, you can assign ports to VLANs.
Example A-24 shows the configuration required on Switch-E to meet the configuration task.

Example A-24   *Configuring VLAN Port Membership on Switch-E*

```
Switch-E# configure terminal
Enter configuration commands, one per line.  End with CNTL/Z.
Switch-E(config)# interface range fa0/3 - 12
Switch-E(config-if-range)# switchport access vlan 200
Switch-E(config-if-range)# exit
Switch-E(config)# interface range fa0/13 - 24
Switch-E(config-if-range)# switchport access vlan 201
Switch-E(config-if-range)# end
```

Once you have completed your configuration, verify the new VLAN port membership settings.
Example A-25 demonstrates verifying VLAN port membership on Switch-E.

Example A-25   *Verifying VLAN Port Membership on Switch-E*

```
Switch-E# show vlan
VLAN Name                             Status    Ports
---- -------------------------------- --------- ------------------------------
1    default                          active
10   management                       active
100  servers100                       active
101  servers101                       active
200  users200                         active    Fa0/3, Fa0/4, Fa0/5, Fa0/6
                                                 Fa0/7, Fa0/8 ,Fa0/9, Fa0/10
                                                 Fa0/11, Fa0/12
201  users201                         active    Fa 0/13, Fa0/14, Fa0/15, Fa0/16
                                                 Fa0/17, Fa0/18, Fa0/19, Fa0/20
                                                 Fa0/21, Fa0/22, Fa0/23, Fa0/24
... <output truncated>
...
```

Step 5   On Switch-F, configure the following VLAN memberships for each
interface:

- VLAN 200—2/3 to 2/12

- VLAN 201—2/13 to 2/24

- Disable ports 2/25 to 2/48

Example A-26 shows the configuration required on Switch-F to meet the configuration task.

Example A-26   *Configuring VLAN Port Membership on Switch-F*

```
Switch-F> (enable) set vlan 200 2/3-12
VLAN 200 modified.
VLAN 1 modified.
VLAN  Mod/Ports
----  ----------------------
200   2/3-12
Switch-F> (enable) set vlan 201 2/13-24
VLAN 201 modified.
VLAN 1 modified.
VLAN  Mod/Ports
----  ----------------------
201   2/13-24
Switch-F> (enable) set port disable 2/25-48
Ports 2/25-48 disabled.
```

Step 6   On all switches, configure all 802.1Q trunks so that any traffic sent on VLAN 10 is not tagged.

On 802.1Q trunks, traffic sent on the native VLAN is not tagged. By default, VLAN 1 is the native VLAN, so you must explicitly configure the native VLAN for each trunk as VLAN 10. To configure the native VLAN on CatOS, you simply change the access VLAN the trunk ports are configured for to the desired native VLAN. On Cisco IOS you must configure the trunking native VLAN as a separate entity, rather than changing the access VLAN of a trunk interface. Example A-27 and Example A-28 demonstrate the configuration required on Switch-C (Cisco IOS) and Switch-F (CatOS).

Example A-27   *Configuring the Native VLAN for Trunks on Switch-C*

```
Switch-C# configure terminal
Enter configuration commands, one per line.  End with CNTL/Z.
Switch-C(config)# interface range FastEthernet 0/1 - 6
Switch-C(config-if-range)# switchport trunk native vlan 10
```

Example A-28   *Configuring the Native VLAN for Trunks on Switch-F*

```
Switch-F> (enable) set vlan 10 2/1-2
VLAN 10 modified.
VLAN 1 modified.
VLAN  Mod/Ports
----  ----------------------
10    2/1-2
```

The configurations just listed must be applied on all 802.1Q trunks between all switches in the network. Once you have completed your configuration, verify the native VLAN settings on all switches. Native VLAN mismatches can cause many headaches and wasted time spent troubleshooting, so if you are changing the native VLAN from the default VLAN 1, make sure you thoroughly verify all trunks in the switched network.

Example A-29 and Example A-30 demonstrate verifying native VLAN configuration on Switch-C (Cisco IOS) and Switch-F (CatOS).

Example A-29 *Verifying Native VLAN Configuration on Switch-C*

```
Switch-C# show interface trunk

Port      Mode         Encapsulation  Status        Native vlan
Fa0/1     on           802.1q         trunking      10
Fa0/2     on           802.1q         trunking      10
Fa0/3     desirable    802.1q         trunking      10
Fa0/4     desirable    802.1q         trunking      10
Fa0/5     desirable    802.1q         trunking      10
Fa0/6     on           802.1q         trunking      10
... <output truncated>
...
```

Example A-30 *Verifying Native VLAN Configuration on Switch-F*

```
Switch-F> (enable) show trunk
* - indicates vtp domain mismatch
Port      Mode         Encapsulation  Status        Native vlan
--------  -----------  -------------  ------------  -----------
 2/1      on           dot1q          trunking      10
 2/2      on           dot1q          trunking      10
... <Output Truncated>
...
```

Spanning Tree Configuration Solution

Step 1 Configure spanning tree so that the Switch-A is the root bridge for all even VLANs and Switch-B is the root bridge for all odd VLANs. Switch-A should be configured as the secondary bridge for all odd VLANs, and Switch-B should be configured as the secondary root bridge for all even VLANs. Configuring spanning-tree timers to ensure that the convergence time of the topology is the most optimal configuration, without placing any additional CPU load on each switch.

For this task, you must ensure that Switch-A is the root for all even VLANs, which includes VLANs 10, 100, 200, and 202. Similarly you must ensure that Switch-B is the root for all odd VLANs (VLANs 1, 101, and 201). You apply this configuration to introduce Spanning Tree Protocol (STP) load sharing; traffic on even VLANs should flow over different ISLs than the odd VLAN traffic flows over.

If you consider the requirements, to minimize the convergence time, you must reduce spanning-tree timers based upon the spanning-tree topology. You can reduce STP timers based upon a network diameter less than seven and/or by reducing the Hello timer from 2 seconds to 1 second. In this lab, the network diameter is four (e.g., Switch A to C to D to E). Notice that you must *not* affect the CPU load on the switch, which means you must *not* configure the Hello timer as a lower value (i.e., 1 second instead of 2 seconds). Use the spanning-tree macro command and specify a network diameter of four to calculate the correct STP timers.

Example A-31 shows the STP configuration required on Switch-A.

Example A-31 *Configuring STP on Switch-A*

```
Switch-A# configure terminal
Enter configuration commands, one per line.  End with CNTL/Z.
Switch-A(config)# spanning-tree vlan 10 root primary diameter 4
% This switch is already the root bridge of the VLAN0010 spanning tree
 vlan 10 bridge priority set to 24576
 vlan 10 bridge max aging time set to 14
 vlan 10 bridge hello time unchanged at 2
 vlan 10 bridge forward delay set to 10
Switch-A(config)# spanning-tree vlan 100 root primary diameter 4
% This switch is already the root bridge of the VLAN0100 spanning tree
 vlan 100 bridge priority set to 24576
 vlan 100 bridge max aging time set to 14
 vlan 100 bridge hello time unchanged at 2
 vlan 100 bridge forward delay set to 10
Switch-A(config)# spanning-tree vlan 200 root primary diameter 4
% This switch is already the root bridge of the VLAN0200 spanning tree
 vlan 200 bridge priority set to 24576
 vlan 200 bridge max aging time set to 14
 vlan 200 bridge hello time unchanged at 2
 vlan 200 bridge forward delay set to 10
Switch-A(config)# spanning-tree vlan 202 root primary diameter 4
% This switch is already the root bridge of the VLAN0202 spanning tree
 vlan 202 bridge priority set to 24576
 vlan 202 bridge max aging time set to 14
 vlan 202 bridge hello time unchanged at 2
 vlan 202 bridge forward delay set to 10
Switch-A(config)# spanning-tree vlan 1 root secondary diameter 4
 vlan 1 bridge priority set to 28672
 vlan 1 bridge max aging time set to 14
 vlan 1 bridge hello time unchanged at 2
 vlan 1 bridge forward delay set to 10
Switch-A(config)# spanning-tree vlan 101 root secondary diameter 4
 vlan 101 bridge priority set to 28672
 vlan 101 bridge max aging time set to 14
 vlan 101 bridge hello time unchanged at 2
 vlan 101 bridge forward delay set to 10
Switch-A(config)# spanning-tree vlan 201 root secondary diameter 4
 vlan 201 bridge priority set to 28672
 vlan 201 bridge max aging time set to 14
 vlan 201 bridge hello time unchanged at 2
 vlan 201 bridge forward delay set to 10
Switch-A(config)# exit
Switch-A# show spanning-tree vlan 10
VLAN0010
  Spanning tree enabled protocol ieee
  Root ID    Priority    24586
             Address     0009.b7aa.9c80
```

Example A-31 *Configuring STP on Switch-A (Continued)*

```
               This bridge is the root
               Hello Time    2 sec  Max Age 14 sec  Forward Delay 10 sec

   Bridge ID  Priority    24586  (priority 24576 sys-id-ext 10)
              Address     0009.b7aa.9c80
              Hello Time    2 sec  Max Age 14 sec  Forward Delay 10 sec
              Aging Time 300

Interface        Port ID                    Designated              Port ID
Name             Prio.Nbr      Cost Sts     Cost Bridge ID          Prio.Nbr
---------------- -------- ----------- --- --------- -------------------- --------
Po1              128.65          4 FWD            0 24586 0009.b7aa.9c80 128.65
Fa2/1            128.65         12 FWD            0 24586 0009.b7aa.9c80 128.3
Fa2/2            128.65         12 FWD            0 24586 0009.b7aa.9c80 128.4
```

In Example A-31, the **show spanning-tree vlan 10** command is used to get the bridge ID of Switch-A in VLAN 10 (0009.b7aa.9c80). You need this information when you verify the spanning-tree topology. Because the designated root matches the local bridge ID, Switch-A is the root bridge for this VLAN.

Notice that the priority of Switch-A for VLAN 10 is 24586, which indicates the extended system ID feature (also known as *MAC address reduction*) is in place. When the extended system ID feature is not used, the root bridge priority is set to 8192, and the secondary root bridge priority is set to 16384 when using the root macro. On Switch-B, the extended system ID feature (referred to as MAC address reduction on CatOS) is not enabled because the Catalyst 6509 Supervisor 2 is assigned 1024 MAC addresses and, therefore, by default does not need MAC address reduction. So, if Switch-B is configured as the secondary root bridge using the root macro command, it actually becomes the root bridge because the priority is to 16384, which is lower than the priority on Switch-A. To ensure that you don't run into situations like this one just mentioned, you should ensure that the MAC address reduction feature is either enabled or disabled on all switches in the network. For this lab, you need to enable MAC address reduction because the Catalyst 3550 switch requires its use. Therefore, on Switch-B and Switch-F (CatOS switches), you should ensure MAC address reduction is enabled.

NOTE   The root and secondary root macro commands are useful tools; however, you should never completely depend on them because they may not operate how you expect in some environments. A good example is provided in the preceding paragraph where MAC address reduction's being enabled on a root bridge but not on a secondary root bridge causes the secondary root bridge to actually become the root bridge. A good way of using the macro commands is to configure them first to ensure the correct timers are configured based upon the Hello time and network diameter of your environment and then manually to configure bridge priority on your root bridge and secondary bridges to a very low value (e.g., 100 for the root, 200 for the secondary). This approach ensures you can be positive that the root and secondary root bridges will be who you expect them to be and also ensures spanning-tree timers will be correctly configured.

Example A-32 shows the spanning-tree configuration required on Switch-B.

Example A-32 *Configuring STP on Switch-B*

```
Switch-B> (enable) set spantree macreduction enable
MAC address reduction enabled
Switch-B> (enable) set spantree root 1,101,201 dia 4
VLANs 1,101,201 bridge priority set to 24576.
VLANs 1,101,201 bridge max aging time set to 14.
VLANs 1,101,201 bridge hello time set to 2.
VLANs 1,101,201 bridge forward delay set to 10.
Switch is now the root switch for active VLANs 1,101,201.
Switch-B> (enable) set spantree root secondary 10,100,200,202 dia 4
VLANs 10,100,200,202 bridge priority set to 28672.
VLANs 10,100,200,202 bridge max aging time set to 14.
VLANs 10,100,200,202 bridge hello time set to 2.
VLANs 10,100,200,202 bridge forward delay set to 10.
Switch-B> (enable) show spantree 1
VLAN 1
Spanning tree mode          PVST+
Spanning tree type          ieee
Spanning tree enabled

Designated Root             00-30-24-48-d4-00
Designated Root Priority    24577
Designated Root Cost        0
Designated Root Port        1/0
Root Max Age   14 sec    Hello Time 2  sec   Forward Delay 10 sec

Bridge ID MAC ADDR          00-30-24-48-d4-00
Bridge ID Priority          24577  (bridge priority: 24576, sys ID ext: 1)
Bridge Max Age 14 sec    Hello Time 2   sec    Forward Delay 10 sec
...
... <Output Truncated>
```

In Example A-32, the **show spantree 1** command is used to get the bridge ID of Switch-B in VLAN 1 (00-30-24-48-d4-00). Because the designated root matches the local bridge ID, Switch-B is the root bridge for VLAN 1. Again, you need this information when you verify the spanning-tree topology.

As a final verification step, verify on another non-root bridge in the network that the correct root bridges and timers have been propagated. Example A-33 demonstrates verifying the STP configuration for an odd and even VLAN on Switch-E.

Example A-33 *Verifying STP on Switch-E*

```
Switch-E# show spanning-tree vlan 1
VLAN0001
  Spanning tree enabled protocol ieee
  Root ID    Priority    24577
             Address     0030.2448.d400
             Cost        38
             Port        1 (FastEthernet0/1)
```

Example A-33 *Verifying STP on Switch-E (Continued)*

```
             Hello Time   2 sec  Max Age 14 sec  Forward Delay 10 sec

  Bridge ID  Priority    32769  (priority 32768 sys-id-ext 1)
             Address     0009.b7ad.2764
             Hello Time   2 sec  Max Age 20 sec  Forward Delay 15 sec
             Aging Time 10

Interface       Port ID                    Designated             Port ID
Name            Prio.Nbr      Cost Sts     Cost Bridge ID         Prio.Nbr
--------------- --------- --------- --- --------- ------------------- --------
Fa0/1             128.1        38 FWD        19 32769 0009.2448.d400  128.5
Fa0/2             128.2        38 BLK        19 32769 0009.7483.aba1  128.5

Switch-E# show spanning-tree vlan 10
VLAN0010
  Spanning tree enabled protocol ieee
  Root ID    Priority    24586
             Address     0009.b7aa.9c80
             Cost        38
             Port        1 (FastEthernet0/1)
             Hello Time   2 sec  Max Age 14 sec  Forward Delay 10 sec

  Bridge ID  Priority    32769  (priority 32768 sys-id-ext 1)
             Address     0009.b7ad.2764
             Hello Time   2 sec  Max Age 20 sec  Forward Delay 15 sec
             Aging Time 10

Interface       Port ID                    Designated             Port ID
Name            Prio.Nbr      Cost Sts     Cost Bridge ID         Prio.Nbr
--------------- --------- --------- --- --------- ------------------- --------
Fa0/1             128.1        38 FWD        19 32769 0009.2448.d400  128.5
Fa0/2             128.2        38 BLK        19 32769 0009.7483.aba1  128.5
```

In Example A-33, you can see that Switch-B (0030.2448.d400) is the root bridge for VLAN 1 (an odd VLAN), while Switch-A (0009.b7aa.9c80) is the root for VLAN 10 (an even VLAN), as indicated by the shaded root bridge IDs. Notice that the timers in use are overriding the configured timers on Switch-E, because all non-root bridges inherit the STP timers sent in each BPDU.

Step 2   Configure the network such that all traffic within even VLANs follows the most optimal path towards the root bridge for even VLANs (Switch-A). Ensure that all traffic within odd VLANs follows the most optimal path towards the root bridge for odd VLANs (Switch-B).

If you refer back to Example A-33, notice that for the odd and even VLANs, the forwarding port (root port) on Switch-E is the same (Fa0/1). This is indicated by the Port description in the section that describes the root bridge for each VLAN, as well as in the section that describes each interface. This setting means that from Switch-E, all non-local traffic (odd and even VLANs) is forwarded over the Fa0/1 link under normal conditions; in other words, load sharing is not occurring.

NOTE For all switches that are directly connected to the root bridges (i.e., Switch-C and Switch-D), load sharing occurs because the root bridge is directly connected and has direct influence over each path.

Because all switches except for Switch-E and Switch-F are directly connected to the root bridges, you need to configure only Switch-E and Switch-F for STP load sharing (however, it is good practice to configure all switches with redundant paths to the root bridge). The recommended approach to implementing STP load sharing is to use per VLAN port cost. Example A-34 demonstrates how to configure Switch-E to enable STP load sharing.

Example A-34 *Configuring STP Load Sharing on Switch-E*

```
Switch-E# configure terminal
Enter configuration commands, one per line.  End with CNTL/Z.
Switch-E(config)# interface FastEthernet 0/1
Switch-E(config-if)# spanning-tree vlan 1 cost 10000
Switch-E(config-if)# spanning-tree vlan 101 cost 10000
Switch-E(config-if)# spanning-tree vlan 201 cost 10000
Switch-E(config-if)# exit
Switch-E(config)# interface FastEthernet 0/2
Switch-E(config-if)# spanning-tree vlan 10 cost 10000
Switch-E(config-if)# spanning-tree vlan 100 cost 10000
Switch-E(config-if)# spanning-tree vlan 200 cost 10000
Switch-E(config-if)# spanning-tree vlan 202 cost 10000
Switch-E(config-if)# end
```

Example A-35 demonstrates how to configure Switch-F to enable STP load sharing.

Example A-35 *Configuring STP Load Sharing on Switch-F*

```
Switch-F> (enable) set spantree portvlancost 2/1 cost 10000 1,101,201
Port 2/1 VLANs 2-100,102-200,202-1005,1025-4094 have path cost 19.
Port 2/1 VLANs 1,101,201 have path cost 10000.
This parameter applies to trunking ports only.
Switch-F> (enable) set spantree portvlancost 2/2 cost 10000 10,100,200,202
Port 2/2 VLANs 1-9,11-99,101-199,201,203-1005,1025-4094 have path cost 19.
Port 2/2 VLANs 10,100,200,202 have path cost 10000.
This parameter applies to trunking ports only.
```

Example A-36 demonstrates how to verify that Switch-E is implementing STP load sharing.

Example A-36 *Verifying STP Load Sharing on Switch-E*

```
Switch-E# show spanning-tree vlan 1
VLAN0001
  Spanning tree enabled protocol ieee
  Root ID    Priority    24577
             Address     0030.2448.d400
             Cost        38
```

Example A-36 *Verifying STP Load Sharing on Switch-E (Continued)*

```
              Port        2 (FastEthernet0/2)
              Hello Time   2 sec  Max Age 14 sec  Forward Delay 10 sec

  Bridge ID  Priority    32769  (priority 32768 sys-id-ext 1)
             Address     0009.b7ad.2764
             Hello Time   2 sec  Max Age 20 sec  Forward Delay 15 sec
             Aging Time 10

Interface        Port ID                 Designated                Port ID
Name             Prio.Nbr    Cost Sts    Cost Bridge ID            Prio.Nbr
---------------- -------- --------- --- --------- ------------------- --------
Fa0/1            128.1       10000 BLK       19 32769 0009.2448.d400  128.5
Fa0/2            128.2          38 FWD       19 32769 0009.7483.aba1  128.5

Switch-E# show spanning-tree vlan 10
VLAN0010
  Spanning tree enabled protocol ieee
  Root ID    Priority    24586
             Address     0009.b7aa.9c80
             Cost        38
             Port        1 (FastEthernet0/1)
             Hello Time   2 sec  Max Age 14 sec  Forward Delay 10 sec

  Bridge ID  Priority    32769  (priority 32768 sys-id-ext 1)
             Address     0009.b7ad.2764
             Hello Time   2 sec  Max Age 20 sec  Forward Delay 15 sec
             Aging Time 10

Interface        Port ID                 Designated                Port ID
Name             Prio.Nbr    Cost Sts    Cost Bridge ID            Prio.Nbr
---------------- -------- --------- --- --------- ------------------- --------
Fa0/1            128.1          38 FWD       19 32769 0009.2448.d400  128.5
Fa0/2            128.2       10000 BLK       19 32769 0009.7483.aba1  128.5
```

If you compare Example A-36 with Example A-33, notice that for VLAN 1 the root port is now the Fa0/2 interface to Switch-D, while for VLAN 10 the root port is still the Fa0/1 interface. This change indicates that spanning tree load sharing has been configured.

Step 3   Ensure that all workstation ports attached to VLAN 201 on Switch-E and Switch-F provide network connectivity within a few seconds after being activated. Configure Switch-E and Switch-F so that BPDUs are not sent out these ports by default.

To provide instant connectivity for workstations, you need to enable spanning tree PortFast, disable DTP, and disable PAgP (on Cisco IOS switches, PAgP is off by default) for all interfaces attached to VLAN 201. This configuration should reduce port activation times to around 3-4 seconds, which is the time taken for a port to negotiate Ethernet speed and duplex settings. You must also ensure that BPDUs are not sent out the workstation ports, which requires you to configure the BPDU Filter option. You can enable BPDU Filter globally or on a per-interface basis. When you globally enable filtering, if a BPDU is received on a PortFast-enabled port, the port is immediately taken out of a PortFast state. If you enable BPDU Filter on a per-interface basis, BPDUs received are simply ignored. Enabling BPDU Filter globally is the safest option and should be used unless you specifically required the behavior of per-interface BPDU Filter.

Example A-37 shows the required configuration on Switch-E.

Example A-37 *Configuring Access Ports on Switch-E*

```
Switch-E# configure terminal
Enter configuration commands, one per line.  End with CNTL/Z.
Switch-E(config)# spanning-tree portfast bpdufilter default
Switch-E(config)# interface range fa0/13
Switch-E(config-if)# switchport mode access
Switch-E(config-if)# spanning-tree portfast
%Warning: portfast should only be enabled on ports connected to a single host.
 Connecting hubs, concentrators, switches,  bridges, etc.to this interface
 when portfast is enabled, can cause temporary spanning tree loops.
 Use with CAUTION
%Portfast has been configured on FastEthernet0/13 but will only
 have effect when the interface is in a non-trunking mode.
Switch-E(config)# interface range fa0/14 - 24
Switch-E(config-if-range)# switchport host
switchport mode will be set to access
spanning-tree portfast will be enabled
channel group will be disabled
```

In Example A-37, BPDU Filter is first enabled globally, after which both methods of configuring workstation ports on Cisco IOS switches are demonstrated. You can manually configure each parameter (configuring a switchport mode of access and enabling PortFast), or you can use the **switchport host** interface configuration command, which is a macro command that configures a switchport mode of access, enables PortFast and ensures EtherChannel is disabled.

On Switch-F, you must also disable PAgP (EtherChannel) because each port is configured with a PAgP mode of auto by default. Example A-38 shows the required configuration on Switch-F. Again, you are recommended to configure BPDU Filter globally, as per the discussion on Switch-E earlier in the chapter.

Example A-38 *Configuring Access Ports on Switch-F*

```
Switch-F> (enable) set spantree global-default bpdu-filter enable
Spantree global-default bpdu-filter enabled on this switch.
Switch-F> (enable) set port channel 2/13 mode off
Port(s) 2/13 channel mode set to off.
Switch-F> (enable) set trunk 2/13 off
Port(s)  2/13 trunk mode set to off.
Switch-F> (enable) set spantree portfast 2/13 enable

Warning: Connecting Layer 2 devices to a fast start port can cause
temporary spanning tree loops. Use with caution.
```

Example A-38 *Configuring Access Ports on Switch-F (Continued)*

```
Spantree port  2/13 fast start enabled.
Switch-F> (enable) set port host 2/14-24
Port(s) 2/14-24 channel mode set to off.

Warning: Connecting Layer 2 devices to a fast start port can cause
temporary spanning tree loops. Use with caution.

Spantree ports 2/14-24 fast start enabled.
Port(s) 2/14-24 trunk mode set to off.
```

In Example A-38, both methods of configuring workstation ports are demonstrated.

Step 4   Configure the network so that Switch-E and Switch-F can recover from direct link failures to Switch-C or Switch-D within 3 seconds. Assume that the MAC address tables of Switch-E and Switch-F hold 600 local MAC addresses.

Switch-E and Switch-F are edge switches and, therefore, can be configured with the Cisco UplinkFast spanning-tree enhancement to provide fast convergence in the event of the direct failure of an uplink to the distribution layer switches in the network. UplinkFast is enabled only on edge switches and uses a dummy multicast mechanism to ensure the bridging tables of other switches in the network are synchronized after a redundant uplink has been activated. The dummy multicast rate by default is 150 multicasts per second, which means it would take 4 seconds to synchronize the 600 local MAC addresses on Switch-E and Switch-F. To provide the 3-second failover time, you must alter the dummy multicast rate to 200 multicasts per second.

Example A-39 and Example A-40 show the configuration required on Switch-E and Switch-F.

Example A-39 *Configuring UplinkFast on Switch-E*

```
Switch-E# configure terminal
Enter configuration commands, one per line.  End with CNTL/Z.
Switch-E(config)# spanning-tree uplinkfast
Switch-E(config)# spanning-tree uplinkfast max-update-rate 200
Switch-E(config)# exit
Switch-E# show spanning-tree uplinkfast
UplinkFast is enabled

Station update rate set to 200 packets/sec.

UplinkFast statistics
-----------------------
Number of transitions via uplinkFast (all VLANs)         : 0
Number of proxy multicast addresses transmitted (all VLANs) : 0

Name                  Interface List
------------------    ------------------------------------
VLAN0001              Fa0/1, Fa0/2(fwd)
VLAN0010              Fa0/1(fwd), Fa0/2
```

continues

Example A-39   *Configuring UplinkFast on Switch-E (Continued)*

```
VLAN0100            Fa0/1(fwd), Fa0/2
VLAN0101            Fa0/1, Fa0/2(fwd)
VLAN0200            Fa0/1(fwd), Fa0/2
VLAN0201            Fa0/1, Fa0/2(fwd)
VLAN0202            Fa0/1(fwd), Fa0/2
```

Example A-40   *Configuring UplinkFast on Switch-F*

```
Switch-F> (enable) set spantree uplinkfast enable rate 20
VLANs 1-4094 bridge priority set to 49152.
The port cost and portvlancost of all ports set to above 3000.
Station update rate set to 20 packets/100ms.
uplinkfast all-protocols field set to off.
uplinkfast enabled for bridge.
Switch-F> (enable) show spantree uplinkfast
Station update rate set to 20 packets/100ms.
uplinkfast all-protocols field set to off.

VLAN            port list
-----------------------------------------------
1               2/1,2/2(fwd)
10              2/1(fwd),2/2
100             2/1(fwd),2/2
101             2/1,2/2(fwd)
200             2/1(fwd),2/2
201             2/1,2/2(fwd)
202             2/1(fwd),2/2
```

In Example A-40, notice that the dummy multicast rate is configured in units of packets per 100 ms on CatOS, unlike Cisco IOS (see Example A-39) where the rate is configured in units of packets per second. The **show spanning-tree uplinkfast** (Switch-E) and **show spantree uplinkfast** (Switch-F) commands verify the update rate is configured correctly and also show the list of candidate root ports for immediate failover (ports with [fwd] next to them are the current active uplinks).

Step 5   Devices in VLAN 100 and VLAN 101 are attached only to the core switches (Switch-A and Switch-B). Ensure that no spanning-tree instance runs for these VLANs on Switch-C, Switch-D, Switch-E, and Switch-F. You cannot explicitly disable spanning tree on any VLAN for this task.

This configuration task is testing your understanding of how far spanning-tree topologies reach when no active hosts are connected to some switches in the network. Although VTP pruning is enabled, which means unknown unicast, broadcast, and multicast traffic for VLANs 100 and 101 is not propagated outside of Switch-A and Switch-B, spanning-tree instances still run on every switch in the network.

NOTE   Because this lab uses multiple VTP domains, VTP pruning will not work as just indicated. For example, Switch-C is in a different VTP domain to Switch-A and Switch-B so no way exists for Switch-C to indicate to Switch-A and Switch-B to prune traffic for VLANs 100 and 101. Similarly, Switch-D is running in VTP transparent mode.

To remove spanning-tree instances on a switch for VLANs that have no active hosts or do not need to act as a transit switch for traffic within the VLAN, you must clear these VLANs from any trunks on the switch. By default, all VLANs are transmitted on trunks, which from the perspective of spanning tree creates a port for each VLAN on the trunk. By removing unnecessary VLANs from trunks, these ports do appear to spanning tree, which removes the spanning-tree instance for the unnecessary VLAN because no ports are active on the switch for the VLAN.

VLAN 100 and VLAN 101 are not required on Switch-C, Switch-D, Switch-E, or Switch-F; hence, all trunks to these switches should have VLANs 100 and 101 cleared. This step requires configuration on all switches in the network (including Switch-A and Switch-B because they have trunks to Switch-C and Switch-D). Example A-41 and Example A-42 demonstrate the configuration required on Switch-C (Cisco IOS) and Switch-B (CatOS). These configurations must be implemented on all trunks on all other switches in the network.

Example A-41   *Clearing VLANs from Trunks on Switch-A*

```
Switch-C# configure terminal
Enter configuration commands, one per line.  End with CNTL/Z.
Switch-C(config)# interface range FastEthernet 0/1 - 6
Switch-C(config-if-range)# switchport trunk allowed vlan 1,10,200-202,1002-1005
```

Example A-42   *Clearing VLANs from Trunks on Switch-B*

```
Switch-B> (enable) clear trunk 2/1 1-1005,1025-4094
Removing Vlan(s) 1-1005,1025-4094 from allowed list.
Port  2/1 allowed vlans modified to .
Switch-B> (enable) set trunk 2/1 1,10,200-202
Adding vlans 1,10,200-202 to allowed list.
Port(s)  2/1 allowed vlans modified to 1,200-202.
VLANs 1-4094 bridge priority set to 49152.
Switch-B> (enable) clear trunk 2/2 1-1005,1025-4094
Removing Vlan(s) 1-1005,1025-4094 from allowed list.
Port  2/2 allowed vlans modified to .
Switch-B> (enable) set trunk 2/2 1,200-202
Adding vlans 1,200-202 to allowed list.
Port(s)  2/2 allowed vlans modified to 1,200-202.
```

Notice on Switch-C (Cisco IOS, Catalyst 3550) that you must include VLANs 1002–1005 in the allowed VLAN list. On Switch-B (CatOS), you must first clear VLANs and then set the permitted VLANs.

Inter-VLAN Routing Configuration Solution

Step 1   Configure the connection to Router-A as an 802.1Q trunk, ensuring that Switch-A is configured with the appropriate DTP mode of operation that is compatible with Router-A.

You need to configure port 2/48 on Switch-B as an 802.1Q trunk with a trunking mode of nonegotiate because Cisco routers do not support DTP. Also ensure you configure VLAN 10 as the native VLAN, as required by this lab for all trunks. Example A-43 shows the required configuration on Switch-B.

Example A-43   *Configuring Trunking on Switch-B*

```
Switch-B> (enable) set vlan 10 2/48
VLAN 10 modified.
VLAN 1 modified.
VLAN  Mod/Ports
----  --------------------
10    1/1-2
      2/1-2,2/48
      15/1
Switch-B> (enable) set trunk 2/48 nonegotiate dot1q
Port(s)  2/48 trunk mode set to nonegotiate.
Port(s)  2/48 trunk type set to dot1q.
```

Step 2   Configure Router-A for inter-VLAN routing. Router-A should use an IP address of 192.168.x.1 on each VLAN, where x represents the VLAN ID. For example, on VLAN 10, Router-A should be configured with an IP address of 192.168.10.1. Also, configure an interface that represents a restricted network attached to Router-A (see Figure 11-1).

Router-A is currently unconfigured and must be configured with a host name and Telnet/enable passwords. Router-A also must be configured with an 802.1Q trunk to Switch-B, and the appropriate inter-VLAN routing configuration as described in the preceding paragraph is required. Example A-44 shows the required configuration on Router-A.

Example A-44   *Configuring Router-A*

```
Router> enable
Router# configure terminal
Enter configuration commands, one per line.  End with CNTL/Z.
Router(config)# hostname Router-A
Router-A(config)# enable secret cisco
Router-A(config)# line vty 0 4
Router-A(config-line)# password cisco
Router-A(config-line)# exit
Router-A(config)# interface FastEthernet0/0
Router-A(config-if)# no shutdown
Router-A(config-if)# exit
Router-A(config)# interface FastEthernet0/0.10
Router-A(config-if)# encapsulation dot1q 10 native
```

Example A-44 *Configuring Router-A (Continued)*

```
Router-A(config-if)# ip address 192.168.10.1 255.255.255.0
Router-A(config-if)# exit
Router-A(config)# interface FastEthernet0/0.100
Router-A(config-if)# encapsulation dot1q 100
Router-A(config-if)# ip address 192.168.100.1 255.255.255.0
Router-A(config-if)# exit
Router-A(config)# interface FastEthernet0/0.101
Router-A(config-if)# encapsulation dot1q 101
Router-A(config-if)# ip address 192.168.101.1 255.255.255.0
Router-A(config-if)# exit
Router-A(config)# interface FastEthernet0/0.200
Router-A(config-if)# encapsulation dot1q 200
Router-A(config-if)# ip address 192.168.200.1 255.255.255.0
Router-A(config-if)# exit
Router-A(config)# interface FastEthernet0/0.201
Router-A(config-if)# encapsulation dot1q 201
Router-A(config-if)# ip address 192.168.201.1 255.255.255.0
Router-A(config-if)# exit
Router-A(config)# interface fa0/.202
Router-A(config-if)# encapsulation dot1q 202
Router-A(config-if)# ip address 192.168.202.1 255.255.255.0
Router-A(config-if)# exit
Router-A(config)# interface loopback0
Router-A(config-if)# ip address 10.0.0.1 255.0.0.0
```

Notice that a loopback interface is created to represent the restricted 10.0.0.0/8 network.

Step 3   Configure all switches in the network with the management IP addressing as
indicated in Figure 11-1. Ensure that all switches can ping any device in the
network.

For this task, you need to configure the management interface on each switch within VLAN 10
and also ensure that you configure a default gateway of 192.168.10.1 (Router-A) to ensure you
can communicate with all devices in the network. Example A-45 to Example A-47 demonstrate
the required configuration on Switch-A (Cisco IOS, Catalyst 6509), Switch-C (Cisco IOS,
Catalyst 3550), and Switch-B (CatOS).

Example A-45 *Configuring IP Management on Switch-A*

```
Switch-A# configure terminal
Enter configuration commands, one per line.  End with CNTL/Z.
Switch-A(config)# interface VLAN 10
Switch-A(config-if)# no shutdown
Switch-A(config-if)# ip address 192.168.10.2 255.255.255.0
Switch-A(config-if)# exit
Switch-A(config)# ip route 0.0.0.0 0.0.0.0 192.168.10.1
```

Example A-46 *Configuring IP Management on Switch-C*

```
Switch-C# configure terminal
Enter configuration commands, one per line.  End with CNTL/Z.
Switch-C(config)# interface VLAN 10
Switch-C(config-if)# no shutdown
Switch-C(config-if)# ip address 192.168.10.9 255.255.255.0
Switch-C(config-if)# exit
Switch-C(config)# ip default-gateway 192.168.10.1
```

Example A-47 *Configuring IP Management on Switch-B*

```
Switch-B> (enable) set interface sc0 10 192.168.10.3 255.255.255.0
Interface sc0 vlan set, IP address and netmask set.
Switch-B> (enable) set ip route default 192.168.10.1
Route added.
```

Notice on Switch-A that you use the **ip route** configuration command to configure the default gateway, while on Switch-C you use the **ip default-gateway** command. Native IOS Catalyst 6500 switches operate as a Layer 3 router by default, meaning IP routing is enabled and the use of routes is required. On the other hand, the Catalyst 3550 operates as a Layer 2 switch by default, which means you cannot configure routes on Switch-C (and also Switch-D and Switch-E), only a default gateway instead.

Once your configurations are complete, verify IP connectivity with all devices using the ping utility.

Management and Security Configuration Solution

Step 1 Configure Simple Network Management Protocol (SNMP) on all switches. Configure a read-only string of "cisco" and enable traps for all events to be sent to an SNMP host at 192.168.100.50.

Example A-48 and Example A-49 demonstrate the required configurations on Switch-B (CatOS) and Switch-C (Cisco IOS).

Example A-48 *Configuring SNMP on Switch-B*

```
Switch-B> (enable) set snmp community read-only cisco
SNMP read-only community string set to 'cisco'.
Switch-B> (enable) set snmp trap enable all
All SNMP traps enabled.
Switch-B> (enable) set snmp trap 192.168.100.50 cisco
SNMP trap receiver added.
Switch-B> (enable) set snmp enable
SNMP enabled.
```

Example A-49 *Configuring SNMP on Switch-C*

```
Switch-C# configure terminal
Enter configuration commands, one per line.  End with CNTL/Z.
Switch-C(config)# snmp-server community cisco ro
Switch-C(config)# snmp-server enable traps
Switch-C(config)# snmp-server host 192.168.100.50 traps cisco
Switch-C(config)# end
```

Step 2 Restrict Telnet access on all switches to only hosts that reside in VLAN 100.
Also, restrict SNMP access to the SNMP host at 192.168.100.50.

VLAN 100 represents the 192.168.100.0/24 subnet; you can restrict access only based upon IP
addressing, not VLANs. Example A-50 and Example A-51 demonstrate the required
configurations on Switch-B (CatOS) and Switch-C (Cisco IOS).

Example A-50 *Restricting Telnet and SNMP Access on Switch-B*

```
Switch-B> (enable) set ip permit 192.168.100.0 255.255.255.0 telnet
192.168.100.0 with mask 255.255.255.0 added to Telnet permit list.
Switch-B> (enable) set ip permit 192.168.100.50 snmp
192.168.100.50 added to Snmp permit list.
Switch-B> (enable) set ip permit enable
Telnet, Snmp and Ssh permit list enabled
```

Example A-51 *Restricting Telnet and SNMP Access on Switch-C*

```
Switch-C# configure terminal
Enter configuration commands, one per line.  End with CNTL/Z.
Switch-C(config)# access-list 1 permit 192.168.100.0 0.0.0.255
Switch-C(config)# line vty 0 15
Switch-C(config-line)# access-class 1 in
Switch-C(config-line)# exit
Switch-C(config)# access-list 2 permit host 192.168.100.50
Switch-C(config)# snmp-server community cisco RO 2
```

Step 3 An Network Time Protocol (NTP) server is available on the network.
Configure all switches so that each has similar clock settings as follows:

- NTP server has an IP address of 192.168.100.50.

- Clock zone is Eastern Standard Time (GMT -5 hours).

Example A-52 and Example A-53 demonstrate the required configurations on Switch-B
(CatOS) and Switch-C (Cisco IOS).

Example A-52 *Configuring NTP on Switch-B*

```
Switch-B> (enable) set timezone EST -5
Timezone set to 'EST', offset from UTC is -5 hours
Switch-B> (enable) set ntp server 192.168.100.50
NTP server 192.168.100.50 added
```

Example A-53 *Configuring NTP on Switch-C*

```
Switch-C# configure terminal
Enter configuration commands, one per line.  End with CNTL/Z.
Switch-C(config)# clock timezone EST -5
Switch-C(config)# ntp server 192.168.100.50
```

Once you have completed your configurations, verify that each switch has synchronized with the NTP server and has the correct time using the **show time** command (CatOS) and **show clock** command (Cisco IOS).

Step 4   To ensure that only IP phones are communicating from VLAN 202, configure the network so that only the communications required to support the IP phones are permitted. All other traffic must be discarded, and you must ensure that unauthorized traffic is discarded as soon as possible. The following lists the protocols that must be permitted from the perspective of communications originating from the IP phones:

- **Skinny Call Control Protocol (SCCP)**—TCP traffic sent to a destination port of 2000

- **Voice traffic**—User Datagram Protocol (UDP) traffic with source and destination ports in the range of 16384–32767

- **HTTP traffic**—TCP traffic sent to a destination port of 80

- **Trivial File Transfer Protocol (TFTP) traffic**—UDP traffic sent to a destination port of 69

- **Dynamic Host Configuration Protocol (DHCP) traffic**—UDP traffic using a source port of 67 and destination port of 68

- **Internet Control Message Protocol (ICMP) traffic (for diagnostic purposes)**—ICMP echo and echo replies

For this task you are required to restrict traffic sent from VLAN 202. You must also ensure that unauthorized traffic is dropped as early as possible upon entry to the network. Because IP phones in VLAN 202 are connected only to Switch-E, to ensure unauthorized traffic sent from this VLAN is dropped immediately you must configure security access control lists (ACLs) on Switch-E to permit only authorized voice traffic and drop any unauthorized traffic. On the Catalyst 3550, you can apply security ACLs on a per-interface basis or on a per-VLAN basis (using VLAN access control lists or VACLs). The requirements clearly state that traffic within VLAN 202 should be restricted; hence, the most efficient configuration is to configure security ACLs on a per-VLAN basis using VACLs.

Example A-54 shows the configuration required on Switch-E.

Example A-54   *Configuring Security ACLs on Switch-E*

```
Switch-E# configure terminal
Enter configuration commands, one per line.  End with CNTL/Z.
```

Example A-54   *Configuring Security ACLs on Switch-E (Continued)*

```
Switch-E(config)# access-list 100 permit tcp any any eq 2000
Switch-E(config)# access-list 100 permit tcp any eq 2000 any
Switch-E(config)# access-list 100 permit udp any range 16384 32767 any range 16384 32767
Switch-E(config)# access-list 100 permit udp any eq 67 any eq 68
Switch-E(config)# access-list 100 permit udp any eq 68 any eq 67
Switch-E(config)# access-list 100 permit udp any any eq 69
Switch-E(config)# access-list 100 permit udp any eq 69 any
Switch-E(config)# access-list 100 permit udp any eq 88 any
Switch-E(config)# access-list 100 permit icmp any any echo
Switch-E(config)# access-list 100 permit icmp any any echo-reply
Switch-E(config)# vlan access-map VLAN202 10
Switch-E(config-access-map)# match ip address 100
Switch-E(config-access-map)# action forward
Switch-E(config-access-map)# exit
Switch-E(config)# vlan filter VLAN202 vlan-list 202
```

In Example A-54, notice that two access control entries (ACEs) are configured for each type of traffic. For example, to permit HTTP traffic, any TCP traffic sent with a destination port of 80 is permitted, as well as any TCP traffic sent with a source port of 80. Because VACLs are applied to traffic as it enters and leaves the VLAN, you must ensure you permit traffic based upon both being sent from client to server and also from server to client. The VACL created has an implicit deny all at the end, which means only traffic defined in ACL 100 is be forwarded in and out of VLAN 202.

Step 5   Configure Switch-E to permit access only to a PC with a MAC address of 0010.0010.0010 on interface Fa0/24. No other devices should be permitted access to the interface. If another device attempts to use the interface, the interface should be shut down immediately.

This task requires port security to be configured, with a MAC address defined that is permitted to attach to interface Fa0/24. Example A-55 shows the configuration required on Switch-E.

Example A-55   *Configuring Port Security on Switch-E*

```
Switch-E# configure terminal
Enter configuration commands, one per line.  End with CNTL/Z.
Switch-E(config)# interface FastEthernet 0/24
Switch-E(config-if)# switchport port-security
Switch-E(config-if)# switchport port-security maximum 1
Switch-E(config-if)# switchport port-security mac-address 0010.0010.0010
Switch-E(config-if)# switchport port-security violation shutdown
Switch-E(config-if)# end
Switch-E# show port-security interface FastEthernet 0/24
Port Security : Enabled
Port status : SecureUp
Violation mode : Shutdown
Maximum MAC Addresses : 1
Total MAC Addresses : 1
Configured MAC Addresses : 1
Sticky MAC Addresses : 0
```

continues

Example A-55 *Configuring Port Security on Switch-E (Continued)*

```
Aging time : 0 mins
Aging type : Absolute
SecureStatic address aging : Disabled
Security Violation count : 0
```

In Example A-55, notice that you must explicitly enable port security on a port by using the **switchport port-security** interface configuration command without any options at all. A common mistake is to configure this command with each of the required options, but to forget to actually enable port security by configuring just the **switchport port-security** command. The **show port-security interface** command is then used to verify the configuration. You can see that port security is enabled, the status of the port is currently up, a security violation causes the port to shut down, and the maximum number of MAC addresses permitted on the port is one. The Security Violation count field can be used to track how many violations have occurred since the switch was last rebooted.

Step 6 Configure the core of the network (Switch-A and Switch-B) to permit communications only between VLANs within the local switching infrastructure, ensuring local devices cannot communicate with the protected network (10.0.0.0/8). Configure these requirements using the least amount of configuration possible.

This task implements security that ensures the devices on the local LAN infrastructure cannot access the restricted network 10.0.0.0/8. To implement this on Switch-A and Switch-B, you can configure a single VACL and apply it to each VLAN. The access defined in the VACL is simple; it simply needs to permit IP communications from any subnet in the 192.168.x.x address space to any other subnet in the 192.168.x.x address space. This access can be defined in a single statement.

Before beginning this configuration, you should be able to ping the loopback interface on Router-A (10.0.0.1) from any switch in the network. After configuring VACLs, you should no longer be able to do this.

Example A-56 and Example A-57 demonstrates the configuration required on Switch-A and Switch-B.

Example A-56 *Configuring VACLs on Switch-A*

```
Switch-A# configure terminal
Enter configuration commands, one per line.  End with CNTL/Z.
Switch-A(config)# access-list 100 permit ip 192.168.0.0 0.0.255.255
  192.168.0.0 0.0.255.255
Switch-A(config)# vlan access-map INTERNAL 10
Switch-A(config-access-map)# match ip address 100
Switch-A(config-access-map)# action forward
Switch-A(config-access-map)# exit
Switch-A(config)# vlan filter INTERNAL vlan-list 1,10,100,101,200-202
```

Example A-57 *Configuring VACLs on Switch-B*

```
Switch-B> (enable) set security acl ip INTERNAL permit ip 192.168.0.0 0.0.255.255
   192.168.0.0 0.0.255.255
INTERNAL editbuffer modified. Use 'commit' command to apply changes.
Switch-A> (enable) commit security acl all
Commit operation in progress.

ACL 'INTERNAL' successfully committed.
Switch-A> (enable) set security acl map INTERNAL 1,10,100,101,200-202
Mapping in progress...

ACL INTERNAL successfully mapped to VLAN 1.
ACL INTERNAL successfully mapped to VLAN 10.
ACL INTERNAL successfully mapped to VLAN 100.
ACL INTERNAL successfully mapped to VLAN 101.
ACL INTERNAL successfully mapped to VLAN 200.
ACL INTERNAL successfully mapped to VLAN 201.
ACL INTERNAL successfully mapped to VLAN 202.
```

Once you have configured, committed, and mapped the VACL, on any switch in the network you should be able to ping any other switch, but you should find that you can no longer ping the loopback interface on Router-A.

Quality of Service Configuration Solution

Step 1   Ensure that all traffic generated by all end devices attached to Switch-E is classified as follows upon entry to the network:

- All voice traffic should be marked with a Differentiated Services Code Point (DSCP) of 46. Voice control traffic (SCCP) should be marked with a DSCP value of 26.

- All SQL server traffic (TCP traffic sent to a destination port of 1433) should be marked with a DSCP of 24.

- All other traffic is marked with a DSCP of 8.

The task requires any traffic received from end devices (interfaces Fa0/3–24) to be classified and marked as indicated in the preceding list. Example A-58 shows the quality of service (QoS) configuration required on Switch-E.

Example A-58 *Configuring QoS Classification and Marking on Switch-E*

```
Switch-E# configure terminal
Enter configuration commands, one per line.  End with CNTL/Z.
Switch-E(config)# mls qos
Switch-E(config)# ip access-list extended VOICE
Switch-E(config-ext-nacl)# permit udp any range 16384 32767 any range 16384 32767
Switch-E(config-ext-nacl)# exit
Switch-E(config)# ip access-list extended VOICE-CONTROL
```

continues

Example A-58   *Configuring QoS Classification and Marking on Switch-E (Continued)*

```
Switch-E(config-ext-nacl)# permit tcp any any eq 2000
Switch-E(config-ext-nacl)# exit
Switch-E(config)# ip access-list extended SQL
Switch-E(config-ext-nacl)# permit tcp any any eq 1433
Switch-E(config-ext-nacl)# exit
Switch-E(config)# class-map match-all VOICE
Switch-E(config-cmap)# match access-group VOICE
Switch-E(config-cmap)# exit
Switch-E(config)# class-map match-all VOICE-CONTROl
Switch-E(config-cmap)# match access-group VOICE-CONTROl
Switch-E(config-cmap)# exit
Switch-E(config)# class-map match-all SQL
Switch-E(config-cmap)# match access-group SQL
Switch-E(config-cmap)# exit
Switch-E(config)# policy-map QOS
Switch-E(config-pmap)# class VOICE
Switch-E(config-pmap-c)# set ip dscp 46
Switch-E(config-pmap-c)# exit
Switch-E(config-pmap)# class VOICE-CONTROL
Switch-E(config-pmap-c)# set ip dscp 26
Switch-E(config-pmap-c)# exit
Switch-E(config-pmap)# class SQL
Switch-E(config-pmap-c)# set ip dscp 24
Switch-E(config-pmap-c)# exit
Switch-E(config-pmap)# class class-default
Switch-E(config-pmap-c)# set ip dscp 8
Switch-E(config-pmap-c)# exit
Switch-E(config-pmap)# exit
Switch-E(config)# interface range FastEthernet 2/3 - 24
Switch-E(config-if-range)# service-policy input QOS
```

In Example A-58, ACLs are first created to define each type of traffic. Each ACL is then referenced in a class map, with each class map configured in a policy map. The policy map configures how the DSCP should be set, based upon each class map.

Step 2   Configure Switch-E so that IP phones connected to interfaces Fa0/3–Fa0/12 transmit voice in VLAN 202 and data from any attached PCs in VLAN 200. Also ensure that any data received from PCs connected to an IP phone has a class of service (CoS) of three.

For this task you must configure the voice VLAN ID (VVID) on ports connected to IP phones. The VVID is passed to Cisco IP phones from the Catalyst 3550 switch in Cisco Discovery Protocol (CDP) messages. The Cisco IP phone tags voice traffic with the VVID, while data from a locally attached PC is not tagged. Consequently, all data from PCs is sent in VLAN 200, as configured earlier. You can also pass the CoS value to apply to data devices attached to each phone, which enables you to specify a CoS of three for non-voice traffic. Example A-59 shows the required configuration.

Example A-59 *Configuring Voice on Switch-E*

```
Switch-E# configure terminal
Enter configuration commands, one per line.  End with CNTL/Z.
Switch-E(config)# interface range FastEthernet 0/7 - 12
Switch-E(config-if-range)# switchport voice vlan 202
Switch-E(config-if-range)# switchport priority extend cos 3
```

Step 3   Web servers are attached to Switch-A and Switch-B. On the client side of
HTTP connections, limit HTTP traffic to 1 Mbps per device (devices
connected to Switch-E are considered client side). On the server side, limit
HTTP traffic to 1 Mbps per connection (devices connected to Switch-A and
Switch-B are considered server side).

As identified in the task, all client-side devices are attached to Switch-E. To configure policing,
you need to modify the current policy map that was configured in Example A-58. Example A-60
shows the required configuration on Switch-E

Example A-60 *Configuring Rate Limiting on Switch-E*

```
Switch-E# configure terminal
Enter configuration commands, one per line.  End with CNTL/Z.
Switch-E(config)# ip access-list extended HTTP
Switch-E(config-ext-nacl)# permit tcp any any eq 80
Switch-E(config-ext-nacl)# exit
Switch-E(config)# class-map match-all HTTP
Switch-E(config-cmap)# match access-group HTTP
Switch-E(config-cmap)# exit
Switch-E(config)# policy-map QOS
Switch-E(config-pmap)# class HTTP
Switch-E(config-pmap-c)# police 1000000 187500 exceed-action drop
```

In Example A-60, you must create a new extended ACL that classifies HTTP traffic. Next, you
create a new class in the existing policy map QOS that is currently applied inbound to interfaces
Fa0/3–24, specifying a rate of 1 Mbps, burst size of 187,500 bytes, and an action of drop for
traffic exceeding the configured parameters. The burst size of 187,500 bytes is calculated by
using Cisco's recommended calculation for burst bytes:

Burst (bytes) = CIR (bps) $* 1.5 / 8 = 1500000/8 = 187,500$

Because the QOS policy map is already applied to each interface, you don't need to reapply the
policy map to each interface.

On the server-side, you must rate limit on Switch-A and Switch-B for ports 2/3–47, which
attach to servers. With a Catalyst 6000/6500 PFC, you can police individual connections or
flows (known as *microflow policing*) as required for this task. Example A-61 shows the required
configuration on Switch-A.

Example A-61 *Configuring Rate Limiting on Switch-A*

```
Switch-A# configure terminal
Enter configuration commands, one per line.  End with CNTL/Z.
Switch-A(config)# mls qos
Switch-A(config)# ip access-list extended HTTP
Switch-A(config-ext-nacl)# permit tcp any eq www any
Switch-A(config-ext-nacl)# exit
Switch-A(config)# class-map match-all HTTP
Switch-A(config-cmap)# match access-group HTTP
Switch-A(config-cmap)# exit
Switch-A(config)# policy-map QOS
Switch-A(config-pmap)# class HTTP
Switch-A(config-pmap-c)# police flow 1000000 187500 conform-action
  set-dscp-transmit 24 exceed-action drop
Switch-A(config-pmap-c)# exit
Switch-A(config-pmap)# exit
Switch-A(config)# interface range FastEthernet 2/3 - 47
Switch-A(config-if-range)# mls qos vlan-based
Switch-A(config-if-range)# exit
Switch-A(config)# interface vlan 100
Switch-A(config-if)# mls qos bridged
Switch-A(config-if)# service-policy input QOS
Switch-A(config-if)# exit
Switch-A(config)# interface vlan 101
Switch-A(config-if)# mls qos bridged
Switch-A(config-if)# service-policy input QOS
Switch-A(config-if)# exit
```

In Example A-61, QoS must first be enabled on Switch-A. Classification of HTTP traffic sent from locally attached Web servers is then configured, after which microflow policing is configured for the HTTP traffic in a policy map called QOS. Because the policing needs to be defined for all Web servers, applying QoS on a per-VLAN basis rather than on the default per-port basis is configured. The **mls qos vlan-based** interface configuration command is required on each interface, after which VLAN 100 and VLAN 101 are configured using the **interface vlan** global configuration command. Notice that the **mls qos bridged** interface configuration command is applied for each VLAN, which enables microflow policing for Layer 2 switched traffic. The QOS policy map defined earlier is then applied for all traffic received in each VLAN.

Example A-62 shows the required configuration on Switch-B.

Example A-62 *Configuring Rate Limiting on Switch-B*

```
Switch-B> (enable) set qos enable
QoS is enabled.
Switch-B> (enable) set qos bridged-microflow-policing enable 100-101
QoS microflow policing is enabled for bridged packets on vlans 100-101
Switch-B> (enable) set qos policer microflow HTTP rate 1000 burst 1500 drop
QoS policer for microflow HTTP created successfully.
Rate is set to 992 and burst is set to 1472 in hardware due to hardware
  granularity.
Switch-B> (enable) set qos acl ip QOS dscp 24 microflow HTTP tcp any eq 80 any
```

Example A-62   *Configuring Rate Limiting on Switch-B (Continued)*

```
QOS editbuffer modified. Use 'commit' command to apply changes.
Switch-B> (enable) commit qos acl all

QoS ACL 'QOS' successfully committed.
Switch-B> (enable) set port qos 2/3-47 vlan-based
Hardware programming in progress...
QoS interface is set to vlan-based for ports 2/3-47.
Switch-B> (enable) set qos acl map QOS 100
Hardware programming in progress...
ACL my_acl is attached to vlan 100.
Switch-B> (enable) set qos acl map QOS 101
Hardware programming in progress...
ACL my_acl is attached to vlan 101.
```

In Example A-62, QoS is first enabled on Switch-B, after which microflow policing is enabled for Layer 2 switched traffic. A microflow policer called HTTP is next created. The rate is specified in kbps; hence, a value of 1000 is configured to reflect 1 Mbps. Similarly, the burst value is configured in kilobits (Kb); to match the 187,500 bytes configured on Switch-E, a value of 1500 (1500 kilobits) is configured. Any traffic that exceeds the rate is dropped. Next, a QoS ACL called QOS is created, which classifies HTTP traffic sent from Web servers, applies the HTTP microflow policer, and also marks the DSCP as 24. VLAN-based QoS ACL mapping is then enabled, which allows the QoS policy to be applied to all ports within VLANs 100 and 101.

Step 4   Configure the network so that the QoS policy configured at the edge is honored throughout the network. Ensure that all voice packets marked with a DSCP of 46 are placed into a priority queue for transmission where possible (assume that the Ethernet modules on Switch-A are WS-X6148-RJ45 with a transmit port type of 2q2t). Trust the IP precedence traffic markings received from Router-A.

For this task, you must configure each switch to honor the QoS marking (DSCP) that has been applied at the edge of the network. This task involves configuring each ISL or trunk to trust the QoS markings of received frames and then to queue traffic on egress ports based upon those markings, which means QoS must be enabled on all switches.

Switch-A and Switch-B must trust the markings of frames received on port 2/1 and port 2/2, and Switch-B must also trust the IP precedence of packets received on port 2/48 (attached to Router-A). Switch-C and Switch-D must trust markings of frames received on interfaces Fa0/1–Fa0/6, with each link to Switch-F configured to trust CoS rather than DSCP because Switch-F does not support DSCP marking. Switch-E must trust markings of frames received on interface Fa0/1 and Fa0/2, while Switch-F must trust markings of frames received on ports 2/1 and 2/2. Switch-F automatically trusts the CoS of any tagged frames received (this is non-configurable) because it is a Catalyst 2900 series switch.

Example A-63 demonstrates the configuration required on Switch-C (Cisco IOS) to ensure the DSCP of frames received on interswitch trunks is trusted.

Example A-63   *Configuring QoS Trust on Switch-C*

```
Switch-C# configure terminal
Enter configuration commands, one per line.  End with CNTL/Z.
Switch-C(config)# mls qos
Switch-C(config)# interface range FastEthernet 0/1 - 5
Switch-C(config-if-range)# mls qos trust dscp
Switch-C(config-if-range)# exit
Switch-C(config)# interface FastEthernet 0/6
Switch-C(config-if)# mls qos trust cos
```

In Example A-63, notice that you must enable QoS explicitly on Switch-C. Also notice that Switch-C is configured to trust the DSCP of received frames on interfaces Fa0/1–5, but configured to trust the CoS of received frames on interface Fa0/6. Interface Fa0/6 is connected to Switch-F (Catalyst 2948G), which does not possess any enhanced QoS intelligence and works only with CoS.

Example A-64 demonstrates the configuration required on Switch-B (CatOS) to ensure the DSCP of frames received on interswitch trunks is trusted, as well as the IP precedence of packets received from Router-A.

Example A-64   *Configuring QoS Trust on Switch-B*

```
Switch-B> (enable) set port qos 1/1 trust trust-dscp
Port 1/1 qos set to trust-dscp
Switch-B> (enable) set port qos 1/2 trust trust-dscp
Port 1/2 qos set to trust-dscp
Switch-B> (enable) set port qos 2/1 trust trust-dscp
Port 2/1 qos set to trust-dscp
Switch-B> (enable) set port qos 2/2 trust trust-dscp
Port 2/2 qos set to trust-dscp
Switch-B> (enable) set port qos 2/48 trust trust-ipprec
Port 2/1 qos set to trust-ipprec
Switch-B> (enable) set port qos 2/1 trust trust-dscp
Port 2/1 qos set to trust-dscp
```

Now that port trust has been configured, you must configure queuing. When a frame is queued for transmission, each switch by default queues frames according to the CoS value of the frame. On all switches except for Switch-F, the CoS value is determined by the internal DSCP assigned to a frame, using a DSCP-to-CoS map. By default, the DSCP value of 46 is mapped to a CoS of 5.

On Switch-A and Switch-B (Catalyst 6509 switches with PFC2), the gigabit uplinks on the Supervisor 2 engines have a transmit port type of 1p2q2t, which represents one strict-priority queue, one high-priority queue, and one standard queue, with two discard thresholds per queue. By default, traffic with a CoS of 5 (i.e., voice in this scenario) is assigned to the strict-priority queue, so no configuration is required on the gigabit uplinks. For the Ethernet ports (tx port type = 2q2t), one high-priority queue and one standard queue exist. By default, traffic with a CoS of 5–8 is assigned to the high-priority queue, so again no configuration is required on Switch-A and Switch-B.

On Switch-C, Switch-D, and Switch-E (Catalyst 3550 switches), all ports have four queues that service in a weighted round robin fashion by default. On the Catalyst 3550, you can change queue 4 into a strict-priority queue, which is required for voice traffic in this scenario. By default, only frames with a CoS of 6 and 7 are placed into queue 4, so you must alter the CoS-to-queue map on each interface to ensure that traffic with a CoS of 5 is placed into the priority queue. Example A-65 shows the configuration required on Switch-C to ensure queuing is configured appropriately for this scenario.

Example A-65 *Configuring Queuing on Switch-C*

```
Switch-C# configure terminal
Enter configuration commands, one per line.  End with CNTL/Z.
Switch-C(config)# interface range FastEthernet 0/1 - 6
Switch-C(config-if-range)# wrr-queue cos-map 4 5 6 7
Switch-C(config-if-range)# priority-queue out
Switch-C(config-if-range)# exit
Switch-C(config)# exit
Switch-C# show mls qos interface FastEthernet 0/1 queueing
FastEthernet0/1
Egress expedite queue: ena
wrr bandwidth weights:
qid-weights
 1 - 25
 2 - 25
 3 - 25
 4 - 25     when expedite queue is disabled
Cos-queue map:
cos-qid
 0 - 1
 1 - 1
 2 - 2
 3 - 2
 4 - 3
 5 - 4
 6 - 4
 7 - 4
```

In Example A-65, the CoS-to-queue map for each interswitch trunk is modified so that frames with a CoS of 5, 6, and 7 are placed into queue 4. Strict priority queuing is then enabled for queue 4 by configuring the **priority-queue out** interface configuration command. Notice in the output of the **show mls qos interface** command that the egress expedite queue (strict priority queue) is enabled and that frames with a CoS of 5 are placed into queue ID #4.

Finally, on all ports of Switch-F (Catalyst 2948G) two queues are supported (one high priority and one low priority). By default, all frames are placed into the low priority queue, so you must modify this behavior to ensure frames with a CoS of 5 are placed into the high-priority queue.

Example A-66 shows the configuration required on Switch-F to enable the high-priority queue for queuing of egress traffic.

Example A-66 *Configuring Queuing on Switch-F*

```
Switch-F> (enable) set qos enable
QoS is enabled.
Switch-F> (enable) set qos defaultcos 3
qos defaultcos set to 3
Switch-F> (enable) set qos map 2q1t 1 1 cos 0-4
Qos tx priority queue and threshold mapped to cos successfully.
Switch-F> (enable) set qos map 2q1t 2 1 cos 5-7
Qos tx priority queue and threshold mapped to cos successfully.
```

In Example A-65, QoS is enabled on Switch-F, and then the default CoS assigned to any untagged frames received by the switch is configured as 3. Next, frames with a CoS of 0–4 are mapped to queue 1, threshold 1 on all ports with 2q1t capabilities (two queues, one threshold per queue), while frames with a CoS of 5–7 are mapped to queue 2, threshold 1, ensuring priority queuing for voice traffic.

Complete Configurations for Self-Study Lab Part I

Example A-67 through Example A-72 show the complete configurations for each switch relevant to Part I of the Self-Study Lab. Refer to Example A-44 earlier for the relevant configuration of Router-A.

On Cisco IOS switches, because all VTP and VLAN configuration is stored in the non-text VLAN database file, you will not see any VTP or VLAN configuration in the configurations shown. The exception to this is on Switch-D because this switch is configured in VTP transparent mode, which stores VTP and VLAN configuration in the switch configuration file.

Example A-67 *Switch-A Configuration*

```
hostname Switch-A
!
enable secret 5 $1$AQcq$SzdT0xVFqoMiV.wuu7qrR.
!
clock timezone EST -5
!
vlan access-map INTERNAL 10
 match ip address 100
 action forward
vlan filter INTERNAL vlan-list 1,10,100,101,200-202
!
mls qos
!
class-map match-all HTTP
 match access-group HTTP
 !
 !
```

Example A-67 *Switch-A Configuration (Continued)*

```
policy-map QOS
 class HTTP
   police flow 1000000 187500 conform-action set-dscp-transmit 24 exceed-action drop
spanning-tree extend system-id
spanning-tree vlan 1 priority 28672
spanning-tree vlan 1 forward-time 10
spanning-tree vlan 1 max-age 14
spanning-tree vlan 10 priority 24576
spanning-tree vlan 10 forward-time 10
spanning-tree vlan 10 max-age 14
spanning-tree vlan 100 priority 28672
spanning-tree vlan 100 forward-time 10
spanning-tree vlan 100 max-age 14
spanning-tree vlan 101 priority 28672
spanning-tree vlan 101 forward-time 10
spanning-tree vlan 101 max-age 14
spanning-tree vlan 200 priority 28672
spanning-tree vlan 200 forward-time 10
spanning-tree vlan 200 max-age 14
spanning-tree vlan 201 priority 28672
spanning-tree vlan 201 forward-time 10
spanning-tree vlan 201 max-age 14
spanning-tree vlan 202 priority 28672
spanning-tree vlan 202 forward-time 10
spanning-tree vlan 202 max-age 14
!
port-channel load-balance src-dst-ip
!
interface range GigabitEthernet1/1 - 2
 switchport
 mtu 9216
 flowcontrol receive on
 flowcontrol send on
 channel-group 1 mode desirable
 switchport trunk encapsulation isl
 switchport mode trunk
 mls qos trust dscp
!
interface range FastEthernet 2/1 - 2
 switchport
 switchport trunk encapsulation dot1q
 switchport trunk allowed vlan 1,10,200-202,1002-1005
 switchport trunk native vlan 10
 switchport mode trunk
 mls qos trust dscp
 speed 100
 duplex full
!
interface range FastEthernet 2/3 - 24
 switchport
 switchport access vlan 100
 mls qos vlan-based
```

continues

Example A-67 *Switch-A Configuration (Continued)*

```
!
interface range FastEthernet 2/25 - 47
 switchport
 switchport access vlan 101
 mls qos vlan-based
!
interface Vlan 10
 ip address 192.168.10.2 255.255.255.0
!
interface Vlan 100
 mls qos bridged
 service-policy input QOS
!
interface Vlan 101
 mls qos bridged
 service-policy input QOS

ip route 0.0.0.0 0.0.0.0 192.168.10.1
!
access-list 1 permit 192.168.100.0 0.0.0.255
access-list 2 permit host 192.168.100.50
access-list 100 permit ip 192.168.0.0 0.0.0.255 192.168.0.0 0.0.255.255
!
ip access-list extended HTTP
 permit tcp any eq www any
!
snmp-server community cisco RO 2
snmp-server enable traps
snmp-server host 192.168.100.50 cisco
!
line con 0
line vty 0 4
 access-class 1 in
 password cisco
 login
line vty 5 15
 access-class 1 in
 password cisco
 login
!
ntp server 192.168.100.50
end
```

Example A-68 *Switch-B Configuration*

```
# ***** NON-DEFAULT CONFIGURATION *****
!
!
#time: Mon Jul 15 2002, 20:59:16 EST
!
#version 7.2(2)
```

Example A-68 *Switch-B Configuration (Continued)*

```
!
set password $2$fX1D$Vwy2IJlXDsFlMudGbU8Wr1
set enablepass $2$DhKF$iZH3NdFq.oOUOJ2XlM0Dv0
!
#system
set system name  Switch-B
!
#mac address reduction
set spantree macreduction enable
!
#snmp
set snmp community read-only cisco
set snmp trap 192.168.100.50 cisco
set snmp enable
!
#vtp
set vtp domain ciscolab
set vtp mode client
set vtp passwd cisco
!
#ip
set interface sc0 10 192.168.10.3 255.255.255.0

set ip route 0.0.0.0/0.0.0.0 192.168.10.1
!
#spantree
#vlan                      <VlanId>
set spantree fwddelay 10    1
set spantree maxage   14    1
set spantree priority 24576 1
set spantree fwddelay 10    10
set spantree maxage   14    10
set spantree priority 28672 10
set spantree fwddelay 10    100
set spantree maxage   14    100
set spantree priority 28672 100
set spantree fwddelay 10    101
set spantree maxage   14    101
set spantree priority 24576 101
set spantree fwddelay 10    200
set spantree maxage   14    200
set spantree priority 28672 200
set spantree fwddelay 10    201
set spantree maxage   14    201
set spantree priority 24576 201
set spantree fwddelay 10    202
set spantree maxage   14    202
set spantree priority 28672 202
!
#ntp
set ntp server 192.168.100.50
set timezone EST -5 0
```

continues

Example A-68 *Switch-B Configuration (Continued)*

```
!
#permit list
set ip permit enable telnet
set ip permit enable ssh
set ip permit enable snmp
set ip permit 192.168.100.0 255.255.255.0 telnet
set ip permit 192.168.100.50 snmp
!
#qos
set qos enable
set qos bridged-microflow-policing enable 100-101
set qos policer microflow HTTP rate 1000 burst 1500 drop
#QOS
set qos acl ip QOS dscp 24 microflow HTTP tcp any eq 80 any
#
commit qos acl all
!
#port channel
set port channel 1/1-2 13
!
#security ACLs
clear security acl all
#INTERNAL
set security acl ip INTERNAL permit arp
set security acl ip INTERNAL permit ip 192.168.0.0 0.0.255.255 192.168.0.0 0.0.255.255
#
commit security acl all
set security acl map INTERNAL 1,10,100-101,200-202
!
# default port status is enable
!
!
#module 1 : 2-port 1000BaseX Supervisor
set trunk 1/1 on isl 1-1005,1025-4094
set trunk 1/2 on isl 1-1005,1025-4094
set port channel 1/1-2 mode desirable silent
set port jumbo 1/1-2 enable
set port flowcontrol 1/1-2 receive on
set port flowcontrol 1/1-2 send on
set port qos 1/1 trust trust-dscp
set port qos 1/2 trust trust-dscp
!
#module 2 : 48-port 10/100 Ethernet
set vlan 10 2/1-2,48
set vlan 100 2/3-24
set vlan 101 2/25-47
clear trunk 2/1-2 1-1005,1025-4094
set trunk 2/1 on dot1q 1,10,200-202
set trunk 2/2 on dot1q 1,10,200-202
set trunk 2/48 nonegotiate dot1q 1-1005,1025-4094
set port duplex 2/1-2 full
set port speed 2/1-2 100
```

Example A-68 *Switch-B Configuration (Continued)*

```
set port qos 2/3-47 vlan-based
set port qos 2/1 trust trust-dscp
set port qos 2/2 trust trust-dscp
set port qos 2/48 trust trust-ipprec
set qos acl map QOS 100
set qos acl map QOS 101
!
end
```

Example A-69 *Switch-C Configuration*

```
hostname Switch-C
!
enable secret 5 $1$AQcq$SzdT0xVFqoMiV.wuu7qrR.
!
clock timezone EST -5
!
mls qos
!
spanning-tree extend system-id
!
interface range FastEthernet 0/1 - 2
 switchport trunk encapsulation dot1q
 switchport trunk allowed vlan 1,10,200-202,1002-1005
 switchport trunk native vlan 10
 switchport mode trunk
 wrr-queue cos-map 4 5 6 7
 priority-queue out
 mls qos trust dscp
 speed 100
 duplex full
!
interface range FastEthernet 0/3 - 4
 channel-group 1 mode desirable
 switchport trunk encapsulation dot1q
 switchport trunk allowed vlan 1,10,200-202,1002-1005
 switchport trunk native vlan 10
 switchport mode trunk
 wrr-queue cos-map 4 5 6 7
 priority-queue out
 mls qos trust dscp
 speed 100
 duplex full
!
interface FastEthernet 0/5
 switchport trunk encapsulation dot1q
 switchport trunk allowed vlan 1,10,200-202,1002-1005
 switchport trunk native vlan 10
 switchport mode trunk
 wrr-queue cos-map 4 5 6 7
 priority-queue out
```

continues

Example A-69 *Switch-C Configuration (Continued)*

```
 mls qos trust dscp
 speed 100
 duplex full
!
interface FastEthernet 0/6
 switchport trunk encapsulation dot1q
 switchport trunk allowed vlan 1,10,200-202,1002-1005
 switchport trunk native vlan 10
 switchport mode trunk
 wrr-queue cos-map 4 5 6 7
 priority-queue out
 mls qos trust cos
 speed 100
 duplex full
!
interface vlan 10
 ip address 192.168.10.9 255.255.255.0
!
ip default-gateway 192.168.10.1
!
access-list 1 permit 192.168.100.0 0.0.0.255
access-list 2 permit host 192.168.100.50
!
snmp-server community cisco RO 2
snmp-server enable traps
snmp-server host 192.168.100.50 cisco
!
line con 0
line vty 0 4
 access-class 1 in
 password cisco
 login
line vty 5 15
 access-class 1 in
 password cisco
 login
!
ntp server 192.168.100.50
end
```

Example A-70 *Switch-D Configuration*

```
hostname Switch-D
!
enable secret 5 $1$AQcq$SzdT0xVFqoMiV.wuu7qrR.
!
clock timezone EST -5
!
mls qos
!
vlan 10
```

Example A-70 *Switch-D Configuration (Continued)*

```
 name management
vlan 100
 name servers100
vlan 101
 name servers101
vlan 200
 name users200
vlan 201
 name users201
vlan 202
 name phones
!
vtp domain ciscolab
vtp mode transparent
vtp version 2
vtp pruning
!
spanning-tree extend system-id
!
interface range FastEthernet 0/1 - 2
 switchport trunk encapsulation dot1q
 switchport trunk allowed vlan 1,10,200-202,1002-1005
 switchport trunk native vlan 10
 switchport mode trunk
 wrr-queue cos-map 4 5 6 7
 priority-queue out
 mls qos trust dscp
 speed 100
 duplex full
!
interface range FastEthernet 0/3 - 4
 channel-group 1 mode desirable
 switchport trunk encapsulation dot1q
 switchport trunk allowed vlan 1,10,200-202,1002-1005
 switchport trunk native vlan 10
 switchport mode trunk
 wrr-queue cos-map 4 5 6 7
 priority-queue out
 mls qos trust dscp
 speed 100
 duplex full
!
interface FastEthernet 0/5
 switchport trunk encapsulation dot1q
 switchport trunk allowed vlan 1,10,200-202,1002-1005
 switchport trunk native vlan 10
 switchport mode trunk
 wrr-queue cos-map 4 5 6 7
 priority-queue out
 mls qos trust dscp
 speed 100
 duplex full
```

continues

Example A-70 *Switch-D Configuration (Continued)*

```
!
interface FastEthernet 0/6
 switchport trunk encapsulation dot1q
 switchport trunk allowed vlan 1,10,200-202,1002-1005
 switchport trunk native vlan 10
 switchport mode trunk
 wrr-queue cos-map 4 5 6 7
 priority-queue out
 mls qos trust cos
 speed 100
 duplex full
!
interface vlan 10
 ip address 192.168.10.10
!
ip default-gateway 192.168.10.1
!
access-list 1 permit 192.168.100.0 0.0.0.255
access-list 2 permit host 192.168.100.50
!
snmp-server community cisco RO 2
snmp-server enable traps
snmp-server host 192.168.100.50 cisco
!
line con 0
line vty 0 4
 access-class 1 in
 password cisco
 login
line vty 5 15
 access-class 1 in
 password cisco
 login
!
ntp server 192.168.100.50
end
```

Example A-71 *Switch-E Configuration*

```
hostname Switch-E
!
enable secret 5 $1$AQcq$SzdT0xVFqoMiV.wuu7qrR.
!
clock timezone EST -5
!
vlan access-map VLAN202 10
 match ip address 100
 action forward
vlan filter VLAN202 vlan-list 202
!
class-map match-all VOICE
```

Example A-71 *Switch-E Configuration (Continued)*

```
 match access-group VOICE
 !
 class-map match-all VOICE-CONTROL
  match access-group VOICE-CONTROL
 !
 class-map match-all SQL
  match access-group SQL
 !
 class-map match-all HTTP
  match access-group HTTP
 !
 policy-map QOS
  class HTTP
   policy 1000000 187500 exceed-action drop
  class VOICE
   set ip dscp 46
 class VOICE
   set ip dscp 26
  class SQL
   set ip dscp 24
  class class-default
   set ip dscp 8
 !
 mls qos
 !
 spanning-tree uplinkfast
 spanning-tree uplinkfast max-update-rate 200
 spanning-tree portfast bpdufilter default
 spanning-tree extend system-id
 !
 interface FastEthernet 0/1
  switchport trunk encapsulation dot1q
  switchport trunk allowed vlan 1,10,200-202,1002-1005
  switchport trunk native vlan 10
  switchport mode trunk
  wrr-queue cos-map 4 5 6 7
  priority-queue out
  mls qos trust dscp
  speed 100
  duplex full
  spanning-tree vlan 1 cost 10000
  spanning-tree vlan 201 cost 10000

 !
 interface FastEthernet 0/2
  switchport trunk encapsulation dot1q
  switchport trunk allowed vlan 1,10,200-202,1002-1005
  switchport trunk native vlan 10
  spanning-tree vlan
  switchport mode trunk
  wrr-queue cos-map 4 5 6 7
  priority-queue out
```

continues

Example A-71 *Switch-E Configuration (Continued)*

```
 mls qos trust dscp
 speed 100
 duplex full
 spanning-tree vlan 10 cost 10000
 spanning-tree vlan 200 cost 10000
 spanning-tree vlan 202 cost 10000
!
interface range FastEthernet 0/3 - 12
 switchport access vlan 200
 switchport host
 switchport voice vlan 202
 switchport priority extend cos 3
 service-policy input QOS
!
interface range FastEthernet 0/13 - 23
 switchport access vlan 201
 switchport host
 service-policy input QOS
!
interface FastEthernet 0/24
 switchport access vlan 201
 switchport host
 switchport port-security
 switchport port-security maximum 1
 switchport port-security mac-address 0010.0010.0010
 switchport port-security violation shutdown
 service-policy input QOS
!
interface vlan 10
 ip address 192.168.10.10
!
ip default-gateway 192.168.10.1
!
access-list 1 permit 192.168.100.0 0.0.0.255
access-list 2 permit host 192.168.100.50
access-list 100 permit tcp any any eq 2000
access-list 100 permit tcp any eq 2000 any
access-list 100 permit udp any range 16384 32767 any range 16384 32767
access-list 100 permit udp any eq 67 any eq 68
access-list 100 permit udp any eq 68 any eq 67
access-list 100 permit udp any any eq 69
access-list 100 permit udp any eq 69 any
access-list 100 permit udp any eq 88 any
access-list 100 permit icmp any any echo
access-list 100 permit icmp any any echo-reply
!
ip access-list extended VOICE
 permit udp any range 16384 32767 any range 16384 32767
!
ip access-list extended VOICE-CONTROL
 permit tcp any any eq 2000
!
```

Example A-71 *Switch-E Configuration (Continued)*

```
ip access-list extended SQL
 permit tcp any any eq 1433
!
ip access-list extended HTTP
 permit tcp any any eq 80
!
snmp-server community cisco RO 2
snmp-server enable traps
snmp-server host 192.168.100.50 cisco
!
line con 0
line vty 0 4
 access-class 1 in
 password cisco
 login
line vty 5 15
 access-class 1 in
 password cisco
 login
!
ntp server 192.168.100.50
end
```

Example A-72 *Switch-F Configuration*

```
# ***** NON-DEFAULT CONFIGURATION *****
!
!
#time: Mon Jul 15 2002, 21:14:37 EST
!
set password $2$f647$Vwy24JlXDsFlMudGbH8Wr1
set enablepass $2$7498F$f7Dl$.OU492JAM0Dv0
!
#system
set system name Switch-F
!
#snmp
set snmp community read-only cisco
set snmp trap 192.168.100.50 cisco
set snmp enable
!
#mac address reduction
set spantree macreduction enable
!
#vtp
set vtp domain ciscolab
set vtp mode client
set vtp passwd cisco
!
#ip
set interface sc0 10 192.168.10.12 255.255.255.0
set ip route 0.0.0.0/0.0.0.0 192.168.10.1
!
```

continues

Example A-72 *Switch-F Configuration (Continued)*

```
#spantree
#portfast
set spantree global-default bpdu-filter enable
!
#uplinkfast groups
set spantree uplinkfast enable rate 20 all-protocols off
!
#vlan                     <VlanId>
set spantree priority 49152  1
set spantree priority 49152  10
set spantree priority 49152  100
set spantree priority 49152  101
set spantree priority 49152  200
set spantree priority 49152  201
set spantree priority 49152  202
!
#ntp
set ntp server 192.168.100.50
set timezone EST -5 0
!
#permit list
set ip permit enable telnet
set ip permit enable ssh
set ip permit enable snmp
set ip permit 192.168.100.0 255.255.255.0 telnet
set ip permit 192.168.100.50 snmp
!
#qos
set qos enable
set qos defaultcos 3
set qos map 2q1t 2 1 cos 0-4
set qos map 2q1t 2 1 cos 5-7
!
#module 1 : 0-port Switching Supervisor
!
#module 2 : 50-port 10/100/1000 Ethernet
set port disable 2/24-48
set port speed 2/1-2 100
set port duplex 2/1-2 full
set vlan 10 2/1-2
set vlan 200 2/3-12
set vlan 201 2/13-24
set spantree portfast 2/48 enable
clear trunk 2/1-2 1-1005,1025-4094
set trunk 2/1 on dot1q 1,10,200-202
set trunk 2/2 on dot1q 1,10,200-202
set trunk 2/3-48 off
set port channel 2/3-48 mode off
set spantree portvlancost 2/1  cost 10000 1,101,201
set spantree portvlancost 2/2  cost 10000 10,100,102,202
!
end
```

Comprehensive Switching Self-Study Lab Part II Solution

Multilayer Configuration Solution

This appendix provides step-by-step solutions for each configuration task required for Part II of the Chapter 11, "Comprehensive Switching Self-Study Study Lab," which continues on from the Part I solution in Appendix A. Each configuration task is listed, followed by the solution for each task. At the end of this appendix, the complete configurations for each network device relevant to Part II of the lab are provided.

Core Layer Configuration Solution

Step 1   To avoid any IP addressing conflicts with Router-A while you convert the network, disconnect Router-A from Switch-B.

There is no configuration required to complete this task.

Step 2   The new multilayer topology has split the Layer 2 domain into smaller pieces. Ensure that Switch-A and Switch-B are configured appropriately to ensure the VTP, VLAN, and spanning-tree parameters configured in the first lab are maintained in the new core Layer 2 domain formed.

In Figure 11-2, notice that all connections to Switch-A and Switch-B from Switch-C and Switch-D are now *routed connections*, which means that Switch-A and Switch-B are essentially in a new Layer 2 domain and, therefore, you must ensure that VLAN Trunking Protocol (VTP), VLANs, trunks, and Spanning Tree Protocol (STP) are configured appropriately for the new Layer 2 domain. In terms of VTP, because Switch-A and Switch-B are in the ciscolab VTP domain and Switch-A is configured as a VTP server, no modification to the VTP configuration is required. In terms of VLANs, VLANs 200, 201, and 202 are no longer required because these VLANs are present only at the edge of the network, which is now separated by a Layer 3 routing domain. In terms of spanning tree, Switch-A and Switch-B are configured as the root/secondary root bridges for odd and even VLANs already, so no configuration of root bridges is required. However, the network diameter has reduced to 2 switch hops, so you can further reduce spanning-tree timers.

Example B-1 and Example B-2 show the VLAN and spanning-tree configuration required on Switch-A and Switch-B for the new Layer 2 domain.

Example B-1 *Switch-A Layer 2 Configuration*

```
Switch-A# configure terminal
Enter configuration commands, one per line.  End with CNTL/Z.
Switch-A(config)# no vlan 200
Switch-A(config)# no vlan 201
Switch-A(config)# no vlan 202
Switch-A(config)# spanning-tree vlan 10 root primary diameter 2
% This switch is already the root bridge of the VLAN0010 spanning tree
 vlan 10 bridge priority unchanged at 24576
 vlan 10 bridge max aging time set to 10
 vlan 10 bridge hello time unchanged at 2
 vlan 10 bridge forward delay set to 7
Switch-A(config)# spanning-tree vlan 100 root primary diameter 2
% This switch is already the root bridge of the VLAN0100 spanning tree
 vlan 100 bridge priority unchanged at 24576
 vlan 100 bridge max aging time set to 10
 vlan 100 bridge hello time unchanged at 2
 vlan 100 bridge forward delay set to 7
Switch-A(config)# spanning-tree vlan 1 root secondary diameter 2
 vlan 1 bridge priority set to 28672
 vlan 1 bridge max aging time set to 10
 vlan 1 bridge hello time unchanged at 2
 vlan 1 bridge forward delay set to 7
Switch-A(config)# spanning-tree vlan 101 root secondary diameter 2
 vlan 101 bridge priority set to 28672
 vlan 101 bridge max aging time set to 10
 vlan 101 bridge hello time unchanged at 2
 vlan 101 bridge forward delay set to 7
```

Example B-2 *Switch-B Layer 2 Configuration*

```
Switch-B> (enable) set spantree root 1,101 dia 2
VLANs 1,101 bridge priority set to 24576.
VLANs 1,101 bridge max aging time set to 10.
VLANs 1,101 bridge hello time set to 2.
VLANs 1,101 bridge forward delay set to 7.
Switch is now the root switch for active VLANs 1,101.
Switch is already the root switch for active VLANs 1,101.
Switch-B> (enable) set spantree root secondary 10,100 dia 2
VLANs 10,100 bridge priority set to 28672.
VLANs 10,100 bridge max aging time set to 10.
VLANs 10,100 bridge hello time set to 2.
VLANs 10,100 bridge forward delay set to 7.
```

In Example B-1, VLANs 200–202 are deleted because they are no longer required in the new Layer 2 domain. Notice that these are deleted only on Switch-A because Switch-A is the VTP server for the ciscolab domain. In Example B-1 and Example B-2, the spanning-tree root macros are used on both switches to generate new timers based upon a network diameter of 2.

Step 3 Configure Switch-A and Switch-B as Layer 3 switches using the IP
addressing indicated in Figure 11-2. Assume a 24-bit subnet mask for all
subnets. Switch-B has an Multilayer Switch Feature Card (MSFC) installed
that provides Layer 3 switching and is to be named "MSFC-B." Ensure that
physical interfaces are configured as routed interfaces wherever possible,
instead of using switch virtual interfaces (SVIs). If required, you are
permitted to create new VLANs.

Switch-A (native IOS) is by default configured as a Layer 3 switch; therefore, no extra
configuration is required to enable this function. The Inter-Switch Links (ISLs) to Switch-C and
Switch-D are now routed links and, therefore, no longer require trunking. On Switch-A, the
interfaces attached to Switch-C and Switch-D can be configured as routed interfaces because
native IOS supports this configuration. Example B-3 shows the configuration required on
Switch-A to configure the new routed interfaces.

Example B-3 *Switch-A Layer 2 Configuration*

```
Switch-A# configure terminal
Enter configuration commands, one per line.  End with CNTL/Z.
Switch-A(config)# interface FastEthernet 2/1
Switch-A(config-if)# no switchport
Switch-A(config-if)# ip address 192.168.1.1 255.255.255.0
Switch-A(config-if)# exit
Switch-A(config)# interface FastEthernet 2/2
Switch-A(config-if)# no switchport
Switch-A(config-if)# ip address 192.168.2.1 255.255.255.0
Switch-A(config-if)# exit
```

In Example B-3, the **no switchport** command configures interfaces Fa2/1 and Fa2/2 as routed
interfaces. The appropriate IP addressing is assigned as per Figure 11-2 in Chapter 11.

On Switch-B (hybrid IOS), the MSFC-2 installed onboard the Supervisor 2 engine provides a
routing component that must be configured separate from the switch operating system to enable
Layer 3 switching. With hybrid IOS, to create a routed interface, you can configure a SVI only
on the MSFC, which attaches to a VLAN. Consequently, a new VLAN must be created for each
link to Switch-C and Switch-D so that the MSFC can communicate with Switch-C and Switch-
D at the end of each link. Notice in Figure 11-2 that a routed link is required to Router-A as
well. Because Switch-A is the VTP server, the VLANs must be created on Switch-A as depicted
in Example B-4.

Example B-4 *Creating VLANs on Switch-A*

```
Switch-A# configure terminal
Enter configuration commands, one per line.  End with CNTL/Z.
Switch-A(config)# vlan 3
Switch-A(config-vlan)# name SwitchB_to_SwitchC
Switch-A(config-vlan)# exit
Switch-A(config)# vlan 4
Switch-A(config-vlan)# name SwitchB_to_SwitchD
Switch-A(config-vlan)# exit
```

continues

Example B-4 *Creating VLANs on Switch-A (Continued)*

```
Switch-A(config)# vlan 5
Switch-A(config-vlan)# name SwitchB_to_RouterA
Switch-A(config-vlan)# exit
Switch-A(config)# spanning-tree vlan 3 root secomdary diameter 2
 vlan 3 bridge priority set to 28672
 vlan 3 bridge max aging time set to 10
 vlan 3 bridge hello time unchanged at 2
 vlan 3 bridge forward delay set to 7
Switch-A(config)# spanning-tree vlan 4 root primary diameter 2
% This switch is already the root bridge of the VLAN0004 spanning tree
 vlan 4 bridge priority set to 28672
 vlan 4 bridge max aging time set to 10
 vlan 4 bridge hello time unchanged at 2
 vlan 4 bridge forward delay set to 7
Switch-A(config)# spanning-tree vlan 5 root secondary diameter 2
 vlan 5 bridge priority set to 28672
 vlan 5 bridge max aging time set to 10
 vlan 5 bridge hello time unchanged at 2
 vlan 5 bridge forward delay set to 7
```

In Example B-4, notice that you must also configure spanning tree for the new VLANs. Once the VLANs have propagated to Switch-B, the appropriate VLANs are in place to begin configuring the MSFC. Example B-5 shows the configuration required on Switch-B to remove trunks, configure spanning tree, assign the appropriate VLANs, and configure the MSFC (MSFC-B) to enable Layer 3 switching.

Example B-5 *MSFC-B Configuration*

```
Switch-B> (enable) set trunk 2/1-2 off
Port(s) 2/1-2 trunk mode set to off.
Switch-B> (enable) set spantree root 3,5 dia 2
VLANs 3,5 bridge priority set to 24576.
VLANs 3,5 bridge max aging time set to 10.
VLANs 3,5 bridge hello time set to 2.
VLANs 3,5 bridge forward delay set to 7.
Switch is now the root switch for active VLANs 1,101.
Switch-B> (enable) set spantree root secondary 4 dia 2
VLANs 4 bridge priority set to 28672.
VLANs 4 bridge max aging time set to 10.
VLANs 4 bridge hello time set to 2.
VLANs 4 bridge forward delay set to 7.
Switch-B> (enable) set vlan 3 2/1
VLAN 3 modified.
VLAN 1 modified.
VLAN  Mod/Ports
----  ----------------------
3       2/1
Switch-B> (enable) set vlan 4 2/2
VLAN 4 modified.
VLAN 1 modified.
VLAN  Mod/Ports
```

Example B-5   *MSFC-B Configuration (Continued)*

```
.... ......................
4     2/2
Switch-B> (enable) session 15
Trying Router-15...
Connected to Router-15.
Escape character is '^]'.

Router> enable
Router# configure terminal
Enter configuration commands, one per line.  End with CNTL/Z.
Router(config)# hostname MSFC-B
MSFC-B(config)# enable secret cisco
MSFC-B(config)# line vty 0 4
MSFC-B(config-line)# password cisco
MSFC-B(config-line)# exit
MSFC-B(config)# interface VLAN 3
MSFC-B(config-if)# ip address 192.168.3.1 255.255.255.0
MSFC-B(config-if)# exit
MSFC-B(config)# interface VLAN 4
MSFC-B(config-if)# ip address 192.168.4.1 255.255.255.0
MSFC-B(config-if)# exit
MSFC-B(config)# interface VLAN 10
MSFC-B(config-if)# ip address 192.168.10.4 255.255.255.0
MSFC-B(config-if)# exit
```

In Example B-5, Switch-B is first cleared of any trunks to Switch-C and Switch-D, spanning tree is configured for each VLAN, and each port is then placed into the appropriate VLAN. The MSFC is next configured with an appropriate host name, and a VLAN 10 SVI is created for management purposes. SVIs are created for VLAN 3 and VLAN 4, which enable IP communications over ports 2/1 and 2/2 to Switch-C and Switch-D.

Step 4   Ensure that devices connected to VLANs 100 and 101 can still connect to the rest of the network without reconfiguration of the IP addressing parameters on any edge device in these VLANs. Traffic for VLAN 100 should be routed through Switch-A, and traffic for VLAN 101 should be routed through MSFC-B. However, should either of the routing engines on either core switch fail, then the remaining working routing engine takes over.

This configuration task requires Hot Standby Router Protocol (HSRP) to be configured on Switch-A and MSFC-B for VLANs 100 and 101, with the virtual IP addresses configured as 192.168.100.1 and 192.168.101.1 (recall from Part I, Router-A was configured with these IP addresses that are used as the default gateway on each VLAN). Example B-6 and Example B-7 show the HSRP configuration required on Switch-A and MSFC-B.

Example B-6   *Configuring HSRP for VLANs 100 and 101 on Switch-A*

```
Switch-A# configure terminal
Enter configuration commands, one per line.  End with CNTL/Z.
Switch-A(config)# interface vlan 100
```

continues

Example B-6   *Configuring HSRP for VLANs 100 and 101 on Switch-A (Continued)*

```
Switch-A(config-if)# ip address 192.168.100.2 255.255.255.0
Switch-A(config-if)# standby ip 192.168.100.1
Switch-A(config-if)# standby priority 150 preempt
Switch-A(config-if)# exit
Switch-A(config)# interface vlan 101
Switch-A(config-if)# no shutdown
Switch-A(config-if)# ip address 192.168.101.2 255.255.255.0
Switch-A(config-if)# standby ip 192.168.101.1
Switch-A(config-if)# standby priority 100
```

Example B-7   *Configuring HSRP for VLANs 100 and 101 on MSFC-B*

```
MSFC-B# configure terminal
Enter configuration commands, one per line.  End with CNTL/Z.
MSFC-B(config)# interface vlan 100
MSFC-B(config-if)# ip address 192.168.100.3 255.255.255.0
MSFC-B(config-if)# standby ip 192.168.100.1
MSFC-B(config-if)# standby priority 100
MSFC-B(config-if)# exit
MSFC-B(config)# interface vlan 101
MSFC-B(config-if)# ip address 192.168.101.3 255.255.255.0
MSFC-B(config-if)# standby ip 192.168.101.1
MSFC-B(config-if)# standby priority 150 preempt
```

In Example B-6 and Example B-7, SVIs are created on both devices to enable access to each server VLAN. Notice that Switch-A is configured as the active (primary) router for VLAN 100 (as its priority is higher than Switch-B), while Switch-B is configured as the active router for VLAN 101. Notice that you must create separate physical IP addresses for each HSRP router.

Distribution and Access Layer Configuration Solution

Step 1   The new multilayer topology has split the Layer 2 domain into smaller pieces. Ensure that Switch-C, Switch-D, Switch-E, and Switch-F are configured appropriately to ensure the VTP, VLAN, and spanning-tree parameters configured in the first lab are maintained in the new Layer 2 topology.

All connections to Switch-A and Switch-B from Switch-C and Switch-D are now routed connections, while the connections to Switch-E and Switch-F are still switched connections. Consequently, Switch-C through Switch-F are essentially in a new Layer 2 domain, and you must ensure that VTP, VLANs, trunks, and STP are configured appropriately for the new Layer 2 domain. In terms of VTP, reconfiguration is required because Switch-D is configured in VTP transparent mode and Switch-F is configured in a different VTP domain. In terms of VLANs, VLANs 100 and 101 are no longer required because these VLANs are present only at the core of the network that is now separated by a Layer 3 routing domain. In terms of spanning tree, Switch-C and Switch-D should be configured as root/secondary bridges for each VLAN.

Example B-8 and Example B-9 show the VTP configuration required on Switch-D and Switch-F to ensure all switches are part of the same VTP domain.

Example B-8 *Switch-D VTP Configuration*

```
Switch-D# configure terminal
Enter configuration commands, one per line.  End with CNTL/Z.
Switch-D(config)# vtp password cisco
Setting device VLAN database password to cisco.
Switch-D(config)# vtp mode client
Setting device to VTP CLIENT mode.
```

Example B-9 *Switch-F VTP Configuration*

```
Switch-F> (enable) set vtp domain ccnp
VTP domain ccnp modified
```

In Example B-9, Switch-F is already configured as a VTP client; hence, you don't need to change the VTP mode.

Example B-10 and Example B-11 show the configuration required for VLANs and spanning tree on Switch-C and Switch-D.

Example B-10 *Switch-C VLAN and Spanning Tree Configuration*

```
Switch-C# configure terminal
Enter configuration commands, one per line.  End with CNTL/Z.
Switch-C(config)# no vlan 100
Switch-C(config)# no vlan 101
Switch-C(config)# spanning-tree vlan 10 root primary diameter 4
% This switch is already the root bridge of the VLAN0010 spanning tree
 vlan 10 bridge priority set to 24576
 vlan 10 bridge max aging time set to 14
 vlan 10 bridge hello time unchanged at 2
 vlan 10 bridge forward delay set to 10
Switch-C(config)# spanning-tree vlan 200 root primary diameter 4
% This switch is already the root bridge of the VLAN0200 spanning tree
 vlan 200 bridge priority set to 24576
 vlan 200 bridge max aging time set to 14
 vlan 200 bridge hello time unchanged at 2
 vlan 200 bridge forward delay set to 10
Switch-C(config)# spanning-tree vlan 1 root secondary diameter 4
 vlan 1 bridge priority set to 28672
 vlan 1 bridge max aging time set to 14
 vlan 1 bridge hello time unchanged at 2
 vlan 1 bridge forward delay set to 10
Switch-C(config)# spanning-tree vlan 201 root secondary diameter 4
 vlan 201 bridge priority set to 28672
 vlan 201 bridge max aging time set to 14
 vlan 201 bridge hello time unchanged at 2
 vlan 201 bridge forward delay set to 10
```

Example B-11 *Switch-D Spanning Tree Configuration*

```
Switch-D# configure terminal
Enter configuration commands, one per line.  End with CNTL/Z.
Switch-D(config)# spanning-tree vlan 1 root primary diameter 4
 vlan 1 bridge priority set to 24576
 vlan 1 bridge max aging time set to 14
 vlan 1 bridge hello time unchanged at 2
 vlan 1 bridge forward delay set to 10
Switch-D(config)# spanning-tree vlan 201 root primary diameter 4
 vlan 201 bridge priority set to 24576
 vlan 201 bridge max aging time set to 14
 vlan 201 bridge hello time unchanged at 2
 vlan 201 bridge forward delay set to 10
Switch-D(config)# spanning-tree vlan 10 root secondary diameter 4
 vlan 10 bridge priority set to 28672
 vlan 10 bridge max aging time set to 14
 vlan 10 bridge hello time unchanged at 2
 vlan 10 bridge forward delay set to 10
Switch-D(config)# spanning-tree vlan 200 root secondary diameter 4
 vlan 200 bridge priority set to 28672
 vlan 200 bridge max aging time set to 14
 vlan 200 bridge hello time unchanged at 2
 vlan 200 bridge forward delay set to 10
```

In Example B-10 and Example B-11, notice that Switch-C is configured as the root bridge for even VLANs, while Switch-D is configured as the root bridge for odd VLANs.

Step 2   Configure Switch-C and Switch-D as Layer 3 switches using the IP addressing shown in Figure 11-2. Ensure that physical interfaces are configured as routed interfaces wherever possible, instead of using SVIs. If required, you are permitted to create new VLANs.

Switch-C and Switch-D are Layer 3–capable switches; however, by default, this functionality is not enabled. The ISLs to Switch-A and Switch-B are now routed links and, therefore, no longer require trunking. The EtherChannel bundle between Switch-C and Switch-D still needs to remain a Layer 2 trunk. On both switches, the interfaces attached to Switch-A and Switch-B can be configured as routed interfaces because Cisco IOS supports this configuration. Example B-12 and Example B-13 show the configuration required on Switch-C and Switch-D to enable Layer 3 switching.

Example B-12 *Configuring Layer 3 Switching on Switch-C*

```
Switch-C# configure terminal
Enter configuration commands, one per line.  End with CNTL/Z.
Switch-C(config)# ip routing
Switch-C(config)# interface FastEthernet 0/1
Switch-C(config-if)# no switchport
Switch-C(config-if)# ip address 192.168.1.2 255.255.255.0
Switch-C(config-if)# exit
Switch-C(config)# interface FastEthernet 0/2
Switch-C(config-if)# no switchport
Switch-C(config-if)# ip address 192.168.3.2 255.255.255.0
```

Example B-13 *Configuring Layer 3 Switching on Switch-D*

```
Switch-D# configure terminal
Enter configuration commands, one per line.  End with CNTL/Z.
Switch-D(config)# ip routing
Switch-D(config)# interface FastEthernet 0/1
Switch-D(config-if)# no switchport
Switch-D(config-if)# ip address 192.168.2.2 255.255.255.0
Switch-D(config-if)# exit
Switch-D(config)# interface FastEthernet 0/2
Switch-D(config-if)# no switchport
Switch-D(config-if)# ip address 192.168.4.2 255.255.255.0
```

In Example B-12 and Example B-13, notice that the **ip routing** global configuration command is required to enable Layer 3 switching. The **no switchport** command configures interfaces Fa2/1 and Fa2/2 as routed interfaces. Also, notice that both switch uplinks to Switch-A and Switch-B are configured as routed physical ports.

At this point, you should be able to ping Switch-A and Switch-B across the ISLs from Switch-C and Switch-D. Example B-14 demonstrates Switch-C successfully pinging Switch-A and Switch-B.

Example B-14 *Verifying IP Connectivity from Switch-C*

```
Switch-C# ping 192.168.1.1

Type escape sequence to abort.
Sending 5, 100-byte ICMP Echos to 192.168.1.1, timeout is 2 seconds:
!!!!!
Success rate is 100 percent (5/5), round-trip min/avg/max = 8/9/16 ms
Switch-C# ping 192.168.3.1

Type escape sequence to abort.
Sending 5, 100-byte ICMP Echos to 192.168.3.1, timeout is 2 seconds:
!!!!!
Success rate is 100 percent (5/5), round-trip min/avg/max = 8/8/10 ms
```

Step 3   Configure the network so that devices connected to VLANs 200, 201, and 202 can still connect to the rest of the network without reconfiguration of the IP addressing parameters on any edge device in these VLANs. You must ensure that edge devices can still connect to the rest of the network within 5 seconds after the failure of either Switch-C or Switch-D. The routed traffic load should be shared for even and odd VLANs by Switch-C and Switch-D, respectively.

This configuration task requires HSRP to be configured on Switch-C and Switch-D for VLANs 200, 201, and 202, with the virtual IP addresses configured as 192.168.200.1, 192.168.201.1, and 192.168.202.1. Example B-15 and Example B-16 show the HSRP configuration required on Switch-C and Switch-D.

Example B-15 *Configuring HSRP for VLANs 200–202 on Switch-C*

```
Switch-C# configure terminal
Enter configuration commands, one per line.  End with CNTL/Z.
Switch-C(config)# interface vlan 200
Switch-C(config-if)# ip address 192.168.200.2 255.255.255.0
Switch-C(config-if)# standby ip 192.168.200.1
Switch-C(config-if)# standby priority 150 preempt
Switch-C(config-if)# exit
Switch-C(config)# interface vlan 201
Switch-C(config-if)# ip address 192.168.201.2 255.255.255.0
Switch-C(config-if)# standby ip 192.168.201.1
Switch-C(config-if)# standby priority 100
Switch-C(config)# interface vlan 202
Switch-C(config-if)# ip address 192.168.202.2 255.255.255.0
Switch-C(config-if)# standby ip 192.168.202.1
Switch-C(config-if)# standby priority 150 preempt
```

Example B-16 *Configuring HSRP for VLANs 200-202 on Switch-D*

```
Switch-D# configure terminal
Enter configuration commands, one per line.  End with CNTL/Z.
Switch-D(config)# interface vlan 200
Switch-D(config-if)# ip address 192.168.200.3 255.255.255.0
Switch-D(config-if)# standby ip 192.168.200.1
Switch-D(config-if)# standby priority 100
Switch-D(config-if)# exit
Switch-D(config)# interface vlan 201
Switch-D(config-if)# no shutdown
Switch-D(config-if)# ip address 192.168.201.3 255.255.255.0
Switch-D(config-if)# standby ip 192.168.201.1
Switch-D(config-if)# standby priority 150 preempt
Switch-D(config)# interface vlan 202
Switch-D(config-if)# no shutdown
Switch-D(config-if)# ip address 192.168.202.3 255.255.255.0
Switch-D(config-if)# standby ip 192.168.202.1
Switch-D(config-if)# standby priority 100
```

In Example B-15 and Example B-16, notice that HSRP priorities are configured so that Switch-C is the active router for even VLANs (200 and 202) and Switch-D is the active router for odd VLANs (201).

Routing and Multicast Routing Configuration Solution

Step 1 Configure Router-A as indicated in Figure 11-2. The FastEthernet0/0 interface should now be configured as a non-trunk port with a single IP address configured, as shown in Figure 11-2. Once complete, reconnect Router-A to Switch-B.

To complete this configuration task, the trunk configuration on Router-A must be removed, as well as the configuration on Switch-B for port 2/48. A new VLAN interface must be configured on MSFC-B to allow MSFC-B to communicate with the 192.168.5.0/24 subnet that is to be configured between Switch-B and Router-A. Example B-17 shows the configuration required on Switch-B and MSFC-B to disable trunking and create the new VLAN interface for communications to Router-A.

Example B-17 *Configuring the Connection Between Switch-B and Router-A*

```
Switch-B> (enable) set trunk 2/48 off
Port(s)  2/48 trunk mode set to off.
Switch-B> (enable) set vlan 5 2/48
VLAN 5 modified.
VLAN 1 modified.
VLAN  Mod/Ports
---- ----------------------
5     2/48
      15/1
Switch-B> (enable) session 15
Trying Router-15...
Connected to Router-15.
Escape character is '^]'.

MSFC-B> enable
MSFC-B# configure terminal
Enter configuration commands, one per line.  End with CNTL/Z.
MSFC-B(config)# interface vlan 5
MSFC-B(config-if)# no shutdown
MSFC-B(config-if)# ip address 192.168.5.2 255.255.255.0
```

Example B-18 shows the configuration required on Router-A.

Example B-18 *Reconfiguring Router-A*

```
Router-A# configure terminal
Enter configuration commands, one per line.  End with CNTL/Z.
Router-A(config)# no interface FastEthernet 0/0.10
% Not all config may be removed and may reappear after reactivating
    the sub-interface
Router-A(config)# no interface FastEthernet 0/0.100
% Not all config may be removed and may reappear after reactivating
    the sub-interface
Router-A(config)# no interface FastEthernet 0/0.101
% Not all config may be removed and may reappear after reactivating
    the sub-interface
Router-A(config)# no interface FastEthernet 0/0.200
% Not all config may be removed and may reappear after reactivating
    the sub-interface
Router-A(config)# no interface FastEthernet 0/0.201
% Not all config may be removed and may reappear after reactivating
    the sub-interface
Router-A(config)# no interface FastEthernet 0/0.202
```

continues

Example B-18 *Reconfiguring Router-A (Continued)*

```
% Not all config may be removed and may reappear after reactivating
    the sub-interface
Router-A(config)# interface FastEthernet 0/0
Router-A(config-if)# ip address 192.168.5.1 255.255.255.0
```

In Router-A, each subinterface is removed because trunking is no longer configured. The physical interface is then configured with an IP address of 192.168.5.1/24. After connecting Router-A back to Switch-B, Router-A should be able to ping 192.168.5.2 on MSFC-B.

Step 2   Ensure that all switches can be managed using the 192.168.10.x addressing used in Part I. The management IP addresses configured on each device cannot be altered, although you may alter the subnet mask and default gateway configuration.

To complete this task, you must split up the 192.168.10.0/24 subnet into smaller subnets so that each subnet fits into the new Layer 3 topology. In the new topology, two Layer 2 domains are separated by a Layer 3 routing domain. The first Layer 2 domain consists of Switch-A and Switch-B, while the second Layer 2 domain consists of Switch-C, Switch-D, Switch-E, and Switch-F. With a 24-bit subnet mask configured, all switches think that all other switches are within the same IP subnet (Layer 2 domain), which, of course, is not the case because routing devices now exist between each Layer 2 domain. To resolve this situation, you must split up the 192.168.10.0/24 subnet into two subnets to represent the fact that two Layer 2 domains now exist. The following lists the new subnets that must be created:

- **192.168.10.0/29**—This subnet consists of devices in the address range of 192.168.10.0–192.168.10.7, which includes Switch-A and Switch-B.

- **192.168.10.8/29**—This subnet consists of devices in the address range of 192.168.10.8–192.168.10.15, which include Switch-C, Switch-D, Switch-E, and Switch-F.

Each subnet can be created by simply altering the subnet mask on each switch from a 24-bit mask (255.255.255.0) to a 29-bit mask (255.255.255.248). After creating the subnets, the next thing that must be configured is an appropriate default gateway for switches that do not possess Layer 3 routing capabilities. These switches include Switch-B (although Switch-B is a Layer 3 switch, MSFC-B provides the separate routing component) and Switch-F. All other switches are now configured for routing, and do not require default gateway configuration. For this lab, Switch-A is configured as the default gateway for Switch-B, and Switch-C is configured as the default gateway for Switch-F.

Example B-19 and Example B-20 demonstrates the configuration required on Switch-A and Switch-B to enable management communications using the same IP addressing.

Example B-19 *Configuring the Management Interface for 192.168.10.0/29 on Switch-A*

```
Switch-A# configure terminal
Enter configuration commands, one per line.  End with CNTL/Z.
Switch-A(config)# interface vlan 10
Switch-A(config-if)# ip address 192.168.10.2 255.255.255.248
```

Example B-20 *Configuring the Management Interface for 192.168.10.0/29 on Switch-B*

```
Switch-B> (enable) set interface sc0 10 192.168.10.3 255.255.255.248
Interface sc0 vlan set, IP address and netmask set.
Switch-B> (enable) clear ip route all
All routes deleted.
Switch-B> (enable) set ip route default 192.168.10.2
Route added.
```

In Example B-20, the default gateway is configured as 192.168.10.2 (Switch-A) instead of 192.168.10.1 because Router-A is no longer configured with this address and Switch-A is providing routing. The same configurations used in Examples B-19 and B-20 are required on the remaining switches. The subnet mask on each switch needs to be configured as a 29-bit (255.255.255.248) mask. On Switch-E and Switch-F, a default gateway of 192.168.10.9 (Switch-C) needs to be configured.

Step 3 Configure Enhanced Interior Gateway Routing Protocol (EIGRP) on all routing devices so that any device in the network can communicate with any other device, regardless of the location in the network.

All routing devices must be configured for EIGRP and should advertise information about all subnets. This configuration can easily be achieved by configuring all 192.168.x.x networks to be included in EIGRP. You must also remove any default routes that point to Router-A from Part I (192.168.10.1) because this address no longer exists, invalidating the route. Example B-21 demonstrates the EIGRP configuration required on Switch-A.

Example B-21 *Configuring EIGRP on Switch-A*

```
Switch-A# configure terminal
Enter configuration commands, one per line.  End with CNTL/Z.
Switch-A(config)# no ip route 0.0.0.0 0.0.0.0 192.168.10.1
Switch-A(config)# router eigrp 1
Switch-A(config-router)# network 192.168.0.0 0.0.255.255
```

The preceding configuration configures EIGRP autonomous system 1 to advertise and operate over any 192.168.x.x network on Switch-A. The same configuration is required on all other routing devices, except for Router-A, which also requires the 10.0.0.0/8 network to be advertised. You must ensure that the same autonomous system number (1) is configured on all EIGRP routers. Once all routing configuration is in place, you should be able to ping any IP address from anywhere in the network (excluding 10.0.0.0/8 because it is a restricted network). Example B-22 shows the routing table on Switch-A after all routing configuration has been completed.

Example B-22 *Displaying the IP Routing Table on Switch-A*

```
Switch-A# show ip route
Codes: C - connected, S - static, I - IGRP, R - RIP, M - mobile, B - BGP
       D - EIGRP, EX - EIGRP external, O - OSPF, IA - OSPF inter area
       N1 - OSPF NSSA external type 1, N2 - OSPF NSSA external type 2
```

continues

Example B-22 *Displaying the IP Routing Table on Switch-A (Continued)*

```
               E1 - OSPF external type 1, E2 - OSPF external type 2, E - EGP
               i - IS-IS, L1 - IS-IS level-1, L2 - IS-IS level-2, ia - IS-IS inter area
               * - candidate default, U - per-user static route, o - ODR
               P - periodic downloaded static route

Gateway of last resort is not set

D    10.0.0.0/8       [90/3072] via 192.168.100.3, 00:00:28, Vlan100
                      [90/3072] via 192.168.101.3, 00:00:28, Vlan100
C    192.168.1.0/24 is directly connected, Fa2/1
C    192.168.2.0/24 is directly connected, Fa2/2
     192.168.10.0/29 is subnetted, 2x subnets
C       192.168.10.2 is directly connected, Vlan10
D       192.168.10.8 [90/3072] via 192.168.1.2, 00:00:28, Fa2/1
                     [90/3072] via 192.168.2.2, 00:00:14, Fa2/2
C    192.168.100.0/24 is directly connected, Vlan100
C    192.168.101.0/24 is directly connected, Vlan101
D    192.168.200.0/24 [90/3072] via 192.168.1.2, 00:00:28, Vlan11
                      [90/3072] via 192.168.2.2, 00:00:14, Vlan11
D    192.168.201.0/24 [90/3072] via 192.168.1.2, 00:00:28, Vlan11
                      [90/3072] via 192.168.2.2, 00:00:14, Vlan11
D    192.168.202.0/24 [90/3072] via 192.168.1.2, 00:00:28, Vlan11
                      [90/3072] via 192.168.2.2, 00:00:14, Vlan11
```

Notice that many routes have two paths available, reflecting the redundant topology of the network. For example, 192.168.200.0/24 is reachable via both 192.168.1.2 (Switch-C) and 192.168.2.2 (Switch-D). Both routes have an equal cost (3072) and, hence, are both installed into the routing table. All traffic routed by the MSFC (in reality, by the L3 engine on the Policy Feature Card [PFC] onboard Switch-A) is load shared over each route, which ensures that the load placed on the redundant paths in your network is being equally distributed, increasing network efficiency and performance.

TIP   Load sharing on the PFC-2 (using Cisco Express Forwarding [CEF]) is performed on a per-destination basis in which packets to a destination always take the same path. This load sharing can result in an uneven distribution of traffic, particularly if you have one heavily used device in the network. Per-packet load sharing load shares by sending each packet over equal cost paths, resulting in a more even distribution of traffic. This feature is supported in CEF for Cisco routers, but is not supported on the PFC-2.

Step 4   Configure multicast routing on all routing devices, which includes all switches except for Switch-E and Switch-F. Configure a shared tree that is rooted at Router-A, which should be used for initial forwarding of multicast traffic. You are not permitted to manually configure Router-A as the root of the shared tree on any other multicast router. Ensure all interfaces enabled for multicast routing are operating in the appropriate mode as recommended by Cisco.

This task requires the configuration of PIM sparse-dense mode, with a rendezvous point (RP) configured at Router-A. Router-A must be configured for Auto-RP, because you cannot manually configure RPs in the task. On Switch-A, Switch-C, Switch-D, and MSFC-B, you must configure multicast routing and enable it for each interface in the network. Example B-23 demonstrates the multicast configuration required on Switch-C.

Example B-23 *Configuring Multicast Routing*

```
Switch-C# configure terminal
Enter configuration commands, one per line.  End with CNTL/Z.
Switch-C(config)# ip multicast-routing
Switch-C(config)# interface range FastEthernet 0/1 - 2
Switch-C(config-if)# ip pim sparse-dense-mode
Switch-C(config-if)# exit
Switch-C(config)# interface vlan 10
Switch-C(config-if)# ip pim sparse-dense-mode
Switch-C(config-if)# exit
Switch-C(config)# interface vlan 200 - 202
Switch-C(config-if)# ip pim sparse-dense-mode
Switch-C(config-if)# exit
```

Router-A must be configured as a RP and must also announce its presence using a protocol such as Auto-RP. Example B-24 shows the configuration required on Router-A.

Example B-24 *Configuring Multicast Routing on Router-A*

```
Router-A# show ip route
Enter configuration commands, one per line.  End with CNTL/Z.
Router-A(config)# ip multicast-routing
Router-A(config)# ip pim send-rp-announce FastEthernet 0/0 scope 5
Router-A(config)# interface FastEthernet 0/0
Router-A(config-if)# ip pim sparse-dense-mode
```

The **ip pim send-rp-announce** command is configured to announce the IP address of the FastEthernet0/0 interface (192.168.5.2) as the RP. The **scope** keyword is configured so that the time-to-live (TTL) of the RP announcements is set to 5 hops.

Step 5 Configure Switch-E to join the multicast group 239.1.1.1 on interface VLAN 10. Ensure that any edge device can ping the 239.1.1.1 address with a response from Switch-E.

Example B-25 shows the configuration required on Switch-E.

Example B-25 *Joining a Multicast Group on Router-E*

```
Switch-E# configure terminal
Enter configuration commands, one per line.  End with CNTL/Z.
Switch-E(config)# interface vlan 10
Switch-E(config-if)# ip igmp join-group 239.1.1.1
```

After the configuration of Example B-25, Switch-E joins the 239.1.1.1 group on VLAN 10. Switch-C and Switch-D are both attached to VLAN 10 and, hence, receive Internet Group Management Protocol (IGMP) Joins sent by Switch-E to join the 239.1.1.1 address.

This action causes Switch-C and Switch-D to join a shared tree rooted at Router-A. As soon as a device starts sending traffic to the 239.1.1.1 address, a shortest path tree (SPT) is formed between the multicast router located closest to the source device and either Switch-C or Switch-D, with the Protocol Independent Multicast (PIM) assert process determining whether Switch-C or Switch-D is the forwarding PIM router for the VLAN 10 subnet. Because all edge devices in this network are reachable over equal cost paths using either Switch-C or Switch-D, the PIM assert process chooses the router with the highest IP address on VLAN 10—in this case, Switch-D (192.168.10.10).

To test the multicast routing topology, attempt to ping 239.1.1.1 from Switch-B. Example B-26 shows the multicast routing table of Switch-D after ping connectivity has been successfully established.

Example B-26 *Viewing the Multicast Routing Table on Switch-D*

```
Switch-D# show ip mroute
IP Multicast Routing Table
Flags: D - Dense, S - Sparse, s - SSM Group, C - Connected, L - Local,
       P - Pruned, R - RP-bit set, F - Register flag, T - SPT-bit set,
       J - Join SPT, M - MSDP created entry, X - Proxy Join Timer Running
       A - Advertised via MSDP, U - URD, I - Received Source Specific Host
          Report
Outgoing interface flags: H - Hardware switched
Timers: Uptime/Expires
Interface state: Interface, Next-Hop or VCD, State/Mode

(*, 239.1.1.1), 01:25:49/00:02:32, RP 192.168.5.1, flags: SJC
  Incoming interface: FastEthernet0/2, RPF nbr 192.168.4.1
  Outgoing interface list:
    FastEthernet0/1, Prune/Sparse, 01:08:34/00:00:00
    Vlan10, Forward/Sparse, 01:08:49/00:00:00, H
    Vlan200, Prune/Sparse, 01:08:44/00:00:00
    Vlan201, Prune/Sparse, 01:08:53/00:00:00
    Vlan202, Prune/Sparse, 01:08:51/00:00:00

(192.168.10.3, 239.1.1.1), 01:18:53/00:01:41, RP 192.168.5.1, flags: CT
  Incoming interface: FastEthernet0/2, RPF nbr 192.168.4.1
  Outgoing interface list:
    FastEthernet0/1, Prune/Sparse, 01:09:34/00:00:00
    Vlan10, Forward/Sparse, 01:25:49/00:00:00, H
    Vlan200, Prune/Sparse, 01:16:04/00:00:00
    Vlan201, Prune/Sparse, 01:16:04/00:00:00
    Vlan202, Prune/Sparse, 01:16:04/00:00:00

(*, 224.0.1.40), 01:40:01/00:02:42, RP 0.0.0.0, flags: SJCL
  Incoming interface: Null, RPF nbr 0.0.0.0
  Outgoing interface list:
    FastEthernet0/2, Forward/Dense, 01:39:54/00:00:00
```

In Example B-26, notice the two shaded multicast route entries. The first, (*,239.1.1.1), is the shared tree that is rooted at the RP. The second, (192.168.10.3,239.1.1.1), is the SPT for Switch-B sending multicast traffic to the 239.1.1.1 group.

Step 6 Ensure that all switches constrain multicast traffic to multicast routers and receivers within each Layer 2 network.

All switches in this lab support IGMP snooping, except for Switch-F, which supports only Cisco Group Management Protocol (CGMP). All switches in this lab have the IGMP snooping feature enabled by default; hence, no extra configuration is required.

To configure CGMP on Switch-F, you must also enable CGMP on each multicast router that is attached to the VLAN 10 subnet Switch-F is attached to. Example B-27 shows the configuration required on Switch-C. This configuration is also required on Switch-D because both are multicast routers attached to Switch-F.

Example B-27 *Configuring CGMP on Switch-C*

```
Switch-C# configure terminal
Enter configuration commands, one per line.  End with CNTL/Z.
Switch-C(config)# interface range vlan 10, vlan 200 - 202
Switch-C(config-if-range)# ip cgmp
```

Example B-28 shows the configuration required on Switch-F, which enables it to receive CGMP messages from Switch-C and Switch-D.

Example B-28 *Configuring CGMP on Switch-F*

```
Switch-F> (config) set cgmp enable
CGMP support for IP multicast enabled.
```

Step 7 Ensure that any access control configurations on the core switches are still compatible with the new topology.

In Part I you configured VLAN access control lists (VACLs) on Switch-A and Switch-B. A VACL called INTERNAL was created that permitted access only between devices within the 192.168.x.x networks. Because the VLANs in use within the core have changed, you must apply the VACL to the new VLANs to maintain security filtering. Example B-29 and Example B-30 shows the configuration required on Switch-A and Switch-B.

Example B-29 *Updating VACLs on Switch-A*

```
Switch-A# configure terminal
Enter configuration commands, one per line.  End with CNTL/Z.
Switch-A(config)# no vlan filter INTERNAL 1, 10, 100, 101, 200-202
Switch-A(config)# vlan filter INTERNAL 1, 3-5, 10, 100, 101
```

Example B-30 *Updating VACLs on Switch-B*

```
Switch-B> (enable)
Switch-B> (enable) clear security acl map all
Map deletion in progress.

Successfully cleared mapping between ACL INTERNAL and VLAN 1.
Successfully cleared mapping between ACL INTERNAL and VLAN 10.
Successfully cleared mapping between ACL INTERNAL and VLAN 100.
Successfully cleared mapping between ACL INTERNAL and VLAN 101.
Successfully cleared mapping between ACL INTERNAL and VLAN 200.
Successfully cleared mapping between ACL INTERNAL and VLAN 201.
Successfully cleared mapping between ACL INTERNAL and VLAN 202.

Switch-B> (enable) set security acl map INTERNAL 1,3-5,10,100,101
Mapping in progress...

ACL INTERNAL successfully mapped to VLAN 1.
ACL INTERNAL successfully mapped to VLAN 3.
ACL INTERNAL successfully mapped to VLAN 4.
ACL INTERNAL successfully mapped to VLAN 5.
ACL INTERNAL successfully mapped to VLAN 10.
ACL INTERNAL successfully mapped to VLAN 100.
ACL INTERNAL successfully mapped to VLAN 101.
```

Complete Configurations for Self-Study Lab Part II

Example B-31 through Example B-38 show the relevant configurations for each switch and router after completing Part II of the Self-Study Lab.

NOTE   On Cisco IOS switches, because all VTP and VLAN configuration is stored in the non-text VLAN database file, you will not see any VTP or VLAN configuration in the configurations shown.

Example B-31 *Switch-A Configuration*

```
hostname Switch-A
!
enable secret cisco
!
clock timezone EST -5
!
vlan access-map INTERNAL 10
 match ip address 100
 action forward
vlan filter INTERNAL vlan-list 1,3-5,10,100,101
 !
```

Example B-31 *Switch-A Configuration (Continued)*

```
mls qos
!
ip multicast-routing
!
class-map match-all HTTP
 match access-group HTTP
!
policy-map QOS
 class HTTP
   police flow 1000000 187500 conform-action set-dscp-transmit 24 exceed-action drop
!
spanning-tree extend system-id
spanning-tree vlan 1 priority 28672
spanning-tree vlan 1 forward-time 7
spanning-tree vlan 1 max-age 10
spanning-tree vlan 3 priority 28672
spanning-tree vlan 3 forward-time 7
spanning-tree vlan 3 max-age 10
spanning-tree vlan 4 priority 24576
spanning-tree vlan 4 forward-time 7
spanning-tree vlan 4 max-age 10
spanning-tree vlan 5 priority 28672
spanning-tree vlan 5 forward-time 7
spanning-tree vlan 5 max-age 10
spanning-tree vlan 10 priority 24576
spanning-tree vlan 10 forward-time 7
spanning-tree vlan 10 max-age 10
spanning-tree vlan 100 priority 28672
spanning-tree vlan 100 forward-time 7
spanning-tree vlan 100 max-age 10
spanning-tree vlan 101 priority 28672
spanning-tree vlan 101 forward-time 7
spanning-tree vlan 101 max-age 10
!
port-channel load-balance src-dst-ip
!
interface range GigabitEthernet1/1 - 2
 switchport
 mtu 9216
 flowcontrol receive on
 flowcontrol send on
 channel-group 1 mode desirable
 switchport trunk encapsulation isl
 switchport mode trunk
 mls qos trust dscp
!
interface FastEthernet 2/1
 ip address 192.168.1.1 255.255.255.0
 ip pim sparse-dense-mode
 mls qos trust dscp
 speed 100
 duplex full
```

continues

Example B-31 *Switch-A Configuration (Continued)*

```
!
interface FastEthernet 2/2
 ip address 192.168.2.1 255.255.255.0
 ip pim sparse-dense-mode
 mls qos trust dscp
 speed 100
 duplex full
!
interface range FastEthernet 2/3 - 24
 switchport
 switchport access vlan 100
 mls qos vlan-based
!
interface range FastEthernet 2/25 - 47
 switchport
 switchport access vlan 101
 mls qos vlan-based
!
interface Vlan 10
 ip address 192.168.10.2 255.255.255.248
 ip pim sparse-dense-mode
!
interface Vlan 100
 ip address 192.168.100.2 255.255.255.0
 standby ip 192.168.100.1
 standby priority 150 preempt
 ip pim sparse-dense-mode
 mls qos bridged
 service-policy input QOS
!
interface Vlan 101
 ip address 192.168.101.2 255.255.255.0
 standby ip 192.168.101.1
 standby priority 100
 ip pim sparse-dense-mode
 mls qos bridged
 service-policy input QOS
!
router eigrp 1
 network 192.168.0.0 0.0.255.255
!
access-list 1 permit 192.168.100.0 0.0.0.255
access-list 2 permit host 192.168.100.50
access-list 100 permit ip 192.168.0.0 0.0.0.255 192.168.0.0 0.0.255.255
!
ip access-list extended HTTP
 permit tcp any eq www any
!
snmp-server community cisco RO 2
snmp-server enable traps
snmp-server host 192.168.100.50 cisco
!
```

Example B-31 *Switch-A Configuration (Continued)*

```
line con 0
line vty 0 4
 access-class 1 in
 password cisco
 login
line vty 5 15
 access-class 1 in
 password cisco
 login
!
ntp server 192.168.100.50
end
```

Example B-32 *Switch-B Configuration*

```
# ***** NON-DEFAULT CONFIGURATION *****
!
!
#time: Mon Jul 15 2002, 20:59:16 EST
!
#version 7.2(2)
!
set password $2$fX1D$Vwy2IJlXDsFlMudGbU8Wr1
set enablepass $2$DhKF$iZH3NdFq.oOUOJ2XlM0Dv0
!
#system
set system name  Switch-B
!
#mac address reduction
set spantree macreduction enable
!
#snmp
set snmp community read-only cisco
set snmp trap 192.168.100.50 cisco
set snmp enable
!
#vtp
set vtp domain ciscolab
set vtp mode client
set vtp passwd cisco
!
#ip
set interface sc0 10 192.168.10.3 255.255.255.248

set ip route 0.0.0.0/0.0.0.0 192.168.10.2
!
#spantree
#vlan                          <VlanId>
set spantree fwddelay 7        1
set spantree maxage   10       1
set spantree priority 24576    1
```

continues

Example B-32 *Switch-B Configuration (Continued)*

```
set spantree fwddelay 7      3
set spantree maxage   10     3
set spantree priority 24576  3
set spantree fwddelay 7      4
set spantree maxage   10     4
set spantree priority 28672  4
set spantree fwddelay 7      5
set spantree maxage   10     5
set spantree priority 24576  5
set spantree fwddelay 7      10
set spantree maxage   10     10
set spantree priority 28672  10
set spantree fwddelay 7      100
set spantree maxage   10     100
set spantree priority 28672  100
set spantree fwddelay 7      101
set spantree maxage   10     101
set spantree priority 24576  101
!
#ntp
set ntp server 192.168.100.50
set timezone EST -5 0
!
#permit list
set ip permit enable telnet
set ip permit enable ssh
set ip permit enable snmp
set ip permit 192.168.100.0 255.255.255.0 telnet
set ip permit 192.168.100.50 snmp
!
#qos
set qos enable
set qos bridged-microflow-policing enable 100-101
set qos policer microflow HTTP rate 1000 burst 1500 drop
#QOS
set qos acl ip QOS dscp 24 microflow HTTP tcp any eq 80 any
#
commit qos acl all
!
#port channel
set port channel 1/1-2 13
!
#security ACLs
clear security acl all
#INTERNAL
set security acl ip INTERNAL permit arp
set security acl ip INTERNAL permit ip 192.168.0.0 0.0.255.255 192.168.0.0 0.0.255.255
#
commit security acl all
set security acl map INTERNAL 1,3-5,10,100-101
!
# default port status is enable
```

Example B-32 *Switch-B Configuration (Continued)*

```
!
!
#module 1 : 2-port 1000BaseX Supervisor
set trunk 1/1 on isl 1-1005,1025-4094
set trunk 1/2 on isl 1-1005,1025-4094
set port channel 1/1-2 mode desirable silent
set port jumbo 1/1-2 enable
set port flowcontrol 1/1-2 receive on
set port flowcontrol 1/1-2 send on
set port qos 1/1 trust trust-dscp
set port qos 1/2 trust trust-dscp
!
#module 2 : 48-port 10/100 Ethernet
set vlan 3 2/1
set vlan 4 2/2
set vlan 5 2/48
set vlan 100 2/3-24
set vlan 101 2/25-47
set port duplex 2/1-2 full
set port speed 2/1-2 100
set port qos 2/3-47 vlan-based
set port qos 2/1 trust trust-dscp
set port qos 2/2 trust trust-dscp
set port qos 2/48 trust trust-ipprec
set qos acl map QOS 100
set qos acl map QOS 101
!
end
```

Example B-33 *Switch-C Configuration*

```
hostname Switch-C
!
enable secret cisco
!
clock timezone EST -5
!
mls qos
!
ip routing
ip multicast-routing
!
spanning-tree extend system-id
spanning-tree vlan 1 priority 28672
spanning-tree vlan 1 forward-time 10
spanning-tree vlan 1 max-age 14
spanning-tree vlan 10 priority 24576
spanning-tree vlan 10 forward-time 10
spanning-tree vlan 10 max-age 14
spanning-tree vlan 200 priority 24576
spanning-tree vlan 200 forward-time 10
```

continues

Example B-33 *Switch-C Configuration (Continued)*

```
spanning-tree vlan 200 max-age 14
spanning-tree vlan 201 priority 28672
spanning-tree vlan 201 forward-time 10
spanning-tree vlan 201 max-age 14
!
interface FastEthernet 0/1
 no switchport
 ip address 192.168.1.2 255.255.255.0
 ip pim sparse-dense-mode
 speed 100
 duplex full
 wrr-queue cos-map 4 5 6 7
 priority-queue out
 mls qos trust dscp
 speed 100
 duplex full
!
interface FastEthernet 0/2
 no switchport
 ip address 192.168.3.2 255.255.255.0
 ip pim sparse-dense-mode
 speed 100
 duplex full
 wrr-queue cos-map 4 5 6 7
 priority-queue out
 mls qos trust dscp
 speed 100
 duplex full
!
interface range FastEthernet 0/3 - 4
 channel-group 1 mode desirable
 switchport trunk encapsulation dot1q
 switchport trunk allowed vlan 1,10,200-202,1002-1005
 switchport trunk native vlan 10
 switchport mode trunk
 wrr-queue cos-map 4 5 6 7
 priority-queue out
 mls qos trust dscp
 speed 100
 duplex full
!
interface FastEthernet 0/5
 switchport trunk encapsulation dot1q
 switchport trunk allowed vlan 1,10,200-202,1002-1005
 switchport trunk native vlan 10
 switchport mode trunk
 wrr-queue cos-map 4 5 6 7
 priority-queue out
 mls qos trust dscp
 speed 100
 duplex full
!
```

Example B-33 *Switch-C Configuration (Continued)*

```
interface FastEthernet 0/6
 switchport trunk encapsulation dot1q
 switchport trunk allowed vlan 1,10,200-202,1002-1005
 switchport trunk native vlan 10
 switchport mode trunk
 wrr-queue cos-map 4 5 6 7
 priority-queue out
 mls qos trust cos
 speed 100
 duplex full
!
interface vlan 10
 ip address 192.168.10.9 255.255.255.248
 ip pim sparse-dense-mode
 ip cgmp
!
interface vlan 200
 ip address 192.168.200.2 255.255.255.0
 ip pim sparse-dense-mode
 ip cgmp
 standby ip 192.168.200.1
 standby priority 150 preempt
!
interface vlan 201
 ip address 192.168.201.2 255.255.255.0
 ip pim sparse-dense-mode
 ip cgmp
 standby ip 192.168.201.1
 standby priority 100
!
interface vlan 202
 ip address 192.168.202.2 255.255.255.0
 ip pim sparse-dense-mode
 ip cgmp
 standby ip 192.168.202.1
 standby priority 150 preempt
!
router eigrp 1
 network 192.168.0.0 0.0.255.255
!
access-list 1 permit 192.168.100.0 0.0.0.255
access-list 2 permit host 192.168.100.50
!
snmp-server community cisco RO 2
snmp-server enable traps
snmp-server host 192.168.100.50 cisco
!
line con 0
line vty 0 4
 access-class 1 in
 password cisco
 login
```

continues

Example B-33 *Switch-C Configuration (Continued)*

```
line vty 5 15
 access-class 1 in
 password cisco
 login
!
ntp server 192.168.100.50
end
```

Example B-34 *Switch-D Configuration*

```
hostname Switch-D
!
enable secret cisco
!
clock timezone EST -5
!
mls qos
!
ip routing
ip multicast-routing
!
spanning-tree extend system-id
spanning-tree vlan 1 priority 24576
spanning-tree vlan 1 forward-time 10
spanning-tree vlan 1 max-age 14
spanning-tree vlan 10 priority 28672
spanning-tree vlan 10 forward-time 10
spanning-tree vlan 10 max-age 14
spanning-tree vlan 200 priority 28672
spanning-tree vlan 200 forward-time 10
spanning-tree vlan 200 max-age 14
spanning-tree vlan 201 priority 24576
spanning-tree vlan 201 forward-time 10
spanning-tree vlan 201 max-age 14
!
interface FastEthernet 0/1
 no switchport
 ip address 192.168.2.2 255.255.255.0
 ip pim sparse-dense-mode
 speed 100
 duplex full
 wrr-queue cos-map 4 5 6 7
 priority-queue out
 mls qos trust dscp
 speed 100
 duplex full
!
interface FastEthernet 0/2
 no switchport
 ip address 192.168.4.2 255.255.255.0
 ip pim sparse-dense-mode
```

Example B-34 *Switch-D Configuration (Continued)*

```
 speed 100
 duplex full
 wrr-queue cos-map 4 5 6 7
 priority-queue out
 mls qos trust dscp
 speed 100
 duplex full
!
interface range FastEthernet 0/3 - 4
 channel-group 1 mode desirable
 switchport trunk encapsulation dot1q
 switchport trunk allowed vlan 1,10,200-202,1002-1005
 switchport trunk native vlan 10
 switchport mode trunk
 wrr-queue cos-map 4 5 6 7
 priority-queue out
 mls qos trust dscp
 speed 100
 duplex full
!
interface FastEthernet 0/5
 switchport trunk encapsulation dot1q
 switchport trunk allowed vlan 1,10,200-202,1002-1005
 switchport trunk native vlan 10
 switchport mode trunk
 wrr-queue cos-map 4 5 6 7
 priority-queue out
 mls qos trust dscp
 speed 100
 duplex full
!
interface FastEthernet 0/6
 switchport trunk encapsulation dot1q
 switchport trunk allowed vlan 1,10,200-202,1002-1005
 switchport trunk native vlan 10
 switchport mode trunk
 wrr-queue cos-map 4 5 6 7
 priority-queue out
 mls qos trust cos
 speed 100
 duplex full
!
interface vlan 10
 ip address 192.168.10.10 255.255.255.248
 ip pim sparse-dense-mode
 ip cgmp
!
interface vlan 200
 ip address 192.168.200.3 255.255.255.0
 ip pim sparse-dense-mode
 ip cgmp
 standby ip 192.168.200.1
```

continues

Example B-34 *Switch-D Configuration (Continued)*

```
 standby priority 100
!
interface vlan 201
 ip address 192.168.201.3 255.255.255.0
 ip pim sparse-dense-mode
 ip cgmp
 standby ip 192.168.201.1
 standby priority 150 preempt
!
interface vlan 202
 ip address 192.168.202.3 255.255.255.0
 ip pim sparse-dense-mode
 ip cgmp
 standby ip 192.168.202.1
 standby priority 100
!
router eigrp 1
 network 192.168.0.0 0.0.255.255
!
access-list 1 permit 192.168.100.0 0.0.0.255
access-list 2 permit host 192.168.100.50
!
snmp-server community cisco RO 2
snmp-server enable traps
snmp-server host 192.168.100.50 cisco
!
line con 0
line vty 0 4
 access-class 1 in
 password cisco
 login
line vty 5 15
 access-class 1 in
 password cisco
 login
!
ntp server 192.168.100.50
end
```

Example B-35 *Switch-E Configuration*

```
hostname Switch-E
!
enable secret cisco
!
clock timezone EST -5
!
vlan access-map VLAN202 10
 match ip address 100
 action forward
vlan filter VLAN202 vlan-list 202
```

Example B-35 *Switch-E Configuration (Continued)*

```
!
class-map match-all VOICE
 match access-group VOICE
!
class-map match-all VOICE-CONTROL
 match access-group VOICE-CONTROL
!
class-map match-all SQL
 match access-group SQL
!
class-map match-all HTTP
 match access-group HTTP
!
policy-map QOS
 class HTTP
  policy 1000000 187500 exceed-action drop
 class VOICE
  set ip dscp 46
class VOICE
  set ip dscp 26
 class SQL
  set ip dscp 24
 class class-default
  set ip dscp 8
!
mls qos
!
spanning-tree uplinkfast
spanning-tree uplinkfast max-update-rate 200
spanning-tree portfast bpdufilter default
spanning-tree extend system-id
!
interface FastEthernet 0/1
 switchport trunk encapsulation dot1q
 switchport trunk allowed vlan 1,10,200-202,1002-1005
 switchport trunk native vlan 10
 switchport mode trunk
 wrr-queue cos-map 4 5 6 7
 priority-queue out
 mls qos trust dscp
 speed 100
 duplex full
 spanning-tree vlan 1 cost 10000
 spanning-tree vlan 101 cost 10000
 spanning-tree vlan 201 cost 10000
!
interface FastEthernet 0/2
 switchport trunk encapsulation dot1q
 switchport trunk allowed vlan 1,10,200-202,1002-1005
 switchport trunk native vlan 10
 spanning-tree vlan
 switchport mode trunk
```

continues

Example B-35 *Switch-E Configuration (Continued)*

```
wrr-queue cos-map 4 5 6 7
priority-queue out
mls qos trust dscp
speed 100
duplex full
spanning-tree vlan 10 cost 10000
spanning-tree vlan 100 cost 10000
spanning-tree vlan 200 cost 10000
spanning-tree vlan 202 cost 10000
!
interface range FastEthernet 0/3 - 12
 switchport access vlan 200
 switchport host
 switchport voice vlan 202
 switchport priority extend cos 3
 service-policy input QOS
!
interface range FastEthernet 0/13 - 23
 switchport access vlan 201
 switchport host
 service-policy input QOS
!
interface FastEthernet 0/24
 switchport access vlan 201
 switchport host
 switchport port-security
 switchport port-security maximum 1
 switchport port-security mac-address 0010.0010.0010
 switchport port-security violation shutdown
 service-policy input QOS
!
interface vlan 10
 ip address 192.168.10.11 255.255.255.248
!
ip default-gateway 192.168.10.9
!
access-list 1 permit 192.168.100.0 0.0.0.255
access-list 2 permit host 192.168.100.50
access-list 100 permit tcp any any eq 2000
access-list 100 permit tcp any eq 2000 any
access-list 100 permit udp any range 16384 32767 any range 16384 32767
access-list 100 permit udp any eq 67 any eq 68
access-list 100 permit udp any eq 68 any eq 67
access-list 100 permit udp any any eq 69
access-list 100 permit udp any eq 69 any
access-list 100 permit udp any eq 88 any
access-list 100 permit icmp any any echo
access-list 100 permit icmp any any echo-reply
!
ip access-list extended VOICE
 permit udp any range 16384 32767 any range 16384 32767
!
```

Example B-35 *Switch-E Configuration (Continued)*

```
ip access-list extended VOICE-CONTROL
 permit tcp any any eq 2000
!
ip access-list extended SQL
 permit tcp any any eq 1433
!
ip access-list extended HTTP
 permit tcp any any eq 80
!
snmp-server community cisco RO 2
snmp-server enable traps
snmp-server host 192.168.100.50 cisco
!
line con 0
line vty 0 4
 access-class 1 in
 password cisco
 login
line vty 5 15
 access-class 1 in
 password cisco
 login
!
ntp server 192.168.100.50
end
```

Example B-36 *Switch-F Configuration*

```
# ***** NON-DEFAULT CONFIGURATION *****
!
!
#time: Mon Jul 15 2002, 21:14:37 EST
!
set password $2$f647$Vwy24JlXDsFlMudGbH8Wr1
set enablepass $2$7498F$f7Dl$.OU492JAM0Dv0
!
#system
set system name Switch-F
!
#snmp
set snmp community read-only cisco
set snmp trap 192.168.100.50 cisco
set snmp enable
!
#mac address reduction
set spantree macreduction enable
!
#vtp
set vtp domain ccnp
set vtp mode client
set vtp passwd cisco
```

continues

Example B-36 *Switch-F Configuration (Continued)*

```
!
#ip
set interface sc0 10 192.168.10.12 255.255.255.248
set ip route 0.0.0.0/0.0.0.0 192.168.10.9
!
#cgmp
set cgmp enable
!
#spantree
#portfast
set spantree global-default bpdu-filter enable
!
#uplinkfast groups
set spantree uplinkfast enable rate 20 all-protocols off
!
#vlan                     <VlanId>
set spantree priority 49152  1
set spantree priority 49152  10
set spantree priority 49152  200
set spantree priority 49152  201
set spantree priority 49152  202
!
#ntp
set ntp server 192.168.100.50
set timezone EST -5 0
!
#permit list
set ip permit enable telnet
set ip permit enable ssh
set ip permit enable snmp
set ip permit 192.168.100.0 255.255.255.0 telnet
set ip permit 192.168.100.50 snmp
!
#qos
set qos enable
set qos defaultcos 3
set qos map 2q1t 2 1 cos 0-4
set qos map 2q1t 2 1 cos 5-7
!
#module 1 : 0-port Switching Supervisor
!
#module 2 : 50-port 10/100/1000 Ethernet
set port disable 2/24-48
set port speed 2/1-2 100
set port duplex 2/1-2 full
set vlan 10 2/1-2
set vlan 200 2/3-12
set vlan 201 2/13-24
set spantree portfast 2/48 enable
clear trunk 2/1-2 1-1005,1025-4094
set trunk 2/1 on dot1q 1,10,200-202
set trunk 2/2 on dot1q 1,10,200-202
```

Example B-36 *Switch-F Configuration (Continued)*

```
set trunk 2/3-48 off
set port channel 2/3-48 mode off
set spantree portvlancost 2/1  cost 10000 1,101,201
set spantree portvlancost 2/2  cost 10000 10,100,102,202
!
end
```

Example B-37 *Router-A Configuration*

```
hostname Router-A
!
enable secret cisco
!
ip multicast-routing
ip pim send-rp-announce FastEthernet0/0 scope 10
!
interface FastEthernet0/0
 ip pim sparse-dense-mode
 ip address 192.168.5.1 255.255.255.0
!
interface loopback0
 ip address 10.0.0.1 255.0.0.0
!
router eigrp 1
 network 10.0.0.0
 network 192.168.0.0 0.0.0.255
!
line vty 0 4
 password cisco
 login
```

Example B-38 *MSFC-B Configuration*

```
hostname MSFC-B
!
enable secret cisco
!
ip multicast-routing
!
interface VLAN 3
 ip address 192.168.3.1 255.255.255.0
 ip pim sparse-dense-mode
!
interface VLAN 4
 ip address 192.168.4.1 255.255.255.0
 ip pim sparse-dense-mode
!
interface VLAN 5
 ip address 192.168.5.2 255.255.255.0
 ip pim sparse-dense-mode
!
```

continues

Example B-38 *MSFC-B Configuration (Continued)*

```
interface VLAN 10
 ip address 192.168.10.4 255.255.255.255
 ip pim sparse-dense-mode
!
interface vlan 100
 ip address 192.168.100.3 255.255.255.0
 ip pim sparse-dense-mode
 standby ip 192.168.100.1
 standby priority 100
!
interface vlan 101
 ip address 192.168.101.3 255.255.255.0
 ip pim sparse-dense-mode
 standby ip 192.168.101.1
 standby priority 150 preempt
!
router eigrp 1
 network 192.168.0.0 0.0.255.255
!
line vty 0 4
 password cisco
 login
```

INDEX

Numerics

C

J

K

L

M

☐ **YES!** I'm requesting a **free** subscription to *Packet*™ magazine.

☐ No. I'm not interested at this time.

☐ Mr.
☐ Ms.

First Name (Please Print) _____ Last Name _____

Title/Position (Required) _____

Company (Required) _____

Address _____

City _____ State/Province _____

Zip/Postal Code _____ Country _____

Telephone (Include country and area codes) _____ Fax _____

E-mail _____

Signature (Required) _____ Date _____

☐ I would like to receive additional information on Cisco's services and products by e-mail.

1. Do you or your company:
A ☐ Use Cisco products   C ☐ Both
B ☐ Resell Cisco products   D ☐ Neither

2. Your organization's relationship to Cisco Systems:
A ☐ Customer/End User   E ☐ Integrator   J ☐ Consultant
B ☐ Prospective Customer   F ☐ Non-Authorized Reseller   K ☐ Other (specify):
C ☐ Cisco Reseller   G ☐ Cisco Training Partner   _____
D ☐ Cisco Distributor   I ☐ Cisco OEM

3. How many people does your entire company employ?
A ☐ More than 10,000   D ☐ 500 to 999   G ☐ Fewer than 100
B ☐ 5,000 to 9,999   E ☐ 250 to 499
c ☐ 1,000 to 4,999   f ☐ 100 to 249

4. Is your company a Service Provider?
A ☐ Yes   B ☐ No

5. Your involvement in network equipment purchases:
A ☐ Recommend   B ☐ Approve   C ☐ Neither

6. Your personal involvement in networking:
A ☐ Entire enterprise at all sites   F ☐ Public network
B ☐ Departments or network segments at more than one site   D ☐ No involvement
C ☐ Single department or network segment   E ☐ Other (specify):
                                                              _____

7. Your Industry:
A ☐ Aerospace   G ☐ Education (K–12)   K ☐ Health Care
B ☐ Agriculture/Mining/Construction U ☐ Education (College/Univ.)   L ☐ Telecommunications
C ☐ Banking/Finance   H ☐ Government—Federal   M ☐ Utilities/Transportation
D ☐ Chemical/Pharmaceutical   I ☐ Government—State   N ☐ Other (specify):
E ☐ Consultant   J ☐ Government—Local   _____
F ☐ Computer/Systems/Electronics

CPRESS

PACKET

PACKET

Packet magazine serves as the premier publication linking customers to Cisco Systems, Inc. Delivering complete coverage of cutting-edge networking trends and innovations, *Packet* is a magazine for technical, hands-on users. It delivers industry-specific information for enterprise, service provider, and small and midsized business market segments. A toolchest for planners and decision makers, *Packet* contains a vast array of practical information, boasting sample configurations, real-life customer examples, and tips on getting the most from your Cisco Systems' investments. Simply put, *Packet* magazine is straight talk straight from the worldwide leader in networking for the Internet, Cisco Systems, Inc.

We hope you'll take advantage of this useful resource. I look forward to hearing from you!

Cecelia Glover
Packet Circulation Manager
packet@external.cisco.com
www.cisco.com/go/packet